W9-BWT-915

Ch	Ethics in Practice Cases	Chs. 1–2	Chs. 3–4	Chs. 5–6	Chs. 7–8	Chs. 9–10	Chs. 11–12–13	Chs. 14–15–16	Chs. 17–18
9	May I Have a "Perk" with That Compensation Package?	X		X		X	X		
9	Should CEOs Raise the Minimum Salary of their Employees?	X		X			X		
9	Facebook and Say on Pay for Directors?	X		X			X		
10	DuPont and Sustainability Reporting	X	X	X				X	
10	Crisis Management: When to Repent? When to Defend?	X				X			
11	Walmart, Amazon, and the $15 Minimum Wage	X		X			X		X
11	The Neglectful Director			X		X	X		
11	Kindness in Firing			X			X		
11	The Serial Whistleblower: Have the Incentives Gone Too Far?	X		X		X			X
11	Whistleblower Waits for Years for Rewards	X				X			X
12	Big Data and Employee Health			X	X	X			
12	Shaming Employees into Good Behavior at Amazon?			X			X		
12	Are Your workers Really Sick When They Take a Sick Day?			X			X		
12	Co-Worker Versus Friendship			X			X		
12	Mental Health, Athletes, and the Pressures to Perform	X		X		X	X		
12	When External Stakeholders Attack	X	X	X			X		
13	Better Check Your Old Yearbooks and Social Media Posts	X		X	X	X	X		
13	What is Reasonable Accommodation for Pregnancy?		X				X		X
13	Using DNA to Catch a Killer			X	X				X
13	Bigotry in the Bakery?		X	X		X		X	
14	Can We Tell the Customer Anything to Make the Sale?		X	X		X		X	
14	What Does the Word *Free* Mean? Should It Be Banned in Advertising?	X	X	X		X		X	
14	Advertising Traps: Do They Represent Ethical Advertising?	X	X	X				X	
14	Food Advertising to Children —Should It Be Banned?	X	X	X		X		X	X
14	Product Names and Racial Bias	X	X	X		X		X	
14	The Growing Business of Return Fraud	X	X	X				X	
15	The Pirated Popcorn	X		X				X	
15	Are Video Games a Harmful Product?	X	X	X	X			X	X
15	Was "Pink Slime" a Victim of Social Media Frenzy? Unethical Reporting?	X			X			X	
15	Sleep Tight and Don't Let the Bedbugs Bite	X		X				X	X
16	Matters of Good Intentions			X				X	

Ch	Ethics in Practice Cases	Chs. 1–2	Chs. 3–4	Chs. 5–6	Chs. 7–8	Chs. 9–10	Chs. 11–12–13	Chs. 14–15–16	Chs. 17–18
16	Competition in the Nonprofit Workplace	X	X	X				X	
17	The NCAA, the Players, and the Government : Should College Athletes Be Paid?	X	X			X			X
17	The Regulatory Dilemma Regarding Marijuana	X	X					X	X
17	To Mask or Not to Mask? COVID-19 Mandates	X	X	X	X			X	X
18	A Scoop of Social Justice with Ice Cream, Please	X	X	X		X		X	
18	The Politics and Business of Blue Jeans	X	X	X		X			X

Summary: 67 Ethics in Practice Cases ; 18 are new.

Business & Society

Ethics, Sustainability, and Stakeholder Management

Eleventh Edition

Archie B. Carroll
University of Georgia

Jill A. Brown
Bentley University

 CENGAGE

Australia • Brazil • Canada • Mexico • Singapore • United Kingdom • United States

Business & Society: Ethics, Sustainability and Stakeholder Management, **Eleventh Edition**
Archie B. Carroll, Jill A. Brown

SVP, Higher Education Product Management: Erin Joyner

VP, Product Management, Learning Experiences: Thais Alencar

Product Director: Joe Sabatino

Product Manager: Heather Mooney and Michael Worls

Product Assistant: Nick Perez

Content Manager: Neha Chawla, MPS Limited

Digital Delivery Quality Partner: Beth Ross

VP, Product Marketing: Jason Sakos

Director, Product Marketing: Danaë April

IP Analyst: Diane Garrity

IP Project Manager: Ilakkiya Jayagopi, Lumina Datamatics Ltd

Production Service: MPS Limited

Designer: Bethany Bourgeois

Cover Image Source: Hildegarde/Getty Images.

For product information and technology assistance, contact us at **Cengage Customer & Sales Support, 1-800-354-9706 or support.cengage.com.**

For permission to use material from this text or product, submit all requests online at **www.copyright.com.**

Library of Congress Control Number: 2021916370

ISBN: 978-0-357-71862-9

Cengage Learning
200 Pier 4 Boulevard
Boston, MA 02210
USA

Cengage is a leading provider of customized learning solutions with employees residing in nearly 40 different countries and sales in more than 125 countries around the world. Find your local representative at **www.cengage.com.**

To learn more about Cengage platforms and services, register or access your online learning solution, or purchase materials for your course, visit **www.cengage.com.**

Printed at CLDPC, USA 09-22

Brief Contents

Preface   xi

About the Authors   xvi

Part 1   Business, Society, and Responsibility   1

Chapter 1

The Business and Society Relationship   2

Chapter 2

Corporate Social Responsibility, Performance, and Impact   18

Part 2   Stakeholders and Sustainability   44

Chapter 3

The Stakeholder Approach to Business, Society, and Ethics   45

Chapter 4

Sustainability and the Natural Environment   68

Part 3   Business Ethics and Leadership   96

Chapter 5

Business Ethics Essentials   97

Chapter 6

Managerial and Organizational Ethics   122

Chapter 7

Ethical Issues in the Global Arena   153

Chapter 8

Business Ethics and Technology: The Digital Enterprise   176

Part 4   Corporate Governance and Strategic Management Issues   199

Chapter 9

Corporate Governance: Foundational Issues   200

Chapter 10

Strategy, Risk, Issues, and Crisis Management   226

Part 5   Internal Stakeholder Issues   250

Chapter 11

Employee Stakeholders and Workplace Issues   251

Chapter 12

Employee Stakeholders: Privacy, Health, Wellness, and Safety   272

Chapter 13

Employment Discrimination, Diversity, and Inclusion   294

Part 6   External Stakeholder Issues   316

Chapter 14

Consumer Stakeholders: Information Issues   317

Chapter 15

Consumer Stakeholders: Product and Service Issues   342

Chapter 16

Community Stakeholders and Corporate Philanthropy   362

Part 7   Business and Government Relations   383

Chapter 17

Business, Government, and Regulation   384

Chapter 18

Busines's Influence on Government and Public Policy   401

Cases   416

Subject Index   523

Name Index   540

Contents

Preface   xi

About the Authors   xvi

Part 1 Business, Society, and Responsibility   1

Chapter 1

The Business and Society Relationship   2

1.1   **Business and Society**   4
   1.1a   Business Defined   4
   1.1b   Society Defined   4

1.2   **Society as the Macroenvironment**   4

1.3   **Pluralistic Societies**   5
   1.3a   Multiple Publics, Systems, and Stakeholders   5
   1.3b   A Special-Interest Society   5

1.4   **Business Criticism and Corporate Response**   6
   1.4a   Factors in the Social Environment   6
   1.4b   A General Criticism of Business: Use and Abuse of Power   10
   1.4c   Balancing Power with Responsibility   12
   1.4d   Business's Response: A Changing Social Contract   12

1.5   **Focus of the Book**   13

1.6   **Structure of the Book**   15

Summary   15

Key Terms   16

Discussion Questions   16

Endnotes   16

Chapter 2

Corporate Social Responsibility, Performance, and Impact   18

2.1   **Corporate Social Responsibility as a Concept**   19
   2.1a   The Beginnings of CSR   20
   2.1b   Evolving Meanings of CSR   21
   2.1c   A Four-Part Definition of CSR   21
   2.1d   The Pyramid of Corporate Social Responsibility   24
   2.1e   CSR in Practice   26

2.2   **Traditional Arguments against and for CSR**   27
   2.2a   Arguments against CSR   28
   2.2b   Arguments in Support of CSR   28
   2.2c   The Business Case for CSR   29

2.3   **CSR Greenwashing**   31

2.4   **Political CSR**   31

2.5   **Corporate Social *Responsiveness, Performance*, and *Impact***   31
   2.5a   Carroll's CSP Model   32

2.6   **Corporate Citizenship**   33
   2.6a   Broad and Narrow Views   33
   2.6b   Stages of Corporate Citizenship   34
   2.6c   Global CSR and Corporate Citizenship   34

2.7   **The Social Performance and Financial Performance Relationship**   35
   2.7a   Three Perspectives on the Social–Financial–Reputation Relationship   35

2.8   **Creating Shared Value, Conscious Capitalism, and Purpose-Driven Business**   37

2.9   **Socially Responsible, Sustainable, ESG Investing**   38

Summary   39

Key Terms   40

Discussion Questions   40

Endnotes   40

Part 2 Stakeholders and Sustainability   44

Chapter 3

The Stakeholder Approach to Business, Society, and Ethics   45

3.1   **Origins of the Stakeholder Concept**   46
   3.1a   What Is the *Stake* in Stakeholder?   46
   3.1b   What Is a Stakeholder?   46

3.2   **Who Are Business's Stakeholders?**   47
   3.2a   Three Views of the Firm: Production, Managerial, and Stakeholder   47
   3.2b   Primary and Secondary Stakeholders   48
   3.2c   Important Stakeholder Attributes: Legitimacy, Power, Urgency   49

3.3   **Strategic, Multifiduciary, and Synthesis: Three Stakeholder Approaches**   51

3.4   **Three Values of the Stakeholder Model**   52
   3.4a   Descriptive Value   52
   3.4b   Instrumental Value   52
   3.4c   Normative Value   52

3.5   **Stakeholder Management: Five Key Questions**   52
   3.5a   Who Are the Organization's Stakeholders?   53
   3.5b   What Are Our Stakeholders' Stakes?   55
   3.5c   What Opportunities and Challenges Do Our Stakeholders Present?   56
   3.5d   What Responsibilities Does a Firm Have toward Its Stakeholders?   56
   3.5e   What Strategies or Actions Should Management Take?   57

3.6   **Effective Stakeholder Management and Engagement**   58
   3.6a   Stakeholder Thinking   59
   3.6b   Developing a Stakeholder Culture   59

3.6c   Stakeholder Management Capability 60
3.6d   Stakeholder Engagement 61
3.6e   The Stakeholder Corporation 62
3.6f   Principles of Stakeholder Management 63

3.7   **Strategic Steps toward Global Stakeholder Management 63**
3.7a   Implementation 63
Summary 63
Key Terms 64
Discussion Questions 64
Endnotes 65

Chapter 4

Sustainability and the Natural Environment 68

4.1   **The Sustainability Imperative: A Call for Business to Step Up 69**

4.2   **The Natural Environment 71**

4.3   **The Impact of Business on the Natural Environment 73**
4.3a   Patagonia 74
4.3b   Apple 74
4.3c   Tesla 74

4.4   **Key Environmental Issues 74**
4.4a   Climate Change and Global Warming 74
4.4b   Air Pollution and Toxins 75
4.4c   Energy and Fossil Fuels 77
4.4d   Water 78
4.4e   Waste Management 79
4.4f   Oceans and Fisheries 79
4.4g   Deforestation and Biodiversity 80

4.5   **Responsibility for Environmental and Sustainability Issues 81**

4.6   **The Role of Governments in Environmental and Sustainability Issues 82**
4.6a   Responses of Governments—United States 82
4.6b   Responses of Governments—International 85

4.7   **Other Environmental and Sustainability Stakeholders 85**
4.7a   Environmental Interest Groups 85
4.7b   Other Sustainability Interest Groups 87
4.7c   Business and Environmental Partnerships-Activists, NGOs, and Interest Groups 88

4.8   **The Future of Business: Greening and/or Growing? 88**
Summary 89
Key Terms 89
Discussion Questions 90
Endnotes 90

Part 3   Business Ethics and Leadership 96

Chapter 5

Business Ethics Essentials 97

5.1   **Business Ethics: Some Basic Concepts 99**
5.1a   Descriptive versus Normative Ethics 100
5.1b   The Conventional Approach to Business Ethics 100
5.1c   Making Ethical Judgments 101
5.1d   Ethics and the Law 103

5.2   **Ethics, Economics, and Law—A Venn Model 104**

5.3   **Three Models of Management Ethics 106**
5.3a   Immoral Management 106
5.3b   Moral Management 108
5.3c   Amoral Management 109
5.3d   Two Hypotheses Regarding the Models of Management Morality 111

5.4   **Developing Moral Judgment 112**
5.4a   Levels of Moral Development 113
5.4b   Different Sources of a Person's Values 115

5.5   **Elements of Moral Judgment 117**
5.5a   Moral Imagination 117
5.5b   Moral Identification and Ordering 117
5.5c   Moral Evaluation 117
5.5d   Tolerance of Moral Disagreement and Ambiguity 118
5.5e   Integration of Managerial and Moral Competence 118
5.5f   A Sense of Moral Obligation 118

5.6   **Rest's Model for Ethical Decision Making and Behavior 119**
Summary 119
Key Terms 119
Discussion Questions 120
Endnotes 120

Chapter 6

Managerial and Organizational Ethics 122

6.1   **Ethics Issues Arise at Different Levels 122**
6.1a   Personal Level 123
6.1b   Managerial and Organizational Levels 123
6.1c   Industry or Profession Level 124
6.1d   Societal and Global Levels 125

6.2   **Managerial Ethics and Ethical Principles 125**

6.3   **Principles Approach to Ethics 125**
6.3a   What Is an Ethics Principle? 125
6.3b   Types of Ethical Principles or Theories 126
6.3c   Principle of Utilitarianism 126
6.3d   Kant's Categorical Imperative (Duty) 126
6.3e   Principle of Rights 127
6.3f   Principle of Justice (Fairness Principle) 128
6.3g   Ethics of Care 129
6.3h   Virtue Ethics 129
6.3i   The Golden Rule 130
6.3j   Servant Leadership 130

6.4   **Ethical Tests Approach to Decision Making 131**
6.4a   Test of Common Sense 131
6.4b   Test of One's Best Self 131
6.4c   Test of Making Something Public (Disclosure Rule) 131
6.4d   Test of Ventilation 132
6.4e   Test of Purified Idea 132
6.4f   Test of the Big Four 132
6.4g   Gag Test 132
6.4h   Use Several Tests in Combination 132

6.5   Managing Organizational Ethics   133
  6.5a   Factors Affecting the Organization's Ethical
          Climate   133
  6.5b   Improving the Organization's Ethical Culture   135

**6.6   Behavioral Ethics—Achieving a Deeper
          Understanding   136**

**6.7   Best Practices for Improving an Organization's
          Ethics   137**
  6.7a   Top Management Leadership
          (Moral Management)   137
  6.7b   Effective Communication of Ethical
          Messages   139
  6.7c   Ethics and Compliance Programs and
          Officers   139
  6.7d   Setting Realistic Objectives   140
  6.7e   Ethical Decision-Making Processes   141
  6.7f   Codes of Ethics or Conduct   141
  6.7g   Disciplining Violators of Ethics Standards   142
  6.7h   Ethics "Hotlines" and Whistle-Blowing
          Mechanisms   143
  6.7i   Business Ethics Training   143
  6.7j   Ethics Audits and Risk Assessments   145
  6.7k   Corporate Transparency   145
  6.7l   Board of Directors Oversight and Leadership   145

6.8   Moral Decisions, Managers, and Organizations   146
Summary   147
Key Terms   147
Discussion Questions   148
Endnotes   148

Chapter 7

Ethical Issues in the Global Arena   153
7.1   Challenges in the Global Environment   154

**7.2   Ethical Issues in the Global Business
          Environment   155**
  7.2a   Questionable Marketing and Plant Safety
          Practices   155
  7.2b   Human Rights, Sweatshops, and Labor
          Abuses   157
  7.2c   Corruption, Bribery, and Questionable
          Payments   161

7.3   Improving Global Business Ethics   165
  7.3a   Balancing and Reconciling the Ethics Traditions of
          Home and Host Countries   165
  7.3b   Strategies for Improving Global Business
          Ethics   166
Summary   170
Key Terms   171
Discussion Questions   171
Endnotes   171

Chapter 8

**Business Ethics and Technology: The Digital
Enterprise   176**
**8.1   The New World of Big Data and Artificial
          Intelligence   177**

8.2   Technology and the Technological Environment   178
8.3   Benefits and Costs of Technology   178

8.4   Technology and Ethics   179
  8.4a   Surveillance   180

8.5   Information Technology   181
  8.5a   Social Media   181
  8.5b   Cybersecurity   181
  8.5c   E-Commerce   182
  8.5d   Invasion of Consumer Privacy via
          E-Commerce   184
  8.5e   The Workplace and Digital Technology   188

8.6   Biotechnology   190
  8.6a   Bioethics   190
  8.6b   Genetic Engineering   191
  8.6c   Genetically Modified Organisms (GMOs)   192
Summary   194
Key Terms   194
Discussion Questions   194
Endnotes   195

**Part 4   Corporate Governance and Strategic
            Management Issues   199**

Chapter 9

Corporate Governance: Foundational Issues   200
9.1   Legitimacy and Corporate Governance   200
  9.1a   The Purpose of Corporate Governance   201
  9.1b   Components of Corporate Governance   201

9.2   Problems in Corporate Governance   204
  9.2a   The Importance of Board Independence   205
  9.2b   Issues Surrounding Compensation   205
  9.2c   The Governance Impact of the Market for Corporate
          Control   208
  9.2d   Insider Trading   208

9.3   Improving Corporate Governance   210
  9.3a   Legislative Initiatives   210
  9.3b   The Securities and Exchange Commission   210
  9.3c   Changes in Boards of Directors   211
  9.3d   Board Diversity   211
  9.3e   Outside Directors   212
  9.3f   Use of Board Committees   212
  9.3g   The Board's Relationship with the CEO   213
  9.3h   Board Member Liability   213

9.4   The Role of Shareholders   214
  9.4a   Shareholder Democracy   214
  9.4b   Shareholder Activism   215
  9.4c   Shareholder Resolutions   215
  9.4d   Shareholder Lawsuits   216

**9.5   Investor Relations and Shareholder
          Engagement   216**

9.6   Alternative Models of Corporate Governance   217
Summary   218
Key Terms   219
Discussion Questions   220
Endnotes   220

Chapter 10

Strategy, Risk, Issues, and Crisis Management 226

10.1 Strategic Management and Corporate Social Policy 226

10.2 Four Key Strategy Levels 227
10.2a Four Strategy Levels Described 228
10.2b Emphasis on Enterprise-Level Strategy 228

10.3 The Strategic Management Process 231
10.3a Strategic Corporate Social Responsibility 232
10.3b Measuring Sustainability and CSR 233

10.4 Public Affairs as a Part of Strategic Management 235

10.5 Risk, Issue, and Crisis Management 236

10.6 Risk Management 236

10.7 Issue Management 237
10.7a Model of the Issue Management Process 238
10.7b Issue Development Process 240

10.8 Crisis Management 241
10.8a The Nature of Crises 241
10.8b Managing Business Crises 242
10.8c Crisis Communications 244

Summary 245
Key Terms 246
Discussion Questions 246
Endnotes 246

Part 5 Internal Stakeholder Issues 250

Chapter 11

Employee Stakeholders and Workplace Issues 251

11.1 The New Social Contract 252

11.2 Employee Engagement 254

11.3 The Employee Rights Movement 254
11.3a The Meaning of Employee Rights 254

11.4 The Right Not to Be Fired without Cause 256
11.4a Employment-at-Will Doctrine 256
11.4b Dismissing an Employee with Care 258

11.5 The Right to Due Process and Fair Treatment 259
11.5a Due Process 259
11.5b Alternative Dispute Resolution 259

11.6 Freedom of Speech in the Workplace 261
11.6a Whistle-Blowing 262
11.6b Consequences of Whistle-Blowing 262
11.6c Government's Protection of Whistle-Blowers 264
11.6d False Claims Act 266
11.6e Management Responsiveness to Potential Whistle-Blowing Situations 266

Summary 267
Key Terms 267
Discussion Questions 268
Endnotes 268

Chapter 12

Employee Stakeholders: Privacy, Health, Wellness, and Safety 272

12.1 Privacy in the Workplace 273
12.1a Collection and Use of Employee Information by Employers 274
12.1b Workplace Monitoring 276
12.1c Integrity Testing 278
12.1d Drug Testing 279

12.2 Health and Wellness in the Workplace 282
12.2a Mental Health in the Workplace 282
12.2b Work-Life Balance and the Family-Friendly Workplace 283
12.2c Smoking, Vaping, Drug, and Alcohol Use in the Workplace 284

12.3 Workplace Safety 285
12.3a The Workplace Safety Problem 285
12.3b Workplace Safety Today 286
12.3c Right-to-Know Laws 286
12.3d Workplace Violence 287

Summary 288
Key Terms 289
Discussion Questions 289
Endnotes 290

Chapter 13

Employment Discrimination, Diversity, and Inclusion 294

13.1 The Civil Rights Movement 295

13.2 Federal Laws Prohibiting Discrimination 296
13.2a Title VII of the Civil Rights Act of 1964 296
13.2b Age Discrimination in Employment Act of 1967 297
13.2c Equal Pay Act of 1963 297
13.2d Rehabilitation Act of 1973, Section 503 298
13.2e Americans with Disabilities Act 298
13.2f Civil Rights Act of 1991 301
13.2g Equal Employment Opportunity Commission 301

13.3 Expanded Meanings of Employment Discrimination 302
13.3a Disparate Treatment 302
13.3b Disparate Impact 302

13.4 Issues in Employment Discrimination 303
13.4a Race, Color, and Ethnicity 303
13.4b Gender 304
13.4c Other Forms of Employment Discrimination 306

13.5 Diversity and Inclusion in the Workforce 308

13.6 Affirmative Action in the Workplace 308

13.7 The Future of Diversity Management 310

Summary 310
Key Terms 311
Discussion Questions 311
Endnotes 311

Part 6   External Stakeholder Issues   316

Chapter 14

Consumer Stakeholders: Information Issues   317

14.1   The Consumer Movement   318
   14.1a Consumerism Today   319
   14.1b Product and Service Information Issues   320
   14.1c Advertising Issues   320
   14.1d Specific Controversial Advertising Issues   322
   14.1e Warranties and Guarantees   331
   14.1f Packaging and Labeling   331
   14.1g Other Product Information Issues   333

14.2   The Federal Trade Commission (FTC)   333

14.3   Consumer Financial Protection Bureau (CFPB)   334

14.4   Self-Regulation in Advertising   335

14.5   Moral Models and Consumer Stakeholders   335
Summary   336
Key Terms   336
Discussion Questions   337
Endnotes   337

Chapter 15

Consumer Stakeholders: Product and Service Issues   342

15.1   The Issue of Quality   343

15.2   The Issue of Safety   345

15.3   Product Liability   349

15.3   Consumer Product Safety Commission   352

15.4   Food and Drug Administration   353

15.5   Business's Response to Consumer Stakeholders   354

15.6   Customer Service Programs   355

15.7   Total Quality Management Programs   356

15.8   Six Sigma Strategy and Other Processes   356
Summary   357
Key Terms   358
Discussion Questions   358
Endnotes   359

Chapter 16

Community Stakeholders and Corporate Philanthropy   362

16.1   Community Involvement and Engagement   363
   16.1a Volunteer Programs   364
   16.1b Managing Community Engagement   365

16.2   Corporate Philanthropy or Business Giving   366
   16.2a A Brief History of Corporate Philanthropy   367
   16.2b A Call for Transparency in Corporate Philanthropy   367
   16.2c Giving to the Nonprofit Sector   368
   16.2d Managing Corporate Philanthropy   369

16.3   Detrimental Impacts on Communities   373
   16.3a Offshoring and Reshoring   374
   16.3b Business and Plant Closings   374

Summary   378
Key Terms   378
Discussion Questions   378
Endnotes   379

Part 7   Business and Government Relations   383

Chapter 17

Business, Government, and Regulation   384

17.1   The Pendulum of Government's Role in Business   385

17.2   The Roles of Government and Business   385

17.3   Interaction of Business, Government, and the Public   386
   17.3a Government–Business Relationship   387
   17.3b Public–Government Relationship   387
   17.3c Business–Public Relationship   387

17.4   Government's Nonregulatory Influence on Business   388
   17.4a Industrial Policy   388
   17.4b Privatization   388
   17.4c Other Nonregulatory Governmental Influences on Business   389

17.5   Government's Regulatory Influences on Business   390
   17.5a Regulation: What Does It Mean?   391
   17.5b Reasons for Regulation   391
   17.5c Types of Regulation   392
   17.5d Issues Related to Regulation   394

17.6   Deregulation   396
   17.6a Purpose of Deregulation   396
   17.6b The Changing World of Deregulation   396

17.7   Self-Regulation as an Alternative?   396
Summary   397
Key Terms   397
Discussion Questions   397
Endnotes   398

Chapter 18

Business Influence on Government and Public Policy   401

18.1   Corporate Political Participation   402

18.2   Corporate Social Activism   402

18.3   Business Lobbying   403
   18.3a Organizational Levels of Lobbying   404

18.4   Corporate Political Spending   408
   18.4a Arguments for Corporate Political Spending   409
   18.4b Arguments against Corporate Political Spending   409
   18.4c Agency Issues   409

18.5   Political Accountability and Transparency   410

18.6   Strategies for Corporate Political Activity   411
   18.6a Financial Performance Outcomes   411

Summary   411

Key Terms   412

Discussion Questions   412

Endnotes   412

Cases   416

Subject Index   523

Name Index   540

Ethics in Practice Cases

Am I Working for My Cup or the House?   10

Does Business Have Too Much Power?   11

Do Small Businesses Have Social Responsibilities?   27

The Socially Responsible Shoe Company   30

Fresh, Local, and Sustainable: Burgers with a Soul   35

Are Plants and Flowers Stakeholders? Does Nature Have Legal Rights?   51

Chickens or Employees? Which Is the Most Important Stakeholder?   59

Something's Rotten in Hondo   62

Carbon Offsets: Are You Ready to Buy Some, When You Rent a Car?   76

Electric Vehicles and Beyond: Can "Supercar" Manufacturers like Ferrari Become Carbon Neutral?   78

A Little Green Lie   82

Who Failed to Protect the Community in Flint, Michigan?   83

Slow Fashion   86

What Would You Do?   102

Little White Lies   103

Is Résumé Inflation and Deception Acceptable?   105

Are People More Ethical When Being "Watched"?   116

Are There Ethical Issues in Self-Checkout?   124

Do More Sales Lead to Lower Ethics?   135

Employees Fired for Cheating on Employer Training Tests   138

Sign the New Ethics Code or Resign   143

Do Ethics Hotlines Always Work?   144

Fair Trade: Is It a Sustainable Movement?   158

Cheating Consultants: Helping Factories to Pass Sweatshop Audits   160

Possible Violations of the Foreign Corrupt Practices Act: Bribes versus Grease Payments   163

Twitter Ethics in Business   182

Zero Trust as a Cybersecurity Model—Don't Trust Anyone   183

Copyright Infringement or Just an Inefficient, Complex System?   187

Using Personal Technology in the Workplace   188

Whole Foods: GMO Transparency or Clever Marketing?   193

May I Have a Little "Perk" with That Compensation Package?   204

Should CEOs Raise the Minimum Salary of their Employees?   207

Facebook and Say on Pay for Directors?   209

DuPont and Sustainability Reporting   235

Crisis Management: When to Repent? When to Defend?   244

Walmart, Amazon, and the $15 Minimum Wage   252

The Neglectful Director   255

Kindness in Firing   258

The Serial Whistle-Blower: Have the Incentives Gone Too Far?   263

Whistle-Blower Waits for Years for Reward   265

Big Data and Employee Health   274

Shaming Employees into Good Behavior at Amazon?   277

Are Your Workers Really Sick When They Take a Sick Day?   278

Co-workers versus Friendship   279

Mental Health, Athletes, and the Pressures to Perform   283

When External Stakeholders Attack   287

Better Check Your Old Yearbooks and Social Media Posts   299

What Is Reasonable Accommodation for Pregnancy?   300

Using DNA to Catch a Killer   301

Bigotry in the Bakery?   307

Can We Tell the Customer Anything to Make the Sale?   321

What Does the Word *Free* Mean? Should It Be Banned in Advertising?   323

Advertising Traps: Do They Represent Ethical Advertising?   324

Food Advertising to Children—Should It Be Banned?   326

Product Names and Racial Bias   330

The Growing Business of Return Fraud   332

The Pirated Popcorn   344

Are Video Games a Harmful Product?   346

Was "Pink Slime" a Victim of Social Media Frenzy? Unethical Reporting?   349

Sleep Tight and Don't Let the Bedbugs Bite   351

Matters of Good Intentions   367

Competition in the Nonprofit Workplace   373

The NCAA, the Players, and the Government: Should College Athletes Be Paid?   387

The Regulatory Dilemma Regarding Marijuana   393

To Mask or Not to Mask? COVID-19 Mandates   394

A Scoop of Social Justice with Ice Cream, Please   402

The Politics and Business of Blue Jeans   404

Cases

Walmart: The Main Street Merchant of Doom   418

Walmart's Labor Practices   423

Chipotle's Struggle with Food Safety: Back on Top Again?   428

The Theranos Story and Fake Blood Testing: Culture, Crime, and Hubris   431

Direct-to-Consumer Advertising for Pharmaceuticals: Is It Ethical?   433

The COVID-19 Pandemic: Herculean Challenges for Business and CSR   435

Volkswagen's Diesel Deception and Its Aftermath   438

Payday Loans: A Needed Product or a Financial Scam?   444

Big Tech's Power Plays   447

An Epidemic of Cheating in College   451

Climate Change and Corporate Activism: Is It All Just Hot Air?   453

Family Business   455

What Makes a Good CEO? The Waiter Rule, Humility, and Amazon   455

Nike, Sweatshops, and Other Issues   458

The Rana Plaza Factory Collapse   463

Big Food, Big Problem: Nestlé in Brazil   467

The Dark Side of Going Green: Tesla's Ethical Dilemma   473

Coke and Pepsi in India: Water, Issues, and Crisis Management   478

An Ethical Dilemma for Chiquita in Colombia   483

Dark Money and Corporate Political Spending on Campaigns   487

Big Pharma's Marketing Tactics   488

Purdue Pharma, OxyContin, and the Opioid Crisis   495

McDonald's: The Coffee Spill Heard 'Round the World   497

Boeing's Two Flight Crashes   501

Should States Woo Big Business with Tax Incentives? Amazon Thinks So!   503

Everlane: Ethical Chic and Radical Transparency in Global Supply Chains   506

Slow and Sustainable Fashion   509

The Perils of Student Loan Debt   510

"Dead Peasant" Life Insurance Policies   513

The Case of the Fired Waitress   516

Two Vets, Two Dogs, and a Deadlock   517

Are Criminal Background Checks Discriminatory?   518

To Take or Not to Take   520

Workplace Spying   520

Preface

Business & Society: Ethics, Sustainability, and Stakeholder Management, Eleventh Edition, provides a conceptual framework, analysis, and discussion of the issues surrounding the business and society relationship. The book's structure, chapters, and cases identify and engage the major topics involved in developing a robust understanding of business *and* society, or business *in* society. The latest research, examples, and cases provide a broad, yet detailed, analysis of the subject matter; they also offer a solid basis for thoughtful learning, reflection, and analysis of the domestic and global issues facing businesses today.

The book employs a managerial perspective that identifies and integrates current and relevant thought and practice. The managerial perspective is embedded within the book's major themes of business ethics, sustainability, and stakeholder management. Each of these themes is essential today. Each theme builds upon its own perspective but is consistent with and overlaps with the others. Taken together, they capture the challenges of the past and provide frameworks for thinking about the current and future role of business in society.

The *business ethics* dimension is central because value considerations continue to be woven into the fabric of the public issues that organizations face today. An emphasis is placed on business ethics essentials and how ethics integrates into managerial and organizational decision making. Special spheres of business ethics discussed include the realms of digital technology, global capitalism, and diversity, equity, and inclusion in the workforce. Additionally, ethical questions are often debated as newer contexts, such as artificial intelligence and remote workplaces, arise. Hence, in this edition, we review these contexts with ethical considerations that are vital to their full treatment.

Sustainability is now one of business's most pressing mandates. It is more evident in the business world today that concerns for natural, social, and financial environments are interconnected and that all three must be maintained in balance for both current and future generations. The context of the United Nations Global Compact and its Sustainable Development Goals (SDGs) is noted in this edition as an overarching framework for business to address sustainability issues. Hence, topics of the triple bottom line, the circular economy, climate change, and business measures of sustainability are highlighted in this edition.

The *stakeholder management* perspective is crucial and enduring and it helps managers (1) identify the various groups or individuals who have stakes in the firm or its actions, decisions, policies, and practices and (2) incorporate the stakeholders' concerns into the firm's daily operations and strategic plans. Stakeholder management is an approach that increases the likelihood decision makers will integrate ethical and management wisdom with respect to all salient parties to the business and society relationship.

As this edition goes to press, the country and world are struggling to deal with the effects of the COVID-19 pandemic. This major outbreak and its consequences will be with us for many years. Major events have the power to change the business and society relationship in significant ways, and we have highlighted many of the immediate effects of the pandemic in this edition. It is essential that the book's topics be read with an ever-present eye on the events breaking in the news each day.

Applicable Courses for Book

This text is appropriate for college and university courses that carry such titles as Business and Society; Business *in* Society; Business and Its Environment; Business Ethics; Business and Public Policy; Social Issues in Management; Business, Government, and Society; Social Responsibility of Business; and Stakeholder Management. The book is appropriate for either a required or an elective course seeking to meet the most recent accrediting standards of the Association to Advance Collegiate Schools of Business (AACSB International). The book has been used successfully in both undergraduate and graduate courses.

Though the AACSB does not require any specific courses in this subject matter, its recently updated (2020) standards specify that a business school's curriculum should include the topics covered throughout this textbook in both undergraduate and graduate degree programs. It should be noted that a new addition to the AACSB's Collective Vision for Business Education is emphasized in its Preamble: the goal is "to transform business education globally for positive social impact," which aligns with the topics in this textbook. The Preamble to the AACSB Standards also focuses on the following values: quality, diversity and inclusion, global mindset, ethics, social responsibility, and community. These topics have been emphasized in the eleventh edition and are integrated throughout the text and the cases.

This book is ideal for coverage of perspectives that form the context for business: ethical and global issues; the influence of political, social, legal, environmental, technological, and regulatory issues; and the impact of diversity and inclusion within and on organizations. The book provides perspectives on business, society, and ethics in the United States as well as other parts of the world. As the world has grown closer due to technology, communications, and transportation, there has been more convergence than divergence in applicability of the ideas presented herein. The book has proved suitable in a number of countries outside of the United States. In previous editions, versions were published in Canada and China. Though often written from the perspective of American society, a special effort has been made to include more global examples and perspectives. Much of the book applies to developed economies around the world including references, examples and applications; however, there are applications to developing economies as well.

Objectives in Relevant Courses

Depending on the placement of a course in the curriculum or the individual instructor's philosophy or strategy, this book has been successfully used for a variety of objectives. The courses for which it is intended typically include several essential goals, including the following:

1. Students should be made aware of the expectations and demands that emanate from the stakeholder environment and are placed on business firms.
2. As prospective managers, students need to understand appropriate business responses and management approaches for dealing with social, political, environmental, technological, and global issues and stakeholders.
3. An appreciation of ethics and sustainability issues and the influence these have on society, management decision making, behavior, policies, and practices is important.
4. The broad question of business's legitimacy as an institution in a global society must be addressed from both business and societal perspectives. These topics are essential to business building trust with society and all stakeholders.
5. The increasing extent to which social, ethical, public, environmental, and global issues must be considered from a strategic perspective is critical in such courses.

New to the Eleventh Edition

This eleventh edition has been updated and revised to reflect recent research, laws, cases, and examples. Material in this new edition includes:

- A complete revision of the sustainability chapter, including a focus on climate change, the United Nations Global Compact and Sustainable Development Goals, and coverage of sustainability reporting and integrated reports
- New research, surveys, and examples throughout all the chapters
- Coverage throughout the text on the most recent ethics scandals and their influence on business, society, organizations, and people
- New concepts and examples on "behavioral ethics," including newer frameworks for understanding ethical decision-making.
- Discussion of recent developments with the COVID-19 pandemic, and newer U.S. federal and state regulations surrounding minimum wage, recreational marijuana, the parameters of social media, endorsements for college athletes, and other laws with significant importance to managers today
- Expanded coverage of social media issues, including issues of usage, privacy, and liability

- Coverage of competing corporate governance perspectives, including the influence of groups like the Business Roundtable
- Updated coverage of social entrepreneurship, social enterprises and impact investing
- Special emphasis is given to Big Tech, its power, its ethical challenges, and the evolving Digital Enterprise features of organizations today.
- Discussion of the emerging topic of Political Corporate Social Responsibility (PCSR)
- Extended coverage of Citizens United, Super PACs, and Dark Money, and the importance of Corporate Political Accountability and Transparency
- Special consideration is given to the topics of diversity, inclusion, employee rights, and discrimination, including LGBT rights and updated protections, updated affirmative action issues, and EEOC reforms
- Updated "Spotlight on Sustainability" features in each chapter, which demonstrate how sustainability is relevant and applicable to each chapter's topics
- Sixty-seven "Ethics in Practice Cases" embedded in chapters throughout the book, many of which are new to this edition
- Thirty-four end-of-text "Cases" that may be assigned with any of the book's chapter topics, 11 of which are brand new to this edition. Review the updated matrices in the front and back cover of the text book.
- A revised and updated Instructor's Manual

"Ethics in Practice" Cases

Integral to this eleventh edition are in-chapter features titled "Ethics in Practice Cases." Interspersed throughout the chapters, these short cases and incidents present

- actual ethical situations faced by companies, managers, consumers, or employees;
- topics currently being discussed in the news; or
- dilemmas faced personally in the work experiences of our former students in university or executive education classes.

These latter types of cases are real-life situations actually encountered in their full- and part-time work experiences. Students and managers wrote some of these cases, and we are pleased they gave us permission to use them. They provide ready examples of the ethical issues people face today as citizens, consumers, and employees. We would like to acknowledge the authors of these for their contributions to the book. Instructors may wish to use these as mini-cases for class discussion when a lengthier case is not assigned. They can be read quickly, but they contain considerable substance for class discussion and analysis.

"Spotlight on Sustainability" Features

The "Spotlight on Sustainability" features in each chapter highlight an important and relevant linkage of sustainability concepts that augment each chapter's text material. The feature sometimes highlights a pertinent organization covered in the chapter and further discusses its activities or issues. Other features highlight a sustainability challenge that a range of organizations face or a sustainability success that organizations or individuals can emulate. These features permit readers to quickly and easily discover how the sustainability theme applies to each topic covered in the text. The concept of sustainability extends to virtually all business, society, and ethics topics and embraces people and profits, as well as the planet.

Structure of the Book

Part 1. Business, Society, and Responsibility
Part 1 of the book provides foundational coverage of pertinent business, society, and stakeholder topics and issues. Because most courses that will use this book relate to the issue of corporate social responsibility (CSR), this concept is discussed at the outset. Part 1 explores vital issues in the business and society relationship and discusses how corporate social responsibility and its complementary concepts—corporate citizenship and sustainability—provide basic frameworks to understanding.

Part 2. Stakeholders and Sustainability
Early coverage is given to the stakeholder management concept because it provides a way of thinking and analyzing all topics in the book, as well as a helpful perspective for thinking about organizations. The stakeholder approach provides three primary values: descriptive value, instrumental value, and normative value. Stakeholder management is characterized by five key questions. Sustainability as a topic has been moved to an early position in the book because it, too, is an overarching theme that permeates all topics covered in the book. The sustainability imperative embraces environmental, social, and ethical domains of thinking about both the present and the future.

Part 3. Business Ethics and Leadership
Four chapters dedicated to business ethics and leadership topics are presented in Part 3. In actual practice, business ethics cannot be separated from the full range of external and internal stakeholder concerns, but the topic's importance merits the more detailed treatment presented here. Part 3 focuses on business ethics essentials, managerial and organizational ethics, ethical issues in the global arena, and business ethics and technology, with particular note of the evolving digital enterprise. Taken together, these chapters examine business and society issues that require ethical thinking.

Part 4. Corporate Governance and Strategic Management Issues
Part 4 consists of two chapters that include corporate governance and strategic management for stakeholder responsiveness. The purpose of this part is to discuss management considerations and implications for dealing with the issues discussed throughout the text. Corporate governance is covered early because in the past decade this topic has been identified as central to effective strategic management. The strategic management perspective is useful because these issues have impacts on the total organization and have become intense ones for many upper-level managers. Special treatment is given to corporate public policy; issue, risk, and crisis management; and public affairs management.

Some instructors may elect to cover Part 4 later in their courses. It could easily be covered after Parts 5 or 6. This option would be most appropriate for those who use the book for a business ethics course or who desire to spend less time on the governance, strategy, and management perspectives.

Part 5. Internal Stakeholder Issues
The primary internal stakeholders addressed in this part are employee stakeholders. Here, we consider workplace issues and the key themes of employee privacy, safety, health, and wellness, as well as employee rights, diversity, employment discrimination, and affirmative action. Two chapters address the new social contract between business and employees and the urgent subjects of employee rights. A third chapter treats the vital topic of diversity, inclusion, and employment discrimination. Owner stakeholders may be seen as internal stakeholders too, but we cover them in Part 4, where the subject of corporate governance has been placed.

Part 6. External Stakeholder Issues
The focus of Part 6 is consumer stakeholders, including information, product, and service issues, which are found in the first two chapters of this section. A final chapter deals with the complex nature of community stakeholders, including business philanthropy. In each of these topic areas, we encounter social and ethical issues and challenges that are integral to business today.

Part 7. Business and Government Relations
Vital topics in Part 7 include business's relations with government and particularly regulation. The business–government relationship is divided into the regulatory initiatives to monitor business practices and business's attempts to influence government.

Case Studies

Throughout each of the chapters, there are "Ethics in Practice" cases, 67 in total, that pertain to the chapter in which they are located but also can be used with other chapters as needed. The 34 end-of-text cases address a broad range of topics and decision situations. The cases are of varying length. They include classic cases (involving such corporate giants as Walmart, Nike, Nestlé, McDonald's, Volkswagen, Chipotle, Coke, Pepsi, Boeing, and Amazon) with ongoing deliberations, as well as new cases touching on issues that have arisen in the past several years.

All the cases are intended to provide instructors and students with real-life situations within which to further analyze course issues, concepts, and topics covered throughout the book. Both the Ethics in Practice cases and the end-of-text cases may be used with various chapters depending on the emphasis of the course. Many of the cases carry ramifications that spill over into several subject areas or issues. Immediately preceding the end-of-text Cases is a set of guidelines for case analysis that the instructor may wish to use in place of or in addition to the questions that appear at the end of each case. A case matrix, located inside the front and back covers of the instructor edition of the textbook and in the instructor's manual, provides guidance as to which of the cases in the book, both Ethics in Practice and end of text, work best with each chapter.

Support for the Instructor

Additional instructor resources for this product are available online. Instructor assets include an Instructor's Manual, PowerPoint® slides, and a test bank powered by Cognero®. Sign up or sign in at www.cengage.com to search for and access this product and its online resources.

Acknowledgments

We would like to express gratitude to our professional colleagues in the Social Issues in Management (SIM) Division of the Academy of Management, the International Association for Business and Society (IABS), and the Society for Business Ethics (SBE). Over the years, members of these organizations have meant a great deal to us and have helped provide a stimulating environment in which we could intellectually pursue these topics in which we have a common interest. Many of these individuals are cited in this book and their work is sincerely appreciated.

Also, we would like to remember our dear friend, co-author on several editions, and colleague, Ann Buchholtz, whose contributions to the study of business and society will remain with us forever, as will our memories of her generous spirit. Ann was someone who stood out among her peers in every dimension of performance and service. She loved the phrase from Mahatma Gandhi, "Be truthful, gentle and fearless," and it described her nature perfectly. Ann left behind many friends, colleagues, and students who will miss her dearly, as well as a beloved brother, Dick Buchholtz, who has been a friend to us over the years. Ann's spirit will live on in this textbook.

We also would like to thank the many reviewers of the ten previous editions who took the time to provide us with helpful critiques. Many of their ideas and suggestions have been used for this edition and led to improvements in the text:

Steven C. Alber, Hawaii Pacific University

Paula Becker Alexander, Seton Hall University

Laquita C. Blockson, Agnes Scott College

Mark A. Buchanan, Boise State University

Peter Burkhardt, Western State College of Colorado

Preston D. Cameron, Mesa Community College

William B. Carper, University of West Florida

George S. Cole, Shippensburg University

Brenda Eichelberger, Portland State University

Jeanne Enders, Portland State University

Joshua S. Friedlander, Baruch College

John William Geranios, George Washington University

Kathleen Getz, Mercyhurst University

Peggy A. Golden, University of Northern Iowa

Russell Gough, Pepperdine University

Michele A. Govekar, Ohio Northern University

Wade Graves, Grayson College

Frank J. Hitt, Mountain State University

Robert H. Hogner, Florida International University

Sylvester R. Houston, University of Denver

Ralph W. Jackson, University of Tulsa

David C. Jacobs, American University

Leigh Redd Johnson, Murray State University

Ed Leonard, Indiana University–Purdue University Fort Wayne

Charles Lyons, University of Georgia

Timothy A. Matherly, Florida State University

Kenneth R. Mayer, Cleveland State University

Douglas M. McCabe, Georgetown University

Douglas McCloskey, Washington University School of Law

Bill McShain, Cumberland University

Geralyn Miller, Indiana University–Purdue University Fort Wayne

Nana Lee Moore, Warner University

Harvey Nussbaum, Wayne State University

Nathan Oliver, University of Alabama Birmingham

E. Leroy Plumlee, Western Washington University

Richard Raspen, Wilkes University

Dawna Rhoades, Embry-Riddle Aeronautical University

William T. Rupp, Austin Peay State University

Robert J. Rustic, The University of Findlay

John K. Sands, Western Washington University

William Sodeman, Seven Hills Foundation

Valarie Spiser-Albert, University of Texas at San Antonio

David S. Steingard, St. Joseph's University

John M. Stevens, The Pennsylvania State University

Diane L. Swanson, Kansas State University

Dave Thiessen, Lewis-Clark State College

Jeff R. Turner, Howard Payne University

Ivan R. Vernon, Cleveland State University

Marion Webb, Cleveland State University

George E. Weber, Whitworth College

Ira E. Wessler, Robert Morris University

We also would like to express our gratitude to our students, who have not only provided comments on a regular basis but also made this eleventh edition even more interesting with the ethical dilemmas they have personally contributed, as highlighted in the Ethics in Practice cases found in many of the chapters or at the end of the text. In addition to those who are named in the Ethics in Practice cases and end-of-text cases and have given permission for their materials to be used, we would like to thank the following individuals for their contributions: Michelle Alen, Kristine Calo, Chad Cleveland, Ken Crowe, Lee Askew Elkins, Charles Lyons, William Megathlin Jr., Madeline Meibauer, Laura Rosario, Paul Rouland Sr., William Sodeman, and Clayton Wilcox. We express grateful appreciation to the authors of the other cases that appear at the end of the text, and their names are mentioned there. Of particular note are Sabine Turley and Bill Turley of Kansas State University for their two new cases on Nestlé in Brazil and Tesla's Ethical Dilemma. Finally, we wish to express our heartfelt appreciation to our family members and friends for their patience, understanding, and support when work on the book altered our priorities and plans.

Archie B. Carroll

Jill A. Brown

About the Authors

Archie B. Carroll

Archie B. Carroll is Robert W. Scherer Chair of Management and Corporate Public Affairs emeritus and professor of management emeritus in the Terry College of Business, University of Georgia. He also served as director of the Nonprofit Management and Community Service Program in the Terry College of Business. Dr. Carroll received his three academic degrees from The Florida State University in Tallahassee. He is the co-author of *Corporate Responsibility: The American Experience* (Cambridge University Press, 2012), which won the Academy of Management, Social Issues in Management, Book of the Year Award in 2014. He was recognized with the first Lifetime Achievement Award in Corporate Social Responsibility (2012) given by the Institute of Management, Humboldt University, Berlin, Germany.

Professor Carroll has published numerous books, chapters, articles, and encyclopedia entries. His research has appeared in the *Academy of Management Journal*, *Academy of Management Review*, *Business and Society*, *Journal of Management*, *Business Ethics Quarterly*, *Journal of Business Ethics*, and many others.

He is former Division Chair of the Social Issues in Management (SIM) Division of the Academy of Management, a founding board member of the International Association for Business and Society (IABS), and past president of the Society for Business Ethics (SBE). He is an elected Fellow of the Southern Management Association (1995), Fellow of the Academy of Management (2005), and Fellow of the International Association for Business and Society (2012).

Other important professional recognitions include the Sumner Marcus Award (1992) for Distinguished Service by the SIM Division of the Academy of Management; Distinguished Research Award by Terry College of Business, University of Georgia; Distinguished Service Award by the Terry College of Business; and the Hunt SMA Sustained Outstanding Service Award (2016) by the Southern Management Association. He was named professor emeritus (2005) at the University of Georgia, and in 2008, he was recognized with the Outstanding PhD Award from the College of Business, Florida State University.

Jill A. Brown

Jill Brown is the Hieken Professor of Business Ethics at Bentley University as well as a Faculty Fellow for the Hoffman Center for Business Ethics. She received her PhD at the University of Georgia; the late Ann Buchholtz served as her Dissertation Chair.

Dr. Brown's research and teaching interests include ethics, corporate social responsibility, corporate governance, and strategic leadership—with a focus on understanding how businesses can create both financial and social value. Brown's work has been published in the *Journal of Business Ethics*, *Business & Society*, *Organization Science*, *Business Ethics Quarterly*, the *Journal of Management Studies*, *Entrepreneurship Theory and Practice*, the *Oxford Handbook of Corporate Social Responsibility*, *Strategic Organization*, *Corporate Governance: An International Review* (*CGIR*), and more. She serves as co-editor of the *Business and Society* journal, which is a journal dedicated to examining issues at the intersection of business and society. Brown served for several years as section editor of the "Teaching Business Ethics" section of the *Journal of Business Ethics*. She is currently an associate editor for *Corporate Governance: An International Review.*

Brown has served in many leadership capacities for the SIM (Social Issues in Management) Division at the Academy of Management, including Program Chair and Division Chair. In her term as Division Chair, she established several new committees to address contemporary issues including the SIM Racial Justice and Communications Committees. She is a former Representative-at-Large of the International Association of Business and Society (IABS), an international organization committed to understanding relationships between business, government, and society. Dr. Brown has received numerous teaching, publishing, and reviewing awards, most recently co-authoring the 2020 Best Paper Runner-Up published in *Business Ethics Quarterly*. She regularly provides ethics training for various organizations, including the Association for Certified Fraud Examiners, the Bentley Global Ethics Training Faculty Workshop, and the Boston CFO Conference.

Part 1

Business, Society, and Responsibility

Chapter 1
The Business and Society Relationship

Chapter 2
Corporate Social Responsibility, Performance, and Impact

1

The Business and Society Relationship

After studying this chapter, you should be able to:

1. Define and explain business and society as foundational concepts. Describe how society is viewed as the macroenvironment.
2. Explain the characteristics of a pluralistic society. Describe pluralism and identify its attributes, strengths, and weaknesses.
3. Clarify what is a special-interest society and how it poses special challenges for business.
4. Identify, discuss, and illustrate the factors leading up to business criticism and corporate response. What is the general criticism of business? How may the balance of power and responsibility be resolved?
5. Identify what is the changing social contract. Is it better or worse for stakeholders?
6. Make clear the major themes characterizing this book: managerial approach, business ethics, sustainability, and stakeholder management.

The year 2020 will be one of those years we all will look back on and remember. The COVID-19 coronavirus pandemic hammered the world and all its institutions and citizens. After the first year of the pandemic, it was reported that the COVID-19 death toll was worse than it looked.[1] At the end of the first year, the worldwide death toll was 2.5 million and the U.S. death toll had reached 50,000.[2] Social distancing, sheltering in place, wearing masks, working at home, taking courses online, living at home with parents, or participating in other life events online had become the norm for more than a year as of this writing.

For the business and society relationship, the pandemic led to the lockdown of many cities and countries, and many businesses had closed or gone out of business. Many employees had lost their jobs and supply chains had been strained as customers went to online shopping for so many of their purchases. A serious shortage of many products occurred. Added to the uncertainty caused by COVID-19 pandemic, it was a year of political and social unrest as well. Protests arose over political issues and social issues such as racism and inequality. This turbulent environment and all the practices it spawned have noticeably altered business and society relationships, and it is against this backdrop that we now think about these topics. This new environment has presented many challenges and complexities to business's relationships with its stakeholders. And, though life as we have known it may continue along its past trajectory, unprecedented changes have occurred, and it is difficult to ascertain which ones will be temporary and which ones will be permanent.

The big hit to the global economy caused by COVID-19 outbreak introduced major issues that business will have to deal with, even though it was not responsible for them occurring. The COVID-19 economy created deep divides between the haves and the have-nots, created added poverty, and will have considerable influence for years to come. A sense of helplessness pervaded societies. When the economy and life return to some version of "normal," the legacy of COVID-19 will have transformed virtually all dimensions of life and business relationships.[3]

The business and society relationship has generated many economic, social, ethical, and environmental challenges over the decades. Though the business system has served most market-based societies well, criticisms of business and its practices have become commonplace. Aided by the media persistently looking for stories of conflict, this may be a reflection of the natural tendency to highlight the negative and to take for granted the beneficial aspects of the relationship. This tendency drives a focus on the stresses and strains of business operating in society.

Business, as an institution, is subject to criticism for a variety of reasons. Business is a more inviting target than government, for example, because it is seen as being motivated only by profit while government is not seeking profits but is charged with acting in the public interest. Particularly in a capitalist system, business has become a primary target of the critics, though flaws in the business-government relationship have played a huge role in the debate. In recent years, more and more commentaries questioning the capitalistic system have emerged, so it appears to be an issue the business community will need to address to repair its bruised image.[4]

Actually, both supporters and critics have weighed in on the capitalistic system. Articles such as "Save the Planet with Capitalism"[5] and "This Is No Time to Go Wobbly on Capitalism"[6] have appeared. On the other side, critics have suggested to "Redesign Capitalism to Incorporate Social Value"[7] and "The Uses and Abuses of 'Capitalism.'"[8] Jamie Dimon, chair and CEO of JPMorgan Chase, thinks businesses and governments must collaborate better to create opportunity for all in order to save capitalism.[9] In light of these different views, it is little wonder that proposals for "conscious capitalism" and "stakeholder capitalism" have become frequently proposed as solutions. Stakeholder capitalism is one of the most popular alternatives set forth, and more will be said about it in Chapter 3.

In the past few years, a number of different business scandals surfaced and damaged the business and society relationship further. These included the Volkswagen emissions scandal, admission by General Motors that it had schemed to conceal deadly safety defects in its ignition switches, revelations that Takata Corporation had been selling defective air bags, and disclosure that Toshiba had engaged in at least $1 billion in accounting irregularities.[10] One of the most serious business disgraces to occur recently was the Wells Fargo scandal. In the most expensive debacle to hit one company ever, Wells Fargo agreed to pay a penalty of $3 billion to settle criminal and civil charges that it had mistreated and defrauded customers systematically over a 14-year period.[11] Another recent scandal involved Purdue Pharma. In 2020, Purdue Pharma admitted that it had marketed and sold its dangerous opioid products to health-care providers even though it knew those providers were diverting them to abusers.[12] At a more general level, a Gallup poll investigating the issue of whether businesses are trusted today found that two-thirds of the worldwide respondents believed that lack of trust in business was widespread.[13]

Other serious questions continue to be raised about a host of ongoing day-to-day business issues: corporate governance, ethical conduct, executive compensation, inequality, human rights, the use of illegal immigrants as employees, healthiness of fast food, international corruption, and so on. The listing of such issues seems endless, but these examples illustrate the enduring tensions between business and society, which in part can be traced to the abundance of recent high-profile incidents, trends, or events.

Undergirding recent scandals and issues, familiar worries embodying social or ethical implications have continued to be debated within the business and society interface. Some of these have included racial justice, equity, businesses moving offshore, downsizing of pension programs, high unemployment, underemployment, level of the minimum wage, reduced health insurance benefits, abuses of corporate power, toxic waste disposal, insider trading, whistle-blowing, product liability, deceptive marketing, and questionable lobbying by businesses to influence the outcome of legislation. These examples of both general and specific issues are typical of today's stories about business and society that one finds on television, in social media, on the Internet, and in newspapers and magazines.

At the broadest level, the role of business in society is the subject of this book. Many key questions will be addressed: the role of business relative to the role of government in the socioeconomic system; what a firm must do to be considered socially responsible; what managers must do to be considered ethical; and what responsibilities companies have to consumers, employees, shareholders, and communities in an age of economic uncertainty and globalization. And, throughout all this, an escalating mandate for sustainability has captured the attention of business leaders, critics, and public policymakers.

As we cope with the third decade of the new millennium, many economic, legal, ethical, and technological issues concerning business and society continue on. This period is turbulent, often chaotic, and has been characterized by significant and rapid changes in the world, the economy, society, technology, and global relationships. Against this setting of flux and ongoing uncertainty in the business and society relationship, some basic concepts and ideas are worth considering first.

Spotlight on Sustainability

Why Is Sustainability Important to the Business and Society Relationship?

- Since sustainability focuses on both the present and the future, it is an indispensable factor for the business and society relationship.
- Sustainability provides a solid foundation for more efficient and effective operations, and it helps lower overall costs. Consumers benefit in the longer term.
- Society's stakeholders have come to realize the necessity for sustainable solutions to public issues. Business is central to addressing many of society's social problems and issues.
- Businesses today have realized the importance of sustainability to their organizations' success and

acceptance in the marketplace. Their reputations are at stake.
- Sustainability creates value for both business and society with a particular concern for protecting and improving the natural environment.
- The quality of a company's relationships with its customers, employees, and the community hinges on its ability to provide stable, long-term resources that are dependable.
- Sustainability is central to businesses fulfilling their social responsibilities to society, and this is central to businesses appropriately relating to their stakeholders.

1.1 Business and Society

There are some foundational concepts that are central to understanding the continuing business and society relationship. Some have chosen to frame the topic as business *in* society. Either way it is thought of, important concepts include our pluralistic and special-interest society, business criticism, corporate power, and corporate social response to stakeholders. First, it is important to address and describe two key terms that are central to the discussion: *business* and *society*.

1.1a Business Defined

Business may be defined as the collection of private, commercially oriented (profit-oriented) organizations, ranging in size from one-family proprietorships (e.g., Bone Dry Roofing Company, Kelly's Jamaican Food, K & K Soul Food, and Barron's Rental Center) to corporate giants (e.g., Microsoft, Apple, Amazon, Coca-Cola, UPS, Google, and Delta Airlines). Between these two extremes are many medium-sized proprietorships, partnerships, and corporations.

When businesses are thought of in this collective sense, all sizes and types of industries are included. In addition, some industries are simply more conducive than others in the creation of visible, social problems. For example, many manufacturing firms by their very nature cause observable air, water, and solid waste pollution and contribute to climate changes. The auto industry with the manufacture of trucks and sport utility vehicles (SUVs) is a specific case in point. Criticisms of Volkswagen, General Motors (GM), and other automakers are raised because of their high profile as manufacturers, the omnipresence of the products they make (which are the largest single source of air pollution), the popularity of their products (many families own multiple cars), and road congestion, which is experienced daily.

Some industries are highly visible because of the advertising-intensive nature of their products (e.g., Nike, Procter & Gamble, PepsiCo, InBev, and Home Depot). Other industries (e.g., tobacco, toys, electronics, and fast foods) are scrutinized because of the possible adverse effects of their products on health or because of their roles in providing health-related products (e.g., pharmaceutical firms, vitamin firms).

For these reasons, when discussing business in its relationship with society, the focus of attention gravitates toward large businesses in well-known industries. However, we should not lose sight of the fact that small- and medium-sized companies increasingly represent settings in which our discussions also apply. In recent years, the social responsibilities of smaller enterprises and the fast-growing movement toward social entrepreneurship have garnered increasing attention.

1.1b Society Defined

Society may be thought of as a community, a nation, or a broad grouping of people with common traditions, values, institutions, and collective activities and interests. As such, when speaking of business and society relationships, this may be referring to business and the local community (business and St. Louis), business and the United States as a whole, global business, or business and a specific group of stakeholders (employees, consumers, investors, environmentalists).

When discussing business and the *total* society, society is thought of as being composed of numerous interest groups, more or less formalized organizations, and a wide variety of institutions. Each of these groups, organizations, and institutions is a purposeful aggregation of people who join together because they represent a common cause or share a set of common beliefs about a particular issue. Examples of special interest groups are numerous: Earthjustice, The Sierra Club, Corporate Accountability, Center for Science in the Public Interest, National Small Business Association, People for the Ethical Treatment of Animals (PETA), Forest Stewardship Council, and Association of Young Americans.

1.2 Society as the Macroenvironment

Understanding the societal environment is a key element in analyzing business and society relationships. At its broadest level, society might be thought of as a **macroenvironment** that includes the total environment outside the firm. The macroenvironment is the comprehensive societal context in which organizations reside. A popular conceptualization of the macroenvironment is to think of it as being composed of four identifiable but interrelated segments: social, economic, political, and technological.[14] These segments are highly interconnected.

The **social environment** focuses on demographics, lifestyles, culture, and social values of the society. Of particular interest here is the manner in which shifts in these factors affect the organization and its functioning. For example, the influx of undocumented workers and immigrants over the past decade has brought changes to the demographic profile of countries. The **economic environment** addresses the nature and direction of the economy in which business operates. Variables of interest include such indices as gross national product, inflation, interest rates, unemployment rates, foreign exchange fluctuations, national debt, global trade, balance of payments, and various other indices of economic activity. Hypercompetition in the world economy has dominated the economic segment of this environment, and global competitiveness is an ongoing issue for businesses.[15]

Businesses moving jobs offshore to lower their labor costs have been a controversial trend. Enduring levels of high unemployment, underemployment, and use of gig workers have been problematic economic issues, exacerbated by the COVID-19 pandemic. Many people have become frustrated about finding jobs and have left the workforce completely. An important overlay to these problems has been the growing belief that a significant income inequality has taken hold in American society and globally.

The **political environment** focuses on the processes by which laws get passed and officials get elected and all other aspects of the interaction between firms, political practices, and government. Of particular interest to business in this segment are the regulatory process, taxation, and the changes that occur over time in business regulation of various industries, products, and different issues. At a global level, issues such as climate change, poverty, an aging population, energy resources, and technology transfer are plaguing governments in many countries. Political polarization has become a widespread issue. A problem that keeps coming to the surface is the inability of congressional bodies to get anything done because of paralysis in the political processes.

Finally, the **technological environment** represents the total set of technology-based advancements taking place in society and the world. This rapidly changing segment includes new products, processes, materials, and means of communication (e.g., social networking), as well as the status of knowledge and scientific advancement. The process and speed of technological change is of significant importance here.[16] The pace of invention, innovation, and diffusion seems to become more dynamic with each passing year. In recent years, Big Data, Business Analytics, and Artificial Intelligence have been hot topics, and businesses are frequently being referred to as digital enterprises.

Understanding that business and society relationships are embedded in a macroenvironment provides us with a constructive way of understanding the kinds of issues that constitute the broad milieu in which business functions. Throughout this book, evidence of these ever-changing environmental segments will become apparent, and it will become easier to appreciate what challenges managers face as they strive to manage effective organizations while interfacing with a complex, sometimes chaotic, society.

1.3 Pluralistic Societies

Today, most societies as macroenvironments are typically pluralistic. Pluralistic societies make for business and society relationships that are complex and dynamic. **Pluralism** refers to a diffusion of power among society's many groups and organizations. A long-standing definition of a pluralistic society is helpful: "A pluralistic society is one in which there is wide decentralization and diversity of power concentration."[17]

The key terms in this definition are *decentralization* and *diversity*. In other words, power is decentralized—dispersed among many groups and people. Power is not held in the hands of any single institution (e.g., business, government, labor, military) or a small number of groups. Pluralistic societies are found all over the world now, and some of the virtues of a pluralistic society are that they prevent power from being concentrated in the hands of a few, freedom of expression and action are maximized, allegiance of individuals to groups is dispersed, and a built-in set of checks and balances are provided.[18]

A weakness of a pluralistic system, however, is that it creates an environment in which diverse institutions pursue their own self-interests with the result that there is no unified direction to bring together individual pursuits. Another weakness is that groups and institutions proliferate to the extent that their goals start to overlap, thus causing confusion as to which organizations best serve which functions. Pluralism forces conflict, or differences in opinions, onto center stage because of its emphasis on autonomous groups, each pursuing its own objectives. In light of these concerns, a pluralistic system does not appear to be very efficient though it does provide a greater balance of power among groups in society.

1.3a Multiple Publics, Systems, and Stakeholders

Knowing that society is composed of so many different semiautonomous and autonomous groups might cause one to question whether we can realistically speak of society in a definitive sense that has a generally agreed-on meaning. Nevertheless, we do speak in such terms, knowing that, unless we specify a particular societal subgroup or subsystem, we are referring to the total collectivity of all those persons, groups, and institutions that constitute society. Thus, references to business and society relationships may refer either to particular segments or *subgroups* of society (consumers, women, minorities, environmentalists, millennials, senior citizens) or to business and some *system* in our society (politics, law, custom, religion, economics). These groups of people or systems also may be referred to in an *institutional* form (business and the courts, business and labor unions, business and the church, business and the Federal Trade Commission, and so on).

Figure 1-1 depicts in graphic form the points of interface between business and some of the publics, systems, or stakeholders with which business interacts. Stakeholders are those groups or individuals with whom an organization interacts or has interdependencies. The stakeholder concept will be developed further in Chapter 3.

If sheer numbers of relationships and interactions are an indicator of complexity, it is easily seen that business's current relationships with different segments of society constitute a truly complex macroenvironment. Today, managers must deal with these interfaces on a daily basis, and the study of business and/in society is designed to improve that understanding.

1.3b A Special-Interest Society

A pluralistic society often transforms into a **special-interest society**. As pluralism expands, a society develops that is characterized by tens of thousands of special-interest groups, each pursuing its own specific agenda. In many parts of the world, these groups form into nonprofit organizations

Figure 1-1 Business and Selected Stakeholder Relationships

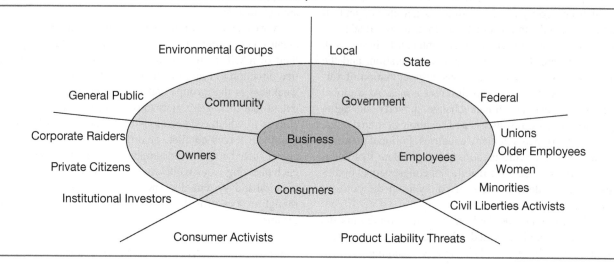

and are frequently called **nongovernmental organizations (NGOs)**. These are citizens' groups that may be organized on a local, national, or international level. Today, many NGOs are long-lived, robust, and ever active watchdogs and actors in the business and society relationship.[19] One newspaper headline noted that "there is a group for every cause." Special-interest groups not only have grown in number at an accelerated pace, but they also have become increasingly activist, intense, and focused on single issues. Such groups are strongly committed to their causes and strive to bring pressure to bear on businesses to meet their needs and on governments to accommodate their agendas.

A major consequence of interest group specialization is that each of these groups has been able to attract a significant following dedicated to the group's specific goals. Increased memberships have meant increased revenues and a sharper focus as each of these groups has more aggressively sought its specific, narrow purposes. The likelihood of these groups working at cross-purposes has made life immensely more complex for the major institutions, such as business and government. But this is how a pluralistic society tends to evolve.

1.4 Business Criticism and Corporate Response

It is inevitable in a pluralistic, special-interest society that the major institutions that make up that society, such as business and government, will become the targets of considerable analysis and criticism. It is important to understand how the process of business criticism has shaped the emergence of the business and society relationship today. Were it not for the fact that individuals and groups have been critical of business and have such high expectations and demands, there would be no articles, books, or courses on this subject,

and fewer improvements would occur in the business and society relationship over time.

Figure 1-2 illustrates how certain factors or social forces that have arisen in the social environment have created an atmosphere in which business criticism has flourished. Though a fair degree of resistance to change has been apparent on business's part, the more positive responses on the part of businesses have been (1) an increased awareness and concern for the social environment in which it operates and (2) a continual changing relationship between business and society. Each of these factors merits closer attention.

1.4a Factors in the Social Environment

Over the decades, many factors in the social environment have created a climate in which criticism of business has taken place and flourished. Some of these factors arise independent of one another, but some are interrelated; that is, they occur and grow hand in hand, often feeding off of one another. Some of the major factors merit discussion.

Affluence and Education. Two factors that have advanced side by side in developed economies are affluence and education. As a society becomes more prosperous and better educated, higher expectations of its major institutions, such as business, naturally follow. These factors now are appearing in developing countries as well.

Affluence refers to the level of wealth, disposable income, and standard of living of the society. Measures of the U.S. standard of living, for example, indicate that it has been rising for decades but leveling off during the recent decade. This same pattern has occurred in many of the developed countries of the world. In the past several years, questions have been raised as to whether successive generations will be better off or not. In spite of recent events, overall affluence remains high, though some think this is changing. This trend toward affluence is found in many of the world's

Figure 1-2 Social Environment Factors, Business Criticisms, and Corporate Responses

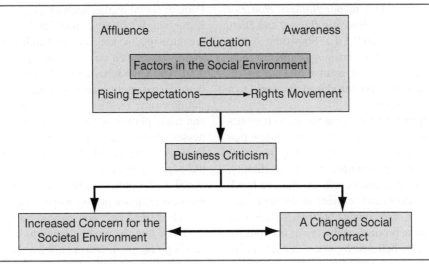

developed countries and also is occurring in emerging economies as global capitalism has spread. Recent worldwide economic data raises valid questions about this continuing affluence, however.[20]

Alongside a relatively high standard of living has been a growth in the average formal **education** of the populace. The U.S. Census Bureau's most recent data report that the number of American adults who were high school graduates has grown to 88 percent, and the numbers who were college graduates increased to 32 percent.[21] At a global level, the number of university graduates is expected to double over this decade, reaching 300 million by 2030.[22] As citizens continue to gain more formal education, these percentages will increase and their expectations of life generally rise. The combination of relative affluence and rising education has formed the underpinning for societies in which criticisms of major institutions, such as business, naturally arise. Moderating factors such as the pandemic and mounting educational costs resulting in huge student debt are also at work. It might also be added that when income and educational levels plateau or decline, business is often singled out as a major culprit. There is significant uncertainty today as to whether past trends will continue.

Awareness through Various Media. Closely related to formal education is the widespread and growing level of public awareness in societies today. Although newspapers and magazines are read by a declining fraction of the population, more powerful media—television, movies, the Internet, and social media—are accessed by virtually entire societies. Through television, the citizenry gets a profusion of information that contributes to a climate of business criticism. For decades, movies have bashed both the capitalist system and businesses. In addition, the Internet and smartphone explosion have brought elevated levels of awareness around the world. Through texts, tweets, e-mails, blogs, and other social media, the average citizen is extraordinarily aware of what is going on in the world on a real-time basis.

24/7 Television Programming There are at least three ways in which information that leads to criticisms of business appear on television. First, there are news shows, such as the ubiquitous 24-hour cable news channels, the evening news on the major networks, and investigative news programs. It is debatable whether or not the major news programs are treating business fairly, but in one major study conducted by Corporate Reputation Watch, senior executives identified media criticism, along with unethical behavior, as the biggest threats to a company's reputation.[23] A serious contender to criticism by TV would be social media activity today.[24]

Business has to deal not only with the scrutiny of 24/7 news coverage but also with myriad investigative news programs, such as *60 Minutes, 20/20, Dateline NBC, American Greed*, and PBS's *Frontline*, that often present exposés of corporate wrongdoings or questionable practices. These shows are enormously popular and influential, and many companies squirm when reporters show up on their premises complete with camera crews.

A second way in which criticisms of business appear on TV is through prime-time programs. More often than not, the businessperson has been portrayed across the nation's television screens as smirking, scheming, cheating, and conniving "bad guys." *The Economist* magazine summed it up nicely in its article in which it declared that "businessmen are always the villains."[25] Even the enormously popular Don Draper on the successful TV series *Mad Men* didn't leave much of a positive reputation behind when he went off the air after eight seasons. One writer called the deeply cynical Draper a "moral vandal" as he let down, abandoned, or lied to every person who had ever loved him and spent his professional advertising life reducing every emotion to a slogan and every desire into slick copy.[26]

A few other TV shows where this hostile portrayal of businesspeople has been evident include *Billions*, *House of Lies*, *Better Call Saul*, *Empire*, *Horrible Bosses*, and *Dirty Money*. Continuing on into 2021, the Showtime drama *Billions* has taken questionable businesspeople to new heights by featuring the unethical executive of a successful hedge fund, Bobby Axelrod, who introduced the world to a ruthlessness that is frightening.[27]

A third way in which television contributes to business criticism is through its own commercials. To the extent that business does not accurately and fairly portray its products and services on TV, it undermines its own credibility. Commercials are a double-edged sword. On the one hand, they may sell more products and services in the short run. On the other hand, they could damage business's long-term credibility if they promote products and services deceptively and dishonestly. It is also believed by many that TV today promotes excessive commercialism as well as sedentary lifestyles.

In sum, news coverage, prime-time programming, and commercials are three ways in which a tense, antibusiness environment is fostered by this "awareness" factor made available through the power and pervasiveness of television.

Movies Movies also are a significant source of business criticisms. Hollywood seems to perceive corporations as powerful, profit-seeking enterprises that have no redeeming values. In these movies, corporate life is depicted as amoral at best and often deadly. The iconic movie *Wall Street* and its sequel—*Wall Street: Money Never Sleeps*—with Michael Douglas again playing the malevolent Gordon Gekko, personifies this trend. Gekko is released from 14 years in prison just in time to witness the financial system's collapse and to revisit his old ways.

Hollywood writers seem to love advancing the "greed is good" portrayal of business, and they go out of their way to perpetuate this image of the corporate community.[28] The release of *The Social Network* did not focus on the positive aspects of Facebook but portrayed its cofounder Mark Zuckerberg as a conniving, antisocial individual who had to make a few enemies to succeed. The movie *Margin Call* cast its characters as flawed and cynical as they sought to save their financial institution from imminent collapse.[29] *Side Effects* portrayed a hotshot trader on Wall Street who's just done time for insider trading. The movie appears to be a modest film about the victims of a greedy pharmaceutical industry, but it turns into a murder mystery set in the world of white-collar crime.[30] And Leonardo DiCaprio's scams in *The Wolf of Wall Street* are especially indicative of the dark side of businesspeople.

Social Media Mentioned last, but perhaps most relevant today, social media now is able to instantaneously bring information, awareness, and criticism to the public's attention. Social media has now made it possible for consumers and employees to communicate with hundreds of thousands of others about companies' products, services, or policies. Popular social media, such as Twitter, Facebook, YouTube, Instagram, WhatsApp, Snapchat, Tik Tok, and many others, are growing by numbers and influence every day. Social media have taken on a new momentum in the digital age. And, while many businesses have been taking advantage of these for promotion purposes, they also have had a potential downside for businesses as customers now have quick and ready platforms for complaining and pointing out businesses' shortcomings, including calling for instant boycotts. Businesses are quickly learning that social media is a double-edged sword and that they are ill prepared to deal with social media criticism. With social media, a new world of business criticism has been opened up, and large businesses as well as small ones now have to be prepared to deal with it.

To be fair, the media are not to blame for most of business's problems. If it were not for the fact that the conduct and practices of some businesses and businesspeople are deeply questionable, the media would not be able to create such an environment. Social media makes the public more aware of questionable practices and should be seen as only one influential factor that contributes to the environment in which business continues to find itself criticized.

Rising Expectations. In addition to affluence, formal education, and awareness through television, movies, social media, and the Internet, other societal trends have fostered a climate in which business criticism has flourished. When these factors work together in concert, one emerging result has been **rising expectations** that are held by many in spite of economic challenges. This is a belief or an outlook that each succeeding generation ought to have a standard of living higher than that of its predecessor. In the United States, another way of phrasing this is whether or not the individual is living the "American dream." Other countries likely have indicators such as this as well. It seems to be a worldwide phenomenon in the developed economies. In one study, 40 percent of American adults *felt* that they were "living the American dream," and this same study found sizable majorities reporting owning their own home, receiving a good education, finding a good job, and giving their children better lives than they themselves had—all characteristics of the "American dream."[31] It is likely, however, that in the face of increasing income inequality, there is some indication that rising expectations have plateaued or declined for some. In fact, *Fast Company* magazine reports that the "new" American dream is just as unattainable as the old one. Their writer argues that "the experience economy is mixing with gig work, an incomprehensible financial system, and unpayable college debt, creating a new set of impossible-to-achieve goals for a new generation."[32]

A mitigating factor for some young people recently is that many of them have had to move back in with their parents because they could not find jobs, they wanted to pay off student loans, or some just wanted to save money so that they could live better once they got out on their own. A study of Millennials found that they still embrace high hopes and expectations for a better life than their predecessors, but that they might define success a little differently than in the past and it may take longer to achieve it.[33] Gen-Z is also feeling good about what their life after COVID-19 is likely to be and they remain optimistic.[34] It is also worth noting that in spite of the tougher economic times, society is still characterized as an "impulse society" wherein many continue to practice instant gratification.[35]

If rising expectations continue as they have in the past, citizens' hopes for major institutions, such as business, should be greater too. Building on this line of thinking, it could be argued that business criticisms continue today because society's rising expectations of business's social performance have outpaced business's ability to meet these growing expectations. To the extent that this has occurred over the past and continues today, business will find itself with a larger social problem.[36] To be balanced, some have observed that we may have entered an era of diminishing economic expectations,[37] but whether this turns out to apply to business's social performance remains doubtful.

One helpful way to think about a **social problem** is that it is a gap between society's expectations of social conditions and the current social realities.[38] From the viewpoint of a business firm, the social problem it faces is experienced as the gap grows between society's *expectations* of the firm's social performance and its *actual* social performance. Rising expectations typically outpace the responsiveness of institutions such as business, thus creating a constant predicament in that it is subject to never-ending criticism for not meeting the public's expectations of it. Figure 1-3 illustrates this larger "social problem" that business faces today. It is depicted by the growing gap between society's expectations of business and business's actual social performance.

Although the general trend of rising expectations may continue, it moderates at times when the economy is not as robust, or in crisis situations, as in a pandemic. One noteworthy outgrowth of the tendency toward rising expectations has been the emergence of what some have called an **entitlement mentality** on the part of some individuals and groups in society. This is the general belief that individuals are owed something (e.g., a job, an education, a living wage, or health care) just because they are a member of society. This impacts businesses because businesses are a central provider for many in society such as consumers, employees, and communities, and citizens blame businesses when expectations are not achieved. To the extent this occurs, much of the entitlement mentality falls on government, but governments have a way of transferring some of these expectations to businesses.

Rights Movement. The pattern of rising expectations and the factors discussed so far have contributed to what has been termed the global **rights movement** that has been evident in societies for many decades now. "Rights" thinking received significant impetus by the adoption of The Universal Declaration of Human Rights by the United Nations in 1948. In the United States, the U.S. Supreme Court has heard increasing numbers of cases aimed at establishing, for some groups, various legal rights that perhaps never occurred to the founders of the nation.[39]

Business, as one of society's prominent institutions, has been affected with an ever-expanding array of expectations as to how people want to be treated, not only as employees but also as shareholders, consumers, environmentally conscious citizens, and members of the community. The rights movement is interrelated with the special-interest society discussed earlier.

In summary, affluence and education, awareness through media, rising expectations, and the rights movements have formed a backdrop against which criticism of business has developed and often flourished. This helps explain why we

Figure 1-3 Society's Expectations versus Business's Actual Social Performance

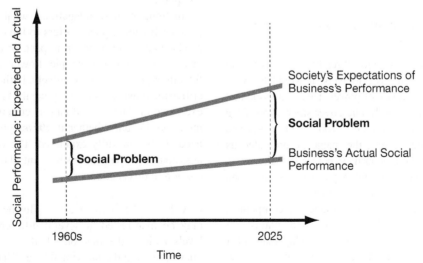

Ethics In Practice Case

Am I Working for My Cup or the House?

In the service industry, employees often are paid minimally by the companies they work for, and their pay rate is determined by the tips received from customers. Consider the case of bartenders. As a bartender, a person is exposed to having to deal with all sorts of peoples' needs as well as co-workers' competition, and standard operating procedures set forth by management. Every time a drink is poured, a decision must be made whether to follow company standards or give away extra alcohol in order to receive a larger tip.

When first being promoted to bartender at an established golf resort, I witnessed firsthand the different factors that can affect one's "pour." A pour can be defined as how much liquor is added to a customer's drink. The three factors that affect one's pour are comparisons to other employees' pours, the requests of customers for extra pours with the promise of a larger tip, and what the company designates as a pour.

When working as a team or having repeat customers, bartenders are compared based on their pour. If one bartender uses two pours and another uses one pour (the latter is the standard for the company), the rule-following bartender is not viewed as favorably as the one using the larger pour. This is clearly reflected in tips from customers. Similarly, the customer might say, "Put a little extra in there and I'll take care of you." The employees are put on the spot to choose between the company and themselves.

The bartender with the heavier pour or who gives away drinks for free may receive more money in the tip cup, but the company suffers from lost revenues. If a bartender makes an average of 100 drinks a night and uses two pours instead of one for each drink, that bartender is giving away 100 drinks worth of alcohol each night, which reduces nightly revenues and has a huge effect on yearly liquor revenues.

In this highly competitive and profitable industry, over pouring is a practice that can cripple a business. As the newest bartender, one wants to fit in with the other bartenders and earn as much money as possible though it costs the company or "house" profits. Which is more important, filling your own tip cup or maximizing the house's profits that do not directly benefit the bartender?

1. Is it ethical to over pour customers' drinks in order to develop better customer relations to earn more tips at the expense of company revenues? Are the bartenders using the "entitlement mentality" here to justify their self-serving actions? Do bartenders have a "right" to take care of their own cups?
2. If the customer wants or expects over pouring, should the companies allow over pouring to satisfy the customers' wants and desires?
3. Is it ethical to witness and not report over pouring on the part of fellow bartenders who have been there longer? Should I inform management what is happening?

Contributed by Matthew DePasquale

---

have a societal environment that is conducive to criticisms of business. Though the U.S. and world economies have been through a battering COVID-19 slump, some of these same general trends are bound to be evidenced but may be moderated if economies improve.

In the next two subsections, some of the general criticisms of business and some of the general responses to such criticisms are identified and discussed.

1.4b A General Criticism of Business: Use and Abuse of Power

If one were to identify a common thread that seems to run through many of the business criticisms, it would be business's use and perceived abuse of power. This is an issue that has been around for decades. In one cover story, *Bloomberg BusinessWeek* posed the question: "Too Much Corporate Power?" In this featured article, the magazine presented its surveys of the public regarding business power. In their survey, nearly two-thirds of Americans said they thought business had too much power over various aspects of their lives.[40]

In the book *Power, Inc.*, the case is made that companies, not kings, now rule the world. The author maintains that global corporations wield greater power today than most nation-states.[41] In Michael Moore's provocative movie, *Capitalism: A Love Story*, the filmmaker continued his assault on business power by laying the blame for the last worldwide recession on both big business and government. Whether at the general level or the level of the firm, questions about business's use or abuse of power continue to be raised. A major *Bloomberg BusinessWeek* article asserted that "fairly or not, Big Business is taking heat for the stagnation of living standards and the widening gap between rich and poor."[42]

In light of these allegations, what exactly is **business power**? Business power refers to the capacity or ability to produce an effect, have an impact, or to bring influence to bear on a situation or people. Power may be perceived or felt either positively or negatively. In the context of business criticism, however, power typically is perceived as being excessive or "abused." Business certainly does have enormous power, but whether it *abuses* power is an issue that needs to be carefully examined. The contention that business abuses power remains the central theme behind the discussion in this section.

Levels of Business Power. Business power exists and may be manifested at several different levels. Four such levels include the macrolevel, the intermediate level, the microlevel, and the individual level.[43] The *macrolevel* refers to the entire corporate system—"Corporate America," Big Business—the totality of business organizations. Power at this level emanates from the sheer size, resources, and dominance of the corporate system over society and our lives. This is a refrain that just does not seem to go away.

The *intermediate level* of business power refers to groups of corporations acting in concert in an effort to produce a desired effect—to set prices, control markets, dominate purchasers, promote an issue, or pass or defeat legislation. Prime examples include Organization of the Petroleum Exporting Countries (OPEC) (gas prices), airlines, cable TV companies, soft drink companies, chicken processors, banks, pharmaceutical companies, and defense contractors pursuing the interests they have in common. Recently, the firms composing Big Tech have come under closer scrutiny because of the power they wield.[44] The combined effect of companies acting in concert is substantial.

The *microlevel* of business power is the level of the individual firm. This might refer to the exertion

of power or influence by any major corporation—for example, Facebook, Google, Walmart, Amazon, Apple, Microsoft, or Nike. The final level at which business power may be manifested is the *individual level*. This refers to the individual corporate leader exerting power—for example, Mark Zuckerberg (Facebook), Guillaume Faury (Airbus), Joseph Papa (Valeant Pharmaceuticals–Canada) Daniel Amos (Aflac), Mary Barra (GM), Tim Cook (Apple), Karen Lynch (CVS; Aetna), Elon Musk (Tesla Motors), Herbert Diess (Volkswagen), Christian Sewing (Deutsche Bank), or Warren Buffett (Berkshire Hathaway).

The key point here is that as one analyzes corporate power, one should think in terms of the different levels at which that power is manifested or felt. When this is done, it is not easy to generalize whether corporate power is excessive or has been abused. The results are often mixed. Specific levels of power need to be delineated and examined before conclusions can be reached.

Ethics In Practice Case

Does Business Have Too Much Power?

The "business system," that totality of all businesses in a nation or the world, is said to be one of the most powerful institutions known to humankind. The other major candidates for this honor are typically government and the military. One of the most often repeated accusations about large businesses is that they have too much power. It is also claimed that they abuse this power.

In 2020, a Big Tech congressional hearing was held featuring bipartisan concurrence. Members of the U.S. House Antitrust Committee were investigating the question of whether Apple, Amazon, Facebook, and Google have too much power. Among the complaints were that they stifle competition, dominate online commerce and communications, engage in practices that have harmful effects, discourage entrepreneurship, destroy jobs, and degrade quality. There seemed to be agreement that these companies had too much power, but no one had suggestions, other than tightening antitrust laws, as to what should be done to curb their power. It is expected that these large companies and others will be carefully scrutinized continually, but this does not necessarily suggest action will be taken.

So, what is business power? Business power is the ability to produce an effect—to get things done and to bring about its desired state of affairs. It's about business getting its way. One way of thinking about business power is to frame it in terms that analysts have claimed are relevant in understanding power. French and Raven have argued that business has five types of power: coercive power, legitimate power, reward power, referent power, and expert power. Each of these may be thought of from the perspective of the executives in a large business and the business itself.

Coercive power occurs when a manager in authority forces someone to do something—usually with some

threat of punishment. Usually, fear is at work. Legitimate power exists when a person in the chain of command has a title or position that implies they have the authority to take some action. Reward power is manifested when a boss uses rewards to get things done. The rewards may not only be monetary, such as pay increases and promotions, but may also be psychological, such as praise. The flip side of reward is punishment, and it is part of the reward power as well. Referent power is gained by leaders due to others admiring them as a role model. Finally, Expert power arises when someone becomes highly regarded due to their superior training, expertise, and/or experience.

1. Which type of power do businesses display the most? Is Big Tech among the most powerful? Give examples.
2. As an employee, with which type of power would you be most concerned? Why?
3. As a consumer, with which type of power would you be most troubled? Why?
4. Have you been the "victim" of business power? Explain.
5. Is business power too great? Does business abuse its power?

Sources: John French and Bertram Raven, "Bases of Social Power." *Studies in Social Power,* edited by Dorwin Cartwright (University of Michigan, Ann Arbor, 1959); Jeffrey Pfeffer, *Power—Why Some People Have It—and Others Don't* (Harper Business, 2010); Quickbase, "The Five Types of Power in Leadership," September 22, 2020, https://www.quickbase.com /blog/the-5-types-of-power-in-leadership, accessed January 26, 2021; Alex Sherman, CNBC, "U.S. Lawmakers Agree Big Tech Has Too Much Power, but What to Do about It Remains a Mystery," July 30, 2020, https://www.cnbc.com/2020/07/30/us -lawmakers-agree-big-tech-has-too-much-power-remedies-unclear.html, accessed February 6, 2021.

Spheres of Business Power. In addition to levels of power, there are also many different spheres or arenas in which business power may be manifested. *Economic power* and *political power* are two spheres that are dominant, but business has other, more subtle forms of power as well. These other spheres include *social and cultural power, power over the individual, technological power,* and *environmental power.*[45]

Is the power of business excessive? Does business abuse its power? Apparently, many people think so. To provide sensible and fair answers to these questions, however, one must carefully specify which level of power is being referred to and in which sphere the power is being exercised. When this is done, it is not simple to arrive at answers that are generalizable. Furthermore, the nature of power is such that it is sometimes wielded unintentionally. Sometimes the use of power is *consequential;* that is, it is not wielded intentionally, but it nevertheless exerts its influence even though no attempt is made to exercise it.[46] Whether business has too much power and abuses its power is a question we will continue to examine and certainly one that the business system and companies need to keep in the forefront of their thinking.

1.4c Balancing Power with Responsibility

Whether or not business abuses its power or allows its use of power to become excessive is a central issue that cuts through many of the topics examined in this book. But power should not be viewed in isolation from responsibility, and this power–responsibility relationship is the foundation for appeals for corporate social responsibility (CSR) and business ethics that are at the heart of business and society discussions.

Iron Law of Responsibility. The **Iron Law of Responsibility** is a concept that addresses this: "In the long run, those who do not use power in a manner which society considers responsible will tend to lose it."[47] Stated another way, whenever power and responsibility become substantially out of balance, forces will be generated to bring them into closer balance.

When power gets out of balance with responsibility, a variety of forces may come to bear on business to be more responsible and more responsive to the criticisms being made against it. Some of these more obvious forces include governmental actions such as increased regulations, or consumer actions such as boycotts or refusing to buy. The investigative news media may become interested in what is going on, and a whole host of special-interest groups may bring pressure to bear. Many citizens think that this power imbalance is what has generated resentment against business firms.

The tobacco industry is an excellent example of an industry that has felt the brunt of efforts to address allegations of abuse of power. After years of business abuse, the Food and Drug Administration (FDA) was given additional authority to address the power imbalance between the industry and customers.

Do consumers have redress when the power–responsibility situation is out of balance? There are a number of different regulatory authorities that consumers may turn to if they believe they have been mistreated. Some of these in the United States include the Federal Trade Commission (FTC), Consumer Financial Protection Bureau (CFPB), Consumer Product Safety Commission (CPSC), and the Food and Drug Administration (FDA). In addition, there are many international agencies, organizations, and resources designed to protect consumers.[48] Many such governmental regulations may have been circumvented by business if it had done a better job of balancing its power with responsibility with consumers, employees, and other stakeholders. This is what CSR is all about, and this topic will be developed further in Chapter 2.

1.4d Business's Response: A Changing Social Contract

Growing out of criticisms of business and unease regarding the power–responsibility imbalance has been an increased concern on the part of business for the stakeholder environment and the evolution of a new business model. The dramatic announcement in 2019 by the Business Roundtable, America's leading CEOs, that the purpose of business is to serve all stakeholders, not just stockholders, represents the most noticeable business response to date regarding a changed social contract.[49] As firms have sensed that the social environment, social values, and the expectations of business have been changing, they have realized that they must adapt as well. Many positive changes have been made by businesses, but as the discussion of the characteristics of a "social problem" indicated, business seldom catches up with stakeholder expectations. As we will see in Chapter 2 and later, businesses' attempts to be socially responsible or sustainable reflect how this concern is increasingly being expressed.

Many major businesses have been expressing their social concern and are seeking to better balance their power with responsibility. *Fortune* magazine recently published a special issue titled "Change the World" in which it featured companies that were striving to tackle society's unmet needs. Its 2020 list emphasized an important corollary—that no business succeeds alone; collaboration among companies, even among rivals, represents a common thread. *Fortune* has gone on to say that as countries face unprecedented collective challenges—a global pandemic, climate change, income inequality—cooperation has become an important power that business can now bring to the table to reflect its sense of responsibility.[50]

Social Contract. An important way of thinking about the business–society relationship is through the concept of a **social contract**. The social contract is a set of reciprocal understandings and expectations that characterize the relationship between major institutions—in our case, business and society. It is also perceived as the understood and tacit agreements that guide behavior in relationships among members of a community or group.[51] The social contract

Figure 1-4 Elements in the Social Contract between Business and Society

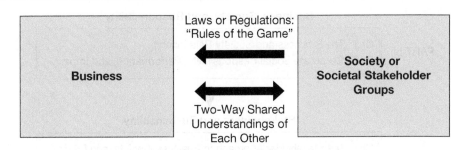

between business and society has been changing, and these changes have been a direct outgrowth of the increased importance of the social environment to many stakeholders. The social contract has been changing to reflect society's expanded expectations of business, especially in the social, ethical, and sustainability realms. Businesses have responded to these changing expectations, though seldom as quickly or as much as the public would like.

The social contract between business and society, as illustrated in Figure 1-4, is articulated or expressed primarily in two main ways:

1. *Laws and regulations* that society has established as the framework within which businesses must operate in their relationships with stakeholders, and
2. *Shared understandings* that evolve over time as to each group's expectations of the other. These are voluntary understandings for mutual benefit.

Laws and regulations spell out the "rules of the game" for business for which they are held accountable. These constitute a formal part of the social contract. Shared understandings, on the other hand, are more subtle and create room for misunderstandings. These two-way shared understandings reflect mutual expectations regarding each other's roles, responsibilities, and ethics. These often-unspoken elements of the social contract represent what might be called the normative perspective on the relationship (i.e., what "ought" to be done by each party to the social contract).[52] The mounting importance of social responsibility, sustainability, and business ethics is reflected here.

If these two-way shared understandings were spelled out, a company might adopt the following hypothetical principles as part of its social contract with consumers:

- We believe our company has a right to innovation, entrepreneurship, and profit-making, whereas our consumers have a right to a healthy society and planet for living.
- We believe that the interests of our company and our customers are best served through a sustainable practice of capitalism—economically, morally, environmentally, and socially.
- We believe that our customers and our company owe each other an equal duty of transparent, authentic, and accountable communication.

- We believe that our company and our customers are duty-bound to serve as custodians of global well-being for this and all future generations.[53]

Unfortunately, a shared understanding of an aspect of the social contract is seldom expressed in clear, written format such as this. Since there are so many of the shared understandings existing in the world of perceptions and expectations, the opportunities for disagreements are always with us.

A *BusinessWeek* editorial commented on the importance of business having a new social contract by asserting, "Listen up, Corporate America. The American people are having a most serious discussion about your role in their lives." The editorial was referring to the criticisms coming out about the abuse of corporate power.[54] Such a statement suggests that changes in the social contract between business and society will be an ongoing process, and in Chapter 2 these changes will be explored further.

1.5 Focus of the Book

Overall, this book takes a **managerial approach** to the business and society relationship. This managerial approach emphasizes three main themes that are of vital importance to managers, organizations, and society today: business ethics, sustainability, and stakeholder management. By viewing issues of social and ethical concern and sustainability from a managerial frame of reference, managers have been able to convert seemingly unmanageable issues into ones that can be dealt with in a balanced and impartial fashion. At the same time, managers have had to integrate traditional economic and financial considerations with ethical and social considerations.

Business ethics is a theme that is integral to the book, and evidences of this may be found in every chapter. Ethical questions inevitably and continuously come into play in management decision making. In the workplace, ethics essentially refers to issues of fairness and justice, and business ethics focuses on ethical issues that arise in the commercial realm. Ethical factors appear throughout our discussion because questions of fairness and justice, no matter how slippery they are to deal with, permeate business's activities as it attempts to interact successfully with major stakeholder

Figure 1-5 Organization and Flow of the Book

Business, Society, and Responsibility

PART I
| Ch1   The Business and Society Relationship |
| Ch2   Corporate Social Responsibility, Performance, and Impact |

Stakeholders and Sustainability

PART II
| Ch3   The Stakeholder Approach to Business, Society, and Ethics |
| Ch4   Sustainability and the Natural Environment |

Business Ethics and Leadership

PART III
| Ch5   Business Ethics Essentials |
| Ch6   Managerial and Organizational Ethics |
| Ch7   Ethical Issues in the Global Arena |
| Ch8   Business Ethics and Technology: The Digital Enterprise |

Corporate Governance and Strategic Management Issues

PART IV
| Ch9   Corporate Governance: Foundational Issues |
| Ch10   Strategy, Risk, Issues, and Crisis Management |

Internal Stakeholder Issues

PART V
| Ch11   Employee Stakeholders and Workplace Issues |
| Ch12   Employees: Privacy, Safety, and Wellness |
| Ch13   Employment Discrimination, Diversity, and Inclusion |

External Stakeholder Issues

PART VI
| Ch14   Consumer Stakeholders: Information Issues |
| Ch15   Consumer Stakeholders: Products and Services |
| Ch16   Community Stakeholders and Corporate Philanthropy |

Business and Government Relations

PART VII
| Ch17   Business, Government, and Regulation |
| Ch18   Business's Influence on Government and Public Policy |

CASES

Subject Index

Name Index

groups. In light of the ongoing ethical scandals in recent years, the ethics theme resonates as one of the most urgent aspects of business and society relationships. Chapters 5–8 deal with business ethics, specifically.

Sustainability is another major theme. The concept of sustainability has become one of businesses' most pressing mandates. Discussions of sustainability began with respect to the natural environment. As time has passed, however, it has become evident that it is a broader concept that applies not only to the natural environment but to the entirety of businesses' operations and processes as well, especially business's global role and development. At a basic level, sustainability is about business's ability to survive and thrive over the long term. The concept of sustainability is derived from the notion of **sustainable development**, which is a pattern of resource use that aims to meet current human needs while preserving the environment so that these needs can be met not only in the present but also for future generations. Today, sustainability is understood to embrace environmental, economic, and social criteria, and this is the general sense in which it will be used in this book.[55] Chapter 4 develops the sustainability theme in more detail, and Spotlights on Sustainability may be found in each chapter of the book.

Stakeholder management is the third major theme characterizing this book. As mentioned throughout this chapter, **stakeholders** are individuals or groups with which business interacts who have a "stake," or vested interest, in the firm. Stakeholders are integral constituents in the business and society relationship. Two broad groups of stakeholders are considered in this book—external and internal. Though all chapters touch on the stakeholder management theme, Chapter 3 develops the concept in detail. Several chapters of the book focus on *internal stakeholders* (Chapters 11–13) and *external stakeholders* (Chapters 14–16). Other stakeholder groups and issues occur throughout the other chapters as well.

1.6 Structure of the Book

The structure and flow of the parts and chapters of this book are outlined in Figure 1-5.

Depending on the emphasis desired in the course, the Parts of the book may be covered in a different sequence or a major Part could be omitted if desired. Taken as a whole, this book strives to take the reader through a building-block progression of foundational and then more developed concepts and ideas that are vital to the business and society relationship and to explore the nature of social and ethical issues and stakeholder groups with which management must interact. It considers the external and internal stakeholder groups in considerable depth.

Summary

The business and society relationship has faced severe testing over the past decades. The COVID-19 pandemic superimposed itself on all business and society relationships beginning in 2020, and the challenges have been immense and continuing. In spite of this, the pluralistic system is still at work, presenting business firms with a variety of trials they must deal with regarding a multitude of stakeholders and an increasingly special-interest society represented by nonprofit organizations and nongovernmental organizations (NGOs).

A major force that shapes the public's view of business is the criticisms that businesses receive from a variety of sources. Factors in the social environment that have contributed to an atmosphere in which business criticism thrives include affluence, education, public awareness developed through the media, rising expectations, an entitlement mentality, and the rights movement. The global economic situation may result in changes in business criticism and its antecedents. In addition, actual questionable practices on the part of business have made it a natural target. The recent ethics scandals involving well-known companies such as Wells Fargo, Boeing, and Theranos have kept business ethics on the front page. Not all firms are guilty, but questionable practices attract negative attention to the entire business system. One result is that the trust and legitimacy of the business system is called into question and the reputational capital of businesses decline.

A common criticism of business is that it has too much power and that it abuses its power. Power operates on four different levels: the level of the entire business system, by groups of companies acting in concert, by the individual firm, and by the individual corporate executive. Business power may be manifested in several different spheres—economic, political, technological, environmental, social, and individual. It is difficult to conclude whether business is actually abusing its power, but it is clear that business has enormous power and that it must exercise it carefully. Power evokes responsibility, and this is the central reason that appeals for corporate responsibility have continued. The Iron Law of Responsibility highlights the need for greater balance in business power and its responsible use. These concerns have led to a changing social environment for business and a changed social contract. The changing terms of the social contract will become evident throughout the book's chapters.

Key Terms

affluence, p. 6
business, p. 4
business ethics, p. 13
business power, p. 10
economic environment, p. 4
education, p. 7
entitlement mentality, p. 9
Iron Law of Responsibility, p. 12
macroenvironment, p. 4

managerial approach, p. 13
nongovernmental organizations
   (NGOs), p. 6
pluralism, p. 5
political environment, p. 5
rights movement, p. 9
rising expectations, p. 8
social contract, p. 12
social environment, p. 4

social problem, p. 9
society, p. 4
special-interest society, p. 5
stakeholder management, p. 15
stakeholders, p. 15
sustainability, p. 15
sustainable development, p. 15
technological environment, p. 5

Discussion Questions

1. In discussions of business and society, why is there a tendency to focus on large-sized rather than small- or medium-sized firms? Have the corporate ethics scandals that have tainted businesses affected small- and medium-sized firms? If so, in what ways have these firms been affected?

2. How will the COVID-19 pandemic alter business and society relationships? Identify and discuss some of the major effects and impacts.

3. Identify and explain the major factors in the social environment that create an atmosphere in which business criticism takes place and prospers. Provide

examples. How are the factors related to one another? Has the pattern of rising expectations run its course? Or is it still a reality among young people today?

4. Give an example of each of the four levels of power discussed in this chapter. Also, give an example of each of the spheres of business power. Is business power excessive?

5. Explain in your own words the Iron Law of Responsibility and the social contract. Give an example of a shared understanding between you as a consumer or an employee and a firm with which you do business or for which you work.

Endnotes

1. Paul Overberg, Jon Kamp, and Daniel Michaels, "COVID-19 Death Toll Is Even Worse Than It Looks," *The Wall Street Journal*, January 15, 2021, A1.

2. Covid-19 Alert, Death Toll, https://www.google.com /search?q=worldwide+deaths+from+covid&rlz =1C1GCEA_enUS751US751&oq=worldwide+deaths &aqs=chrome.0.0i20i263i433j69i57j0i20i263j0l7 .9709j0j15&sourceid=chrome&ie=UTF-8. Accessed February 26, 2021.

3. Nicholas Christakis, "The Long Shadow of the Pandemic: 2024 and Beyond," *The Wall Street Journal*, October 17-18, 2020, C1–C2.

4. Lynn Forester de Rothschild and Adam S. Posen, "How Capitalism Can Repair Its Bruised Image," *The Wall Street Journal*, January 2, 2013, A17.

5. D. A. Shaywitz, "Save the Planet with Capitalism," *The Wall Street Journal*, October 9, 2019, A15.

6. Nikki Haley, "This Is No Time to Go Wobbly on Capitalism," *The Wall Street Journal*, February 27, 2020, A17.

7. "Redesign Capitalism to Incorporate Social Value," *Time*, November 2 and 9, 2020, 5.

8. Barton Swaim, "The Uses and Abuses of Capitalism," *The Wall Street Journal*, February 27–28, 2021, C9.

9. Jamie Dimon, "How to Save Capitalism," *Time*, February 3, 2020, 62.

10. Charles Moore, "The Middle Class Squeeze," *The Wall Street Journal*, September 26–27, 2015, C1.

11. Emily Flitter, "The Price of Wells Fargo's Fake Account Scandal Grows by $3 Billion," *The New York Times*, February 1, 2020, https://www.nytimes.com/2020/02/21/business /wells-fargo-settlement.html. Accessed November 9, 2020.

12. U.S. Department of Justice, "Opioid Manufacturer Purdue Pharma Pleads Guilty to Fraud and Kickback Conspiracies," November 24, 2020, https://www.justice .gov/opa/pr/opioid-manufacturer-purdue-pharma-pleads -guilty-fraud-and-kickback-conspiracies. Accessed January 26, 2021.

13. Gallup, "Are Businesses Worldwide Suffering from a Trust Crisis?" February 6, 2019, https://www.gallup.com /workplace/246194/businesses-worldwide-suffering-trust -crisis.aspx. Accessed November 9, 2020.

14. Liam Fahey and V. K. Narayanan, *Macroenvironmental Analysis for Strategic Management* (St. Paul: West, 1986), 28–30.

15. Michael Porter and Jan Rivkin, "What Business Should Do to Restore U.S. Competitiveness," *Fortune*, October 29, 2012, 168–171.

16. Porter and Rivkin, 2012, Ibid.

17. Joseph W. McGuire, *Business and Society* (New York: McGraw-Hill, 1963), 130.

18. Keith Davis and Robert L. Blomstrom, *Business and Society: Environment and Responsibility*, 3rd ed. (New York: McGraw-Hill, 1975), 63

19. Bob Lurie, *BloombergBusiness*, "A New Social Contract for Green Business,". https://www.bloomberg.com/news/articles/2009-05-12/a-new-social-contract-for-green-business. Accessed November 11, 2020.

20. T. Wiedmann, M. Lenzen, L. Keyber, and J. Steinberger, "Scientist's Warning on Affluence," Nature Communications, June 19, 2020, https://www.nature.com/articles/s41467-020-16941-y. Accessed February 26, 2021.

21. United States Census Bureau, USA Quickfacts, https://www.census.gov/quickfacts/fact/table/US/EDU635218#EDU635218. Accessed November 9, 2020.

22. ICEF Monitor, "Number of Degree Holders Worldwide Will Reach 300 Million by 2030," July 17, 2019, https://monitor.icef.com/2019/07/oecd-number-of-degree-holders-worldwide-will-reach-300-million-by-2030/. Accessed February 26, 2021.

23. "Executives See Unethical Behavior, Media Criticisms as Threats," *Nashville Business Journal* (June 11, 2002).

24. I-Scoop, "Businesses Remain Unprepared for Social Media Criticism," https://www.i-scoop.eu/businesses-remain-unprepared-social-media-criticism/. Accessed February 26, 2021.

25. "Businessmen Are Always the Villains," *The Economist*, October 16, 2015.

26. Gina Berreca, "What Did Don Draper Really Leave Behind?" *Athens Banner-Herald*, May 22, 2015, A6.

27. "Billions," https://www.sho.com/billions. Accessed November 9, 2020.

28. Michael Medved, "Hollywood's Business-Bashing: Biting the Hand That Is You," *USA Today* (February 3, 2010), 9A.

29. Rachel Dodes, "Hollywood's Favorite Villain," *The Wall Street Journal*, October 14, 2011, D1.

30. Logan Hill, "Movie Math," *Bloomberg Businessweek*, February 11–17, 2013, 70.

31. Everett Rosenfeld, *USA Today*, July 5, 2014, http://www.usatoday.com/story/money/business/2014/07/05/american-dream-unrecognized/12047675/. Accessed October 26, 2015.

32. Jon Kolko, "The New American dream Is Just as Unattainable as the Old One," *Fast Company*, August 7, 2020, https://www.fastcompany.com/90476099/the-new-american-dream-is-just-as-unattainable-as-the-old-one. Accessed November 9, 2020.

33. Susan Page and Jenny Ung, "American Dream Survives among Millennials, Poll Finds," *USA Today*, March 16, 2016, 2A.

34. Mark Perna, "Why Is Gen-Z Feeling So Good about Life after COVID-19?" June 23, 2020, Why Is Gen-Z Feeling So Good About Life After COVID-19? (forbes.com). Accessed February 26, 2021.

35. Paul Roberts, *The Impulse Society: America in the Age of Instant Gratification* (New York: Bloomsbury USA, 2014).

36. Robert J. Samuelson, *The Good Life and Its Discontents: The American Dream in the Age of Entitlement, 1945–1995* (New York: Times Books, 1996).

37. "The Age of Diminished Expectations," *The Economist*, February 20, 2013. Accessed March 18, 2013.

38. Neil H. Jacoby, *Corporate Power and Social Responsibility* (New York: Macmillan, 1973), 186–188.

39. Charlotte Low, "Someone's Rights, Another's Wrongs," *Insight* (January 26, 1987), 8.

40. Aaron Bernstein, "Too Much Corporate Power?" *Business Week*, September 11, 2000, https://www.bloomberg.com/news/articles/2000-09-10/too-much-corporate-power. Accessed January 26, 2021.

41. David Rothkopf, *Power, Inc.: The Epic Rivalry between Big Business and Government—and the Reckoning that Lies Ahead* (New York: Farrar, Straus & Giroux, 2012).

42. Peter Coy, "Open Season on Big Business," *Bloomberg Businessweek*, February 25, 2016, 11.

43. Edwin M. Epstein, "Dimensions of Corporate Power: Part I," *California Management Review* (Winter 1973), 11.

44. Gallup.com, Megan Brenan, "Views of Big Tech Worsen, Public Wants More Regulation," February 18, 2021; "Views of Big Tech Worsen; Public Wants More Regulation." Accessed February 26, 2021.

45. Epstein, ibid.

46. Ibid.

47. Keith Davis and Robert L. Blomstrom, *Business and Its Environment* (New York: McGraw-Hill, 1966), 174–175.

48. Consumer World, "Consumer Agencies and Organizations," https://www.consumerworld.org/pages/agencies.htm. Accessed February 26, 2021.

49. Business Roundtable, "Business Roundtable Redefines the Purpose of the Corporation to Promote an Economy That Serves all Americans," August 19, 2019, Business Roundtable Redefines the Purpose of a Corporation to Promote "An Economy That Serves All Americans." Accessed February 26, 2021.

50. "Change the World," *Fortune*, October 2020, 81–116.

51. BusinessDictionary.com, "Social Contract," http://www.businessdictionary.com/definition/social-contract.html. Accessed March 28, 2016.

52. Thomas Donaldson and Thomas W. Dunfee, "Toward a Unified Conception of Business Ethics: Integrative Social Contracts Theory," *Academy of Management Review* (April 1994), 252–253.

53. Simon Mainwaring, "The Corporate Social Contract," *CR Corporate Responsibility Magazine*, http://www.thecro.com/topics/business-ethics/the-corporate-social-contract/. Accessed March 28, 2016.

54. "New Economy, New Social Contract," *BusinessWeek* (September 11, 2000), 182.

55. International Institute for Sustainable Development, "What Is Sustainable Development?" https://www.iisd.org/about-iisd/sustainable-development. Accessed November 11, 2020.

2

Corporate Social Responsibility, Performance, and Impact

Chapter Learning Outcomes

After studying this chapter, you should be able to:

1. Describe some early views of corporate social responsibility (CSR). Explain how CSR evolved and encompasses economic, legal, ethical, and philanthropic components. Explain the Pyramid of CSR. How is it a unified whole, dynamic, and sustainable? How does ethics permeate the pyramid? Will the pyramid vary globally?
2. Articulate the traditional arguments both against and for CSR. Explain how the business case for CSR has strengthened the concept's acceptance.
3. Describe how the concept of corporate social *responsiveness* differs from CSR.
4. Explain how corporate social *performance* (CSP) became more popular. Describe how it is different than CSR. What does corporate social *impact* address?

5. Describe how corporate citizenship is a valuable way of thinking about CSR. Explain its broad and narrow views.
6. Summarize the three perspectives on the relationship between corporate social performance (CSP) and corporate financial performance (CFP).
7. Define CSR Greenwashing and how it may lead to misleading reputational profiles of companies.
8. Describe and characterize the socially responsible investing movement. Differentiate between negative and positive screens that are used in investment decisions.

Corporate social responsibility (CSR) is a concept that has grown in importance over the past half century. One of the primary reasons for its popularity is because during this time, business has been undergoing the most intense scrutiny it has ever received from the public. Business has been charged with a variety of allegations—that it has little concern for the consumer, exploits employees, cares nothing about the deteriorating social order, has no concept of principled ethical decision making, and is indifferent to the problems of minorities and the environment. Issues about what responsibilities business has to society continue to be raised. These claims have generated an unprecedented number of pleas for companies to be more socially responsible. Not only is the public concerned with questionable business practices, but it also has rising expectations about businesses making a positive social impact, particularly since the COVID-19 pandemic.

For some, the concept of corporate social responsibility (CSR) has been embraced in the broader term *corporate citizenship*. Other terms that have been derived from CSR include corporate social *responsiveness*, corporate social *performance*, and corporate social *impact*. Today, many business executives prefer the term *sustainability* as an inclusive reference to social responsibility issues. The term *conscious capitalism* is preferred by others.

Some arguments have been made for the expression *creating shared value* (CSV) and others have preferred *purpose-driven business*. These terms are often employed as synonyms for CSR. For others, they represent similar but somewhat distinct expressions. In the final analysis, these terminologies are often overlapping in their meanings and have more similarities than differences. Though the terms are frequently used interchangeably, a careful examination of each is needed to understand the user's intent. In this book, the terminology of CSR will continue to be used and other terms and frameworks will be invoked when appropriate. The CSR concept remains the centerpiece of competing and complementary frameworks being used.[1]

CSR has been a "front-burner" issue within the business and society relationship and continues to grow in importance each year. An important landmark in its growth was the formation of an organization called **Business for Social Responsibility (BSR)**. BSR was formed to fill an urgent need for a national business alliance that fosters socially responsible corporate policies. In 2021, BSR claimed more than 250 member corporations and reported among its membership such recognizable names as Apple, Inc., Abbott Laboratories, Amazon, Coca-Cola Co., Google, Inc., Johnson & Johnson, Target Corp., Michelin, Microsoft, and hundreds of others. The mission statement of BSR is illuminating: "We work with business to create a just and sustainable world."[2] Today many of the world's leading corporations have an upper echelon officer who is responsible for the firm's corporate social responsibility, corporate citizenship, or sustainability.[3]

This chapter is dedicated to CSR-related issues, concepts, and practices that have emerged because it is a core idea that undergirds most business/society relationships. It is important to explore the meaning of the CSR concept in more detail.

2.1 Corporate Social Responsibility as a Concept

Chapter 1 described how criticisms of business have led to increased concern for the social environment and a changed social contract between business and society. Out of these developments has grown the notion of CSR. It is useful to consider some early definitions of CSR to develop a sense of perspective.

An early view of CSR stated: "**Corporate social responsibility (CSR)** is seriously considering the impact of the company's actions on society."[4] Another early definition held that "social responsibility … requires the individual to consider [their] acts in terms of a whole social system, and holds [them] responsible for the effects of [their] acts anywhere in that system."[5] Both of these early definitions provide useful insights into the idea of social responsibility.

Figure 2-1 illustrates the business criticism–social response cycle, depicting partially how the concept of CSR evolved out of the ideas introduced in Chapter 1—business criticism, the increased concern for the social environment, and the changed social contract. Figure 2-1 also clarifies that businesses' commitment to CSR has led to increased corporate *responsiveness* toward stakeholders and improved social (stakeholder) *performance*—ideas that are developed more fully in this chapter.

To be sure, the growth of social responsibility practices has brought about a society more satisfied with business. However, this satisfaction, despite reducing the number of factors leading to business criticism, has at the same time led to increased expectations that have resulted in *more*

Figure 2-1 Business Criticism–Social Response Cycle

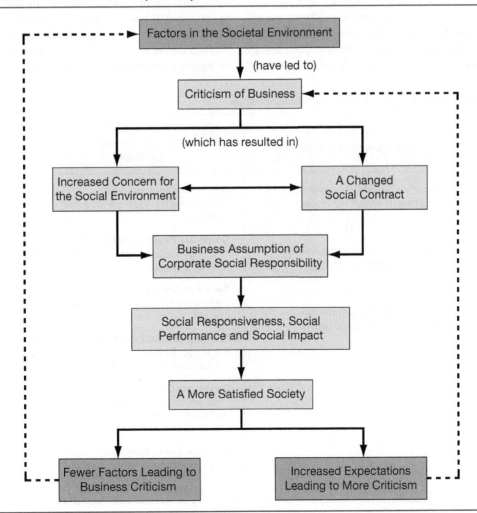

criticism. Figure 2-1 illustrates this double effect. The net result is that overall levels of business social performance, impact, and societal satisfaction should increase with time in spite of this interplay of positive and negative influences. Should business not be responsive to societal expectations, it could conceivably enter a downward spiral, resulting in significant deterioration in the business and society relationship. The tidal wave of corporate fraud beginning in 2001 (Enron scandal), followed by the Wall Street financial collapse beginning in 2008, has seriously called businesses' concern for society into question, and this concern continues today as ethical controversies at major companies such as Volkswagen, Wells Fargo, Boeing, Facebook, and Google have captured the public's attention. Additionally, the COVID-19 pandemic, beginning in 2020, has put businesses under more stress to improve their social performance.

Many academics and practitioners today use the terms **corporate citizenship, corporate responsibility, sustainability, creating shared value (CSV), conscious capitalism, purpose-driven business**, and others to collectively embrace the host of concepts related to CSR. For now, a simple summary of the themes or emphases of each of these concepts helps clarify how the flow of ideas has extended as these concepts have developed. In Figure 2-2, a summary of the various terminologies that are in use today is presented along with a brief indication of their emphases. These terms will be developed further in later discussions.

From a practicing manager's point of view, companies use an assortment of position titles for the lead CSR position in their companies. Following are some that were in use by companies as recently as 2021:

Executive Vice President and Chief Sustainability Officer (Walmart)

Vice President, Global Policy, Environmental Sustainability, & Social Impact, (Coca Cola Company)

Director, Corporate Social Responsibility (Adobe)

Corporate Social Responsibility & Chief Sustainability Officer (AT&T)

Head of CSR and Sustainability (Gap, Inc.)

Chief, Corporate Social Responsibility (Verizon)

2.1a The Beginnings of CSR

The concept of business responsibility that prevailed in the United States and among free-market societies since the Industrial Revolution of the 1800s has been fashioned after the traditional, or classical, *economic model*.[6] Adam Smith's concept of the "invisible hand" was its major starting point. The classical view holds that a society could best determine its needs and wants through the marketplace. In this view, the invisible hand of the market transforms self-interest into societal interest. Although the marketplace has done a fairly good job in deciding what goods and services should be produced, it had not fared quite as well in ensuring that businesses always acted fairly and ethically.

Over the decades, when laws constraining business behavior began to proliferate, a *legal model* emerged. Society's

Figure 2-2 Corporate Social Responsibility Related Concepts

Traditional CSR Concepts	Competing and Complementary Concepts
Corporate Social Responsibility (CSR) *Emphasizes obligation, accountability* ⬇ **Corporate Social Responsiveness** *Emphasizes action, activity* ⬇ **Corporate Social Performance** *Emphasizes outcomes, results*	**Corporate Citizenship (CC)** *companies are citizens and all this implies* **Corporate Responsibility (CR)** *broadly focuses on all categories of responsibility* **Sustainability (SUS)** *embraces longer term concern for people, planet, and profits* **Creating Shared Value (CSV)** *how companies generate economic value while producing societal value* **Conscious Capitalism** *four key principles: higher purpose; stakeholder orientation; conscious leadership; conscious culture* **Purpose-Driven Business** *higher purpose; company purpose is broader than products, services, and profits*

expectations of business changed from being strictly economic in nature to encompassing issues that had been previously at a business's discretion, and eventually laws were passed to reflect these concerns. Over time, a *social model*, focusing more on society's expectations beyond what was legally required, and business ethics emerged, eventually transforming to a *stakeholder model*. Throughout, there has continued to be a tension between the interests of shareholders and other stakeholders. In the stakeholder model, sustainability has become a prominent focus. This idea will be developed further in Chapter 4.

The concept of CSR has gained universal acceptance and a broadening of meaning. The emphasis has moved from little more than a general awareness of social and ethical concerns to a period in which specific issues, such as corporate governance, product safety, honesty in advertising, employee rights, affirmative action, environmental sustainability, ethical behavior, and global CSR, took center stage. More recently, issues of diversity and inclusion and human rights have been emphasized. An *issue* orientation eventually gave way to the more recent focus on corporate social *performance*, corporate *citizenship*, *sustainability*, and *social impact*. It is helpful to expand on the evolving views of CSR by examining a few definitions or understandings of this term that have developed over the years.

2.1b Evolving Meanings of CSR

Let's return to the basic question: What does CSR really mean? Up to this point in the chapter, a rather simple definition of social responsibility has been used: *Corporate social responsibility is seriously considering the impact of the company's actions on society.*

Although this definition has inherent ambiguities, most of the evolving definitions also have limitations. A second definition is more specific: *Social responsibility is the obligation of decision makers to take actions that protect and improve the welfare of society as a whole along with their own interests.*[7]

This description suggests two active aspects of social responsibility: *protecting* and *improving*. To protect the welfare of society implies the *avoidance of negative impacts* on society. To improve the welfare of society implies the *creation of positive benefits* for society. Like the first definition, this second characterization is unavoidably vague.

A third definition that has been useful is also rather general. But, unlike the previous two, it places social responsibilities in context vis-à-vis economic and legal objectives of business: *The idea of social responsibility supposes that the corporation has not only economic and legal obligations, but also certain responsibilities to society that extend beyond these obligations.*[8]

This description is attractive in that it acknowledges the importance of economic objectives (e.g., sustainable profits) side by side with legal obligations while also encompassing a broader conception of the firm's responsibilities. It is limited, however, in that it does not clarify what the *certain*

responsibilities that extend beyond these are. Over the years, a number of different definitions or views on CSR have evolved.[9] One study found 37 different definitions of CSR that have appeared since 1980, and that is why it is important that we focus on one comprehensive definition that will be helpful to us in moving through the book.[10]

2.1c A Four-Part Definition of CSR

Each of the definitions of CSR presented earlier is valuable. At this point, it is useful to present Carroll's four-part definition of CSR that focuses on the *types* of social responsibilities embedded in the concept. This definition helps us identify and understand the component obligations that make up CSR, and it is the definition that will be used most frequently throughout this book:

> The social responsibility of business encompasses the economic, legal, ethical, and discretionary (philanthropic) expectations that society has of organizations at a given point in time.[11]

This four-part definition places economic and legal expectations of business in context by linking them to more socially oriented concerns. These social concerns include ethical responsibilities and philanthropic (voluntary/discretionary) responsibilities. This set of four responsibilities, creating a total CSR perspective, creates a foundation or infrastructure that helps delineate and frame businesses' responsibilities to the society of which it is part.

Economic Responsibilities. At a foundational level, business has **economic responsibilities**. It may seem odd to call an economic responsibility a social responsibility, but, in effect, this is what it is. First and foremost, free enterprise systems call for business to be an economic institution; that is, as an institution, it should have the objective to produce goods and services that society needs and wants and to sell them at fair prices—prices that societal members think represent the value of the goods and services delivered and that provide business with profits sufficient to ensure its survival and growth and to reward its investors. The economic responsibility is also foundational because it helps provide jobs for societal members. As seen in the recent pandemic, business's economic role is critical to the survival of society and the provision of jobs.

While thinking about its economic responsibilities, business employs many management concepts that are directed toward financial effectiveness—attention to revenues, costs, investments, strategic decision making, and the host of business concepts focused on augmenting the long-term financial performance of the organization. Today, global hypercompetition in business has underscored the importance of business's economic responsibilities. The COVID-19 pandemic has made economic sustainability an urgent topic. Though economic responsibilities are indispensable, they are not enough; without them, other responsibilities become moot because firms go out of business. With them, this is just part of what businesses must do to meet society's expectations of them.

Legal Responsibilities. Business also has **legal responsibilities.** Just as society has sanctioned economic systems by permitting businesses to assume the productive role, as a partial fulfillment of the social contract, it has also established the ground rules—the laws and regulations—under which businesses are expected to operate. Legal responsibilities reflect society's view of "codified ethics" in the sense that they articulate basic notions of fair practices that are established by lawmakers. It is business's responsibility toward society to comply with these laws. It is not an accident that compliance officers now have an important role on company organization charts.

If business does not agree with laws or regulations that have been passed or are about to be passed, however, society has provided an approach by which dissenters can be heard through the political process. In past decades, societies witnessed a proliferation of laws and regulations striving to monitor and control business practices. A memorable *Newsweek* cover story titled "Lawsuit Hell: How Fear of Litigation Is Paralyzing Our Professions" emphasized the burgeoning role that the legal responsibility of organizations has assumed.[12] And, with the proliferation of technological innovations, regulations affecting the digital economy are becoming a more urgent topic.[13] The legal aspect of the business and society relationship will be examined further in other chapters as pertinent applications arise.

As important as legal responsibilities are, they do not capture the full range of standards and practices expected of business by society. On its own, the law is inadequate for at least three reasons. First, the law cannot possibly address all the topics or issues that business may face. New issues endlessly emerge in realms such as digital issues, technology, e-commerce, artificial intelligence, robotics, and genetically modified foods—just to mention a few examples. Stakeholders' privacy is a major issue that cuts through all these. Second, the law often lags behind more recent standards of what is considered appropriate practice. For example, as technology permits more precise measurements of climate change, laws based on measures made by previous methods become quickly outdated. Third, laws are made by elected lawmakers and often reflect the personal interests and political motivations of legislators rather than appropriate ethical justifications. A wise sage once said, "Never go to see how sausages or laws are made. It may not be a pretty picture." Although we would like to believe that lawmakers are focusing on "what is right and best for society," the history of political maneuvering, compromising, and self-interested decision making often suggests otherwise. Hence, laws and regulations, on their own, are not enough.

Ethical Responsibilities. Because laws are essential but not sufficient, **ethical responsibilities** are needed to embrace those activities, standards, and practices that are expected or

prohibited by society even though they are not codified into law. Ethical responsibilities embody the full scope of norms, standards, values, and expectations that reflect what consumers, employees, shareholders, and the community regard as fair, just, and consistent with respect for or protection of stakeholders' moral rights.[14]

Over time, changes in the public's concept of ethics or values precede the establishment of new laws and they become the driving forces behind the initial creation of laws and regulations. For example, the civil rights, environmental, and consumer movements activated in the 1960s reflected basic alterations in societal values and thus were ethical bellwethers foreshadowing and leading to later legislation. Second, ethical responsibilities may be seen as embracing and reflecting newly emerging values and norms that society expects business to meet, and they may reflect a higher standard of performance than that previously or currently required by law. Ethical responsibilities in this sense are continually evolving—usually rising and expanding. As a result, debate about their acceptability continues. Regardless, business is expected to be responsive to newly emerging concepts of what constitutes ethical practices. One example might be Whole Foods Market and other stores selling only those foods it considers organic and free from genetically modified organisms (GMOs). These practices are not required by law, but many consumers expect companies today to engage in these practices. In recent years, ethics issues in the global arena have multiplied and extended the study of acceptable business norms and practices.

Superimposed on these ethical expectations originating from societal and stakeholder groups are the implicit levels of ethical performance suggested by a consideration of the great universal ethical principles of moral philosophy, such as justice, rights, virtue, and utilitarianism.[15] Because ethical responsibilities are so important, Part 3 of this textbook, composed of four chapters, is dedicated to the subject of business ethics. For the moment, it is useful to think of ethical responsibilities as encompassing those decision and practice arenas in which society expects certain levels of moral or principled performance but for which it has not yet been articulated or codified into law.

Philanthropic Responsibilities. Finally, there are business's voluntary, discretionary, or **philanthropic responsibilities.** Though not responsibilities in the literal sense of the word, these are perceived and understood as responsibilities because they reflect current expectations of business by the public. The amount and nature of these activities are voluntary or discretionary, guided only by business's desire to engage in social activities that are not mandated, not required by law, and not necessarily expected of business in an ethical sense. Nevertheless, the public has an expectation that business will "give back," and thus this category has become a part of the implied social contract between business and society. Such activities might include corporate giving, scholarships to universities, product and service donations, employee volunteerism, community development, and any other kind of voluntary use of the organization's resources and its employees with the community or other stakeholders.

Examples of companies expressing their philanthropic responsibilities, and "doing well by doing good," are many:

- **Chick-fil-A**, the fast-food restaurant, through the WinShape Centre® Foundation, operates foster homes, sponsors a summer camp that hosts more than 1,900 campers every year, and has provided college scholarships for thousands of students.[16]

- For two decades, **Aflac, Inc.**, the supplement insurance provider, has raised and contributed more than $100 million for the treatment and research of childhood cancer and has made the Aflac Cancer Center and Blood Disorders Service at Children's Healthcare of Atlanta its primary philanthropic cause.[17] It is little wonder the Aflac Duck has become an international icon.

- **General Mills**, the food company, goes the extra mile to support community causes. During the COVID-19 pandemic, General Mills made food, boxed it up, and sent it directly to Feeding America and to hundreds of food banks.[18]

- **Timberland**, the products company, has created two programs for its employees to get involved in transforming communities. Their Path of Service Program provides employees up to 40 hours per year of paid volunteer time to serve in their communities. Their Pillar Service Events Program helps employees to use their service hours by organizing events such as on Earth Day each year.[19]

Although there is sometimes an ethical motivation for companies to get involved in **philanthropy**,[20] it typically is a practical way for the company to demonstrate that it is a good corporate citizen. A major distinction between ethical and philanthropic responsibilities is that the latter typically are not *expected* in a moral or an ethical sense. Communities desire and expect business to contribute its money, facilities, and employee time to humanitarian programs or purposes, but they do not regard firms as unethical if they do not provide these services at the desired levels. Therefore, these responsibilities are more discretionary, or voluntary, on business's part, although the societal expectation that these be provided has been around for some time. This category of responsibilities is often referred to as good "corporate citizenship" because it entails the company giving back to the community just because it is a member of the community.

To summarize, the four-part CSR definition forms a comprehensive conceptualization or framework that includes the economic, legal, ethical, and philanthropic expectations society places on organizations at a given point in time. In turn, these expectations are understood by businesses as "responsibilities" for which they need to provide some positive, accountable, responses. Figure 2-3 summarizes the four components, society's expectation regarding each component, and explanations.

The four-part definition of CSR provides us with a structure or framework within which to identify and situate the different expectations that society has of business. With each of these four categories considered to be an indispensable facet of the total social responsibility of business, they comprise a conceptual model that more completely and specifically describes the kinds of expectations that society has of business. A major advantage of the four-part definitional model is its ability to accommodate those who have argued against CSR by characterizing an economic emphasis as separate from a social emphasis. This four-part definition includes these two categories (economic, legal) along with two others (ethical, philanthropic) that collectively make up CSR. Other writers sometimes limit CSR to initiatives that companies take that go beyond what is economically and legally required. Sometimes the term is used only for those activities that are philanthropic, but the four-part model more comprehensively, and more realistically, characterizes business' total responsibilities to society today.

Figure 2-3 The Four Types of CSR: Expectations and Explanations/Examples

Type of Responsibility	Societal Expectations	Explanations/Examples
Economic responsibility	REQUIRED of business by society	Be profitable. Maximize sales, minimize costs. Make sound strategic decisions. Be attentive to dividend policy. Provide investors with adequate and attractive returns on their investments. Provide jobs.
Legal responsibility	REQUIRED of business by society	Obey all laws, adhere to all regulations. Environmental and consumer laws. Laws protecting employees. Fulfill all contractual obligations. Honor warranties and guarantees.
Ethical responsibility	EXPECTED of business by society	Avoid questionable practices. Respond to spirit as well as to letter of law. Assume law is a floor on practice, operate above minimum required. Do what is right, fair, and just. Assert ethical leadership.
Philanthropic responsibility	DESIRED/EXPECTED of business by society	Be a good corporate citizen. Give back. Make corporate contributions. Provide programs supporting community—education, health or human services, culture and arts, and civic. Provide for community betterment. Engage in volunteerism.

2.1d The Pyramid of Corporate Social Responsibility

A useful way of graphically depicting the four-part definition of CSR is to envision it as a pyramid with four layers or levels. This **Pyramid of Corporate Social Responsibility (CSR)** is shown in Figure 2-4.[21]

The CSR Pyramid portrays the four types or components of CSR, beginning with the basic building block of economic responsibility at the base. The infrastructure of CSR begins at the point of a successful, profit-making enterprise that has demonstrated its economic sustainability. At the same time, business is expected to obey the law because the law is society's codification of acceptable and unacceptable practices. Additionally, there is business's responsibility to be ethical. At its most basic level, this is the obligation to do what is right, just, and fair and to avoid or minimize harm to stakeholders (employees, consumers, the environment, and others). Finally, business is expected to be a good corporate citizen—to fulfill its philanthropic responsibilities by contributing financial and human resources to the community and improving the quality of life.

No metaphor is perfect, and the Pyramid of CSR is no exception. It intends to illustrate that the *total* social responsibility of business is composed of four distinct types or components that, when taken together, make up the whole. Although the types/components have been treated as separate concepts for discussion purposes, they are not mutually exclusive and are not intended to juxtapose a firm's economic responsibilities

with its other responsibilities. At the same time, a consideration of the separate components helps the manager see more clearly that the different types or kinds of obligations are in constant and dynamic tension with one another. The most critical tensions are those between economic and legal, economic and ethical, and economic and philanthropic. Some might see this as a conflict between a firm's "concern for profits" and its "concern for society," but it is suggested here that this is an oversimplification because the two are so intertwined. Their reconciliation is what CSR is all about.

Pyramid as a Unified Whole. A CSR or stakeholder perspective would focus on the total pyramid as a unified whole and on how the firm should engage in decisions, actions, policies, and practices that *simultaneously* fulfill its four component parts. This pyramid should *not* be interpreted to mean that business is expected to fulfill its social responsibilities in some sequential fashion, starting at the base. Rather, business is expected to fulfill *all* its responsibilities simultaneously. The positioning of economic, legal, ethical, and philanthropic strives to portray the fundamental or basic nature of these four categories to business's existence in capitalistic economic systems. Economic and legal responsibilities are *required* by society; ethical and philanthropic responsibilities are *expected* and *desired* by society. In non-capitalistic economic systems, the sequencing of the four responsibilities might be seen differently by those societies. For example, Wayne Visser has maintained that

Figure 2-4 The Pyramid of Corporate Social Responsibility

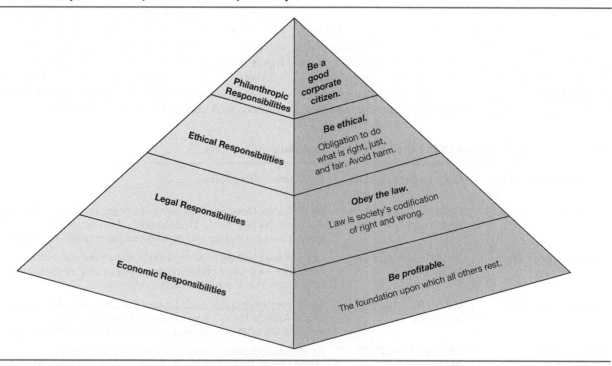

Sources: Adapted from Archie B. Carroll, "The Pyramid of Corporate Social Responsibility: Toward the Moral Management of Organizational Stakeholders," *Business Horizons* (July–August 1991), 42. Copyright © 1991 by the Foundation for the School of Business at Indiana University. Used with permission. Also see Archie B. Carroll, "Managing Ethically with Global Stakeholders: A Present and Future Challenge," *Academy of Management Executive*, Vol. 18, No. 2, May 2004, 114–120.

developing countries present a distinctive set of CSR agenda challenges that are collectively different to those faced in the developed world.[22]

In summary, the total social responsibility of business entails the concurrent fulfillment of the firm's economic, legal, ethical, and philanthropic responsibilities. This might be illustrated in the form of an equation, as follows:

Economic Responsibilities + Legal Responsibilities + Ethical Responsibilities + Philanthropic Responsibilities = Total Corporate Social Responsibility

Stated in more practical and managerial terms, the socially responsible firm should strive to

- Make a profit
- Obey the law
- Be ethical
- Be a good corporate citizen

CSR Pyramid Is a Dynamic, Sustainable, Stakeholder Model. It is especially important to note that the four-part CSR definition and the Pyramid of CSR represent dynamic, sustainable, stakeholder models. Each of the four components of responsibility addresses different stakeholders in terms of the varying priorities in which the stakeholders are affected, and these responsibilities may change over time. Economic responsibilities most dramatically impact owners, shareholders, and employees (because if the business is not financially sustainable, owners, shareholders, and employees will be directly affected). When the global COVID-19 pandemic hit, many owners and shareholders lost money, went out of business, and employees were displaced and significantly affected. The pandemic has demonstrated how critical the economic responsibilities are to societies.

Legal responsibilities are certainly crucial with respect to owners and shareholders, but in today's society, the threat of litigation against businesses arises most frequently from employees and consumer stakeholders. Ethical responsibilities affect all stakeholder groups, but an examination of the ethical issues business faces today suggests that they involve consumers, employees, and the natural environment most frequently. Finally, philanthropic responsibilities most affect the community, but it could be reasoned that employees are next affected because some research has suggested that a company's philanthropic performance significantly affects its employees' morale and satisfaction. The CSR definition and pyramid are sustainable in that they represent long-term responsibilities that overarch into future generations of stakeholders as well.

The role of stakeholders in discussions of CSR is inseparable. In fact, there have been recent calls for CSR to be redefined as corporate "stakeholder" responsibilities, rather than corporate "social" responsibilities.[23] Others have suggested that CSR should stand for corporate "sustainability" responsibilities. These views would be entirely consistent with the models presented in this chapter because a concern for stakeholders and sustainability is implicit in their understanding and application.

As business's major areas of social and stakeholder concerns are presented in various chapters in the book, it will be seen how the model's four facets (economic, legal, ethical, and philanthropic) provide a useful framework for conceptualizing the issue of CSR. The social contract between business and society is, to a large extent, formulated from mutual understandings that exist and evolve in each of these areas. But it should be noted that the ethical and philanthropic categories, taken together, more frequently capture the essence of what many people generally mean today when they speak of the social responsibility of business. Situating these two categories relative to the legal and economic obligations, however, keeps them in proper perspective and provides a more comprehensive understanding of CSR.

Ethics and Global Applications Permeate. Two additional comments of explanation regarding the Pyramid of CSR should be made. First, it should be emphasized that even though there is a separate ethics category in the model, the ethical dimension cuts through and permeates all categories in the model. Ethical considerations are involved in the economic category in that in capitalistic societies, it is believed that profitability is the ethically acceptable system for the production and distribution of goods and services. That is, in free-enterprise societies, such as capitalism, the economic responsibility is seen as the ethically best form of economic system. Regarding the legal responsibility category, it should be emphasized that practically all laws were predicated on an ethical rationale before they became formalized into law. The ethical category stands on its own, of course, but the philanthropic responsibility has historically, and ideally by some, been seen as an ethical concern for others, and thus ethics sometimes permeates philanthropic giving. However, many companies have seen philanthropy not from an ethical point of view but from a practical, public relations, or reputation-building perspective that reflects good citizenship. In short, ethics permeates and cuts through all four of the levels in the pyramid.

Concerning global applications, in other countries, continents, and cultures, the CSR pyramid may not as accurately reflect the priorities present there. The four categories do exist in other cultural environments but their sequence may not adhere to the CSR pyramid that was developed primarily based on American-styled, primarily capitalistic, economies. In Europe, for example, many countries are social democracies and the government plays a much larger role in providing goods and services than in the United States, and thus CSR and the levels in the pyramid might have a different significance and be interlinked in a somewhat different manner.[24] Or, as stated earlier, in developing countries or emerging economies, it may be argued that responsibilities in the pyramid may occur in a different foundational sequence.[25] To the extent that countries' socioeconomic systems become more similar to free-market capitalism, however, it would be expected that the pyramid as presented would more accurately reflect CSR in those countries.

2.1e CSR in Practice

CSR in practice is seen both in those firms that are generally perceived to be socially responsible and also in firms that are beginning to be known as CSR Exemplar firms.

Practices of Socially Responsible Firms. What do companies have to do to be seen as socially responsible? A study by Walker Information, a research organization, sought to discover what the general public perceived to be the activities, characteristics, or practices of socially responsible companies. Figure 2-5 summarizes what the sample said were the top 20 activities or characteristics of socially responsible companies.[26] The items in this listing are quite compatible with our discussion of CSR. Most of these activities would be representative of the legal, ethical, and philanthropic or discretionary components of our four-part CSR definition.

Rise of CSR Exemplar Firms. In the past several decades, a number of different socially responsible firms have become models for other firms. These may be called **CSR exemplar firms** because they have tended to go well beyond the typical and established patterns for business firms in terms of their social responsibility excellence. These firms have taken the lead in advocating or integrating social, environmental, or sustainability dimensions to their missions. Many of them today claim they are purpose-driven. Though larger firms typically get most of the attention with respect to CSR, as indicated earlier, medium-sized and smaller firms

are also organizational types in which CSR is important and practiced.[27] There are at least three main categories of socially responsible firms addressed here: social entrepreneurship firms, social intrapreneurship firms, and mainstream adopters.

Social entrepreneurship firms, also known as **social enterprises**, are those that began their CSR initiatives at their founding and strategically carried it forward. A social enterprise typically has at least two goals: to achieve social, cultural, or community outcomes; and to earn revenue.[28] Social entrepreneurship firms are aggressively moving into the mainstream and may be found in such realms as clothing and fashion, food and drink, home, health and lifestyle, travel, professional services, finance, and tech.[29]

A large part of their initial mission was to bring about social change or to reflect certain social values as a part of their organization's character. Porter and Kramer have argued that social entrepreneurship has been moving capitalism toward the creation of "shared value" in which economic value is created in a way that also creates value for society by "addressing its needs and challenges."[30] Three well-known examples of social entrepreneurship firms would be The Body Shop International, founded by social activist Anita Roddick; Ben & Jerry's, also founded by two social activists, Ben Cohen and Jerry Greenfield; and Toms, founded by Blake Mycoskie. Since its beginning, Toms has sought not only to produce and sell quality products but also to bring about social change by giving away to poor children a pair of shoes for every pair it sells: "one for one."[31]

A new organizational form, called the benefit corporation, or B Corp, is an emerging area of social entrepreneurship and enterprise wherein states permit companies to charter themselves on both a social and economic mission.

Figure 2-5 Top 20 Activities, Characteristics, or Practices of Socially Responsible Companies

The following are activities, characteristics, or practices of socially responsible companies as identified by citizens.

- Makes products that are safe.
- Does not pollute air or water.
- Obeys the law in all aspects of business.
- Promotes honest or ethical employee behavior.
- Commits to safe workplace ethics.
- Does not use misleading or deceptive advertising.
- Upholds stated policy banning discrimination.
- Utilizes "sustainable" packaging.
- Protects employees against sexual harassment.
- Recycles within company.
- Shows no past record of questionable activity.
- Responds quickly to customer problems.
- Maintains waste reduction program.
- Provides or pays portion of medical costs.
- Promotes energy conservation program.
- Helps displaced workers with placement.
- Gives money toward charitable or educational causes.
- Utilizes only biodegradable or recyclable materials.
- Employs friendly or courteous or responsive personnel.
- Tries continually to improve quality.

Source: Walker Information. Used with permission.

Ethics In Practice Case

Do Small Businesses Have Social Responsibilities?

When we speak about CSR, it is usually targeted toward large corporations or firms. But what about small businesses? During the best of times, many if not most small businesses are living on the ragged edge of survival. Think of the small businesses you are familiar with. How many seem to be prospering?

The U.S. Small Business Administration defines small businesses in one way, but the ones we are interested in here are typically much, much smaller. These are the small businesses we deal with in our local communities: grocery stores, gift shops, barber shops, restaurants, bars, movie theaters, dry cleaners, fast-food vendors, repair shops, and so on. Researchers often lump together small and medium-sized enterprises (SMEs) into one group, and they all face many of the same challenges.

During the recent pandemic, the pressures on small businesses were especially stressful because of economic lockdowns in many states and cities. Also, with more and more families sheltering-in-place, they are only going out to spend money on necessities. If a small business has tough times when the economy is good, how is it to fare when the economy is down?

On the one hand, small businesses and SMEs do not have the resources to direct toward CSR as large corporations do. But on the other hand, how are they to compete if they are not socially responsible? Maybe the question pertains to the nature and types of social responsibilities small businesses are able to provide.

1. Are small businesses expected to be socially responsible, or is CSR a concept best served by large businesses with ample resources?
2. What are the specific responsibilities small businesses might be expected to perform regarding the four-part CSR definition? In other words, what are their economic, legal, ethical, and philanthropic responsibilities? How would their implementation differ from a large, well-known, successful business?
3. Think of a couple small businesses you use. Evaluate their social responsibilities using the Pyramid of CSR.

Sources: Dale Cudmore, Digital.com, "Should Your Small Business Care about CSR? Here's the Honest Answer," October 7, 2020, https://digital.com/blog/csr-small-business/, accessed February 6, 2021; Laura Spence, "Small Business Responsibility: Expanding Core CSR Theory," *Business & Society*, April 25, 2014; Bridget Pollack, U.S. Small Business Administration, "Corporate Social Responsibility: What Your Small Business Needs to Know," July 6, 2017, https://www.sba.gov/blog/corporate-social-responsibility-what-your-small-business-needs-know, accessed February 6, 2021.

B Corps are permitted by charter to pursue both societal welfare and shareholder welfare, so the social mission is "built into" the business from the beginning.[32] B Corporations will be discussed further in Chapter 9.

Social intrapreneurship firms are companies that did not have a specific social agenda as part of their *initial* formation but later developed from within a highly visible social agenda or program. Social intrapreneurs are people who work inside major companies to develop and promote innovative, practical solutions to social, environmental, or sustainability challenges as a part of their financial missions. *Sustainability*, a leading nonprofit advocacy organization, says, "These corporate change makers work inside big business, often against the prevailing status quo, to innovate and deliver market solutions to some of the world's most pressing social and environmental challenges."[33] Companies today that might illustrate this model include Timberland, Starbucks, Panera Bread, Microsoft, and Patagonia. As a result of innovation and risk taking, these firms have become high-profile exemplars of social responsibility and sustainability.

Mainstream adopters, a third group of CSR exemplar firms, would include all other conventional businesses that have adopted, practiced, and achieved some degree of distinction or recognition for socially responsible policies and practices. Their motives might include one or more of the following: gaining competitive advantage, reducing costs, enhancing their reputations, emulating what other firms are doing, or fulfilling their own concept of corporate citizenship. Firms that would fall into this third category might include, but are not limited to, Apple, General Electric, Xerox, Aflac, Coca-Cola, Unilever, DuPont, AT&T, UPS, General Mills, and Walmart. While it is not always easy to clearly identify which category each firm is in, because some overlaps occur, the three types do offer a good way of understanding the range of strategies by which different business firms have taken on a socially conscious mission and have become highly visible CSR role models for other firms seeking to integrate social responsibility and sustainability into their everyday operations.[34]

2.2 Traditional Arguments against and for CSR

In an effort to provide a balanced, historically accurate view of CSR, it is useful to consider the arguments that traditionally have been raised against and for it.[35] It should be stated clearly at the outset, however, that those who argue *against* CSR are not using in their considerations the comprehensive four-part CSR definition and model presented in this chapter. Rather, it appears that the critics are viewing CSR more narrowly—as only the businesses' voluntary efforts to pursue social goals (primarily the philanthropic category). Some critics equate CSR with only the philanthropic category because they think of this as "giving away" the shareholders' money.

Today, few businesspeople and academics argue against the fundamental notion of CSR. The debate among businesspeople more often centers on the kinds and degrees of CSR and on subtle ethical questions, rather than on the basic question of whether or not business should be socially responsible, sustainable, or a good corporate citizen. Today, few resist CSR on the grounds of economic theory. The following arguments have historically been cited regarding CSR, and it is helpful to understand them to appreciate CSR's development over the years.

2.2a Arguments against CSR

Classical Economics. This traditional view holds that management has one responsibility—to maximize shareholder wealth. This classical economic school of thought, often attributed to the late Milton Friedman, argued that social issues are not the concern of businesspeople and that these problems should be resolved by the unfettered workings of the free-market system.[36] Further, this view holds that if the free market cannot solve the social problem, then it falls upon government and legislation to do the job.

A careful reading of Friedman's writings, however, reveals that he softened his argument somewhat by his assertion that management is "to make as much money as possible *while conforming to the basic rules of society, both those embodied in the law and those embodied in ethical customs*"[37] (italics added). Thus, when Friedman's entire statement is considered, it appears that he accepts three of the four categories of the four-part model: economic, legal, and ethical. The only category not specifically embraced in his quote is the voluntary or philanthropic category. It is clear that the classical economic argument views CSR more narrowly than depicted in the four-part model. Though not held my many today, the classical economic argument against CSR continues to be discussed, mostly by academics.[38] Deep down, however, some business practitioners may still think this way.

Business Is Not Equipped. This objection to CSR holds that managers are oriented toward finance and operations and do not have the necessary expertise (social skills) to make social decisions.[39] Although this may have been true at one point in time, it is less true today as CSR has become integral to business school education and executive education and has been integrated into corporate strategic decisions.

Dilutes Business Purpose. Closely related to business not being equipped is a third issue: If managers were to pursue CSR vigorously, it would tend to dilute business's primary purpose.[40] The objection here is that CSR would put business into fields not related to its "proper aim."[41] There is little practical evidence, however, that this dilution has been realized. Moreover, the rise of social enterprises documents that some entrepreneurs see the decision to pursue social goals as a desirable choice, not a dilution of business

purpose. Ironically, today's popular usage of the term *purpose driven* supposes that businesses do have a higher purpose than profits only.

Too Much Power Already. A fourth argument against CSR is that business already has enough power—economic, environmental, political, and technological—and so why place in its hands the opportunity to wield additional power?[42] In reality, today, business has this social power regardless of CSR. Further, this view tends to ignore the potential use of business's social power for the public good.

Global Competitiveness. Another argument that merits consideration is that by encouraging business to assume social responsibilities, businesses might be placed in a weakened position in terms of global competition. The increase in the costs of products caused by inclusion of social or environmental considerations in the price structure might necessitate raising the prices of products, thereby making them less competitive in international markets. This once prominent argument fades considerably when we consider the reality that today social responsibility has become widespread globally, not one restricted to domestic firms and operations. Indeed, today, firms must be socially responsible to be competitive because most countries now expect it and the global community is watching carefully.

2.2b Arguments in Support of CSR

In response to the traditional arguments presented against CSR, a number of arguments have been presented in support of the concept. These arguments are still valid.

Enlightened Self-Interest. The long-term self-interest of business view, sometimes referred to as "enlightened self-interest," holds that if business is to have a healthy climate in which to operate in the future, it must take actions now to ensure its long-term sustainability. The reasoning behind this view is that society's expectations are such that if business does not respond on its own initiative, its role in society may be altered by the public—for example, through government regulations or, more dramatically, through alternative economic systems for the production and distribution of goods and services.

Business must be responsive to society's expectations over the long term if it is to survive in its current form or in a less restrained form. This concern for the long-term viability of business and society is the primary driver in the current emphasis on sustainability, which has become a synonym for CSR in the minds of many.

Warding Off Government Regulations. One of the most practical reasons for business to be socially responsible is to ward off government intervention and regulations. Today, there are numerous areas in which government intervenes with an expensive, elaborate regulatory apparatus to fill a void left by business's self-regulatory inaction or inattention to CSR. To the extent that business polices itself with self-disciplined standards and guidelines, and strives to be socially responsible, future government intervention can be somewhat forestalled.

Resources Available and Let Business Try. Two arguments supporting CSR deserve mention together: "Business has the resources" and "Let business try."[43] These two views maintain that because business has a reservoir of management talent, functional expertise, and capital, and because so many others have tried and failed to solve societal problems, business should be given a chance. These arguments have considerable merit, because there are some social problems that best can be handled, in the final analysis, only by business. Examples include creating a fair and equitable workplace, providing safe products, and engaging in fair advertising. Admittedly, government can and does assume a role in these areas, but business has primary responsibility for these decisions.

Proaction Better than Reaction. Another argument supporting CSR is that "proaction is better than reaction." This position holds that *proacting* (anticipating and initiating) is more practical, and less costly, than simply *reacting* to problems that have already occurred. Environmental pollution is a good example, particularly business's experience with attempting to clean up solid waste, rivers, lakes, and other waterways that have been neglected for decades. A wiser and more cost-effective approach would have been to prevent environmental degradation in the first place. *Proaction* is a basic idea that undergirds the notion of **sustainable development.**

Public Support. A final argument in favor of CSR is that the public strongly supports it.[44] A recent Nielsen survey has revealed what has been frequently found in recent years—consumers are increasingly more willing to pay more for products and services that are provided by companies committed to positive environmental and social impact.[45] This public support for CSR has grown over the years.[46]

2.2c The Business Case for CSR

After considering the pros and cons of CSR, most businesses and managers today embrace the idea. Society's stakeholders clearly benefit from CSR. But what do businesses get out of it? Some are satisfied that it is the right thing to do. Others want more specific, tangible benefits to their companies. Therefore, in recent years, the "business case" for CSR has been unfolding.[47] Though overlapping, the business case for sustainability has been advancing as well.[48] The **Business Case for CSR** refers to the reasons why businesspeople believe that CSR brings distinct benefits or advantages to their organizations as well as to the business community. In this line of thinking, CSR directly benefits the company's "bottom line." The astute business guru Michael Porter, perhaps the most respected consultant today in upper-level management circles and boardrooms, has pointed out how corporate and social

initiatives are intertwined. According to Porter, "Today's companies ought to invest in corporate social responsibility as part of their business strategy to become more competitive." In a competitive context, "the company's social initiatives—or its philanthropy—can have great impact, not only for the company but also for the local society."[49]

In his perceptive book, *The Civil Corporation*, Simon Zadek has identified four ways in which firms respond to CSR pressures, and he argues that these form a composite business case for CSR. His four approaches are as follows[50]:

1. *Defensive approach.* This is an approach designed to alleviate negative consequences. Companies will do what they have to do to avoid pressure that makes them incur costs.
2. *Cost–benefit approach.* This traditional approach holds that firms will undertake those activities if they can identify direct benefits that exceeds costs.
3. *Strategic approach.* In this approach, firms will recognize the changing social environment and engage with CSR as part of a deliberate, emergent corporate strategy.
4. *Innovation and learning approach.* In this approach, an active engagement with CSR provides new opportunities to understand the marketplace, provide innovative products and services, and enhance organizational learning, which leads to competitive advantage.

A relevant study published by the Harvard Business School has provided specific findings as to how CSR has produced documentable business results. In this study, respondents reported that CSR initiatives improved their companies' social standing, created important solutions to social/environmental problems, and addressed senior managers' social/environmental missions. The business impacts included increased revenues and reduced costs.[51] Business in the Community Ireland also has documented benefits to firms from CSR initiatives. They found that CSR drives innovation, trust, and transparency; boosts long-term profitability; and engages the workforce.[52] Project ROI, an initiative spearheaded by IO Sustainability, a research and advisory services firm, has made the case for the return-on-investment of corporate responsibility. The project has established firm linkages between social responsibility and measurable business outcomes. They carefully make the case that fit, commitment, management, and connection are essential for payoffs to occur.[53] Some research has documented that if companies use pro-social initiatives just to increase productivity, however, it may backfire on them if people think their motivations are not appropriate.[54]

Companies may vary as to why they pursue a CSR strategy, but these approaches, taken together, build a strong bottom-line, business rationale for the pursuit of socially responsible business. It must be noted that some CSR experts do not always support the "business case" and believe company efforts need to be more ethically or altruistically motivated to succeed.[55] Figure 2-6 summarizes some of the business case (reasons and benefits) for CSR taken from two different studies.

Figure 2-6 Reasons and Benefits Supporting the Business Case for CSR

Six Business Reasons for Engaging in CSR

Companies that understand CSR are using it to push the following business processes in the organization:

1. Customer engagement
2. Employee engagement
3. Brand differentiation
4. Long-term plans
5. Cutting costs
6. Innovation

Benefits to Businesses of Corporate Social Responsibility Policies

Carefully implemented CSR policies can help the organization:

1. Win new business
2. Increase customer retention
3. Develop and enhance relationships with customers, suppliers, and networks
4. Attract, retain, and maintain a happy workforce and be an Employer of Choice
5. Save money on energy and operating costs and manage risk
6. Differentiate itself from competitors
7. Improve its business reputation and standing
8. Provide access to investment and funding opportunities
9. Generate positive publicity and media opportunities due to media interest in ethical business activities

Sources: "Six Reasons Companies Should Initiate Plans for CSR," https://www.midas-pr.com/six-reasons-companies-should-initiate-plans-for-csr/, accessed January 28, 2021; Simply CSR, "Business Benefits of CSR," http://www.simplycsr.co.uk/the-benefits-of-csr.html, accessed January 28, 2021.

Ethics In Practice Case

The Socially Responsible Shoe Company

When Blake Mycoskie was on a visit to Argentina in 2006, a bright idea struck him. He was wearing alpargatas—resilient, lightweight, canvas slip-ons—shoes typically worn by Argentinian farmworkers, during his visit to poor villages where many of the residents had no shoes at all. He formulated the plan to start a shoe company and give away a pair of shoes to some needy child or person for every shoe the company sold. This became the basic mission of his company.

Initially, Blake had to self-finance his company. He decided to name his company "Toms: Shoes for Tomorrow." Blake is from Texas, and he liked to read books about such business success stories as those of Ted Turner, Richard Branson, and Sam Walton. He appends the following message to his e-mails: "Disclaimer: you will not win the rat race wearing Toms."

In the summer of 2006, he unveiled his first collection of Toms shoes. By fall, the company had sold 10,000 pairs and he was off to the Argentinian countryside, along with several volunteers, to give away 10,000 pairs of shoes. In an article in *Time*, Blake was quoted as saying, "I always thought I'd spend the first half of my life making money and the second half giving it away. I never thought I could do both at the same time."

By February 2007, Blake's company had orders from 300 stores for 41,000 of his spring and summer collection of shoes, and he had big plans to go international by entering markets in Japan, Australia, Canada, France, and Spain in the summer of 2008. In 2012, the company also launched its Toms Eyewear line and adopted a program called "One for One," in which "with every pair you purchase, Toms will give sight to a person in need. One for One." By 2015, Toms had given away 50 million shoes. By 2021, Toms had created its Global Giving Fund focused on COVID-19 and had generated $2 million in support of global relief efforts.

1. How would you assess Toms' CSR using the four-part CSR definition? The company's website does not discuss CSR but focuses on "Impact." Explain and discuss.
2. Is Blake Mycoskie a social entrepreneur, intrapreneur, or mainstream adopter? Is his company a social enterprise? Explain.
3. Do you believe Blake's twin goal of economic and social success is sustainable? Review the company's website to see additional information: www.toms.com.
4. What challenges do you foresee for the company's future?

Sources: Nadia Mustafa, "A Shoe That Fits So Many Souls," *Time* (February 5, 2007), C2; Blake Mycoskie, *Start Something That Matters*, 2011; Philip Broughton, "Doing Good by Shoeing Well," *The Wall Street Journal*, September 9, 2011, A17; Toms Shoes, http://www.toms.com/improving-lives, accessed March 30, 2016; Toms Global Giving Fund COVID-19, https://www.toms.com/us/impact.html, accessed January 28, 2021.

2.3 CSR Greenwashing

As an addendum to the discussion of CSR and its related terms, it is important to point out that not all companies that promote their CSR images are serious about being responsible to stakeholders. Some are attempting to convey an image of responsibility when in fact they are conducting business as usual—focusing on their own profits with superficial attention given to responsible business practices. Greenwashing, an offshoot of the term *whitewashing*, is a concept that originated when it was observed that some companies sought to convey to the public that they were "green," that is, environmentally friendly, when in fact it was all a facade. According to one consulting firm that has studied the phenomenon, TerraChoice, 95 percent of the products that are marketed as eco-friendly have committed at least one of the greenwashing sins, ranging from using weak data to support marketing claims to more deliberate deceptions such as inventing bogus certifications.[56]

In a similar way, some companies may be participating in a more generalized version of the environmental subterfuge that we might call **CSR Greenwashing**—that is, intentionally seeking to convey the image of a socially responsible firm when the evidence of their practices does not support this conclusion. Companies do this in a variety of ways including deceptive public relations, making claims without evidence to support it, misleading labeling, executive speeches that are more PR than fact, and promoting a relatively unimportant but visible CSR initiative and hoping that observers will not notice their overall record or that there may be acts of irresponsibility taking place behind the scenes. CSR Greenwashing is a form of "virtue signaling" that has become popular today. Examples of greenwashing are evident in the fashion industry today among fast-fashion brands that are popular with college students. The companies claim their products are environmentally friendly when they are not.[57]

The conclusion we must reach concerning CSR and sustainability is that in order to truly understand companies' motives and strategies, we have to carefully analyze the consistency of their practices and policies with their stated missions and aspirations particularly in the CSR arena. There are no 100 percent pure CSR companies, but some do much better than others. In any event, we need to examine carefully company practices and claims lest they be exposed as CSR Greenwashing. Stakeholders need to watch carefully if companies start parading their virtues when their internal standards or other practices may not be consistent with the image they are seeking to convey.

2.4 Political CSR

In the past decade, there has been developing a concept known as political corporate social responsibility, or *Political CSR* (*PCSR*), an emerging version of CSR that has gained more attention and application especially in European or similar contexts where the government historically has assumed a larger role in providing societal benefits. Scherer, Rasche, Palazzo, and Spicer have defined PCSR as follows:

> PCSR entails those responsible business activities that turn corporations into political actors, by engaging in public deliberations, collective decisions, and the provision of public goods or the restriction of public bads in cases where public authorities are unable or unwilling to fulfil this role.[58]

In some countries, companies have increasingly taken on responsibilities traditionally left to governments. In addition, some businesses have engaged in political activity via philanthropy, often seen as lobbying, to help bring about a more beneficial business or social environment. Political CSR is a concept that emphasizes activities that have an intended or unintended political impact. Among the CSR activities of companies that might have a political dimension include companies as providers of community services (e.g., health and education) that previously have been seen as the purview of the state. Another aspect of PCSR occurs when companies try to usurp government regulations or be responsive to government policies.[59]

Some see Political CSR more as a governance mechanism wherein corporations contribute to global regulation and in providing public goods.[60] One goal of those advocating political CSR has been to integrate corporate political activity with traditional CSR theory and practice.[61] The field of Political CSR is defined differently by experts and is still in its early stages; we will consider many of these same topics in Chapter 17 when business, government, and regulation are addressed and in Chapter 18 when businesses' influences on government and public policy are discussed. Clearly, governments are important stakeholders and business-government relations are a vital topic of importance.

2.5 Corporate Social *Responsiveness*, Performance, and *Impact*

It is now worthwhile to consider extensions to the core concept of CSR that have arisen over the years. First, there is the issue of the distinction between the terms *responsibility* and *responsiveness* in the evolution of the CSR field. While **corporate social responsibility (CSR$_1$)** focuses on accountability or obligations of business, **corporate social responsiveness (CSR$_2$)** represents an *action-oriented* variant of CSR.

Early on, it was held that the term *responsibility* is too suggestive of efforts to pinpoint accountability or obligation. Therefore, it is not dynamic enough to fully describe business's willingness and activity—apart from obligation—to *respond* to social demands. Ackerman and Bauer criticized

CSR_1 by stating, "The connotation of 'responsibility' is that of the process of assuming an obligation. It places an emphasis on motivation rather than on performance." They go on to say, "Responding to social demands is much more than deciding what to do. There remains the management task of *doing* what one has decided to do, and this task is far from trivial."[62] They maintain that "social responsiveness" (CSR_2) is a more appropriate description of what is essential in the social arena.

This point has some merit. Responsibility, taken quite literally, does imply more of a state or condition of having assumed an obligation, whereas *responsiveness* connotes a dynamic, action-oriented condition. It should not be over-looked, however, that much of what business has done and is doing has resulted from a particular motivation—an assumption of an obligation—whether assigned by government, forced by special-interest groups, or voluntarily assumed. Accordingly, the corporate social responsiveness dimension is, practically speaking, an *action phase* of management's CSR response in the social sphere.

For many years now, there has been a trend toward making the concern for social, environmental, and ethical issues more and more *practical and results-oriented*. The responsiveness thrust was a step in this direction. Another step has been to emphasize what flows from the responsiveness idea—corporate social *performance*. The **corporate social performance (CSP)** focus addresses the accomplishment of an initiative. CSP suggests that what really matters is what companies are able to achieve—the results or outcomes of their acceptance of CSR, including the adoption of a responsiveness viewpoint. CSP is a bottom-line concept concerned with results.

A conceptual framework or model for CSP, as developed by Carroll, sought to identify three important dimensions of CSP. First, it is important to specify the nature (economic, legal, ethical, or philanthropic) of the responsibility. Next, it is important to identify a strategy, philosophy, pattern, or mode of responsiveness. Finally, it is important to identify the social or stakeholder issues to which these responsibilities are manifested and applied. The issues, and especially the degree of organizational interest in the issues, are always in a state of flux. As times change, so does the emphasis on the range of social or ethical issues and stakeholders that business feels compelled to address.

If corporate social *performance* identifies, typically from the company's point of view, what social programs have been able to achieve in terms of its objectives, results, or measures, another concept, that of **corporate social impact (CSI)**, carries this one step further and addresses what impact or effect is being realized or felt by the recipients of the firm's performance initiatives. Researchers have observed that most studies of CSR have stopped short of actually assessing impacts, especially toward the broader society. Their conclusion is that CSR initiatives need to be designed for greater social impact.[63] A concern for social impact would involve looking at the social initiative more from the point of view of the recipient of the social initiative

than from the perspective of the company. The distinction between performance and impact is subtle, but this distinction is likely to be further developed in the future. The emphasis on impact would necessitate that the stakeholders affected would be involved in the assessment of results.

2.5a Carroll's CSP Model

It is helpful to consider further Carroll's CSP model referenced above. Figure 2-7 presents Carroll's corporate social performance (CSP) model, which brings together the three major dimensions described above in a graphical depiction:

Dimension 1. Social responsibility categories—economic, legal, ethical, and discretionary (philanthropic).

Dimension 2. Philosophy (or mode) of social responsiveness—strategies ranging from reaction, defense, accommodation, and proaction.

Dimension 3. Social (or stakeholder) issues involved—consumers, environment, employees, community, shareholders, and others.[64]

The first dimension of this CSP model pertains to all that is included in the *definition of social responsibility* presented earlier—the economic, legal, ethical, and discretionary (philanthropic) components. The second is a *social responsiveness continuum* or dimension. This references the company's strategy, philosophy, or mode of responsiveness (e.g., reaction, defense, accommodation, proaction). The third dimension concerns the *scope or range of social or stakeholder issues* (e.g., consumerism, environment, product safety, and discrimination) that management must address in the first two dimensions.

The CSP model is intended to be useful to both academics and managers. For academics, the model is primarily a conceptual aid to understanding the distinctions among the various concepts of CSR that have appeared in the literature (responsibility, responsiveness, performance). What were previously regarded as separate explanations of CSR are treated here as three separate aspects or dimensions of CSP.

For the manager, the model provides a template to systematically think through major stakeholder issues. Although it does not provide guidance as to how far the organization should go, it does provide a framework that may lead to more effective social performance and impact. Companies may vary in which issues are most critical to them and what strategies of responsiveness they decide to pursue. An applicable example of this is the bold decision of CVS pharmacy to discontinue selling tobacco products. CVS decided that selling tobacco was no longer ethically consistent with selling pharmaceuticals and that proactive action (the discontinuance of tobacco sales) was needed.

In addition, the CSP model could be used as a planning and diagnostic problem-solving tool. It can assist the analysts or managers by identifying categories within which the organization and its decisions can be situated. There have been several extensions, reformulations, or reorientations of

Figure 2-7 Carroll's Corporate Social Performance Model

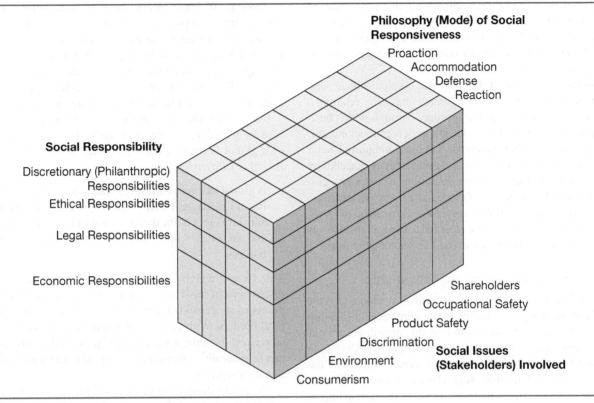

Philosophy (Mode) of Social Responsiveness
Proaction
Accommodation
Defense
Reaction

Social Responsibility
Discretionary (Philanthropic) Responsibilities
Ethical Responsibilities
Legal Responsibilities
Economic Responsibilities

Shareholders
Occupational Safety
Product Safety
Discrimination
Environment
Consumerism

Social Issues (Stakeholders) Involved

Source: Archie B. Carroll, "A Three-Dimensional Conceptual Model of Corporate Social Performance," *Academy of Management Review* (Vol. 4, No. 4, 1979), 503. Reproduced with permission.

the CSP model over the years, and these efforts have doubtless improved the CSP model.[65]

Though corporate social *responsibility, responsiveness, performance,* and *impact* each represent periods in the development of CSR, today most believe that when CSR is mentioned it implicitly embraces the responsibility, responsiveness, and performance/impact dimensions of the concept. That will be our assumption as we move forward with CSR discussions in this book. At the same time, moreover, many use the concepts of corporate citizenship and sustainability interchangeably.

2.6 Corporate Citizenship

Many business practitioners and academics alike have grown fond of the term **corporate citizenship** in reference to businesses' CSR and CSP. Earlier in the chapter, corporate citizenship was presented as another term used synonymously with *corporate social responsibility/responsiveness/performance* and *sustainability*. A careful look at the concept and its literature shows that although it is a useful and attractive term, it is not dissimilar to the other terminologies, except in the eyes of some writers who have attempted to give it a specific, narrow meaning. Nevertheless, it is a popular term and one worth briefly exploring.

If one thinks about companies as "citizens" of the countries and communities in which they reside, corporate citizenship means that these companies have certain duties or responsibilities they must fulfill to be perceived as good corporate citizens. In today's global business environment, some have argued that multinational enterprises are citizens of the world. Windsor has argued that corporate citizenship has become an important practitioner-based movement and that it conveys a sense of responsibility for social impacts or a sense of neighborliness in local communities.[66]

2.6a Broad and Narrow Views

Corporate citizenship has been described by some as a broad, inclusive term that essentially embraces all CSR-related issues. Corporate citizenship has been defined as "serving a variety of stakeholders well."[67] Reputation researcher Charles Fombrum proposed a broad conception. He holds that corporate citizenship is composed of a three-part view that encompasses (1) a reflection of shared moral and ethical principles, (2) a vehicle for integrating individuals into the communities in which they work, and (3) a form of enlightened self-interest that balances all stakeholders' claims and enhances a company's long-term value.[68]

Also in the broad view, the four-part definition of CSR may be seen as embracing the "four faces of corporate citizenship"—economic, legal, ethical, and philanthropic.

Each face, aspect, or responsibility category reveals an important facet of corporate citizenship that contributes to the whole. It is suggested that "just as private citizens are expected to fulfill these responsibilities, companies are as well."[69] This view essentially equates the concepts of CSR and corporate citizenship.

At the narrow end of the spectrum, corporate citizenship is often viewed simply as "corporate community relations." In this view, it embraces the functions through which business intentionally interacts with nonprofit organizations, citizen groups, and other stakeholders at the community level.[70] The focus in the narrow view is on one primary stakeholder group—the community. Other definitions of corporate citizenship fall between these broad and narrow perspectives, and some refer to global corporate citizenship as well, because today companies are expected to conduct themselves appropriately wherever they do business around the world.[71]

2.6b Stages of Corporate Citizenship

Like individual development, companies develop and grow in their maturity for dealing with corporate citizenship issues. A major contribution to how this growth occurs has been presented by researchers at the Center for Corporate Citizenship at Boston College. The center holds that the essence of corporate citizenship is how companies deliver on their core values in a way that minimizes harm, maximizes benefits, is accountable and responsive to key stakeholders, and supports strong financial results.[72] This definition is quite compatible with the four-part definition of CSR presented earlier. The center's **stages of corporate citizenship** concept helps to explain these points.

The development of the corporate citizenship model reflects a stage-by-stage process in which seven dimensions (*citizenship concept, strategic intent, leadership, structure, issues management, stakeholder relationships,* and *transparency*) evolve as companies move through five stages and become more sophisticated in their approaches to corporate citizenship. The five stages include *elementary, engaged, innovative, integrated,* and *transforming.*

The stages of corporate citizenship framework effectively present the challenges of credibility, capacity, coherence, and commitment that firms move through as they come to grips with developing more comprehensive and integrated citizenship agendas. From the researchers' work, it is apparent that corporate citizenship is not a static position but is one that progresses through different themes and challenges as firms get better and better over time.[73]

2.6c Global CSR and Corporate Citizenship

Global CSR and **global corporate citizenship** are topics that have become extremely important and relevant today. As global capitalism has become the marketplace stage for large- and medium-sized enterprises, the expectations that they address citizenship issues at a world level also multiply. Chapter 7 examines global business ethics in detail. Here, it is noted that there are also challenges for global CSR and global citizenship. To some extent, these are international extensions of the concepts treated throughout this book. Because cultures have features that are both divergent and common, however, adaptations of traditional CSR and corporate citizenship concepts often are necessary. Since there is no one-size-fits-all model of CSR, over time, countries are adapting CSR versions to best fit their local cultures and economies.

Two items illustrate the kind of thinking behind the idea of global corporate citizenship. First is a definition of a global business citizen presented in the book *Global Business Citizenship*:

> A global business citizen is a business enterprise (including its managers) that responsibly exercises its rights and implements its duties to individuals, stakeholders, and societies within and across national and cultural borders.[74]

This view of a global business citizen is consistent with the discussions of this topic from a domestic perspective, but it points to its expanded application across national and cultural borders. With this working definition, it can be understood how the citizenship concepts presented in this chapter can be naturally expanded and adapted to embrace multinational enterprises.

A second illustration of the global reach is provided by a distinction between frameworks for understanding CSR in America versus Europe. Earlier we discussed these differences with respect to the Pyramid of CSR. This distinction illustrates how CSR around the world has much in common, but specific, national contexts must be considered to fully grasp the topic. Matten and Moon maintain that CSR (and corporate citizenship) is more "explicit" in America, whereas it is more "implicit" in Europe. In their distinctions, they argue that **explicit CSR** would normally consist of voluntary, self-interest-driven policies, programs, and strategies as is typical in U.S.-based understandings of CSR.

By contrast, **implicit CSR** would embrace the entirety of a country's formal and informal institutions that assign corporations an agreed-on share of responsibility for society's concerns. Implicit CSR, such as that seen in the United Kingdom and Europe, would embrace the values, norms, and rules evident in the local culture.[75] The authors contend that CSR is more implicit, or understood, in Europe because it is more a part of the culture than in the United States. In Europe, some aspects of CSR are decreed or imposed by institutions, such as government, whereas in the United States, CSR is more voluntary, often pressured, and driven by companies' specific, explicit actions. And, when thinking about CSR and corporate citizenship in the global context, a special case must be made for their applications in developing countries.[76]

In short, although CSR and corporate citizenship have much in common in terms of their applicability around the world and in diverse countries, national differences are also likely to exist, which might suggest divergent or dissimilar strategies depending on where business is being conducted. One study of firms from 42 countries found that the *political* system followed by the *labor* and *education* systems and the *cultural* system were the most important variables that affected corporate social performance and citizenship in different countries.[77] Following this, Political CSR, discussed earlier, would be more applicable in Europe and other social democracies. As the world economic stage becomes more of a common environment within which businesses function, convergence in CSR approaches seems predictable.

2.7 The Social Performance and Financial Performance Relationship

An issue that surfaces frequently in considerations of CSR-related concepts is whether there is a demonstrable relationship between a firm's social responsibility performance and its financial performance. Attempts to measure this relationship have typically been hampered by definitional and measurement problems. The appropriate performance criteria for measuring financial performance and social responsibility are subject to debate. Furthermore, the accurate measurement of social responsibility is difficult at best.

Over the years, many studies on the social responsibility–financial performance relationship have produced mixed results.[78] In a comprehensive meta-analysis, one review of research on the relationship supports the conclusion that social and financial performance are positively related. The researchers conclude by saying, "portraying managers' choices with respect to CSP and CFP as an either/or trade-off is not justified in light of 30 years of empirical data."[79] In another study, the conclusion was reached that "there is a small, but positive relationship between corporate social performance and company financial performance."[80] Finally, other studies have concluded that research supports a positive association between corporate social and financial performance.[81]

2.7a Three Perspectives on the Social–Financial–Reputation Relationship

To understand the relationship between social performance, financial performance, and reputation, it is important to note

---

Ethics In Practice Case

Fresh, Local, and Sustainable: Burgers with a Soul

Burgerville sells not only burgers but also good works. But if you don't live in Oregon or the state of Washington, you may have never heard about Burgerville, a company founded in 1961 in Vancouver, Washington. As of 2021, there were 40 Burgerville restaurants spanning those two states with more scheduled to come.

In the 1990s, when Burgerville began losing sales of its burgers to the national chains, Chief Executive Tom Mears decided to differentiate his product and sell "burgers with a soul." Mears, the son-in-law of the founder, decided to combine good food with good works. The company began to build its strategy around three key words—"fresh, local, and sustainable." It pursued this strategy through partnerships with local businesses, farms, and producers. *Gourmet* magazine once recognized Burgerville as the home of the nation's freshest fast food.

According to the company's website, "At Burgerville, doing business responsibly means doing business sustainably. One example of this is our commitment to purchasing 100 percent local wind power equal to the energy use of all our restaurants and corporate office." The company purchases its electricity from local windmills. Burgerville uses "sustainable agriculture," which means that its meat and produce are free from genetically modified seeds or livestock. In its cooking, the company avoids trans-fats, and once the cooking oils are used up, they are converted into biodiesel. The company buys its antibiotic- and hormone-free beef locally.

In addition to burgers, Burgerville offers a wild Coho salmon and Oregon hazelnut salad. Meals for children often come with seeds and gardening tools rather than the usual cheap toy offered at the national chains.

Burgerville extends its good works to its employees. The company pays 95 percent of the health insurance for its hundreds of workers. This adds $1.5 million to its annual compensation expense. To get its affordable health care, employees have to work a minimum of 20 hours a week for at least six months, a more generous arrangement than most provided by stores.

Being a good corporate citizen is expensive when done the Burgerville way. Though the company won't reveal its financial bottom line, one industry consultant estimated that its margin is closer to 10 percent compared with McDonald's 15 percent. Like many other fast-food restaurants, Burgerville has had to adapt to a changing world during the COVID-19 pandemic period, but it hopes to restore its status when the critical period of the pandemic passes.

1. Is the world ready for a socially responsible, sustainable hamburger? How much extra would you be willing to pay, assuming the burgers really taste good?
2. What tensions among its economic, legal, ethical, and philanthropic responsibilities do you think are most pressing to Burgerville?
3. Does Burgerville sound like a business that might work in Oregon and Washington, but maybe not elsewhere? What is the future of Burgerville?

Sources: "Fast Food: Want a Cause with That?" *Forbes* (January 8, 2007), 83; "4 Secrets from HR Experts on Engaging Employees in Workplace Wellness," *Washington Business Journal*, https://www.bizjournals.com/washington/how-to/human-resources/2015/10/4-secrets-from-hr-experts-on-workplace-wellness.html, accessed March 1, 2021; "About Burgerville," http://www.burgerville.com/about/, accessed January 29, 2021.

that there have been at least three different perspectives that have dominated discussions and research.

Perspective 1. The most popular view is the belief that *socially responsible firms are more financially profitable.* To those who advocate the concept of social performance, it is apparent why they would like to think that social performance is a driver of financial performance and, in addition, a corporation's reputation. If it could be demonstrated that socially responsible firms, in general, are more financially successful and have better reputations, this would significantly bolster the CSP view, even in the eyes of its critics. Perspective 1 has been studied extensively. The findings of many of the studies that have sought to demonstrate this relationship have been inconclusive.[82] Alternatively, other studies have concluded that CSR positively affects the firm's financial performance by developing a positive image among the stakeholders and decreasing overall costs.[83] Barnett and Salomon studied different degrees of CSP and found that firms with high CSP have the highest CFP.[84]

Perspective 2. This view, which has not been studied as extensively, argues that a firm's financial performance is a driver of its social performance. This perspective is built somewhat on the notion that social responsibility is a "fair weather" concept. That is, when times are good and companies are enjoying financial success, higher levels of social

performance are observed. In one major study, it was found that financial performance either precedes or is contemporaneous with social performance. This evidence supports the view that social–financial performance correlations are best explained by positive synergies or by "available funding."[85]

Perspective 3. A third perspective argues that there is an *interactive* relationship between and among social performance, financial performance, and corporate reputation. In this symbiotic view, the three major factors influence each other, and, because they are so interrelated, it is not easy to identify which factor is driving the process. In one major study, researchers concluded that the relationships flow in each direction; that is, what is profitable performance is social performance and what is social is profitable, thereby resulting in a positive feedback circle.[86] Regardless of the perspective taken, each view advocates a significant role for CSP, and it is expected that researchers will continue to explore these perspectives for years to come using different methodologies. Further, if business leaders believe there are positive and interactive effects between CSR, CSP, and reputation, and they do, they will continue to pursue these social-stakeholder strategies.[87] Figure 2-8 depicts the essentials of each of these views.

Related to this, it should be mentioned that a "contingency" view suggests that CSP should be seen as a function of the "fit" between specific strategies and structures and the nature of the social issue. According to Husted's

Figure 2-8 Relationships among Corporate Social Performance (CSP), Corporate Financial Performance (CFP), and Corporate Reputation (CR)

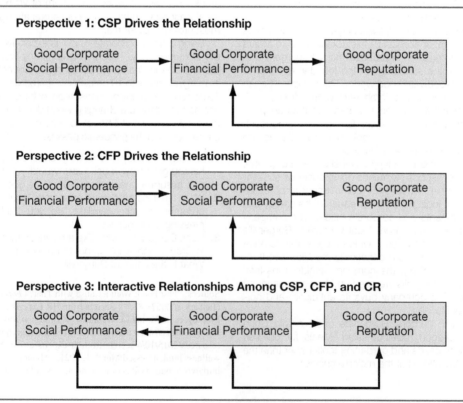

Spotlight on Sustainability

Myths about Sustainability

There are many myths and misconceptions about sustainability. Often these misconceptions, or myths, serve as barriers to companies pursuing sustainable development. Myths about sustainability are eliminated when the experiences of leading companies are considered. Following are some insights running counter to some of these misconceptions.

1. *Sustainability is a cost we can't afford right now.* Former Xerox CEO Anne Mulcahy said that being "a good corporate citizen" saved the company from bankruptcy.
2. *There's no money to be made from sustainability.* Johnson & Johnson has undertaken 80 sustainability projects since 2005 and achieved $187 million in savings with an ROI of nearly 19 percent, and rising.
3. *It's just for big companies.* Actually, smaller companies have an advantage because their competitiveness often depends on being lean, resourceful, and nimble, which sustainability makes possible.

4. *We'll be accused of greenwashing if we pursue sustainability.* Companies that set and achieve meaningful goals have the right to publicize their successes.
5. *Since we don't make things, we don't have to worry about the supply chain.* Walmart doesn't make things, but it has developed a supplier index for its thousands of suppliers to gauge the carbon impact from supplies they sell to the business.

Sources: Vijay Kanal, "The Eight Biggest Myths about Sustainability in Business," https://www.greenbiz.com/article/eight-biggest-myths-about-sustainability-business, accessed February 15, 2021; Michael D. Lemonick, "Top 10 Myths about Sustainability," July 2, 2020, https://rubberform.com/top-10-myths-about-sustainability, accessed February 15, 2021; Stockholm Environment Institute, "Dispelling Myths about Sustainability and People," https://www.sei.org/events/dispelling-myths-on-sustainability-and-people/, accessed February 15, 2021.

---

research, the social issue is determined by the expectation gaps between the firm and its stakeholders that occur within or between views of what is and/or ought to be, and high CSP is achieved by closing these expectation gaps with the appropriate strategy and structure.[88]

A basic premise of all these perspectives is that there is only one "bottom line"—a corporate *financial* bottom line—that addresses primarily the shareholders' investments in the firm. An alternative view is that the firm has "multiple bottom lines" that benefit from CSP. This **stakeholder–bottom line** perspective maintains that the impacts or benefits of social performance cannot be fully measured or appreciated by considering only the impact on the firm's financial bottom line.

To truly employ a stakeholder perspective, companies need to accept the stakeholder–bottom line view as reflective of reality. Thus, CSP cannot be fully comprehended unless its impacts on stakeholders, such as consumers, employees, the community, and other stakeholder groups, are recognized and measured. Research may never conclusively demonstrate a simple relationship between CSP and financial performance. If a stakeholder perspective is taken, however, it may be more straightforward to assess the impact of CSP on multiple stakeholders.

2.8 Creating Shared Value, Conscious Capitalism, and Purpose-Driven Business

In addition to CSR, corporate citizenship, and sustainability, which will be further addressed in Chapter 4, three other concepts have become popular in recent years: creating shared value, conscious capitalism, and purpose-driven business. Since they overlap significantly with the earlier presented CSR-related frameworks, their treatment here will be brief.

Creating Shared Value (CSV). The CSV concept was introduced by Porter and Kramer as a response to what they saw as too narrow a view of value creation on the part of businesses. They argued that business and society could be brought back together again if businesses redefined their basic purpose as creating shared value, that is, generating economic value in a way that also produces value for society by addressing its challenges. They argued that companies could do this in three ways: by reconceiving products and markets, by redefining productivity in the value chain, or by building supportive industry clusters at the company's locations. They believed that CSV has the potential to reshape capitalism and improve the business and society relationship.[89] Their concept has gained a lot of attention. Some critics, however, have pointed out shortcomings of CSV, saying it is an unoriginal idea and is based on a shallow conception of the corporation's role in society.[90]

Conscious Capitalism. The concept of conscious capitalism was developed by John Mackey, cofounder of Whole Foods. According to Mackey, "conscious capitalism is a more complex form of capitalism that reflects and leverages the interdependent nature of life and all of the stakeholders in business."[91] Companies that practice conscious capitalism are said to be ones that follow the four pillars guiding their practice. These four basic pillars include a *higher purpose, stakeholder orientation, conscious leadership*, and a *conscious culture*.[92] It is significant to observe that the companies that are embracing either CSV or conscious capitalism are typically the same companies that have been identified as high on CSR, corporate citizenship, and sustainability characteristics. Examples include Whole Foods, Starbucks,

Figure 2-9 The CSR Evolutionary Trajectory

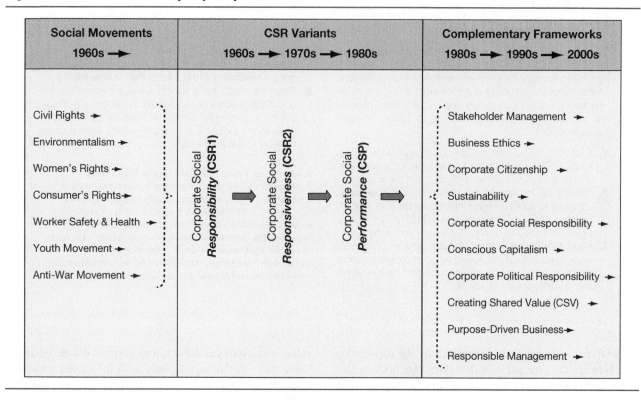

Chipotle, Costco, Panera, and The Container Store.[93] The overlapping characteristics of CSV and conscious capitalism with concepts already presented are numerous and, therefore, they will not be treated in more detail. A careful consideration of the features of all these frameworks, however, is worthwhile as each has something important to contribute to the improvement of business and society relationships.

Purpose-Driven Business. *Purpose* is a buzzword that has captured considerable attention in the past several years. It is being maintained that purpose-driven companies are outperforming profit-driven companies.[94] For the most part, the notion of purpose-driven appears to be a fashionable nomenclature for CSR and conscious capitalism. The "purpose" behind the concept replicates the basic pillar of "higher purpose" that characterizes conscious capitalism. It suggests that companies should operate with all important stakeholders in mind, not just shareholders. This makes it duplicative with the idea of CSR. Three mistakes about the usage of purpose have been set forth: (1) using a vague purpose, as saying "we strive to make a difference" is too vague; (2) equating purpose with philanthropy—this is the same mistake made with CSR, indicating it only pertains to business giving; and (3) the mistake of making purpose a project, as purpose is not a "one and done" project and requires a total commitment to a restyled corporate culture to be effective.[95] In a recent Porter Novelli study of purpose, 90 percent of business leaders believed that leading with purpose gives them an advantage in today's marketplace.[96]

Figure 2-9 presents an evolutionary trajectory of corporate social responsibility concepts and variants, including an indication of the social movements that started them all and the complementary frameworks that have evolved over time. It is expected that most of the alternative frameworks will continue to be popular because they all have their own supporters and advocates.

2.9 Socially Responsible, Sustainable, ESG Investing

Special-interest groups, business, the media, and academics are not alone in their interest in business's social performance. Investors are increasingly interested. The **socially responsible, sustainable, or ethical investing** movement arrived on the scene in the 1970s and has continued to grow and prosper. Like the CSR movement, it has taken on different names. Today it is sometimes called **impact investing**, ethical investing, or **environmental, social, and governance (ESG) investing**. Socially responsible investing (SRI) has matured into a comprehensive investing approach complete with social and environmental screens, shareholder activism, and community investment, accounting for about $17 trillion of investments in the United States, according to the Forum for Sustainable and Responsible Investing.[97] The SRI Forum refers to it as sustainable, responsible, impact investing that considers environmental, social, and corporate governance (ESG) criteria aimed at generating long-term competitive financial returns and positive societal impact.

Socially conscious investments have been continuing to grow.[98] Today, about one-third of professional management investments are categorized as sustainable investments. Over the years 2018–2020, the leading issues with ESG investing have been corporate political activity; labor and equal employment opportunity; climate change; executive pay; and independent board chairs.[99]

As expected, managers of socially conscious mutual funds do not use only ethical or social responsibility criteria to decide which companies to invest in. They consider a company's financial health before all else. Moreover, a growing corps of brokers, financial planners, and portfolio managers are available to help people evaluate investments for their social impacts.[100] The steady flow of money into ESG funds is notable because they have logged better-than-average returns especially during the highly volatile market in 2020. The evidence seems clear: social investing is here to stay.[101]

The concept of *social screening* is the backbone of the socially conscious investing movement. Investors seeking to put their money into socially responsible firms want to *screen out* those firms they consider to be socially irresponsible or to actively *screen in* those firms they think of as socially responsible or sustainable. Thus, there are negative social screens and positive social screens. Some of the *negative social screens* that historically have been used include the avoidance of investing in tobacco manufacturers, gambling casino operators, and defense or weapons contractors.[102]

It is more difficult, and thus more challenging, to implement *positive social screens*, because these require the potential investor to make judgment calls as to what constitutes an acceptable or a strong level of social performance on social investment criteria. Criteria that may be used as either positive or negative screens, depending on the firm's performance, might include the firm's demonstrated record on issues such as equal employment opportunity and affirmative action, diversity, environmental sustainability, treatment of employees, corporate citizenship (broadly defined), and treatment of animals.[103]

Today, two basic strategies are used for sustainable investing. First is the traditional use of ESG criteria in portfolio construction across a wide range of asset classes. Community investing, which represents an important segment, seeks to finance projects or institutions that serve poor and underserved communities. The second strategy involves the filing of shareholder resolutions and practicing other forms of shareholder engagement aimed at social or sustainable objectives. These two basic strategies combine together to encourage responsible business practices and to allocate capital for social benefits across the economy.[104]

Regardless of what it is called, it is clear that social or impact investing has "arrived" on the scene and has become a major part of the mainstream. Socially responsible investing is growing globally as well.[105] Socially conscious mutual funds will continue to be debated in the investment community. The fact that they exist, have grown, and have prospered, however, provides evidence that the practice is a serious one and that there truly are investors in the real world who take the social responsibility and sustainability issues quite seriously.

Summary

Corporate social responsibility, responsiveness, performance, impact and corporate citizenship, sustainability, purpose-driven businesses are important and related concepts. The CSR concept and its variants have a rich history. It has grown out of many diverse views. A four-part conceptualization was presented that broadly conceives CSR as encompassing economic, legal, ethical, and philanthropic obligations. The four responsibilities were also depicted as part of the Pyramid of CSR—building upon the basic economic foundations of business.

The concern for CSR has been expanded to include a concern for social responsiveness, social performance, and social impact. A CSP model was presented that brought the responsibility and responsiveness dimensions together into a framework that also identified categories of social or stakeholder issues that must be considered.

The concept of CSR Greenwashing alerts us to be careful about companies' claims. Political CSR (PCSR) was identified as a topic that is growing in importance, especially in Europe. The term *corporate citizenship* arrived on the scene to embrace a whole host of socially conscious activities and

practices on the part of businesses. This term has become quite popular in the business community. It is not clear that the concept is different than the emphases on corporate social responsibility, responsiveness, and performance, but it is a terminology being frequently used. Other popular terminologies that share support include *conscious capitalism*, *creating shared value*, and *purpose-driven business*. These concepts align nicely with other CSR-related ideas discussed.

Three possible perspectives on the relationship between and among corporate social performance, financial performance, and corporate reputation were explored. The positive relationships among these concepts have been found to be modest, and research continues to flesh out more definitive conclusions. Whether the relationships can be empirically proven is one issue. More important is the fact that many business executives believe the relationships are valid for a multitude of "business case for CSR" justifications. Today, a concern for sustainability has taken its place at the table. The language of sustainability has become quite popular among businesses, academics, and the media. This topic is the primary subject in Chapter 4.

Finally, the socially responsible, ESG, or impact investing movement is flourishing. This success documents that there is a growing body of investors who are sensitive to business's social and ethical (as well as financial) performance. Studies of social or ESG investing have demonstrated that investors do not have to give up financial performance to achieve social performance and impact. The industry has been growing exponentially and is now considered to be a vital part of the mainstream of investing.

Key Terms

Business Case for CSR, p. 29
Business for Social Responsibility (BSR), p. 18
conscious capitalism, p. 20
corporate citizenship, p. 20
corporate social impact (CSI), p. 32
corporate social performance (CSP), p. 32
corporate social responsibility (CSR), p. 19
corporate social responsibility (CSR₁), p.31
corporate social responsiveness (CSR₂), p. 31

creating shared value (CSV), p. 20
CSR exemplar firms, p. 26
CSR Greenwashing, p. 31
economic responsibilities, p. 21
environmental, social, and governance (ESG) investing, p. 38
ethical responsibilities, p. 22
explicit CSR, p. 34
global corporate citizenship, p. 34
impact investing, p. 38
implicit CSR, p. 34
legal responsibilities, p. 22
mainstream adopters (of CSR), p. 27
philanthropic responsibilities, p. 22

philanthropy, p. 23
purpose-driven business, p. 20
Pyramid of Corporate Social Responsibility (CSR), p. 24
social enterprises, p. 26
social entrepreneurship, p. 26
social intrapreneurship, p. 27
socially responsible, sustainable, or ethical investing, p. 38
stages of corporate citizenship, p. 34
stakeholder–bottom line, p. 37
sustainability, p. 20
sustainable development, p. 29

Discussion Questions

1. Generally speaking, what does CSR mean? What are some of the earlier definitions of CSR? Why were they sometimes ambiguous?

2. Explain the Pyramid of Corporate Social Responsibility. Define each category and provide several examples of each "layer" of the pyramid. Identify and discuss some of the tensions among and between the layers or components. In what sense do the different layers of the pyramid "overlap" with each other?

3. In what sense is the Pyramid of CSR a unified whole, dynamic, and sustainable? How is it stakeholder inclusive?

4. Explain what makes a CSR exemplar firm. Distinguish among social entrepreneurship, social intrapreneurship, and mainstream adopters.

5. In your view, what is the single strongest argument *against* the idea of corporate social responsibility?

What is the single strongest argument *for* corporate social responsibility? Briefly explain.

6. Differentiate between corporate social *responsibility*, social *responsiveness*, and social *performance*. How does corporate social *impact* relate to these terms?

7. What is unique about the following alternative frameworks to CSR: corporate citizenship, sustainability, creating shared value, conscious capitalism, and purpose-driven business? Why do businesspeople and academicians like to create or adopt faddish terms?

8. Does socially responsible investing seem to you to be a legitimate way in which the average citizen might demonstrate concern for CSR? Why is it also called impact investing? Discuss.

Endnotes

1. Archie B. Carroll, "Corporate Social Responsibility: The Centerpiece of Competing and Complimentary Frameworks," *Organizational Dynamics* (2015), 44: 87–96.

2. Business for Social Responsibility, https://www.bsr.org/en/about. Accessed December 1, 2020.

3. Robert Strand, "The Chief Officer of Corporate Social Responsibility: A Study of Its Presence in Top Management Teams," *Journal of Business Ethics* (2013), 112: 721–734.

4. Quoted in John L. Paluszek, *Business and Society: 1976–2000* (New York: AMACOM, 1976), 1.

5. Keith Davis, "Understanding the Social Responsibility Puzzle," *Business Horizons* (Winter 1967), 45–50.

6. For a more complete history of corporate responsibility in the United States, see Archie B. Carroll, Kenneth J. Lipartito, James E. Post, Patricia H. Werhane, and Kenneth E. Goodpaster, executive editor, *Corporate Responsibility: The American Experience* (Cambridge, MA: Cambridge University Press, 2012).

7. Keith Davis and Robert L. Blomstrom, *Business and Society: Environment and Responsibility*, 3rd ed. (New York: McGraw-Hill, 1975), 39.

8. Joseph W. McGuire, *Business and Society* (New York: McGraw-Hill, 1963), 144.

9. For a more complete history of the CSR concept, see Archie B. Carroll, "Corporate Social Responsibility: Evolution of a Definitional Construct," *Business and Society,* 38(3), September 1999, 268–295.

10. Alexander Dahlsrud, "How Corporate Social Responsibility Is Defined: An Analysis of 37 Definitions," *Corporate Social Responsibility and Environmental Management*, 15, 2008, 1–13.

11. Archie B. Carroll, "A Three-Dimensional Conceptual Model of Corporate Social Performance," *Academy of Management Review,* 4(4), 1979, 497–505. Also see Archie B. Carroll, "The Pyramid of Corporate Social Responsibility: Toward the Moral Management of Organizational Stakeholders," *Business Horizons* (July–August 1991), 39–48.

12. Stuart Taylor Jr. and Evan Thomas, "Civil Wars," *Newsweek* (December 15, 2003), 43–53.

13. Brian Armstrong, "The Digital Economy Is Becoming Ordinary, Best We Understand It," *The Conversation*, January 24, 2020, https://theconversation.com/the-digital -economy-is-becoming-ordinary-best-we-understand -it-130398#:~:text=The%20best%20example%20of%20 this,between%20strangers%20in%20new%20ways. Accessed December 10, 2020.

14. Archie B. Carroll, "The Pyramid of Corporate Social Responsibility: Toward the Moral Management of Organizational Stakeholders," *Business Horizons* (July–August 1991), 39–48. Also see Archie B. Carroll, "The Four Faces of Corporate Citizenship," *Business and Society Review*, 100–101, 1998, 1–7.

15. Ibid. Also see Mark S. Schwartz, *Corporate Social Responsibility: An Ethical Approach* (Peterborough, Ontario: Broadview Press, 2011).

16. Winshape Foundation, https://winshape.org/. Accessed December 12, 2020.

17. Aflac, https://www.choa.org/medical-services/cancer-and -blood-disorders/aflac-cancer-and-blood-disorder-center. Accessed December 12, 2020.

18. General Mills, https://blog.generalmills.com/2020/04/were -making-food-and-giving-it-away/. Accessed December 12, 2020.

19. Timberland, "Community Service," https://images. timberland.com/is/content/TimberlandBrand/ Responsibility/downloads/2020/q3/Community_Q3_2020. pdf. Accessed December 12, 2020.

20. Mark Schwartz and Archie Carroll, "Corporate Social Responsibility: A Three Domain Approach," *Business Ethics Quarterly*, 13(4), 2003, 503–530.

21. Carroll, 1991, 1–7.

22. Wayne Visser, "Corporate Social Responsibility in Developing Countries," in Andrew Crane, Abagail McWilliams, Dirk Matten, Jeremy Moon, and Donald S. Siegel (eds.), *The Oxford Handbook of Corporate Social Responsibility* (Oxford: Oxford University Press, 2008), 473–499.

23. R. Edward Freeman, S. Ramakrishna Velamuri, and Brian Moriarty, "Company Stakeholder Responsibility: A New Approach to CSR," *Business Roundtable Institute for Corporate Ethics Bridge Paper* (2006), 10.

24. Dirk Matten and Jeremy Moon, "Implicit and Explicit CSR: A Conceptual Framework for Understanding CSR in Europe," *Research Paper Series, International Centre for CSR* (Nottingham University Business School, U.K., 2004), 9. Also see N. A. Dentchey, M. Balen, and E. Haezendonck, "On Voluntarism and the Role of Governments in CSR: Towards a Contingency Approach," *Business Ethics: A European Review*, 2015.

25. Wayne Visser, "Corporate Social Responsibility in Developing Countries," in Andrew Crane, Abagail McWilliams, Dirk Matten, Jeremy Moon, and Donald Siegel (eds.), *The Oxford Handbook of Corporate Social Responsibility* (Oxford: Oxford University Press, 2008), 473–502. Also see D. Jamali, "CSR in Developing Countries through an Institutional Lens." *Corporate Social Responsibility and Sustainability: Emerging Trends in Developing Economies (Critical Studies on Corporate Responsibility, Governance and Sustainability,* Volume 8) Emerald Group Publishing Limited, 2014, *8*, 21–44.

26. Walker Group, "Corporate Character: It's Driving Competitive Companies: Where's It Driving Yours?" Unpublished document, 1994.

27. Laura J. Spence, "Small Business Social Responsibility: Expanding Core CSR Theory," *Business and Society*, 55(1), 2016, 23–55.

28. Social Enterprise Alliance, "What Is Social Enterprise?" https://socialenterprise.us/about/social-enterprise/. Accessed February 15, 2021.

29. Cory Ames, ""50 Social Entrepreneurs Changing the World," Grow Ensemble, April 25, 2020. Accessed January 28, 2021.

30. M. E. Porter and M. R. Kramer, "Creating Shared Value," *Harvard Business Review* (January–February 2011), 64.

31. Toms, https://www.toms.com/. Accessed February 15, 2021.

32. Certified B Corporation, "About B Corps," https:// bcorporation.net/about-b-corps. Accessed February 15, 2021.

33. MovingWorlds, "Social Intrapreneurship: Creating Change from Inside," https://movingworlds.org/social -intrapreneurship. Accessed December 12, 2020.

34. Carroll et al., 2012, 373–374.

35. For further discussion, see Duane Windsor, "Corporate Social Responsibility: Cases for and against It," in Marc J. Epstein and Kirk O. Hanson, eds., *The Accountable Corporation: Corporate Social Responsibility,* Vol. 3 (Westport, CN and London: Praeger, 2006), 31–50.

36. Milton Friedman, "The Social Responsibility of Business Is to Increase Its Profits," *The New York Times* (September 1962), 126. Also see "Special Report: Milton Friedman," *The Economist* (November 25, 2006), 79.

37. Ibid, 33 (emphasis added).

38. Aneel Karnani, "The Case against Corporate Social Responsibility," *The Wall Street Journal*, August 23, 2010, R1; R4.

39. Christopher D. Stone, *Where the Law Ends* (New York: Harper Colophon Books, 1975), 77.

40. Keith Davis, "The Case for and against Business Assumption of Social Responsibilities," *Academy of Management Journal* (June 1973), 312–322.

41. F. A. Hayek, "The Corporation in a Democratic Society: In Whose Interest Ought It and Will It Be Run?" in H. Ansoff (ed.), *Business Strategy* (Middlesex: Penguin, 1969), 225.

42. Davis, 320.

43. Davis, 316.

44. Businesswire, "Consumers Expect the Brands They Support to Be Socially Responsible," October 2, 2019,

https://www.businesswire.com/news/home
/20191002005697/en/Consumers-Expect-the
-Brands-they-Support-to-be-Socially-Responsible.
Accessed December 13, 2020.

45. Nielsen, "Global consumers Are Willing to Put Their
Money Where Their Heart Is When It Comes to Goods
and Services from Companies Committed to Social
Responsibility," https://www.nielsen.com/us/en/press
-releases/2014/global-consumers-are-willing-to-put-their
-money-where-their-heart-is/. Accessed December 10,
2020.

46. Solitaire Townsend, "88% of Consumers Want
You to Help Them Make a Difference," *Forbes*,
November 21, 2018, https://www.forbes.com/sites
/solitairetownsend/2018/11/21/consumers-want-you
-to-help-them-make-a-difference/?sh=46991a7d6954.
Accessed December 10, 2020.

47. Archie B. Carroll and Kareem M. Shabana, "The Business
Case for Corporate Social Responsibility: A Review of
Concepts, Research and Practice," *International Journal of
Management Reviews*, 12(1), March 2010, 85–105.

48. Archie B. Carroll and K. M. Shabana, "The Business Case
for Sustainability," in *Sustainability Matters: Why and
How Corporate Boards Should Become Involved*," Matteo
Tonello (ed.), Research Report R-1481-11-RR (New York:
The Conference Board, 2011), 21–26.

49. Reported in "CSR—A Religion with Too Many Priests,"
European Business Forum (Issue 15, Autumn 2003).

50. Simon Zadek, *The Civil Corporation: The New Economy
of Corporate Citizenship* (London: Earthscan, 2001). See
also Lance Moir, "Social Responsibility: The Changing
Role of Business," Cranfield School of Management, U.K.

51. Kasturi Rangan, Lisa Chase, and Sohel Karim, "The Truth
about CSR," *Harvard Business Review* (January–February
2015), 41–49.

52. Business in the Community Ireland, "The Business
Case for CSR," https://www.bitc.ie/join-the-network/the
-business-case-for-csr/. Accessed March 1, 2021.

53. Babson College, "Project ROI: Making the Case for
Responsible Business Practices," https://www.babson
.edu/academics/centers-and-institutes/the-lewis-institute
/thought-leadership/project-roi/#. Accessed December 10,
2020.

54. Stephan Meier and Lea Cassar, "Stop Talking about How
CSR Helps Your Bottom Line," *Harvard Business Review*
(January 31, 2018), https://hbr.org/2018/01/stop-talking-about
-how-csr-helps-your-bottom-line. Accessed March 1, 2021.

55. Michael Barnett, "The Business Case for Corporate Social
Responsibility: A Critique and a Path Forward," *Business
& Society*, 58(1), 2019, 167–190.

56. David Gelles, "Social Responsibility That Rubs Right
Off," *The New York Times*, October 18, 2015, BU 3.

57. Harrison Vogt, "Fashion Companies Use Greenwashing to
Lie to Consumers," *The Daily Orange,* http://dailyorange
.com/2020/03/fashion-companies-use-greenwashing-lie
-consumers/. Accessed March 1, 2021.

58. A. G. Scherer, A. Rasche, G. Palazzo, and A. Spicer,
"Managing for Political Corporate Social Responsibility—
New Challenges and Directions for PCSR 2.0," *Journal
of Management Studies*, 53, 2016. Also see BOS Business
and Society, "What Do We Mean by Political CSR—
Towards a Definition," http://blog.cbs.dk/BOS/2016/03/19
/what-do-we-mean-by-political-csr-towards-a-definition/.
Accessed March 30, 2016.

59. Jedrzej George Frynas and Sian Stephens, "Political
Corporate Social Responsibility: Reviewing Theories
and Setting New Agendas," *International Journal of
Management Reviews*, 17, 2015, 483–509.

60. A. G. Scherer and G. Palazzo, "The New Political Role
of Business in a Globalized World: A Review of a New
Perspective on CSR and Its Implications for the Firm,
Governance, and Democracy," *Journal of Management
Studies,* 48, 2011, 899–931.

61. Frynas and Stephens, ibid.

62. Robert Ackerman and Raymond Bauer, *Corporate Social
Responsiveness: The Modern Dilemma* (Reston, VA:
Reston Publishing Company, 1976), 6.

63. Michael L. Barnett, Irene Henriques, and Bryan Husted,
"Beyond Good Intentions: Designing CSR Initiatives for
Greater Social Impact," *Journal of Management,* 46(6),
July 2020, 937–964.

64. Carroll, 1979, 502–504.

65. Steven L. Wartick and Philip L. Cochran, "The Evolution
of the Corporate Social Performance Model," *Academy of
Management Review,* 10, 1985, 765–766; Donna J. Wood,
"Corporate Social Performance Revisited," *Academy
of Management Review,* October 1991, 691–718; D. L.
Swanson, "Addressing a Theoretical Problem by Reorienting
the Corporate Social Performance Model," *Academy of
Management Review,* 20(1), 1995, 43–64; D. L. Swanson,
"Toward an Integrative Theory of Business and Society:
A Research Strategy for Corporate Social Performance,"
Academy of Management Review, 24(3), 1999, 596–521.

66. Duane Windsor, "Corporate Citizenship: Evolution and
Interpretation," in Jörg Andriof and Malcom McIntosh
(eds.), *Perspectives on Corporate Citizenship* (Sheffield,
UK: Greenleaf Publishing, 2001), 39–52.

67. Samuel P. Graves, Sandra Waddock, and Marjorie Kelly,
"How Do You Measure Corporate Citizenship?" *Business
Ethics* (March/April 2001), 17.

68. Charles J. Fombrum, "Three Pillars of Corporate
Citizenship," in Noel Tichy, Andrew McGill, and Lynda
St. Clair (eds.), *Corporate Global Citizenship* (San
Francisco: The New Lexington Press), 27–61.

69. Archie B. Carroll, "The Four Faces of Corporate Citizenship,"
Business and Society Review, 100/101, 1998, 1–7.

70. Barbara W. Altman, *Corporate Community Relations
in the 1990s: A Study in Transformation*, unpublished
doctoral dissertation, Boston University.

71. Andreas G. Scherer and Guido Palazzo (eds.),
Handbook of Research on Global Corporate Citizenship
(Cheltenham, UK: Edward Elgar Publishing, 2008).

72. Philip Mirvis and Bradley K. Googins, *Stages of
Corporate Citizenship: A Developmental Framework*
(monograph) (Boston: The Center for Corporate
Citizenship at Boston College, 2006), i.

73. Ibid., 1–18.

74. Donna J. Wood, Jeanne M. Logsdon, Patsy G. Lewellyn,
and Kim Davenport, *Global Business Citizenship: A
Transformative Framework for Ethics and Sustainable
Capitalism* (Armonk, NY: M. E. Sharpe, 2006), 40.

75. Dirk Matten and Jeremy Moon, "Implicit and Explicit
CSR: A Conceptual Framework for Understanding CSR in
Europe," *Research Paper Series, International Centre for
Corporate Social Responsibility* (Nottingham University
Business School, United Kingdom, 2004), 9.

76. Wayne Visser, "Corporate Social Responsibility in
Developing Countries," in Andrew Crane, Abagail

McWilliams, Dirk Matten, Jeremy Moon, and Donald Siegel (eds.), *The Oxford Handbook of Corporate Social Responsibility* (Nottingham University Business School, United Kingdom, 2004), 9.

77. Ioannis Ioannou and George Serafeim, "What Drives Corporate Social Performance? The Role of Nation-Level Institutions," *Journal of International Business Studies*, 43, December 2012, 834–864. Cited on Harvard Business Review Faculty and Research, https://www.hbs.edu/faculty /Pages/item.aspx?num=42921. Accessed March 1, 2021.

78. See, for example, Mark Starik and Archie B. Carroll, "In Search of Beneficence: Reflections on the Connections between Firm Social and Financial Performance," in Karen Paul (ed.), *Contemporary Issues in Business and Society in the United States and Abroad* (Lewiston, NY: The Edwin Mellen Press, 1991), 79–108; and I. M. Herremans, P. Akathaporn, and M. McInnes, "An Investigation of Corporate Social Responsibility, Reputation, and Economic Performance," *Accounting, Organizations, and Society,* 18(7/8), 1993, 587–604.

79. Marc Orlitzky, Frank Schmidt, and Sara Rynes, "Corporate Social and Financial Performance: A Meta-Analysis," *Organization Studies,* 24(3), 2003, 369–396. Also see Marc Orlitzky, "Payoffs to Social and Environmental Performance," *Journal of Investing* (Fall 2005), 48–51. Also see Lee E. Preston and Douglas P. O'Bannon, "The Corporate Social–Financial Performance Relationship: A Typology and Analysis," *Business and Society,* 36(4), December 1997, 419–429; Sandra Waddock and Samuel Graves, "The Corporate Social Performance– Financial Performance Link," *Strategic Management Journal,* 18(4), 1997, 303–319; Jennifer Griffin and John Mahon, "The Corporate Social Performance and Corporate Financial Performance Debate," *Business and Society,* 36(1), March 1997, 5–31; Ronald Roman, Sefa Hayibor, and Bradley Agle, "The Relationship between Social and Financial Performance," *Business and Society,* 38(1), March 1999, 121. For a reply to this study, see John Mahon and Jennifer Griffin, "Painting a Portrait: A Reply," *Business and Society,* 38(1), March 1999, 126–133.

80. John Peloza, "The Challenge of Measuring Financial Impacts from Investments in Corporate Social Performance," *Journal of Management* (December 2009), 1518–1541.

81. Heli Wang and Jaepil Choi, "A New Look at the Corporate Social-Financial Performance Relationship: The Moderating Roles of Temporal and Interdomain Consistency in Corporate Social Performance," *Journal of Management*, February 2013, 416–441.

82. Orlitzky, Schmidt, and Rynes, 2005, and Peloza, 2009. For an excellent overview of this research see Marc Orlitzky, "Corporate Social Performance and Financial Performance," Chapter 5, in Crane et al. (eds.), 2008, 113–136.

83. A. Y. Ali, R. Q. Danish, and M. Asar-ul-Haq, "How Corporate Social Responsibility Boosts Firm Financial Performance: The Mediating Role of Corporate Image and Customer Satisfaction." *Corporate Social Responsibility and Environmental Management*, June 10, 2019.

84. Michael Barnett and Robert Salomon, "Does It Pay to Be Really Good? Addressing the Shape of the Relationship between Social and Financial Performance," *Strategic Management Journal,* 33(11), June 2011, 1.

85. Preston and O'Bannon, 428.

86. Mercedes Rodriguez-Ferandez, "Social Responsibility and Financial Performance: The Role of Good Governance," *BRQ Business Research Quarterly*, September 2015. Also see A. Awaysheh, R. A. Heron, T. Perry, and J. I. Wilson, "On the Relation between Corporate Social Responsibility and Financial Performance," *Strategic Management Journal*, January 3, 2020, https://onlinelibrary.wiley.com /doi/epdf/10.1002/smj.3122. Accessed March 1, 2021.

87. Porter Novelli, *The 2020 Porter Novelli Executive Purpose Study*, September 2020, p. 5

88. Bryan Husted, "A Contingency Theory of Corporate Social Performance," *Business and Society,* 39(1), March 2000, 24–48, 41. Also see A. Awaysheh, R. A. Heron, T. Perry, and J. I. Wilson, "On the Relation between Corporate Social Responsibility and Financial Performance," *Strategic Management Journal*, January 3, 2020, https://onlinelibrary.wiley.com/doi/epdf/10.1002 /smj.3122. Accessed March 1, 2021.

89. Michael E. Porter and Mark R. Kramer, http://www .sustainability-index.com/. Accessed March 30, 2016.

90. A. Crane, G. Palazzo, L. Spence, and D. Matten, "Contesting the Value of 'Creating Shared Value'," *California Management Review*, February 1, 2014, https:// journals.sagepub.com/doi/10.1525/cmr.2014.56.2.130. Accessed February 15, 2021.

91. Conscious Capitalism, https://www.consciouscapitalism .org/credo. Accessed February 15, 2021.

92. Ibid.

93. Susan Berfield, "The Clutter in Kip Tindell," *BloombergBusinessweek*, February 19, 2015, 41–45.

94. McLeod & More, "The Purpose-Driven Business," https:// www.mcleodandmore.com/purpose-driven-business/. Accessed January 29, 2021.

95. McLeod & More, ibid.

96. Porter Novelli, *The 2020 Porter Novelli Executive Purpose Study*, September 2020, p. 5.

97. The Forum for Sustainable and Responsible Investment, https://www.ussif.org/. Accessed January 29, 2021.

98. Domini Impact Investments, https://www.domini.com/. Accessed February 15, 2021.

99. The Forum for Sustainable and Responsible Investment, https://www.ussif.org/. Accessed January 29, 2021.

100. Meir Statman, "What You Need to Know about Social-Impact Investing," *Wall Street Journal*, October 4, 2020, https://www.domini.com/. Accessed February 15, 2021.

101. Caitlin McCabe, "Do-Good Funds Shine Amid Wider Slump," *The Wall Street Journal*, May 13, 2020, B13.

102. William A. Sodeman, *Social Investing: The Role of Corporate Social Performance in Investment Decisions,* unpublished Ph.D. dissertation, University of Georgia, 1993. See also William A. Sodeman and Archie B. Carroll, "Social Investment Firms: Their Purposes, Principles, and Investment Criteria," in *International Association for Business and Society 1994 Proceedings*, edited by Steven Wartick and Denis Collins, 339–344.

103. CNote, "Positive and Negative Investment Screening Explained," https://www.mycnote.com/blog/positive -and-negative-investment-screening-explained/. Accessed February 15, 2021.

104. US | SIF, "Sustainable Investing Basics," https://www .ussif.org/sribasics. Accessed January 29, 2021.

105. Global Impact Investing Network, https://thegiin.org /about/. Accessed February 15, 2021.

Part 2

Stakeholders and Sustainability

Chapter 3

The Stakeholder Approach to Business, Society, and Ethics

Chapter 4

Sustainability and the Natural Environment

3

The Stakeholder Approach to Business, Society, and Ethics

Chapter Learning Outcomes

After studying this chapter, you should be able to:

1. Describe stakeholder capitalism and its characteristics. How does it differ from traditional capitalism?
2. Identify the origins of the stakeholder concept by explaining what is a stake and what is a stakeholder.
3. Who are business's stakeholders in primary and secondary terms? What is a marginalized or fringe stakeholder?
4. Differentiate among the three stakeholder approaches: strategic, multifiduciary, and synthesis.

5. Identify and explain the three values of the stakeholder model. Which combination of these values makes the most sense for stakeholder management?
6. Name and describe the five key questions that capture the essence of stakeholder management.
7. Explain major concepts in effective stakeholder management to include stakeholder thinking, stakeholder culture, stakeholder management capability, and stakeholder engagement.
8. Describe the three strategic steps toward global stakeholder management.

The business organization today, especially the modern corporation, is the institutional centerpiece of a multifaceted, complex society. Society today consists of many people with many different interests, expectations, and demands regarding what major organizations ought to provide to accommodate people's jobs, lives, and lifestyles. Business responds to many of the expectations placed on it. There has been an ever-changing social contract. There have been many assorted legal, ethical, and philanthropic expectations and demands being met by organizations willing to change if the economic incentives were present and honored. What was once viewed as a specialized means of providing profit through the manufacture and distribution of goods and services has become a multipurpose social institution that people and groups depend on for their livelihoods, prosperity, and fulfilment.

Even in uncertain economic times, we live in societies expecting a quality, sustainable lifestyle, with more individuals and groups every day laying claim to their share of the good life. Business organizations today have found it necessary to be responsive to individuals and groups they once viewed as powerless and unable to make such claims on them. We call these individuals and groups **stakeholders**. The stakeholder approach to management is a recognized framework constantly undergoing development, especially in the business-and-society arena. In the academic and business communities, advances in stakeholder theory have illustrated the crucial development of the stakeholder concept.[1]

As suggested in Chapter 1, we have entered a period in which there have been calls for a new form of capitalism: **stakeholder capitalism**. This movement has been underway for some time, but its biggest boost came in 2019 when the Business Roundtable, an organization of large company CEOs, officially embraced a new model of capitalism that takes into account the interests of all businesses' stakeholders, not just its shareholders or owners.[2] Klaus Schwab, founder and executive chair of the World Economic Forum (WEF), says in his recent book, *Stakeholder Capitalism* (2021), that we need a global economy that works for progress, people, and the planet.[3] Perhaps that is why multistakeholder initiatives have become an important governance mechanism in the global economy.[4]

Though there is some scepticism that stakeholder capitalism is just a fashionable new expression intended mostly for show,[5] if one looks at the top-performing firms in the Business Roundtable espousing this new form of free enterprise, it is apparent that most of them are doing a strong job of serving all or most stakeholders well. Among the top performers in this group include Apple, Amazon, Accenture, IBM, Salesforce.com, Cisco Systems, and Home Depot.[6] It is too early to write the obituary for traditional capitalism in which the shareholder is number one, but stakeholder capitalism appears to be a reset of this model and is making it more inclusive and popular. It certainly creates an economic environment in which stakeholder management, the topic of this chapter, may flourish even more.

In terms of corporate applications, we are proposing in this chapter a **stakeholder approach** to the business-and-society relationship so that harmony with stakeholders may be maintained and sustained. Others have called it a **stakeholder view of the firm**. In this approach or view, it is maintained that to generate and sustain wealth, the firms' relationships with its stakeholders are the critical factor.[7] Along these lines, a model for the "stakeholder corporation" has already been proposed, and it has been argued that "stakeholder inclusion" is the key to company success in the 21st century.[8] In *Redefining the Corporation: Stakeholder Management and Organizational Wealth*, the authors argue that the corporate model needs redefinition because of business size and socioeconomic power and the inadequacy of the "ownership" model and its implications.[9] Yet another book, titled simply *Stakeholders*, traces the theory and practice of the concept and brings us up to date on both strategic and ethical perspectives on stakeholders.[10]

An outgrowth of these developments is that it has become apparent that business organizations must address the legitimate needs and expectations of stakeholders if they want to be effective and sustainable.[11] Businesses must use a stakeholder approach because it represents an ethical course of action in which all those affected by company policies and decisions are considered. Businesses must recognize and factor in their stakeholders' needs, expectations, claims, and rights to achieve balanced performance. For sustainable development to become a reality, the stakeholder approach offers the best opportunity whether it be in the form of stakeholder capitalism or stakeholder management. It is for these reasons that the stakeholder concept and orientation have become central to the vocabulary and thinking in the study of business, society, and ethics.

3.1 Origins of the Stakeholder Concept

The stakeholder concept has become central to the understanding of business and society relationships. The term *stakeholder* is a variant of the more familiar and traditional concepts of *stockholders* or *shareholders*—the investors in or owners of businesses. Just as an individual might own a private house, automobile, or iPhone, a stockholder owns a portion or a share of one or more businesses. Thus, a shareholder is also a type of stakeholder. However, it is now apparent that shareholders are just one of many legitimate stakeholders that business and organizations must deal with today to be successful.

3.1a What Is the *Stake* in Stakeholder?

To appreciate the concept of stakeholders, it helps understand the idea of a stake. A **stake** is an interest in or a share in an undertaking. If a group plans to go out to dinner and a movie for the evening, each person in the group has a stake, or interest, in the group's decision. No money has been spent yet, but each member sees his or her interests (preference, taste, priority) in the decision. A stake may also be a **claim**. A claim is a demand for something due or believed to be due. We can see clearly that an owner or a shareholder has an interest in and an ownership of a share of a business. But now, we are including others in the management approach.

The idea of a stake can range from simply an interest in an undertaking at one extreme to a legal claim of ownership at the other. Between these extremes might be a "need" for something or a "right." It might be a legal right to certain treatment rather than a legal claim of ownership, such as that of a shareholder. Legal rights might include the right to fair treatment or the right to privacy (not to have one's privacy invaded or abridged). A right also might be thought of as a moral right, such as that expressed by an employee: "I've got a right not to be fired because I've worked here 30 years, and I've given this firm the best years of my life." Or a consumer might say, "I've got a right to a safe product after all I've paid for this."

In short, stakeholders have a stake in the "value" they expect to receive from firms with which they interact. Harrington and Wicks have contended that stakeholders, in general, desire utility associated with (1) the actual goods and services companies provide, (2) organizational justice (fair treatment), (3) affiliating with companies that exhibit practices consistent with the things they value, and (4) getting a good deal from the company based on the opportunity costs they spend compared with value received from other companies.[12] When stakeholders perceive that they have shared utility in a relationship, they will be more cooperative and more inclined to govern themselves, rather than rely on the government or other institutional bodies.[13] Stakeholders, thus, have an important stake in the value provided them by firms.

Stakes take on a variety of different forms. Figure 3-1 summarizes various categories or types of stakes and provides examples.

3.1b What Is a Stakeholder?

It follows, then, that a stakeholder is an individual or a group that has one or more of the various kinds of stakes in the organization. Just as stakeholders may be *affected by* the actions, decisions, policies, or practices of the business firm, these stakeholders may also *affect* the organization's actions, decisions, policies, or practices. With stakeholders, therefore, there is an actual two-way interaction or exchange of influence. In short, a stakeholder may be thought of as "any individual or group who can affect or is affected by the actions, decisions, policies, practices, or goals of the organization."[14]

Figure 3-1 Types of Stakes

	An Interest	**A Right**	**Ownership**
Definitions	When a person or group will be *affected by* a decision, it has an *interest* in that decision.	(1) Legal right: When a person or group has a *legal claim* to be treated in a certain way or to have a particular right protected.	When a person or group has a *legal title* to an asset or a property; ownership.
Examples	This plant closing will affect the community. This TV commercial demeans women, and I'm a woman. I'm concerned about the environment for future generations.	Employees are entitled to due process, privacy; customers or creditors have certain legal rights.	"This company is mine. I founded it, and I own it," or "I own 5,000 shares of this corporation."
Definitions		(2) Moral right: When a person or group thinks it has a *moral or ethical right* to be treated in a certain way or to have a particular right protected.	
Examples		Fairness, justice, equity	

3.2 Who Are Business's Stakeholders?

In today's hypercompetitive, global business environment, many different individuals and groups may be business's stakeholders. From the business point of view, certain individuals and groups have more *legitimacy* in the eyes of the management; that is, they have a legitimate (authentic, justified), direct interest in, or claim on, the operations of the firm. The most obvious of these groups are shareholders, employees, and customers.

However, from the point of view of a highly pluralistic society, stakeholders include not only these groups but other groups as well. These other groups include the community, competitors, suppliers, government, special-interest groups, the media, and society, or the public at large. Regulators, activists, and geographic communities also have been identified as stakeholders.[15] Marc Benioff, CEO of Salesforce .com, has asserted that "My customers are my stakeholders. My partners are my stakeholders. My employees are my stakeholders. I have other stakeholders, too. I even consider the communities that we live in are stakeholders. The environment is a stakeholder. We cannot do our business without that."[16] The list of related stakeholders obviously extends beyond these major groups.

Since sustainability is one of the key themes in this book, special attention is called to the natural environment and economic and social environments as stakeholders. When the concept of sustainability first became popular, however, it was the natural environment that was primarily discussed. In keeping with sustainability, Mark Starik has reasoned that the natural environment, nonhuman species, and future generations should be considered among business's important stakeholders.[17] However, one reason these groups often have been neglected is that there has never been a direct spokesperson for them. Who is to speak for the mountain ranges, the biosphere, the oceans, and the flora and fauna? The answer is interest groups such as Greenpeace, Friends of the Earth, and other environmental groups.[18] But these nonprofit organizations and nongovernmental organizations (NGOs) are *indirect* stakeholders, and consequently there has been a reluctance to fully incorporate their concerns by some organizations. Therefore, explicit consideration of the natural environment is emphasized in this stakeholder chapter.

3.2a Three Views of the Firm: Production, Managerial, and Stakeholder

From a historical perspective, the advancement of the stakeholder concept parallels the growth and expansion of the business enterprise. In what has been termed the traditional **production view of the firm**, owners thought of stakeholders as only those individuals or groups that supplied resources or bought products or services.[19] Later, as we witnessed the growth of corporations and the resulting separation of ownership from control, business firms began to see their responsibilities toward other major constituent groups to be essential if they were to be successful. In addition to suppliers of goods and users of goods, the owners and employees were acknowledged as stakeholders. Thus, the **managerial view of the firm** emerged. Finally, as major internal and external changes occurred in business and its environment, managers were required to undergo a radical conceptual shift in how they perceived the firm and its multilateral relationships with constituent or stakeholder groups. The result was the **stakeholder view of the firm**.[20] Figure 3-2 depicts the evolution from the production view to the managerial view of the firm, and Figure 3-3 illustrates the stakeholder view of the firm. The stakeholder view encompasses numerous different individuals and groups that are embedded in

Figure 3-2 The Production View and Managerial Views of the Firm

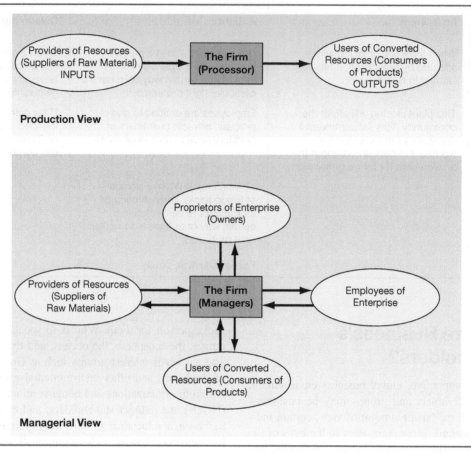

Source: Adapted from Freeman's *Strategic Management: A Stakeholder Approach*, Copyright © 1984 by R. Edward Freeman. Reprinted with permission from Pitman Publishing Company.

the firm's internal and external environments. The diagram in Figure 3-3 is called a **stakeholder map** because it charts out a firm's stakeholders.

In the stakeholder view of the firm, the management must perceive as stakeholders not only those groups that the management *thinks* have some stake in the firm but also those individuals and groups that themselves think or perceive they have a stake in the firm. This is an essential perspective that the management must take, at least until it has had a chance to weigh carefully the legitimacy of the claims and the power of various stakeholders. Of particular note is that each stakeholder group may be thought of as being composed of subgroups; for example, the government stakeholder group includes federal, state, and local government subgroups as stakeholders. Similarly, employees may be classified into subgroups such as women, minorities, older workers, and union members.

3.2b Primary and Secondary Stakeholders

A useful way to categorize stakeholders is to think of them as *primary* and *secondary* as well as *social* and *nonsocial*.[21]

Primary social stakeholders have a *direct* stake in the organization and its success and, therefore, are most influential. Examples would include shareholders and investors; employees and managers; customers; local communities; and suppliers and other business partners. **Secondary social stakeholders** may be extremely influential as well, especially in affecting reputation and public standing, but their stake in the organization is more *indirect* or *derived*. Examples would include government and regulators; civic organizations; social activist groups; media and commentators; trade bodies; and competitors. A firm's responsibility toward secondary stakeholders may be less but is not always avoidable. These groups quite often represent legitimate public concerns or wield significant power, and this makes it impossible for them to be ignored.[22] By contrast, there also are secondary social stakeholders who are frequently ignored or assumed away. This group includes marginalized, **fringe stakeholders**, who have little voice, power, or urgency. Often, the fringe stakeholders include the poor, the weak, the less literate, those who are isolated or enslaved, indigenous peoples, and others. Sometimes this group's views are expressed through NGOs or community organizations, but often they are ignored.[23]

Primary nonsocial stakeholders also exist, and these might include the natural environment, future generations, and nonhuman species. **Secondary nonsocial stakeholders**

Figure 3-3 The Stakeholder View of the Firm

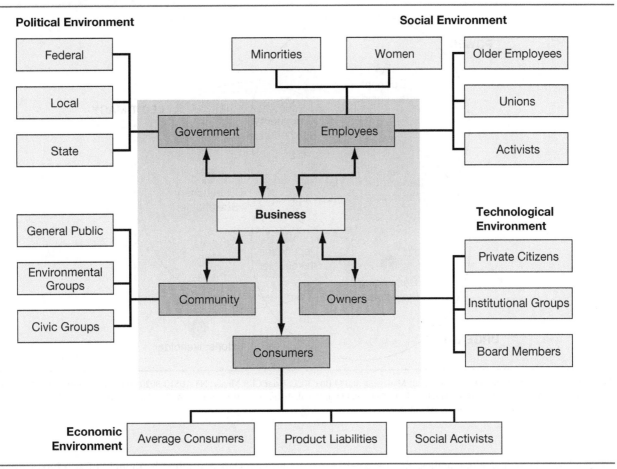

might include those who represent or speak for the primary nonsocial stakeholders. They might include environmental interest groups such as Friends of the Earth or Greenpeace, or animal welfare organizations such as People for the Ethical Treatment of Animals (PETA) or American Society for the Prevention of Cruelty to Animals (ASPCA). The secondary social and nonsocial stakeholders have also been termed *nonmarket players* (NMPs) by strategy experts, and they may include activists, environmentalists, and NGOs. Often these groups are hostile to the firm because they hold competing ideologies such as conflicting beliefs and attitudes regarding social, ecological, ethical, or political issues. This often puts them on a collision course with company managements.[24]

The terms *primary* and *secondary* may be defined differently depending on the situation. Secondary stakeholders can quickly become primary, for example. This often occurs through social media or special-interest groups when a claim's *urgency* (as in a boycott or demonstration) takes precedence over its legitimacy. In today's business environment, the media and social media have the power to instantaneously transform a stakeholder's status within minutes or hours. Thus, it may be useful to think of primary and secondary classes of stakeholders for discussion purposes,

but we should understand their categories are fluid and how easily and quickly those categories can shift.

One overriding point that should be made concerning the question of who businesses' stakeholders are, and what are their stakes, is that it is the perception of the management group that drives decisions. Regardless of the actual status of stakeholders, the management group may not accurately *perceive* who are their stakeholders and their importance to the firm. Additionally, managers can also inaccurately assess stakeholders' stakes, and this poses a real challenge in stakeholder analysis.[25]

3.2c Important Stakeholder Attributes: Legitimacy, Power, Urgency

How do managers decide which stakeholders deserve their attention? Stakeholders have attributes such as legitimacy, power, and urgency. A typology of stakeholders has been developed based on these three attributes.[26] When these three attributes are superimposed, as depicted in Figure 3-4, seven stakeholder categories may be created.

The three attributes of legitimacy, power, and urgency help us see how stakeholders may be thought of and analyzed in terms of their characteristics. The stakeholders are

Figure 3-4 Stakeholder Typology: One, Two, or Three Attributes Present

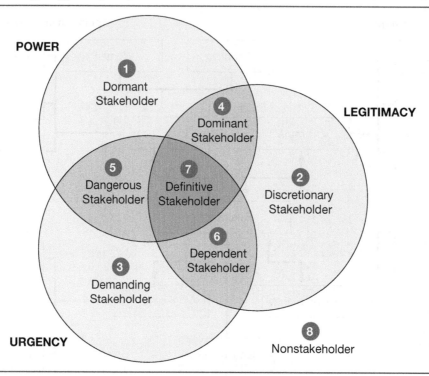

Source: Reprinted with permission of Academy of Management, PO Box 3020, Briar Cliff Manor, NY 10510-8020. Stakeholder Typology: One, Two, or Three Attributes Present (Figure), R. K. Mitchell, B. R. Agle, and D. J. Wood, *Academy of Management Review*, October 1997. Reproduced by permission of the publisher via Copyright Clearance Center, Inc.

more or less salient depending on these factors. **Legitimacy** refers to the perceived validity or appropriateness of a stakeholder's claim to a stake. Therefore, owners, employees, and customers represent a high degree of legitimacy due to their explicit, formal, and direct relationships with a company. Stakeholders that are more distant from the firm, such as social activist groups, NGOs, competitors, or the media, might be thought to have less legitimacy.

Power refers to the ability or capacity of the stakeholder(s) to produce an effect—to get something done that otherwise may not be done. Therefore, whether one has legitimacy or not, power means that the stakeholder could affect the business. For example, with the help of the media and social media, a large, vocal, activist group such as PETA could wield extraordinary power over a business firm. In recent years, PETA has been successful in influencing the practices and policies of virtually all fast-food restaurants regarding their suppliers' treatment of chickens and cattle. Examples follow later in the chapter.

Though not referring to it as power, several researchers have highlighted the importance of stakeholder "pressure" in implementing CSR in companies. They have defined stakeholder pressure as "the ability and capacity of stakeholders to affect an organization by influencing its organizational decisions."[27] This sounds like the concept of power, but they assert that the pressure they are referring to occurs regardless of the legitimacy, power, or urgency of different

groups. Hence, it might be thought of as a broader concept that occurs regardless of a stakeholder's attributes. In other words, stakeholders could exert *pressure* whether based on legitimacy, power, or urgency.

Urgency refers to the degree to which the stakeholder's claim on the business calls for the business's *immediate* attention or response. Urgency may imply that something is critical—it really needs to get done. Or it may imply that something needs to be done immediately, or on a timely basis. A management group may perceive a union strike, a consumer boycott, a contaminated product, or a social-activist group criticizing the company on social media as urgent. With social media today, the concept of urgency has taken on new meaning.

Other research has suggested that **proximity** is another stakeholder attribute that should be considered in addition to legitimacy, power, and urgency.[28] The spatial distance between the organization and its stakeholders refers to proximity, and it is a relevant consideration in evaluating stakeholders' importance and priority. Stakeholders that share the same physical space or are adjacent to the organization may affect and be affected by the organization more than those farther away. In a global example, nation-states may share borders, introducing spatially-related stakeholders. It is evident, therefore, that the greater the proximity, the greater the likelihood of relevant and important stakeholder interactions and relationships.[29]

An excellent example of a stakeholder action that illustrated both power and urgency occurred in several dozen Home Depot stores around the country. In each of the stores, strange announcements began blaring from the intercom systems: "*Attention shoppers, on aisle seven you'll find mahogany ripped from the heart of the Amazon.*" Shocked store managers raced through the aisles trying to apprehend the environmental activists behind the stunt. The activists had apparently gotten the access codes to the intercoms. After months of similar antics, Home Depot bowed to the demands of the environmental group and announced that it would stop selling wood from endangered forests and, instead, stock wood products certified by the Forest Stewardship Council (FSC).[30] This group of environmental activists was not even on Home Depot's stakeholder radar screen and then, all of a sudden, the company was "persuaded" it had to sell only FSC-certified wood. This was a bold display of stakeholder power.

The typology of stakeholder attributes suggests that managers must attend to stakeholders based on their assessment of the extent to which competing stakeholder claims reflect legitimacy, power, and urgency and are therefore salient, or outstandingly prominent. Using the categories shown in Figure 3-4, the stakeholder groups represented by overlapping circles (e.g., those with two or three attributes such as Categories 4, 5, 6, and 7) are highly "salient" to the management and would likely receive priority attention. Like any typology, it is important to recognize that it is a static model subject to interpretation and change. For example, some have argued that urgency may not be as relevant (as legitimacy and power) for identifying stakeholders, whereas "legitimacy" may be defined as "moral legitimacy."[31] Nevertheless, these stakeholder attributes are a helpful tool for assessing stakeholder claims.

3.3 Strategic, Multifiduciary, and Synthesis: Three Stakeholder Approaches

A major challenge embedded in the stakeholder approach is to determine whether it should be seen primarily as a way to *manage better* or as a way to *treat more ethically* those groups known as stakeholders. Both concerns have sustainability implications. This issue may be addressed by considering the stakeholder approach used. Kenneth Goodpaster has suggested three approaches: the strategic approach, the multifiduciary approach, and the stakeholder synthesis

---

Ethics In Practice Case

Are Plants and Flowers Stakeholders? Does Nature Have Legal Rights?

Scientists in Switzerland for years have created genetically modified foods, such as rice, corn, and apples. In fact, the question has been raised as to whether they ever stopped to think that their experiments may be "humiliating" to plants. A constitutional rule was passed after the Swiss Parliament asked a panel of philosophers, geneticists, theologians, and lawyers to establish the "meaning" of a flora's dignity. The panel wrote a lengthy treatise on the "moral consideration of plants for their own sake." The document argued that vegetation has an inherent value and that it is immoral to harm plants arbitrarily. One example of this would be the "decapitation of wildflowers at the roadside without any apparent reason."

Defenders of the law state that it reflects a broader, progressive effort to protect the sanctity of all living things and to promote sustainability. Switzerland also granted new rights to all "social animals." For example, prospective dog owners now have to take a four-hour course on pet care before they can acquire a dog. Anglers now have to learn how to catch fish humanely. Goldfish can no longer be flushed down the toilet as a means of disposal. First, they must be anesthetized with special chemicals.

One Swiss scientist recently exclaimed, "Where does it stop? Should we now defend the dignity of microbes and viruses?" In a related decision, the people of Ecuador passed a new constitution that is said to be the first to recognize ecosystem rights enforceable in a court of law. Now, the nation's rivers, forests, and air are right-bearing entities with "the right to exist, persist, and regenerate."

Other actions that have been taken suggest the lengths to which the stakeholder status for nature has been established. A court in India has given the status of "legal persons" to the Himalayan glaciers in a quest to halt environmental deterioration. Also in India, the polluted Ganges and Yamuna rivers were given the same status as human beings so that legal guardians can now represent them in court. In New Zealand, the Whanganui River became designated as a legal person. In Ecuador, the South American country gave nature rights like those of humans arguing that ecosystems have the right to exist, persist, maintain, and regenerate.

1. Are plants and flowers stakeholders? Are they primary or secondary stakeholders? Does vegetation have rights? What about insects, dogs, and goldfish?
2. Are the Swiss, Indian, New Zealand, and Ecuadorian decisions too extreme? What are the limits of stakeholders' rights? Is this taking sustainability too far or pushing the idea to unrealistic limits?
3. What are the implications for business decisions of the Swiss and Ecuadorian decisions? Are these unique to these countries and won't apply elsewhere?

Sources: "Swiss Government Issues Bill of Rights for Plants," https://www.treehugger.com/swiss-government-issues-bill-of-rights-for-plants-4854568, accessed February 6, 2020; RationalWiki.org "Plant Rights," https://rationalwiki.org/wiki/Plant_rights, accessed February 6, 2020; NPR, "Recognizing the Rights of Plants to Evolve?" October 26, 2012, https://www.npr.org/2012/10/26/160940869/recognizing-the-right-of-plants-to-evolve, accessed February 6, 2020; "The Legal Rights of Nature," *Time*, April 6, 2017, https://time.com/4728311/the-legal-rights-of-nature/feed/, accessed February 6, 2020.

approach.[32] The **strategic approach** views stakeholders primarily as factors to be taken into consideration and managed while the firm pursues profits for its shareholders. The **multifiduciary approach** views stakeholders as more than just individuals or groups who can wield economic or legal power. This view holds that the management has a fiduciary, or trust, responsibility toward stakeholders just as it has this same responsibility toward shareholders. An innovative, **synthesis approach to stakeholders** is preferred because it holds that business does have moral responsibilities to stakeholders but that they should not be seen as part of a fiduciary obligation. As a consequence, the management's basic fiduciary responsibility toward shareholders is kept intact, but it is also expected to be implemented within a context of ethical responsibility toward other stakeholders.[33] The result is the same in the multifiduciary and stakeholder synthesis views. However, the reasoning or rationale is different.

As we continue our discussion of stakeholder management, it should become clear that we are pursuing it from a balanced perspective, which suggests that we are integrating the strategic approach with the stakeholder synthesis approach. We should be managing strategically and morally at the same time.[34] The stakeholder approach should not be just a better way to manage. It also should be a more ethical and sustainable way to manage.

3.4 Three Values of the Stakeholder Model

In addition to the strategic, multifiduciary, and stakeholder synthesis approaches, the stakeholder model of the firm has three aspects or *values* that should be appreciated. Although interrelated, these include the descriptive, instrumental, and normative values.[35]

3.4a Descriptive Value

First, the stakeholder model has value because it is **descriptive**; that is, it provides language and concepts to effectively explain the corporation or organization in stakeholder inclusive terms. The business organization is a constellation of cooperative and competitive interests, or stakes, possessing both instrumental and intrinsic value. Understanding organizations in this way allows us to have a more complete description and explanation of how they function. The language and terms used in the stakeholder model are useful in helping us understand organizations. As a result, stakeholder language and concepts are being used more and more in many fields of endeavor today— business, government, politics, education, nonprofit organizations, and so on.

3.4b Instrumental Value

Second, the stakeholder model has value because it is **instrumental** in that it is useful in portraying the relationship between the practice of stakeholder management and the resulting achievement of corporate performance goals. The fundamental premise here is that practicing effective stakeholder management should lead to the achievement of important business goals, such as profitability, stability, and growth.[36] This is similar to the *strategic approach* discussed earlier. Business school courses in strategic management and human resource management often employ the instrumental model of stakeholders.

3.4c Normative Value

Third, the stakeholder model has value because it is **normative**, wherein stakeholders are seen as possessing value irrespective of their instrumental use to management. This is often considered the moral or ethical view because it emphasizes how stakeholders *should* be treated. The "principle of stakeholder fairness" has been suggested as the moral underpinning, or normative justification, for the stakeholder model.[37] Thus, the normative value of stakeholder thinking is of central importance in business ethics and business and society.

In summarizing, stakeholder theory is *managerial* in the broad sense of the term in that it not only describes or predicts but also recommends attitudes, structures, and practices that constitute effective stakeholder management. Successful stakeholder management requires simultaneous attention to the legitimate interests of all salient stakeholders in the creation of organizational structures and policies and in decision making.[38]

3.5 Stakeholder Management: Five Key Questions

The managers of a business firm are responsible for establishing the firm's overall direction (its governance, mission, strategies, goals, and policies) and ensuring implementation of these plans. The challenge of **stakeholder management** is to see to it that while the firm's primary stakeholders achieve their objectives, the other stakeholders are dealt with ethically and are also relatively satisfied. At the same time, the firm's profitability must be ensured. This is the classic "win–win" situation. The management's second-best alternative is to meet the goals of its primary stakeholders, keeping in mind the important role of its owner-investors. Without economic sustainability, all other stakeholders' interests become unresolved.

With these perspectives in mind, it is possible to approach stakeholder management with the idea that managers can become successful stewards of their stakeholders' resources by gaining knowledge about stakeholders and using this knowledge to predict and improve their company's decisions, policies, and actions. Thus, the important functions of stakeholder management are to identify, to describe, to analyze, to understand, and, finally, to manage. The quest for stakeholder management embraces social, legal, ethical, and economic considerations. Normative as well as instrumental objectives and perspectives are essential.

Five key questions are critical to capturing the essential information needed for effective stakeholder management:

1. *Who* are our organization's stakeholders?
2. What are our stakeholders' *stakes*?
3. What *opportunities and challenges* do our stakeholders present to the firm?
4. What *responsibilities* (economic, legal, ethical, and philanthropic) does the firm have to its stakeholders?
5. What *strategies or actions* should the firm take to best address stakeholder challenges and opportunities?[39]

Figure 3-5 presents a schematic of the decision process outlining the five questions and key issues with respect to each. The feedback loop suggests that this is an ongoing process.

3.5a Who Are the Organization's Stakeholders?

To manage effectively, each firm and its management group must ask and answer this question: *Who are our stakeholders?* This stage is often called **stakeholder identification**.

Figure 3-5 Stakeholder Management: Five Key Questions

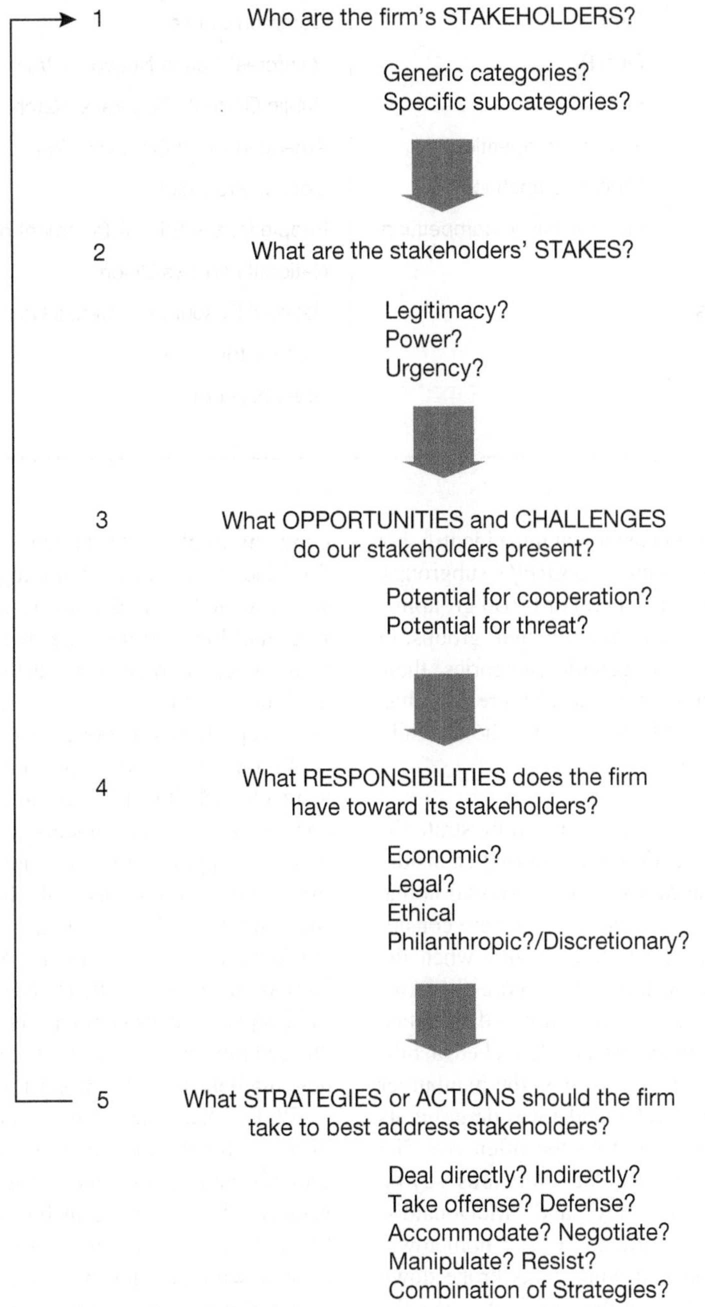

1 Who are the firm's STAKEHOLDERS?

Generic categories?
Specific subcategories?

2 What are the stakeholders' STAKES?

Legitimacy?
Power?
Urgency?

3 What OPPORTUNITIES and CHALLENGES
do our stakeholders present?

Potential for cooperation?
Potential for threat?

4 What RESPONSIBILITIES does the firm
have toward its stakeholders?

Economic?
Legal?
Ethical
Philanthropic?/Discretionary?

5 What STRATEGIES or ACTIONS should the firm
take to best address stakeholders?

Deal directly? Indirectly?
Take offense? Defense?
Accommodate? Negotiate?
Manipulate? Resist?
Combination of Strategies?

Figure 3-6 Some Generic and Specific Stakeholders of a Large Firm

Owners	Employees	Governments	Customers
Trusts	Young employees	Federal	Business purchasers
Foundations	Middle-aged employees	• EPA	Government purchasers
Mutual funds	Older employees	• FTC	Educational institutions
Universities	Women	• OSHA	Global markets
Board members	Minority groups	• CPSC	Special-interest groups
Employee pension funds	People with disabilities	State	Internet purchasers
Management owners	Special-interest groups	Local	
Individual owners	Unions		

Community	Competitors	Social Activist Groups	
General fundraising	Firm A	Common Cause	
United Way	Firm B	Rainforest Action Network (RAN)	
YMCA/YWCA	Firm C	Public Citizen's Congress Watch	
Middle schools	Indirect competition	American Civil Liberties Union	
Elementary schools	Global competition	Consumers Union	
Residents who live close by	Internet-based competition	People for the Ethical Treatment of Animals (PETA)	
All other residents		National Farmers Union	
Neighborhood associations		National Resources Defense Council	
Local media		Citizens for Health	
Chamber of Commerce		Greenbiz.com	
Environments			

To answer this question fully, management must identify not only *generic* stakeholder groups but also *specific* subgroups. A generic stakeholder group is a general or broad grouping, such as employees, shareholders, environmental groups, or consumers. Within each of these generic categories, there may be a few or many specific subgroups. Figure 3-6 illustrates some of the generic and specific stakeholder subgroups of a large organization.

McDonald's Continuing Experience. To illustrate the process of stakeholder identification, it is helpful to consider some events in the life of the McDonald's Corporation that resulted in their broadening significantly who were considered their stakeholders. This case study begins when the social activist group PETA, which claims more than two million members and supporters, decided it was dissatisfied with some of McDonald's practices and launched a billboard and bumper sticker campaign against the hamburger giant.[40] PETA, convinced that McDonald's was dragging its feet on animal welfare issues, went on the offensive. The group announced that it would put up billboards saying "The animals deserve a break today" and "McDonald's: Cruelty to Go" in Norfolk, Virginia, PETA's hometown. The ad campaign was announced when talks broke down between PETA and McDonald's on the subject of ways the

company might foster animal rights issues within the fast-food industry. Using terminology introduced earlier, PETA was a secondary social or nonsocial stakeholder and, therefore, had low legitimacy. However, its power and urgency were extremely high as it was threatening the company with a highly visible, potentially harmful campaign that was being reported by a cooperative and empathetic media.

PETA's pressure tactics continued and escalated. As a result, McDonald's eventually announced significant changes in the requirements it was placing on its chicken and egg suppliers. Egg suppliers were required to improve the "living conditions" of their chickens. Specifically, McDonald's insisted that its suppliers no longer cage its chickens wingtip to wingtip. Suppliers were required to increase the space allotted to each hen from 48 square inches to 72 square inches per hen. They were also required to stop "forced molting," a process that increases egg production by denying hens food and water for up to two weeks.[41]

PETA then escalated its pressure tactics against the firm by distributing "*unhappy* meals" at restaurant playgrounds and outside the company's shareholder meeting venues. The kits came in boxes similar to that of Happy Meal™, McDonald's meal for children, but were covered instead with pictures of slaughtered animals. These also depicted a bloody, knife-wielding "Son of Ron" doll that resembled the Ronald McDonald clown, as well as toy farm animals with slashed throats. One image featured a bloody cow's head and the familiar fast-food phrase "Do you want fries with that?"[42] PETA continued to aggressively pursue McDonald's and other firms, such as Burger King and KFC, for their chicken slaughter methods and other animal treatment issues. PETA had become the stakeholder that refused to go away. PETA continues its ongoing campaign against McDonald's with its criticism of McDonalds for suggesting customers add bacon to their sandwiches. PETA protestors have brandished signs showing pigs in transport trucks alongside the words "I am not bacon. I'm an individual." And "These were my last moments on earth."[43]

In this example, it can be seen how the set of stakeholders that McDonald's had to deal with grew markedly from its traditional stakeholders to include a powerful, special-interest group such as PETA. With the cooperation of the media stakeholders, especially social media, PETA moved from being a secondary stakeholder to a primary stakeholder with great power and urgency in McDonald's life.

Not only has McDonald's had to deal with PETA's protests, but other companies and issues have caught their attention as well. PETA's protests have been targeted toward the following issues: experimentation, food, clothing, entertainment, companion animals, and wildlife. The actual experiences of the companies targeted by PETA illustrate the evolving nature of the question, "Who are our stakeholders?" In actuality, stakeholder identification is an unfolding process. However, by recognizing early the potential of failure if one does not think in stakeholder terms, the value and usefulness of stakeholder thinking can be readily seen. Had McDonald's, KFC, Benetton, and other firms perceived PETA as a stakeholder with power, urgency, and some moral legitimacy earlier on, perhaps it could have dealt with these situations more effectively. These firms should have been aware of one of the basic principles of stakeholder responsibility: "Recognize that stakeholders are real and complex people with names, faces, and values."[44]

Getting to know a company's stakeholders requires managers to go beyond simple list making of their characteristics. It means getting to know your stakeholders just like you get to know your customers. A McKinsey study found a strong positive correlation between in-depth profiling of stakeholders and success in engaging them.[45] But, many businesses do not carefully identify their generic stakeholder groups, much less their specific stakeholder groups. "Who are our stakeholders?" is an essential first question, however, if the management is to be in a position to address the second major question, "What are our stakeholders' stakes?"

3.5b What Are Our Stakeholders' Stakes?

Once stakeholders have been identified, the next step is to address the question: *What are our stakeholders' stakes?* Even groups in the same generic category frequently have different specific interests, concerns, perceptions of rights, and expectations. Management's challenge is to identify the

nature, legitimacy, power, urgency, and saliency of a group's stake(s) and their potential to affect the organization.

Nature or Legitimacy of a Group's Stakes. Stakeholders may possess varying types of stakes. Think about a large corporation with several hundred million shares of stock outstanding. Among the shareholder population of this corporation are these more specific subgroups:

1. Institutional owners (trusts, foundations, pension funds, churches, universities)
2. Large mutual fund organizations (Fidelity, Vanguard, Pax World)
3. Board of director members who own shares
4. Members of management who own shares
5. Millions of small, individual shareholders

For all these subgroups, the nature of stakeholder claims on this corporation is *ownership*. All these groups have legitimate claims—they are all owners. Because of other factors, such as power or urgency, however, these stakeholders may have to be dealt with differently. Increasingly, however, special interest groups are claiming moral legitimacy for the actions they take. Examples might include PETA, as described earlier, civil rights groups, immigration rights groups, criminal justice groups, children advocacy groups, worker's rights groups, and consumer rights groups.

Power of a Group's Stakes. When power is considered, significant differences become apparent. Which of the groups in the previous list are the most powerful? Certainly not the small, individual investors, unless they have found a way to organize and thus wield power. The powerful stakeholders in this case are (1) the institutional owners and mutual fund organizations, because of the sheer magnitude of their investments, and (2) the board and management shareholders, because of their dual roles of ownership and management (control). Increasingly today, utilizing social media, many of the special interest groups named above can wield considerable power.

Subgroups within a Generic Group. Consider a manufacturing firm in an industry in Ohio that is faced with a generic group of environmental stakeholders. Within the generic group of environmental stakeholders might be the following specific subgroups:

1. Residents living within a 25-mile radius of the plant
2. Other residents in the city
3. Residents who live in the path of the jet stream hundreds of miles away (some in Canada) who are being impacted by acid rain
4. Environmental Protection Agency (federal government)
5. Ohio's Environmental Protection Division (state government)
6. Sierra Club (environmental activist group)
7. Ohio Environmental Council (special interest group)

It would require some degree of time and care to identify the nature, legitimacy, power, and urgency of each of these specific groups. However, it could and should be done if the firm wants to better engage and manage its environmental stakeholders. Furthermore, it should be stressed that companies have an ethical responsibility to be sensitive to legitimate stakeholder claims even if the stakeholders have no power or leverage with the management.

Return for a moment to the fast-food industry, and especially the McDonald's example. One may conclude that PETA, as a special-interest, animal welfare group, did not have much *legitimacy* vis-à-vis these companies. It did claim animals' rights and treatment as a moral issue and thus had some moral legitimacy through the issues it represented. Unfortunately for PETA, not all of the public shares its concerns or degree of concern with these issues. However, PETA has and continues to have tremendous power and urgency. It was this power, wielded in the form of adverse publicity, media attention, and tenacity, that without a doubt played a significant role in bringing about changes in these companies' policies as the companies sought to maintain their reputational capital.

3.5c What Opportunities and Challenges Do Our Stakeholders Present?

Opportunities and challenges represent opposite sides of the coin when it comes to stakeholder analysis. The opportunities are for businesses to build decent, productive working relationships with the stakeholders. Challenges, on the other hand, usually present themselves in such a way that the firm must handle the stakeholders acceptably or be harmed in some way—financially (short term or long term) or in terms of its public image or reputation in the community.

Stakeholder challenges typically take the form of varying degrees of expectations, demands, boycotts, or threats. In most instances, they arise because stakeholders think or believe that their needs or points of view are not being met adequately. The stakeholder groups may hold competing ideologies or conflicting beliefs. The example of PETA illustrated this point quite well. The challenges also arise when stakeholder groups think that any crisis that occurs is the responsibility of the firm or that the firm caused the crisis in some way.

Another example of a stakeholder crisis illustrates this point:[46] A campaign to transform the entire logging industry was launched by Rainforest Action Network (RAN). RAN, an environmental activist group, campaigns "for the forests, their inhabitants and the natural systems that sustain life by transforming the global marketplace though education, grassroots organizing and nonviolent direct action."[47] RAN directed their campaign against Boise, Inc., an international distributor of office supplies and paper and an integrated manufacturer and distributor of paper, packaging, and building materials. As a result, Boise implemented a domestic old-growth policy and committed to "no longer harvesting timber from old-growth forests in the United States." To catch up with public values and meet the new marketplace standards, Boise became the first U.S. logging

and distribution company to commit to "eliminate the purchase of wood products from endangered areas."[48] RAN's aggressive protection of rainforests continues to this day. Currently, RAN has campaigns focused on climate change, fossil fuels, shale, and rainforest destruction.[49]

If one looks at the recent experiences of businesses, including the crises mentioned here, it is evident that there is a need to think in stakeholder terms to understand fully the potential threats and challenges those businesses of all kinds face on a daily basis.

Potential for Cooperation or Threat. Opportunities and challenges might also be viewed in terms of *potential for cooperation* and *potential for threat* to enable managers to identify strategies for dealing with stakeholders.[50] In terms of potential for threat, managers need to consider stakeholders' relative power and its relevance to a particular issue facing the organization. In terms of potential for cooperation, the firm needs to be sensitive to the possibility of joining forces with stakeholders for the advantage of all parties involved. Several companies have entered into cooperative partnerships with the sustainability group Environmental Defense Fund (EDF). Climate change is one of its most important issues today.[51] In an example of collaboration, EDF and FedEx joined together in a cooperative relationship to launch the first "street ready" hybrid trucks ever built. Today, hundreds of these trucks are in the corporate fleets of UPS, Coca-Cola, and the U.S. Postal Service.

3.5d What Responsibilities Does a Firm Have toward Its Stakeholders?

The next logical question after identifying and understanding stakeholders' threats and opportunities is *"What responsibilities does a firm have in its relationships with its stakeholders?"* One way of answering this question might be to state what different stakeholder groups might logically expect from companies. If this is done, a list such as the following might be the result, and it would certainly embrace at least one major outcome each group might expect:

- Shareholders—good to excellent returns on their investment
- Employees—fair pay, good working conditions, strong benefits, trusted leadership
- Customers—fair prices, safe products, excellent service
- Local community—jobs, stability, and minimal disruption
- Suppliers—regular business and prompt payment[52]

Responsibilities to stakeholders also might be thought of in terms of the corporate social responsibility framework presented in Chapter 2. What economic, legal, ethical, and philanthropic responsibilities does management have toward each stakeholder? Because most of the firm's economic responsibilities are principally to its owners or shareholders, the analysis naturally turns to legal, ethical, and philanthropic questions. The most pressing threats are typically presented as legal and ethical issues. Often, opportunities

Figure 3-7 Stakeholder Responsibility Matrix

Stakeholders	Types of Responsibilities			
	Economic	Legal	Ethical	Philanthropic
Owners				
Customers				
Employees				
Community				
Public at Large				
Social Activist Groups				
Others				

are reflected in areas of philanthropy or "giving back" to the community.

It should be pointed out, however, that the firm itself has an economic stake in most legal and ethical issues it faces. For example, when Johnson & Johnson (J&J) faced the Tylenol poisoning crisis, it had to decide what legal and ethical actions to take and what actions were in the firm's best economic interests. In this classic case, J&J concluded that recalling the tainted Tylenol products was not only the ethical choice but also one that would preserve its reputation for being concerned about consumers' health and well-being. Figure 3-7 illustrates the **stakeholder responsibility matrix** that management might face when assessing the firm's responsibilities to stakeholders. The matrix is a template that managers might use to systematically think through its various responsibilities to each stakeholder group.

3.5e What Strategies or Actions Should Management Take?

Once responsibilities have been assessed, an organization must contemplate strategies and actions for addressing its stakeholders. In every decision situation, a number of alternative courses of action are available, and management must choose one or several that seem best. Important questions or decision choices that management has before it in dealing with stakeholders include the following:

- Do we deal *directly* or *indirectly* with stakeholders?
- Do we take the *offense* or the *defense* in dealing with stakeholders?
- Do we *accommodate, negotiate, manipulate,* or *resist* stakeholder overtures?
- Do we employ a *combination of the aforementioned* strategies or pursue a *singular course* of action?[53]
- Do we *engage with a partner to cooperate* on dealing with stakeholders or *do it alone*?

In actual practice, managers need to prioritize stakeholder expectations and demands before deciding the appropriate strategy to employ.[54] In addition, strategic thinking in terms of forms of communication, degree of collaboration, development of policies or programs, and allocation of resources would need to be thought through carefully.[55] The development of specific strategies could be based on a classification of stakeholders' *potentials for cooperation and threat* discussed earlier. If these two factors are used, four stakeholder types and resultant generic strategies emerge: supportive, marginal, nonsupportive, and mixed blessing.[56]

Type 1: Supportive **Stakeholder.** The **supportive stakeholder** is high on potential for cooperation and low on potential for threat. This is the ideal stakeholder. To a well-managed organization, supportive stakeholders might include its board of directors, managers, employees, and loyal customers. Others might be suppliers and service providers. The strategy with supporters is one of *involvement.* An example of this might be the strategy of engaging employee stakeholders through participative management or employee volunteerism. Stakeholder inclusion and engagement are primary strategies with supportive stakeholders.

Type 2: Marginal **Stakeholder.** The **marginal stakeholder** is low on both potential for threat and potential for cooperation. For large organizations, these stakeholders might include professional associations of employees, inactive consumer interest groups, or shareholders—especially those that hold few shares and are not organized. The strategy here is for the organization to *monitor* the marginal stakeholder. Monitoring is especially called for to make sure circumstances do not change.

Type 3: Nonsupportive **Stakeholder.** The **nonsupportive stakeholder** is high on potential for threat but low on

Figure 3-8 Stakeholder Types, Examples, and Recommended Strategies and Actions

Stakeholder Type	Examples of Stakeholder Type	Stakeholder *Potential* for Threat	Stakeholder *Potential* for Cooperation	Strategy/Action Recommended
Supportive Stakeholder	Board of directors, some employees	Low	High	Involve; take offense, accommodate, proact; keep satisfied
Marginal Stakeholder	Professional associations, interest groups	Low	Low	Monitor; watch carefully; minimal effort; offense or defense
Nonsupportive Stakeholder	Competitors, unions, governments, some activist groups	High	Low	Defend; be prepared; guard against; negotiate
Mixed-Blessing Stakeholder	Employees, clients, customers	High	Medium to High	Collaborate; take offense, partnership, pool resources; keep informed

Sources: Compiled from multiple sources: Grant T. Savage, Timothy W. Nix, Carlton J. Whitehead, and John D. Blair, "Strategies for Assessing and Managing Organizational Stakeholders," *Academy of Management Executive* (Vol. V, No. 2, May 1991), 61–75; Ian C. MacMillan and Patricia E. Jones, *Strategy Formulation: Power and Politics* (St. Paul, MN: West, 1986), 66.

potential for cooperation. Examples of this group could include competing organizations, unions, federal or other levels of government, the media, and social media. Special-interest groups or NGOs often fall in this category. The recommended strategy here is to *defend* against the nonsupportive stakeholder.

An example of a special-interest group that many would regard as nonsupportive is the Earth Liberation Front (ELF), a movement that originated in the Pacific Northwest. It claimed responsibility for a string of arsons in the suburbs of Los Angeles, Detroit, and Philadelphia. ELF's attacks targeted luxury homes and sports utility vehicles (SUVs), the suburban status symbols that some environmentalists regard as despoilers of the Earth. Many such radical environmental groups have been called "eco-terrorists."[57] Such organizations do not seem interested in establishing positive, or supportive, relationships with companies and industries. In the examples discussed earlier, PETA and RAN typically came across as nonsupportive stakeholders because of their high potential for threat and reticence toward cooperation.

Type 4: Mixed-Blessing **Stakeholder.** The **mixed-blessing stakeholder** is high on both potential for threat and potential for cooperation. Examples of this group, in a well-managed organization, might include employees who are in short supply, clients, or customers. A mixed-blessing stakeholder could become a supportive or a nonsupportive stakeholder. The recommended strategy here is to *collaborate* or engage with the mixed-blessing stakeholder. By maximizing collaboration, the likelihood that this stakeholder will remain supportive is enhanced. Today, many companies regard sustainability groups as mixed blessings rather than nonsupportive. These firms are turning environmentalists into allies by building alliances with them for mutual gain.[58]

Figure 3-8 summarizes an analysis of stakeholder types and recommended strategies and actions.

A summary guideline regarding these four stakeholder types might be stated in the following way:[59]

Managers should attempt to satisfy minimally the needs of marginal stakeholders and to satisfy maximally the needs of supportive and mixed blessing stakeholders, enhancing the latter's support for the organization.

The four stakeholder types and recommended strategies illustrate what was referred to earlier in this chapter as the "strategic" or instrumental view of stakeholders. It also could be argued that by taking stakeholders' needs and concerns into consideration, businesses' ethical treatment of them should be improved. It takes more than just consideration, however. Management still has an ethical responsibility toward stakeholders that extends beyond the strategic view. A fuller appreciation of this ethical responsibility is developed in Chapters 5–8.

3.6 Effective Stakeholder Management and Engagement

Effective stakeholder management and engagement is at the top of the list in terms of executive priorities today. This process requires a strong commitment on the part of management and demands a careful assessment of the five key questions posed in this chapter. Business has been and will continue to be subjected to careful scrutiny of its actions, practices, policies, and ethics. Stakeholder management and engagement helps deal with these issues.

Criticisms of business and calls for better corporate citizenship have been the consequences of the changes in the business-and-society relationship, and the stakeholder approach to viewing the organization has become one essential response. To do less is to deny the realities of

Ethics In Practice Case

Chickens or Employees? Which Is the Most Important Stakeholder?

Tyson Foods, Inc., the largest U.S. chicken processor, fired two of its employees at a Mississippi meatpacking plant. The firing occurred after an animal rights group, Mercy for Animals, released an undercover 2 ½-minute video that showed the workers mistreating the birds at the slaughterhouse. Mercy for Animals accused the firm of cruelty to chickens.

As a result of this disclosure, six Tyson employees and the company faced possible criminal charges of animal cruelty. A spokesman for Tyson said that the firm does not believe the behavior shown in the video represents the thousands of workers it employs across the country.

Mercy for Animals secretly recorded employees tossing, punching, throwing, and dismembering birds that had been improperly shackled and missed the blade designed to slaughter them.

The investigation at Tyson's plant was the fourth such probe by Mercy for Animals and the group was calling for Tyson to implement "meaningful animal welfare requirements" at its farms and plants.

The practice of exposing animal cruelty by way of undercover videos has become a controversial issue and some states ban the practice that some opponents call "ag-gag laws." The animal rights groups say that these videos are the only way to expose wrongdoing. Opponents of the practice say that the filmmakers get their jobs under false pretenses and that the videos misrepresent the meatpacking industry.

In another major case, Mercy for Animals is exposing Costco for extreme animal suffering as it seeks to supply itself with cheap chickens. This case also was exposed via a hidden camera.

1. Are chickens stakeholders? Are animal rights groups stakeholders? If so, what is the nature of their stake? Do they have legitimacy as stakeholders? If not, what is the nature of their stake?
2. What are the stakes of the company and employees in this type of situation? Are their stakes more important than those of the social interest groups?
3. Is it ethical for special interest groups, such as Mercy for Animals, to use undercover video techniques such as this?
4. What responsibilities does the company have toward its employees in this situation? To its chickens and special interest groups?
5. What strategies or actions should Tyson and Costco take to address their stakeholders in this case?

Sources: Mercy for Animals, https://mercyforanimals.org/, accessed February 9, 2021; Mercy for Animals, Tyson Foods, 2015, http://www.mercyforanimals.org/investigations, accessed March 31, 2016; "Tyson Fires Workers over Cruelty," *The Wall Street Journal*, October 29, 2015, B4; "Tyson Fires Two Workers after Video Shows Cruelty to Chickens," *BloombergBusiness*, October 28, 2015, https://www.bloomberg.com/news/articles/2016-05-25/tyson-investigates-chicken-farm-where-group-alleges-abuse-iomz9r5v, accessed February 9, 2021; Mercy for Animals, "Costco Exposed," https://mercyforanimals.org/, accessed March 2, 2021.

business's plight in the modern world, which is increasingly global in scope, and to fail to see the kinds of adaptations that are essential if businesses are to prosper now and in the future.

3.6a Stakeholder Thinking

Stakeholder thinking undergirds stakeholder management and is the process of always reasoning in stakeholder terms throughout the management process, and especially when organizations' decisions and actions have important implications for others. It is aligned with a **stakeholder mindset,** or **stakeholder orientation,** whereby managers look at the world as they start with a stakeholder "script" to create value for a wide array of stakeholders within their value chain.[60] However, some managers continue to think in shareholder terms because it is simpler. To think in stakeholder terms increases the complexity of decision making, and it is quite taxing for some managers to assess which stakeholders' claims take priority in a given situation. Despite its complexity, however, the stakeholder view is most consistent with the environment that business faces today, and "stakeholder thinking" has become a vital characteristic of effective stakeholder management.

In fairness, we should also note that there are criticisms and limitations of the stakeholder approach. One major criticism relates to the complexity and time-consuming nature of identifying, assessing, and responding to stakeholder claims, which constitute an extremely demanding process. Also, the ranking of stakeholder claims is no easy task. Finally, the question of the legitimacy of various stakeholder issues calls to mind normative questions such as, are some stakeholders more legitimate than others, and therefore should receive more attention?[61] These challenges must be kept in mind as the approach is used in practice.

In addition to stakeholder thinking, effective stakeholder management is facilitated by a number of other useful concepts. The following concepts—stakeholder culture, stakeholder management capability, the stakeholder corporation model, and principles of stakeholder management—round out a useful approach to stakeholder management effectiveness. Each of these is considered in more detail.

3.6b Developing a Stakeholder Culture

In management circles, the importance of developing a strong, values-based corporate culture has been recognized as a key to successful enterprises. Corporate culture refers to the taken-for-granted beliefs, functional guidelines, ways of doing things, priorities, and values important to managers.[62] Within that context, developing a strong **stakeholder culture** is a major factor supporting

Figure 3-9 A Continuum of Stakeholder Cultures

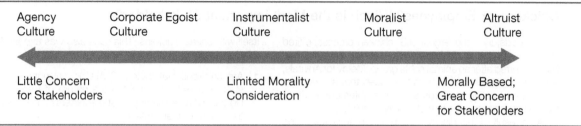

Agency Culture	Corporate Egoist Culture	Instrumentalist Culture	Moralist Culture	Altruist Culture

Little Concern for Stakeholders   Limited Morality Consideration   Morally Based; Great Concern for Stakeholders

successful stakeholder management. Stakeholder culture embraces the beliefs, values, and practices that organizations have developed for addressing stakeholder issues and relationships.

There are at least five categories of stakeholder cultures that reside on a continuum from little concern to great concern for stakeholders.[63] First is an **agency culture**, which basically is not concerned with others. Next are two cultures characterized by limited morality considerations—**corporate egoist culture** and **instrumentalist culture**—which focus mostly on the firm's shareholders as the important stakeholders. These cultures focus on short-term profit maximization. Finally, there are two cultures that are broadly moral—**moralist culture** and **altruist culture**. Both of these cultures are morally based and provide the broadest concern for stakeholders.[64] Figure 3-9 illustrates the categories of stakeholder cultures depicted on a continuum. Effective stakeholder management requires the development of a robust corporate culture that broadly conceives of responsibilities to others. In the above scheme, the moralist and altruist cultures would be most compatible with stakeholder management and a stakeholder corporation.

3.6c Stakeholder Management Capability

Effective stakeholder management is also greatly affected by the extent to which the organization has developed its **stakeholder management capability (SMC)**.[65] Stakeholder management capability describes an organization's integration of stakeholder thinking into its processes and it may reside at one of three levels of increasing sophistication: rational, process, and transactional. The **rational level** of SMC simply entails the company identifying who their stakeholders are and what their stakes happen to be. This is the level at which management might create a basic stakeholder map, such as that depicted in Figure 3-3. This represents a beginning or entry level of SMC. This first level has also been termed by Mark Starik as the element of *familiarization* and *comprehensiveness*, because the management operating at Level 1 is seeking to become familiar with their stakeholders and to develop a comprehensive assessment of their identification and stakes.[66]

Spotlight on Sustainability

Engaging Stakeholders on Sustainability

Enlightened companies have discovered that engaging stakeholders on their sustainability initiatives is vitally important and have concluded there are important guidelines for making this happen. Some of these guidelines include the following:

- Stakeholders need to be "on board" with your sustainability initiatives.
- Engage your stakeholders *sooner* rather than later. It is important to understand their perspectives and to be able to integrate them into your strategies and practices.
- Identify an *internal champion* who can help to align the interests of high-priority stakeholders with high-level internal decision makers.
- Employ *internal education*. It is important to identify and prioritize internal stakeholders and get them on board.
- Identify and engage your *most vocal critics*. It is important to find common ground early. These stakeholders can impact others both positively and negatively.
- Use *social media*. This will help engagement with stakeholders earlier and on a timelier basis.

- Use social media *openly and authentically*. Stakeholders will trust you more.
- Pay close attention to *consumer stakeholders*. They are frequently confused about sustainability messages. Many consumers are suspicious of green claims due to greenwashing.
- Pay close attention to *employees, NGOs, and the community stakeholders*. Employee engagement is critical to the success of engaging those outside the organization. Make it easy for them to participate.
- Face-to-face feedback and interactions are critical to success. Social media is important but not enough.

Sources: *Greenbiz*, "How to Engage Stakeholders on Sustainability," https://www.greenbiz.com/article/how-engage-stakeholders-sustainability, accessed February 9, 2021; Gap, Inc. "Engaging Stakeholders," https://www.gapincsustainability.com/strategy/sustainability-strategy/engaging-stakeholders, accessed February 9, 2021; EMG, "Benefits of Engaging Stakeholders," https://www.emg-csr.com/benefits-engaging-stakeholders/, accessed February 9, 2021.

At Level 2, the **process level**, organizations go a step further and actually develop and implement processes—approaches, procedures, policies, and practices—by which the firm may scan the environment and gather pertinent information about stakeholders, which is then used for decision-making purposes. A relevant stakeholder principle here is "constantly monitoring and redesigning processes to better serve stakeholders."[67] This second level has been described as *planning integrativeness*, because the management does focus on planning processes for stakeholders and integrating a consideration for stakeholders into organizational decision making.[68]

Level 3 is the **transactional level**. It is the highest and most developed of the three levels. This is the utmost goal for stakeholder management—the extent to which managers actually engage in transactions (relationships) with stakeholders.[69] At this highest level of SMC, in which a *transformation* of the business and society relationship occurs, management must take the initiative in meeting stakeholders face to face and attempting to be responsive to their needs. The transactional level may require actual negotiations with stakeholders.[70] Level 3 is the *communication* level, which is characterized by *communication proactiveness, interactiveness, genuineness, frequency, satisfaction*, and *resource adequacy*. Resource adequacy refers to the management actually spending resources on stakeholder transactions.[71] Regarding stakeholder communications, a relevant principle is that business must "engage in intensive communication and dialogue with (all) stakeholders, not just those who are friendly."[72]

An example of successful Level 3 SMC was the relationship established between General Motors Corporation (GM) and the Coalition for Environmentally Responsible Economies (Ceres). These two organizations actually began to talk with one another, and the result was a mutually beneficial collaboration. The arrangement became a high-profile example of an important trend within the sustainability movement—that of using quiet discussions, engagement, and negotiations rather than noisy protests to change corporate behavior.

3.6d Stakeholder Engagement

Recently, there has been growing interest in the topic of stakeholder engagement. **Stakeholder engagement** may be seen as an approach by which companies successfully implement the transactional level (Level 3) of strategic management capability. Business for Social Responsibility (BSR), a global industry group, strongly advocates stakeholder engagement as a process for achieving sustainable organizations.[73] Companies may employ different strategies in terms of the degree of engagement with their stakeholders, but best practices suggest that interaction with stakeholders should be integrated into every level of decision making in the organization.[74]

Ladder of Stakeholder Engagement. A ladder of stakeholder engagement, which depicts a number of steps from low engagement to high engagement, represents a continuum of engagement postures that companies might

follow.[75] *Lower* levels of stakeholder engagement might be used for informing and explaining. Formats at this level might include news coverage, publications, or reports. *Middle* levels of engagement would focus on communicating by way of formats such as conferences, social media, mass e-mails, newsletters, or surveys. *Higher* levels of stakeholder engagement might be active or responsive attempts to involve stakeholders in company decision making. At the highest level, processes such as *involvement, collaboration, partnership,* or *joint ventures* might be appropriate descriptions of the high-priority relationship established.

An example of this highest level would be when a firm enters into a strategic alliance with a stakeholder group to seek the group's opinion of a product design that would be sensitive to the group's concerns, such as environmental impact, employee safety, or product safety. This was illustrated when McDonald's entered into an alliance with the Environmental Defense Fund to eliminate polystyrene packaging that was not biodegradable.[76] In another collaboration, McDonald's agreed with PETA to implement a less cruel chicken slaughter method by 2024.[77]

Transparency. The concept of stakeholder engagement is relevant to developing what Tapscott and Ticoll refer to as *The Naked Corporation*. In their book, they argue that in the characteristics of the open enterprise, "environmental engagement" and "stakeholder engagement" are two critical factors. Environmental engagement calls for an open operating environment: sustainable ecosystems, peace, order, and good public governance. Stakeholder engagement calls for these open enterprises to put resources and effort into reviewing, managing, recasting, and strengthening relationships with stakeholders, old and new.[78] The "open enterprise" with an emphasis on "transparency" has become crucial because of the ongoing threats of corporate scandals. Transparency is becoming an increasingly important attribute of successful stakeholder engagements.

Engaging on Sustainability. One of the most important concerns today is engaging stakeholders on sustainability. The idea here is to involve stakeholders such as the social media, consumers, NGOs, and communities as early as possible on sustainability developments and initiatives. "Sustainability Stakeholder Engagement" conferences have been held to facilitate this process. One of the unique aspects of these conferences has been the increasing use of social media technologies, such as Twitter, to engage stakeholders in a timelier fashion.[79]

The Coca-Cola Company employed stakeholder engagement on sustainability with a variety of its stakeholders. Examples of their stakeholders and how they have engaged them include the following:

- Bottling partners. Day-to-day interactions with business partners, joint projects, participation in Global Environment Council.
- Consumers. Hotlines, consumer websites, plant tours, surveys, focus groups.

Ethics In Practice Case

Something's Rotten in Hondo

George Mackee thought of himself as bright, energetic, and with lots of potential. *So why is this happening to me?* he thought. George, with his wife, Mary, and his two children, had moved to Hondo, Texas, from El Paso four years earlier and was now the manager of the Ardnak Plastics plant in Hondo, a small plant that manufactured plastic parts for small equipment. The plant employed several hundred workers, which was a substantial portion of the population of Hondo. Ardnak Plastics Inc. had several other small plants the size of Hondo's. George had a good relationship with Bill, his boss, in Austin, Texas.

The Emissions Problem. One of the problems George's plant had was that the smokestack emissions were consistently above Environmental Protection Agency (EPA) guidelines. Several months ago, George got a call from Bill stating that the EPA had contacted him about the problem and fines would be levied. George admitted the situation was a continual problem, but because headquarters would not invest in new smokestack scrubbers, he didn't know what to do. Bill replied by saying that margins were at their limits and there was no money for new scrubbers. Besides, Bill commented, other plants were in worse shape than his and they were passing EPA standards.

A Questionable Solution. George ended the conversation by assuring Bill that he would look into the matter. He immediately started calling his contemporaries at other Ardnak plants. He found they were scheduling their heavy emissions work at night so that during the day when the EPA took their sporadic readings they were within standards. George contemplated this option even though it would result in increasing air contamination levels.

The Double Bind. A month went by, and George still had not found a solution. The phone rang; it was Bill. Bill expressed his displeasure with the new fines for the month and reminded George that there were very few jobs out in the industry. That's when Bill dropped the whole thing into George's lap. Bill had been speaking to the Mexican government and had received assurances that no such clean air restrictions would be imposed on Ardnak if they relocated 15 miles south of Hondo in Mexico. However, Ardnak must hire Mexican workers. Bill explained that the reason for relocating would be to eliminate the EPA problems. Bill told George he had one week to decide whether to eliminate the fines by correcting the current problems or by relocating.

George knew that relocating the plant on the Mexican side would devastate the infrastructure of the city of Hondo and would continue to put contaminants into the air on the U.S. side. When he mentioned the possibility to Mary, she reinforced other concerns. She did not want him to be responsible for the loss of the jobs of their friends and extended families.

1. Use the Stakeholder Typology in Figure 3-4 to identify, who are the stakeholders in this situation, and what are their stakes? How does proximity fit into this decision? Who are the most salient stakeholders?
2. What social responsibility, if any, does Ardnak Plastics Inc. have to the city of Hondo?
3. What are the ethical issues in this case?
4. Based on what you identify in question #1, what should George do? Why?

Source: This case was written by Geoffrey P. Lantos, Stonehill College. Permission to reprint granted by Arthur Andersen & Co., SC.

- Communities. Meetings, plant visits, partnerships on common issues, sponsorships.
- Employees. Engagement surveys, town hall meetings, individual development plans, employee well-being projects.

Other stakeholders engaged in the process include governments and regulatory bodies, NGOs, shareholders, analysts, suppliers, and trade associations. Two of their primary engagement topics have included water sustainability/stewardship and sustainable agriculture, ongoing issues. Coke's engagement with stakeholders has helped produce their Sustainable Agriculture Guiding Principles (SAGP) and the company believes that their stakeholder engagement initiatives on sustainability have reaped significant benefits. Coca-Cola believes that continuous dialogue and engagement is critical to respecting human and workplace rights within their system.[80]

Another element in stakeholder engagement is **stakeholder dialogue**. Stakeholder dialogue is primarily focused on exchanging communications with stakeholder groups and thus it is one form of engagement. When considering stakeholder dialogue among global stakeholders, it is worth noting that different countries are characterized by different approaches. In one major study, for example, it was found that stakeholder dialogue varied among three major countries—Germany,

Italy, and the United States. Germany and Italy employed a more *implicit* approach, whereas the United States used a more *explicit* approach.[81] The approaches to stakeholder dialogue were more *focused* in Germany, more *engaging* in Italy, and more *strategic* in the United States. A major conclusion of this study was that stakeholder dialogue has to be tailored to the national business system and that attempts to develop universal principles or guidelines may be imprudent.

3.6e The Stakeholder Corporation

An idealistic form or goal of the stakeholder approach or stakeholder management might be called the "**stakeholder corporation**." The central element of this concept is **stakeholder inclusiveness**.[82] Wheeler and Sillanpää say the following about this:

In the future, development of loyal relationships with customers, employees, shareholders, and other stakeholders will become one of the most important determinants of commercial viability and business success. Increasing shareholder value will be best served if your company cultivates the support of all who may influence its importance.

Advocates of the stakeholder corporation would embrace the idea of **stakeholder symbiosis**, which recognizes that all stakeholders depend on each other for their success and financial well-being.[83] It is the acceptance of this mutuality of interests that makes the difference in a firm becoming a stakeholder corporation. As James Post has summarized, "The stakeholder corporation is characterized by leaders who understand the need to balance, prioritize, and adjust to the needs of all constituencies."[84]

3.6f Principles of Stakeholder Management

After years of observation and research, a set of "**principles of stakeholder management**" was developed for use by managers and organizations. These principles, also known as the **Clarkson Principles**, were named after the late Max Clarkson, a dedicated researcher on the topic of stakeholder management. The principles are intended to provide managers with guiding precepts regarding how stakeholders should be treated. The key words in the principles are action words that reflect the kind of cooperative spirit that should be used in building stakeholder relationships: *acknowledge, monitor, listen, communicate, adopt, recognize, work, avoid,* and *acknowledge potential conflicts.* These principles serve as guidelines for successful stakeholder management.[85]

3.7 Strategic Steps toward Global Stakeholder Management

The global competition that characterizes business firms in the 21st century necessitates a stakeholder approach for effective and ethical management. The stakeholder approach requires that stakeholders be moved to the center of management's vision. Three strategic steps may be taken that can lead today's global competitors toward the more balanced view that is needed in today's dynamic business environment.[86]

1. **Governing Philosophy**. *Integrate stakeholder management into the firm's governing philosophy.* Boards of directors and top management teams should move the organization from the idea of "shareholder agent" to "stakeholder trustee." Long-term shareholder value, along with sustainability, will be the objective of this transition in corporate governance.
2. **Values Statement**. *Create a stakeholder-inclusive "values statement."* Various firms have done this under several

titles. Twitter calls this a "mission statement" focusing on sharing ideas instantly. Whole Foods Market has its "Higher Purpose Statement" that calls for courage, integrity, and love. L. L. Bean has a "core values statement" that focuses on customer stakeholders being treated well so they will always come back. Regardless of what such a values statement is called, such a pledge publicly reinforces the organization's commitment to stakeholders.

3. **Measurement System**. *Implement a stakeholder performance measurement system.* Such a system should be integrated, monitored, and auditable as stakeholder relations are improved. Measurement is evidence of serious intent to achieve results, and such a system will motivate a sustainable commitment to the stakeholder view. One recent example of a measurement system has been Walmart's creation of a Sustainability Index System (THESIS). With this initiative, the company is helping create a more transparent supply chain, driving product innovation, and ultimately providing customers with information they need to assess products' sustainability.[87]

3.7a Implementation

Regardless of the strategic approaches used, the acid test of effective stakeholder management is in its successful *implementation.* Implementation implies the following key activities: execution, application, operationalization, and enactment. Corporate social responsibility and sustainability are made operable when companies translate their stakeholder dialogue into practice.[88] After studying three large, successful companies in detail—Cummins Engine Company, Motorola, and the Royal Dutch/Shell Group— prominent researchers concluded that the key to effective implementation is in recognizing and using stakeholder management as a *core competence.*[89]

When this is done, at least four indicators or manifestations of successful stakeholder management will be apparent. First, stakeholder management results in *survival.* Second, there are many *avoided costs.* Third, there was *continued acceptance and use* in the companies studied, implying success. Fourth, there was evidence of *expanded recognition and adoption* of stakeholder-oriented policies by other companies and consultants.[90] These indicators suggest the value and practical benefits that may be derived from implementing the stakeholder approach. Finally, it should be noted that organizations develop learning processes over time in implementing their changing or evolving stakeholder orientations.[91]

Summary

Increasingly, societies are moving toward some variation of stakeholder capitalism. In this context, a stakeholder is an individual or a group that claims to have one or more stakes in an organization. Stakeholders may affect the organization and, in turn, be affected by the organization's actions, policies, practices, and decisions. The stakeholder approach extends beyond the traditional production and managerial views of the firm and warrants a much broader conception of the parties involved in the organization's functioning and success. Both primary and secondary social and nonsocial stakeholders assume significant roles in the eyes of management. A typology of stakeholders suggests that three attributes are especially important: legitimacy, power, and urgency. Proximity also is often a salient factor.

Strategic, multifiduciary, and stakeholder synthesis approaches help us appreciate the strategies that may be adopted with regard to stakeholders. The stakeholder synthesis approach is encouraged because it highlights the ethical responsibility business has to its stakeholders. The stakeholder view of the firm has three values that make it useful: descriptive, instrumental, and normative. In a balanced perspective, managers are concerned with both company goal achievement and ethical treatment of stakeholders.

Five key questions assist managers in stakeholder management: (1) Who are the firm's stakeholders? (2) What are our stakeholders' stakes? (3) What challenges or opportunities are presented to a firm by stakeholders? (4) What responsibilities does a firm have to its stakeholders? (5) What strategies or actions should a firm take with respect to its stakeholders? Effective stakeholder management requires the assessment and appropriate response to these five questions. In addition,

the use of other relevant stakeholder thinking concepts is helpful. Identifying **stakeholder utility**, or value, is important.

Approaching stakeholder relationships with a mindset to creating value, and developing a stakeholder culture, is also vital. The concept of stakeholder management capability (SMC) illustrates how firms can grow and mature in their approach to stakeholder management. Stakeholder engagement emphasizes carefully selecting an engagement approach—informing, communicating, or actually engaging. The stakeholder corporation is a model that represents stakeholder thinking in its most advanced form and stakeholder inclusion is the central element.

Principles of stakeholder management are helpful in guiding managers toward more effective stakeholder thinking. Although the stakeholder management approach is quite complex and time consuming, it is a way of managing that is in tune with the complex, dynamic environment that business organizations face today. Strategic steps in global stakeholder management include making stakeholders a part of the guiding philosophy, creating corporate value statements, and developing measurement systems that monitor results. In the final analysis, implementation is the key to effective stakeholder management.

Key Terms

agency culture, p. 60

altruist culture, p. 60

claim, p. 46

Clarkson Principles, p. 63

corporate egoist culture, p. 60

descriptive value (of stakeholder model), p. 52

five key questions, p. 53

fringe stakeholders, p. 48

instrumental value (of stakeholder model), p. 52

instrumentalist culture, p. 60

legitimacy, p. 50

managerial view of the firm, p. 47

marginal stakeholder, p. 57

mixed-blessing stakeholder, p. 58

moralist culture, p. 60

multifiduciary approach to stakeholders, p. 52

nonsupportive stakeholder, p. 57

normative value (of stakeholder model), p. 52

power, p. 50

primary nonsocial stakeholders, p. 48

primary social stakeholders, p. 48

principles of stakeholder management, p. 63

process level, p. 60

production view of the firm, p. 47

proximity, p. 50

rational level, p. 60

secondary nonsocial stakeholders, p. 48

secondary social stakeholders, p. 48

stake, p. 46

stakeholders, p. 45

stakeholder approach, p. 46

stakeholder capitalism, p. 45

stakeholder corporation, p. 62

stakeholder culture, p. 59

stakeholder dialogue, p. 62

stakeholder engagement, p. 61

stakeholder identification, p. 53

stakeholder inclusiveness, p. 62

stakeholder management, p. 52

stakeholder management capability (SMC), p. 60

stakeholder map, p. 48

stakeholder mindset, p. 59

stakeholder orientation, p. 59

stakeholder responsibility matrix, p. 57

stakeholder symbiosis, p. 63

stakeholder thinking, p. 59

stakeholder utility, p. 64

stakeholder view of the firm, p. 47

strategic approach, p. 52

strategic approach to stakeholders, p. 52

supportive stakeholder, p. 57

synthesis approach to stakeholders, p. 52

transactional level, p. 61

urgency, p. 50

Discussion Questions

1. Explain how stakeholder capitalism has evolved to be a governing system in many advanced nations of the world. Have business firms adapted to this evolving system?

2. Explain the concepts of stake and stakeholder from your perspective as an individual. What kinds of stakes and stakeholders do you have? Discuss.

3. Explain in your own words the differences between the production, managerial, and stakeholder views of the firm. Which view is most realistic and why?

4. Differentiate between primary and secondary social and nonsocial stakeholders in a business situation. Give examples of each.

5. What are the five key questions that must be answered for stakeholder management to be successful?

6. What are the three levels of stakeholder engagement that a company might use? Explain each.

7. Is the stakeholder corporation a realistic model for business firms? Will stakeholder corporations become more prevalent in the 21st century? Why or why not?

Endnotes

1. See, for example, Jill A. Brown and William R. Forster, "CSR and Stakeholder Theory: A Tale of Adam Smith," *Journal of Business Ethics* (Vol. 112, 2013), 301–312; Robert A. Phillips, "Stakeholder Theory and a Principle of Fairness," *Business Ethics Quarterly* (Vol. 7, No. 1, January 1997), 51–66; Sandra A. Waddock and Samuel B. Graves, "Quality of Management and Quality of Stakeholder Relations," *Business and Society* (Vol. 36, No. 3, September 1997), 250–279; James P. Walsh, "Taking Stock of Stakeholder Management," *Academy of Management Review* (Vol. 30, No. 2, 2005), 426–438; Thomas Jones and Andrew Wicks, 1999, "Convergent Stakeholder Theory," *Academy of Management Review* (Vol. 20, 1999), 404–437.

2. Rick Wartzman and Kelly Tang, "Companies' Broader Mission," *The Wall Street Journal* (October 28, 2019), R6.

3. Klaus Schwab, *Stakeholder Capitalism: A Global Economy that Works for Progress, People and Planet* (New Jersey: John Wiley & Sons, 2021).

4. Kristin Huber and Maximilian J. L. Schormair, "Progressive and Conservative Firms in Multistakeholder Initiatives: Tracing the Construction of Political CSR Identities within the Accord on Fire and Building Safety in Bangladesh," *Business & Society,* 60(2), 2021, 454–495.

5. Lucian Bebchuck and Roberto Tallarita, "Stakeholder Capitalism Seems Mostly for Show," *The Wall Street Journal* (August 7, 2020), A15.

6. Wartzman and Tang, 2020, R6.

7. James E. Post, Lee E. Preston, and Sybille Sachs, "Managing the Extended Enterprise," *California Management Review,* 45(1), Fall 2002, 8–9.

8. David Wheeler and Maria Sillanpää, *The Stakeholder Corporation: A Blueprint for Maximizing Stakeholder Value* (London: Pitman Publishing, 1997).

9. James E. Post, Lee E. Preston, and Sybille Sachs, *Redefining the Corporation: Stakeholder Management and Organizational Wealth* (Stanford: Stanford University Press, 2002).

10. Robert Phillips and R. Edward Freeman, *Stakeholders* (Edward Elgar Pub, 2010). Also see Ed Freeman, Jeffrey Harrison, Bidhan Parmar, and Simone De Colle, *Stakeholder Theory: The State of the Art*, (New York: Cambridge University Press, 2010).

11. Jeanne M. Logsdon, Donna J. Wood, and Lee E. Benson, "Research in Stakeholder Theory, 1997–1998: The Sloan Foundation Minigrant Project" (Toronto: The Clarkson Centre for Business Ethics, 2000).

12. Jeffrey S. Harrison and Andrew C. Wicks, "Stakeholder Theory, Value and Firm Performance," *Business Ethics Quarterly* (January 2013), 97–124.

13. Vivek Soundararajan and Jill Brown, "Voluntary Governance Mechanisms in Global Supply Chains: Beyond CSR to a Stakeholder Utility Perspective," *Journal of Business Ethics* (2014), 1–20. DOI: 10.1007/s10551-014-2418-y.

14. This definition is similar to that of R. Edward Freeman in *Strategic Management: A Stakeholder Approach* (Boston, MA: Pitman, 1984), 25.

15. George Kassinis, "The Value of Managing Stakeholders," in Pratima Bansal and Andrew Hoffman (eds.), *The Oxford Handbook of Business and the Natural Environment* (Oxford: Oxford University Press, 2012).

16. "The Many Stakeholders of Salesforce.com," *The Wall Street Journal* (October 27, 2015), R2.

17. Mark Starik, "Is the Environment an Organizational Stakeholder? Naturally!" *International Association for Business and Society (IABS) 1993 Proceedings*, 466–471.

18. David Woodward, "Is the Natural Environment a Stakeholder? Of Course It Is (No Matter What the Utilitarians Might Say)," in *Critical Perspectives on Accounting Conference*, New York (April 25–27, 2002), New York: Baruch College, City University of New York.

19. Freeman, 5.

20. Freeman, 24–25. Also see James E. Post, Lee E. Preston, and Sybille Sachs (2002); Freeman, 5.

21. Wheeler and Sillanpää (1997), 167.

22. Ibid., 168.

23. Lauren McCarthy and Judy Muthuri, "Engaging Fringe Stakeholders in Business and Society Research: Applying Visual and Participatory Research Methods," *Business and Society,* 57(1), 2018, 131–173.

24. Gideon D. Markman, Theodore L. Waldron, and Andreas Panagopoulos, "Organizational Hostility: Why and How Nonmarket Players Compete with Firms," *Academy of Management Perspectives,* 30(1), 2016, 74–92.

25. Donna J. Wood, Ronald K. Mitchell, Bradley R. Agle, and Logan M. Bryan, "Stakeholder Identification and Salience After 20 Years: Progress, Problems and Prospects," *Business & Society*, 60(1), 2021, p. 234.

26. Ronald K. Mitchell, Bradley R. Agle, and Donna J. Wood, "Toward a Theory of Stakeholder Identification and Salience: Defining the Principle of Who and What Really Counts," *Academy of Management Review* (October 1997), 853–886.

27. Bernd Helmig, Katharina Spraul, and Diana Ingenhoff, "Under Positive Pressure: How Stakeholder Pressure Affects Corporate Social Responsibility Implementation," *Business and Society,* 55(2), 2016, 151–187.

28. Mark Starik and Cathy Driscoll, "The Primordial Stakeholder: Advancing the Conceptual Consideration of Stakeholder Status for the Natural Environment," in

A. J. Zakhem, D. E. Palmer, and M. L. Stoll (eds.), *Stakeholder Theory: Essential Readings in Ethical Leadership and Management* (Amherst, NY: Prometheus Books, 2007), 219–222.

29. Ibid.

30. Jim Carlton, "How Home Depot and Activists Joined to Cut Logging Abuse," *The Wall Street Journal* (September 26, 2000), A1; Greenpeace, "Activists Target Home Depot's Destruction of Ancient Forests," July 6, 2010, https://www.greenpeace.org/usa/news/activists-target-the-home-depo/. Accessed February 16, 2021.

31. Benjamin A. Neville, Simon J. Bell, and Gregory J. Whitwell, "Stakeholder Salience Revisited: Refining, Redefining, and Refueling an Underdeveloped Conceptual Tool," *Journal of Business Ethics,* 102(1), 2011, 357–378.

32. Kenneth E. Goodpaster, "Business Ethics and Stakeholder Analysis," *Business Ethics Quarterly,* 1(1), January 1991, 53–73.

33. Ibid.

34. Johanna Kujala, Anna Heikkinen, and Hanna Lehtimaki, "Understanding the Nature of Stakeholder Relationships: An Empirical Examination of a Conflict Situation," *Journal of Business Ethics,* 109, 2012, 53–65.

35. Thomas Donaldson and Lee Preston, "The Stakeholder Theory of the Corporation: Concepts, Evidence, Implications," *Academy of Management Review,* 20(1), 1995, 65–91.

36. Ibid.

37. Robert Phillips, *Stakeholder Theory and Organizational Ethics* (San Francisco: Berrett-Koehler Publishers, Inc., 2003), 85–118.

38. Donaldson and Preston.

39. Parallel questions are posed with respect to corporate strategy by Ian C. MacMillan and Patricia E. Jones, *Strategy Formulation: Power and Politics* (St. Paul, MN: West, 1986), 66.

40. "Animal Rights Group Aims Ad Attack at McDonald's," *The Wall Street Journal* (August 30, 1999), B7. Also see http://www.mccruelty.com/why.aspx. Accessed March 31, 2016.

41. Marcia Yablon, "Happy Hen, Happy Meal: McDonald's Chick Fix," *U.S. News & World Report* (September 4, 2000), 46.

42. Ibid.

43. PETA, "McDonald's Bacon Hour Giveaway Sparks PETA Protest," January 28, 2019, https://www.peta.org/media/news-releases/mcdonalds-bacon-hour-giveaway-sparks-peta-protest/. Accessed February 8, 2021.

44. R. Edward Freeman, S. R. Velamuri, and Brian Moriarty, "Company Stakeholder Responsibility: A New Approach to CSR," Business Roundtable Institute for Corporate Ethics, Bridge Paper (2006), 11.

45. John Browne and Robin Nuttall, "Beyond Corporate Social Responsibility: Integrated External Engagement," *McKinsey Quarterly* (March 2013), http://www.mckinsey.com/insights/strategy/beyond_corporate_social_responsibility_integrated_external_engagement. Accessed March 31, 2016.

46. Rainforest Action Network, "Illegal logging and road construction," https://www.ran.org/?s=logging. Accessed February 8, 2021.

47. Rainforest Acton Network, "Fighting for People and Planet," https://www.ran.org/mission-and-values/. Accessed February 8, 2021.

48. Rainforest Action Network, "Forests," https://www.ran.org/issue/forests/. Accessed February 8, 2021.

49. Rainforest Action Network, "Campaigns," https://www.ran.org/publications/. Accessed February 8, 2021.

50. Grant T. Savage, Timothy W. Nix, Carlton J. Whitehead, and John D. Blair, "Strategies for Assessing and Managing Organizational Stakeholders," *Academy of Management Executive,* V(2), May 1991, 61–75.

51. Environmental Defense Fund, "Our key priorities," https://www.edf.org/. Accessed February 8, 2021.

52. Dennis Hammer, Career.pm, "What do stakeholders really want from you?" April 1, 2019, https://www.career.pm/posts/what-do-stakeholders-really-want-from-you/. Accessed February 8, 2021.

53. MacMillan and Jones, 66–70.

54. John F. Preble, "Toward a Comprehensive Model of Stakeholder Management," *Business and Society Review,* 110(4), 2005, 421–423.

55. Ibid., 415.

56. Savage, Nix, Whitehead, and Blair, 65.

57. Seth Hettena and Laura Wides, "Eco-Terrorists Coming Out of the Wild," *USA Today* (October 3, 2003), 22A. Also see Anti-Defamation League, "Extremism in America," http://archive.adl.org/learn/ext_us/default.html?LEARN_Cat=Extremism&LEARN_SubCat=Extremism_in_America&xpicked=1&item=0. Accessed March 31, 2016.

58. Marilyn Geewax, "Business Forges Unusual Alliances," *Cox News Service,* https://www.businessforafairminimumwage.org/news/0034/cox-news-service-business-forges-unusual-alliances. Accessed February 22, 2021.

59. Savage, Nix, Whitehead, and Blair, 72.

60. Andrew C. Wicks, Adrian. C. Keevil, and Bidhan Parmar, "Sustainable Business Development and Management Theories," *Business and Professional Ethics Journal,* 31(3/4), 2012, 375–398; S. L. Berman, Andrew Wicks, Suresh Kotha, and Thomas Jones, "Does Stakeholder Orientation Matter? The Relationship Between Stakeholder Management Models and Firm Financial Performance," *Academy of Management Journal* 42(5), November 2017; Vivek Soundararajan, Jill A. Brown, and Andy Wicks, "Can Multi-Stakeholder Initiatives Improve Global Supply Chains? Improving Deliberative Capacity with a Stakeholder Orientation," *Business Ethics Quarterly*, February 7, 2019.

61. Robert Phillips, "Stakeholder Legitimacy," *Business Ethics Quarterly*, 13(1), 2005, 25–41.

62. C. Geertz, *The Interpretation of Cultures: Selected Essays* (New York: Basic Books, 1973). See also M. J. Hatch, "The Dynamics of Organizational Culture," *Academy of Management Review,* 18, 1993, 657–693.

63. Thomas M. Jones, Will Felps, and Gregory A. Bigley, "Ethical Theory and Stakeholder-Related Decisions: The Role of Stakeholder Culture," *Academy of Management Review,* 32(1), 2007, 137–155.

64. Ibid.

65. Freeman, 53.

66. Mark Starik, "Stakeholder Management and Firm Performance: Reputation and Financial Relationships to U.S. Electric Utility Consumer-Related Strategies," unpublished Ph.D. dissertation, University of Georgia, 1990, 34.

67. Freeman, Velamur, and Moriarty (2006), 11.

68. Starik (1990), 36.

69. Freeman, 69–70.

70. Freeman, Velamur, and Moriarty (2006), 11.
71. Starik (1990), 36–42.
72. Freeman, Velamur, and Moriarty (2006), 11.
73. Business for Social Responsibility (BSR), "Five-Step Approach for Stakeholder Engagement" (April 29, 2019), https://www.bsr.org/en/our-insights/report-view /stakeholder-engagement-five-step-approach-toolkit. Accessed February 22, 2021.
74. Browne and Nuttall (2013); Freeman, Velamur, and Moriarty (2006), 11.
75. Andrew L. Friedman and Samantha Miles, *Stakeholders: Theory and Practice* (Oxford: Oxford University Press, 2006), 160–179.
76. Ibid., 175. Also see Laura Dunham, R. Edward Freeman, and Jeanne Liedtka, "Enhancing Stakeholder Practice: A Particularized Exploration of Community," *Business Ethics Quarterly,* 16(1), 2006, 23–42.
77. PETA, "McDonald's Finally Agrees to Use Less Cruel Slaughter Method in 2024," https://www.peta.org/blog /mcdonalds-finally-agrees-to-use-less-cruel-slaughter -method-in-2024/. Accessed February 10, 2021.
78. Don Tapscott and David Ticoll, *The Naked Corporation: How the Age of Transparency Will Revolutionize Business* (Free Press, 2003).
79. Perry Goldschein and Beth Bengston, "How to Engage Stakeholders on Sustainability," *GreenBiz.com*, https:// www.greenbiz.com/article/how-engage-stakeholders -sustainability. Accessed February 16, 2021.
80. Coca-Cola Company, "Stakeholder Engagement," https:// www.coca-colahellenic.com/en/a-more-sustainable-future /our-approach/stakeholder-engagement. Accessed February 10, 2021.
81. Lorenzo Patelli, "Stakeholder Dialogue in Germany, Italy, and the United States," *Director Notes, The Conference Board,* New York: The Conference Board (July 2012), https://corpgov.law.harvard.edu/2012/08/18/stakeholder -dialogue-in-germany-italy-and-the-united-states/. Accessed February 10, 2021.
82. Wheeler and Sillanpää (1997), book cover.
83. "Stakeholder Symbiosis," *Fortune* (March 30, 1998), S2–S4, special advertising section.
84. James Post, "Governance and the Stakeholder Corporation: New Challenges for Global Business," Corporate Public Affairs Oration, Melbourne, June 24, 2004. https://www .econbiz.de/Record/governance-and-the-stakeholder -corporation-new-challenges-for-global-business-post -james/10003402870. Accessed February 10, 2021.
85. *Principles of Stakeholder Management* (Toronto: The Clarkson Centre for Business Ethics, School of Management, 1999), University of Toronto, 4.
86. "Measurements," *Measuring and Managing Stakeholder Relationships* (Indianapolis: Walker Information Global Network, 1998).
87. Walmart Sustainability Hub, "Walmart's THESIS Index," https://www.walmartsustainabilityhub.com/sustainability -index. Accessed February 10, 2021.
88. Esben Rahbek Pedersen, "Making Corporate Social Responsibility (CSR) Operable: How Companies Translate Stakeholder Dialogue into Practice," *Business and Society Review,* 111(2), 2006, 137–163, https://onlinelibrary.wiley .com/doi/abs/10.1111/j.1467-8594.2006.00265. Accessed February 23, 2021.
89. Post, Preston, and Sachs (2002), 22.
90. James E. Post, Lee E. Preston, and Sybille Sachs, "Managing the Extended Enterprise: The New Stakeholder View," *California Management Review,* 45(1), Fall 2002, 22–25.
91. Marc Maurer and Sybille Sachs, "Implementing the Stakeholder View," *Journal of Corporate Citizenship,* 17, Spring 2005, 93–107.

4

Sustainability and the Natural Environment

After studying this chapter, you should be able to:

1. Identify the components of the triple bottom line and how it relates to sustainability.
2. Discuss the concept of sustainability and its imperative.
3. Discuss the UN Global Compact and its sustainability goals.
4. Describe the natural environment, the impact of business on the natural environment, and major natural environment issues.
5. Identify and discuss the issues that arise for businesses in their responsibility for the environment and sustainability.
6. Discuss the role of governments in environmental and sustainability issues.
7. Describe other environmental stakeholders, including interest groups, employees, and investors.
8. Discuss business environmentalism, sustainability goals, and the future of the business/environment relationship.

In the Walt Disney movie *WALL-E*, a solitary robot named WALL-E finds itself on a deserted Earth, navigating a world of trash and barren landscape. The movie provides a clear message: take care of the world you inhabit, because if you do not, the consequences are dire. In essence, it is a movie about sustainability.

Climate change, recycling, energy, pollution, solar panels, carbon emissions, carbon footprint, fair trade, deforestation, water, plastics, pesticides, biodiversity, sustainable eating, sustainable fashion, sustainable finance, ecotourism ... the list of topics that fall under sustainability is wide and varied, and we explore many of these in this chapter. But what does it mean for a company to be sustainable? There are so many definitions and measures of sustainability that it can be hard to answer that question. In fact, one article pointed out that in one year, a large company was recognized as a top-ten sustainable company by one data provider and a bottom-ten performer by another.[1] However, assessing the sustainability of a company involves understanding how it is broadly defined, how it is important to business, how it translates into sustainability goals and measures, and what stakeholders might be involved.

While the natural environment is considered an external stakeholder group and might be considered alongside other external stakeholders like government, consumers, and the community, we introduce it in this chapter, and early in the book, to emphasize its importance to business and society relationships. Additionally, as you will see below, sustainability encompasses not only the natural environment but also broader environments including the economy and society. All of these things are important to understanding the concept of sustainability and business.

Most businesses now include measures of sustainability in their **key performance indicators (KPIs)**. As the sustainability movement grows, creative businesspeople are developing new ways of doing business that benefit all aspects of the **triple bottom line**—people, planet, profits. The concept seeks to encapsulate for business the three key spheres of **sustainability** that it must attend to—*economic*, *social*, and *environmental*. The economic bottom line refers to the firm's creation of material wealth, including financial income and assets. The emphasis is on *profits*. The social bottom line is about the quality of people's lives and about equity between people, communities, and nations. The emphasis is on *people*. The environmental bottom line is about protection and conservation of the natural environment.[2] The emphasis is on the *planet*.

In spite of the fact that sustainability refers broadly to each of these three areas, many practitioners and academics continue to speak as though sustainability is only about business and its natural environment. Each of these three—profits, people, and planet—is implicit in the Pyramid of corporate social responsibility (CSR) and represents a version of the stakeholder–bottom line concept. At its narrowest, *triple bottom line* is used as a framework for measuring and reporting corporate performance in terms of economic, social, and environmental indicators. At its broadest, the concept is used to capture the whole set of values, issues, and processes that companies must address to minimize harm resulting from their activities and to create economic, social, and environmental value.[3]

Corporate sustainability is the goal of the triple bottom line approach. The goal of sustainability is to create long-term stakeholder value by taking advantage of opportunities and managing risks related to economic, environmental, and social developments. Leaders in this area try to take advantage of the market's demand for sustainable products and services while successfully reducing and avoiding sustainability costs and risks. To help achieve these goals, indices such as the Dow Jones Sustainability Indexes were created to monitor and assess the sustainability of corporations.[4] As will become apparent throughout the book, the concept of sustainability is intertwined with other social responsibility concepts and terminology, and it has become so important in business and academic usage that it needs to be emphasized in various contexts.

We draw from the Brundtland Commission (formerly the World Commission on Environment and Development [WCED]) to define **sustainable business** as "business that meets the needs of the present without compromising the ability of future generations to meet their own needs."[5] Put another way, the focus of sustainability is the creation of a good quality of life for both current and future generations of humans and nonhumans by achieving a balance between economic prosperity, ecosystem viability, and social justice.[6] The concept is akin to walking lightly on the earth, taking only what is needed, and leaving behind enough for future generations to have access to the same resources.

The focus on sustainability for business has been swift as businesses become more and more convinced that it is not only the right thing to do but also something that can drive revenues, savings, and be a source of competitive advantage. In a recent comprehensive survey of more than 1,000 top executives across 21 industries and 99 countries, fully 95 percent of CEOs say that they are personally committed that their companies lead on sustainable development goals.[7]

The growth of attention to sustainability is not surprising when one considers the strong business case for sustainability. In *Green to Gold*, Daniel Esty and Andrew Winston offer three basic reasons for incorporating sustainability into a business's core strategy.[8] First, there are upside benefits. Sustainability requires innovation and entrepreneurship that can help a firm to move ahead of competitors through new ideas, lower costs, and stronger intangibles such as trust and credibility. Sustainable companies can even carry less risk, resulting in lower lending rates. Second, companies that ignore the sustainability imperative run the risk of incurring society's wrath once they step over the line. Companies such as DuPont Chemical and municipalities like the city of Flint, Michigan, experienced significant stakeholder backlash following their pollution issues, and Coca-Cola, PepsiCo, and Nestlé continue to receive criticism for their association with plastic waste. Finally, sustainability is the right thing to do. As the sign in Patagonia headquarters says, "There is no business to be done on a dead planet."[9]

This chapter begins by discussing the concept of sustainability and its importance to business, that is, a sustainability imperative. An overview of the growth of the sustainability movement and the drivers of corporate

sustainability will follow. We highlight Schneider Electric, an energy company that moved away from high-voltage electric distribution to focus on data centers and smart solutions to make the world more energy efficient, renewable, and digital. Consequently, Schneider earned the number-one spot in the *Corporate Knights* ranking for sustainability in 2021 and the Global 100 index as the world's most sustainable company.[10] We discuss how companies are assessed on their sustainability goals, with a focus on the UN Global Compact's principles on sustainability.

The focus is then narrowed to environmental sustainability and the top environmental issues facing business today. The section on environmental ethics begins a discussion of individual and collective responsibility for sustaining the environment. We explore the role of the government and environmental interest groups in promoting change, and we offer ways in which businesses can develop a strategy aimed at achieving environmental sustainability. In sum, with a broad view of sustainability that encompasses the environment, economy, and society, we then move on in the rest of the book chapters to identify and discuss specific stakeholder groups that are involved in the business and society relationship.

4.1 The Sustainability Imperative: A Call for Business to Step Up

Several years ago, a discussion of sustainability would have had to include strong arguments about why businesses would benefit from sustainable practices. Today, the need for sustainability is a "given" as businesses now integrate sustainability into their business strategies.

The sustainability imperative has been, in large part, driven by large-scale initiatives like the **United Nations Global Compact (UNGC)**, whose members total more than 12,000 companies in more than 160 countries. In 2015, the UNGC launched a global initiative for member businesses to agree to commit to ten principles regarding human rights, labor, environment, and anticorruption, and 17 **sustainable development goals (SDGs)** in support of the principles. These are outlined in Figure 4-1. The goals were developed as part of the UNGC 2030 Agenda for Sustainable Development, which set out a 15-year plan to achieve its goals.[11]

Figure 4-1 presents the UNGC's 17 SDGs. The UNGC's goals are designed to help unite global stakeholders to "transform the world to end extreme poverty, fight inequality and injustice, and protect the planet."[12] Each goal is accompanied by a variety of resources for businesses to implement actions designed to address the goal, including an SDG Compass to navigate the tools, as well as an SDG Industry matrix that showcases industry-specific examples and ideas for corporate action.

Annual reports regarding the UNGC 2030 agenda up to 2020 indicate that while some progress has been made

Figure 4-1 The UN Global Compact's Sustainable Development Goals (SDGs)

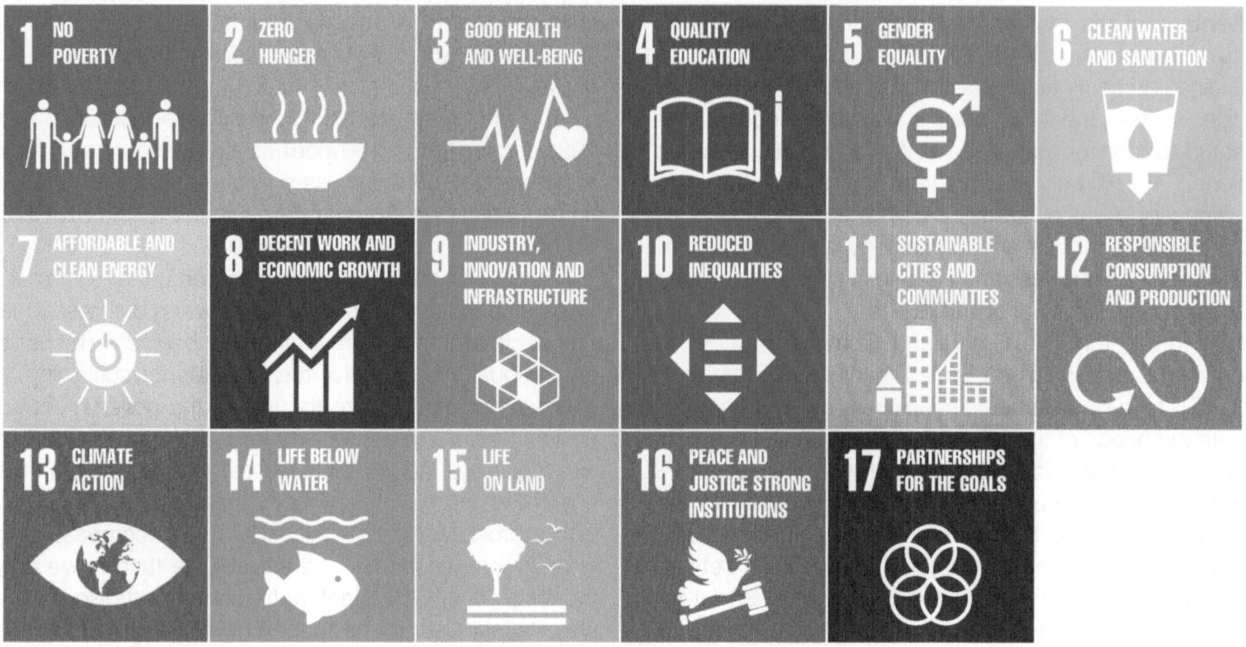

Source: 17 Goals to Transform Our World, https://www.unglobalcompact.org/sdgs/17-global-goals, accessed January 28, 2021.

in accomplishing the goals, it has been uneven. Therefore, unless changes are made, the agenda's promise might not be fulfilled.[13] Additionally, the COVID-19 global pandemic resulted in some devastating impacts of the pandemic on specific goals and targets. Nevertheless, UN Secretary-General Antonio Guterres rallied UNGC members in 2021 with the message, "Everything we do during and after this crisis [COVID-19] must be with a strong focus on building more equal, inclusive and sustainable economies and societies that are more resilient in the face of pandemics, climate change, and the many other global challenges we face."[14]

One company, Schneider Electric, attributes its sustainability successes to an original commitment to the UNGC principles. Schneider was one of the first companies to endorse the principles, including asking their suppliers to be sustainable.[15] Schneider develops systems that manage electricity for businesses. While it began in high-voltage electrical distribution, it transformed over the years to a renewable energy company, curbing its own emissions by 250,000 metric tons of CO_2 in 24 months, committing to net-zero operational emissions by 2030, and offering a suite of energy-efficient technologies that could save 120 million metric tons of CO_2 on their customers' behalf.[16] As expressed by CEO Jean-Pascal Tricoire, "We have two competing objectives which are essential. The first one is that everybody gets access to energy, because energy gives you access to a decent life. But at the same time, we need to reduce emissions by a factor of two in the next 20 years."[17]

Another factor in support of businesses' commitment to sustainability is the media attention to companies who "do well by doing good," like those highlighted in *Fortune*

magazine's Change the World (CTW) rankings.[18] Each year, *Fortune* publishes a list of companies that have had a positive social impact through activities that are part of their core business strategy. Interestingly, the *Fortune* focus is built on the premise that "the profit motive can inspire companies to tackle society's unmet needs."[19] Recent winners include Alibaba Group Holding and Nvidia. Vaccine makers including Pfizer and Moderna have also been highlighted for their important role in the race for a COVID-19 vaccine.

Activism, and in particular youth activism, is another source of incentives for business to take on sustainability challenges. In 2018, for example, then 15-year-old Greta Thunberg started a school strike in Sweden to draw attention to climate change. Since then, her message has taken off as a global social movement, where young people across the world join her rally.[20] Since 2018, she has addressed the United Nations, met with the Pope, exchanged words with the president of the United States, addressed the World Economic Forum in Davos, Switzerland, and inspired four million people to join a global climate strike in September 2019.[21] Her activism seems to provide results as well. After she spoke to Parliament and demonstrated with the British environmental group Extinction, the United Kingdom passed a law requiring that the country eliminate its carbon footprint.[22]

In sum, the concept of sustainability has been institutionalized as a form of CSR, with a critical mass of supporters that point to its benefits.[23]

Ceres, a Boston-based sustainability nonprofit organization that works with many institutional investors, identifies several key drivers that underscore the imperative toward sustainability, presenting both risks and opportunities that parallel the UNGC initiatives: [24]

1. Competition for Resources—Demand for resources is growing more quickly than they can be replaced.
2. Climate Change—Businesses must be prepared to not only respond to new policies and regulations regarding emissions but also take advantage of opportunities to profit from new technologies that reduce emissions or create solutions.
3. Economic Globalization—Wide disparities in social and environmental standards bring risks as well as opportunities.
4. Connectivity and Communications—Stakeholders can monitor and react to sustainability efforts more quickly and effectively. Reputations are more easily and quickly built and destroyed.

The attention to sustainability inevitably begins at the top ranks of any organization. Schneider Electric's CEO, for example, has been described as "something of an electricity evangelist," and he champions sustainability with the edict, "All you need is a change of mentality."[25] One of the foremost advocates of corporate sustainability is Paul Polman, former CEO of Unilever, the British multinational consumer goods company. During his tenure as CEO from 2009–2019, Polman helped turn around Unilever while developing its reputation as a sustainable company. For example, concerned that a focus on shareholder wealth maximization would lead to a short-term outlook at odds with the long-term perspective needed for sustainability, Polman banned quarterly earnings reports, which lowered his percentage of hedge fund investors from 15 percent to 5 percent in three years.[26] Not sorry to see the hedge fund investors go, he then actively courted more long-term-oriented investment funds. It is not surprising that following his stint at Unilever, Polman went on to cofound a social venture, *IMAGINE*, designed to accelerate business leadership to achieve global goals.[27]

Company leadership teams are increasingly populated with a chief sustainability officer (CSO), as seen in companies such as Procter & Gamble, Nike, and H&M.[28] According to the *GreenBiz Group*, corporate engagement at the executive levels is the key for businesses to move beyond the "low hanging fruit" of finding control inside their operations, such as facilities and fleets, which have attractive financial paybacks.[29]

4.2 The Natural Environment

Similar to other broad terms, **environment** means many things to many people—trees in the backyard, a family's favorite vacation spot, a mare and her colt in a pasture, a trout stream in the mountains, earth and the other planets, and our solar system. Broadly speaking, it is anything that is external or internal to an entity. For humans, the environment

can include external living, working, and playing spaces and natural resources, as well as internal physical, mental, and emotional states.

This chapter focuses on the **natural environment**—all living and nonliving things occurring naturally (i.e., not artificial). We discuss why it is important, how it has become a major concern, and what businesses and other organizations have done both to and for it—making it one of the most significant societal issues of our time. The chapter also describes the variety of responses human organizations, including businesses, have developed to address this issue. Throughout the chapter, the emphasis is on two themes: that humans are a part of their natural environment, and that the environment itself is extremely complex, defying simple analyses.

In spite of the recent progress described in the introduction, for years businesses conducted their operations with little concern about environmental consequences. Virtually every sector of business in every country was responsible for consuming significant amounts of materials and energy and causing waste accumulation and resource degradation. For instance, forestry firms and companies that process raw materials, such as uranium, coal, and oil, have caused major air, water, and land pollution problems in their extraction, transportation, and processing stages. Manufacturing firms, such as those in steel, petrochemicals, and paper products, have been major sources of air and water pollution. Consumer products companies, such as those who produce bottled water, have contributed toxins to the environment and created a plastics waste problem that has endangered marine life. Most major industry sectors have contributed significant levels of pollution with relatively little concern. Businesses have looked the other way, simply labeling the negative consequences of their actions as *externalities*.[30] **Externalities** are side effects or by-products of actions that are not intended and often disregarded.

By labeling the environmental consequences as external to the process, businesses in the past were able to both acknowledge and dismiss the problems they created. In some ways, those days are ending. Companies that were once infamous for the damage they did to the environment are now scrambling to lead the way in environmental initiatives as they realize that such initiatives not only increase efficiency but also satisfy stakeholders and perhaps even help to invent entirely new businesses. Companies like Tesla (electric cars), First Solar (utility-scale solar energy), and Everlane (ethical fashion) are examples of businesses that were developed from environmental initiatives like alternative energy and ethical sourcing.

Nevertheless, businesses still pose hazards to the environment, as evidenced by recent large-scale pollution examples. One of the most notorious examples is the decades-long damage to the air and drinking water in West Virginia due to chemical giant DuPont's use of the toxin PFOA for manufacturing Teflon. The story is portrayed in the 2019 movie *Dark Waters*, directed by Todd Haynes and starring Mark

Ruffalo as attorney Robert Bilott, who takes on the DuPont Corporation. After years of legal battling, DuPont agreed to pay $671 million in cash to settle thousands of lawsuits alleging links to six diseases in the local population, including testicular and kidney cancers.[31] It is no wonder that in a recent poll by *Just Capital* of more than 4,500 adults in the United States, respondents felt that businesses are almost twice as likely to consider their shareholders more than other stakeholders like the environment and their employees.[32]

Waves of Environmentalism. Businesses are said to have encountered different "waves" of environmental policy, although exact timelines and characteristics vary widely in reports.[33] Currently, environmentalism is said to be in the fourth wave. The following periods and characteristics are generally acknowledged by environmental scientists and historians:

- First wave, 1700s–1800s: Environmental laws were intended to promote settlement and the extraction and use of natural resources.
- Second wave, 1800s–early 1900s: Environmental laws were aimed at mitigating some of the problems associated with western expansion. Land conservation movement.
- Third wave, 1900s: Environmental laws were triggered by awareness of environmental priorities and public policy. Anti-pollution laws and rise of powerful market-based solutions and corporate partnerships.
- Fourth wave, currently: Environmental policy focuses on sustainable development and finding ways to safeguard natural resources drawing on technological innovations, new public policy, and new ways to collaborate and communicate.

The fourth wave that we are currently experiencing provides hope in combating pollution and environmental problems with new technologies that, in combination with data analytics, are lower priced and affordable. In sum, the fourth wave offers promise in addressing problems that have plagued our natural environment for years. For example, the Environmental Defense Fund (EDF) partnered with Google Earth Outreach to put sensors on Google Street View cars to map and measure methane leaks from natural gas lines in more than a dozen cities.[34]

One term that has surfaced in the fourth wave is **circular economy**, which is a term applied to the system that businesses use to recycle—it involves keeping resources and extracting value from them as long as possible and then recovering and regenerating the resources and products at the end of each life cycle.[35] It is an alternative to a "take-make-dispose" approach for lower energy use that some say offers as much as a $4.5 trillion value opportunity for businesses should they convert to a circular approach.[36] More broadly, when companies work with their ecosystems partners to improve resource efficiency and achieve environmental benefits, they are employing a **circular business model**.[37]

Patagonia is a company that uses a circular economy strategy and business model. Through an initiative called Worn Wear, they provide support for their customers to repair damaged clothing and equipment themselves.[38] Alternatively, they provide a way for customers to send clothing to the company for repair or recycling. They also urge their customers to buy only what they need and avoid "relentless consumption." At the same time, Patagonia established a fund to invest in other "circular leaning" companies, and they support secondary markets for their products through partnerships with eBay in the United States and United Kingdom and through investment in Yerdle, an app that lets people give away items.[39] Other businesses who have found success with circular innovations include the beer giant AB InBev, whose innovations have led them to achieve an average 98 percent recycling rate for packaging material, and Winnow, whose technology reduces food waste in large-scale kitchens.[40]

Figure 4-2 provides a diagram of how the circular economy works.

Environmental literacy, whether for business, government, or individual decision making, requires, at minimum, some

Figure 4-2 The Circular Economy

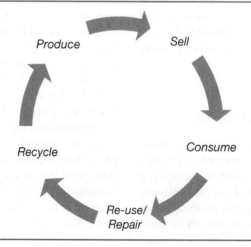

Figure 4-3 Glossary of Important Environmental Terms

Bio-based Product	A product (other than food or feed) that is composed, in whole or in part, of biological products or renewable agricultural or forestry materials
Biofuel	Transportation fuels made from biomass materials including ethanol (made from corn or sugarcane), biodiesel (made from vegetable oils and liquid animal fats), green diesel (from algae and plant sources), and biogas (methane from animal manure)
Carbon Dioxide (CO_2)	A colorless gas with a density about 53% higher than that of dry air
Carbon Emission	The release of carbon into the atmosphere
Carbon Footprint	The total amount of greenhouse gases a person, product, or company emits directly or indirectly
Carbon Neutral	The maintenance of a balance between producing and using carbon dioxide
Carbon Offset	A reduction in emissions of carbon dioxide or other greenhouse gases made to compensate for emissions made elsewhere. Every metric ton of offsets reduces one metric ton (2,205 lbs) of CO_2 emissions.
Carrying Capacity	The volume of and intensity of use by organisms that can be sustained in a particular place and at a particular time without degrading the environment's future suitability for that use
Chlorofluorocarbon (CFC)	Any of several gaseous compounds that are believed to be a major cause of stratospheric ozone depletion
Circular Economy	A system of keeping resources and extracting value from them for as long as possible and then recovering and regenerating the resources and products at the end of each life cycle. It is an alternative to a "take-make-dispose" approach.
Ecosystem	All living and nonliving substances present in a particular place, often interacting with others
Entropy	A measure of disorder of energy, indicating its unavailability for recycling for the same use
Environment	Anything that is external or internal to an entity. For humans, the environment can include external living, working, and playing spaces and natural resources, as well as internal physical, mental, and emotional states.
Fossil Fuel	A natural fuel such as coal, natural gas, petroleum, and Orimulsion, formed in the geological past
Fracking	The process of injecting liquid at high pressure into subterranean rocks so as to force open existing fissures and extract oil or gas
Greenhouse Gas	A gas that contributes to the greenhouse effect by absorbing infrared radiation (e.g., CO_2 and chlorofluorocarbons)
Greenwashing	Information disseminated by a company so as to present an environmentally responsible public image. The term is also used in conjunction with false and/or unsubstantiated environmental claims issued by companies.
Internal Carbon Tax	A tax on individual business units within the company based on energy usage that goes into a common fund that invests in environmental sustainability projects
Irreversibility	The inability of humans and nature to restore environmental conditions to a previous state within relevant time frames
Photovoltaic (PV) Panels	Solar panels that convert sunlight into energy

rudimentary knowledge of environmental issues. Without at least some basic technical information, would-be stakeholder managers abdicate their responsibility to make wise choices, which are potentially critical to the survival of their organizations, as well as to the survival of humans and other species in the natural environment. Figure 4-3 presents definitions of a few of the most important environmental terms.

4.3 The Impact of Business on the Natural Environment

Corporate environmental responsibility, a subset of CSR, has evolved over the decades to become institutionalized in business practice. Reducing environmental impact is a

large part of businesses' sustainability imperative as stakeholders from consumers to suppliers to regulators and others are looking for businesses to commit to actions to mitigate the effects of climate change and other environmental hazards.

Now that caring for the natural environment has become good business, there are countless examples of firms demonstrating that sustainable business practices can not only help the planet but also be a source of competitive advantage. Several companies that are "shaking up" sustainability are worth mentioning, and we briefly discuss them below. These companies—Patagonia, Apple, and Tesla—are considered to have taken "principled stances" and/or led innovative programs for better social and environmental conditions. We outline their sustainability initiatives below.

Spotlight on Sustainability

50 Years of Earth Day

Earth Day is celebrated on April 22nd every year, and on April 22, 2020, Earth Day turned 50 years old. As one of the original social movement initiatives focusing on the environment, it inspired 20 million Americans in 1970—10 percent of the population at the time—to demonstrate against oil spills, polluting factories, and other sources of environmental degradation. Its founders, most notably Senator Gaylord Nelson from Wisconsin, were inspired by the 1962 publication of the book *Silent Spring* by Rachel Carson that exposed the harmful effects of chemicals like DDT pesticides on the environment. Today, Earthday.org represents the movement and works with more than 75,000 partners in more than 190 countries to drive action for the planet.

The New York Times came up with a list of 10 big environmental victories and failures since Earth Day's 1970 origin. Some of the big victories included the following: "renewable energy is suddenly serious business," "oil spills are rarer (if still big, sometimes)," and "the bald eagle soars again." These were offset by failures like "clean energy isn't yet growing fast enough," "humans remain addicted to oil," and "an extinction crisis looms." The message is clear—while much progress has been made, there is still much work to be done to address the "wicked problems" of sustainability and the environment.

Sources: Earthday.org, https://www.earthday.org/, accessed February 15, 2021; Brad Plumer and John Schwartz, "50 Years of Earth Day: What's Better Today, and What's Worse," *The New York Times* (April 21, 2020), https://www.nytimes.com/interactive/2020/climate/earth-day-history.html, accessed February 15, 2021.

4.3a Patagonia

Patagonia has received a variety of accolades, including the UN Champions of the Earth Award.[41] This is not surprising because one cannot discuss business sustainability without mentioning Patagonia, the outdoor lifestyle company that is said to be "arguably one of the most environmentally focused companies in the world."[42] Decades before most businesses considered the possibility of recycling, Patagonia had made it an integral part of operations.[43] After discovering Patagonia could make their outdoor gear out of discarded plastic soda bottles, founder-owner Yvon Chouinard set about to do an environmental assessment of all their materials. He found that cotton was particularly damaging due to its dependencies on pesticides, insecticides, and defoliants. "To know this and not switch to organic cotton would be unconscionable," says Chouinard.[44] Today, it is considered a prime example of how the circular economy works, as we noted above.[45]

4.3b Apple

In 2014, Apple CEO Tim Cook made some bold statements to investors about how Apple does not pursue environmental improvements solely for return on investments.[46] He was angered by questions at the annual meeting about the profitability of investing in renewable energy.[47] Since then, Apple has continued to push their sustainability initiatives, powering all of their stores, data centers, and offices in 44 countries with 100 percent renewable energy, for example.[48] Along with Apple's commitment to recycling, Apple partners with multiple initiatives to avoid conflict minerals and unfair labor conditions in the production chain. Although it receives some criticism for the short life cycle of its products, Apple continues to work toward using only recycled and renewable materials in both products and packaging, and it is the electronics brand with the highest use of renewable energy, according to one sustainability ranking group.[49]

4.3c Tesla

Tesla is well known for its innovation in the development of the electric vehicle. However, its sustainable reach goes beyond this mission. Like Apple, Tesla is building what is generally called an **ecosystem** of sustainable brands—a group of interconnected elements, formed by interactions with others in its community and environment. Tesla's commitment to sharing technology under a "common, rapidly-evolving technology platform" is almost unprecedented, as Tesla announced in 2014 that it would not pursue lawsuits against anyone who wants to use its technology to improve transport.[50] Most recently, it developed a Powerwall solar battery pack for home renewable energy that doubles battery pack usage and allows enough energy to be stored to power an entire house.

4.4 Key Environmental Issues

What are some of the key environmental issues that businesses face? We look at each of the following environmental topics next:

a. Climate Change and Global Warming
b. Air Pollution and Toxins
c. Energy and Fossil Fuels
d. Water
e. Waste Management
f. Oceans and Fisheries
g. Deforestation and Biodiversity

4.4a Climate Change and Global Warming

No environmental issue has been more contentious than the subject of **climate change**, which is also known as **global warming** because it is associated with the precipitation of **greenhouse effects** (i.e., the prevention of solar heat absorbed by our atmosphere from returning to space) that can persist in the atmosphere for centuries.[51]

The debate about climate change's existence poses "alarmists against deniers"[52] in the realm of climate science, which has been termed "a veritable cornucopia of unanswered questions."[53] Debated issues include the evidence and rate of global warming, the extent to which human activity contributes to it, as well as the resolutions and safeguards that might be put in place to thwart forecasted warming trends. Melting glaciers, the decline of crop yields, and the effects of sea-level rise are presented as evidence of climate change. The evidence is hard to refute, with the world already warming 1.1°C since the Industrial Revolution,[54] and the earth losing 28 trillion metric tons of ice between 1994 and 2017.[55] In fact, most agree that the world is at a "climate crossroads."[56]

While some debate the science, climate change has become a hot-button issue for businesses. In late 2020, for the first time in the history of the World Economic Forum's survey of more than 750 CEOs, industry experts, and global leaders, environmental concerns occupied all five of the top spots of global risks.[57] In early 2021, in the midst of the COVID-19 pandemic, CEO Larry Fink of the large institutional shareholder BlackRock Investments announced his company would drop investments that have high sustainability-related risks.[58] He framed it with the quote, "I believe that the pandemic has presented such an existential crisis—such a stark reminder of our fragility—that it has driven us to confront the global threat of climate change more forcefully and to consider how, like the pandemic, it will alter our lives."[59]

Regulations and initiatives, like the U.S. Environmental Protection Agency's Clean Air Act, have been put forward to address climate change issues. In his first few days in office, President Biden took a series of steps to address climate change, including committing the United States to a path to achieve net-zero emissions, economy-wide, by no later than 2050—paralleling similar goals by Britain's amended Climate Change Act and the European Union's Green Deal.[60]

On a global scale, the 2016 Paris Agreement on Climate Change, which followed its 2015 conference, brought together 190 countries with an overall aim to limit global warming to below 2°C above preindustrial levels, and preferably 1°C. Early reports on progress are varied, but there is some evidence of improvements as countries make climate change a top concern.[61]

In an effort to address these concerns, businesses like Microsoft are leading a movement to offset emissions with an **internal carbon tax**—a tax on individual business units within the company based on energy usage that goes into a common fund that invests in environmental sustainability projects.[62] Also known as **carbon pricing**, the tactic seems to be working, as Microsoft has reported more than $10 million in energy cost savings each year and emissions reductions of nearly 10 million tons since 2012.[63] Microsoft is not the only company to do this, with nearly 1,400 companies, including Disney and Shell, voluntarily charging themselves as well.[64]

Carbon footprints and **carbon offsets** are also in the radar of business. Carbon footprint is the total amount of greenhouse gases (like CO_2) a person, product, or company emits directly or indirectly. In 2021, for example, Exxon vowed to reduce its carbon footprint in lowering the "intensity" of its emissions in its oil and gas operations by 15 percent to 20 percent by 2025, including its methane emissions. This was in response to investors like BlackRock that singled out Exxon as moving too slowly to address climate risks.[65]

Carbon offsets are certificates for purchase that pay a company to reduce emissions elsewhere in the world. One offset represents the reduction of one metric ton (2,205 lbs) of CO_2 emissions. Microsoft, for example, bought 1.3 million carbon offsets for 2021 as part of a drive to become carbon negative by 2030. A total of 1.1 million were linked to forestry projects, with the remaining were linked to bioenergy and soil projects.[66]

Offsets can be somewhat controversial in the fight against climate change. As noted in the Ethics in Practice case on carbon offsets, there are concerns that offsets create **moral hazard,** allowing polluters to keep polluting and transferring the burden to others to do the work. Additionally, in the pledge to be carbon neutral, companies can pay big money to reduce their carbon footprint rather than using the money to develop the technology and infrastructure to truly reduce emissions. Finally, some view offset purchases as **greenwashing,** particularly when they come from fossil fuel companies. For example, the oil company BP PLC (formerly BP Amoco) is one of the world's biggest buyers of forest carbon-offset credits and recently bought a controlling stake in Finite Carbon, which creates and sells offset credits on behalf of landowners, who are paid not to cut their trees down.[67]

Figure 4-4 shows growth in global carbon dioxide emissions projected out to 2025, measured in million metric tons.

4.4b Air Pollution and Toxins

The short- and long-term effects of both outdoor and indoor **air pollution** are wide-ranging and severe.[68] Air pollution leads to acid rain, global warming, smog, the depletion of the ozone layer, and other serious conditions. It also causes serious respiratory and other illnesses, so it is not surprising that it rates high in concern according to public opinion polls.[69] In late 2020, a young girl who suffered a fatal asthma attack in 2013 was the first person in Great Britain to officially have air pollution listed as a cause of death.[70] In fact, according to World Health Organization (WHO), the effects of air pollution kill an estimated 7 million people across the world every year.[71]

Record-setting wildfires in the last few years, many linked to prolonged heat waves and climate conditions, have also contributed to air pollution concerns. In California in 2020, more than 9,000 fires burned over 4 million acres of land.[72] Also in 2020, following months-long wildfires, parts of Australia recorded the worst-ever air quality to date, reaching "hazardous" pollution levels.[73]

Figure 4-4 World Fossil Carbon Dioxide Emissions

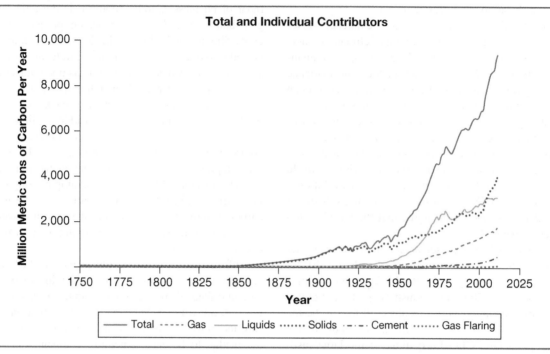

What can business do to address air pollution issues? The World Economic Forum (WEF) cites five actions that business can take to tackle pollution[74]:

1. Add air quality to their CSR activities and reporting.
2. Quantify air pollution down the supply chain and/or manufacturing processes.
3. Collect the data required to develop emissions inventories for key major pollutants.
4. Establish programs that reduce air pollution from their own operations and their suppliers.
5. Promote awareness campaigns to communicate and be transparent about the levels of emission caused by their operations and explain what they will do to address them.

Ethics In Practice Case

Carbon Offsets: Are You Ready to Buy Some, When You Rent a Car?

Rental car giants like Enterprise, National, and Alamo have offered carbon offsets for purchase since early 2008 so that customers can purchase credits that offset the greenhouse gases they put in the air when driving their cars. They partner with TerraPass, a San Francisco-based company, to supply the offsets, and the agencies usually match the donations up to a combined $1 million. When the car rental companies first piloted the program, they found that 1,000 customers a day were willing to pay the $1.25 fee per rental for an offset. Hertz waited until 2017 to begin offering offsets.

Carbon offsets are not without debate, however. Some environmentalists equate offsetting to a "pay some money and the guilt is scrubbed away" philosophy. Also, one study showed that 85 percent of offset projects would have gone ahead even without the purchase of offsets. Another study found that if countries had actively cut their pollution instead of buying offsets, global emissions would have been 600 million tons lower. Finally, there have been incidences of scams, companies that purport to be legitimate offset companies, but are not. Fortunately, third-party agencies, like the Gold Standard, are available to ensure the efficacy of carbon offset programs.

1. Would you consider purchasing carbon offsets the next time you rent a car?
2. How might your decision about purchasing offsets depend on (a) the type of car you are renting and (b) the environmental causes the offsets support?
3. To what extent is your decision related to the (low) pricing of the offset?

Sources: Bernadine Williams, "Car Rental Agencies Offer 'Carbon Offsets' to Customers," *Automotive News* (January 16, 2009), https://www.autonews.com/article/20080116/RETAIL/301169992/car-rental-agencies-offer-carbon-offsets-to-customers, accessed February 4, 2021; "Hertz Launches Carbon Offset Program for Corporate Sales Customers," *Hertz.com* (April 18, 2017), https://ir.hertz.com/2017-04-18-Hertz-Launches-Carbon-Offset-Program-for-Corporate-Sales-Customers, accessed February 4, 2021; Nikita Andester, "Carbon Offsetting Companies Comparted," *Ethical.net* (May 24, 2019), https://ethical.net/climate-crisis/carbon-offsetting-companies-compared/, accessed February 4, 2021; Umair Irfan, "Can You Really Negate Your Carbon Emissions? Carbon Offsets, Explained," Vox (February 27, 2020), https://www.vox.com/2020/2/27/20994118/carbon-offset-climate-change-net-zero-neutral-emissions, accessed February 14, 2021.

On September 7, 2020, the WEF announced an annual "International Day for Clean Air for Blue Skies" to raise awareness and promote solutions. Companies like IKEA, Johnson & Johnson, the global tech company Danfoss, Novo Nordisk, Siemens Mobility, and the Philips Foundation were all cited as exemplars of businesses who have already taken steps to address air pollution.[75]

While most people are familiar with outdoor air pollution, indoor air pollution is another environmental problem that is becoming an increasing concern, because most people spend the majority of their lives indoors. Indoor air pollution comes from a variety of sources, including oil, gas, kerosene, coal, wood, and tobacco products, and building materials and furnishings such as asbestos-containing insulation, damp carpets, household cleaning products, and lead-based paints.[76] The immediate effects of indoor air pollution are typically short term and treatable; however, longer-term effects that might show up years after exposure can be severely debilitating or fatal.[77] For example, the company Lumber Liquidators recently had to pay $2.5 million to settle claims that some of its products violated California air standards. Its laminate flooring made in China had high levels of the carcinogen formaldehyde that could harm users.[78]

The production of **toxic substances**, whether as constituents of intended products or as unwanted by-products, is an important issue because of its potential for harm. The EPA defines toxic substances as chemicals or compounds that may present an unreasonable threat to human health and the environment. Human exposure to toxic substances can cause a variety of health effects, including damage to the nervous system, reproductive and developmental problems, cancer, and genetic disorders.[79]

Ozone is an oxygen-related gas that is harmful to life near the earth's surface but is vital in the stratosphere in blocking dangerous ultraviolet radiation from the sun. More than 20 years ago, NASA scientists observed a huge decrease in ozone over Antarctica. They then discovered a "hole" in the ozone layer that had grown as large as the North American continent. Their measurements showed that the flow of ultraviolet (UV) light had increased directly under the ozone hole. This phenomenon was attributed to human-produced chemicals—**chlorofluorocarbons (CFCs)**, used in refrigeration, and halons, used in fire extinguisher systems, as well as other ozone-depleting chemicals. A thinner layer of ozone is associated with a higher rate of skin cancer and other illnesses, as well as an increase in problems with agricultural production.

In 1987, 46 countries came together to agree to the **Montreal Protocol**, an international treaty designed to protect the ozone layer by phasing out the production of substances that are responsible for ozone depletion.[80] While companies like DuPont, who manufactured CFC, were initially opposed to any regulation, by the time the Montreal Protocol was gathering traction, they backed the plan, as they had already begun exporting CFC alternatives to Europe. In sum, many see the success of the Montreal Protocol as providing hope for other multilateral initiatives for global environmental challenges.[81]

Ozone hole observers were cautiously optimistic in 2013 when the hole in the ozone layer was at its second smallest point in 20 years.[82] More recently, the National Aeronautics and Space Administration (NASA) observed that ozone depletion was significantly worse than in 2019, but better than in the early 2000s—largely due to ongoing declines in the atmospheric concentration of ozone-depleting chemicals like chlorine and bromine.[83]

Nevertheless, as anyone who has travelled to Australia knows, Australia's ozone layer was severely thinned as a result of heavy use of substances like chlorofluorocarbons, and the path to recovery has been slow, particularly as they have the highest rate of skin cancer in the world.[84] In fact, full recovery is not expected until at least the end of the century.[85]

For those interested in observing the hole in process, NASA provides "Ozone Watch" (http://ozonewatch.gsfc. nasa.gov/), a website with pictures created from satellite images that enable observers to check on the latest status of the ozone layer over the South Pole.

4.4c Energy and Fossil Fuels

A major environmental issue is **energy inefficiency**, or the wasting of precious nonrenewable sources of energy. Nonrenewable energy sources, such as coal, oil, and natural gas, were formed millions of years ago under unique conditions of temperature, pressure, and biological phenomena (hence the term **fossil fuels**). Once these are depleted, they will be gone forever. In addition, because these fuels are not equally distributed around the world, they are the cause of significant power imbalances worldwide, with associated armed conflicts that are typically disastrous for both humans and the natural environment in general.[86] As India, China, and other fast-growth areas in the developing world increase their demand for energy, the depletion of fossil fuels is occurring at a quickening pace.

Additionally, there are concerns about the mining and extraction techniques used to capture fossil fuels. For example, **fracking** is a process of injecting liquid at high pressure into rocks and shale to open up fissures and extract oil or gas. Proponents of fracking point to its efficiencies and lower costs in extracting fuels, particularly in relation to the costs of the global oil market. Additionally, they note that natural gas has fewer CO_2 emissions and can serve as a "bridge fuel" in the transition to renewable energy.[87] It is controversial for several reasons, however, including pollution threats to sensitive lands when it causes leaks and contaminates groundwater, as well as other harms to communities close to extraction operations.[88]

The answer to the nonrenewability problem is to use as little as possible of these energy sources through implementation of sound energy conservation practices, while also shifting to renewable energy sources. Several technologies for tapping these renewable, low-polluting energy sources

Ethics In Practice Case

Electric Vehicles and Beyond: Can "Supercar" Manufacturers like Ferrari Become Carbon Neutral?

Phasing out gasoline and diesel-powered vehicles is another move toward rethinking energy efficiencies. Although Tesla is perhaps the most well-known company in the U.S. electric vehicle market, other global automakers have joined suit in the quest to eliminate emissions. Companies including Renault-Nissan, The Volkswagen Group, and China's BYD Auto have had great success in the electric vehicle market. In a striking departure from its business model, General Motors set a 2035 target date to go all-electric with its vehicles, albeit hinging on government incentives and support to "nudge" consumers toward plug-in cars. Ford soon followed with a similar commitment for its cars in Europe.

Other auto companies like Ferrari, however, are more challenged when it comes to lowering emissions. "Supercars" such as Ferrari models produce a disproportionate number of carbon emissions per mile, so going carbon neutral is tough for the company, even with the development of its first hybrid model, the SF90 Stradale, in 2020. Going fully electric for Ferrari means rethinking its brand, which is known for its eight- and 12-cylinder engines. In 2018, Ferrari CEO Louis Camilleri committed to produce an all-electric supercar by 2025 or 2030; however, in early 2020 he reversed his position. Camilleri said he did not see Ferrari ever committing to a 100 percent electric vehicle, particularly since the hybrid SF Stradale, with its 4.0-liter V-8 engine and three electric motors, can take a car from zero to 60 mph in 2.5 seconds and reach a top speed of 211 mph. When CEO Camilleri retired in 2021, acting CEO John Elkann said he was still committed to making the company carbon neutral by 2030, but there were no clear plans for a pure battery-electric Ferrari anytime soon.

1. Do you think Ferrari should consider manufacturing a 100 percent electric vehicle?
2. What responsibilities does Ferrari have to work toward lower emissions?
3. What do you think of the CEO's change of perspective? Is a hybrid vehicle good enough for Ferrari's electrification?
4. Can a company, like Ferrari, ever really be sustainable?

Sources: "Ferrari's Road to Lower Emissions Has Bumps," *The Wall Street Journal* (February 3, 2021), B14; Bryan Hood, "Ferrari Will Never Go Fully Electric, CEO Says," *Robb Report* (November 4, 2020), https://robbreport.com/motors/cars/ferrari-not-going-fully-electric-yet-1234579269/, accessed February 14, 2021; Stephen Wilmot, "Ferrari Wants to Save the Planet, Too," *The Wall Street Journal* (February 4, 2020), https://www.wsj.com/articles/ferrari-wants-to-save-the-planet-too-11580841033, accessed February 14, 2021; Mike Colias, "GM Aims to Go All Electric by 2035," *The Wall Street Journal*, (January 29, 2021), B1; William Boston, "Ford to Go All Electric in Europe by 2030," *The Wall Street Journal* (February 18, 2021), B3.

are becoming economically competitive with nonrenewable sources and so, for business, the energy issue represents not only a challenge but also an opportunity.[89] Companies like Facebook, Google, Amazon, and Apple have successfully invested in renewable energy technology, in part due to a boost in government incentives and declining systems costs.[90]

Solar and wind are alternatives to fossil fuels as energy sources, and companies like Ikea have been able to capitalize on these alternatives. As an early adopter of rooftop solar, Ikea's parent company Ingka Group recently announced that its wind and solar assets generate 132 percent more energy than it needs for its own operations.[91] And while the COVID-19 pandemic agitated energy markets in 2020, the push for clean energy continued as more than 130 global corporations bought a record-setting total of 23.7 gigawatts in wind and solar.[92] In Europe, increasing use of wind and solar resulted in a 32 percent drop in electricity generated from coal across the European Union (EU) in 2020.[93]

With the money now flowing into "clean tech" funds that focus mainly on renewable sources of energy like hydropower, wind, and solar, firms are scrambling to determine how to capitalize on this sustainability trend. **Exchange-traded funds (ETFs)** that specialize in alternative energies have been growing in popularity, as have clean energy bonds. SolarCity is among the most popular of solar-backed bonds, perhaps because of its association as a subsidiary of Tesla.[94] Regardless of where investments are directed, the global renewable energy section is expected to see ongoing growth as companies and governments work to achieve new mandates.

4.4d Water

Water presents problems in both quality and quantity. It is no wonder that the United Nations Global Compact committed to SDG No. 6, which calls on members to "ensure availability and sustainable management of water and sanitation for all" by 2030.[95]

The developed world has made significant progress in the quality of water—no longer are waterways so polluted that they risk catching on fire as the Cuyahoga River did in Cleveland in 1969.[96] However, more recent incidences like the Flint, Michigan, water contamination crisis, which identified lead poisoning in the community as a result of changing the water supply from Detroit's system to the Flint River, is evidence of ongoing problems with water pollution that can affect the health and welfare of communities for decades.[97] We discuss this in more detail in the Ethics in Practice case in section 4.6a.

Municipal sewage, industrial wastes, urban runoff, agricultural runoff, atmospheric fallout, and overharvesting all continue to contribute to the degradation of the world's oceans and waterways. So, too, do dam sedimentation, deforestation, overgrazing, and over-irrigation. The quality of the developing world's water quality is in far worse shape than that in the developed world. A staggering 80 percent of the world's wastewater is untreated as it flows into rivers, lakes, and oceans.[98] More than 2 billion people worldwide lack clean water, and the problem shows no signs of abating.[99]

Beyond the problem with pollution, experts now warn that the world is facing a "water bankruptcy."[100] More than four billion people, or two-thirds of the world's population, face severe water shortages during at least one month every year.[101] In the United States, the state of California has faced severe droughts for many years in a row. As a result, the state developed its own website (http://drought.ca.gov/) and developed conservation actions and recovery efforts to address dry conditions and devastating wildfires.

For business, the consequences of water scarcity are dire. Recently, Coca Cola, Nestlé, and Kraft Heinz noted that water shortages posed a real threat to their agricultural supply chains.[102] However, corporate action seems sparse in addressing concerns of both water shortages and quality. In a recent survey of more than 2,400 companies by CDP, a corporate disclosure company, less than half of the corporate respondents said they regularly meter and monitor the quality of their discharges, while just 12 percent had a water pollution reduction goal or target.[103]

World Water Day, first launched by the United Nations Conference on Environment and Development in 1992, is held annually to draw attention to these issues, as governments and companies around the world unveil their latest plans to tackle water quality and scarcity.[104] As more companies sign on to invest in water technologies, improve water protections, and address groundwater depletion, the hope is that developed and developing countries can work together to address some of these issues. Researchers point out that water quality and quantity are not only important to basic human needs but also to the safety and security of agriculture, industry, and ecosystems that can even undermine national security.[105]

4.4e Waste Management

Reduce, Reuse, and Recycle is the waste management mantra. The first goal is to *reduce* the amount of waste discarded, which is source reduction; this is the best form of waste management because in using this method the waste is never generated in the first place. The next best option is to *reuse* containers and products—either repairing anything that is broken or giving it to someone who can repair it. Reusing is preferable to recycling because it does not require reprocessing to make the item usable again. *Recycling* is the third best option but still valuable. **Recycling** transforms what once might have been waste into a valuable resource. Business can profit greatly from the boon in recycling. By recycling, businesses are able to cut costs—producing less garbage means lower landfill fees. Apple is a company that

embraces the recycling process with strict factory standards for recycling the iPhone, both to protect its technology and benefit the bottom line. They have a "full-destruction" policy that partners them with a network of recyclers to grind the iPhone to bits and allows recycling partners to share in the sale of extracted materials like gold and copper.[106]

Recognizing these advantages, companies like Gap have developed lofty goals for diverting waste away from landfills.[107] The company is trying to reduce packaging weight and even change the materials to allow for greater recycling. Similarly, PepsiCo has pledged to make 100 percent of its packaging recyclable, compostable, or biodegradable with the help of a new technology from Pulpex Limited that produces paper pulp bottles made from wood along with other renewable sources.[108] Even the Danish toy maker Lego, which has been making building blocks from petroleum-based plastic since 1963, is searching to reduce its carbon footprint with bio-based plastics.[109]

When companies begin to adopt new waste management practices, take on circular business models, and practice a circular economy, there is an opportunity for a "win-win," when business can gain value while also helping the environment.

Special consideration must be given to waste that is hazardous. Hazardous waste has properties that make it harmful or potentially harmful to human health or the environment. As defined by the EPA, the large and diverse world of hazardous waste includes liquids, solids, contained gases, or sludges.[110] Hazardous wastes can be generated by manufacturing processes, or they can simply result from discarded commercial products, such as cleaning fluids or pesticides.[111] The risk posed by these wastes creates countless causes for concern. Exposure to these wastes in the environment, whether in air, water, food, or soil, can cause cancer, birth defects, and a host of other problems.[112]

4.4f Oceans and Fisheries

UN Global Compact SDG No. 14 sets out the goal to conserve and sustainably use ocean resources. The EPA expresses it well by saying we all live in a **watershed**—an area that drains to a common waterway, such as a stream, lake, estuary, wetland, aquifer, or ocean.[113] Our actions affect waterways, and so far, they have not been for the better. Each year, trillions of gallons of sewage and industrial waste are dumped into marine waters. These and other pollutants, such as oil and plastics, have been associated with significant damage to a number of coastal ecosystems, including salt marshes, mangrove swamps, estuaries, and coral reefs. The result has been local and regional shellfish bed closures, seafood-related illnesses, and reduced shoreline protection from floods and storms. The amount of plastic in the ocean has created such a large problem that the WEF in 2016 pronounced that there will be more plastic than fish in terms of weight in the world's oceans by 2050.[114]

But the problem for oceans and fisheries does not just revolve around waste. Once it would have been inconceivable that the vast oceans would ever run short of fish to meet human needs. However, a 2008 report found that 85 percent of the world's fisheries were either at capacity, over capacity, or had collapsed.[115] Fast forward to 2020, and the issue still remains. As National Geographic noted, overfishing is draining the oceans, in large part due to government subsidies that fuel overfishing.[116]

Although more work is needed, efforts to reclaim the waters have met with some success. A recent study pointed to substantial progress in the recovery of marine populations following conservation interventions.[117] The return of the Chesapeake blue crab is a regional example. A variety of efforts such as shortening the crabbing season, instituting a crabber license buyback program, and not permitting the raking of hibernating pregnant females from the bay floor have yielded promising results over the years.[118]

4.4g Deforestation and Biodiversity

Although humans depend on forests for building materials, fuel, medicines, chemicals, food, employment, and recreation, the world's forests can be quickly depleted by a variety of human factors. **Deforestation** adds to soil erosion problems and is a major cause of the greenhouse effect. Felled trees are no longer able to absorb carbon dioxide and are sometimes burned for land clearing and charcoal, thereby releasing rather than absorbing carbon dioxide.

Deforestation plays a key role in global warming. Trees, and particularly older trees, provide the largest stores of

---

Ethics In Practice Case

Who Failed to Protect the Community in Flint, Michigan?

In April 2014, the city of Flint, Michigan, switched its water supply from Detroit's system to the Flint River under the control of a state-appointed emergency manager. The decision was made as a cost-saving measure because of Flint's dire economic situation. But, not too long after the switch was made, residents began complaining about the taste, color, and odor of the water. Some began to have concerns about the water quality. By October 2014, coliform bacteria had been detected in some of the tap water, but the Michigan Department of Environmental Quality blamed it on cold weather, aging pipes, and a population decline. Over the next few months, there were rising concerns about the water quality, including statements from the local General Motors factory about the water's corrosive effects on auto parts and statements from local residents and private testing companies about higher levels of lead in the water. The City of Detroit offered to reconnect Flint back to the city system in January 2015, waiving the reconnection fee, but the Flint emergency manager declined the offer.

In September 2015, a professor at Virginia Tech reported that the corrosiveness of the river water was causing lead to leach into the supply, and shortly thereafter, a group of doctors in Flint urged the city to stop using the river water after finding high levels of lead in the blood of local children, which could cause learning disabilities, behavior problems, and additional illness. The results of tests showed lead levels running from 11 parts per billion to as high as 397 parts per billion. At this point, the "blame game" began.

An official at the U.S. Environmental Protection Agency said her department knew as early as April 2015 about the lack of corrosion controls in Flint's water supply, but she said she could not bring the information to the public and override state control. EPA Administrator Gina McCarthy blamed Flint's lead problems on state regulators who prescribed the wrong chemical treatments to keep corrosive river water from leaching the lead pipes. She said she did not have enough evidence of state delays to show that the EPA needed to move in and take control. Some observers point out that the EPA did everything it was required to do under the law because there is no policy or regulation that required the EPA to tell the public what it knew about the lead in Flint's drinking water system.

In October 2015, Flint reconnected to Detroit's water supply after the governor got involved; however, residents still could not drink the water unfiltered. Four years later, after nearly $400 million in state and federal spending, Flint finally secured a clean water source, but residents remain angry and mistrustful. In 2020, the state of Michigan agreed to pay $600 million to the 95,000 victims of the water crisis, with a focus on the disconcerting health effects on children of Flint in particular. In January 2021, former governor Rick Snyder was charged with two counts of willful neglect of duty.

1. Who are the stakeholders in this case, and what are their stakes?
2. Where does the responsibility for the Flint, Michigan, water crisis belong?
3. When would it have been the appropriate time for the EPA to notify Flint residents, even if not required by law? Would it have mattered?
4. What would you have done if you were the "official" at the EPA who knew about the problem back in April 2015?
5. How is this an example of the tensions between law and ethics? Explain.
6. How can sustainability be a state and federal objective if cases such as the Flint River are permitted to occur?

Sources: Flint Water Advisory Task Force Report (March 21, 2016), http://mediad.publicbroadcasting.net/p/michigan/files/201603/taskforce_report.pdf?_ga=1.147700144.609033 213.1458749402, accessed February 16, 2021; Julie Bosman, "Michigan to Pay $600 Million to Victims of Flint Water Crisis," *The New York Times* (August 19, 2020), https://www.nytimes.com/2020/08/19/us/flint-water-crisis-settlement.html, accessed February 16, 2021; Brakkton Booker, "Former Michigan Governor Rick Snyder Charged in Flint Water Crisis," NPR (January 13, 2021), https://www.npr.org/2021/01/13/956592508/new-charges-in-flint-water-crisis-including-former-michigan-gov-rick-snyder, accessed February 15, 2021; Derek Robertson, "Flint Has Clean Water Now. Why Won't People Drink It?," *Politico Magazine* (December 23, 2020), https://www.politico.com/news/magazine/2020/12/23/flint-water-crisis-2020-post-coronavirus-america-445459; accessed February 16, 2021.

carbon on land, helping to mitigate global warming. In fact, the loss of primary forest in 2019 (the older trees that have been undisturbed by humans for more than 140 years) has been associated with 1.8 gigatons of carbon-dioxide emissions— equivalent to that produced annually by 400,000 cars. And unfortunately, older trees are dying at a faster rate than in the past. Some losses are due to forest-harvesting, but also rising temperatures have produced more droughts, wildfires, and insect infestations that have killed trees.[119]

While many companies have pledged to address deforestation issues, progress remains slow. Hence, shareholder advocacy groups have gotten involved in pushing businesses to improve their "no deforestation" practices. Much of forest destruction is linked to commodities such as palm oil, beef, leather, timber, and pulp. Hence, companies including Tyson Foods and Procter & Gamble have been pushed to look at their supply chains and operate in regions with no deforestation risk.[120]

An ecosystem's **biodiversity**, that is, the variation of life forms inside the system, serves as a key indicator of its health. Ecosystem and habitat destruction through agricultural and urban development activities and pollution have put at risk both wildlife and beneficial plants. Species used to die off at a natural rate of one to five in a year; now dozens become extinct each day.[121]

What does this mean for business? In a McKinsey study, a majority of executives see biodiversity as more of an opportunity than a risk.[122] Preserving biodiversity through new products from renewable natural resources and communicating with stakeholders about these ideas were noted to boost their company's reputation. Hence, McKinsey and other consulting firms publish guidance for companies on how to best address their impact on biodiversity. In 2020, the United Nations held its first Biodiversity Summit, featuring an online platform, "Voices of Nature," which features statements and commitments from a wide variety of stakeholders.[123] Areas of concern for companies and biodiversity include water scarcity, infectious disease, food insecurity, flooding, droughts and desertification, and soil degradation. While much progress has been made, as the population of the world continues to grow, the problems created by these issues will only increase.

4.5 Responsibility for Environmental and Sustainability Issues

Environmental problems such as smog, toxic waste, and acid rain can be described as **"wicked problems"**—that is, problems with characteristics such as interconnectedness, complexity, uncertainty, ambiguity, conflict, and societal constraints. Every wicked problem seems to be a symptom of another problem.[124] Responsibility for such messy situations is difficult to affix, because solutions to wicked problems are seldom complete and final and, therefore, credit for these solutions is seldom given or taken. Chlorofluorocarbons, or

CFCs, for example, were once considered safe alternatives to other, more toxic refrigerants, which is why these ozone destroyers are so ubiquitous in our society's technologies.

When no one takes responsibility for adverse environmental effects, a phenomenon called the **tragedy of the commons** is likely to occur.[125] A "commons" is a plot of land available to all. When the commons are large enough to accommodate the needs of everyone, no problems occur. However, as herders continue to add animals to their herds, the carrying capacity of the commons becomes strained. It is in the self-interest of each herder to allow the animals to graze, even though the cumulative grazing will inevitably destroy the commons. The analogy of a "commons" can be applied to the environment as a whole as well as its many constituent parts. In the absence of constraints, self-interest is likely to lead individuals and organizations to behave in ways that will not sustain our shared resources. [126]

Environmental Ethics. Nature itself is a polluter and destroyer. The earth's core is continually polluting many bodies of water and airsheds with a full range of toxic heavy metals. Species have been going extinct since life evolved as, in a continuous cycle of life and death, nature acts as its own destroyer. Given this fact, there are many ethics questions to be raised regarding the environment. For example:

- What does absolute human environmental sensitivity mean? Humans must consume at least some plants and water to survive. If humans and their organizations need to pollute and destroy at least some of nature for their survival, what is the relative level of degradation that is ethical?

- Do nonhuman species have any "rights," and, if so, what are they, and how can they be reconciled with human rights?

- Concerning human rights and the environment, how do we assess the claims of indigenous cultures to the use of their respective environments? Is there any connection between the domination of humans by humans (e.g., the domination of one nation, race, or gender by another) and the domination of nature by humans? This latter question is especially central to several schools of environmental ethical thought, including social ecology, ecofeminism, and environmental justice. Whose standards will determine what is or is not ethical? How clean do the air and water need to be, and how much is the public willing to pay to meet these standards?

As we will discuss in our chapters on business ethics, values play a major role and can be highly variable in breadth and depth across perspectives, situations, and time. In *Who Speaks for the Trees*, authors Sama, Welcomer, and Gerde show that integrating sustainability into a firm's philosophy is a natural extension of stakeholder theory.[127] They expand the concept of the natural environment beyond living things to the entire ecological system from which the firm obtains resources and to which it bears responsibility for the impacts, both positive and negative, that firm actions have on it. They invoke the ethic of care, discussed in Chapter 6,

---

Ethics In Practice Case

A Little Green Lie

I am employed by Telecommunication Company as a sales consultant. The work environment is very competitive and as "salespeople," we are always required to surpass our quotas and "make money." Lately the company has decided to "go green," which is good for the environment. However, the true motive behind the company's initiative is to save money on paper bills, as the managers have confessed to us. As a way of making us convert customers to paperless billing, they have factored paperless billing conversion into our performance evaluation metrics, which means that if we do not perform, we can be reprimanded or fired. One of the area managers suggested we tell customers that the company is no longer sending out paper bills and that if they wish to still receive a paper bill, they will be charged a fee (which is completely false, as paper bills are free to customers). I see customers fall for this explanation and go paperless in order to save money, and the sales consultants who have applied this method are usually our top rankers. The manager said it is not really lying, especially if you are helping self-interested customers to help the environment.

1. Global warming and environmental issues have become serious problems. Keeping this in mind, is it right to deceive customers if your main motive is to save the environment and help save trees?
2. Is it ethical for the area manager to demand that sales representatives lie?
3. Would it be ethical for the sales representative to follow the directions of the manager?
4. Would it be fair for the company to start charging (e.g., $1.50) for those who want to keep receiving paper bills?
5. What would you do if you were in this position, and what would be your motive behind it?

Contributed Anonymously

---

and explain that organizations that follow a practice of care would treat the natural environment, which they call the "silent stakeholder," with respect.[128] Many other ethics concepts and principles discussed in our next chapters apply to the natural environment and sustainability discussions.

4.6 The Role of Governments in Environmental and Sustainability Issues

As mentioned earlier, governments have played major roles in environmental matters since the inception of such issues. Governments have procured, distributed, and developed habitable lands and other resources; protected, taxed, and zoned natural environment-based areas; and, more recently, exercised regulatory control over how those environments could be used. This section looks at how governments have dealt with environmental challenges and then identifies what has been done in several other countries and at the international level.

4.6a Responses of Governments—the United States

Although the U.S. federal government has influenced environmental policy since at least 1899, with its permit requirement for discharge of hazardous materials into navigable waters, the major entrance of the U.S. government into environmental issues occurred in 1970 with the signing of the **National Environmental Policy Act (NEPA).** The second section of this act spells out its purposes: "To declare a national policy which will encourage productive and enjoyable harmony between man and his environment; to promote efforts which will prevent or eliminate damage to the environment and biosphere and stimulate the health and welfare of man; and to enrich the understanding of the ecological systems and natural resources important to the Nation."[129] In 2020, the NEPA regulations were updated for the first time in more than 40 years to reflect current technologies and agency practices and to improve the readability of the regulations.[130]

Also, in 1970, the U.S. **Environmental Protection Agency (EPA)**[131] was created as an independent agency to research pollution problems, aid state and local government environmental efforts, and administer many of the federal environmental laws. These laws can be categorized into three areas—air, water, and land. The roles and responsibilities of the EPA include a wide range of functions to protect the environment, but it is also important to remember that it is a federal agency that must work with state agencies. This can often be difficult in enforcing pollution and other environmental problems, which can cross over state and federal jurisdictions. This challenge is evidenced in the Flint City, Michigan water crisis, which, as noted earlier in the Ethics in Practice case, involved city, state, and federal agencies.

Air Quality Legislation. The key piece of federal air quality legislation is the **Clean Air Act.**[132] The overall approach of this act is similar to that used in other areas of federal regulation, such as safety and health legislation, in that standards are set and timetables for implementation are established. The EPA has set standards for a variety of air pollutants. Businesses that directly produce these substances must reduce their emissions to within the set standards.[133] Fines levied under the Clean Air Act can be pretty substantial. In 2021, Toyota paid the largest ever civil penalty under the act, agreeing to pay $180 million for violations that went on between 2005 and 2015 related to timely reporting of defects that interfered with some cars' tailpipe emission regulation systems.[134]

Spotlight on Sustainability

There's an App for That

Sustainability software has become a huge growth market. With increased interest in sustainability reporting and major buyers such as Walmart requiring suppliers to show proof of sustainable practices, companies are looking for ways to improve and monitor their environmental impacts.

At the same time, individuals are increasingly interested in achieving a more sustainable lifestyle. Software manufacturers have been designing apps for smartphones to make that task easier. The following apps are free and available for both iPhone and Android users.

FoodKeeper

The Foodkeeper app provides guidance on the safe handling, preparation, and storage of foods. It is a free app from the U.S. Department of Agriculture (USDA) Food Safety and Inspection Service that provides information about how you can buy food at its peak quality so you can reduce food waste.

Giki

For consumers in the United Kingdom, the Giki app has a built-in scanner to check items for eco-friendly features. The app awards badges based on how sustainable the product is. If the product does not score well, Giki offers alternatives.

GoodGuide

GoodGuide helps consumers find products that are safe, healthy, green, and ethical. The app has the capability to scan bar codes, enabling consumers to decide between products based on their environmental, health, and social impact. Main ratings are provided by qualified scientists, but users may also comment on and review products.

iRecycle

Local recycling options can be hard to locate. iRecycle provides users with the collection points for recycling a range of materials, as well as directions, hours, and the materials collected at each location. Interested users can also connect with other recyclers through Facebook and Twitter.

Locavore

Eating local food is not only a way to enjoy the freshest food available but also a way to reduce one's carbon footprint by minimizing transportation. Locavore identifies the foods that are currently in season, as well as those that are coming into season soon. They also provide information about the food, in-season recipes, and directions to local farmer's markets.

Paper Karma

Use your phone to stop unwanted paper mail (coupons, flyers, catalogs, magazines, yellow pages, etc.). Simply take a photo of the mail you do not want and Paper Karma takes care of the rest. Paper Karma contacts the mailer and asks to have your name removed from the distribution list.

Seafood Watch

The Seafood Watch app lets consumers search for seafood and sushi so that they can make sustainable seafood choices. It also provides alternatives to seafood on the "Avoid" list. Project Fishmap lets users add names of restaurants and stores where they found sustainable seafood and find out where others have found it.

Tap

Plastic pollution is a huge problem for the planet. Replacing plastic bottles with a reusable bottle is easy with the Tap app, which can help you find refill stations on the go.

Think Dirty

Think Dirty helps consumers find eco-friendly cosmetics and beauty products. The app rates products on the Dirty Meter, taking into consideration ingredients, certifications, and health impacts.

Sources: https://www.paperkarma.com/; http://www.goodguide.com/; https://giki.earth/; http://www.getlocavore.com/; http://www.earth911.com/eco-tech/food-waste-foodkeeper-app/; http://www.earth911.com/eco-tech/irecycle-now-on-android/; https://www.seeker.com/earth-conservation/the-tap-app-is-a-drinking-water-search-engine-for-refillable-bottles; http://www.seafoodwatch.org/seafood-recommendations/our-app; https://www.thinkdirtyapp.com/, accessed February 15, 2021.

The Clean Air Act introduced the concept of **emissions trading** (i.e., **"cap and trade"**) to the United States. This approach is intended to reduce a particular pollutant over an entire industrial region by treating all emission sources as if they were all beneath one bubble. A business can increase its emissions of sulphur dioxide in one part of a plant or region if it reduces its sulphur dioxide pollution by as much or more in another part of the plant or region. In addition, businesses that reduce their emissions can trade these rights to other businesses that want to increase their emissions.

Proponents of emissions credit trading hail these policies as free-market environmentalism, whereas opponents ridicule them as licenses to pollute. The emissions trading system is part of the **Kyoto Protocol**, an international agreement that set legally binding targets and deadlines for cutting the greenhouse gas emissions of industrialized countries.[135]

Water Quality Legislation. U.S. government involvement in water quality issues has followed a pattern similar to that of air quality issues. The **Clean Water Act** was passed in the early 1970s with broad environmental quality goals and an implementation system, involving both the federal and state governments, designed to attain those goals. The ultimate purpose of the act was to achieve water quality consistent with protection of fish, shellfish, and wildlife and with safe conditions for human recreation in and on the water. The more tangible goal was to eliminate discharges of pollutants into navigable waters, which include most U.S. rivers, streams, and lakes.

In August 2015, the Clean Water Act was updated with the Clean Water Rule, otherwise known as **"Waters of the United States" (WOTUS)** rule. The rule, to be jointly enforced by the U.S. EPA and the U.S. Army, more precisely defines the streams and wetlands to be protected as well as the permitting requirements for agriculture.[136] Another act—the Marine Protection, Research, and Sanctuaries Act of 1972—sets up a similar system for control of discharges into coastal ocean waters within U.S. territory. A third water quality law administered by the EPA, the Safe Drinking Water Act of 1974, establishes maximum contaminant levels for drinking water.[137]

Land-Related Legislation. Land pollution and degradation issues differ from air and water quality issues, because land by definition is far less fluid and therefore somewhat more visible than air and water and is more amenable to local or regional problem-solving approaches. Consequently, the U.S. federal government, in the Solid Waste Disposal Act of 1965, recognized that regional, state, and local governments should have the main responsibility for nontoxic waste management. A 1976 amendment to this act, called the Resource Conservation and Recovery Act (RCRA), set up a federal regulatory system for tracking and reporting the generation, transportation, and eventual disposal of hazardous wastes by businesses responsible for creating these wastes.[138]

The U.S. government has staked out a much larger role for itself in the area of toxic wastes, which often end up in the ground. The 1976 **Toxic Substances Control Act** requires manufacturing and distribution businesses in the chemical industry to identify any chemicals that pose "substantial risks" of human or other natural environment harm. This legislation was seminal to the indictment of DuPont in the chemical PFOA scandal we described above. Because there are more than 70,000 chemicals already in use in the United States and more than 1,000 new chemicals introduced every year, the EPA has prioritized the substances that must be tested to focus on those that might cause cancer, birth defects, or gene mutations.[139]

The other major U.S. government activity in toxic wastes, which is a major type of land pollution, is known as **Superfund** or, more formally, the Comprehensive Environmental Response, Compensation, and Liability Act of 1980 (CERCLA). Superfund is an effort to clean up more than 2,000 hazardous waste dumps and spills around the country, some dating back to the previous century. Funded by taxes on chemicals and petroleum, this program has established a National Priorities List to focus on the most hazardous sites and places legal and financial responsibility for the proper remediation of these sites on the appropriate parties. In addition, CERCLA requires that unauthorized hazardous waste spills be reported and can order those responsible to clean up the sites.[140] In 2020, CERCLA celebrated 40 years of cleaning up and transforming communities, with a record of cleaning up hundreds of Superfund sites since its origin.[141]

One of the most important amendments to the Superfund law, the Emergency Planning and Community Right-to-Know Act of 1986, requires manufacturing companies to report to the federal government annually all of their releases into the environment of any of more than 500 toxic chemicals and chemical compounds. The EPA accumulates these reports and makes them available to the public (at https://iaspub.epa.gov/triexplorer/tri_release.chemical) with the intention that an informed public will pressure manufacturers to reduce these toxic releases.[142]

Endangered Species and Biodiversity Legislation. The world's species are disappearing at an alarming rate, according to the World Conservation Union, which releases an annual Red List of endangered species.[143] Their 2020 report shows that nearly 35,000 species are now considered threatened with extinction—a quarter of the total number of species they assessed.[144] Another study in 2020 noted that approximately 173 species went extinct between 2001 and 2014—25 times more than one would expect under a normal extinction rate.[145] These measures of biodiversity suggest that things are not going well. More broadly, environmentalists refer to the "sixth mass extinction" or the **Anthropocene extinction** when referring to the ongoing extinction of species as a result of human activity—for example, in the overkilling of big mammals, which led to the extinction of mammoths. A decade ago, countries united under a ten-year plan supervised by the United Nations, to protect and conserve natural systems and fight extinction of species, but to date, most of the targets have not been met.[146]

Responsibility for endangered species in the United States is shared by two agencies, the U.S. Interior Department's Fish and Wildlife Service and the Commerce Department's National Marine Fisheries Act. They administer the 1973 **Endangered Species Act (ESA)**. Protection of species sometimes means moving them to safe areas when their original habitats have been destroyed by human activities, but it can also mean prevention of these activities, such as mining, construction, and fishing, before such habitat deprivation occurs. This restriction of business activities can be expected to continue as the extinction rate for species climbs, resulting in sometimes intense political conflicts between business interests and environmental groups. [147]

4.6b Responses of Governments— International

Sustainable development has been mainstreamed outside of the United States through many different regulatory forms. In Europe, for example, sustainable development has been part of the European Union since it was included in the Treaty of Amsterdam as an overarching goal of EU policies.[148] The European Commission oversees policies and targets related to green initiatives. In 2021, national sustainability plans had to be submitted by EU member states to the commission before being allowed to tap into the bloc's €750 billion recovery fund from the coronavirus pandemic.[149] India's National Action Plan on Climate Change (NAPCC) charts a low carbon development path focusing on eight areas including solar and energy efficiency. Key regulations include the Environment Protection Act of 1986 (EP Act), the Air Act of 1981, and the National Green Tribunal Act of 2010, which reiterates strict enforcement of measures for pollutants.[150] In Denmark, a new ambitious climate law was recently passed by the government that has legally binding climate targets and does not allow for backsliding of targets.[151]

More broadly, the **United Nations Environment Programme (UNEP)** has led the way in identifying global environmental and sustainability problems and in working toward their resolution. The UNEP sets the global environmental agenda within the United Nations system. This includes working with the UN Global Compact, which we discussed at the beginning of this chapter as the world's largest voluntary corporate sustainability initiative. The UNEP has also been instrumental in laying the groundwork and continuing to support the Montreal Protocol, which we noted earlier has led to significant accomplishments in addressing ozone layer depletion.

The **Global Reporting Initiative (GRI)**, which we discuss again in Chapter 7, is a collaborating center of the UNEP. GRI spearheaded the development of a sustainability reporting framework that has become the most widely used standard in the world. The reporting framework outlines the principles and indicators that organizations can use to measure and report their economic, environmental, and social performance.[152]

As we noted above, The U.N.'s 2015 Paris Climate Conference (otherwise known as the 21st Conference of the Parties or **COP21**), is considered to have created an "unprecedented global mandate to arrest climate change."[153] Developed countries at the Paris Climate Conference agreed to provide $100 billion annually through 2020 as a "floor" of financial assistance for developing countries to adapt to climate change and reduce emissions while growing their clean energy economies.[154]

To date, significant challenges remain in the implementation of the Paris Climate Agreement. According to the Organisation for Economic Co-operation and Development (OECD), which manages the finances, the developed countries were close to achieving the $100 billion target, but several member nations have raised doubts over whether this is true. Arguments over funding data have made it difficult to assess exactly how much has been collected, with several studies suggesting that they have fallen short, particularly in light of the COVID-19 pandemic.[155] Additionally, the U.S. withdrawal from the Paris Climate Conference during the Trump administration in November 2020, and then its subsequent re-entry under President Biden in early 2021, also created confusion about funding.[156] Nevertheless, there are signs that progress has been made toward the agreement, with 25 countries and the EU working toward net-zero commitment dates, as well as several Asian economic powers like South Korea, Japan and China (the world's largest emitter).[157]

4.7 Other Environmental and Sustainability Stakeholders

4.7a Environmental Interest Groups

Perhaps no force in today's societies is more responsible for the "greening" of nations around the world than are the many environmental interest groups making up what has come to be known as "the environmentalist movement." This collection of nonprofit membership and think-tank organizations has been credited with moving the world's governments and businesses, as well as publics, in the direction of environmental sustainability through a host of activities, including demonstrations, boycotts, public education, lobbying, and research.

The history of the environmental movement is instructive. While a few U.S. groups (the National Audubon Society, the Sierra Club) were formed in the early 1900s during the second green wave, many of the largest national and international environmental groups, such as the Environmental Defense Fund (EDF), Greenpeace, and the National Resources Defense Council (NRDC), were created during the third environmental wave, in the late 1960s and early 1970s. Since that time, all of these groups and hundreds of other smaller, more locally focused environmental organizations have grown in size and clout.

Environmental interest groups have been instrumental in significantly influencing business environmental policy. For example, EDF has worked with Federal Express on building a new generation of vehicles, with DuPont on developing nanotech standards, and with PHH Arval on becoming the first carbon neutral fleet.[158] Other outcomes of relationships between environmental interest groups and business stakeholders have included the following:

- Corporate selection of environmental group representatives for corporate boards and top management positions.
- Mutual participation in environmental "cleanup" projects.
- Corporate donations of time and money to environmental groups for their environmental conservation programs.

This trend toward cooperation between otherwise adversarial groups is a characteristic of the third environmental or green wave, and it continues into the fourth wave that we experience today. These cooperatives also illustrate concepts from Chapter 3 on stakeholders—the transactional level of stakeholder management capability and higher levels of stakeholder engagement.

The former chair of the Sierra Club identified three types of major U.S. environmental organizations based on this criterion of cooperation with business. He labeled groups characterized by confrontational behaviors as "radicals,"

groups that seek pragmatic reform through a combination of confrontation and cooperation as "mainstreamers," and groups that avoid confrontation and are more trusting of corporations as "accommodators."[159] As we mentioned earlier, the differences between the types of groups are beginning to blur as business and environmental activists collaborate increasingly on shared goals. Nevertheless, it is instructive to look at some of the groups that have taken and still sometimes take a more radical approach, often powered by their use of social media.

One group that falls into the radical camp is the Rainforest Action Network (RAN). RAN has been particularly successful in getting large corporations to change their ways. The ways in which RAN has accomplished their goals are described in Figure 4-6. RAN began as a small organization, with a budget of only $2.4 million and a staff of just 25. Nevertheless, they have garnered the attention of big business in a way that the larger, more established environmental organizations have never managed. Most recently, they publicly weighed in when Goldman Sachs declared it will no longer finance new coal mines, coal power plants, or oil exploration in the Arctic.[160] RAN responded, "Now other major U.S. banks, especially JPMorgan Chase—the world's worst banker of fossil fuels by a wide margin—must improve on what Goldman has done."[161] RAN has been described as a mosquito in a tent, "just a nuisance when it starts, but you can wake up later with some serious welts."[162]

In addition to environmental groups, businesses are paying closer attention to sustainability's green wave because of

---

Ethics In Practice Case

Slow Fashion

Fast fashion is a term that has been applied to clothing that goes from the high fashion catwalk to mainstream clothing stores in record time, enabling the average buyer to wear the latest trends. Zara and H&M are examples of retailers that have made their mark with fast fashion identities, but other retailers have joined the rush to fast fashion in order to provide their customers with the trendiest clothes to wear at moderate prices. The consumer can then afford to get new clothes in the next season when fashion trends inevitably change. Because the expected lifespan is short, fast fashion clothing tends to be made with less care and lower quality materials, cutting corners to make it cheaply and quickly.

Slow fashion has entered the scene and is endeavoring to change consumer habits. Slow fashion uses traditional methods of sewing and weaving, quality materials that are natural in origin, and quality handcrafting. As noted by a cofounder of the slow fashion line Zady: "It's about understanding the process or the origins of how things are made .... where our products come from, how they're constructed and by whom. Slow fashion is really indicative of a movement of people who want to literally slow down." The clothing is made to last and consumers repair rather than replace clothing that is slightly damaged. Like the slow food movement, slow fashion promotes a more thoughtful

approach to living on the earth in a sustainable way. To that end, Zady founder Maxine Bedat founded the New Standard Institute to "turn the fashion industry into a force for good."

1. Is the criticism of fast fashion fair? Should an industry be held accountable for the waste its consumers generate?
2. Do you think slow fashion will become "fashionable" in the way that fast fashion has? If it does, will its popularity persist or just end up being another fashion trend?
3. What responsibilities do consumers have for sustainability?

Sources: http://www.hearts.com/ecolife/join-slow-fashion-movement/, accessed April 2, 2016; Maureen Dickson, Carlotta Cataldi, and Crystal Glover, "The Show Fashion Movement: Reversing Environmental Damage," http://www.notjustalabel.com/editorial/the_slow_fashion_movement, accessed February 16, 2021; Elizabeth Blair, *NPR* (April 24, 2015), "Slow Fashion Shows Consumers What It's Made Of," http://www.npr.org/2015/04/24/401764329/slow-fashion-shows-consumers-what-its-made-of, accessed February 16, 2021; Emily Farra, "Can This Group Put an End to Fake News about Sustainable Fashion?, *Vogue* (April 25, 2019), https://www.vogue.com/article/maxine-bedat-new-standard-institute-sustainable-fashion-resource, accessed February 16, 2021; *New Standard Institute*, https://www.newstandardinstitute.org/communitymain, accessed February 17, 2021.

Figure 4-6 The Mosquito in the Tent Strategy

Street Theater	During the holiday season, Rainforest Action Network (RAN) carolers sang "Oil Wells" to the tune of "Jingle Bells" in front of the Citigroup headquarters on Park Avenue. RAN obtained the access code to the Home Depot intercom and announced to shoppers that they should step carefully, because the wood on Aisle 13 had been ripped from the Amazon Basin and there might be blood on the floors. They had actors, dressed up as Minnie and Mickey Mouse, locked to Walt Disney headquarters with a banner that read, "Disney is destroying Indonesia's rainforest."
Celebrity Endorsements	The night before Citigroup's annual shareholder meeting, RAN began airing commercials showing Ed Asner, Susan Sarandon, Darryl Hannah, and Ali MacGraw cutting up their Citibank credit cards.
Coalitions	RAN doesn't go it alone. They work with other environmental organizations, socially responsible investors, liberal philanthropists, and even sympathetic insiders (which is how they got the Home Depot access code).
Internet Organizing	RAN uses the Internet to both launch their own initiatives and support those of other groups. They urge individuals to contact those whose behavior they want to change and thank those who responded to RAN's requests for action.

Sources: Marc Gunther, "The Mosquito in the Tent," *Fortune* (March 31, 2004), 158–162; Lisa Gerwitz, "It's Not Easy Being Green," *Deal.com* (March 8, 2004), 1; Dan Murphy, "Stunning Reversal? Why 'Big Paper' Just Went Green in Indonesia," *Christian Science Monitor* (February 19, 2013), http://www.csmonitor.com/Environment/2013/0219/Stunning-reversal-Why-big-paper-just-went-green-in-Indonesia, accessed February 17, 2021; see also http://www.ran.org/take-action-online, accessed February 17, 2021.

at least three other sustainability stakeholder groups: green consumers, green employees, and green investors.

4.7b Other Sustainability Interest Groups

Green Consumers. Individuals referred to as **green consumers** are actual and potential customers of retail firms, usually in developed countries, who express preferences for products, services, and companies that are perceived to be more environment friendly than other competitive products, services, and firms. For example, a rise in "eco-athleisure" workout gear has been embraced by consumers who look for environmentally friendly fibers and logos.[163] Of course, brands such as Nike and Patagonia belong to trade groups like the **Sustainable Apparel Coalition** that follow brand-specific sustainability indices that consumers know about. However, green consumers purchasing sportswear will also look for logos like *Recycled PET*, which show that materials like plastic bottles have been recycled for fabrics. Additionally, *organic cotton labeling*, certifying that the cotton has not been treated with toxins, is popular with green consumers, as well as *Cradle-to-Cradle Fashion Positive certification*, which points to reuse and recycling opportunities.[164]

It seems that consumers, overall, are willing to pay more for green products—or at least products from companies that are committed to sustainability. In a 2020 study of more than 18,000 consumers in 28 different countries, 71 percent of those surveyed said they are willing to pay extra for products and services that come from companies that are committed to positive social and environmental impact, and 57 percent were willing to change their purchasing habits to help reduce negative environmental impact.[165]

Green Employees. A second stakeholder interest group with which most businesses are concerned is **green employees**. Although the popular press has not focused as much attention on green employees as it has on green consumers, there is

evidence that employees are playing a major role in promoting environmentalism at work. In addition to union and general employee environmental concerns with plant, warehouse, and office safety and health, employees in many companies have assisted management in going beyond these traditional concerns into areas such as pollution prevention, recycling, energy and environmental audits, and community environmental projects. In fact, a recent survey of Generation Z employees, those born between 1996 and 2015, shows that 93 percent believe their companies and brands have an obligation to take a stand on environmental issues.[166]

Green Investors. Another important business stakeholder involved in environmental issues is the **green investor**. As we mentioned in Chapter 2, these are investors who are interested in advancing social causes. These individuals and organizations want to put their money where their environmental values are by identifying and utilizing financial instruments that are associated with environmentally oriented companies. A growing number of mutual funds, stock and bond offerings, money market funds, and other financial instruments have included environmental components in recent years. In fact, environmental, social, and governance (**ESG**) **investing** is flourishing, with the S&P 500 ESG Index leading the way in outperforming the standard S&P 500 index over one-, three-, and five-year time frames to 2020.[167] Global investors driving businesses to take necessary action on climate change include the **Climate Action 100+**, a group of more than 540 investors responsible for more than $52 trillion in assets under management. The group was formed in 2017 in large response to the 2015 Paris Climate Change Conference.[168]

Shareholder resolutions address concerns that range from toxic emissions to recycling and waste to nuclear power plants and climate change. According to *Proxy Preview*, shareholder resolutions regarding environmental and sustainable governance resolutions combined represented 66 percent of the proxies filed in 2020, with a focus

Spotlight on Sustainability

Living "The Other Low-Carb Life"

Have you calculated your personal carbon and/or ecological footprint? Many individuals have begun to make a commitment to the "carbon neutral" lifestyle by tracking and paying for the CO_2 that they spend. Carbon neutrality can be achieved through a combination of minimizing carbon emissions where possible (it is possible to book a carbon neutral flight or have carbon neutral groceries delivered to your home) and then purchasing offsets for the emissions that remain. For example, environmental consultant Guy Dauncey tallies his annual carbon spending when he tallies his taxes. He found that his personal activities caused 13.5 tons of carbon emissions. The going rate for carbon was $10 a ton, and so he arranged to do $135 of work for the Solar Electric Light Fund, a group that helps African villagers use solar power instead of kerosene.

The Nature Conservancy (http://www.nature.org) provides a free carbon footprint calculator that measures how many tons of carbon dioxide and greenhouse gasses are generated by the different choices an individual makes each year; see https://www.nature.org/en-us/get-involved/how-to-help/carbon-footprint-calculator/. They provide advice on how to evaluate carbon offset options, and they offer carbon offset options, such as contributing to the Tensas

River Basin Project on the Mississippi River. Their website also provides a range of information on global warming along with ways in which individuals can become involved in the issue.

The U.S. Environmental Protection Agency also provides a free carbon footprint calculator: https://www3.epa.gov/carbon-footprint-calculator/. You can find your car's rated fuel efficiency along with other useful information.

Even organizations like the National Hockey League have embraced the idea of reducing their carbon footprints. Citing its deep connection to the natural environment, the NHL was named the Environmental Protection Agency's Green Partner of the Year in 2015 after successful implementation of LED lighting in its arenas, among other initiatives.

Sources: "The 50 Best Inventions of the Year," *Time* (November 23, 2009), 57–92; Danylo Hawaleshka, "The Other Low-Carb Life," *Maclean's* (June 21, 2004), 54; http://www.nature.org, accessed February 16, 2021; Skinner Bachs, "NHL Green Week Highlights Initiatives to Reduce Hockey's Carbon Footprint," http://www.inquisitr.com/2891425/nhl-green-week-highlights-initiatives-to-reduce-hockeys-carbon-footprint/, accessed February 16, 2021.

on political activity and climate change.[169] Perhaps as a result of this attention from shareholders, tech companies like Apple have begun to issue "green bonds" to finance clean energy projects across its global business operations. As noted by Apple's vice president of environment, policy, and social initiatives, "This will allow investors to show they will put their money where their hearts and concerns are."[170]

4.7c Business and Environmental Partnerships-Activists, NGOs, and Interest Groups

In the past several years, a shift in the relationship between business and environmental activists, **nongovernmental organizations (NGOs)**, and interest groups has occurred. Accommodation and cooperation are replacing antagonism as the parties begin to recognize their mutual dependence. Business needs environmental partners to both inform and validate their environmental efforts and activists, NGOs, and interest groups need business to change the way it operates in order to protect the planet.[171]

More and more, businesses are partnering with these groups to accomplish their sustainability objectives. For example, a *GreenBiz* survey showed that large corporations view NGO partners in four ways, as:[172]

- Trusted Partners—Corporate-friendly, highly credible, long-term partners
- Useful Resources—Highly credible organizations known for creating helpful frameworks and services for corporate partners

- Brand Challenged—Credible, but not influential, organizations
- The Uninvited—Less broadly known groups, or those viewed more as critics than partners

Despite the obvious challenges of working with the "brand challenged" and the "uninvited," the corporations acknowledged that all four types of partners need to be addressed—to get their perspectives and attempt to address their concerns, particularly regarding climate change, community engagement, and energy (both renewables and efficiency).[173] Evidence of such stakeholder collaborations shows that these partnerships can be successful. For example, in 2019 farmers, food companies, policymakers, and environmental advocates came together through the Environmental Defense Fund to reduce greenhouse gas emissions and environmental impacts across the supply chains of Smithfield Foods, the world's largest pork processor. The common theme was shared value in the growing demand for climate change.[174]

4.8 The Future of Business: Greening and/or Growing?

The salient environmental question business and citizens may need to address in the future is this: "How much is enough?" A common business and, indeed, public policy goal in most human societies has been economic growth. Typically, businesses and societies have needed increasing amounts of either materials or energy, or both, to achieve that economic growth. Limits on growth, similar to limits on human reproduction, at either the macro or micro level, have not been widely popular. This has led to what one magazine called "The Environmentalists' Civil War," with "pro-energy, pro-density humanists" on the one side and "anti-energy, pro-sprawl absolutists" on the other.[175]

However, one potential problem with unrestrained economic growth worldwide is that, unless technology or people change significantly within a generation, environmental problems could change in degree from significant to severe. Individual governments and international organizations like the United Nations can certainly help to identify and address environmental problems, but businesses must be proactive in caring for the environment, and they will need to work with various allies to accomplish sustainability goals.

The pressures on the environment come from many directions. However, world population is projected to continue to grow, creating greater demands on food and fuel resources. Large countries such as China and India are industrializing, and they will use increasing amounts of materials and energy. The already industrialized countries continue to maintain the highly consumptive lifestyles that have strained the environment. As the name implies, the sustainability imperative is of the essence. Business no longer has the luxury of deciding whether or not to respond to it—societies in general and the natural environment in particular cannot wait.

Summary

The concept of sustainability is complex and includes the natural environment and broader environments including the economy and society. After defining sustainability, we discuss how sustainability and business are now linked by performance expectations like the triple bottom line that include the economic, social, and environmental spheres that link to the concept of sustainability. Large-scale initiatives like the UN Global Compact provide principles and goals that help businesses integrate sustainability into their business strategies. Expectations that business has an imperative to address sustainability issues are part of a fourth wave of environmentalism that focuses on technological innovations, public policy, and new ways for business and government to collaborate to address environmental problems. The circular economy and circular business models are examples of newer approaches to tackle sustainability issues. We also highlight several businesses that exhibit top sustainability practices today.

Although there is a growing consensus about the importance of sustainability, there remain significant differences of opinion on how problems will develop in the future and what should be done to resolve them. The natural environment is crucial for human survival, and a number of complex and interconnected human-induced activities are threatening this environment. We discuss seven key environmental issues that businesses face. Problems such as those profiled in this chapter are potentially endangering nonhuman species and ecosystems and reducing the quality of human life. Individuals and their organizations, including businesses, are directly or indirectly responsible for this situation. We discuss the responses of all governments in exercising regulatory control to address some of these issues.

The recent growth in partnerships between business and environmental activists, NGOs, and interest groups is a promising sign, as we note, but more changes must come. A minimum baseline of sustainability—meeting the needs of the present without compromising the ability of future generations to meet their needs—should be the bottom line for business as it moves into the future.

Key Terms

air pollution, p. 75

Anthropocene extinction, p. 84

biodiversity, p. 81

biofuel, p. 73

cap and trade, p. 84

carbon dioxide, p. 73

carbon emission, p. 73

carbon footprints, p. 75

carbon neutral, p. 73

carbon offsets, p. 75

carbon pricing, p. 75

Ceres' Roadmap to Sustainability, p. 70

chlorofluorocarbons (CFCs), p. 77

circular business model, p. 72

circular economy, p. 72

Climate Action 100+, p. 87

climate change, p. 74

Clean Air Act, p. 82

Clean Water Act, p. 84

corporate sustainability, p. 68

COP21, p. 85

deforestation, p. 80

ecosystem, p. 74

emissions trading, p. 84

Endangered Species Act (ESA), p. 85

energy inefficiency, p. 77

environment, p. 71

Environmental Protection Agency (EPA), p. 82

ESG investing, p. 87

exchange-traded funds (ETFs), p. 78

externalities, p. 71

fossil fuels, p. 77

fracking, p. 77

Global Reporting Initiative (GRI), p. 85

global warming, p. 74
green consumers, p. 87
green employees, p. 87
green investor, p. 87
greenhouse effect, p. 74
greenwashing, p. 75
internal carbon tax, p. 75
key performance indicators (KPIs), p. 68
Kyoto Protocol, p. 84
Montreal Protocol, p. 77
moral hazard, p. 75
National Environmental Policy Act (NEPA), p. 82

natural environment, p. 71
NGOs, p. 88
ozone, p. 77
recycling, p. 79
shareholder resolutions, p. 87
Superfund, p. 84
Sustainable Apparel Coalition, p. 87
sustainability, p. 68
sustainable business, p. 69
sustainable development goals (SDGs), p. 69
toxic substances, p. 77
Toxic Substances Control Act, p. 84

tragedy of the commons, p. 81
triple bottom line, p. 68
United Nations Environment Programme (UNEP), p. 85
United Nations Global Compact (UNGC), p. 69
"Waters of the United States" (WOTUS), p. 84
watershed, p. 79
wicked problems, p. 81

Discussion Questions

1. What is the triple bottom line? How does it relate to sustainability?
2. What is sustainability? How does sustainability relate to environmentalism?
3. What are the waves of environmentalism? What is new in the fourth wave?
4. What are several of the most important environmental issues now receiving worldwide attention?
5. Who has responsibility for addressing environmental issues?
6. How can ethics be applied in response to environmental issues?
7. Should businesses and societies continue to focus on unlimited economic growth?

Endnotes

1. Alex Davidson, "What's a Sustainable Company? It's Hard to Define," *The Wall Street Journal* (April 3, 2016), http://www.wsj.com/articles/whats-a-sustainable-company-its-hard-to-define-1459735511. Accessed January 14, 2021.
2. Simon Zadek, *The Civil Corporation: The New Economy of Corporate Citizenship* (London: Earthscan, 2001); see also Lance Moir, "Social Responsibility: The Changing Role of Business," Cranfield School of Management, U.K.
3. Sustainability, "Environmental, Social and Governmental Goals," https://www.sustainability.com/. Accessed February 22, 2021.
4. Dow Jones Sustainability Indices, https://www.spglobal.com/esg/csa/indices/index. Accessed February 22, 2021.
5. "Report of the World Commission on Environment and Development," http://www.un.org/documents/ga/res/42/ares42-187.htm. Accessed January 15, 2021.
6. W. Edward Stead and Jean Garner Stead with Mark Starik, *Sustainable Strategic Management* (Armonk, NY: M. E. Sharpe, Inc., 2004).
7. UNGC-Accenture Strategy CEO Study on Sustainability, https://www.accenture.com/us-en/insights/strategy/ungcceostudy. Accessed January 25, 2021.
8. Daniel C. Esty and Andrew S. Winston, *Green to Gold: How Smart Companies Use Environmental Strategy to Innovate, Create Value, and Build Competitive Advantage* (New Haven, CT: Yale University Press, 2006).
9. Susan Casey, "Éminence Green," Fortune (April 2, 2007), 62–70.

10. Mike Scott, "Top Company Profile: Schneider Electric Leads Decarbonizing Megatrend," Corporate Knights (January 25, 2021), Winter Issue, https://www.corporateknights.com/reports/2021-global-100/top-company-profile-schneider-electric-leads-decarbonizing-megatrend25289-16115328/. Accessed January 26, 2021.
11. United Nations SDGs, https://sdgs.un.org/goals. Accessed February 22, 2021.
12. Ibid.
13. "The Sustainable Development Goals Report 2020," UNGC, https://unstats.un.org/sdgs/report/2020/. Accessed January 28, 2021.
14. Ibid.
15. Mike Scott, "Top Company Profile: Schneider Electric Leads Decarbonizing Megatrend," *Corporate Knights* (January 25, 2021), https://www.corporateknights.com/reports/2021-global-100/top-company-profile-schneider-electric-leads-decarbonizing-megatrend25289-16115328/. Accessed January 28, 2021.
16. Ibid.
17. David Vetter, "'All You Need Is a Change of Mentality': CEO of Schneider Electric, Rated World's Most Sustainable Company, on Going Carbon-Free," *Forbes* (January 27, 2021), https://www.forbes.com/sites/davidrvetter/2021/01/27/all-you-need-is-a-change-of-mentality-ceo-of-schneider-electric-rated-worlds-most-sustainable-company-on-going-carbon-free/?sh=1d259ea47156. Accessed January 29, 2021.

18. See "Companies Changing the World," *Fortune*, https://www.sharedvalue.org/community/fortune-change-the-world-list/. Accessed January 29, 2021.

19. https://fortune.com/change-the-world/2020/

20. See Suylin Haynes, *Time* Special Climate Issue (September 23, 2019), p. 48.

21. Charlotte Alter, Suyin Haynes, and Justin Worland, "One Teen's Race to Save the Planet," *Time Special Edition Sustainability: The Practical Sustainable Life* (2020), p. 68.

22. Ibid.

23. Kareem Shabana, Ann Buchholtz, and Archie Carroll, "The Institutionalization of Corporate Social Reporting," *Business & Society* (2016), doi:10.007/0007650316628177, 1–16.

24. "Ceres Roadmap for 2030," Ceres (Boston, MA: 2020), https://roadmap2030.ceres.org/. Accessed January 3, 2021.

25. Vetter, 2021.

26. Ibid.

27. IMAGINE, https://imagine.one/.

28. "The Growth of the Chief Sustainability Officer in the Workplace," *Open Access Government* (February 7, 2020), https://www.openaccessgovernment.org/the-growth-of-the-chief-sustainability-officer-in-the-workplace/82140/. Accessed January 29, 2021.

29. Joel Makower, "The State of Green Business 2015" (February 23, 2015), *GreenBiz* Report, https://www.greenbiz.com/article/state-green-business-2015. Accessed May 6, 2016.

30. Paul R. Ehrlich, Anne H. Ehrlich, and Gretchen C. Daily, *The Stork and the Plow: The Equity Answer to the Human Dilemma* (New Haven, CT: Yale University Press, 1997), 24.

31. Arathy Nair, "DuPont Settles Lawsuits over Leak of Chemical Used to Make Teflon, *Reuters* (February 13, 2017), https://www.reuters.com/article/us-du-pont-lawsuit-west-virginia/dupont-settles-lawsuits-over-leak-of-chemical-used-to-make-teflon-idUSKBN15S18U. Accessed February 1, 2021.

32. *JUST Capital* 2020 Survey, https://justcapital.com/reports/just-capital-2020-survey-results/. Accessed February 2, 2021.

33. Note: Environmental science scholars seem to define waves beginning in the 1800s, while environmental history scholars begin in the 19th and early 20th centuries. We combine the two in the characteristics and draw from Fred Krupp, "Welcome to the Fourth Wave: A New Era of Environmental Progress," *Environmental Defense Fund* (March 21, 2018), https://www.edf.org/blog/2018/03/21/welcome-fourth-wave-new-era-environmental-progress. Accessed February 17, 2021.

34. Fred Krupp, "Harnessing the Fourth Wave of Environmentalism," Medium (March 20, 2018), https://medium.com/the-fourth-wave/harnessing-the-fourth-wave-of-environmentalism-c71afa14eb11. Accessed February 23, 2021.

35. See Marcus Zils, "Moving towards a Circular Economy," *McKinsey & Company Report 2014*, http://www.mckinsey.com/business-functions/sustainability-and-resource-productivity/our-insights/moving-toward-a-circular-economy. Accessed February 15, 2021.

36. See Peter Lacy and Jakob Rutgvist, *Waste to Wealth: The Circular Economy Advantage* (Springer, 2016); Jessica Long and Wesley Spindler, *The Circular Economy*

Handbook (Palgrave Macmillan, 2020); Amy Brown, "Can the Circular Economy Save Us? Experts Are Betting on It," *Triple Pundit* (August 18, 2020), https://www.accenture.com/us-en/services/sustainability-index. Accessed February 15, 2021.

37. John Frishammar and Vinit Parida, "Circular Business Model Transformation: A Roadmap for Incumbent Firms," *California Management Review*, 61/2: 5–29.

38. The Ethical Corporation, "Patagonia Circular Economy Strategy: A Case Study," http://1.ethicalcorp.com/LP=8770?utm_source=Abhishek%20&utm_medium=Abhishek%20&utm_campaign=Abhishek. Accessed February 15, 2021.

39. Ibid.

40. Amy Brown, 2020.

41. United Nations Environment Programme, "US Outdoor Clothing Brand Patagonia Wins UN Champions of the Earth Award" (September 24, 2019), https://www.unep.org/news-and-stories/press-release/us-outdoor-clothing-brand-patagonia-wins-un-champions-earth-award. Accessed February 17, 2021.

42. Esty and Winston, 25.

43. Susan Casey, "Éminence Green," *Fortune* (April 2, 2007), 62–70.

44. Ibid., 67.

45. Anne Brock, "Patagonia Leads by Example in the Circular Economy," *TriplePundit* (February12, 2016), http://www.triplepundit.com/2016/02/patagonia-leads-example-circular-economy/. Accessed February 17, 2021.

46. "Tim Cook Tells Climate Change Sceptics to Ditch Apple Shares," *The Guardian* (March 3, 2014), http://www.theguardian.com/environment/2014/mar/03/tim-cook-climate-change-sceptics-ditch-apple-shares. Accessed February 17, 2021.

47. Ibid.

48. Apple 2020 Progress Report on Sustainability, https://www.apple.com/environment/. Accessed February 17, 2021.

49. http://rankabrand.org/electronics/Apple. Accessed February 17, 2021.

50. Geoff Ledford, "Powered by Purpose: What Tesla's Model 3 Says about the Future of Sustainability," *TriplePundit*, http://www.triplepundit.com/2016/04/tesla-model-3-sustainability/. Accessed February 17, 2021.

51. William Collins, Robert Colman, James Haywood, Martin R. Manning, and Philip Mote, "The Physical Science behind Climate Change," *Scientific American* (August 2007), 64–71.

52. Ted Nordhaus, "Ignore the Fake Climate Debate," *The Wall Street Journal* (January 23, 2020), https://www.wsj.com/articles/ignore-the-fake-climate-debate-11579795816. Accessed February 2, 2021.

53. John Steele Gordon, "The Unsettling, Anti-Science Certitude on Global Warming," *The Wall Street Journal* (July 21, 2015), A11.

54. Justin Worland, "The Defining Year," *Time* (July 20/27, 2020), p. 36.

55. Yereth Rosen, "Earth Is Losing Ice Faster Today Than in the mid-1990's, Study Suggests," Thomson Reuters (January 25, 2021), https://www.reuters.com/article/us-climate-change-ice/earth-is-losing-ice-faster-today-than-in-the-mid-1990s-study-suggests-idUSKBN29U0U0. Accessed March 4, 2021.

56. Worland, p. 36.

57. See *World Economic Forum*, "The Global Risks Report 2020," https://www.weforum.org/reports/the-global -risks-report-2020 Accessed February 2, 2021; Katherine Dunn, "World Leaders Finally Accept the Economic Risk of Climate Change, but Business Chiefs Are a Holdout, *Fortune* (January 17, 2020), https://fortune .com/2020/01/17/world-economic-forum-climate-change -zurich-insurance/. Accessed February 1, 2021.

58. "Larry Fink's 2021 Letter to CEOs," https://www .blackrock.com/corporate/investor-relations/larry-fink-ceo -letter. Accessed February 1, 2021.

59. Ibid.

60. See "Executive Order on Tackling the Climate Crisis at Home and Abroad," *The White House Briefing Room* (January 27, 2021), https://www.whitehouse.gov/briefing -room/presidential-actions/2021/01/27/executive-order-on -tackling-the-climate-crisis-at-home-and-abroad/. Accessed February 2, 2021; "How Is the UK Tackling Climate Change?" *Energy and Climate Intelligence Unit*, https:// eciu.net/analysis/briefings/uk-energy-policies-and-prices /how-is-the-uk-tackling-climate-change. Accessed February 4, 2021; "EU Climate Action and the European Green Deal," *European Union Website*, https://ec.europa.eu/clima /policies/eu-climate-action_en. Accessed February 4, 2021.

61. Ibid.

62. Joseph E. Aldy and Gianfranco Gianfrate, "Future-Proof Your Climate Strategy," Harvard Business Review (May–June 2019), https://hbr.org/2019/05/future-proof -your-climate-strategy. Accessed February 2, 2021. Also, David Gelles, "Microsoft Leads Movement to Offset Emissions with Internal Carbon Tax," *The New York Times* (September 26, 2015), http://www.nytimes. com/2015/09/27/business/energy-environment/microsoft -leads-movement-to-offset-emissions-with-internal -carbon-tax.html?_r=0,m Accessed February 4, 2021.

63. Ibid.

64. Ibid.

65. Christopher Matthews, "Exxon Vows to Reduce Its Carbon Footprint," *The Wall Street Journal* (December 15, 2020, p. B1.

66. "Microsoft Buys $1.3 Million Carbon Offsets in 2021 Portfolio," *S&P Global* (January 29, 2021), https://www .spglobal.com/platts/en/market-insights/latest-news /coal/012921-microsoft-buys-13-million-carbon-offsets -in-2021-portfolio. Accessed February 4, 2021.

67. Ryan Dezember, "BP Taps into Carbon Trade on Trees," *The Wall Street Journal*, (December 17, 2020), B1.

68. "Air Pollution Effects," https://www.epa.gov/air-research /research-health-and-environmental-effects-air-quality. Accessed January 15, 2021.

69. Mark Dolliver, "Environmental Worries Will Never Be Extinct," *Adweek* (March 26, 2007), 35.

70. Elian Peltier, "In Landmark Ruling, Air Pollution Recorded as a Cause of Death for British Girl," *The New York Times*, (December 16, 2020), https://www.nytimes. com/2020/12/16/world/europe/britain-air-pollution-death .html. Accessed February 4, 2021.

71. World Health Organization, https://www.who.int/health -topics/air-pollution#tab=tab_1. Accessed March 1, 2021.

72. Tim Stelloh, "California Exceeds 4 Million Acres Burned by Wildfires in 2020," *NBC News* (October 4, 2020), https://www.nbcnews.com/news/us-news/california -exceeds-4-million-acres-burned-wildfires- 2020-n1242078. Accessed February 4, 2021.

73. "Smoke from Australian Bushfires Was More Deadly Than the Fires Themselves," *Airqualitynews.com* (March 25, 2020), https://airqualitynews.com/2020/03/25/smoke -from-australian-bushfires-was-more-deadly-than-the -fires-themselves/. Accessed February 4, 2021.

74. Roderick Weller and Eleni Michalopoulou, "Pollution Costs Lives and Is Bad for Business," *World Economic Forum* (September 7, 2020), https://www.weforum.org /agenda/2020/09/pollution-costs-lives-here-are-5-ways -companies-can-clean-up-the-air/. Accessed February 2, 2021.

75. Ibid.

76. "Air Pollution: Current and Future Challenges," https:// www.epa.gov/clean-air-act-overview/air-pollution-current -and-future-challenges. Accessed February 14, 2021.

77. Air Pollution: Current and Future Challenges.

78. "Lumber Liquidators to Settle Air Safety Allegations," *The New York Times* (March 23, 2016), B2.

79. http://nationalatlas.gov/mld/efct17x.html. Accessed February 15, 2021.

80. U.S. Department of State, "The Montreal Protocol on Substances that Deplete the Ozone Layer," https://www .state.gov/key-topics-office-of-environmental-quality-and- transboundary-issues/the-montreal-protocol-on-substances -that-deplete-the-ozone-layer/. Accessed February 4, 2021.

81. https://www.rapidtransition.org/stories/back-from-the -brink-how-the-world-rapidly-sealed-a-deal-to-save-the -ozone-layer/

82. Linda Marsa, "Is the Ozone Hole Shrinking?" *Discover Magazine* (April 5, 2013), http://discovermagazine. com/2013/may/02-is-the-ozone-hole-shrinking. Accessed January 28, 2021.

83. "Large Deep Antarctica Ozone Hole in 2020," *NASA Earth Observatory* (September 20, 2020), https:// earthobservatory.nasa.gov/images/147465/large-deep -antarctic-ozone-hole-in-2020. Accessed February 4, 2021.

84. Joshua O'Reilly, "The Global Climate & Health Alliance," https://climateandhealthalliance.org/resources/impacts /skin-cancer-in-australia/. Accessed February 4, 2021.

85. Ibid.

86. "How a Market Heats Up," *Fortune* (May 29, 2006), 74–75.

87. Richard Eidlin, "The Business Case for Rethinking Fracking," *Greenbiz*, (October 29, 2014), https://www .greenbiz.com/article/business-case-rethinking-fracking. Accessed February 14, 2021.

88. See "The Truth about Franking and the Environment," *The Wilderness Society*, https://www.wilderness.org/articles /article/truth-about-fracking-and-environment. Accessed February 14, 2021; Tala Hadavi, "How Fracking Changed America Forever," *CNBC* (January 7, 2020), https://www .cnbc.com/2020/01/06/the-impact-of-fracking-on -us-consumers-and-local-communities.html. Accessed February 14, 2021.

89. Wolfram Krewitt, Sonja Simon, Wina Graus, Sven Teske, Arthouros Zervos, and Oliver Schafer, "The 2°C Scenario: A Sustainable World Energy Perspective," *Energy Policy* (October 2007), 4969–4980.

90. Claire Groden, "The New Power Added to U.S. Grids in 2015 Was Mostly Renewable," *Fortune* (February 4, 2016), http://fortune.com/2016/02/04/electricity -renewable-energy/. Accessed January 31, 2021.

91. Tina Casey, "Ikea Has More Renewable Energy Than It Can Use, and That's Just the Beginning," *Triple Pundit*

(February 4, 2021), https://www.triplepundit.com/story/2021/ikea-renewable-energy/718146. Accessed February 14, 2021.

92. Tina Casey, "Despite the Global Pandemic, Clean Energy Just Had a Banner Year," *Triple Pundit* (January 28, 2021), https://www.triplepundit.com/story/2021/pandemic-clean-energy/717891, Accessed February 14, 2021.

93. Vetter, 2020.

94. Justin Kuepper, "Investing Tin the Global Renewable Energy Sector," *The Balance* (January 27, 2021), https://www.thebalance.com/how-to-invest-in-the-global-renewable-energy-sector-4056875. Accessed February 14, 2021.

95. United Nations, 2015.

96. Esty and Winston, 2006.

97. See Jeremy C.F. Lin, Jean Rutter, and Haeyoun Park, "Events That Led to Flint's Water Crisis," *The New York Times* (January 21, 2016), http://www.nytimes.com/interactive/2016/01/21/us/flint-lead-water-timeline.html?_r=0. Accessed February 14, 2021; Jonathan Lapook, "Doctors Explain the Long-Term Health Effects of the Flint Michigan Crisis," *CBS News* (January 19, 2016), http://www.cbsnews.com/news/doctors-explain-the-long-term-health-effects-of-flint-water-crisis/. Accessed February 14, 2021.

98. "Wastewater a Resource that Can Pay Dividends for People, the Environment, and Economies, Says World Bank," *The World Bank* (March 1, 2020), https://www.worldbank.org/en/news/press-release/2020/03/19/wastewater-a-resource-that-can-pay-dividends-for-people-the-environment-and-economies-says-world-bank. Accessed February 15, 2021.

99. Ibid.

100. Geoffrey Lean, "Water Crisis Now Bigger Threat Than Financial Crisis," *The Independent* (March 15, 2009), http://www.independent.co.uk/environment/climate-change/water-scarcity-now-bigger-threat-than-financial-crisis-1645358.html. Accessed February 15, 2021.

101. Nicholas St. Fleur, "Two-Thirds of the World Faces Severe Water Shortages," *The New York Times* (February 12, 2016), http://www.nytimes.com/2016/02/13/science/two-thirds-of-the-world-faces-severe-water-shortages.html?_r=0. Accessed February 15, 2021.

102. Bruno Sarda, "Companies Blind to Risks of Water Pollution and Scarcity, and the Untappled Opportunity to Address It," *Greenbiz* (May 11, 2020), https://www.greenbiz.com/article/companies-blind-risks-water-pollution-and-scarcity-and-untapped-opportunity-address-it. Accessed February 15, 2021.

103. CDP Global Water Report 2019, https://www.cdp.net/en/research/global-reports/cleaning-up-their-act. Accessed February 15, 2021.

104. Mary Mazzoni, "3p Weekend: Governments, Companies Tackle Water Scarcity," *TriplePundit* (March 25, 2016), http://www.triplepundit.com/2016/03/3p-weekend-governments-companies-tackle-water-scarcity/. Accessed February 15, 2021.

105. Julie Padowski, Steven Gorelick, Barton Thompson, Scott Rozelle, and Scott Fendorf, "Assessment of Human–Natural System Characteristics Influencing Global Freshwater Supply Vulnerability," *Environmental Research Letters,* 10(10), 2015.

106. Tim Culpan Olga Kharif, "Where Phones Go to Die," *Bloomberg Businessweek* (March 7–13, 2006), 35.

107. See Gina Marie Cheeseman, "Gap Wants to Halve Its Greenhouse Gas Emissions by 2020," *TriplePundit* (January 27, 2016), http://www.triplepundit.com/2016/01/gap-wants-halve-greenhouse-gas-emissions-2020/?utm_source=Daily+Email+List&utm_campaign=5ca7092b82-RSS_EMAIL_CAMPAIGN&utm_medium=email&utm_term=0_9dedefcee3-5ca7092b82-220417273. Accessed February 15, 2021; Gap, Inc Global Sustainability, https://www.gapincsustainability.com/environment/protecting-our-shared-environment/diverting-waste. Accessed February 15, 2021.

108. Tina Casey, "This Johnnie Walker Bottle Is Actually Made of Paper," *Triple Pundit* (July 23, 2020), https://www.triplepundit.com/story/2020/johnnie-walker-paper-bottle/120986. Accessed February 15, 2021.

109. See Loretta Chao, "Lego Tries to Build a Better Brick," *The Wall Street Journal* (July 14, 2015), B4; Rachel Cooper, "Lego to Ban Plastic Blocks by 2030," *Climate Action* (September 13, 2018), https://www.climateaction.org/news/lego-to-ban-plastic-blocks-by-2030. Accessed February 15, 2021.

110. http://www.epa.gov/wastes/. Accessed February 15, 2021.

111. Ibid.

112. Ibid.

113. https://www.epa.gov/healthywatersheds. Accessed March 1, 2021.

114. Ivana Kottasova, "More Plastic Than Fish in Oceans by 2050," CNN Business (January 19, 2016). https://money.cnn.com/2016/01/19/news/economy/davos-plastic-ocean-fish/index.html. Accessed February 15, 2021.

115. B. Freitas, L. Delagran, E. Griffin, K. L. Miller, and M. Hirshfield, "Too Few Fish: A Regional Assessment of the World's Fisheries," May 2008, *Oceana,* http://oceana.org/sites/default/files/reports/toofewfish41.pdf. Accessed February 15, 2021.

116. "The Sea Is Running Out of Fish, Despite Nations' Pledges to Stop It," *National Geographic* (October 8, 2019), https://www.nationalgeographic.com/science/2019/10/sea-running-out-of-fish-despite-nations-pledges-to-stop/. Accessed February 15, 2021.

117. Roya Sabri, "A Glimmer of Hope: We Can Restore Marine Health by 2050," *Triple Pundit* (April 15, 2020), https://www.triplepundit.com/story/2020/glimmer-hope-we-can-restore-marine-health-2050/87226. Accessed March 1, 2021.

118. http://www.chesapeakebay.net/issues/issue/blue_crabs#inline. Accessed February 15, 2021. Accessed February 15, 2021.

119. "The World Is Losing Its Big Old Trees," *The Economist* (August 19, 2020), https://www.economist.com/graphic-detail/2020/08/19/the-world-is-losing-its-big-old-trees. Accessed February 15, 2021.

120. Heather Clancy, "Fighting Deforestation Should Be a Top Priority for 2021, and Here Is How It Can Be," (January 11, 2021), https://www.greenbiz.com/article/fighting-deforestation-should-be-top-priority-2021-and-heres-how-it-can-be. Accessed February 15, 2021.

121. Center for Biological Diversity, http://www.biologicaldiversity.org/programs/biodiversity/elements_of_biodiversity/extinction_crisis/. Accessed February 6, 2021.

122. "The Next Environmental Issue for Business: McKinsey Global Survey Results," http://www.mckinsey.com/business-functions/sustainability-and-resource-productivity/our-insights/the-next-environmental-issue-for-business-mckinsey-global-survey-results. Accessed March 30, 2016.

123.   United Nations Summit on Biodiversity-Summary, (September 30, 2020), https://www.un.org/pga/75/united-nations-summit-on-biodiversity-summary/. Accessed February 16, 2021.

124.   David C. Wagman, "Wicked Problems," *Power Engineering* (May 2006), 5.

125.   Garrett Hardin, "The Tragedy of the Commons," *Science* (Vol. 162, 1968), 1243–1248.

126.   Ibid.

127.   Linda M. Sama, Stephanie A. Welcomer, and Virginia W. Gerde, "Who Speaks for the Trees? Invoking an Ethic of Care to Give Voice to the Silent Stakeholder," in S. Sharma and M. Starik (eds.), *Stakeholders, the Environment and Society* (Cheltenham, UK: Edward Elgar, 2004), 140–165.

128.   Ibid.

129.   Public Law 91-190 (1969), 42 U.S.C. Section 4331 et seq.

130.   National Environmental Policy Act, "CEQ NEPA Regulations," https://ceq.doe.gov/laws-regulations/regulations.html. Accessed February 16, 2021.

131.   U. S. Environmental Protection Agency, EPA, https://www.epa.gov/. Accessed February 18, 2021.

132.   Overview of the Clean Air Act and Air Pollution, http://www.epa.gov/air/caa/. Accessed February 16, 2021.

133.   Ibid.

134.   The United States Department of Justice Office of Public Affairs (January 14, 2021), https://www.justice.gov/opa/pr/toyota-motor-company-pay-180-million-settlement-decade-long-noncompliance-clean-air-act. Accessed February 16, 2021.

135.   "Kyoto Protocol," http://unfccc.int/kyoto_protocol/items/2830.php. Accessed February 17, 2021.

136.   https://www.epa.gov/cleanwaterrule. Accessed February 17, 2021.

137.   T. McAdams, *Law, Business & Society*, 3rd ed. (Homewood, IL: Irwin, 1992), 784–787, http://www.epa.gov. Accessed February 17, 2021.

138.   Summary of the Toxic Substances Control Act, http://www2.epa.gov/laws-regulations/summary-toxic-substances-control-act. Accessed February 17, 2021.

139.   Ibid.

140.   Summary of Superfunds, http://www.epa.gov/superfund/. Accessed February 17, 2021.

141.   U.S. Environmental Protection Agency, "EPA Celebrates Superfund – 40 Years of Cleaning Up and Transforming Communities Across the Country," https://www.epa.gov/newsreleases/epa-celebrates-superfund-40-years-cleaning-and-transforming-communities-across-country. Accessed February 23, 2021.

142.   Superfunds, http://www.epa.gov/superfund/. Accessed February 17, 2021.

143.   IUCN 2020. IUCN Red List of Threatened Species. https://www.iucnredlist.org/resources/summary-statistics. Accessed February 16, 2021.

144.   Ibid.

145.   Ivana Kottasova, "The Sixth Mass Extinction Is Happening Faster Than Expected. Scientists Say Its Our Fault," *CNN* (June 1, 2020), https://www.cnn.com/2020/06/01/world/sixth-mass-extinction-accelerating-intl/index.html. Accessed February 16, 2021.

146.   "The United Nations Must Get Its New Biodiversity Targets Right," *Nature* (February 18, 2020), https://www.nature.com/articles/d41586-020-00450-5. Accessed February 16, 2021.

147.   Ibid.

148.   European Commission, "Environment," https://ec.europa.eu/environment/sustainable-development/. Accessed February 16, 2021.

149.   Frederic Simon, "2021: Another Decisive Year for Europe's Climate Ambitions," *Euractiv* (January 7, 2021), https://www.euractiv.com/section/energy-environment/news/2021-another-decisive-year-for-europes-climate-ambitions/. Accessed February 16, 2021.

150.   Els Reynaers Kini, Gautambala Nandeshwar, and MV Kini, "Environmental Law and Practice in India: Overview," *Thomson Reuters*, https://uk.practicallaw.thomsonreuters.com/0-503-2029?transitionType=Default&contextData=(sc.Default)&firstPage=true. Accessed February 16, 2021.

151.   Jocelyn Timperley, "The Law That Could Make Climate Change Illegal," *BBC* (July 7, 2020), https://www.bbc.com/future/article/20200706-the-law-that-could-make-climate-change-illegal. Accessed February 16, 2021.

152.   Ibid.

153.   Carlos Pascual and Antonia Bullard, "Impact of Paris 2015," *The Wall Street Journal* (February 23, 2016), A12.

154.   Thomas Schueneman, "COP21, the Paris Agreement and the Art of the Possible," *TriplePundit* (December 15, 2015), http://www.triplepundit.com/2015/12/cop21-paris-agreement-art-possible/#. Accessed February 16, 2021.

155.   Jess Shankleman, "Rich Countries Missing the $100 Billion Climate Finance Goal," *Bloomberg Green*, (November 6, 2020), https://www.bloomberg.com/news/articles/2020-11-06/rich-countries-are-missing-the-100-billion-climate-finance-goal. Accessed February 16, 2021.

156.   Ibid.

157.   Molly Bergen and Helen Mountford, "6 Signs of Progress Since the Adoption of the Paris Agreement," World Resources Institute, (December 8, 2020), https://www.wri.org/blog/2020/12/paris-agreement-progress-climate-action. Accessed February 16, 2021.

158.   The Environmental Defense Fund, "Partnerships: The Key to Scalable Future," http://www.edf.org/approach/partnerships/corporate. Accessed April 3, 2016.

159.   M. E. Kriz, "Shades of Green," *National Journal* (July 28, 1990).

160.   "Climate of Investment Fear," *The Wall Street Journal* (January 6, 2020), https://www.wsj.com/articles/climate-of-investment-fear-11578355653. Accessed February 17, 2021.

161.   Ibid.

162.   Mark Gunther, "The Mosquito in the Tent," *Fortune* (March 31, 2004), 158–162; Lisa Gerwitz, "It's Not Easy Being Green," Deal.com (March 8, 2004), 1.

163.   Lauren Newton, "The Rise of Eco-Athleisure," *TriplePundit* (April 15, 2016), http://www.triplepundit.com/2016/04/rise-eco-athleisure/. Accessed February 21, 2021.

164.   Ibid.

165.   Karl Haller, Jim Lee, and Jane Cheung, "Meet the 2020 Consumers Driving Change," *IBM Insights* (June 24, 2020), https://www.google.com/url?sa=t&rct=j&q=&esrc=s&source=web&cd=&ved=2ahUKEwjYsbj8jfHuAhVPBs0KHTFjCDYQFjAMegQIBBAC&url=https%3A%2F%2Fwww.ibm.com%2Fdownloads%2Fcas%2FEXK4XKX8&usg=AOvVaw2VxwnCjaEkTr5an5Y8qHJN. Accessed February 21, 2021.

166. Isabel LoDuca, "Why Gen Z Voices Matter in Making Business Sustainable," *Greenbiz* (October 19, 2020), https://www.greenbiz.com/article/why-gen-z-voices -matter-making-business-sustainable. Accessed February 17, 2021.

167. Catherine Brock, "3 ESG Funds to Round Out Your Investment Portfolio," *The Motley Fool* (January 19, 2021), https://www.fool.com/investing/stock-market/types-of -stocks/esg-investing/2021/01/19/3-esg-funds-to-round -out-your-investment-portfolio/. Accessed February 17, 2021.

168. Climate Action 100+, https://www.climateaction100.org /about/. Accessed February 15, 2021.

169. See https://www.proxypreview.org/2020/report-cover. Accessed February 17, 2021; Peter Reali, Christina Gunnell, and Jennifer Grzech, Harvard Law School Forum on Corporate Governance (April 27, 2020), https:// corpgov.law.harvard.edu/2020/04/27/2020-proxy-season -preview/. Accessed February 17, 2021.

170. Reuters, "Apple Just Issued $1.5 Billion in Bonds to Help the Environment," *Fortune* (February 17, 2016), http:// fortune.com/2016/02/17/apple-green-bonds/. Accessed February 17, 2021.

171. John Carey and Michael Arndt, "Hugging the Tree-Huggers," *Businessweek* (March 12, 2007), 66–68.

172. GreenBiz, "How Companies Rate Activists as Partners" (2014), http://info.greenbiz.com/rs/greenbizgroup/images /greenbiz-ngo-report.pdf. Accessed February 17, 2021.

173. Ibid.

174. Tom Murray, "This Unlikely Partnership Drives Positive Change in the Food Sector," *Triple Pundit* (November 1, 2019) https://www.triplepundit.com/story/2019/unlikely -partnership-drives-positive-change-food-sector/85471. Accessed February 17, 2021.

175. Robert Bryce, "The Environmentalists' Civil War," *National Review* (April 17, 2015), http://www .nationalreview.com/article/417070/environmentalists -civil-war. Accessed February 17, 2021.

Part 3

Business Ethics and Leadership

Chapter 5
Business Ethics Essentials

Chapter 6
Managerial and Organizational Ethics

Chapter 7
Ethical Issues in the Global Arena

Chapter 8
Business Ethics and Technology: The Digital Enterprise

5

Business Ethics Essentials

Chapter Learning Outcomes

After studying this chapter, you should be able to:

1. Describe the public's opinion of business ethics.
2. Define business ethics, explain the conventional approach to business ethics, and identify the sources of ethical norms in individuals.
3. Analyze the economic, legal, and ethical aspects of a decision by using a Venn model.
4. Identify, explain, and illustrate three models of management ethics.

5. In terms of making moral management actionable, describe and discuss Kohlberg's three levels of moral development and Gilligan's ethics of care.
6. Identify and discuss six major elements of moral judgment. How does Rest's four component model of ethical decision-making build upon these elements?

The public's interest in business ethics continues at a high level. Certainly, there has been an ebb and flow of interest on society's part, but in recent years this interest has grown to a preoccupation or, as some might say, an obsession. With the ethics scandal tsunami of the early 2000s, beginning with Enron, we witnessed the birth and accelerated maturation of the "ethics industry."[1] The Enron scandal is considered to be the most notorious in American history as it involved massive misrepresentations of earnings, the creation of a fraudulent energy crisis, and embezzlement.

The Enron collapse ushered in an avalanche of ethics scandals that brought down several other companies, including the accounting firm Arthur Andersen and the telecom company WorldCom. The magnitude of CEO greed and contempt for the law seemed unprecedented. And, it wasn't until the Wall Street financial crisis beginning in 2008 that the country realized that the difficulties with corporate ethics had not been fixed.

The Wall Street financial crisis and scandals, commencing in 2008, ushered in a new set of corporate characters, and it has been mostly companies and not CEOs or CFOs accused of questionable dealings.

Occurring at about the same time as the Wall Street financial scandals was the exposure of Bernard L. Madoff's infamous Ponzi scheme. The world economy has improved since the Wall Street financial scandals, but it has continued to be difficult for trust in business to be restored. With each passing day, it seems, some new business ethics scandal hits the news. Some are more serious than others. But in recent years, companies such as Wells Fargo with its fake accounts scandal, Volkswagen with its emissions scandal, Equifax with its inadequate security leading to hacker theft of millions, Theranos and the health-care start-up selling blood tests that did not work, and Boeing with its flawed

MAX pilot software leading to two airline crashes, and many others, have assured us that business ethics trials deserve their front-page status and that businesses still have much to do to restore the public's trust in them.

What the scandals of the past couple of decades have revealed is that the issue of business ethics has both macro and micro effects. At the macro level, the entire business system has been polluted and called into question. This is the level of capitalism and Big Business, as an institution, maintaining its legitimacy in a complex world. At the micro level, individual companies, managers, and employees still face the continuing onslaught of ethics challenges that occur regularly. Using a managerial perspective, business ethics education is more focused on this latter category of ethics challenges. The broad environment, which deals with business and society relationships, however, continues to be a confounding backdrop against which these daily challenges occur. This has been complicated by the implications of the COVID-19 pandemic, the effects of which may be felt for years.

Figure 5-1 summarizes some of the major business ethics scandals that have occurred in recent years. The effects of these continue to the present day. Many of these companies and executives have claimed their innocence, and allegations and trials are at various stages of completion.

The public's view of business ethics has never been very high. Some observers have claimed that business ethics is essentially a contradiction in terms, an oxymoron, and sometimes suspect that there is only a fine line between a business executive and a crook. Each of us as consumers, employees, or citizens can easily recall some problem that occurred in our everyday lives that involved suspected unethical behavior on the part of businesses. Over many years now, public opinion polls have revealed the public's deep concerns about the honesty and ethical standards of

Figure 5-1 Major Business Ethics Scandals

Companies Implicated	Legal/Ethical Charges and Accusations
Airbus of Europe	Bribed to secure contracts around world
Boeing	Flawed software leading to two major airline crashes
Purdue Pharma	Felonies selling OxyContin; kickbacks and fraud
Theranos	Fraud and falsification of blood testing machinery
Facebook	Accused of revenue approaches resulting in privacy lapses
Credit Suisse	Execs turned blind eye to banker's wrongdoing; failing to prevent money laundering
Houston Astros	Devised a sign-stealing scheme for decoding opposing catcher's signs
Wells Fargo	Sales employees pressured to create fake customer accounts
Volkswagen	Emissions scandal; illegal pollution control defeat-devices installed on cars
Wirecard	Inflated company's results by booking fake income
Takata	Faulty airbags leading to consumer deaths/recalls
Pilgrim's Pride Corporation	Indicted for fixing price of chickens sold to restaurants and grocery stores
Peanut Corporation of America	Deadly salmonella outbreak leading to deaths; fraud

business. In their 2020 poll, for example, Gallup found that only 17 percent of the public rated the ethics of business executives very high or high.[2]

In the third decade of the 2000s, it appears that society is clamoring for a renewed emphasis on values, morals, and ethics, and the business ethics discussions during this period reflect an ongoing societal concern. Whether the business community will be able to close the trust gap and ratchet up its reputation to a higher plateau remains to be seen. One thing is certain: There is a continuing interest in business ethics, and the proliferation of business ethics courses, blogs, and tweets, along with the revitalized interest on the part of the business community, paints an encouraging picture for the "ethics industry" of the future.

Sometimes it is difficult to tell whether business ethics have really deteriorated or if the media, including social media, are doing a more thorough job of reporting on ethics violations. There is no doubt that the media are reporting

ethical problems more frequently and fervently. Spurred on by the continuing supply of scandals, the media have found business ethics and, indeed, ethics questions among all institutions to be subjects of mounting and sustaining interest.

As maintained in Chapter 1, society is always changing. Due to affluence, education, awareness, and other factors, society is not just changing but raising its expectations of business's integrity and ethical performance. Many business managers subscribe to this belief—that it is society that is changing, not just them.

Figure 5-2 illustrates one way of looking at the ethical problem in business today compared to earlier periods. It depicts the growing disconnect between society's expectations of business ethics and ethics in practice. Note in the figure that actual business ethics is assumed to be slightly improving but not at the same pace as public expectations are rising. In this analysis, the magnitude of the current ethics problem is seen partially to be a function of rising

Figure 5-2 Business Ethics Today versus Earlier Periods

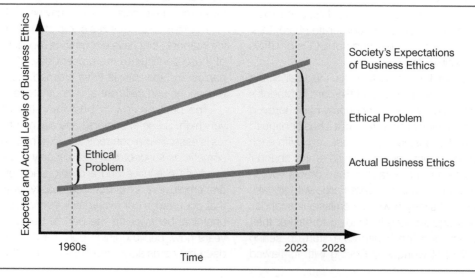

Figure 5-3 Examples of Ethical Issues Businesses Face Today

Stakeholder Group	Examples of Ethical Issues
Customers	Product safety/healthfulness Advertising/marketing honestly Packaging fairly/accurately Labeling accurately/completely Pricing fairly relative to quality Protecting consumer privacy
Employees	Fair compensation practices Fair day's work and pay; living wage Compliance with employment laws Avoidance of employment discrimination Safe working conditions Avoiding employee theft/embezzlement Protecting employees' privacy Dealing with distracted employees
Community/Environment	Environmental protection/sustainability Adherence to legal mandates Good corporate citizenship Philanthropy/supporting causes Adapting to foreign cultures Avoidance of bribery
Shareholders	Protecting shareholders' interests Fair compensation for executives Quality boards of directors Protection of company assets Fair returns on investments Communicating accurately Transparency

societal expectations about business behavior compared with smaller increases, declines, or stability in actual business ethics. It is difficult to accurately say whether business ethics are definitely getting better, worse, or staying the same, but perceptions and expectations are significantly driving businesses' reputations.

Not all business ethics issues turn into major scandals. But the range of business issues within which ethical problems continue to reside are numerous. To gain an appreciation of the kinds of issues that are important on a day-to-day basis under the rubric of business ethics, Figure 5-3 presents a list of business ethics issues that companies typically have to face with major stakeholder groups. Against this backdrop, we plan to begin our business ethics discussion in this chapter and the next three chapters. This chapter introduces essential business ethics concepts. Next, Chapter 6 extends the discussion by considering managerial and organizational ethics. Then Chapter 7 turns to the international sphere as ethical issues in the global arena are examined. Finally, Chapter 8 focuses on business technology issues and the digital enterprise.

5.1 Business Ethics: Some Basic Concepts

In Chapter 2, ethical responsibilities of business were alluded to in an introductory way. The contrast between ethics, economics, law, and philanthropy were discussed. To be sure,

we all have a general idea of what business ethics means, but now it is important to probe the topic more deeply. To understand business ethics, it is useful to comment on the relationship between ethics and morality.

The terms *ethics* and *morals* often are used interchangeably by commentators on business ethics. Both have to do with the standards of right or wrong, fairness, or justice. One distinction holds that **ethics** are standards of conduct, which originate from some external group or source such as society, in general, or business, in particular. Ethics in this view would be governed by society, professions, or organizations and may appear as principles, standards, or codes.

By contrast, **morals** are frequently seen as standards of conduct that originate within the individual. Morality, in this view, is often viewed as one's personal compass regarding right or wrong.[3] One complication is that some experts define these terms in the opposite manner to that expressed above. Another complication is that it is often difficult for persons to sort out the origins of their standards of behavior or conduct, that is, whether their standards are coming from outside the individual or from within the individual. For this reason, we will take the position that both ethics and morality are so similar to one another that we may use the terms interchangeably to refer to the study of fairness, justice, and behavior.

Business ethics, therefore, is concerned with the rightness, wrongness, fairness, or justice of actions, decisions, policies, and practices that take place within a business context or in the workplace. Business ethics is often seen as a set of principles or code of conduct by which activities are judged to be appropriate or questionable. Business ethics is a field of study in which the practices in organizations are analyzed to determine whether they are acceptable or not. Business ethics is also a field of study and topic that is of interest to the public, academics, students, and managers. Many stakeholders have much at stake in issues of business ethics.

5.1a Descriptive versus Normative Ethics

Two key branches of moral philosophy, or business ethics, are *descriptive* ethics and *normative* ethics. Each takes a different perspective that is important to understand.

Descriptive ethics is concerned with describing, characterizing, and studying the morality of people, an organization, a culture, or a society. It also compares and contrasts different moral codes, systems, practices, beliefs, and values.[4] In descriptive business ethics, the focus is on learning what *is* occurring in the realm of behavior, actions, decisions, policies, and practices of business firms, managers, or, perhaps, specific industries. Public opinion polls frequently give us glimpses into descriptive ethics—what people believe is going on as the basis of their perceptions and understandings.

Descriptive ethics focuses on "what is"—the prevailing set of ethical standards and practices in the business community, specific organizations, or on the part of specific managers. The major danger in using descriptive ethics is that some people may adopt the view that "if everyone is doing it," it must be acceptable. For example, if a survey reveals that 70 percent of employees are padding their expense accounts, this describes what they say *is* taking place, but it does not describe what *should* be taking place. Just because many employees are participating in this questionable activity does not make it an acceptable practice. This is why normative ethics is important.

Normative ethics, by contrast, is concerned with supplying and justifying a coherent moral system of thinking and judging. Normative ethics seeks to uncover, develop, and justify basic moral principles that are intended to guide behavior, actions, and decisions.[5] Normative business ethics, therefore, seeks to propose some principle or principles for distinguishing what is ethical from what is unethical in the business context. It deals more with "what ought to be" or "what should be" in terms of business practices. Normative ethics is concerned with establishing norms or standards by which business practices might be guided or judged.

Normative business ethics might be based on moral common sense (be fair, honest, truthful), or it might require critical thinking and the pursuit of different types of ethical analysis (interest based, rights based, duty based, virtue based).[6] In our study of business ethics, we need to be ever mindful of this distinction between descriptive and normative perspectives. It is tempting to observe the prevalence of a particular practice in business (e.g., discrimination or deceptive marketing) and conclude that because so many are *doing it* (descriptive ethics), it must be acceptable behavior. Normative ethics would insist that a practice be justified on the basis of some ethical principle, argument, philosophy, or rationale before being considered acceptable. Normative ethics demands a more meaningful moral anchor than just "everyone is doing it." Normative ethics is our primary concern in this book.

5.1b The Conventional Approach to Business Ethics

In this chapter and the next, we will present three approaches to business ethics: the **conventional approach** (Chapter 5), the **principles approach** (Chapter 6), and the **ethical tests approach** (Chapter 6). The conventional approach to business ethics, discussed in this chapter, is to compare a decision, practice, or policy being used in practice with prevailing norms of acceptability in society, and then trying to decide whether it is ethical or not. We call this the conventional approach because it is thought that this is the way conventional or general society thinks. The conventional approach relies on the use of common sense and a widely held sense of what is ethical. The major challenge in this approach is answering the questions "*Whose* ethical norms do we use?" in making the ethical judgment and "What ethical norms are *prevailing*?" This approach may be depicted by highlighting the major variables to be compared with one another:

Decisions, Behaviors, or Practices ↔ Prevailing Norms of Acceptability

There is considerable room for variability on both of these questions. With respect to whose/which norms should be used as the basis for ethical judgments, the conventional approach would consider as legitimate those norms emanating from a variety of sources—family, friends, religious beliefs, the local community, one's employer, law, the profession, and so on. This approach might also employ what is in one's own judgment or best self-interest as a guideline. If one was deciding whether to deduct a certain expense on one's taxes, for example, the conventional approach might cause one to look at what the law says; or, it may lead one to ask friends how they are handling the expense. The problem arises, of course, because different decisions may be made based on *whose* standard is used.

One's conscience, one's personal judgment, or one's self-interest would be seen by many to be a legitimate source of ethical norms in the conventional approach. Two classic *Frank & Ernest* comic strips poke fun at the use of one's conscience, however. In the first panel, a sign on the wall reads "Tonight's Lecture: Moral Philosophy." In the second panel, it shows Frank saying to Ernest, "I'd let my conscience be my guide, but I'm in enough trouble already!" In a second comic strip, Frank says to Ernest, while they are standing at a bar, "I always use my conscience as my guide. But, fortunately, it has a terrible sense of direction."

Figure 5-4 Sources of Ethical Norms Transmitted to Individuals

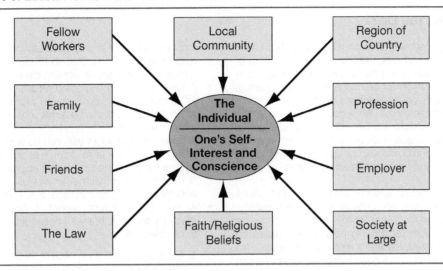

These comic strips reveal the often-limiting nature of using one's conscience.

Figure 5-4 illustrates some of the sources of ethical norms that may come to bear on the individual and that might be used in various circumstances, and over time, using the conventional approach. These different sources compete in their influence on what constitutes the "prevailing norms of acceptability" in society today.

In many circumstances, the conventional approach to ethics may be useful and applicable. What does a person do, however, if norms from one source conflict with norms from another source? Also, how can we be sure that societal norms are really appropriate or defensible? Society's culture today sends us many and often conflicting messages about what is appropriate ethical conduct. We get these messages from television, movies, books, music, politics, the Internet, social media, and other sources in the culture, and they do not always convey high ethical standards.

Popular TV shows such as *Survivor* and *The Amazing Race* have run episodes in which questionable ethics have been depicted and sometimes celebrated. On *Survivor*, the participants are forever creating alliances (agreements of trust) with others and then breaking them (violating trust) in the interest of winning the game. These same patterns are also seen on *The Amazing Race*.

Another example of the conflicting messages people get today from society occurs in the realm of sexual harassment in the workplace. On the one hand, today's television, movies, advertisements, and music are replete with sexual innuendo and the treatment of people as sex objects. This would suggest that such behavior is normal, acceptable, even desired. On the other hand, the law and the courts are stringently prohibiting sexual gestures or innuendo in the workplace. As we will see in Chapter 13, it does not take much sexual innuendo to constitute a "hostile work environment" and a sex discrimination charge under Title VII of the Civil Rights Act. In this example, we see a norm that is prevalent in culture and society clashing with a norm arising from employment law and business ethics. These examples serve to illustrate how views of ethics that may be seen as acceptable to many in conventional society would not be accepted in more rigorous forms of ethical analysis.

5.1c Making Ethical Judgments

Making business decisions that have an ethical dimension to them is something faced by managers and employees every day. When a decision is made about what is ethical (right, just, fair) using the conventional approach, there is room for variability on several counts (see Figure 5-5). Three key elements compose such a decision. First, we observe or participate in the *decision*, *action*, or *practice* that has taken place in the workplace setting. Second, we *compare the practice with prevailing norms of acceptability*—that is, society's or some other group's standard of what is acceptable or unacceptable. Third, we must recognize that *value judgments are being made* by someone as to what really occurred (the actual behavior) and what the prevailing norms of acceptability actually are.

This means that two different people could look at the same behavior or practice, compare it with their understandings of what the prevailing norms are, and reach different conclusions as to whether the behavior was ethical or not. In fact, this happens all the time and really is the basis of much ethical analysis that takes place. This judgment process becomes quite complex as perceptions of what is ethical inevitably lead to the difficult task of ranking different values against one another.

If we can put aside for a moment the fact that perceptual differences about an incident do exist, and the fact that we might differ among ourselves because of our personal values and philosophies of acceptable behavior, we are still left with the challenging task of determining society's prevailing norms of acceptability of business practice.

Ethics In Practice Case

What Would You Do?

A popular U.S. TV show is titled *What Would You Do?* Using actors and hidden cameras, the show presents a variety of scenarios of people acting out in situations, usually conflicts or poor treatment of someone, in a public setting. The show focuses on the reactions of the people watching what is being acted out, while not knowing that those engaged in the scenario are just actors. The reactions of those watching the scenarios are recorded and later the show's anchor, John Quiñones, comes out from hiding and confronts those who have reacted and asks them why they did what they did.

Some of the show's episodes have featured situations such as racial profiling occurring in a restaurant, parents publicly disapproving of their child's interracial dating, a pompous club promoter denying people entry based on how they are dressed, teenagers taunting a homeless man on the street, and a grocery bagger being insulted because of a disability.

If you observed the following scenarios, what would you do? Why would you react the way you did?

- Several young men and women are stealing items from an open house you are attending. You do not know the hosts very well but you know most of those who are stealing.
- A waitress is being hassled by her supervisor who is using verbal sexual innuendo at the restaurant where you are trying to enjoy your meal. You are a regular customer but you don't know the waitress because she is new.
- You observe a man accidentally dropping an expensive bottle of wine in a liquor store when the manager is not

looking. The man turns to those around him and denies responsibility; he even tries to blame a Latino maintenance employee who is working cleaning up the store.
- A transgender woman named Amelia works as a server at a restaurant and proceeds to inform a regular customer that she used to be a man named Bill. The customer begins to harass Amelia.
- A good friend of yours tells you he is planning to omit certain important facts from his résumé before he applies for the same job you are applying for. He says, "it's not important that they know I just lived off my parents for two years after college. Hey, I needed a break."
- At your place of employment, a customer paid too much for an order, but your boss told you not to call it to his attention.

1. What would you do in each of these situations if you observed them occurring?
2. Would your actions reflect "conventional" thinking about business ethics? Would you react differently than most people? Why?
3. What would be the primary source of ethical norms that would be at work in your thinking (see Figure 5-4)?

Sources: Wikipedia, "What would you do?" https://en.wikipedia .org/wiki/What_Would_You_Do%3F, accessed March 20, 2021; ABC News, "What would you do?" https://abcnews .go.com/WhatWouldYouDo, accessed March 20, 2021; A&E, "What would you do?" https://www.facebook.com /watch/?v=10153715709439799, accessed March 20, 2021.

As a whole, members of society generally agree at a high level of abstraction that certain practices are inappropriate. However, the consensus tends to disintegrate as we move from the general situation to specific details.

This may be illustrated with a business example. We might all agree with the general belief that "You should not steal someone else's property." As a general precept, we likely would have consensus on this. But, as we look at specific situations, our consensus may tend to disappear. Is it acceptable to take home from work such things as pencils, pens, paper clips, paper, staplers, jump drives, and calculators? Is it acceptable to use company-bought gasoline for

private use or to pad one's expense accounts? Is it acceptable to use company-owned computers for personal e-mail or Web browsing? What if everyone else is doing it?

What is important in these examples is that we are more likely to reach consensus in principle than in practice. Some people who would say these practices are not acceptable might privately engage in them and rationalize them. Furthermore, a person who would not think of shoplifting even the smallest item from a local store might take pencils and paper home from work on a regular basis. A comic strip depicting the "Born Loser" illustrates this point. In the first panel, the father admonishes his son Wilberforce as follows:

Figure 5-5 Elements Involved in Making Ethical Judgments

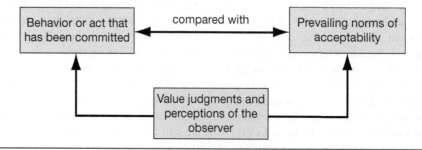

"You know how I feel about stealing. Now tomorrow I want you to return every one of those pencils to school." In the second panel, Father says to Wilberforce: "I'll bring you all the pencils you need from work." This is an example of the classic double standard, and it illustrates how actions may be perceived differently by the observer or the participant.

Thus, when using the conventional approach to business ethics, determinations of what is ethical and what is not require judgments to be made on at least three counts:

1. What is the *true nature* of the practice, behavior, or decision that occurred?
2. What are society's (or business's) *prevailing norms* of acceptability?
3. What *value judgments* are being made by someone about the practice or behavior, and what are that person's *perceptions* of applicable norms?

The human factor in the situation thus introduces the problem of perception, rationalization, and values and makes the decision process depicted in Figure 5-5 more complex than it first appears.

The conventional approach to business ethics can be valuable because we all need to be aware of and sensitive to the total culture and environment in which we exist. We need to be aware of how society regards ethical issues. It has limitations, however, and we need to be cognizant of these

as well. The most serious danger is that of falling into an **ethical relativism** where we pick and choose which source of norms we wish to apply on the basis of what will justify our current actions or maximize our freedom. A relevant comic strip illustrates this point. In a courtroom, while swearing in, one witness stated, "I swear to tell the truth … *as I see it.*"

In the next chapter, Chapter 6, we present a principles approach that is needed to augment the conventional approach to business ethics. The principles approach represents *normative ethics* and considers general guidelines to ethical decision making that managers should consider in practice. We also present an ethical tests approach, which is more of a practical approach to ethical decision making.

5.1d Ethics and the Law

The issue of ethics as compared to the law arises often in discussions of business ethics. In Chapter 2, we said that ethical behavior is typically thought to reside *above* behavior required by the law. This is the generally accepted view of ethics. We should make it clear, however, that in many respects the law and ethics overlap and are intertwined. To appreciate this, it is important to recognize that the law embodies notions of ethics. That is, the law may be seen as

Ethics In Practice Case

Little White Lies

Little white lies seem harmless, but they represent deceptions that can adversely affect others as well as ourselves. According to one study, most people tell two to four lies daily. In other words, lying is fairly common. Telling little white lies in the workplace can have serious consequences for employees, employers, and other stakeholders. Telling little lies outside of work can also be problematic.

What are some of the reasons why employees tell little white lies? Once people get inside organizations, the little white lies are often easy to justify or rationalize. Lying to get ahead is common, as is lying to get a raise or promotion. Taking credit for someone else's work is also not uncommon. Covering up one's mistakes is another motive for a little white lie. Telling a little white lie to avoid hurting someone's feelings seems logical and justified.

Some people lie to achieve a better work-life balance, for example, when they claim to be working when they are actually taking time off. This is not uncommon, particularly when working from home. During the recent pandemic, the number of rounds played on golf courses increased significantly, raising questions about whether employees who were supposed to be working from home were darting out for four hours of golf, with their smartphones in hand in case someone called.

Telling little white lies (exaggerations? deceptions?) on job applications is also commonplace. Other little white lies are given when people are leaving a job. Why be honest about why you are leaving? Lying during exit interviews are one way this happens.

The following are some of the little white lies many of us are guilty of using:

"My phone died."
"I'm just five minutes away."
"Traffic was bad; that's why I'm late."
"I'm never on social media at work."
"Of course, I remember you!"
"I can't come in today, I'm sick."
"Oh well, everyone's doing it. What's the problem?"

1. How would you define a "little white lie"? How small does it need to be to be called "little"?
2. How might a little white lie by you be perceived as a very serious misgiving at work?
3. If a small lie is justified in your mind, can you just ignore it and move on?
4. What are the consequences or damages as a result of little white lies?

Sources: Tessa West, "The Lies We Tell at Work—and the Damage They Do." *The Wall Street Journal*, March 30, 2020, R12; Duke TIP, "Ethics and the Little White Lie," https://tip.duke.edu/programs/summer-studies/courses/ethics-and-little-white-lie, accessed March 11, 2021; Bob Larkin, "60 White Lies We Tell Every Day." March 27, 2019, https://bestlifeonline.com/white-lies/, accessed March 11, 2021.

a reflection of what society thinks are minimal standards of conduct and behavior.

Both law and ethics have to do with what is deemed appropriate or acceptable, but law reflects society's *codified* ethics. Therefore, if people break a law or violate a regulation, they also are probably behaving unethically. We should be open to the possibility, however, that in some rare cases the law may not be ethical, in which case standing up to the law might be the principled course of action. A case in point might have been when Rosa Parks, a black woman, stood up to the authorities and refused to move to the back of the bus because she thought this was racial discrimination. In retrospect, Parks was doing the principled thing, and civil rights history has borne this out.

In spite of the frequent intermixing of law and ethics, we continue to talk about desired ethical behavior as behavior that extends beyond what is required by law. The *spirit* of the law often extends beyond the *letter* of the law and often taps into the ethical dimension. Viewed from the standpoint of minimums, we would certainly say that obedience to the law is generally regarded to be a minimum standard of ethical behavior.

In addition, it should be noted that the law does not address all realms in which ethical questions might be raised. Thus, there are clear roles for both law and ethics to play.[7] In the realm of rapidly changing technological or social advances, for example, it is hard for lawmakers to keep laws and regulations up to date; therefore, ethics plays an important role in situations such as this. An example of this situation occurs in the case of drones. Drone technology and their recreational uses are way ahead of laws regulating and protecting the public's safety regarding them; therefore, we all depend on the good consciences of their users until laws are passed to help protect us. Marijuana is another case in point. It is still illegal at the federal level, but the state laws are changing at a dizzying pace. And, laws aside, employers have the authority to implement drug-free workplaces in some states.[8]

Research on illegal corporate behavior has been conducted for some time. Illegal corporate behavior comprises business practices that are in direct defiance of law or public policy. This research has focused on two dominant questions: (1) Why do firms behave illegally or what leads them to engage in illegal activities? (2) What are the consequences of behaving illegally?[9] We will not deal with these studies of lawbreaking in this discussion; however, we should acknowledge this body of studies and investigations as being relevant to our interest in business ethics because it represents a special case of business ethics (illegal behavior).

5.2 Ethics, Economics, and Law—A Venn Model

Following on our discussion of ethics versus law, it is important to note that in many business decisions, ethics,

economics, and the law all come into play. When we focus on ethics and ethical decision making, it is useful to consider these primary elements that come into tension while making ethical judgments. In Chapter 2, these were introduced as part of the four-part definition of corporate social responsibility, and they were depicted in the Pyramid of corporate social responsibility (CSR). When we discuss a firm's CSR, philanthropy commonly enters the discussion. This is because philanthropic initiatives are one of the primary ways many companies display their CSR in the community—through good and charitable works.

In ethical decision-making situations, however, we tend to set aside philanthropic expectations and focus on ethical expectations and, especially, those elements that primarily come into tension with ethics—economics (the quest for profits) and law (society's codified ethics). Thus, in most decision-making situations, ethics, economics, and law become the central variables that must be considered and balanced against each other in the quest to make wise and sensible decisions.

A firm's economic, legal, and ethical responsibilities may be depicted in a Venn diagram model illustrating how certain actions, decisions, practices, or policies fulfill one, two, or three of these responsibility categories. Figure 5-6 presents this Venn diagram model, illustrating the overlapping potential of these three responsibility categories.

In Area 1 of the diagram, where the decision, action, or practice fulfils all three responsibilities, the management prescription is to "go for it." That is, the action is profitable, in compliance with the law, and represents ethical behavior. In Area 2a, the action under consideration is profitable and legal, but its ethical status may be uncertain. The guideline here is to "proceed cautiously." In these kinds of situations, the ethics of the action needs to be carefully considered. In Area 2b, the action is profitable and ethical, but perhaps the law does not clearly address the issue or is ambiguous. If it is ethical, there is a good chance it is also legal, but the guideline again is to "proceed cautiously."

In Area 3 of the diagram, the action is legal and ethical but not profitable. Therefore, the strategy here would be to avoid this action or "find ways to make it profitable." However, there may be a compelling case to take the action if it is legal and ethical and, thus, represents the right thing to do. Schwartz and Carroll have presented a three-domain approach to CSR that employs a Venn diagram format similar to that presented in Figure 5-6. They provide corporate examples to illustrate each section of the Venn diagram.[10]

By taking philanthropy out of the picture, the Venn model serves as a useful template for thinking about the more immediate expectations that society has on business in a situation in which the ethical dimension plays an important role. It illustrates clearly that many business decisions boil down to trade-offs between the influences of economics, law, and ethics.

Figure 5-6 A Venn Model for Ethical Decision Making

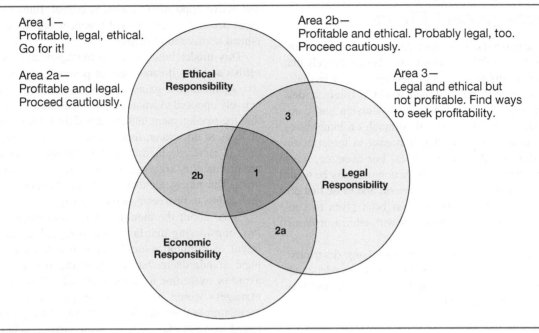

Area 1—
Profitable, legal, ethical.
Go for it!

Area 2a—
Profitable and legal.
Proceed cautiously.

Area 2b—
Profitable and ethical. Probably legal, too.
Proceed cautiously.

Area 3—
Legal and ethical but
not profitable. Find ways
to seek profitability.

Ethics In Practice Case

Is Résumé Inflation and Deception Acceptable?

According to Steven Levitt, author of *Freakonomics*, a small bit of inflation on one's résumé is universal. Levitt estimates that at least half the people engage in this deception to some degree. Typically, the small edits to one's résumé are done to disguise some unaccounted-for time between jobs. There may be nothing to hide except the fact that an unexplained time period looks suspicious. On other occasions, the deceptions have been more substantial, for example, claiming an academic degree one almost acquired but didn't: "Well, I was just two courses short!" It has also been said that based on one study, the average American tells two to four lies a day, often at work. A survey of 2,500 hiring managers by CareerBuilder found that 30 percent of them find false or misleading information on applicants' résumés.

A résumé controversy with significant consequences occurred when the then-Yahoo CEO, Scott Thompson, was questioned about a statement on his company's website, which reported that he had a degree in computer science. A dissident shareholder went public with the revelation that Thompson couldn't have a degree in computer science because the small college he graduated from didn't have a computer science *major* until *after* he graduated. The company's regulatory filing indicated that Thompson had a degree in accounting and computer science. Thompson claimed the website information was an inadvertent error without providing more information. According to his college, Thompson graduated with a bachelor's of science degree in business administration.

Days after this information came out, a person close to Yahoo's board reported that in absence of information

that Thompson intentionally misled, the company probably would not force him out, indicating that his importance as CEO to the company was more important than whether he had a computer science degree or not. In spite of this, CEO Scott Thompson resigned his position soon thereafter amid the controversy over his résumé discrepancy.

1. In light of the prevalence of these practices, is résumé inflation and deception acceptable? Is it okay "up to a point" as long as the distortion doesn't get too big? Is a small amount of puffery on one's résumé just expected as part of the game of getting a job and getting ahead? What would the conventional approach to business ethics say about this?
2. Some small schools don't have official majors but people sometimes claim them anyway because they took several courses in a specialized area. Is this an acceptable practice?
3. If you had been on Yahoo's board, would you have supported keeping Thompson?
4. Why do you suppose Thompson resigned?

Sources: Steven Levitt, *Freakonomics*, 2005; David Wescott, "The Truth Won't Set You Free," *Bloomberg Business Week*, February 4–10, 2013; "Imaginary Friends," *Bloomberg Businessweek*, January 21–27, 2013, 68; Amir Efrati and J. S. Lublin, "Résumé Trips Up Yahoo's Chief," *Wall Street Journal*, May 5–6, 2012, A1, A12; Peter Yang, "The Most Outrageous Resume Lies Employers Have Seen," March 19, 2019, https://www.cnbc.com/2019/03/19/the-most-outrageous-resume-lies-and-4-secret-tactics-hiring-managers-use-to-catch-a-liar.html, accessed March 12, 2021.

5.3 Three Models of Management Ethics

In striving to understand the basic concepts of business ethics, it is useful to think in terms of key ethical models that might describe different types of management or business ethics found in the organizational world.[11] These models provide some useful base points for discussion and comparison. The media have focused so much on immoral or unethical business behavior that it is easy to forget about the possibility of other ethical types. For example, scant attention has been given to the distinction that may be made between those activities that are *immoral* and those that are *amoral*. Similarly, little attention has been given to contrasting these two forms of behavior with ethical or *moral* management.

Believing that there is value in discussing descriptive models, or frameworks, for purposes of clearer understanding, here we describe, compare, and contrast three models or types of ethical management:

- Immoral management
- Moral management
- Amoral management

A major goal in this section is to develop a clearer understanding of the range of management postures in which ethics or morality is a defining characteristic. By seeing these approaches come to life through description and example, prospective managers will be in an improved position to assess their own ethical approaches and those of other organizational members (supervisors, subordinates, and peers). Another important objective is to identify more completely the amoral management model, which often is overlooked in the everyday rush to classify things as good or bad, moral or immoral. In a later section, we discuss the **elements of moral judgment** that must be developed if the transition to moral management is to succeed. A more detailed development of each management model is valuable in coming to understand the range of ethics that leaders may intentionally or unintentionally display. The two extremes will be considered first—immoral and moral management—followed by amoral management.

5.3a Immoral Management

Using *immoral* and *unethical* as synonyms, **immoral management** is defined as an approach that is devoid of ethical principles or precepts and at the same time implies a positive and active opposition to what is ethical. Immoral management decisions, actions, and practices are discordant with ethical norms and principles.

This model holds that the management's motives are selfish and that it cares only or primarily about its own or its organization's gains. If the management's activity is actively opposed to what is regarded as ethical, this suggests that the management understands right from wrong and yet chooses to do wrong; thus, its motives are deemed greedy or self-centered. In this model, the management's goals are profitability and organizational success at virtually any price. The management does not care about other stakeholders' claims to be treated fairly or justly.

What about the management's orientation toward the law, considering that law is often regarded as an embodiment of minimal ethics? Immoral management regards legal standards as barriers that the management must avoid or overcome to accomplish what it wants. Immoral managers would just as soon engage in illegal activity as in immoral or unethical activity. This point is illustrated in a popular *Dilbert* comic strip. Dogbert, the VP of Marketing, announces at a meeting: "It's my job to spray paint the road kill." In panel 2, he says: "I'll use a process the experts call 'dishonesty.'" In panel 3, Dilbert concludes: "My motto is 'If it isn't immoral, it probably won't work.'"[12]

Operating Strategy. The operating strategy of immoral management is focused on exploiting opportunities for corporate or personal gain. An active opposition to what is moral would suggest that managers cut corners anywhere and everywhere it appears useful. Thus, the key operating question guiding immoral management is, "Can we make money with this action, decision, or behavior, *regardless of what it takes*?" Implicit in this question is that nothing else matters, at least not very much. A business ethics course probably would not help them. Figure 5-7 summarizes some of the major characteristics of immoral managers.

Illustrative Cases. Examples of immoral management abound. The Enron scandal is one that is illustrative and enduring. It goes to show how immoral management is often lasting and impossible to come back from.

Enron Few business scandals stand out as clearly as a classic example of immoral management as much as that of

---

Figure 5-7 Characteristics of Immoral Managers

- These managers intentionally do wrong.
- These managers are *self-centered* and *self-absorbed*.
- They care only about themselves or the organization's profits or success.
- They actively oppose what is right, fair, or just.
- They *exhibit no concern* for stakeholders.
- These are the "bad guys."
- An ethics course probably would not help them.

Enron Corporation. The two major players in the Enron scandal were CEO Jeffrey Skilling and president Ken Lay, now convicted felons. Though Enron imploded in 2001, it was not until 2006 that Skilling and Lay were brought to justice and convicted.[13] Ken Lay, founder and CEO of Enron, died on July 5, 2006, before he had a chance to serve his prison sentence that would have taken him to the end of his life.[14]

Lay and Skilling were both convicted of securities fraud and conspiracy to inflate profits, along with a number of other charges. They used off-the-books partnerships to disguise Enron's debts, and then they lied to investors and employees about the company's disastrous financial situation while selling their own company shares.[15] In addition, Enron traders manipulated California's energy market to create phony shortages. This forced the state to borrow billions to pay off artificially inflated power bills. Voters in California were so fearful of brownouts, skyrocketing power bills, and rising state debt that they recalled Gov. Gray Davis and replaced him with Arnold Schwarzenegger.[16]

In 2013, Skilling, though in prison, was still trying to convince the courts that he was not given a fair trial and that his conviction should be overturned.[17] In 2016, Enron CFO Andy Fastow finished his prison sentence and quietly made amends. Lay, Skilling, and Fastow were clearly immoral managers. Volkswagen's cheating on emissions testing and Wells Fargo's creation of fake consumer accounts would also be cases of immoral management.

Everyday Questionable Practices In a "Deloitte & Touche USA Ethics & Workplace" survey, respondents identified a number of everyday questionable behaviors observed in the workplace that they thought were unacceptable. This list reveals commonplace practices that would illustrate the model of immoral management:[18]

- Stealing cash from a cash box at work
- Cheating on expense reports
- Lying on time sheets about hours worked
- Coming into work hung over
- Telling a demeaning joke (e.g., racist)
- Taking office supplies for personal use

In this same Deloitte & Touche survey, respondents provided what they considered to be other unethical behaviors.[19] These practices also would be characterized as immoral management:

- Showing preferential treatment toward certain employees
- Taking credit for another person's accomplishments
- Rewarding employees who display wrong behaviors
- Bullying a fellow employee (e.g., verbally, sexually, racially)

All of these are examples of immoral management wherein executives' decisions or actions were self-centered, actively opposed to what is right, focused on achieving organizational success at whatever the cost, and cutting corners where it was useful. These decisions were made without regard to the possible consequences of such concerns as honesty or fairness to others. What is apparent from the survey findings is that immoral management can occur on an everyday basis and does not need to be in the league of the mega scandals such as Enron or Wells Fargo to be unacceptable behavior.

Spotlight on Sustainability

Ray Anderson's Conversion Experience

Many managers have a conversion experience before they become moral managers. In other words, they had to transition from, probably, an amoral condition to a moral style. Often this comes as a result of an epiphany, a sudden realization in understanding what they experience. A prominent example is that of Ray Anderson, former CEO of Interface Carpet, who had been ranked as one of the leading sustainable CEOs. Anderson had a special moment occur when he was reading Paul Hawken's *Ecology of Commerce* in which he came to the conclusion that he, personally, was an environmental villain.

"It was an epiphanic spear in my heart, a life-changing moment; a new definition of success flooded my mind," he told the U.K.'s *Guardian* newspaper about the revelation. He went on to report: "I realized I was a plunderer and it was not a legacy I wanted to leave behind. I wept."

Anderson then made it his new mission to change that legacy and proceeded to, as the *Guardian* puts it, "turn the company into a champion of environmental sustainability." By taking this courageous step, Anderson played a leadership role in getting many other companies into the conversation about sustainability. Without his ethical leadership, it is questionable when or if this would have occurred.

Anderson was a sought-after international speaker who gave nearly 100 talks each year to audiences hungry for a message about the company that was proving the business model for sustainability works. One of his most important talks was a TED Talk titled "The Business Logic of Sustainability." Mr. Anderson died in 2011, but his memory serves as a constant reminder of the importance of sustainability and moral management.

Sources: "Ray's Legacy Is Alive at Georgia Tech," https://www.raycandersonfoundation.org/georgia-tech-center-for-business-strategies-for-sustainability, accessed March 12, 2021; Center for American Progress, "It's Easy Being Green: The Legacy of Ray Anderson," https://www.americanprogress.org/issues/green/news/2011/08/10/10190/its-easy-being-green-the-legacy-of-ray-anderson/, accessed March 20, 2021; Ted.com, "The Business Logic of Sustainability," https://www.ted.com/talks/ray_anderson_the_business_logic_of_sustainability?language=en, accessed March 12, 2021.

5.3b Moral Management

At the opposite extreme from immoral management is **moral management**. Moral management conforms to the highest standards of ethical behavior or professional standards of conduct. Although it is not always apparent what level of ethical standards prevail, moral management strives to be highly ethical in terms of its focus on exemplary ethical norms and professional standards of conduct, motives, goals, orientation toward the law, and general operating strategy.

In contrast to the selfish motives in immoral management, moral management aspires to succeed, but only within the confines of sound ethical precepts, that is, standards predicated on such norms as honesty, fairness, justice, respect for rights, and due process. Moral management's motives would be termed fair, balanced, or unselfish. Organizational goals continue to stress profitability, but only within the confines of legal compliance and responsiveness to ethical standards.

Moral management pursues its objectives of profitability, legality, and ethics as both required and desirable. Moral management would not pursue profits at the expense of the law and sound ethics. Indeed, the focus here would be not only on the letter of the law but on the spirit of the law as well. The law would be viewed as a minimal standard of ethical behavior because moral management strives to operate at a level above what the law mandates.

Operating Strategy. The operating strategy of moral management is to live by sound ethical standards, seeking out only those economic opportunities that the organization or management can pursue within the confines of ethical boundaries. The manager or organization assumes a leadership position when ethical dilemmas arise. The central question guiding moral management's actions, decisions, and practices is, "Will this action, decision, or practice be fair to all stakeholders involved as well as to the organization?"

Lynn Sharp Paine advocates an "integrity strategy" that closely resembles the moral management model.[20] The **integrity strategy** is characterized by a conception of ethics as the driving force of an organization. Ethical values shape management's search for opportunities, the design of organizational systems, and the decision-making process.

Ethical values in the integrity strategy provide a common frame of reference and serve to unify different functions, lines of business, and employee groups. Organizational ethics, in this view, helps to define what an organization is and what it stands for.

Habits of Moral Leaders Closely related to moral management is the topic of moral leadership. Carroll has set forth what he refers to as the "Seven Habits of Highly Moral Leaders."[21] Adapting the language used by Stephen Covey in his bestselling book *The Seven Habits of Highly Effective People*,[22] these qualities would need to be so common in the leader's approach that they become habitual as a leadership approach. The seven habits of highly moral leaders are as follows:

1. They have a passion to do right.
2. They are morally proactive.
3. They consider all stakeholders.
4. They have a strong ethical character.
5. They have an obsession with fairness.
6. They undertake principled decision making.
7. They integrate ethics wisdom with management wisdom.[23]

Figure 5-8 summarizes the important characteristics of moral managers.

Illustrative Cases. Two cases of moral management illustrate how this model of management might be played out in actual practice.

CVS Health CVS Caremark, the giant retail pharmacy chain, made a bold strategic decision when it decided to discontinue selling tobacco products, foregoing around $2 billion in annual sales. CVS has 7,600 stores in the United States and also is striving to create more in-store health clinics. After its purge of tobacco products, the company renamed itself CVS Health.[24] The company indicated that some customers were not happy with the decision but they thought it was the right decision to make. The company also decided it would not sell e-cigarettes because those, too, would be inconsistent with their new store model. The company claimed that one of the primary reasons it was dropping tobacco sales was because it really does care about the

Figure 5-8 Characteristics of Moral Managers

- These managers conform to a *high level of ethical or right behavior* (moral rectitude).
- They conform to a high level of personal and professional *standards*.
- *Ethical leadership* is commonplace—they search out where people may be hurt.
- Their goal is to succeed but only within the confines of *sound ethical precepts* (honesty, fairness, due process).
- *High integrity* is displayed in *thinking, speaking*, and *doing*.
- These managers embrace the letter and *spirit* of the law. Law is seen as a *minimal* ethical level. They prefer to operate *above* legal mandates.
- They possess an acute *moral sense* and *moral maturity*.
- Moral managers are the "good guys."

health and well-being of its customers and the public.[25] The company apparently wanted to become more of a health-care company, and they thought selling tobacco products was not consistent with that mission.

In supporting CVS's decision, Dr. Ronald Depinho of the Anderson Cancer Center applauded the company for making the decision. Dr. Depinho said that CVS was sending a strong message to other retailers that tobacco is a dangerous product and that it "extracts a very significant social and economic toll on society that is responsible for about 20 percent of deaths in the United States and about 30 percent of cancer deaths." He continued, "They have placed people before profits."[26]

Merck Another well-known case of moral management, that has become a classic, occurred when Merck & Co., the pharmaceutical firm, invested millions of dollars to develop a drug for treating "river blindness," a Third World disease that was affecting almost 18 million people. Seeing that no government or aid organization was agreeing to buy the drug, Merck pledged to supply the drug for free forever. Merck's recognition that no effective mechanism existed to distribute the drug led to its decision to go far beyond industry practice and organize a committee to oversee the drug's distribution.[27]

It should be emphasized that not all organizations now engaging in moral management have done so all along. These companies sometimes arrived at this posture after years or decades of rising consumer expectations, increased government regulations, lawsuits, and pressure from social and consumer activists. By the same token, some moral management companies may slip from this status due to actions or practices taken. One of the most puzzling examples is that of the Volkswagen scandal. For years VW had been building its reputation as a socially responsible company; then, out of the blue, we learn about its emissions scandal wherein its actions were wholly inconsistent with the image and reputation it had spent years developing.

We must think of moral management, therefore, as a desirable posture that in many instances has evolved over periods of several years. If we hold management to an idealistic, 100 percent historical moral purity test, no management or company will meet the standard. Rather, we should consider moral those managements that now see the enlightened self-interest of responding in accordance with the moral management model rather than alternatives, and are able to sustain this approach.

5.3c Amoral Management

Amoral management is not just a middle position on a continuum between immoral and moral management. Conceptually it has been positioned between the other two, but it is different in nature and kind from both. Being amoral means being unaware or indifferent to questions of right or wrong.[28] Here we distinguish between two kinds of amoral management: **intentional amoral management** and **unintentional amoral management**.

Intentional Amoral Management. Intentionally amoral managers do not factor ethical considerations into their decisions, actions, and practices because they believe business activity resides outside the sphere to which moral judgments apply. They simply think that different rules apply in business than in other realms of life. Intentionally amoral managers are in a distinct minority today. At one time, however, as managers first began to think about reconciling business practices with sound ethics, some managers adopted this stance. A few intentionally amoral managers are still around, but they are a vanishing breed in today's ethically conscious world.

Unintentional Amoral Management. Like intentionally amoral managers, unintentionally amoral managers do not think about business activity in ethical terms, but for different reasons. These managers are simply casual about, careless about, or indifferent to the fact that their decisions and actions may have negative or deleterious effects on others. These managers lack ethical perception and moral awareness. They have no "moral sense." That is, they blithely go through their organizational lives not thinking that what they are doing has an ethical dimension or facet. These managers are generally thought to be well intentioned but are either too insensitive or too self-absorbed to consider the effects of their decisions and actions on others. These managers normally think of themselves as ethical managers, as do most managers, but they are frequently overlooking these unintentional, subconscious, or unconscious aspects. As it turns out, they are more amoral than moral.

Unconscious Biases Sometimes amoral managers may be unconscious of hidden biases that prevent them from being objective. Researchers have found that many business people go through life deluded by the illusion of objectivity. Unconscious or implicit biases can run contrary to our consciously held, explicit beliefs.[29] Though most managers think they are ethical, sometimes even the most well-meaning person unwittingly allows unconscious thoughts and biases to influence what appear to be objective decisions. Four sources of unintentional, or unconscious, influences include implicit forms of prejudice, bias that favors one's own group, conflict of interest, and a tendency to overclaim credit.[30]

Unconscious biases were believed to be at work among accountants in some of the major accounting scandals in years past. Three *structural aspects* of accounting bias include ambiguity, attachment, and approval. When *ambiguity* exists, people tend to reach self-serving conclusions. For example, subjective interpretations of what constitutes a deductible expense may be made in a self-serving fashion. *Attachment* occurs when auditors, motivated to stay in their clients' good graces, approve things they might otherwise not approve. With respect to *approval*, external auditors may be reviewing the work of internal auditors, and self-serving biases may become even stronger when other people's biases are being endorsed or approved, especially if those judgments align with one's own biases.[31]

In addition, three aspects of human nature may amplify unconscious biases: familiarity, discounting, and escalation.

- *Familiarity* is noted when people may be more willing to harm strangers (anonymous investors) than individuals they know (clients).
- *Discounting* refers to the act of overlooking or minimizing decisions that may not have immediate consequences.
- *Escalation* occurs when an accountant or businessperson allows small judgments to accumulate and become large and then decides to cover up the unwitting mistakes through concealment. Thus, small indiscretions escalate into larger ones, and unconscious biases grow into conscious corruption.[32]

These unconscious biases have been exposed in research within the general realm of behavioral ethics, which will be explored in further detail in Chapter 6. For now, they are considered because they can be the source of unintentional amorality.

Amoral management pursues profitability as its goal but does not consciously or cognitively attend to moral issues that may be intertwined with that pursuit. If there is an ethical guide to amoral management, it would be the marketplace as constrained by law—the letter of the law, not the spirit. The amoral manager sees the law as the parameters within which business pursuits take place but is not particularly concerned with the spirit of the law.

Operating Strategy. The operating strategy of amoral management is to not bridle managers with excessive ethical structure but to permit free rein within the supposedly unspoken but understood tenets of the free enterprise system. Personal ethics may periodically or unintentionally enter into managerial decisions, but it does not preoccupy management. Furthermore, the impact of decisions on others is an afterthought, if it ever gets considered at all.

Amoral management represents a model of decision making in which the managers' ethical mental gears, to the extent that they are present, are stuck in neutral. The key management question guiding decision making is, "Can we make money with this action, decision, or behavior?"

Note that the question does not imply an active or implicit intent to be either moral or immoral.

Lynn Sharp Paine has articulated a "compliance strategy" that is consistent with the characteristics of amoral management. The **compliance strategy**, as contrasted with her integrity strategy discussed earlier, is more focused on acceptance of the law as its driving force. The compliance strategy is lawyer-driven and is oriented not toward ethics or integrity but more toward conformity with existing regulatory and criminal law. The compliance approach depends on deterrence as its underlying monitoring device. This approach envisions managers as rational maximizers of self-interest, responsive to the personal costs and benefits of their choices, yet indifferent to the moral legitimacy of those choices.[33] Figure 5-9 summarizes the major characteristics of amoral managers.

Illustrative Cases. Unintentionally amoral management seems to be built into many decision-making applications.

Examples When police departments first stipulated that recruits must be at least 5'9" tall and weigh at least 180 pounds, they were making an amoral decision, because they were not considering the detrimental exclusion this would impose on women and other ethnic groups who do not, on average, attain that height and weight. When companies decided to use scantily clad people to advertise autos, cologne, and other products, these companies were not thinking of the degrading and demeaning characterization of people that would result from what they thought was an ethically neutral decision. When Domino's initially decided to deliver pizza orders within 30 minutes or the food was free, they didn't think about how such a policy might induce their drivers to speed and, sometimes, cause auto accidents. This policy was later dropped.

Wells Fargo A definitive illustration of unintentionally amoral management involved the case of Wells Fargo Bank—giving the company the benefit of the doubt when managers say they were only trying to set high goals for their employees to render superior performance. Considered in isolation, the setting of high-performance goals seems to be an acceptable management practice.

Figure 5-9 Characteristics of Amoral Managers

Intentionally Amoral Managers
- These managers don't think ethics and business should "mix."
- Business and ethics are seen as existing in *separate* spheres. Ethics is seen as too "Sunday schoolish" and not applicable to business.
- These managers are a vanishing breed. There are few managers like this left in the world.

Unintentionally Amoral Managers
- These managers forget to consider the *ethical dimension* of decision making and practice.
- They just don't "*think ethically.*"
- They may lack *ethical perception* or awareness; they have no "ethics buds" that help them sense the ethical dimension.
- They may be well-intentioned but morally casual or careless; may be morally *unconscious*.
- Their ethical gears, if they exist, are in *neutral*.

However, what it led to at Wells Fargo was a culture in which the employees felt pressured to engage in cross-selling or pushing account holders to open new accounts even though they did not need them or were unaware they had been opened.[34] To respond to their supervisors' high-pressure sales tactics, many employees were led to opening multiple fraudulent accounts for customers even though they did not ask for or want them. The pressure apparently came from higher up in the bank. Some branch managers were told they would end up "working for McDonald's" if they missed their sales quotas. As it turned out, bank employees said they felt strongly pressured to open what turned out to be 2.1 million phony deposit accounts and credit cards for unwitting customers.[35] What made this case, at least early on, an example of unintentional amoral management is that the managers involved where not thinking ethically about what consequences might result from their setting high sales goals and then pressuring employees into reaching them or be punished. All the managers were concerned about were company profits or their own status in the bank.

Today, many companies do not think carefully about the effects employee rewards systems might have on customers and others. In addition to problems revealed at Wells Fargo, some research has shown that the effects of rewards and recognitions often backfire and work against employee motivation and productivity.[36]

Figure 5-10 provides a summary of the major characteristics of immoral, amoral, and moral management. It compares the three in terms of ethical norms, motives, goals, orientation toward the law, and operating strategy.

5.3d Two Hypotheses Regarding the Models of Management Morality

A thorough study has not been conducted to ascertain precisely what proportions of managers each model of morality represents in the total management population. However, two plausible hypotheses regarding the moral management models are worthy of consideration.

Population Hypothesis. The **population hypothesis** is that the distribution of the three models might approximate a normal curve within the management *population*, with the amoral group occupying the large middle part of the curve and the moral and immoral categories occupying the smaller tails of the curve. It is difficult to research this question. If you asked managers what they thought they were or what others thought they were, a self-serving bias would likely enter in and you would not get an accurate, unbiased answer. Another approach would be to observe management actions. This would be nearly impossible because it is not possible to observe all management actions for any sustained period. Therefore, the supposition remains a hypothesis based on

Figure 5-10 Three Models of Management Ethics

Organizational Characteristics		Immoral Management	Amoral Management	Moral Management
	Ethical Norms	Management decisions, actions, and behavior imply a positive and active opposition to what is moral (ethical). Decisions are discordant with accepted ethical principles. An active negation of what is moral is implied.	Management is neither moral nor immoral, but decisions lie outside the sphere to which moral judgments apply. Management activity is outside or beyond the moral order of a particular code. May imply a lack of ethical perception and moral awareness.	Management activity conforms to a standard of ethical, or right, behavior. Conforms to accepted professional standards of conduct. Ethical leadership is commonplace on the part of management.
	Motives	Selfish. Management cares only about its or the company's gains.	Well-intentioned but selfish in the sense that impact on others is not considered.	Good. Management wants to succeed but only within the confines of sound ethical precepts (fairness, justice, due process).
	Goals	Profitability and organizational success at any price.	Profitability. Other goals are not considered.	Profitability within the confines of legal obedience and ethical standards.
	Orientation Toward Law	Legal standards are barriers that management must ignore or overcome to accomplish what it wants.	Law is the ethical guide, preferably the letter of the law. The central question is what we can do legally.	Obedience toward letter and spirit of the law. Law is a minimal ethical behavior. Prefer to operate well above what law mandates.
	Strategy	Exploit opportunities for corporate gain. Cut corners when it appears useful.	Give managers free rein. Personal ethics may apply but only if managers choose. Respond to legal mandates if caught and required to do so.	Live by sound ethical standards. Assume leadership position when ethical dilemmas arise. Enlightened self-interest.

Source: Archie B. Carroll, "In Search of the Moral Manager," *Business Horizons* (March/April 1987), 8. Copyright © 1987 by the Foundation for the School of Business at Indiana University. Used with permission.

Figure 5-11 Three Models of Management Morality and Emphases on CSR

Models of Management Morality	Components of the CSR Definition			
	Economic Responsibility	Legal Responsibility	Ethical Responsibility	Philanthropic Responsibility
Immoral management	XXX	X		
Amoral management	XXX	XX	X	X
Moral management	XXX	XXX	XXX	XXX

Weighting code:
X = token consideration (appearances only)
XX = moderate consideration
XXX = significant consideration

one person's judgment of what is going on in the management population.

This proposed normal curve distribution is similar to behavioral economist Dan Ariely's belief that 1 percent of people would *never* steal, 1 percent would *always* try to steal, and 98 percent would be honest as long as they were not tempted. Ariely believes that most of us are 98-percenters. One of Ariely's students told him the story about a locksmith who helped him when he locked himself out of his house. Being amazed at how easily and quickly the locksmith was able to pick the lock, the locksmith told him that the locks were there to keep the honest people from stealing. The locks remove the temptation for most people.[37] It is uncertain whether the large middle group of amoral managers would cheat or not if tempted, but the normal curve distribution pattern is strikingly similar.

Individual Hypothesis. Equally disturbing as the belief that the amoral management style is common among the managerial population today is an alternative hypothesis, the **individual hypothesis**, which holds that within each *individual* manager, these three models may operate at various times and under various circumstances. That is, the average manager may be amoral most of the time but may slide into a moral or an immoral mode on occasion, based on a variety of impinging factors. Like the population hypothesis, this view cannot be empirically supported at this time, but it does provide an interesting perspective for managers to ponder. This perspective would be somewhat similar to the situational ethics argument that has been around for some time. Is the individual hypothesis more likely valid than the population hypothesis? Could it be that both may exist at the same time?

Amoral Management Is a Serious Organizational Problem. With the exception of the major ethics scandals witnessed in the past couple decades, it could be argued that the more insidious ethical problem in organizations today seems to be that group of managers who for one reason or another subscribe to or live out the amoral management ethic pattern. These are managers who are driven primarily by profitability or a bottom-line ethos, which regards economic success as the exclusive barometer of organizational and personal achievement. These amoral managers are not necessarily bad people, but they essentially see the competitive business world as ethically neutral. Until this group of managers moves toward the moral management ethic, we will continue to see businesses and other organizations criticized as they have been in the past.

To connect the three models of management morality with concepts introduced earlier, we show in Figure 5-11 how the components of corporate social responsibility (Chapter 2) would likely be viewed by managers using each of the three models of management morality.

5.4 Developing Moral Judgment

The characteristics of immoral, moral, and amoral management discussed in this chapter should provide some useful benchmarks for managerial self-analysis because self-analysis and introspection significantly help managers recognize the need to move from the immoral or amoral ethic to the moral ethic. To make moral management actionable, both immoral and amoral management must be discarded and the process of developing moral judgment begun.

As a manager, it is helpful to know something about how people, whether they are managers or employees, develop moral (or ethical) judgment. Perhaps if we knew more about this maturation process, we could better understand our own behavior and the behavior of those around us and those we manage. Further, we might be able to better design reward systems for encouraging ethical behavior if we knew more about how employees and others think and process issues about ethics. A good starting point is to appreciate what psychologists have to say about how we as individuals develop morally. The major research on this issue is **Kohlberg's levels of moral development**.[38] After this discussion, we consider other sources of a manager's values, especially those emanating from both societal sources and from within the organization itself. At the conclusion of this chapter, we will discuss further the elements involved in moral judgment and James Rest's stages of moral decision making that encompass moral judgment.

Figure 5-12 Kohlberg's Levels of Moral Development

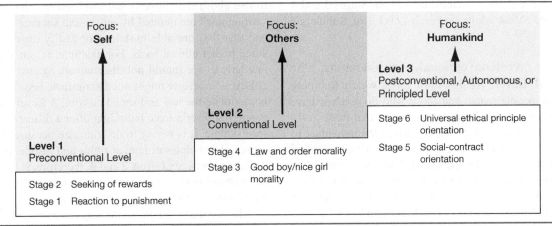

5.4a Levels of Moral Development

The psychologist Lawrence Kohlberg conducted extensive research into the topic of **moral development**. He concluded, on the basis of more than 20 years of research, that there is a general sequence of three levels (each with two stages) through which individuals progress in learning to think or develop morally. There is widespread academic and practical usage of his levels of moral development, and this suggests a general if not unanimous consensus that it is valuable. Figure 5-12 illustrates Kohlberg's three levels and six stages. There it can be seen that as one develops morally, the focus moves from the *self*, to *others*, and then to *humankind*. Understanding this progression is of great value in developing a basic foundation in business ethics and leadership.

Level 1: Preconventional Level. At the **preconventional level of moral development**, which is typically characteristic of how people behave as infants and children, the focus is mainly on the *self*. As infants start to grow, their main behavioral reactions are in response to punishments and rewards. Stage 1 is the *reaction-to-punishment stage*. If you want a child to do something (such as stay out of the street) at a very early age, scolding or disciplining often is needed. The child's orientation at this stage is toward the avoidance of pain.

As the youngster gets a bit older, rewards start to work. Stage 2 is the *seeking-of-rewards stage*. The youngster begins to see some connection between being "good" (i.e., doing what parents want the child to do) and some reward that may be forthcoming. The reward may be parental praise or something tangible, such as ice cream, extra computer screen time, or getting to use a parent's iPad. At this preconventional level, children do not completely understand the moral idea of "right" and "wrong" but rather learn to behave according to the consequences—punishments or rewards—that are likely to follow.

Though we normally associate the preconventional level with the moral development of children, many adults in organizations are significantly influenced by rewards and

punishments. Consequently, the preconventional level of motivation may be observed in adults as well as children and is relevant to a discussion of adult moral maturity. Like children, adults in responsible positions react to punishments (organizational sanctions) or seek rewards (approval). In fact, some adults get stuck at this level of moral development, and this is why rewards and punishments work.

Level 2: Conventional Level. As people mature, they learn that there are *others* whose ideas or welfare ought to be considered. Initially, these others include family and friends. At the **conventional level of moral development**, the individual learns the importance of conforming to the conventional norms of the group or society. This is the level at which social relationships form and become dominant.

The conventional level is composed of two stages. Stage 3 has been called the *"good boy/nice girl" morality stage*. The young person learns that there are some rewards (such as feelings of acceptance, trust, loyalty, or friendship) for living up to what is expected by family and peers, so the individual begins to conform to what is generally expected of a good child, sibling, friend, and so on.

Stage 4 is the *law-and-order morality stage*. Not only does the individual learn to respond to family, friends, the school, and the church, as in Stage 3, but also the individual now recognizes that there are certain norms in society (in school, in the theater, in stores, in the car, waiting in line) that are expected or needed if society is to function in an orderly fashion. Thus, the individual becomes socialized or acculturated into what being a good citizen means. These "law-and-order" rules for living include not only the actual laws (don't run a red light, don't walk until the "Walk" light comes on, don't text or talk while driving) but also other, less official norms (don't break into line, be sure to tip the server, mute your mobile phone in restaurants).

At Stage 4, people see that they are part of a larger social system and that to function in and be accepted by this social system requires a considerable degree of acceptance of and conformity to the norms and standards of society. Therefore, many organizational members are strongly influenced by society's conventions as manifested in both Stages 3 and 4 as described. Most adults do reach Level 2 of Kohlberg's levels.

Level 3: Postconventional, Autonomous, or Principled Level. At this third level, which Kohlberg argues few people reach, and those who do reach it have trouble staying there, the focus moves beyond those "others" who are of immediate importance to the individual to *humankind* as a whole. At the **postconventional level of moral development**, the individual develops a concept of ethics that is more mature than the conventionally articulated situation. Thus, it is sometimes called the level at which moral principles become self-accepted, not because they are held by society but because the individual now perceives and embraces them as "right."

Kohlberg's third level consists of two stages that differ by whether the individual can just follow rules established by society or others, or engage in the individual's moral reasoning. Stage 5 is the *social-contract orientation.* At this stage, right action is thought of in terms of general individual rights and standards that have been critically examined and agreed on by society as a whole. Social contracts have influence. There is a clear awareness of the relativism of personal values and a corresponding emphasis on fair processes for reaching consensus.

Stage 6 is the *universal-ethical-principle orientation.* Here, individuals use their thinking and consciences in accord with self-chosen ethical principles that are anticipated to be universal, comprehensive, and consistent. These universal principles (e.g., the Golden Rule, fairness, rights) might be focused on such ideals as justice, human rights, reciprocity, and social welfare. At this stage, individuals are motivated by a commitment to universal principles or guidelines for humankind.

Kohlberg suggests that at Level 3, individuals are able to rise above the conventional level where "rightness" and "wrongness" are defined by others and societal institutions and that they are able to defend or justify their actions on some higher ethical basis. For example, in our society the law tells us we should not discriminate against minorities. A Level 2 manager might not discriminate because to do so is to violate the law and social custom. A Level 3 manager would not discriminate but might offer a different reason—for example, it is wrong to discriminate because it violates universal principles of human rights and justice. Part of the difference between Levels 2 and 3, therefore, is traceable to the motivation for the course of action taken. The authenticity of one's motives is crucial at Level 3.

The discussion to this point may have suggested that we are at Level 1 as infants, at Level 2 as youths, and, finally, at Level 3 as adults. There is some approximate correspondence between chronological age and Levels 1 and 2, but the important point should be made that Kohlberg thinks many of us as adults never get beyond Level 2. The idea of getting to Level 3 as managers or employees is desirable because it would require us to think about people, products, and markets at a higher ethical level than that generally attained by conventional society. However, even if we never get there, Level 3 urges us to continually ask, "What ought to be?" The first two levels tell us a lot about moral development that should be useful to us as managers. There are not many people who consistently operate according to Level 3 principles. Sometimes a manager or employee may dip into Level 3 on a certain issue or for a certain period of time. Sustaining that level, however, is quite challenging.

If we frame the issue in terms of the question, "Why do managers and employees behave ethically?" we might infer conclusions from Kohlberg that look similar to those presented in Figure 5-13. These conclusions attempt to generalize about people's reactions to various factors.

Figure 5-13 Why Managers and Employees Behave Ethically

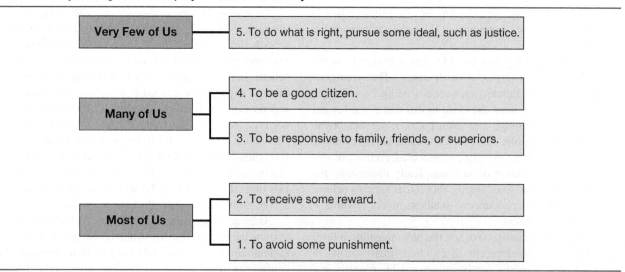

Ethics of Care as an Alternative to Kohlberg. One of the major criticisms of Kohlberg's research was set forth by psychologist Carol Gilligan. Gilligan argued that Kohlberg's conclusions may accurately depict the stages of moral development among men, whom he used as his research subjects, but that his findings are not generalizable to women.[39] According to Gilligan's view, men tend to deal with moral issues in terms that are impersonal, impartial, and abstract. Examples might include the principles of justice and rights that Kohlberg argues are relevant at the postconventional level. According to Gilligan, women, on the other hand, perceive themselves to be part of a network of relationships with family and friends and thus are more focused on *relationship maintenance* and *hurt avoidance* when they confront moral issues. For women, then, morality is often more a matter of caring and showing responsibility toward those involved in their relationships than in adhering to abstract or impersonal principles, such as justice. This alternative view of ethics has been called the **ethics of care**.

According to Gilligan, women move in and out of three moral levels.[40] At the first level, the *self* is the sole object of concern. At the second level, the chief desire is to *establish connections and participate* in social life. In other words, maintaining relationships or directing one's thoughts toward others becomes dominant. Gilligan says that this is the conventional perception of women. At the third level, women recognize their own needs and the *needs of others*—those with whom they have relationships. Gilligan goes on to say that women never settle completely at one level. As they attain moral maturity, they do more of their thinking and make more of their decisions at the third level. This level requires care for others as well as care for oneself. In this view, morality moves away from the legalistic, self-centered approach that some say characterizes traditional ethics.

The value of this research is the idea that moral development levels and stages do occur and that managers need to be aware of and sensitive to this in their approaches to dealing with people and ethics challenges in their organizations. Research on this topic is ongoing.

5.4b Different Sources of a Person's Values

In addition to considering the levels of moral development as an explanation of how and why people behave ethically, it is also useful to look at the different *sources of a manager's (employee's) values*. Ethics and values are intimately related. We referred earlier to ethics as the set of moral principles or values that drives behavior. Thus, the rightness or wrongness of behavior, sense of fairness, and sense of justice really turns out to be a manifestation of the ethical beliefs held by the individual. Values, on the other hand, are the individual's concepts of the relative worth, utility, or importance of certain ideas. Values reflect what the individual considers important in the larger scheme of things. One's values, therefore, shape one's ethics. They are closely interrelated. Because this is so, it is important to understand the many different value-shaping forces that influence employees and managers.

The increasing pluralism of the society in which we live has exposed managers to a large number of values of many different kinds, and this has resulted in ethical diversity. One way to examine the sources of a manager's values is by considering both forces that originate from *outside the organization* to shape or influence the manager and those that emanate from *within the organization*. This is not as simply done as we would like because some sources are difficult to pinpoint. This discussion expands on and organizes some of the sources of ethical norms depicted earlier in Figure 5-4.

Sources External to the Organization: The Web of Values. The external sources of a person's values refer to those broad sociocultural values that have emerged in society over a long period of time. Although current events (scandals, fraud, deception, bribery) seem to affect these historic values by bringing specific ones into clearer focus at a given time, these values are rather enduring and change slowly. It has been stated that "every executive resides at the center of a web of values" and that there are five principal repositories of values influencing businesspeople. These five include religious, philosophical, cultural, legal, and professional values.[41] Each deserves brief consideration.

Religious Values. Religion and faith have long been a basic source of morality in most societies. Religion and morality are so intertwined that William Barclay related them for definitional purposes: "Ethics is the bit of religion that tells us how we ought to behave."[42] The biblical tradition of Judeo-Christian theology forms the core for much of what Western society believes today about the importance of work, the concept of fairness, and the dignity of the individual. Other religious traditions also inform management behavior and action.[43]

Philosophical Values. Philosophy and various philosophical systems are also external sources of the manager's values. Beginning with preachments of the ancient Greeks, philosophers have claimed to demonstrate that *reason* can provide us with principles or morals in the same way it gives us the principles of mathematics. John Locke argued that morals are mathematically demonstrable, although he never explained how.[44] Aristotle presented his Golden Rule and his doctrine of the mean, Kant presented his categorical imperative, Bentham argued for his pain and pleasure calculus, and modern-day existentialists have shown us the influence of various kinds of reasoning for ethical choice. Today, the strong influences of moral relativism and postmodernism have influenced some people's values.

Cultural Values. Culture is that broad synthesis of societal norms and values emanating from everyday living. Culture has also had an impact on the manager's and employees' thinking. Modern sources of culture include

Ethics In Practice Case

Are People More Ethical When Being "Watched"?

Most people would probably say they would be more honest if they were being watched. This is human nature, isn't it? A team of researchers at Newcastle University in the United Kingdom decided to test this proposition by creating an experiment.

The setting for the experiment was the often-used coffee station set up in a department break room where faculty and staff could help themselves to coffee, tea, or milk during the day and then place their payment for the refreshments in a jar or a box. The "honor system" was requested because there was no one at the station to monitor whether people actually paid or not. The department had been using an "honesty box" for people to place their money in for years.

The researchers decided to post the prices for the coffee, tea, and milk on a poster that featured a banner across the top that contained images that were alternated without announcement from week to week. The poster was placed above the coffee station. The alternating images included a set of eyes and a picture of flowers. The image of eyes was varied in their gender and position, but they were always situated so that they appeared to be looking directly at the person.

The research team collected the money each week and recorded how much had been placed in the box. The team calculated that, on average, the amount collected when the "eyes poster" was present was 2.76 times the amount collected when the flowers poster was there. The researchers concluded that the effect of being "watched" had the subconscious effect of improving people's honesty. The researchers were surprised at how large an effect resulted from being watched.

Later, the question was raised whether using "watching eyes" could curb dishonest behaviors in other settings.

The researchers hung signs with the watching eyes and a poster warning about bicycle thefts near some campus bike racks. After two years they calculated that the racks with signs above them experienced a 62 percent drop in bicycle theft. Unfortunately, they discovered that bike thefts increased in other places on campus where signs were not posted. Police in Nottingham, UK, used the technique and reported that they had a 40 percent decrease in small crimes such as shoplifting when they posted similar signs.

1. Do the results of these experiments surprise you? What ethical phenomena were at work here?
2. Evaluate the experiment using Kohlberg's levels of moral development. Does the experiment tend to support or refute Kohlberg's findings? Do you think it would make a difference whether the coffee drinkers were men or women? What would Gilligan say?
3. How could managers use the conclusions reached in this experiment?
4. Was it unethical for the research team to conduct this experiment without telling people it was going on?

Sources: "Big Brother Eyes Encourage Honesty," ABC Science, https://www.abc.net.au/science/articles/2006/06/28/1673749.htm, accessed March 15, 2021; Steve Conner, "Watchful Gaze That Can Keep You Honest," https://www.independent.co.uk/news/science/watchful-gaze-that-can-keep-you-honest-6096951.html, accessed March 15, 2021; Danny Lewis, "Putting Eyeballs on Billboards Might Stop Crime," Smithsonian Magazine, August 25, 2015, https://www.smithsonianmag.com/smart-news/putting-eyeballs-billboards-might-help-stop-crime-180956394/, accessed March 15, 2021.

music, movies, television, video games, social networking, and the Internet. The melting-pot culture of many countries today is a potpourri of norms, customs, and rules that defy summarization. In recent years, it has become difficult to summarize what messages the culture is sending people about ethics. In an influential book, Alan Wolfe's *Moral Freedom: The Search for Virtue in a World of Choice*, the author argues that in the United States and in many Western nations, the traditional values that our culture once looked upon with authority (churches, families, neighborhoods, civic leaders) have lost the ability to influence people as they once did.[45] Supporting this, Mark Smith, in his book *Secular Faith*, argues that culture now trumps religion and that today culture is influencing religion and philosophy so much more than it once did as a source of values.[46]

Legal Values. The legal system has been and continues to be one of the most powerful forces defining what is ethical and what is not for managers and employees. As stated earlier, the law represents the codification of what the society considers right and wrong or fair. Although we as members of society

do not completely agree with every law in existence, there often is more consensus for law than for ethics. Law, then, "mirrors the ideas of the entire society."[47] Law represents a minimum ethic of behavior but does not encompass all the ethical standards of behavior. In recent years, it has become an understatement to observe that we live in a litigious society. This trend toward suing someone to bring about justice has clearly had an impact on management decision making. Therefore, it is easy to see how laws and regulations are among the most influential drivers of business ethics.[48]

Professional Values. These include those values emanating from professional organizations and societies that represent various jobs and positions. As such, they presumably articulate the ethical consensus of the leaders of those professions. For example, the Public Relations Society of America has a code of ethics that public relations executives have imposed on themselves as their own guide to behavior. Though there is not a generally accepted code of conduct or ethics for general managers, in recent years The Oath Project has sought to establish enhanced professionalization of management by proposing and gaining signatories to a form of a "Hippocratic oath for business," which would help integrate professional conduct and social responsibility into the culture, core values, and day-to-day operations of corporations and academic institutions.[49]

In sum, several sources of values are external to the organization and they come to bear on the manager and employees and influence their ethics. In addition to those mentioned, people are influenced by family, friends, acquaintances, and social events and current events of the day as depicted earlier in Figure 5-4.

Sources Internal to the Organization. The external forces constitute the broad background or milieu against which a manager or an employee behaves or acts. There are, in addition, a number of more immediate factors that help to channel the individual's values and behavior. These values grow out of the specific organizational experience itself. These internal (within the organization) sources of a manager's values constitute more immediate and direct influences on one's actions and decisions.

When an individual goes to work for an organization, a *socialization process* takes place in which the individual comes to learn and adopt the predominant values of that organization. The individual learns rather quickly that to survive and to succeed, certain norms must be internalized, honored, and perpetuated. This is a process of learning and adapting to the organization's culture. These "internal" norms that are prevalent in business organizations include the following:

- Respect for the authority structure
- Loyalty to bosses and the organization
- Conformity to principles, practices, and traditions
- Performance counts above all else
- Results count above all else

Each of these norms may take on a major influence in people who subordinate their own standard of ethics to those of the organization. In fact, research suggests that these internal sources play a much more significant role in shaping business ethics than do the host of external sources we considered first. *Respect for the authority structure, loyalty, conformity, performance*, and *results* have been historically synonymous with survival and success in business. When these influences are operating together, they form a composite **bottom-line mentality** that is remarkably influential in its impact on individual and group behavior. These values form the central motif of organizational activity and direction.

The impact of the bottom-line mentality is explored further in Chapter 6 when we discuss the powerful influence leaders have over employees and peers. Only recently are some managers and organizations starting to respond to the "multiple bottom line" or "triple-bottom-line" perspectives introduced earlier. From the standpoint of ethics, sustainability, and stakeholder management, managers will increasingly need to think and practice beyond that which is dictated by the short-term obsession with quarterly earnings.

5.5 Elements of Moral Judgment

It is important to consider what it takes for moral or ethical judgment to develop. For growth in moral judgment to take place, it is necessary to appreciate the key elements involved in making moral judgments. This is a notion central to the transition from the amoral management position to the moral management position. Powers and Vogel have suggested that there are six major elements or capacities that are essential to making moral judgments: (1) moral imagination, (2) moral identification and ordering, (3) moral evaluation, (4) tolerance of moral disagreement and ambiguity, (5) integration of managerial and moral competence, and (6) a sense of moral obligation.[50] Each reveals an essential ingredient in developing moral judgment, which then forms the basis for managerial and organizational ethics to be examined in the next chapter.

5.5a Moral Imagination

Moral imagination refers to the ability to perceive that a web of competing economic relationships is, at the same time, a web of moral or ethical relationships. Business and ethics are not separate topics but occur side by side in organizations. Those with moral imagination are able to perceive more clearly the presence of ethical issues and develop creative ways for dealing with them. Developing moral imagination means not only becoming sensitive to ethical issues in business decision making but also developing the perspective of *searching out* subtle places where people are likely to be harmfully affected by adverse decision making or behaviors of managers.[51]

5.5b Moral Identification and Ordering

Moral identification and ordering refers to the ability to discern the relevance or nonrelevance of moral factors that are introduced into a decision-making situation. Are the moral issues actual or just rhetorical? The ability to see moral issues as issues that can be dealt with is at stake here. Once moral issues have been identified, they must be ranked, or ordered, just as economic or technological issues are prioritized during the decision-making process. A manager must not only develop this skill through experience but also finely hone it through repetition and the application of ethics principles.

5.5c Moral Evaluation

Once issues have been imagined, identified, and ordered, evaluations must be made. *Moral evaluation* is the practical, decision phase of moral judgment and entails essential skills, such as coherence and consistency, that have proved to be effective principles in other contexts. What managers need to do here is to understand the importance of clear principles, develop processes for weighing ethical factors, and develop the ability to identify what the likely moral as well as economic outcomes of a decision will be. The real challenge in moral evaluation is to integrate the concern for others into organizational goals, purposes, and legitimacy.

5.5d Tolerance of Moral Disagreement and Ambiguity

An objection that managers often have to ethics discussions is the amount of disagreement generated and the volume of ambiguity that must be tolerated. This must be accepted, however, because it is a natural part of ethics discussions. To be sure, managers need closure and precision in their decisions. But the situation is not always clear in moral discussions, just as it is in many traditional and more familiar decision contexts of managers, such as introducing a new product based on limited test marketing, choosing a new executive for a key position, deciding which of a number of excellent computer systems to install, or making a strategic decision based on instincts. The *tolerance of moral disagreement and ambiguity* includes the ability to hear, discuss, and be respectful toward other people's views.[52]

5.5e Integration of Managerial and Moral Competence

The *integration of managerial and moral competence* is a necessary capability to make ethical decisions in organizations. The scandals that major corporations face today did not occur independently of the companies' economic activities but were embedded in a series of decisions made at various points in time and culminated from those earlier decisions. Therefore, moral competence is an integral part of managerial competence. Managers are learning—some the hard way—that there is a significant corporate and, in many instances, personal price to pay for their amorality.

The amoral manager sees ethical decisions as isolated and independent of managerial decisions and competence, but the moral manager sees every evolving decision as one in which an ethical perspective must be integrated.

5.5f A Sense of Moral Obligation

The foundation for all the capacities we have discussed is a *sense of moral obligation*[53] and integrity. This wisdom is the key to the process but is the most difficult to acquire. Developing a sense of moral obligation requires the intuitive or learned understanding that moral threads—a concern for fairness, justice, and due process to people, groups, and communities—are woven into the fabric of managerial decision making and are the integral components that hold systems together.

The late Milton Friedman, our modern-day Adam Smith, even alluded to the importance of ethics when he stated that the purpose of business is "to make as much money as possible while conforming to the basic rules of society, both those embodied in the law and *those embodied in ethical custom.*"[54] The moral manager develops a sense of moral obligation and integrity that is the glue that holds together the decision-making process in which human welfare is inevitably at stake. Indeed, the sense of moral obligation is what holds society and the business system together as an ethical, sustainable enterprise.

Figure 5-14 summarizes the six elements of moral judgment as they might be perceived by amoral and moral managers. The contrast between the two perspectives should be helpful in understanding each element of moral judgment.

Figure 5-14 Elements of Moral Judgment in Amoral and Moral Managers

Amoral Managers	Moral Managers
Moral Imagination	
See a web of competing economic claims as just that and nothing more.	Perceive that a web of competing economic claims is simultaneously a web of moral relationships.
Are insensitive to and unaware of the hidden dimensions of where people are likely to get hurt.	Are sensitive to and hunt out the hidden dimensions of where people are likely to get hurt.
Moral Identification and Ordering	
See moral claims as squishy and not definite enough to order into hierarchies with other claims.	See which moral claims being made are relevant or irrelevant; order moral factors just as economic factors are ordered.
Moral Evaluation	
Are erratic in their application of ethics if it gets applied at all.	Are coherent and consistent in their normative reasoning.
Tolerance of Moral Disagreement and Ambiguity	
Cite ethical disagreement and ambiguity as reasons for forgetting ethics altogether.	Tolerate ethical disagreement and ambiguity while honestly acknowledging that decisions are not precise like mathematics but must finally be made nevertheless.
Integration of Managerial and Moral Competence	
See ethical decisions as isolated and independent of managerial decisions and managerial competence.	See every evolving decision as one in which a moral perspective must be integrated with a managerial one.
A Sense of Moral Obligation	
Have no sense of moral obligation and integrity that extends beyond managerial responsibility.	Have a sense of moral obligation and integrity that holds together the decision-making process in which human welfare is at stake.

5.6 Rest's Model for Ethical Decision Making and Behavior

In concluding our chapter on business ethics essentials it is useful to see how both the ideas of developing moral judgment as presented by Kohlberg, and the elements of moral judgment presented by Powers and Vogel in the previous section, may be combined into to a process of moral or ethical decision making. James Rest, a cognitive-development researcher, who also happened to have been a student of Kohlberg's, developed a **four-component model**

for **ethical decision making and behavior** that built upon these ideas.[55] His research argued that there are four steps in moral development that lead to ethical action.[56] Rest's four components that involve cognitive or psychological processes included (1) **moral awareness** wherein a moral issue must be recognized, (2) making a **moral judgment**, (3) establishing **moral intent**, that is, resolving to place moral issues ahead of other concerns, and (4) **moral action** (taking action on the moral concerns).[57] We introduce this model as we close out Chapter 5 because it ties together some of the concepts presented to this point, and it urges us to think about the process of ethical decision making that will be further pursued in Chapter 6.

Summary

Business ethics has become a serious challenge for the business community. Business ethics concerns the rightness, wrongness, and fairness of managerial practices and policies, and these are not easy judgments to make. Multiple norms compete as to which standards of business behavior should be compared. It is not easy to say whether business's ethics have declined in recent years or just seem to have done so because of increased media coverage and rising public expectations. The major ethics scandals of the early 2000s have affected the public's trust of executives and major business institutions, and polls indicate that the public does not have a high regard for the ethics of business or managers.

The conventional approach to business ethics was introduced as the way that average people on the street or in organizations might reason through ethical situations. They typically look to society's norms as a primary indicator of what is acceptable or not. One major challenge with this approach is that it is not clear which standards or norms should be used, and thus conventional thinking is susceptible to ethical relativism and misjudgment. Though conventional thinking has value, the varied sources of norms informing decision making can often result in confusion and conflicting expectations. In the next chapter we will turn to the principles approach and the ethical tests approaches to business ethics.

A Venn diagram model was presented as an aid to making decisions when economics, law, and ethics expectations compete with each other and are in tension. Three models of management ethics were presented that include: (1) immoral management, (2) moral management, and (3) amoral management. Amoral management is further classified into intentional and unintentional categories.

There are two hypotheses about the presence of these three moral types: their presence in the management population and their presence in individuals themselves.

Understanding how moral judgment develops is helpful to aspiring managers. A generally accepted view is that the moral judgment process develops similar to the pattern described by Lawrence Kohlberg. His three levels of moral development reflect how individuals progress in their thinking: (1) preconventional, (2) conventional, and (3) postconventional, autonomous, or principled. Gilligan and others have suggested that men and women use different perspectives as they perceive and deal with moral issues. Care must be exercised in generalizing about the process of moral development.

In addition to moral maturity, managers' ethics are affected by sources of values originating from external to the organization and from sources within the organization. This latter category includes respect for the authority structure, loyalty, conformity, and a concern for financial performance and results. Taken together, they represent the "bottom line" mentality that is so prevalent in organizations today.

Six elements in developing moral judgment were presented. These six elements include (1) moral imagination, (2) moral identification and ordering, (3) moral evaluation, (4) tolerance of moral disagreement and ambiguity, (5) integration of managerial and moral competence, and (6) a sense of moral obligation. If the moral management model is to be sustained, these six elements need to be developed and successfully integrated. Building upon Kohlberg's work and the elements of moral judgment, we conclude with Rest's four component model of ethical decision making that entails moral awareness, moral judgment, moral intention, and moral action.

Key Terms

amoral management, p. 109

bottom-line mentality, p. 117

business ethics, p. 99

compliance strategy, p. 110

conventional approach,
   p. 99

conventional level of moral development (level 2), p. 113

descriptive ethics, p. 100

elements of moral judgment, p. 106
ethical relativism, p. 103
ethical tests approach, p. 100
ethics, p. 99
ethics of care, p. 115
four-component model for ethical
 decision making and behavior
 (Rest's model), p. 119
individual hypothesis, p. 112
immoral management, p. 106

integrity strategy, p. 108
intentional amoral management, p. 109
Kohlberg's levels of moral
 development, p. 112
moral action, p. 119
moral awareness, p. 119
moral development, p. 113
moral intent, p. 119
moral judgment, p. 119
moral management, p. 108

morals, p. 99
normative ethics, p. 100
population hypothesis, p. 111
postconventional level of moral
 development, (level 3) p. 114
preconventional level of moral
 development (level 1), p. 113
principles approach, p. 100
unintentional amoral management,
 p. 109

Discussion Questions

1. Provide a definition of ethical business behavior, explain the components involved in making ethical decisions, and give an example from your personal experience of the sources of ethical norms that affect you while making these determinations.

2. To demonstrate that you understand the three models of management ethics—moral, immoral, and amoral—give an example, from your personal experience, of each type. Do you agree that amorality is a serious problem? Why? Explain.

3. Give examples, from your personal experience, of Kohlberg's Levels 1, 2, and 3. If you believe you have ever gotten to Level 3, give an example of what it was.

4. How does Gilligan's research about the process of moral development differ from that of Kohlberg's? Have you seen these differences in your personal experiences? Explain by way of example.

5. Compare your motivations to behave ethically with those listed in Figure 5-13. Do the reasons given in that figure agree with your personal assessment? Discuss the similarities and differences between Figure 5-13 and your personal assessment.

6. From your personal experience, give an example of a situation you have faced that would require one of the six elements of moral judgment. Which of these six elements are most important and why?

7. Is everyone capable of recognizing a moral issue in stage one (moral awareness) of Rest's moral decision-making model? Do you think that people can get "stuck" in a stage, for example, imparting moral judgment but incapable of thinking with moral intent?

Endnotes

1. For a history of business ethics, see Richard T. DeGeorge, "The History of Business Ethics," in Marc J. Epstein and Kirk O. Hanson (eds.), *The Accountable Corporation, Business Ethics,* Vol. 2 (Westport, CT: Praeger Publishers, 2006), 47–58.

2. Linda Saad, Gallup, "U. S. Ethics Ratings," https://news .gallup.com/poll/328136/ethics-ratings-rise-medical -workers-teachers.aspx. Accessed March 20, 2021.

3. Diffen, "Ethics vs. Morals," diffen.com/difference/Ethics _vs_Morals#:~:text=Morals,-Diffen%20›%20English%20 Language&text=While%20they%20are%20sometimes%20 used,principles%20regarding%20right%20and%20wrong. Accessed March 17, 2021.

4. Richard T. DeGeorge, *Business Ethics*, 4th ed. (New York: Prentice Hall, 1995), 20–21. See also Rogene A. Buchholz and Sandra B. Rosenthal, *Business Ethics* (Upper Saddle River, NJ: Prentice Hall, 1998), 3.

5. DeGeorge, 15.

6. Kenneth E. Goodpaster, "Business Ethics," in Patricia H. Werhane and R. Edward Freeman (eds.), *The Blackwell Dictionary of Business Ethics* (Malden, MA: Blackwell Publishers, 1997), 51–57.

7. For more on ethics and the law, see William A. Wines, *Ethics, Law, and Business* (Mahwah, NJ: Lawrence Erlbaum Associates, 2006).

8. Tamara Lytle, "Marijuana and the Workplace: It's Complicated." August 28, 2019, https://www.shrm.org/hr -today/news/hr-magazine/fall2019/pages/marijuana-and -the-workplace-its-complicated.aspx. Accessed March 11, 2021.

9. See, for example, Melissa Baucus and Janet Near, "Can Illegal Corporate Behavior Be Predicted? An Event History Analysis," *Academy of Management Journal* (Vol. 34, No. 1, 1991), 9–36; and P. L. Cochran and D. Nigh, "Illegal Corporate Behavior and the Question of Moral Agency," in William C. Frederick (ed.), *Research in Corporate Social Performance and Policy*, Vol. 9 (Greenwich, CT: JAI Press, 1987), 73–91.

10. Mark S. Schwartz and Archie B. Carroll, "Corporate Social Responsibility: A Three-Domain Approach," *Business Ethics Quarterly,* 13(4), October 2003, 503–530.

11. Most of the material in this section comes from Archie B. Carroll, "In Search of the Moral Manager," *Business Horizons,* March/April 1987, 7–15. See also Archie B. Carroll, "Models of Management Morality for the New Millennium," *Business Ethics Quarterly,* 11(2), April 2001, 365–371.

12. *Dilbert* comic strip, by Scott Adams (September 15, 2007), https://dilbert.com/. Accessed March 17, 2021.

13. Allan Sloan, "Laying Enron to Rest," *Newsweek* (June 5, 2006), 25–30, http://www.readabstracts.com/News -opinion-and-commentary/Laying-Enron-to-rest-Shes-a -criminal-Give-me-a-break.html. Accessed March 17, 2021.

14. "Kenneth Lay," *The Economist* (July 8, 2006), 81.

15. Andrew Dunn, "Lay, Skilling Assets Targeted by U.S. After Guilty Verdicts" (May 26, 2006), http://Bloomberg.com. Accessed May 26, 2006.

16. Kim Clark and Marianne Lavelle, "Guilty as Charged," *U.S. News & World Report* (June 5, 2006), 44–45.

17. The Enron Blog, "Status of Jeff Skilling," January 10, 2013, http://caraellison.wordpress.com/2013/01/10/status -of-jeff-skilling/. Accessed March 4, 2013.

18. "Deloitte & Touche USA 2007 Ethics & Workplace" survey, 2007, Deloitte Development LLC, 16. Also see Deloitte, Leadership Counts, https://community.corporatecompliance .org/HigherLogic/System/DownloadDocumentFile. ashx?DocumentFileKey=076bc9f2-89a3-4aad-bfa6 -d0d18daee212. Accessed March 16, 2021.

19. Ibid., 15.

20. Lynn Sharp Paine, "Managing for Organizational Integrity," *Harvard Business Review* (March–April 1994), 106–117.

21. Archie B. Carroll, "The Moral Leader: Essential for Successful Corporate Citizenship," in Jorg Andriof and Malcolm McIntosh (eds.), *Perspectives on Corporate Citizenship* (Sheffield, UK: Greenleaf Publishing Co., 2001), 139–151.

22. Stephen Covey, *The Seven Habits of Highly Effective People* (New York: Simon & Schuster, 1989).

23. Carroll (2001), ibid., 145–150.

24. Paul Ziobro, "CVS Renames Itself CVS Health as It Ends Its Sale of Tobacco Products," *The Wall Street Journal*, September 3, 2014. Accessed March 12, 2021.

25. BusinessEthicsCaseBlogspot, "CVS Bans Tobacco Products," February 15, 2014, http://businessethicscases .blogspot.com/2014/02/cvs-bans-tobacco-products.html. Accessed March 12, 2021.

26. PBS News Hour, "Considering the Ethics and Economics of CVS Stores Ending Tobacco Sales," February 5, 2014, https://www.pbs.org/newshour/show/considering-ethics -economics-cvs-stores-ending-tobacco-sales. Accessed March 12, 2021.

27. Business Enterprise Trust, 1994, "The Business Enterprise Trust Awards (1991 Recipients)," unpublished announcement; Zicklin School of Business, "People, Not Profit: Merck's Battle against River Blindness," http:// zicklin.baruch.cuny.edu/centers/zcci/zcci-events/the -merck-river-blindness-case. Accessed February 11, 2016.

28. Dictionary.com, "Amoral," https://www.dictionary.com /browse/amoral. Accessed March 12, 2021.

29. Mahzarin R. Banaji, Max H. Bazerman, and Dolly Chugh, "How (Un) Ethical Are You?" *Harvard Business Review* (December 2003), 56–64, https://hbr.org/2003/12/how -unethical-are-you. Accessed March 12, 2021.

30. Ibid.

31. Max Bazerman, George Loewenstein, and Don A. Moore, "Why Good Accountants Do Bad Audits," *Harvard Business Review* (November 2002).

32. Ibid.

33. Paine, 109–113.

34. Emily Glazer, "Wells Slams Former Bosses' High-Pressure Sales Tactics," *Wall Street Journal*, April 11, 2017, A1.

35. Geoff Colvin, "Can Wells Fargo Get Well?" *Fortune*, June 15, 2017, 138–146.

36. Dina Gerdeman, "How to Demotivate Your Best Employees," Harvard Business School Working Knowledge, https:// hbswk.hbs.edu/item/how-to-demotivate-your-best -employees. Accessed March 16, 2021.

37. Dan Ariely, *The (Honest) Truth about Dishonesty*, Harper: 2012; also see Gary Belsky, "Why (Almost) All of Us Cheat and Steal," *Time Business*, June 18, 2012, 40.

38. Lawrence Kohlberg, "The Claim to Moral Adequacy of a Highest Stage of Moral Judgment," *The Journal of Philosophy,* 52, 1973, 630–646.

39. Carol Gilligan, *In a Different Voice: Psychological Theory and Women's Development* (Cambridge, MA: Harvard University Press, 1982). Also see Goodtherapy, "Carol Gilligan," https://www.goodtherapy.org/famous -psychologists/carol-gilligan.html. Accessed March 15, 2021.

40. Manuel G. Velasquez, *Business Ethics,* 3rd ed. (Englewood Cliffs, NJ: Prentice Hall, 1992), 30. See also Brian K. Burton and Craig P. Dunn, "Feminist Ethics as Moral Grounding for Stakeholder Theory," *Business Ethics Quarterly,* 6(2), 1996, 136–137.

41. George A. Steiner, *Business and Society* (New York: Random House, 1975), 226.

42. William Barclay, *Ethics in a Permissive Society* (New York: Harper & Row, 1971), 13. http://www.princeton. edu/~achaney/tmve/wiki100k/docs/Ethic_of_reciprocity .html.

43. "Ethic of Reciprocity," http://www.princeton. edu/~achaney/tmve/wiki100k/docs/Ethic_of_reciprocity .html. Accessed February 20, 2016.

44. Marvin Fox, "The Theistic Bases of Ethics," in Robert Bartels (ed.), *Ethics in Business* (Columbus, OH: Bureau of Business Research, Ohio State University, 1963), 86–87.

45. Alan Wolfe, *Moral Freedom: The Search for Virtue in a World of Choice* (New York: W.W. Norton & Co., 2001).

46. Mark A. Smith, *Secular Faith* (Chicago, IL: University of Chicago Press, 2015).

47. Carl D. Fulda, "The Legal Basis of Ethics," in Bartels, 43–50.

48. American Management Association, "The Ethical Enterprise: Doing the Right Things in the Right Ways, Today and Tomorrow—A Global Study of Business Ethics 2005–2015," http://www.amanet.org/images /HREthicsSurvey06.pdf. Accessed February 20, 2016.

49. "The Oath Project," http://theoathproject.org /professionals/. Accessed March 15, 2021.

50. Charles W. Powers and David Vogel, *Ethics in the Education of Business Managers* (Hastings-on-Hudson, NY: The Hastings Center, 1980), 40–45. Also see Patricia H. Werhane, *Moral Imagination and Management Decision Making* (New York: Oxford University Press, 1999).

51. Patricia Werhane, "Moral Imagination," Volume 2, *Business Ethics*, Wiley Online Library, online published January 21, 2016. Accessed February 20, 2016.

52. Powers and Vogel, ibid.

53. Powers and Vogel, ibid.

54. Milton Friedman, "The Social Responsibility of Business Is to Increase Its Profits," *The New York Times* (September 1962), 126 [italics added].

55. James R. Rest, *Moral Development: Advances in Research and Theory* (New York: Praeger).

56. Ethics Sage, "How Do We Make Ethical Decisions: An Essay," October 23, 2018, https://www.ethicssage. com/2018/10/how-do-we-make-ethical-decisions-an-essay .html. Accessed March 16, 2021.

57. Thomas Jones, "Ethical Decision Making by Individuals in Organizations: An Issue-Contingent Model," *Academy of Management Review*, 16(2), 1991, 368.

6

Managerial and Organizational Ethics

Chapter Learning Outcomes

After studying this chapter, you should be able to:

1. Identify and explain the different levels at which business ethics may occur and be addressed.
2. Enumerate and discuss the principles of managerial ethics and ethical tests for guiding ethical decisions.
3. In terms of managing organizational ethics, identify the factors affecting an organization's ethical culture and provide examples of these factors at work.
4. Identify and explain concepts from "behavioral ethics" that affect ethical decision making and behavior in organizations.
5. Describe the best practices that management may take to improve an organization's ethical culture. What are the three most important and why?
6. Explain the cascading effect of moral decisions, moral managers, and moral organizations.

The ethical issues on which managers must make decisions are numerous and varied. The news media tends to focus on the major ethical scandals involving well-known corporate names. Therefore, Purdue Pharma, Theranos, Boeing, Wells Fargo, Volkswagen, Takata, and other such high-visibility firms have attracted considerable attention. As a consequence, many of the day-to-day ethical challenges that managers and employees face in medium-sized and small organizations are often overlooked or underreported. People today face ethical issues in a variety of settings, but our concern in this chapter is limited to managerial and organizational ethics.

Managers encounter day-to-day ethical challenges in arenas such as conflicts of interest, sexual harassment, discrimination, inappropriate gifts to corporate personnel, unauthorized payments, customer dealings, evaluation of personnel, and pressure to compromise their personal standards. But often these managers have no experience or training in business ethics or ethical decision making to tackle such quandaries.

The ethical challenge in business is a daunting one, and progress on this front is vital to sustainable businesses. An ethics officer for a large corporation once said that there are three types of organizations: those that *have had* ethics problems, those that *are having* ethics problems, and those that *will have* ethics problems. Ethical issues appear through all levels of management, in many different types of jobs, and in organizations of all sizes.

A study of managers' desired leadership qualities was conducted by consultant and writer Lee Ellis, who concluded that *integrity* is the quality most sought after in leaders.[1] Furthermore, sustaining a company's integrity requires constant vigilance.[2] A retired corporate executive, now business school lecturer, Bill George, former CEO of

Medtronic, asserted that today we need corporate leaders with integrity.[3] But how does one get personal integrity, and as a manager, how do you instill it in yourself and your organization to create an ethical organizational climate? These topics will be explored in this chapter.

Some of the significant challenges managers face today include the following: How do you keep your own managerial ethics focused in such a way that you avoid immorality and amorality? What principles, concepts, or guidelines are available to help you to be ethical? What specific strategies, approaches, or best practices might be emphasized to bring about an ethical culture in companies and organizations? How is "behavioral ethics" affecting decision making?

6.1 Ethics Issues Arise at Different Levels

As individuals and as managers, we experience ethical pressures or dilemmas in a variety of settings and at different levels of occurrence, including the personal level, the managerial and organizational level, the industry level, the societal level, and the global level. These levels ripple out from the individual level to the global level. In an analogous manner, Epstein and Hanson have recently described that ethical failures in business have occurred using the following metaphor: Some people are bad—this is their *bad-apple theory*. Some companies are bad—this is their *bad-barrel theory*. The economic system itself is bad—this is their *bad-orchard theory*.[4] Indeed, poor business ethics does occur because of "bad apples" (people), "bad barrels" (organizations), and "bad orchards" (industries, societies, global). In this chapter, we will focus on people and organizations, for they are the levels about which action may be more readily taken by managers.

Some observers believe that "ethics are ethics" regardless of whether they are applied at the personal, managerial, or organizational level. In many respects this is true. However, each level of application also introduces distinct challenges. To help understand the types of decision situations that are faced at the various levels, it is worth considering them in terms of the types of issues that may arise in different contexts.

6.1a Personal Level

First, we all experience *personal-level* ethical challenges. This is where the possibility of "bad apples" occurs. These challenges include situations we face in our personal lives that are generally outside the context of our employment but may have implications for our jobs. Questions or dilemmas that we might face at the personal level include the following examples:

- Should I cheat on my income tax return by overinflating my charitable contributions?
- Should I tell the professor I need this course to graduate this semester when I really don't?
- Should I download music from the Internet although I realize it is someone else's intellectual property?
- Should I connect to Netflix using a friend's logon information rather than paying for my own account?

Wanda Johnson, a 34-year-old single mother of five from Savannah, Georgia, faced a personal-level ethical dilemma when temptation came knocking in the form of a bagful of money that contained $120,000. True story: Johnson, a low-paid custodian at a local hospital, was on her lunch break when she witnessed the money bag falling off an armored truck. She could have used the money to pay her outstanding bills. She had recently pawned her television set to procure enough cash to keep the bill collectors at bay. The bag contained small bills and nobody saw her find it. Johnson's experience is not uncommon. Others, in Salt Lake City, Utah, Harvey, Louisiana, and San Jose, California, have similarly found bags of money that have fallen off armored trucks. What should she do? What would you do?

Johnson later confessed that she knew she had to turn it in. After consulting with her pastor, she turned in the money to the police. Johnson reported that her religious upbringing had taught her that was the right thing to do. Later she was rewarded by the SunTrust Bank with $5,000 and was also promised an unspecified sum by EM Armored Car Service, Inc.[5] So, in addition to bad apples there are good apples, like Wanda, at the personal level. Would everyone react to this personal, ethical dilemma in the same fashion as did Johnson? We all face hundreds of such dilemmas throughout our lives, and how we respond to them doubtless has a bearing on what we would do in our organizational lives.

6.1b Managerial and Organizational Levels

Individuals also encounter ethical issues at the *organizational (company) level* in their roles as employees, managers, or entrepreneurs. This is where the possibility of "bad barrels" occurs. Many of these issues are similar to those we face personally. However, managerial- and organizational-level issues carry consequences for an individual's status in the organization, for the company's reputation and success in the community, and also for the kind of ethical culture that will prevail on a day-to-day basis at the workplace. In addition, how the issue is handled may have serious managerial or organizational consequences. Examples of issues faced by employees and managers at the organizational level include the following:

- Should I set high performance goals for my work team to benefit the organization, even though I know it may cause them to cut corners to achieve such goals?
- Should I over-report the actual time I worked on this project, hoping to get overtime pay or additional recognition?
- Should I authorize a subordinate team member to sidestep company policy so that we can close the deal and be rewarded by month's end?
- Should I misrepresent the warranty time on some product I'm selling in order to get the sale?

A recent example of an organizational-level ethical and legal fraud involved the company Theranos, the blood testing company that started out as a Silicon Valley darling and ended up facing fraud charges and going out of business. The company and its founder, Elizabeth Holmes, were charged with conducting an elaborate, years-long fraud against its investors and the public. Before her company collapsed, Holmes became a media favorite, appeared on magazine covers, and was being compared with Apple cofounder Steve Jobs. Holmes and the company's president, Ramesh Balwani, were eventually charged with conspiracy to commit wire fraud and attempting to defraud doctors and patients even though they knew they could not consistently produce reliable results for certain blood tests.[6] It was also reported that their lab chief faced pushback from management when he questioned the technology's accuracy.[7] This case, which is ongoing, was so egregious that HBO presented a documentary about it, *The Inventor: Out for Blood in Silicon Valley*.[8] Actress Jennifer Lawrence plays the role of Holmes in the movie *Bad Blood*, also chronicling the Theranos fraud.

Not all companies collapse like Theranos. Companies that continue to operate must deal with ethical culture issues often. When thinking about the managerial and organizational level of ethics, the presence or absence of unethical practices goes a long way toward revealing the climate or culture of ethics that exists within that organization. To illustrate the types of questionable practices that are evident in organizations, a 2020 survey published by the Ethics & Compliance Initiative documented some of the situations that managers and employees often face. In this survey of employees, the following were some of the types of misconduct observed and reported along with the percentage of time these items were mentioned:[9]

Favoritism toward certain employees (35 percent)

Management lying to employees (25 percent)

Conflicts of interest (23 percent)

Improper hiring practices (22 percent)

Abusive behavior (22 percent)

Health violations (23 percent)

In all cases, the number of observations were higher than when this same survey was taken three years prior. Each of these categories reveals the array of questionable practices that employees and managers face every day in their work lives. How they respond to these ethical issues often carries serious consequences for themselves and their organizations.

6.1c Industry or Profession Level

A third level at which a manager or an organization might experience business ethics issues is the *industry or profession level*. This level would be part of the "bad orchard." At this level, the industry might be stock brokerage, real estate,

health care, insurance, financial services, telemarketing, electronics, or a host of others. Related to the industry might be the *profession* of which an individual is a member—accounting, engineering, pharmacy, medicine, journalism, or law. Examples of questions that might pose ethical dilemmas at this level include the following:

- Is this safety standard we electrical engineers adopted really adequate for protecting the consumer in this age of do-it-yourselfers?
- Is this standard contract we realtors have adopted actually in keeping with the financial disclosure laws that have recently been strengthened?
- Is it ethical for telemarketers to make cold calls to prospective clients during the dinner hour when we suspect they will be at home?
- Is it ethical for accountants to allow a restatement of earnings that can cause investors to lose money and confidence in the market?

An industry that faces ethical challenges every day is the health-care industry. Their simple maxim of "first, do no harm" turns out to be far more complex in the context of rapidly changing technology, continuous budget constraints, and novel health-care crises such as pandemics. Some of

---

Ethics In Practice Case

Are There Ethical Issues in Self-Checkout?

Self-checkouts, where customers scan their own items, bag them, and pay without the assistance of a cashier, are not only prominent today but often are preferred by many. At grocery chains, big box stores, fast-food restaurants, and chain retailers, the self-checkouts increasingly are outnumbering the human-staffed checkout lanes. Self-checkouts have many benefits. They often save time. They reduce labor costs. Many consumers love them. Self-checkouts also have their disadvantages. They involve high upfront costs to the retailer. They increase the risk of theft. Customers are sometimes confused and experience technical difficulties. They limit human contact, which many customers enjoy. Regardless of the pros and cons, self-service seems to be here to stay, and we are seeing more of it every day.

The increased incidence of self-checkout theft poses a major ethics issue for the retailers and for the customers (assuming they have a conscience). In one survey of 2,600 people, almost 20 percent revealed they had cheated while using the self-checkouts in grocery stores. Most of those surveyed said they did it because they thought there was low risk of being caught. In another study of self-checkouts using hand scanners, out of sales of $21 million, it was discovered that $850,000 worth of goods were not paid for. Several methods are often employed. In the "switcheroo," the customer peels off a sticker from a less expensive item and places it on top of the actual barcode. In the "pass around," the customer simply passes the item by without it actually being scanned. Surely there are other approaches.

In an online discussion of this issue, one person said that anyone who pays for more than half of their stuff is

a moron. Another comment was that there's no ethical issue here; the store is just making you work for them. One spokesperson for a national shoplifting prevention association thinks that self-checkouts are tempting to people who are already predisposed to shoplifting by creating rationalizations for it. Others think the offenders have "thrill" personalities and that doing it makes their routine lives more exciting. Others think these are ordinarily honest people who are taking advantage of the false sense of anonymity in dealing with a mechanical cashier.

1. Why do some shoppers try to take advantage of self-checkout opportunities?
2. Is this a personal level or organizational level ethical issue? Explain.
3. Why don't companies try to monitor against these issues more carefully?
4. If you were the store manager, what steps would you take to ensure honest checking-out?
5. If you worked at a store and "caught" a violator, what action would you take and why?

Sources: Ben Dwyer, CardFellow, "Self-Checkout: Should You Implement It?" https://www.cardfellow.com/blog/self-checkout-should-you-implement-it/, November 7, 2019, accessed February 10, 2021; Jack Marshall, Ethics Alarms, "Self-Checkout Ethics," February 10, 2021, https://ethicsalarms.com/2021/02/10/self-checkout-ethics/, accessed February 10, 2021; Sophia Harris, CBC News, "A Crime of Opportunity: Why Some Shoppers Steal at Self-Checkout," November 17, 2019, https://www.cbc.ca/news/business/self-checkout-shoplifting-retail-theft-1.5361316, accessed February 10, 2021.

the issues the industry faces in which ethics are embedded include the following: testing the efficacy of new medical technology without harming patients; taking advantage of Big Data without dehumanizing patients; safeguarding patient privacy while using population health data; ensuring equal access to customized medicine; reconciling patient care decisions with financial management; implementing artificial intelligence and robotics ethically; and devising fair responses to pandemics and other widespread medical emergencies.[10] This industry combines the ethical issues faced by the industry itself and its primary decision makers (physicians, nurses, and technicians).

Other industries facing serious ethical questions in recent years include the college admissions industry and the student loan industry. In the college admissions industry, the recent Netflix movie *Operation Varsity Blues: The College Admissions Scandal* documented the bribery-for-admission issues being faced. In the student loan industry, educational debt today is seen by many to be a ticking time bomb inasmuch as there is now more than $1.6 trillion in outstanding loan balances.[11] Weak job prospects as well as rising costs for basic living expenses have meant that many college students are not earning enough to pay back their loans. Default rates have been climbing for more than ten years. According to many analysts, the student loan industry is facing serious problems, and they have been brought about by questionable loans in the industry.[12] The student loan situation is examined in closer detail in Case 28 at the end of the text.

6.1d Societal and Global Levels

At the *societal* and *global levels*, also possible parts of the "bad orchard," it becomes difficult for the individual manager to have a direct effect on business ethics. Managers acting in concert through their companies and industries and professional associations can certainly bring about high standards and constructive changes. Because the industry, societal, and global levels are quite removed from the actual practicing manager, in this chapter we will focus our attention primarily on the managerial and organizational levels. Managers' greatest impact can be felt through what they do personally or as a member of the management team.

In Chapter 7, we will deal with business ethics at the global level, and in Chapter 8 we will explore ethics and technology as firms increasingly are becoming digital enterprises.

6.2 Managerial Ethics and Ethical Principles

In thinking about managerial ethics, it is anticipated that most individuals want to behave ethically or improve their ethical conduct in organizational situations. Our discussion here focuses on those who desire to be ethical and are looking for help in doing so. All the difficulties with making ethical judgments that we discussed in the previous chapter are applicable in this discussion as well.

Managerial ethics, for the most part, entails making decisions that have ethical implications or consequences. Difficult decisions typically present the individual with a conflict-of-interest situation. Conflicts of interest are at the heart of ethics and ethical decision making. A **conflict of interest** is usually present when the individuals have to choose between their interests and the interests of someone else or some other group (their organization, other stakeholders). What it boils down to in the final analysis is answering the question, "What is the ethical course of action to take in this situation?" In other instances, practices that managers and organizations employ are embedded with ethical implications. Someone else most likely first introduced the practices at an earlier time, so some managers do not see that each time they continue a questionable practice, they are implicitly deciding that it is appropriate.

In answering the question about the right or fair course of action, it often seems that individuals think about the situation briefly and then go with their instincts. There are, however, guidelines for ethical decision making that employees or managements might turn to if they really want to make the best ethical decisions. Some of these guidelines are discussed in the next several sections of this chapter.

In Chapter 5, we discussed business ethics using the conventional approach. The **conventional approach** entailed making a comparison between a decision, action, or policy and prevailing norms of acceptability. In this chapter, we introduce two approaches to managerial ethics or ethical decision making that serve as additional guidance: (1) the principles approach and (2) the ethical tests approach.

6.3 Principles Approach to Ethics

The **principles approach** to ethics or ethical decision making is based on the idea that employees and managers desire to anchor their decisions, actions, or policies on a more solid foundation than that provided with the conventional approach. Several principles of ethics have evolved over time as moral philosophers and ethicists have attempted to organize and codify their thinking and guidelines. These principles are normative in nature as they offer guidance regarding what one "ought to do" in a situation.

6.3a What Is an Ethics Principle?

From a practical point of view, a principle of business ethics is an ethical concept, guideline, or rule that, if applied when you are faced with an ethical decision or practice, will assist you in taking the ethical course of action.[13] Ethics principles or guidelines have been around for centuries. The Golden Rule, presented in various forms, has been around for several millennia. In the 16th century, Miguel de Cervantes, the Spanish novelist and author of *Don Quixote*, uttered an important ethics principle that is still used today and seldom attributed to him: *Honesty is the best policy.*

6.3b Types of Ethical Principles or Theories

Moral philosophers customarily divide ethics principles or theories into two categories: teleological and deontological. **Teleological theories** focus on the *consequences* or results of the actions they produce. Utilitarianism is the major principle in this category. It recommends taking the action that results in the greatest good for the greatest number. For example, it could be argued that the workplace would be better off if only college graduates were hired, even though not everyone needs a college degree to do our work. **Deontological theories**, by contrast, focus on *duties*. For example, it could be argued that managers have a duty or an obligation to tell the truth when they are doing business. The principles of rights and of justice, two major ethics theories we will discuss, seem to be nonteleological in character.[14]

Aretaic theories are a third, less-known category of ethics, put forth by Aristotle. The term comes from the Greek word *arete*, which means "goodness" (of function), "excellence" (of function), or "virtue." Aristotle saw the individual as essentially a member of a social unit and moral virtue as a behavioral habit, a character trait that is both socially and morally valued. Virtue theory is the best example of an aretaic theory.[15] Other principles, such as the principle of caring, the Golden Rule, and servant leadership, reflect concerns for duty, consequences, and virtue, or a combination of several principles.

Many different principles of ethics have been promulgated, but we must limit our discussion to those that have been regarded as most useful in business applications. Therefore, we will concentrate on the following major principles: *utilitarianism* (consequences based) and *Kant's categorical imperative, rights*, and *justice* (duty based). In addition, we will consider the principles of *care, virtue ethics, servant leadership*, and the *Golden Rule*—approaches that are popular and relevant today.

The basic idea behind the principles approach is that managers may improve the wisdom of their ethical decision making if they factor into their proposed actions, decisions, behaviors, and practices a consideration of certain principles or philosophies of ethics.

6.3c Principle of Utilitarianism

Many ethicists have held that the correctness or fairness of an action can best be determined by looking at its overall results or **consequences**. If the consequences are good, the action or decision is considered good. If the consequences are bad, the action or decision is considered wrong. An example of utilitarianism might be in the case of a pharmaceutical firm that has released a new drug that has been approved by the government but it does have side effects. But, the drug is able to help more people than are bothered by the side effects, so it is considered a good drug though it has problems for some.

The **principle of utilitarianism** is therefore a *consequential* principle, or as stated earlier, a *teleological* principle. In its simplest form, **utilitarianism** asserts: "we should always act so as to produce the greatest ratio of good to evil for everyone."[16] Another way of stating utilitarianism is to say that one should take the course of action that represents the "greatest good for the greatest number."[17] Two of the most influential philosophers who advocated this consequential view were Jeremy Bentham (1748–1832) and John Stuart Mill (1806–1873).

The attractiveness of utilitarianism is that it forces the decision maker to think about the general welfare, or the common good. It proposes a standard outside of self-interest by which to judge the value of a course of action. To make a cost-benefit analysis is to engage in utilitarian thinking. Utilitarianism forces us to think in stakeholder terms: What would produce the greatest good in our decision, considering stakeholders such as owners, employees, customers, and others, as well as ourselves?

A weakness of utilitarianism is that it ignores actions that may be inherently wrong. A strict interpretation of utilitarianism might lead a manager to fire certain minorities and older workers because they "do not fit in" or to take some other drastic action that contravenes public policy and other ethics principles. In utilitarianism, by focusing on the ends (consequences) of a decision or an action, one may ignore the means (the decision or action itself). This leads to a problematic situation wherein one may argue that the end justifies the means, using utilitarian reasoning. Therefore, the action or decision is considered objectionable only if it leads to a lesser ratio of good to evil.

Another problem with the principle of utilitarianism is that it may come into conflict with the concepts of justice or rights. Critics of utilitarianism say that the mere increase in total good is not good in and of itself because it ignores the *distribution* of good, which is also an important issue. Another stated weakness is that when using this principle, it is difficult to formulate satisfactory rules for decision making. Therefore, utilitarianism, like most ethical principles, has its advantages and disadvantages.[18] Like many ethics principles, utilitarianism seems to work best when used in combination with other ethics principles.

6.3d Kant's Categorical Imperative (Duty)

Immanuel Kant's **categorical imperative** is a *duty-based* principle of ethics or, as stated earlier, it is a deontological principle.[19] A **duty** is an obligation; that is, it is an action that is morally obligatory. The duty approach to ethics refers both to the obligatory nature of particular actions and to a way of reasoning about what is right and what is wrong.[20] Kant's categorical imperative argues that a sense of duty arises from *reason* or *rational nature*, an internal source. By contrast, the Divine Command principle maintains that God's law is the source of duties. Thus, we can conceptualize both internal and external sources of duty.

Kant proposed three formulations in his theory or principle. The categorical imperative is best known in the following form: "Act only according to that maxim by which you can at the same time *will* that it should become a universal law." Stated another way, Kant's principle is that a person should act only on rules (or maxims) that you would be willing to see everyone follow.[21] Kant's second formulation, referred to as the *principle of ends*, is "so act to treat humanity, whether in your own person or in that of any other, in every case as an *end* and never as merely a means." This has also been referred to as the *respect for person's principle*.[22] This means that each person has dignity and moral worth and should never be exploited or manipulated or merely used as a means to another end; therefore, we have a duty to respect persons.[23]

The third formulation of the categorical imperative invokes the *principle of autonomy*. It basically holds that "every rational being is able to regard oneself as a maker of universal law. That is, we do not need an external authority—be it God, the state, our culture, or anyone else—to determine the nature of the moral law. We can discover this for ourselves."[24] Kant argues that this view is not inconsistent with Judeo-Christian beliefs, his childhood heritage, but one must go through a series of logical leaps of faith to arrive at this point.[25] Like all ethical principles, Kant's principles have strengths, weaknesses, supporters, and detractors. In the final analysis, it is his emphasis on *duty*, as opposed to consequences, that merits their discussion here. Further, the notion of universalizability and respect for persons are key ideas. The principles of rights and of justice, which we discuss next, seem more consistent with the duty-based perspective than with the consequences-based perspective.

6.3e Principle of Rights

One major problem with utilitarianism is that it does not handle the issue of **rights** very well. That is, utilitarianism implies that certain actions are morally right (i.e., they represent the greatest good for the greatest number) when in fact they may violate another person's rights.[26] The **principle of rights** maintains that persons have both moral and legal rights that should be honored and respected. **Moral** rights are important, justifiable claims or entitlements. They do not depend on a legal system to be valid. They are rights that people ought to have based on moral reasoning. The right to life or the right not to be killed by others is a justifiable claim in our society. The Declaration of Independence referred to the rights to life, liberty, and the pursuit of happiness. John Locke had earlier spoken of the right to property. Today we speak of human rights, some of which are legal rights and some moral rights. **Legal rights** are rights that some governing authority (the Constitution, the Bill of Rights, or federal, state, or local government) have formalized as rights.

An important aspect of the principle of rights is that a right can only be overridden by a more basic or important right. Consider the problem of applying the principle of utilitarianism when it collides with the principle of rights. For example, if we accept the basic right to human life, we are precluded from considering whether taking someone's life might produce the greatest good for the greatest number. To use a business example, if a person has the right to equal treatment (not to be discriminated against), we could not argue for discriminating against that person to produce greater good for others (e.g., a more harmonious workplace).[27]

The principle of rights expresses morality from the point of view of the individual or group of individuals, whereas the principle of utilitarianism expresses morality in terms of the group or society as a whole. The rights view forces us in our decision making to ask what is due each individual and to promote individual welfare. It also limits the validity of appeals to numbers and to society's aggregate benefit.[28] However, a central question that is not always easy to answer is: "What constitutes a legitimate right that should be honored, and what rights or whose rights take precedence over others?"

Figure 6-1 provides a listing of many types of rights that are being claimed in our society today. Some of these already are legally protected, whereas others are "claimed" as moral rights but are not legally protected. Managers are

Figure 6-1 Various Legal Rights and Claimed Moral Rights in Today's Society

Civil rights	AIDS victims' rights
Minorities' rights	Children's rights
Women's rights	Fetal rights
Disabled people's rights	Embryo rights
Older people's rights	Animal's rights
Religious affiliation rights	Right to burn the American flag
Employee rights	Right of due process
Consumer rights	Right to choose
Shareholder rights	Right to health care
Privacy rights	Gay rights
Right to life	Transgender rights
Right to work	Victims' rights
Criminals' rights	Rights based on looks
Smokers' rights	Right to free expression
Nonsmokers' rights	

expected to be attentive to both legal and moral rights, but clear guidelines are not always available to help one sort out which claimed moral rights should be protected, to what extent they should be protected, and whose rights should take precedence over others. Sometimes politics gets intertwined in this determination. This is one of the limitations of the rights theory.

Rights may be subdivided further into two types: negative rights and positive rights.[29] A **negative right** is the right to be left alone. It is the right to think and act free from the coercion of others; for example, freedom from false imprisonment, freedom from illegal search and seizure, and freedom of speech are all forms of negative rights.[30] A **positive right** is the right to something, such as the right to food, to health care, to clean air, to a certain standard of living, or to education.[31] In business, as in all walks of life, both negative and positive rights are played out in both legal and morally claimed forms.

Competing Rights and Ethical Dilemmas. A special problem arises with the rights approach to ethical decision making when the situation is not a clear "right versus wrong" but is more nearly "right versus right." This represents the special case of dealing with the dilemma of **competing rights**.[32] We know that when right faces wrong, we need to choose that which is right. Nevertheless, sometimes the decision will be between two apparent rights, and then it is harder to choose. Here are some examples of competing rights:

- It is right to tell the truth, but it is also right to be kind and considerate of people's feelings.
- It is right to offer job security, but as a manager you may have to lay off employees to balance your accounts.
- It is right to apply rules and procedures without favoritism, but it is also right to give special consideration to hardworking, dependable employees.[33]

A high-profile debate occurred between Apple Computers and the FBI that illustrated competing rights that led to an ethical dilemma. The case involved two rights—the right to homeland security (safety) and the right to data security/privacy. In this debate, the FBI wanted Apple to provide it with access to an iPhone that had been used by a terrorist, but Apple didn't want to give them access, arguing that their customers' security and privacy were at stake.[34] This case was finally resolved when the FBI discovered a way to unlock the iPhone without Apple's help.[35] This case was very complex and we will not resolve it here, but it is an excellent example of how two apparent "rights" may compete with each other.

In a dilemma involving competing rights, there are no easy solutions. Two general approaches are to (1) eliminate the conflict by reframing it or (2) decide what is "more right." In deciding what is more right, identify which competing right is more in line with laws, regulations, and organizational policies; which is most in sync with organizational

values; which provides the greatest good for the greatest number of stakeholders; or which establishes the best precedent for guiding similar situations in the future.[36] In the final analysis, someone may still be dissatisfied with the resolution.

6.3f Principle of Justice (Fairness Principle)

Just as the principle of utilitarianism does not handle well the idea of rights, it does not deal effectively with the principle of justice either. One way to think about the **principle of justice** is to say that it involves the fair treatment of each person. This is why it is often called the "fairness principle."[37] Most would accept that we have a duty to be fair to employees, consumers, and other stakeholders. But how do you decide what is fair to each person? How do you decide what is "due" each person? Often it is hard to say because people might be expecting their due according to their *type of work*, their *effort expended*, their *merit*, their *need*, *time spent*, or other criteria. Each of these measures could be reasoned to be appropriate in different situations. Today the question of what constitutes fairness has divided people to such an extent that it has been argued that we have a new culture war over fairness.[38]

To use the principle of justice, we also must ask, "What is meant by justice?" There are several kinds of justice (or fairness) that come into play in organizations. **Distributive justice** refers to the distribution of benefits and burdens in societies and organizations. **Compensatory justice** involves compensating someone for a past injustice. **Procedural justice**, or *ethical due process*, refers to fair decision-making procedures, practices, or agreements.[39]

Procedural justice, or **ethical due process**, is especially relevant to business and professional organizations. Employees, customers, owners, and all stakeholders want to be treated fairly. They want to believe that they have been treated rightly and fairly in decision situations. They want their side of the issue to be heard, and they want to believe that the managers or decision makers took all factors into consideration and weighed them carefully before making a decision that affected them. The term **process fairness** has also been used to describe ethical due process.[40] Three factors have been identified that help to decide whether process fairness has been achieved. First, have people's (employees, customers) input been included in the decision process? Second, do people believe the decisions were made and implemented in an appropriate manner? Third, people watch their managers' behavior. Do they provide explanations when asked? Do they treat others respectfully? Do they actively listen to comments being made?[41] Ethical due process, or process fairness, works effectively with all stakeholders, whether they are employees, customers, owners, or others. Almost everyone responds positively to being treated fairly.

Rawls's Principle of Justice. John Rawls, a political philosopher who died in 2002 at the age of 81, became well known for his own version of ethical due process.[42] He provided what some have referred to as a comprehensive **principle of justice**.[43] Rawls's concept is based on the idea that what we need first is a fair method by which we may choose the principles through which conflicts will be resolved. The two principles of justice that underlie his theory are as follows:[44]

1. Each person has an equal right to the most extensive basic liberties compatible with similar liberties for all others.
2. Social and economic inequalities are arranged so that they are both (a) reasonably expected to be to everyone's advantage and (b) attached to positions and offices open to all.

According to Rawls's first principle, each person should be treated equally. In other words, it holds that each person should enjoy equally a full array of basic liberties.[45] The second principle is more controversial. It is often misinterpreted to imply that public policy should raise as high as possible the social and economic well-being of society's worst-off individuals. It is criticized by both those who argue that the principle is too strong and those who think it is too weak. The former think that, as long as people enjoy equal opportunity, it is not a case of injustice if some people benefit from their own work, skill, ingenuity, or assumed risks. Therefore, such people are more deserving and should not be expected to produce benefits for the least advantaged. The latter group thinks that the inequalities that may result could be so great as to be clearly unjust. Therefore, the rich get richer and the poor get only a little less poor.[46] The "income inequality" movement that is in the news today is essentially based on this latter explanation.

In developing further his second principle, Rawls imagined people gathered behind a "veil of ignorance," unaware of whether they, personally, were rich or poor, talented or incompetent. He then asked what kind of society they would create. He reasoned that the rule everyone would be able to agree on would be to maximize the well-being of the worst-off person, partially out of fear that any of them could wind up at the bottom.[47] This view has its critics, and it represents a situation that could not likely be brought about especially in a meritocracy—a system based on ability rather than need.

Supporters of the principle of justice claim that it preserves the basic values—freedom, equality of opportunity, and a concern for the disadvantaged—that have become embedded in societies' moral beliefs. Critics object to various parts of the theory and would not subscribe to Rawls's principles at all.

6.3g Ethics of Care

The **ethics of care** or the **principle of caring** is being discussed just after our discussion of utilitarianism, rights, and justice because this alternative view is critical of many traditional views. Some traditional views, it has been argued, embrace a masculine approach to perceiving the world and advocate rigid rules with clear lines.[48] The "care" perspective builds on the work of Carol Gilligan, whose reservations about Kohlberg's theory of moral development were discussed in Chapter 5. Gilligan asserted that women often spoke in "a different voice" that was more reflective of responsibility to others and on the continuity of interdependent relationships.[49]

The care perspective maintains that traditional ethics like the principles of utilitarianism and rights focus too much on the individual self and on cognitive thought processes. In the traditional view, "others" may be seen as threats, so rights become important. Resulting moral theories then tend to be legalistic or contractual.

Caring theory is founded on wholly different assumptions. Proponents of this perspective view the individual person as essentially relational, not individualistic. These persons do not deny the existence of the self but hold that the self has relationships that cannot be separated from the self's existence. This caring view emphasizes the relationships' moral worth and, by extension, the responsibilities inherent in those relationships, rather than in rights, as in traditional ethics.[50]

Several writers have argued that caring theory is consistent with stakeholder theory, or the stakeholder approach, in that the emphasis is on a more cooperative, caring type of relationship. In this view, firms should seek to make decisions that satisfy stakeholders, leading to situations in which all parties in the relationship gain. Robbin Derry elaborates: "In the corporate environment, there is an increasing demand for business to be attentive to its many stakeholders, particularly customers and employees, in caring ways. As organizations attempt to build such relationships, they must define the responsibilities of initiating and maintaining care. The ethics of care may be able to facilitate an understanding of these responsibilities."[51]

Jeanne Liedtka, by contrast, has questioned whether organizations can care in the sense in which caring theory proposes. Liedtka takes the position that caring people could lead to a caring organization that offers new possibilities for simultaneously enhancing the effectiveness and the moral quality of organizations.[52] The principle of caring offers a different perspective to guide ethical decision making—a perspective that clearly is thought provoking and valuable.

6.3h Virtue Ethics

The major principles discussed to this point have been more action-oriented. That is, they were designed to guide our actions and decisions and they involved the manager or leader "doing something." Another ethical tradition, often referred to as **virtue ethics**, merits consideration. Virtue ethics, rooted in the thinking of Plato and Aristotle, and many Eastern philosophies, is a school of thought that focuses on the individual becoming imbued with virtues (e.g., honesty, fairness, truthfulness, trustworthiness, benevolence, respect, and nonmalfeasance).[53] Virtue ethics is sometimes referred to as an aretaic theory of ethics, as defined earlier.[54]

Virtue ethics is a system of thought centered in the heart of the person—the manager, the employee, the competitor, and so on. This is in contrast to the principles we have discussed, which see the heart of ethics in *actions* or *duties* being carried out. Action-oriented principles focus on *doing*. Virtue ethics emphasizes *being*. The underlying assumption of virtue ethics is that the actions of a virtuous person will also be virtuous. Traditional ethical principles of utilitarianism, rights, and justice focus on the question, "What should I do?" Virtue ethics focuses on the question, "What sort of person should I *be* or *become*?"[55]

Ethics programs that have developed from the notion of virtue ethics have sometimes been called *character education* because this particular approach emphasizes character development. Many observers think that one reason why business and society are witnessing moral decline today is that we have failed to teach our young people universal principles of good character. The Character Counts program promotes the Six Pillars of Character: trustworthiness, respect, responsibility, fairness, caring, and citizenship.[56] Character education is needed not only in schools but in corporations as well. Corporate well-being demands character and business leaders are a vital and necessary force for putting character back into business.[57]

Virtue ethicists have brought back to the public debate the idea that virtues are important whether they be in the education of the young or in management training programs. Virtues such as honesty, integrity, loyalty, promise keeping, fairness, and respect for others are completely compatible with the major principles we have been discussing. The principles, combined with the virtues, form the foundation for effective ethical action and decision making.

6.3i The Golden Rule

The **Golden Rule** merits consideration because of its history and popularity as a basic and strong principle of ethical living and decision making. A number of studies have found it to be the most powerful and useful to managers.[58] The Golden Rule—"Do unto others as you would have them do unto you"—is a straightforward, easy-to-understand principle. Further, it guides the individual decision makers to behaviors, actions, or decisions that they should be able to express as acceptable or not based on some direct comparisons with what they would consider ethical or fair.

The Golden Rule, also known as the **ethic of reciprocity**, argues that if you want to be treated fairly, treat others fairly; if you want your privacy protected, respect the privacy of others. The key is impartiality. According to this principle, we are not to make an exception of ourselves. In essence, the Golden Rule personalizes business relations and brings the idea of self-perceived fairness into business deliberations.[59]

The popularity of the Golden Rule is linked to the fact that it is rooted in history and religious traditions and is among the oldest of the principles of living. Further, it is universal in that it requires no specific religious belief or faith. Since time began, religious leaders and philosophers have advocated the Golden Rule in one form or another.

Leadership expert John C. Maxwell published an insightful book titled *There's No Such Thing as "Business" Ethics: There's Only One Rule for Making Decisions.* The one rule Maxwell advocates is the Golden Rule. According to Maxwell, there are four reasons why managers and all decision makers should adopt the Golden Rule.

1. The Golden Rule is accepted by most people.
2. The Golden Rule is easy to understand.
3. The Golden Rule is a win–win philosophy.
4. The Golden Rule acts as a compass when you need direction.[60]

As one considers the ethics principles and concepts presented, no single principle is recommended for use always. The more one gets into each principle, the more one realizes how difficult it would be for a person to use each principle consistently as a guide to decision making. On the other hand, to say that an ethical principle is imperfect is not to say that it has not raised important criteria that should be addressed in personal or business decision making. The major principles and approaches we have discussed have raised to our consciousness the importance of the collective good, individual rights, caring, character, serving others first, and fairness.

6.3j Servant Leadership

An increasingly popular approach to organizational leadership and thinking today is **servant leadership**. It is an approach to ethical leadership and decision making based on the moral principle of *serving others first*. Can these two roles—servant and leader—be fused in one person—a manager or leader? What are the basic tenets of servant leadership?

Servant leadership is a model or principle of ethical management—an approach to ethical decision making—based on the idea that serving others such as employees, customers, community, and other stakeholders is the first priority. The modern era of servant leadership is marked primarily by the works of Robert K. Greenleaf, who spent 38 years of his career working for AT&T. Greenleaf takes the strong position that the servant leader is "servant first." Froto Baggins, the fictional character in *The Lord of the Rings,* often has been said to be a servant leader. Froto gave up himself and put his life on the line for the fellowship, and in the process he helped the members of the fellowship to flourish and discover their gifts.[61]

Ten key characteristics essential for the development of servant leaders have been culled from Greenleaf's writings. Each of these is worth noting because, collectively, they paint a portrait of servant leadership in terms of leader behaviors and characteristics. These characteristics are as follows:[62] listening; empathy; healing; persuasion; awareness; foresight; conceptualization; commitment to the growth of people; stewardship; and building community.

Each of these characteristics is based on the ethical principle of putting the other person first—whether that other person is an employee, a customer, or some other important stakeholder. Some of these characteristics could be stated as virtues and some as behaviors. Thus, servant leadership embraces several of the ethical perspectives discussed earlier. Servant leadership builds a bridge between the ideas of business ethics and those of leadership. Joanne Ciulla has observed that people follow servant leaders because they can trust them, and this invokes the ethical dimension.[63]

In summary, the principles approach to ethics focuses on guidelines or concepts that have been created to help people and organizations make wise, ethical decisions. Two ethical categories include the teleological (ends-based) and the deontological (duty-based). Both duty and consequences are important ethical concepts. In our discussion, we have treated the following as important components of the principles-based approach: utilitarianism, rights, justice, caring, virtue, the Golden Rule, and servant leadership. Such principles, or principle-based approaches, cause us to think deeply and to reflect carefully on the ethical decisions we face in our managerial and organizational lives. For the most part, these principles are rooted in moral philosophy, logic, and religion. On a more pragmatic level, we turn now to a series of practical ethical tests that constitute another major approach to ethics.

6.4 Ethical Tests Approach to Decision Making

In addition to the principles approach to ethics in guiding personal and managerial decision making, a more practical **ethical tests** approach represents a more practical alternative. While the principles have almost exclusively been generated by moral philosophers and business ethicists, the ethical tests presented here have been culled from the real-world experiences of many. The ethical tests are more practical or hands-on in orientation and do not require the depth of moral thinking that the principles do. The ethical tests are posed as questions that should provide useful guidance. No single test is recommended as a universal answer to the question, "What action or decision should I take in this situation?" However, people may find one or several tests that will be beneficial in helping them to clarify the appropriate course of action in a decision situation.

To most of us, the notion of a test invokes the thought of questions posed that need to be answered. Indeed, each of these tests for managerial ethical decision making requires the thoughtful deliberation of a central query that gets to the heart of the ethics issue. The answer to the question should help the decision maker decide whether the course of action, practice, or decision should be pursued or not. No single test is fool proof, but each should be helpful. Often, several tests can be used in conjunction with one another.

6.4a Test of Common Sense

With this first ethical test, the individual simply asks, "Does the action I am getting ready to take really make sense?" When you think of behavior that might have ethical implications, it is logical to consider the practical consequences. If, for example, you would surely get caught engaging in a questionable practice, the action does not pass the **test of common sense.** Many unethical practices have come to light when one is led to ask whether individuals really used their common sense at all. This test has limitations. For example, if you conclude that you would not get caught engaging in a questionable practice, this test might lead you to think that the questionable practice is an acceptable course of action, when in fact it is not. In addition, there may be other aspects of the situation that you have overlooked. Some have called the test of common sense the **"smell" test.** If a proposed course of action stinks, do not do it.

6.4b Test of One's Best Self

Psychologists tell us that each person has a self-concept. Most people can envision a scenario of themselves *at their best*. This ethics test requires the individual to pose the question, "Is this action or decision I'm getting ready to take compatible with my concept of myself *at my best*?" This test addresses the notion of the esteem with which we hold ourselves and the kind of person we want to be known as. Naturally, this test would not be of much value to those who do not hold themselves in high esteem. To those concerned about their esteem and reputation, however, this could be a powerful guide preventing one from taking a questionable course of action.

6.4c Test of Making Something Public (Disclosure Rule)

The test of making something public, sometimes called the disclosure rule, is one of the most powerful tests.[64] If you are about to engage in a questionable practice or action, you might pose the following questions: "How would I feel if others knew I was doing this? How would I feel if I knew that my decisions or actions were going to be featured on the national evening news tonight for the entire world to see?" This test addresses the issue of whether your action or decision can withstand public disclosure and scrutiny. How would you feel if all your friends, family, and colleagues knew you were engaging in this action? If you feel comfortable with this thought, you are probably on solid footing. If you feel uncomfortable with this thought, you might need to rethink your position. A variation of this test has been called the "Grandma test." Here the question would be, "If my grandmother saw what I was doing, would she approve?" Another version of this test is called the "viral news test." To use this test, ask yourself how your proposed decision or action would be viewed if it went viral on social media. A disadvantage of this test is that it is only as good as the society in which we live.[65]

6.4d Test of Ventilation

The test of ventilation is to "expose" your proposed action or decision to others and get their thoughts on it before acting. This test works best if you get opinions from people who you know might not see things your way. The important point here is that you do not isolate yourself with your ethical dilemma but seek others' views. After you have subjected your proposed course of action to other opinions, you may find that you have not been thinking clearly or fairly. In other words, ventilate—or share—your ethical quandary, rather than keeping it to yourself. Someone else may say something of value that will help you in making your decision.

6.4e Test of Purified Idea

An idea or action might be thought to be "purified"—that is, cleansed or made acceptable—when a person with authority says or implies it is appropriate. Such a person of authority might be a supervisor, a manager, or a lawyer. The central question here is, "Am I thinking this action or decision is right just because someone with appropriate or higher authority or knowledge says it is right?" Be careful about this type of thinking. If you look hard enough, you always can find a lawyer or an accountant to endorse almost any idea if it is phrased right.[66] However, these other persons are not the final arbiter of what is right or wrong. Similarly, just because a superior says an action or a decision is ethical does not make it so. The decision or course of action may still be questionable or wrong even though others have sanctioned it with their approval. This is one of the most common ethical errors people make, and people must constantly be reminded that they themselves ultimately will be held accountable if the action is indefensible.[67]

6.4f Test of the Big Four

Another test of your ethical behavior is to question whether it has fallen victim to "the Big Four." The Big Four are four characteristics of decision making that may lead you astray or toward the unethical course of action. The four factors are greed, speed, laziness, and haziness.[68] *Greed* is the drive to acquire more and more in your own self-interest. *Speed* refers to the tendency to rush things and cut corners because you are under the pressure of time. Do not confuse "cutting corners" with efficiency. *Laziness* may lead you to take the easy course of action that requires the least amount of effort. This can lead to mental errors. *Haziness* may lead you to acting or reacting without a clear idea of what is going on. It is critical to understand the situation before taking action. All four of these factors represent temptations that, if succumbed to, might lead to unethical behavior.[69]

6.4g Gag Test

This test was provided by a judge on the Louisiana Court of Appeals. He argued that a manager's clearest signal that a dubious decision or action is going too far is when you simply "gag" at the prospect of carrying it out.[70] Admittedly, this test can capture only the grossest of unethical behaviors, but there are some managers who may need such a crude kind of test. Actually, this test is intended to be more humorous than serious, but a few might be helped by it. Figure 6-2 summarizes the practical ethical guidelines that may be extracted from these ethical tests.

6.4h Use Several Tests in Combination

None of the previously mentioned ethics tests alone offers a perfect way to determine whether a decision, act, or practice is ethical or unethical. If several tests are used in combination, especially the more powerful ones, they do provide a means of practically examining proposed actions before engaging in them. To repeat, this assumes that the individual really wants to do what is right and fair and is looking for guidance. To the fundamentally unethical person, however, these tests would not be of much value.

Figure 6-2 Practical Guidelines Derived from Key Ethical Tests Approach to Business Ethics

Ethical Test	Practical Ethical Guideline
Common Sense	If the proposed course of action violates your "common sense," don't do it. If it doesn't pass the "smell" test, don't do it.
One's Best Self	If the proposed course of action is not consistent with your perception of yourself at your "best," don't engage in it.
Making Something Public	If you would not be comfortable with people knowing you did something, don't do it. Don't take a course of action if you think your grandma might disapprove.
Ventilation	Expose your proposed course of action to others' opinions. Don't keep your ethical dilemma to yourself. Get a second opinion.
Purified Idea	Don't think that others in authority such as an accountant, a lawyer, or a boss can "purify" your proposed action by saying they think it is okay. It still may be wrong. You will still be held responsible.
Big Four	Don't compromise your action or decision by tempting behaviors, such as greed, speed, laziness, or haziness.
Gag Test	If you "gag" at the prospect of carrying out a proposed course of action, don't do it.

Figure 6-3 Three Major Approaches to Business Ethics or Ethical Decision Making

Approaches to Business Ethics	Description
Conventional Approach *(Chapter 5)*	Compare a decision, practice, or policy with society's prevailing norms of acceptability. This is the way conventional societies think.
Principles Approach *(Chapter 6)*	Be guided by principles or guidelines, anchored in moral philosophy, that have been around for centuries. Examples include the principles of rights, justice, utilitarianism, care, virtue, Golden Rule, and servant leadership.
Ethical Tests Approach *(Chapter 6)*	Ethical tests are practical questions you might ask yourself that might direct you to pursue ethical courses of action. Examples include the tests of common sense; one's best self; making something public (disclosure rule); ventilation, purified idea, Big Four, gag test.

Based on a five-year study of ethical principles and ethical tests, Phillip Lewis asserted that there is high agreement on how a decision maker should behave when faced with a moral choice. He presents a general process:

> In fact, there is almost a step-by-step sequence. Notice: One should (1) look at the problem from the position of the other person(s) affected by a decision; (2) try to determine what virtuous response is expected; (3) ask (a) how it would feel for the decision to be disclosed to a wide audience and (b) whether the decision is consistent with organizational goals; and (4) act in a way that is (a) right and just for any other person in a similar situation and (b) good for the organization.[71]

Implicit in Lewis's recommendation is evidence of stakeholder theory, virtue theory, servant leadership, the Golden Rule, the disclosure rule, and Rawls's principle of justice. It is this type of combining of ethics principles that may prove to be most useful.

Figure 6-3 summarizes the three major approaches to ethics and ethical decision making presented in Chapter 5 (conventional approach) and Chapter 6 (principles approach and ethics tests approach).

6.5 Managing Organizational Ethics

To this point, our discussion has centered on principles, guidelines, and approaches to ethical decision making that employees and managers might use. Clearly, ethical decision making is at the heart of business ethics, and we cannot stress enough the need to sharpen decision-making skills if amorality is to be eradicated and moral management is to be achieved. Now, we shift our attention to the *organizational context* in which decision making occurs. Actions and practices that take place within the organization's structure, processes, culture, or climate are vital in bringing about ethical business practices and results. Based on his research, Craig VanSandt has concluded, "Understanding and managing an organization's ethical work climate may go a long way toward defining the difference between what a company does and what kind of organization it is."[72]

To manage ethics in an organization, a manager must appreciate that the organization's ethical climate is just one part of its overall corporate culture. When McNeil Laboratories, a subsidiary of Johnson & Johnson, voluntarily withdrew Tylenol from the market immediately after the reports of tainted, poisoned products, some people wondered why they made this decision. An often-cited response was, "It's the J & J way."[73] This statement conveys a noteworthy message about the firm's ethical work climate or corporate culture. It also raises the question of how organizations and managers should deal with, understand, and shape business ethics through actions taken, policies established, and examples set. The organization's moral climate is a complex entity, and we can discuss only some facets of it in this section.[74]

Figure 6-4 portrays several levels of moral climate and some of the key factors that may come to bear on managers as they make decisions. What happens within organizations, as Figure 6-4 depicts, is nested in industry's, business's, and society's moral climate. But, our focus in this section is on the organization's moral climate. Regardless of the ethics of individuals, organizational factors prove to be powerful in shaping ethical or unethical behavior and practices. The following three major questions drive the consideration of managing organizational ethics:

1. What factors contribute to ethical or unethical behavior in the organization?
2. What actions, strategies, or best practices might the management team use to improve the organization's ethical climate?
3. What psychological and organizational processes revealed through "behavioral ethics" come into play when ethical decision making and behavior are pursued?

6.5a Factors Affecting the Organization's Ethical Climate

For managers to be able to create an ethical work climate, they must first understand the factors at work in the organization that influence whether or not other managers and employees behave ethically. It is clear that both individual and contextual factors influence the ethical climate in the organization. More than a few studies have been conducted that have sought to identify and to rank the sources

Figure 6-4 Factors Affecting the Morality of Managers and Employees

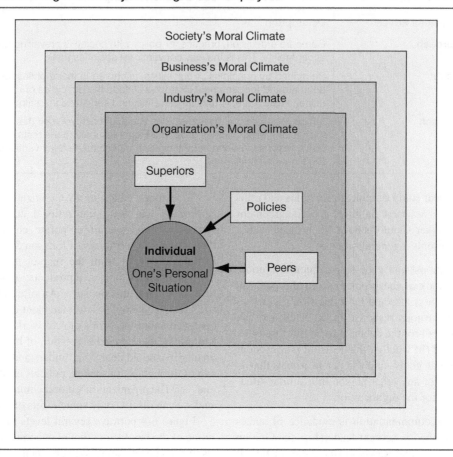

of ethical behavior in organizations. In other words, why do employees and managers sometimes engage in questionable behavior? Is it because they are "bad apples," as Epstein and Hanson suggested? Or is it because of a "bad barrel" (the organization)? Even when the organizational context is not bad, per se, there continue to be influences that arise within the organization that affect behaviors.

What are these influences? Although there is some variation in the rankings of studies, findings from three influential studies are worthy of note[75]:

- *Behavior of superiors* was ranked as the primary influence on unethical behavior in three studies examined. In other words, the influence of bosses is powerful.
- *Behavior of one's peers* was ranked high in two of the three studies. People do pay attention to what their peers are doing and expecting.
- *Industry or professional ethical practices* ranked in the upper half in all three studies. These contextual factors are influential.
- *Personal financial need* ranked last in all three studies. But let's not assume it does not matter because for some people it does.

What stands out in these studies, from an organizational perspective, is the powerful influence of the behavior of one's superiors and peers. Also notable about these findings

is that quite often it is assumed that society's moral climate has a lot to do with managers' morality, but this factor was ranked low in the two studies in which it was considered. Apparently, society's moral climate serves as a background factor that does not have a direct and immediate impact on organizational ethics. Furthermore, it is enlightening to know that personal financial need ranked so low. But we should not assume that personal needs and wants are irrelevant. Sometimes personal financial needs and greed are at work. What these findings suggest is that there are factors at work over which managers can exercise some discretion. One of the primary factors is the pressure bosses put on their subordinates to achieve and perform. Thus, we begin to see the managerial dimension of business ethics.

Pressures Exerted on Employees by Superiors. One major consequence of the behavior of superiors and peers is that pressure is placed on subordinates and/or other organizational members to achieve results, and this often requires that they compromise their ethics. In one early national study of this topic, managers were asked to what extent they agreed with the following proposition: "Managers today feel under pressure to compromise personal standards to achieve company goals."[76] It is insightful to consider the management levels of the 64.4 percent of the respondents who agreed with the proposition.

The *pattern of response* is what is especially insightful about these findings. It appears that the lower that managers, or employees, are in the hierarchy, the more they perceive pressures to engage in unethical conduct. These varying perceptions at different levels in the managerial hierarchy suggest that higher-level managers may not be tuned in to how pressure is perceived or "felt" at lower levels. This breakdown in understanding, or lack of sensitivity by higher management to how far subordinates will go to please them, can be conducive to lower-level subordinates behaving unethically out of a real or perceived fear of reprisal, a misguided sense of loyalty, or a distorted concept of their jobs.[77]

In the 2020 Global Busines Ethics Survey, it was found that employees report that the pressure to compromise standards is as high as it ever has been.[78] Regarding the management level reporting pressure, it is now discovered that middle management is feeling this pressure the most followed by top management. It has been argued that this new pattern may be attributable to the increase in organizational transitions that are taking place, largely due to COVID-19 and its impact. While not the only reason for the increase in pressure, top and middle management's awareness of and/or involvement in changes appears to now be a key driver in the higher rates experienced recently.[79]

6.5b Improving the Organization's Ethical Culture

Because the *behavior of managers* has been identified as the most important influence on the ethical behavior of organization members, it should come as no surprise that most actions and strategies for improving the organization's ethical culture must originate from top management and other management levels as well. Organizational ethical culture refers to the shared values, beliefs, behaviors, and ways of doing things in the organization. It has been found that positive corporate cultures help a company's bottom line, but the reverse is not necessarily true—a company's success is not enough to ensure a positive culture.[80] Therefore, intended initiatives to improve the organization's culture are needed; it does not just happen because the business is successful.

The process by which managers strive to improve on the organization's ethical culture has sometimes been referred to as "institutionalizing ethics" into the organization.[81] According to the Ethics & Compliance Initiative, critical aspects of an organization's ethical culture include management's trustworthiness, whether managers at all levels talk about ethics and model ethical behavior, and the extent to which employees value and support ethical conduct, accountability, and transparency. Ethics culture includes the tone set by top management leaders, supervisor reinforcement of ethical behavior, and peer commitment—supporting one another in doing the right thing.[82]

In its 2020 study of ethical business cultures, the Global Business Ethics Survey found there were key drivers to improving ethical culture. These included (1) employee awareness of program elements that helped employees navigate potential ethical problems; (2) employee perceptions of the organization's culture based on commitment, modeling, and communications from superiors; and (3) key ethics outcomes such as pressure to compromise standards, observed misconduct, the reporting of misconduct, and retaliation against those reporting misconduct.[83]

Ethics In Practice Case

Do More Sales Lead to Lower Ethics?

At my recent job, I held a position as a Customer Service and Sales Representative for a well-recognized bank. My responsibility was to help customers solve issues and concerns they might have on their accounts, but mainly I was to concentrate on selling them bank products. I started out as a teller and worked my way up to a Sales Rep. As I went through training, they instructed us to concentrate on customer service before anything else, but they also mentioned that sales were an important part of the position, yet never mentioning that it would be the primary goal. The goal setting level in the bank is determined by the amount of sales the bank needs quarterly. However, these goals differ from the requirements of each individual's position. There is also a big emphasis on meeting daily sales goals to reach your numbers by the end of the quarter.

As I started working, I realized that it was difficult to meet the daily goals that are expected. The bank sets goals that are somewhat unrealistic to most of us, particularly because we have the same customers visiting the bank. It is very difficult to sell other products to the same customers since they already have every bank product they need. By the bank setting these high goals, we are pushed to sell to some customers extra checking or savings accounts that sometimes were unnecessary for them to have. Yet, to achieve our goals we encourage them to open the new accounts by saying it would somehow benefit them. I am not pleased with doing this, since we could easily just convert the existing product to the new one without having to open another account for them. The customers have more trouble keeping track of all these extra accounts rather than just keeping the existing ones with the new benefits. However, not selling them the new products sometimes makes it impossible to meet our sales goal for the quarter.

1. Is it ethical for the bank to keep raising our goals and expect that we keep selling these extra accounts that customers might not really need?
2. What are the ethical issues facing the company?
3. Is it right for us not to disclose to the customer the idea of keeping the same account and just convert it instead of opening a new one?
4. Should I give in to the pressure of the company to meet the company's goal? What should I do?

Contributed by Catalina Vargas

Another factor important to an ethical culture is whether the organization has a compliance or an ethics orientation.

Compliance versus Ethics Orientation. An organization with a culture of ethics is most likely a mixture of an emphasis on compliance and on such values as integrity or ethics. Compliance emphases took a huge step forward when the U.S. Sentencing Commission (USSC), an independent agency of the judicial branch of the federal government, passed guidelines that were most recently revised and updated in 2015. These Organizational Sentencing Guidelines began a partnership between companies and the federal government to prevent and deter corporate illegal/unethical practices.[84] The guidelines gave companies incentives for creating strong compliance and ethics programs. It is little wonder, then, that we have seen such programs increase in number and become vital parts of companies' corporate cultures.

An ongoing discussion is whether a **compliance orientation** or an **ethics orientation** should prevail in companies' ethics programs.[85] Historically, more emphasis has been placed on legal compliance than on ethics. Several concerns articulated about a compliance focus have been identified.[86] A pure compliance focus could undermine the ways of thinking or habits of mind that are needed in ethics thinking. It also has been argued that compliance can squeeze out ethics by focusing too much on what is legal. The issue of a "false consciousness" also has been raised. This means that managers may become accustomed to addressing issues in a mechanistic, rule-based way, and this may cause them to not consider tougher issues that a more ethics-focused approach might require.[87]

Because of the rule of law and growing litigation, a compliance focus cannot be eliminated. The approach recommended here is toward developing organizational cultures and programs that aspire to be ethics-focused. The importance of both has been emphasized in the observation that the ethics perspective is needed to give a compliance program "soul," while compliance features may be necessary to give ethics programs more "body."[88] In short, both are essential.

6.6 Behavioral Ethics—Achieving a Deeper Understanding

To this juncture, we have discussed ethics principles and managing organizational ethics. It now is helpful to focus on a relatively new field of thought that has been termed **behavioral ethics**. For the most part, our discussions have been normative in nature. Behavioral ethics, by contrast, helps us to augment our understanding at a deeper level of many of the behavioral processes that research has shown are taking place in people and organizations. Thus, most of these learnings are descriptive in nature as they strive to capture insights into processes that have been observed to

be taking place in actual practice. An awareness of these behavioral phenomena greatly adds to our understanding of business ethics and should help us to better design ethics initiatives in organizations.

Behavioral ethics has been defined as "the study of systematic and predictable ways in which individuals make ethical decisions and judge the ethical decisions of others that are at odds with intuition."[89] This approach embraces both intentional and unintentional unethical behaviors. It also has been noted that behavioral ethics embraces individual, group, and organizational influences.[90] Behavioral ethics gives us insights into how people actually behave in organizations as a result of psychological processes or as a consequence of organizational factors at work. These insights help us overcome problems or better design organizations to offset detrimental consequences.

Some of the phenomena that have been observed that would fit into the category of behavioral ethics are worth briefly noting. They should be seen as helpful insights into understanding behaviors observed. **Bounded ethicality** tends to occur when managers and employees find that even when they aspire to behave ethically, it is difficult due to a variety of organizational pressures and psychological tendencies that intervene.[91] There are limits on people's abilities to be ethical. Tendencies toward bounded ethicality might include claiming credit for a group's work without realizing you are doing it, engaging in implicit discrimination and in-group favoritism, and falling prey to the influence of conflicts of interest.[92]

Conformity bias is a behavioral pattern that has also been observed. This is the tendency people have to take their cues for ethical behavior from their peers rather than exercising their own independent ethical judgment. Another predisposition is **overconfidence bias**. This is the tendency for people to be more confident of their own moral character or behavior than they have objective reason to be. **Self-serving bias** is similar; this is the propensity people have to process information in a way that serves to support their preexisting beliefs and their perceived self-interest.[93]

Other important behavioral ethics patterns include framing, incrementalism, role morality, and moral equilibrium. **Framing** refers to the fact that people's ethical judgments are affected by how a question or issue is posed (framed). It has been found, for example, that when people are prompted to think of an issue as an "ethical" issue, they will tend to make more ethical decisions than if they had been prompted to think of the issue as a "business" issue.[94] **Incrementalism** is the predisposition toward the slippery slope. It has been noted that there is a tendency toward making a series of minor ethical misjudgments that can lead to major ethical mistakes.

Role morality is the tendency some people have to use different ethical standards as they move through different roles in life. For example, a person might make more questionable decisions at work when job and profits are at stake than they would at home or in their family. Finally, **moral equilibrium** has been observed. This is the penchant for people to keep an ethical scoreboard in their heads and use this information when making future decisions. While seeking equilibrium, for example, a person might take moral license on an issue if they think they are running a moral surplus in their overall behavior.[95] While seeking balance, people may rationalize future behavior rather than judging each decision situation on its own merits.

Related to some of these concepts, there are ethical breakdowns or barriers that organizational members may experience even as they see themselves as "good people" striving to do what is right.[96] Five barriers to an ethical organization include the following: **Ill-conceived goals** are poorly set goals that encourage negative behaviors such as sales goals emphasized too frequently or set too high. **Motivated blindness** is the process of overlooking the questionable actions of others when it is in one's own best interest. This is the self-serving bias described earlier. **Indirect blindness** occurs when one holds others less accountable for unethical behaviors when they are carried out through third parties. The **slippery slope**, mentioned earlier as incrementalism, causes people to not notice others' unethical behavior when it gradually occurs in small increments. Finally, **overcoming values** is the act of letting questionable behaviors pass if the outcome is good. This can occur when managers overemphasize results rather than how the results were achieved. It could be played out as the ends justifying the means.

Research into behavioral ethics gives us deeper and richer insights into the challenges of being ethical within our managerial and organizational roles and the difficulties of creating an ethical organizational culture while implementing many of the best practices and principles to be discussed next. Behavioral ethics may be seen as an overlay of real-world experience on the normative strategies of improving business ethics using ethics training, ethics principles, and other decision-making approaches. Consequently, they must

be taken into consideration when striving to manage business ethics or improving the organization's ethics.

6.7 Best Practices for Improving an Organization's Ethics

Best practices are those approaches, programs, policies, or guidelines that experience has shown produce the most effective results. In the following sections, we will discuss some of the best practices that experts have concluded are vital to improving an organization's ethical culture or climate. Figure 6-5 summarizes these best practices for creating such an ethical organization. Top management leadership in the pursuit of moral management is at the hub of these initiatives. Board of Directors' oversight has become especially vital in recent years as corporate governance has been discovered to be an integral part of an ethical culture.

6.7a Top Management Leadership (Moral Management)

It has become an established principle of ethical leadership that the **moral tone** of an organization is set by top management. The linkage between the "tone at the top" and business fraud has received international attention over the past several years. Tone at the top refers to the ethical atmosphere that is created by the organization's leadership.[97] The tone that top management sets will have a trickle-down effect on the rest of the organization. If the tone set by management focuses on ethics and integrity, employees can be expected to follow these values. On the other hand, if top management is casual or unconcerned and focused more on the bottom-line results, employees might be more inclined to engage in questionable behavior because they will think

Figure 6-5 Best Practices for Improving an Organization's Ethical Culture

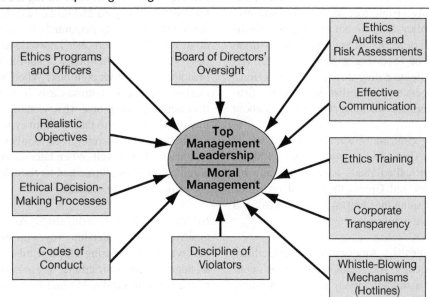

Ethics In Practice Case

Employees Fired for Cheating on Employer Training Tests

During one of its tests for new employee analysts, Goldman Sachs Group, Inc. fired about 20 new employees for cheating on tests during their training period. The employees had been working with the investment bank's securities division and included analysts from its New York and London offices. The topics on the tests were the employees' knowledge of important industry and regulatory information, including information about compliance, gift-giving policies, and anti-money laundering policies. JPMorgan Chase had fired ten employees a month earlier for similar violations.

Goldman Sachs has been one of the most selective employers on Wall Street, and during the previous year the company hired only 3 percent of its 267,000 applicants. The firm's CEO has referred to his company as the employer of choice in their industry. They typically recruit the best and the brightest from some of the nation's most elite business schools. One observer said that getting a job at Goldman was harder than being accepted into Harvard.

Apparently, the tests had never been received well by the new employees. The tests are seen as time consuming, repetitive, and annoying, and some of the test takers saw them as a waste of time and put them off until the last minute. Some observers remarked that cheating on these types of tests had been an accepted part of finance training in the industry.

How the employees got caught cheating was somewhat surprising in its lack of complexity. The employees who cheated used their Goldman-issued computers to look up terms that appeared on the exam. They took their tests on these computers and also used them to search on Google for some of the answers. The company was able to trace the cheating activity on their computers. Some of the cheaters shared answers, a practice said to be a routine way to save time during the hectic workweek.

The tests taken were not seen as difficult and a person had to score a 70 to pass on the one-hour test. If they failed, they would have been given another chance to take the test, and they would not have been fired (at least the first time). However, they might have evoked disappointment and ire by their supervisors.

A Goldman Sachs spokesperson said, "this conduct was not only a clear violation of the rules, but completely inconsistent with the values we foster at the firm."

1. If these were bright, young employees who had survived a very competitive hiring process, why do you think they risked it all by cheating?
2. Did the topics covered by the test make firing a more likely outcome? Should the test takers have seen this?
3. Was firing a fair consequence in this situation? Should the company have used some other penalty? If so, what?

Sources: Julia La Roche, "This Is How the Goldman Sachs Analysts Who Got Fired Cheated," https://www.yahoo.com/entertainment/s/goldman-sachs-analysts-got-fired-162922277.html, accessed March 22, 2021; Justin Baer, "Goldman Firing about 20 Junior Staffers for Cheating on Tests," *The Wall Street Journal*, October 17–18/2016, B2, https://www.wsj.com/articles/goldman-firing-about-20-junior-staffers-for-cheating-on-tests-1445010241, accessed March 22, 2021; Sofia Horta e Costa and Ruth David, "Goldman, J. P. Morgan Said to Fire 30 Analysts for Cheating on Tests," October 16, 2015, accessed March 22, 2021.

that management is not concerned with ethical conduct. Employees are more likely to engage in the same practices they observe their managers doing.[98]

Top management, therefore, through its capacity to set a personal example and to shape policy, is in the ideal position to provide a highly visible role model. The authority and ability to shape policy, both formal and implied, forms one of the vital aspects of the job of any leader in any organization. This aspect of becoming a moral manager has been referred to as "role modeling through visible action." Effective moral managers recognize that they live in a fishbowl and that employees are watching them for cues about what's important.[99]

There is a striking contrast between weak and strong ethical leadership in business practice today. Indeed, weak leaders are often called "bad" leaders and, according to researchers Gini and Green, they could be called "*mis-leaders*."[100] Examining the contrast between weak and strong ethical leadership is revealing.

Weak Ethical Leadership. An example of weak ethical leadership (or role modeling) was found in one author's consulting experiences in a small company where a long-time employee was identified as having embezzled about $20,000 over a 15-year period. When the employee was questioned as to why she had done this, she explained that she thought it was all right because the president of the company had led her to believe it was okay by actions he had taken. She further explained that any time during the fall, when the leaves had fallen in his yard and he needed them raked, he would simply take company personnel off their jobs and have them do it. When he needed cash, he would take it out of the company's cash box in her office or get the key to the soft drink machine and raid its coin box. When he needed stamps to mail his personal Christmas cards, he would take them out of the company stamp box. The woman's perception was that it was okay for her to take the money because the president did it frequently. Therefore, she thought it was an acceptable practice for her as well. When later questioned, the president admitted this was all true and he thought the woman should not be dealt with too harshly.

Strong Ethical Leadership. An example of strong, positive ethical leadership was seen in the case of a firm that was manufacturing electron tubes. One day the plant manager called a hurried meeting to announce that a sample of the tubes in production had failed a critical safety test. This meant that the safety and performance of the batch of

10,000 tubes was highly questionable. The plant manager wondered aloud, "What are we going to do now?" Ethical leadership was shown by the vice president for technical operations, who looked around the room at each person and then declared in a low voice, "Scrap them!" According to an employee who worked for this vice president, that act set the tone for the corporation for years, because every person present knew of situations in which faulty products had been shipped under pressures of time and budget.[101]

These cases provide vivid examples of how a leader's actions and behavior communicated important messages to others in the organization. In the absence of knowing what to do, most employees look to the behavior of their leaders for cues as to what conduct is acceptable. In the second case, another crucial point is illustrated. When we speak of management providing ethical leadership, it is not just restricted to top management. Vice presidents, plant managers, supervisors, and, indeed, all managerial personnel share the responsibility for ethical leadership. This was reinforced in one ethics survey when employees were asked to identify their "leaders" and quite often they identified their direct supervisors as top management more often than the CEO or president.[102] This finding reinforces the critical role that all managers play in ethical leadership. To workers, what all their superiors in the organization do is important.

Two Pillars of Ethical Leadership. It has been contended that a manager's reputation for ethical leadership is founded on two pillars: perceptions of the manager both as a moral person *and* as a moral manager. Being a *moral person* requires three major attributes: traits, behaviors, and decision making. Important traits are stable personal attributes, such as integrity, honesty, and trustworthiness. Critical behaviors—what you do, not what you say—include doing the right thing, showing concern for people, being open, and being personally ethical. Decision making by the moral person needs to reflect a solid set of ethical values and principles. In this activity, the manager would hold to values, be objective/fair, demonstrate concern for society, and follow ethical decision rules.[103]

The idea of the second pillar, being a *moral manager*, was developed and discussed in the previous chapter. According to researchers, moral managers recognize the importance of proactively putting ethics at the forefront of their ethical agenda. To them, good leadership necessarily consists of a moral ingredient.[104] Putting ethics at the forefront involves three major activities. First, the moral manager must engage in *role modeling* through visible action. Second, the moral manager *communicates about ethics and values*. Third, the moral manager needs to *use rewards and discipline effectively*. This is a powerful way to send signals about desirable and undesirable conduct in the workplace.[105]

6.7b Effective Communication of Ethical Messages

Management also carries a profound burden in terms of providing ethical leadership in the area of effective communication.

We have seen the importance of communicating through acts, principles, and organizational climate. Later we will discuss further the communication aspects of setting realistic objectives, codes of conduct, and the decision-making process. Here, however, we want to stress the importance of communicating principles, techniques, and practices. If organization members do not clearly understand what the ethical standards, values, and expectations are, this creates a major impediment to their use.

Conveying the importance of ethics through communication includes both written and verbal forms of communication. It also includes nonverbal communications. In each of these settings, management should operate according to certain key ethical principles. Candor, fidelity, and confidentiality are three important communication principles. *Candor* requires that a manager be forthright, sincere, and honest in communication transactions. It requires the manager to be fair and free from prejudice and malice in the communication. *Fidelity* in communication means that the communicator should be faithful to detail, should be accurate, and should avoid deception or exaggeration. *Confidentiality* is another principle that ought to be stressed. Ethical managers must exercise care in deciding what information they disclose to others. Trust can be easily shattered if the manager does not have a keen sense of what is confidential in a communication.[106]

6.7c Ethics and Compliance Programs and Officers

One of the most important strategies in creating an ethical workplace culture is the use of ethics and compliance programs along with officers to lead them in their initiatives and responsibilities. Ethics and compliance programs are typically organizational units, people or departments that have been assigned the responsibility for monitoring and improving ethics in the organization. There are several certification programs for ethics and compliance officers. One of the most popular is the LPEC—Leading Professional in Ethics and Compliance—which is available through the Ethics and Compliance Initiative. Recognized at the international level, LPEC-certified professionals represent more than 60 countries and range across all industries.[107]

Based on common practice, ethics and compliance programs typically include the following features:[108]

- Written standards of ethical workplace conduct (e.g., codes of conduct/ethics)
- Ethics training on the standards
- Mechanisms to seek ethics advice or information
- Methods or means for reporting misconduct anonymously
- Performance evaluations of ethical conduct
- Systems to discipline violators
- A set of guiding values or principles

In addition to this list of common practices, other important features of successful ethics and compliance programs include the ethical tone set at the top, and the organization's culture, risk assessments, and ethics testing.[109]

Figure 6-6 Essential Elements in an Effective Ethics and Compliance Program

The U.S. Sentencing Commission has identified seven key elements that companies should have in their ethics and compliance programs to satisfy the commission's review. If a company has these important elements, it will be dealt with less harshly should violations arise. If companies follow the guidelines, they may receive reduced fines, reduced sentences, or deferred prosecutions. Organizations should consider adopting Governance, Risk Management and Compliance (GRC) software applications to serve as foundations for their programs.

STRUCTURE. Establish Policies, Procedures, and Controls. Organizations must establish these to serve as standards to prevent and detect unethical conduct.

OVERSIGHT. Exercise Effective Compliance and Ethics Oversight. Multiple layers of management need to be involved to ensure the effectiveness of programs. Designated individuals at the various levels must be knowledgeable of the program.

DUE DILIGENCE. Exercise Due Diligence to Avoid Delegation of Authority to Unethical Individuals. Reasonable efforts need to be made to be sure that individuals with a history on unethical behavior are avoided.

COMMUNICATION. Communicate and Educate Employees on Programs. Practical steps must be taken periodically by the organization to be sure that all employees understand the policies, procedures, and standards.

MONITORING. Monitor and Audit Programs for Effectiveness. Mechanisms must be created for ensuring that the ethics and compliance program is being followed by all employees and that the program is effective.

PROMOTION AND ENFORCEMENT. Ensure Consistent Promotion of Program and Enforcement of Violations. Organizations should reward those actions that demonstrate adherence to an ethical culture and discipline violators of ethical standards.

RESPONSE. Respond to Incidents and Take Steps to Prevent Future Incidents. Organizations should take appropriate investigative actions to look into possible violations and should preserve the confidentiality of such investigations.

Sources: United States Sentencing Commission, "2018 Guidelines Manual Annotated," https://www.ussc.gov/guidelines, accessed March 24, 2021; "Seven Elements of an Effective Compliance Program," https://institutinalo-initiatives.utdallas.edu/compliance/resources/seven-elements-of-an-effective-compliance-program/, accessed March 24, 2021.

A key finding in business ethics research has been that ethics and compliance programs are increasing in number and that they do make a difference.[110]

Figure 6-6 summarizes the elements that ought to exist in companies' ethics programs in order to comply with the U.S. Sentencing Commission's Organizational Guidelines for effective programs. Two major benefits accrue to organizations that follow these guidelines. First, following the guidelines mitigates severe financial and oversight penalties. Second, some prosecutors are choosing not to pursue some actions when the companies in question already have sound programs in place if they follow these guidelines.[111]

The Ethics and Compliance Initiative has said that it will eventually make available a self-assessment tool to help organizations gauge where they are in the process of developing a strong program.[112]

Ethics and Compliance Officers. Ethics and compliance programs are often headed by an individual with the title **ethics and compliance officer, ethics officer,** or **compliance officer,** who is in charge of implementing the array of ethics and compliance initiatives in the organization. In some cases, the creation of ethics programs and designation of ethics and compliance officers has been in response to the Federal Sentencing Guidelines, which reduced penalties to those companies with ethics programs that were found guilty of ethics violations.[113] Many companies have created ethics and compliance programs and hired officers to lead them because of the Sarbanes–Oxley law or because they were seeking to improve the organization's ethics.

Just as ethics programs have proliferated in companies, the number of ethics officers occupying important positions in major firms has grown significantly. In addition, they are now scrutinized more carefully because some have been found personally liable for mistakes taking place within their firms.[114] These officers are increasingly getting a direct line to their company's boss as many companies are now responding more assertively to government enforcement efforts. Major firms such as Johnson & Johnson, Alcatel-Lucent, Pfizer, and Tenet Healthcare have decided that their chief compliance officer would report directly to the CEO and Board rather than the chief legal or finance officer.[115] The purpose of such moves is to elevate their importance and authority over compliance and ethics matters.

As valuable as ethics and compliance programs and officers are, there is some possible downside danger in their existence. By holding individuals and organizational units responsible for the company's "ethics and compliance," there is some possibility that managers may tend to "delegate" to these persons or units the responsibility for the firm's ethics. Ethics is everyone's job, however, and specialized units should not be used as a substitute for the assumption of ethical responsibility by everyone in leadership positions.

6.7d Setting Realistic Objectives

Closely related to all ethics initiatives and programs being implemented by top management is the necessity that managers at all levels set realistic objectives or goals. A manager may quite innocently and inadvertently create a condition leading to unethical behavior on a subordinate's part. Take the case of a marketing manager setting a sales goal of a 20 percent increase for the next year when a 10 percent increase is all that could be realistically and honestly expected, even with outstanding performance. In the absence of clearly established and communicated ethical norms, it is easy to see how subordinates might believe that they should go to any lengths to achieve the 20 percent goal. With the goal having been set too high, the salespeople face a situation that is conducive to unethical behavior in order to please the superior. This is, in fact, what happened in the Wells Fargo scandal when higher managers were setting objectives at unreasonable levels.[116]

Managers need to be keenly sensitive to the possibility of unintentionally creating situations in which others may perceive a need or an incentive to cut corners or do the wrong thing. Unrealistic expectations are the primary driver of employees perceiving excessive pressure to achieve goals. This kind of knowledge is what justifies business ethics being a management and leadership topic.

6.7e Ethical Decision-Making Processes

Decision making is at the heart of the management process. If there is any practice or process that is synonymous with management, it is decision making. Decision making usually entails a process of stating the problem, analyzing the problem, identifying the possible courses of action that might be taken, evaluating these courses of action, deciding on the best alternative, and then implementing the chosen course of action.

Ethical decision making is not a simple process but rather a multifaceted one that is complicated by multiple alternatives, mixed outcomes, uncertain and extended consequences, and personal implications.[117] It would be nice if a set of ethical principles was readily available for the manager to "plug in" and walk away from, with a decision to be forthcoming. However, that was not the case when we discussed principles that help managerial decision making in Chapter 5, and it is not the case when we think of organizational decision making. The ethical principles discussed earlier are applicable here, but there are no simple formulas revealing easy answers. The key is that managers establish decision-making processes that will yield the most appropriate ethical decisions.

An Ethics Screen. Although it is difficult to portray graphically the process of ethical decision making, it is possible as long as we recognize that such an effort cannot totally capture reality. Figure 6-7 presents one conception of the ethical decision-making process. In this model, the manager is asked to identify the action, decision, or behavior that is being considered and then work through the steps in the process. The decision maker is asked to subject the proposed course of action to an **ethics screen**, which consists of several select standards such as those presented in the last chapter, which included the conventional, principles, and ethical

tests approaches. The goal is that unethical alternatives will be "screened out" and ethical ones will be "screened in." By using all or a combination of these ethical standards, it is expected that more ethical decisions will be made than would have been made otherwise.

6.7f Codes of Ethics or Conduct

Top management has the responsibility for establishing standards of behavior and for effectively communicating those standards to all managers and employees in the organization. The most formal way by which companies and ethics officers have fulfilled this responsibility is through the use of **codes of ethics** or **codes of conduct**. According to Joan Dubinsky, Chief Ethics Officer for the International Monetary Fund (IMF), "a Code of Conduct is the single most important element of your ethics and compliance program. It sets the tone and direction for the entire function. Often, the Code is a standalone document, ideally only a few pages in length. It introduces the concept of ethics and compliance and provides an overview of what you mean when you talk about ethical business conduct."[118]

Some corporate codes are designed around stakeholders. Others are designed around issues.[119] The content of corporate codes typically addresses the following topics: employment practices; employee, client, and vendor information; public information/communications; conflicts of interest; relationships with vendors; environmental issues; ethical management practices; and political involvement.[120] Increasingly, corporate codes of conduct are addressing global issues and relationships with other firms, communities, and governments.[121] Recent research has found that the *quality of code content* plays a crucial role in the effectiveness of codes of conduct and in their ability to transform organizational cultures. Those companies maintaining high-quality codes were found to be more often associated with high rankings of corporate social responsibility, ethical behavior, sustainability, and public perception.[122]

Following are a few statements that major companies have to say about their codes of conduct:[123]

> Google—"The code underscores the importance of speaking up and taking action against wrongdoing."
> Coca-Cola—"A quick glance at the Coca-Cola Code of Business Conduct reveals a clear underlying theme—integrity."
> Hershey Company—"This code of conduct does an excellent job of promoting Hershey's culture while clearly indicating how employees should act."
> Microsoft—"Microsoft provides its employees with a visually appealing, easy to read document that is reflective of the organization's values."

Both successes and failures have been reported with organizational codes of conduct, but the acid test seems to be whether or not such codes actually become "living documents," not just platitudinous public relations statements that are put into a file drawer upon dissemination. Codes

Figure 6-7 A Process of Ethical Decision Making Using an Ethics Screen

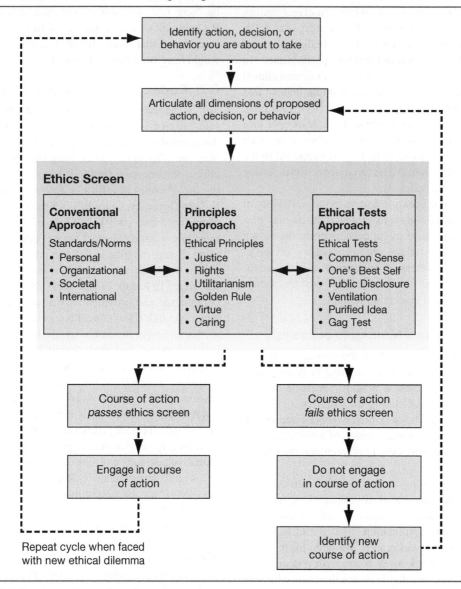

may not be a panacea for management, but when properly developed, administered, and communicated, they serve to raise the level of ethical behavior in the organization by clarifying what is meant by ethical conduct, encouraging moral behavior, and establishing a standard by which accountability may be measured.

6.7g Disciplining Violators of Ethics Standards

To instill an ethical climate that all organizational members will believe in, management must discipline violators of its accepted ethical norms and standards. A major reason the general public, and even employees in many organizations, have questioned business's sincerity in desiring a more ethical environment has been business's reluctance to discipline violators. There are numerous cases where top management officers have behaved unethically and yet were

retained in their positions. At lower levels, there have been cases of top management overlooking or failing to penalize the unethical behavior of subordinates. This evidence of inaction on management's or the board's part signals implicit approval of the individual's behavior. To be fair, organizations need to communicate their ethics standards clearly and convincingly before taking disciplinary action. But then, an organization needs to respond forcefully to the individual who is guilty of deliberately or flagrantly violating its code of ethics.

Based on their research, Treviño, Hartman, and Brown have argued, "The moral manager consistently rewards ethical conduct and disciplines unethical conduct at all levels in the organization, and these actions serve to uphold the standards and rules."[124] The effort on the part of management has to be complete in communicating to all, by way of disciplining offenders, that unethical behavior will not be tolerated in the organization.

Ethics In Practice Case

Sign the New Ethics Code or Resign

Barclay's PLC, the major U.K. bank, was fined £290 million by regulators in the United Kingdom and United States after it was found guilty of manipulating the interbank lending rate Libor. A new CEO, Anthony Jenkins, took over after his predecessor resigned in the wake of the allegations and fines.

As an early order of business, Jenkins decided it was time to change the ethics culture of the bank and to improve the bank's ethics. Jenkins sent a memo to the bank's 140,000 employees informing them that from now on employee performance would be evaluated on a set of ethical standards. The new standards would be part of the bank's code of conduct, and it would be built around five key values: respect, integrity, service, excellence, and stewardship. Jenkins was quoted as saying that "We must never again be in a position of rewarding people for making the bank money in a way which is unethical or inconsistent with our values."

Jenkins said that the bank's culture has been "too short-term focused, too aggressive and on occasions too self-serving." Some of the changes being introduced include the following: the reward structure will be altered so that it upholds the company's values; a new code of conduct will be issued and expected to be signed off on by everyone; a new role called head of compliance will help redesign the bank's compensation policies.

Jenkins's message to those who don't desire to make the changes is simple—Barclay's is not the place for you—the rules have changed and you will no longer feel comfortable at Barclay's, and we will not be comfortable with you as our colleagues.

1. What is your evaluation of Jenkins's proposed approach to changing the ethics culture at Barclays?
2. Can an ethics culture change of the magnitude desired be initiated effectively by a memo? What else is necessary and why?
3. Is a threat of discharge the best way to frame a desire for new, ethical values? How would you recommend the bank take on such a gargantuan ethics program?

Sources: Jill Treanor, "Barclay's Branch Chief Vows Culture Change at Scandal-Hit Bank," *The Guardian*, August 20, 2013, https://www.theguardian.com/business/2013/aug/20/barclays-chief-culture-change-vaswani, accessed March 24, 2021; "Barclays Boss Anthony Jenkins Tells Staff to Sign up to Ethical Code or Quit," HuffPost Business United Kingdom, January 17, 2013, https://www.huffingtonpost.co.uk/2013/01/17/barclays-ethical-code-anthony-jenkins-quit-libor-_n_2494463.html, accessed March 24, 2021; Rachel Straus, "The Rules Have Changed: Barclays New Boss Tells New Staff to Sign Up New Ethics Code or Quit the Bank," This is money.co.uk, https://www.thisismoney.co.uk/money/saving/article-2263903/Barclays-new-boss-tell-staff-sign-new-ethics-code-quit-bank.html, accessed March 24, 2021.

6.7h Ethics "Hotlines" and Whistle-Blowing Mechanisms

One problem that frequently leads to the covering up of unethical acts by people in an organization is that they do not know how to respond when they witness or suspect a questionable practice. An effective ethical culture is contingent on employees having a mechanism for, and top management support of, reporting violations or "blowing the whistle" on wrongdoers. One corporate executive summarized this point as follows: "Employees must know exactly what is expected of them in the moral arena and how to respond to warped ethics."[125]

The Association of Certified Fraud Examiners report that ethics hotlines are the most frequent way employees blow the whistle on fraud or related infractions.[126] Such hotlines may be telephone, Web, or e-mail based. In addition, they are typically used without alerting anyone in management about the problem ahead of time. The fraud examiners report that anonymous tips they receive on ethics hotlines are by far the most common way that fraud is detected in organizations. In their survey, 37.8 percent of frauds were detected based on these anonymous tips, while only 17 percent were identified through management reviews and 14 percent by management audits. They conclude that ethics hotlines are clearly one of the best practices for detecting fraud and helping to create an ethical work culture.[127]

Ethics hotlines can have a downside risk, however. Business ethicist Barbara Ley Toffler has argued that ethics hotlines have the potential to do harm. She suspects that many of the reported wrongdoings are false accusations and that if the company does not handle these issues carefully, it may do a lot of damage to employee morale.[128]

In lieu of ethics hotlines and other whistle-blowing mechanisms, some companies now opt to have an **ethical ombudsperson** investigate reported ethics violations. An ethical ombudsperson, often called an "ombuds," is a neutral person who is appointed or employed by an organization to investigate and help resolve ethical and other violations that have been reported.[129]

6.7i Business Ethics Training

Today, business ethics and compliance training and training programs are considered to be one of the most important best practices in improving organizational ethics. What are the goals of ethics training? Different companies set different goals, but a typical set of goals for ethics training might include the following:

- To learn the fundamentals of business ethics
- To learn to solve ethical dilemmas
- To learn to identify causes of unethical behavior
- To learn about common managerial ethical issues

Ethics In Practice Case

Do Ethics Hotlines Always Work?

Ethics and compliance "hotlines" are designed to give employees an opportunity to internally "blow the whistle" on wrongdoing. Many of them are designed by corporate compliance and ethics offices, and some of them are contracted out to independent firms to give employees a greater sense of confidentiality when they report what they see or think is going wrong in the company.

A major corporation that created such a compliance hotline was Olympus Corporation, the Japanese camera maker. Olympus Corporation started its compliance hotline (now called an Integrity Hotline) soon after Japan passed a whistleblower protection law. The hotline office was to handle the receipt of phone calls, letters, e-mails, and other forms of reporting from employees. These were to be reports of violations of the law or the company's code of conduct.

On investigation, the *Wall Street Journal* learned that the company created an independent panel to look into the use of the hotline and other company irregularities. It was discovered that there were significant problems with how the hotline was being used. It was found, for example, that the two executives who were in charge of the company's hotline were also allegedly behind the concealment of $1.5 billion in company losses.

The panel's report noted that the company's corporate culture was characterized by serious problems. The panel observed a suffocating atmosphere that inhibited employees from speaking openly. The panel concluded that compliance systems were significantly disabled. One employee who used the hotline to report on wrongdoing claimed they were transferred to a less desirable job after issuing a complaint via the hotline. The hotline required employees to report their names in case complaints needed to be investigated further.

When the hotline was initially set up, some recommended that it be administered by external parties so that those reporting complaints would feel more secure about their anonymity. The manager in charge strongly opposed using an outside party to administer the hotline. It was later revealed by a Japanese consumer affairs agency that about two-thirds of the large firms did use outside parties to administer their hotlines.

1. What ethics issues do you see in this company's culture and administration of the hotline?
2. As an employee, would you feel uncomfortable filing an ethics complaint in a system run by the company itself? Could anything be done to ensure your confidentiality?
3. What principles should be followed in designing a company ethics or compliance hotline?

Sources: Juro Osawa, "Olympus Hotline Didn't Blow Whistle," *The Wall Street Journal*, https://www.wsj.com/articles/SB1000142405 29702038995045771298634189598828#:~:text=TOKYO%E2% 80%94To%20understand%20why%20it,oversaw%20the% 20company's%20whistleblowing%20hotline, accessed March 24, 2021; "Ethics Hotlines," In Touch, https://getintouch.com/ solutions/compliance-hotlines/?gclid=CjwKCAjwxuuCBhAT EiwAIIIz0V-L-yp-2zJqPBILboPxZTmXCv9tKKpTTrySOx-OAcU7Y1ju0S_efBoCWiUQAvD_BwE, accessed March 24, 2021; Olympus, Compliance and Ethics, https://www.olympusamerica. com/corporate/ethics_corporate_compliance.asp#:~:text=The%20 OCA%20Compliance%20Department%20can,to%20 management%20in%20good%20faith, accessed March 24, 2021.

- To learn whistle-blowing criteria and risks
- To learn to develop a code of ethics and execute an internal ethical audit[130]

Though it is not easy designing ethics training programs, and there are limits to how much ethics may be taught in programs, a set of recommendations set forth by AccountingWeb for designing an effective ethics training program include the following nine steps:[131]

- Make it specific. Be sure specific behaviors are targeted.
- Make it a two-way conversation. There must be Q & A between employees and managers.
- Make it interactive. This is so employees may learn first hand how to make ethical decisions.
- Make it memorable and situational. Use quizzes targeted toward specific situations.
- Make it relatable. Use examples of good and bad behavior that employees can relate to.
- Reinforce training. This is an important role for ethics trainers to continue communicating with trainees.
- Repeat the program. Ongoing programs that are repeated annually or quarterly will be most effective and memorable.

- Make it a visible program. Principles should be highlighted during strategic planning sessions and also during employee performance reviews.
- Enforce the ethics hotline. Employees need to be armed with the proper tools for when they observe questionable behaviors or have questions themselves.

A well-designed ethics training program will help embed the company's code of conduct into the culture of the organization. A well-implemented program will strive to align an employee's personal and professional ethics with the expected business ethics of the employer.

One former ethics officer of a major corporation has criticized much ethics training done by companies. He said that most of this training is being done in the form of a mandatory annual compliance exercise, typically one hour in duration. Often, it is a "check the box" exercise in that management can check off that it is completed for the year. He goes on to say that if such training is not done well, it turns out to be indistinguishable from all the other meetings employees have to attend.[132] In addition to general ethics training, today companies are offering training on special ethics-related topics. Among the most important in recent years are the following: diversity training, workplace safety, data protection, and privacy training.[133]

Business ethics training is a costly investment, so companies need to know whether they work or not. Recent research does suggest that training programs are having a positive effect. However, research also has revealed that there is considerable variability in their effectiveness.[134] Therefore, companies need to carefully investigate approaches and results before investing their time and money in ethics training.

6.7j Ethics Audits and Risk Assessments

In increasing numbers, companies today are beginning to appreciate the need to follow up on their ethics initiatives and programs. Ethics audits are mechanisms or approaches by which a company may assess or evaluate its ethical climate or programs. **Ethics audits** are intended to carefully review ethics initiatives such as ethics programs, codes of conduct, hotlines, and ethics training programs to determine their effectiveness and results. A major purpose is to identify any gaps that may exist between what is intended and what is actually occurring. In addition, they are intended to examine other management activities that may add to or subtract from the company's ethics initiatives. This might include management's sincerity, communication efforts, incentive and reward systems, and other activities. Ethics audits may employ written instruments, committees, outside consultants, and employee interviews.[135] A popular variation on the ethics audit is the **sustainability audit**. More companies today are employing this approach for identifying and managing sustainability issues within their organizations. They want to improve the credibility of their sustainability reports and provide greater confidence to all stakeholders.[136]

Spurred on by the revised Federal Sentencing Guidelines and other legislation, companies are increasingly designing and conducting fraud risk assessments of their operations. **Fraud risk assessments** are the review processes designed to identify and monitor conditions and events that may have some bearing on the company's exposure to compliance/misconduct risk and to review the company's methods for dealing with these concerns. Risk, in this context, is typically focused on the company's exposure to possible compliance, misconduct, and ethics issues.

According to recent surveys, the top five subjects of ethics program risk analyses include internal policies and processes, employee awareness and understanding of compliance and ethics issues, anonymous reporting systems, disciplinary systems as prevention tools, and employee intent or incentives.[137] Typically arising from outside the firm, but becoming an important fraud issue today, has been *cyber risk.* Cyberattacks at Target, Sony, JPMorgan, Zoom, Marriott, and Anthem have surfaced as dramatic examples of technology-based vulnerabilities to fraud companies face today.[138] Since companies have a legal

and ethical responsibility to keep information secure and private, this is an important reason why fraud risk assessments are crucial.

6.7k Corporate Transparency

One of the most important best practices in the improvement of ethics programs and ethical conduct in the organization is that of **transparency. Corporate transparency** refers to a quality, characteristic, or state in which activities, processes, practices, and decisions that take place in companies become *open or visible to the outside world.* A common definition of transparency is the degree to which an organization provides public access to information; accepts responsibility for its actions; makes decisions more openly; and establishes incentives for leaders to uphold these standards.[139]

The three characteristics that seem to dominate the concept of transparency are openness, ongoing communication, and accountability.[140] The opposite of transparency is **opacity**, or an opaque condition in which activities and practices remain obscure or hidden from outside scrutiny and review.

Pressures toward transparency have come both from the outside and from within companies. From the outside, various stakeholders such as consumers, environmentalists, government, and investors want to know more clearly what is going on within the organizations. Over the years, business scandals have served as an added outside force. The Sarbanes–Oxley Act also mandated greater transparency. The importance of transparency is that it leads to accountability.

6.7l Board of Directors Oversight and Leadership

One would think that oversight and leadership of ethics initiatives by the boards of directors of businesses would be a "given." That has not been the case, however, in many instances.[141] The primary impetus for board involvement in and oversight of ethics programs and initiatives has been the mega scandals of the past couple decades that have impacted many major companies. This has been coupled with the passage of the Sarbanes–Oxley Act, which has overhauled federal securities laws to improve corporate governance. Corporate governance will be discussed in detail in Chapter 9, but here we want to emphasize the board's role in oversight of corporate ethics, one of the most urgent issues in recent years.

Corporate boards, like top managers, should provide strong ethical leadership. Former SEC chair William Donaldson said that it is not enough for a company to profess a code of conduct. According to Donaldson, "the most important thing that a board of directors should do is determine the elements that must be embedded in the company's moral DNA."[142] In other words, strong leadership from the board and CEOs is still the most powerful force in improving the company's ethical culture.

Spotlight on Sustainability

Effective Transparency: How to Make It Happen

The importance of transparency in developing ethical business cultures has been established. But, how is this done? There are several important criteria that are needed to be sure transparency is done right. Lorraine Smith has proposed six essential criteria for successful transparency. First, there is the need to get and make available the right information. Accurate information about organizational practices is essential. Second, the right stakeholders need to be reached. Whether the stakeholders are customers or special interest groups, the right information needs to be targeted to the right stakeholders. Third, the right format for organizing and presenting information needs to be selected. Reports, news releases, text messages, Facebook pages, Web pages—there are many options for making information available. Communicating information in the right format is essential for effective transparency.

Fourth, the right time for release of information is essential. Historically, yearly or monthly publication of information once was adequate. This is no longer true in a high-tech, high-communications world. Stakeholders expect information on a more timely basis now—this week, today, right now! Rumors can get started quickly if companies are not transparent in the time frame people expect today. Fifth, the right frequency is essential, and this is related to the right format and the right time.

Finally, the right intentions must be at work. Management needs to be genuine about why information is being made available. Is it in reaction to an issue or a demand? Has someone requested the information? Is it a proactive response to a set of standards the company is now following, such as the Global Reporting Initiative or the Caux Principles? Is management striving to create an authentic culture of transparency? Stakeholders can figure motive out so it is best if management has the best intentions to begin with.

In short, companies need to pay close attention to scope, disclosure, and timing in their transparency efforts. Giving stakeholders fair and equitable access will help build a culture of integrity. Following standards of professionalism, a culture of transparency may be developed. If these recommendations are used, companies will be in a stronger position to convey their honesty and trustworthiness with respect to transparency. In the long term, such a strategy will make the overall culture of the organization more sustainable.

Sources: Olympus, "Principle of Transparency Guidelines," https://www.olympus-global.com/company/philosophy/code/pdf/code_en_20200109.pdf, accessed March 25, 2021; OECD, "Openness and Transparency," https://www.oecd.org/governance/opennessandtransparency-pillarsfordemocracytrustandprogress.htm, accessed March 25, 2021; Sustainability, Lorraine Smith, "Six Elements of Effective Transparency," http://www.justmeans.com/blogs/six-elements-of-effective-transparency, accessed March 25, 2021.

Many ethics and compliance (E&C) officers at large companies will tell you that the board's involvement in providing ethical leadership is average at best. In one study, it was revealed that E&C officers estimate that boards spend less than two hours a year on ethics and compliance.[143] Only 40 percent of the E&C officers believed that their boards would be willing to hold senior executives accountable for misconduct. The E&C officers thought that, at a minimum, the boards should view E&C as foundational to the business, hold leadership accountable for E&C outcomes, and develop long-term plans and rigorous metrics for behavior and outcomes, not just activities.[144]

6.8 Moral Decisions, Managers, and Organizations

In the last two chapters, we have discussed ethical or moral acts, decisions, practices, managers, and organizations. Though the goal of ethics initiatives is to develop moral organizations, sometimes all we get are isolated ethical acts, decisions, or practices, or, if we are fortunate, a few moral managers. Achieving the status of moral standing in organizations is a goal, whatever the level on which it may be achieved. Sometimes all we can do is bring about **moral decisions**, acts, or practices. A broader goal is to create **moral managers**, in the sense in which they were discussed in Chapter 5 and this chapter. Finally, the highest-level goal for managers may be to create **moral organizations**, for which many of the best practices discussed in this chapter will need to be successfully implemented.

The important point here is to emphasize that the goal of managers should be to create *moral decisions, moral managers*, and, ultimately, *moral organizations* while recognizing that what we frequently observe in business is the achievement of moral standing at only one of these levels. The ideal is to create a moral organization that is fully populated by moral managers making moral decisions (and practices, policies, and behaviors), but this is seldom achieved. Figure 6-8 depicts the sequencing and goals of each of these levels. Once moral organizations are achieved, the stories and successes feed back in such a way that they augment the creation of moral managers and moral decisions. Over time, the overall level of moral development and maturity should rise when this process is repeated over several cycles. These challenges become even more specialized when we consider global business ethics in Chapter 7 and ethical issues and technology in Chapter 8.

Figure 6-8 Moral Decisions, Moral Managers, and Moral Organizations

Summary

The subject of business ethics may be addressed at several different levels: personal, managerial–organizational, industry, societal, and global. This chapter focuses on the managerial and organizational levels—the levels at which managers can have the most direct impact.

A number of different ethical principles serve as guides to managerial decision making. Ethics principles may be categorized as teleological (ends-based), deontological (duty-based), or aretaic (virtue-based). One of the major deontological principles is the categorical imperative. Major philosophical principles of ethics include utilitarianism, rights, and justice. The Golden Rule was singled out as a particularly powerful ethical principle among various groups studied. Virtue ethics was identified as an increasingly popular concept. Servant leadership was presented as an approach to management that embraced an ethical perspective of putting others first. Seven practical tests were proposed to assist the manager in making ethical decisions: the test of common sense, the test of one's best self, the test of making something public, the test of ventilation, the test of purified idea, the test of the Big Four, and the gag test.

At the organizational level, factors were discussed that affect the organization's moral culture or climate. It was concluded that the behavior of one's superiors and peers and industry ethical practices were the most important influences on an organization's ethical culture. Society's moral climate and personal needs were considered to be relevant factors but less important. Behavioral ethics is a maturing field based on empirically observed phenomena describing psychological processes that occur when managers and employees strive to do the right thing in their decision making and in their design of an ethical organizational culture. Our knowledge from behavioral ethics serves as a reality check on the implementation of normative processes in business ethics.

Best practices for improving the firm's ethical climate include providing leadership from top management, ethics and compliance programs, and ethics and compliance officers; setting realistic objectives; infusing the decision-making process with ethical considerations; utilizing codes of conduct; disciplining violators; creating whistle-blowing mechanisms or hotlines; training managers in business ethics; using ethics audits and risk assessments (which often include sustainability audits); adopting the concept of transparency; and board of director oversight of ethics initiatives.

The goal of ethics initiatives is to achieve a status that may be characterized not just by isolated and intermittent moral decisions but also by the presence of moral managers and the ultimate achievement of a moral organization. When a moral organization is achieved, the successes will feed back into the process and greatly improve decisions, practices, and managers themselves.

Key Terms

aretaic theories, p. 126

behavioral ethics, p. 136

bounded ethicality, p. 136

categorical imperative, p. 126

codes of conduct, p. 141

codes of ethics, p. 141

common sense, test of, p. 131

compensatory justice, p. 128

competing rights, p. 128

compliance officer, p. 140

compliance orientation, p. 136

conflict of interest, p. 125

conformity bias, p. 136

consequences, p. 126

conventional approach, p. 125

corporate transparency, p. 145

deontological theories, p. 126

distributive justice, p. 128

duty, p. 126

ethic of reciprocity, p. 130

ethical due process, p. 128

ethical ombudsperson, p. 143
ethical tests, p. 131
ethics and compliance officer, p. 140
ethics audits, p. 145
ethics of care, p. 129
ethics officer, p. 140
ethics orientation, p. 136
ethics screen, p. 141
framing, p. 136
fraud risk assessments, p. 145
Golden Rule, p. 130
ill-conceived goals, p. 137
incrementalism, p. 136
indirect blindness, p. 137
legal rights, p. 127
moral decisions, p. 146

moral equilibrium, p. 136
moral managers, p. 146
moral organizations, p. 146
moral rights, p. 127
moral tone, p. 137
motivated blindness, p. 137
negative right, p. 128
opacity, p. 145
overcoming values, p. 137
overconfidence bias, p. 136
positive right, p. 128
principle of caring, p. 129
principle of justice, p. 128
principle of rights, p. 127
principle of utilitarianism, p. 126
principles approach, p. 125

procedural justice, p. 128
process fairness, p. 128
Rawls's principle of justice, p. 128
rights, p. 127
role morality, p. 136
self-serving bias, p. 136
servant leadership, p. 130
slippery slope, p. 137
"smell" test, p. 131
sustainability audit, p. 145
teleological theories, p. 126
test of common sense, p. 131
transparency, p. 145
utilitarianism, p. 126
virtue ethics, p. 129

Discussion Questions

1. From your personal experience, give two examples of ethical dilemmas you have experienced as a member of an organization.
2. Using the examples you provided for question 1, identify one or more of the guides to decision making or ethical tests that you think would have helped you resolve your dilemmas. Describe how it would have helped.
3. Which is more important in ethics principles: consequences or duty? Discuss.
4. Assume that you are in your first managerial position. Identify five ways in which you might provide ethical leadership. Rank them in terms of importance, and be prepared to explain your ranking.
5. What do you think about codes of conduct? Give three reasons why an organization ought to have

a code of conduct and three reasons why an organization should not have a code of conduct. On balance, how do you assess the value of codes of conduct?
6. An ongoing debate concerns whether business ethics can and should be taught in business schools. Do you think ethics can be taught in business school? Substantiate your point with reasons. Can top managers and board members be taught business ethics in training programs?
7. Identify and prioritize the best practices for improving the organization's ethical climate. What are the strengths and weaknesses of each?
8. Which three of the concepts under the field of behavioral ethics appear to be the most powerful? Explain why and give examples.

Endnotes

1. Lee Ellis, *Leading Talents, Leading Teams* (Chicago, IL: Northfield Publishing, 2003), 201–204.
2. Eugene Soltes, "Where Is Your Company Most Prone to Lapses in Integrity?" *Harvard Business Review*, July–August 2019, 51–54.
3. Bill George, *Authentic Leadership: Rediscovering the Secrets to Creating Lasting Value* (San Francisco: Jossey-Bass, 2003).
4. Marc J. Epstein and Kirk O. Hanson, *Rotten: Why Corporate Misconduct Continues and What to Do about It* (Los Altos, California, CA: Lanark Press, 2021), ix–x.
5. Dan Chapman, "Woman Rewarded for Act of Honesty," *The Atlanta Journal-Constitution* (September 8, 2001).
6. The U. S. Attorney's Office Northern District of California, "U.S. vs. Holmes, et al" https://www.justice .gov/usao-ndca/us-v-elizabeth-holmes-et-al. Accessed March 29, 2021.

7. Sara Randazzo, "Theranos Official Disputed Testing," *The Wall Street Journal*, February 18, 2021, B4.
8. Patrick Ryan, "Elizabeth Holmes: Six Burning Questions after HBO's Theranos Documentary, 'The Inventor'" *USA Today*, March 15, 2019, https://www.usatoday.com /story/life/tv/2019/03/15/inventor-everything-you-need -know-hbos-crazy-theranos-doc/3161952002/. Accessed March 29, 2021.
9. Ethics & Compliance Initiative, The State of Ethics and Compliance in the Workplace: A Look at Global Trends, Vienna, Virginia: E & CI, 2021, 16–17. Also see https:// www.ethics.org/global-business-ethics-survey/. Accessed March 18, 2021.
10. Advent Health University, "Six Ethical Issues in Healthcare in 2020." May 5, 2020, https://online.ahu.edu /blog/ethical-issues-in-healthcare/. Accessed March 18, 2021.

11. John Mitchell, "The Long Road to the Student Debt Crisis," *The Wall Street Journal*, June 8–9, 2019, C1–C2.

12. CNBC, Abigail Johnson Hess, "How Student Debt Became a $1.6 Trillion Crisis," Make It, https://www.cnbc.com/2020/06/12/how-student-debt-became-a-1point6-trillion-crisis.html. Accessed March 18, 2021.

13. Archie B. Carroll, "Principles of Business Ethics: Their Role in Decision Making and an Initial Consensus," *Management Decision,* 28(28), 1990, 20–24.

14. John R. Boatright, *Ethics and the Conduct of Business,* 7th ed. (Pearson Higher Education, 2012).

15. Tom L. Beauchamp, *Philosophical Ethics: An Introduction to Moral Philosophy,* 3rd ed. (New York: McGraw-Hill, 2001).

16. William H. Shaw and Vincent Barry, *Moral Issues in Business,* 12th ed. (Cengage Learning, 2013).

17. Michael Shermer, "Does the Philosophy of 'the Greatest Good for the Greatest Number' Have Any Merit?" *Scientific American*, May 1, 2018, https://www.scientificamerican.com/article/does-the-philosophy-of-the-greatest-good-for-the-greatest-number-have-any-merit/. Accessed March 19, 2021.

18. Shaw and Barry, 45–46.

19. I. Kant, *Groundwork of the Metaphysic of Morals*, trans. H. J. Paton (New York: Harper and Row, 1964).

20. Victoria S. Wike, "Duty," in Patricia H. Werhane and R. Edward Freeman (eds.), *The Blackwell Encyclopedic Dictionary of Business Ethics* (Malden, MA: Blackwell Publishers, Ltd, 1997), 180–181.

21. Boatright, 53.

22. Scott J. Reynolds and Norman E. Bowie, "A Kantian Perspective on the Characteristics of Ethics Programs," *Business Ethics Quarterly,* 14(2), April 2004, 275–292.

23. Louis P. Pojman, *Ethics: Discovering Right and Wrong,* 7th ed. (Cengage Learning, 2012).

24. Ibid., 150.

25. Ibid., 152–153.

26. Manuel C. Velasquez, *Business Ethics: Concepts and Cases,* 7th ed. (Pearson Education Limited, 2014).

27. Richard T. DeGeorge, *Business Ethics,* 5th ed. (Upper Saddle River, NJ: Prentice Hall, 1999), 69–72.

28. Velasquez, 73.

29. "Rights: What Are They Anyway?" http://dspace.dial.pipex.com/town/street/pl38/rights.htm. Accessed July 18, 2007.

30. "Negative and Positive Rights," https://www.libertarianism.org/media/around-web/negative-rights-vs-positive-rights. Accessed March 19, 2021.

31. Ibid.

32. Jed Blackburn, "How to Balance Competing Rights?" February 25, 2014, https://www.martindale.com/labor-employment-law/article_Cassels-Brock-Blackwell-LLP_2088856.htm. Accessed March 19, 2021.

33. Eric Harvey and Scott Airitam, Ethics 4 Everyone, Walk the Talk Company, 2002, 24–27.

34. Jon Swartz, "Split Opinion on Apple-FBI Standoff," *USA Today*, February 22, 2016, 4B.

35. Katy Benner and Eric Lichtblau, "U.S. Says It Has Unlocked iPhone without Apple," *New York Times*, March 16, 2016, https://www.nytimes.com/2016/03/29/technology/apple-iphone-fbi-justice-department-case.html?action=click&contentCollection=Technology&region=Footer&module=WhatsNext&version=WhatsNext&contentID=WhatsNext&moduleDetail=undefined&pgtype=Multimedia. Accessed March 19, 2021.

36. Harvey and Airitam, 26–27.

37. M. Valasquez, C. Andre, T. Shanks, and M. Meyer, "Justice and Fairness," https://www.scu.edu/ethics/ethics-resources/ethical-decision-making/justice-and-fairness/. Accessed March 19, 2021.

38. Jonathan Haidt, "The New Culture War Over Fairness," *Time*, October 22, 2012, 25, http://content.time.com/time/subscriber/article/0,33009,2126664,00.html. Accessed March 19, 2021.

39. Ibid; also see "Four Types of Justice," http://changingminds.org/explanations/trust/four_justice.htm. Accessed February 22, 2016.

40. Joel Brockner, "Why It's So Hard to Be Fair," *Harvard Business Review* (March 2006), 122–129.

41. Ibid., 123.

42. "John Rawls," *The Economist* (December 7, 2002), 83.

43. John Rawls, *A Theory of Justice* (Cambridge, MA: Harvard University Press, 1971).

44. DeGeorge, 69–72.

45. Michael M. Weinstein, "Bringing Logic to Bear on Liberal Dogma," *The New York Times* (December 1, 2002), 5.

46. Ibid., 72.

47. Ibid., 5.

48. Dahlia Lithwick, "Women: Truly the Fairer Sex," *Newsweek* (April 20, 2009), 13, https://law.stanford.edu/press/women-truly-the-fairer-sex/. Accessed March 19, 2021.

49. Robbin Derry, "Ethics of Care," in Werhane and Freeman (1997), 254.

50. Brian K. Burton and Craig P. Dunn, "Feminist Ethics as Moral Grounding for Stakeholder Theory," *Business Ethics Quarterly,* 6(2), 1996, 133–147; see also A. C. Wicks, D. R. Gilbert, and R. E. Freeman, "A Feminist Reinterpretation of the Stakeholder Concept," *Business Ethics Quarterly,* 4, 1994, 475–497; Craig Dunn and Brian Burton, "Ethics of Care," in Robert Kolb, *The Sage Encyclopedia of Business Ethics and Society*, 2nd ed. (Los Angeles: Sage Reference), 1251–1254.

51. Derry (1997), 256.

52. Jeanne M. Liedtka, "Feminist Morality and Competitive Reality: A Role for an Ethic of Care?" *Business Ethics Quarterly,* 6, 1996, 179–200. See also John Dobson and Judith White, "Toward the Feminine Firm," *Business Ethics Quarterly,* 5, 1995, 463–478.

53. Alasdair MacIntyre, *After Virtue* (University of Notre Dame Press, 1981); see also Louis P. Pojman, *Ethics: Discovering Right and Wrong,* 7th ed. (Cengage Learning, 2012).

54. Beauchamp, 2001.

55. Pojman, 161; see also Bill Shaw, "Sources of Virtue: The Market and the Community," *Business Ethics Quarterly,* 7, 1997, 33–50; and Dennis Moberg, "Virtuous Peers in Work Organizations," *Business Ethics Quarterly,* 7, 1997, 67–85; "Virtue Ethics," *Internet Encyclopedia of Philosophy*, https://iep.utm.edu/virtue/. Accessed March 19, 2021.

56. Character Counts! "Six Pillars of Character," https://charactercounts.org/program-overview/six-pillars/. Accessed February 22, 2016.

57. "Aspects of Leadership: Good Character and Good Choices," Josephson Institute, http://business.josephsoninstitute.org/blog/2016/02/02/build-your-future-by-building-your-character-character-is-a-matter-of-choices-not-fate/. Accessed February 22, 2016.

58. Carroll, 1990, 22; also see Archie B. Carroll, "One Rule Can Best Guide Practices," in Archie B. Carroll, *Business Ethics: Brief Readings on Vital Topics* (New York and London: Routledge Publishers, 2009), 170–171.

59. Barry, 50–51.

60. John C. Maxwell, *There's No Such Thing as "Business" Ethics: There's Only One Rule for Making Decisions* (Warner Books, 2003), 24–29.

61. Nilda Perez, "The Analogy of Frodo Baggins as Servant Leader," July 1, 2013, http://foresightstrategiesgroup.com/the-analogy-of-frodo-baggins-as-servant-leader/#:~:text=A%20servant%20leader%20is%20committed,purpose%20to%20achieve%20their%20goal. Accessed March 19, 2021.

62. Larry C. Spears (ed.), *Reflections of Leadership* (New York: John Wiley & Sons, 1995), 4–7.

63. Joanne B. Ciulla, *The Search for Ethics in Leadership Business and Beyond* (Springer, 2020).

64. Gordon L. Lippett, *The Leader Looks at Ethics* (Washington, DC: Leadership Resources, 1969), 12–13.

65. Ethics Ops, "Ethics Tests," https://www.ethicsops.com/viral-news-test. Accessed March 19, 2021.

66. "Stiffer Rules for Business Ethics," *BusinessWeek* (March 30, 1974), 88.

67. Lippett, 12–13.

68. Eric Harvey and Scott Airitam, *Ethics 4 Everyone: The Handbook for Integrity-Based Business Practices* (Dallas, TX: The Walk the Talk Company, 2002), 31.

69. Ibid., 31.

70. Frederick Andrews, "Corporate Ethics: Talks with a Trace of Robber Baron," *The New York Times* (April 18, 1977), C49–C52.

71. Phillip V. Lewis, "Ethical Principles for Decision Makers: A Longitudinal Study," *Journal of Business Ethics,* 8, 1989, 275.

72. Craig V. VanSandt, "The Relationship between Ethical Work Climate and Moral Awareness," *Business & Society,* 42(1), March 2003, 144–151.

73. Cited in John B. Cullen, Bart Victor, and Carroll Stephens, "An Ethical Weather Report: Assessing the Organization's Ethical Climate," *Organizational Dynamics* (Autumn 1989), 50.

74. For an excellent discussion, see Deborah Vidaver Cohen, "Creating and Maintaining Ethical Work Climates: Anomie in the Workplace and Implications for Managing Change," *Business Ethics Quarterly,* 3(4), October 1993, 343–355; see also B. Victor and J. Cullen, "The Organizational Bases of Ethical Work Climates," *Administrative Science Quarterly,* 33, 1988, 101–125; and H. R. Smith and A. B. Carroll, "Organizational Ethics: A Stacked Deck," *Journal of Business Ethics,* 3, 1984, 95–100.

75. Barry Posner and Warren Schmidt, "Values and the American Manager: An Update," *California Management Review* (Spring 1984), 202–216; Steve Brenner and Earl Molander, "Is the Ethics of Business Changing?" *Harvard Business Review*, (January–February 1977); Raymond Baumhart, "How Ethical Are Businessmen?" *Harvard Business Review*, (July–August 1961), 6ff. Also see Alison Taylor, "How Companies Can Create an Ethics Program for a New Era," *The Wall Street Journal*, September 23, 2020, https://www.wsj.com/articles/how-companies-can-create-an-ethics-program-for-a-new-era-11600869601. Accessed March 29, 2021.

76. Archie B. Carroll, "Managerial Ethics: A Post-Watergate View," *Business Horizons* (April 1975), 75–80.

77. Carroll, 1975, 75–80.

78. *Global Business Ethics Survey*, "The State of Ethics and Compliance in the Workplace," Vienna, Virginia: Ethics & Compliance Initiative, 2021, 13.

79. Ibid., 14.

80. Alina Dizik, "Corporate Culture Affects a Company's Results—But in Surprising Ways," *The Wall Street Journal* (February 22, 2016), R6.

81. T. V. Purcell and James Weber, *Institutionalizing Corporate Ethics: A Case History, Special Study No. 71* (New York: The President's Association, American Management Association, 1979); see also James Weber, "Institutionalizing Ethics into Business Organizations: A Model and Research Agenda," *Business Ethics Quarterly,* 3(4), October 1993, 419–436.

82. Ethics & Compliance Initiative, https://www.ethics.org/global-business-ethics-survey/?highlight=culture. Accessed March 22, 2021; T. V. Purcell and James Weber, *Institutionalizing Corporate Ethics: A Case History, Special Study No. 71* (New York: The President's Association, American Management Association, 1979); see also James Weber, "Institutionalizing Ethics into Business Organizations: A Model and Research Agenda," *Business Ethics Quarterly,* 3(4), October 1993, 19.

83. Ethics & Compliance Initiative, https://www.ethics.org/global-business-ethics-survey/?highlight=culture. Accessed March 22, 2021.

84. United States Sentencing Guidelines, "Overview of the Guidelines," https://www.ussc.gov/guidelines/organizational-guidelines. Accessed March 22, 2021.

85. Archie B. Carroll, "Ethics Programs Go Beyond Compliance Strategy," *Business Ethics: Brief Readings on Vital Topics* (New York and London: Routledge Publishers, 2009), 184–185.

86. Ronald E. Berenbeim and Jeffrey M. Kaplan, "Ethics and Compliance … The Convergence of Principle- and Rule-Based Ethics Programs: An Emerging Trend," *The Conference Board, Executive Action Series*, No. 231, March 2007.

87. Ibid., 2.

88. Berenbeim and Kaplan, 4.

89. Max H. Bazerman and Francesca Gino, "Behavioral Ethics: Toward a Deeper Understanding of Moral Judgment and Dishonesty," *Annual Review of Law and Social Science, December 2012,* https://hbswk.hbs.edu/item/behavioral-ethics-toward-a-deeper-understanding-of-moral-judgment-and-dishonesty. Accessed March 26, 2021.

90. Linda Treviño, Gary Weaver, and Scott Reynolds, "Behavioral Ethics in Organizations: A Review," *Journal of Management,* 32, 2006, 951.

91. Robert S. Benchley, "Answering an Ethical SOS," *McCombsToday.org/Magazine*, Fall 2012, 16–21, https://www.mccombs.utexas.edu/News/McCombs-Magazine. Accessed March 26, 2021.

92. Ann E. Tenbrunsel, Kristina A. Diekmann, Kimberly A. Wade-Bezoni, Max H. Bazerman, "The Ethical Mirage: A Temporal Explanation as to Why We Are Not as Ethical as We Think We Are," *Research in Organizational Behavior,* 30, 2010, 153–173.

93. Benchley, 2012, 21.

94. Benchley, 2012, 21.

95. Benchley, 2012, 21.

96. Max H. Bazerman and Ann E. Tenbrunsel, "Ethical Breakdowns," *Harvard Business Review* (April 2011), 58–65.

97. Association of Certified Fraud Examiners, "Tone at the Top," https://www.acfe.com/uploadedFiles/ACFE_ Website/Content/documents/tone-at-the-top-research.pdf. Accessed March 22, 2021.

98. Ibid.

99. Linda Klebe Treviño, Laura Pincus Hartman, and Michael Brown, "Moral Person and Moral Manager: How Executives Develop a Reputation for Ethical Leadership," *California Management Review,* 42(4), Summer 2000, 134, http://homepages.se.edu/cvonbergen/files/2012/12 /Moral-Person-and-Moral-Manager_How-Executives -Develop-a-Reputation-for-Ethiccal-Leadership1.pdf. Accessed March 22, 2021.

100. Al Gini and Ronald M. Green, *Ten Virtues of Outstanding Leaders: Leadership and Character* (Malden, MA: Wiley-Blackwell, 2013).

101. Harvey Gittler, "Listen to the Whistle-Blowers Before It's Too Late," *The Wall Street Journal* (March 10, 1986), 16.

102. Ethics Resource Center. "National Business Ethics Survey of the U. S. Workforce" 2013, https:// lowellmilkeninstitute.law.ucla.edu/wp-content /uploads/2015/10/Thomas-Jordan_Ethics-Resource-Center -National-Business-Ethics-of-the-U.S.-Workplace.pdf. Accessed March 22, 2021.

103. Treviño, Hartman, and Brown, 128–142.

104. Gini and Green, 2013; Treviño, Hartman, and Brown, 128–142.

105. Treviño, Hartman, and Brown, Gini and Green, 2013, 133–136.

106. Aaron Mandlebaum, "Ethical Communication: The Basic Principles," October 23, 2020, https://www.smbadvisors. com/capabilities/knowledge-management/insights/ethical-communication-the-basic-principles#:~:text=Ethical%20 communication%20is%20a%20type,words%20and%20 the%20resulting%20actions. Accessed March 22, 2021.

107. Ethics & Compliance Initiative, "Leading Professional in Ethics & Compliance (LPEC)," https://www.ethics.org/ leadership-professional-in-ethics-compliance/. Accessed March 24, 2021.

108. Ethisphere Magazine, 2013 National Business Ethics Survey, 16, https://magazine.ethisphere.com/2013 -national-business-ethics-survey-of-the-u-s-workforce/. Accessed March 24, 2021.

109. Ethical Systems, "Five Key Features of a Good Ethics and Compliance Program," https://www.ethicalsystems. org/five-key-features-of-a-good-ethics-and-compliance -program/. Accessed March 24, 2021.

110. "Large Companies Can Boost Ethical Performance and Cut Business Risk," Corporate Board, May–June 2015, 27. Business Insights: Essentials. Web. March 2, 2016.

111. United States Sentencing Commission, "2018 Guidelines Manual Annotated," https://www.ussc.gov /guidelines/2018-guidelines-manual-annotated. Accessed March 24, 2021.

112. Ibid.

113. Susan Gaines, "Handing Out Halos," *Business Ethics* (March/April 1994), 20–24.

114. Emily Glazer, "The Most Thankless Job on Wall Street Gets a New Worry," *The Wall Street Journal*, February 11, 2016. Accessed March 24, 2021.

115. Gregory Millman and Ben DiPietro, "For Compliance Chiefs, Who's the Boss?" *The Wall Street Journal* (January 16, Vol. 2014), B7, https://www.wsj.com/articles /SB10001424052702303330204579250723925965180. Accessed March 24, 2021.

116. Harvard Law School Forum on Corporate Governance, "The Wells Fargo Cross-Selling Scandal," February 6, 2019, https://corpgov.law.harvard.edu/2019/02/06/the-wells-fargo -cross-selling-scandal-2/. Accessed March 24, 2021.

117. LaRue T. Hosmer, *The Ethics of Management,* 7th revised ed. (McGraw Hill Book Company, 2011), 12–14.

118. Joan Dubinsky, "Code Redux Part One: Updating your code of conduct," https://i-sight.com/resources/code -redux-part-one-updating-your-corporate-code-of-conduct/. Accessed March 24, 2021.

119. Institute of Business Ethics, "Codes of Ethics," https:// www.ibe.org.uk/knowledge-hub/ibe-business-ethics -framework/code-of-ethics.html. Accessed March 24, 2021.

120. "Common Ethics Code Provisions," http://www.ethics.org /eci/research/free-toolkit/code-provisions. Accessed March 11, 2016.

121. Cynthia Stohl, Michael Stohl, and Lucy Popova, "A New Generation of Corporate Codes of Ethics," *Journal of Business Ethics,* 90, 2009, 607–622.

122. Patrick Erwin, "Corporate Codes of Conduct: The Effects of Code Content and Quality on Ethical Performance," *Journal of Business Ethics,* 99(4), April 2011, 535–548.

123. I-sight, "18 of the Best Code of Conduct Examples," https://i-sight.com/resources/18-of-the-best-code-of -conduct-examples/. Accessed March 24, 2021.

124. Treviño, Hartman, and Brown, op. cit., 136.

125. Allen, 16.

126. Lighthouse, "Why Ethics Hotlines Are Considered a Best Practice," https://www.lighthouse-services.com/Newsletters /Why%20Ethics%20Hotlines%20Are%20Considered%20 a%20Best%20Practice.pdf. Accessed March 24, 2021.

127. Ibid.

128. Jim Brennan, "Having an Ethics Hotline Is a Really, Really Bad Idea," December 14, 2015, The Compliance and Ethics Blog, https://complianceandethics.org/having -an-ethics-hotline-is-a-really-really-bad-idea-really/. Accessed March 24, 2021.

129. International Ombudsman Association, "What Is an Organizational Ombudsman?" https://www .ombudsassociation.org/what-is-an-organizational-ombuds. Accessed March 24, 2021.

130. "Business Ethics Training," Webucator, https://www .webucator.com/business-skills-training/course/business -ethics-training.cfm. Accessed March 25, 2021.

131. AccountingWeb, "Nine Steps to Make Your Company's Ethics Training Program Stick," April 8, 2015, https:// www.accountingweb.com/practice/practice-excellence/ nine-steps-to-make-your-companys-ethics-training- program-stick. Accessed March 25, 2021.

132. Francis J. Daly, "An Ethics Officer's Perspective," in Marc J. Epstein and Kirk O. Hanson (eds.), *The Accountable Corporation: Business Ethics,* Vol. 2 (Westport, CT: Praeger Publishers, 2006), 186.

133. Knnit, "Everything You Need to Know about Corporate Training in 2021," March 26, 2021, https://knnit.com /everything-you-need-to-know-about-corporate-training-in -2021/?__cf_chl_jschl_tk__=669a5f21b204733b0411e4c 32d932e85bc1894b3-1616765524-0-AWv043MPnjQjK 9BRvjRXoQW-hAFC7dgsmtm1QK2XbkuExxk8BjLBzuv

QNg3GqBvoIUoBLVKUC42yIs6HFU4UHLA-kVZ70Eot
_AmbzGHMSdgFPZFgkwHLgwRCT2RssCp6N2k0IKNT
ZGIH5br695e8m7qG1XDTB6DiZY4xxo1RTSLafcVu
8WEEPT8I2Syu_MerFLYjwgLghpZmsoGd2kcgByD5Mn
UookKHB_Tx_uZduCfr0789KPpg5HMjmcXAwXfXtPe
XPSgbOomwKYpLbn_QmRDtlecJXd3yxFL9swJdEg
YlRytgnTkRMm8m34K8qoB6Qfn6b2T6dtSNcwjief2wyk
10fym9kalHxobdEMJliaVeViXioONwo9hzVwZsczpx
QLBsKx0aWV9higUf-nEmQ-s. Accessed March 26, 2021.

134.   Logan Steele, Tyler Mulhearn, Kelsey Medieros, Logan
Watts, and Shane Connelly, "How Do We Know What
Works? A Review and Critique of Current Practices in
Ethics Training Evaluation," *Accountability in Research,*
23(6), 2016, https://www.tandfonline.com/doi/abs/10.1080
/08989621.2016.1186547. Accessed March 25, 2021.

135.   Eric Krell, "How to Conduct an Ethics Audit," *HR
Magazine*, April 2010, https://www.shrm.org/hr-
today/news/hr-magazine/Pages/0410agenda_social.
aspx#:~:text=An%20ethics%20audit%20is%20
a,Develop%20metrics. Accessed March 25, 2021.

136.   *Sustainability-Reports.com*, "Big Four Audit Firms Lead
Sustainability Assurance Services," June 22, 2011, https://
www.sustainability-reports.com/titel-1108/. Accessed
March 25, 2021.

137.   Ronald E. Berenbeim, "Ethics Programs and Practices: A
20-Year Retrospective," The Conference Board, https://

www.conference-board.org/publications/publicationdetail
.cfm?publicationid=1207. Accessed March 25, 2021;
Association of Certified Fraud Examiners, "Fraud
Risk Assessment Tool," https://www.acfe.com/frat
.aspx?id=6797. Accessed March 25, 2021.

138.   The Conference Board, "Emerging Practices in Cyber
Risk Governance," https://conference-board.org/topics
/cyber-risk-governance. Accessed March 25, 2021.

139.   Maggie Campbell, "Transparency in Business: Mean What
You Say," April 29, 2020, https://elementthree.com/blog
/transparency-in-business-mean-what-you-say/. Accessed
March 25, 2021.

140.   Peter Levesque, "What Do We Mean by Transparency?"
Institute for Knowledge Mobilization, http://www
.knowledgemobilization.net/what-do-we-mean-by
-transparency/. Accessed March 25, 2021.

141.   Archie B. Carroll, "Slack Corporate Governance Costs Us
All," *Business Ethics: Brief Readings on Vital Topics* (New
York and London: Routledge Publishers, 2009), 86–87.

142.   Quoted in Curtis C. Verschoor, "Unethical Workplace Is
Still with Us," *Strategic Finance* (April 2004), 16.

143.   David Greenberg, "Board Oversight of Ethics and
Compliance: The Real Dynamics," NACD BoardTalk,
October 9, 2018, https://blog.nacdonline.org/posts/ethics
-compliance-real-dynamics. Accessed March 25, 2021.

144.   Ibid.

7

Ethical Issues in the Global Arena

Chapter Learning Outcomes

After studying this chapter, you should be able to:

1. Describe the ethical and social challenges faced by multinational corporations (MNCs) operating in the global business environment.
2. Summarize the key implications for managers of the following ethical issues: infant formula controversy, Bhopal tragedy, factory collapses, sweatshops, and human rights abuses.
3. Define corruption and differentiate between bribes and grease payments, and outline the major features of the Foreign Corrupt Practices Act.
4. What are the major global business ethics codes created by international organizations? Which two seem most important and why?
5. Identify and discuss strategies companies may employ for improving global business ethics.

The growth of global business as a critical element in the world economy is one of the most important developments of the past half century, but it also has been an increasingly fertile ground for corruption and ethical challenges. Epstein and Hanson refer to the global level as potentially part of the "Bad Orchard" level. At this competitive, global level, ethical behavior is much more challenging and misconduct is more likely.[1] In the United States and elsewhere, domestic issues have been made immensely more complex by the escalating international growth of commerce. At the same time, the **internationalization** of business has created unique challenges of its own. With the rise of global business, international markets have been seen as natural extensions of an ever-expanding global marketplace that must be pursued if firms are to remain competitive.

This expanded global marketplace has been referred to also as the **transnational economy**.[2] A useful definition of the transnational or global economy is as follows: trade in goods, a much smaller trade in services, the international movement of labor, and international flows of capital and information.[3]

Most observers have assumed that international business would continue its rapid growth of the past two decades and that, increasingly, companies and countries would become more integrated with the rest of the world. Global trade statistics, however, suggest that after a burst of **globalization** about a decade ago, world business has been more in a period of consolidation, possibly even retrenchment.[4] Beginning with the global financial crisis of 2009, growth in international trade has become sluggish. With the global pandemic serving as a significant overlay beginning in 2020, the challenges have been even greater.[5] French President Emmanuel Macron has said that the coronavirus "will change the nature of globalization, with which we have lived for 40 years."[6]

This is why some business experts have begun to think that the globalization moment is over. Why, for example, would one want to offshore jobs to China when Chinese workers are demanding and getting large pay raises? Why would a company want to expand its supply chain when it might be interrupted by terrorists?[7] These and other important questions are being asked.

Not only has world economic growth slowed, but global instability in the form of geopolitics has become more intense than in any recent period.[8] Geopolitical issues that have now intertwined governments with business include global migration patterns, tariffs, trade wars, terrorism, and corruption. In spite of this, the most recent survey of CEOs says that they expect global economic growth to improve beginning in 2021.[9] McKinsey & Company has observed that "the resilience that businesses have developed in the face of disruption (the pandemic) can provide a new foundation for growth."[10]

Some companies are beginning to question the breadth of their operations and are worried about their vulnerability to regional instabilities.[11] Not only has business growth slowed in the global economy, but it has also been getting more complex and subject to increasing disruptive changes. Researchers at the McKinsey Global Institute have observed that there are four trends or forces that are transforming the nature of the global economy and, hence, global business: the rise of emerging markets, the accelerating rate of technological change on market competition, an aging world population, and greater connectedness in movements of trade, capital, people, and data.[12] These trends have been ushering in a dynamic, new phase of globalization.

The complexity and intricacies of the transnational economy and the globalization of business are seen visibly when social or ethical issues arise. At best, business ethics is difficult when we are dealing with one culture. Once two or more cultures intersect, along with the rapid changes in each of them, it gets extremely complex. Managers have to deal not only with differing customs, protocols, and ways of operating but also with differing concepts of law and standards of acceptable business practices. All of this is then exacerbated by the fact that world political issues become intertwined. What might be intended as an isolated corporate attempt to bribe a foreign government official, in keeping with local custom, could readily explode into major international political tensions between two or more countries.

7.1 Challenges in the Global Environment

There are five major challenges that virtually all businesses face in doing business internationally. These include language barriers, cultural differences, managing global teams, currency exchange and inflation rates, and nuances of foreign politics, policy, and relations.[13] Underlying these challenges as they operate in a multinational, business environment, companies also have to deal with several complex issues. One is that of achieving *corporate legitimacy* as the **multinational corporation (MNC)**, or **multinational enterprise (MNE)**, seeks to be recognized and accepted in an unfamiliar society. A second and related problem is the fundamentally *differing philosophies* that may exist between the firm's home country and the host country in which it seeks to operate.[14] For firms to be perceived as legitimate in the eyes of a host country, they must fulfill their social responsibilities and be good corporate citizens abroad just as they were expected to do so at home. Sometimes being socially responsible has different meanings in different countries.

Closely related to the legitimacy issue is the dilemma of MNCs that have quite different cultural or philosophical perspectives from those of their host countries. The philosophy of Western industrialized nations, and thus their MNCs, has focused on economic growth, efficiency, specialization, free trade, and comparative advantage. By contrast, many developing countries

or emerging economies have different priorities. Other important objectives for them might include a more equitable income distribution or increased economic self-determination. In this context, the economically advanced nations may appear to be inherently exploitative in that their presence may perpetuate the dependency of the poorer nation.[15] Very large MNCs have budgets that exceed those of many small countries. Thus, critics of MNCs say they have too much power and undue political influence over governments and can exploit developing nations.[16] These basic challenges set the stage for examining how ethical problems arise in the global environment.

An important topic that has come up in recent years has to do with the diverse views about corporate social responsibility (CSR) relative to business–government relationships that occur in different regions of the world. For example, Scherer and Palazzo have noted that under conditions of globalization, the strict division of responsibilities between private businesses and nation-state governments do not hold as much everywhere.[17] They observe that many business firms have begun to assume social and political responsibilities that extend beyond legal requirements and fill some vacuums in global governance. Thus, there is an emerging, politicized concept of CSR that is occurring in some parts of the world.[18] We discussed this notion of political CSR in Chapter 2, and we continue the conversation in Chapter 18 when we discuss business's influence on government. Though this changing relationship between business and government is not occurring everywhere, it is a factor that needs to be considered in some regions of the world. It is in the global business environment where it has become most applicable.

Social, cultural, and ethical tensions are built into global business. MNCs attempt to bridge the cultural gaps between two or more cultures; yet, as they attempt to adapt to local customs and business practices, they are assailed at home for not adhering to the standards, practices, laws, or ethics of their home country.

Figure 7-1 graphically depicts the dilemma of MNCs caught between the characteristics and expectations of their

Figure 7-1 The Dilemma of the Multinational Corporation

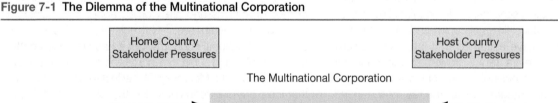

| Home Country Stakeholder Pressures | | Host Country Stakeholder Pressures |

The Multinational Corporation

Standards → ← Standards
Practices → ← Practices
Ethics → ← Ethics
Laws → ← Laws
Culture → ← Culture
Customs → ← Customs
System of Government → ← System of Government
Socioeconomic System → ← Socioeconomic System

Spotlight on Sustainability

A Global Sustainability Movement: Earth Hour

The celebration known as Earth Hour was started in Australia in 2007 by the World Wide Fund for Nature (WWF). The organization's mission is to stop degrading Earth's natural environment and to create a low-carbon future for planet Earth.

Earth Hour is a global sustainability movement that was initiated with the hope that each year will bring about a continued celebration. The first Earth Hour was held in Australia, and after national acclaim, it gained high international interest, with more and more cities beginning to sign up for the next Earth Hour campaign.

Held each year on the last Saturday of March, Earth Hour engages millions of concerned citizens in 180 countries and territories to turn off their lights and show support for the planet. Beyond the switching-off event, Earth Hour has become a catalyst for positive sustainability impact. You can learn more about Earth Hour's mission and events in your country by going to https://www.earthhour.org /take-part/events.

Sources: Earth Hour, https://www.earthhour.org/our-mission, accessed March 26, 2021; "Earth Hour 2021," https://www .worldwildlife.org/pages/earth-hour, accessed March 26, 2021; Earth Hour, Facebook, @earthhour, https://www.facebook.com /earthhour/, accessed March 26, 2021.

home country and those of one or more host countries. They often find themselves in an almost unmanageable situation but cannot be deterred from finding sustainable solutions if they desire to expand to markets abroad.

7.2 Ethical Issues in the Global Business Environment

The challenges for companies operating in the global business environment include issues of corporate social responsibility, generally, and business ethics, specifically. Our primary focus in this chapter will be on business ethics, but the issues related to the global dimension of CSR should not be forgotten. For many companies, most of the ethical problems that arise in the global environment are in the same categories as those that arise in their domestic environments. These ethical issues reside in all of the functional areas of business: operations, marketing, finance, accounting, and management. These issues embrace the fair treatment of stakeholders—employees, customers, the community, and competitors—and involve product safety, plant safety, advertising practices, human resource management, human rights, environmental problems, business practices, and so on.

These ethical issues may seem to be somewhat fewer in developed countries, but they exist there as well. The ethical challenges seem to be more acute in less-developed countries (LDCs) or emerging economies because these countries are at earlier stages of economic development and often do not have a legal or ethical infrastructure in place to help protect their citizenry. This situation creates an environment in which there is temptation to operate with lower standards, or perhaps no standards, because fewer government regulations or activist groups exist to protect the stakeholders' interests. In the LDCs, the opportunities for business exploitation and the engagement in questionable practices (by developed countries' standards) are abundant.

It is useful to identify some prominent categories of ethical issues in the global sphere to provide some appreciation of the development of these kinds of issues for business. First, we will discuss questionable marketing and plant safety practices. Then, we will address the issue of human rights and labor abuses often found in "sweatshops" (the use of cheap labor in developing countries)—a topic that has dominated international business discussions for the past couple decades. Then, we will consider the special challenges of corruption, bribery, and questionable payments. From these prominent examples, we should be able to develop an appreciation of the kinds of ethical challenges that confront all MNCs doing business globally. Finally, we will consider some strategies for companies seeking to improve their global business ethics.

7.2a Questionable Marketing and Plant Safety Practices

The process of marketing either domestically or abroad creates many ethical and legal challenges for businesses. The most obvious marketing issues are those embedded in the product itself and its promotion. A classic example of a *questionable marketing practice* is the now-infamous infant formula controversy that has spanned many decades and continues even today. The *plant safety issue* is best illustrated by considering the Union Carbide Bhopal crisis that began in 1984, continued into the 1990s, and is not completely resolved today. Following Bhopal was the factory fire and building collapse in Dhaka, Bangladesh, and this was followed by the disastrous Rana Plaza building collapse in Bangladesh.

These tragedies are significant and representative because they illustrate the endless problems companies can face as a result of mistakes made in global business ethics and how their effects can be felt for decades.

The Infant Formula Controversy. The **infant formula controversy** is a classic example that illustrates ethical questions that can arise while marketing products abroad.[19]

For decades, there was a realization among physicians working in tropical lands (many of which were LDCs) that severe health risks were posed to infants from bottle-feeding as opposed to breast-feeding. Such countries typically had neither refrigeration nor sanitary conditions. Water supplies were not pure, and powdered infant formula mixed with bacteria-infected water likely led to disease and diarrhea in the bottle-fed infant.

Because people in these developing countries are typically poor and often uneducated, mothers tended to overdilute the powdered formula, trying to make it last longer, thus diminishing significantly the amount of nutrition the infant receives. Once a mother begins bottle-feeding, her capacity for breast-feeding quickly diminishes. Poverty also leads the mother to put less-expensive substitute products such as powdered whole milk and cornstarch in the bottle. These products are nutritionally inadequate and unsatisfactory for the baby's digestive system.

It eventually became apparent that in LDCs there was increased bottle-feeding, decreased breast-feeding, and a dramatic increase in the numbers of malnourished and sick babies because of this. The problems surfaced when several of the infant formula companies, aware of the conditions just described, were promoting their products and, therefore, promoting bottle-feeding in an intense way. Such marketing practices as mass advertising, billboards, radio jingles, and free samples became commonplace. These promotional devices typically portrayed the infants who used their products as healthy and robust, in sharp contrast with the reality that was brought about by the conditions mentioned.

Although several companies were engaging in these questionable marketing practices, the Swiss conglomerate Nestlé was singled out by a Swiss social activist group in an article titled "Nestlé Kills Babies." At about the same time, an article appeared in Great Britain titled "The Baby Killers."[20] From this point on, a protracted controversy developed, with Nestlé and other infant formula manufacturers on one side and a host of organizations on the other side filing shareholder resolutions and lawsuits against the company.

Among the groups that were actively involved in the controversy were groups such as the National Council of Churches and its Interfaith Center on Corporate Responsibility (ICCR), United Nations Children's Fund (UNICEF), the World Health Organization (WHO), and the Infant Formula Action Coalition (INFACT). Nestlé was singled out because it had the largest share of the world market and because it aggressively pushed sales of its infant formula in developing countries, even after the WHO developed a sales code to the contrary.[21]

INFACT and ICCR organized and began a national boycott in 1977 against Nestlé that continued for almost seven years.[22] In 1984, after spending tens of millions of dollars resisting the boycott, Nestlé finally reached an accord with the protesters. The company agreed to make some changes in its business practices. The protesters, in return, agreed to end their boycott but to continue monitoring Nestlé's performance.[23] The infant formula controversy continued well into the 1990s and 2000s.

The infant formula controversy illustrates the character of questionable marketing practices by firms pursuing what might be called normal practices were it not for the fact that they were being pursued in foreign countries where local circumstances made them suspect.[24] The infant formula controversy also illustrates the endurance of certain ethical issues, particularly in the global arena.

Even today, the International Baby Food Action Network (IBFAN) (http://www.ibfan.org/) continues to advocate safety in feeding babies and lobbies against companies that continue engaging in questionable business and marketing practices.[25] By 2013, the infant formula issue was flaring anew in China where it has been alleged that formula makers pay doctors and medical staff to motivate them to get newborns hooked on infant formula.[26] In addition, because many more well-to-do families in China do not trust the quality and safety of their own brands, they have been buying up infant formula from Australia that because of its proximity to the product can be delivered more quickly.[27] In 2020, although many improvements had been made, Nestlé was still struggling to win over its baby formula critics.[28]

Plant Safety and the Bhopal Tragedy. The Union Carbide **Bhopal tragedy** brought into sharp focus the challenges of multinationals conducting manufacturing operations in a foreign, less-developed business environment. On December 3, 1984, the leakage of methyl isocyanate gas caused what many have termed the "worst industrial accident in history." The final death toll was between 15,000 and 20,000, and a half million survivors suffering from related maladies.[29] The tragedy raised numerous legal, ethical, social, and technical questions for MNCs.[30] Forty years later, many issues related to the Bhopal, India, disaster remain unresolved.[31]

Interviews with experts just after the accident revealed a belief that the responsibility for the accident had to be shared by the company and the Indian government. According to Union Carbide's inspector, the Bhopal plant did not meet U.S. standards and had not been inspected in more than two years. In addition, the Indian government allowed thousands of people to live dangerously near the plant, and there were no evacuation procedures.[32]

Many important questions that have implications for manufacturing abroad have been raised by the Bhopal disaster. Among the more important of these issues are the following:[33]

1. To what extent should MNCs maintain identical standards at home and abroad regardless of how lax laws are in the host country?
2. How advisable is it to locate a complex and dangerous plant in an area where the entire workforce is basically unskilled and uneducated, and where the populace is ignorant of the inherent risks posed by such plants?
3. How wise are laws that require plants to be staffed entirely by local employees?

4. What is the responsibility of corporations and governments in allowing the use of otherwise safe products that become dangerous because of local conditions? (This question applies to the infant formula controversy also.)
5. After reviewing all the issues, should certain kinds of plants even be located in developing nations?

At the heart of these questions is the issue of differing safety standards in various parts of the world. Additionally, it is unclear to what extent MNC businesses are responsible for their suppliers across the world.

The complexity and tragedy of the Bhopal gas leak case for its victims, the Indian government, and Union Carbide are attested to by the fact that this issue remains a topic of discussion today. In 1989, Union Carbide extricated itself from relief efforts by agreeing to pay the Indian government $470 million to be divided among victims and their families. Dow Chemical Company bought Union Carbide in 2001. By 2020, victims of the Bhopal tragedy said that the pandemic had worsened their health and living conditions and were demanding more accountability. Dow Chemical continues to deny liability, saying that Union Carbide settled the case back in 1989.[34]

Factory Fire in Dhaka. In a factory fire reminiscent of the Bhopal tragedy, 112 workers were killed in a Tazreen Fashions, Ltd., factory near Dhaka, Bangladesh, in November 2012. This disaster was especially newsworthy because more than 500 Bangladeshi garment workers had died in fires in the previous six years according to labor groups. The fire has been called the country's worst industrial accident, and it received high-profile news coverage when it was discovered that garments for Wal-Mart Stores were being manufactured there at the time.[35]

Walmart says it had found serious fire-safety concerns at the plant in an inspection conducted in 2011 and that it had removed Tazreen from its list of authorized factories "months ago" but that one of its suppliers used the plant without its authorization.[36] A Bangladesh government committee investigation found that the incident was an act of sabotage. In addition, the committee's report disclosed that three mid-level executives from Tazreen Fashions were suspected of stopping workers from leaving during the fire because they wanted to prevent employee theft.[37] Companies such as Walmart were under pressure to police the safety concerns of factories used. Although 45 cases were filed against the Tazreen Fashions factory owners, as of 2016 no action had been taken against them.[38] By 2020, victims' friends and family continued to fight for justice through protests and media campaigns.[39]

Rana Plaza Factory Collapse. Just five months after the fire at Tazreen Fashions, in April 2013, a garment factory known as the Rana Plaza Building collapsed in Bangladesh, killing more than 1,100 workers and injuring some 3,000 more. The building housed 5,000 workers in five textile firms. This incident continued the spotlight on Western

companies that use factories for low-cost clothes manufacturing, though these companies have not been identified as the guilty parties.[40] The building that collapsed was owned by a local politician who had the building built six years earlier without the required permits.

The public in Bangladesh had been upset over the lack of safety regulations governing buildings and the ease with which politicians get these structures built.[41] In 2015, police finally filed homicide charges against 42 people, including the building owner, former mayor of the local council, owners of the five garment factories located in the complex, and dozens of council officials and engineers. This was considered to be a remarkable legal step in a country where past industrial accidents were rarely pursued or prosecuted.[42]

After the 2013 Rana Plaza disaster, global corporations not held to be responsible in the disaster formed two parallel, corporate-backed groups to address safety issues in Bangladesh's garment industry. Twenty-six North American–based companies formed the Alliance for Bangladesh Worker Safety (Alliance). In addition, 189 mostly European retailers and global workers' unions formed the Accord on Fire and Building Safety in Bangladesh (Accord).[43] These groups were formed to help monitor and improve working conditions in the Bangladeshi garment industry. In 2018, the Alliance announced that it was ending its tenure in Bangladesh and that it would turn over to a local company the role of monitoring factory conditions. The Alliance indicated that 93 percent of the faults identified were corrected while 428 factories completed 100 percent of remediation works.[44] The Accord's five-year agreement was due to conclude in 2018 as well, but as of 2021 it was continuing its monitoring and reporting progress. The Accord reported results similar to those of the Alliance.[45]

The lessons from Bhopal, Dhaka, and Rana Plaza are many and will continue to be analyzed. In companies around the globe, these disasters have stimulated continued discussions in the issue of how to operate abroad, as well as the extent to which businesses are responsible for their supply chain suppliers. To be sure, legal and ethical issues are central to the discussions. What are at stake, however, are not just the practices of businesses abroad but also the very question of their presence. Depending on the final outcome of these cases, MNCs may decide that the risks of doing certain types of business abroad are just too great.

7.2b Human Rights, Sweatshops, and Labor Abuses

The concept of global human rights is anchored in many of the rights principles discussed in Chapter 6. The range of human rights expected from businesses primarily encompasses those affecting employees and consumer stakeholders. Labor rights and abuses is one of the top issues. Consumers have more freedom of choice, but employees are often stuck in their jobs without sufficient mobility. No issue has been more consistently evident in the global business ethics realm than the use and alleged abuse of women, children, and workers in cheap-labor factories, often called "sweatshops," in developing countries. For example, a report by the Associated Press (AP) found that slavery persists in the seafood industry, though Thai businesses and government have repeatedly vowed to clean up the nation's multi-billion-dollar seafood exporting industry. One factory was found to be housing dozens of enslaved workers and runaway migrants. Children and their parents were found to be working side by side in a warehouse that had overflowing toilets and the stench of sewage.[46]

The investigation found shrimp peelers who were working 16-hour days for little or no pay while the company monitored them to prevent their escape. They also found that the farmed shrimp entered the supply chains of major food stores and retailers including Walmart, Whole Foods, and Target, as well as the supply chains of popular restaurant chains such as Red Lobster and Olive Garden. Although most of these companies denied that this was happening, they condemned the reported labor practices and said they were striving to eliminate human rights and labor abuses that

were taking part in the industry.[47] A 2018 report by Human Rights Watch documented that there continue to be rights abuses and forced labor in Thailand's fishing industry.[48] To its credit, Thailand has become the first Asian country pledging to adhere to international standards set forth in the International Labor Organization's (ILO) Work in Fishing Convention, which sets out binding rules for conditions on fishing vessels.[49]

In the Tazreen factory fire, it was reported that even though Bangladesh has become the world's second largest exporter of garments behind China, it also pays some of the lowest wages in the world.[50] The major players in this controversy, large corporations, have highly recognizable names—Nike, Walmart, Gap, Kmart, Reebok, J. C. Penney, and Disney, to name just a few. The countries and regions of the world that have been involved are also recognizable—Southeast Asia, Pakistan, Indonesia, Honduras, Dominican Republic, Thailand, China, Bangladesh, the Philippines, Mexico, and Vietnam. Sweatshops have not been totally eliminated in the United States either, but the most serious problems seem to be in the developing countries.[51]

Ethics In Practice Case

Fair Trade: Is It a Sustainable Movement?

After the collapse of the Rana Plaza factory in Bangladesh, killing more than 1,100 workers, the fair-trade movement for apparel and home furnishings took off. The Fair-Trade Movement had begun with coffee, and Starbucks was one of the first companies to sign on to the idea to help farmers and workers in less-developed countries. Fair trade is an alternative approach to conventional trade and is based on partnerships being developed between producers and traders, businesses and consumers. The global fair-trade system is represented by Fairtrade International (FTI) and its member organizations.

FTI carries out its mission of empowering producers and combating poverty by certifying factories that meet certain standards that include employee safety and health, acceptable wages and working conditions, environmental impact, worker's rights, and other pertinent criteria.

Fair Trade USA (FTUSA) audits and certifies transactions between U.S. companies and their international suppliers to ensure that rigorous fair-trade standards have been met. Fair Trade USA is a 501(c)(3) nonprofit organization that seeks to inspire the rise of conscious consumers and eliminate exploitation. FTUSA now certifies 20 brands and includes companies such as Patagonia, Williams-Sonoma, and Bed Bath & Beyond. Before Rana Plaza, FTUSA only certified a handful of brands. Whole Foods Market got into apparel when it began carrying fair-trade certified T-shirts made by Pact Apparel.

Fair trade does not come without higher costs. The average total cost to the brands to get certification including third-party factory audits comes to about 1 to 5 percent of what the brands pay to factories. Brands are also expected to pay more based on the volume of purchases from factories.

As a concept, the fair-trade movement appears to be the epitome of CSR. The fair-trade movement has its detractors, however. Among the criticisms: (1) little money actually reaches the developing world, (2) less money actually reaches the farmers and workers, (3) evidence of impact has not been adequately assessed, (4) fair trade is profitable to traders in rich countries, (5) fair trade hurts other farmers and producers, (6) fair-trade criteria presuppose a set of political values that everyone does not agree with, (7) some supporters of fair trade use bullying and misleading selling techniques, (8) people who volunteer to work on free trade are misled, (9) there is failure to monitor standards, and (10) corruption is in the process. In another criticism of fair trade, it was pointed out that it may increase revenues to some farmers, but it is mostly about redistribution rather than expanding the overall amount of value created.

1. Do consumers today support the idea of paying more for a product just to help workers in emerging economies?
2. Why did the fair-trade movement explode in popularity after the Rana Plaza collapse? Will the movement continue to grow once working conditions get better?
3. What are the global ethical issues embedded in the concept and implementation of fair trade?
4. Do the "certified" companies really care, or are they simply interested in their reputations?
5. Is the fair-trade movement sustainable? Or will it plateau and decline over time?

Sources: Fair Trade USA, https://www.fairtradecertified.org/about-us, accessed March 31, 2021; Fairtrade International, https://www.fairtrade.net/, accessed March 31, 2021; Robert Lamb, "How Fair-Trade Works," https://money.howstuffworks.com/fair-trade.htm, accessed March 31, 2021.

Though **sweatshops**, characterized by child labor, low pay, poor working conditions, worker exploitation, and health and safety violations, have existed for decades, they have grown in number in the past couple decades as global competition has heated up and corporations have gone to the far reaches of the world to lower their costs and increase their productivity. The problem has become so serious that there now is a growing interest in what is being called "modern slavery" in business, which embraces a multitude of different forms of forced labor exploitation.[52]

The Nike Corporation was an early lightning rod for social activists concerned about overseas manufacturing conditions, standards, and ethics. A major reason for this was the company's high profile and visibility, extensive advertising using athletic superstars, as well as the stark contrast between the tens of millions of dollars Nike icons Michael Jordan and Tiger Woods were earning and the several dollars of daily wage rate the company's subcontractors once paid their Indonesian workers.[53] The continuing challenges faced by Nike are developed further in Case 14 in the Case section at the end of the book.

Critics of sweatshop labor practices, including social activist groups, labor unions, student groups, and grassroots organizations, have been speaking out, criticizing business abusers, and raising public awareness for decades. These critics claim many businesses are exploiting children and women by paying them poverty wages, working them to exhaustion, punishing them for minor violations, violating health and safety standards, and tearing apart their families. Many of these companies counter that they offer the children and women workers a superior alternative. They say that although their wage rates may be embarrassing by developed-world standards, those rates frequently equal or exceed local legal minimum wages, or average wages.[54]

A number of different programs, organizations, and initiatives have begun seeking to redress these problems in sweatshops. Two that merit closer consideration include The Fair Labor Association and SA8000.

Fair Labor Association (FLA). The **Fair Labor Association (FLA)** has been working to improve sweatshop conditions and human rights violations for more than 20 years. FLA claims that its mission "is to combine the efforts of business, civil society organizations, and colleges and universities to promote and protect workers' rights and to improve working conditions globally through adherence to international standards."[55] Some of its participating companies include well-known names such as Adidas Group, Cutter & Buck, Patagonia, Under Armour, Barnes & Noble, Puma, and many affiliate universities. FLA uses a multistakeholder approach to improving workers' lives. They have employed a three-step process that entails setting standards through a code of conduct, monitoring and reporting, and supporting compliance.[56] In 2020, FLA launched its Fair Compensation Strategy in which it proposes that workers in affiliate supply chains earn a compensation that

is sufficient to meet their basic needs and have some discretionary income.[57]

Social Accountability 8000 (SA8000). Another major initiative to improve sweatshop and human rights conditions was created by **Social Accountability International (SAI).** SAI is a nongovernmental, multistakeholder organization whose mission is to advance the human rights of workers around the world. SAI convenes key stakeholders in an effort to develop consensus-based standards, conduct cost-benefit research, accredit auditors, provide training and technical assistance, and assist corporations in improving social compliance in their supply chains.[58]

SAI has developed one of the world's preeminent social standards—Social Accountability 8000 or SA8000—designed to piggyback on the ISO8000 quality-auditing system of the International Standards Organization (ISO).

The SA8000 initiative involves a broad spectrum of U.S. and international companies, such as Gucci, General Mills, Walt Disney Company, Chiquita Brands, VF, and Carrefour, plus a number of labor and human rights groups. The current standards for SA8000 include those in the following categories:[59]

1. *Child Labor:* No use or support of child labor.
2. *Forced or Compulsory Labor:* No use of forced or compulsory labor.
3. *Health and Safety:* Provide a safe and healthy work environment; prevent potential occupational accidents.
4. *Freedom of Association and Right to Collective Bargaining:* Respect the right to form and join trade unions and bargain collectively.
5. *Discrimination:* No discrimination in hiring, remuneration, access to training, promotion, termination, or retirement based on many different factors.
6. *Discipline:* No corporal punishment, mental or physical coercion, or verbal abuse. No harsh or inhumane treatment is allowed.
7. *Working Hours:* Comply with the applicable law but, in any event, no more than 48 hours per week with at least one day off for every seven-day period; voluntary overtime paid at a premium rate and not to exceed 12 hours per week on a regular basis.
8. *Remuneration:* Respect right of personnel to living wage; all workers paid at least the minimum wage; wages sufficient to meet basic needs and provide discretionary income.
9. *Management Systems:* Facilities seeking to gain and maintain certification must go beyond simple compliance to integrate the SA8000 standard into their management systems and practices.[60]

As of 2020, more than 4,600 SA8000 companies were operating in 58 countries covering 2.2 million employees.[61]

Another strategy being used by companies seeking to improve working conditions in factories is to create **ethical supply chains**, also called **sustainable supply chains**. This practice involves companies that have pledged to only do business with suppliers who agree to adhere to social and environmental standards. These MNCs usually ask their main suppliers to comply with these standards and that they also ask their own suppliers to comply with the standards as well. The purpose in this process is to create a cascade of ethical and sustainable practices that permeate the supply chain or supply network.[62] As an example, we provide the case of Everlane, a clothing company that evidences best practices in global supply chains, in Case 26 in the Case section at the end of the book.

Individual Company Initiatives. In addition to the initiatives by such industry organizations as the FLA and the SAI (SA8000), it is important to note that some individual companies are striving on their own behalf to address the issues surrounding sweatshops and other forms of labor exploitation. A number of companies have developed *global outsourcing guidelines* and codes as parts of their sustainability initiatives and have made important strides in attempts at self-monitoring of their production facilities in developing countries. Companies such as Nike, Levi Strauss & Co., and Gap are notable examples.[63]

Despite the best efforts of some companies to improve factory conditions in emerging countries, there is growing evidence that some suppliers have learned how to conceal abuses and continue to get away with unacceptable practices. It has been disclosed that many factories, especially in China, have learned how to "game the system" through questionable practices. Some of these practices include keeping double sets of books; scripted responses wherein managers and employees are tutored how to answer auditors' questions about hours, pay, and safety practices; and hidden production, whereby plants meet U.S. demands by secretly shifting work to subcontractors that violate pay and safety standards, but these subcontractors are hidden from the auditors.[64]

Sweatshops and labor abuses sharply contrast the haves and the have-nots of the world's nations. Consumers in developed countries have benefited greatly from the lower prices made possible by cheap labor. It remains to be seen how supportive those consumers will be when prices rise because MNCs improve wage rates and conditions in developing countries. The MNCs face a continuing and volatile ethical issue that will not go away. In the age of transparency, we should expect more revelations in the years to come.

Alien Tort Claims Act and Human Rights Violations. Looking beyond possible human rights violations in sweatshops, claims that companies may have violated the human rights of foreign nationals could come back to haunt firms that have been accused of more serious human rights abuses. At stake is the U.S. courts' interpretation of an obscure piece of legislation known as the **Alien Tort Claims Act (ATCA).**[65] Though researchers cannot determine why Congress passed this little-known act in 1789, recently it has

---

Ethics In Practice Case

Cheating Consultants: Helping Factories to Pass Sweatshop Audits

A growing number of consulting firms in China now advertise that they can help Chinese factories pass labor audits being conducted by Western companies. These firms claim they can help generate two sets of books—real ones and fake ones. These consultants are part of a rising cottage industry in China that helps factories "appear" to pass the increasingly stringent audits being used to help clean up sweatshops and labor abuses in that country.

Auditors of working conditions in low-wage plants have also said they have found documents that might have been used in factories to prep workers with the answers the factory wanted the auditors to hear—this is according to the Fair Labor Association (FLA) that conducted an investigation.

The Ethical Trading Initiative, a London-based group, is concerned that audit fraud is a serious problem. Fake payroll books have become so common that auditors now assume there are (at least) two sets of books.

One Chinese consulting firm even advertised on the Internet that it has software available to generate fake factory books. The software also allows the factories to adjust their employee data to present the type of profile the auditors are expecting. The demand for the services of these consulting firms seems to be rising as factories seek to pass the increasingly difficult audit standards.

In their defense, some factory owners in China say it's impossible to meet the MNC's demands for better working conditions while also keeping prices low.

1. Is it ethical to operate a consulting firm that helps factories to lie, cheat, and deceive auditors seeking to monitor working conditions? Could you imagine firms such as this succeeding in your country?
2. What are the implications for the business system in countries that permit this to occur? What happens to the business and society relationship?
3. Should the MNCs striving to create ethical supply chains attempt to interact with and lobby the governments to outlaw consulting firms such as these?
4. Have we now reached the point that working conditions cannot be improved while keeping prices low? If so, what comes next?

Sources: Jane Moyo, "Can Audits Build Confidence in Company Supply Chains?," Ethical Trading Initiative, July 5, 2018, https://www.ethicaltrade.org/blog/can-audits-build-confidence-company-supply-chains, accessed March 31, 2021; Kathy Chu, "A Look at How Some Chinese Factories Lie to Pass Audits," China Labor Watch, http://www.chinalaborwatch.org/newscast/168, accessed March 31,2021; QualityInspection.org, "3 Common Ways Factories Try to Cheat Inspectors/Auditors," March 19, 2019, https://qualityinspection.org/factories-try-cheat-inspector-auditor-china/, accessed March 31, 2021.

been the centerpiece of a controversy that may have widespread implications for American firms operating abroad.

In the past decade, efforts have been made to use the ATCA to sue transnational companies for violations of international law in countries outside the United States. Plaintiffs have argued that ATCA could be used by foreign individuals seeking to sue U.S. firms in U.S. courts for companies' actions abroad. If these suits were to succeed, the ATCA could become a powerful tool to increase corporate accountability around the globe.[66] Some of the companies that have been targeted under this law include Occidental Petroleum of Los Angeles, Del Monte, Chevron, Caterpillar, Ford, IBM, and GM.

Many of the companies have said that they have been unfairly targeted by activists who are using the law to try to remedy the injustices of foreign governments. Many of the lawyers for these companies also say the companies are being blamed for crimes they deplore and know nothing about.

In a significant 2013 judgment, the U.S. Supreme Court reined in the scope of the Alien Torts Act. The Court held that the statute cannot be applied to actions that take place overseas, thus weakening a device some human rights groups have used against alleged violators in their home countries. The Court held that the ATCA only applies to actions that take place in the United States. The Supreme Court's ruling will shut down many cases that have been ongoing for decades. Several justices expressed the concern that affirming liability in events which took place overseas would make American courts a magnet for distressed foreign plaintiffs for acts unrelated to the United States and could invite foreign courts to encourage judging U.S. corporations for actions outside their own borders.[67] In 2018, the U.S. Supreme Court ruled against the use of the ATCA in suing corporations.[68] Just when it was thought that the ATCA was no longer viable, in December 2020 the Supreme Court began hearing oral arguments in two other possible violations of the act.[69]

7.2c Corruption, Bribery, and Questionable Payments

The most frequent and highly publicized ethical problems with respect to global business have most recently been corruption, bribes, and questionable payments. These acts of fraud are as old as history itself, but in recent decades, governments around the world have escalated their attempts to eliminate them.

Corruption in global business continues to be an overarching problem. It starts with outright bribery of government officials and the giving of questionable political contributions. Beyond these, there are many other corrupt activities: the misuse of company assets for political favors, kickbacks and protection money for police, free junkets for government officials, secret price-fixing agreements, and insider dealing, just to mention a few. All of these activities have one thing in common: they are attempts to influence

the outcomes of decisions in cases when the nature and extent of the influence are not made public. In essence, these activities are abuses of power.[70]

Though one seldom hears an official definition of *corruption*, such synonyms as *dishonesty, sleaze, fraud, deceit*, and *cheating* are typically invoked. Transparency International, the global coalition against corruption, defines corruption as follows: the abuse of "entrusted power for private gain." They go on to say that corruption erodes trust, weakens democracies, hampers economic development, and further exacerbates inequality, poverty, social division, and the environmental crisis.[71]

Bribery is the primary form of corruption found in global business, and its practice merits closer examination. Simply speaking, bribery is the practice of offering something (usually money, but also other monetary benefits) in order to gain an illicit advantage.[72] Bribes are illegal in most places and generally held to be unethical, but it is informative to consider the ongoing debate about bribery. Some businesspeople continue to contend that bribery is necessary in some parts of the world, and some countries of the world continue to assert that they are culturally obligatory or defensible.

Opinions for and against Bribery in Global Settings. Opinions typically given in favor of permitting bribery have included the following:

- bribes are necessary for profits in order to do business;
- everybody does it—it will happen anyway;
- bribery is an accepted practice in many countries—it is normal and expected;
- bribes are forms of commissions, taxes, or compensation for conducting business between cultures.

Reasons frequently cited against giving bribes include the following:

- bribes are inherently wrong and cannot be accepted under any circumstances;
- bribes are illegal in the United States and most developed nations and, therefore, unfair elsewhere;
- one should not compromise one's own beliefs;
- managers should not deal with corrupt governments;
- such demands, once started, never stop;
- one should take a stand for honesty, morality, and ethics;
- those receiving bribes are the only ones who benefit;
- bribes create dependence on corrupt individuals and countries, and bribes deceive stockholders and pass on costs to customers.[73]

The costs of bribes and other forms of corruption are seldom fully understood or described. The World Economic Forum (WEF) estimates that the cost from global graft is more than 5 percent of world domestic product, and this probably underestimates it. In addition, bribes and corruption retard economic growth, especially in emerging economies.[74]

When government officials accept "speed" money or "grease payments" to issue licenses, the economic cost is

3 to 10 percent above the licensing fee. When tax collectors permit underreporting of income in exchange for a bribe, income tax revenues may be reduced by up to 50 percent. When government officials take kickbacks, goods and services may be priced 20 to 100 percent higher than they actually could have been. In addition to these direct economic costs, there are many indirect costs—demoralization and cynicism and moral revulsion against politicians and the political system. Due to bribery and corruption, politicians have been swept from office in many countries including Zimbabwe, Brazil, Italy, Japan, and Korea.[75]

The Foreign Corrupt Practices Act (FCPA). One of the first initiatives by a major government to address the problem of corruption and bribery in international business was the passage of the U.S. **Foreign Corrupt Practices Act (FCPA)** in 1977. Before this, many of the payments and bribes made by U.S.-based MNCs were not illegal. Even so, firms could have been engaging in illegal activities depending on whether and how the payments were reported to the Internal Revenue Service (IRS).

With the passage of the FCPA, however, it became a criminal offense for a representative of an American corporation to offer or give payments to the officials of other governments for the purpose of getting or maintaining business. The FCPA specifies a series of fines and prison terms that can result if a company or management is found guilty of a violation.[76]

The FCPA differentiates between bribes and facilitating payments, also called **grease payments**. The law does not prohibit so-called grease payments, or minor, facilitating payments to officials, for the primary purpose of getting them to do whatever they are supposed to do anyway. Such payments are commonplace in many countries. The real problem with questionable payments is that some forms of payments are prohibited (e.g., bribes), but other payments (e.g., grease payments) are not prohibited. The law is sometimes ambiguous on the distinctions between the two.[77]

To violate the FCPA, payments (other than grease payments) must be made corruptly to obtain business. This suggests some kind of quid pro quo. The idea of a corrupt quid pro quo payment to a foreign official may seem clear in the abstract, but the circumstances of the payment may easily blur the distinction between what is acceptable "grease" (e.g., payments to expedite mail pickup or delivery, to obtain a work permit, border crossings, or to process paperwork) and what is illegal bribery. The safest strategy for managers to take is to be careful and to seek a legal opinion when questions arise. It also is helpful for companies to have clear policies on such payments.[78] The year 2020 was a record setting year for FCPA enforcement.[79]

Figure 7-2 presents a basic distinction, with examples, between bribes (which are prohibited) and grease (or facilitating) payments (which are not prohibited) based on the FCPA.

The FCPA was intended to have and has had a significant impact on the way U.S. and many developed country's firms do business globally. A number of firms that paid bribes to foreign officials have been the subject of criminal and civil enforcement actions, resulting in large fines and, sometimes, suspension and debarment from federal procurement contracting. Sometimes their employees and officers have been imprisoned as well.[80] The Department of Justice (DOJ) has been cracking down on bribery at an accelerating pace in recent years. The DOJ's crackdown on corrupt practices has been broadened in that it is now attempting to catch both U.S. and foreign-based companies. For the past 20 years, the anti-bribery provisions of the FCPA now apply to foreign firms and persons doing business in the United States. Further, foreign companies whose securities are publicly traded in the United States now are also subject to the FCPA.[81]

Figure 7-3 summarizes several examples of the major cases involving violations of the FCPA due to charges made by the U. S. Securities and Exchange Commission (SEC).

The Global Anticorruption Movement. Corruption and bribery in global business is a significant and ongoing topic. With substantial increases in global trade and competition,

Figure 7-2 Bribes Compared to Grease Payments

Definitions	Examples
Grease Payments	
Relatively small sums of money given for the purpose of getting minor officials to: • Do what they are supposed to be doing • Do what they are supposed to be doing faster or sooner • Do what they are supposed to be doing better than they would otherwise do	Money given to minor officials (clerks, attendants, or customs inspectors) for the purpose of expediting. This form of payment helps get goods or services through red tape or administrative bureaucracies.
Bribes	
Relatively large amounts of money given for the purpose of influencing officials to make decisions or take actions that they otherwise might not take. If the officials considered the merits of the situation only, they might take some other action.	Money given, often to high-ranking officials. Purpose is often to get these people to purchase goods or services from the bribing firm. May also be used to avoid taxes, forestall unfavorable government intervention, secure favorable treatment, and so on.

Figure 7-3 Major Examples of Violations of the Foreign Corrupt Practices Act Charged by the U.S. Securities and Exchange Commission (SEC)

Company Charged	Violations of FCPA
Goldman Sachs (2020)	Violations of the Foreign Corrupt Practices Act (FCPA) in connection with the 1Malaysia Development Berhad (1MDB) bribe scheme, and as part of coordinated resolutions, it has agreed to pay more than $2.9 billion, which includes more than $1 billion to settle the SEC's charges.
Herbalife (2020)	The SEC's order finds that Herbalife's Chinese subsidiaries made payments and provided meals, gifts, and other benefits to Chinese officials in connection with obtaining sales licenses, curtailing government investigations of Herbalife China, and removing negative coverage of Herbalife China in state-owned media. Herbalife China managers asked employees to falsify expense documents in an effort to conceal the improper payments.
Novartis (2020)	The SEC's order finds that local subsidiaries or affiliates of Novartis or its former subsidiary Alcon Inc. engaged in schemes to make improper payments or to provide benefits to public and private health-care providers in South Korea, Vietnam, and Greece in exchange for prescribing or using Novartis or Alcon products.
Walmart (2019)	Walmart failed to sufficiently investigate or mitigate certain anti-corruption risks and allowed subsidiaries in Brazil, China, India, and Mexico to employ third-party intermediaries who made payments to foreign government officials without reasonable assurances that they complied with the FCPA. The SEC's order details several instances when Walmart planned to implement proper compliance and training only to put those plans on hold or otherwise allow deficient internal accounting controls to persist even in the face of red flags and corruption allegations.

Source: U.S. Securities and Exchange Commission, "SEC Enforcement Actions: FCPA Cases," https://www.sec.gov/spotlight/fcpa/fcpa-cases.shtml, accessed April 5, 2021.

Ethics In Practice Case

Possible Violations of the Foreign Corrupt Practices Act: Bribes versus Grease Payments

Following are some hypothetical situations that involve payments while doing international business. Do these represent bribes, which are illegal under the Foreign Corrupt Practices Act (FCPA), or are they "grease payments" intended to facilitate work getting done?

Situation 1

Healthy Forever, an infant formula manufacturer, has a subsidiary in Korea. The subsidiary makes payments to health-care professionals to get them to recommend Healthy Forever's products to new and expectant mothers.

Has a violation of the FCPA occurred in this situation?

Situation 2

QualityCom, a St. Louis–based technology company, hired several relatives of Chinese officials who were deciding whether to select the company's products.

Has a violation of the FCPA occurred in this situation?

Situation 3

Dynamic Products Co. (DP) of Augusta, Georgia, is attending a trade show in Beijing, China, because it wants to penetrate the Asian market. While at the trade show, a DP manager takes some prospective customers out for dinner and drinks and picks up the tab. The customers were midlevel managers at several different companies that were regulated by the government of China.

Have violations of the FCPA occurred in this situation?

Situation 4

While at the trade show in Beijing, Dynamic Products Co. (DP) decides it wants to invite some executives from one of China's state-owned utilities to the United States to engage in talks about a lucrative contract with the utility on which it plans to

make a bid. DP desperately wants the contract and offers to fly the officials and their wives first class to the United States and put them up at Augusta, Georgia's nicest hotel for a week and offers them tickets to The Masters, one of the premier golf events in the world. On the final day of their visit, DP organizes a meeting at which they discuss the possible contract.

Have violations of the FCPA occurred in this situation?

Situation 5

Big Mining Corp. (BMC), a major company listed on the New York Stock Exchange, recently discovered a quartz deposit in Kuwait. To get access to the deposit, BMC needs to construct a road from the deposit site to the nearest port. BMC hires an agent to help it get this job done, especially the securing of the required permits and documents from government officials. The agent informed BMC that he will need to make a small cash payment to an administrative clerk in Kuwait so that he will process the permit application speedily. In their previous experiences, BMC learned that permit approvals such as this could take months to get approved. BMC's director of projects is anxious to get the road permit approved, so she gives the agent permission to make the payment to the clerk.

Is this payment a violation of the FCPA?

Sources: U.S. Securities and Exchange Commission, "Foreign Corrupt Practices Act," https://www.investor.gov/introduction-investing/investing-basics/glossary/foreign-corrupt-practices-act-fcpa, accessed April 1, 2021; "Is It a Bribe…or Not?" *The Wall Street Journal*, July 22, 2013, R3, https://www.wsj.com/articles/SB10001424127887324021104578551251640574378, accessed April 1, 2021;"The WSJ Blogger," https://www.thewsjblogger.com/tag/bribe/, accessed April 1, 2021. U.S. Securities and Exchange Commission, "SEC Enforcement Actions: FCPA Cases," https://www.sec.gov/spotlight/fcpa/fcpa-cases.shtml, accessed April 1, 2021.

free markets, and democracy over the past decade, this comes as no surprise.[82] Several powerful developments are worthy of mention. Each has contributed to what has been called a growing **anticorruption movement**. By all accounts, the fight against corruption has been a long and continuing march, but progress is being made.[83]

The major players in the anticorruption movement include these initiatives: Transparency International, OECD Antibribery Initiatives, UN Convention against Corruption, and individual country initiatives.

Transparency International. An innovative special-interest group—**Transparency International (TI)**—was modeled after the human rights group Amnesty International. TI has established itself as the world's foremost anticorruption organization. TI states its mission in the following way: "Our mission is to stop corruption and promote transparency, accountability, and integrity at all levels and across all sectors of society."[84]

TI maintains more than 100 national chapters of locally established, independent organizations that fight corruption in their respective countries.[85] The primary tool that TI uses to combat corruption worldwide is its Corruption Perception Index. Their Bribe Payers Index appears to be discontinued.

Corruption Perception Index (CPI) The primary tool that TI uses to combat corruption is its now-famous annual **Corruption Perception Index (CPI)**. The annual CPI has been widely credited with putting TI and the issue of corruption on the international policy agenda. The CPI, which ranks 180 countries and territories by their perceived level of public sector corruption, according to experts and businesspeople, uses a scale of 0 to 100 where zero is highly corrupt and 100 is very clean. In 2021, TI reported that like previous years, two-thirds of countries score below 50 and the average score is 43. TI's data show that despite some progress, most countries still fail in tackling corruption effectively.[86]

In TI's 2020 rankings, the most recent available, the "highly clean" (less corrupt) countries included

- Denmark
- New Zealand
- Finland
- Singapore
- Sweden
- Switzerland

The bottom ranked (more corrupt) countries included

- Venezuela
- Yemen
- Syria
- Somalia
- South Sudan

The United States was ranked 25th from the top with a score of 67. TI makes the point that in spite of excellent records, no country is exempt from corruption. They have

reported that many "clean" countries have dodgy records overseas.[87] In its corruption reporting, TI pointed out that corruption was undermining an equitable response to COVID-19 pandemic and other crises, highlighting the importance of transparency and anti-corruption measures in emergency situations.

OECD Antibribery Initiatives. Another major ongoing program in the anticorruption movement is an antibribery treaty and initiative that the 29 industrialized nations of the Organisation for Economic Co-operation and Development (OECD) and five other countries agreed to in 1997. By 2020, 44 OECD member countries and seven non-member countries were subscribed to the OECD Antibribery Convention.[88] The OECD member nations agreed to ban international bribery and to ask each member nation to introduce laws patterned after the U.S. FCPA in its country. The main thrust of the treaty was to criminalize offering bribes to foreign officials who have sway over everything from government procurement contracts and infrastructure projects to privatization tenders.

In spite of good intentions, the OECD has been criticized for not doing enough quickly enough. It has also been criticized for dramatically failing to live up to its own governance and anti-sleaze standards. The broader criticism is that the OECD antibribery signatories have failed to follow through on their plans. Implementation and execution, often problems in effective management, have been serious issues for the OECD initiatives.

It may be some years before the OECD Antibribery Convention is fully implemented. However, the OECD represents a noteworthy initiative by a number of major countries in the global battle to eliminate corruption from commercial transactions.

UN Convention against Corruption (UNCAC). Another major initiative to combat corruption around the world is the **UN Convention against Corruption (UNCAC)**, which was created and implemented in December 2005.[89] It created the opportunity to develop a global language about corruption and a coherent implementation strategy. A multitude of international anticorruption agreements already exist; however, their implementation has been uneven and only moderately successful. The UNCAC gives the global community the opportunity to address both of these weaknesses and begin establishing an effective set of benchmarks for effective anticorruption strategies.[90]

From a business perspective, UNCAC claims to hold the potential to become the global framework for combating corruption, which will pave the way for the establishment of a level playing field for all market participants. A central objective of UNCAC is to bring a higher degree of uniformity in the formulation and application of anticorruption rules across the world.[91] As of 2020, there were 187 signatory countries to UNCAC.[92] UNCAC builds upon the UN Global Compact, which, as noted in Chapter 4, presents ten principles of conduct in the areas of human rights, labor standards, and environment. These will be covered later in the chapter under the topic of Global Codes of Conduct.

7.3 Improving Global Business Ethics

It is clear from the discussion up to this point that business ethics is much more complex at the global level than at the domestic level. The complexity arises from the fact that a wide variety of value systems, stakeholders, cultures, forms of government, socioeconomic conditions, and standards of ethical behavior exist throughout the world. Recognition of diverse standards of ethical behavior is important, but if we assume that firms from developed countries should operate in closer accordance with developed countries' ethical standards than with those of developing countries, the strategy of ethical leadership in the world will indeed be a challenging one.

Because the United States and European multinationals have played such a leadership role in world affairs—usually espousing fairness and human rights—these firms have a heavy responsibility, particularly in underdeveloped countries and developing nations. The power–responsibility equation and the Iron Law of Responsibility (see Chapter 1) suggest that these firms have a serious ethical responsibility

in global markets. That is, the larger sense of ethical behavior and social responsibility derives from the enormous amount of power these countries have.

In the following section, we will first discuss the challenge of honoring and balancing the ethical traditions of a business's home country with those of its host country. Next, we will discuss four recommended strategies for conducting business in foreign environments.[93] We will conclude by taking a look at some other steps companies are taking to improve their global ethics.

7.3a Balancing and Reconciling the Ethics Traditions of Home and Host Countries

One of the greatest challenges that businesses face while operating globally is achieving some kind of reconciliation and balance in honoring both the cultural and moral standards of their home and host countries. Should a business adhere to its home country's ethical standards for business practices or to the host country's ethical standards? There is no simple answer to this question. The diagram presented in Figure 7-4 frames the extreme decision choices businesses face when they consider operating globally. At one extreme, firms may engage in ethical imperialism by adhering to their home country's standards. At the other extreme, they may engage in cultural relativism by adapting to the host country's standards. These extreme alternatives deserve further discussion.

Figure 7-4 Ethical Choices in Home versus Host Country Situations

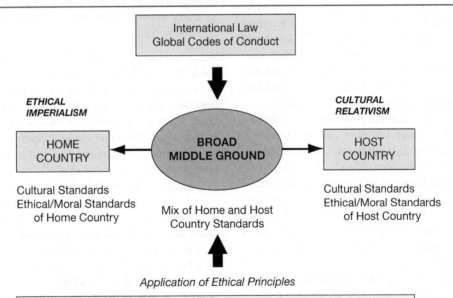

Ethical Imperialism. At one extreme in Figure 7-4 is a position often called **ethical imperialism**. This position holds that the business firm should continue to follow its home country's ethical standards even while operating in another country. Because U.S. and Western standards for treating employees, consumers, and the natural environment have been quite high relative to the standards in many developing countries, it is easy to see how managers might find this posture appealing.

As reliance on internationally based factories has soared in recent years and harsh conditions have been documented by the media, an increasing number of companies, such as Levi Strauss, Walmart, and Reebok, have espoused higher standards for foreign factories that cover issues such as wages, safety, and workers' rights to organize. Such higher standards could be seen by other countries, however, as the United States and the Western world attempting to impose its standards on the host country—thus the name "ethical imperialism" resides at one end of the continuum. Fortunately, the business world seems to be moving in the direction of eliminating corruption and operating according to higher ethical standards.

Cultural Relativism. At the other extreme in Figure 7-4 is a position often called **cultural relativism**. This position is characterized by foreign direct investors such as MNCs following the host country's ethical standards. This is the posture reflected in the well-known saying "When in Rome, do as the Romans do." This position would maintain that the investing firm should set aside its home country's ethical standards and adopt the ethical standards of the host country. For example, if a country holds that it is illegal to hire women for most managerial positions, the investing MNC would accept and adopt this standard, even if it runs counter to its home country's standards. Or if the host country has no environmental protection laws, this position would argue that the multinational need not be sensitive to environmental standards.

It has been argued that cultural relativism holds that no culture's ethics are better than any other's and that there are, therefore, no international rights or wrongs. If Thailand tolerates the bribery of government officials, then Thai tolerance is no worse than Japanese or German intolerance. If Switzerland does not find insider trading morally repugnant, then Swiss liberality is no worse than American restrictiveness.[94] Most ethicists find cultural relativism to be a case of moral or ethical relativism and, therefore, an unacceptable posture for companies to take.

Presented in Figure 7-4 is a series of questions management needs to ask to help it determine its stance on home versus host country ethics. Depending on the issue (e.g., worker safety versus minimum pay), companies may be more inclined to follow their home country's ethics. Key questions that must be posed and answered include the following: Which ethical standards will be used? Which ethical standards will transcend national boundaries? What constitutes moral minimums with respect to each category of ethical issue?

It may sound like a simplistic solution to say that the MNC needs to operate in some broad middle ground where a mix of home and host country ethical standards may be used. The challenge for managers will be to determine what mix of ethical standards should be used and how this decision should be made. As mentioned earlier, managers will need to ask themselves which moral standards are applicable in the situations they face. Which ethical standards best protect stakeholders and their rights?

Use of ethical principles such as those articulated in the previous chapters—rights, justice, utilitarianism, and the Golden Rule—still apply. Managers will need to decide which ethical standards should transcend national boundaries and thus represent **hypernorms** (transcultural values).[95] Hypernorms can be thought of as standards that are so basic that they are universally accepted. Examples might be health, safety, and freedom—but some cultures would not accept these examples. Donaldson and Dunfee have argued that for hypernorms to be established to help guide global business ethics, certain evidences are needed to confirm their legitimacy. For example, they maintain that hypernorms are more justified or confirmed when they meet some of the following conditions:

- widespread consensus that the principle is universal;
- a component of well-known global industry standards;
- supported by prominent NGOs;
- supported by regional governmental organizations such as the European Community, the OECD, or the Organization of American States;
- supported by global business organizations such as the Caux Round Table and the International Chamber of Commerce.[96]

When it is not possible to identify hypernorms that may guide ethical practices, the safest course of action would be to operate based on the higher of home versus host ethical standards, though this is not always easy to determine especially when a host country invokes a standard as being part of its culture. The home and host country's stage of maturity on economic development and culture are also important factors that must be considered.[97]

Managers also need to decide what will represent their **moral minimums** with respect to these and other issues. It would be nice to think that international laws and global codes of conduct will make these decisions easier. Though several such sets of codes and principles are available, they may be challenging to apply. In the interim, managers will need to be guided by the ethical concepts at their disposal, possibly with help from some of the strategies to which we now turn.

7.3b Strategies for Improving Global Business Ethics

In many instances, major companies work to improve their global business ethics through their global social responsibility programs.[98] Often, however, additional strategies must be used when operating globally. Four major strategies or categories of action that could help MNCs conduct global business while maintaining an ethical sensitivity in their practices include the following, and each deserves some explanation and discussion:

1. global codes of conduct,
2. linking ethics with global strategy,
3. suspension of business activities in certain countries, and
4. ethical impact statements and audits.[99]

(1) Global Codes of Conduct. Global codes of conduct seek to establish universal principles or guidelines that should be followed while doing business around the world. These would be closely related to the hypernorms discussed in the previous section. There are two types of global codes of conduct of interest here. First, there are specific corporate global codes that individual companies have developed. Second, there are global codes or guidelines that have been developed by various international organizations. Each of these deserves some consideration.

Corporate Global Codes In Chapter 6, we discussed codes of conduct, and that discussion applies in the global sphere as well. While operating on the world stage, MNCs have been severely criticized for employing divergent ethical standards in different countries, thus giving the impression that they are attempting to exploit local circumstances. A growing number of MNCs, for example, Chiquita Brands International, Caterpillar Tractor, Allis Chalmers, Coca-Cola, Johnson's Wax, Medtronic, and others, have developed and used codes geared toward worldwide operations.

One of the first and most well-known of the corporate global codes is that of Caterpillar, Inc., one of the world's leading manufacturers of construction and mining equipment. Their code is now titled "Code of Conduct: Our Values in Action."[100] Caterpillar has been building work machines that have been used the world over for close to 100 years. The code goes into considerable detail and has major sections that cover the following important values that Caterpillar aspires toward: integrity, excellence, teamwork, commitment, and sustainability. In addition, on its website, its code of conduct is presented as downloads in 20 different languages.[101]

Other companies give employees advice in their codes of conduct as they address global considerations. For example, Coca-Cola, truly a global corporation, has a detailed 41-page code of conduct. Coke's code gives the following advice to its worldwide associates: "Sometime you might face a situation where the right thing to do is not obvious. That is where our Code of Conduct can help. It is always here as your guide to preserving our reputation and living our values."[102]

Global Codes Created by International Organizations In addition to individual corporate codes, global codes or standards have been developed by a number of international

organizations that anticipate companies will adopt and follow. Some of these codes focus on one specific issue; many provide standards across a number of issue areas. Two of the most recent global codes have been developed by the International Standards Organization (ISO), an independent NGO with a membership of 163 national standards bodies, with its headquarters in Geneva, Switzerland.

ISO created a global standard known as **ISO 26000—Social Responsibility**. ISO 26000 provides guidance on how businesses and organizations can operate in a socially responsible way. This encompasses acting in an ethical and transparent way that contributes to the health and welfare of society.[103] The standard was launched after five years of work by many different stakeholders, including governments, NGOs, industry, consumer groups, and labor organizations. The core subjects and issues addressed in ISO 26000 include organizational governance, human rights, labor practices, the environment, fair operating practices, consumer issues, and community involvement and development.[104]

In 2016, ILO launched **ISO 37001—Anti-Bribery Management Systems**, a new standard designed to specifically address bribery and corruption. In addition to addressing bribery and corruption, the new standard was designed to help companies instill a culture of honesty, transparency, and integrity. ISO 37001 is designed to instill an anti-bribery culture within an organization and implement appropriate controls, which will in turn increase the chance of detecting bribery and reduce its incidence in the first place. The measures required by ISO 37001 are designed to be integrated into existing management processes and controls.[105]

Figure 7-5 summarizes brief information about some of the more prominent of the global codes and principles that have been created by international organizations. Among them are the UN Global Compact, Caux Round Table Principles, Global Sullivan Principles, OECD Guidelines for Multinational Enterprises, Global Reporting Initiatives, and ILO standards.

Two of the most widely used global standards are the **UN Global Compact** and the **Caux Round Table Principles**. The UN Global Compact took an important step by issuing its Sustainable Development Goals (SDGs) that lay out a path to end extreme poverty, fight injustice and inequality, and protect the planet. The 17 Sustainable Development Goals (Agenda 2030), which were presented in Chapter 4, also address the most important business ethics topics to include human rights, labor standards, and anticorruption.[106] The Caux Round Table Principles were launched more than 20 years ago and are seen as the precursor to the UN Global Compact that was developed soon after.[107] The seven principles are rooted in the recognition that neither the law nor market forces are sufficient enough to ensure positive and productive conduct. Figure 7-6 summarizes the seven principles.

(2) Ethics and Global Strategy. The major recommendation regarding ethics and global strategy is that the ethical dimensions of multinational corporate activity should be

Figure 7-5 Global Ethics Codes and Standards Developed by International Organizations

Codes, Standards, or Guidelines	Brief Description and Website
UN Global Compact	The Global Compact's operational phase was launched at UN headquarters in 2000. Today, thousands of companies from all regions of the world and international labor and civil society organizations are engaged in the Global Compact, working to advance ten universal principles in the areas of human rights, labor, the environment, and anticorruption. https://www .unglobalcompact.org/what-is-gc/mission/principles. Accessed April 2, 2021.
Caux Round Table Principles for Business	The CRT Principles for Responsible Business are a worldwide vision for ethical and responsible corporate behavior and serve as a foundation for action for business leaders worldwide. As a statement of aspirations, the CRT Principles aim to express a world standard against which business behavior can be measured. https://www.cauxroundtable.org/principles/. Accessed April 2, 2021.
Global Sullivan Principles of Social Responsibility	The objectives of the Global Sullivan Principles are to support economic, social, and political justice by companies where they do business; to support human rights and to encourage equal opportunity at all levels of employment, including racial and gender diversity on decision-making committees and boards; and to train and advance disadvantaged workers for technical, supervisory, and management opportunities. https://sustainabilitydictionary.com/2006/02/17/the -global-sullivan-principles-gsp/. Accessed April 2, 2021.
OECD Guidelines for Responsible Business Conduct	The guidelines are recommendations addressed by governments to multinational enterprises operating in or from adhering countries. They provide voluntary principles and standards for responsible business conduct in a variety of areas including employment and industrial relations, human rights, environment, information disclosure, combating bribery, consumer interests, science and technology, competition, and taxation. http://mneguidelines.oecd.org/guidelines/. Accessed April 2, 2021.
Global Reporting Initiative Guidelines	GRI's guidelines have been updated over the years. They address three major categories of reporting: Human Rights and Reporting, Reporting on Community Impacts, and Gender Reporting. https://www.globalreporting.org/how-to-use-the-gri-standards/gri-standards-english -language/. Accessed April 2, 2021.
ISO Standards	ISO 26000 addresses Social Responsibility and ISO 37001 addresses corruption and bribery. ISO 26000 was launched in 2010 and ISO 37001 was launched in 2016. https://www.iso.org /iso-37001-anti-bribery-management.html. Accessed April 2, 2021.

considered as significant inputs into top-level strategy formulation and implementation.[108] At the top level of decision making in the firm, corporate strategy is established, as discussed in Chapter 10. At this level, especially through enterprise level strategy, commitments are made that will define the underlying character and identity of the organization. The overall moral tone of the organization and all decision making and behaviors are set at the strategic level, and management needs to ensure that social and ethical factors do not get lost in the preoccupation with market opportunities and competitive factors. The maxim that ethics should be global, not local, is a driving force for engaging in international business.[109]

A more proactive stance is needed for dealing with ethical issues at the global level. Strategic decisions that may be influenced by ethical considerations in the global sphere include, but are not limited to, product/service decisions, plant location, operations policy, supply chain configurations, marketing policy and practices, and human resource

Figure 7-6 Caux Round Table Principles

Principle Number	Principle
1	Respect stakeholders beyond shareholders
2	Contribute to economic and social development
3	Build trust by going beyond the letter of the law
4	Respect rules and conventions
5	Support responsible globalization
6	Respect the environment
7	Avoid illicit activities

Source: Caux Round Table, https://www.cauxroundtable.org/principles/, accessed April 5, 2021.

management policies. More and more companies are employing departments and strategies with respect to global corporate social responsibility and global business citizenship.[110] Two companies illustrate how ethical considerations may be factored into global business decisions: Levi Strauss & Co. and Starbucks.

Levi Strauss & Co. A valuable illustration of ethics being factored into strategic decision making is provided by Levi Strauss & Co. Because the company operates in many countries and diverse cultures, it believes that it must take special care in selecting its contractors and the countries where its goods are produced in order to ensure that its products are being made in a manner consistent with its values and reputation. Years ago, the company developed a set of *global sourcing guidelines* that established standards its contractors must meet.[111]

Faced with global competition, Levi Strauss took the unprecedented action of publishing on its website a list of all active owned-and-operated and contract factories producing the company's branded products. The company's senior vice president for global sourcing said, "We believe that greater transparency within the supply chain will provide additional momentum for our efforts to improve working conditions in apparel factories worldwide. Our hope is that this level of transparency will become standard across the apparel sector, fostering greater collaboration among brands in shared factories."[112] Levi Strauss & Co.'s *Sustainability Guidebook* discusses the company's core values that it employs as it strives to be socially and ethically responsible in its global operations.[113] As a part of its overall global strategy, Levi's also has an extensive 23-page Worldwide Code of Business Conduct that addresses virtually every conceivable ethics issue it might face at the global level.[114]

Starbucks Another example of a company integrating ethical concerns into its corporate strategies is that of Starbucks Coffee Co., the Seattle-based firm. Starbucks' global strategy encompasses initiatives that might best be described as a combination of corporate social responsibility policies and a code of conduct that more specifically addresses global business ethics. Starbucks' Standards of Business Conduct indicate they are Living their Values.[115] As a part of its strategy, Starbucks maintains that since it is a global company, it is subjected to the highest standards of ethical business conduct. The standards apply to all partners, officers, and the board of directors as well as temporary service workers and independent contractors. Starbucks also has an anti-retaliation policy stating that the company does not tolerate retaliation against or the victimization of any partner who raises concerns or questions regarding a potential violation of the Standards of Business Conduct or any Starbucks policy that they reasonably believe to have occurred.[116]

As an additional dimension of its international business endeavors, the company states that their partners must comply with all local and foreign laws regarding customs and trades.[117] Ethical Consumer, a not-for-profit, multistakeholder

cooperative, states that Starbucks' comprehensive global business ethics strategy embraces climate change, environmental reporting, habitats and resources, palm oil, military and arms supply, human rights, worker rights, and supply chain management, just to mention a few.[118]

Though Starbucks sounds like a righteous company, like virtually all corporations doing business globally, it gets accused of questionable practices. In the case of Starbucks, the company found itself in hot water in 2020 when a TV exposé of child labor in Guatemala revealed that children under the age of 13 were working on farms that supplied coffee beans to the company. In its defense, Starbucks said that these farms were certified in 2019 as meeting their ethical sourcing guidelines and that they would continue their investigation of this reported incident.[119] Despite strong policies and good intentions, it is challenging for global corporations to monitor activities worldwide with perfection.

(3) Suspension of Activities. A multinational enterprise may sometimes encounter unbridgeable gaps between the ethical values of its home country and those of its host country. When this occurs, and reconciliation does not appear to be in sight, the responsible company might consider suspending activities in the host country. For example, years ago IBM and Coca-Cola established a precedent for this activity by suspending their activities in India because of that country's position on the extent of national ownership and control.[120] In a fight against corruption, Procter & Gamble even closed a Pampers diaper plant in Nigeria rather than pay bribes to customs inspectors.[121] We discuss the case of Chiquita that resulted in their closing a banana plant in Colombia, South America, in Case 19 in the case section at the end of the book.

The case of Google provides an example of the challenges between home and host country values. In 2010, Google decided to move its search engine out of China because it no longer thought it to be appropriate to censor searches at the request of the Chinese government. Google is credited with a clever, strategic decision by moving its search engine to Hong Kong, which is a special administrative region that has broader free-speech protections. This decision allowed Google to adhere to its own privacy principles while also allowing the Chinese government to save face.[122] By 2016, however, Google was planning to return to China while thinking of ways it could live with local laws and yet still provide some services.[123] By 2020, Google's on-and-off policy with respect to China continued; however, it was revealed that the Google parent company, Alphabet, was back in China (because it never left). Though the company had been widely credited as "having left China," Google still operates a significant in-country Chinese presence and through its parent company continues to launch new projects.[124]

Other technology companies such as Twitter and Facebook have also faced challenges in working in repressive regimes while seeking balance between their standards and those of their host countries that will allow them to expand their markets. In 2021, a military coup in Myanmar and a bloody crackdown on protestors put significant pressure on foreign companies operating in the country to suspend operations. Some of the firms began scaling back, others choosing to depart, and those that had linkages to the military were being urged to cut them.[125]

Suspension of business in a foreign country is not a decision that can or should be taken too hastily, but it must be regarded as a viable option for those firms that desire to travel on the higher moral road of free trade and human rights advocacy. Each country is at liberty to have its own standards, but this does not mean that other country's firms must do business in that country. Ethical leadership means that a company needs to express a willingness to take a moral stand when the occasion merits.

(4) Ethical Impact Statements and Audits. MNCs need to be constantly aware of the impacts they are having on society, particularly foreign societies. One way to do this is to periodically assess the company's impacts. Companies have a variety of impacts on foreign cultures, and ethical impacts represent only a few of these. The impact statement idea derived, in part, from the practice of environmental impact statements pioneered years ago. **Ethical impact statements** are an attempt to assess the underlying moral justifications for corporate actions and the consequent results of those actions. The information derived from these actions would permit the MNCs to modify or change their business practices if the impact statement suggested that such changes would be necessary or desirable.

One form of ethical impact assessment is some firms' attempts to monitor their compliance with their companies' global ethics codes. For example, Mattel Toy Company developed an independent audit and monitoring system for its code. Mattel's monitoring program was headed by an independent panel of commissioners who selected a percentage of the company's manufacturing facilities for annual audits. In one audit, for example, Mattel terminated its relationship with three contractor facilities for refusing to meet company-mandated safety procedures.[126] Today,

Mattel claims to be continuing its auditing of compliance to its code of conduct through its Responsible Supply Chain Commitment (RSCC). Mattel's RSCC embraces standards with respect to ethical sourcing, manufacturing, and its Anti-Slave Labor Policy.[127]

A major problem with Mattel's and others' auditing processes of their operations is that maintaining them in the face of competitors who are not doing the same gets to be time consuming and expensive.[128] The Mattel example highlights the challenges involved in monitoring a company's social impact in international markets.

Many companies today are issuing sustainability audits and reports in which they attempt to report on their global activities. For the most part, however, these reports feature the positive impacts and do not carefully examine the questionable practices of the firm. The major challenge in global business today is monitoring supply chains. This is where unethical practices are likely to occur. Although there are some violators, many companies today are doing a better job of monitoring their global operations and working environments. As consumers and the public are becoming better educated and aware of overseas operations, companies are sensing greater pressure to build more sustainable supply chains.[129]

The reports revealed that there were five vital steps among anticorruption programs that seemed to work best for companies[130]:

1. High-level commitment by top management
2. Detailed statements of policies and operating procedures
3. Training and discussion of policies and procedures
4. Hotlines and help lines for all organizational members
5. Investigative follow-up, reporting, and disclosure

These essential steps, which mirror ethics programs discussed in Chapter 6, when combined with the strategies for improving global business ethics discussed earlier, go a long way toward establishing a solid foundation for fighting bribery and corruption, the most insidious issues in global business ethics. The good news is that companies are now aware of these issues, and most are moving to address them.

Summary

Ethical dilemmas pose difficulties, in general, for businesses, and those arising in connection with doing business in global markets are among the most complex. An examination of major issues that have arisen in global business ethics over the past several decades shows that they rank right up there with the most well-known news stories about business performance. The infant formula controversy, the Bhopal tragedy, factory fires and collapses in Bangladesh, corruption and bribery, concern about human rights and sweatshops, and the supply chain issues of MNCs in Third World countries have all provided an opportunity for business critics to assail corporate ethics in the international sphere. These problems arise for a multiplicity of reasons, but differing cultures, value systems, forms of government, socioeconomic systems, and underhanded and ill-motivated business exploits have all been contributing factors.

Steps taken by the United States and other major countries to address the issues of corruption and bribery include the Foreign Corrupt Practices Act, the OECD Antibribery Convention, and the UN Convention against Corruption (UNCAC). Individual country initiatives also have been vital, as are the efforts of nonprofit organizations such as Transparency International. A number of different approaches to improving global business ethics were presented. The balancing of home and host country standards were discussed with the extreme options of ethical imperialism or cultural relativism presented and contrasted.

Four strategies for improving global business ethics were set forth: (1) global codes of conduct, encompassing corporate codes, and global codes created by international organizations; (2) the integration of ethical considerations into corporate strategy; (3) the suspension of activities in the host country; and (4) the use of ethical impact statements and audits. These strategies offer some hope that global business can be better managed.

In spite of the worldwide global pandemic and questions being raised about the future of international business, current trends point to a modest growth in business activity in the transnational economy, and though there is some evidence of a backlash against globalization, the ethical issues associated with international business remain. Indeed, it could easily be argued that business's greatest ethical challenges in the future will be on the global stage.

Key Terms

Alien Tort Claims Act (ATCA), p. 160
anticorruption movement, p. 164
Bhopal tragedy, p. 156
bribery, p. 161
Caux Round Table Principles, p. 167
corruption, p. 161
Corruption Perception Index (CPI), p. 164
cultural relativism, p. 166
ethical impact statements, p. 170
ethical imperialism, p. 166
ethical supply chains, p. 159
Fair Labor Association (FLA), p. 159

Foreign Corrupt Practices Act (FCPA), p. 162
globalization, p. 153
grease payments, p. 162
hypernorms, p. 166
infant formula controversy, p. 155
internationalization, p. 153
ISO 26000—Social Responsibility, p. 167
ISO 37001—Anti-Bribery Management Systems, p. 167
moral minimums, p. 166
multinational corporations (MNCs), p. 154

multinational enterprises (MNEs), p. 154
Social Accountability International (SAI), p. 159
sustainable supply chains, p. 159
sweatshops, p. 159
transnational economy, p. 153
Transparency International (TI), p. 164
UN Convention against Corruption (UNCAC), p. 164
UN Global Compact, p. 167

Discussion Questions

1. Drawing on the notions of moral, amoral, and immoral management introduced in Chapter 5, categorize your impressions of (a) Nestlé, in the infant formula controversy; (b) Union Carbide, in the Bhopal tragedy; and (c) Google, in moving its search engine out of China.

2. As an MNC seeks to balance and honor the ethical standards of both the home and host countries, conflicts inevitably will arise. What criteria do you think managers should consider as they try to decide whether to use home or host country ethical standards? Does the use of hypernorms help? Explain.

3. Differentiate between a bribe and a grease payment. Give an example of each.

4. Conduct research for purposes of updating the latest rankings of Transparency International and the activities of the OECD, UNCAC, and individual country initiatives. How could countries that now rank lowest most effectively improve their TI rankings?

5. What are the major strategies companies might employ in improving global business ethics? What are the key steps research has shown are important to successful company anticorruption efforts?

Endnotes

1. Marc Epstein and Kirk Hanson, *Rotten: Why Corporate Misconduct Continues and What to Do about It* (Los Angeles: Lanark Press, 2021).

2. Peter F. Drucker, "The Transnational Economy," *The Wall Street Journal* (August 25, 1987), 38. See also Tammie S. Pinkston and Archie B. Carroll, "Corporate Citizenship Perspectives and Foreign Direct Investment in the U.S.," *Journal of Business Ethics*, 13, 1994, 157–169.

3. Paul Krugman, cited in Alan Farnham, "Global—Or Just Globaloney?" *Fortune* (June 27, 1994), 97–98.

4. William Mauldin, "Worries Rise over Global Trade Slump," *The Wall Street Journal*, September 14, 2015, https://www.wsj.com/articles/worries-rise-over-global-trade-slump-1442251590. Accessed April 13, 2021.

5. Douglas Irwin, "Globalization in Retreat," *The Wall Street Journal*, December 17, 2020, R13.

6. Ibid.

7. Adrian Woolridge, "Made Everywhere and Nowhere," *The Wall Street Journal*, April 19, 2016, A11.

8. Chrystia Freeland, "Globalization Bites Back," *The Atlantic*, May 2015, 82.

9. PWC, "PWC 24th Annual Global CEO Survey," 2021, https://www.pwc.com/gx/en/ceo-agenda/ceosurvey/2021.html?WT.mc_id=CT3-PL300-DM1-TR2-LS4-ND30-TTA9-CN_CEO-Survey2021-GlobalCEOSurvey-Google&gclsrc=aw.ds&&gclid=Cj0KCQjwgtWDBhDZARIsADEKwgMdqGr4ObCg3-cWKwwvIVT42ZFIyW76bC2_vXzWw7aG9ylxGYJFnMUaArKREALw_wcB. Accessed April 13, 2021.

10. McKinsey & Co., "Rethinking Operations in the Next Normal," April 12, 2021, https://www.mckinsey.com/business-functions/operations/our-insights/rethinking-operations-in-the-next-normal. Accessed April 13, 2021.

11. Ibid.

12. Richard Dobbs, James Manyika, and Jonathan Woetzel, *No Ordinary Disruption: The Four Forces Breaking All the Trends* (Public Affairs, 2015).

13. Catherine Cote, "Five Common Challenges of International Business You Should Consider," Harvard Business School Online, November 24, 2020, https://online.hbs.edu/blog/post/challenges-of-international-business. Accessed March 26, 2021.

14. Stephen Brammer, Geoffrey Williams, and John Zinkin, "Religion and Attitudes to Corporate Social Responsibility in a Large Cross-Country Sample," *Journal of Business Ethics,* 71(3), 2007, 229–243.

15. Ibid., 172.

16. Investopedia, "What Is a Multinational Corporation (MNC)?" http://www.investopedia.com/terms/m/multinationalcorporation.asp. Accessed April 6, 2016.

17. Andreas Scherer and Guido Palazzo, "The New Political Role for Business in a Globalized World: A Review of the New Perspective on CSR and Its Implications for the Firm, Governance, and Democracy," *Journal of Management Studies,* 48(4), 2011, 899–931.

18. Ibid.

19. See Livia Gershon, "The Continuing Controversy over Baby Formula," JStorDaily, July 20, 2018, https://daily.jstor.org/the-continuing-controversy-over-baby-formula/. Accessed March 30, 2021; for background, see James E. Post, "Assessing the Nestlé Boycott: Corporate Accountability and Human Rights," *California Management Review* (Winter 1985), 115–116.

20. Rogene A. Buchholz, William D. Evans, and Robert Q. Wagley, *Management Response to Public Issues* (Englewood Cliffs, NJ: Prentice Hall, 1985), 80.

21. Ibid., 81–82.

22. Oliver Williams, "Who Cast the First Stone?" *Harvard Business Review* (September–October, 1984), 155.

23. "Nestlé's Costly Accord," *Newsweek* (February 6, 1984), 52.

24. For further discussion, see S. Prakash Sethi, *Multinational Corporations and the Impact of Public Advocacy on Corporate Strategy: Nestlé and the Infant Formula Case* (Boston: Kluwer Academic, 1994).

25. The International Baby Food Action Network, https://www.ibfan.org/. Accessed March 30, 2021.

26. Laurie Burkitt, "Infant Formula Issue Flares Anew in China," *The Wall Street Journal*, September 17, 2013, B4.

27. Rebecca Puddy and Rhett Burnie, "China's Thirst for Baby Formula Creating Problems for Australian Shoppers and Staff," December 10, 2018, https://www.abc.net.au/news/2018-12-11/abc-investigation-uncovers-chinese-baby-formula-shoppers/10594400. Accessed March 30, 2021.

28. SwissInfo.ch, "Nestle Struggles to Win over Its Baby Formula Critics," January 10, 2020, https://www.swissinfo.ch/eng/milk-for-older-babies_nestl%C3%A9-struggles-to-win-over-infant-formula-critics/45473338. Accessed March 30, 2021.

29. *Brittanica*, "Bhopal," https://www.britannica.com/place/Bhopal-India#ref1022123. Accessed March 30, 2021.

30. Stuart Diamond, "The Disaster in Bhopal: Lessons for the Future," *The New York Times* (February 3, 1985), https://www.nytimes.com/1985/02/03/world/the-disaster-in-bhopal-lessons-for-the-future.html. Accessed March 30, 2021; see also Russell Mokhiber, "Bhopal," *Corporate Crime and Violence* (San Francisco: Sierra Club Books, 1988), 86–96.

31. International Business Times, "30 Years after the Bhopal Disaster, India Has Not Learned the Lessons of the World's Worst Industrial Tragedy," December 2, 2014, https://www.ibtimes.com/30-years-after-bhopal-disaster-india-has-not-learned-lessons-worlds-worst-industrial-1731816. Accessed March 30, 2021.

32. Stuart Diamond, "Disaster in India Sharpens Debate on Doing Business in Third World," *The New York Times* (December 16, 1984, 1), https://www.nytimes.com/1984/12/16/world/disaster-india-sharpens-debate-doing-business-third-world-corporation-forced.html. Accessed March 30, 2021.

33. Ibid.

34. Reuters, "Victims of Bhopal Gas Tragedy Say Pandemic Has Worsened Their Plight," December 3, 2020, https://www.reuters.com/article/us-india-bhopal-anniversary/victims-of-bhopal-gas-tragedy-say-pandemic-has-worsened-their-plight-idUSKBN28D2HN. Accessed March 30, 2021.

35. Rebecca Prentice and Geert de Neve, "Five Years after Deadly Factory Fire, Bangladesh's Garment Workers Are Still Vulnerable," The Conversation, November 23, 2017, https://theconversation.com/five-years-after-deadly-factory-fire-bangladeshs-garment-workers-are-still-vulnerable-88027. Accessed March 30, 2021.

36. Syed Al-Mahmood, Tripti Lahiri, and Dana Mattioli, "Fire Warnings Went Unheard," *The Wall Street Journal*, December 11, 2012, B1.

37. Syed Zan Al-Mahmood, "Bangladesh Probe Calls Fatal Fire Act of Sabotage," *The Wall Street Journal*, December 18, 2012, B4, https://www.wsj.com/articles/SB10001424127887323723104578185260860346712. Accessed March 30, 2021.

38. Sushmita S. Preetha, "A Lesson on Lessons Not Learnt," *The Daily Star*, April 11, 2016, https://www.thedailystar.net/op-ed/politics/lesson-lessons-not-learnt-1207150. Accessed March 30, 2021.

39. Peoples Dispatch, "Despite Eight Year Struggle, Tazreen Fire Victims in Bangladesh Yet to Get Justice," November 27, 2020, https://peoplesdispatch.org/2020/11/27/despite-eight-year-struggle-tazreen-fire-victims-in-bangladesh-yet-to-get-justice/. Accessed March 30, 2021.

40. Syed Zain Al-Mahmood and Shelly Banjo, "Deadly Collapse," *The Wall Street Journal*, April 25, 2013, A1, http://online.wsj.com/public/resources/documents/pageone042613.pdf. Accessed March 30, 2021.

41. Syed Zain Al-Mahmood and Tom Wright, "Collapsed Factory Was Built without Permit," *The Wall Street Journal*, April 26, 2013, A9, https://www.wsj.com/articles /SB10001424127887323789704578444280661545310. Accessed March 30, 2021.

42. Syed Zain Al-Mahmood, "Bangladeshi Police Charge 42 in Collapse of Factory Complex," *The Wall Street Journal*, June 2, 2015, B6, https://www.wsj.com/articles /bangladeshi-police-charge-42-with-homicide-for-2013 -garment-factory-collapse-1433181270. Accessed March 30, 2021.

43. Syed Zain Al-Mahmood, "Alliance Sets Plan to Finance Bangladesh Factory Upgrades," *The Wall Street Journal*, December 5, 2014, https://www.wsj.com/articles /alliance-sets-plan-to-finance-bangladesh-factory -upgrades-1417791607. Accessed March 30, 2021.

44. Business and Human Rights Resource Centre, "Bangladesh: Alliance for Bangladesh Workers Safety Announces End of Its Tenure," December 14, 2018, https:// www.business-humanrights.org/en/latest-news/bangladesh -alliance-for-bangladesh-workers-safety-announces-end-of -its-tenure/. Accessed March 30, 2021.

45. Accord, "January 2021 Quarterly Aggregate Report," https://bangladeshaccord.org/updates/2021/02/12/january -2021-quarterly-aggregate-report. Accessed March 30, 2021.

46. Kevin McCoy, "Slave-Peeled Shrimp Exported to U.S. Stores," *USA Today*, December 15, 2015, 4B, https://www .usatoday.com/story/money/business/2015/12/14 /slave-peeled-shrimp-exported-major-us-stores/77279762/. Accessed March 30, 2021.

47. Ibid.

48. Human Rights Watch, "Hidden Chains: Rights Abuses and Forced Labor in Thailand's Fishing Industry," January 23, 2018, https://www.hrw.org/report/2018/01/23/hidden -chains-rights-abuses-and-forced-labor-thailands-fishing -industry. Accessed March 30, 2021.

49. Michael Taylor, "U.N. Urges Asian Countries to Follow Thailand on Fishing Pledge," January 31, 2019, https:// www.reuters.com/article/idUSL3N1ZV2OA. Accessed March 30, 2021.

50. Syed Zain Al-Mahmood, Kathy Chu, and Tripti Lahiri, "Bangladesh Fire Raises Pressure to Improve Factory Safety," *The Wall Street Journal*, December 13, 2012, https://www.wsj.com/articles/SB10001424127887324296 604578176983283834310. Accessed March 31, 2021.

51. Ashok Kumar, "Sweatshops Aren't Going to Last Forever," March 23, 2020, https://jacobinmag.com/2020/03 /sweatshops-labor-globalization-gap-nike-adidas -monopsony. Accessed March 31, 2021.

52. Robert Caruana, Andrew Crane, Stefan Gold, and Genevieve LeBaron, "Modern Slavery in Business: The Sad and Sorry State of a Non-Field," *Business & Society,* 60(2), 2021, 251–287.

53. Mark Clifford, Michael Shari, and Linda Himelstein, "Pangs of Conscience: Sweatshops Haunt U.S. Consumers," *Businessweek* (July 29, 1996), 46–47, https:// www.bloomberg.com/news/articles/1996-07-28/pangs-of -conscience-over-sweatshops. Accessed March 31, 2021.

54. "Fast Fashion Creates Misery—and That's Always a Bad Look," *The Guardian*, July 7, 2020, https://www .theguardian.com/commentisfree/2020/jul/07/fast-fashion -clothing-brands-leicester-boohoo-consumers. Accessed March 31, 2021; also see Kumar, 2020, ibid.

55. Fair Labor Association, "About Us," https://www.fairlabor .org/about-us. Accessed March 31, 2021.

56. Ibid.

57. Fair Labor Association, "2020 Fair Compensation Strategy," https://www.fairlabor.org/report/2020-fair -compensation-strategy. Accessed March 31, 2021.

58. Social Accountability International, "About SAI," https:// sa-intl.org/about/. Accessed March 31, 2021.

59. The SA8000 Standard, https://sa-intl.org/programs /sa8000/. Accessed March 31, 2021.

60. Ibid.

61. SA8000 Certified Organizations, http://www .saasaccreditation.org/?q=node/23. Accessed March 31, 2021.

62. Veronica Villena and Dennis Gioia, "A more sustainable supply chain," *Harvard Business Review*, March–April 2020, https://hbr.org/2020/03/a-more-sustainable-supply -chain. Accessed March 31, 2021.

63. Levi Strauss & Company, "Remaining Committed to Sustainability in These Hard Times," April 22, 2020, https://www.levistrauss.com/2020/04/22/sustainability -hard-times/. Accessed March 31, 2021; Gap, Inc. "Global Supply Chains," https://www.gapinc.com/en-us/careers /global-supply-chain. Accessed March 31, 2021; Nike, Inc. "FY20, Nike Inc. Impact Report," https://purpose.nike. com/fy20-nike-impact-report. Accessed March 31, 2021.

64. Business & Human Rights Centre, "Secrets, Lies, and Sweatshops [China]," https://www.business-humanrights. org/en/latest-news/secrets-lies-and-sweatshops-china/. Accessed March 31, 2021; also see Finbar Bermingham and Cissy Zhou, "Bribes, Faked Factories and Forged Documents: The Buccaneering Consultants Pervading China's Factory Audits," January 22, 2021, https://www .scmp.com/economy/china-economy/article/3118683 /bribes-fake-factories-and-forged-documents- buccaneering. Accessed March 31, 2021.

65. David Golove, "The Alien Tort Statute and the Law of Nations," November 17, 2020, JustSecurity, https://www .justsecurity.org/73376/the-alien-tort-statute-and-the -law-of-nations-new-historical-evidence-of-founding-era -understandings/. Accessed March 31, 2021.

66. "Alien Tort Claims Act," *Global Policy Forum*, https:// archive.globalpolicy.org/international-justice/alien-tort -claims-act-6-30.html. Accessed March 31, 2021.

67. Jess Bravin, "High Court Reigns in Scope of Alien Torts Act," *The Wall Street Journal*, April 17, 2013, https:// www.wsj.com/articles/BL-LB-44750. Accessed March 31, 2021; for further information, see "The Alien Tort Statute," Center for Justice and Accountability, https://cja.org /what-we-do/litigation/legal-strategy/the-alien-tort-statute/. Accessed March 31, 2021.

68. "The U.S. Supreme Court Delivers a Death Knell to the Alien Tort Statute," June 13, 2018, https://cmmllp.com/the -u-s-supreme-court-delivers-a-death-knell-to-the-alien-tort -statute/. Accessed March 31, 2021; also see Jess Bravin, "Court Shields Corporations in Abuse Suits," *Wall Street Journal*, April 25, 2018, A2.

69. John Beisner, "Supreme Court Mulls Scope of Alien Tort Statute in *Nestle, Cargill*," December 22, 2020, https:// www.skadden.com/insights/publications/2020/12/insights -special-edition-us-supreme-court-term/scotus-mulls -scope-of-alien-tort-statute. Accessed March 31, 2021.

70. The World Bank, "Combating Corruption," https://www .worldbank.org/en/topic/governance/brief/anti-corruption. Accessed March 31, 2021.

71. Transparency International, "What Is Corruption?" https://www.transparency.org/en/what-is-corruption. Accessed March 31, 2021.

72. Transparency International UK, "What Is bribery?" https://www.antibriberyguidance.org/guidance/5-what-bribery/guidance. Accessed March 31, 2021.

73. Ian I. Mitroff and Ralph H. Kilmann, "Teaching Managers to Do Policy Analysis: The Case of Corporate Bribery," *California Management Review* (Fall 1977), 50–52, https://journals.sagepub.com/doi/abs/10.2307/41164737. Accessed March 31, 2021; also see Debate.org, "Debate: Is Bribery Ever Acceptable?" https://www.debate.org/opinions/is-bribery-ever-acceptable. Accessed March 31, 2021.

74. Acemonglu and Robinson, 2015, ibid.

75. See United Nations, "Global Cost of Corruption at Least 5 Percent of World Gross Domestic Product," September 10, 2018, https://www.un.org/press/en/2018/sc13493.doc.htm#:~:text=The%20World%20Economic%20Forum%20estimates,trillion%20in%20bribes%20every%20year. Accessed March 31, 2021; "The Destructive Costs of Greasing Palms," *Businessweek* (December 6, 1993), https://www.bloomberg.com/news/articles/1993-12-05/the-destructive-costs-of-greasing-palms. Accessed March 31, 2021; Michelle Gavin, "New Report Shines Spotlight on Corruption in Zimbabwe," Council on Foreign Relations, February 19, 2021, https://www.cfr.org/blog/new-report-shines-spotlight-corruption-zimbabwe. Accessed March 31, 2021.

76. "Foreign Corrupt Practices Act," *Department of Justice*, https://www.justice.gov/criminal-fraud/foreign-corrupt-practices-act. Accessed March 31, 2021.

77. Matthew Stephenson, "The FCPA's Facilitating Payments Exception: Mostly Harmless," June 17, 2014, https://globalanticorruptionblog.com/2014/06/17/the-fcpas-facilitating-payments-exception-mostly-harmless/. Accessed March 31, 2021.

78. U.S. Department of Justice Archives, "Intent of the Parties," https://www.justice.gov/archives/jm/criminal-resource-manual-834-intent-parties#:~:text=In%20essence%2C%20a%20bribe%20requires,offense%20of%20receiving%20a%20bribe.&text=%C2%A7%20201%2C%20which%20prohibit%20the,an%20intended%20quid%20pro%20quo. Accessed March 31, 2021.

79. National Law Review, "FCPA Year in Review 2020." March 15, 2021, https://www.natlawreview.com/article/fcpa-year-review-2020. Accessed April 13, 2021.

80. "DOJ and SEC Issue Long-Awaited Update to FCPA Resource Guide," July 3, 2020, https://www.morganlewis.com/pubs/2020/07/doj-and-sec-issue-long-awaited-update-to-fcpa-resource-guide. Accessed March 31, 2021.

81. U.S. Department of Justice, "Foreign Corrupt Practices Act," https://www.justice.gov/criminal-fraud/foreign-corrupt-practices-act. Accessed March 31, 2021.

82. "Global Bribery Offenses Guide," DLA Piper, December 4, 2019, https://www.dlapiper.com/en/us/insights/publications/2019/09/bribery-offenses-guide/. Accessed March 31, 2021.

83. U.S. Department of State, "Recognizing Anticorruption Champions around the World," February 23, 2021. https://www.state.gov/dipnote-u-s-department-of-state-official-blog/recognizing-anticorruption-champions-around-the-world/. Accessed March 31, 2021.

84. Transparency International, "What We Do," https://www.transparency.org/en/what-we-do. Accessed March 31, 2021.

85. Ibid.

86. Transparency International, "Corruption Perception Index 2020," https://www.transparency.org/en/news/cpi-2020-global-highlights. Accessed March 31, 2021.

87. Ibid.

88. OECD, OECD Bribery Convention, http://www.oecd.org/corruption-integrity/explore/oecd-standards/anti-bribery-convention/. Accessed April 1, 2021.

89. United Nations, "United Nations Convention Against Corruption," https://www.unodc.org/unodc/en/treaties/CAC/. Accessed April 1, 2021.

90. United Nations, "State of Implementation of UN Convention Against Corruption," https://www.unodc.org/unodc/en/corruption/tools_and_publications/state_of_uncac_implementation.html. Accessed April 1, 2021.

91. Ibid.

92. United Nations, "Signature and Ratification Status," https://www.unodc.org/unodc/en/corruption/ratification-status.html. Accessed April 1, 2021.

93. Gene R. Laczniak and Jacob Naor, "Global Ethics: Wrestling with the Corporate Conscience," Business (July–September 1985), 3–10; also see Jolene Lampton, "Ethics Must Be Global," *Strategic Finance*, February 1, 2020, https://sfmagazine.com/post-entry/february-2020-ethics-must-be-global/. Accessed April 1, 2021.

94. Tom Donaldson, "Global Business Must Mind Its Morals," *The New York Times* (February 13, 1994), F-11, https://www.nytimes.com/1994/02/13/business/viewpoints-global-business-must-mind-its-morals.html. Accessed April 1, 2021; see also Tom Donaldson, "Values in Tension: Ethics Away from Home," *Harvard Business Review* (September–October, 1996), https://hbr.org/1996/09/values-in-tension-ethics-away-from-home. Accessed April 1, 2021.

95. Tom Donaldson and Thomas W. Dunfee, "When Ethics Travel: The Promise and Peril of Global Business Ethics," *California Management Review,* 41(4), Summer 1999, 48–49; also see Markus Scholz, Gaston de la Reyes Jr., and N. Craig Smith, "The Enduring Potential of Justified Hypernorms," *Business Ethics Quarterly*, March 6, 2019, https://www.cambridge.org/core/journals/business-ethics-quarterly/article/enduring-potential-of-justified-hypernorms/803B53E25841F9B6E77CA939D8992EC1. Accessed April 1, 2021.

96. T. Donaldson and T. Dunfee, "Toward a Unified Conception of Business Ethics: Integrative Social Contracts Theory," *Academy of Management Review,* 19, 1994, 252–284.

97. Clark and Brown, 2015, ibid.

98. Archie B. Carroll, "Managing Ethically with Global Stakeholders: A Present and Future Challenge," *Academy of Management Executive*, 18(2), May 2004, 114–120, https://www.jstor.org/stable/4166070?seq=1. Accessed April 1, 2021.

99. Laczniak and Naor, 3–10.

100. Caterpillar, "Code of Conduct: Our Values in Action," https://www.caterpillar.com/en/company/code-of-conduct.html. Accessed April 1, 2021.

101. Ibid.

102. The Coca-Cola Company, "Code of Business Conduct," https://www.coca-colacompany.com/policies-and-practices/code-of-business-conduct. Accessed April 2, 2021.

103. ISO, ISO 2600 Social Responsibility, https://www.iso.org/iso-26000-social-responsibility.html. Accessed April 2, 2021.

104. ISO, "ISO 26000: Seven Core Subjects," https://www.iso.org/files/live/sites/isoorg/files/store/en/PUB100259.pdf. Accessed April 2, 2021.

105. ISO, "ISO 37001 – Anti-Bribery Management Systems," https://www.iso.org/publication/PUB100396.html. Accessed April 2, 2021.

106. UN Global Compact, "The Power of Principles," https://www.unglobalcompact.org/what-is-gc/mission/principles. Accessed April 2, 2021.

107. Caux Roundtable for Moral Capitalism, "Principles for Responsible Business," https://www.cauxroundtable.org/principles/. Accessed April 2, 2021.

108. Laczniak and Naor, 7–8. Also see Allen C. Amason and Andrew Ward, *Strategic Management: From Theory to Practice*, 2nd ed. (New York: Routledge, 2021).

109. Jolene Hampton, "Ethics Must Be Global," February 1, 2020, *Strategic Finance*, https://sfmagazine.com/post-entry/february-2020-ethics-must-be-global/. Accessed April 2, 2021.

110. Donna J. Wood, Jeanne M. Logsdon, Patsy G. Lewellyn, and Kim Davenport, *Global Business Citizenship: A Transformative Framework for Ethics and Sustainable Capitalism* (Armonk, NY: M.E Sharpe, 2006).

111. Levi Strauss Global Sourcing and Operating Guidelines, https://www.levistrauss.com/wp-content/uploads/2019/03/Global-Sourcing-and-Operating-Guidelines.pdf. Accessed April 2, 2021.

112. GreenBiz, "Levi Strauss & Co. Publishes List of Active Suppliers," https://www.greenbiz.com/article/levi-strauss-publishes-list-active-suppliers. Accessed April 2, 2021.

113. Levi Strauss & Co., *Sustainability Guidebook*, http://levistrauss.com/wp-content/uploads/2017/12/2017-Sustainability-Guidebook_December2017.pdf. Accessed April 2, 2021.

114. Levi Strauss & Co., *Worldwide Code of Business Conduct*, Revised 2019, https://www.levistrauss.com/wp-content/uploads/2020/06/Code-of-Conduct-English.pdf. Accessed April 2, 2021.

115. Starbucks Standards of Business Conduct, "Living Our Values," https://livingourvalues.starbucks.com/en-us/living-our-values. Accessed April 5, 2021.

116. Ibid.

117. Starbucks, "International Business," https://livingourvalues.starbucks.com/en-us/business-practices. Accessed April 5, 2021.

118. Ethical Consumer, "Starbucks Corporation," https://www.ethicalconsumer.org/company-profile/starbucks-corporation. Accessed April 5, 2021.

119. UpWorthy.com, "Starbucks Caught in Child Labor Scandal: Children as Young as 8 Picked Coffee Beans on Farms," https://scoop.upworthy.com/starbucks-guatemala-child-labor-scandal-channel-4-dispatches. Accessed April 5, 2021.

120. Laczniak and Naor, 8.

121. "The Short Arm of the Law," *The Economist* (March 2, 2002), 63–65.

122. L. Gordon Crovitz, "Google's Search Result: Hong Kong," *The Wall Street Journal* (March 29, 2010), A21.

123. Kaveh Waddell, "Why Google Quit China—and Why Its Heading Back," *The Atlantic*, January 19, 2016.

124. SupChina, "Google Parent Company Alphabet Is Back in China (because it never left)," https://supchina.com/2020/06/18/google-parent-company-alphabet-is-back-in-china-because-it-never-left/. Accessed April 5, 2021.

125. Reuters Wire Service, USNews, "Factbox: the Foreign Firms doing business in Myanmar," March 9, 2021, https://www.usnews.com/news/world/articles/2021-03-09/factbox-the-foreign-firms-doing-business-in-myanmar. Accessed April 5, 2021.

126. Mattel press release (November 20, 1997).

127. Mattel, "Responsible Supply Chain," https://corporate.mattel.com/en-us/citizenship/responsible-supply-chain. Accessed April 5, 2021.

128. S. Sethi, Emre Veral, H. Jack Shapiro, and Olga Emelianova, "Mattel, Inc.: Global Manufacturing Principles (GMP)–A Life Cycle Analysis of a Company-Based Code of Conduct in the Toy Industry," *Journal of Business Ethics*, April 1, 2011, https://link.springer.com/article/10.1007/s10551-010-0673-0. Accessed April 5, 2021.

129. SupplyChainBrain, "Ethics Issues Are at the Heart of Supply-Chain Management," https://www.supplychainbrain.com/articles/6907-ethics-issues-are-at-the-heart-of-supply-chain-management#:~:text=Few%20companies%20set%20out%20deliberately%20to%20commit%20unethical%20practices%2C%20says%20Grackin.&text=The%20public's%20growing%20awareness%20of,is%20yet%20another%20powerful%20motivator. Accessed April 5, 2021.

130. Ibid.

8

Business Ethics and Technology: The Digital Enterprise

Chapter Learning Outcomes

After studying this chapter, you should be able to:

1. Identify and describe what the new world of Big Data and artificial intelligence is all about and the implications it holds for businesses.
2. What makes an organization a digital enterprise? How does this relate to business ethics?
3. Explain how social media have changed the world of business and technology.
4. Discuss how surveillance is a new dimension to being a consumer and an employee and what its implications are for stakeholders.

5. Articulate an understanding of technology and the technological environment.
6. Identify the characteristics of technology to include their benefits, side effects, and challenges in business.
7. Comment on the relationship between technology and ethics.
8. Define information technology and discuss the issues relating to e-commerce in business.
9. Define biotechnology. Identify the ethical issues involved in genetic engineering and genetically modified organisms (GMOs).

We live in an age dominated and driven by rapidly advancing technology. As Nancy Gibbs, editor of *Time* magazine, observed, "technology ... accelerates and complicates."[1] In fact, technological change is significantly outpacing generational time spans. The world can look different in the span of a few years, as businesses have come to realize. At one time it was common for chief financial officers to be strongly positioned to become CEOs. Today, it is the chief technology officer (CTO) of major firms. We are now in the digital era, the era of the digital enterprise, and strong technology leadership has become the key to business success.[2]

The latest working generation, called the iGeneration or Generation Z, is said to have no "off switch" when it comes to technology. For this new group of post-Millennials, technology is said to be a "part of their DNA."[3] To understand the present and to see the future, we need to pay attention to the findings of *Common Sense Media*, which has reported that "screen addiction" is now a serious phenomenon among young people. On average, more than six and a half hours a day are spent by youth on devices using screens—TVs, tablets, phones, video games, computers—for nonschool purposes. Digital citizenship is now a topic being discussed in schools, particularly following the coronavirus pandemic, where most students learned online for a year or more.[4] Now and in the future, we live in a world driven by technology—for companies, consumers, employees, and life in general.

Technology and its rapid innovations have been leading businesses toward becoming digital enterprises. A **digital enterprise** is an organization in which digital technology is at the center of all its business processes. It affects the way the organization operates, develops products and services, generates revenues, and engages with customers. It greatly affects its relationships with its employees. In short, a digital enterprise leverages technology in support of its mission, values, and operations.[5] Though many organizations use digital technology in one form or another, many have not yet become digital enterprises, but most of them are on the way toward digital transformation.[6] **Digital transformation** is a process in many companies currently as they strive to integrate digital technology into all areas of their businesses, resulting in fundamental changes in how the businesses operate and deliver value to their customers.[7] It is safe to say that most successful businesses today are on the road toward digitalization, converting their processes toward computer-driven systems.

Beyond organizations, technology is how we sustain life and make it comfortable. But technology, as many have observed, is a two-edged sword. Many positive benefits flow from technological advances. By the same token, many new problems or challenges are posed by advancing technology, especially in the arena of business ethics. Futurist John Naisbitt, for example, has questioned whether advancing technology is a "liberating" or "destructive" force in society. He has said that, at best, technology supports and improves human life, and at its worst it alienates, isolates, distorts, and destroys.[8]

Thinking positively, dynamic technological advances have become such a central part of our lives and doing business in the third decade of the 21st century that they must be carefully considered. More and more ethical issues for business and for society have arisen as a result of technological advances. Many believe that technology has developed at a speed that significantly outstrips the capacity of society, government, or business to grasp its consequences or ethical implications. In this chapter, we will explore some of these issues, knowing full well that other aspects related to technology will be touched on in other chapters as specific stakeholder groups are considered in more detail. As we brainstorm about what new technologies may have in store for business, one observer has even called it an "idolatry of data," which has been enabled by the almost unimaginable data-gathering capabilities of new technology.[9]

8.1 The New World of Big Data and Artificial Intelligence

Digital enterprises and most organizations depend on Big Data and increasingly on artificial intelligence to function today. This new information world, called by most experts **Big Data**, describes the infinite sea of facts, opinions, trends, surveys, and analyses that inundate business on a day-to-day basis. Big Data can be analyzed for insights that can lead to better decisions and more successful strategic business moves.[10] Businesses employ **business analytics**, which are the processes of using statistical methods for analyzing historical and current data in order to gain new insights and improve decision making[11] Artificial intelligence is another vital component of increasingly digital enterprises. **Artificial intelligence (AI)** is the ability of computers or computer-controlled devices to perform tasks that are commonly associated with human beings, and developing systems that are endowed with the intellectual processes characteristic of humans, such as the ability to reason, discover meaning, generalize, or learn from past experience.[12] Exploring Big Data and AI further helps us understand what is happening today in the budding digital enterprise movement.

As we have indicated, the term *Big Data* describes the multitude of information that is available and how businesses are striving to put such information to work. Information comes from many more sources than ever before, and businesses can get access to it as quickly as it is generated.[13] Using powerful computers, ubiquitous sensors, monitoring devices, and the Web, it is now possible to analyze mountains of raw data, which yields previously unknown insights that increasingly are being used by business, government, and others.[14] Big Data is characterized by the 3Vs—high *volume*, high *velocity*, and high *variety*. It has been in the commercial world where Big Data has seen its greatest impact to date.[15]

For companies, the advantages of Big Data have been accompanied by a host of new issues, among them, data security, privacy, and cybercrime, which have become huge threats to, and responsibilities of, business. For all of its advantages, Big Data has its downsides as well, and many of them are riddled with ethical challenges. Business analytics, a process of analyzing and interpreting diverse data, started with relatively simple algorithms such as tracking our online behavior and using this information to insert commercials or ads for products or services we've mentioned in e-mails, or searched for on the Web, into our online business. But more than one observer has noted that some of what is taking place becomes "creepy."[16]

Hugh Watson, an MIS expert, has even gone so far as to create what he has called, only semi-humorously, the Creepiness Scale to reflect how business analytics can cross over from being surprising and helpful to becoming scary, or wrong, in its variance from the norm.[17] Let's say you meet someone new at a conference and soon thereafter they become a Facebook friend recommendation. Or, let's say you go to a hospital emergency room and then start receiving ads from personal injury attorneys. Or, what about airlines quickly raising their fares when you attempt to flee an impending hurricane? These are creepy, Professor Watson would say.[18] Plotting the use of personal data and algorithms against a creepiness dimension, Watson says that incidences move from "helpful" to "creepy" to "so wrong."[19] In other words, at some point the use of Big Data moves from being creepy to being wrong or unethical. Recently, for example, we learned that creepy firms such as Cambridge Analytica actually use data mining to extract information from websites such as Facebook, using "psychographic microtargeting" to alter public opinion, spread falsehoods, and influence elections. *The Wall Street Journal* contributor Gregg Easterbrook has said that Facebook itself seems increasingly creepy when it lies to the public about what happens to the data it collects.[20]

If Big Data were not enough, the challenges presented by artificial intelligence combine to create many issues involving the use and misuse of information. Using Big Data and business analytics, artificial intelligence combines with them to alter the business world in more ways than we can describe. Not only will products and services be altered, but AI has great potential for transforming workplaces and operations. AI is changing the way managers do their jobs. The same technology that helps us navigate from one place on a map to another, or lets an online store recommend products based on our previous purchases, is now helping managers to make personnel decisions: who to hire, who to promote, and who to fire. For example, a company can provide a job description and AI algorithms will gather and crunch data from numerous sources to find people with the right skills, experience, or perspectives.[21]

AI can also help companies analyze their worker's e-mails to determine if they are feeling satisfied with their jobs so that managers can give them more attention before their productivity declines or they lose interest in the company.

If companies are worried about high turnover, they can use AI to find employees who may be inclined to leave based on variables such as length of time they have been with the company, their physical distance from colleagues, or how many managers they have had in the past. AI can overcome managers' prejudices but can reflect its own biases such as favoring candidates whose characteristics are similar to those it has analyzed before.[22] Another problem: automated decision making may tempt managers to defer to AI's recommendations as they abdicate using their own judgment. In addition, AI systems' thirst for data may lead companies to push against the boundaries of a worker's privacy.[23]

It becomes quickly obvious how the use and dependency on AI can raise ethical issues in the workplace for managers. For example, can AI be useful in a situation, and should it be? Managers will need to take the initiative in raising key ethical questions regarding its application. Major issues include exploring how to avoid biases in AI algorithms, when to disclose the use of AI to consumers and employees, and to address the effects on privacy and people's fears about AI's impacts on their lives as employees and consumers. Approaching AI from an ethical perspective necessitates that managers develop a long-term understanding of the values the company wants to see reflected in the technology and creating rules that produce confidence, not fear.[24]

As the use of Big Data and AI increasingly present ethical issues, it is not surprising that recommendations for accountability, transparency, and ethical use arise. Several principles for Big Data/AI ethics have arisen:

- Private customer data and identity should remain private.
- Shared private information should be treated confidentially.
- Customers should have a transparent view as to how their data are being used or sold.
- Big data should not interfere with human will, employing inferences and predictions belying who we are as persons.
- Big Data should not institutionalize unfair biases such as racism or sexism.[25]

There are many lists for improving the business ethics of technology, but these will suffice at this stage in the discussion. At this juncture, we should back off from these cutting-edge applications and consider technology and the technological environment more generally.

8.2 Technology and the Technological Environment

We have begun this chapter considering the power and influence of Big Data and artificial intelligence. Now it is time to consider the topic of technology, generally, because it does expand beyond the topics discussed so far. Technology means many things to many people. In this chapter, **technology** will refer to the "totality of the means employed to provide objects necessary for human sustenance and comfort."[26] It also is seen as a scientific method used in achieving a

practical purpose.[27] Technology refers to all the ways people use or apply their inventions, discoveries, data, and information to satisfy their needs and desires. Taken together, these technological advances have made work easier and more productive.[28] But technology has also introduced new challenges, many of them social or ethical in nature.

In Chapter 1, we discussed the macroenvironment of business and how this total environment was composed of several significant and interrelated segments such as the social, economic, political, and technological. The **technological environment**, our current topic of concern, represents *the total set of technology-based advancements or progress taking place in society*. Pertinent aspects of this segment include new products, processes, materials, states of knowledge, and scientific advancements in both theoretical and applied senses. The rate of change and complexity of the technological environment have made it of special interest to business today. In the exploding information technology realm and the burgeoning field of biotechnology, the shape of how we are living, what products we are using, and what processes we are being exposed to is changing at an accelerating pace.

8.3 Benefits and Costs of Technology

Whatever the technological level of advancement, there are general benefits and undesirable side effects, or costs, of technology, and ethical challenges inherent in these technological advancements.

Few would dispute that society has benefited greatly from technology and innovation. We live better lives today as employees, consumers, and members of the community due to technology. Technology has helped us gain control over nature and to build for ourselves a civilized life. Through the ages, technology has benefited society in four main ways.[29] It has increased society's production of goods and services; it has reduced the amount of labor needed to produce goods and services; it has made labor easier and safer; and higher standards of living have been a direct result of labor-saving technology.[30]

Though technologies have benefited people in many ways, there have also been some unanticipated costs and side effects as well—problems, issues, or effects not anticipated before technologies were designed and implemented. One major reason for this is that technologies are often implemented before much thought is given to possible costs, side effects, ethical problems, or downside risks. In fact, almost "every technology is used before it is completely understood. There is always a lag between an innovation and the apprehension of its consequences," and we always are living in that lag.[31] A major problem during this lag is that ethical issues and challenges are only later perceived and faced.

Four categories of undesirable side effects of technology are representative of the issues we face in business today. First, there is *environmental pollution*. Second, there is *depletion of natural resources*. Third, there is *technological unemployment*. The most common form of technological unemployment occurs when machines take the place of humans, as we experience in automation and now in the robotic movement. Fourth, there is the *creation of unsatisfying jobs* due to technology as jobs are broken down into smaller components and workers are further removed from the finished product that might provide a greater sense of fulfillment and pride. Monotony and boredom can easily set in when jobs are significantly shaped by certain technological processes.[32]

Another cost or side effect of new and growing technology use has been termed **digital amnesia**. In a digital economy, this forgetfulness phenomenon has affected young and old, consumers and employees, as we are outsourcing our brainwork to digital devices.[33] A study by Kapersky Labs concluded that the majority of digital consumers are no longer able to recall critical contact information even for those closest to them; they suggest there is now a direct link between data available at the click of a button and a failure to remember that information anymore. Related to this, our average attention spans have fallen from 12 seconds in 2000 to 8.25 seconds today.[34]

This is similar to the **Google Effect**, which holds that just knowing that some bit of data can easily be retrieved on the Internet makes us less likely to now remember it. In fact, one report on the Google Effect concludes that losing our Internet connection has become more and more like losing a friend. In addition, there is an amazing amount of research that identifies the effects of communications technology on our brains, nervous systems, social abilities, relationships, mental health, physical health, and family structures.[35] To these undesirable effects, we can surely add others, many of which are replete with ethical issues.

8.4 Technology and Ethics

As we consider technology and ethics, we must say that technology unquestionably has many benefits for humankind. Our perspective at this juncture, however, is to raise the ethical questions that may be related to business development and use of technology and innovation. To do so does not mean that one is against technology. It simply means that one is concerned about the ethical use and implications of technology. Like management decision making and globalization of business, the actions of the business community with respect to technology have ethical implications that should be identified, discussed, and factored into decision making. Management needs to ask who will be hurt and in what ways by technology; what are the risks and problems that may arise? Management's goal should be to avoid immoral and amoral practices with respect to technology and to move toward an ethically sustainable posture with respect to this potent business resource.

Applying ethics analysis to questions involving technology is essentially an extension of our discussions of business ethics up to this point. The goal of managers and businesses striving to be ethical should be to avoid harm and to do what is morally justified and fair. In making ethical judgments, the prevailing norms of acceptability regarding technology must

---

Spotlight on Sustainability

Technoethics: An Interdisciplinary Field

It is not surprising that the field of study known as *technoethics* has arrived and has become popular and important. **Technoethics** is an interdisciplinary field concerned with ethical issues and the ethical dimension of technology in society. Technoethics conceives of technology and ethics as socially embedded fields that specialize in the ethical use of technology, guarding against the misuse of technology, and striving to develop principles to guide new technological developments and applications that will be beneficial to society. Technology and ethics are perceived as interconnected topics that are ever present in life and society. Technoethics describes a wide range of ethical issues revolving around technology that include people working and shopping in organizations to broader concerns such as the social, ethical, and legal aspects of technology and its use in society.

Just a few of the issues with which technoethics is concerned today include digital copyrights, cyber-criminality, privacy versus security, GPS technologies and privacy, genetically modified organisms (GMOs), surveillance cameras at work and at stores, computer monitoring devices, biotech issues, and information and communication issues.

Organizational technoethics is a rapidly growing subfield. This subfield focuses on how information spreads within organizations and is shared among managers and colleagues around the world in global organizations. The technological means by which organization members communicate with one another today have proliferated and have raised many ethical concerns. As a consequence, there is a growing need for more study and analysis of its implications.

Figuring out what is ethical in the Internet age has added impetus to the expansion of technoethics. Companies that are on the leading edge are finding that they can quickly find themselves in trouble with some offended public. It could be about privacy, free speech, marketing tactics, or a range of other issues.

Sources: Encyclopedia.com, "Technoethics," https://www.encyclopedia.com/science/encyclopedias-almanacs-transcripts-and-maps/technoethics, accessed April 8, 2021; IGI Global, "What Is Technoethics?" https://www.igi-global.com/dictionary/technoethics-education-twenty-first-century/37932; R. Luppicini, *Technoethics and the Evolving Knowledge Society* (Hershey: Idea Group Publishing), 2010; David Freedman, Inc., "The Technoethics Trap," https://www.inc.com/magazine/20060301/column-freedman.html, accessed April 8, 2021.

be tested by the principles of fairness and justice, protection of rights, utilitarianism, and other applicable ethical guidelines. The goal should be to reconcile and build bridges over the gap between "what is" and "what ought to be." Beyond this, the challenge of business ethics and technology is to identify the major issues in which an ethical dimension may reside, and apply ethical analysis to them. Many of these issues arise in chapters throughout the book. Here, however, our focus is on taking a more focused look at technology, in general, and issues that arise due to technology in business.

Two prominent ethical issues in the realm of technology seem to underlie considerations of technology and ethics. First is the idea of technological determinism. **Technological determinism** is the imperative that "what *can* be developed *will* be developed." When someone once asked, "why do we want to put men on the moon?" the answer was always "because we *can* put men on the moon." In other words, scientists and those who work with advanced technologies are driven to push back the frontiers of technological development without consideration of ethical issues, social problems, or side effects. This is true with information technology as well as with science.

A second important concept undergirding this topic is that of ethical lag. **Ethical lag** occurs when the speed of technological change far exceeds that of ethical development.[36] As stated earlier, we always seem to be living in the condition of ethical lag. Throughout our consideration of technology and ethics, these two phenomena are evident and influential.

Beyond these two factors, which touch all technologies, we might ask how we can make ethics a priority in today's digital organizations. In fact, an entire field of study has arisen around this question. The ethical use of technology, often called **ethical tech**, is a key part of working successfully with technology today. To be tech savvy, today's managers need to move beyond analyzing Big Data and implementing AI; it means being able to understand the potential dilemmas that designing and using these technologies can present.[37] The notion of ethical tech requires a set of values that govern the organization's overall approach to using technology driving strategy and operations. Ethical tech is a concept that embraces a wide range of issues from data privacy to surfacing bias in algorithms to replacing humans with machines and committing to use data fairly.[38] Ethical tech requires creating an appropriate organizational culture, a deeper commitment to social impact, a readiness to embrace change, and embracing an ethics tech mindset. The characteristics of this ethical tech mindset, according to Brenna Sniderman at Deloitte, include the following:[39]

- A drive toward a shared, inclusive, cross-functional responsibility;
- Being ethically driven from the start;
- Making ethical tech part of a holistic, tech-savvy approach;
- Making the ethical tech mindset relevant, specific, and flexible;

- Making sure it's more than compliance;
- Equipping your people with resources to respond; and
- Ensuring your approach can evolve.

So many of the ideas presented in Chapters 5 and 6 apply here; the fundamental concepts of business ethics and the way managers and organizations make these principles useful for decision making and policy making are broadly applicable, especially to issues involving technology.

There are a number of arenas in which specific issues of business ethics and technology might be explored. Research over the past few years reveals two broad categories of issues that now merit consideration in this chapter: **information technology (IT)** and **biotechnology**. Each is broad and deep, so we can consider them only in an introductory way in this chapter. Each, however, significantly involves business, either directly or indirectly. Within each, there are thousands of technologies that raise ethical questions. Our purpose, therefore, will be to focus on a few that give us a representative sampling of ethical issues we face with technology.

8.4a Surveillance

Another issue in the realm of ethics and technology has been the rising extent to which companies are using video camera surveillance mounted in stores to monitor customers' and employees' actions. We know we are being watched, but do we know how smart these technologies have become? For example, Amazon has embraced smart technologies in installing machine learning-powered surveillance cameras in its delivery vans in early 2021. However, workers at the company have balked at the invasion of privacy, and the company is now requiring all employees to agree to be surveyed by AI or lose their jobs.[40] In another example, a few Macy's, CVS Pharmacy, and Babies 'R' Us stores have used a system called the Video Investigator. This advanced surveillance software can monitor a customer's movements and compare them between video images and recognize any type of unusual activity. If the shopper removes ten items at once from a shelf, for example, or opens a case that is normally kept closed and locked, the system alerts security guards of the activity. The system can also predict where a shoplifter is likely to hide (e.g., at the end of aisles or behind floor displays).[41] In short, surveillance provided by technological advances now addresses a variety of business issues, including theft, substance abuse, vandalism, corporate espionage, and other illegal, unethical, or unauthorized activities.[42] We are, indeed, being watched and recorded—more and more. Much of this is for the good. But there can be possible abuses as well.

It is obvious that technology has become an integral aspect of our work and consumer lives. In this next section, we will consider technology in different contexts, including social media, e-commerce, and workplace digital technology. Then, we will discuss the biotechnology industry, which is a unique context ripe with new technologies.

8.5 Information Technology

Information technology (IT) is the use of any computers, storage, networking, and other physical devices, infrastructure, and processes to create, process, store, secure, and exchange all forms of electronic data.[43] Information technology is deeply entrenched in all businesses and stakeholders involved in those businesses. Before we address two broad business areas that typically characterize IT, electronic commerce, and computer technology in the workplace, we address a topic that has come to be quite important to business today, that of social media.

8.5a Social Media

Though not typically thought to be a part of businesses' internal information technology components, social media seems to fit here as it is driven by information and serves as a bridge or connection between the organization and the external environment. In the sea of Big Data, one of the hottest topics in technology these days is social media. **Social media** is a computer-based technology that facilitates the sharing of ideas, thoughts, and information through the building of virtual networks and communities.[44] Globally, there are more than 3.8 billion social media users, and many of them are companies. The largest social media platforms include Facebook, YouTube, WhatsApp, and Instagram.[45] In addition, businesses and their representatives frequently use Twitter and LinkedIn. Social media represent the cutting edge of business communication based on technology. Consumers want to use it and companies want to exploit it, especially for marketing purposes. A relevant question is, What possible social and ethical implications will social media tools create?[46] On the positive side, most popular tools in social networking provide a cyber-meeting space for people wanting to network. Networking tools provide a space where individuals can describe themselves and connect with others. Companies and their representatives use it for these purposes.

However, social media has a dark side in which social and ethical issues arise as companies and others try to take advantage of the technology. For example, many websites as well as individuals have become wary of Facebook's tracking techniques.[47] Others have objected to Facebook, in collaboration with researchers, attempting to manipulate news feeds to gauge the emotional reactions of users. Some have felt they were being treated by Facebook as "lab rats."[48] Twitter has also raised some ethical issues that appear to be ongoing. The company has tried to scrub sensitive content from its websites, but it walks a fine line between free expression and an aversion to being held legally accountable for the actions of its users.[49]

For companies, unfair reviews of products or services and how to respond to these pose a constant challenge. The public should expect accurate information about companies and products, but often this does not happen when "tweets" are flying based on emotional reactions rather than facts.

Social media frequently places more emphasis on instantaneous rather than accurate information, and this can unfairly put companies on the defensive, sometimes for reasons based on inaccurate information.[50] The challenge of social media as a technology is to promote freedom within an ethical context of responsibility. More information is good, but only if it promotes truth-telling.[51]

Many companies are now experiencing the reality that the use of social media in the workplace poses many risks and potentially serious compliance and ethical challenges. Companies that plan to use social media for business purposes must set standards and expectations for all users. Among the issues businesses need to consider are the following:[52]

- Collecting and using personal and corporate information
- Creating and maintaining company discussion boards, blogs, chat rooms, and marketing activities
- Reviewing company information to be posted on social media
- Disclosing company sponsorship and ownership of posted materials
- Disclosing company conflicts of interest with information posted on social media

Social media is a powerful tool for sharing company stories and projecting values into the community. But companies always need to remember that if social media topics enter into gray ethical areas, they should think seriously about the business ethics guidelines that are available before committing to action.[53]

8.5b Cybersecurity

Cybercrime and data security are important issues companies are facing today in the new world of Big Data. It is little wonder that chief information officers have trouble sleeping at night as cybersecurity threats are relentless, getting stronger and coming from more directions than ever before.[54] The consequences of data breaches can be disastrous involving staggering losses of customer data and corporate secrets followed by huge costs to strengthen security as well as deal with lawsuits and regulatory scrutiny.[55] The costs of cybercrime, which are driving the need for enhanced cybersecurity, include damage and destruction of data, stolen money, lost productivity, theft of intellectual property, theft of personal and corporate data, embezzlement, fraud, post-attack disruptions to the normal course of business, restoration and deletion of hacked security systems, and reputational harm.[56]

Attention to critical topics like cybersecurity are often heightened by major hacks of systems. Recently, the Solar-Winds hack was determined by security experts to be among the two or three most serious cyber-espionage intrusions in U.S. history.[57] In September 2019, SolarWinds, an Austin-based software company, was compromised. Hackers implanted malware into an update for Orion, an IT and cybersecurity dashboard product made by SolarWinds. This malware, called

Ethics In Practice Case

Twitter Ethics in Business

Twitter is one of the most frequently used social media. It may be because it is so easy and fast to use. Maybe it's because tweets are so brief. Knocking out a few tweets does not take much time or thought.

Twitter has been used for a number of nefarious and malicious reasons. Though most people who tweet do it responsibly, there are thousands of misleading, deceptive, criminal, or maligned tweets that go out daily. Though young people use social media more than anyone, Twitter has caught on in business too. Entertainment and sports personalities, employees, public relations personnel—all use Twitter extensively, most often to promote a product or a cause to rally support for.

Angela Dwyer has suggested that there are at least four categories of tweeters, and they all face ethical challenges. First, there are *paid tweeters*. Sometimes these are celebrities or sports stars that are paid by companies to tweet as a form of advertising. They typically do not disclose that they are being paid to tweet. The Federal Trade Commission (FTC) has said that celebrities in this category should disclose their relationships with advertisers when making endorsements, but it is hard to enforce.

Second, there are *company tweeters*. These individuals write reviews or tweets about promotional offers for their own companies. Some company tweeters are enthusiastic about their own companies and products and want the world to know. Others are tweeting because their boss has asked them to do so, or they want to be viewed favorably come raise and promotion time.

Third, there are *out-of-context tweeters*. Sometimes while attending events, these tweeters tweet hurried reactions or impressions that contain unverified or false information. Or, they do not present the context in which something was said or done. In other words, they do not provide the big picture. Tweets such as this have the potential to misinform or distort. To make matters worse, they are often retweeted before fuller or more accurate information is given.

Fourth, there are *ghost tweeters*. When someone is paid to write tweets on behalf of someone else, the ghost writer, or ghost tweeter may put out information without any confidence about whether the information is factual or accurate. Politicians, executives, sports stars, and other highly placed businesspeople may use ghost tweeters who are simply following a script without knowing for sure about the accuracy of its information.

In short, there are many opportunities and ways by which social media such as Twitter may be abused, misused, or be implicated in questionable practices by businesses and businesspeople.

1. Are these forms of tweeting ethical? How do you draw the fine line between ethical and unethical in each of these categories of tweeting? Which category faces the most ethical challenges in business?
2. Are there other categories of tweeters you can think of? Do they face ethical challenges?
3. Some people may say, "Hey, don't sweat it, it's only a tweet! You need to be on guard yourself!" Is this a reasonable response to business use of Twitter or other social media? Who cares?!
4. Are there other forms of social media that business uses that are more ethically challenging than Twitter? Describe them.
5. Should companies that use Twitter have a code of conduct for guidance in what represents ethical tweets? What key ethical principles should guide the use of Twitter?

Sources: Twitter, "The Twitter Rules," https://help.twitter.com/en/rules-and-policies/twitter-rules, accessed April 8, 2021; The Ethics of Writing, "Is Tweeting Ethical?" November 23, 2018, https://ethicsofwriting.com/2018/11/is-tweeting-ethical/; Charlie Warzel, "Scientists May Have Figured Out Twitter Ethics," BuzzFeed News, https://www.buzzfeednews.com/article/charliewarzel/scientists-may-have-figured-out-twitter-ethics, accessed April 8, 2021; Ethics Sage, "The Twitter Golden Rule: Tweet Others the Way You Want to Be Tweeted," October 27, 2020, https://www.ethicssage.com/2020/10/the-twitter-golden-rule-tweet-others-the-way-you-want-to-be-tweeted.html, accessed April 8, 2021.

"Sunburst," was a backdoor that allowed hackers to monitor and further infiltrate networks on which it was installed. By June 2020, SolarWinds believed that 18,000 Orion customers had downloaded a software-update patch that included the Sunburst backdoor. By December, Microsoft announced that the SolarWinds hackers had accessed the internal source code that underlies some of its software. In January 2021, a group of U.S. intelligence agencies announced that they thought they had identified who had engaged in the hack. As it turned out, federal agencies of the government indicated they were impacted by the compromised Orion patch and that Microsoft e-mail accounts were also compromised.[58] The SolarWinds debacle revealed that the U.S. government as well as many companies were exposed and unprepared to deal with a cyberattack of this magnitude.

In 2020, a survey of corporate technology officers revealed that most companies are worried about all sorts of cyberthreats, but they do not think they are prepared to defend against them.[59] Smaller companies, in particular, say they are less confident about the risks they face though they know that ransomware, malware, credential theft, and attacks on supply chains, and Internet of Things devices are serious exposures they face.[60] Actions companies are taking include installing in-house cybersecurity programs, dedicating a budget for cybersecurity, hiring dedicated employees, conducting ongoing cybersecurity training, developing incident response plans, purchasing cybersecurity insurance, and providing the leadership team with advanced training.[61]

8.5c E-Commerce

Electronic commerce, often referred to as **e-commerce,** *e-business*, or *Web-based marketing*, is one of the most significant technological phenomena of our day. It primarily

Ethics In Practice Case

Zero Trust as a Cybersecurity Model—Don't Trust Anyone

The Zero Trust approach to cybersecurity was once mocked as crazy. Over the past decade, however, the developer of Zero Trust has gained followers. In spite of all security measures put in place, the Zero Trust model assumes that anyone logging into a system is suspicious and they are required to authenticate their credentials each time they connect. Zero Trust assumes that organizations should automatically not trust anything inside or outside of its perimeters and instead must verify anything and everything trying to gain access to the system.

The SolarWinds cybersecurity hack is one of the major attacks convincing many that zero trust might be needed. It might not have stopped the SolarWinds attack, but it might have allowed the so-called experts to detect the hack sooner.

In addition to the federal government looking seriously at Zero Trust, Microsoft Corporation, which has advocated for the model for some time, found that targeted victims in the SolarWinds attack whose systems had embraced the model were more resilient afterwards.

Zero Trust models are expensive and time-consuming, because in some cases it requires the company to tear out existing systems and replace them to ensure the deletion of malware. Even the developer of the Zero Trust approach, John Kindervag, who still works in cybersecurity and continues to promote his method across both public and private sectors, recommends moving gradually. Ripping out and replacing systems should only be approached after considering easier and less expensive measures.

In spite of these warnings about being cautious, CIOs and many other corporate executives are implementing Zero Trust systems at a quickened pace. One expert has observed that very soon Zero Trust will be cited as the one-time big framework in cybersecurity.

1. Who are the stakeholders and what are their stakes in using the Zero Trust model? What are the ethical issues in this case? Explain.
2. Is the Zero Trust approach to cybersecurity an ethical approach to cybersecurity? By what ethical premises might this approach be justified?
3. Trust has always been held up as a key factor in successful leadership. Isn't the idea of "not trusting anyone" in defiance of contemporary approaches to management and leadership today?
4. How would a highly ethical leader justify and explain the use of Zero Trust?
5. If Zero Trust is the best available, why not just install it immediately rather than fooling around with less sophisticated approaches?

Sources: Mary Pratt, "What Is Zero Trust? A Model for More Effective Security," CSOonline, January 16, 2018, https://www.csoonline.com/article/3247848/what-is-zero-trust-a-model-for-more-effective-security.html, accessed April 9, 2021; "Don't Trust Anyone," *Bloomberg Businessweek*, March 29, 2021, 24; Microsoft, "Enable a Remote Workforce by Embracing Zero Trust Security," https://www.microsoft.com/en-us/security/business/zero-trust, accessed April 10, 2021.

affects consumer stakeholders and competitors of the e-commerce firms. Most experts today know that the Internet has reshaped the way business is conducted around the world. Part of this is firms selling products and services online. Beyond this, companies are integrating the Internet into every aspect of their businesses, and many products are being interconnected through the Internet of Things (IoT). IoT refers to the development of the Internet in which everyday objects (computers, thermostats, appliances, smartphones, etc.) have network connectivity allowing them to receive and send data.[62]

Business transactions via e-commerce total trillions of dollars, and the majority of it comes from business-to-business (B2B) sales.[63] However, consumer transactions are huge and growing, particularly following the coronavirus pandemic, when so many relied on online ordering. In fact, may retail businesses attribute their ability to staying open in the "catastrophic year" of 2020 to e-commerce sales.[64] Companies are spending billions of dollars linking customers, sales, and marketing over the Web, increasingly through social networking and apps such as Instagram, TikTok, and Clubhouse to connect directly to consumers. In short, electronic commerce is a flourishing business, and the opportunity for questionable practices arises along with this growth.

Along with the growth of electronic commerce, business ethics problems have arisen as well. The major category of problems for consumers is **online scams**. According to Fraud!Alert, a project of the National Consumer League, con artists are taking advantage of the Internet's growth in popularity to scam the unwary. During one recent year, for example, the top frauds over the Internet included fake check scams, prizes/sweepstakes/free gifts, phishing/spoofing, advance fee loans, friendship scandals, money offers, Internet auctions, family/friend imposters, and scholarships/grants.[65] Other scams included credit card fraud, travel and vacation scams, pyramid schemes, and bogus investment opportunities. In 2020–2021, the largest scams involved stimulus check scams, investment scams, fake check scams, and prizes and sweepstakes scams. Virtually all of these scams are delivered via telephone and e-mail using technologies such as wire transfers, credit cards, bank account debits, and bank debit cards.[66]

Many of the ongoing issues in e-commerce ethics include the following:[67] access, intellectual property, privacy and informed consent, protection of children, security of information, and trust. These ethical issues are not restricted to e-commerce. They also occur in brick-and-mortar businesses. The manifestations and scope of these issues, however, differ from those of traditional businesses.

Access refers to the differences in computer access between the rich and the poor. *Intellectual property*, in e-commerce, is illustrated by the ethics of downloading music or books. *Privacy and informed consent* differ in e-commerce. An illustration is the novel ways companies place cookies on our computers without informed consent. In addition, firms collect online information and merge it with offline information. *Protection of children* is an ongoing ethical issue, and it is illustrated in the issue of pornography and the dangers of children getting hooked up with sexual predators. E-commerce makes porn more accessible than through traditional businesses. *Security* is such a major issue that even today some are reluctant to do business on the Web for fear their credit card numbers will be intercepted by someone not associated with the e-commerce business. Finally, *trust* is the basis for practically all business transactions, and it is especially crucial in e-commerce.[68]

8.5d Invasion of Consumer Privacy via E-Commerce

The average person encounters two forms of Internet electronic commerce: business-to-consumer (B2C) transactions and business-to-business (B2B) transactions. Most of us are quite familiar with B2C transactions when we do personal business on the Internet—buying products and services, arranging credit cards, accessing travel websites, and doing financial business such as personal banking. In terms of Web-based marketing to consumers, consumer stakeholders are primarily affected by such issues as database sharing, identity theft, and invasion of privacy. Invasion of privacy is a legitimate concern in all business transactions; however, the case of e-commerce deserves special attention because

of the ease with which data can be accessed, stored, and transmitted in electronic form.

One of the most important ethical issues with respect to doing business over the Internet is the question of invasions of consumer privacy.[69] Figure 8-1 summarizes some of the concerns that privacy advocates and law enforcement experts have about the Internet's threat to privacy.

Some of the most prevalent technological means by which companies invade consumers' privacy include the use of cookies and spam. **Cookies** are identification tags that websites drop on our personal computer hard drives so they can recognize repeat visitors the next time we visit their websites.[70] **Spam**, which crowds our inboxes daily, is unsolicited commercial e-mail. It is sent through "open relays" to millions of persons. A major problem is that spammers have begun to send advertisements via text messages to cell phones.[71] Most consumers interpret the receipt of *spam* as a rude and annoying invasion of their privacy. Interestingly, dozens of companies make programs that protect our e-mail privacy, block cookies, and filter spam and porn, but few consumers bother to use them.[72]

Collection and use of personal information is a serious invasion of privacy with respect to electronic commerce. Though non-Internet companies have engaged in this practice for years, everything seems magnified in the e-world in which we now live. None of us really knows how much personal information is collected, saved, swapped, or sold in e-commerce. Thousands of retailers, from online stores to catalog companies, collect and store personal information, from asking customers for their zip codes to collecting names, addresses, household income, and purchasing patterns through a store credit card. In short, the average consumer has little control over what is done with personal data

Figure 8-1 Examples of Threats to Consumers' Privacy Posed by the Internet

Threats to Privacy	Description
Social networks	Social networks allow individuals to establish connections and store information remotely. Default privacy settings provide too much personal information online. This information creates a field day for identity thieves, hackers, scammers, debt collectors, employers, marketers, data miners, and governments.
Hackers	Organized cybercriminals known as hactivists participate in phishing, online shopping fraud, banking fraud, and other deceptions.
Behavioral advertising	Behavioral advertising is a technique used by advertisers to present targeted ads to consumers by collecting information about their browsing behavior. These techniques create a behavioral profile of you that is then used for exploitation.
Data stealing	Done through rogue applications on social networking sites—computers that harbor botnets (Coreflood) and smartphone malware (DroidDream) are a couple that may be after you.
Facial-recognition technology	Once used for security and surveillance. Facebook deployed facial-recognition software that allows Facebook to gather data or recognize your face. Then people can be searched for using a picture.
GEO-Tags	Used when photos or videos are taken with a GPS-equipped device (e.g., smartphone). Photos are embedded with a geo-tag revealing the exact location of where taken. Revelation of geo-locational data on social networking sites creates danger of social surveillance and stalking.

Source: Wired, "Privacy and Security in the Internet Age," https://www.wired.com/insights/2015/01/privacy-and-security-in-the-internet-age/, accessed April 12, 2021, Jason Aten, "Here Are the Biggest Online Privacy Threats Facing Companies and Consumers," Inc., https://www.inc.com/jason-aten/here-are-biggest-online-privacy-threats-facing-companies-consumers-and-covering-your-webcam-wont-solve-them-all.html, accessed April 12, 2021.

once it is collected.[73] An ongoing concern is **identity theft** or someone tampering with one's financial accounts. Less serious is the inundation of marketing attempts, both online and offline, which consumers are subjected to as a result of information being distributed.

Phishing. One of the most common and serious problems in the realm of computer scams against consumers and companies continues to be the ongoing scam identified as **phishing**. Phishing is an attempt to obtain financial or other confidential, personal information from Internet users, typically by way of an e-mail that looks like it is from a legitimate organization, such as a financial institution, but contains a link to a fake website that replicates the real one.[74] The technique is called "phishing" because it lures prey (computer users) with convincing bait into revealing passwords and other private data. The Anti-Phishing Working Group reports that phishers are using a variety of techniques to fool users. These include domain names chosen to avoid detection, encryption designed to lull users into a false sense of security, and deceptive e-mail addresses used to spoof trusted companies.[75]

Botnet scams, one of the latest techniques by which hackers get access to personal and corporate information, are exploding in numbers. *Bots* are computers that have been compromised by unethical hackers. A network of bots, called a **botnet**, is created by e-mails that get distributed by these compromised computers, and these are controlled by a central computer called the command-and-control server.[76] Botnets are not only the way our personal information is compromised, but they represent the greatest threat to data security for businesses and governments today.[77]

Government's Involvement in Consumer Privacy Protection.

The federal government has gotten involved in protecting consumers' privacy, but many observers believe it is not doing enough. Over the past several years, a number of different bills designed to protect consumer privacy on the Internet have been filed but have not yet been passed. Many of the legislators have been uncertain whether a broad privacy bill is even needed or what it should look like. Like so many proposals, the proposed Privacy Bill of Rights has not yet been adopted into law by Congress. However, it does contain some important privacy principles that ethical companies should consider.[78] California has passed the California Consumer Privacy Act of 2018 that gives consumers more control over the personal information companies collect from them.[79] In 2015, the General Data Protection Regulation (GDPR) was passed by the European Commission, and it was implemented in 2016. The regulation is an important step in protecting individuals' rights in the digital age and by clarifying rules for business.[80]

The U.S. Federal Trade Commission annually reports its summary of consumer complaints. Many of the complaints involve the Internet and invasion of privacy. The FTC is the primary government agency concerned with protecting consumers' privacy today. Under the FTC Act, the commission guards against unfairness and deception. The primary legislation now governing consumers' privacy includes the Financial Services Modernization Act (Gramm–Leach–Bliley Act), concerned with financial privacy; the Fair Credit Reporting Act; and the Children's Online Privacy Protection Act.[81] Other legislation regulating consumer and employee privacy may come soon in the wake of such accelerated e-commerce growth.

The FTC has issued a report on what it considers to be the "best practices" companies should follow in protecting consumer privacy. Each of these recommended best practices is just one part of the FTC's suggested privacy framework:[82]

1. *Privacy by Design.* Companies should "build in" privacy at every stage of product development.
2. *Simplified Choice for Consumers and Businesses.* Consumers should be given the ability to make decisions about their data at a relevant time and context, including a Do Not Track mechanism, while reducing the burden on businesses of providing unnecessary choices.
3. *Greater Transparency.* Make information collection and use practices transparent.

With this report, the FTC has called on companies to take action to implement best practices in protecting consumers' privacy. The FTC argues that privacy protection should be the default setting for commercial data practices and has again called on Congress to enact baseline privacy legislation.[83]

Business Initiatives to Protect Consumer Privacy.

There are a number of different ways companies are striving to protect the privacy of their customers in electronic commerce.

Ethical Leadership First, businesses need to recognize the potential ethical issues involved in electronic commerce and be committed to treating customers and all affected stakeholders in an ethical fashion. This commitment and ethical leadership from the top undergirds all other initiatives. Ethical leadership must begin with the board of directors, the CEO, and top management. Every principle discussed in Chapter 6 about top management leadership applies to this discussion as well.

Privacy Policies Companies may take the initiative with their own carefully crafted privacy policies designed to protect customers. An example of this might be a company deciding to do more than the law requires. A company that has gone to great lengths to explain its privacy policy to customers and guests is the Walt Disney Company. On its website, it provides the following statement regarding its privacy policy:

> We are dedicated to treating your personal information with care and respect. Our privacy policy is designed to provide transparency into our privacy practices and

principles, in a format that our guests can navigate, read and understand.[84]

Companies would do well to listen to consumers' opinions on their privacy protection. A recent survey conducted by McKinsey & Company found that consumers trust companies that limit the use of their personal data and respond quickly to hacks and breaches.[85]

Chief Privacy Officers An innovative approach to protecting consumers' privacy has been the increasing use of a **chief privacy officer (CPO)** in a number of major companies. Though companies began using CPOs several decades ago, the job has grown in importance since then. CPOs share the common objective of finding ways to protect consumers and achieve legal compliance while still enabling companies to innovate and grow. More and more, CPOs are called on to supervise "privacy by design" by providing continuous input during the R&D process so that potential privacy issues are identified and remedied early before they create costly problems.[86]

It is the primary responsibility of the CPO to keep a company out of trouble, whether in a court of law or in the court of public opinion. This includes developing Internet policies, helping their companies avoid consumer litigation, creating methods of handling and resolving consumer complaints, and assessing the risk of privacy invasion of company activities and practices.[87] The job is a challenging one. CPOs must balance their customers' right to privacy with their employer's need for information for financial purposes.[88]

CPOs also play a critical role in ensuring employee as well as consumer privacy. CPOs are relevant to the section of this chapter on the workplace and they are brought up again in Chapter 12, where employees' rights to privacy are discussed further.

Data Security One of the clearest ways companies can protect the information of their customers is through data security systems and practices. Yet, data breaches (also called "hacks") are on the rise. **Data security** is the process of protecting corporate data from unauthorized access, corruption, or loss. It involves putting protective measures in place to ensure that data are available to those in the company authorized to use them and to prevent those from outside the company getting access to it. Data security is intended to protect against the following types of threats: cyber-fraud, ransomware attacks, malware attacks, and other malevolent intrusions.[89] A robust data security system provides the following benefits that are crucial to companies today: preventing automated attacks, protecting consumers' privacy, data backup, ensuring data integrity, protecting brand loyalty and reputation, and ensuring business continuity.[90]

A few data breaches of 2020 and 2021 illustrate the threats posed by data breaches.[91]

Estee Lauder (2020): An unsecured database belonging to the company exposed 440 million customer records. E-mail addresses and IP addresses were exposed.

MGM Resorts (2020): More than 10.6 million hotel guests had their personal information exposed on a hacking forum. The data dump exposed home addresses, phone numbers, e-mail addresses, and dates of birth.

Zoom (2020): The credentials of more than 500,000 Zoom accounts were found for sale on the dark web and hacker forums for as little as $0.02 per account.

Facebook (2021): The personal data of 533 million Facebook users from 106 countries were posted online for free in a low-level hacking forum.

T-Mobile (2021): An undisclosed number of customers were affected by SIM swap attacks, or SIM hijacking, when scammers took control of and switched phone numbers using engineering techniques.

It is obvious that data security and cybercrime are among the biggest threats companies face today. Some believe that cyber-espionage and computer crime could soon surpass terrorism as the primary threat facing Americans and developed nations.[92] Data breaches that have occurred in recent years point out the strong need for companies, governments, and individuals to make data security a number-one priority. Companies have an ethical responsibility to protect data in spite of the lack of severe penalties for failing to do so.

Questionable Businesses and Practices. Several questionable businesses and practices have been made possible by electronic commerce and the use of the Internet. These include Web-based pornography, Internet gambling, and Web-based downloading of music, movies, books, and other copyrighted digital materials.

Illegal Downloading The illegal or uncompensated downloading of music, movies, television shows, and other copyrighted works continues to be a serious, questionable practice because it represents theft of intellectual property. Bringing this problem to the public's attention in 2015, Taylor Swift made headlines with her social media assault on Apple in response to the company's failure to pay her and others for their music during the free trial period downloads. After Ms. Swift's tirade, Apple changed its position and said it would pay artists for streaming even during customers' free trial period.[93]

For several years now, the Recording Industry Association of America (RIAA), the music industry trade group, has found university campuses to be hotbeds of file-sharing activity. It has become more aggressive in seeking violations. The mission of RIAA is to protect the intellectual property and First Amendment rights of artists and music labels.[94] In reflecting on this issue, one student observed that downloading was so easy and there is so much free content on the Internet that it's hard to discriminate between illegal downloading, streaming free content, and just copying something from a friend's laptop. The student went on to observe that when a product is digital, it does not feel like stealing. Over the past decade,

Ethics In Practice Case

Copyright Infringement or Just an Inefficient, Complex System?

Spotify, the music streaming company, faced a $150 million class action lawsuit led by David Lowery, the frontman for Cracker, the alternative rock band, and Camper Van Beethoven, an American rock band. The musicians maintained that Spotify had not been securing the proper licenses for all of the music it offered and had not been paying royalties to all of the appropriate parties. The implication emerging from the lawsuit was that the company that claimed to be providing an alternative to online piracy was not living up to its own legal obligations. In short, it was a case of copyright infringement, and some might say it involved stealing another person's intellectual property.

A license for a piece of music involves two separate copyrights. First is the recording, which is typically owned by the performer's label and, second, is the underlying composition, which is often owned by the songwriter or their publisher. So, to use a recording, a streaming company such as Spotify would have to get two licenses. This is done by negotiating with the publisher or by sending the rights holder a notice and paying a royalty.

Lowery claimed that Spotify frequently skipped the second part. He claimed that there may be hundreds or thousands of artists who have not been paid for their work, including him. Spotify did not argue against this but said that tracking down the proper rights holders is a complex process and hard to do. The company said it has royalties set aside for cases where royalty rights are not clear, and it stands ready to pay the royalties if the affected artists make a rightful claim. But, one of Lowery's lawyers argued that artists should not have to track down royalties owed them and that it is Spotify's responsibility to secure the license and pay the royalty.

Spotify, in its defense, said that the laws and copyright infrastructure that exists does not fully factor in the scope and speed with which digital music services operate. The company maintained that securing advance permissions for each track is inefficient and possibly crippling for a company trying to stay competitive. In January 2016, Spotify was hit with a second lawsuit over the alleged systemic and willful copyright infringement. In 2018, a federal judge consolidated the Lowery case with that of Melissa Ferrick's and approved a settlement of $112 million, including an immediate cash payment of $44 million to class members and a pledge to pay ongoing royalties.

1. Who are the stakeholders affected and what are the ethical issues in this case?
2. Was Spotify justified in saying it was prepared to pay but claimants would have to come to them and present a rightful claim? Or, did Spotify have the responsibility to find the artists and secure permission and pay the appropriate royalty before they streamed the music?
3. How do you evaluate the company's claim that the system is too complex and inefficient and that the laws and copyright infrastructure are the problem in the digital music industry?
4. Is the issue in this case that the law is not keeping up with the high-tech music streaming industry or that Spotify is using this as an excuse to take shortcuts and engage in a questionable practice?

Sources: Adrian Covert, Vocativ, "Spotify Is Facing a $150 Million Lawsuit over Unpaid Royalties," https://www.vocativ.com/news/265949/spotify-is-facing-a-150-million-lawsuit-over-unpaid-royalties/index.html, accessed April 13, 2021; Ed Christman, Billboard, "Spotify Hit with Second Lawsuit Over Copyright Infringement," https://www.billboard.com/articles/business/6836439/spotify-hit-with-second-copyright-infringement-lawsuit-melissa-merrick-david-lowery/, accessed April 13, 2021; Eriq Gardner, "Spotify Wins Approval of $112.5 Deal to Settle Copyright Class Action," Hollywood Reporter, May 23, 2018, https://www.hollywoodreporter.com/thr-esq/spotify-wins-approval-1125-million-deal-settle-copyright-class-action-1114307, accessed April 13, 2021.

peer-to-peer technology companies have transformed continuously and speedily, making it more complicated to police.[95] In spite of this, laws and ethics are being violated, and these examples illustrate how Internet technology has threatened legitimate businesses.

It should be noted, however, that it is not only individuals who are taking advantage of the creative works of others. In 2004, Google entered into an agreement with major libraries to take about 20 million books, make digital copies of them, and make them available online to users. Google made no payments to authors of these works. The Authors Guild filed suit against Google, but in October 2015, a New York Court of Appeals ruled that Google was protected in doing this under the doctrine of fair use.[96]

Monitoring Technology It's one thing if your employer is monitoring your practices, but what about companies that monitor consumers without their knowing about it? Thousands of companies now monitor, analyze, and influence the lives of millions of people. What is being monitored or tracked? Consumer behavior, movements, social relationships, and interests are often recorded, evaluated, and analyzed in real time. Companies exploiting personal information has become a multi-billion-dollar industry. Most of what we know, however, is just the tip of the iceberg, and much of it we do not know about.[97]

Real-time monitoring is now taking place in online platforms, advertising technology providers, data brokers, and businesses in virtually all industries are now taking advantage of monitoring and surveillance without people knowing about it. A major reason that business tracking and monitoring, including profiling, has become so pervasive is because almost all websites, mobile app providers, and device vendors share behavioral data with other companies.[98] In terms of devices, smartphones have become the primary source of data collection. Virtually everyone has a smartphone today and the information collected often provides insights into the user's personality and, certainly, buying behavior.

Platforms such as Google, Apple, or Microsoft are some of the primary collectors of information.[99]

These are just a sampling of the kinds of controversial ethical and legal issues that arise in connection with electronic commerce. As the Smart Revolution takes over all our consumer products, there will be plenty to worry about in the realm of consumer privacy as monitoring technology advances.[100]

8.5e The Workplace and Digital Technology

While computer-based information technology creates ethical issues for consumer stakeholders with respect to electronic commerce and Web-based marketing and other aspects of their lives, employee stakeholders also are significantly affected by technology in the workplace. We will discuss these issues in more detail, especially employee surveillance and privacy, in Chapter 12. Though computers have provided workers with countless benefits and easier access to information, there have been many adverse effects. Included among these have been communication breakdowns, increased stress, distractions, disconnectedness, and health issues.[101]

In this section, we will discuss several workplace technology issues: biometrics, robotics, cell phone use and texting, unethical employee activities, and company actions.

Biometrics. The developing field of biometrics has begun to take off, especially in commercial applications. **Biometrics** is the use of body measurements, such as eye scans, fingerprints, or palm prints, for determining and confirming identity. The technology of biometrics typically conjures up images of Big Brother surveillance tactics, and it has met resistance in cases where the government has wanted to use it for identification purposes. What seems to be speeding up its use, however, are commercial applications that provide assistance for consumers.[102] Popular types of biometric devices in use today include face scanners, hand scanners, fingerprint scanners, retina or iris scanners, voice recognition scanners, keystroke dynamics, and signature recognition.[103]

In the past several years, there has been an explosion of applications in the commercial use of biometrics.[104] In some businesses now, consumers can scan their fingers or wave their palms over a scanner to gain access to accounts, safe deposit boxes, or to make purchases. Already one can purchase laptop computers and mobile phones that come with built-in finger scanners. Other domestic applications include biometric door locks, garage locks, and safe locks. Even online services now respond to the rhythm and other characteristics of a person's typing, using a template of your "keystroke dynamics." There are flash drives that work only when activated by your thumbprint.[105] In short, biometrics

---

Ethics In Practice Case

Using Personal Technology in the Workplace

Increasingly, especially in small businesses, companies are permitting employees to use their own personal technology devices on the job. Smartphones, laptops, and tablets are the primary technologies being used. This has created a social movement known as BYOD—"bring your own device" to work.

The benefits to small businesses are several. If companies allow personal technologies at work, this means they have to spend much less on technology resources themselves. Plus, many employees are more comfortable using their own equipment and it is portable so they can take it with them. Companies also benefit because the employees in possession of their personal devices are "always working." Some productivity gains may be expected.

But the use of many gadgets leads to many risks. One major risk is lost or stolen devices, which can lead to huge headaches for companies. Once lost or misplaced, others can access company information, some of which may be confidential or proprietary. Companies, in general, do not implement basic policies such as requiring lock codes on the personal devices when they are used at work.

Another big issue is misappropriation of information. Personal devices make it much easier for employees to take information when they leave work. Thus, private information could get in the hands of competitors or thieves. Viruses and other malware are another troubling issue. Often, employees do not keep virus protection on their personal devices up to date, and an infected device could create problems throughout a company's network. Other

issues include ownership, ability to monitor, technical challenges, and unanticipated costs.

As work steadily spills into personal lives, as it especially did during the pandemic, and companies continue to allow personal devices to be used on the job, the dividing line between work lives and personal lives continues to blur. This will pose additional problems for organizations and their staff in the future.

1. What are the ethical issues at stake when companies permit employees to use personal technologies on the job? What are the implications for all stakeholders?
2. On balance, should companies continue to allow personal technological devices on the job, or should they disallow them? If they allow them, what policies should be put in place?

Sources: Suzanne Lucas, "The Pros and Cons of a Bring Your Own Device (BYOD) to work policy," September 17, 2020, https://www.thebalancecareers.com/bring-your-own-device -byod-job-policy-4139870, accessed April 14, 2021; Oasis Blog, "Technology in the Workplace: Should Employees Use Personal Devices for Work?" https://www.oasisadvantage.com/knowledge -center/technology-in-the-workplace-should-employees-use -personal-devices-for-work, accessed April 14, 2021; Sandra Melo, "Advantages and Disadvantages of BYOD (Bring Your Own Device)," March 5, 2020, https://mydatascope.com/blog/en /advantages-and-disadvantages-of-byod-bring-your-own-device/, accessed April 14, 2021.

is revolutionizing the way business is conducted and is expected to grow faster in the future.

Like most technologies, biometrics has many advantages and some possible risks. For the most part, the focus has not been on the legal and ethical risks associated with biometrics, but this is an issue that companies, consumers, and employees will need to watch carefully in the future. Fortunately, international standards are being developed by the International Organization for Standardization (ISO).[106] The potential abuses and misuses of biometrics are many and must be factored into decisions about the treatment of all stakeholders, especially customers and employees.

Automation and Robotics. It is difficult today to speak about automation and robotics without reference to artificial intelligence that is now combining forces to bring dramatic changes to our lives. At one time discussions about automation centered around the question of humans *versus* machines. Today, humans *plus* machines have become the norm. The highest performing organizations today have been able to seamlessly embed digital technologies aimed at boosting human productivity.[107]

Most advanced economies have become "automation nations," as predictions for automation and robotics takes off significantly in part due to the 2020 pandemic. Autonomous robots took on expansive roles in stores and warehouses in 2020 and are expected to gain momentum in the immediate years ahead. Robots that collect data and share real-time inventory updates and accurately pinpoint product locations are becoming commonplace.[108] Other important advances include (1) multipurpose robots expert at multitasking, (2) sensors, drones, and cameras that are becoming the ideal robot accessories, and (3) 5G connectivity that will allow massive machine-type communications. Additionally, the supply shortages evidenced during the COVID-19 pandemic have proven that automation will play a huge role in supply chain management going forward.[109]

The public's opinions about automation are a key factor companies will need to address as they plan for a more highly automated future for consumers and employees. The Pew Research Center has reported how Americans see automation, and it is expected these same finding are representative of worldwide opinions. Some of the public's expectations about future automation include the following:[110]

- Widespread automation will advance in the coming decades.
- There will be more negative than positive effects from widespread job automation
- Automation has hurt more people than it has helped.
- Automation will disrupt a number of professions.
- Young and part-time workers will be personally affected.
- There should be limits on job automation.
- There is a split on whether it is government's duty to help machine-displaced workers.

The opportunities and challenges facing companies as worldwide growth in automation and robotics continue

will be huge. Robots are no longer just on assembly lines. Collaborative robots that work alongside humans, called **cobots**, are getting cheaper and easier to program, and this is encouraging businesses to put them to work at new tasks in many different industries. It is estimated that cobot sales will be around 27 percent of all robot sales by 2025 as their popularity increases.[111] In terms of challenges, a concern for robotics and ethics will become more important than it has been so far. A new field, **roboethics**, has emerged, but it has been more in theory than in practice. The purpose of roboethics is ensuring that machines with artificial intelligence behave in ways that prioritize human safety above their assigned tasks and that their behavior is in accordance with generally accepted ethical standards.[112]

An important editorial in *The Economist* has argued that society needs to move quickly in developing ways of dealing with the ethics of robotics. It points out three areas where progress is needed in regulating the development and use of autonomous robots.[113] First, laws are needed to clarify who is at fault if a robotic device causes harm—the designer, programmer, manufacturer, or operator. Second, when ethical systems are embedded into robots, they need to be decision-making schemes that would seem right to most people. Third, collaboration is needed among engineers, ethicists, lawyers, and policymakers who left on their own might come up with widely divergent rules.[114] The rise of robotics and its impact on the workplace will need to be monitored closely in the years to come.

Cell Phones and Texting. It has been estimated that citizens have been mashing out more than six billion text messages a day in the United States and probably a few billion more on services such as WhatsApp and Facebook Messenger.[115] Although e-mail and the Internet most often create ethical problems in the workplace, the use of company-sponsored cell phones by employees represents one of the fastest growing technologies with increasing ethical and legal implications. The use of a cell phone is no longer a private matter as job pressures are tempting more and more employees to use the phones while driving. Because some companies now make cell phones available to their employees, this issue spills over into the business arena and becomes a business ethics and legal topic.

According to the U.S. National Highway Safety Transportation Agency (NHSTA), the broader issue is distracted driving, and it includes texting while driving, using a smartphone, using a navigation system, talking to passengers, watching videos, and adjusting music. Smartphone use and texting are the two primary problems. In 2019, distracted driving claimed more than 3,000 lives, and the number is growing each year. Already most states ban texting while driving and many states restrict cell phone use.[116]

A trend with enormous implications for employers is the growing number of employees—managers, salespeople, consultants, lawyers, ad executives, and others—who are questionably using cell phones for talking and texting while driving and chalking up sales or billable hours. Every year in the United States over a half a million people are injured or killed in traffic accidents attributed to a combination of texting and driving. The statistics are shocking especially considering that this danger could be completely avoided. These numbers are far higher than similar calculations in Europe and the United Kingdom.[117]

Plaintiffs are more frequently claiming that the employer is partly to blame because it presses employees to work long hours from distant locations, often encouraging them to use cell phones without setting safety guidelines. A study by an insurance company found that chatty drivers suffered slower reaction times, took longer to stop, and missed more road signs than drivers who were legally drunk. A new term has been coined for accidents caused by cell phone–using drivers—*DWY* (driving while yakking).[118]

Cell phone use—linked to technology—is raising red flags for employers and individuals concerned about their careers. Not enough companies have the needed policies on cell phone use at this time. It appears that as high-tech tools extend the workplace into every corner of life, too many companies have been leaving the responsibility entirely up to the employees. These cases are tragic examples of what can happen when employees, using technology, become too distracted, pressured, or overfocused on their work.[119]

To address the legal and ethical challenges they face, companies need to develop bring your own device (BYOD) policies that take into account both the employer and the employee. While these policies can be complicated to craft, they can work well when employers balance security, compliance, and privacy concerns of all parties.[120]

Unethical Activities by Employees involving Technology. In most of the instances described to this point, the employer has had responsibility for the use of technology and its implications. There is another area that should be identified: questionable activities involving technology that originate from the employees. In a major study of workers, the following are unethical activities employees said they had engaged in during the previous year.[121] All these items were related to technology.

- Created a potentially dangerous situation by using new technology while driving
- Wrongly blamed an error the employee made on a technological glitch
- Copied the company's software for home use
- Used office equipment to shop on the Internet for personal reasons
- Used office equipment to network/search for another job
- Accessed private computer files without authorization
- Used new technologies to intrude on co-workers' privacy
- Visited porn websites using office equipment

As can be seen by the activities in this list, employee-related issues involving the use or misuse of technology is another significant category of challenges that must be monitored by management.

Company Actions. Companies have many options for addressing the kinds of ethical issues described to this point. A major survey of *Fortune* 500 nonmanagement employees revealed that management should clearly define guidelines for ethical computer use by employees. Options for doing this include company management making these decisions, using the Information Systems Society's code of ethics, and involving employees and users in a collaborative attempt to decide on computer ethics policies.[122] Beyond this, companies should carefully think about the ethical implications of their use of technology and integrate decisions designed to protect employees into their policies and practices, especially their codes of conduct.

We earlier discussed the importance of companies addressing the ethics of technology: ethical tech. To repeat an important point, leaders of organizations need to be sure their technology ethics conforms to their overarching organizational values. Their approach must address the use of technology as a whole and not be focused on just one technology. Companies need to proactively consider and evaluate how they can use technology in a responsible manner so that they can develop trust with all their stakeholders.[123]

8.6 Biotechnology

The 20th century's revolution in information technology is merging with the 21st century's revolution in biotechnology. Indeed, Walter Isaacson labeled the 2000s as the "biotech century."[124] The field of biotechnology involves "using biology to discover, develop, manufacture, market, and sell products and services."[125]

The field of biotechnology carries with it significant implications for business and for business ethics, and we can only touch on these issues here. In fact, we now have a burgeoning growth industry—the biotechnology industry. The biotech industry today consists of small entrepreneurial start-up companies funded largely by venture capitalists, along with dozens of larger, more established companies. Most of the applications of biotechnology are in health care, the pharmaceutical industry, and agriculture.[126] From a sustainability perspective, biotechnology is striving to *heal*, *fuel*, and *feed* the world.[127]

In this section, we will discuss bioethics, genetic engineering, and genetically modified organisms (GMOs).

8.6a Bioethics

The field of **bioethics** deals with the ethical issues embedded in the commercial use of biotechnology, especially in medicine and health care. As new biotech products are developed, thorny ethical issues inevitably arise. Unfortunately, ethicists and bioethicists ask relevant questions more than they are able to provide definite answers. The questions asked are rather straightforward and typify ethical inquiries: What is the right thing to do and how to do it? What is worthwhile? Who is responsible to whom and for what?[128]

Spotlight on Sustainability

Is Biotech Agriculture Sustainable?

When we think of sustainable agriculture, we typically think of food products that have been organically grown. However, sustainable agriculture is not limited to organic production according to the Biotechnology Industry Organization (BIO). According to BIO, there is currently a new standard being developed under the auspices of the American National Standards Institute that will incorporate any technology that will increase agriculture sustainability. In BIO's perspective, biotech crops are sustainable and also good for the environment. They require fewer pesticides and employ farming techniques that improve soil health and retention of water. Through biotechnology, global pesticide use is down, soil erosion has been reduced, and fuel consumption has been reduced.

According to the Seed Biotechnology Center, genetically engineered (GE) crop varieties offer promising traits that will help increase health and nutrition, sustain farming

on marginal lands, and decrease concerns with pests and disease. Currently, there are more than 100 agricultural crops that have been genetically modified in research stations around the world, and five of the most promising traits that are being analyzed in numerous crops include herbicide tolerance, insect resistance, stress tolerance, nitrogen use efficiency, and nutritional traits.

Sources: Clara Rodriguez Fernandez, "Ten Ways Biotechnology Makes the World More Sustainable," October 22, 2019, https://www.labiotech.eu/best-biotech/sustainable-biotechnology/, accessed April 15, 2021; Team Linchpin, "The Environmental Biotechnology Industry Trends for 2021," https://linchpinseo.com/trends-in-the-environmental-biotechnology-industry/, accessed April 15, 2021; Bio, "The Sustainability of Biotechnology," https://archive.bio.org/articles/sustainability-biotechnology, accessed April 15, 2021.

One of the primary tool bioethicists use is *proceduralism*. This involves elaborate protocols being established that ensure that certain classical worries, such as informed consent, are not violated. The focus is on being sure that appropriate procedures are being followed rather than on the actual ethical content of the decisions. This sounds similar to the concept of ethical due process discussed in an earlier chapter. The worry continues, however, over whether corporate executives and scientists are deceiving their own consciences by focusing on the *how* rather than the *why*, or the *means* rather than the *end*.[129]

Both critics and supporters say that the use of bioethicists lends companies an air of credibility. The real question is, "Can they really be objective if they are on a company's payroll?" Supporters say that yes, they function like a newspaper ombudsperson that gets paid by the paper to criticize coverage and prevent potential conflicts. Detractors say no, there's no way around a conflict of interest if money is changing hands. A real danger is that the participation of bioethicists may be interpreted as a stamp of approval.[130] If properly used, bioethicists can significantly add to the effectiveness of decision making in the biotechnology arena, just as ethics and compliance officers can add value in other organizations.

Of special interest in this section are two broad realms of biotechnology that help us appreciate some of the challenges in business ethics: genetic engineering and genetically modified organisms (GMOs). Genetic engineering, primarily of humans, and genetic engineering of agricultural and food products are both part of genetic science and have significant implications for business. For discussion purposes, however, we will treat them separately.

8.6b Genetic Engineering

Genetic engineering is defined as "the development and application of scientific methods, procedures, and technologies

that permit direct manipulation of genetic material in order to alter the hereditary traits of a cell, organism, or population."[131] The most controversial aspect of genetic engineering involves the applications to human beings. Two major areas of genetic engineering, or genetic science, seem to capture the public's imagination today. One is stem cell research and the second is cloning. Both pose enormous and interesting challenges for business and business ethics. Because these topics are so wide, deep, and specialized, we will turn our attention to topics that have much more significance in business today, cloning of animals for food and genetic testing and profiling.

Cloning Animals for Food. An important issue on the **cloning** front is that of companies wanting to clone animals for food. Scientists and consumer experts in the United States have been debating whether the country should become the first in the world to allow food from cloned animals onto supermarket shelves. Scientists and companies strongly support cloning for food, indicating they see the technology as an effective, important way to produce higher quality, healthier food. In the United States, the primary regulatory body for animal cloning is the Food and Drug Administration (FDA). After decades of study and analysis, the FDA has concluded that meat and milk from clones of cattle, swine, and goats, as well as their offspring, are as safe to consume as from conventionally bred animals.[132] The FDA continues to supervise regulations pertaining to this process. A related issue is whether food from cloned animals should be labeled as such. The FDA does not seem to think such labeling is necessary, but opponents say such labels are essential.

Opponents of cloning animals for food come from a large number of different consumer and scientific groups. Consumer advocate organizations such as the Center for Food Safety (CFS), Consumers Union, and the Consumer Federation of America, along with environmental and animal welfare groups, have raised issues with the idea. The CFS is representative of these groups. The CFS still urges further studies to ascertain the long-term risks and environmental threats associated with cloned animals. They continue to urge a moratorium on cloned animals into the food supply until adequate studies have been completed and the products are declared to be safe. They also think that cloned foods that are already in the food supply should be labelled to ensure public awareness.[133] The European Commission, which is the Executive Branch of the European Union (EU), has been more cautious about permitting cloned food items into the food supply, though they believe the cloned products to be as safe as conventionally bred animals.[134] The EU Novels Food Regulation 2015/2283 remains the applicable legislation, and it requires a pre-market authorization to be sold or imported into the EU.[135] It appears that this is likely to be an emotionally debated ethical issue for some time.

Genetic Testing and Profiling. Many questions have been raised about applications of biotechnology in **genetic testing**. Genetic testing became popular as a consumer product due to services offered by such firms as Ancestry and 23andMe. Beginning in 2020, it seems their popularity began to diminish somewhat, however. This may be because people's fears have been raised about companies using their personal information for targeted advertising, without their knowledge, and they have become sensitive about their health information.[136] Genetic testing has raised many questions, especially from both legal and ethical perspectives.[137] It has been speculated that someday each of us will have implanted in our bodies a DNA chip that contains all our genetic information. There are some positives associated with this. It will help each person manage personal health risks. It will also help a physician predict how well a patient will respond to various therapies. Future drugs will be developed using genetic information so that the therapy will be coupled with the DNA information. The privacy invasion implications are staggering, however, and this continues to be a debated topic.[138]

One result of genetic testing can be genetic profiling. **Genetic profiling** involves the use of biotechnology in identification of the unique characteristics of a person's DNA for forensic or diagnostic purposes. It is also referred to as DNA profiling.[139] Genetic profiling has proven to be acceptable and useful in cases such as diagnosing a disease for medical purposes or for forensic purposes in law enforcement.[140] It provides a perfect means for identifying a person and thus raises questions of privacy and possible discrimination based on genetic factors.[141] Though few companies actually use genetic profiling or genetic screening, the fear that this type of personal information might be used or abused for purposes of employment selection or other workplace decisions has elevated this topic to one of ethical concern.[142]

In terms of legal protections in the United States, the *Genetic Information Nondiscrimination Act* (*GINA*) was passed and took effect in 2009. Under GINA, it is illegal to discriminate against employees or applicants because of genetic information.[143] Other countries have developed or are rapidly developing similar laws as well.

8.6c Genetically Modified Organisms (GMOs)

Another highly debated category of biotechnology that carries important and more frequent ethical implications and debates for business is that of **genetically modified foods (GMFs)**, **genetically engineered foods (GEFs)**, or more frequently referred to as **genetically modified organisms (GMOs)**. GMOs are plants or animals created through the gene-splicing techniques of biotechnology (also called genetic engineering).[144] Products that are not used with GMOs are typically referred to as "organic." GMOs have been deeply embedded in the global food supply for decades. In the United States, for example, almost all corn, cotton, and soybeans have been genetically modified or engineered. In spite of this, issues have continued to be raised by environmental groups about GMOs and the processes of producing them. Some of the continuing concerns include lack of proper regulations, destruction of ecosystems, soil degradation, and community health impacts.[145]

Polls in the United States indicate that Americans remain divided over the safety of GMO products.[146] Similarly, the Pew Research Center reports that about half of many publics around the world doubt the safety of GMOs.[147]

Supporters of GMOs have emphasized that consumers have been eating foods containing them for more than 15 years and that there has been no credible evidence that people have been harmed. Critics say that just because there is no evidence of harm is not the same as saying they have been proved safe.[148]

The FDA has not determined that GMOs are unsafe but they continue to be monitored. The FDA, the Environmental Protection Agency (EPA), and the U.S. Department of Agriculture (USDA) have responsibility for ensuring that GMOs are safe for humans, the planet, and animal health.[149]

In addition to consumers who have a stake in GMOs, the multi-billion-dollar agribusiness industry has much at stake. What decisions are made regarding GMOs have significant implications for them and their investors as well.

The debate seems to hinge on whether the perceived pros or cons of GMOs will win out as the arguments are presented and experience is gained.

Labeling of GMOs. Since the safety of GMOs does not seem to be the major issue according to scientific research, the more urgent issue has become the question of whether foods that contain GMOs should be labeled when they are sold in grocery stores or served elsewhere. Many consumer activists think that, at a minimum, foods that contain genetically modified ingredients ought to be labeled as such. The Consumer

Ethics In Practice Case

Whole Foods: GMO Transparency or Clever Marketing?

Whole Foods Market, long known to be a reformist, sustainability-oriented supermarket chain selling natural products, startled the industry in early 2013 by announcing that it was embarking on a five-year plan to require labeling of genetically modified foods (GMFs) in its stores by 2018. Its decision came months after Proposition 37 in California was narrowly defeated in November 2012. Proposition 37 would have required disclosure labels on all foods that contained genetically engineered ingredients.

The FDA in the United States has found no research to support allegations that genetically engineered ingredients raise safety concerns greater than those found in traditionally grown products. And the FDA has not yet issued any regulations requiring GMF labeling, though some is being prepared. The World Health Organization (WHO) and the National Academy of Sciences (NAS) have found no evidence that GMFs are unsafe. But critics persist and say that there still may be some unknown harmful effects that in time will be revealed.

In the California battle, many of the large mainstream companies opposed the labeling measure. Supporters included smaller, natural foods companies such as Stonyfield Farm, Annie's, Clif Bar, Nature's Path Foods, and Whole Foods. Opponents of GMO labeling fear that such labeling will cause many consumers to think their products containing GMOs are unsafe.

Whole Foods has taken the position that the consumer has a right to know how its foods were produced and whether GMOs are present in any of its foods. The company already has seven stores in the United Kingdom, which already requires GMO labeling. According to Whole Foods, it is close to completely meeting the labeling standard of the USDA, and it requires its suppliers to comply with the standard as well. Plus, they expect that all non-GMO label claims be third-party verified or certified.

1. Do consumers have a right to know whether GMOs are present in products even if research has never found dangers associated with them? Why?
2. Will GMO labeling unfairly raise fears among consumers that such foods are unsafe when research has shown them not to be? Is this unfair to the grocer?
3. Do you believe Whole Foods honestly thinks GMO labeling is ethically justified, or is the company doing this as a strategic marketing decision to promote its sustainability image and reputation?
4. Is the Whole Food's approach a sustainable standard? Explain.

Sources: Whole Foods Market, "GMO Labeling," https://www.wholefoodsmarket.com/quality-standards/gmo-labeling, accessed April 15, 2021; RetailDetail, "Whole Foods Expands to Continental Europe," November 1, 2019, https://www.retaildetail.eu/en/news/food/whole-foods-expands-continental-europe, accessed April 15, 2021; Whole Foods Market, U.K., https://www.wholefoodsmarket.co.uk/, accessed April 15, 2021.

Federation of America Foundation, for example, continues to raise concerns about the current regulatory regime in the United States and whether enough is being done to protect consumer safety. They are especially critical of a proposal by the FDA to allow genetically engineered plant developers to self-determine whether the regulations apply to them and to keep secret the entry of GE products on the market. The FDA has not mandated labeling of GMOs, but it has issued a position statement regarding voluntary labeling.[150] In December 2018, the USDA published its National Bioengineered Food Disclosure Standard (the USDA Standard) requiring food manufacturers to disclose the presence of bioengineered (BE) ingredients by January 1, 2022.[151]

In spite of slow movement on the part of the regulators, the labeling issue will not go away. Proponents of mandatory labeling argue that the consumer has a right to full disclosure about product contents and that the consumers' right to safety holds that such knowledge should be available to them. Of special concern, the organic and natural foods market segment fears that genetically modified crops may be slipping into its products. This market segment strongly supports the Non-GMO Project.[152] The Non-GMO Project is a nonprofit collaboration of manufacturers, retailers, processors, distributors, farmers, seed companies, and consumers. The project's shared belief is "that everyone deserves an informed choice about whether or not to consume genetically modified products and our common mission is to ensure the sustained availability of non-GMO choices."[153] As of June 2020, 25 U.S. states either had passed GMO labeling requirements or were currently considering them with bills having been submitted to state legislative bodies.[154]

The issues of safety and labeling of GMOs continue unabated. Special-interest activist groups on both sides of the debate continue to be energetic in advocating their points of view. The agribusiness industry continues to argue that the foods are safe and that mandatory testing and labeling are not necessary and are needlessly expensive. The FDA does not seem inclined to impose any strenuous requirements on producers. Consumer activists, however, have brought together environmentalists, organic farmers, chefs, and religious leaders, and they continue to lobby for rigorous safety testing and labeling.[155] Some are wondering whether GMO foods are the answer to world hunger.[156]

As economies improve, the organic and natural foods market segment will start to grow again, and with it is likely to continue the expectation that these products will be differentiated by their non-GMO characteristic.

Summary

Business use of technology today is so dramatic that the topic merits this separate chapter. Big Data, artificial intelligence, and business analytics have become prominent issues. Basic concepts such as technology and the technological environment were introduced and defined. The benefits and costs of technology were considered. Questions regarding the ethics of technology were raised and the issue of surveillance was treated. Two broad areas of technology were raised: information technology and biotechnology.

In the realm of information technology, characterized by companies moving toward digital enterprises, the category with the most widespread current impact in business, topics included social media, cybersecurity, e-commerce, e-commerce ethics, invasion of consumer privacy, and workplace and computer ethics. Federal and state initiatives are in place to protect consumer privacy, while businesses' initiatives to protect consumer privacy include ethical leadership,

chief privacy officers, and data security. Questionable business practices included illegal downloading and monitoring technology. Computer technologies in the marketplace and workplace have had significant application, influence, and impact. Topics to watch closely include biometrics, robotics, use of cell phones, and texting.

The field of biotechnology was discussed with respect to social and ethical implications. A key topic in this sphere included the new field of bioethics. Arenas of biotechnology were identified and discussed. Included were the topics of genetic engineering, which included a discussion of cloning and genetic testing and profiling; also discussed was the topic of GMOs. It is anticipated that the debate over food safety and labeling will continue for years as different interest groups raise questions about the appropriateness and safety of GMOs. Newer regulations being passed in the United States, Europe, and around the world may quell some of the debate.

Key Terms

Artificial intelligence (AI), p. 177
Big Data, p. 177
bioethics, p. 190
biometrics, p. 188
biotechnology, p. 180
botnet scams, p. 185
botnets, p. 185
business analytics, p. 177
chief privacy officer (CPO), p. 186
cloning, p. 191
cobots, p. 189
cookies, p. 184
data security, p. 186
digital amnesia, p. 179
digital enterprise, p. 176

digital transformation, p. 176
e-commerce, p. 182
electronic commerce, p. 182
ethical lag, p. 180
ethical tech, p. 180
genetic engineering, p. 191
genetic profiling, p. 192
genetic testing, p. 192
genetically engineered foods (GEFs), p. 192
genetically modified foods (GMFs), p. 192
genetically modified organisms (GMOs), p. 192
Google Effect, p. 179

identity theft, p. 185
information technology (IT), p. 180
online scams, p. 183
phishing, p. 185
roboethics, p. 189
social media, p. 181
spam, p. 184
technoethics, p. 179
technological determinism, p. 180
technological environment, p. 178
technology, p. 178

Discussion Questions

1. Are there any benefits or negative side effects of technology in business that have not been mentioned in this chapter? Identify and discuss.

2. Is society intoxicated with technology? Does this pose special problems for business with respect to the ethics of technology? Will such intoxication blind people to ethical considerations in business?

3. Do you think business is abusing its power with respect to invasion of privacy of consumers? Is surveillance of consumers in the marketplace a fair and justified practice? Which particular practice do you think is the most questionable?

4. Is it an exaggeration to question the ethical implications for business of cell phone and text-messaging use? Discuss both sides of this issue.

5. Do you think genetically modified organisms (GMOs) raise a legitimate safety hazard? Should government agencies such as the FDA and USDA take more action to require safety testing? Do you think labeling unfairly stigmatizes GMOs and makes consumers question their safety?

Endnotes

1. Nancy Gibbs, "The Privacy Debate," *Time*, March 28, 2016, 6.
2. MIT Technology Review, "From Chief Technology Officer to CEO," September 29, 2020, https://www.technologyreview.com/2020/09/29/1008974/from-cto-to-ceo/. Accessed April 6. 2021.
3. Sharon Jayson, "iGeneration Has No Off Switch," *USA Today* (February 10, 2010), 1D, https://www.benton.org/headlines/igeneration-has-no-switch. Accessed April 6, 2021.
4. "Spotlight: Kids and Technology," *Time*, November 16, 2015, 25; also see "Nonprofit Spotlight: Kids-N-Technology," October 7, 2020, https://www.wbtv.com/video/2020/10/07/nonprofit-spotlight-kids-n-technology/. Accessed April 6, 2021.
5. Frederik Rosseel, "Is Your Business a Digital Enterprise?" Docbyte, https://www.docbyte.com/blog/is-your-business-a-digital-enterprise. Accessed April 7, 2021.
6. McKinsey Digital, "The Digital Enterprise," https://www.mckinsey.com/business-functions/mckinsey-digital/our-insights/the-digital-enterprise. Accessed April 7, 2021.
7. The Enterprisers Project, "What Is Digital Transformation?" https://enterprisersproject.com/what-is-digital-transformation#q1. Accessed April 7, 2021.
8. John Naisbitt, Nana Naisbitt, and Douglas Phillips, *High Tech/High Touch: Technology and Our Search for Meaning* (Nicholas Brealey Publishing Co, 1999).
9. Leon Wieseltier, "Among the Disrupted," *The New York Times Magazine* (January 18, 2015), 14.
10. SAS, "Big Data: What It Is and Why It Matters," https://www.sas.com/en_us/insights/big-data/what-is-big-data.html. Accessed April 7, 2021.
11. Omnisci, "Business Analytics," https://www.omnisci.com/technical-glossary/business-analytics. Accessed April 7, 2021.
12. B. J. Copeland, "Artificial Intelligence," *Brittanica*, https://www.britannica.com/technology/artificial-intelligence. Accessed April 7, 2021.
13. Steven Rosenbush and Michael Totty, "How Big Data Is Changing the Whole Equation for Business," *The Wall Street Journal* (March 11, 2013), R1, https://www.wsj.com/articles/SB10001424127887324178904578340071261396666. Accessed April 7, 2021.
14. Michael S. Malone, "The Big-Data Future Has Arrived," *The Wall Street Journal* (February 23, 2016), A17.
15. David Gewirtz, "Volume, Velocity, and Variety: Understanding the 3 V's of Big Data," ZDNet, March 21, 2018, https://www.zdnet.com/article/volume-velocity-and-variety-understanding-the-three-vs-of-big-data/. Accessed April 7, 2021.
16. Hugh J. Watson, "Avoid Being Creepy in the Use of Personal Data and Algorithms," *Business Intelligence Journal*, 24(1), March 2020.
17. Ibid.
18. Ibid.
19. Ibid.
20. Gregg Easterbrook, "Big Data, Big Problems," *Wall Street Journal*, April 23, 2018, A17.
21. Ted Greenwald, "How AI Is Transforming the Workplace," *The Wall Street Journal*, March 13, 2017, R1.
22. Kirsten Martin, "Ethical Implications and Accountability of Algorithms," *Journal of Business Ethics,* 160(4), 2019, 835–850.
23. Greenwald, 2017.
24. Stephen A. Schwarzman, "Can We Make Artificial Intelligence Ethical?" *Athens Banner Herald*, January 24, 2019, A4.
25. Pedro Uria-Recio, "5 Principles for Big Data," Toward Data Science, September 14, 2018, https://towardsdatascience.com/5-principles-for-big-data-ethics-b5df1d105cd3. Accessed April 8, 2021.
26. *Webster's Ninth New Collegiate Dictionary* (Springfield, MA: Merriam-Webster, Inc., 1983), 1211.
27. Ibid.
28. *"Technology,"* Dictionary.com, https://www.dictionary.com/browse/technology. Accessed April 8, 2021.
29. "Technology," *The World Book Encyclopedia* (Chicago, WorldBook, Inc., 2016).
30. Ibid.
31. Leon Wieseltier, "Among the Disrupted," *The New York Times Magazine*, January 18, 2015, 15.
32. "Technology," 2016, ibid, 80.
33. Dick Meyer, "Technology Creating World of 'Digital Amnesiacs,'" *Athens Banner Herald* (October 9, 2015), A4, https://www.onlineathens.com/article/20151009/OPINION/310099962. Accessed April 8, 2021.
34. Ibid.
35. Ibid.
36. Beverly Kracher and Cynthia L. Corritore, "Is There a Special E-Commerce Ethics?" *Business Ethics Quarterly* (January 23, 2015), 77, https://www.cambridge.org/core/journals/business-ethics-quarterly/article/abs/is-there-a-special-ecommerce-ethics/910C266F5FCD021233B266131F3D9568. Accessed April 8, 2021.
37. Brenna Sniderman, "Ethical Tech: Making Ethics a Priority in Today's Digital Organization," Digital Agenda, February 21, 2020, https://digitalagenda.io/insight/ethical-tech-making-ethics-a-priority/. Accessed April 8, 2021.
38. Ibid.
39. Ibid.
40. James Vincent, "Amazon Delivery Drivers Have to Consent to AI Surveillance in Their Vans or Lose Their Jobs," *The Verge*, (March 24, 2021), https://www.theverge.com/2021/3/24/22347945/amazon-delivery-drivers-ai-surveillance-cameras-vans-consent-form. Accessed April 16, 2021.
41. Elizabeth Woyke, "Attention Shoplifters: With $30 Billion in Theft, There's a Revolution in Surveillance Systems," *Business Week* (September 11, 2006), 46; also see Cognitech, https://www.cognitech.com/. Accessed March 11, 2016.
42. "Ethics and Morality of Video Surveillance," http://felenasoft.com/xeoma/en/articles/video-surveillance-ethics/. Accessed March 14, 2016.
43. Rich Castagna and Stephen Bigelow, "Information Technology (IT)," TechTarget, https://searchdatacenter.techtarget.com/definition/IT. Accessed April 9, 2021.
44. Investopedia, "What Is Social Media?" March15, 2021, https://www.investopedia.com/terms/s/social-media.asp. Accessed April 9, 2021.

45.   Ibid.

46.   CampusQuad, "The Evolution of Social Media Use among College Students," http://www.campusquad.co/evolution -social-media-use-among-college-students-2/. Accessed March 14, 2016.

47.   Reed Albergotti, "Websites Wary of Facebook Tracking," *The Wall Street Journal* (September 24, 2014), B1, https:// www.wsj.com/articles/websites-are-wary-of-facebook -tracking-software-1411513056. Accessed April 9, 2021.

48.   Reed Albergotti and Elizabeth Dwoskin, "Facebook Study Spurs Ethical Questions," *Wall Street Journal* (July 1, 2014), B1, https://www.wsj.com/articles/facebook-study -sparks-ethical-questions-1404172292. Accessed April 9, 2021.

49.   Yoree Koh and Reed Albergotti, "Twitter Faces Free-Speech Dilemma," *The Wall Street Journal* (August 22, 2014), B1, https://www.wsj.com/articles/twitter-is -walking-a-fine-line-confronted-with-grisly-images -1408659519. Accessed April 9, 2021.

50.   Jeremy Harris Lipschultz, *Huffpost Business*, "The Ethics of Social Media Accuracy," December 6, 2017, https://www.huffpost.com/entry/the-ethics-of-social -media_b_7489280. Accessed April 9, 2021.

51.   Ibid.

52.   Jason Lunday, "Managing the Workplace Ethics of Social Media," Corporate Compliance Insights, https:// www.corporatecomplianceinsights.com/managing-the -workplace-ethics-of-social-media/. Accessed April 9, 2021.

53.   Business Ethics Resource Center, "Five Principles for Avoiding Ethics Pitfalls on Social Media," https://www .businessethicsresourcecenter.org/five-principles-for -ethical-social-media/. Accessed April 9, 2021.

54.   "What Keeps CIOs Up at Night?" *The Wall Street Journal*, May 30, 2018, R1.

55.   Ibid.

56.   Steve Morgan, "Cybercrime to Cost the World $10.5 Trillion Annually by 2025," *Cybercrime Magazine*, November 13, 2020, https://cybersecurityventures.com /hackerpocalypse-cybercrime-report-2016/. Accessed April 9, 2021.

57.   David Morris and Robert Hackett, "After SolarWinds: Untangling America's Cybersecurity Mess," *Fortune*, February/March 2021, 63.

58.   Ibid, p. 64.

59.   Rob Sloan, "The Industries Most Vulnerable to Cyberattacks," *The Wall Street Journal*, June 22, 202, R1.

60.   Ibid., R4.

61.   Ibid., R4.

62.   Matt Burgus, "What Is the Internet of Things" https:// www.wired.co.uk/article/internet-of-things-what-is -explained-iot. Accessed April 12, 2021.

63.   TechTarget, "E-Commerce," https://searchcio.techtarget. com/definition/e-commerce. Accessed April 12, 2021.

64.   Amy Haimerl, "When You're a Small Business, e-Commerce is Tougher Than It Looks," *The New York Times* (March 7, 2021), https://www.nytimes.com/2021 /03/07/business/small-business-e-commerce.html. Accessed April 16, 2021.

65.   Fraud!Org, "Common Scams," https://fraud.org/common -scams/. Accessed April 12, 2021.

66.   Ibid.

67.   Kracher and Corritore, 71–94.

68.   Ibid., 78–82.

69.   To appreciate the different issues in which privacy arises, go to the website of Privacy Rights Clearinghouse, https:// privacyrights.org/. Accessed April 12, 2021.

70.   The EPIC Cookies Page, http://epic.org/privacy/internet /cookies/. Accessed March 16, 2016.

71.   Epic.org., "Spam," https://epic.org/privacy/junk_mail /spam/. Accessed April 12, 2021.

72.   Ibid.

73.   TED Blog, "What Data Is Being Collected on You? Some Shocking Information," https://blog.ted.com/what-data -is-being-collected-on-you-some-shocking-info/. Accessed April 12, 2021.

74.   "Phishing," Dictionary.com, https://www.dictionary.com /browse/phishing. Accessed April 12, 2021.

75.   APWG, "Phishing Activity Trends Report, 2020," https:// apwg.org/trendsreports/. Accessed April 12, 2021.

76.   SentinelOne, "What Is a Botnet (and Why They Are Dangerous)?" https://www.sentinelone.com/blog/what-is-a -botnet-and-why-are-they-dangerous/?utm_adgroup =118513729154&utm_type=b&utm_target=dsa -19959388920&utm_device=c&utm_medium=cpc&utm _source=google&utm_campaign=11908692948&utm _content=488210496953&utm_term=&gclid =Cj0KCQjw38-DBhDpARIsADJ3kjldRQzX_n _RDiKDI3i2aX2z3xAswieoMLnd5X-t-wR9GhPGE _giv1oaAhHtEALw_wcB. Accessed April 12, 2021.

77.   Ibid.

78.   Iapp, "An Overview of the Senate's Proposed Privacy Bill of Rights Act," https://iapp.org/news/a/an-overview-of-the -u-s-senates-proposed-privacy-bill-of-rights-act/. Accessed April 12, 2021.

79.   State of California Office of the Attorney General, "California Consumer Privacy Act," https://oag.ca.gov /privacy/ccpa. Accessed April 12, 2021.

80.   European Commission, "Data Protection in the EU," https://ec.europa.eu/info/law/law-topic/data-protection /data-protection-eu_en. Accessed April 12, 2021.

81.   Federal Trade Commission, "Protecting Consumer's Financial Privacy," https://www.ftc.gov/news-events /media-resources/protecting-consumer-privacy/financial -privacy. Accessed April 12, 2021.

82.   Federal Trade Commission, *Protecting Consumer Privacy in an Era of Rapid Change: Recommendations for Businesses and Policy Makers*, January 12, 2015, https:// www.amazon.com/Protecting-Consumer-Privacy-Rapid -Change/dp/1507525419. Accessed April 12, 2021.

83.   Ibid.

84.   The Walt Disney Company, "Privacy Policy," https://privacy .thewaltdisneycompany.com/en/. Accessed April 12, 2021.

85.   McKinsey & Co., "The Consumer-Data Opportunity and the Privacy Imperative," April 27, 2020. Accessed April 12, 2021.

86.   Stanford Lawyer, "Chief Privacy Officers," June 25, 2020, https://law.stanford.edu/stanford-lawyer/articles/chief -privacy-officers/. Accessed April 12, 2021.

87.   The Conference Board, "Chief Privacy Officers Council," https://conference-board.org/councils/chief-privacy -officers. Accessed April 12, 2021.

88.   Ibid.

89.   EastIdahoNews.Com, "Why Data Security Is Even More Crucial to Your Business in 2021," April 12, 2021, https:// www.eastidahonews.com/lifestyles/why-data-security-is -even-more-crucial-to-your-business-in-2021/. Accessed April 13, 2021.

90. Ibid.

91. IdentityForce, "2021 Data Breaches – The Worst So Far," https://www.identityforce.com/blog/2021-data-breaches. Accessed April 13, 2021.

92. Chuck Brooks, "Alarming Cybersecurity Stats: What You Need to Know for 2021." Forbes, March 2, 2021, https://www.forbes.com/sites/chuckbrooks/2021/03/02/alarming-cybersecurity-stats-------what-you-need-to-know-for-2021/?sh=40ed5fa758d3. Accessed April 13, 2021.

93. John Jurgensen and Barbara Chai, "Apple to Pay Artists after Taylor Swift's Protests," *The Wall Street Journal* (June 22, 2015), https://www.wsj.com/articles/taylor-swift-withholds-album-from-apple-music-1434916050#:~:text=AAPL%201.92%25%20backed%20off%20its,powerhouse%20pop%20star%20Taylor%20Swift.&text=Swift%20released%20an%20open%20letter,included%20in%20the%20streaming%20service. Accessed April 13, 2021.

94. RIAA, "About RIAA," https://www.riaa.com/about-riaa/. Accessed April 13, 2021.

95. Ibid.

96. Roxana Robinson, "How Google Stole the Work of Millions of Authors," *The Wall Street Journal* (February 8, 2016), A13, https://www.wsj.com/articles/how-google-stole-the-work-of-millions-of-authors-1454880410#:~:text=In%202004%20Google%20sent%20its,books%20not%20covered%20by%20copyright.&text=The%20Authors%20Guild%20challenged%20what%20Google%20was%20doing%20in%20Authors%20Guild%20v. Accessed April 13, 2021.

97. Wolfi Christl, Cracked Labs, "Corporate Surveillance in Everyday Life," June 2017, https://crackedlabs.org/en/corporate-surveillance. Accessed April 14, 2021.

98. Ibid.

99. Ibid.

100. Matt Smith, "Ethical Data Collection Strategies for a Digital World," Cazbah, https://www.cazbah.net/proper-data-collection/. Accessed April 14, 2021.

101. Miki Markovich, "Negative Effects of Computers in the Workplace," Chron., March 6, 2019, https://smallbusiness.chron.com/negative-effects-computers-workplace-22023.html. Accessed April 14, 2021.

102. *The Economist*, "Biometrics Gets Down to Business," https://www.economist.com/technology-quarterly/2006/12/02/biometrics-gets-down-to-business. Accessed April 14, 2021.

103. Amiram Pinto, "Understanding the Types of Biometrics," November 12, 2019, https://www.nice.com/engage/blog/rta-understanding-the-types-of-biometrics-2513/. Accessed April 14, 2021.

104. Ibid.

105. Ibid.

106. Biometrics Institute, "International Standards," https://www.biometricsinstitute.org/what-is-biometrics/standards/. Accessed April 14, 2021.

107. Susan Galer, "The Four Most Important Digital Automation Trends Circa 2021." Fortune, February 16, 2021, https://www.forbes.com/sites/sap/2021/02/16/the-four-most-important-digital-automation-trends-circa-2021/?sh=51edb21f3e74. Accessed April 14, 2021.

108. Greg Nichols, "Automation Nation: 9 Robotic Predictions for 2021," December 30, 2020, https://www.zdnet.com/article/automation-nation-9-robotics-predictions-for-2021/. Accessed April 14, 2021.

109. Ibid.

110. A. W. Geiger, "How Americans See Automation and the Workplace in 7 Charts," Pew Research Center, April 8, 2019, https://www.pewresearch.org/fact-tank/2019/04/08/how-americans-see-automation-and-the-workplace-in-7-charts/. Accessed April 14, 2021.

111. Natasha Khan, "Robots Shift from Factories to New Jobs," *The Wall Street Journal*, June 11, 2018, B4.

112. WhatIs.com, "Roboethics (robot ethics)," https://whatis.techtarget.com/definition/roboethics-robot-ethics. Accessed April 14, 2021.

113. "Robot Ethics: Morals and the Machine," *The Economist*, June 2, 2012, https://www.economist.com/leaders/2012/06/02/morals-and-the-machine. Accessed April 15, 2021.

114. Ibid; also see Jerry Kaplan, "Can We Create an Ethical Robot?" *The Wall Street Journal* (July 24, 2015), https://www.wsj.com/articles/can-we-create-an-ethical-robot-1437758519. Accessed April 14, 2021.

115. Clive Thompson, "Texting Isn't the First Technology Thought to Impair Social Skills," Smithsonian Magazine, March, 2016, https://www.smithsonianmag.com/innovation/texting-isnt-first-new-technology-thought-impair-social-skills-180958091/. Accessed April 14, 2021.

116. NHTSA, "Distracted Driving," https://www.nhtsa.gov/risky-driving/distracted-driving. Accessed April 14, 2021.

117. Bankrate, "Distracted Driving Statistics and Facts, 2021," March 10, 2021, https://www.bankrate.com/insurance/car/distracted-driving-statistics/. Accessed April 14, 2021.

118. YourLegalGuide.com, "Cell Phone Car Accidents," http://www.yourlegalguide.com/cell-phone-accidents/. Accessed April 14, 2021.

119. Paul Lannon and Phillip Schreiber, "BYOD Policies: What Employers Need to Know," February 1, 2016, https://www.shrm.org/hr-today/news/hr-magazine/Pages/0216-BYOD-policies.aspx. Accessed April 14, 2021.

120. Ibid.

121. Amanda Mujica, Edward Petry, and Dianne Vickery, "A Future for Technology and Ethics," *Business and Society Review*, 104(3), https://onlinelibrary.wiley.com/doi/abs/10.1111/0045-3609.00055. Accessed April 14, 2021.

122. Thomas Hilton, "Information System Ethics: A Practitioner Survey," *Journal of Business Ethics* (December, 2000), 279–284, https://link.springer.com/article/10.1023/A:1006274825363. Accessed April 15, 2021.

123. Catherine Bannister, "Ethical Technology and Trust," Deloitte, January 15, 200, https://www2.deloitte.com/us/en/insights/focus/tech-trends/2020/ethical-technology-and-brand-trust.html. Accessed April 14, 2021.

124. Walter Isaacson, "The Biotech Century," *Time* (January 11, 1999), 42–43.

125. Bio, "What Is Biotechnology?" https://www.bio.org/what-biotechnology. Accessed April 15, 2021.

126. Ibid.

127. Ibid.

128. Center for Practical Bioethics, "What Is Bioethics?" https://www.practicalbioethics.org/what-is-bioethics. Accessed April 15, 2021.

129. "Bioethics: Wanna Buy a Bioethicist?" *Christianity Today* (October 1, 2001), 32–33, https://www.christianitytoday.com/ct/2001/october1/24.32.html; also see M. D. Taylor, "Reconceiving Bioethical Proceduralism," EuropePMC, May 1, 2019, https://europepmc.org/article/med/31206294. Accessed April 15, 2021.

130. Nell Boyce, "And Now, Ethics for Sale," Institute for Agriculture & Trade Policy, https://www.iatp.org/news/and-now-ethics-for-sale. Accessed April 15, 2021.

131. "Genetic Engineering," Dictionary.com, https://www.dictionary.com/browse/genetic-engineering. Accessed April 15, 2021.

132. Food and Drug Administration, "Animal Cloning and Food Safety," https://www.fda.gov/consumers/consumer-updates/animal-cloning-and-food-safety. Accessed April 15, 2021,

133. Center for Food Safety, "About Cloned Animals," https://www.centerforfoodsafety.org/issues/302/animal-cloning/about-cloned-animals. Accessed April 15, 2021.

134. "Biotechnology: Cloning Animals for Food to Be Banned in the E.U." September 8, 2015, http://news.discovery.com/tech/biotechnology/cloning-animals-for-food-to-be-banned-in-eu-150908.htm. Accessed March 25, 2016.

135. USDA, "Animal Cloning," https://www.usda-eu.org/topics/animal-cloning/#:~:text=The%20EU%20Novel%20Foods%20Regulation,or%20sold%20in%20the%20EU. Accessed April 15, 2021.

136. Christina Farr, "Consumer DNA Testing Hits a Rough Patch: Here's How Companies Like Ancestry and 23andMe Can Survive," August 26, 2020, https://www.usda-eu.org/topics/animal-cloning/#:~:text=The%20EU%20Novel%20Foods%20Regulation,or%20sold%20in%20the%20EU. Accessed April 15, 2021.

137. Medscape, "Ethical Issues in Genetic Testing," https://www.medscape.com/viewarticle/505222_4. Accessed April 15, 2021.

138. Ibid.

139. The Free Dictionary, "genetic profiling," https://www.thefreedictionary.com/genetic+profiling#:~:text=Noun,genetic%20fingerprinting. Accessed April 15, 2021.

140. Lindsey Van Ness, "DNA Databases Are a Boon to Police, but a Menace to Privacy," February 20, 2020, https://www.pewtrusts.org/en/research-and-analysis/blogs/stateline/2020/02/20/dna-databases-are-boon-to-police-but-menace-to-privacy-critics-say. Accessed April 15, 2021.

141. Taunton-Rigby, 18–19.

142. Claire Andre and Manuel Valasquez, "Genetic Screening in the Workplace," November 13, 2015, https://www.scu.edu/ethics/focus-areas/bioethics/resources/read-my-genes-genetic-screening-in-the-workplace/. Accessed April 15, 2021.

143. U.S. Equal Employment Opportunity Commission, "Genetic Information Discrimination," https://www.eeoc.gov/genetic-information-discrimination. Accessed April 15, 2021.

144. Green America, ""Genetically Engineered Crops 7 GMOs," https://www.greenamerica.org/gmos-stop-ge-wheat/better-sources-wheat-genetic-engineering-gmos-organic-food-farmers-stop-ge-wheat/genetic-. Accessed April 15, 2021.

145. "Ibid.

146. Helen Christophi, "Poll: Americans Divided over Safety of GMO Products," November 19, 2018, https://www.courthousenews.com/poll-americans-divided-over-safety-of-gmo-products/. Accessed April 15, 2021.

147. Brian Kennedy and Cary Lynne Thigpen, "Many Publics Around the World Doubt Safety of Genetically Modified Foods," Pew Research Center, November 11, 2020, https://www.courthousenews.com/poll-americans-divided-over-safety-of-gmo-products/. Accessed April 15, 2021.

148. Ibid.

149. U.S. Food and Drug Administration, "How GMOs Are Regulated for Food and Plant Safety in the United States," April 22, 2020, https://www.fda.gov/food/agricultural-biotechnology/how-gmos-are-regulated-food-and-plant-safety-united-states. Accessed April 15, 2021.

150. U.S. Food and Drug Administration, ibid.

151. Whole Food Markets, "GMO Labeling," https://www.wholefoodsmarket.com/quality-standards/gmo-labeling. Accessed April 15, 2021.

152. Non-GMO Project,

153. Non-GMO Project, https://www.nongmoproject.org/. Accessed April 15, 2021.

154. National Conference of State Legislatures, "State Legislation Addressing Genetically Modified Organisms," June 2, 2020, https://www.ncsl.org/research/agriculture-and-rural-development/state-legislation-addressing-genetically-modified-organisms-report.aspx. Accessed April 15, 2021.

155. ibid.

156. National Geographic, "Are Genetically Modified Crops the Answer to World Hunger?" January 28, 2020, https://www.nationalgeographic.org/article/are-genetically-modified-crops-answer-world-hunger/. Accessed April 15, 2021.

Part 4

Corporate Governance and Strategic Management Issues

Chapter 9
Corporate Governance: Foundational Issues

Chapter 10
Strategy, Risk, Issues, and Crisis Management

9

Corporate Governance: Foundational Issues

Chapter Learning Outcomes

After studying this chapter, you should be able to:

1. Link the issue of legitimacy to corporate governance.
2. Discuss the problems that have led to the recent spate of corporate scandals and problems in corporate governance.
3. Discuss the principal ways in which companies can improve corporate governance.
4. Discuss the role of shareholders and the idea of strengthening shareholder voice. What are some of the mechanisms that enable this?
5. Discuss the role of the Securities and Exchange Commission (SEC) in protecting investors.

6. Identify and discuss the principal ways in which shareholder activists exert pressure on corporate management to improve governance.
7. Why are investor relations and shareholder engagement important? Discuss.
8. Compare and contrast the shareholder-primacy, director-primacy, and stakeholder governance models of corporate governance. What are their respective strengths and weaknesses? Which do you prefer and why?
9. In the realm of corporate governance, what should companies do to ensure effective corporate social responsibility (CSR), sustainability, and business ethics?

In Part IV of this book, we more closely examine how management has responded, and *should* respond, to the social, ethical, and stakeholder issues developed throughout this book. This chapter explores the ways in which company boards of directors and top managers govern the corporation. In Chapter 10, the view expands to look at how these social, ethical, and stakeholder issues fit into not only the strategy of the firm but also the management of risk, issues, and crises.

We begin by examining the concept of legitimacy and the part that corporate governance plays in establishing the legitimacy of business. Then, the role of social activism is introduced as both establishing and challenging the legitimacy of business. We then explore how good corporate governance can mitigate the problems created by the separation of ownership and control and examine some of the specific challenges facing those involved in corporate governance today. All of these concepts help to improve businesses' CSR, sustainability, and business ethics.

9.1 Legitimacy and Corporate Governance

Corporate governance took center stage at the dawn of the 21st century. The bankruptcy of Enron, once the seventh-largest company in the United States, as well as those of corporate giants WorldCom and Parmalat, sent shock waves through the corporate world. When a host of firms subsequently issued earnings restatements, investors throughout the world began wondering where they could place their trust. A few years later, the global financial crisis struck and investors were stunned as they watched their life savings shrivel.

More recently, the Wells Fargo fraud/fake accounts scandal, Purdue Pharma's role in the opioid drug crisis, the Nissan CEO's alleged financial misconduct, and Theranos' fake blood-testing kits further chip away at the public's trust. Events like these threaten the institution of business as a whole by calling the legitimacy of the institution of business into question. For example, in a 2020 Gallup poll, people had more confidence in the military, the public schools, and even the newspapers than they had in big business.[1] As noted by one governance expert, "We can do better. And with trillions of dollars of wealth governance by these rules of the game, we must do better."[2]

More and more, the upper echelons of business, which include board members and executives, are also expected to take on social issues. Environmental, social, and governance issues (ESG), which we discussed in Chapter 4, are now a regular part of a board's agenda, but much more work needs to be done in these areas. In fact, in PwC's annual Corporate Directors survey, which includes responses from more than 600 public board directors, only half (51 percent) say their board fully understands ESG issues impacting the company.[3]

To understand corporate governance, it is important to understand the idea of **legitimacy**. Legitimacy is a somewhat abstract concept, but it is vital in that it helps explain the importance of the relative roles of a corporation's charter, shareholders, board of directors, management, and employees—all of which are components of the modern corporate governance system. Legitimacy is a condition that prevails when there is congruence between the organization's activities and society's expectations.[4] Thus, whereas legitimacy is a condition, **legitimation** is a dynamic process by which business seeks to perpetuate its acceptance by the public. We emphasize the dynamic process aspect because society's norms and values change, and business must change if its legitimacy is to continue. It is also useful to consider legitimacy at both the micro, or company, level and the macro, or business system, level.

At the *micro level of legitimacy*, we refer to individual business firms achieving and maintaining legitimacy by conforming to societal expectations. Companies seek legitimacy in several ways. First, a company may adapt its methods of operating to conform to what it perceives to be the prevailing standard. For example, a company may discontinue door-to-door selling if that marketing approach comes to be viewed in the public mind as a shoddy sales technique,[5] or a pharmaceutical company may discontinue offering free drug samples to physicians if this practice begins to take on the aura of a bribe. Second, a company may try to change the public's values and norms to conform to its own practices by advertising and other techniques.[6] For example, vitamin retailer GNC Holdings, Inc. has been successful at this in their promotion of nutritional supplements.[7]

Finally, an organization may seek to enhance its legitimacy by identifying itself with other organizations, people, values, or symbols that have a powerful legitimate base in society.[8] This occurs at several levels. At the national level, companies proudly announce appointments of celebrities, former politicians, or other famous people to managerial positions or board directorships. For example, a recent study found that more than 45 percent of senators who have left office since 1992 have served on the board of a publicly traded firm.[9] At the community level, a company may ask the winning local football coach to provide an endorsement by sitting on its board or promoting its products.[10]

The *macro level of legitimacy* is the level with which we are most concerned in this chapter. The macro level refers to the corporate system—the totality of business enterprises. It is difficult to talk about the legitimacy of business in pragmatic terms at this level. Business is such a potpourri of institutions of different shapes, sizes, and industries that saying anything conclusive about it is difficult. Yet, this is an important level at which business needs to be concerned about its legitimacy. What is at stake is the acceptance of the form of business as an institution in our society.

Business must now accept that it has a **fragile mandate**. It must realize that its legitimacy is constantly subject to ratification, and it must realize that it has no inherent right to exist. Business exists solely because society has given it that right.[11] In this sense, business is a public institution as well as a private entity.[12] When the legitimacy of business as an

institution in society is in question, political and social factors may overshadow economic factors to change the future of the institution of business in profound ways.[13]

Social activism plays a role in the fragile mandate of business. Social activists work to promote or impede changes in business or government policies and influence the actions of individuals and groups. Social activists can enhance a company's legitimacy when they throw their support behind a company, or they can cause a company to lose legitimacy when they publicly criticize or critique a company's actions. Hence, executives are often faced with aligning their firms with popular social causes and asked to show leadership on social problems such as racial inequity, racial justice, and climate change.[14] Should the company come down on the wrong side of the issue, however, its legitimacy could be called into question. **Corporate social activism** occurs when businesses advocate that government change public policies on social or moral issues, and we discuss this in more depth in Chapters 11 and 12.

In comparing the micro view of legitimacy with the macro view, it is clear that, although specific business organizations try to perpetuate their own legitimacy, the corporate or business system as a whole rarely addresses the issue at all, and it is often up to social activists to remind business leaders of the fragility of business in society. This is unfortunate because the spectrum of powerful issues regarding business conduct clearly indicates that such institutional introspection is necessary if business is to survive and prosper. If business is to continue to justify its right to exist, we must remember the question of legitimacy and its operational ramifications.

9.1a The Purpose of Corporate Governance

The purpose of corporate governance is a direct outgrowth of the question of legitimacy. The word *governance* comes from the Greek word for steering.[15] The way in which a corporation is governed determines the direction in which it is steered. Owners of small private firms can steer the firm on their own; however, the shareholders who are the owners of public firms must count on boards of directors to make certain that their companies are steered properly in their absence. For business to be legitimate and to maintain its legitimacy in the eyes of the public, it must be steered in a way that corresponds to the will of the people.

Corporate governance refers to the method by which a firm is being governed, directed, administered, or controlled and to the goals for which it is being governed. Corporate governance is concerned with the relative roles, rights, and accountability of such stakeholder groups as owners, boards of directors, managers, employees, and others who have a stake in the firm's governance.

9.1b Components of Corporate Governance

This chapter focuses on the **Anglo-American model**, which we explain in detail below, is characterized as having outside directors, following common law, with a market-oriented and shareholder-oriented governance. This is often contrasted with the **Continental-European** (or "Rhineland") **model**, where inside directors and civil law dominate, as well as block ownership and bank-orientation and stakeholder-coordinated governance.[16] We focus on the Anglo-American model because forces for a global convergence on this model are notably strong, albeit debatable.[17] These forces include support from global institutional investors, as well as accountants and regulators who feel comfortable with rules-based accounting standards.[18]

The Anglo-American model has historically been considered a shareholder-primacy model because shareholders have primary importance. However, recently, there has been a movement in the United States to redefine the purpose of the corporation to a more stakeholder-oriented model. This shift was legitimized with a 2019 announcement by the **Business Roundtable (BRT)**, a group representing more than 181 CEOs of large publicly traded companies, that affirmed that their businesses are committed to meeting the needs and providing long-term value to all of their stakeholders, not just shareholders.[19] The challenge of implementing a more stakeholder governance model is difficult at best, particularly as CEO compensation models are often aligned with share price; hence, the BRT announcement was met with much speculation.[20] Additionally, a year after the announcement, one report found that most of the companies whose CEOs signed the commitment did not follow through with increased stakeholder commitments relative to their peers, as well as their pledges.[21] Therefore, it remains to be seen whether stakeholder capitalism discussed in Chapter 3 will become a reality.

However, there is a growing trend in the United States and Europe toward increasing the scope of the board of directors and management discretion, as regulators begin to embrace a principles-based accounting framework, which provides fewer exceptions to accounting issues than a traditional rules-based system.[22] Hence, it is not surprising that there are shifting views about shareholder primacy. Additionally, the COVID-19 pandemic has been seen as an inflection point for corporate governance, as boards face demands from a variety of stakeholders with heightened expectations for corporate citizenship.[23] Later in this chapter we will discuss a director-primacy model of corporate governance that aligns with this trend and is receiving increasing attention.[24]

Roles of Four Major Groups. The four major groups we need to discuss in setting the stage for the shareholder-primacy model of corporate governance are the shareholders (owner-stakeholders), the board of directors, the managers, and the employees. Overarching these groups is the **charter** issued by the state, giving the corporation the right to exist and stipulating the basic terms of its existence, including corporate governance practices. Figure 9-1 presents these four groups, along with the state charter, in a hierarchy of corporate governance authority.

Shareholders own stock in the firm and, according to the shareholder-primacy model, this gives them ultimate control over the corporation as the firm's owners. This control is manifested in the right to select the board of directors of the company and to vote on shareholder resolutions that are proposed at annual meetings. Generally, the number of shares of stock owned determines the degree of each shareholder's right. The individual who owns 100 shares of Apple Computer, for example, has 100 "votes" when electing the board of directors. By contrast, the large public pension fund that owns 10 million shares has 10 million "votes."

Because large organizations may have hundreds of thousands of shareholders, they elect a smaller group, known as the **board of directors**, to govern and oversee the management of the business. Under the shareholder-primacy model, the purpose of the board is to ascertain that the manager puts the interests of the shareholders first. The third major

Figure 9-1 The Corporation's Hierarchy of Authority

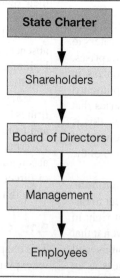

group in the authority hierarchy is the **management**—the group of individuals hired by the board to run the company and manage it on a daily basis. Along with the board, the top management team establishes the overall policy. Middle- and lower-level managers carry out this policy and conduct the daily supervision of the operative employees. **Employees** are those hired by the company to perform the actual operational work. Managers are employees, too, but in this discussion, we use the term *employees* to refer to non-managerial employees.

Separation of Ownership from Control. The major condition embedded in the Anglo-American model of modern corporations that has contributed to the corporate governance problem has been the **separation of ownership from control**. This problem did not exist before corporations came into being. In the precorporate period, owners were typically the managers themselves; thus, the system worked the way it was intended, with the owners also controlling the business. Even when firms grew larger and managers were hired, the owners were often on the scene to hold the management group accountable. For example, if a company got in trouble, the Carnegies, or Mellons, or Morgans, as owners, were always there to fire the president.[25]

As the public corporation grew and stock ownership became widely dispersed, shareholders (owners) became more distant from managers (including the CEO) and a separation of ownership from control became the prevalent condition. Figure 9-2 illustrates the precorporate and corporate periods. The dispersion of ownership into hundreds of thousands or millions of shares meant that essentially no one person or group owned enough shares to exercise control. This being the case, the most effective control that owners could exercise was the election of the board of directors to serve as their representatives and watch over the management.

The problem with this evolution was that true authority, power, and control began to rest with the group that had the most concentrated interest at stake—the management. The shareholders were owners in a technical sense, but most of them did not perceive themselves as owners. If you owned 100 shares of Walt Disney Company and there were 10 million shares outstanding, you would be more likely to see yourself as an investor than you would be to see yourself as an owner. With just a telephone call issuing a sell order to your stockbroker, your "ownership" stake could be gone. Furthermore, with stock ownership so dispersed, no real supervision of corporate boards was possible.

The other factors that added to management's power were the corporate laws and traditions that gave the management group control over the proxy process—the method by which the shareholders elected boards of directors. Technically, the board hires and fires managers, but eventually managers were able to subvert that process. Over time, managers, especially CEOs, were able to influence board member selection so that boards of directors became filled with like-minded executives who would too often defer to the management on whatever it wanted. The result of this process was the opposite of what was originally intended: power, authority, and control began to flow upward from the management rather than downward from the shareholders (owners).

Agency problems developed in the separation of ownership and control when the interests of the shareholders were not aligned with the interests of the managers, and the managers (who are hired *agents* with the responsibility of representing the owners' best interests) began to pursue self-interest instead of the owners' best interests. Managers as agents have the ability to do this because they have more information about the workings of the organization than the shareholders do. For example, managers of the corporation may try to grow the company to avoid a firm's takeover

Figure 9-2 Precorporate versus Corporate Ownership and Control

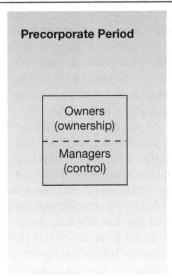
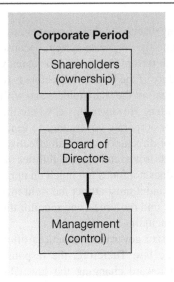

Ethics In Practice Case

May I Have a Little "Perk" with That Compensation Package?

Perquisites, otherwise known as "perks," are benefits, money, or goods that an employee is entitled to, based on a particular status. Perks can include a membership to a club, a parking benefit, payment of life insurance premiums, or complimentary access to an athletic club, among other benefits. They are commonly included in executive packages and can play an important role in recruiting and retaining executives. For example, Alphabet CEO Sundar Pichai has access to personal use of a company aircraft including on-board catering, while IBM CEO Ginni Rometty has access to personal security and the ability to have her family attend business-related events at the company's expense.

When are perks considered excessive? While CEO Schiller of Energy XXI (now Cox Oil) had use of a company card, he submitted business expenses that the SEC ended up investigating, including $40,000 for a bottle of wine, $36,000 for a shopping trip for board members' and senior officers' partners, and $43,000 for the use of company aircraft to attend a college football game. More than half of the Fortune 100 executives can use a company jet for their personal use or to bring partners, families, or friends along on a business trip with them; additionally, nearly 10 percent of this group can also get reimbursements of the taxes they accrue by flying on the aircraft. According to a recent Equilar survey, shareholders do not often object to perks, but they want to understand the business need. Perhaps most controversial are "Flex Perks," which are allowances that executives can use for almost anything they want.

1. Do you believe that executives are entitled to these perks? What are the arguments on either side of this debate?
2. How much is too much? What might determine the number of perks awarded to a CEO or top management team member?
3. What stakeholders are involved, when considering the potential benefits/harms of executive perks?
4. Why do boards give CEOs such generous perks? Could it be because they, too, receive generous perks (like attending meetings at nice resorts)? What is the conflict of interest here?

Sources: Catey Hill, "8 CEO Perks That Will Make You Angry," *MarketWatch* (January 18, 2017), https://www.marketwatch.com /story/8-ceo-perks-that-will-make-you-angry-2016-01-28, accessed March 4, 2021; "What Are Perquisites and What Role Do They Play in Executive Compensation Packages?," *Veritas* (August 25, 2020), https://veritasecc.com/insights/what-are-perquisites-and-what-role-do-they-play-in-executive-compensation-packages/, accessed March 4, 2021. Laura Woods, "The Most Outrageous CEO Salaries and Perks," *GOBanking Rates* (August 3, 2020), https://www.gobankingrates.com/net-worth/business-people /outrageous-ceo-salaries-perks/#15, accessed March 4, 2021; "Executive Benefits and Perquisites," Equilar (January 27, 2016), https://www.equilar.com/reports/31-executive-benefits-and-perquisites.html, accessed March 4, 2021.

attempt in an effort to increase their own job security. However, a takeover may be in the shareholders' best interests. Similarly, managers may consume corporate resources in the form of perquisites ("perks") like extra vacation time or the use of the company's jet.

9.2 Problems in Corporate Governance

It is clear from the preceding discussion that a potential governance problem is built into the corporate system because of the separation of ownership from control and the agency problems that result. The duty of the board of directors is to oversee management on behalf of the shareholders and with full regard for the stakeholders. However, this is where the system can break down. For corporate governance to function effectively, the board of directors must be an effective, potent body carrying out its roles and responsibilities. It must create a culture that does not focus too much on maximizing short-term results, and it must attract the right mix of directors that can advise, find resources, and monitor the behavior of management, including the CEO.

Surprisingly, bad corporate governance practices often fall within the letter of the law. Therefore, the response to them has been geared toward changing the law. The Sarbanes–Oxley Act (SOX) was a response to the problems that stemmed from Enron and WorldCom and the like, and the Dodd–Frank Wall Street Reform and Consumer Protection Act were a response to the global financial crisis. We will discuss them later in this chapter.

To be fair, corporate governance is a complex process, and even a well-designed board is no guarantee of success. Nevertheless, boards have improved, and they continue to improve in many ways. In the 2020 *PwC* survey of corporate directors, director sentiment seems to have shifted toward a longer-term focus, even under the shadow of the COVID-19 pandemic crisis.[26] More than half said their company had established protocols and practices around preparing for director-shareholder interactions—a newer corporate governance issue surrounding shareholder engagement, which we discuss later in the chapter.[27]

As we discuss the failings of corporate governance in the past decades, we must keep in mind that boards share in the blame but are not responsible for all of it. They are not superheroes, and we should not expect them to be.[28] This is particularly true during times of crisis, like the COVID-19 pandemic, where board turnover has created a void of experienced directors who have navigated through other crises, like the global financial crisis.[29] However, even many directors themselves believe that their boards are falling short in creating value for their stakeholders.[30]

9.2a The Importance of Board Independence

Board independence from management is a crucial aspect of good governance. It is here that the difference between inside directors and outside directors becomes most pronounced. **Outside directors** are independent from the firm and its top managers. They can come from a variety of backgrounds (e.g., top managers of other firms, academics, former government officials), but the one thing they have in common is that they have no other substantive relationship to the firm or its CEO. In contrast, **inside directors** have ties of some sort to the firm. They can be top managers in the firm, family members, or others with a professional or personal relationship to the firm or to the CEO. To varying degrees, inside directors may be "beholden" to the CEO and less objective in decision making; therefore, they might be hesitant to speak out when necessary. Since the implosion of Enron and its aftermath, changes in public policy and public opinion have led to an increase in the percentage of independent directors.

9.2b Issues Surrounding Compensation

The issue of executive pay is a lightning rod for those who think that CEOs are placing their own interests over those of their shareholders. For example, people became outraged when they heard that Wall Street firms gave out $18.2 billion as bonuses in 2008 as the economy crumbled. In 2017, the Securities and Exchange Commission (SEC) approved a new rule, the **CEO Pay Ratio**, that would require most public companies to regularly reveal the ratio of chief executive's pay to that of employees.[31] However, outrage over the widening pay gap between CEOs and rank-and-file employees continues today, with the Economic Policy Institute reporting in 2020 that CEOs in the top 350 firms earn 320 times as much as a typical worker.[32] These numbers were upsetting before the COVID-19 crisis but particularly upsetting in the midst of the pandemic, when many companies were said to be slashing executive salaries and many workers lost jobs.[33] While some companies like Walt Disney and McDonald's began reducing executive salaries in response to COVID-19, one report concluded that these reductions were largely insignificant and merely window dressing.[34] Two issues remain at the heart of the CEO pay controversy: (1) the extent to which CEO pay is tied to firm performance and (2) the overall size of CEO pay.

The CEO Pay–Firm Performance Relationship. The move to tie CEO pay more closely to firm performance grew in momentum when shareholders observed CEO pay rising as firm performance fell, particularly following the economic crisis in 2008–2009. Many executives had received staggering salaries, even while profits were falling, workers were being laid off, and shareholder returns were dropping. Since then, shareholders have focused not only on limiting the pay initially rewarded but also on taking back pay that, in retrospect, seems undeserved.

However, the failure to link CEO pay to performance seems to continue. In a recent analysis looking at the past five years of CEO pay compared to their companies' total returns, executives in the top pay quartile made 12 times what those in the bottom quartile did, but produced financial returns only twice as good.[35] Across different industries, CEOs continue to get paid high dollars even when companies underperform. For example, J.C. Penney filed for bankruptcy protection and paid out millions of dollars for top executives right before it happened, including a $4.5 million bonus for CEO Jill Soltau, and $1 million each for three other top executives.[36] In another example, Boeing's former CEO Dennis Muilenburg walked away with over $58.5 million after being fired when Boeing was accused of selling its 737 Max jets with faulty software leading to the crash of two airplanes that killed hundreds.[37] One might readily ask why boards of directors permitted these patterns to occur.

Efforts to strengthen the CEO pay–firm performance relationship have historically focused on the use of **stock options**. While they have improved the pay–performance relationship, they have also created a host of new problems. Stock options are designed to motivate the recipient to improve the value of the firm's stock. Put simply, an option allows the recipient to purchase stock in the future at the price it is today, that is, "at the money." If the stock value rises after the granting of the option, the recipient will make money. The logic behind giving CEOs stock options is that those CEOs will want to increase the value of the firm's stock so that they will be able to exercise their options, buying stock in the future at a price that is lower than it's worth. This logic only works if the option is granted at the true "at-the-money" price. The possibility of quick gains through misrepresentation of the pricing has led to numerous abuses. The following are the ones most frequently in the news.

Stock option **backdating** occurs when the recipient is given the option of buying stock at yesterday's price, resulting in an immediate and guaranteed wealth increase. This puts the stock option "in the money" rather than "at the money," which is where an option should be granted. Backdating results in an immediate gain and is not in keeping with the purpose of stock options. This is not the only stock option abuse that has been observed. Even stock options granted "at the money" can be problematic when coupled with inside knowledge that the stock price is soon going to change. **Spring-loading** is the granting of a stock option at today's price but with the inside knowledge that something good is about to happen that will improve the stock's value. **Bullet-dodging** is the delaying of a stock option grant until right after bad news.

Backdating is not inherently illegal but can be deemed so if documents were falsified to conceal the backdating. The backdating of grant dates has considerably slowed down since the Sarbanes–Oxley Act of 2002 changed the reporting requirements for stock option grants. Additionally, stock options in general have declined as part of a CEO's total compensation, with companies instead favoring performance-based plans.[38] However, they are still prevalent in over half of long-term incentive plans in the S&P 1500.[39]

To a certain extent, **restricted stock** has replaced stock option plans in attempts to incentivize CEOs, managers, and directors and align them with owners. Unlike stock options, restricted stock always has value, even in a down market, and it can deliver the same value with fewer shares than options because it does not have an exercise price. It also incentivizes executives to think for the long term because the essence of restricted stock is that the employee must remain employed until the stock vests to receive its value. For example, the music streaming and media company Pandora Media has shifted almost all of its stock options to restricted stock, even for rank-and-file employees, to create less risk and less dilution.[40]

Excessive CEO Pay. Concern about the size of executive compensation has been around for a long time. In ancient Greece, Plato recommended that no one in a community receives a wage higher than five times that of the lowest paid worker. Today, CEO salaries have skyrocketed while worker salaries have waned. Median pay for CEOs in the Standard & Poor's (S&P) 500 companies increased 6 percent in 2019, reaching $12.2 million.[41] While in the 1950s CEO average pay was just 20 times more than the average pay of workers, this has blossomed to more than 300 times, as we noted above.[42] Typically, the issue of excessive executive pay is a U.S. phenomenon. However, in 2020 it was reported that London's Financial Times Stock Exchange (FTSE) top 100 CEOs' total pay was, on average, 84 times the average earnings of their employees, further prompting the European Commission to look at new rules over executive pay disclosures and executive/worker pay gaps.[43]

The topic of excessive CEO pay is not without debate, however. Economist Tyler Cowen argues that overall CEO compensation for top companies rises in lockstep with the value of those companies on the stock market, and that CEOs have "upped their game" relative to many other workers.[44] Additionally, he points out, the main driver of income inequality are superstar firms like Google, Facebook, and Verizon that pay more than executives at their more traditional counterparts.[45] Nevertheless, concerns about excessive pay have led institutional shareholders, like BlackRock, to increasingly vote against egregious pay schemes.[46]

The **Say on Pay movement** evolved from concerns over excessive executive compensation and failures to link CEO pay to performance. It began in the United Kingdom in 2002, with regulations that included the requirement to submit a remuneration report to a shareholder vote at each annual meeting.[47] Soon after the United Kingdom instituted its regulations, Say on Pay requirements spread through Europe and Australia, with the Netherlands making the vote binding on the company.[48] In the United States, the Dodd–Frank Wall Street Reform and Consumer Protection Act requires companies to submit their executive pay packages to a nonbinding shareholder vote at least once every three years.[49]

Evidence suggests that the additional transparency has caught the eyes of shareholders, and it may be working in

curbing CEO pay.[50] Executive pay also has begun to have an impact on a firm's larger reputation.[51] In the Corporate Knight's ranking of the Global 100 most sustainable firms, executive pay is a part of two clean capitalism key performance indicators: the ratio of CEO to average employee pay and the linking of executive pay to clean capitalism goals.[52] Corporate Knights defines **clean capitalism** as "an economic system in which prices fully incorporate social, economic, and ecological costs and benefits, and actors are clearly aware of the consequences of their marketplace actions."[53]

When an executive's high level of pay results from dubious practices, such as financial misconduct or the exercising of options in a questionable way, shareholders have a right to try to recover those funds, but in the past, they have lacked a mechanism for doing so. This has changed due to the increasing adoption of **clawback provisions**, which are compensation recovery mechanisms that enable a company to recoup compensation funds, typically in the event of a financial restatement or executive's misbehavior.[54] Today, about 90 of the 100 largest publicly traded companies write clawback provisions into executive contracts.[55]

However, clawback provisions are not without controversy, as companies find it difficult to recoup the money, once it has been released.[56] The **Council of Institutional Investors (CII)**, a nonprofit association of corporate, public, and union employee benefit funds, issued a policy that both current and former executive officers should be subject to clawback in cases of financial misstatements, fraud, personal misconduct, or ethical lapses that could cause reputational harm.[57] The CII does not have power over listings, but its members are large shareholders with voting power.[58]

Individual investors and other parties concerned do not have to wade through proxy statements to learn about CEO compensation. The AFL-CIO sponsors CEO PayWatch (https://aflcio.org/paywatch), a website that is an "online center for learning about the excessive salaries, bonuses, and perks of the CEOs of major corporations."[59] Visitors to the website can enter their pay and a firm's name and find out how many years they would have to work to make what the CEO of that firm makes in one year (or how many workers are at your salary that the CEO's pay could support). The website also provides instructions for assessing the pay of CEOs at public corporations and beginning a campaign of shareholder activism in any company.

Executive Retirement Plans and Exit Packages. Executive retirement packages have traditionally flown under the radar, escaping the notice of shareholders, employees, and the public. However, as details of some retirement packages have become public, those packages have come under increased scrutiny. The packages are negotiated well in advance and so they often are unrelated to performance. For example, many were upset when former CEO of Genesis Healthcare, George Hager Jr., retired and was given a $5.2 million "retention payment" at the height of the pandemic. Genesis operates more than 300 nursing homes in the United States, and at the time of his retirement the death toll in Genesis nursing homes had reached 2,800 and the company was relying on federal emergency aid to survive financially.[60] Many see the CEO-worker retirement divide as an even greater contributor to the wider economic divide than basic pay—with the 100 largest U.S. CEO retirement packages at one point worth a combined value of $4.9 billion, equal to the retirement account savings of 41 percent of American families.[61]

Part of the public's frustration is that these CEO retirement packages stand in stark contrast to the retirement packages that workers receive. Many of today's workers do not have retirement packages, and those who do are far more likely to have the less-lucrative defined contribution plans (that specify what will be put into the retirement fund) rather than the defined benefit plans (that specify the benefit the retiree will receive).[62]

Outside Board Director Compensation. Paying board members is a relatively recent idea. Ninety years ago, it was illegal to pay nonexecutive board members. The logic was that because board members represented the shareholders, paying them out of the company's (i.e., shareholders') funds would be self-dealing.[63] Today, outside board members are paid for their efforts. Recently, median pay for board members in the top 100 largest publicly traded companies was reported to be more than $300,000, not including meeting fees that may be also be paid for meeting attendance.[64] Unlike executive compensation, there is no Say on Pay option for shareholders to approve director compensation, but in general, there have been relatively few shareholder protests over director compensation. One exception to this has been a shareholder suit brought against Facebook directors who awarded themselves additional Facebook stock (see Ethics in Practice case on page 209).

Transparency. SEC rules on disclosure of executive compensation are designed to address some of the more obvious problems by making the entire pay packages of top executives transparent. They are designed not just to have companies disclose their pay packages but also to explain them, including the degree of alignment between pay and relevant measures of performance. Investors not satisfied with aspects of compensation can register their disapproval with negative Say on Pay votes, votes against (or withheld from) members of the board compensation committee, or both.

The Dodd–Frank Wall Street Reform and Consumer Protection Act includes provisions intended to have the SEC improve the transparency of firm operations. The CEO pay ratio, discussed above, is one example of such a provision—although it took eight years following the Dodd-Frank Act for the SEC to implement it. Another Dodd–Frank requirement focuses on the transparency of the compensation

---

Ethics In Practice Case

Should CEOs Raise the Minimum Salary of their Employees?

In 2015, Dan Price, the 31-year-old CEO of Seattle-based financial services company Gravity, Inc., established a $70,000 minimum wage for his 120 employees. As noted by one observer, "Grown men cried. Profits soared."

Price decided to do this after an employee boldly told Price that his conservative wage setting, based on market rates, translated into the employees not making enough money to lead "a decent life." Price realized the employee was correct. He acknowledged that he had been "so scarred by the recession that I was proactively, and proudly, hurting my staff." For three years after the employee encounter, Price handed out 20 percent annual raises, and then, after the company continued to realize profit growth, he announced in 2015 that he would phase in a minimum wage of $70,000, and he immediately cut his own salary from $1.1 million to $70,000 to help fund it. The move doubled the pay of about 30 of his workers and gave another 40 significant raises. In 2019, Price repeated his pledge, saying that all of the employees in the company's new Idaho office would earn a minimum salary of $70,000 by 2024. During the COVID-19 pandemic, Price had to tell his employees that company revenues had plummeted and something needed to be done. Nearly every employee agreed to a voluntary pay cut so that no worker would be laid off. Gravity took out a federal Paycheck Protection loan, and by 2021, workers had their full salaries restored and the company paid them what they lost in July from pay cuts.

1. If you were a CEO, would you consider raising the minimum salary of your employees, as Price did? What are the benefits? What are the costs?
2. What are the ethical issues involved in this decision?
3. Does your answer to #1 change if you learned that a research study shows that increases in income up to $75,000 can significantly improve a person's emotional well-being?

Sources: Paul Keegan, "Here's What Really Happened at That Company That Set a $70,000 Minimum Wage," *Inc.* (November 2015), https://www.inc.com/magazine/201511/paul-keegan /does-more-pay-mean-more-growth.html, accessed March 7, 2021; Denis Collins, "This CEO Raised the Minimum Salary of His Employees to $70K and Now He's Doing it Again," https:// deniscollins.tumblr.com/post/187950465398/this-ceo-raised-the-minimum-salary-of-his, accessed March 7, 2021; *Gravity,* https://gravitypayments.com/blog/new-digs-new-era-for-gravitys-boise-team/, accessed March 7, 2021; John Sowell, "He Employs 50 Boise Workers. They Took Pay Cuts to Avoid Layoffs. The Choice Paid Off," Idaho Statesmen (August 20, 2020), https:// www.idahostatesman.com/news/business/article244968805.html, accessed March 9, 2021.

setting process. In 2012, the SEC approved new exchange listing standards rules to include issues such as the independence of compensation committee members, the compensation adviser hiring process, and the nature of the relationship between the compensation adviser and the committee.[65] In 2015, the SEC proposed to supplement its Dodd–Frank disclosure rules to require companies to calculate and present information highlighting the company's executive compensation practices relative to its financial performance.[66] In sum, the Dodd–Frank Act continues to provide for rules to be designed for more transparency for shareholders.

9.2c The Governance Impact of the Market for Corporate Control

Mergers and acquisitions are another issue of corporate governance, one that comes from outside the corporation. The expectation from the Anglo-American shareholder-primacy perspective is that the threat of a possible takeover will motivate top managers to pursue shareholder, rather than self, interest (the expectation of the director-primacy perspective will be explained later in the chapter). The merger, acquisition, and hostile takeover craze of the 1980s motivated many corporate CEOs and boards to go to great lengths to protect themselves from these takeovers, and these continued with some of the "mega" mergers and acquisitions of the early 2000s.

Today, hostile takeovers have been making a comeback, fueled by market downturns and the COVID-19 pandemic, which have made some companies more affordable now for competitors.[67] Two of the controversial practices associated with hostile takeovers are poison pills and golden parachutes. We briefly consider each of these and see how they fit into corporate governance issues. Then we examine the issue of insider trading.

Poison Pills. A **poison pill** is intended to discourage or prevent a hostile takeover. It works much like its name suggests—when an acquirer tries to swallow (i.e., acquire) a company, the poison pill makes the company very difficult for them to ingest. Poison pills can take a variety of forms but, typically, when a hostile suitor acquires more than a certain percentage of a company's stock, the poison pill provides that other shareholders be able to purchase shares, thus diluting the suitor's holdings and making the acquisition prohibitively expensive (i.e., difficult to swallow). In 2012, for example, Netflix adopted a poison pill to fend off a corporate takeover by corporate raider Carl Icahn.[68] In 2020, HP adopted a poison pill to fend off a takeover by Xerox.[69]

Poison pills have fallen out of favor, largely due to institutional shareholder pressures.[70] Nevertheless, they remain within the corporate arsenal, and in early 2020 at least 45 firms adversely affected by the pandemic (including Hilton, Barnes & Noble, and Spirit Airlines) announced the adoption of poison pills, leading to them being renamed "crisis pills."[71] Poison pills have also taken on a new role as a strategy to fend off shareholder activists who want to change the direction of the company.[72] Although activist campaigns

tapered off in the COVID-19 pandemic, poison pills adopted in response to a company being approached by an activist investor historically represented over one quarter of all adoptions.[73] The motivation is different from that of a hostile takeover—instead of preventing a hostile suitor that might hurt shareholders and end a company's independence, the "low-threshold" poison pill is designed to limit ownership by any single investor for a short period, subject to renewal, and the company's future survival is not in question.[74]

Golden Parachutes. A **golden parachute** is a provision in an employment contract in which a corporation agrees to make payments to key officers in the event of a change in the control of the corporation.[75] One of the more infamous examples of a golden parachute is the buyout of WeWork cofounder and former CEO Adam Neumann, who was scheduled to receive a $1.7 billion golden parachute that included a $185 million consulting contract and a $500 million loan to repay a credit line when the company was sold in large part to SoftBank Group.[76] WeWork's valuation collapsed after the company's plans for an IPO were thwarted following media attention to Neumann's alleged self-dealing, erratic behavior, and drug use.[77] In April 2020, Softbank pulled out of a $3 billion share buyout plan, taking away nearly $1 billion of Neumann's golden parachute payout. At this writing, Neumann was planning on suing Softbank over the bank's cancellation.

Advocates argue that golden parachutes provide top executives involved in takeover battles with an incentive for not fighting a shareholder wealth-maximizing takeover attempt in an effort to preserve their employment. However, a study of more than 400 takeover attempts found that golden parachutes had no effect on takeover resistance.[78] Critics argue that executives are already being paid sufficiently well and that these parachutes essentially reward them for failure.[79] Others argue that lavish exit packages might make CEOs too eager to accept a takeover offer.[80] The trend in the percentage of executives awarded packages is holding steady, particularly as Say on Pay regulations now invite shareholder votes on golden parachutes proposals.[81]

9.2d Insider Trading

Insider trading is the practice of buying or selling a security by someone who has access to material information that is not available to the public. **Material information** is information that a reasonable investor might want to use and that is likely to affect the price of a firm's stock once that information is released to the public. Although insider trading is typically thought of as illegal conduct, insider trading can be legal or illegal.[82] Whether or not insider trading is legal depends on when the trade occurs. If the trade is made while the information is still not public, then it is illegal because members of the public do not have access to that information.[83]

Information can be passed along in many forms, including in social media. In 2018, Elon Musk of Tesla was sued by the SEC after he tweeted on August 7 that he had "funding

Figure 9-3 An Insider Trading Quiz

Which of the following are considered to be illegal inside trading, prosecutable by the SEC?

1. A lower-level employee of the company learns the company will have higher-than-expected earnings in the next quarterly statement and buys shares of the company's stock before the statement is released to the public. Can that employee be prosecuted by the SEC?
2. The above employee who learned the information does not trade on the information but tells his or her spouse and that spouse buys company stock shares before the information goes public. Can the spouse be prosecuted by the SEC?
3. In the above example (#2), can the employee who did not trade be prosecuted by the SEC?
4. While playing basketball on the weekend, the employee shares the information with a casual friend. That friend then buys shares of the company's stock before the statement is released to the public. Can the friend be prosecuted by the SEC?

The answer to all the questions in this quiz is "yes."

secured" to take Tesla private at $420/share.[84] The tweet sent Tesla's share price up as much as 13.3 percent and was considered to violate securities laws in manipulating the market. Musk settled with the SEC and agreed to step down as chair and have the company's lawyers preapprove written communications. However, more tweets in 2019 put Musk in potential contempt of the settlement when he discussed Tesla's production.[85]

The market system is based on trust and fair play. Investor confidence relies on fairness and integrity in the securities markets and illegal insider trading erodes that confidence (see Figure 9-3).[86]

The SEC has brought charges against people who received or revealed inside information in a variety of ways. One can be a **tipper** who provides that information or a **tippee** who receives the information. Both types are prosecutable and both have been prosecuted by the SEC.[87] Data analytics have made it much easier to catch illegal inside traders, perhaps contributing to an overall decline in the number of insider trading cases in the United States since the early 2000s.[88]

Ethics In Practice Case

Facebook and Say on Pay for Directors?

In 2014, a shareholder derivative suit was filed in the State of Delaware Courts alleging that the Facebook Board of Directors violated their duties to their shareholders by paying its nonexecutive directors an average $461,000 per director, which was 43 percent more than peers like Adobe, Amazon, Cisco, eBay, and Yahoo!, among others. The lawsuit, *Espinoza v. Zuckerberg*, further noted that the Facebook Board granted its board members an unlimited amount of stock as part of their annual compensation, with the only limit being a $2.5 million share limit per director in a single year (worth approximately $145 million at the time of filing). The lawsuit claimed breach of fiduciary duty, waste of corporate assets, and "unjust enrichment." The issue accelerated in late 2014, when Jan Koum, WhatsApp cofounder and CEO, joined the board and received a salary of $1 but stock awards worth over $1.9 billion when Facebook acquired WhatsApp.

The Facebook Board at the time consisted of eight individuals, six of whom were "outside" (i.e., nonemployee) directors who benefited from the compensation plan, including Lead Independent Director Donald Graham and Directors Peter Thiel, Marc Andreessen, Reed Hastings, Erskine Boles and Desmond-Hellman. Inside directors included founder and CEO/Chairman Mark Zuckerberg and COO Sheryl Sandberg. Zuckerberg, who had 60 percent of the voting power, allegedly approved the stock grants in a written affidavit, rather than at a stockholder meeting—thereby circumventing shareholders by signing off on directors' stock grants instead of presenting it at a shareholders' meeting.

Facebook ended up settling the lawsuit—agreeing to submit its non-employee director compensation program to shareholder vote in the future. However, the vote of Facebook's shareholders was a mere formality, as Mr. Zuckerberg held voting control of Facebook's shares. Nevertheless, the lawsuit brought up issues of Say on Pay—this time for not just company executives but also for company directors.

1. Should directors have the right to approve their own compensation without taking it to shareholder vote? Please justify your answer and explain what might or might not warrant this.
2. Did Zuckerberg break the law by not bringing the compensation issue up in a stockholder meeting?
3. What is an appropriate level of director pay? Is the proposed compensation in the Facebook situation excessive? How might this be determined?
4. Institutional Shareholder Services, a proxy advisory firm, has noted that there is "too much work and too much time" required of directors; could this justify higher director pay?[89]

Sources: Jonathan Stempel, "Zuckerberg, Other Facebook Directors Are Sued Over Pay Plan," *Reuters* (June 9, 2014), http://www.reuters.com/article/us-facebook-lawsuit-idUSKBN0EK1YO20140609, accessed March 7, 2021; Paul Hodgson, "Facebook Director Pay Not Getting Many Shareholder 'Likes'," *Fortune* (December 15, 2015), http://fortune.com/2015/12/15/facebook-director-pay/, accessed March 7, 2021; Matt Chiappardi, "Facebook Agrees to Settle Chancery Suit Over Director Pay," *Law 360*, (January 26, 2016), https://www.law360.com/articles/750892/facebook-agrees-to-settle-chancery-suit-over-director-pay, accessed March 7, 2021.

Insider trading allegations cause the general public to lose faith in the stability and security of the financial industry because **information asymmetry** (one party having information that another does not) favors one group over another. Information asymmetry can also arise if companies release information to one group before another receives it. If large investors can act on information that smaller investors do not have, the playing field is not level. To prop up investor confidence, the SEC instituted disclosure rules designed to aid the small investor. **Regulation FD (fair disclosure)** ensures that when companies disclose meaningful information to a limited group of individuals like large shareholders and securities professionals, they must do so publicly so that small investors can enjoy a more level playing field.[90]

9.3 Improving Corporate Governance

Legislative initiatives to improve corporate governance are first discussed. SOX was passed in response to the public outcry for greater protection following the Enron and other financial scandals of 2001. The Dodd–Frank Wall Street Reform and Consumer Protection Act was passed in response to the global financial crisis. We then proceed to other efforts to improve corporate governance through changes in the composition, structure, and functioning of boards of directors.

9.3a Legislative Initiatives

The **Accounting Reform and Investor Protection Act of 2002**, also known as the **Sarbanes–Oxley Act of 2002 (aka SOX or Sarbox)**, amended the securities laws to provide better protection to investors in public companies by improving the financial reporting of companies. According to the Senate committee report, "the issue of auditor independence is at the center of [SOX]."[91] Some of the ways the act endeavors to ensure auditor independence are by:

- Limiting the nonauditing services an auditor can provide.
- Requiring auditing firms to rotate the auditors who work with a specific company, and making it unlawful for accounting firms to provide auditing services where conflicts of interest (as defined by the act) exist.
- Enhancing financial disclosure with requirements such as the reporting of off-balance-sheet transactions, the prohibiting of personal loans to executives and directors, and the requirement that auditors assess and report on the internal controls employed by the company.
- Requiring that audit committees have at least one financial expert, that CEOs and chief financial officers (CFOs) certify and be held responsible for financial representations of the company, and that whistle-blowers are afforded protection.

- Requiring that corporations must disclose whether they have adopted a code of ethics for senior financial officers, and, if they have not, provide an explanation for why they have not.[92]

The penalties for noncompliance with SOX are severe. A CEO or CFO who misrepresents company finances may face a fine of up to $1 million and imprisonment for up to ten years. If that misrepresentation is willful, the fine may go up to $5 million with up to 20 years of imprisonment.[93]

Since the passage of SOX, debate has continued regarding its costs and benefits, but research points to the effectiveness of SOX, particularly as compliant firms are seen to have a reduced risk of accounting fraud, lower risk of financial restatements, and higher investor confidence.[94]

The **Dodd–Frank Wall Street Reform and Consumer Protection Act** was passed in the wake of the global financial crisis and signed into law on July 21, 2010. This comprehensive legislation covers 16 major areas of reform affecting banks, credit card companies, credit rating agencies, insurance companies, hedge funds, and futures trading. Legislative efforts are important and governments have a responsibility to respond when crises such as the Enron and WorldCom bankruptcies and global economic crises occur. Government has a responsibility to protect the public interest, but no amount of legislative oversight will fully protect the public from the next crisis. In their study of the global financial crisis, Michael Santoro and Ronald Strauss acknowledge that government has a crucial role to play but conclude, "No amount of government regulation can succeed where the moral core is corrupt… Unless Wall Street itself formulates a coherent moral response to the crisis, no amount of regulatory oversight will prevent another, potentially more destabilizing, crisis from occurring."[95]

9.3b The Securities and Exchange Commission

The role of the SEC in the United States is clear; the commission is responsible for protecting investor interests; maintaining fair, orderly, and efficient markets; and facilitating capital formation.[96] Press releases about actions taken by the SEC reveal a host of issues the SEC regularly addresses, including suspending trading on companies where insider trading may have occurred, investigating and charging fraud, investigating auditors, and awarding monies for whistle-blowers who "blow the whistle" on illegal activity (which we discuss further in Chapter 13).[97]

Beyond monitoring firms for compliance related to accounting activities, board duties, and executive compensation issues, the SEC is also focused on climate and ESG issues. In 2021, the SEC announced the creation of a Climate and ESG Task Force to develop initiatives and identify ESG-related misconduct. As noted by SEC Acting Chair of the Task Force Allison Herren Lee, "Climate risks and sustainability are critical issues for the investing public and our capital markets."[98]

However, many critics argue that the SEC often appears more focused on the needs of business than on those of investors. In the one of the worst scandals in the SEC's 75-year history, the SEC failed to stop the Bernard Madoff Ponzi scheme that cost investors around the world tens of billions of dollars. A **Ponzi scheme** lures investors in with the fake promise of profit but actually pays earlier investors with later investors' money until the scheme collapses.

The SEC failed to stop Madoff in spite of having been warned of the scheme nearly a decade earlier. Harry Markopolos, an independent financial fraud investigator, provided the SEC with both the reasons and the roadmap for investigating Madoff, but they failed to stop the scheme. According to Markopolos, "I gift wrapped and delivered the largest Ponzi scheme in history to them and somehow they couldn't be bothered to conduct a thorough and proper investigation because they were too busy on matters of higher priority."[99] The first substantive complaint the SEC received about Madoff was in 1992, 16 years before the scheme imploded.[100] A 2011 movie, *Chasing Madoff,* about Markopolos's ten-year quest to catch Madoff draws heavily from his aptly named book, *No One Would Listen.*[101]

By all accounts, the failure to catch Madoff would be unlikely to happen today. In fact, the SEC has a whole page on their website devoted to "Post-Madoff Reforms" about revitalizing and improving internal controls and enforcement.[102]

9.3c Changes in Boards of Directors

Because of the growing belief that CEOs and executive teams need to be made more accountable to shareholders and other stakeholders, boards have been undergoing a variety of changes. There are several key areas that need change as well as some of the recommendations that were set forth for improving board functioning. Figure 9-4 presents a list of nine "red flags" that signal that a board member should increase his or her involvement and a roadmap for board repair.

9.3d Board Diversity

Do diverse boards make a difference? Given the diversity of stakeholders, a diverse board is better able to hear their concerns and respond to their needs.[103] Diverse boards are also less likely to fall prey to groupthink because they would have the range of perspectives necessary to question the assumptions that drive group decisions.[104] And there is considerable evidence of board diversity being associated with better financial and social performance.[105]

Increasing board diversity is front and center in corporate governance these days. Despite decades of understanding that a more diverse board can help the firm, a significant percentage of boards are still composed of exclusively white, male directors.[106] In 2019, the S&P 500 reached a milestone in that there was elected at least one female director to the last remaining all-male boards, but the total percentage of women on boards continues to be less than one-quarter of all board members.[107] And while ethnic minorities on boards across all companies on the Russell 3000 index surpassed 10 percent for the first time in 2019, *PwC*'s 2020 annual corporate directors survey found that only 34 percent of directors believe it is important to have racial diversity on their board.[108]

The Alliance for Board Diversity tracks increases in representation for women and minorities but has noted that "the raw numbers (of boardroom diversity) are still small."[109] Despite some efforts by organizations to increase board diversity and ongoing academic research on how to bring change in gender diversity on boards,[110] representation of Hispanic, Asian, African American, and female directors on boards continues to grow modestly. As one article noted, "Latinos are 18 percent of the U.S. population…but only 3 percent of corporate directors."[111] However, the pressure

Figure 9-4 Red Flags That Signal Board Problems and Steps to Take for Board Repair

Red Flags	Steps to Take for Board Repair
1. Company has to restate earnings	1. Spread risk oversight among multiple committees
2. Poor employee morale	2. Seek outside help in identifying potential risks
3. Adverse Sarbanes-Oxley 404 or Dodd-Frank opinion	3. Deepen involvement in corporate strategy
4. Poor customer satisfaction track record	4. Align board size and skill mix with strategy
5. Management misses strategic performance goals	5. Revamp executive compensation
6. Company is target of employee lawsuits	6. Pick compensation committee members who will question the status quo
7. Stock price declines	7. Use independent compensation consultants
8. Quarterly financial results miss analysts' expectations	8. Evaluate CEO on grooming potential successors
9. Low corporate governance quotient rating	9. Know what matters to your investors

Sources: "What Directors Think 2015," *SpencerStuart* (February 2015), https://www.spencerstuart.com/research-and-insight/what-directors-think-2015, accessed March 7, 2021. Joanne S. Lublin, "Corporate Directors Give Repair Plan to Boards," *The Wall Street Journal* (March 24, 2009), B4; "What Directors Think 2015," SpencerStuart (February 2015), https://www.spencerstuart.com/research-and-insight/what-directors-think-2015, accessed March 7, 2021; Joanne S. Lublin, "Corporate Directors Give Repair Plan to Boards," *The Wall Street Journal* (March 24, 2009), B4.

is growing for companies to address these shortcomings. In California, state legislators passed a bill that requires every publicly traded company based in California to have at least one woman on their board, and for larger boards, more than one. Companies that do not comply face fines starting at $100,000.[112] Institutional investors like State Street and BlackRock are pressuring companies to disclose the diversity of their boards.[113] More recently, the second largest exchange in the world, the U.S. NASDAQ, asked the SEC for permission to impose a quota system on the boards of its listed companies such that each board have a minimum of one-woman director and one who is minority or LGBTQ.[114]

What can business do to increase board diversity? Many companies are considering adopting a policy resembling the National Football League's Rooney Rule, which requires organizations to interview a minority candidate for every open leadership position, including board seats. And many companies adopting tenure limits and mandatory retirement ages aim to refresh their boards with more diverse directors as other directors retire.[115]

Problems with achieving board diversity are not confined to the United States, but mandates in Europe have pushed firms to bring more diversity into the boardroom. As a result, in Italy, Germany, and several other European nations, the number of women on boards has tripled and, in some cases, quadrupled in recent years.[116] In Norway, high numbers are directly linked to a government mandate to increase the number of women on boards. The 500 publicly traded firms in Norway were told they would face closure if they did not meet a January 2008 deadline for achieving 40 percent female representation on their boards.[117] By 2008, every major Norwegian corporation was in compliance. In fact, the number of women on Norway's corporate boards almost quadrupled in five years.[118] Not surprisingly, this dramatic shift ignited a fierce debate about the use of quotas to create change and the role of women in the workplace.[119] Spain, Iceland, Italy, Belgium, the Netherlands, and France have now followed Norway's lead, with their regulators making compulsory or quasi-compulsory recommendations for female representation.[120]

9.3e Outside Directors

As we discussed earlier, legislative, investor, and public pressure have led firms to seek a greater ratio of outside to inside board members. Do outside board members make a difference for both shareholders and stakeholders? As with diversity, a relationship between the proportion of outside directors and financial performance is difficult to find. For that reason, scholars have looked to more targeted measures. One study found outside directors to be associated with fewer shareholder lawsuits.[121] Another study found that outside directors were associated with better social performance.[122] A recent study suggests that outside directors have the ability to be objective, and therefore, it is one of the core attributes needed for a director to be an effective monitor of management.[123]

Some have suggested that a lack of outside directors on the board of Volkswagen led to a "clannish board" that did not allow for the objectivity that might have stopped its engineers from purposefully circumventing U.S. emissions standards.[124] Board independence can come at a cost, however, as inside directors have greater knowledge of the firm because of their connections to it. Additionally, some observers have expressed concern that the drive for more outside directors has pushed CFOs off the board. Finally, it is unclear that a board made up of outsiders truly brings objectivity in decision making when the CEO often remains a powerful insider of the organization.[125]

Outside directors are a heterogeneous group and so the impact of appointing more outside directors to boards can be expected to vary with the characteristics of the directors who are appointed. Arguably, the most important characteristic for outside directors is the ability to ask difficult questions and speak truthfully about concerns, without letting ties to the firm get in the way.

9.3f Use of Board Committees

The **audit committee** of the board is responsible for assessing the adequacy of internal control systems and the integrity of financial statements that are prepared by management. SOX mandates that the audit committee be composed entirely of independent board members and that there be at least one identified financial expert, as defined in SOX.[126] The principal responsibilities of an audit committee are as follows[127]:

1. To ensure that published financial statements are not misleading
2. To ensure that internal controls are adequate
3. To follow up on allegations of material, financial, ethical, and legal irregularities
4. To ratify the selection of the external auditor

While the audit committee has taken center stage in the current corporate governance environment, other committees still play key roles. The **nominating committee**, which should be composed of outside directors, has the responsibility of ensuring that competent, objective board members are selected. The function of the nominating committee is to nominate candidates for the board and for senior management positions. The suggested role and responsibility of this committee notwithstanding, in most companies, the CEO continues to exercise a powerful role in the selection of board members. This is because the CEO is part of the upper echelon of businesspeople that share social clubs, business groups, and government policy forums.[128] The danger in this practice is that a too cozy relationship between the CEO and the board may develop over time.

The **compensation committee** has the responsibility of evaluating executive performance and recommending terms and conditions of employment. Both the New York Stock Exchange (NYSE) and NASDAQ require that the compensation committee be composed of independent board members. Together, the audit, nominating, and compensation committees are considered to be the principal monitoring committees in an organization.[129] Additionally, many companies, particularly in the financial services industry, have formed board-level **risk committees** to provide oversight about risks regarding strategy and tactics across operational, financial, and compliance areas.

Finally, each board has committees that respond to the needs of their industries and that address public policy and social issues. They have a variety of names. For example, Johnson & Johnson has a regulatory, compliance, and governmental affairs committee as well as a science, technology, and sustainability committee.[130] Unilever has a corporate responsibility and reputation committee.[131] Most major companies today have **corporate responsibility committees** or **corporate sustainability committees** that typically deal with such issues as diversity, equal employment opportunity, environmental affairs, employee health and safety, consumer affairs, political action, and other areas in which public or ethical issues are present.

9.3g The Board's Relationship with the CEO

Boards of directors have always been responsible for monitoring CEO performance and dismissing poorly performing CEOs. Historically, however, CEOs were protected from the axe that hit other employees when times got rough. Post Sarbanes–Oxley, this was no longer true, with the rising vigilance of outside directors and the increasing power of large institutional investors causing average CEO tenure in the 1000 largest U.S. companies to hit its lowest, at 6.9 years, in 2020.[132]

"You have to perform or perish," according to John A. Challenger, CEO of outplacement firm Challenger, Gray & Christmas Inc. "If you don't produce immediate results, you just don't have much room to move."[133] Research has shown that there is a considerable "CEO effect" on firm performance, supporting the idea that the CEO is ultimately responsible for the fate of the business.[134] Nevertheless, the optimal time for a CEO or board member to serve on a board is a subject of much debate. As noted by one expert, "There is no simple answer to the question of CEO tenure. A firm can perform well with leaders enjoying a wide spectrum of terms of office … If there was an automatic formula we could apply we would not need boards with independent judgment."[135]

Part of the protection that CEOs once felt came from **CEO duality**, which occurs when the CEO serves a dual function, being both CEO and chair of the board. As is true with outside directors, CEO duality is "a double-edged sword."[136] CEOs who also serve as chairs are able to provide important inside information to the board and act decisively in responding to a competitive marketplace; however, that comes at the cost of a reduced ability of the board to monitor the CEO effectively.[137] Activist shareholders have been succeeding in getting companies to split the CEO and board chair function. In 2020, more than half of the S&P 500 companies split the chair and CEO role compared to 40 percent and 29 percent in 2010 and 2005, respectively.[138]

9.3h Board Member Liability

Concerned about increasing legal hassles emanating from stockholder, customer, and employee lawsuits, directors have been quitting board positions or refusing to accept them in the first place. In the past, courts rarely held board members personally liable in the hundreds of shareholder suits filed every year. Instead, the **business judgment rule** prevailed. The business judgment rule holds that courts should not challenge board members who act in good faith, making informed decisions that reflect the company's best interests instead of their own self-interest. The argument for the business judgment rule is that board members need to be free to take risks without fear of liability. The determination of good faith is central here because the rule was never intended to absolve board members completely from personal liability. In cases where the good faith standard was not upheld, board members have paid a hefty price. For example, when Dole Food Company went private, the Delaware Court of Chancery held two directors of the company jointly and severally liable for $148 million because they breached their duty of loyalty by spinning off high-margin businesses prior to going private that did not allow for a "fairer price" for the stockholders.[139]

The Caremark case then further heightened directors' concerns about **personal liability**. Caremark, a home health-care company now merged with CVS, paid substantial civil and criminal fines for submitting false claims and making illegal payments to doctors and other health-care providers. The Caremark board of directors was then sued for breach of fiduciary duties because the board members had failed in their responsibility to monitor effectively the Caremark employees who violated various state and federal laws. The Delaware Chancery Court ruled that it is the duty of the board of directors to ensure that a company has an effective reporting and monitoring system in place. If the board fails to do this, individual directors can be held personally liable for losses that are caused by their failure to meet appropriate standards.[140]

Although the "Caremark Law" is still seen as one of the hardest claims for plaintiffs to win, recent cases have brought it to the forefront, including a 2019 Blue Bell Creameries listeria outbreak, where shareholders alleged that two officers of the company had breached their duties of care and loyalty by knowingly disregarding contamination risks.[141]

The reality of director liability, however, is that most directors are protected with **Directors & Officers (D&O)** insurance, and they are rarely called on to contribute out of their own personal financial assets in response to private civil litigations. The insurance premiums are paid for by the companies where the directors serve on boards, and directors with state-of-the-art insurance policies face little out-of-pocket liability risk.[142]

9.4 The Role of Shareholders

Shareholders are a varied group with a range of interests and expectations. They, however, have one aspect in common: in the Anglo-American system of corporate governance, they are the owners of the corporation. As such, they have a right to have their voices heard. Putting that right into practice, however, has presented an ongoing challenge for shareholders and managers.

Our discussion begins with an overview of the state of shareholder democracy, which relates to strengthening shareholder voice and participation in corporate governance. We then discuss shareholder activism, shareholder resolutions, and shareholder lawsuits—all of which give voice to the shareholders in governance. We close with recommendations for improved shareholder relations.

9.4a Shareholder Democracy

Throughout the world, shareholders have been fighting to have their voices heard in corporate governance. This **shareholder democracy** movement stems from the lack of power shareholders have felt, particularly in board elections prior to recent reforms. In the United States, shareholders have been frustrated in the past when votes against board members were meaningless without a majority vote and corporations have been free to ignore shareholder resolutions.[143] Similarly, many European firms have not had one vote for each share issued.[144] Of course, the ability of shareholders to elect board members is central to the governance process because the elected board members will be governing the corporation.[145] However, pundits and scholars disagree over the value of the recommended reforms.

Proponents of shareholder democracy argue that if shareholders do not have more voice in the governance and operations of the company, the board is likely to become a self-perpetuating oligarchy.[146] They contend that increased shareholder power and involvement will lead to improved firm performance.[147] Opponents counter that shareholders are not "owners" in the traditional sense of the word because they can exit their ownership relatively easily by simply selling their shares.[148] They contend that increased shareholder power will lead to inefficient and short-term-oriented decision making, as well as infighting among competing interests.[149]

Shareholder democracy begins with board elections and so we focus our discussion there. Three key issues that have arisen are majority vote, classified boards, and proxy access.

Majority vote is the requirement that board members be elected by a majority of votes cast. This is in contrast to the previously prevailing norm of plurality voting. With plurality voting, the board members with the greatest number of "yes" votes are elected to the available seats on the board. The "no" and withheld votes are not counted. With "plurality plus," board members who receive less than a majority of votes cast must submit their resignation; however, boards of directors have not always accepted the resignations.[150]

Classified boards (also known as **staggered boards**) are those that elect their members in staggered terms. For example, in a board of 12 members, four might be elected each year, and each would serve a three-year term. It would then take three years for the entire board slate to be replaced. Classified boards are popular, with companies like Facebook and Tesla choosing to operate with such boards. Many shareholder activists oppose classified boards because of the time required to replace the board. Proponents of classified boards argue that board members need a longer period to make longer-term-oriented strategic decisions. However, it is still up for debate as to whether classified boards are

---

Spotlight on Sustainability

Shareholder Resolutions and Sustainability

Shareholder resolutions, proposals submitted by shareholders for a vote at the company's annual meeting, can appear to be frustrating propositions. Boards of directors and top management usually oppose them, and, even when resolutions are put forth, they typically get only a fraction of the votes needed to pass. In spite of these discouraging statistics, shareholders often can have a greater impact than one would first believe.

Proxy Preview 2020, for example, found that out of 429 shareholder resolutions filed on environmental, social, and sustainable governance (ESG) issues in 2020, 300 were put to vote at annual meetings, with shareholders and companies reaching agreements more often. Two-thirds of the proposals address issues of climate change, fair treatment for women on boards and in the workplace, and corporate political spending. Shareholder resolutions continue to move companies to action, with examples like Starbucks agreeing to shift from single-use packaging to reusable packaging and Verizon agreeing to conduct

a child risk assessment to help protect kids from sexual predators online. In another notable success, 53 percent of shareholders at Chevron Corporation voted in 2020 for a resolution that would push the oil company to make sure that its climate-change lobbying aligned with the Paris Agreement, a legally binding international treaty on climate change. It was the first time that a climate proposal won a majority of the company's shareholder votes.

Sources: "Proxy Preview 2020 Shows Jump in ESG Shareholder Proposals as SEC Prepares to Restrict Shareholder Rights," As You Sow (March 19, 2020), https://www.globenewswire.com /news-release/2020/03/19/2003481/0/en/Proxy-Preview-2020- Shows-Jump-in-ESG-Shareholder-Proposals-as-SEC-Prepares-to- Restrict-Shareholder-Rights.html, accessed March 7, 2021; Rob Berridge, "How Climate Proposals Fared During the 2020 Proxy Season," *GreenBiz* (September 14, 2020) https://www.greenbiz .com/article/how-climate-proposals-fared-during-2020-proxy- season/, accessed March 7, 2021.

better or worse for stakeholders than unitary boards, where shareholders vote on board members every year.[151]

Proxy access provides shareholders with the opportunity to propose nominees for the board of directors and put them on the company's proxy card (ballot) for the company's annual shareholder meeting. In 2010, the Dodd–Frank Act allowed shareholders to nominate directors to a company's board and have their nominees included in the proxy materials if they own at least 3 percent of the company's shares continuously for at least the prior three years—but the implementation of this provision became difficult when the SEC unsuccessfully sought to adopt a market-wide proxy access rule.[152] Since 2015, however, proxy access has been adopted by the majority of the S&P 500 companies.[153]

9.4b Shareholder Activism

One major reason that relations between management groups and shareholders have heated up is that shareholders have discovered the benefits of organizing and wielding power. **Shareholder activism** is not a new phenomenon. It goes back over 60 years to 1932, when Lewis Gilbert, then a young owner of ten shares, was appalled by the absence of communication between the New York–based Consolidated Gas Company's management and its owners. Supported by a family inheritance, Gilbert decided to quit his job as a newspaper reporter and "fight this silent dictatorship over other people's money." He resolved to devote himself "to the cause of the public shareholder."[154] Today, shareholder activism is thriving. Shareholder activists have put forth a record number of proposals that have led to a shift toward greater shareholder power, but have also created tensions between shareholders and board members.[155]

Church groups were the early mainstay of the corporate social responsibility movement and were among the first shareholder groups to adopt the strategy of raising social issues with corporations. Church groups began examining the relationship between their portfolios and corporate practices, and they remain among the largest groups of institutional stockholders willing to take on the management and press for what they think is right. Many churches' activist efforts are coordinated by the Interfaith Center on Corporate Responsibility (ICCR), which coordinates the shareholder advocacy of about 300 religious orders with about $500 billion in investments. For example, the ICCR was instrumental in convincing Kimberly-Clark to divest the cigarette paper business and pressuring PepsiCo to move out of Myanmar.[156]

Shareholder activists have historically been socially oriented; that is, they want to exert pressure to make the companies in which they own stock more socially responsive. While that remains true for many, activist shareholders are now also driven by a concern for profit. In late 2015, DuPont CEO Ellen Kullman faced a very public and controversial proxy battle against activist investor Nelson Peltz, cofounder of an $11 billion hedge fund. Peltz wanted Kullman to step down as CEO because he believed the company was

underperforming, and his group had plans for dividing and spinning off parts of the company.[157] Kullman eventually won the proxy battle, at a cost of $15 million to the company in defending itself. However, Kullman resigned shortly after the battle, and within a few months, DuPont merged with Dow Chemical.[158]

The growth of shareholder activism shows no signs of abating.[159] Activist shareholders, known also as **corporate gadflies**, are no longer dismissed as nuisance and are instead viewed as credible, powerful, and a force with which to be reckoned.[160] In fact, money managers and hedge funds advertise their activist orientation in the belief that being seen as aggressive gives them an edge.[161] Some of the top activist investors and (their founders) in the United States include Elliott Management (Paul Singer), Carl Icahn, Third Point Partners (Dan Loeb), Starboard Value (Jeffrey Smith), ValueAct Capital (Jeff Ubben), and Trian Partners (Nelson Peltz). Collectively, these activists have targeted hundreds of companies since 2017, with assets under management totalling over $200 billion.[162]

9.4c Shareholder Resolutions

One of the major vehicles by which shareholder activists communicate their concerns to management groups is through the filing of **shareholder resolutions**. Several of the shareholder resolutions filed in 2021 included the following: Disclosure of Plans and Policies Aligned with Achieving Racial Equality (Abbott Labs); Give Each Share an Equal Vote (Alphabet, Inc.); and Executive Pay and Sustainability Metrics (Apple Computer).[163] To file a resolution, a shareholder or a shareholder group must obtain a stated number of signatures to require management to place the resolution on the proxy statement so that all the shareholders can vote it on. Resolutions that are defeated (fail to get majority votes) may be resubmitted provided they meet certain SEC requirements for such resubmission.

Although an individual could initiate a shareholder resolution, she or he probably would not have the resources or means to obtain the required signatures to have the resolution placed on the proxy. Thus, most resolutions are initiated by large institutional investors that own large blocks of stock or by activist groups that own few shares of stock but have significant financial backing. Additionally, **proxy advisory firms**, like **Glass Lewis** and **Institutional Shareholder Services (ISS)**, also have considerable influence in the resolution process—providing research, data, and recommendations on management and shareholder proxy proposals that are voted on at a company's annual meeting. Their role is controversial, however, as on the one hand they can facilitate a proxy vote, and on the other, they advise companies on how to manage them. One study reflected the proxy firms' tremendous influence as they found that in a sample of 175 asset managers with over $5 trillion in assets, the firms voted with ISS recommendations 95 percent of the time.[164]

It is apparent that these proxy firms might have a **conflict of interest**, particularly as the two firms control 97 percent of the proxy market and have a deep relationship with public pension funds, their biggest clients.[165] Hence, the SEC in 2019 voted to approve guidance that requires more transparency of proxy firms, although it is unclear how this might affect their level of influence.[166]

Foundations, religious groups, universities, and other such large shareholders are in the best position to initiate resolutions. The issues on which shareholder resolutions are filed vary widely, but they typically concern some aspect of a firm's social performance. In 2020, a record number of social and environmental resolutions were filed, with political spending and climate change at the heart of most of the activity.[167]

As suggested earlier, most shareholder resolutions never pass, and even those that pass are typically nonbinding. However, they often foster constructive engagement and push companies to action. In 2020, 462 proposals were filed, and 44 percent were withdrawn, but the majority were withdrawn after companies and proponents reached agreements.[168]

9.4d Shareholder Lawsuits

Shareholder lawsuits are another form of activism that allow shareholders to pursue claims against the corporation in which they hold shares. When shareholders feel that a board has not met their **fiduciary duties** of care, loyalty and good faith, they can take legal action. As we noted above, however, the business judgment rule protects boards and board members from lawsuits for simply making bad choices. Shareholder lawsuits vary by topic. For example, in 2013, Bank of America shareholders received a $2.4 billion settlement in their lawsuit against the bank to settle claims that the bank hid crucial information from shareholders when it bought Merrill Lynch & Co. at the height of the financial crisis.[169] In 2019, the cosmetics company Coty was sued by shareholders for allegedly overpaying for Kylie Jenner's Kylie Cosmetics line.[170] In 2020, Alphabet was sued by shareholders related to their alleged mishandling of sexual harassment allegations against senior executives. Alphabet settled the suit, agreeing to establish a $310 million fund to support diversity, equity, and inclusion practices, and preventing employees under investigation for sexual misconduct or harassment from accelerating sales of stock.[171]

The **Private Securities Litigation Reform Act of 1995** was intended to rein in excessive levels of private securities litigation. New concerns over COVID-19 pandemic-related events that might foster additional shareholder and securities litigation has also caused stakeholders like the U.S. Chamber Institute for Legal Reform to petition the SEC for additional rule-making.[172]

In sum, it is clear that shareholders have evolved to expect more "voice" on issues that are important to them. These go beyond expectations of higher share price and now include environmental, social, and governance issues in which shareholders show a growing concern. In the next section, we discuss how business might engage more with shareholders, both to acknowledge their voices and to address their concerns.

9.5 Investor Relations and Shareholder Engagement

Over the years, corporate boards have neglected their shareholders. As share ownership has dispersed, there are several legitimate reasons why this inattention has taken place. However, the tide seems to be turning, as boards seem to be communicating more with their major investors. **Shareholder engagement**, an example of stakeholder engagement discussed in Chapter 3, is becoming part of many boards' policies—a strategy and set of formal procedures for opening communication between shareholders and a company on a variety of issues, including executive compensation, CEO succession, and company financial and ESG performance. In 2014, independent directors and representatives of the world's largest institutional investors formed the **Shareholder-Director Exchange (SDX)** working group to develop protocols for director-shareholder engagement for U.S. public companies. However, despite such initiatives, the concept of shareholder engagement is still emerging, with some resistance from companies that worry about less-than-legitimate investor concerns that might require time and attention away from key issues.[173]

Public corporations have obligations to existing shareholders as well as potential shareholders. **Full disclosure** (also known as **transparency**) is one of these responsibilities. Disclosure should be made at regular and frequent intervals and should contain information that might affect the investment decisions of shareholders. This information might include the nature and activities of the business, financial and policy matters, tender offers, and special problems and opportunities in the near future and in the longer term.[174] Board members should avoid conflicts between personal interests and the interests of shareholders. Company executives and directors have an obligation to avoid taking personal advantage of information that is not disclosed to the investing public and to avoid any personal use of corporation assets and influence.

Shareholder engagement and transparency can take many different forms. For example, Berkshire Hathaway Inc. is known for attending to its shareholders, and CEO Warren Buffett is praised by shareholders in return.[175] One indication of Berkshire Hathaway's relationship with shareholders is the annual meeting. Buffett calls the annual shareholders' meeting "Woodstock weekend for capitalists."[176] Of course, communicating is easier when you have Buffett's record of serving his shareholders well. Companies that have incidents to explain like Massey Energy's coal facility explosion or BP's Deepwater Horizon rig explosion make communication with shareholders more challenging.[177]

Technology has made investor relations easier to accomplish, and companies have begun to take advantage of it. Intel Corporation was the first company to let shareholders use the Internet to vote and submit questions to the annual meeting, and Walmart provides live Twitter and video updates from their annual meetings.[178] The COVID-19 pandemic shifted traditional in-person annual meetings to virtual shareholder meetings in the traditional voting season from April through June. In 2019, when the world went virtual with meetings due to the pandemic, virtual shareholder meetings were termed a "resounding success."[179] One study summarized the benefits to the board of increased shareholder engagement including: (1) it socializes shareholders, (2) it showcases board expertise, (3) it creates board self-awareness and increases understanding of expectations, and (4) it builds trust and personal capital.[180]

With good investor relations, greatly enhanced with stakeholder engagements, many serious problems can be averted and those that are unavoidable are less likely to fester. If shareholders are able to make their concerns heard outside the annual meeting, they are less likely to confront managers with hostile questions when the meeting is in session. If their recommendations receive serious consideration, they are less likely to put them in the form of a

formal resolution. Constructive engagement is easier for all involved.[181]

In sum, holding corporations accountable requires the orchestration of many different stakeholders including the board of directors, the CEO, senior management, employees, shareholders, regulators, whistle-blowers, and other stakeholder groups—supported by legislation that helps to increase transparency. Figure 9-5 presents a summary of these various participants.

9.6 Alternative Models of Corporate Governance

As mentioned in the beginning of this chapter, the material presented so far is based on the Anglo-American model of corporate governance: It is one of shareholder primacy, that is, it considers shareholders to be of primary importance. As discussed previously, the **shareholder-primacy model** asserts that maximizing share value is the ultimate firm goal and that improving corporate governance entails reducing board power, maximizing shareholder power, and tying incentives to share price. Activist shareholders have been

Figure 9-5 Holding Corporations Accountable

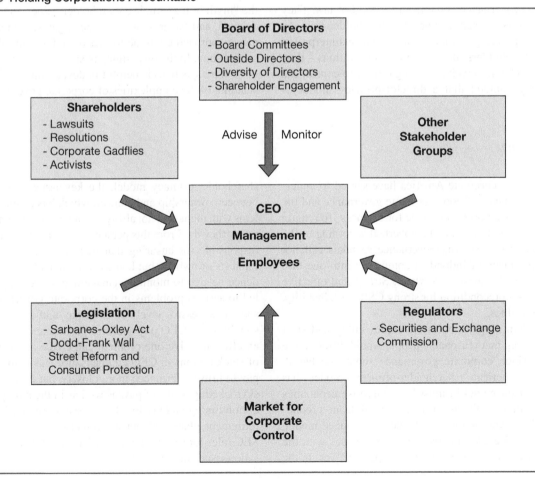

pursuing these goals with some success, but sometimes that pursuit has strained relations between shareholders and the board.[182]

A newer perspective, the **director-primacy model**, challenges the traditional model of shareholder primacy and suggests the balance of power in corporate governance should favor board members (versus shareholders), because board members are elected by shareholders and therefore represent their interests.[183] A director-primacy model of corporate governance is based on the concept of a corporation that is not owned, but instead is an independent legal entity that owns itself.[184] In it, boards are "mediating hierarchs" who are responsible for balancing the often-competing interests of a variety of stakeholders. From this perspective, board members should be given the autonomy and discretion needed to balance demands that sometimes conflict with each other.[185]

Instead of a principal-agent based model, the director-primacy view is distinct, but it stems from a **team production model** of corporate governance. Team production notes that the work of a corporation requires the combined input of two or more individuals or groups.[186] From this perspective, corporations are cooperative teams charged with the responsibility of not only creating new wealth but also attending to the interests and needs of stakeholders—and boards should be reflective of that cooperative team.[187]

Many of the proponents for a director-primacy model of corporate governance come from the field of law. They argue that the laws used to support a shareholder-primacy model of corporate governance have been misinterpreted and that shareholders do not own corporations—they only own stock and thus have no legal right to control the firm.[188] They contend that a director-primacy model of corporate governance will ultimately serve shareholders best because it provides boards of directors the autonomy needed to do what is in the long-term best interests of the corporation.[189] These proponents contend that focusing on share value promotes short-termism, which eventually can cause harm to firms and all their stakeholders, including shareholders.[190]

The Business Roundtable's 2019 call for a commitment to long-term value creation by focusing on stakeholders has prompted even more debate about the optimal governance model. Some have proposed a new **stakeholder governance model**, which reimagines corporate governance as a cooperative exercise between and among a corporation's stakeholders.[191] However, the specifics on this newer paradigm are still evolving, and many governance experts are speculative about how this would work in practice. In fact, governance experts Lucian Bebchuk and Stephen Bainbridge, who have frequently disagreed over shareholder versus director primacy, align in skepticism about stakeholder governance that they see as imposing significant costs on shareholders, stakeholders, and society at large.[192]

Regardless of the type of governance model embraced by practitioners, the pursuit of share value is coming under question by practitioners as well as academics. As noted by *PwC*, "The dichotomy between long-term and short-term thinking has had a polarizing effect on corporate boardrooms and investors in recent years."[193] Recent controversies over the "myth of maximizing shareholder value" continue to be debated, and the arguments for and against the ideal governance approach continue to evolve and are not likely to be settled soon. In the meantime, awareness and understanding of both perspectives is helpful in developing a richer understanding of the complexities of corporate governance.

Summary

Recent events in corporate America have served to underscore the importance of good corporate governance and the legitimacy it is supposed to provide for business. To remain legitimate, corporations must be governed according to the intended and legal pattern. Governance scandals call not only the legitimacy of individual companies into question but also that of business as a whole. Strong and effective governance is a precondition for strong CSR, sustainability, and business ethics.

The modern corporation is a complex entity and so it is not surprising that reasonable people would differ on the model by which corporate governance should be based. The Anglo-American shareholder-primacy model has been a dominant model in most free enterprise economies for years, but the director primacy-based team production model, as well as the stakeholder governance model, are making noticeable inroads in U.S. businesses with the idea that they offer broader stakeholder perspectives. In the shareholder-primacy model, the key issue is a separation between ownership and control, which has resulted in problems with managers not always doing what the owners would rather they do. From this perspective, boards of directors are responsible for ensuring that managers represent the best interests of owners, but boards sometimes lack the independence needed to monitor management effectively. This has led to serious problems in the corporate governance arena, such as excessive levels of CEO pay and a weak relationship between CEO pay and firm performance. And at times an effort to solve one problem can create another. The use of stock options in CEO compensation has helped tie CEO pay to firm performance more closely, but it has resulted in skyrocketing levels of pay, as well as in the manipulation of option timing and pricing. Other issues are lavish executive retirement plans and outside director compensation. New SEC rules for transparency may have an impact on compensation issues in the future.

In the director-primacy model, the board is a mediating hierarch, responsible for balancing the needs of all the stakeholders. In the stakeholder governance model, multiple stakeholders are expected to have direct input into board decision-making. At times, the varying models of corporate governance converge but more often, they diverge. The market for corporate control is an example. From the shareholder-primacy perspective, the market for corporate control should rein in CEO excesses. The threat of a takeover should motivate a CEO to represent shareholders' best interests. Poison pills become problems because they can blunt the takeover threat by making it prohibitively expensive for an acquirer. In contrast, the director-primacy model would see poison pills as an opportunity to slow the speed of a hostile takeover attempt, providing an opportunity to assure that all stakeholders are well represented. And under a stakeholder governance model, poison pills would be assessed based on their impact on stakeholders beyond just those in primary contact with the company, like local communities.

SOX was a landmark piece of legislation, drafted in response to the financial scandals of the early 2000s. The global financial crisis ushered in the Dodd–Frank Wall Street Reform Act, which brought comprehensive financial regulatory reform, and new requirements that affected the oversight of financial institutions and corporate governance practices. The COVID-19 pandemic will likely have repercussions for governance and regulations, as we will see proposals to address pandemic event-related litigation against companies for years to come.

In many ways, corporate governance has improved. CEOs no longer enjoy complete job security when firm performance suffers. Corporations can no longer release false or misleading reports without threat of consequences. The growth in CEO pay has tapered off, although it remains at extremely high levels. These improvements are worthy of note, but they are insufficient to protect the legitimacy of business. Continual vigilance must be maintained if corporate governance is to realize its promise and its purpose, that of being responsive to the needs of shareholders and the many individuals and groups who have a stake in the firm, as well as enabling business to be a positive force in society.

Key Terms

Accounting Reform and Investor Protection Act of 2002, p. 210
agency problems, p. 203
Anglo-American model, p. 201
audit committee, p. 212
backdating, p. 205
board of directors, p. 202
bullet-dodging, p. 205
business judgment rule, p. 213
Business Roundtable (BRT), p. 202
CEO duality, p. 213
CEO Pay Ratio, p. 205
charter, p. 202
classified boards (also known as staggered boards), p. 214
clawback provisions, p. 206
clean capitalism, p. 206
compensation committee, p. 212
conflict of interest, p. 215
Continental-European (or "Rhineland") model, p. 202
corporate gadflies, p. 215
corporate governance, p. 201
corporate responsibility committee, p. 213
corporate social activism, p. 201
corporate sustainability committee, p. 213
Council of Institutional Investors (CII), p. 206

Directors & Officers (D&O), p. 213
Dodd–Frank Wall Street Reform and Consumer Protection Act, p. 210
director-primacy model, p. 218
employees, p. 203
fiduciary duties, p. 216
fragile mandate, p. 201
full disclosure (also known as transparency), p. 216
Glass Lewis, p. 215
golden parachute, p. 208
information asymmetry, p. 210
inside directors, p. 205
insider trading, p. 208
Institutional Shareholder Services (ISS), p. 215
legitimacy, p. 200
legitimation, p. 201
majority vote, p. 214
management, p. 203
material information, p. 208
nominating committee, p. 212
outside directors, p. 205
personal liability, p. 213
poison pill, p. 208
Ponzi scheme, p. 211
Private Securities Litigation Reform Act of 1995, p. 216
proxy access, p. 215
proxy advisory firms, p. 215

Regulation FD (fair disclosure), p. 210
restricted stock, p. 206
risk committees, p. 213
Sarbanes–Oxley Act of 2002 (aka SOX or Sarbox), p. 210
Say on Pay movement, p. 206
separation of ownership from control, p. 203
shareholder activism, p. 215
shareholder democracy, p. 214
Shareholder-Director Exchange (SDX), p. 216
shareholder engagement, p. 216
shareholder lawsuit, p. 216
shareholder-primacy model, p. 217
shareholder resolutions, p. 215
shareholders, p. 202
social activism, p. 201
spring-loading, p. 205
staggered boards, p. 214
stakeholder governance model, p. 218
stock options, p. 205
team production model, p. 218
tippee, p. 209
tipper, p. 209
transparency, p. 216

Discussion Questions

1. Explain the evolution of corporate governance. What problems developed? What are the current trends?
2. What are the major criticisms of boards of directors? Which single criticism do you find to be the most important? Why?
3. How do companies lose legitimacy? Explain how governance failures could happen. How might they be avoided?
4. How has shareholder activism changed the practices of business and corporate governance?

5. Outline the major suggestions that have been set forth for improving corporate governance. In your opinion, which suggestions are the most important? Why?
6. Discuss the pros and cons of the shareholder-primacy, director-primacy, and shareholder governance models of corporate governance. Which do you prefer and why?

Endnotes

1. Gallup Confidence in Institutions, https://news.gallup.com /poll/317135/amid-pandemic-confidence-key-institutions -surges.aspx. Accessed March 3, 2021.
2. Guhan Subramanian, "Corporate Governance 2.0," *Harvard Business Review* (March, 2015, p. 98).
3. Pamela Gordon and Leilani Latimer, "5 Steps Boards Can Take to Be ESG-Ready for 2021," *Greenbiz*, (January 21, 2021), https://www.greenbiz.com/article/5-steps-boards -can-take-be-esg-ready-2021. Accessed March 9, 2021.
4. Cited in Edwin M. Epstein and Dow Votaw (eds.), *Rationality, Legitimacy, Responsibility: Search for New Directions in Business and Society* (Santa Monica, CA: Goodyear Publishing Co., 1978), 72.
5. Ibid., 73.
6. Ibid.
7. "Miracle Healers," *The Economist* (September 19, 2015), 57.
8. Epstein and Votaw, 1978.
9. Maxwell Palmer and Benjamin Schneer, "How and Why Retired Politicians Get Lucrative Appointments on Corporate Boards," *Washington Post Monkey Cage* Post (February 1, 2015), https://www.washingtonpost.com /blogs/monkey-cage/wp/2015/02/01/how-and-why-retired -politicians-get-lucrative-appointments-on-corporate -boards/. Accessed March 9, 2021.
10. Epstein and Votaw, 1978.
11. William R. Dill (ed.), *Running the American Corporation* (Englewood Cliffs, NJ: Prentice Hall, 1978), 11.
12. Richard C. Warren, "The Evolution of Business Legitimacy," *European Business Review* (Vol. 15, No. 3, 2003), 153–163.
13. Ibid.
14. Ross Kerber, Helen Coster, and Arriana McLymore, "U.S. Companies Vow to Fight Racism but Face Critics on Diversity," *Thomson Reuters* (June 10, 2020), https://www .reuters.com/article/us-minneapolis-police-companies -insight/u-s-companies-vow-to-fight-racism-but-face -critics-on-diversity-idUSKBN23H1KW. Accessed March 3, 2021.
15. "Special Report: Corporate America's Woes, Continued— Enron: One Year On," *The Economist* (November 30, 2002).
16. Ruth V. Aguilera and Gregory Jackson, "The Cross-National Diversity of Corporate Governance: Dimensions and Determinants," *Academy of Management Review* (2003), 28, no. 3, 447–465.

17. R.I. (Bob) Tricker, "The Cultural Dependence of Corporate Governance," (November 7, 2011), https:// corporategovernanceoup.wordpress.com/page/2/. Accessed March 8, 2021.
18. Ibid.
19. The Business Roundtable, "Statement of the Purpose of the Corporation" (August 19, 2019), https://opportunity. businessroundtable.org/ourcommitment/. Accessed March 7, 2021.
20. John D. Stoll, "Shareholders Are Still King," *The Wall Street Journal* (September 7–8, 2019), P. B2.
21. Catherine Thorbecke, "Stakeholder Capitalism Commitments Mostly for Show Amid COVID-19, Report Finds," *ABC News* (September 22, 2020), https://abcnews .go.com/Business/stakeholder-capitalism-commitments -show-amid-covid-19-report/story?id=731655. Accessed March 7, 2021.
22. David A. Katz and Laura A. McIntosh, "Corporate Governance Update: The Broadening Basis for Business Judgment," *Law.com* (September 23, 2020), https://www .law.com/newyorklawjournal/2020/09/23/corporate -governance-update-the-broadening-basis-for-business -judgment/?slreturn=20210203140923. Accessed March 3, 2021.
23. Lynn Paine, "COVID-19 Is Rewriting the Rules of Corporate Governance," *Harvard Business Review* (October 6, 2020), https://hbr.org/2020/10/covid-19-is -rewriting-the-rules-of-corporate-governance. Accessed March 5, 2021.
24. Lynn Stout, *The Shareholder Value Myth* (San Francisco, CA: Berrett-Koehler Publishers, Inc., 2012).
25. Carl Icahn, "What Ails Corporate America—And What Should Be Done," *Businessweek* (October 17, 1986), 101.
26. PwC's 2020 Annual Corporate Directors Survey, "Turning Crisis into Opportunity," *PwC*, https://www.pwc.com/us /en/services/governance-insights-center/library/annual -corporate-directors-survey.html. Accessed March 4, 2021.
27. Ibid.
28. Jack Welch and Suzy Welch, "How Much Blame Do Boards Deserve?" *Businessweek* (January 14, 2009), http:// www.businessweek.com/stories/2009-01-13/how-much -blame-do-boards-deserve. Accessed March 8, 2021.
29. John D. Stoll, "Corporate Boards Suffer from an 'Experience Gap' as the Coronavirus Upends Business,"

The Wall Street Journal (March 20, 2020), https://www
.wsj.com/articles/corporate-boards-suffer-experience-gap
-as-coronavirus-upends-business-11584716400. Accessed
March 4, 2021.

30. See Paula Loop, Paul DeNicola, and Leah Malone, "2020
Annual Corporate Directors Survey," Harvard Law School
Forum on Corporate Governance, https://corpgov.law
.harvard.edu/2020/11/01/2020-annual-corporate-directors
-survey/. Accessed March 4, 2021; Dominic Barton and Mark
Wiseman, "Where Boards Fall Short," *Harvard Business
Review* (January–February 2015), https://hbr.org/2015/01
/where-boards-fall-short. Accessed March 4, 2021.

31. Peter Eavis, "S.E.C. Approves Rule on C.E.O. Pay
Ratio," *The New York Times* (August 5, 2015). https://
gravitypayments.com/blog/new-digs-new-era-for-gravitys
-boise-team/. Accessed March 4, 2021.

32. Lawrence Mishel and Jori Kandra, " CEO Compensation
Surged 14% in 2019 to $21.3 Million," *Economic
Policy Institute* (August 18, 2020), https://www.epi.org
/publication/ceo-compensation-surged-14-in-2019-to-21
-3-million-ceos-now-earn-320-times-as-much-as-a-typical
-worker/. Accessed March 4, 2021.

33. "How CEO Pay in America Got Out of Whack," *The
Economist* (July 11, 2020), https://www.pwc.com/us
/en/services/governance-insights-center/library/annual
-corporate-directors-survey.html. Accessed March 4, 2021.

34. See *CGLytics*, "Will the Dust Settle?," (February 10,
2021), https://insights.diligent.com/white-paper/russell
-3000-pandemic-report-vol-2-will-the-dust-settle. Accessed
March 4, 2021; *Equilar*, "CEO Pay Did Not Increase in
2019- What Will Be the Effects of COVID-19?" https://
www.equilar.com/press-releases/122-ceo-pay-and
-impacts-of-covid19.html. Accessed March 5, 2021.

35. Ibid.

36. Jack Kelly, "CEOs are Making Millions While Laying
off Thousands of Workers and Filing for Bankruptcy,"
Forbes, (June 10, 2020), https://www.forbes.com
/sites/jackkelly/2020/06/10/ceos-are-making-millions
-while-laying-off-thousands-of-workers-and-filing-for
-bankruptcy/?sh=a1b5ee053f30. Accessed March 5, 2021.

37. Ibid.

38. See Aubrey Bout, Brian Wilby, and Perla Cruz, "S&P
500 CEO Compensation Increase Trends," *Harvard Law
School Forum on Corporate Governance* (February 11,
2020), https://corpgov.law.harvard.edu/2020/02/11
/sp-500-ceo-compensation-increase-trends-3/. Accessed
March 4, 2021; Willis Towers Watson, "2020 S&P 1500
CEO Pay Study," https://www.willistowerswatson.com
/en-US/Insights/2020/08/2020-S-P-1500-CEO-pay-study.
Accessed March 4, 2021.

39. Ibid.

40. Emily Chasan, "Last Gasp for Stock Options?" *The Wall
Street Journal CFO Report* (August 16, 2013), http://
blogs.wsj.com/cfo/2013/08/26/last-gasp-for-stock
-options/. Accessed March 5, 2021.

41. Willis Towers Watson, "2020 S&P 1500 CEO Pay
Study," https://www.willistowerswatson.com/en-US
/Insights/2020/08/2020-S-P-1500-CEO-pay-study.
Accessed March 4, 2021.

42. Michel and Kandra, 2020.

43. See CIPD, "Executive Pay in the FTSE 100: 2020 Review"
(August 5, 2020), https://www.cipd.co.uk/knowledge
/strategy/reward/executive-pay-ftse-100-2020#gref.
Accessed March 5, 2021; Alex Barker, David Oakley, and

Brian Groom, "EU Eyes New Rules over Executive Pay,"
The Financial Times, March 8, 2014 (London Edition), 2.

44. Tyler Cowen, "CEOs Are Not Overpaid," *Time* (April 22,
2019), p. 22.

45. Ibid.

46. "How CEO Pay in America Got Out of Whack," *The
Economist* (July 11, 2020), https://www.economist.com
/business/2020/07/11/how-ceo-pay-in-america-got-out-of
-whack. Accessed March 5, 2021.

47. Paul Hodgson, "A Brief History of Say on Pay," *Ivey
Business Journal* (September/October 2009), http://www
.iveybusinessjournal.com/topics/leadership/a-brief-history
-of-Say on Pay. Accessed March 5, 2021.

48. Ibid.

49. Diane Brady, "Say on Pay: Boards Listen When
Shareholders Speak," *Bloomberg Businessweek* (June 7,
2012), http://www.businessweek.com/articles/2012-06-07
/Say on Pay-boards-listen-when-shareholders-speak.
Accessed March 5, 2021.

50. Paul Hodgson, "Surprise Surprise: Say on Pay Appears to
Be Working," *Fortune* online (July 8, 2015), http://fortune
.com/2015/07/08/Say on Pay-ceos/. Accessed March 5,
2021.

51. Joann Lublin, "How Much the Best-Performing and
Worst-Performing CEOs Got Paid," *The Wall Street
Journal* online (June 25, 2015), http://www.wsj.com
/articles/how-much-the-best-and-worst-ceos-got
-paid-1435104565. Accessed March 5, 2021.

52. Corporate Knights 2015 Global 100 Methodology, http://
www.global100.org/methodology/selection-criteria.html.
Accessed March 5, 2021.

53. Corporate Knights, Clean Capitalism, http://www
.corporateknights.com/us/about-us/. Accessed March 5, 2021.

54. Gretchen Morgenson, "Making Managers Pay, Literally,"
The New York Times (March 25, 2007), 1.

55. Theo Francis, "Clawbacks Are Hard, So Companies
Try Postponing Pay Instead," *The Wall Street Journal*
(February 7, 2021), https://www.wsj.com/articles
/clawbacks-are-hard-so-companies-try-postponing-pay
-instead-11612693801. Accessed March 5, 2021.

56. Ibid.

57. Randy Diamond, "CII Gets Specific on Its Clawback
Recommendations," *Pensions & Investments* (October 5,
2012), http://www.pionline.com/article/20121005
/DAILYREG/121009896. Accessed March 5, 2021.

58. Ibid.

59. ALF-CIO. Executive PayWatch, https://aflcio.org
/paywatch. Accessed March 7, 2021.

60. Will Englund, "Senator Warren Calls Genesis
Healthcare Executive Bonus Act of 'Unfathomable Greed'"
(February 2, 2021), https://www.washingtonpost.com
/business/2021/01/20/genesis-nursing-homes-ceo-bonus/.
Accessed March 9, 2021.

61. Kevin McCoy, "Retirement Benefit Gap: CEOs Have
Platinum Pension Packages," USA Today (October 28,
2015), http://www.usatoday.com/story/money/2015/10/28
/ceo-retirement-packages-dwarf-employee-benefits
/74681692/. Accessed March 7, 2021.

62. Stephanie Costo, "Trends in Retirement Plan Coverage
over the Last Decade," *Bureau of Labor Statistics*
(February, 2006), http://www.bls.gov/opub/mlr/2006/02
/art5full.pdf. Accessed March 7, 2021.

63. Geoffrey Colvin, "Is the Board Too Cushy?" *Director*
(February 1997), 64–65.

64. Daniel Laddin, Matthew Vnuk, and Whitney Cook, "2019–2020 Director Compensation: Board Pay Flat, Leadership Pay Up," *Compensation Advisory Partners* (August 27, 2020), https://www.capartners.com/cap-thinking/2019-20-director-compensation-board-pay-flat-leadership-pay-up/. Accessed March 5, 2021.

65. Matt Orsagh, "SEC: 'More Transparency Please' on Executive Compensation," *Market Integrity Insights* (June 22, 2012), http://blogs.cfainstitute.org /marketintegrity/2012/06/22/sec-more-transparency-please -on-executive-compensation/. Accessed March 8, 2021.

66. Statement by SEC Commissioner Luis A. Augilar at an Open Meeting on Pay Versus Performance Disclosures (April 29, 2015), http://www.sec.gov/news/statement /improving-transparency-for-executive-pay-practices.html. Accessed March 8, 2021.

67. Kai Liekefett, "The Comeback of Hostile Takeovers," Harvard Law School Forum on Corporate Governance (November 8, 2020), https://corpgov.law.harvard .edu/2020/11/08/the-comeback-of-hostile-takeovers/. Accessed March 7, 2021.

68. Dealbook, "Netflix Adopts Poison Pill," DealB%k (November 5, 2012), http://dealbook.nytimes. com/2012/11/05/netflix-adopts-poison-pill/. Accessed January 31, 2016.

69. Serge Klebnikov, "Xerox Fires Back at HP's 'Poison Pill' Plan to Slow Takeover Bid," *Forbes* (February 21, 2020), https://www.forbes.com/sites/sergeiklebnikov/2020/02/21 /xerox-fires-back-at-hps-poison-pill-plan-to-slow-takeover -bid/?sh=32521038254a. Accessed March 8, 2021.

70. Heidi N. Moore, "The Demise of Poison Pills?: Why Takeover Defenses Have Been on the Wane; Shareholders vs. Boards," *The Wall Street Journal* (February 24, 2009), C4.

71. Ofer Eldar and Michael Wittry, "The Return of Poison Pills: A First Look at 'Crisis Pills'," *Harvard Law School Forum on Corporate Governance*, (May 6, 2020), https:// corpgov.law.harvard.edu/2020/05/06/the-return-of-poison -pills-a-first-look-at-crisis-pills/. Accessed March 7, 2021.

72. Steven Davidoff Solomon, "Poison Pill's Relevance in the Age of Shareholder Activism," DealBook (April 18, 2014), http://dealbook.nytimes.com/2014/04/18/poison -pills-relevance-in-the-age-of-shareholder-activism/?_r=0. Accessed March 7, 2021.

73. John Laide, "2014 Poison Pill Impetus: Why Are U.S. Companies Adopting Poison Pills? FactSet Insight (January 2, 2015), http://www.factset.com /insight/2015/01/2014-poison-pill-impetus-why-are -u.s.-companies-adopting-poison-pills#.VwEjl3qUQmR. Accessed March 7, 2021.

74. Solomon, 2014.

75. Philip L. Cochran and Steven L. Wartick, "Golden Parachutes: Good for Management and Society?" in S. Prakash Sethi and Cecilia M. Falbe (eds.), *Business and Society: Dimensions of Conflict and Cooperation* (Lexington, MA: Lexington Books, 1987), 321.

76. See Rosabeth Moss Kanter, "WeWorks Saga Is a Cautionary Tale about Golden Parachutes and CEO Pay," *CNN Business* (November 7, 2019), https://www.cnn .com/2019/11/05/perspectives/adam-neumann-golden -parachute-wework. Accessed March 7, 2021; Amy Chozick, "Adam Neumann and the Art of Failing Up," (November 2, 2019, updated May 18, 2020), https://www .nytimes.com/2019/11/02/business/adam-neumann -wework-exit-package.html. Accessed March 7, 2021.

77. Nicholas Vega, "Ex-WeWork CEO Adam Neumann Didn't Get a $1.7B Golden Parachute, Chairman Says," *The New York Post* (February 10, 2020), https://nypost .com/2020/02/10/ex-wework-ceo-adam-neumann-didnt -get-a-1-7b-golden-parachute-successor-says/. Accessed March 7, 2021.

78. Ann K. Buchholtz and Barbara A. Ribbens, "Role of Chief Executive Officers in Takeover Resistance: Effects of CEO Incentives and Individual Characteristics," *Academy of Management Journal* (June 1994), 554–579.

79. Cochran and Wartick, 325–326.

80. Chris Gay, "Can Huge CEO Golden Parachutes Hurt You?" U.S. News Money (November 4, 2012), http:// money.usnews.com/money/personal-finance/mutual-funds /articles/2012/11/14/can-huge-ceo-golden-parachutes-hurt -you. Accessed March 8, 2021.

81. Brian Breheny, Joseph Yaffe, and Caroline Kim, "Say-on-Pay Votes and Compensation Disclosures," Harvard Law School Forum on Corporate Governance, (January 6, 2021), https://corpgov.law.harvard.edu/2021/01/06/say -on-pay-votes-and-compensation-disclosures/. Accessed March 5, 2021.

82. U.S. Securities and Exchange Commission "Insider Trading," http://www.sec.gov/answers/insider.htm. Accessed March 8, 2021.

83. Josh Clark, "How Insider Trading Works," *howstuffworks*, http://money.howstuffworks.com/insider-trading.htm. Accessed March 8, 2021.

84. "Tesla's Elon Musk Reaches Deal with SEC Over Twitter Use," *The Guardian* (April 26, 2019), https://www .theguardian.com/technology/2019/apr/26/tesla-elon -musk-sec-twitter-deal. Accessed March 7, 2021.

85. David Gelles, "Elon Musk Becomes Unlikely Anti-Establishment Hero in GameStop Saga," *The New York Times* (January 29, 2021), https://www.nytimes .com/2021/01/29/business/elon-musk-gamestop-twitter .html. Accessed March 7, 2021.

86. U.S. Securities and Exchange Commission, "Insider Trading," http://www.sec.gov/answers/insider.htm. Accessed March 7, 2021.

87. Reem Heakal, "Defining Illegal Insider Trading," Investopedia (July 26, 2013), http://www.investopedia .com/articles/03/100803.asp. Accessed March 7, 2021.

88. Tom Dreisbach, "Under Trump, SEC Enforcement of Insider Trading Dropped to Lowest Point in Decades," NPR (August 14, 2020), https://www.npr .org/2020/08/14/901862355/under-trump-sec -enforcement-of-insider-trading-dropped-to-lowest -point-in-decade. Accessed March 7, 2021.

89. Christopher H. Schmitt, "The SEC Lifts the Curtain on Company Info," *Businessweek* (August 11, 2000).

90. Liz Moyer, "Study Finds Director Pay Rising Sharply," *DealB%k* (December 9, 2015), http://www.nytimes .com/2015/12/10/business/dealbook/study-finds -director-pay-rising-sharply.html?_r=0. Accessed March 8, 2021.

91. Michael Schlesinger, "2002 Sarbanes–Oxley Act," *Business Entities* (November/December 2002), 42–49.

92. Ibid.

93. Jonathon A. Segal, "The Joy of Uncooking," *HR Magazine* (November 2002), 52–57.

94. Gretchen Morgenson, "Sarbanes-Oxley, Bemoaned as a Burden, Is an Investor's Ally," *The New York Times*, (September 8, 2017), https://www.nytimes

.com/2017/09/08/business/sarbanes-oxley-investors.html. Accessed March 7, 2021.

95. Michael Santoro and Ronald Strauss, *Wall Street Values: Business Ethics and the Financial Crisis* (New York: Cambridge University Press, 2013), p. 19.

96. U.S. Securities and Exchange Commission, Investor.gov, https://www.investor.gov/introduction-investing/investing -basics/role-sec. Accessed March 9, 2021.

97. U.S. Securities and Exchange Commission, Press Releases, https://www.sec.gov/news/pressreleases. Accessed March 9, 2021.

98. "SEC Announces Enforcement Task Force Focused on Climate and ESG Issues," https://www.sec.gov/news /press-release/2021-42. Accessed March 9, 2021.

99. Allan Chernoff, "Madoff Whistleblower Blasts SEC," CNNMoney.com (February 4, 2009), http://money .cnn.com/2009/02/04/news/newsmakers/madoff_ whistleblower/. Accessed March 8, 2021.

100. Ibid.

101. Daniel M. Gold, "The High Human Cost of Following the Money in the Madoff Fraud Case," *The New York Times* (August 25, 2011), http://movies.nytimes.com/2011/08/26 /movies/chasing-madoff-a-documentary-of-a-fraud-review .html?_r=0. Accessed March 8, 2021.

102. The Securities and Exchange Commission Post-Madoff Reforms, https://www.sec.gov/spotlight /secpostmadoffreforms.htm. Accessed March 8, 2021.

103. Thomas W. Joo, "A Trip through the Maze of 'Corporate Democracy': Shareholder Voice and Management Composition," *St. John's Law Review* (Fall, 2003), 735–767.

104. Steven A. Ramirez, "A Flaw in the Sarbanes–Oxley Reform: Can Diversity in the Boardroom Quell Corporate Corruption?" *St. John's Law Review* (Fall, 2003), 837–866.

105. See Jared Landaw, "Maximizing the Benefits of Board Diversity: Lessons Learned from Activist Investing," Harvard Law School Forum on Corporate Governance (July 14, 2020), https://corpgov.law.harvard .edu/2020/07/14/maximizing-the-benefits-of-board -diversity-lessons-learned-from-activist-investing/. Accessed March 9, 2021; Toyah Miller and Maria Carmen Triana, "Demographic Diversity in the Boardroom: Mediators of the Board Diversity–Firm Performance Relationship," *Journal of Management studies*, 46(5), 2009, 755–786; Maria Carmen Triana, Toyah Miller, and Tiffany Trzebiatowski, "The Double-Edged Nature of Board Gender Diversity: Diversity, Firm Performance, and the Power of Women Directors as Predictors of Strategic Change," *Organization Science*, 25(2), 2014, 609–632; Niclas L. Erhardt, James D. Werbel, and Charles B. Shrader, "Board of Director Diversity and Firm Financial Performance," *Corporate Governance: An International Review* (April 2003), 102–111.

106. Matteo Tonello, "Corporate Board Practices in the Russell 3000 and S&P 500, 2020 Edition," The Conference Board, https://conferenceboard.esgauge.org/boardpractices/report. Accessed March 7, 2021.

107. Ibid.

108. PwC, "Turning Crisis into Opportunity," 2020 Annual Corporate Directors Survey, https://www.pwc.com/us /en/services/governance-insights-center/library/annual- corporate-directors-survey.html. Accessed March 7, 2021.

109. Alliance for Board Diversity, "Missing Pieces Report: Industry View" (January 2020), https://www2.deloitte

.com/us/en/pages/center-for-board-effectiveness/articles /missing-pieces-report-industry-view.html. Accessed March 7, 2021.

110. See for example, Susan Adams, Patricia Flynn, and Toni Wolfman, "Orchestrating the Demise of All-Male Boards," *Journal of Management Inquiry* (DOI 1056492614546264, 2014).

111. James Ellis, "Latinos are 18% of the U.S. Population...," *Bloomberg Businessweek*, (January 11, 2021), 10–12.

112. Rachel Feintzeig, "Women Get Bigger Share of Board Seats," *The Wall Street Journal* (September 12, 2019), B6.

113. Ibid.

114. Chip Cutter, "Pressures Rise to Diversify Boards," *The Wall Street Journal* (December 8, 2020), B1.

115. Russell Reynolds Survey on Board Diversity, http://www .russellreynolds.com/insights/thought-leadership/minority -female-representation-on-fortune-250-boards-executive -teams. Accessed March 8, 2021.

116. Vanessa Fuhrmans, "Pressure Tactics Diversify Boards," *The Wall Street Journal* (April 26, 2018), B6.

117. Joan Warner, "Get Ready for a Red-Hot Season," *Directorship* (December 2006–January 2007), 1–27.

118. Stephanie Holmes, "Smashing the Glass Ceiling," *BBC News* (January 11, 2008), http://news.bbc.co.uk/2/hi /business/7176879.stm. Accessed January 4, 2016.

119. Claire Cain Miller, "Women on the Board: Quotas Have Limited Success," *The Upshot* (June 19, 2014), http://www .nytimes.com/2014/06/20/upshot/women-on-the-board -quotas-have-limited-success.html?_r=0. Accessed March 8, 2021.

120. Ibid.

121. Eric Helland and Michael Sykuta, "Who's Monitoring the Monitor? Do Outside Directors Protect Shareholders' Interests?" *Financial Review* (May 2005), 155–172.

122. Richard A. Johnson and Daniel W. Greening, "The Effects of Corporate Governance and Institutional Ownership Types on Corporate Social Performance," *Academy of Management Journal* (October 1999), 564–576.

123. Donald C. Hambrick, Vilmos Misangyi, and Chuljin Park, "The Quad Model for Identifying a Corporate Director's Potential for Effective Monitoring: Toward a New Theory of Board Sufficiency," *Academy of Management Review* (Vol. 40, No. 3, 2015), 323–344.

124. James B. Stewart, "Problems at Volkswagen Start at the Boardroom," *The New York Times* (September 24, 2015), B1.

125. John Joseph, William Ocasio, and Mary-Hunter McDonnell, "The Structural Elaboration of Board Independence: Executive Power, Institutional Logics, and the Adoption of the CEO-Only Board Structures in U.S. Corporate Governance," *Academy of Management Journal* (Vol. 57, No. 6, 2014), 1834–1858.

126. The Sarbanes–Oxley Act 2002, http://www.legalarchiver .org/soa.htm. Accessed March 5, 2021.

127. Charles A. Anderson and Robert N. Anthony, *The New Corporate Directors: Insights for Board Members and Executives* (New York: John Wiley & Sons, 1986), 141.

128. Sydney Finkelstein and Donald Hambrick, "Boards of Directors and Corporate Governance," in *Strategic Leadership: Top Executives and Their Effects on Organizations* (MN: West Publishing, 1996), 216.

129. Olubunmi Faleye, Rani Hoitash, and Udi Hoitash, "The Costs of Intense Board Monitoring," *Journal of Financial Economics* (Vol. 101, 2011), 160–181.

130.   Johnson & Johnson, http://www.investor.jnj.com /governance/committee.cfm. Accessed March 7, 2021.

131.   Unilever Investor Relations, http://www .unilever.com/investorrelations/corp_governance /boardandmanagementcommittees/. Accessed March 7, 2021.

132.   Dave Magnani, "Average C-Suite Tenure and Other Important Executive Facts," M&A Executive Search (November 19, 2020), https://maexecsearch.com/average -c-suite-tenure-and-other-important-executive-facts/. Accessed March 5, 2021; Korn Ferry, "Where Have All the Long-Tenured CEOs Gone?" https://www.kornferry .com/insights/articles/where-have-all-the-long-tenured -ceos-gone. Accessed March 5, 2021.

133.   Nanette Byrnes and David Kiley, "Hello, You Must Be Going," *Businessweek* (February 12, 2007), 30–32.

134.   Donald Hambrick and Timothy Quigley, "Toward a More Accurate Contextualization of the CEO Effect on Firm Performance," *Strategic Management Journal, 35*(4), 2014, 473–491.

135.   Jeffrey Sonnenfeld, "CEO Exit Schedules: A Season to Stay, a Season to Go," *Fortune* online (May 6, 2015), http://fortune.com/2015/05/06/ceo-tenure-cisco/. Accessed January 2, 2016.

136.   Sydney Finkelstein and Richard D'Aveni, "CEO Duality as a Double-Edged Sword: How Boards of Directors Balance Entrenchment Avoidance and Unity of Command," *Academy of Management Journal, 37*(5), 1994, 1079–1106.

137.   Ibid.

138.   SpencerStuart, "2020 SpencerStuart Board Index," https:// www.spencerstuart.com/research-and-insight/2020-q3 -ceo-transitions. Accessed March 5, 2021.

139.   Court of Chancery of the State of Delaware Memorandum Opinion In Re Dole Food Co., Inc Stockholder Litigation, In Re Appraisal of Dole Food Company, Inc. (August 15, 2015), http://courts.delaware.gov/opinions/download .aspx?ID=228790. Accessed March 8, 2021.

140.   Paul E. Fiorella, "Why Comply? Directors Face Heightened Personal Liability after Caremark," *Business Horizons* (July/August 1998), 49–52.

141.   Kevin M. LaCroix, "Another Delaware Breach of the Duty of Oversight Case Survives Dismissal Motion," *The D&O Diary* (May 5, 2020), https://www.dandodiary .com/2020/05/articles/director-and-officer-liability /another-delaware-breach-of-the-duty-of-oversight-case -survives-dismissal-motion/. Accessed March 9, 2021.

142.   Kevin LaCroix, The 'Myth' of Outside Director Liability," The D&O Diary (October 20, 2015), https://www.dandodiary .com/2015/10/articles/director-and-officer-liability/the-myth -of-outside-director-liability-and-the-critical-importance-of -do-insurance/. Accessed March 9, 2021.

143.   "Ownership Matters," *The Economist* (March 11, 2006), 10.

144.   "What Shareholder Democracy?" *The Economist* (March 26, 2005), 62.

145.   "Who Selects, Governs," *Directorship* (May 2004), 6.

146.   Dennis M. Ray, "Corporate Boards and Corporate Democracy," *Journal of Corporate Citizenship* (Winter, 2005), 93–105.

147.   Lucien A. Bebchuk, "The Case for Increasing Shareholder Power," *Harvard Law Review* (January 2005), 835–914.

148.   Iman Anabtawi and Lynn A. Stout, "Fiduciary Duties for Activist Shareholders," *Stanford Law Review* (February 2008), 1255–1329.

149.   Lynn A. Stout, "Corporations Shouldn't Be Democracies," *The Wall Street Journal—Eastern Edition* (September 27, 2007), A17.

150.   Joann S. Lublin, "Directors Lose Elections but Not Seats: Staying Power of Board Members Raises Questions about Investor Democracy," *The Wall Street Journal* (September 28, 2009), B4.

151.   Ann Buchholtz and Jill Brown, "Shareholder Democracy as a Misbegotten Metaphor," in M. Goranova and L. Ryan (Eds.), *Shareholder Empowerment* (New York: Palgrave-MacMillan, 2015), 81–102.

152.   Holly J. Gregory, Rebecca Grapsas, and Claire Holland, "The Latest on Proxy Access," Harvard Law School Forum on Corporate Governance, (February 1, 2019), https://corpgov.law.harvard.edu/2019/02/01/the-latest-on -proxy-access/. Accessed March 7, 2021.

153.   Ibid.

154.   Lauren Tainer, *The Origins of Shareholder Activism* (Washington, DC: Investor Responsibility Research Center, July 1983), 2.

155.   Jennifer G. Hill, "The Rising Tension between Shareholder and Director Power in the Common Law World," *Corporate Governance: An International Review* (July 2010), 344–359.

156.   "Religious Activists Raise Cain with Corporations," *Chicago Tribune* (June 7, 1998), Business Section, 8.

157.   Jeffrey Sonnenfeld, "Another Suicidal Board? How DuPont's Directors Failed Ellen Kullman," Fortune (October 13, 2015), http://fortune.com/2015/10/13/dupont -board-ellen-kullman/. Accessed March 8, 2021.

158.   Stephen Gandel, "How Dupont Went to War with Activist Investor Nelson Peltz," *Fortune* online (May 11, 2015), http://fortune.com/2015/05/11/how-dupont-went-to-war. Accessed March 8, 2021.

159.   David Benoit, "Activism's Long Road from Corporate Raiding to Banner Year," *The Wall Street Journal Online* (December 26, 2015), http://www.wsj.com/articles /activisms-long-road-from-corporate-raiding-to-banner -year-1451070910. Accessed March 8, 2021.

160.   Duhigg, 2007.

161.   Ibid.

162.   Investopedia, "Top 10 Activist Investors in the U.S," https://www.investopedia.com/top-10-activist-investors-in -the-us-5083258. Accessed March 7, 2021.

163.   Exchange ICCR. "2021 Shareholder Resolutions." https:// exchange.iccr.org/resolutions/public. Accessed March 8, 2021.

164.   "Meet the Biggest 'Stakeholders'," *The Wall Street Journal* (August 28, 2019), A14.

165.   Ibid.

166.   Ibid.

167.   *Proxy Preview*, 2020, https://www.proxypreview.org/2020 /report. Accessed March 8, 2021.

168.   Deborah Nason, "Shareholders Challenge the Companies They Invest in to Promote Good in the World," *CNBC* (November 30, 2020) https://www.cnbc.com/2020/11/30 /shareholders-challenge-firms-they-invest-in-to-promote -good-in-the-world.html. Accessed March 9, 2021.

169.   Justin Fox, "Ending the Shareholder Lawsuit Gravy Train," *Harvard Business Review* (February 27, 2014). https://hbr.org/2014/02/ending-the-shareholder-lawsuit -gravy-train/. Accessed March 8, 2021.

170.   "Coty Being Sued for Allegedly Overpaying for 'Inflated' Kylie Cosmetics, Deceiving Shareholders," *The Fashion Law* (September 14, 2020), https://www .thefashionlaw.com/coty-is-being-sued-for-allegedly -overpaying-for-inflated-kylie-cosmetics/. Accessed March 8, 2021.

171. Jennier Elias, "Alphabet Settles Shareholder Lawsuit Over Alleged Mishandling of Sexual Misconduct by Executives," *CNBC* (September 25, 2020), https://www.cnbc.com/2020/09/25/alphabet-settles-shareholder-lawsuit-.html. Accessed March 8, 2021.

172. See Petition for Rulemaking on COVID-19 Related Litigation (October 30, 2020) https://www.google.com/url?sa=t&rct=j&q=&esrc=s&source=web&cd=&ved=2ahUKEwijtLD6-qDvAhVvRTABHRCJCIgQFjAPegQIIRAD&url=https%3A%2F%2Fwww.sec.gov%2Frules%2Fpetitions%2F2020%2Fpetn4-766.pdf&usg=AOvVaw2VszdPyNFcP3vuRVoLlM6M. Accessed March 8, 2021.

173. Matt Orsagh, "Shareholder Engagement: Bridging the Divide between Boards and Investors," CFA Institute Market Integrity Insights (March 26, 2014), https://blogs.cfainstitute.org/marketintegrity/2014/03/26/shareholder-engagement-bridging-the-divide-between-boards-and-investors/. Accessed March 8, 2021.

174. "The Responsibility of a Corporation to Its Shareholders," *Criteria for Decision Making* (C. W. Post Center, Long Island University, 1979), 14.

175. Mel Duvall and Kim S. Nash, "Auditing an Oracle: Shareholders Nearly Deify Warren Buffett for the Way He Manages His Diverse Holding Company, Berkshire Hathaway of Omaha," *Baseline* (August 1, 2003), 30.

176. "Recap: The 2015 Berkshire Hathaway Annual Meeting" (May 2, 2015), *The Wall Street Journal* online Moneybeat, http://blogs.wsj.com/moneybeat/2015/05/02/live-analysis-the-2015-berkshire-hathaway-annual-meeting/. Accessed March 8, 2021.

177. Michael McGinn, "Disclose No Evil," *Newsweek* (February 28, 2011), 5.

178. Curran, 2009.

179. Marc Gerber, Richard Grossman and Khadija Lalani, "Virtual Shareholder Meetings in the 2021 Proxy Season," Harvard Law School Forum on Corporate Governance (October 13, 2020), https://corpgov.law.harvard.edu/2020/10/13/virtual-shareholder-meetings-in-the-2021-proxy-season/. Accessed March 8, 2021.

180. Amy Freedman, Wes Hall, and Ian Robertson, "The Director-Shareholder Engagement Guidebook," Harvard Law School Forum on Corporate Governance" (March 2, 2019), https://corpgov.law.harvard.edu/2019/03/02/the-director-shareholder-engagement-guidebook/. Accessed March 9, 2021.

181. Warner, 2007.

182. Hill, 2010.

183. See Stephen Bainbridge, "Long-Term Bias and Director Primacy," *UCLA School of Law, Law-Econ Research Paper* (20-04). Columbia Margaret M. Blair and Lynn A. Stout, "A Team Production Theory of Corporate Law," *Virginia Law Review* (March, 1999), 247–329; Stephen M. Bainbridge, "Director Primacy and Shareholder Disempowerment," *Harvard Law Review* (April 2006), 1735–1758; Luh Luh Lan and Loizos Heracleous, "Rethinking Agency Theory: The View from the Law," *Academy of Management Review* (April 2010) 223–239.

184. Stout, 2012.

185. Blair and Stout, 1999.

186. Ibid.

187. Allen Kaufman and Ernie Englander, "A Team Production Model of Corporate Governance," *Academy of Management Executive* (August 1, 2005), 9–22.

188. Stout, 2010.

189. Stout, 2012.

190. Ibid.

191. See Martin Lipton and William Savitt, "Stakeholder Governance – Issues and Answers," *Harvard Law School Forum on Corporate Governance* (October 25, 2019), https://corpgov.law.harvard.edu/2019/10/25/stakeholder-governance-issues-and-answers/. Accessed March 8, 2021.

192. See ProfessorBainbridge.com, "Lucian Bebchuk Comes Out Against Stakeholder Governance," https://www.professorbainbridge.com/professorbainbridgecom/2020/03/lucian-bebchuk-comes-out-against-stakeholder-governance.html. Accessed March 8, 2021; Lucian Bebchuck and Roberto Tallarita, "The Illusory Promise of Stakeholder Governance," https://papers.ssrn.com/sol3/papers.cfm?abstract_id=3544978. Accessed March 8, 2021.

193. PwC Annual Corporate Directors Survey (2015), http://www.pwc.com/us/en/corporate-governance/annual-corporate-directors-survey/assets/pwc-2015-annual-corporate-directors-survey.pdf. Accessed March 7, 2021.

10

Strategy, Risk, Issues, and Crisis Management

Chapter Learning Outcomes

After studying this chapter, you should be able to:

1. Describe and differentiate between the concepts of strategic management and corporate social policy.
2. Articulate the four major strategy levels and explain enterprise-level strategy, social entrepreneurship, and the benefit corporation.
3. Explain the strategic management process and the role that sustainability reports and integrated reports play in the process.
4. Distinguish between risk management, issue management, and crisis management.

5. Describe the major categories of risk management and some of the factors that have characterized risk management in actual practice.
6. Define issue management and the stages in the issue management process. How is issue management a bridge to crisis management?
7. Define crisis management and the types of crises.
8. List and discuss the major stages or steps involved in managing business crises. Why is crisis communications so important?

The overriding goal of this chapter is to focus on planning for the turbulent social/ethical stakeholder environment. We begin by providing a broad overview of *strategic management* and discuss how social and ethical issues fit into this concept. We introduce the term *corporate social policy* to describe that component of management decision making that embraces these issues. Then we discuss corporate public affairs as the formal organizational approach some companies use in implementing these initiatives.

In previous chapters, we have mentioned companies that have had challenges in managing issues ranging from product safety to financial fraud. These issues require different managerial decision-making processes that include risk management, issue management, and crisis management. We discuss these concepts and introduce the major steps involved in managing business crises.

Businesses responding to a turbulent environment becomes even more relevant in the wake of the COVID-19 pandemic. Beyond the economic challenges of trying to stay competitive amid a global recession, businesses had to make quick decisions regarding approaches to customers, employees, suppliers, the government, and communities. Many CEOs, like Enrique Lores of HP, carried a message of "weathering the storm" and taking the time to "reinvent" their businesses.[1]

A year into the pandemic, a survey by *PwC* identified several steps that businesses had taken to tackle their business challenges, including (1) modifying the layouts

of physical space, (2) addressing employee well-being, including mental health and morale, (3) making appropriate updates to business continuity plans, and (4) successfully on-boarding new employees.[2] Another study by McKinsey noted the need for businesses to adapt their workplace practices for working parents who were forced to supervise the education of their children at home during the pandemic, which notably affected women adversely.[3] The COVID-19 pandemic tested the strategies, risk, issues, and crisis management of businesses in a way that required quick action and, for many, a crash course in crisis management.

In sum, this chapter points to the idea that businesses must plan for, and be prepared for, managing social/ethical issues. Some of these issues might be anticipated and planned for, while others may catch businesses by surprise; therefore, companies must find a way to plan and respond in an ethical way to satisfy their stakeholders as best they can.

10.1 Strategic Management and Corporate Social Policy

Strategic management refers to the overall management process that strives to identify corporate purpose and position a firm to succeed in its market environment by achieving competitive advantage. A business relates to its market environment through the products and services it produces and the markets in which it chooses to participate. Strategic management therefore incorporates sustainability and ethical concerns, with the realization that the long-term viability of a firm is linked inextricably with its impact on the economy, society, and the environment.

Corporate social policy refers to a firm's posture, stance, strategy, or position regarding the environmental, social, global, and ethical aspects of stakeholders and corporate functioning. It can also be called *corporate sustainability policy*, and it might be identified in organizations under the *corporate public affairs* function, or within the concept of *corporate citizenship*. While the impact of the environmental/social/ethical/global stakeholder environment on business organizations has always been powerful, it seems to grow stronger each year. What started as a simple awareness of social issues and social responsibility in business has matured into a focus on the management of sustainability, reflected in the triple bottom line. As we noted in Chapter 4, sustainability is now a strategic issue with far-reaching implications for organizational purpose, direction, and functioning.

Many businesses formalize their concerns under the rubric of **corporate public affairs**, corporate affairs, or **public affairs management**. Businesses encounter situations daily that involve highly visible public and ethical issues, including those that are subject to intensive public debate for specific periods before being institutionalized. Examples of such issues have included sexual harassment, racial justice, equal employment opportunities, product safety, and employee privacy. Other issues that are more philosophical might include the broad role of business in society, issues of corporate governance, and the relative balance of business versus government that is best for our society.

The idea behind corporate social policy is that a firm must give specific attention to issues in which basic questions of justice, fairness, ethics, or social policy reside. Today's dynamic stakeholder environment necessitates that managers employ a policy perspective to these issues. At one time, the social environment was thought to be a relatively constant backdrop against which the real work of business took place. Today, these issues are central, and managers at all levels must address them. Corporate social policy is the process by which management addresses these significant concerns.

Corporate social policy incorporates sustainability as that part of the overall strategic management of the organization that focuses on the environmental, economic, social, and ethical stakeholder issues that are embedded in the decision processes of the firm. Therefore, just as a firm needs to develop policy in functional areas such as human resources, operations, marketing, or finance, it also must develop corporate *social* policy to address proactively the host of issues discussed throughout this book.

Ben & Jerry's is an ice cream maker that has long been known for its public social policies as well as its popular ice cream flavors. Its acquisition by Unilever in 2015 only solidified its commitment to a values-based social policy. For example, in the 2016 election season, it launched an "Empower Mint" ice-cream flavor in support of a voting-rights campaign. CEO Jostein Solheim summed up the company's corporate social policies as follows: "Many people are feeling a tremendous lack of trust in [public] institutions around them. We need organizations, including businesses, to step forward more than ever."[4]

Relationship of Ethics to Strategic Management. A consideration of ethics is implicit in corporate social policy discussions, but it is useful to make this relationship more explicit. Over the years, a growing number of observers have stressed this point. The leadership challenge of determining future strategy in the face of rising moral and ethical standards may be the most strenuous in strategic decision making, particularly stressful within the inherently amoral corporation.[5] However, a shift is taking place in business as more companies attempt to integrate ethics, social responsibility, sustainability, and strategic management. In fact, consulting firms like *KPMG* now offer services on how to integrate environmental, social, and governance (ESG) issues into strategy, as businesses realize that good ESG practices can drive business results.[6]

The focus of linking ethics and strategy moved to center stage in the book *Corporate Strategy and the Search for Ethics*, which argued that if business ethics were to have any meaning beyond pompous moralizing, it should be linked to business strategy. The theme was that the concept of corporate strategy could be revitalized by linking ethics to strategy. This linkage permits addressing the most pressing management issues of the day in ethical terms. The book introduces the idea of *enterprise strategy* as the one that best links these two vital notions, and this concept is examined in more detail in the next section.[7]

The concept of corporate social policy and the linkage between ethics and strategy are better understood when we think about the

1. four key levels at which strategy decisions arise and
2. steps in the strategic management process in which these decisions are embedded.

We discuss these important concepts in sections 10.2 and 10.3 below.

10.2 Four Key Strategy Levels

Because organizations are hierarchical, it is not surprising to find that strategic management also is hierarchical in nature; that is, the firm has several different levels at which strategic decisions are made, or at which the strategy process occurs. These levels range from the broadest or highest levels, where missions, visions, goals, and decisions entail higher risks and are characterized by longer time horizons, more subjective values, and greater uncertainty, to the lowest levels (where planning is done for specific functional areas characterized by shorter time horizons, less complex information needs, and less uncertainty).

10.2a Four Strategy Levels Described

Four key strategy levels are important to corporate social responsibility (CSR), ethics, sustainability, and stakeholder issues: (1) enterprise-level strategy, (2) corporate-level strategy, (3) business-level strategy, and (4) functional-level strategy.

Enterprise-Level Strategy. The broadest level of strategic management is known as *societal-level strategy* or *enterprise-level strategy*. **Enterprise-level strategy** is the overarching strategy level that poses such basic questions as, "What is the role of the organization in society?" and "For what do we stand?" As will be evident from the detailed discussion later, this encompasses the development and articulation of corporate social policy and may be considered the first and most important level at which ethics and strategy are linked. Corporate governance is one of the most important topics at this level.

Corporate-Level Strategy. **Corporate-level strategy** addresses what are often posed as the most defining business question for a firm, "In what business(es) should we be?" Thus, mergers, acquisitions, and divestitures, as well as whether and how to participate in global markets, are examples of decisions made at this level. A host of issues related to ethics and sustainability arise at this level as well.

Business-Level Strategy. **Business-level strategy** is concerned with the question, "How should we compete in a given business or industry?" Thus, a company whose products or services take it into many different businesses, industries, or markets will need a business-level strategy to define its competitive posture in each of them. A competitive strategy might address whether a product should be low cost or differentiated, as well as whether it should compete in broad or narrow markets and how to do so in a sustainable way.

Functional-Level Strategy. **Functional-level strategy** addresses the question, "How should a firm integrate its various subfunctional activities and how should these activities be related to changes taking place in the diverse functional areas (finance, marketing, human resources, IT and operations)?"[8] Companies need to be certain that their functional areas conduct themselves in ways that are consistent with the values for which the firm stands.

The purpose of identifying the four strategy levels is to clarify that corporate social policy is primarily a part of enterprise-level strategy, which, in turn, is but one level of strategic decision making that occurs in organizations. In terms of its implementation, however, the other strategy levels inevitably come into play, and all levels play a part in fulfilling a firm's commitment to its purpose and values. Figure 10-1 illustrates that enterprise-level strategy is the broadest strategy level and that the other levels are narrower concepts that cascade from it.

10.2b Emphasis on Enterprise-Level Strategy

The term *enterprise-level strategy* is not used frequently in the business community, but it is helpful here. Although many firms address the issues with which enterprise-level strategy is concerned, use of this terminology is concentrated primarily in the academic community. This terminology describes the level of strategic thinking necessary if firms are to be fully responsive to today's complex and dynamic stakeholder environment. Most organizations today convey their enterprise or societal strategy in their vision, missions, or values statements. Others embed their enterprise strategies in codes of conduct. Increasingly, these strategies are reflecting a global level of application, like the UN Global Compact principles and Sustainable Development Goals (SDGs), which we noted in Chapter 4.

Figure 10-1 The Hierarchy of Strategy Levels

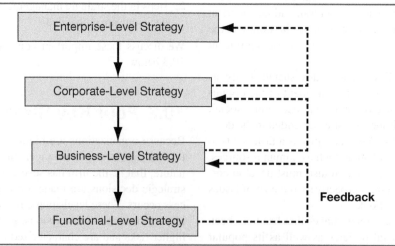

Enterprise-level strategy needs to be thought of as a concept that more closely aligns "social and ethical concerns" with traditional "business concerns."[9] In setting the direction for a firm, a manager needs to understand the impact of changes in business strategy on the underlying values of the firm and the new stakeholder relationships that will consequently emerge and take shape. Thus, at the enterprise level, the task of setting strategic direction involves understanding the role in society of a particular firm as a whole and its relationships to other social institutions. Important questions that help flesh out enterprise strategy then become:

- What is the role and purpose of our organization in society?
- How do our stakeholders perceive our organization?
- What principles or values does our organization represent?
- What obligations do we have to society, including to the world?
- What are the broad implications for our current mix of businesses and allocation of resources?

Many firms have addressed some of these questions—perhaps only in part or in an ad hoc way. The point of enterprise-level strategy, however, is that the firm needs to address these questions intentionally, specifically, and cohesively in such a way that a corporate social policy is articulated.

How have business firms addressed these questions? How are these reflected in enterprise-level thinking and corporate social policy? The manifestations show up in various ways in different companies, such as a firm's response when faced with public crises. Does it respond to its stakeholders in a positive, constructive, and sensitive way or in a negative, defensive, and insensitive way? Corporate decisions and actions reveal the presence or absence of soundly developed enterprise-level strategy. Companies also demonstrate the degree of thinking that has gone into public issues by the presence or absence and use or non-use of codes of ethics, codes of conduct, mission statements, purpose statements, values statements, vision statements, or other such policy-oriented codes and statements. Special topics of importance in enterprise-level strategy include social entrepreneurship, bottom of the pyramid, the benefit corporation, and the importance of core values. We discuss each of these next.

Social Entrepreneurship. Although enterprise strategy is relevant for all firms, it holds special applicability in **social entrepreneurship**. Social entrepreneurship is a cultural phenomenon that has been growing exponentially.[10] In spite of its popularity, it remains a term that is ill-defined.[11] Social entrepreneurs, as discussed in Chapter 2, differ from traditional entrepreneurs in that the social enterprise has a mission of societal value creation, and that mission is its reason for being. Social entrepreneurs must create wealth to survive and thrive as well, but it is a means to an end of social value creation. The social mission is fundamental to social entrepreneurship. In contrast, socially responsible businesses may create social value en route to creating

wealth, but wealth creation remains that business's ultimate goal. J. Gregory Dees, an expert on this topic, provides the following elements of social entrepreneurship[12]:

Social entrepreneurs play the role of change agents in the social sector, by:
- Adopting a mission to create and sustain social value (not just private value)
- Recognizing and relentlessly pursuing new opportunities to serve that mission
- Engaging in a process of continuous innovation, adaptation, and learning
- Acting boldly without being limited by resources currently in hand
- Exhibiting heightened accountability to the constituencies served and for the outcomes created

Social entrepreneurship can address a range of societal goals, including education, the environment, and the arts. However, alleviating poverty has been a central focus of many social entrepreneurs. During the COVID-19 pandemic, for example, social entrepreneurs banded together under the World Economic Forum-sponsored coalition, the COVID Response Alliance for Social Entrepreneurs, to take on 21 projects related to issues of health care, education, and more.[13]

Bottom of the Pyramid (BOP). **Bottom of the pyramid** is a term used to characterize the largest and poorest socioeconomic group of people, the billions of people who live on just a few dollars a day.[14] C. K. Prahalad and Stuart L. Hart introduced the concept that businesses could make a fortune by engaging with this typically forgotten segment of society because it contains innovative entrepreneurs as well as value-demanding customers.[15] They envisioned large, multinational corporations (MNCs) being the ones that would be able to take advantage of the BOP concept. A review of the work that has happened in the decade since they highlighted this potential market shows that only a small number of MNCs have been involved.[16] Instead, smaller enterprises and social entrepreneurs have led the effort.[17]

Social entrepreneurship helps to highlight the enterprise strategy of business and to provide a mechanism by which entrepreneurial individuals can draw on their business-based skills to make a positive difference in the world. At the same time, social entrepreneurship holds a mirror up to traditional business, showing the potential the marketplace has for creating societal as well as economic value.

As mentioned in Chapter 2, Porter and Kramer have proposed the concept of **shared value** that holds that economic and social goals are not mutually exclusive—business can pursue profit while also promoting the common good.[18] In an interview about social entrepreneurship, Porter talked about the "crisis of purpose" that he was seeing in his work with the CEOs of the world.[19] He said, "The profit that comes from benefitting society is a higher form of profit that corporations should aspire to," and that redefining aspirations in this way will lead to " a sense of much greater purpose."[20]

Spotlight on Sustainability

Enterprise-Level Strategy in Action

One of the best ways to appreciate a company's social policy or enterprise-level strategy is to examine its posture on sustainability. Wegmans, a regional U.S. supermarket chain with stores in the Mid-Atlantic region, has made a formal and effective commitment to promoting sustainability through a sustainability mission statement, a sourcing philosophy, and a sustainability coordinator.

Wegmans' mission statement begins with the Native American proverb, "We do not inherit the earth from our ancestors; we borrow it from our children." It goes on to say, "There are no simple solutions to these challenges. Still, we all have a responsibility to be aware and be accountable. We promise to take steps to protect our world for future generations—it's part of our commitment to make a difference in every community we serve."

To learn more about Wegmans' commitment to sustainability, check out its website: http://www.wegmans.com.

The Benefit Corporation. A new corporate form has arisen that helps companies that wish to emphasize enterprise-level strategy. This new corporate form is designed to aid companies that have found it challenging to fulfill their social good–oriented missions in traditional for-profit corporations that entail a fiduciary duty for profit maximization and shareholder primacy. **Benefit corporations**, as mentioned in Chapter 2, permit corporations to pursue stakeholder and societal welfare maximization as well as shareholder wealth maximization because benefit corporations (**B Corps**) have a broader mission that includes having a positive impact on society. Benefit corporations give managers the opportunity to build, investors the opportunity to finance, and customers the opportunity to patronize businesses that promise to make social responsibility, or purpose, an important goal.

A new law grew out of B Lab, a nonprofit group that certifies companies as **B Corporations**, based on their accountability, transparency, and social responsibility.[21] Notable B Corporations include Ben & Jerry's, Etsy, Allbirds, and Patagonia, which altered its bylaws and went through a rigorous assessment to reincorporate as a benefit corporation in 2011.[22] Patagonia made the decision to do so because the designation codified and made more transparent the company's efforts to be environmentally friendly, while also providing them access to more than 1,300 global companies that share similar values.[23] As noted by one journalist, B corporations are "companies willing to bet on a different conceptualization of 'good business.'"[24]

In the United States, individual states have the authority to create and charter corporations and so the benefit corporation movement is growing state by state. The popularity of the B Corps certification is not just contained in the United States. The United Kingdom has more than 60 companies that are benefit corporations, and the certification process is also available in South America, Canada, Australia, and other parts of Europe.[25]

Benefit corporation status does not give firms tax or other incentives; however, it offers companies some legal protection to make decisions for reasons other than maximizing profits.[26] Hence, the decision to pursue B Corp status is one way that companies can take bring enterprise-level goals to the business level in the strategic planning process.

Patagonia has helped guide numerous other companies through the process of becoming B Corps over the years. However, the process of becoming a B Corp is not without controversy. Figure 10-2 outlines some of the pros and cons of being a B Corporation.[27]

Figure 10-2 The Pros and Cons of B Corporation Status

Pros:

- **Built-In Commitment.** It builds social commitment directly into governance to support the corporation and protect it.
- **Good Publicity.** It offers reputational effects with best practices.
- **Protection from Investor Pressures.** It can protect the company from pressures by capital markets to capitalize short-term profits.
- **Partners with Similar Values.** It offers the chance set a high benchmark for stakeholders with B Lab screenings for certain requirements on working conditions, supply chain management, and relationships with local communities.

Cons:

- **Lack of Oversight.** The rigorous B Corp certification process involves annual self-reports with a "third-party standard" for assessing performance, but only 10 percent of applicants receive on-ground verification.
- **Legal Uncertainty and Brand Erosion.** The B Corp represents a certification, whereas the benefit corporation is an actual legal entity. Neither is required to adhere to the same standards—inviting legal questions and this could erode the brand.
- **Investor Wariness.** Some investors could balk at the emphasis on social good over shareholder returns.

Sources: Ryan Bradley, "The Tao of Rose," *Fortune* (September 15, 2015), 155–162; Jonathan Crew, "The Good and Bad of Being a B Corp," *Fortune* (September 15, 2015), 160; James Surowiecki, "Companies with Benefits," *The New Yorker* (August 4, 2014), http://www.newyorker.com/magazine/2014 /08/04/companies-benefits, accessed March 18, 2021; Heather Clancy, "To Be or Not to Be? More Tech Companies Should Ask Themselves that Question," Greenbiz (June 25, 2020), https://www.greenbiz.com/article/b-or-not-b-more-tech-companies-should-ask-themselves-question, accessed March 19, 2021.

Figure 10-3 Unilever Purpose and Principles

Purpose and Principles

Our corporate purpose states that to succeed requires "the highest standards of corporate behavior toward everyone we work with, the communities we touch, and the environment on which we have an impact."

Always Working with Integrity

Conducting our operations with integrity and with respect for the many people, organizations, and environments, our business touches has always been at the heart of our corporate responsibility.

Positive Impact

We aim to make a positive impact in many ways: through our brands, our commercial operations and relationships, through voluntary contributions, and through the various other ways in which we engage with society.

Continuous Commitment

We're also committed to continuously improving the way we manage our environmental impacts and are working toward our longer-term goal of developing a sustainable business.

Setting Out Our Aspirations

Our corporate purpose sets out our aspirations in running our business. It's underpinned by our code of Business Principles, which describes the operational standards that everyone at Unilever follows, wherever they are in the world. The code also supports our approach to governance and corporate responsibility.

Working with Others

We want to work with suppliers who have values similar to our own and work to the same standards we do. Our Business Partner code, aligned to our own Code of business principles, comprises ten principles covering business integrity and responsibilities relating to employees, consumers, and the environment.

Source: https://www.unileverusa.com/about/who-we-are/purpose-and-principles/, accessed March 19, 2021. Reproduced with kind permission of Unilever PLC and group companies.

Importance of Core Values. In enterprise level strategy, it is crucial that firms not only have values statements that provide guidance but also that these values "mean something." **Core values** are the deeply ingrained principles that guide all of a company's actions and decisions, and they serve as cultural cornerstones.[28] Though many companies have written publicly proclaimed values statements, many have been sullied because they are not followed. To be effective, companies need to weave core values into everything they do. If a company's core values are not upheld, they become hollow or empty and may do more harm than good.

Deeply felt and strongly held values have the power to transform. Apple has long been known for infusing progressive values like inclusion, equality, and environmentalism into their brands, while still being considered a "ruthless competitor."[29] Apple touts its values very openly, even given the potential risk that its existing and potential customers might not share the same values.[30]

In what do value-based companies believe? It has been argued that three basic organizational values undergird all others: transparency, sustainability, and responsibility.[31] A good example of a values-based business is Unilever, and these values are reflected in their purpose and principles statement shown in Figure 10-3. Just as the character of a person will be evident in that person's actions, the values of an organization can be seen in that organization's activities.

More and more, superior performers are those companies that meet both the social and financial expectations of their stakeholders, a theme we are developing in this chapter and book. Following is a discussion of how corporate social policy is integrated into the **strategic management process**.

10.3 The Strategic Management Process

To understand how corporate social policy is just one part of the larger system of management decision making, it is useful to identify the major steps that make up the strategic management process. Boards and top management teams are responsible for activating the process. One conceptualization includes six steps: (1) goal formulation, (2) strategy formulation, (3) strategy evaluation, (4) strategy implementation, (5) strategic control, and (6) environmental analysis.[32] Figure 10-4 graphically portrays an expanded view of this process.

The environmental scanning component requires collection of information on trends, events, and issues that occur in the stakeholder environment, and this information is then fed into the other steps of the process. Although the tasks or steps are presented sequentially, they are in fact interactive and do not always occur in a neatly ordered pattern or sequence.

Figure 10-4 The Strategic Management Process and Corporate Social Policy

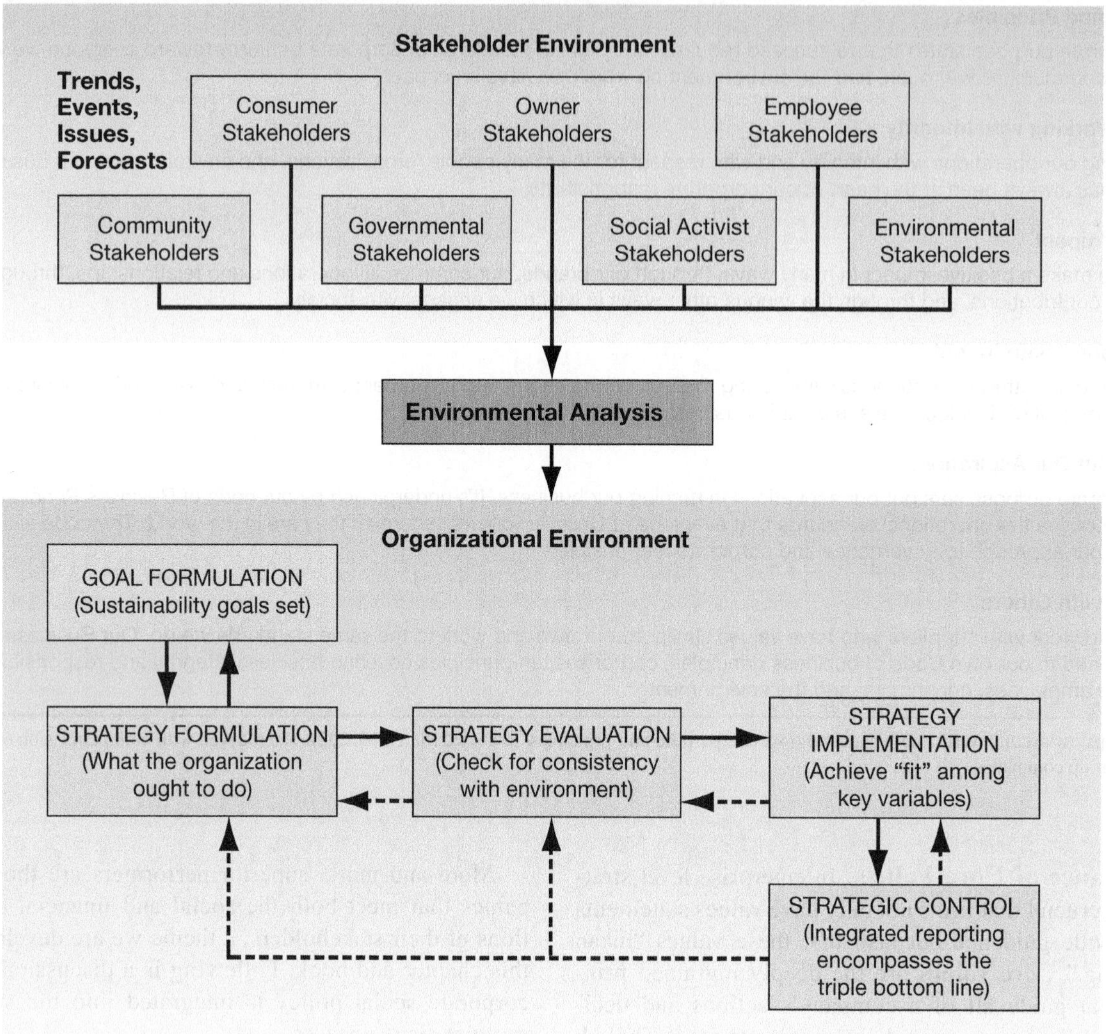

10.3a Strategic Corporate Social Responsibility

In recent years, the term **strategic corporate social responsibility** has captured the idea of integrating a concern for society into the strategic management processes of the firm.[33] Such a perspective ensures that CSR is fully integrated into the firm's strategy, mission, and vision. **Strategic CSR** and the firm's level of strategic management reflect a firm's enterprise-level strategy discussed earlier.

Porter and Kramer Framework. The notion of strategic CSR got a huge boost when strategy expert Michael Porter began advocating the importance of the linkage between competitive advantage, a crucial strategy concept, and CSR.[34] He and co-author Mark Kramer argued that the interdependence between business and society takes two forms: "inside-out linkages," wherein company operations affect society, and "outside-in linkages," wherein

external societal forces affect companies.[35] To prioritize social issues, they categorize three broad ways corporations intersect with society and two primary modes of corporate involvement:[36]

Type of Intersection:
1. Generic Social Issues – Social issues not material to long-term competitiveness
2. Value Chain Social Impacts – Normal operations that significantly affect society
3. Social Dimensions of Competitive Context – Social issues that affect the drivers of a company's competitiveness.

These types of social issues prompt different modes of corporate involvement including *responsive CSR*, which addresses generic issues and value chain social impacts through good corporate citizenship and by mitigating harm from negative corporate impacts on society. *Strategic CSR* transforms value chain social impacts into activities that benefit society, while simultaneously reinforcing corporate strategy, as well as advancing strategic philanthropy that leverages relevant areas of competitiveness.[37]

These ideas are integrated into a series of steps that intend to integrate business and society strategically and contribute to a firm's **value proposition**—the services or features intended to make a company or product attractive to customers. These steps include:

1. Identifying the points of intersection (inside-out and outside-in)
2. Choosing which social issues to address (generic, value chain social impacts, and social dimensions of competitiveness)
3. Creating a corporate social agenda (responsive and strategic)
4. Integrating inside-out and outside-in practices (getting practices to work together)
5. Creating a social dimension to the value proposition (the company adds a social dimension to its value proposition, thus making social impact integral to the overall strategy)[38]

The Porter–Kramer framework is useful because it applies strategic thinking to both leverage positive social and environmental benefits and mitigate negative social and environmental impacts in ways that enhance competitive advantage. From all indications, companies are beginning to accept this way of thinking. However, challenges remain. While companies are increasingly engaging in ESG activities, one study found that few of them are using those activities to differentiate themselves strategically.[39] The challenge for companies, therefore, is to find the ways in which the environmental and social dimensions can be incorporated into the business as part of the whole rather than a separate part. Integrated reporting, as we explain next, represents a major step in that direction.

10.3b Measuring Sustainability and CSR

Achieving sustainability requires accountability for performance and that necessitates a change in the way many firms operate. Organizations can only perform well financially, socially, and environmentally if performance information and performance accountability reflect those goals.[40] When firms only measure financial performance and the board holds them responsible for only maximizing shareholder value, environmental and social considerations become side issues. To achieve sustainable corporate performance, corporations need a "fundamental change in their goals and how they achieve them."[41] The triple bottom line must be reflected in every aspect of the firm's operations to achieve sustainability.

Sustainability Reporting. Sustainability reports, also known as **social responsibility reports, social audits, ESG reports,** and **integrated reports (IRs),** represent an effort to measure a firm's overall value creation and to spur integrated thinking that recognizes the interconnections of the range of business functions, as well as the multiple business bottom lines.[42] The movement toward sustainability reports continues to gain momentum, particularly as there is greater demand from investors for reliable, high-quality, and comparable data.[43] The International Integrated Reporting Council (IIRC) is spearheading the development of a global framework for IR. The IIRC group is composed of regulators, investors, businesses, NGOs, standard setters, and representatives from the accounting profession.[44] According to Professor Mervyn King, chair of the IIRC:

We define Integrated Reporting as the language evidencing sustainable business. It is the means by which companies communicate how value is created and will be enhanced over the short, medium and long term... The journey toward Integrated Reporting therefore also entails a mindset change about how the company makes its money.[45]

Global organizations like the IIRC are supported by regional organizations like the European Union Directive, the U.S.-based Sustainability Accounting Standards Board (SASB), and other organizations that guide and provide metrics for preparing sustainability reports. As a result, the KPMG Survey of Corporate Responsibility Reporting 2020 concluded that over 96 percent of the world's largest 250 companies now report on corporate responsibility, with three in five companies including this information in their annual financial reports.[46]

IR does not necessarily replace other reports. Firms may still issue financial statements, environmental impact reports, social responsibility reports, and so on. However, by pulling that information together into an integrated format, decision makers become more aware of the interconnectedness of decisions and the fact that sustainability considerations cut across all the individual areas. The goal is to provide a single comprehensive report that connects ESG (environmental, social, governance) metrics with the standard annual report to encourage long-term value creation.

Sustainability reports are important to the context of strategic control. When sustainability goals are developed, these goals serve as standards in the process of measuring, disclosing, and documenting progress on economic, environmental, social, and governance goals. Following the development of goals, actual sustainability performance results are compared to the established goals, and then corrective action is taken to make sure that actual performance and goals are aligned. For example, Cisco's 2020 sustainability report sets strategic sustainability goals for 2025 and beyond, with five-year planning cycles and reviews.[47]

Strategic control is a process of managing the execution of strategic plans. It tracks strategic plan implementation to ensure that goals are achieved. As a part of strategic control, the sustainability report can assume a role much like that portrayed in Figure 10-5. This figure is similar to the

Figure 10-5 The Sustainability Report in the Context of Strategic Control

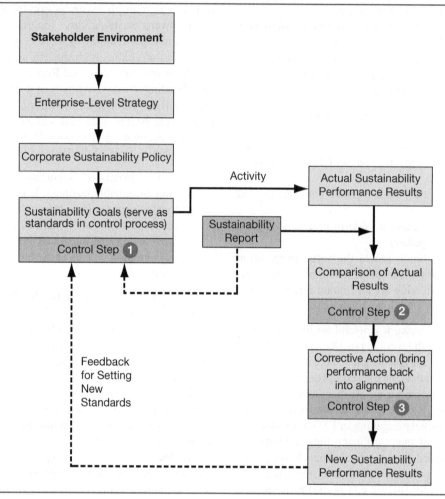

diagram of the strategic management process and corporate social policy shown in Figure 10-4, but it is modified somewhat to highlight sustainability goals and the first three steps in the strategic control process.

The impetus for sustainability reports in recent years has come both from inside the firm and from societal and public interest groups' expectations that firms be transparent and report their achievements in the triple bottom line. Such reports typically require monitoring and measuring progress, and this is valuable to management groups wanting to track their own progress as well as be able to report it to other interested parties.

Globalization is another driver for sustainability reports. As more and more companies do business globally, they need to document their achievements when critics raise questions about their contributions, especially in developing countries. Companies such as Nike, Walmart, and many others have been criticized for their use of sweatshops abroad, so they have an added incentive to issue such reports. Sustainability reports can also help companies to engage with stakeholders. Ford Motor Company, for example, works with stakeholder committees to inform and shape their reporting approach and materiality analysis, but these

forums have also allowed them to address problems on human rights and carbon dioxide reduction.[48]

Global Reporting Initiative. One of the major impediments to the advancement of effective sustainability reporting has been the absence of standardized measures. According to the Global Initiative for Sustainability Ratings (GISR), there are more than 100 ratings agencies that produce sustainability ratings and research on companies. These include Bloomberg, MSCI, RepRisk, Sustainalytics, and Thomson Reuters.[49]

Standardization is a challenge that has been undertaken by a consortium of over 300 global organizations called the **Global Reporting Initiative (GRI)**. Ceres, a nongovernmental, national network of investors that has been mentioned in earlier chapters, launched the GRI in conjunction with the U.N. Environment Programme (UNEP) with the mission of developing globally applicable guidelines for reporting on the economic, environmental, and social performance of corporations, governments, and nongovernmental organizations (NGOs).[50]

GRI is now considered the de facto international standard for comprehensive sustainability reporting, encompassing

Ethics In Practice Case

DuPont and Sustainability Reporting

The 2020 Sustainability Report for DuPont reads, "Our purpose—to empower the world with the essential innovations to thrive—evokes how we use our passion and proven expertise in science and innovation to create sustainable solutions for the complex challenges facing our world. Over the course of DuPont's existence, we have proven repeatedly that the most valuable and enduring business outcomes are the ones that are beneficial to society and help the planet thrive."

However, it was only a few years earlier that an article was published disclosing that for years DuPont had been using the chemical PFOA in the manufacturing of Teflon, a product used in nonstick pots and pans. PFOA at the time was not regulated by the Environmental Protection Agency, but after animals began getting sick near DuPont's Parkersburg, West Virginia, facility, lawyer Rob Bilot pursued an investigation. Samples from the Ohio River at the time showed toxicity levels near the facility eight times higher than normal, which had made its way into the drinking water supply of residents in Ohio and West Virginia. Many DuPont employees and local residents were subsequently diagnosed with cancer and leukaemia. In 2017, DuPont settled more than 3,500 PFOA lawsuits for $671 million but denied any wrongdoing. In 2021, the lawsuit settlements reached $4 billion across several DuPont affiliates. As noted earlier, this DuPont story is portrayed in the 2019 movie *Dark Waters*, with actor Mark Ruffalo as the attorney who brought the civil suit against DuPont.

1. To what extent does sustainability reporting address the future, rather than the past? What is a company to do when their sustainability report is positive but they later are found not to live up to their past report? Can sustainability reports work against a company in this regard?

2. In its sustainability report, the DuPont chair and CEO noted, "DuPont has come a long way since the 1970s when our focus was on our environmental compliance." How can newer sustainability reports address these issues?

3. How can DuPont bring more consistency between its stated commitments in its sustainability reports and later reported violations?

Sources: Nathaniel Rich, "The Lawyer Who Became Dupont's Worst Nightmare," *The New York Times Magazine* (January 6, 2016), https://www.nytimes.com/2016/01/10/magazine/the-lawyer-who-became-duponts-worst-nightmare.html, accessed March 21, 2021; Michael Kourabas, "The Case of DuPont's Pollution and the Importance of CSR" (January 11, 2016), *Triple Pundit*, http://www.triplepundit.com/2016/01/case-duponts-pollution-importance-csr/?utm_source=Daily+Email+List&utm_campaign=ddd5cb046f-RSS_EMAIL_CAMPAIGN&utm_medium=email&utm_term=0_9dedefcee3-ddd5cb046f-220417273, accessed March 20, 2021; *Dupont 2020 Sustainability Progress Report*, https://www.dupont.com/about/sustainability.html, accessed March 20, 2021; Monica Amarelo, Environmental Working Group (EWG), (January 21, 2021), "DuPont, Chemours and Corteva Reach $4 Billion Settlement on 'Forever Chemicals' Lawsuits," https://www.ewg.org/release/dupont-chemours-and-corteva-reach-4-billion-settlement-forever-chemicals-lawsuits, accessed March 20, 2021.

the "triple bottom line" of economic, environmental, and social issues. The mission of GRI is to maintain, enhance, and disseminate the guidelines through ongoing consultation and stakeholder engagement.[51]

As firms develop enterprise-level strategies and corporate social policies, the potential and expectation for sustainability reporting remains high. Sustainability reporting is best appreciated not as an isolated, periodic attempt to assess social performance but rather as an *integral part* of the overall strategic management process as it is described here.

10.4 Public Affairs as a Part of Strategic Management

In a comprehensive management system, which this chapter describes, the overall flow of activity would be as follows: A firm engages in strategic management, part of which includes the development of enterprise-level strategy, which poses the question, "For what do we stand?" Some companies today are referring to this as their "purpose," and we covered this in Chapter 2. The answers to this question help the organization form a corporate social policy, which is a more specific posture on the public, social, or stakeholder environment or specific issues within this environment. Some firms call this **public affairs** or **corporate affairs strategy**.

Public affairs (PA) and **corporate affairs (CA)** are umbrella terms that some companies use to describe the management processes that focus on the formalization and institutionalization of corporate social policy. The PA/CA function is a logical component of the overall strategic management process. PA/CA experts argue that it has grown to be one of the most important parts of strategic management and today may be seen as the strategic core business function for companies wanting to compete successfully internationally.[52]

The public affairs function took on new meaning during the COVID-19 pandemic as businesses took stock of their resources to determine how to best tackle the global challenge. More frequent and timely communication, strategic use of digital media, a continued focus on sustainability, and regular communication with employees all became highlighted during the pandemic. Employees were anxious to understand what was going on, and it was the public affairs (or corporate affairs) offices that would direct communications. As noted by the consulting group *SpencerStuart*, "Covid-19 'shone a light' on corporate affairs' vital role in engaging with external and internal stakeholders that will outlive the crisis itself."[53]

As an overall concept, PA/CA management embraces corporate social policy, discussed earlier, along with **issues management** and **crisis management**, which we cover below. Corporate PA/CA also embraces the broad areas of governmental relations, including lobbying, and corporate communications. In sum, an integrated model of PA/CA suggests that it is the interface of multiple disciplines, including business and society, ethics, CSR, ecological systems, ethics, economics, sociology, political science, reputational management, and strategic management.[54]

The PA/CA function as we know it today is an outgrowth of the social activism begun decades ago. An important element of the public affairs function is the influence it has on corporate strategy and planning. If the public affairs function is to be effective in representing the "noncommercial" factors and issues affecting business decision making, it is important that public affairs has influence at the top management level. Public affairs can help identify and prioritize issues, as well as provide input on emerging social and political trends. For public affairs to fulfill this function, it is important that they have a seat at the table for corporate planning sessions.

In short, the PA/CA function within firms is strategically positioned to wield more and better influence in the years ahead to help business build bridges between its strategic management and its corporate social performance. It must be added, however, that many firms have decided not to use traditional PA departments for these issues but have begun separate corporate citizenship, CSR, sustainability and ethics offices to organize their corporate-level handling of these issues.

10.5 Risk, Issue, and Crisis Management

In previous chapters, we have mentioned companies that have had challenges in managing issues and crises ranging from product safety issues to financial fraud. Food safety, highlighted with far-reaching *Escherichia coli (E. coli)* outbreaks like that at Chipotle, is an example of an issue that shocked consumers into being fearful of "fresh" food.[55] Other continuing issues, such as employee rights, racial equity, sexual harassment, workplace safety, sweatshops, bribery, corruption, and deceptive advertising, contribute to the negative opinion many people hold of business.

Not all issues are caused by business. External events are sometimes unavoidable, but firms must still prepare for their possibilities and manage their repercussions effectively. The COVID-19 global pandemic is an example of this. Throughout this book, we discuss major social and ethical issues that have become controversies in the public domain. Some have been caused by external events, whereas the roots of others can be traced back to the businesses themselves.

Managerial decision-making processes known as risk management, issue management, and crisis management are three major ways by which businesses respond to these situations. These three approaches symbolize the extent to which the environment has become turbulent and the public sensitized to business's responses to the issues that have emerged from this turbulence. In today's environment of instantaneous and global communication, no event is too small to be noticed by everyone.

In an ideal situation, risk, issue, and crisis management might be seen as the natural and logical by-products of a firm's development of enterprise-level strategy and overall corporate social policy, but this is not always the case. Some firms do not think seriously about social and ethical issues until they face a crisis. However, even those firms that have not experienced major crises themselves have seen what major business crises can do to companies. Such firms should still be concerned with risk, issue, and crisis management in preparing for an uncertain future because no company is immune from the threat of a crisis.

Relationships between Risk, Issue, and Crisis Management. Differentiating between risk, issue, and crisis management is problematic, even for the professionals who work in those fields. As is true with all planning processes, risk, issue, and crisis management have many characteristics in common as well as differences. Though they are interrelated, we have chosen to treat them separately for discussion purposes.

We begin with a discussion of risk management, which involves efforts to keep issues from arising—*potential* issues that may or may not occur.[56] Then, we explore issue management, which is a process by which organizations identify issues in the stakeholder environment, analyze and prioritize those issues in terms of their relevance to the organization, plan responses to the issues, and then evaluate and monitor the results. Thus, an issue is something that already exists. Finally, crisis management is the management of issues that have become major threats—those that have escalated into a critical state.

A common thread is that all three processes focus on improving stakeholder management and enabling the organization to be more ethically responsive to stakeholders' expectations. It is helpful to think of these management approaches in connection with concepts introduced earlier in the chapter, such as the sustainable strategic management process, enterprise-level strategy, corporate social policy, and integrated reporting.

10.6 Risk Management

Risk management concerns potential issues—addressing potential issues that have not yet occurred and endeavoring to keep issues from arising. The act of identifying and preparing for potential issues is difficult for the human psyche, as our bounded rationality is not geared toward envisioning the future.[57] Scholars Robert Kaplan and Anette Mikes argue that, too often, managers adopt a compliance approach to the management of risk by basing it on rules.[58] This can be effective in controlling preventable, internal risks but not in controlling risks that stem from a company's strategy or risks caused by major disruptions in the external environment.

Kaplan and Mikes provide a useful framework for risk management that divides it into three categories[59]:

- *Preventable risks*—internal risks that offer no strategic benefits
- *Strategic risks*—risks taken to achieve greater returns
- *External risks*—external threats that cannot be controlled

Preventable risks can cause serious damage and so risk managers should eliminate them whenever possible. The Boeing 777 engines made by Pratt & Whitney aircraft that have been shown to be consistent with metal fatigue is an example of a preventable risk because they have been associated with a need to step up inspections.[60] Because they are internal and foreseeable, preventable risks lend themselves to a rule-based compliance approach. A corporate mission that defines the company's values, clear boundaries for employee behavior, and effective monitoring procedures usually is effective at preventing this category of risks.[61] However, oftentimes, even the savviest of companies fails to anticipate and prevent risks.

Strategic risks, unlike preventable risks, are not necessarily bad. Because risk and return are related, companies might take on additional risk in order to pursue a company strategy that promises higher returns. Facebook took on additional risk when it began engaging with third parties and their apps that could grab Facebook user data. Even after the Cambridge Analytica scandal, where the political data-analytics firm had purchased the personal information of millions of Facebook users without their knowledge through quiz apps, Facebook continued to face situations where third parties could grab user information.[62] In this instance, a two-pronged risk management approach is needed to curtail the risk:

1. Reducing the probability of the risk event occurring, and
2. Developing the capability to manage the risk event should it occur.

A strategic risk management program does not prevent a firm from taking on strategic risks; it simply enables the firm to do so more effectively.[63]

External risks are beyond the firm's control: They originate from outside the company and include events such as natural disasters and economic shocks. The COVID-19 pandemic would illustrate this. These usually cannot be controlled and they can be the most difficult to predict. Methods of identifying external risks should include techniques like scenario analysis to assist risk managers in foreseeing the unforeseeable. Some external risk events have a low probability of occurrence and so are difficult for managers to envision.[64]

Risk Management and Sustainability. Sustainability involves living in the present in a way that does not compromise the future. Risk management involves taking action today that will mitigate or prevent a problem that could arise in the future. As such, sustainability and risk management share a connection in that both are concerned with the future consequences of present-day actions. Sustainability is concerned both with not harming and with benefitting future generations. Risk management can provide a mechanism for avoiding, or at least mitigating, future harm to stakeholders and avoiding or mitigating the risk of not benefitting stakeholders in the future.[65] Such is the case, for example, of a company's environmental goals to reduce carbon emissions to address climate change. As noted in Chapter 4, Microsoft and other companies like Disney are leading a movement to offset emissions with an internal carbon tax, called "carbon pricing," by voluntarily charging themselves and using that money to build solar panels and wind farms.[66]

Risk shifting is an issue that merits attention in this regard. In the pursuit of sustainability for the business enterprise, some managers may use management techniques that shift risk from the firm to other parties. For example, some techniques can shift risks to the customer base, eroding the economic sustainability of the consumer.[67] This underscores the importance of a holistic approach to sustainability. Risk managers must take care not to promote the sustainability of the firm in such a way that it threatens the sustainability of stakeholders.

10.7 Issue Management

The Issue Management Council defines an issue as "a gap between [a firm's] actions and stakeholder expectations" and issue management as "the process used to close that gap."[68] Many of the crises companies face today arise out of issues that are being monitored and prioritized through issue management systems. In addition, effective issue management is a vital component of postcrisis management. For example, after dealing with an oil spill crisis, a company must continue to address the issue of environmental degradation.[69] Figure 10-6 provides examples of major *issue* categories and specific *crises* that have occurred within these issue categories.

The emergence of "company issue management groups" and "issue managers" has been a direct outgrowth of the changing mix of issues that managers have had to handle. The growth of technology has presented business with other issues to address, such as cybersecurity and data management issues, as we noted above with Facebook's issues with data sharing.

For most firms, social, ethical, political, and technological issues are at the same time economic issues, because firms' success in handling them frequently has a direct bearing on their financial statuses, reputations, and well-being. Over time, management groups face an escalating challenge as a changing mix of issues creates a cumulative effect.

Figure 10-6 Issue Categories and Sample Crises Within Categories

Issue Categories		
Food, Beverage, and Products	**Health-Related Issues**	**Corporate Fraud and Ethics**
Crises	**Crises**	**Crises**
Tyson and Pilgrim's Pride: Pled guilty to price fixing and bid-rigging chicken/broiler meat (2020–2021)	COVID-19: The largest pandemic to affect the world since the 1918 influenza epidemic (2019–2021)	Purdue Pharmaceuticals: Pled guilty to charges of fraud and kickback conspiracies in marketing and sales of opioids (2020–2021)
Chipotle: *E. coli* and norovirus outbreaks closed stores nationwide (2015–2016)	Theranos: CEO Elizabeth Holmes charged with fraud and conspiracy for marketing blood testing devices that did not work and gave false information (2020–2021)	Valeant Pharmaceuticals: Accounting fraud and price gouging (2015–2016)
Horsemeat Scandal in the United Kingdom: Millions of burgers and beef products recalled across Europe for containing horsemeat (2013)	U.S. National Football League: Investigation into head and brain injuries from occupational hazard of the sport (2016)	Volkswagen: Guilty of "diesel dupe" with deceptive emissions testing software (2015–2016)
Peanut Corporation of America: Over 125 varieties of products recalled due to salmonella contamination (2008–2009)	Ebola: The largest outbreak of Ebola in history, beginning in West Africa, but with multiple countries affected (2014)	Turing Pharmaceuticals: CEO Shkreli found guilty of price gouging the drug Daraprim (2015)
Taco Bell: Outbreak of *E. coli* closed outlets nationwide (2006)	H1N1: A possible flu pandemic led to crises for companies and questions of how to treat employees (2009)	Bernie Madoff: Ponzi scheme cost major foundations millions of dollars jeopardizing critical medical research (2008–2009)
Coca-Cola and Pepsi: Allegations that soft drinks in India contained pesticide residue (2004–2007)		

10.7a Model of the Issue Management Process

The issue management process discussed here has been extracted from many of the conceptualizations previously developed. Like the strategic management process, which entails a multitude of sequential and interrelated steps or stages, many different authorities including companies, academics, consultants, and associations have conceptualized the issue management process in a variety of ways. Figure 10-7 presents a model of the issue management process that depicts the elements or stages that seem to be common to most issue management process models. It is also consistent with the stakeholder orientation we have been developing and using. It contains *planning aspects* (identification, analysis, ranking or prioritization of issues, and formulation of responses) and *implementation aspects* (implementation of responses and evaluation, monitoring, and control of results). Although we discuss the stages in the issue management process as though they are discrete, in reality, they may be interrelated and overlap one another. Each of these steps are worthy of further consideration.

Identification of Issues. Many names have been assigned to the process of issue identification. The terms *social forecasting*, *futures research*, *environmental scanning*, and *public issues scanning* have been used at various times, and many techniques have been employed too. All of these approaches or techniques are similar, but each has its own unique characteristics. Common to all of them, however, is the need to scan the stakeholder environment and identify emerging issues or trends that might later be determined to have some relevance

to or impact on the organization. In recent years, examples of identified issues that may have widespread ramifications for many organizations include natural disasters, acts of terrorism, potential pandemics, and economic events.

Issue identification, in its most rudimentary form, involves the assignment to some individual in the organization the tasks of continuously scanning social media and a variety of publications to build a comprehensive inventory of issues. One result of this scanning is an internal report that is circulated throughout the organization. The next step in this evolution may be for the company to subscribe to a trend information service that is prepared by a private individual or consulting firm that specializes in environmental or issue scanning.[70]

Analysis of Issues. The next two steps in the issue management process (analysis and ranking of issues) are closely related. To analyze an issue means to carefully study, dissect, break down, classify, or engage in any specific process that helps management understand the nature or characteristics of the issue. An analysis requires that you look beyond the obvious manifestations of the issue and strive to learn more of its history, development, current nature, and potential for future relevance to the organization. It is clear that this is a very important part of the issues management process, and yet, companies often fail in this step.

For example, a *PwC* report noted that in 2015 Toyota failed to address their "sticky" accelerator defects, denying and postponing the issue, which resulted in more accidents.[71] In contrast, when Fitbit (now owned by Google) discovered that their activity-monitoring wristbands resulted in some customers experiencing irritated skin, they immediately

Figure 10-7 The Issue Management Process

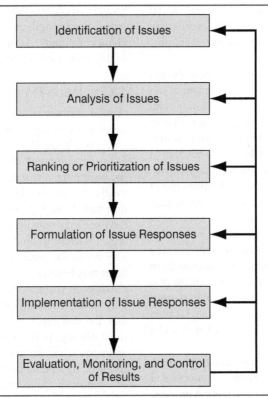

launched an internal investigation with independent experts to analyze and address the issue.[72]

A series of key questions that focus on stakeholder groups in attempting to analyze issues has been proposed:[73]

- Who (which stakeholder) is affected by the issue?
- Who has an interest in the issue?
- Who is in a position to exert influence on the issue?
- Who has expressed opinions on the issue?
- Who ought to care about the issue?

In addition to these questions, the following key questions help with issue analysis:[74]

- Who started the ball rolling? (historical view)
- Who is now involved? (contemporary view)
- Who will get involved? (future view)

Answers to these questions place management in a better position to rank or prioritize the issues so that it will have a better sense of the urgency with which the issues need to be addressed.

Ranking or Prioritization of Issues. Issues vary in the extent to which they matter to an organization, and so determining which issues matter most is essential in determining which ones should receive the most organizational resources, such as time and money. Of the many ways to analyze issues, two essential questions are (1) *How likely is the issue to affect the organization?* and (2) *How much impact will the issue have?*[75]

Once these questions are answered, it is necessary to rank issues in some form of a hierarchy of importance or relevance to the organization. Those listed as top priority will receive the most attention and resources, whereas those at the bottom may even be removed from consideration because of their low likelihood or potential impact. The prioritization stage may involve a simple grouping of issues into categories ranging from the most urgent to the least important. Alternatively, a more elaborate or sophisticated scoring system may be employed.[76]

Other techniques that have been used in issues identification, analysis, and prioritization include polls or surveys, expert panels, content analysis, the Delphi technique, trend extrapolation, scenario building, and the use of precursor events or bellwethers. Teams of company experts are also used. For example, Baxter International, a U.S.-based health-care and biotech firm, uses multidisciplinary teams because its main issues are in bioethics, and expertise in this subject cuts across a number of different knowledge-based lines of business.[77]

While the analysis and ranking stages could be done by an individual, more often, the company moves up to a next stage of formalization. This next stage involves assignment of the issue management function to a team, often as part of a public or corporate affairs department, which begins to specialize in the issue management function.

Formulation and Implementation of Responses. Formulation and implementation of responses are two steps in the issue management process combined here for discussion purposes. Again, we point out that the formulation and implementation stages in the issue management process are quite similar to the stages of the strategic management process as a whole.

Formulation in this case refers to the response design process. Based on the analysis conducted, companies can then identify options that might be pursued in dealing with the issues, in making decisions, and in implementing those decisions. Strategy formulation refers not only to the formulation of the actions that the firm intends to take but also to the creation of the overall strategy, or degree of aggressiveness, employed in carrying out those actions. Options might include aggressive pursuit, gradual pursuit, or selective pursuit of goals, plans, processes, or programs.[78]

Formulation is a key stage for rebuilding trust with stakeholders as well. As noted by *PwC*, a credible commitment to change, with a plan of action, can reverse any mistrust from the initial incident.[79] Again, Fitbit provides an example of a company that, while dealing with customer complaints, contracted with external dermatologists and formulated a plan to address the skin irritation issues in their wristbands and a plan for next-generation trackers.[80]

Once plans for dealing with issues have been formulated, *implementation* becomes the focus. Many organizational aspects need to be addressed in the implementation process, including the clarity of the plan itself, resources needed to implement the plan, top management support, organizational structure, technical competence, and timing.[81]

Evaluation, Monitoring, and Control. The steps of evaluation, monitoring and control in the issue management process also parallel steps in the strategic management process; however, in the current discussion, they suggest that companies should continually evaluate the results of their responses to the issues and ensure that these actions are kept on track. This stage requires careful monitoring of stakeholders' opinions. A form of stakeholder audit—something derivative of the social audit discussed earlier—might be used. Stakeholder engagement might also be used at this stage. The information gathered during this final stage in the issue management process is then fed back to the earlier stages in the process so that changes or adjustments might be made as needed. Evaluation information may be useful at each stage in the process.

The issue management process has been presented as a complete system. In practice, companies apply the stages across various degrees of formality or informality as needed or desired. It is helpful here to provide an example. The Chipotle *E. coli* outbreak case, which we discuss in more detail in Case 4, began with Chipotle's attention to a growing issue in food quality, the need and desire to provide customers with healthier, nonartificial, high-quality food in chain restaurants. The company capitalized on an issue that had been highlighted in polls and in the media—the need for healthier fast-food options—and implemented resources including relying on local farms to create a new business model and address the issue. Chipotle's business model that began as a strength quickly became a weakness with supply chain constraints. As one columnist noted, "All of a sudden, highly processed industrial food doesn't look so bad."[82]

10.7b Issue Development Process

A vital attribute of issue management is that issues tend to develop according to an evolutionary pattern and a life cycle emerges. Figure 10-8 presents a simplified view of what an **issue development life cycle process** might look like. In the beginning, a nascent issue emerges in the press or social media, is enunciated by public interest organizations, and is detected through public opinion polling. During this time, the issue may reflect a felt need, receive media coverage, and attract interest group development and growth. A typical firm may notice the issue but take no action. More issue-oriented firms may become more active in their monitoring and in their attempts to shape or help "define the issue."[83] Active firms may have the capacity to prevent issues from going any further, through either effective responses to the issues or effective lobbying. In the next stage of the cycle, local, regional, and national media attention may address the issue, quickly followed by leading political jurisdictions (e.g., cities, states, or countries). Quite often, federal government attention is generated in the form of studies and hearings; legislation, regulation, and litigation follow. In today's societies, the politicization of an issue may expedite its growth curve.

This life cycle process is simply an example of a sequence. Issues vary, and so the stages in the process, especially the early stages, might occur in a different sequence or in an iterative pattern. Further, not all issues complete the process; some are resolved before they reach the stage of legislation or regulation. It is important not to oversimplify the issue development process. The paths issues follow vary with the nature of the issues and the intensity and variety of stakeholder interests and values. The complex interactions of all the variables make it unlikely issues will follow a straight line.[84]

Consider the issue of data protection, which provides an example of issue development. To date, because the United States does not have federal law to handle such issues like Europe's General Data Protection Regulation (GDPR), it has been left to the companies themselves to determine how customers' data should be handled. Facing growing public concern about the collection and trade of personal data, U.S. states have taken the lead in proposing a series of privacy laws including protecting the privacy of student data, and sharing customer data, even as they wait for federal legislation to address these issues and move through the issue development life cycle.[85] Meanwhile, companies like Facebook, Apple, and Google form their own policies, often publicly squaring off against each other as they debate "opt in" data collection for targeted ads.[86] Alert companies will be proactive and take actions earlier to head off or shape future government regulations that may emerge.

Figure 10-8 Issue Development Life Cycle Process

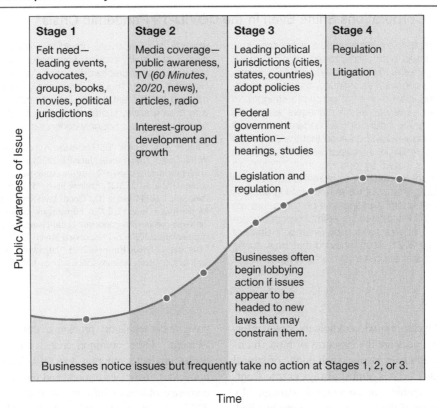

Stage 1	Stage 2	Stage 3	Stage 4
Felt need— leading events, advocates, groups, books, movies, political jurisdictions	Media coverage— public awareness, TV (*60 Minutes*, *20/20*, news), articles, radio Interest-group development and growth	Leading political jurisdictions (cities, states, countries) adopt policies Federal government attention— hearings, studies Legislation and regulation Businesses often begin lobbying action if issues appear to be headed to new laws that may constrain them.	Regulation Litigation

Public Awareness of Issue

Businesses notice issues but frequently take no action at Stages 1, 2, or 3.

Time

10.8 Crisis Management

Airlines, unfortunately, have experience with crisis management as the grim reality is that although there are relatively few air accidents, when they happen, they often kill customers. Such was the case for Southwest 1380 in April 2018 when an engine ruptured on a New York to Dallas trip and shrapnel broke a window, leading to the loss of a passenger. While tragic, Southwest's response is considered an exemplar of crisis management.[87] The airline immediately sent a plane to Philadelphia, where the flight made its emergency landing. The plane was filled with Southwest employees trained to be part of an accident response team to provide grief counseling, travel arrangements, and resources for the passengers. It was the first time the airline had a passenger fatality, but CEO Gary Kelly was quick to get on video and deliver a 40-second video apology that came across as honest and heartfelt. The airline also quickly pulled advertising from social media. The airline gave checks for $5,000 to each passenger on the flight, as well as a $1,000 voucher for future travel.

Contrast this case with the crisis of the disappearance of the Malaysian flight MH370 in April 2014 following its departure from Kuala Lumpur. While this crisis was handled quite well by Malaysia Airlines (which released five public statements during the day MH370 disappeared and communicated regularly and publicly with stakeholders), the Malaysian government did not handle the crisis as well. They mishandled information, attacked the foreign media when journalists asked to verify conflicting statements, failed to include a senior official who could speak Mandarin, and mistreated the relative of a missing passenger with security staff that ejected the relative during a press conference.[88] The way the Malaysian government mishandled the crisis became an international issue that created a crisis of confidence in the country itself.[89]

Unfortunately, crises occur with regularity, making them almost routine. However, the fallout from a crisis is not routine in any way. Boeing, for example, was plagued with software problems related to its Boeing 737 MAX series that led to two plane crashes in 2018 and 2019 that killed 346 people. In 2021, they agreed to pay more than $2.5 billion to settle criminal charges related to the faulty flight control system, but Boeing's initial responses to the crises were less than ideal, and as a result, Boeing's reputation suffered.[90] Crises can topple organizations if top management does not respond quickly, decisively, and effectively.[91] At the same time, a strong and effective response to a crisis can strengthen an organization in the end. Businesses need to find ways to prepare, learn, communicate, and manage situations of crises to keep their stakeholders informed and assume responsibility when they should.

10.8a The Nature of Crises

There are many kinds of business crises. Those mentioned here have all been associated with major stakeholder groups and have achieved high-visibility status. Hurt or killed

Spotlight on Sustainability

Sustainable Corporations Shine Even in the COVID-19 Pandemic Crisis

The COVID-19 pandemic crisis sparked a global economic downturn that closed businesses, raised unemployment, and created long lines at food banks. And yet, ESG investing in sustainable companies continued, as many considered ESG an important marker of corporate strength. In a *Financial Times* survey of wealth managers across the United Kingdom at the height of the pandemic, almost 9 in 10 wealth managers polled believed that the COVID-19 pandemic would result in increased investor interest in ESG investing. As noted by one manager, "COVID-19 presents us with the opportunity to retire the ESG label in favor of recognizing that what we're really talking about is Finance 101. That is, the management of issues that are self-evident and influence good long-term corporate financial outcomes." This was echoed by *Greenbiz*'s State of Green Businesses 2021, which showed that even during the pandemic, sustainability targets actually grew in the majority of companies, providing evidence that companies' sustainability profiles were becoming "baked into its stock price and creditworthiness." As summed up in the *Greenbiz* report, "Such turmoil easily could have spelled the end, or at least the pause, of anything having to do with business and sustainability. But it didn't. The forward march of progress not only continued but accelerated."

Sources: Amy Brown, "ESG Investing Appears Pandemic-Proof: Will It Last?" *TriplePundit* (June 22, 2020) https://www.triplepundit.com/story/2020/esg-investing-pandemic/120646, accessed March 22, 2021; Andrew Perry, "How the Coronavirus Pandemic Could Change 'Do-Good' Investing for the Better," *MarketWatch* (June 15, 2020), https://www.marketwatch.com/story/how-the-coronavirus-pandemic-could-change-do-good-investing-for-the-better-2020-06-15, accessed March 22, 2021; Joel Makower, "The State of Green Business 2021," https://www.greenbiz.com/article/state-green-business-2021, accessed March 21, 2021.

customers, hurt employees, injured stockholders, stolen information, and unfair practices are the concerns of modern crisis management. Not all crises involve such public or ethical issues, but these kinds of crises almost always ensure front-page status. Major companies can be seriously damaged by such episodes, especially if the episodes are poorly handled. In today's climate of active social media, crises become even more urgent as the harm done can occur quickly.

What is a crisis? Dictionaries state that a **crisis** is a "turning point for better or worse," an "emotionally significant event," or a "decisive moment." We all think of crises as being emotionally charged, but we do not always think of them as turning points for better or for worse. The implication here is that a crisis is a decisive moment that, if managed one way, could make things worse but, if managed another way, make things better, or not as bad. From a managerial point of view, a line needs to be drawn between a problem and a crisis. Problems, of course, are common in business. A crisis, however, is not as common. A useful way to think about a crisis is as follows:

A crisis is an extreme event that may threaten your very existence. At the very least, it causes substantial injuries, deaths, and financial costs, as well as serious damage to your reputation.[92]

Figure 10-9 presents a "how *not* to do it" case in crisis management as experienced by golf star Tiger Woods. At the time, Woods was under fire for allegations of serial infidelity that were at odds with the family-oriented image he had cultivated.

Types of Crises. A variety of situations leave companies vulnerable to crises. These include industrial accidents, environmental problems, union problems or strikes, product recalls, investor relations, hostile takeovers, proxy fights, rumors or media leaks, government regulatory problems, acts of terrorism, and embezzlement.[93] Other common crises include information system hacks, product tampering, executive kidnapping, work-related homicides, malicious rumors, and natural disasters that destroy corporate offices or information bases.[94] Since September 11, 2001, terrorist attacks, we have had to add terrorism to this list.

Crises may be grouped into seven families[95]:

- *Economic crises* (recessions, hostile takeovers, stock market crashes)
- *Physical crises* (industrial accidents, product failures, supply breakdown)
- *Personnel crises* (strikes, exodus of key employees, workplace violence)
- *Criminal crises* (product tampering, kidnappings, acts of terrorism)
- *Information crises* (theft of proprietary information, cyberattacks)
- *Reputational crises* (rumormongering or slander, logo tampering)
- *Natural disasters* (earthquakes, tornadoes, floods, fires)

After major crises, companies report the following outcomes: The crises escalated in intensity, were subjected to media and government scrutiny, interfered with normal business operations, and damaged the company's bottom line. Reputational crises may be particularly difficult for businesses to rebound from as they attempt to reintegrate and rebuild trust with their stakeholders.[96] However, it is not impossible. For example, Volkswagen rebounded from its emissions testing scandal within just a few years to become the second largest seller of vehicles in the world.[97]

10.8b Managing Business Crises

Five Practical Steps in Managing Crises. The following five steps, synthesized from the actual experiences of

Figure 10-9 Crisis Management and Tiger Woods, Inc.: How Not to Do It

In 2009, when Tiger Woods crashed his Cadillac Escalade into a fire hydrant and a tree in his gated Florida community, the world's media converged on him. Allegations of serial infidelity soon arose that set the pro-golfer's personal and professional life into a tailspin. As the man behind a billion-dollar financial empire and the personification of the brand it sells, Woods' personal trouble quickly developed into an organizational crisis. His management of the crisis held implications not only for him but also for the businesses that had been built around him, including his major sponsors.

Most crisis management experts fault his management of the crisis. Woods waited days to issue a statement, and the statement that finally appeared spoke only vaguely of "transgressions." Robbie Vorhaus, a crisis reputation adviser in New York, believes Woods should have spoken more quickly, "If you don't tell your story first, then you're letting someone else tell your story. Now he has to react and respond to what everyone else is saying." It has been suggested that Woods broke three basic rules of crisis management when he failed to follow his own advice:

- **Rule No. 1: Don't Wait.** After the car crash, Woods issued a statement acknowledging the accident but nothing else. Two days later, Woods issued another statement, but it was vague and the story was shaped by others in the interim.
- **Rule No. 2: Don't Run from the Truth.** Woods' first statement pleaded for privacy and claimed that "false, unfounded and malicious rumors" were circulating, giving the impression that the rumors were untrue. Three days later, he changed his story but admitted only to unspecified "transgressions."
- **Rule No. 3: Don't Hide.** Woods hid away long after the accident, leaving the women who alleged that they had relationships with him as the only voices telling the story.

In an odd twist of fate, in 2021 Woods was involved in another terrible car crash, but this time there was no evidence of personal altercation or any type of impairment. The initial response of the public this time was empathy, with many of golf's top golfers wearing Tiger's signature red shirt and black pants in support of Woods at a tournament following the crash. Woods tweeted a humble note of thanks to all his supporters—a significant change in tone from his responses to his prior car crash.

Sources: Dana Mattoli, "Tiger Bungles Crisis Management 101," *The Wall Street Journal* (December 8, 2009), A31; Ryan Ballingee, "Tiger's Own Words May Be Cause for Concern about Anthony Galea," *Waggle Room* (December 18, 2009); Blair Bernstein, "Crisis Management and Sports in the Age of Social Media," *Elon Journal of Undergraduate Research in Communications*, 2012, 3/2, 1–3; Amir Vera, "Here's What We Know about Tiger's Car Wreck and Injuries," *CNN* (February 24, 2021), https://www.cnn.com/2021/02/24/us/tiger-woods-car-accident-what-we-know-intl-spt/index.html, accessed March 22, 2021; Des Bieler and Cindy Boren, "Tiger Woods Thanks Golfers Who Wore Red and Black," *The Washington Post* (March 1, 2021), https://www.washingtonpost.com/sports/2021/02/28/golfers-tiger-woods-red-black/, accessed March 22, 2021.

companies going through crises, are summarized and discussed next. They are (1) identifying areas of vulnerability, (2) developing a plan for dealing with threats, (3) forming crisis teams, (4) simulating crisis drills, and (5) learning from experience. These steps are similar to those identified in our discussions of risk and issues management.

First: Identifying Areas of Vulnerability In this first step, some areas of vulnerability are obvious, such as potential chemical spills, whereas others are more subtle. The key seems to be in developing a greater consciousness of how things can go wrong and get out of hand. At Chipotle, following *E. coli* incidences that sickened at least 53 people in nine states, one critic noted that Chipotle failed to identify the areas of vulnerability in their newer business model: "If Chipotle is going to continue to provide an alternative model to processed, industrial food, it needs to also be at the forefront of creating systems to support that new approach, such as offering its employees paid sick days."[98]

A key to identifying areas of vulnerability is "recognizing the threat." Recognizing low-probability but high-consequence events is a challenge, but planning for them can help a company to survive major crises.[99] Some ways that companies can identify areas of vulnerability include the following:[100]

- *Scenario planning.* Create scenarios for crises that could occur over the next two years.
- *Risk analysis.* Estimate the probabilities and costs/benefits of estimated future events.
- *Incentives.* Reward managers for information sharing.

- *Networks.* Build formal coalitions to mobilize internal and external information suppliers.

Pfizer and other drug manufacturers were tested about recognizing threats during the COVID-19 crisis, as did others when supply chain woes mounted worldwide. Just-in-time manufacturing and inventory systems, which are usually beneficial to businesses, fell behind, and incentives linked to short-term objectives could not be fulfilled.[101] As businesses reflect on the pandemic, they will inevitably revisit their areas of vulnerability with lessons learned about risk analysis and short-termism in incentive plans. As noted by one journalist, "The world is learning that a just-in-time inventory system and a short-term focus on maximizing return on investment is no match for a restive Mother Nature."[102]

Second: Developing a Plan for Dealing with Threats A plan for dealing with the most serious crisis threats is a logical next step. One of the most crucial issues is communications planning. Chipotle founder and co-chief executive Steve Ells acknowledged that the cost of new safety programs to prevent future outbreaks of *E. coli* and norovirus were "very, very expensive," but CFO John Hartung said, "We're not trying to make this cost-effective. We're just doing it."[103] Most of us would agree that paying for something now is infinitely better for the safety and well-being of others.

Third: Forming Crisis Teams Another step that can be taken as part of an overall planning effort is the formation of **crisis teams**, especially in large organizations. Such teams have played key roles in many well-managed disasters. As noted above in the Southwest Airlines 1380 disaster, a crisis team was deployed to the area where the flight was rerouted. That evening, in the hotel where many passengers were staying, the crisis team slipped notes under the doors to remind them that people were onsite to offer assistance.

Another task in assembling crisis teams is identifying managers who can cope effectively with stress. Not every executive can handle the fast-moving, high-pressured, ambiguous decision environment that is created by a crisis, and early identification of executives who can is important. The COVID-19 pandemic caused a number of alert companies to form crisis teams. Just outside of Paris, a team of executives from Peugeot, the French carmaker, gathered daily at 8:00 a.m. to plot a path out of the massive supply-and-demand crisis caused by the coronavirus ripping through the global economy. For PSA Group, the parent company, a shortage of key parts could have devasting consequences for their manufacturing plants. Hence, the company's "war room" staffed by key executives helped the company deal with this major economic disruption.[104]

Fourth: Simulating Crisis Drills Some companies have gone so far as to run crisis drills in which highly stressful situations are simulated so that managers can "practice" what they might do in a real crisis. As a basis for conducting crisis drills and experiential exercises, a number of companies

have adopted a crisis management software package. This software allows companies to centralize and maintain up-to-date crisis management information and allows company leaders to assign responsibilities to their crisis team, target key audiences, identify and monitor potential issues, and create crisis-response processes.[105]

Fifth: Learning from Experience The final stage in crisis management is learning from experience. At this point, managers need to ask themselves exactly what they have learned from past crises and how that knowledge can be used to advantage in the future. Part of this stage entails an assessment of the effectiveness of the firm's crisis-handling strategies and identification of areas where improvements in capabilities need to be made. Without a crisis management system of some kind in place, the organization will find itself reacting to crises after they have occurred. If learning and preparation for the future are continuous, however, the firm may engage in more proactive behavior.[106]

10.8c Crisis Communications

Virtually all crisis management plans call for effective **crisis communications**, but they are not always effectively executed. There are a number of different stakeholder groups with whom effective communications are critical, especially the media and those immediately affected by the crisis. Many companies have failed to manage their crises successfully

Ethics In Practice Case

Crisis Management: When to Repent? When to Defend?

When facing a crisis, especially one in which the organization is implicated, many experts on crisis management take the approach that management or the firm needs to quickly repent of its malfeasance or wrongdoing, ask for forgiveness, and promise to do better in the future. This soft approach argues for engaging in careful communications and apologizing, if necessary. This approach, some believe, is the best route to limiting damage and restoring the public's confidence in the company and its leaders.

In their book *Damage Control: Why Everything You Know about Crisis Management Is Wrong*, authors Eric Dezenhall and John Weber argue that this soft approach is often wrong. According to the authors, if you are facing a lawsuit, a scandal, a defective product, or allegations of insider trading, experts may tell you to stay positive, get your message out, and everything will be just fine. But, Dezenhall and Weber conclude, this kind of cheery talk does not help much during a real crisis, and it's easy to lose sight of your genuine priorities. If your case goes to trial, for example, you might want the public to think you're a wonderful company, but all that matters is what the jury thinks.

The authors support a political model of crisis management, which means you may have to fight back and defend yourself. When the company has done wrong, repentance is in order. When the company has been wronged, a strong defense is recommended. The authors recommend not admitting guilt and meeting each accusation with a counterclaim.

They say this is how Martha Stewart turned her public image around after serving a jail sentence. They also cite how successful the mobile phone industry was in mounting a defense against the consumer complaints that the phones were causing brain tumors. The key, they say, is determining when to be conciliatory and when to defend aggressively.

1. What are the relevant issues in this debate over the best response to a crisis?
2. Is it best to apologize, repent and move on, or stand firm and aggressively defend?
3. What is the downside risk of mounting a rigorous defense?
4. If a company apologizes for minuscule mistakes, does it risk angering customers by drawing attention to what otherwise might have been a nonissue?
5. Review the case about the Chipotle crisis. Did the company repent or defend?

Sources: Eric Dezenhall and John Weber, *Damage Control: Why Everything You Know about Crisis Management Is Wrong* (New York: Portfolio Hardcover, 2007); Howcast, "Damage Control and Crisis Management in PR," http://www.howcast.com/videos/508056-damage-control-crisis-management-public-relations/, accessed March 22, 2021; American Marketing Association, Steve Heisler, "Is a Company Apology Always Necessary?" April 9, 2020. https://www.ama.org/marketing-news/is-a-company-apology-always-necessary/, accessed March 23, 2021.

because of inadequate or failed communications with key stakeholder groups. It is axiomatic that *prepared* communications will be more helpful than *reactive* communications. There are ten steps of crisis communication that are worth summarizing:[107]

1. Identify your crisis communications team.
2. Identify key spokespersons who will be authorized to speak for the organization.
3. Train your spokespersons.
4. Establish communications protocols.
5. Identify and know your audience.
6. Anticipate crises.
7. Assess the crisis situation.
8. Identify key messages you will communicate to key groups.
9. Decide on communications methods.
10. Be prepared to ride out the storm.

A brief elaboration on the importance of identifying key messages that will be communicated to key groups is useful (point 8). It is important that companies communicate with internal stakeholders first because rumors are often started there, and uninformed employees can do great damage to a successful crisis management effort. Additionally, with the popularity of social media and the use of outlets like Twitter and smartphones to report eyewitness accounts about disasters, terrorist attacks, and other social crises, it is important to squelch misinformation and provide localized information to assist in decision making. Internal stakeholders are a company's best advocates and can be supportive during a crisis. Uniformity of response is of vital importance during a crisis and so it is important to have a key spokesperson (point 2).[108]

The Centers for Disease Control and Prevention (CDC) states as part of its crisis communications training that the first 48 hours of a crisis are the most important. The program's mantra is reported as "be *first*, be *right*, be *credible*."[109] This became known in their efficient handling of the Ebola outbreak in West Africa in 2014. In 2020, however, the CDC was criticized for COVID-19 guidelines issued, resulting in them reversing their position, so even the best of efforts can be subject to extreme public scrutiny amid crises.[110]

Being first means getting your message out first, which allows you to control its accuracy and content. Being right means saying and doing the right thing. This is the ethical dimension of communications. This is done after the management team has gathered all the facts and understands exactly what has happened in the crisis. Being credible means being open, honest, and speaking with one consistent voice. Mixed messages from mixed sources can lead to disaster. The company's spokesperson should be sincere, be empathetic, be accountable, demonstrate competence, display expertise, and put forth consistent facts.[111] For all this to happen, careful crisis communications must be a priority in the crisis plan.

Summary

Corporate social policy is a firm's posture or stance regarding the public, social, or ethical aspects of stakeholders and corporate functioning. It is a part of strategic management, particularly enterprise-level strategy. Enterprise-level strategy is the broadest, overarching level of strategy, and its focus is on the role of the organization in society. A major aspect of enterprise-level strategy is the integration of important core values into company strategy. The other strategy levels include the corporate, business, and functional levels. The strategic management process entails six stages, and a concern for social, ethical, and public issues may be seen at each stage. In the control stage, the social audit, social performance, sustainability report is crucial.

Social entrepreneurship holds the mission of the firm as its ultimate purpose. Creating wealth is necessary for social entrepreneurs if they are to survive and thrive, but wealth is more of a means to an end that benefits society. The benefit corporation is a new corporate form that makes it possible for social entrepreneurs and other like-minded business people to promote the social good as well as wealth creation. Sustainability reports, otherwise known as ESG or social responsibility reports, measure how well the firm achieves the triple bottom line of planet, people, and profit. Integrated reporting is becoming increasingly prevalent as firms try to pull their reporting together into a comprehensive format.

Public affairs can be described as the management function that is responsible for monitoring and interpreting a corporation's noncommercial environment and managing its response to that environment. PA is intimately linked to corporate social policy, environmental analysis, issues management, and crisis management. The major functions of PA departments today include government relations, political action, community involvement or responsibility, issues management, global PA, and corporate philanthropy. Some companies do not use public affairs departments but choose to organize these activities into different departments such as sustainability, CSR, and ethics offices.

Risk, issue, and crisis management are key approaches by which companies may plan for the turbulent stakeholder environment. These approaches are frequently found housed in a company's department of public/corporate affairs or in their own departments. Risk management identifies and prepares for potential issues that have not yet occurred in order to keep the issues from arising. Issue management is a process by which an organization identifies issues in the stakeholder environment, analyzes and prioritizes those issues in terms of their relevance to the organization, plans responses to the issues, and then evaluates and monitors the results. Issue management requires knowledge of the changing mix of issues, as well as a comprehensive understanding of the issue management process, the issue development process, and the implementation of issue management. In sum, issue management serves as a bridge to crisis management.

Crisis management, like issue management, is not a panacea for organizations. In spite of well-intended efforts by management, not all crises will be resolved in the company's favor. Nevertheless, being prepared for the inevitable makes sense, especially in today's world of instantaneous global communications and obsessive media coverage. A crisis has a number of different stages, and managing crises requires a number of key steps before, during, and after the crisis. These steps include identifying areas of vulnerability, developing a plan for dealing with threats, forming crisis teams, using crisis drills, and learning from experience. Crisis communications is critical for successful crisis management. When used in tandem, risk, issue, and crisis management can help managers fulfill their economic, legal, ethical, and philanthropic responsibilities to stakeholders.

Key Terms

B Corporation (B Corps), p. 230
benefit corporation, p. 230
bottom of the pyramid, p. 229
business-level strategy, p. 228
core values, p. 231
corporate affairs (CA), p. 235
corporate affairs strategy, p. 235
corporate-level strategy, p. 228
corporate public affairs, p. 227
corporate social policy, p. 227
crisis, p. 242
crisis communications, p. 244
crisis management, p. 236
crisis teams, p. 243

enterprise-level strategy, p. 228
ESG reports, p. 233
external risks, p. 237
functional-level strategy, p. 228
Global Reporting Initiative (GRI), p. 234
integrated report (IR), p. 233
issue development life cycle process, p. 240
issues management, p. 236
preventable risk, p. 237
public affairs (PA), p. 235
public affairs management, p. 227
public affairs strategy, p. 235

risk management, p. 236
risk shifting, p. 237
shared value, p. 229
social audit, p. 233
social entrepreneurship, p. 229
social responsibility report, p. 233
strategic corporate social responsibility (strategic CSR), p.232
strategic management, p. 226
strategic management process, p. 231
strategic risks, p. 237
sustainability report, p. 233
value proposition, p. 233

Discussion Questions

1. Which of the four strategy levels is most concerned with social, ethical, or public issues? Discuss the characteristics of this level.
2. Identify and explain the steps involved in the strategic management process.
3. What is the difference between integrated reporting and a social performance report?
4. What is social entrepreneurship and how is it related to the Bottom of the Pyramid (BOP)?

5. Why are integrated reports increasing in popularity?
6. Describe the corporate public affairs function today.
7. Which of the major stages in the issue management process do you think is the most important? Why?
8. Following the approach presented in Figure 10-7, identify a new issue category not listed in Figure 10-7.
9. Identify several examples of "crises" that have occurred in recent years under each issue category.

Endnotes

1. John D. Stoll, "A Crash Course in Crisis Management," *The Wall Street Journal* (March 28–29, 2020), B2.
2. PwC, "Emerging Stronger from COVID-19," *PwC. com*, https://www.pwc.com/us/en/library/covid-19.html. Accessed March 18, 2021.
3. McKinsey COVID-19 Briefing Note #45, (March 10, 2021), https://www.mckinsey.com/business-functions/risk /our-insights/covid-19-implications-for-business. Accessed March 18, 2021.

4. Vanessa Fuhrmans, "New Ben & Jerry's CEO Plans to Stir Social Activism," *The Wall Street Journal* (August 18, 2018), B5.
5. Kenneth R. Andrews, *The Concept of Corporate Strategy*, 3d ed. (Homewood, IL: Irwin, 1987), 68–69.
6. See KPMG, https://boardleadership.kpmg.us/relevant -topics/articles/2017/esg-strategy-and-the-long-view.html. Accessed March 18, 2021; Stuart Levine, "Smart ESG Drives Business Results," Forbes (February 22, 2021),

https://www.forbes.com/sites/stuartrlevine/2021/02/22 /smart-esg-drives-business-results/?sh=71a654052413. Accessed March 18, 2021.

7. See R. Edward Freeman and Daniel R. Gilbert Jr., *Corporate Strategy and the Search for Ethics* (Englewood Cliffs, NJ: Prentice Hall, 1988), 20; aR. Edward Freeman, Daniel R. Gilbert Jr., and Edwin Hartman, "Values and the Foundations of Strategic Management," *Journal of Business Ethics* (Vol. 7, 1988), 821–834; Daniel R. Gilbert Jr., "Strategy and Ethics," in *The Blackwell Encyclopedic Dictionary of Business Ethics* (Malden, MA: Blackwell Publishers Ltd., 1997), 609–611.

8. See Charles W. Hofer, Edwin A. Murray Jr., Ram Charan, and Robert A. Pitts, *Strategic Management: A Casebook in Policy and Planning*, 2nd ed. (St. Paul, MN: West Publishing Co., 1984), 27–29; Gary Hamel and C. K. Prahalad, *Competing for the Future* (Boston: Harvard Business School Press, 1994).

9. R. Edward Freeman, *Strategic Management: A Stakeholder Approach* (Boston: Pittman, 1984), 90.

10. Tina Saebi, Nicolai J. Foss, and Stefan Linder, "Social Entrepreneurship Research: Past Achievements and Future Promises," *Journal of Management, 45*(1), 2019, pp. 70–95.

11. See Peter A Dacin, M. Tina Dacin, and Margaret Matear, "Social Entrepreneurship: Why We Don't Need a New Theory and How We Move Forward from Here," *Academy of Management Perspectives, 24*(3), 2010, pp. 37–57.

12. George Dees, "The Meaning of Social Entrepreneurship and Duke's CASE," Social Innovations Solutions, https:// socinnovation.wordpress.com/2010/09/20/duke-case/. Accessed March 19, 2021.

13. World Economic Forum, https://www.weforum.org/covid -alliance-for-social-entrepreneurs. Accessed March 18, 2021.

14. C. K. Prahalad and Stuart L. Hart. "The Fortune at the Bottom of the Pyramid," *Strategy+Business* (Vol. 20, 1998), 1–13.

15. Ibid.

16. Ans Kolk, Miguel Rivera-Santos, and Carlos R. Rufin, "Reviewing a Decade of Research on the 'Base/Bottom of the Pyramid' (BOP) Concept," *Business & Society*, Forthcoming, DOI 10.1177/0007650312474928. Available at SSRN: http://ssrn.com/abstract=2193938. Accessed March 18, 2021.

17. Ibid.

18. Michael E. Porter and Mark R. Kramer, "Creating Shared Value," *Harvard Business Review* (January/February 2011), 62–77.

19. Michaela Driver, "An Interview with Michael Porter: Social Entrepreneurship and the Transformation of Capitalism," *Academy of Management Learning and Education*, *11*(3), 2012, p. 436.

20. Ibid.

21. Shira Schoenberg, "Massachusetts Companies Create Socially Responsible 'Benefit Corporations,'" Masslive. com (December 4, 2012), https://www.masslive.com /politics/2012/12/massachusetts_companies_create.html. Accessed March 18, 2021.

22. Ryan Bradley, "The Tao of Rose," *Fortune* (September 15, 2015), 155–162.

23. Ibid.

24. Mara Leighton and Jacquelin Saguin, "B Corps Are Businesses Committed to Using Their Profit for Good," *Business Insider* (February 23, 2021). Accessed March 18, 2021.

25. Catherine Clifford, "B Corp Movement Gets Its Wings in Europe," *Entrepreneur* (April 22, 2015), https://www .entrepreneur.com/article/245403. Accessed March 18, 2021.

26. Clifford, 2015.

27. Jonathan Chew, "The Good and Bad of Being a B Corporation," *Fortune* (September 15, 2015), 160.

28. James C. Collins and Jerry I. Porras, *Built to Last: Successful Habits of Visionary Companies* (HarperBusiness, 1994).

29. Christopher Mims, "Apple Hopes Values Can Create Value," *The Wall Street Journal* (March 27, 2019), B4.

30. Ibid.

31. Mark Albion, *True to Yourself: Leading a Values-Based Business* (San Francisco, CA: Berrett-Koehler, 2006).

32. Thomas L. Wheelen, J. David Hunger, Alan Hoffman, and Charles Bamford, *Essentials of Strategic Management* (Boston, MA: Pearson, 2017).

33. William B. Werther Jr. and David Chandler, *Strategic Corporate Social Responsibility: Stakeholders in a Global Environment,* 2nd ed. (Thousand Oaks, CA: SAGE Publications), 2011.

34. Michael E. Porter and Mark R. Kramer, "Strategy and Society: The Link between Competitive Advantage and Corporate Social Responsibility," *Harvard Business Review* (December 2006), 80–92.

35. Ibid., 84.

36. Ibid., 85

37. Ibid., 83–90.

38. Ibid., 90–91.

39. George Serafeim, "Social-Impact Efforts That Create Real Value," *Harvard Business Review* (September–October 2020), https://hbr.org/2020/09/social-impact-efforts-that -create-real-value. Accessed March 18, 2021.

40. Edward E. Lawler III and Christopher G. Worley, *Management Reset: Organizing for Sustainable Effectiveness* (John Wiley & Sons, 2011), 10–12.

41. Ibid.

42. IIRC, Integrated Reporting, https://integratedreporting .org/. Accessed March 18, 2021.

43. Thomas Singer, "Four Things You Should Know about Sustainability Reporting Practices," *Greenbiz* (March 2, 2020), https://www.greenbiz.com/article/4-things-you -should-know-about-sustainability-reporting-practices. Accessed March 18, 2021.

44. IIRC, http://integratedreporting.org/. Accessed March 18, 2021.

45. "Sustainability and Reporting Trends in 2025—Preparing for the Future," Global Reporting Initiative First Analysis Paper (May 2015), https://www.globalreporting.org /resourcelibrary/Sustainability-and-Reporting-Trends -in-2025-1.pdf, 4. Accessed March 18, 2021.

46. KPMG Survey of Sustainability Reporting 2020, https:// home.kpmg/be/en/home/insights/2020/12/sus-the-kpmg -survey-of-sustainability-reporting-2020.html. Accessed March 18, 2021.

47. Cisco 2020 Sustainability Report, https://www.cisco .com/c/en/us/about/csr.html. Accessed March 18, 2021.

48. Ford Sustainability 2020, https://corporate.ford.com /microsites/sustainability-report-2020/index.html. Accessed March 19, 2021.

49. Polly Ghazi, "Sustainability Reporting by the Largest U.S. Companies Hits New Highs," *TriplePundit* (July 27, 2020), https://www.triplepundit.com/story/2020

/sustainability-reporting-new-highs/121006. Accessed March 22, 2021.

50. Ceres, https://www.ceres.org/. Accessed March 22, 2021.

51. Ibid.

52. Phil Harris and Craig S. Fleisher (eds), *The Handbook of Public Affairs* (Thousand Oaks, CA: Sage Publications, 2005), 561–562. See also "Public Affairs at the Head of Corporate Strategy," *Corporate Public Affairs*, *16*(2), 2006, 1–2.

53. Sabine Aigner, Philip Dedrijvere, Matthias Fritton, Jonathan Harper, and Rebekah Orchard, "Influence at the Top: The Expanding Role of the Corporate Affairs Officer," SpencerStuart (December 2020), https://www.spencerstuart .com/research-and-insight/influence-at-the-top-role-of-the -corporate-affairs-leader. Accessed March 24, 2021.

54. Harris and Fleisher, 2005.

55. Roberto Ferdman and Ana Swanson, "Chipotle Sales and Profits Plunge as Fears of Food Poisonings Grow," *The Washington Post* (February 2, 2016), https://www .washingtonpost.com/news/wonk/wp/2016/02/02/chipotle -sales-and-profits-plunge-as-fears-of-food-poisonings -grow/. Accessed March 23, 2021.

56. Risks vs. Issues, *The Engineer Leader* (August 6, 2012), http://engineeringcareercoach.com/2012/08/16/risks-vs -issues/. Accessed March 20, 2021.

57. Louis Anthony Cox Jr., "Community Resilience and Decision Theory Challenges for Catastrophic Events," *Risk Analysis: An International Journal* (November 2012), 1919–1934.

58. Robert S. Kaplan and Anette Mikes, "Managing Risks: A New Framework," *Harvard Business Review* (June 2012), 48–60.

59. Ibid.

60. Andrew Tangel, Alison Sider, and Doug Cameron, "Boeing 777 Engines Made by Pratt & Whitney Already Faced Scrutiny," *The Wall Street Journal* (February 21, 2021), https://www.wsj.com/articles/boeing-777 -engines-made-by-pratt-whitney-already-faced-new -scrutiny-11614044828. Accessed March 20, 2021.

61. Kaplan and Mikes, 2012.

62. Kurt Wagner and Bloomberg, "Facebook Admits Another Blunder with Users," *Fortune* (July 1, 2020), https:// fortune.com/2020/07/01/facebook-user-data-apps -blunder/. Accessed March 20, 2021.

63. Kaplan and Mikes, 2012, 48.

64. Ibid.

65. Frank C. Krysiak, "Risk Management as a Tool for Sustainability," *Journal of Business Ethics* (April 2009, Supplement 3), 483–492.

66. David Gelles, "Microsoft Leads Movement to Offset Emissions with Internal Carbon Tax," *The New York Times* (September 26, 2015), http://www.nytimes. com/2015/09/27/business/energy-environment/microsoft -leads-movement-to-offset-emissions-with-internal-carbon -tax.html?_r=0. Accessed March 20, 2021.

67. Diane B. MacDonald, "When Risk Management Collides with Enterprise Sustainability," *Journal of Leadership, Accountability & Ethics* (January 2011), 56–66.

68. Issue Management Council, https://issuemanagement.org /learnmore/clarification-of-terms/. Accessed March 20, 2021.

69. Tony Jaques, "Issue Management as a Post-Crisis Discipline: Identifying and Responding to Issue Impacts beyond the Crisis," *Journal of Public Affairs* (February 2009), 35–44.

70. Ibid., 32.

71. *PwC* Report, "Rebuilding Trust after Times of Crisis: A Practical Guide" (February 2015), https://www.pwc.nl /nl/assets/documents/pwc-rebuilding-trust.pdf. Accessed March 20, 2021.

72. Ibid.

73. William R. King, "Strategic Issue Management," in William R. King and David I. Cleland (eds.), *Strategic Planning and Management Handbook* (New York: Van Nostrand Reinhold, 1987), 259.

74. James K. Brown, *This Business of Issues: Coping with the Company's Environment* (New York: The Conference Board, 1979), 45.

75. Elizabeth Dougall, "Issues Management," *Essential Knowledge Project* (December 12, 2008), http://www .instituteforpr.org/issues-management/. Accessed March 22, 2021.

76. Brown, 33.

77. Cited in Heugens, 2005, 488

78. I. C. MacMillan and P. E. Jones, "Designing Organizations to Compete," *Journal of Business Strategy* (Vol. 4, No. 4, Spring 1984), 13.

79. *PwC* Report, 2015, 8.

80. Paul Lamkin, "Fitbit Still Plagued with Skin Irritation Complaints," *Forbes* (April 27, 2015), http://www.forbes .com/sites/paullamkin/2015/04/27/fitbit-still-plagued -with-skin-irritation-complaints/#56de5a81487b. Accessed March 22, 2021

81. Roy Wernham, "Implementation: The Things That Matter," in King and Cleland, 1987, 453.

82. Craig Giammona and Leslie Patton, "Small Suppliers, Big Problems," *Businessweek* (December 14–20, 2015), 21.

83. Mahon, 81–82.

84. Barbara Bigelow, Liam Fahey, and John Mahon, "A Typology of Issue Evolution," *Business & Society* (Spring 1993), 28. For another useful perspective, see John F. Mahon and Sandra A. Waddock, "Strategic Issues Management: An Integration of Issue Life Cycle Perspectives," *Business & Society* (Spring 1992), 19–32. Also see Steven L. Wartick and Robert E. Rude, "Issues Management: Fad or Function," *California Management Review* (Fall 1986), 134–140.

85. Somini Sengupta, "No U.S. Action, So States Move on Privacy Laws," *The New York Times* (October 30, 2013), https://www.nytimes.com/2013/10/31/technology/no- us-action-so-states-move-on-privacy-law.html. Accessed March 23, 2021.

86. Greg Bensinger, "Goliath vs. Goliath: Facebook and Apple's Fighting Over Data Privacy Rights Doesn't Help Consumers Much, Until It Does," *The New York Times*, (December 19, 2020), https://www.nytimes. com/2020/12/19/opinion/facebook-apple-privacy.html. Accessed March 22, 2021.

87. Scott McCartney, "The Minutes after Disaster Struck," *The Wall Street Journal* (April 25, 2018), A9.

88. Wayne Burns, "Off Course: The Baffling Case of MH370 and the Crisis Management That Survived It," *Corporate Public Affairs* (2014, 24, 1), 1–4.

89. Ibid.

90. David Schaper, "Boeing to Pay $2.5 Billion Settlement Over Deadly 737 Max Crashes," *NPR* (January 8, 2021), https://www.npr.org/2021/01/08/954782512/boeing-to -pay-2-5-billion-settlement-over-deadly-737-max-crashes. Accessed March 24, 2021.

91. Ken Brumfield, "Succeeding in Crisis Leadership," *Financial Executive* (October 2012), 45–47.

92. Ian Mitroff, "Crisis Leadership: Seven Strategies of Strength," *Leadership Excellence, 22*(1), 2005, 11.

93. Ibid., 68. For further discussion of types of crises, see Ian Mitroff, "Crisis Management and Environmentalism: A Natural Fit," *California Management Review* (Winter 1994), 101–113.

94. Pearson and Clair, 60.

95. Ian I. Mitroff and Mural C. Alpaslan, "Preparing for Evil," *Harvard Business Review* (April 2003), 3–9.

96. See Nicole Gillespie, Graham Dietz, and Steve Lockey, "Organizational Reintegration and Trust Repair after an Integrity Violation: A Case Study," *Business Ethics Quarterly, 24*(3), 2014, 371–410; Jonathan Bundy and Michael D. Pfarrer, "A Burden of Responsibility: The Role of Social Approval at the Onset of a Crisis," *Academy of Management Review, 40*(3), 2015, 345–369; Michael Pfarrer, Katherine DeCelles, Ken Smith, and M. Susan Taylor, "After the Fall: Reintegrating the Corrupt Organization," *Academy of Management Review, 33*, 2008, 730–749.

97. Christopher Steitz and Jan Schwartz, "Volkswagen Sees Strong Rebound After Containing COVID," Reuters (February 22, 2021), https://www.reuters.com/article /us-volkswagen-results/volkswagen-sees-strong-rebound -after-containing-covid-idUSKBN2AQ1VQ. Accessed March 22, 2021.

98. Nancy Gagliardi, "A Tough Year Is Ahead for Chipotle," *Forbes* (January 6, 2016), http://www.forbes.com/sites /nancygagliardi/2016/01/06/looks-like-a-tough-year- ahead-for-chipotle/#7f44395761f9. Accessed March 20, 2021.

99. Ibid.

100. Watkins and Bazerman, 2003.

101. Charley Grant, "Losing Dollars by Pinching Pennies: When Short-Termism Goes Bad," *The Wall Street Journal* (March 19, 2021), https://www.wsj.com/articles/losing -dollars-by-pinching-pennies-when-short-termism-goes -bad-11616165999. Accessed March 25, 2021.

102. Ibid.

103. Susan Berfield, "Chipotle's Crisis," *Bloomberg Businessweek* (December 28–January 10, 2016), 49.

104. Tara Patel and Chad Thomas, "Peugeot Creates a War Room to Battle Coronavirus Disruption," *Bloomberg Businessweek*, March 11, 2020, https://www.bloomberg .com/news/articles/2020-03-11/how-does-a-company -prepare-for-a-crisis. Accessed March 23, 2021.

105. PwC, "Global Crisis Centre: Crisis Management and Response" *PwC.com*, (2021), https://www.pwc.com/gx/en /issues/crisis-solutions.html. Accessed March 25, 2021.

106. Ian Mitroff, Paul Shrivastava, and Firdaus Udwadia, "Effective Crisis Management," *Academy of Management Executive* (November 1987), 285.

107. Johnathan L. Bernstein, "The Ten Steps of Crisis Communications," *Crisisnavigator* (January 2013), http:// www.crisisnavigator.org/The-Ten-Steps-of-Crisis -Communications.490.0.html. Accessed March 20, 2021.

108. Richard Wm. Brundage, "Crisis Management—An Outline for Survival," *Crisisnavigator* (January 2013), http://www.crisisnavigator.org/Crisis-Management-An -Outline-for-Survival.454.0.html?&no_cache=1&sword _list[]=Brundage. Accessed March 25, 2021.

109. Cited in Irene Rozansky, "Communicating in a Crisis," *Board Member* (March/April 2007), 2.

110. "After Criticism, C.D.C. Reverses Covid-19 Guidelines on Testing People Who Were Exposed," *New York Times*, (September 18, 2020), https://www .nytimes.com/2020/09/18/world/covid-coronavirus .html?searchResultPosition=1. Accessed March 23, 2021.

111. Rozansky, Ibid.

Part 5

Internal Stakeholder Issues

Chapter 11
Employee Stakeholders and Workplace Issues

Chapter 12
Employee Stakeholders: Privacy, Health, Wellness, and Safety

Chapter 13
Employment Discrimination, Diversity, and Inclusion

11

Employee Stakeholders and Workplace Issues

Chapter Learning Outcomes

After studying this chapter, you should be able to:

1. Discuss the implications of new workplace trends.
2. Outline the characteristics of the new social contract between employers and employees.
3. Explain the concept of employee engagement and the actions companies are taking to make the workplace friendlier.
4. Explain the employee rights movement and its underlying principles.
5. Describe what is entailed with the right not to be fired without cause and discuss the employment-at-will doctrine and its role in employee rights.
6. Discuss the right to due process and fair treatment.
7. Elaborate on the freedom-of-speech issue and whistleblowing.

We begin this next section examining internal stakeholder issues and, specifically, the approach of businesses to their employees. Employees are essential to the creation of firm value and the financial success it provides, and so companies have a moral responsibility to create value for employees in their workplace experience and lives. Doing so is also cost effective because increasing morale and reducing turnover improves the bottom line.[1]

A renewed focus on employee stakeholder issues has been a direct outgrowth of the kinds of social changes that have brought other societal issues into focus. Today's issues are quite unlike the historical concerns of higher pay, shorter hours, more job security, and better working conditions. These expectations still exist, but they now embrace more complex workplace trends and issues. A continued post-pandemic recovery, an influx of Generation Z talent, the growth of the "sharing economy," work-at-home alternatives, and the expectation of a 24/7 work environment have created new challenges for employee engagement in the workforce.[2] Combined with macroenvironmental issues like globalization, digitization, and the growing number of part-time workers, it becomes obvious that the relationship between employees and employers has evolved to one that can be fractious at times.[3] These issues highlight the continued importance of pay levels and employee healthcare and retirement benefits, particularly as companies try to reduce costs to stay competitive and employees strive to maintain their standard of living. In sum, employee stakeholders and workplace issues are complex, challenging, and vital to effective stakeholder management.

Some say a "**new workplace**" has evolved based on the effects of the 2020 global pandemic and changing societal conditions. For many organizations, this includes how to respond to social justice movements, how to shift to a full-time remote staff, how to support employees' well-being and how to manage a hybrid workforce.[4] A recent *Harvard Business Review* article noted the following trends that comprise this new workplace:[5]

- Employers shifting from managing employee experience to managing the life experience of their employees.
- More companies adopting stances on current societal and political debates.
- More companies addressing gender-wage gaps.
- New regulations limiting employee monitoring.
- Flexibility will shift from location to time (e.g., when employees are expected to work).
- Disputes will ensue regarding vaccine requirements for employees.
- Mental health support will be the "new normal" for businesses and employees.
- Employees will look to "rent" talent to fill skills gaps.
- States will compete to attract individual talent rather than trying to get companies to relocate.

It becomes apparent that these workplace trends require businesses to adapt to changing societal conditions. Employers have an opportunity to react to these changes with an increased awareness of employees' personal lives and the consideration of issues like fairness and equity in the workforce. It is therefore imperative that businesses regularly examine their operations and policies to ensure they meet the needs of their employees as primary internal stakeholders.[6]

Because the subject of employee stakeholders and workplace issues is extensive, we dedicate three chapters to these topics. In this chapter, three major themes or trends characterize the modern relationship between employees and their employers: the evolution of the social contract, the practice of employee engagement, and the expansion of employee rights. First, we will discuss the evolving social contract between organizations and workers, which is different from social contracts of the past. Second, we will consider the continuing trend toward more and better employee engagement in the workforce. Third, we will examine the concept of employee rights, and we will describe how the changes in the workplace have precipitated a renewal in the employee rights movement. In particular, we focus on the right not to be fired without good cause, the right to due process and fair treatment, and the right to freedom of speech in the workplace.

In Chapter 12, we will extend our discussion to the expectations and rights of employees to privacy, safety, and health. In Chapter 13, we discuss employment diversity and discrimination. These three chapters should be considered a continuous discussion of employee stakeholders wherein economic, legal, and ethical responsibilities are all taken into consideration.

11.1 The New Social Contract

In Chapter 1, we discussed the concept of the **social contract**—a set of reciprocal understandings that characterize the relationship between business and society. We noted that the social contract has been changing to reflect society's expanded expectations of business, and this may certainly be seen in the expectations surrounding employer–employee relationships. Fifty years ago, the trend was that employees stayed in the same job in the same company for

---

Ethics In Practice Case

Walmart, Amazon, and the $15 Minimum Wage

For almost ten years now, there has been a movement in the United States to have businesses pay at least $15 an hour as a minimum wage. The current federal minimum wage, at $7.25 an hour, has not been raised since 2009. A 2021 study by *The Economic Policy Institute* notes that this increase is long overdue, as they show that raising the federal minimum wage to $15 by 2025 would lift the pay of 32 million workers, of which 19 million are essential and front-line workers.

Walmart, the U.S.'s largest employer with more than 1.5 million workers, steadfastly refuses to raise its minimum wage, which is currently $11 an hour, despite protests from current employees and a group called United for Respect. In its defense, Walmart cites the perks it offers entry-level workers that are career boosters such as enrollment in online academic degree programs for $1 per day, good maternity leave benefits, and developmental upskills training for career opportunities. It also notes that it raised its average associate wage to more than $15 an hour. Walmart CEO Doug McMillon said that raising wages to a blanket $15 minimum would compromise the "ladder of opportunity" that encourages employees to strive to earn more as they climb the ranks. He also noted that a $15 minimum is an "important target," but it should be "paced in a way that's good for the U.S. economy." Meanwhile, rival Costco Wholesale Corporation recently set its minimum wage at $16 an hour.

The Walmart example is part of a larger conversation on the pros and cons of raising federal minimum wage. Opponents of raising the minimum wage point to potential job losses that will result, as well as an overall increase in the prices of goods and services. For example, a recent report from the Congressional Budget Office (CBO) estimated 1.4 million jobs would be lost if the federal minimum wage were to be raised. Proponents of an increase dispute these numbers and argue that while prices may increase, the increases would be spread out among many consumers and few would feel the effects. Adding to the debate is that each state has its own minimum wage requirements,

so a federal minimum wage increase would have disparate impact across different states.

Amazon was an early proponent of raising the federal minimum wage; in 2018 they implemented the $15 minimum wage. A recent study found that following Amazon's actions, local companies followed suit, and in areas where Amazon operates, low-wage workers at other businesses saw significant wage growth beyond what might have been expected and no significant job losses. The message of the study: wage increases by large corporate employers appear to drive up other companies' wages without driving down employment.

1. What are the ethics issues involved with raising the federal minimum wage? What values are at play here?
2. How might decisions about raising the minimum wage differ for small versus large businesses?
3. What do you think about Walmart's arguments regarding overall employee benefits and opportunities versus minimum wage increases?
4. Do you think the federal minimum wage should be raised?

Sources: Thomas Buckley, "Walmart's Fight Against a $15 Minimum Wage Could Thrust It Into the Inequality Debate," *Bloomberg Businessweek* (Aril 27, 2021), https://www.bloomberg .com/news/articles/2021-04-27/walmart-wmt-fights-against-15 -minimum-wage-as-inequality-debate-rages, accessed April 29, 2021; David Cooper, Zane Mokhiber, and Ben Zipperer, "Raising the Federal Minimum Wage to $15 by 2025 Would Lift the Pay of 32 Million Workers," *Economic Policy Institute* (March 9, 2021), https://www.epi.org/publication/raising-the-federal-minimum -wage-to-15-by-2025-would-lift-the-pay-of-32-million-workers/, accessed April 29, 2021; Kelly Anne Smith, "What You Need to Know about the Minimum Wage Debate," *Forbes* (February 26, 2021), https://www.forbes.com/advisor/personal-finance /minimum-wage-debate/, accessed April 29, 2021; Ben Casselman and Jim Tankersley, "When Amazon Raises Its Minimum Wage, Local Companies Follow Suit," *The New York Times* (March 5, 2021), accessed April 29, 2021.

years and those companies rewarded employees' loyalty by offering job stability, a decent wage, and good benefits. As we note above, however, today's employees have different expectations and different needs in the current workplace.

The workforce of today is more mobile, less loyal, and more diverse. From CEOs to factory workers, employees have come to know that their jobs are vulnerable, and so they have come to view themselves as free agents, bearing sole responsibility for their own careers.[7] The trend is captured in the term **gig economy**, characterized by work consisting of a series of short-term jobs coordinated through a mobile app.[8] In fact, a recent PwC study noted that organizations are planning on using more gig-based employees in their organizations over the next three to five years.[9] Of course, the gig economy brings a whole host of issues related to employees and their social contracts with employers.

A gathering of experts, policymakers, and activists at the Aspen Institute sought to understand the new social contract, captured in what they call the "**1099 economy**" of contingent workers.[10] The "1099" refers to one of several tax forms used for reporting income other than wages to the Internal Revenue Service; those who are self-employed use it. The concern is that workers will not be able to earn a living wage under this new social contract, without access to stable and adequate incomes, protections from abuse, and basic benefits like health care and retirement.[11] As noted in the following Ethics in Practice case, this concern becomes evident in discussions around raising the minimum wage, with companies like Walmart, the U.S. largest employer, defending its treatment of employees even as it resists a $15/hour minimum wage.

Even today's full-time employees do not look for a promise for lifetime employment. Instead, they seek competitive pay and benefits coupled with opportunities for professional growth. At the same time, they want meaningful work, a vision they can share with the company, an ethical organization that supports corporate social responsibility, clear performance feedback, and a strong, supportive organizational culture.[12] Some analysts argue that a key driver of an organization's ability to survive and thrive into the future will be the social contract that the firm has with its employees.[13] Figure 11-1 presents some of the characteristics of the historical and new social contract between employers and employees.

Surveys of **Generation Z** workers reflect the expectations of the new social contract. About 17 million members of Generation Z, born in 1997 or later, are now in the workforce. According to recent surveys, early signs suggest that Gen Z members are more competitive and pragmatic, but also more anxious and reserved. Hence, they reflect desires for financial security as well as making work a central part of their lives.[14] They have similar viewpoints with the **Millennials** ahead of them, although quite a few Gen Z workers experienced job loss and/or pay cuts during the COVID-19 pandemic.[15] Nevertheless, 38 percent of Gen Z workers consider **work-life balance** as their number-one factor in choosing an employer. Many of the Gen Z workers have faced challenges in the transition to working from home during the pandemic, especially in the areas of productivity, boredom, mental health, and skill development.[16] However, they continue to look for collaborative and team-friendly work environments.[17] Finally, although Gen Z members love technology, they also crave human interaction, and therefore employers must understand that they desire to "know" the people they work with.[18]

More than anything else, the expectations of employees and the new social contract represent an adaptation to the changing world of work and changing business circumstances. Going forward, we can expect free-agent employees to be more proactive about their work environments than the loyal employees of the past once were. Therefore, businesses will need to be proactive as well with employee

Figure 11-1 The Changing Social Contract between Employers and Employees

Historical Social Contract	New Social Contract
Job security; long, stable career and employment relationships	Few tenure arrangements; jobs constantly "at risk"; employment as long as you "add value" to the organization
Lifetime careers with one employer	Fewer life careers; changing employer common; careers more dynamic
Stable positions/job assignments	Temporary project assignments
Loyalty to employer; identification with employer	Loyalty to self and profession; diminished identification with employer
Paternalism; family-type relationships	Relationships far less warm and familial; no more parent–child relationships
Employee sense of entitlement	Personal responsibility for one's own career/job future
Stable, rising income	Pay that reflects contributions; pay for "value added"
Job-related skill training	Learning opportunities; employees in charge of their own education and updating
Focus on individual job accomplishments	Focus on team building and projects
Personal face-to-face communication	Communication through technologies

engagement programs that foster loyalty and dedication. It is likely that employee stakeholders' expectations of fair treatment will also continue to rise, and we will witness continuing growth in the employee rights movement.

11.2 Employee Engagement

When businesses invest in **employee engagement**, the benefits are clear. Companies with active employee engagement programs have higher customer ratings, profitability, and productivity than those who do not have such programs.[19] Additionally, they have significantly less turnover, less shrinkage, less absenteeism, fewer safety incidents, and fewer quality defects.[20] Engaged employees are those who identify and have an emotional commitment to the organization and are enthusiastic and committed to their work and their workplace. They consistently bring extra effort to their roles in the organization in support of its goals. In fact, year after year, the best managed companies are those that excel in employee engagement.[21]

What can companies do to encourage their employees to be engaged with their work? Most businesses first assess employee engagement through surveys that are done regularly to measure and assess how motivated and engaged their employees are.[22] Thanks to technology and Big Data, it is easier to identify key employee issues through new, sophisticated, sentiment-analysis software that allows companies to drill deeper into employee motivations and job satisfaction.[23] Companies then create action plans to support employee engagement through mentoring programs, career training, relationship management strategies, and targeted communication initiatives to stay on top of employee engagement issues.[24] It is easy to see how an active employee engagement program aligns with good stakeholder management, and specifically the supportive stakeholder approach, which we discussed in Chapter 3.

Employee engagement suffered perhaps its most challenging time during the height of the COVID-19 pandemic in 2020. However, following a turbulent year, a Gallup poll of employee engagement in the United States found that employee engagement actually increased to 39 percent in January 2021, representing a new record level of such engagement.[25] How did this happen? Employees reported that they were getting more feedback from their manager either daily or a few times per week. Notably, employees who worked remotely at least some of the time had the highest levels of engagement. These findings point to the importance of meaningful feedback from employers, even as more employees work remotely or in a hybrid format.

11.3 The Employee Rights Movement

For decades now, the employee rights movement, driven by employee expectations, has characterized worker concerns in the changing social contract. Employees want to be treated fairly, and promoting the idea of employee rights is a major way in which they have sought to improve employee-employer relationships from their perspective. In our discussion of employee rights, we focus on employees in the private sector because of the underlying public sector–private sector dichotomy. The public sector is subject to constitutional control of its power, and so government employees have more protections. In contrast, the private sector generally has not been subject to constitutional control because of the concept of **private property**, which holds that individuals and private organizations are free to use their property as they desire. As a result, private corporations historically and traditionally have not had to recognize employee rights to the same degree because society honored the corporation's private property rights. The underlying issues for the private sector and its stakeholders then become why and to what extent the private property rights of business should be changed or diluted.

A brief comment on the role of labor unions is appropriate here. In general, although labor unions have been quite successful in improving the material conditions of life at work in the United States—pay, fringe benefits, and working conditions—they have not been as active in pursuing civil liberties. We must give unions credit for the gains they have made in converting what were typically regarded as management's rights or prerogatives into issues in which labor could participate. However, we should note that labor unions seem to be disappearing from the U.S. business scene. In 1953, union representation reached its highest proportion of the private employment workforce, at 36 percent.[26] In 2020, the percent of wage and salary workers who were members of unions in the United States was 10.8 percent.[27] Compared to other countries, the U.S. unionization rate is low, but Organisation for Economic Co-operation and Development (OECD) statistics suggest that union membership is declining worldwide as well.[28]

There is always speculation about a new groundswell of support for labor unions, particularly when economic downturns, political influence, and corporate actions prompt employee concerns. In 2020, a Gallup poll found that 65 percent of Americans surveyed were in favor of labor unions, representing the highest percentage of support since 2003.[29] Simultaneously, Amazon workers in an Alabama warehouse attempted to form a union with complaints about grueling workload demands and the company's monitoring of employees.[30] The turnout for the vote was low and did not pass, but Amazon CEO Jeff Bezos acknowledged that more needed to be done to listen and respond to worker demands, noting, "It is clear to me that we need a better vision for how we create value for employees."[31]

11.3a The Meaning of Employee Rights

Before we consider specific employee rights issues, we should discuss briefly what we mean by **employee rights**. A lawyer might look at employee rights as claims that one can enforce in a court of law. For many economists as well, rights are only creations of the law. For our purposes, we will approach employee rights from the "principle of rights" perspective discussed in Chapter 6, and viewed from this perspective, rights are justifiable claims that utility cannot override. While we will focus on employee ethical rights, we will also consider employee legal rights.

Employee rights can be positive or negative. Said differently, they can focus on achieving desired outcomes or on prohibiting unwanted outcomes. Richard Edwards has grouped employee rights into three categories based on the fact that these rights find their source in *law, union contracts*, or *employers' promises*. Rights provided by the law are called **statutory rights**. These include, for example, the rights established by the Civil Rights Act of 1964 (at a national level) or by the Massachusetts Right to Know Law (at the state level), which grant production workers the right to be notified of specific toxic substances they may be exposed to in the workplace. Union contracts, by contrast, provide workers with rights established through the process of **collective bargaining**. Examples of these rights are seniority preferences, job security mechanisms, and grievance procedures.[32]

Employer promises are the third source of employees' rights. These employer grants or promises are called **enterprise rights**. Typical examples of such enterprise rights might include the right to petition beyond one's immediate supervisor, the right to be free from physical intimidation, the right to a grievance or complaint system, and the right

to due process in discipline. Other enterprise rights include the right to have express standards for personnel evaluation, the right to have one's job clearly defined, the right to a "just cause" standard for dismissal, and the right to be free from nepotism and unfair favoritism.[33]

Management provides and justifies enterprise rights, and so the rationale for those rights can be as varied as the managers who implement them. They might reflect the prevailing customs and norms of a company's industry. They might extend above and beyond those offered by competing firms and thus be used as a type of recruiting tool. They may also be given on the basis of some normative ethical principle or reasoning (e.g., "This is the way workers ought to be treated"). In this situation, the ethical principles of justice, rights, and utilitarianism, as well as notions of virtue ethics, may be the rationales. Enterprise rights also might arise out of two-way shared understandings that develop through the evolving social contract, as discussed in Chapter 1.

To summarize, employee rights may be based on economic, legal, and/or ethical sources of justification. In this way, management may provide the employee rights as part of an effort to be socially responsible or to display moral management, as discussed in Chapter 5. To illustrate this point further, Figure 11-2 characterizes how moral managers, as well as amoral and immoral managers, might view employee stakeholders.

The following discussions focus on job-related rights that are often claimed by employees and thus merit further

---

Ethics In Practice Case

The Neglectful Director

I was hired as a temporary employee of a toy manufacturing company, and the department I was assigned to was going through some rough changes. Their director had recently quit and the new director, from a similar company that had just recently filed for bankruptcy, took her place. She said she had about 20 years in the imports business and knew it like the back of her hand. Naturally, her new employees were relieved and hoped that business would continue as usual.

Months passed and I learned a lot about the important aspects of our company. In those months, my co-workers and I noticed that our boss was not doing much work. We were used to a hands-on director who was not afraid to pull up her sleeves and dive into the deepest piles of papers. Soon, work that we thought our new director was supposed to be handling started piling up. We also gained a huge customer whose orders were the task equal to the amount of work we had already. She also put me, the temporary employee, in charge of the new customer. Because huge amounts of work were getting cranked out of our department, we worked 10-hour shifts and Saturdays to get it all done. Then my co-workers started complaining. "All she does is watch YouTube videos all day," one said. "She's always talking on her cell phone," another co-worker said. Another temp was hired to help us out so that we wouldn't have to work on Saturdays.

I was finally hired as a permanent employee. I was elated for about two months to have a job that I could call "home" and co-workers that I could get to know. However, alas, the company started laying off employees. They began to fire most of the temporary employees; then, they fired 11 regular employees. In all, we lost both of our temps and a regular employee in our department. I can't help but feel that it was our director's fault that we had lost these employees.

1. The reason I was hired was my director's strong push to keep me. Should I let her continue to neglect her responsibilities just because I owe her some kind of thanks? Should my loyalty be with my company in general or to the person that hired me?
2. Even after one of my co-workers spoke to our director about her wasteful spending, she continued to do so. Should my co-worker have gone above her to let her boss know what was going on?
3. As an employee, do I have any rights in this situation? If so, what would they be?
4. What would you have done in this situation? Why?

Contributed Anonymously

Figure 11-2 Three Models of Management Morality and Their Orientations toward Employee Stakeholders

Model of Management Morality	Orientation toward Employee Stakeholders
Moral Management	Employees are a human resource that must be treated with dignity and respect. Employees' rights to due process, privacy, freedom of speech, and safety are maximally considered in all decisions. Management seeks fair dealings with employees. The goal is to use a leadership style, such as consultative/participative, that will result in mutual confidence and trust. Commitment is a recurring theme.
Amoral Management	Employees are treated as the law minimally requires. Attempts to motivate focus on increasing productivity rather than satisfying employees' growing maturity needs. Employees are still seen as factors of production, but a remunerative approach is used. The organization sees self-interest in treating employees with minimal respect. Organization structure, pay incentives, and rewards are all geared toward short- and medium-term productivity.
Immoral Management	Employees are viewed as factors of production to be used, exploited, and manipulated for gain of individual managers or the company. No concern is shown for employees' needs/rights/ expectations. Managers pursue a short-term focus in a coercive, controlling, and alienating environment.

consideration here. These include (1) the *right not to be fired without good cause*, (2) the *right to due process and fair treatment*, and (3) the *right to freedom, particularly freedom of expression and freedom of speech*. In Chapter 12, we will consider the rights to privacy, safety, and health in the workplace.

11.4 The Right Not to Be Fired without Cause

A **good cause norm**, the belief that employees should be discharged only for good reasons (i.e., just cause dismissal), prevails in the United States today. This normative belief persists in spite of the fact that it does not match the descriptive reality of what often happens. From a legal perspective, most U.S. employees can be fired for any reason, or for no reason, as long as the firing is not in violation of any discrimination laws. Belief in the good cause norm stands in direct opposition to the employment-at-will doctrine, which many private employers believe is their right based on current laws. With employers and employees holding such contradictory views, it is easy to see why so many disputes occur, and terms like *unjust dismissals* and *wrongful discharge* have become part of today's employment language.

11.4a Employment-at-Will Doctrine

The central issue in the movement to protect workers' job-related rights involves changing views of the **employment-at-will doctrine**. In the industrialized world, the United States is unique in adhering to this doctrine, which is based on the private property rights of the employer and the principle that the relationship between employer and employee is a voluntary one that can be terminated at any time by either party for any reason. This doctrine holds that

just as employees are free to quit a company any time they choose, employers can discharge employees for any reason, or no reason, as long as they do not violate federal discrimination laws, state laws, or union contracts. What this doctrine means is that unless employees are protected by a union contract (the vast majority of the workforce is not), or by one of the discrimination laws, an employer is free to let an employee go anytime, for any reason. This doctrine is not widely understood by the workforce because it appears to be counterintuitive to fair treatment.

Recently, the concept of employment-at-will was tested in New York City, when Mayor Bill de Blasio barred fast-food employers from firing workers without a good reason and required employers to prove the reason if a worker contests their termination.[34] The COVID-19 pandemic appeared to give a boost to such "just cause" policies with concerns about unfair firings in retaliation for workers complaining about hard working conditions. However, most agree that the New York law will be difficult for employers to satisfy as they struggle to provide justification every time they fire an employee.

As previously mentioned, most employees in the United States believe that employment law not only should follow a good cause norm but also should reinforce this in practice.[35] However, most private employees in the United States are in an at-will employment relationship and can be discharged at any time by their employers.[36]

Legal Challenges to Employment-at-Will. Three broad categories of issues that illustrate the legal challenges that have arisen with regard to employment-at-will discharges are (1) public policy exceptions, (2) implied contract exceptions, and (3) breach of good faith actions.[37] States vary in their adoption of exceptions to employment-at-will, creating a patchwork of employment situations around the country.

A major exception to the long-standing employment-at-will doctrine is known as the **public policy exception**, which is recognized by most states (exceptions are Alabama, Florida, Georgia, Louisiana, Maine, Nebraska, New York, and Rhode Island).[38] This exception protects employees from being fired because they refuse to commit crimes or because they try to take advantage of privileges to which they are entitled by law. The courts have held that management may not discharge an employee who refuses to commit an illegal act or performs a public obligation, such as serving on a jury or supplying information to the police. This exception sometimes covers whistle-blowers. We will further discuss the case of whistle-blowers later in the chapter.

Workers who believe they have contracts or implied contracts with their employers are protected in the 36 states and the District of Columbia that recognize the **implied contract exception**.[39] In some instances, the courts hold employers to promises they do not even realize they have made. For example, statements in employee handbooks or personnel manuals, job-offer letters, and even oral assurances about job security can be interpreted as implied contracts that the management is not at liberty to violate. In one example, a Connecticut woman and her husband worked for the same company and the company laid off the husband after undergoing a restructuring. The company promised the woman that she would not be fired, even if her husband went to work for a competing company. When he did, the company terminated the woman. She sued for breach of implied contract and the court awarded her $850,000.[40] As another example, if an employee can prove in court that the hiring manager said, "We do not fire people without a good reason," that can be enough to create an implied contract. Even the use of the term *permanent employee* to mean an employee who had worked beyond a six-month probationary period may be construed as a promise of continuous employment.

Courts have also recognized that employers should hold themselves to a standard of fairness and good faith dealings with employees. This concept is the broadest restraint on employment-at-will terminations. The **good faith principle** suggests that employers may run the risk of losing lawsuits to former employees if they fail to show that employees had every reasonable opportunity to improve their performance before termination. Only 11 states recognize the good faith principle.[41] As previously noted, however, the good faith principle reflects what many already believe is the responsibility of businesses toward their employees. The principle is not a problem for companies if they simply employ fair ways of taking disciplinary measures and mechanisms for reviewing grievances that provide employees with due process. We will discuss such due-process mechanisms later in the chapter.

Moral and Managerial Challenges to Employment-at-Will. As previously mentioned, the United States is unique in its adherence to the employment-at-will doctrine, and most people in the United States believe a norm of good cause should apply to employment decisions, so it is not surprising that employment-at-will has been criticized on moral as well as legal grounds. The argument generally used in favor of employment-at-will is that employers invoke their property rights when they terminate an employee. Researchers Werhane, Radin, and Bowie derive three objections to employment-at-will. First, they argue that employees deserve respectful treatment, which includes explaining the reasons for termination when it occurs. Second, employees do not have the option of being arbitrary or capricious with employers, and so employers should bear the same responsibility in their treatment of employees. The third issue is based on the concept of reciprocity: Employees are expected to be trustworthy, loyal, and respectful in their interactions with employers, and so employers should show employees the same consideration.[42]

Spotlight on Sustainability

Sustainability in the Hiring and Retention of Employees

A study by the National Environmental Education Foundation (NEEF) found educating employees in environmental and sustainability (E&S) initiatives can attract and retain good talent while also increasing profitability and reducing environmental impact. The study presents a variety of case studies including eBay. eBay's green team convinced the company to build the largest commercial solar installation in San Jose, California. They reduced CO_2 emissions by over one million pounds a year and saved more than $100,000. In a statement, Diane Wood, president of NEEF, said that past environmental education programs focused on employees involved in safety and health. Now they realize they must involve the entire workforce. Human resource management has a critical role to play through the recruitment and selection of the right people and the establishment of policies and incentives that support a sustainability orientation.

This idea is also supported by research that shows that Millennials are likely to choose to work for, and stay

with, a company that has a strong sustainability plan. According to *Fast Company*, companies have a high chance of attracting and retaining employees if they can demonstrate a strong commitment to sustainability. Additionally, when employees are engaged and interested in sustainability, it is easier for sustainability initiatives to succeed.

Sources: Grace Olupinyo, "Benefits of Sustainability: Improved Employee Attraction, Engagement and Retention," *GreenBusiness Bureau* (June 23, 2020), https://greenbusinessbureau.com/blog /how-sustainability-benefits-companies-by-increasing-employee -attraction-and-retention/, accessed April 20, 2021; Greenbiz Staff, "Why Bringing Employees on Board Helps Sustainability Projects Succeed," *Greenbiz.com* (February 22, 2010), http:// www.greenbiz.com/news/2010/02/22/bringing-employees-board -makes-sustainability-projects-success#ixzz0pS7n8RUA, accessed April 20, 2021.

Ethics In Practice Case

Kindness in Firing

In February 2019, a worker who had just been dismissed at a factory in Aurora, Illinois, opened fire and killed five colleagues before he was killed by police. Any time we read or hear about a workplace shooting in response to an employee's firing, employers are forced to think about the ways they manage the dismissal process. The ways that employers approach terminations vary considerably, with much of the process up for debate including the proper day to let an employee go, whether or not to have security escorts present, and how long to maintain a fired worker's benefits.

Many HR managers employ empathy and compassion during the process, as they say that it can help keep the integrity of the person intact. Some even offer to assist the fired employee in finding another job and provide a phone number for the employee to text them with questions. Extending benefits for a period of time can be particularly helpful to terminated employees because it gives them time to schedule doctors' appointments for family members. When the termination gets contentious, HR consultants suggest finding a neutral place to conduct the firing and prepping security personnel before the meeting. Fortunately, most terminations do not result in violence. With a little sensitivity in the process, adequate prep work before the meeting, and a clear message, employers may be able to fire employees while still preserving the employee's dignity.

1. Should all managers be trained on termination practices, or just HR personnel? If yes, what kind of training should they receive?
2. It is often been said that a termination "should never be a surprise" to the employee. What does that mean? What are best practices leading up to a termination?
3. Have you ever had to fire someone, or have you ever been fired? Was it done respectfully?

Sources: Chip Cutter, "Bosses Seek a Kinder Way to Fire People," *The Wall Street Journal* (April 11, 2019), B5; Julie Bosman and Mitch Smith, "Aurora Shooting Updates: 5 Killed and Several Others Wounded," *New York Times* (February 15, 2019), https://www.nytimes.com/2019/02/15/us/aurora-shooting.html, accessed April 20, 2021; Joel Peterson, "Firing with Compassion," *Harvard Business Review* (March/April 2020), 98(2), pp. 135–139.

Employment-at-will can present managerial problems as well. We should not forget the impact that an employment-at-will environment can have on the culture of an organization. Most bad reasons for firing employees, such as discrimination, are already illegal, and managers can always fire an employee for good justifiable reasons. From this perspective, employment-at-will is not needed because it simply protects the right of the employer to fire an employee for no reason at all. This creates an odd dynamic. Trust and loyalty are important to effective workplaces, but they are reciprocal relationships. For managers to be able to trust their employees, they must be willing to be trustworthy in return.[43]

11.4b Dismissing an Employee with Care

With respect to employee dismissals, management needs to be aware not only of the content of the decision to dismiss but also of the *process* for doing it. Treating employees responsibly, with care, is important not only to the terminated employee but also to the survivors of the process, who then expect they will be treated with care if they face a similar situation. A positive corporate culture can be preserved even in difficult times with thoughtful treatment of employees, especially in dismissal situations. Steve Harrison offers some dos and don'ts for dismissing employees in a responsible manner. The following are some specific recommendations for actions[44]:

1. *Fire employees in a private space.* Do not terminate an employee in a way that enables co-workers to see what is happening or that forces them to "walk a gauntlet" in front of them.
2. *Be mindful of employees' logistics.* How will they get closure on their projects? How will they get home that day?

3. *Preserve employees' dignity.* If you must lay off a trusted and valuable employee for economic reasons, don't confiscate IDs and cell phones immediately or cancel passwords immediately.
4. *Choreograph the notification in advance.* The purpose of the meeting should not be a surprise.
5. *Use transparent criteria for layoffs.* The rationale for terminations should be clear both to those laid off and to the survivors.

The following are some of the actions managers should *not* take when dismissing employees[45]:

1. *Do not fire on a Friday.* Terminated employees would not have access to support services on weekends and so would have to cope on their own.
2. *Do not say that downsizing is finished.* It is impossible to know for sure that the downsizing has ended and being wrong about that would make subsequent layoffs more difficult for all concerned.
3. *Do not terminate an employee via e-mail.* Although this advice seems obvious, firms have done so to the detriment of employees as well as their reputations.
4. *Stick to the topic and avoid platitudes.* For example, do not say, "This is as hard for me as it is for you"—it isn't.
5. *Do not rush through the meeting.* Being willing to give a person time is a way of communicating that the person matters. Not to give the employee the time needed for the termination puts salt in the wound.

For effective stakeholder management, organizations must always consider their obligations to employee stakeholders and their rights and expectations with respect to their jobs. Companies that aspire to emulate the tenets of the moral management model will need to re-examine continuously their attitudes, perceptions, practices, and policies with respect to this issue and take care to dismiss employees only for justified economic-related or performance-related reasons, not arbitrary reasons. Further, if employee discharges are handled carefully and in accordance with the above recommendations, employees are more likely to believe they received fair treatment, a topic we address next, and this will benefit everyone in the organization.

11.5 The Right to Due Process and Fair Treatment

One of the most frequently proclaimed employee rights issues of the past decade has been the right to due process. **Due process** is the right to receive an impartial review of one's complaints or opinions and to be dealt with fairly. In the context of the workplace, the right to due process involves the rights of employees to have impartial third parties review the decisions that adversely affect them. The right not to be fired without just cause would fall into this category of fair treatment; however, in this section we will expand on this concept and discuss other applications.

One major obstacle to the due-process idea is that to some extent it is a bit contrary to the employment-at-will principle discussed earlier. Due process is consistent with the democratic ideal that undergirds the universal right to fair treatment, and so one can argue that without due process, employees do not receive fair treatment in the workplace. Furthermore, the fact that the courts are gradually eroding the employment at-will principle might serve as an indication that employment-at-will is thought to be unfair. If this is true, the due-process concept makes more sense.

11.5a Due Process

All employees have the right to be evaluated in a fair and effective manner. Affording due process for employees can range from the expectation that the company treat employees fairly to the position that employees deserve a fair system of decision making when their status in the organization is at stake.[46]

Sometimes unfair treatment happens in such a subtle way that it is difficult to know that it has taken place. What do you do, for example, if your supervisor refuses to recommend you for promotion or permit you to transfer because your supervisor considers you to be exceptionally good at your job and doesn't want to lose you? How do you prove that a manager has given you a low performance appraisal because you resisted sexual advances? The issues over which due-process questions may arise can be quite difficult and subtle and often challenging to prove.

Due process, when formalized, is a system for ascertaining that organizational decisions have been fair.[47] As such, it aligns closely with the concept of procedural justice, or

ethical due process, that we discussed in Chapter 6. The following are the main requirements of a due-process system in an organization:[48]

1. It must be a procedure; it must follow rules. It must not be arbitrary.
2. It must be sufficiently visible and so well known that potential violators of employee rights and victims of abuse are aware of it.
3. It must be predictably effective.
4. It must be institutionalized—a relatively permanent fixture in the organization.
5. It must be perceived as equitable.
6. It must be easy to use.
7. It must apply to all employees.

Procedural due process is a concept derived from the Fifth and Fourteenth Amendments of the U.S. Constitution. In law, due process requires a balancing act between the interests of the government and those of the individual. In organizations, a similar balancing act occurs. The challenge is to balance the interests of the individual employee with those of the organization.[49]

The increased use of contract and gig workers puts another spin on the concept of due process in the workforce. As we noted earlier, the U.S. contingent, or temporary workforce, is growing at an alarming rate and is creating a new form of the social contract between employers and employees. The concern is that employers are avoiding the costs of full-time workers (health care benefits, retirement benefits) by using temporary workers. U.S. Department of Labor (DOL) Wage and Hour Division director David Weil calls this trend **fissuring**.[50] He believes that many of the companies using temporary workers should really be considered "joint employers" together with the contractors that sign the checks, making them liable for violations.[51]

Additionally, gig workers face challenges in due process because their job performance is often assessed by ratings, which can be arbitrary. As noted in a recent article in *The Economist*, people might give an Uber driver a poor rating because they are in a bad mood or they got stuck in traffic during the ride.[52] Similarly, a TaskRabbit employee who has been contracted for odd jobs might be rated poorly by someone who wanted them to do a task outside of the described job. And because gig workers' income is linked to their ratings, the impact of poor ratings can be an unfair assessment of the worker's performance.

Due process is a cornerstone for treating employees fairly. However, with new types of businesses, workers, and technology, companies will be challenged to find novel ways to make sure that employees continue to be valued for their services and that contingent workers are treated fairly in their employment.

11.5b Alternative Dispute Resolution

Many companies can and do provide due process for their employees in several ways. **Alternative dispute resolution (ADR)** is a term that refers to ways of resolving disputes that avoid litigation. It is a popular, and yet controversial, form of conflict resolution because the practice of ADR can vary widely and there are constant calls for more standardization in ADR approaches.[53] Yet, it is a popular choice for businesses—even during the global pandemic when in-person ADR became challenging, ADR remained an effective and popular means of resolving dispute.[54] The approaches described here represent some of the ADR methods that have been employed by companies.

Common Approaches. One of the most often-used mechanisms to resolve differences is the **open-door policy**. This approach typically relies on senior-level executives who assert that their "door is always open" for those who think they have been treated unfairly. Alternatively, the organization might assign to an executive of the human resources department the responsibility for investigating employee grievances and either handling them or reporting them to higher management.

From the employee's standpoint, the major problems with these approaches are that (1) the process is closed (seldom reviewed by someone else), (2) one person is reviewing what happened, and (3) there is a tendency in organizations for one manager to support another manager's decisions. The process is opened up somewhat by companies that use a **hearing procedure**, which permits employees to be represented by an attorney or another person, with a neutral company executive deciding the outcome based on the evidence. Similar to this approach is the use of a management **grievance committee**, which may involve multiple executives in the decision process.

The Ombudsman. A due-process mechanism that has become popular for dealing with employee problems is the use of a corporate **ombudsman**, also known as **ombuds** or **ombudsperson**. The term developed from a Swedish word that refers to one who investigates reported complaints and helps to achieve equitable settlements. The Swedish term "ombuds" means "representative" and "man" means "the people," so the terms *ombudsman*, *ombudsperson*, and *ombuds* are used interchangeably. Most major corporations have an ombudsman, with many joining after Sarbanes–Oxley (SOX) was passed.[55] SOX contains a lesser-known provision that encourages employees to report wrongdoing and prohibits corporate retaliation against those employees.[56] The ombudsman's task is quite different from that of the human resources manager. Ombudsmen are formally and officially neutral and promise client confidentiality.[57] Ombudsmen can handle the concerns of employees who believe they have witnessed wrongdoing and do so in a way that keeps the problem from getting out of hand.[58]

According to a recent *Harvard Business Review* article, the success of an ombuds program is said to be dependent on getting the right person for the role, including someone who (1) is a good listener, (2) establishes trust in people at

all levels, (3) is skilled at thinking through problems, and (4) has an understanding of the corporate culture and who has influence in the organization.[59] In fact, the ombudsperson can be seminal to an organizational turnaround. In the mid-2000s, the Pacific Investment Management Company (Pimco) had a reputation as a cutthroat bond investment company. Some say Pimco enjoyed that reputation and wore it "as a badge of honor."[60] When a spate of lawsuits alleging gender discrimination and harassment surfaced, Pimco decided to overhaul how employees were evaluated, promoted, and trained. Key to the turnaround were workplace surveys as well as the appointment of an employee ombudsperson. The company hoped that the ombudsperson might help transform the company culture, including fostering more transparency and promoting more diversity.[61]

The Peer Review Panel. The **peer review panel** is another due-process mechanism currently in use. The Society for Human Resource Management (SHRM) notes that it can be an effective way to resolve workplace conflict, providing that the aggrieved employees present their side of a dispute to a small panel of employees and that supervisors are selected from a pool of employees trained in dispute resolution.[62] As Ann Reesman, former general counsel of the Equal Employment Advisory Council, put it, "The benefit of using peer review rather than some external decision maker is that the peer review panel is well-versed in the company culture and how the company operates."[63] In addition, peers tend to find decisions handed down by peers to be trustworthy.[64]

In an interesting twist on the peer-review process, Amazon introduced a new employee grievance process with a platform called Pivot. Employees placed in Pivot are cited for performance issues and have the option of an appeals process that includes a "career ambassador" and the choice of either one manager or three nonmanagers for the employee's jury. Amazon sees this as a process that helps it retain more of its 500,000 workers, but to date, panel members have been seen to side with their peers only about 30 percent of the time.[65]

The key to a successful peer review panel or committee is to make sure that the people involved in the process are respected members of the organization. Election rather than appointment of committee members helps participants to trust the independence of the process. Ideally, everyone involved in peer review should receive training in relevant areas such as dispute resolution, discrimination, fairness, legalities, and ethics. Representatives of both employees and management should be involved in the decision-making process.[66] We examine the peer review process in more detail in Case 30, "The Case of the Fired Waitress," in the cases at the end of the book.

The Future of ADR. The trend toward using ADR is growing, spurred partly by the time and money saved by avoiding costly litigation. Viewed from the "ethics of care" standpoint, alternative dispute resolution is preferable to the adversarial strategies that preceded it.[67] However, ADR is not without problems. In particular, many observers have expressed concern that some employers were requiring new hires to sign contracts, waiving their right to sue the firm and accepting pre-dispute **mandatory arbitration** as the alternative. Arbitration is a process where a neutral party resolves a dispute between two or more parties and the resolution is binding. In mandatory arbitration, the parties must agree to arbitration prior to any dispute. Critics of this practice argue that this robs employees of their right to due process, thereby favoring the organization and not the employee.

And without the strict judicial rules against conflicts of interest, companies can steer cases to friendly arbitrators. In turn, interviews and records show that some arbitrators cultivate close ties with companies to get business.[68] In one investigation into the use of arbitration by businesses for both consumers and employees, investigators discovered what they called "an alternate system of justice."[69] Reporters found that when it comes to federal class actions, arbitration clauses come into play most often in employment cases. Most of these involve wage disputes, but companies are also pursuing arbitration in discrimination claims.[70]

Supporters contend that the arbitration process is just as fair as a jury trial while costing much less in time and money. The popularity of ADR to resolve employee disputes continues, and employees are often unaware that they agree to this form of conflict resolution when they sign their employment documents. To avoid this, one attorney advises that employees carefully read all of their employment documents, including the handbook.[71] If the employer insists on ADR, the employee might be able to negotiate several points, but it is best to do it through an attorney.[72]

11.6 Freedom of Speech in the Workplace

It has been said that the workplace is a place where "free speech goes to die.[73] In the United States, people are free to say whatever they like, unless they are at work."[74] Political speech is an example. The U.S. Constitution protects an individual's political free speech from governmental interference. However, employers and those who work under them are not equal when it comes to free-speech legal claims. Employers have the right to take action against any employee who engages in political speech that company leaders find offensive. With a few narrow exceptions, the Constitution and the federal laws derived from it only protect a person's right to expression from government interference, not from the restrictions a private employer may impose.[75] In fact, companies like General Motors have introduced conduct codes in which they can police workers' speech even when they are not at work.[76]

In such a restrictive environment, it is easy to see how much courage is needed for employees to speak up when they

see something wrong. However, private employers may also feel that they have a duty to speak up and monitor the free speech of their employees. A few high-profile cases over the years have highlighted the delicate balance between the right of free speech for employees and the rights of other individuals when an employee acts and speaks on behalf of a private corporation, or even appears to do so.[77] For example, Donald Sterling, former owner of the Los Angeles Clippers basketball team, was fined $2.5 million and banned from the National Basketball Association for remarks he made that were deemed racist.[78] More recently, University of Tennessee–Chattanooga (UTC) assistant coach Chris Malone was fired over a tweet mocking Georgia politician and voting rights activist Stacey Abrams.[79] However, the UTC is a public institution, not private, and it remains to be seen whether or not the firing was legal under the First Amendment.

As one attorney explained, the concept of free speech is particularly tricky when it comes to management because the employer must consider how the statements have an actual and material effect on its employees and on the workplace.[80] At issue is that private employers may feel they have a duty to curb free speech that is potentially discriminatory; however, by putting restrictions on employee speech, they may themselves be discriminatory.

The use of social media as an outlet for free speech also complicates these issues. Twitter and Facebook have become important forums for public conversation and debate, and with this has come a considerable responsibility, and power, regarding free speech parameters.[81] Following the 2020 U.S. presidential election, for example, President Donald Trump was banned from these platforms and others based on what the platforms considered "inflammatory messages" on the day of the stampede and violence on the Capitol building.[82] Many were left wondering about whether or not the social media companies themselves were limiting free speech.[83]

What is the solution? Some have argued that the best option may be to allow social media companies to self-regulate by creating internal speech policies. Others suggest that laws should be put in place requiring that media companies abide by basic nondiscrimination and due-process obligations such that they do not limit the range of ideas and viewpoints that the public can hear.[84] Regardless of what may develop regarding social media and free speech, it is obvious that employer/employee relationships will be challenged by free speech issues on social media platforms for some time to come.

For an employer, they must be careful not to interfere with employee rights under the **National Labor Relations Act (NLRA)**. Even social media postings may be protected from retaliation for employees of private employers if the discussions involve terms and conditions of their employment.[85] In 2021, Amazon felt the effects of the NLRA when the National Labor Relations Board found that Amazon violated labor law when it fired two high-profile employees who were vocal about concerns about Amazon's treatment of warehouse workers during the pandemic.[86]

The bottom line is that employees have ideas, opinions, and voices about things that are going on at work.

Figure 11-3 Two Views of Employee Responsibility in a Potential Whistle-Blowing Situation

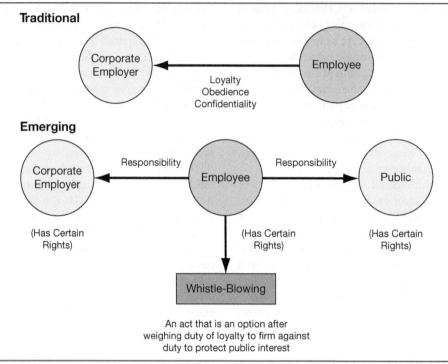

They often possess valuable information that can actually improve the operations, the morale, and the ethical climate of a company. Good employers will be receptive to constructive feedback from their employees; in the end, it is the fair and ethical thing to do.[87]

11.6a Whistle-Blowing

As stated earlier, the current generation of employees has a different concept of loyalty to and acceptance of authority than those of past generations. The result is unprecedented numbers of employees "blowing the whistle" on their employers. A **whistle-blower** is a former or current organization member who discloses "illegal, immoral, or illegitimate practices under the control of their employers, to persons or organizations that may be able to effect action."[88] Four key elements comprise the whistle-blowing process: the whistle-blower, the act or complaint about which the whistle-blower is concerned, the party to whom the complaint or report is made, and the organization against which the complaint is made.[89]

What is at stake is the employees' right to speak out in cases where they think the company or management is engaging in an unacceptable practice. Whistle-blowing is contrary to the cultural tradition that an employee does not question a superior's decisions and acts, especially in public. The former view held that the employee owes loyalty, obedience, and confidentiality to the corporate employer; however, the current view of employee responsibility holds that the employee may have a duty not only to the employer but also to the public and to their own conscience. Whistle-blowing, in this latter situation, becomes an important option for the employee

should management not be responsive to expressed concerns. Figure 11-3 depicts these two views of employee responsibility.

Most whistle-blowers engage in these acts out of a genuine or legitimate belief that certain actions in their organizations are wrong and that they are doing the right thing by reporting them. They may have learned of the wrongful acts by being asked or coerced to participate in them, or through observation or examination of company records.

The genuinely troubled employee may initially express concern to a superior or to someone else within the organization. Other potential whistle-blowers may be planning to make their reports for the purpose of striking out or retaliating against the company or a specific manager for some reason. In a survey of studies of whistle-blowers, however, Near and Miceli found the latter to be uncommon. Whistle-blowers were on average more highly paid, with higher job performance than inactive observers were. They were more likely to hold supervisory or professional status, and they have both the role and responsibility to report wrongdoing and the knowledge of channels for doing so.[90]

Figure 11-4 depicts a checklist to be followed by whistle-blowers before blowing the whistle.

11.6b Consequences of Whistle-Blowing

Unfortunately, whistle-blowers are not always rewarded for their contributions to the public interest. Although they are now more likely to get some form of protection than they were in the past, whistle-blowers can still pay dearly for their actions. In fact, the Ethics and Compliance Initiative (ECI) reported in 2021 under its Global Business Ethics Survey (GBES) that rates of retaliation against employees

Figure 11-4 A Checklist to Follow before Blowing the Whistle

The following should be considered before an employee blows the whistle:

1. Is there any alternative to blowing the whistle? Make sure you have tried to remedy the problem by reporting up the normal chain of command and have had no success.
2. Does the proposed disclosure advance public interest rather than personal or political gain? Don't act out of frustration or because you feel mistreated.
3. Have you thought about the outcomes of blowing the whistle for yourself and your family? Be prepared for the possibility of disapproval from friends, family, and fellow workers.
4. Have you identified the sources of support both inside and outside the organization on which you can rely during the process? Make sure you know your legal rights and have enlisted the help of others.
5. Do you have enough evidence to support your claim? Even more evidence is needed if you plan to remain anonymous. Be thorough but do not break the law.
6. Have you identified and copied all supporting records before drawing suspicion to your concerns? Remember to keep a factual log both before and after blowing the whistle.

Sources: The Government Accountability Center, http://www.afscmeinfocenter.org/blog/2008/06/courage-without-martyrdom-the.htm#.V0Q7rY-cHIU, accessed April 20, 2021; Kenneth K. Humphreys, "A Checklist for Whistleblowers to Follow," *Cost Engineering* (October 2003), 14; Stephen Martin Kohn, *A Whistleblower's Handbook* (Lyons Press: Guilford, CT, 2011).

for reporting wrongdoing in the United States reached a high of 79 percent—an increase of 35 percentage points from the prior year.[91] Various types of corporate retaliation are often taken against whistle-blowers by their employers. The following table includes top forms of retaliation and their respective incidence levels.[92]

- Excluded from decisions and work activity   64 percent
- Cold shoulder from co-workers   62 percent
- Verbal abuse from management   62 percent
- Almost lost job   56 percent
- Not given promotion or raise   55 percent
- Verbal abuse from co-workers   51 percent
- Cut in hours or pay   46 percent
- Relocated or reassigned   44 percent

Whistle-blowing is not easy, and despite regulatory protections, retaliation can occur. Employees who believe that they have been retaliated against for engaging in protected conduct may file a complaint with the secretary of labor to request an investigation by OSHA's Whistleblower Protection Program.

Ethics In Practice Case

The Serial Whistle-Blower: Have the Incentives Gone Too Far?

When the False Claims Act was instituted in 1863, the motivations of the government were pretty clear: penalize companies or people who defraud the government. When the government enacted higher potential rewards and easier filing procedures in 1986 and then again in 2009, the number of whistle-blower filings exploded, with annual filings nearly doubling over ten years from 2009 to 2019. However, something else exploded as well—the growth of serial whistle-blowers.

Serial whistle-blowers are people who file suit after suit in the hopes of landing the "big one." Often these are health-care–related cases. Since 1986, more than 25 people or groups fall into this category of serial whistle-blowers with five suits or more filed in the last two decades. The phenomenon is also reflected in the number of frivolous lawsuits that do not result in any settlement or judgment, which were 74 percent of suits filed from 1987 to 2010, according to the Justice Department.

One investigation into a serial whistle-blower found that a physician who received $38 million, and was praised by a federal prosecutor for this "good citizenry," had filed 12 suits against different laboratories with a string of allegations surrounding unfair drug pricing practices and false performance claims. While the physician claims that all his

filings were based on "nonpublic" documents and his original sources, many have been thrown out or abandoned because of deficient allegations. However, the government continues to see value in the whistle-blowing incentives, particularly in the health-care industry. From 2009 to 2019, it collected over $16 billion in civil recoveries due to the actions of whistle-blowers.

1. Is it appropriate to file more than one whistle-blower claim?
2. Are the incentives too high for whistle-blowers, thus putting some people into the whistle-blowing "business"?
3. Beyond the whistle-blower, who benefits from the pursuit and settlement of these claims?

Sources: Debra Cassens Weiss, "18 Repeat Whistleblowers Reap Millions of Dollars in False-Claim Suits," *ABA Journal* (July 24, 2014), http://www.abajournal.com/news/article/repeat_whistleblowers_reap_millions_of_dollars_in_false_claims_suits/, accessed April 20, 2021; Peter Loftus, "Meet the Serial Whistleblowers," *The Wall Street Journal* (July 24, 2014), A1; Andrew Ward, "Pharma Whistleblower Takes Total Payouts Close to $100m," *Financial Times* (February 16, 2016), http://www.ft.com/cms/s/0/25277046-d4c3-11e5-8887-98e7feb46f27.html#axzz49Tc2Y0IY, accessed April 20, 2021.

Figure 11-5 Whistle-Blowers Get the Hollywood Treatment

Movie	Stars	Story	Inspiration
The Report (2019)	Adam Driver, Annette Bening	The movie follows Senate staffer Daniel Jones who led an investigation into the CIA's use of torture in the wake of 9/11	Directed by Scott Burns; an investigation into CIA's Detention and Interrogation Program
Dark Waters (2019)	Mark Ruffalo	Lawyer takes on decades-long battle with DuPont over the company's environmental contamination and cover-up	Based on real-life lawyer Robert Bilott who took on the big chemical company
The Snowden Files (2016)	Joseph Gordon-Levitt	Chronicles the life of NSA whistle-blower Edward Snowden	Directed by Oliver Stone and titled after the book by *Guardian* journalist Luke Harding
The Whistleblower (2010)	Rachel Weisz, Vanessa Redgrave	Nebraska police officer serves as peacekeeper in post-war Bosnia and blows whistle on U.N. cover-up of sex trafficking scandal	Based on the experiences of Kathryn Bolkovac who worked with the U.N. International Police at a U.K. security company
The Informant! (2009)	Matt Damon, Scott Bakula, Joel McHale	Mark Whitacre, an employee at Archer Daniels Midland (ADM), blows the whistle on the lysine price-fixing conspiracy	This dark comedy is based on *The Informant*, a book by journalist Kurt Eichenwald.
The Insider (1999)	Russell Crowe, Al Pacino, Christopher Plummer	A successful scientist is fired from a major tobacco company for taking a principled stand. *60 Minutes* is due to report the story, but they cave to corporate pressure.	Based on a *Vanity Fair* article, "The Man Who Knew Too Much." The movie tells the true story of Jeffrey Wigand, who was fired from Brown & Williamson tobacco company.

Figure 11-5 chronicles Hollywood's treatment of some famous whistle-blowers.

11.6c Government's Protection of Whistle-Blowers

Just as employees are beginning to get some protection from the courts through the public policy exception to the employment-at-will doctrine, the same is true for whistle-blowers. The U.S. federal government was one of the first organizations to attempt to protect its own whistle-blowers. A highlight of the **1978 Civil Service Reform Act** was protection for federal employees who expose illegal, corrupt, or wasteful government activities.

It is difficult to protect whistle-blowers against retaliation because so often the reprisals are subtle. An added boost for federal employees came in 1989, when Congress passed the **Whistleblower Protection Act** and the president signed it into law. The effect of this act was to reform the Merit System Protection Board and the Office of General Counsel, the two offices that protect federal employees.[93]

Protection for private employees began to arrive at that point. The U.S. Congress introduced a range of protections for workers in various industries.[94] Typically, the whistle-blower protections were contained in various pieces of legislation that dealt with a range of issues, of which whistle-blowing was just one. As a result, no one piece of legislation provides an umbrella of protection for all whistle-blowers across the country. Even more recent whistle-blower protections are limited. The Sarbanes–Oxley (SOX) whistle-blower protections apply only to employees in publicly held firms. The Dodd–Frank Wall Street Reform and Consumer Protection whistle-blower protections apply only to employees in the financial industry.

Current legislation attempts to address these limitations. In 2015, the **Motor Vehicle Safety Whistleblower Act** was passed by Congress to provide incentives to bring to light safety-related problems. In 2016, the **Defend Trade Secrets Act** was passed into law, which includes strong and much needed protections for corporate whistle-blowers, establishing clear procedures for immunity for employees who disclose trade secrets to the government as part of a whistle-blower case.[95] Also in 2016, the **FBI Whistleblower Protection Enhancement Act** was signed into law, providing compensatory damages for whistle-blowers, expanding the scope of protected activity, ending bureaucratic delays in processing cases, and allowing for case review by independent administrative law judges. The motivation for this bill stemmed from the case of whistle-blower Jane Turner, who fought for 15 years for justice after reporting theft from Ground Zero and the victims of the 9/11 attacks by FBI agents.[96] Figure 11-6 lists the federal laws that include whistle-blower protections.

Of all these, SOX whistle-blower protections are the most stringent in preventing wrongful discharge. In addition to protecting employees who were fired, the law has four other important whistle-blower protections for employees in publicly traded corporations:[97]

1. The corporations are required to form independent audit committees and develop confidential procedures for whistle-blowers to follow.
2. The law establishes ethical standards for attorneys who practice before the SEC that include specification for when the attorney is required to blow the whistle on the client.

Figure 11-6 Federal Laws with Whistle-Blower Protections

Affordable Care Act	International Safe Container Act
Asbestos Hazard Emergency Response Act	Longshore and Harbor Workers' Compensation Act
Clean Air Act	Migrant and Seasonal Agricultural Worker Protection Act
CERCLA (Superfund Act)	Motor Vehicle Safety Whistleblower Act
Commercial Motor Vehicle Safety Act	Moving Ahead for Progress in the 21st Century Act
Consumer Product Safety Act	National Transit Security Act
Department of Defense Authorization Act	Occupational Safety and Health Act
Dodd–Frank Wall Street Reform and Consumer Protection Act	Pipeline Safety Improvement Act
Energy Reorganization Act	Safe Drinking Water Act
Fair Labor Standards Act	Sarbanes–Oxley Act
FBI Whistleblower Protection Enhancement Act	Seaman's Protection Act
FDA Food Safety Modernization Act	Solid Waste Disposal Act
Federal Mine Safety and Health Act	Surface Mining and Control Act
Federal Railroad Safety Act	Toxic Substances Control Act
Federal Water Pollution Control Act	Wendell H. Ford Aviation Investment and Reform for the 21st Century Act

Source: U.S. Department of Labor Occupational Safety and Health Administration, "The Whistleblower Protection Program," https://www.whistleblowers.gov/, accessed April 20, 2021.

3. In a provision that applies to all employees, not only those in publicly held corporations, SOX criminalized retaliation against whistle-blowers who give truthful information to a law enforcement officer by amending the federal obstruction of justice statute.
4. SOX gives the SEC jurisdiction over every aspect of the law, including the whistle-blower provisions, and allows for criminal penalties.

The states vary even more widely in the whistle-blower protections they provide. **Michigan's Whistleblowers Protection Act of 1981** was the first state law designed to protect any employee in private industry against unjust reprisals for reporting alleged violations of federal, state, or local laws to public authorities. The burden was placed on the employer to show that questionable treatment was

justified based on proper personnel standards or valid business reasons.[98] The Michigan act spurred similar laws in other states, but the progress has been slow. As noted above, most state courts have recognized a public policy exception to employment at-will, and therefore whistle-blowers have some limited protection from discharge.

The crazy quilt of whistle-blower protections makes it difficult for employees to shed light safely on corporate wrongdoing. In some states, whistle-blowers could be fired at will; in other states, they would have to sort through a bewildering assortment of statutes to determine what, if any, protection existed for them. People vary in their need to know they have protection before blowing the whistle. Figure 11-7 describes a study that looks at the differences between people who do the right thing in spite of great personal danger and others who choose not to act.

Figure 11-7 Giving Voice to Values

Giving Voice to Values, spearheaded by Professor Mary Gentile, is an innovative curriculum development designed to help business students and practitioners to strengthen their abilities to voice their values when situations call them into conflict. The focus is not on determining what the right thing to do is, but rather on determining how to do it. Giving Voice to Values is designed to help students build a tool kit that will enable them to voice their values when ethical challenges arise.

Gentile cites a study of World War II rescuers that shows that moral courage can be strengthened through anticipating ethical challenges that might occur and formulating a response

to them. In this study, researchers looked for commonalities among individuals who protected others from the Nazis even when they put their own lives at risk by doing so. They found that people who acted with moral courage when confronted with real danger tended to have earlier life experiences where they anticipated situations in which their values would be challenged and had a respected listener with whom they discussed how they would handle that situation. This act of practicing a response before being put in the difficult situation seemed to strengthen their subsequent ability to handle ethical challenges that occurred.

Sources: Mary C. Gentile, *Giving Voice to Values: How to Speak Your Mind When You Know What's Right* (New Haven: Yale University Press, 2010); Mary C. Gentile, "Giving Voice to Values: Way of Thinking about Values in the Workplace," The Aspen Institute Center for Business Education (September 2008).

Ethics In Practice Case

Whistle-Blower Waits for Years for Reward

Kim Gwang-ho was a safety engineer at the Korean auto-maker Hyundai Motor Co. when he discovered that his employer failed to address a design flaw linked to engines seizing up and catching fire. Mr. Kim agonized over what to do when he failed to get sufficient action from the company's internal auditors, including his request for a full recall of all vehicles with the faulty engines. Finally, in 2016, Mr. Kim flew from Seoul to Washington, D.C., to meet with the National Highway Traffic Safety Administration (NHTSA) to discuss the safety issues. After going public with his concerns, he lost his job, was sued by Hyundai for allegedly leaking business secrets, and had his house, outside of Seoul, searched by police.

The NHTSA eventually launched an investigation. Hyundai and its sister firm, Kia Corporation, ended up settling with the NHTSA and agreed to a record $210 million in fines and committed expenditures for new safety procedures. They also settled a class-action lawsuit from owners in 2019. In October 2020, the carmakers set aside another $2.5 billion for engine problems.

What happened to Mr. Kim? Well, Mr. Kim was under the assumption that he would be entitled to a reward as part of a whistle-blower program that Congress ordered the NHTSA to create in 2015. In fact, Mr. Kim had learned about the U.S. whistle-blower law through company-provided training at Hyundai. However, for years, the NHTSA has been stalled in red tape in setting up the "rules" that might award whistle-blowers for auto cases like this 10 to 30 percent of the penalties collected from a successful investigation. Several lawmakers have tried to push the agency to move forward in setting up the process. Meanwhile, Mr. Kim continues to wait at home for some remuneration, stating, "I have hope that all these pains and all these hard days will be finally rewarded."

1. Is it appropriate for delays of this sort to exist in federal agencies when whistle-blowers come forward?
2. What are the ethics involved in this situation? What values are involved here?
3. How does a case like this affect future whistle-blowers?

Sources: Ben Foldy, "Whistleblower Waits Years for Reward," *The Wall Street Journal* (April 5, 2021), B1; Gregg Gardner, "Hyundai, Kia to Pay $210 Million for Delayed Recalls," *Forbes* (November 27, 2020), https://www.forbes.com/sites/greggardner/2020/11/27/hyundai-kia-to-pay-210-million-for-delayed-recalls/?sh=3b1497657d40, accessed April 20, 2021; Tom Krisher, "Hyundai, Kia Fined for Delaying U.S. Engine Failure Recalls," *ABC News* (November 27, 2020), https://abcnews.go.com/US/wireStory/hyundai-kia-fined-delaying-us-engine-failure-recalls-74430341, accessed April 20, 2021.

11.6d False Claims Act

A provocative piece of federal legislation that was passed to add an incentive for whistle-blowers in the public interest is the **False Claims Act (FCA)**. The act has *qui tam* (Latin shorthand for "he who sues for the king as well as himself") provisions that allow employees to blow the whistle about contractor fraud and share with the government in any financial recoveries realized by their efforts. The 1986 act grew out of outrage in the mid-1980s over reports of fraud and abuse on the part of military contractors, such as the infamous $600 toilet seats and country club memberships billed to the government.[99]

What is particularly controversial about the FCA is the magnitude of the financial incentives that individual employees may earn as a result of their whistle-blowing efforts. The law allows individuals to be awarded as much as 15 to 25 percent of the proceeds in cases where the government joins in the action and from 15 to 30 percent of the proceeds in actions that the government does not join.[100]

Whistle-blowers have been instrumental in identifying and assisting the recovery of funds, particularly in the health-care area, where fraud has been rampant. In 2020 alone, the Justice Department recovered more than $2.2 billion from False Claims Act cases, with the majority involving the health-care industry.[101] The FCA has also inspired other similar programs. Twenty-nine states, three large cities, and one country have FCAs that are modeled after the federal law, although few offer monetary awards for whistle-blowers and instead focus on identity and retaliation protections.[102]

11.6e Management Responsiveness to Potential Whistle-Blowing Situations

Normally, employees pursue whistle-blowing options after regular, less dramatic channels of communication have failed. Ideally, employees should always feel free to open up to management about any concerns they have. Even in the best of organizations, however, people hesitate to speak up. Employee self-censorship is common, particularly surrounding ethical issues. As noted by Professor James Detert, "Ethical situations at work can be cause for alarm, *and* are also a normal part of doing business. The key is to not let either of those realities prevent you from making a rational decision."[103]

In a study of whistle-blower protections, workers in a leading high-technology organization were asked if they felt safe speaking up about problems in the firm. In spite of the fact that this organization had a variety of formal mechanisms such as an ombudsperson and grievance procedures, half the employees indicated that they did not feel safe speaking up.[104] Their overall concern was with self-preservation. They perceived a risk to speaking up that lead them to conclude, "When in doubt, keep your mouth shut."[105] As noted above, this aligns with recent surveys about an increase in rates of retaliation among employees.

In rare instances, employees were afraid to speak out because they had experiences with managers who responded badly to past suggestions. More often, the reticent employees were simply responding to a vague perception of a threat in the work environment. Sometimes they were put off by organizational stories about people who had spoken up and then suddenly were no longer there. Typically, their silence stemmed from untested assumptions.[106]

The findings of these studies have clear implications for encouraging free and open speech in the workplace. It is not enough to remove barriers or put formal mechanisms in place. Significant changes in the organizational culture must occur if organizations want to deal fairly with employee stakeholders. The following are suggestions for how to accomplish that goal[107]:

1. Managers must not only accept suggestions—they must also invite them. Managers cannot implement all suggestions, but it is important for managers to acknowledge each one.
2. Managers must refute commonly held assumptions and organizational myths that discourage communication.

For example, they can counter the commonly held belief that employees should give managers suggestions in private by explaining that openly discussed ideas are likely to be useful.
3. Managers should tailor rewards so that employees share more directly in any cost savings or sales increase from ideas they offer. Tangible rewards can help employees to overcome intangible concerns.

In an ideal world, employees would automatically speak freely to managers if they saw something wrong happening or had an idea to improve operations. Unfortunately, the work world is not ideal. However, whistle-blowers are integral to keeping firms healthy. In fact, one study found that companies that have more complaints from whistle-blower hotlines actually have fewer lawsuits, smaller bills from legal settlements, and fewer fines.[108] It is incumbent upon managers to design organizations that enable and empower employees to come forward with information that will either stop wrongdoing or improve company operations long before whistle-blowing is needed.

Summary

Employee stakeholders today are more sensitive about their roles and their rights for a variety of reasons. Underlying this new concern are changes in the historical social contract between employers and employees that have been driven by global competition and a changing economy, including more contingent workers and a new generation of workers called Generation Z. This has spurred the growth of employee engagement programs to assist employees in their personal and career development. Employee engagement efforts help both the employee and the employer. Central among the growing employee rights issues discussed in this chapter are (1) the right not to be fired without good cause, (2) the right to due process and fair treatment, and (3) the right to freedom of speech.

The basis for the argument that we may be moving toward an employee's right not to be fired is the erosion by the courts of the employment-at-will doctrine. More and more, the courts are making exceptions to this longstanding common-law principle. Additionally, changes in the workforce to include more contingent workers challenge businesses in the ways they implement employment-at-will. Three major exceptions to employment-at-will are the public policy exception, the idea of an implied contract, and breach of good faith. Society's concept of what represents fair treatment to employees is constantly changing.

The employees' right to due process is concerned primarily with fair treatment. Common approaches for management responding to this concern such as the open-door policy and traditional grievance procedures have been disappointing, and so newer methods such as the ombuds approach and peer review are becoming more prevalent; however, freedom of speech issues continue to challenge employers and employees alike. Whistle-blowers in the private sector now enjoy some of the protections once accorded only to public sector employees; however, those protections are not a guarantee. Whistle-blowers continue to face many obstacles as they seek to speak out on their concerns. Managers should be genuinely attentive to employees' rights in this realm if they wish to avert major scandals and prolonged litigation. A stakeholder approach that emphasizes ethical relationships with employees can create an organizational environment in which employees feel freer to express their concerns openly, lessening the need to blow a whistle.

Key Terms

1099 economy, p. 253
1978 Civil Service Reform Act, p. 264
alternative dispute resolution (ADR), p. 259
collective bargaining, p. 255
Defend Trade Secrets Act, p. 264

due process, p. 259
employee engagement, p. 254
employee rights, p. 254
employment-at-will doctrine, p. 256
enterprise rights, p. 255
False Claims Act (FCA), p. 266

FBI Whistleblower Protection Enhancement Act, p. 264
fissuring, p. 259
Generation Z, p. 253
gig economy, p. 253
good cause norm, p. 256

good faith principle, p. 257
grievance committee, p. 260
hearing procedure, p. 260
implied contract exception, p. 257
mandatory arbitration, p. 261
Michigan's Whistleblowers Protection
 Act of 1981, p. 265
Millennials, p. 253

Motor Vehicle Safety Whistleblower
 Act, p. 264
National Labor Relations Act (NLRA),
 p. 261
new workplace, p. 251
ombuds/ombudsman/ombudsperson,
 p. 260
open-door policy, p. 260

peer review panel, p. 260
private property, p. 254
public policy exception, p. 257
social contract, p. 252
statutory rights, p. 255
whistleblower, p. 262
Whistleblower Protection Act, p. 264
work-life balance, p. 253

Discussion Questions

1. What changes in employees in the workplace will be brought about by organizations becoming digital enterprises? What changes will be brought about as a result of the worldwide pandemic?

2. Rank the various changes that are occurring in the workplace in terms of their importance to the growth of the employee rights movement. Briefly explain your ranking.

3. Explain the employment-at-will doctrine, and describe how it is being eroded. Do you think its existence is leading to a healthy or an unhealthy employment environment in the United States? Justify your reasoning.

4. Discuss the new gig economy and the implications for employee engagement.

5. In your own words, explain the right to due process. What are some of the major ways management is attempting to ensure due process in the workplace?

6. If you could choose only one, which form of alternative dispute resolution would be your choice as the most effective approach to employee due process? Explain.

7. How do you feel about whistle-blowing now that you have read about it? Are you now more sympathetic or less sympathetic to whistle-blowers? Explain.

8. What is your assessment of the value of the False Claims Act? What is your assessment of the value of the whistle-blower protections?

9. What other steps can managements take to be responsive to potential whistle-blowing situations?

Endnotes

1. Naina Dhingra, Andrew Samo, Bill Schaninger, and Matt Schrimper, "Help Your Employees Find Purpose— Or Watch Them Leave" (April 5, 2021), *McKinsey & Company*, https://www.mckinsey.com/business-functions /organization/our-insights/help-your-employees-find -purpose-or-watch-them-leave. Accessed April 19, 2021.

2. PwC, "Productivity 2021 and Beyond: Five Pillars for a Better Workforce," https://www.pwc.com/gx/en/industries /financial-services/publications/productivity-agenda.html. Accessed April 19, 2021.

3. Ibid.

4. Brian Knopp, "9 Trends That Will Shape Work in 2021 and Beyond," *Harvard Business Review* (January 14, 2021), https://hbr.org/2021/01/9-trends-that-will-shape -work-in-2021-and-beyond. Accessed April 29, 2021.

5. Ibid.

6. Beth Tyner Jones, "The Future of Work: Workplace Trends for 2021 and Beyond," *The National Law Review* (February 22, 2021), https://www.natlawreview.com /article/future-work-workplace-trends-2021-and-beyond. Accessed April 29, 2021.

7. Michelle Conlin, "Job Security, No. Tall Latte, Yes," *Businessweek* (April 2, 2001), 62–64.

8. Irwin, 2016.

9. PwC, 2021.

10. See John Morrison, "Could 2020 Be the Year We Finally Rewrite the Social Contract?", Reuters Events, (May 2, 2020), https://www.reutersevents.com/sustainability/could -2020-be-year-we-finally-rewrite-social-contract. Accessed April 20, 2021; "The 1099 Economy: Exploring a New Social Contract for Employers, Employees, & Society," The Aspen Institute (September 10, 2015), http://www .aspeninstitute.org/video/1099-economy-exploring-new -social-contract-employers-employees-society-0. Accessed April 20, 2021.

11. Ibid.

12. See Mark Horoszowski, "We Interviewed 50 Corporate Responsibility Leaders with Big Plans for 2021," *TriplePundit* (March 11, 2021), https://www .triplepundit.com/story/2021/corporate-responsibility -leaders-2021/719546. Accessed April 29, 2021; Morrison, 2020.

13. Ibid.

14. Janet Adamy, "Your New Workers Are Gen Z—Get Ready," *The Wall Street Journal* (September 7, 2018), A1-9.

15. Kim Parker and Ruth Igielnik, "On the Cusp of Adulthood and Facing an Uncertain Future: What We Know about Gen Z So Far," Pew Research Center (May 14, 20200, https://www.pewresearch.org/social -trends/2020/05/14/on-the-cusp-of-adulthood-and-facing

-an-uncertain-future-what-we-know-about-gen-z-so
-far-2/. Accessed April 19, 2021.

16. Mark Perna, "4 Huge Challenges for Remote Gen-Z
Workers—And How to Overcome Them," *Forbes*
(February 2, 2021), https://www.forbes.com/sites/
markcperna/2021/02/02/4-huge-challenges-for-
remote-gen-z-workers-and-how-to-overcome-
them/?sh=391e3b17d1c4. Accessed April 29, 2021.

17. See Marcie Merriman, "How Contradictions Define
Generation Z," EY (January 28, 2020), https://www
.ey.com/en_us/consulting/how-contradictions-define
-generation-z. Accessed April 19, 2021; Rea Regan,
"Everything You Need to Know about Generation Z in
the Workplace in 2021," *Connecteam* (October 21, 2020),
https://connecteam.com/generation-z-in-the-workplace/.
Accessed April 19, 2021.

18. Ibid.

19. Erica Volini, Kraig Eaton, and Jeff Schwartz, "Diving
Deeper: Five Workforce Trends to Watch in 2021,"
Deloitte (December 9, 2020), https://www2.deloitte
.com/us/en/insights/focus/human-capital-trends/2021
/workforce-trends-2020.html. Accessed April 19, 2021.

20. Ibid.

21. Rick Wartzman and Lawrence Crosby, "The Key Factor
Driving a Company's Results: Its People," *The Wall Street
Journal* (August 13, 2018), R5.

22. Jess Bell, "Pulse Surveys in 2021: Predicting the Future
of Employee Feedback," *Human Resources Director*,
(March 4, 2021), https://www.hcamag.com/au
/specialisation/employee-engagement/pulse-surveys
-in-2021-predicting-the-future-of-employee-feedback
/248204. Accessed April 20, 2021.

23. Ibid.

24. Society for Human Resource Management, "Developing
and Sustaining Employee Engagement," https://www
.shrm.org/resourcesandtools/tools-and-samples/toolkits
/pages/sustainingemployeeengagement.aspx. Accessed
April 29, 2021.

25. Jim Harter, "U.S. Employee Engagement Rises Following
Wild 2020," *Gallup* (February 26, 2021), https://www
.gallup.com/workplace/330017/employee-engagement
-rises-following-wild-2020.aspx. Accessed April 19, 2021.

26. Leo Troy, *The End of Unionism: An Appraisal* (St. Louis:
Center for the Study of American Business, Washington
University, September 1994), 1–2.

27. *U.S. Bureau of Labor Statistics*, "Union Members
Summary" (January 22, 2021), https://www.bls.gov/news
.release/union2.nr0.htm. Accessed April 20, 2021.

28. "Trade Union Density," OECD (2020), https://stats.oecd
.org/Index.aspx?DataSetCode=TUD. Accessed April 20,
2021.

29. CNN Newsource, "Here's Why 2021 Could Be a Big Year
for Labor Unions," https://keyt.com/news/money-and
-business/2021/03/01/heres-why-2021-could-be-a-big
-year-for-labor-unions/. Accessed April 20, 2021.

30. Karen Weise and Noam Scheiber, "Why Amazon
Workers Sided with the Company Over a Union," *The
New York Times* (April 16, 2021), https://www.nytimes
.com/2021/04/16/technology/amazon-workers-against
-union.html. Accessed April 20, 2021.

31. Ibid.

32. Richard Edwards, *Rights at Work* (Washington, D.C.: The
Brookings Institution, 1993), 25–26.

33. Ibid., 33–35.

34. Chris Marr, "NYC Fast-Food Worker Law Shines Light on
'Just Cause' Policies," *Bloomberg Law* (February 1, 2021),
https://news.bloomberglaw.com/daily-labor-report/nyc
-fast-food-worker-law-shines-light-on-just-cause-policies.
Accessed April 20, 2021.

35. Ellen Dannin, "Why At-Will Employment Is Bad for
Employers and Just Cause Is Good for Them," *Labor Law
Journal* (Spring 2007), 5–16.

36. Tara J. Radin and Patricia H. Werhane, "Employment
-At-Will, Employee Rights, and Future Directions for
Employment," *Business Ethics Quarterly* (April 2003),
113–130.

37. See "At Will Employment: Complete Guide with State
Information and Definition," *Betterteam,* (2021), https://
www.betterteam.com/at-will-employment#:~:text=All%20
states%20in%20the%20U.S.,do%20not%20allow%20
any%20exceptions. Accessed April 29, 2021; David H.
Autor, John J. Donohue III, and Stewart J. Schwab, "The
Employment Consequences of Wrongful-Discharge
Laws: Large, Small, or None at All?" *American Economic
Review* (May 2004), 440–446.

38. Shelbie Watts, "At-Will Employment: What Are the
Exceptions?" *Homebase,* (March 5, 2021), https://
joinhomebase.com/blog/at-will-employment-exceptions/.
Accessed April 29, 2021.

39. Ibid.

40. Ibid.

41. Ibid.

42. Patricia H. Werhane, Tara J. Radin, and Norman E.
Bowie, *Employment and Employee Rights* (Malden, MA:
Blackwell Publishing, 2004).

43. Dannin, 5–16.

44. Steve Harrison, *The Manager's Book of Decencies: How
Small Gestures Build Great Companies* (Columbus, OH:
McGraw-Hill, 2007).

45. Ibid.

46. Paul Falcone, "The Elements of Due Process," Society
for Human Resource Management (September 6, 2017),
https://www.shrm.org/resourcesandtools/hr-topics
/employee-relations/pages/the-elements-of-due-process.
aspx. Accessed May 3, 2021.

47. William M. Haraway, "Employee Grievance Programs:
Understanding the Nexus between Workplace
Justice, Organizational Legitimacy and Successful
Organizations," *Public Personnel Management* (Winter
2005), 329–342.

48. See Falcone, 2021; David W. Ewing, *Freedom inside the
Organization: Bringing Civil Liberties to the Workplace*
(New York: McGraw-Hill, 1977), 11.

49. Richard A. Posthuma, "Procedural Due Process and
Procedural Justice in the Workplace: A Comparison and
Analysis," *Public Personnel Management* (Summer 2003),
181–195.

50. Lydia DePillis, "Department of Labor Sends Warning Shot
to Clients of Temp Staffing Agencies," *The Washington
Post* (January 20, 2016), https://www.washingtonpost
.com/news/wonk/wp/2016/01/20/department-of-labor
-sends-warning-shot-to-clients-of-temp-staffing-agencies/.
Accessed April 20, 2021.

51. Ibid.

52. "How Modern Workers Are at the Mercy of Ratings," *The
Economist* (February 8, 2020), https://www.economist
.com/business/2020/02/06/how-modern-workers-are-at
-the-mercy-of-ratings. Accessed April 20, 2021.

53.   International Institute for Conflict Prevention & Resolution, https://www.cpradr.org/. Accessed April 20, 2021.

54.   David Slossberg, "Today's Business: Refining the Process of Alternative Dispute Resolution During a Pandemic," *New Haven Register* (November 27, 2020), https://www.nhregister.com/business/article/Today-s-Business-Refining-the-process-of-15747946.php. Accessed April 20, 2021.

55.   Allen Church, "Ombudsmen Ease Governance Compliance," *Claims* (December 2004), 63–65.

56.   Ibid.

57.   See International Ombudsman Association, "What Is an Organizational Ombudsman?" https://www.ombudsassociation.org/what-is-an-organizational-ombuds. Accessed May 1, 2021; Carolyn Hirschman, "Someone to Listen," *HR Magazine* (January 2003), 47–50.

58.   Ibid.

59.   Charles L. Howard, "What Happens When an Employee Calls the Ombudsman?," *Harvard Business Review*, (May/June 2020), 98 (3), 59–60.

60.   Justin Baer, "Bond Giant Pimco Attempts to Change Its Culture," *The Wall Street Journal* (April 17, 2021), https://www.wsj.com/articles/bond-giant-pimco-attempts-to-change-its-culture-11618651802. Accessed April 20, 2021.

61.   Ibid.

62.   Society for Human Resource Management, "Problem Resolution and Peer Review Policy," *SHRM* https://www.shrm.org/ResourcesAndTools/tools-and-samples/policies/Pages/cms_000515.aspx. Accessed April 20, 2021.

63.   Ibid.

64.   Ibid.

65.   "Inside Amazon's People's Court," *Bloomberg Businessweek* (July 2, 2018), 22–24.

66.   "Peer-Review Policy Provides Protection," *Credit Union Directors Newsletter* (April 2004), 7–8.

67.   Marc Lampe, "Mediation as an Ethical Adjunct of Stakeholder Theory," *Journal of Business Ethics* (May 2001), 165–173.

68.   Jessica Silver-Greenburg and Michael Corkery, "In Arbitration, a 'Privatization of the Justice System,'" *The New York Times* (November 1, 2015), http://www.nytimes.com/2015/11/02/business/dealbook/in-arbitration-a-privatization-of-the-justice-system.html. April 20, 2021.

69.   Ibid.

70.   Ibid.

71.   Lisa Guerin, "Signing an Arbitration Agreement with Your Employer," *NOLO.com* http://www.nolo.com/legal-encyclopedia/signing-arbitration-agreement-with-employer-30005.html. Accessed May 3, 2021.

72.   Ibid.

73.   Michael Dolgow, "Where Free Speech Goes to Die: The Workplace," *Bloomberg Businessweek* (August 3, 2012), http://www.cnbc.com/2015/04/30/why-did-the-us-pay-this-former-swiss-banker-104m.html. Accessed April 20, 2021.

74.   Ibid.

75.   Genevieve Lakier, "The Great Free Speech Reversal," *The Atlantic* (January 27, 2021), https://www.theatlantic.com/ideas/archive/2021/01/first-amendment-regulation/617827/. Accessed May 1, 2021.

76.   "The Case for Free Speech at Work," *The Economist* (February 2, 2020), https://www.economist.com/leaders/2020/02/27/the-case-for-free-speech-at-work. Accessed April 20, 2021.

77.   Martin Berman-Gorvine, "Employer Ability to Silence Employee Speech Narrowing in Private Sector," *Bloomberg BNA* (May 19, 2014), http://www.bna.com/employer-ability-silence-n17179890580/. Accessed April 20, 2021.

78.   Robert Windrem, "Clippers Owner Donald Sterling Fined $2.5M and Banned for Life by NBA," *NBC News*, (April 29, 2014), https://www.nbcnews.com/storyline/nba-race-furor/clippers-owner-donald-sterling-fined-2-5m-banned-life-nba-n92671. Accessed May 3, 2021.

79.   Neil Vigdor, "'Hateful' Tweet about Stacey Abrams Costs University Football Coach His Job," *The New York Times* (January 8, 2021), https://www.nytimes.com/2021/01/08/us/coach-fired-stacey-abrams.html. Accessed May 3, 2021.

80.   Berman-Gorvine, 2014.

81.   Lakier, 2021.

82.   Kate Conger, Mike Isaac, and Sheera Frenkel, "Twitter and Facebook Lock Trump's Accounts After Violence on Capitol Hill," *The New York Times* (January 14, 2021), https://www.nytimes.com/2021/01/06/technology/capitol-twitter-facebook-trump.html. Accessed May 2, 2021.

83.   Ibid.

84.   Ibid.

85.   "Social Media Posts During Turbulent Times: FAQs on Employee Rights and Employer Responsibilities," The National Law Review (June 22, 2020), https://www.shrm.org/ResourcesAndTools/tools-and-samples/policies/Pages/cms_000515.aspx. Accessed April 20, 2021.

86.   Matt Day, "Amazon Violated Law in Firing Employee Activists, NLRB Says," *Fortune* (April 5, 2021), https://fortune.com/2021/04/05/amazon-violated-law-in-firing-employee-activists-nlrb-says/. Accessed May 3, 2021.

87.   Shari Lava, "Voicing Your Opinion in the Workplace," *Chron.com*, http://work.chron.com/voicing-opinion-workplace-4397.html. Accessed April 20, 2021.

88.   Marcia P. Miceli and Janet P. Near, *Blowing the Whistle: The Organizational and Legal Implications for Companies and Employees* (New York: Lexington Books, 1992), 15.

89.   Janet P. Near and Marcia P. Miceli, *The Whistle-Blowing Process and Its Outcomes: A Preliminary Model* (Columbus, OH: The Ohio State University, College of Administrative Science, Working Paper Series 83–55, September, 1983), 2. See also Miceli and Near, 15.

90.   Janet P. Near and Marcia P. Miceli, "Whistleblowing— Myth and Reality," *Journal of Management* (1996 Special Issue), 507–526.

91.   Global Business Ethics Survey Report 2020, "The State of Ethics Compliance in the Workforce" (March 2021), https://www.ethics.org/global-business-ethics-survey/. Accessed April 20, 2021.

92.   Ibid.

93.   Ana Radelat, "When Blowing the Whistle Ruins Your Life," *Public Citizen* (September/October 1991), 16–20.

94.   Jon O. Shimabukuro and L. Paige Whitaker, "Whistleblower Protections under Federal Law: An Overview," Congressional Research Service (September 13, 2012), 1–21.

95.   National Whistleblowers Legal Defense and Education Fund, "Obama Strengthens Key Corporate Whistleblower Protections" (May 11, 2016), http://www.whistleblowersblog.org/2016/05/articles/corporate-whistleblowers/obama-strengthens-key-corporate-whistleblower-protections/. Accessed April 20, 2021.

96. National Whistleblower Center, "Jane Turner," https://www.whistleblowers.org/team/jane-turner/. Accessed May 3, 2021.

97. Stephen M. Kohn, "Sarbanes-Oxley Act: Legal Protection for Corporate Whistleblowers," National Whistleblower Center, http://www.whistleblowers.org/index.php?option=com_content&task=view&id=27. Accessed April 20, 2021.

98. Alan F. Westin, "Michigan's Law to Protect the Whistle Blowers," *The Wall Street Journal* (April 13, 1981), 18. Also see Daniel P. Westman, *Whistle-blowing: The Law of Retaliatory Discharge* (Washington, D.C.: The Bureau of National Affairs, 1991); Robert L. Brady, "Blowing the Whistle," *HR Focus* (February 1996), 20.

99. See Marisa Sanfilippo, "Wrongful Termination Lawsuits," *Business.com* (September 1, 2020), https://www.business.com/articles/avoiding-wrongful-termination-lawsuits/. Accessed May 1, 2021; Andrew W. Singer, "The Whistle-Blower: Patriot or Bounty Hunter?" *Across the Board* (November 1992), 16–22.

100. "False Claims Act Developments: 2020 Year in Review," TAF Education Fund (February 17, 2021), https://www.taf.org/post/2020review. Accessed April 20, 2021.

101. The United States Department of Justice, "Justice Department Recovers Over $2.2 Billion from False Claims Act Cases in Fiscal Year 2020," *The U.S. Dept of Justice* (January 14, 2021), https://www.justice.gov/opa/pr/justice-department-recovers-over-22-billion-false-claims-act-cases-fiscal-year-2020#:~:text=21%2C%202020%2C%20the%20department%20reached,arising%20from%20its%20conduct%20in. Accessed May 3, 3021.

102. "International Whistleblowing Legislation and America's False Claim Act," *JD Supra* (March 5, 2021), https://www.jdsupra.com/legalnews/international-whistleblowing-7519162/. Accessed May 3, 2021.

103. Amy Gallo, "How to Speak Up about Ethical Issues at Work," *Harvard Business Review* (June 4, 2015), https://hbr.org/2015/06/how-to-speak-up-about-ethical-issues-at-work. Accessed April 20, 2021.

104. See Relias Media, "Handle Whistleblower Complains with Care," https://www.reliasmedia.com/articles/146281-handle-whistleblower-complaints-with-care. Accessed May 1, 2021; James R. Detert, Ethan R. Burris, and David A. Harrison, "What's Really Silencing Your Employees," *Harvard Business Review* (June 8, 2010), https://hbr.org/2010/06/whats-really-silencing-your-em. Accessed May 3, 2021; James R. Detert and Amy C. Edmondson, "Why Employees Are Afraid to Speak," *Harvard Business Review* (May 2007), 23–25.

105. Detert and Edmondson, 24.

106. Ibid.

107. Ibid.

108. Kyle Welch and Stephen Stubben, "Throw Out Your Assumptions about Whistleblowing," *Harvard Business Review* (January 14, 2020), https://hbr.org/2020/01/throw-out-your-assumptions-about-whistleblowing. Accessed May 3, 2021.

12

Employee Stakeholders: Privacy, Health, Wellness, and Safety

After studying this chapter, you should be able to:

1. Articulate the issues in the new workplace that are changing traditional employer/employee relationships.
2. Understand concerns surrounding the employee's right to privacy in the workplace, including the use of employee information.
3. Recognize the issues surrounding workplace monitoring, including concerns with data collection, technology, and the effects of being monitored.

4. Describe the issues related to integrity and drug testing in the workplace.
5. Elaborate on the right to health in the workplace, with particular reference to mental health in the workplace, work-life balance, and smoking, vaping, and opioid use in the workplace.
6. Understand safety issues, including violence in the workplace.

In this chapter, we extend the concept of employee rights and discuss employees' rights to privacy, a healthy work environment, and safety. As we noted in Chapter 11, the nature of work changed during the global COVID-19 pandemic, and this, combined with newer technologies, has created a new workforce defined by virtual, remote workplaces, a growing reliance on digital enterprises, and different expectations surrounding employee/employer relationships. As of March 2021, workers were supplying about 45 percent of their labor services from home, which was down from the beginning of the pandemic, but still almost ten times the pre-pandemic rate.[1] Additionally, recent surveys have indicated that over half of employees would like the option to continue to work remotely even as the pandemic slows down—and most workers say they would take up to an 8 percent pay cut to maintain the ability to work from home.[2]

Not all employees have had an easy time transitioning to remote work. For remote working mothers, the struggle to balance work and life has taken its toll, with their levels of well-being much lower than those of remote working fathers.[3] Additionally, not all jobs can be adapted for remote work, and the ability to offer remote options seems to break along lines of class, education, and ethnicity, posing challenges for employers in approaching issues of diversity, equity, and inclusion.[4]

During the pandemic, many employees experienced **"Zoom fatigue"**—the exhaustion associated with videoconferencing for work—which has significant implications for employees' well-being and productivity.[5] Interestingly, one study surveying more than 10,000 virtual employees across the globe found that Zoom fatigue is worse for women than men, as women tend to have longer meetings and shorter breaks between them.

Another issue that continues to challenge employer/employee relationships is an employee's right to privacy, which is ill defined at best and particularly challenging with regard to workplace surveillance and the use of Big Data. During the pandemic, employers turned to digital tools to monitor employees' activities at home, taking screenshots of workers' computers, tracking keystrokes, monitoring instant messaging, sending alerts when keyboards are idle, and allowing remote control takeover of the computer.[6] These newer forms of monitoring employees highlight ethical issues of privacy and transparency. Employers using these programs need to be transparent with employees and make sure that they do not cross the line and invade an employee's privacy.

Constitutional protection of privacy applies only to the actions of government, not to those of private sector employers. From a legal standpoint, the meager amount of privacy protection that exists, as with so many employee rights, is a collection of diverse statutes, varying from issue to issue and from state to state. Hence, there is a genuine need for management groups to apply ethical thinking and standards to this increasingly important area.

Employee rights to safety and health is an area of growing intensity, too. The pandemic has introduced new cleaning procedures, temperature checks, health surveys, and sick time policies to the workplace.[7] Many employees will face employers that are requiring they be vaccinated with the COVID-19 vaccine, and while the **Equal Employment Opportunity Commission (EEOC)** has published guidelines for private employers, a variety of social, legal, and ethical factors come into play.[8] For example, how should employers respond to an employee who objects to complying with a vaccination requirement? What if the employee has a disability that precludes them from complying with a vaccination requirement? When is an unvaccinated employee a direct threat to a workplace?

Additional threats to employee safety are also at issue. Today's workplace, whether in a manufacturing facility or in an office complex, can expose workers to a variety of hazards, risks of accidents, and occupational diseases. If regular internal workplace hazards were not enough, the phenomenon of violence is a serious threat to workplace peace and stability that requires managerial attention. Management should also be aware of the issues affecting employee mental health in the workplace, as well as the need for family-friendly workplaces and the legal rights employees have under the Family and Medical Leave Act (FMLA).

In sum, it is clear that if managers are to be successful in dealing with employees' needs and treating them fairly as stakeholders, they must address these concerns of employee privacy, health, wellness, and safety now and in the future. Google is a company that is addressing the new workplace with big plans to reinvent offices to cope with the new "workplace sensibilities" changed by the pandemic. To facilitate a safe and productive work environment for employees coming back to the office, they have been (1) encouraging (but not mandating) that employees be vaccinated, (2) developing portable "team pods" that can be rearranged and wheeled into different arrangements, (3) employing "privacy robots" equipped with sensors to come over to desks and inflate a translucent, cellophane balloon wall to keep prying eyes away, and (4) implementing a flexible work week.[9] Yet even Google may have a hard time addressing stressful issues of work-life balance and mental health challenges that continue to increase in the new workplace. The workplace environment today poses a number of ethical and social challenges for employers to consider when managing and engaging with employee stakeholders.

12.1 Privacy in the Workplace

As noted above, even though employees may not have legal rights to privacy in various circumstances, managers should understand that employees do have ethical expectations of privacy and that these expectations, whenever possible, should be honored as well.

Technological developments have made surveillance simpler and less expensive—not only in public places but also in the workplace. What was once only an option for large corporations now is available to practically every work environment, along with the ethical issues it brings. **Privacy in the workplace** is in flux as the implications of new

technological options are considered. A majority of employers monitor their employees. There are no clear legal definitions of what constitutes privacy or invasion of privacy, but everyone seems to have an opinion when one personally experiences such a situation. **Workplace privacy** is the extent to which employers monitor and collect information on the activities, communications, and private lives of others.[10] Business ethicist Patricia Werhane opts for a broader definition. She says that privacy includes (1) the right to be left alone, (2) the related right to autonomy, and (3) the claim of individuals and groups to determine for themselves when, how, and to what extent information about them is communicated to others.[11] Not all employers agree with this definition, however, and that is when the challenges begin.

We gain great efficiencies from computers and new technologies, but we also pay a price. Part of that price is that information about us is stored in dozens of places, including federal agencies (the Internal Revenue Service and the Social Security Administration), state agencies (courts and motor vehicle departments), and many local departments and businesses (school systems, credit bureaus, banks, life insurance companies, and direct-mail companies).

The only federal level of privacy protection in the United States is the **Electronic Communication Privacy Act (ECPA) of 1986**. The interception or unauthorized access of a wire, oral, or electronic communication where there is a reasonable expectation of privacy is illegal under this act unless it is covered by one of the statutory exceptions or required by government compulsion. One of the statutory exceptions is the business use exception: The act does not apply if the interception or access occurs as part of the "ordinary course of business." It also does not apply if the person gives consent. The one clear protection for employees is that employers may not listen to purely personal phone conversations; however, they can monitor a conversation for the time required to determine that the call is personal.[12]

States have tried to enact laws to strengthen workplace privacy, with states like California, Maryland, New York, and Washington leading the charge, but the result is a patchwork of state laws.[13] To address this, the Uniform Law Commission, which provides states with legislation to provide clarity to critical areas of state law, enacted the **Employee and Student Online Privacy Protection Act (ESOPPA)** that prohibits employers and educational institutions from requiring employees or students to provide them with access to their accounts or to "friend" the institution.[14]

Efforts to enact a U.S. law specifically geared toward workplace privacy have always been stymied. However, employee data privacy lawsuits continue to grow, and these court cases may have implications for workplace privacy in the future. One of the key issues is the phrase "reasonable expectation of privacy." In one case, the New Jersey Supreme Court ruled in favor of an employee whose company read e-mails that she sent to her attorney using her personal, password-protected, e-mail account on the company's computer.[15] The court unanimously found that the use of a password that she did not save on the employer's hard drive, as well as the

Ethics In Practice Case

Big Data and Employee Health

Companies like Walmart and JPMorgan are more actively involving themselves in employee wellness. They are paying firms to collect and crunch employee data to identify employee health problems and guide them toward doctors or services like weight-loss programs. Although health-privacy laws do not give employers the authority to view workers' personal health information, they are able to get aggregated data on employees through wellness firms who have access to workers' health data. For example, Cigna Corporation analyzed claims data for JPMorgan to identify employees who lacked primary-care physicians.

Another company, Castlight, can identify segments of an employee population and tell an employer how many women are currently trying to have children through data that tracks women who have stopped filling birth-control prescriptions and/or who have made fertility-related searches on their app. While employees have to "opt in" to its services, some say that this option is hidden because it is linked to the use of a search function for in-network doctors and the ability to track health-care spending. Nevertheless, some employees see the benefit of being alerted to "at-risk" situations, like rising glucose levels that might indicate diabetes, or options to surgery for a given condition. In sum, the use of employee data to track employee health issues continues to be controversial.

1. What are the pros and cons of the use of employee data for health tracking?
2. Are you comfortable with the idea of employers using your data to predict your future? Is this an invasion of your privacy?
3. What, if any, health areas would you consider "off-limits" to employee wellness firms and employers?
4. Is there any potential conflict of interest between the wellness firms and employers?
5. Is there a utilitarian logic to the collection of health information (i.e., for the greater good)?

Sources: "Big Data in Healthcare," Artemis Health (January 21, 2020), https://www.artemishealth.com/blog/big-data-in-healthcare-how-employers-providers-and-brokers-are-using-healthcare-analytics, accessed May 12, 2021; Rachel Emma Silverman, "Bosses Tap Big Data to Flag Workers' Ills," *The Wall Street Journal* (February 15, 2016), B1; Valentina Zarya, "Employers Are Quietly Using Big Data to Track Employee Pregnancies," *Fortune* (February 17, 2016), http://fortune.com/2016/02/17/castlight-pregnancy-data/, accessed May 12, 2021; Aimee Picchi, "The 'Big Data' App That Predicts Employees' Health," CBS News (February 18, 2016), http://www.cbsnews.com/news/the-big-data-app-that-predicts-employees-health/, accessed May 12, 2021.

attorney client privilege, gave her a reasonable expectation of privacy.[16] The Justices further noted that the company's e-mail policy said, "Occasional personal use is permitted."[17]

The workplace privacy issue creates dilemmas that are not easily resolved. At this writing, over half of the states have enacted laws that protect employee privacy by prohibiting employers from demanding that employees provide them with Facebook and other social media usernames and passwords, and other states are considering similar bills.[18] However, employers have a good deal of freedom in writing their human resource policies about social media, provided that they obey applicable laws.

As we discussed in Chapter 8, the use of technology, Big Data, and the rise of digital enterprises have serious ethical implications for society. To develop a deeper understanding, next we focus on four employee privacy issues that are particularly important in today's workforce:

- Collection and use of employee information
- Employee monitoring
- Preemployment testing
- Drug testing

12.1a Collection and Use of Employee Information by Employers

The collection, use, and possible abuse of employee information are serious public policy issues that warrant scrutiny. With a majority of Americans believing their online and offline activities are being tracked and monitored, it is obvious that this is a hot-button issue in today's digital workforce. In fact, a recent survey disclosed that 81 percent of the public say that the potential risks they face because of data collection by companies outweigh the benefits.[19]

Today's government databases, with various agencies mixing and matching data, form a cohesive web of information on individual citizens. In the United States, the **Privacy Act of 1974** set certain controls on the right of the government to collect, use, and share data about individuals. These restrictions were relaxed when the **USA Patriot Act** was signed into law in 2001 in response to the attack on the World Trade Center (WTC) towers. However, few laws protect the privacy of individuals in the workplace. Many privacy advocates say, "You check your privacy rights at the door when you enter the workplace."[20]

The necessity for guidelines regarding the collection of information became abundantly clear when one employee in Illinois sued his employer for violating an Illinois state law, the Biometric Information Privacy Act (BIPA), when it required employees to "clock in" using their fingerprints.[21] The employee alleged that the company violated BIPA by not giving proper notice, not obtaining informed consent, and not publishing its data retention and destruction policies concerning fingerprint data. The state of Illinois is one of the few states that developed a law specifically to protect biometric data and is evidence of a growing trend for increased scrutiny on employers to keep employee data safe.

Some companies claim that there are nobler intentions to the gathering of data than just an attempt to lower costs—particularly regarding health care. These include identifying health risks for workers, encouraging them to join weight-loss programs, and helping them find treatment. However, there are also risks in the safeguarding of consumer data, as hackers continue to raid data. The Identity Theft Resource Center noted that in 2019 alone, there were 525 medical and health-care data breaches, compromising more than 39 million records.[22]

Background checks of both applicants and current employees have become another source of concern for privacy advocates. States vary in the latitude they allow employers when checking employee backgrounds, but many states, with the notable exception of California, give employers relatively free rein. Some state and local laws also limit the use of criminal history in employment decisions. Hawaii, Illinois, Massachusetts, Minnesota, New Jersey, and Rhode Island, and over a dozen cities and localities, support "**ban-the-box**"—that is, banning the check box on employment applications asking whether the candidate has ever been convicted of a crime.[23] And new federal law also seems to be embracing this, as seen in the **Fair Chance to Compete for Jobs Act of 2019**, which bans federal agencies and contractors from inquiring about a job applicant's criminal history until the applicant receives a conditional job offer.[24] It is okay, however, for employers to inquire about criminal history (within limits) later in the hiring process.[25]

Guidelines on the Use of Background Checks.

As odd as it may sound to be considered for employees, **consumer reports** is the official term for employment background checks. They can include credit reports, criminal background reports, and other information from a range of sources. The use of consumer reports in the United States is governed under the **Fair Credit Reporting Act (FCRA)** by the **Federal Trade Commission (FTC)**. The FCRA requires employers to do a few things before getting information relative to background checks. These include:[26]

1. Inform the individual in writing (but not in the application) that the information may be used for employment decisions.
2. Inform the individual about their right to an investigation description if the background check includes an investigative report.
3. Get written permission from the individual to do the background check.
4. Certify to any outside background check provider (i.e., credit bureaus like Equifax or Experian, or private agencies like GoodHire) that permission was obtained from the individual and that FCRA requirements were followed.

However, two significant loopholes exist in the protections that allow employers to bypass the FCRA. First, employers can opt to do the background checks themselves instead of using outside providers. If so, the restrictions do not apply.[27] Second, the restrictions do not apply if an adverse employment decision was made for reasons other than the contents of the background check, and so employers can bypass the requirements by citing different reasons.[28]

The overriding principle that should guide corporate decision making with regard to the collection and use of employee information is that companies should collect only necessary information from employees and use it only in ways that are appropriate. Companies should be careful not to misuse this information by employing it for purposes for which it was not intended. Employers have a duty to treat their employee's private information with care, neither releasing it to others nor allowing it to become public through careless management. Employers also have a responsibility to allow employees to correct any inaccurate information.

Another problem is that the FCRA does not cover the interview process and so, depending on state law, an employer might be able to obtain some information by simply asking. For example, a background check may not contain information on an arrest that happened more than seven years earlier. However, in some states, an employer may be able to ask an employee, verbally or in writing, "Have you *ever* been arrested?"[29] There is no doubt that the details behind the FCRA make it challenging for businesses and employees alike. Companies like Whole Foods, Dollar General, Publix, and Panera have all been sued over their use of background checks. Most often, the "clear and conspicuous" contingency is the problem. This means that the notice of a background check must stand out from the rest of the job application.[30]

The EEOC monitors employer use of background checks, too, stepping in when discriminatory practices are thought to have occurred. Two background check practices have caused the most problems for the EEOC and, by extension, the employers who are brought into court: (1) blanket no-hire policies based on criminal records or negative credit scores, and (2) lack of a correlation between the information from the background check and the actual job for which the person would have been hired.[31]

Recently, Uber was sued in a class action lawsuit filed in New York alleging that the company's use of background checks discriminates against black and Latino/Latina drivers.[32] The plaintiff claimed that his criminal history consisted of a single 2013 misdemeanor speeding violation, which Uber discovered in a 2020 background check, despite the fact that he had been driving for them without incident from 2014–2020. One day after they did the background check, he was deactivated. FCRA and its state equivalents require employers using consumer reports to provide notice to individuals before taking adverse action, and the New York City Human Rights Law (NYCHRL) requires employers to evaluate employees' and applicants' criminal history on an individualized basis, with the job kept open until the employee has a chance to respond.[33] It is unclear what the outcome of the lawsuit will be, but it is easy to see how background checks require a balance of due diligence and fairness on the part of the employer.

Although there are still few guidelines for the collection of information in most professions, the health-care industry has developed stronger guidelines for the way that collected information is handled in general, and those guidelines cover the use of medical information in employment. Medical information supplied to employers must be relevant to the job and requires the applicant's specific written consent.[34] An employer may require a preemployment physical, but the **Americans with Disabilities Act (ADA)** requires that the physical exam be requested only *after* a job offer. The act requires employers to protect the confidentiality of applicant and employee medical information, while also making it illegal to base employment decisions on a medical condition that does not affect the employee's ability to perform the essential functions of the job. We will discuss the ADA in more detail in Chapter 13.

The U.S. federal government has tightened up screening practices. The EEOC provides guidance regarding the use of criminal background checks in hiring. People with criminal backgrounds are not a protected class, that is, federal anti-discrimination laws do not protect them. However, minorities account for a disproportionate percentage of the jail population and so the EEOC is concerned that criminal background checks will have a disparate impact on minority applicants.[35]

In one of the first cases filed by the EEOC following its updated guidance, a federal court in South Carolina approved a settlement in which BMW Manufacturing agreed to pay $1.6 million and offer jobs to aggrieved African American former employees and applicants. The EEOC argued that BMW's prior screening for arrest and conviction records disproportionately screened out African Americans from employment.[36] In 2019, Dollar General paid $6 million to settle a class race discrimination lawsuit brought by the EEOC for denying employment to African Americans at a significantly higher rate than white applicants for failing the company's broad criminal background check.[37]

The EEOC guidance asks employers to make an individualized assessment of each case when considering arrest and conviction records in employment decisions.[38] The biggest problem for businesses is that they are conflicted because they are still subject to EEOC lawsuits if they require background checks in circumstances where state law requires that the firm not hire someone with a felony conviction.[39] One law group recommends that employers carefully review their background screening policies to ensure that their requirements are job related and consistent with business necessity, and be prepared to demonstrate the existence of a legitimate business reason that justifies the policy should it result in a disproportionate disqualification of minority applicants.[40]

12.1b Workplace Monitoring

In the old days, supervisors monitored employees' work activities by peeking over their shoulders and judging how things were going. Technology changed all that by providing other tracking options for employee monitoring. Privacy advocates are concerned about the use of technology to gather information about workers on the job and with good reason. During the pandemic, more than one out of four companies purchased new technology for the first time to passively track and monitor employees.[41]

Even before COVID-19 pandemic, employers were increasing their monitoring of employee productivity, with a Gartner report revealing that of 239 large corporations, 50 percent were monitoring the content of employee e-mails and social media accounts, along with who they met with and how they used their workspaces.[42] Amazon, for example, has been said to rely on such employee tracking tools as navigation software, item scanners, thermal cameras, security cameras, and recorded footage.[43] The reasons for surveillance are many, including monitoring for employee theft as well as tracking for productivity; however, Amazon has also been accused of using such data to potentially limit unionization efforts.[44]

An employee working for a company that has disclosed that it will monitor its employees is considered to have given implicit consent. With broad exceptions like this, it is not surprising that the Electronic Communication Privacy Act (ECPA) has been ineffective in regulating the monitoring of employees in the workplace.[45] Employer monitoring of employees has become the norm in businesses today, and there are no incentives for employers to remove surveillance once it is installed. The consequence is that millions of workers are laboring under the relentless gaze of electronic supervision. For example, as noted in the Ethics in Practice case below, Amazon was using digital bulletin boards and videotapes to shame workers fired for alleged theft and to warn other employees to behave.

Interestingly, recent research points to the fact that employees are more likely to pretend they are working (instead of actually working) when employers track their productivity.[46] Employers must therefore consider whether their employee monitoring is helping or hindering, taking into consideration human behaviors, particularly as many have shifted to more hybrid forms of working remotely.

What Can Be Monitored? As was discussed in Chapter 8, the introduction of new technologies creates new opportunities for surveillance by employers. Global positioning system (GPS) technology has made it possible to monitor worker location and movement patterns. In 2018, Amazon pushed GPS technology even further when it won two patents for wristband trackers, which proposed technology to emit ultrasonic sound pulses and radio transmission to track where an employee's hands were in relation to inventory bins and provide "haptic feedback" to steer workers to the correct bin.[47]

With more workers working from home during the pandemic, employee monitoring software is now prevalent on computers. According to one employment lawyer,

---

Ethics In Practice Case

Shaming Employees into Good Behavior at Amazon?

Amazon is a company with warehouses full of small, valuable items and a workforce that has relatively high turnover. In an effort to curb theft, Amazon put up flatscreen TVs that display examples of alleged on-the-job theft, including silhouettes of employees stamped with the words "terminated" or "arrested" with details about how they stole, how much they stole, and how they got caught. In addition, Amazon was reported to display information about firings related to workplace violence and "cheerier" announcements about updates on incentive bonuses and holidays. In warehouses without flatscreens, firings were allegedly posted on sheets of paper on a bulletin board or taped to the wall.

Some have accused Amazon of having "two faces," with a customer-focused, revolutionizing e-commerce platform on one side and a tougher, internal-focused workplace with punishing hours and stressful conditions on the other side. However, nobody disputes that loss prevention is a persistent concern for Amazon, and extra vigilance may be required as a result. Yet, recent actions by Amazon workers to unionize in select states seemed to provide evidence that Amazon might need to do a fairer job addressing employee concerns. When the union vote did not go through, former CEO and founder Jeff Bezos even acknowledged, "I think we need to do a better job for our employees. It's clear to me that we need a better vision for how we create value for our employees."

1. There is nothing illegal with Amazon's method of broadcasting bad behavior. Is it unethical or unadvisable? Why?
2. How would you feel about this as an employee of Amazon? How would you feel if you were one of the unaffected employees?
3. Are you more comfortable with broadcasts about theft than violence in the workforce? Are there any other employee behaviors that should or should not be broadcast this way?

Sources: Phil Wahba, "Bezos Defends Amazon Worker Treatment but Acknowledges 'Need to Do Better,'" *Fortune* (April 15, 2021), https://fortune.com/2021/04/15/jeff-bezos-amazon-workers-union-election-bessemer-alabama/, accessed May 13, 2021; BBC News, "Amazon Uses Shock Tactic to Stop Thefts at Warehouses," *BBC .com,* http://www.bbc.com/news/technology-35763908, accessed May 13, 2021; Emily Jane Fox, "Amazon Reportedly Has Scorecards to Shame Its Workers," *Vanity Fair* (March 8, 2016), http://www.vanityfair.com/news/2016/03/amazon-warehouse-theft, accessed May 13, 2021.

---

employees working from home can expect employers to monitor them by:[48]

- keeping track of what they type,
- recording Internet activity,
- taking screenshots,
- using a device's webcam,
- noting which employees access what files and when,
- monitoring an employee's physical location using GPS, and
- measuring the employee's productivity, such as noting idle time.

Technology works both ways. Webcams and phone cams can possibly serve as a tool that employees can use to monitor their employers. Some companies have moved to ban them from the workplace due to fear of corporate espionage.[49]

Effects of Being Monitored. Invasion of privacy is one major consequence of employee monitoring. Another is potential unfair treatment. Employees working under such systems complain about stress and tension resulting from their being expected and pressured to be more productive now that their efforts can be observed. The pressure of being constantly monitored is also producing low morale and a sense of job insecurity in many places. Employees have good reason to be concerned. One technology research firm estimates that the employee monitoring solutions industry will be worth more than $3.8 billion by 2023.[50]

Guidelines on the Issue of Monitoring. Researcher Reid Blackman notes that the problem with monitoring is that it comes with a real risk that it will erode trust between employers and employees.[51] Employees suffer mental distress and become fearful, which ironically decreases productivity. And while there may be some good to monitoring—for example, for employee health issues—employers must be careful to always respect employees and their privacy. Blackman suggests six recommendations for "walking the tightrope" of employee monitoring and privacy issues:[52]

1. Choose metrics carefully by involving all relevant stakeholders, including new and old hiring managers, supervisors, and those who are actually being monitored.
2. Be transparent with your employees about what you're monitoring and why.
3. Offer carrots as well as sticks to link to productivity and reward "hustle."
4. Accept that very good workers will not always be able to do very good work all the time—especially under present circumstances.
5. Monitor your own systems to ensure that people of color and other vulnerable groups are not disproportionately affected.
6. Decrease monitoring when and where you can.

Blackman points out that employees are a company's most valuable asset. Significant resources are invested in their hiring and development, so treating them with respect—and acknowledging their right to privacy—is

Ethics In Practice Case

Are Your Workers Really Sick When They Take a Sick Day?

In their "Working in America: Absent Workforce" study, Kronos Inc. found that nearly 40 percent of employees have taken sick days when they are not actually sick, and 61 percent of the respondents said their work did not get done when they were absent. Another study highlighted that this phenomenon is only getting worse over time. The arrival of COVID-19 presented even more of a challenge as many workers began calling in sick: how were employers really supposed to know if a worker was telling the truth about testing positive, or being exposed to someone with COVID-19, which required them to stay at home for several weeks? In April 2020, the Federal Bureau of Investigation (FBI) warned employers to be alert for employees who submit fraudulent COVID-19 claims. The warning described a Fortune 500 manufacturing facility worker who faked a positive COVID-19 test result and his employer shut down their facility and incurred a $175,000 loss.

In an effort to curb the resultant losses, some businesses are hiring detectives to spy on employees who have called in sick but might be playing hooky. Investigators are looking to determine if the illness or injury actually exists and, if it does, whether it is serious enough to justify the absence.

Rick Raymond is a private detective who has taken on a variety of these cases. He tracked one woman to a theme park where they take rider pictures as they round a sharp turn. He brought the pictures as proof she was there. He has tracked others to bowling alleys, pro football games,

and weddings. He estimates that about 80 to 85 percent of the people he is hired to follow end up being guilty.

1. The courts have ruled that this practice is legal. Is it ethical?
2. Should limits be placed on the use of private detectives in following employees when they are outside of the office? Explain what these might be.
3. How would you react if your boss had you followed when you called in sick?
4. If you were an employer or a manager, would you hire a private detective to follow one of your employees?

Sources: Lynne Curry, "Here's What to Do if You Suspect Your Employee Is Lying about Testing Positive for COVID-19," *Anchorage Daily News* (July 6, 2020), https://www.adn.com/business-economy/2020/07/06/heres-what-to-do-when-you-suspect-your-employee-is-lying-about-testing-positive-for-covid-19/, accessed May 13, 2021; "Working in America: Absent Workforce," *Kronos*, http://www.workforceinstitute.org/wp-content/themes/revolution/docs/Workingin-Amer-Survey.pdf, accessed May 13, 2021; Thomas Chan, "Employers and Insurers Hire Private Eyes to Probe Sick Leave Scams," *South China Morning Post* (May 2, 2013), http://www.scmp.com/news/hong-kong/article/1227821/employers-and-insurers-call-private-investigatorsroot-out-sick-leave, accessed May 13, 2021; Eric Spitznagel, "The Sick Day Bounty Hunters," *Bloomberg Businessweek* (December 8–12, 2010), 93–95.

not only the right thing to do but also important to the success of any business.

12.1c Integrity Testing

Integrity testing, sometimes referred to as honesty testing, is another area in which employee privacy issues need careful consideration. With one study finding that 75 percent of hiring managers have caught a candidate lying on a résumé, it is easy to see why employers might be interested in testing the integrity of their applicants.[53] In the invasion-of-privacy arena, one of the most controversial issues has been the use of the **polygraph**, or lie detector, in business. The **Employee Polygraph Protection Act (EPPA)** of 1988 banned most uses in the private sector of the lie detector, but it can still be used by private employers that provide security services, protection of nuclear facilities, shipment or storage of radioactive or toxic waste, public water supply facilities, public transportation, precious commodities, or propriety information. In addition, employers that manufacture, distribute, or dispense controlled substances may use polygraph tests for some of their positions. Government employers are also exempt from the prohibitions on polygraph testing, as are private consultants or experts under contract to various government departments, agencies, or bureaus.[54]

Many companies now use question-and-answer **integrity tests** (also known as *honesty tests*), which are a specific type

of **personality test**. However, integrity tests receive the same criticisms that led to severe restriction of lie detector testing. Critics of integrity tests claim they are intrusive and invade privacy by the nature of their inquiries. Some critics also say that they are unreliable and that employers use them as the sole measure of the fitness of an applicant. In fact, one study found that integrity tests had accuracy rates between 37 and 59 percent, and instead of finding good candidates, they erred on the side of disqualifying honest candidates.[55]

In a recent survey by the consulting group EY, most managers expressed interest in reestablishing the importance of personal integrity in business, particularly in the wake of the COVID-19 pandemic and the ethical issues that accompany it.[56] Hence, integrity tests may be making a comeback. Management and testing companies claim the tests are useful in weeding out potentially dishonest applicants, particularly when they are combined with cognitive ability assessments.[57] They claim that each question asked has a specific purpose. They also argue that hiring by "gut feeling" is problematic, and integrity tests provide a more objective assessment.[58] In fact, the U.S. Office of Personnel Management endorses integrity/honesty tests as valid measures of overall job performance.[59]

Integrity tests are subject to the same kinds of legal hurdles and ethical considerations that affect polygraph and drug tests. The Civil Rights Act (to be discussed in Chapter 13) makes it unlawful for any test to have a particularly negative impact on a protected subgroup. From the ADA perspective, medical examinations can be given only after a conditional offer of employment has been made. The EEOC has ruled that integrity tests are not medical examinations, and so they can be given to applicants.[60]

Companies are increasingly turning to the use of broader personality tests, of which the integrity test is a specific form: Personality tests cover areas such as conscientiousness, sociability, introversion, extraversion, emotional stability, maturity, and openness to new ideas.[61] More than 75 percent of large companies use assessment and personality tests to screen applicants.[62] However, a recent HBO Max documentary, *Persona: The Dark Truth Behind Personality Tests*, provided insight into how these tests may discriminate against many potential employees. The documentary reveals how the tests can be "junk science" in assuming that people's self-reported moods accurately correlate to future job performance. Additionally, many of the tests are driven by artificial intelligence (AI) screening tools that unfairly exclude candidates with disabilities. It seems that this may be an important issue going forward. In 2020, ten members of the U.S. Senate asked the EEOC for clarification about their authority to investigate bias in AI-driven hiring technologies.[63] With such rising concerns, the EEOC has reported that it plans to pay more attention to them in the future.[64]

Guidelines on the Use of Integrity Tests. Even when legal issues surrounding integrity and personality tests are resolved, ethical issues are likely to remain. A test that will identify many of those who would behave unethically at a cost to the firm will also yield "false positives," people labeled as unethical who would have been good, honest employees. In statistics, this is called a **type 1 error**, finding an innocent person to be guilty. In contrast, a **type 2 error** finds a guilty person to be innocent. The nature of testing is such that an effort to decrease one type of error will lead to an increase in the other. In other words, the more strictly a test is used to rule out any person who would be guilty of unethical behavior, the greater is the chance that innocent people will be judged unethical. One human resource expert suggests the following attributes of strong personality assessments:[65]

1. They measure stable traits that will not change once the candidate has been working for some length of time.
2. They are normative in nature, which allows you to compare one candidate's scores against another.
3. They have a "candidness" or "lie detector" scale so you understand how likely it is that the results accurately portray the test-taker.
4. They have high reliability and have been shown to be valid predictors of job performance.

It is important, therefore, that integrity tests be used judiciously and that they not be the primary criterion on which employment is based.

12.1d Drug Testing

Drug testing is an umbrella term intended to embrace drug and alcohol testing and employer testing for any suspected substance abuse. The issue of drug testing in the workplace has many of the same characteristics as the lie detector and integrity testing issues. Companies say they need to do

---

Ethics In Practice Case

Co-workers versus Friendship

I worked in retail for a handful of years, and during that time, I have made great lifelong friends. Because I am a hardworking, committed employee, my boss, the owner, took notice, and she promoted me to manager at age 17. During my fifth year working at the store, we hired a new employee, Lindsey, and we instantly became great friends. We became so close that we were hanging outside of work, and Lindsey introduced me to her group of friends. My new group of friends and I became super close, where I would see them every day.

Lindsey had a lot of health problems, and she would frequently call out sick. Being a manager, I had to take responsibility and cover her shifts, even though I would have other obligations. I requested the Fourth of July weekend off to go to my lake house with my family. At the last minute, however, Lindsey called out sick, and I received a phone call from my boss begging me to cover her shifts, which I did.

On July 3, my friend Rob invited me to come over to his family BBQ, because he knew I was missing my family BBQ. He told me all of our friends would be there as well, so I planned to head over there after I got out of work. I worked ten hours that day, I was exhausted, but I wanted to see

my friends. I pulled up to his house, and I saw Lindsey's car there. I was extremely confused because Lindsey called out sick for the whole weekend, so why was she there?

Lindsey did not seem the least bit sick; in fact, she was socializing and having the time of her life. I could not believe Lindsey just put me in this horrible position—I missed my family vacation because she did not "feel" like working that weekend. If I ratted her out, I would lose the new friends with whom I had become extremely close. As her manager, should I tell my boss that Lindsey was faking it, even though we are friends outside of work? Where does the line end between friends and employees?

1. What are the ethical issues in this case?
2. Should I have just gone on my family vacation and not have covered the shift?
3. Should I report Lindsey's behavior? Is there some other action I should take?
4. How should I deal with Lindsey in the future, professionally and personally?

Contributed by Madeline Meibauer

such testing to protect themselves and the public, but opponents claim that drug tests are not accurate and invade the employee's privacy. Concerns about drug testing include the implications for employee privacy, the inaccuracy of tests, and the impact of drug testing on employee morale. If management desires to create a favorable workplace for employee stakeholders, they should pay close attention to the legalities and ethics of drug testing, which could be perceived as privacy invasions by their employees if not judiciously used.

Quest Diagnostics, a major provider of employment-related drug-testing services, releases an annual index that shows that workforce positive drug tests climbed to its highest rate in 2020.[66] Marijuana continues to have the highest positivity rates, and that trend is likely to continue. Various state marijuana legalization developments have created a confusing situation for companies, as we will note in Chapter 17.

The U.S. Drug Enforcement Administration continues to consider marijuana to be a Schedule 1 controlled substance, but the Department of Justice is reviewing the states that have legalized marijuana and is reviewing recommendations on how to monitor the effects of state legislation.[67] As the issue of state versus federal law about marijuana use continues to evolve, companies will have to sort out how best to respond to the continuous shifts in the legal landscape.

Arguments for Drug Testing. Proponents of drug testing argue that the costs of drug abuse on the job are staggering. The consequences range from accidents and injuries to theft, bad decisions, and ruined lives. The greatest concern is in industries where mistakes can cost lives—for example, the railroad, airline, aerospace, nuclear power, and hazardous equipment and chemicals industries. Thus, the primary ethical argument for employers conducting drug tests is the responsibility they have to their own employees and to the general public to provide safe workplaces, secure asset protection, and safe places in which to transact business. This is an example of the trade-offs that are often at the core of ethical decisions, as we noted in Chapter 6. In this case, drug testing places the employee's right to privacy against everyone else's right to safety.

Arguments against Drug Testing. Opponents of drug testing see it as both a due-process issue and an invasion-of-privacy issue. The due-process issue relates to the sometimes-questionable accuracy of drug tests. Common foods and medications can lead to a false positive, giving the appearance of drug use when the person being tested is innocent. This can create a downward spiral for that employee, causing reputational damage, lost income, and considerable expense to try to rebut the allegation of drug use.[68]

Beyond the rights issues of drug testing, many employers are finding it a difficult hurdle in hiring because they cannot find enough workers to pass a drug test, particularly in areas that enjoy low-to-moderate unemployment levels.[69]

And with the number of states legalizing cannabis increasing, the pool of qualified, drug-free candidates is narrowing and forcing many companies to stop testing for marijuana completely.[70]

Many legitimate questions arise in the drug-testing issue. Do employers have a right to know if their employees use drugs off the job? Are employees performing on the job satisfactorily? Obviously, a delicate balance is necessary, because employers and employees alike have legitimate interests that must be protected. If companies are going to engage in some form of drug testing, they should think carefully about developing policies that not only will achieve their intended goals but also will be fair to the employees and will minimize invasions of privacy. Such a balance will not be easy to achieve but must be sought. To do otherwise will guarantee decreased employee morale, more lawsuits, and new government regulations.

Guidelines for Drug Testing. If management perceives the need to conduct a drug-testing program to protect other stakeholders, it should carefully design and structure the program so that it will be minimally intrusive of employees' privacy rights. Guidelines have been developed by the American College of Occupational and Environmental Medicine (ACOEM) to reflect the ethical aspects of drug testing. These are included in Figure 12-1.[71]

State and Federal Legislation. Some states and cities have enacted laws or are considering doing so to restrict workplace drug testing. Generally, these laws restrict the scope of testing by private and public employers and establish privacy protections and procedural safeguards. Some states do not completely ban drug testing but restrict the circumstances (e.g., for reasonable cause) under which it may be used. They may also restrict drug testing to reasonable suspicion and place limits on the disciplinary actions employers may take. Other states provide discounts on worker's compensation and/or incentives of another kind to organizations that implement drug testing. This patchwork of incongruous state laws complicates drug testing for employers.

Employee Assistance Programs. One of the most significant strategies undertaken by corporate America to deal with the growing alcohol- and drug-abuse problem in the workplace has been **Employee Assistance Programs (EAPs).** EAPs extend into a variety of employee problem areas such as compulsive gambling, financial stress, emotional stress, marital difficulties, aging, legal problems, AIDS, and other psychological, emotional, and social difficulties. The term **broad brush EAP** describes this comprehensive model.[72] A recent major concern of EAPs has been to integrate them into the company's general health management strategy so that it can become a core strategic component.[73]

EAPs represent a positive and proactive step companies can take to deal with these serious problems. EAPs are

Figure 12-1 Ethical Aspects and Guidelines for Drug Testing

Guidelines for drug testing shift over time, and so exceptions to these might be considered and/or new guidelines may develop. The major point is that management needs to think through its policies and their consequences very carefully when designing and conducting drug-testing programs. The following are suggested guidelines from the American College of Occupational and Environmental Medicine (ACOEM):

1. A written company policy and procedure concerning substance abuse and screening should exist and be applied impartially.
2. The reason for any requirement for the drug testing program should be clearly documented. Reasons might involve safety for the individual, other employees, or the public; security needs; or requirements related to job performance.
3. Any employees or applicants who will be affected should be informed in advance of the company's drug use, misuse, and testing policies, as well as their right to refuse to be tested and the consequences of refusal.
4. Employees should have a clear understanding of—and the company's policy should state—the possible consequences of a nonnegative test result including, but not limited to, refusal to hire, firing, suspension, rehabilitation, referral to substance abuse counseling, and not entering a facility.

5. Where special safety or security needs justify testing for the presence of drugs on an unannounced and random basis, employees should be made aware of all aspects of the drug-testing program.
6. All tests should be done in a uniform and impartial manner.
7. A licensed physician (MD/DO) should supervise the collection, transportation, and analysis of the specimens, as well as the reporting of results. Stringent legal, technical, and ethical requirements should be observed when reporting results.
8. A licensed and appropriately qualified physician should be designated as the medical review officer (MRO) and should evaluate positive results before a report is made to the employer.
9. An employee or applicant who tests positive should be informed of the positive results by the physician and should have the opportunity to explain and discuss the results before the employer is notified. The procedure for this should be clearly outlined.
10. Any report to the employer should provide only the information needed for work placement purposes or as required by government regulations. The employer should not be told of the specific types or levels of drug found unless required by law. A trained and qualified physician should make that report.

Source: ACOEM, "Ethical Aspects of Drug Testing" (July 22, 2019), https://acoem.org/Guidance-and-Position-Statements/Guidance-and-Position-Statements/Ethical-Aspects-of-Drug-Testing-en, accessed May 14, 2021; Substance Abuse and Mental Health Services Administration, "Drug-Free Workplace Guidelines and Resources," Drug-Free Workplace Guidelines and Resources | SAMHSA, accessed May 18, 2021; Oschmann Employee Screening Service, "Ensuring Your Employee Drug Testing Program Is Ethical," Ensuring Your Employee Drug Testing Program Is Ethical - Oschmann Employee Screening Services (oschmannscreening.com), accessed May 18, 2021.

designed to be confidential and nonpunitive, and they affirm three important propositions: (1) employees are valuable members of the organization, (2) it is better to help troubled employees than to discipline or discharge them, and (3) recovered employees are better employees.

Unfortunately, most human resource professionals say that EAP programs are significantly underutilized and undervalued.[74] Additionally, when employees seek support (most often through a hotline), the program provides inappropriate or substandard solutions. Fortunately, with a shift in the acceptance of mental health in recent years, EAPs are being utilized for mental health and crisis support. A selling point of many EAPs is that they have global reach, and that seems to be a driver for many organizations keeping them in place right now.[75] In an era when employees are increasingly exerting their workplace rights, enlightened companies are offering EAPs in an effort to help solve their mutual problems. More information on EAPs can be found at the Employee Assistance Professionals Association website, https://www.eapassn.org/.[76]

Summary Guidelines on the Issue of Privacy. During our discussion of various privacy issues, we have indicated steps that management might consider taking in an attempt to be responsive to employee stakeholders and to treat them fairly. Frederick S. Lane III, a law and technology expert and author of *The Naked Employee: How Technology Is*

Compromising Workplace Privacy, offers an "Employee Privacy Bill of Rights" that sets forth guidelines for developing privacy policies and procedures that uphold the dignity of the employee.[77] He maintains that to preserve employee rights, firms should:

1. Obtain informed consent from employees and applicants before acquiring information about them.
2. Disclose the nature of any surveillance that will occur.
3. Set controls so as to avoid casual and unauthorized spread of information.
4. Limit the collection and use of medical and health data to that which is relevant to the job.
5. Require reasonable suspicion before doing drug tests.
6. Respect and preserve the boundary between work and home.

Business's concern for protection of the privacy of its employees, customers, and other stakeholders is increasing. It is not surprising, therefore, that a new form of corporate executive came on the horizon. As we discussed in Chapter 8, **chief privacy officers (CPOs)** are high-ranking executives responsible for monitoring and protecting the private information held by firms. They differ from security personnel in that they determine what data should be protected while the security department determines how it will be protected. CPOs are responsible for ensuring that the privacy of individuals in the workplace is respected.

12.2 Health and Wellness in the Workplace

Though the terms *health* and *wellness* are often used interchangeably, the World Health Organization (WHO) maintains that they are similar but not the same. The WHO defines *health* as "a state of complete physical, mental and social well-being and not merely the absence of disease or infirmity (illness)." Then, WHO defines *wellness* as "the optimal state of health of individuals and groups," and wellness is usually expressed in terms of a positive approach to living. The primary difference between the two is that health is the goal and wellness is more the active process of achieving it.[78] Today, companies are emphasizing both the overall goal and the process.

The COVID-19 pandemic has forever changed the way human resources professionals and businesses approach health and wellness in the workforce. From feelings of isolation to health-care and childcare worries, employees faced increasing levels of stress associated with their jobs. In fact, a recent American Psychological Association survey found that 70 percent of 3,000+ respondents said work was a "significant source of stress in their lives" compared to 64 percent in 2019.[79] In another survey of more than 300 organizations, 46 percent of employees said their work-life balance had decreased.[80] And this is worse in the United States than in other countries, with a recent index showing that the United States ranks 30th out of 40 countries in terms of time devoted to leisure and personal care.[81]

Fortunately, companies in the United States have become increasingly more sensitive about health and wellness issues. Even before the pandemic struck, nine out of ten employers were planning to invest more in mental health to address issues of loneliness, burnout, Zoom fatigue, and work-life balance.[82] Starbucks, for example, initiated a comprehensive training program called Mental Health Fundamentals for its employees, designed to address employee mental health issues before they get too severe.[83]

In addition to addressing mental health, many companies offer health insurance that includes weight loss, smoking cessation, or lifestyle coaching programs; however, the results have been mixed.[84] In 2021, the EEOC proposed restrictions on the incentives for these programs amid concerns that they discriminated against older employees and violated the ADA, among other issues.[85] Instead of financial motivations, the EEOC proposal reducing incentives to things like T-shirts and water bottles. Yet, research has shown that employees participate in these programs only when they are highly incentivized or forced to make a choice between more or less attractive health benefits.[86] Hence, employers continue to be challenged with finding the right mix of health-care benefits to help employees stay healthy and well.

Smoking, vaping, and drug use are controversial issues related to health in the workplace and so they merit special attention. Like other issues we have examined, smoking and vaping in the workplace have employee rights, privacy, and due-process ramifications. With evolving marijuana laws, and the potential to decriminalize marijuana, it is possible that employers will have to review their drug policies. Additionally, the growing opioid crisis, as we will discuss in Chapter 15, has affected the workplace with industries such as the construction industry being hit particularly hard.[87] Overall, it is clear that employers will have to find ways to continue to motivate employees to stay healthy and be well, while also addressing newer health issues that employees face with evolving regulations, as well as new remote workplace routines.

12.2a Mental Health in the Workplace

Mental health in the workforce has been on the radar of human resources professionals for decades. Issues of workplace-related stress, anxiety, burnout, and depression are included in this broad category. However, the coronavirus pandemic highlighted these issues as never before. In fact, one mental health expert at Johns Hopkins commented, "There's no doubt that the coronavirus pandemic will be the most psychologically toxic disaster in anyone's lifetime."[88] One survey by Qualtrics found that 44 percent of newly remote workers said their mental health had declined since the outbreak of the pandemic.

Unfortunately, however, employees are often reluctant to discuss their mental health issues, either for fear of retaliation or firing, or simply because they are uncomfortable with discussing personal issues. Mental health conditions are covered under the American with Disabilities Act, and employers must make reasonable accommodations for workers with such disorders, but employees have to be willing to disclose their need for accommodations.

The stigma of mental health issues pervades workplaces and beyond. In 2020, professional athletes jumped into the fray to raise consciousness and address the stigma of mental health issues that holds many people back from seeking help. An HBO special, *Weight of Gold*, further highlighted the link between mental health depression and pressures to perform, with 2016 Summer Olympic champion swimmer Michael Phelps speaking candidly about the mental health toll caused by the immense pressure to do well.[89] We discuss this in the nearby Ethics in Practice case.

The accessibility of wellness programs for mental health was a problem during the pandemic, but many companies jumped quickly to offering online programs including meditation and virtual therapy that proved beneficial to employees. Reorganizing workspaces to make employees feel safer as they return to work will also be important to employee mental health going forward. According to the consulting group EY, employers that prioritize their workers' mental health as we emerge from the pandemic will gain an edge in the fight for top talent going forward.[90] While the pandemic challenged business/stakeholder relationships on many fronts, it is possible that one upside is that it has caused businesses to reimagine and reshape their platform of mental-health-care benefits.

Ethics In Practice Case

Mental Health, Athletes, and the Pressures to Perform

For decades there has been stigma associated with discussing mental health issues that include behavioral, personality, mood, or emotional disorders, as people fear they will be viewed negatively, or even lose their jobs. As a result, many suffer quietly with anxiety, depression, and even suicidal thoughts overshadowing their lives. This can have terrible consequences for the individual and their families, friends, and organizations.

To address this, in 2020, Indianapolis Colts' linebacker Darius Leonard went online and on TV to open up about his struggles with depression and anxiety. This led to the team's Kicking the Stigma campaign that became notable for its positive impact, particularly during the pandemic. Other athletes then followed with disclosures about their mental health struggles. In the HBO documentary *The Weight of Gold*, athletes share their stories about mental health struggles and pressures to perform, including such athletes as Apolo Ohno, Shaun White, Sasha Cohen, Lolo Jones, and Steve Holcomb.

The stigma of mental health goes beyond athletes. A recent survey revealed rising levels of mental health concerns among workers, some due to the pandemic but also some due to productivity pressures. In fact, the two are correlated, as employers were surprised to see productivity rise during the early stages of the pandemic but they did not realize that employees were pushing themselves to their limits and suffering mental health distress as a result. In fact, the survey revealed that 68 percent were worried that reaching out about a mental health issue could affect their job security.

1. Is it ethical for employers to be concerned about employees' mental health or is this just a personal issue? How might employers help employees feel comfortable with seeking help for mental health issues?
2. How might technology enhance or impede the organization's ability to address employees' mental health?
3. What ethical theories apply here?

Sources: A. J. Horch, "Coronavirus Stress: Mental Health Issues Are Rising Among Workers, but Help Is Available," *CNBC* (October 5, 2021), https://www.cnbc.com/2020/10/05 /coronavirus-stress-mental-health-issues-rising-among-workers-.html, accessed May 16, 2021; Halle Kiefer, "Michael Phelps, Fellow Athletes Discuss 'Post Olympic Depression' in HBO's Weight of Gold Trailer," *New York Magazine* (July 20, 2020), https://www.vulture.com/2020/07/athletes-discuss-mental-health-hbo-weight-of-gold-trailer.html, accessed May 16, 2021; Alex Janin, "How to Deal with Stress at Work," *The Wall Street Journal* (January 8, 2021), https://www.wsj.com/articles/how-to-deal-with-stress-at-work-11610122418, accessed May 16, 2021.

12.2b Work-Life Balance and the Family-Friendly Workplace

One of the most notable trends among employers for making the workplace a more desirable and healthy venue is the movement toward helping employees balance their work lives and their personal lives, including developing family-friendly workplaces. Employees are increasingly less willing to spend every waking hour at work and are more committed to having time to spend at home with family. However, despite an increase in family-friendly policies at businesses, the pressure of a round-the-clock work culture has taken its toll on the workforce. One study shows that in the United States, 85.8 percent of males and 66.5 percent of females work more than 40 hours per week, and that Americans work hundreds more hours a year than Japanese, British, German, and French workers.[91] In a 2020 study of 310 U.S. organizations by the Conference Board, 46 percent of respondents said their work-life balance has decreased, particularly during the coronavirus pandemic.[92]

With fewer employees commuting to work, many workers have been using the time to work even more, leading many to feel burned out. The phenomenon of **burnout** is so pervasive that just two years ago the World Health Organization categorized it as an occupational phenomenon resulting from workplace stress.[93] During the pandemic, women suffered burnout disproportionately, especially black and Latina mothers who are more likely to be their families' sole breadwinners.[94]

Despite the challenges of a 24/7 workplace culture, companies are searching for more ways to help employees achieve **work-life balance**—how working people manage their time spent at and outside of work.[95] Companies are endeavoring to maintain **family-friendly** benefits while striving to reduce costs. These benefits include flex time, paid time off, advancement opportunities, and child care.

One expert suggests it is time for employees to take control and negotiate their work-life balance by asking employers to focus on things like output instead of how much they work. They go on to suggest if employers then follow with empowering employees with the equivalent of two-day deliveries and leveraging technology to allow employees to pick their own schedules, true transformation can happen.[96] Another expert suggests that work-life balance is a cycle, not an achievement, that requires employees to be self-aware of imbalances and make moves to correct, including the following actions:[97]

- Pause and ask, "What is causing me stress or imbalance, and how are these circumstances affecting how I engage with my job?"
- Pay attention to your emotions.
- Reprioritize—reflect on your activities and work on addressing priorities and ask, "What am I willing to sacrifice, and for how long?"
- Consider your alternatives and what can be changed, recognizing that improving the situation takes time and experimentation.

- Implement changes and make a "public" change that explicitly shifts your colleagues' expectations.
- Revisit the cycle again as part of a regular re-valuation for improvement.

Although not everyone thinks that companies are becoming as family friendly as they claim to be, it is clear that many workers, especially younger generations, are talking more about the importance of work-life balance that affords employees a better, family-friendly environment, and many leading companies are responding. Even through the pandemic, many companies continued to offer virtual events and online gatherings designed to build relationships and familiarity between co-workers that were designed to make work more friendly and "fun." Both directly and indirectly, family-friendly workplaces positively contribute to the physical and mental health of employees.

It is in the context of organizations and better work-life balance that we next discuss a law aimed at health-related issues in the workplace—the FMLA. The FMLA is important to the health and well-being of employees because it helps employees to take care of their families and health situations while still maintaining their jobs and careers.

Family and Medical Leave Act. The **Family and Medical Leave Act (FMLA)** was made into law in 1993, but it has become increasingly more relevant today. This act was designed to make life easier for employees with family or health problems and is continually revisited as the workplace changes. In 2010, the law was expanded to include employees with family members on active military duty.[98] In 2020, in response to the coronavirus pandemic, the **Families First Coronavirus Response Act (FFCRA)** expanded paid sick leave or expanded family medical leave for certain COVID-19 related reasons. Other changes to the FMLA include a revised definition of "spouse" to include same-sex married couples in all 50 states.[99] Figure 12-2 provides details about the benefits that the FMLA grants employees.

The Department of Labor regularly surveys the public about the FMLA. The most recent survey showed that the corporate views on the FMLA are mixed—generally positive but with some issues that merit concern. The good news is that the law seems to work well when employees take up to 12 weeks of unpaid leave for a close relative's sickness or the birth or adoption of a child. Additionally, the portion of employees having heard of FMLA has risen over the years to 76 percent of employees. However, more than half believe that FMLA covers more situations than it does, like care for a sibling or a grandchild. Additionally, problems arise when employees take unscheduled intermittent leave. In addition, defining a *serious medical condition* has been a challenge.[100] In sum, the FMLA has accomplished much good for employees' psychological health. However, clarifying terminology is important if it is to continue to provide workers with the opportunity to fulfill their family responsibilities without sacrificing their careers.

12.2c Smoking, Vaping, Drug, and Alcohol Use in the Workplace

The importance of the health and wellness of employees is hard to argue against. However, some of the most controversial areas regarding employees is how employers can help employees with some of their "vices" that can negatively impact their work. These include smoking and its newer counterpart, vaping, as well as the use of drugs and alcohol in the workforce.

Smoking and Vaping at Work. Most states regulate smoking in the workplace to some degree, but there is no federal law that governs smoking at work. Few states have statewide bans on smoking electronic cigarettes or vapor devices indoors; however, in many cases, electronic smoking devices are included in the smoke-free laws of the states. The issue of **smoking in the workplace** began in the 1980s in the United States. The idea that smoking ought to be curtailed or restricted in the workplace is a direct result of

Figure 12-2 The Family Medical Leave Act

The Family Medical Leave Act (FMLA) entitles eligible employees of covered employers to take unpaid, job-protected leave for specified family and medical reasons.

- An employee may take up to 12 weeks of unpaid leave in any 12-month period for the birth or adoption of a child or for the care of a child, spouse, or parent with a serious health condition that limits the employee's performance.
- Employees must be reinstated in their old jobs or be given equivalent jobs upon returning to work; the employer does not have to allow employees to accrue seniority or other benefits during the leave periods.
- Employers must provide employees with health benefits during leave periods.
- Employees are protected from retaliation in the same way as under other employment laws; an employee cannot

be discriminated against for complaining to other people (even the newspapers) about an employer's family leave policy.

Employers also have rights under the FMLA. These rights include the following:

- Companies with fewer than 50 workers are exempt.
- Employers may demand that employees obtain medical opinions and certifications regarding their needs for leave and may require second or third opinions.
- Employers do not have to pay employees during leave periods, but they must continue health benefits.
- If an employee and a spouse are employed at the same firm and are entitled to leave, the total leave for both may be limited to 12 weeks.

Source: The U.S. Department of Labor, "Family Medical Leave Act," https://www.dol.gov/agencies/whd/fmla/factsheets, accessed May 17, 2021.

the growing antismoking sentiment in society in general. Evidence of the need to control smoking in the workplace continues to mount, particularly regarding vaping. A recent study of more than 1,000 employees showed that the majority observed co-workers vaping at work and 12.1 percent reported vaping at work themselves.[101] These employees vaped for a variety of reasons, including as a partial or complete substitute for cigarettes, a belief that e-cigs are less harmful than cigarettes, and the ability to vape in workplaces where other types of tobacco are prohibited.

Research has also demonstrated that allowing smoking and/or vaping in the workplace has several strong disadvantages that relate to health and safety that managements need to consider. It is not surprising, therefore, that many companies have adopted smoke-free workplace programs and are continuing to do so. Not only are the programs an increased protection for all employees, but the employers receive many benefits as well, including lower medical costs for their health plans.[102]

Drugs in the Workplace. Unfortunately, according to a recent Quest Diagnostic report, workforce substance abuse continues to rise, driven by increase in illicit drug use of cocaine, marijuana, and methamphetamines.[103] This has significant implications for workplace safety, particularly when the upswing includes employees in safety-sensitive jobs with federally mandated testing. The construction industry has been particularly hard hit as workers seeking relief from their pain from manual labor get hooked on prescription drugs. One recent study showed that construction workers are six times more likely than workers in other manufacturing, industrial, and service industries to become addicted to opioids.[104]

And the rise of addiction has only increased amid the isolation and limited access to support clinics during the pandemic. Marijuana continues to top the list of the most commonly detected illicit substances across all workforce categories and specimen types.[105] While the national debate on drug misuse has focused primarily on marijuana, increasing positivity rates for cocaine and methamphetamine are also cause for concern, according to the Quest report.[106]

Alcohol in the Workplace. An increase in substance use in the workforce is not just limited to drugs. Alcohol use during work hours skyrocketed during the COVID-19 lockdowns when employees began working from home. With work-from-home employees and social distancing it was increasingly difficult to recognize signs of employee substance abuse.[107] In 2020, the National Safety Council (NSC) called for employers to not only be ready for a workforce with increased substance misuse problems and mental health concerns but also to understand how to help workers.[108]

Guidelines on the Issues of Smoking, Vaping, and Drug Use. What can an employer do to address these issues? There is sufficient evidence to conclude that regular drug testing works, both as a powerful deterrent and as an effective way to identify people who need help. For other substance abuse issues, the NSC recommends employers build both short- and long-term responses to these considerations and ensure mental health continues to be prioritized.[109] Employers need buy-in and engagement from leadership, management, human resources, communications, and employees, which is critical for success. Finally, employers must develop a comprehensive identification and treatment plan to build tobacco-free and vape-free workplace policies, alongside a drug-free workplace, to promote employee health and safety.

12.3 Workplace Safety

Workers Memorial Day is sponsored by the U.S. union organization, the AFL-CIO, and it is observed every year on April 28 to honor those workers who have died on the job. That date also is the anniversary of the Occupational Safety and Health Administration and the Federal Coal Mine Health and Safety Act. Sadly, 2.78 million deaths per year around the world can be attributable to occupational accidents or work-related diseases.[110] Additionally, there are some 374 million non-fatal work-related injuries each year. The human cost is vast and estimated at an economic burden of 3.94 percent of global Gross Domestic Product (GDP) each year. In the United States, workplace fatalities have hit their highest levels since 2008, with more than 5,333 fatal worker injuries in 2019.[111]

The primary law that protects the safety and health of workers in the United States is the Occupational Safety and Health Act. This act requires the Secretary of Labor to set safety and health standards that protect employees and their families. Every private employer who engages in interstate commerce is subject to the regulations promulgated under this act.[112] The federal agency responsible for overseeing the safety and health of America's workers is the **Occupational Safety and Health Administration (OSHA)**. Examining the workplace safety problem includes understanding the right-to-know laws that have evolved from it, and so we turn to these issues next.

12.3a The Workplace Safety Problem

As we discussed in Chapter 7, the dramatic and catastrophic poisonous gas leak at the Union Carbide plant in Bhopal, India, highlighted the issue of safety in the workplace for all to see. The death toll topped 2,000, and tens of thousands more were injured. People around the globe were startled and shocked at what the results of one major industrial accident could be. Lawsuits sought damages that quickly exceeded the net worth of the company.[113] More than 30 years after the disaster, survivors of the accident and their supporters continue to push for damages for unmet medical bills and toxic cleanup. This incident foreshadowed the need to take steps to protect worker health and safety. What this incident clearly signaled is not only that employees have a legal and moral right to a safe working environment but also that businesses

Spotlight on Sustainability

It's All Connected

Workplace safety is not always mentioned in discussions of business sustainability, but that is beginning to change. Sustainability initiatives encompass environmental, social, and economic (ESG) considerations—and safety hinges on all three. The lean and green movement combines eliminating waste with respecting people and the environment. For example, a recent study of ergonomics discovered that the muscle pain and stress experienced by workers in one department of the company stemmed from root causes in another department. Furthermore, factors that were the source of the muscle pain had also affected employees in still other departments.

Sustainability's focus on systemwide thinking lends itself to seeing the connections in complex systems and recognizing the resulting interactions and their consequences.

However, employee safety and health have received relatively little attention in the sustainability movement, and so the Center for Safety and Health Sustainability was launched with the purpose of bringing safety and health into the discussion and practice of sustainability.

Sources: Occupational Safety and Health Organization, "Sustainability in the Workforce," https://www.osha.gov/sustainability, accessed May 17, 2021; Ash M. Genaidy, Reynold Sequeira, Magda M. Rinder, and Amal D. A-Rehim, "Determinants of Business Sustainability: An Ergonomics Perspective," *Ergonomics* (March 2009), 273–301; Michael A. Taubitz, "Lean, Green, and Safe," *Professional Safety* (May 2010), 39; Center for Safety and Health Sustainability, http://centershs.org/index.php, accessed May 17, 2021.

and their managers can face significant legal costs if they do not ensure that employees are protected.

12.3b Workplace Safety Today

It is almost unbelievable that we still have to be concerned about workplace safety with all of the protections that employers must provide for their employees. However, an examination of OSHA reports reveals that many accidents are deemed "preventable workplace tragedies."[114] These include such incidences as the strangulation death of a bowling center mechanic working on an automatic bowling pinsetter, the crushing of an auto parts worker inside a stamping machine, and the fatal fall of a construction worker on a building site.[115] One safety group provides the following seven most common causes of workplace accidents:[116]

- Shortcuts
- Overconfidence
- Poor or lack of housekeeping
- Starting a task before getting all necessary information
- Neglecting safety procedures
- Mental distractions
- Lack of preparation

Beyond a legal obligation, it is an employer's ethical duty and obligation to provide a safe work environment, free of any conditions or activities that might cause harm. Each of the seven causes listed is preventable, and so it is the obligation of businesses to provide training and development to ensure the safety of its employees.

12.3c Right-to-Know Laws

Prompted by the Union Carbide tragedy in Bhopal (India) and other, less dramatic industrial accidents, workers have demanded to know more about the thousands of chemicals and hazardous substances they are being exposed to daily in the workplace. Experts argue that employers have a duty to provide employees with information on the hazards of workplace chemicals and to make sure that workers understand what the information means in practical terms.

To address this concern, many states have passed **right-to-know laws** and expanded public access to this kind of information by employees and even communities. Although the states took the initiative on the right-to-know front, OSHA followed suit by creating a Hazard Communication Standard, supported by the Environmental Protection Agency's Emergency Planning and Community Right-to-Know Act (EPCRA) that preempted state regulations. This standard requires covered employers to identify hazardous chemicals in their workplaces and to provide employees with specified forms of information on such substances and their hazards. Specifically, manufacturers, whether they are chemical manufacturers or users of chemicals, must take certain steps to achieve compliance with the standard.[117] These steps include the following:

1. Update inventories of hazardous chemicals present in the workplace.
2. Assemble material safety data sheets (MSDSs) for all hazardous chemicals.
3. Ensure that all containers and hazardous chemicals are properly labeled.
4. Provide workers with training on the use of hazardous chemicals.
5. Prepare and maintain a written description of the company's hazard communication program.
6. Consider any problems with trade secrets that may be raised by the standard's disclosure requirements.
7. Review state requirements for hazard disclosure.

Despite such right-to-know laws, companies have been known to withhold information from employees. For example, in Chapter 4, we discussed the issue of DuPont's failure to tell workers and affected communities about the high concentrations of the toxin PFOA, used for manufacturing Teflon by DuPont, which employers and community members were exposed to in the 1970s and 1980s.

Employees have certain workplace rights with respect to safety and health on the job that OSHA provides by law. As in our discussion of the public policy exceptions to the employment-at-will doctrine in the preceding chapter, it should be clear that workers have a right to seek safety and health on the job without fear of punishment or recrimination.

12.3d Workplace Violence

Another issue that has become a major problem and is posing challenges to management is escalating violence in the workplace. **Workplace violence** is one of the four leading causes of death in the workplace and the leading cause of death for women.[118] It falls into two categories: (1) violence from an outside source and (2) violence stemming from co-workers. Workplace violence from co-workers cuts across all industries, while certain industries have a greater likelihood of workplace violence from the general public.[119] For example, workplace violence injury rate in private hospitals and home health services has more than doubled since 2009.[120] Most recently, issues of Uber and Lyft drivers being assaulted have highlighted the violence that employees of ride-sharing services are subject to, and the limitations of the protections afforded to them because they are considered to be independent contractors.[121]

In the United States, nearly two million workers report that they are victims of workplace violence each year, and many more victims never report it.[122] Workplace deaths due to violence continue to rise each year, and as of 2019, they were the second leading cause of job death.[123] Overall, companies are making few efforts to address it. Despite the seriousness of this issue, the majority of workplaces do not have a formal program that addresses workplace violence.[124]

The problem of workplace violence shows no sign of abating. Experts note that a variety of factors promote continued violence including an overall greater tolerance for violence, easily available weapons, economic stress, a difficult job market, and insufficient support systems.[125] In the United States, gun law battles are complicating an already difficult situation. Businesses have historically been able to keep guns out of the workplace with a posted sign, but gun advocates have been testing that in the courts.[126]

Who Is Affected? Although no workplace is immune from workplace violence, some workers are at increased risk of workplace violence from the general public. According to OSHA, the workers who are more likely to experience workplace violence include the following[127]:

- Workers who exchange money with the public
- Workers who deliver passengers, goods, or services
- Workers who work alone or in small groups
- Workers who work late at night or very early in the morning
- Workers who work in community settings and homes where they have extensive contact with the public
- Workers who work in high-crime areas

The workers who are direct targets of the violence are not the only people affected. Not only are the family and friends of the victims affected, but also those employees in the workplace who escaped the violence also experience long-term effects. These survivors often spend years dealing with

Ethics In Practice Case

When External Stakeholders Attack

Both customers and employees are primary stakeholders, and so when one begins to attack the other, stakeholder management becomes even more challenging. The problem of customer violence is real and appears to be growing. One form of workplace homicide is on the rise: assaults on employees by customers. The number is relatively low in terms of overall workplace fatalities, but the upward trend is a concern. In a survey of workplace violence, the Institute of Finance and Management (IOFM) found that 61 percent of the 307 organizations surveyed believe that abuse of employees by customers has become significantly worse. Sometimes the abuse is simply verbal, but other times it can result in serious injury and sometimes death. And this only became worse during the pandemic when security guards and employees were trying to enforce mask-wearing mandates. In one notable case, a Family Dollar security guard was shot and killed for trying to enforce mask-wearing.

1. Business cannot refer a customer to an EAP as it can with an employee. It also is not possible to screen and select,

much less train, customers as one does for employees. What can a business do to protect its employees from violent customers?
2. Why is customer violence on the increase? Is it the fault of the customer, the employees or organization, and/or society?
3. What actions or policies do you recommend that managers initiate to stem this growing problem?

Sources: Andrea Lebron, "The Latest on Workplace Violence Statistics," *Rave Mobile Safety* (February 8, 2021), https://www.ravemobilesafety.com/blog/latest-workplace-violence-statistics, accessed May 17, 2021; "The Customer Isn't Always Right," *Security Director's Report* (June 2013), 1–11; "Master Guide to Workplace Violence," *IOFM* (2013), http://www.iofm.com/research/view/master-guide-toworkplace-violence (cited in *Security Director's Report*, 2013), accessed May 17, 2021.

Figure 12-3 OSHA's Recommendations for Preventing Workplace Violence

The best protection employers can offer is to establish a zero-tolerance policy toward workplace violence against or by their employees. The employer should establish a workplace violence prevention program or incorporate the information into an existing accident prevention program, employee handbook, or manual of standard operating procedures. It is critical to ensure that all employees know the policy and understand that all claims of workplace violence will be investigated and remedied promptly. In addition, employers can offer additional protections such as the following:

1. Provide safety education for employees so they know what conduct is not acceptable, what to do if they witness or are subjected to workplace violence, and how to protect themselves.
2. Secure the workplace. Where appropriate to the business, install video surveillance, extra lighting, and alarm systems and minimize access by outsiders through identification badges, electronic keys, and guards.

3. Provide drop safes to limit the amount of cash on hand. Keep a minimal amount of cash in registers during evenings and late-night hours.
4. Equip field staff with cellular phones and hand-held alarms or noise devices, and require them to prepare a daily work plan and keep a contact person informed of their location throughout the day. Keep employer-provided vehicles properly maintained.
5. Instruct employees not to enter any location where they feel unsafe. Introduce a "buddy system" or provide an escort service or police assistance in potentially dangerous situations or at night.
6. Develop policies and procedures covering visits by home health-care providers. Address the conduct of home visits, the presence of others in the home during visits, and the worker's right to refuse to provide services in a clearly hazardous situation.

Source: "What Can These Employers Do to Help Protect These Employees," *Workplace Violence OSHA Fact Sheet.* http://www.osha.gov/OshDoc/data_General_Facts/factsheet-workplace-violence.pdf, accessed May 17, 2021.

the after-effects.[128] Many fear returning to work, and some never do. They will often play the event over in their minds, unable to forget what happened. Victoria Spang is a marketing director who hid in the personnel office when a client of her law firm came in with assault weapons, killing eight people and wounding six. "No one ever forgets. You'd walk by people's cubicles, and they would keep pictures of the victims up. It's a moment in life you'll always remember."[129]

Guidelines on Prevention of Violence. The federal OSHA has a "general duty clause" that mandates employers to provide safe workplaces; however, it does not set forth specific standards or requirements addressing violence and has stated it will not try to regulate "random antisocial acts."[130] OSHA will apply the general duty clause to determine whether the violent act arose from events that should have been foreseen by the company. Specifically,

the company will be liable when (1) the employer neglected to keep the workplace free from a hazard, (2) the hazard was one that is generally recognized by the employer or the industry, (3) the hazard was already causing or was likely to cause serious harm, and (4) elimination or removal of the hazard was feasible.[131]

Management has both the legal and moral duty to address the problem of workplace violence. Companies have barely begun to put meaningful safety measures into place, but such measures will become more important in the future. Programs that deal with crises, and long-range efforts to bring about safer workplace environments, will be essential. Figure 12-3 lists OSHA's recommendations for what employers can do to protect their employees from workplace violence. Beyond this, there are a number of different recommended actions companies may take to anticipate and prevent workplace violence before it occurs.[132]

Summary

Critical employee stakeholder issues include the rights to and expectations of privacy, safety, and health and wellness. These issues should be seen as extensions of the issues and rights outlined in Chapter 11. With the rapid development of new technologies, workplace privacy has increasingly become a serious issue. The wealth of available technology presents new challenges for companies as they weigh the importance of knowing their workers' activities against the importance of maintaining trust and morale. The collection and use of employee information, as well as the issue of employee monitoring, require employers to assess the need for such information, including whether and how much

to invest in the sophisticated technologies and how their employees might react. Other privacy issues include the use of integrity and drug testing in the workplace and the controversies with using these when state laws vary.

Of equal, if not more, importance to employee stakeholders are the issues of workplace health and wellness, including mental health and work-life balance, which have only become more challenging in the wake of the coronavirus pandemic and the Zoom fatigue that many experience in working remotely. The need for employees to take family leave also impacts the work environment. While many might think that smoking, vaping, and drug/alcohol use in the workforce might have declined with remote work, the opposite is in fact the case. Hence, employers would be wise to develop a comprehensive framework for addressing these issues to protect the health and well-being of their employees. Wise managers will develop policies for dealing with these issues, as well as their privacy and due-process implications.

The workplace safety problem, when it was more fully realized, led to the creation of OSHA. OSHA is the federal government's major instrument for protecting workers on the job. State-promulgated right-to-know laws, as well as federal statutes, have been passed in recent years to provide employees with an added measure of protection, especially against harmful effects of exposure to chemicals and toxic substances, as happened with the DuPont PFOA disaster. However, existing laws and regulations deal only with known problems.

As the world changes, so do the threats to worker health and safety. Unexpected or undetected threats to workers' health and safety are certain to occur and will represent new challenges for managers. Another issue affecting employees is the growing issue of violence in the workplace, which is exacting a heavy toll, and businesses must be responsive. Socially responsible companies will strive to move beyond what is being required by law and to do what is right and fair for their employee stakeholders.

Key Terms

Americans with Disabilities Act (ADA), p. 276
background checks, p. 275
ban-the-box, p. 275
broad brush EAP, p. 280
burnout, p. 283
chief privacy officers (CPOs), p. 281
consumer reports, p. 275
drug testing, p. 279
Electronic Communication Privacy Act (ECPA) of 1986, p. 273
Employee and Student Online Privacy Protection Act (ESOPPA), p. 273
Employee Assistance Programs (EAPs), p. 280
Employee Polygraph Protection Act (EPPA), p. 278

Equal Employment Opportunity Commission (EEOC), p. 273
Fair Chance to Compete for Jobs Act of 2019, p. 275
Fair Credit Reporting Act (FCRA), p. 275
Families First Coronavirus Response Act (FFCRA), p. 284
Family and Medical Leave Act (FMLA), p. 284
family-friendly, p. 283
Federal Trade Commission (FTC), p. 275
integrity tests (also known as *honesty tests*), p. 278
Occupational Safety and Health Administration (OSHA), p. 285

personality test, p. 278
polygraph, p. 278
Privacy Act of 1974, p. 274
privacy in the workplace, p. 273
right-to-know laws, p. 286
smoking in the workplace, p. 284
type 1 error, p. 279
type 2 error, p. 279
USA Patriot Act, p. 274
work-life balance, p. 283
workplace privacy, p. 273
workplace violence, p. 287
Zoom fatigue, p. 272

Discussion Questions

1. In your own words, describe what privacy means and what privacy protection companies should give employees.

2. How has technology affected workplace privacy? What are the implications for the social contract between firms and their employees?

3. Enumerate the strengths and weaknesses of integrity tests as a management tool for decision making. Under what circumstances could management most legitimately argue that integrity testing is necessary?

4. Should employers continue to do drug testing for things like marijuana, which continues to be controversial with varying state laws? Why or why not?

5. Which two of the six policy guidelines on the issue of privacy presented in this chapter do you think are the most important? Why?

6. Identify work-life balance issues that affect employees today. How has technology helped or hindered the balancing act?

7. Describe some of the challenges for employers assisting with mental health issues in the workplace. How is this different from other health issues such as smoking, vaping, and drug use? Should employers provide comprehensive health and wellness assistance for all of these issues?

8. What are some of the central issues affecting workplace safety today?

9. Identify the privacy, health, and due-process ramifications of violence in the workplace.

Endnotes

1. See Jose Maria Barrero, Nicholas Bloom, and Steven J. Davis, "Why Working from Home Will Stick," *Becker Friedman Institute at the University of Chicago*, https://bfi.uchicago.edu/insight/finding/why-working-from-home-will-stick/?campaign_id=134&emc=edit_db_20210506&instance_id=30347&nl=debatable&regi_id=47538893&segment_id=57421&te=1&user_id=7dcb7294be513e5616998f4c8360a9ce. Accessed May 10, 2021; Spencer Bokat-Lindell, "Debatable: Get Back to Work!" *The New York Times* (May 6, 2021), https://static.nytimes.com/email-content/DB_sample.html. Accessed May 10, 2021.

2. Ibid.

3. Jess Huang, Alexis Krivkovich, Ishanaa Rambachan, and Lareina Yee, "For Mothers in the Workplace, a Year (and Counting) Like No Other," *McKinsey & Company* (May 5, 2021), https://www.mckinsey.com/featured-insights/diversity-and-inclusion/for-mothers-in-the-workplace-a-year-and-counting-like-no-other. Accessed May 10, 2021.

4. Bokat-Lindell, 2021.

5. "A New Study Suggests that 'Zoom Fatigue' Is Worse for Women than Men," *The Economist* (April 17, 2021), https://www.economist.com/graphic-detail/2021/04/17/a-new-study-suggests-that-zoom-fatigue-is-worse-for-women-than-men. Accessed May 12, 2021.

6. Nexsen Pruet, PLLC, "2021: We Thought You Would Never Get Here and Now that You Are, What Can Employers Expect," *JDSupra* (January 7, 2021), https://www.jdsupra.com/legalnews/2021-we-thought-you-would-never-get-5301925/. Accessed May 10, 2021.

7. Carrie Schochet, "10 Workplace Trends to Watch for in 2021," *Forbes* (January 11, 2021), https://www.forbes.com/sites/forbesbusinesscouncil/2021/01/11/10-workplace-trends-to-watch-for-in-2021/?sh=75a3e9f13ddf. Accessed May 11, 2021.

8. Pruet, 2021.

9. Daisuke Wakabayashi, "Google's Plan for the Future of Work: Privacy Robots and Balloon Walls," *The New York Times* (May 3, 2021), https://www.nytimes.com/2021/04/30/technology/google-back-to-office-workers.html?te=1&nl=debatable&emc=edit_db_20210510. Accessed May 10, 2021.

10. Gregory Hamel, "Definition of Workplace Privacy," *Small Business Chronicle*, https://smallbusiness.chron.com/definition-workplace-privacy-15419.html. Accessed May 11, 2021.

11. Patricia H. Werhane, *Persons, Rights, and Corporations* (Englewood Cliffs, NJ: Prentice Hall, 1985), 118.

12. Ibid.

13. Electronic Privacy Information Center, "Workplace Privacy," http://www.epic.org/privacy/workplace. Accessed May 17, 2021.

14. "State Social Media Privacy Laws," National Conference of State Legislatures (April 7, 2021), https://www.ncsl.org/research/telecommunications-and-information-technology/state-laws-prohibiting-access-to-social-media-usernames-and-passwords.aspx. Accessed May 12, 2021.

15. Susan K. Livio, "N.J. Supreme Court Upholds Privacy of Personal E-Mails Accessed at Work," *NJ.com* (March 30, 2010), http://www.nj.com/news/index.ssf/2010/03/nj_supreme_court_sets_new_ruli.html. Accessed May 17, 2021.

16. Ibid.

17. Ibid.

18. See "State Social Media Privacy Laws," National Conference of State Legislatures (April 7, 2021), https://www.ncsl.org/research/telecommunications-and-information-technology/state-laws-prohibiting-access-to-social-media-usernames-and-passwords.aspx. Accessed May 12, 2021; Gauri Punjabi, "Main Social Media Employee Privacy Law Goes into Effect October 15, 2015," Mintz Levin (September 20, 2015), https://www.employmentmattersblog.com/2015/09/maine-social-media-employee-privacy-law-goes-into-effect-october-15-2015/. Accessed May 12, 2021.

19. Brooke Auxier, Lee Rainie, Monica Anderson, Andrew Perrin, Madhu Kumar, and Erica Turner, "Americans and Privacy: Concerned, Confused and Feeling Lack of Control," *Pew Research Center* (November 15, 2019), https://www.pewresearch.org/internet/2019/11/15/americans-and-privacy-concerned-confused-and-feeling-lack-of-control-over-their-personal-information/. Accessed May 13, 2021.

20. Privacy Rights Clearinghouse, "Privacy Today: A Review" (May 5, 2016), http://www.privacyrights.org/ar/Privacy-IssuesList.htm#D. Accessed May 17, 2021.

21. Tom Spiggle, "Can Employers Monitor Employees Who Work from Home Due to the Coronavirus?," *Forbes* (May 21, 2020), https://www.forbes.com/sites/tomspiggle/2020/05/21/can-employers-monitor-employees-who-work-from-home-due-to-the-coronavirus/?sh=1c5037222fb7. Accessed May 13, 2021.

22. Identity Theft Resource Center, "Data Breaches in the Healthcare Industry Continue Due to Availability of Valuable Information," ITRC (August 11, 2020), https://www.idtheftcenter.org/data-breaches-in-the-healthcare-industry-continue-due-to-availability-of-valuable-information/. Accessed May 13, 2021.

23. Beth Avery and Han Lu, "Ban the Box: U.S Cities, Counties, and States Adopt Fair Hiring Policies," *National Employment Law Project* (September 30, 2020), https://www.nelp.org/publication/ban-the-box-fair-chance-hiring-state-and-local-guide/. Accessed May 13, 2021.

24. Ibid.

25. Ibid.

26. Shelbie Watts, "State Background Check Laws that Are New in 2021," *Homebase* (December 17, 2020), https://joinhomebase.com/blog/background-check-laws-2021/. Accessed May 13, 2021.

27. Privacy Rights Clearinghouse, "Employment Background Checks" (January 17, 2019), https://privacyrights.org/consumer-guides/employment-background-checks-jobseekers-guide. Accessed May 13, 2021.

28. Ibid.

29. Tony Guerra, "Can You Ask if Someone Committed a Crime During an Interview?" *Houston Chronicle.com*, https://work.chron.com/behaviorbased-openended-interview-questions-9390.html. Accessed May 13, 2021.

30. Claire Zillman, "Why Whole Foods, Dollar General, and Panera Have All Been Sued over a Tiny Hiring Technicality," *Fortune* (January 16, 2015), http://fortune.com/2015/01/16/whole-foods-dollar-general-panera-hiring-lawsuit/. Accessed May 28, 2016.

31. Jim Giuliana, "Recruiting: EEOC Warns about Background Checks," *HR Morning* (January 6, 2010), http://www.hrmorning.com/recruiting-eeoc-warns-aboutbackground-checks/. Accessed May 22, 2016.

32. "Gig Employer Hit with Background Check Class Action," *Hunton Employment & Labor Perspectives* (April 14, 2021), https://www.huntonlaborblog.com/2021/04/articles/criminal-background-checks/gig-employer-hit-with-background-check-class-action/. Accessed May 13, 2021.

33. Ibid.

34. Privacy Rights Clearinghouse, 2016.

35. EEOC, "Enforcement Guidance on the Consideration of Arrest and Conviction Records in Employment Decisions under Title VII of the Civil Rights Act," https://www.eeoc.gov/laws/guidance/enforcement-guidance-consideration-arrest-and-conviction-records-employment-decisions. Accessed May 17, 2021.

36. Rachel Burke, "The Use of Background Checks to Make Employment Decisions Is not Without Peril," *Employer Law Report* (October 14, 2015), https://www.lexology.com/library/detail.aspx?g=67ef74bc-357f-4e12-9c0d-7c927f96df00. Accessed May 17, 2021.

37. U.S. Equal Opportunity Commission, "Dollar General to Pay $6 Million to Settle EEOC Class Race Discrimination Suit," *EEOC.gov* (November 18, 2019), https://www.eeoc.gov/newsroom/dollar-general-pay-6-million-settle-eeoc-class-race-discrimination-suit. Accessed May 13, 2021.

38. U.S. Equal Opportunity Commission, "What You Should Know: The EEOC and Arrest and Conviction Records, *EEOC.gov*, https://www.eeoc.gov/laws/guidance/what-you-should-know-eeoc-and-arrest-and-conviction-records. Accessed May 13, 2021.

39. Ibid.

40. Burke, 2015.

41. Brian Kropp, "9 Work Trends that HR Leaders Can't Ignore in 2021," *Gartner* (January 21, 2021), https://www.gartner.com/smarterwithgartner/9-work-trends-that-hr-leaders-cant-ignore-in-2021/. Accessed May 13, 2021.

42. Reid Blackman, "How to Monitor Your Employees—While Respecting Their Privacy," *Harvard Business Review* (May 28, 2020), https://hbr.org/2020/05/how-to-monitor-your-employees-while-respecting-their-privacy. Accessed May 11, 2021.

43. Nandita Bose, "Amazon's Surveillance Can Boost Output and Possibly Limit Unions—Study," *Reuters* (September 15, 2020), https://www.reuters.com/article/amazon-com-workers-surveillance/amazons-surveillance-can-boost-output-and-possibly-limit-unions-study-idUSKBN25S3F2. Accessed May 11, 2021.

44. Ibid.

45. Nancy J. King, "Electronic Monitoring to Promote National Security Impacts Workplace Privacy," *Employee Responsibilities and Rights Journal* (September 2003), 127–147.

46. Kristin Stoller, "When Employers Track Their Productivity: Here's Why," *Forbes* (May 5, 2021), https://www.forbes.com/sites/kristinstoller/2021/05/05/employees-are-more-likely-to-pretend-theyre-working-when-employers-track-their-productivity-heres-why/?sh=506ef8fb49c2. Accessed May 13, 2021.

47. Ceylan Yeginsu, "If Workers Slack Off, the Wristband Will Know (And Amazon Has a Patent for It)," *The New York Times* (February 1, 2018), https://www.nytimes.com/2018/02/01/technology/amazon-wristband-tracking-privacy.html. Accessed May 13, 2021.

48. Tom Spiggle, "Can Employers Monitor Employees Who Work from Home Due to the Coronavirus?," *Forbes* (May 21, 2020), https://www.forbes.com/sites/tomspiggle/2020/05/21/can-employers-monitor-employees-who-work-from-home-due-to-the-coronavirus/?sh=1c5037222fb7. Accessed May 13, 2021.

49. John P. Mello Jr., "Camera Phones a Flashpoint of Concern," *Boston Works* (April 11, 2004), G7.

50. "Employee Monitoring Solution Market to Garner $3.84 Bn Worth by 2023," *GlobeNewswire* (July 31, 2019), https://www.globenewswire.com/news-release/2019/07/31/1894451/0/en/Employee-Monitoring-Solution-Market-to-Garner-3-84-Bn-Worth-by-2023-Workforce-Balance-to-Initiate-Growth-for-Employee-Monitoring-Solution-Market.html. Accessed May 13, 2021.

51. Blackman, 2020.

52. Ibid.

53. Tessa West, "The Lies We Tell at Work—and the Damage They Do," *The Wall Street Journal* (March 27, 2020), https://www.wsj.com/articles/the-lies-we-tell-at-workand-the-damage-they-do-11585319160. Accessed May 13, 2021.

54. David E. Terpstra, R. Bryan Kethley, Richard T. Foley, and Wanthanee Limpaphayom, "The Nature of Litigation Surrounding Five Screening Devices," *Public Personnel Management* (Spring 2000), 43–54.

55. "Integrity Tests: Not Predictive and Only 37–64% Accurate," *Converus*, https://converus.com/integrity-tests/. Accessed May 13, 2021.

56. "Is This the Moment of Truth for Corporate Integrity?," *EY Global Integrity Report 2020*, https://www.google.com/url?sa=t&rct=j&q=&esrc=s&source=web&cd=&ved=2ahUKEwiDnqG3-sfwAhVEGs0KHaBnBV0QFjAPegQIFRAD&url=https%3A%2F%2Fassets.ey.com%2Fcontent%2Fdam%2Fey-sites%2Fey-com%2Fen_gl%2Ftopics%2Fassurance%2Fassurance-pdfs%2Fey-is-this-the-moment-of-truth-for-corporate-integrity.pdf&usg=AOvVaw3SDFEWjhK2IONRKNEamAE3. Accessed May 13, 2021.

57. Dori Meinert, "What Do Personality Tests Really Reveal?" *Society for Human Resource Management* (June 1, 2015), https://www.shrm.org/publications/hrmagazine/editorialcontent/2015/0615/pages/0615-personality-tests.aspx. Accessed May 13, 2017.

58. Gregory M. Lousig-Nont, "Seven Deadly Hiring Mistakes," *Supervision* (April 2003), 18–19.

59. U.S. Office of Personnel Management, https://www.opm.gov/policy-data-oversight/assessment-and-selection/other-assessment-methods/integrityhonesty-tests/. Accessed May 13, 2021.

60. Larry R. Seegull and Emily J. Caputo, "When a Test Turns into a Trial," *ABA Business Law Section* (January/February, 2006), http://apps.americanbar.org/buslaw/blt/2006-01-02/caputo.html. Accessed May 13, 2021.

61. Bill Roberts, "Your Cheating Heart," *SHRM HR Magazine* (June 1, 2011), https://www.shrm.org/publications/hrmagazine/editorialcontent/2011/0611/pages/0611roberts.aspx. Accessed May 13, 2021.

62. Henry Claypool, "Job Hiring Increasingly Relies on Personality Tests, but That Can Bar People with Disabilities," *NBC News* (March 4, 2021), https://www.nbcnews.com/think/opinion/job-hiring-increasingly-relies-personality-tests-they-can-bar-people-ncna1259466. Accessed May 13, 2021.

63. Thomas Ahearn, "EEOC Asked to Clarify Authority to Investigate Bias in AI Hiring Technologies," *Employment Screening Services* (December 9, 2020), https://www.esrcheck.com/wordpress/2020/12/09/eeoc-bias-ai-hiring-technologies/. Accessed May 13, 2021.

64. Ibid.

65. Whitney Martin, "The Problem with Using Personality Tests for Hiring," *Harvard Business Review* (August 27, 2014), https://hbr.org/2014/08/the-problem-with-using-personality-tests-for-hiring. Accessed May 13, 2021.

66. Quest Diagnostics, "Workforce Drug Testing Positivity Climbed to Highest Rate in 16 Years, New Quest Diagnostics Drug Testing Index Analysis Finds," *Questdiagnostics.com* (August 25, 2020), https://www.questdiagnostics.com/home/physicians/health-trends/drug-testing/. Accessed May 14, 2021.

67. U.S. Government Accountability Office, GAO-19-9, https://www.gao.gov/products/gao-19-9. Accessed May 13, 2021.

68. Jim Akin, "The Truth About False Positives and Employment Drug Screens," *GoodHire* (July 16, 2020), https://www.goodhire.com/blog/the-truth-about-false-positives-and-employment-drug-screens/. Accessed May 14, 2021.

69. Valentina Sanchez, "Is Cannabis Use the Same as Off-Duty Drinking by Workers? Many Companies Still Say No," *CNBC* (July 27, 2019), https://www.cnbc.com/2019/07/27/will-cannabis-use-soon-be-the-same-as-off-duty-drinking-by-workers.html. Accessed May 14, 2021.

70. Ibid.

71. ACOEM, "Ethical Aspects of Drug Testing," https://acoem.org/Guidance-and-Position-Statements/Guidance-and-Position-Statements/Ethical-Aspects-of-Drug-Testing-en (July 22, 2019). Accessed May 14, 2021.

72. Eileen Smith, "How to Choose the Right EAP for Your Employee," *Employee Benefit News* (November 1, 2000).

73. Sean Fogarty, "EAPs New Role: A Core Strategic Element," *Employee Benefits Advisor* (April 2010), 40–46.

74. Katie Lynch, "Is it Finally Time to Reconsider Employee Assistance Programs?," *Forbes* (January 19, 2021), https://www.forbes.com/sites/forbeshumanresourcescouncil/2021/01/19/is-it-finally-time-to-reconsider-employee-assistance-programs/?sh=1fd9c4c028b7. Accessed May 14, 2021.

75. Ibid.

76. International Employee Assistance Professionals Association, https://www.eapassn.org/. Accessed May 14, 2021.

77. Frederick S. Lane III, *The Naked Employee* (New York: AMACOM, 2003).

78. Rohini Radhakrishnan, "What Is Health and Wellness?" (January 27, 2021), What Is Health and Wellness? (medicinenet.com). Accessed May 18, 2021.

79. Alex Janin, "How to Deal with Stress at Work," *The Wall Street Journal* (January 8, 2021), https://www.wsj.com/articles/how-to-deal-with-stress-at-work-11610122418. Accessed May 16, 2021.

80. Allison Pohle, "How to Improve Your Work-Life Balance," *The Wall Street Journal* (March 31, 2021), https://www.wsj.com/articles/how-to-improve-your-work-life-balance-11608244271?mod=article_inline. Accessed May 16, 2021.

81. Ibid.

82. AIHR Digital, "9 Workplace Trends to Watch Out for in 2021," *AIHR DigitalHRtech.com*, https://www.digitalhrtech.com/workplace-wellness-trends/. Accessed May 16, 2021.

83. Ibid.

84. See AIHR Digital, 2021; Michelle Andrews, "Why Employers' Incentives for Weight Loss Fall Flat with Workers," *South Carolina NPR* (January 8, 2016), http://www.npr.org/sections/health-shots/2016/01/08/462380096/why-employers-incentives-for-weight-loss-fall-flat-with-workers. Accessed May 17, 2021.

85. Scott Kobil, "Well Done? EEOC's New Proposed Rules Would Limit Employer Wellness Programs to De Minimis Incentives—with Significant Exceptions," *The National Law Review* (January 12, 2021), https://www.natlawreview.com/article/well-done-eeoc-s-new-proposed-rules-would-limit-employer-wellness-programs-to-de. Accessed May 16, 2021.

86. Al Lewis, "New EEOC Wellness Rules are Already Dead," *BenefitsPro* (January 22, 2021), https://www.benefitspro.com/2021/01/22/new-eeoc-wellness-rules-are-already-dead/?slreturn=20210416090056. Accessed May 16, 2021.

87. Vipal Monga, "Opioid Use Hits Construction Industry as Overdoses Soar," *The Wall Street Journal* (January 5, 2021), https://www.wsj.com/articles/opioid-use-hits-construction-industry-as-overdoses-soar-11609855200. Accessed May 16, 2021.

88. Naz Beheshti, "10 Eye-Opening Statistics on the Mental Health Impact of the Coronavirus Pandemic," *Forbes* (May 28, 2020), https://www.forbes.com/sites/nazbeheshti/2020/05/28/10-eye-opening-statistics-on-the-mental-health-impact-of-the-coronavirus-pandemic/?sh=1f01560c2df0. Accessed May 16, 2021.

89. Halle Kiefer, "Michael Phelps, Fellow Athletes Discuss 'Post Olympic Depression' in HBO's Weight of Gold Trailer," *New York Magazine* (July 20, 2020), https://www.vulture.com/2020/07/athletes-discuss-mental-health-hbo-weight-of-gold-trailer.html. Accessed May 16, 2021.

90. Pamela Spence, "How Covid-19 Reshapes the Mental Health Needs of Workers," *EY* (July 29, 2020), https://www.ey.com/en_us/health/how-covid-19-reshapes-the-mental-health-needs-of-workers. Accessed May 16, 2021.

91. See G. E. Miller, "The U.S. Is the Most Overworked Developed Nation in the World," *Something Finance* (January 13, 2020), https://20somethingfinance.com/american-hours-worked-productivity-vacation/. Accessed May 16, 2021; Stacy Weckesser, "Americans Are Now Working More Hours than any Country in the World," *Blue Water Credit* (July 21, 2020), https://bluewatercredit.com/americans-now-working-hours-country-world/. Accessed May 16, 2021.

92. Allison Pohle, "How to Improve Your Worklife Balance," *The Wall Street Journal* (March 31, 2021), https://www.wsj.com/articles/how-to-improve-your-work-life-balance-11608244271?mod=article_inline. Accessed May 16, 2021.

93. Christopher Mullen, "Work-Life Balance Is a Thing of the Past: Now It's All About Work-Life Negotiation," *Forbes* (March 16, 2021), https://www.forbes.com/sites/forbescoachescouncil/2021/03/16/work-life-balance-is-a-thing-of-the-past-now-its-all-about-work-life-negotiation/?sh=4967bd9751ab. Accessed May 15, 2021.

94. Ibid.

95. Alan Kohll, "The Evolving Definition of Work-Life Balance," *Forbes* (March 27, 2018), https://www.forbes.com/sites/alankohll/2018/03/27/the-evolving-definition-of-work-life-balance/?sh=5fa710ce9ed3. Accessed May 19, 2021.

96. Mullen, 2021.

97. Ioana Lupu and Mayra Ruiz-Castro, "Work-Life Balance Is a Cycle, Not an Achievement," *Harvard Business Review* (January 29, 2021), https://hbr.org/2021/01/work-life-balance-is-a-cycle-not-an-achievement. Accessed May 17, 2021.

98. "Military Expansions in FMLA Are Now Law," *HR Focus* (January 2010), 2.

99. U.S. Department of Labor, "2018 Employee and Worksite Perspectives of the Family Medical Leave Act National Surveys," https://www.dol.gov/agencies/oasp/evaluation/fmla2018. Accessed May 17, 2021.

100. Ibid.

101. Alexa Rombert, Megan Diaz, Jodie Briggs, Daniel Stephens, Basmah Rahman, Amanda Graham, and Barbara Schillo, "Vaping in the Workplace: Prevalence and Attitudes Among Employed US Adults," *Journal of Occupational and Environmental Medicine* (January 2021), Vol 63 (1), pp. 10–17.

102. The Centers for Disease Control, "Smoking by Industry, Occupation & Gender," *CDC.gov*, https://www.cdc.gov/niosh/topics/tobacco/tobaccosmoking.html. Accessed May 17, 2021.

103. "Workforce Drug Use on the Rise," *EHS Today* (May 31, 2017), https://www.ehstoday.com/safety/article/21919044/workforce-drug-use-on-the-rise-infographic. Accessed May 17, 2021.

104. Vipal Monga, "Opioid Use Hits Construction Industry as Overdoses Soar," *The Wall Street Journal* (January 5, 2021), https://www.wsj.com/articles/opioid-use-hits-construction-industry-as-overdoses-soar-11609855200. Accessed May 17, 2021.

105. Quest, "Workforce Drug Testing Positivity Climbed to Highest Rate in 16 Years," *Quest Diagnostics* (August 20, 2020), https://newsroom.questdiagnostics.com/2020-08-25-Workforce-Drug-Testing-Positivity-Climbed-to-Highest-Rate-in-16-Years-New-Quest-Diagnostics-Drug-Testing-Index-TM-Analysis-Finds. Accessed May 17, 2021.

106. Ibid.

107. Joanne Sammer, "Employers Respond to Rising Substance Abuse with Treatment, Support," *SHRM* (March 5, 2021), https://www.shrm.org/resourcesandtools/hr-topics/benefits/pages/employers-respond-to-rising-substance-abuse-with-treatment-and-support.aspx. Accessed May 17, 2021.

108. Occupational Health and Safety, "NSC Calls for Employers to Brace for Increased Employee Substance Abuse," *OHS Online* (June 12, 2020), https://ohsonline.com/articles/2020/06/12/nsc-calls-for-employers-to-brace-for-increased-employee-substance-abuse.aspx. Accessed May 17, 2021.

109. Ibid.

110. International Labor Organization, "Safety and Health at Work," http://www.ilo.org/global/topics/safety-and-health-at-work/lang--en/index.htm. Accessed May 17, 2021.

111. U.S. Department of Labor, Occupational Safety and Health Administration, https://www.osha.gov/data/commonstats. Accessed May 17, 2021.

112. Legal Information Institute, "Workplace Safety," http://www.law.cornell.edu/wex/workplace_safety. Accessed May 17, 2021.

113. "Union Carbide Fights for Its Life," *Businessweek* (December 24, 1984), 52–56.

114. National Council for Occupational Safety and Health, "Not an Accident: Preventable Deaths 2015," http://www.coshnetwork.org/sites/default/files/Not-an-Accident-2015.pdf. Accessed May 17, 2021.

115. OSHA Regional News Release (September 2, 2015), https://www.osha.gov/pls/oshaweb/owadisp.show_document?p_table=NEWS_RELEASES&p_id=28662. Accessed May 17, 2021.

116. Safety Partners, "7 Most Common Causes of Workplace Accidents," http://www.safetypartnersltd.com/7-most-common-causes-of-workplace-accidents/#.V1TJYOSUQmR. Accessed May 17, 2021.

117. U.S. Department of Labor, OSHA, "Hazard Communication," http://www.osha.gov/pls/oshaweb/owadisp.show_document?p_table=FEDERAL_REGISTER&p_id=13349. Accessed May 17, 2021.

118. U.S. Department of Labor, OSHA, "Workplace Violence," https://www.osha.gov/workplace-violence. Accessed May 17, 2021.

119. Ibid.

120. AFL-CIO, "Death on the Job: The Toll of Neglect" (October 6, 2020), https://aflcio.org/reports/death-job-toll-neglect-2020. Accessed May 17, 2021.

121. See "Rough Ride Share: Why Drivers Are also at Risk of Violence," *The Guardian* (February 6, 2020), https://www.theguardian.com/us-news/2020/feb/06/uber-rideshare-lyft-safety-crime. Accessed May 17, 2021; Molly McHugh, "Uber and Lyft Drivers Work Dangerous Jobs—But They're on Their Own," *Wired* (March 10, 2016), http://www.wired.com/2016/03/uber-lyft-can-much-keep-drivers-safe/. Accessed May 17, 2021.

122. U.S. Department of Labor, OSHA, "Workplace Violence," http://www.osha.gov/SLTC/workplaceviolence/. Accessed May 17, 2021.

123. Ibid.

124. Joy Stephenson-Laws, "Increase Workplace Wellness to Decrease Workplace Violence," *EHS Today* (April 19, 2018), https://www.ehstoday.com/safety/article/21919595/increase-workplace-wellness-to-decrease-workplace-violence. Accessed May 17, 2021.

125. Susan Ladika, "Surging Gun Sales Could Soon Become a Workplace Concern," *SHRM*, https://www.shrm.org/hr-today/news/all-things-work/pages/surging-guns-sales-could-soon-become-a-workplace-concern.aspx. Accessed May 17, 2021.

126. "Workplace Violence: New Regulation, Threats and Best Practices," *Security Director's Report* (May 2010), 1–11.

127. OSHA Fact Sheet, http://www.osha.gov/OshDoc/data_General_Facts/factsheet-workplace-violence.pdf. Accessed May 17, 2021.

128. Stephanie Armour, "Companies, Survivors Suffer Years after Violence at Work," *USA Today* (July 9, 2003), 3A.

129. Ibid., 3A.

130. Cole A. Wist and Hugh C. Thatcher, "Workplace Violence: An American Secret," *Labor and Employment Law Center* (Winter 2010), p. 6.

131. Wist and Thatcher, 6.

132. Prevent Violence at Work, "Basic Recommendations for Preventing Violence in the Workplace," http://www.prevention-violence.com/en/int-210.asp. Accessed May 17, 2021.

13

Employment Discrimination, Diversity, and Inclusion

Chapter Learning Outcomes

After studying this chapter, you should be able to:

1. Discuss the concept of discrimination in the workforce and the evolution of its current paradigm.
2. Chronicle the U.S. civil rights movement and progress regarding protected employee groups in the past 50 years.
3. Outline the essentials of federal discrimination laws.
4. Define and provide examples of the expanded meanings of employment discrimination including disparate treatment and disparate impact and issues in employment discrimination relating to race, color, national origin, sex, age, religion, sexual orientation, genetic information, and disability.
5. Understand and discuss the concepts of diversity and inclusion in the workforce.
6. Discuss the concept of affirmative action and current issues related to diversity management.

In 2020, it seemed that the world reached a tipping point about discrimination. The killing of George Floyd, a black man, by a white Minneapolis police officer provided fuel for an antidiscrimination social movement that had been arguably languishing for decades. And while this sparked a swell of protests about race discrimination, other forms of discrimination, including gender, ethnic, and religious discrimination, were also highlighted in the protests. Under pressure for change, businesses pledged billions of dollars toward new initiatives for diversifying their workforce and training their employees.[1] And yet, a recent Gallup poll showed that about one in four black and Hispanic employees in the United States report having been discriminated against at work in the past year.[2] Additionally, 16 percent of Asian employees reported experiencing discrimination as well.[3]

In the two preceding chapters, we discussed employee rights issues that affect virtually everyone in the workplace. In this chapter, we explore the concept of discrimination in the workforce and then focus on those groups of stakeholders whose employment rights and circumstances are protected by discrimination laws. In the United States, there are **protected groups** who have federal legal protection from discrimination based on aspects such as race, color, religion, national origin, sex (including pregnancy, sexual orientation, or gender identity), age (40 or older), disability, and genetic information (including family medical history).[4] In addition to these federal protections, 22 states and the District of Columbia have laws that protect individuals from employment discrimination based on sexual orientation and gender identity.[5] Many of the issues we review in this chapter have grown out of the general belief that certain employees may face discrimination and that they have workplace rights that should be protected. It is true that the protected groups are protected from discrimination by the law. However, we must remember that legal protection is often not enough. It is very difficult to identify and prove discrimination even though there are laws prohibiting it. Hence, ethical practices are always advocated in the treatment of all employees.

Diversity is the presence of differences within a given setting, including differences in race, ethnicity, gender, or any other number of characteristics.[6] **Inclusion** is the practice of ensuring that people feel a sense of belonging, respect, and support from the organization. Managing diversity and inclusion in the workforce continues to evolve from the days when diversity was approached from an idea of promoting people from groups that continue to be affected by a legacy of discrimination (i.e., affirmative action).

Diversity and inclusion are top priorities in businesses today because they are not only the right thing to do from ethical and stakeholder management perspectives, but they also reflect good business. While most people know this intuitively, the numbers back this up. For example, a recent *McKinsey* study shows that gender-diverse companies are 25 percent more likely to outperform their peers, and ethnically diverse companies are 36 percent more likely to do the same.[7] In another study, *The Wall Street Journal* found that the stocks of companies that score well on diversity outperform their low scoring peers by almost 6 percent.[8] As noted by CEO, president, and chair of

Procter & Gamble, David Taylor, "A diverse team supported by an inclusive environment that values each individual will outperform a homogenous team every time."[9]

In this chapter we examine the legal, moral, and ethical issues related to discrimination, as well as the effective management of diversity in the workplace. To explore these and related issues, we will cover the following major topics in this chapter: the civil rights movement, federal laws that protect against employment discrimination, the types of discrimination (i.e., disparate treatment and disparate impact), a variety of issues related to employment discrimination, diversity in the workforce, and, finally, affirmative action in the workplace.

13.1 The Civil Rights Movement

In the United States, federal antidiscrimination laws date back to the U.S. Constitution—in particular, the First, Fifth, and Fourteenth Amendments, which were designed to forbid religious discrimination and deprivation of employment rights without due process. There were also the Civil Rights Acts of 1866, 1870, and 1871, which were based on these amendments. However, none of these acts was ever effective. Most authorities agree that the Civil Rights Act of 1964 was the effective beginning of the employee protection movement, particularly for those special groups that we will be discussing in this chapter. It would take volumes to trace thoroughly the historical events that led ultimately to passage of this first significant piece of civil rights legislation in the modern period. The act grew out of conflict that had been apparent for years but that erupted in the 1950s and 1960s in the form of protests and boycotts.[10]

Equal opportunity was supposed to be everyone's birthright, but not everyone shared this American dream. Things began to change because of individuals who had the courage to stand up for their rights as U.S. citizens. These individuals include Mrs. Rosa Parks, a black department store worker who was arrested for refusing to yield her bus seat to a white man. One of the leaders of the boycott in protest about the treatment of Mrs. Parks was a young minister, Dr. Martin Luther King Jr., who became one of the most visible spokespersons for the civil rights movement until he was assassinated in 1968. Against this backdrop of minorities being denied access to the American ideal of equal opportunity in employment, Congress finally passed the Civil Rights Act of 1964.[11]

While legislation can promote change, activism also plays a role. For example, the women's movement began in the 1970s. Women's groups began to see that the workplace situation was little better for women than for black Americans and other minorities. Despite the fact that the labor participation rate for women was growing, women were still occupying low-paying jobs. They were making some minor inroads into managerial and professional jobs, but progress was slow.

The 1990s began with the next major civil rights movement, the disability rights movement. The Americans with Disabilities Act (ADA) of 1990 was designed not only to stop discrimination against people with disabilities but also to open up access to buildings and transportation, which in turn opened up access to employment. Around the same time, the transgender movement began to gain ground, with the first international conference on transgender law and employment policy taking place in 1992.

Jump to fall of 2018, and the #MeToo movement exploded as women and allies shared their experiences of sexual harassment in the workplace and called on companies to rethink their leadership. Currently, the Black Lives Matter movement garners international attention in its quest for racial justice and equity in the wake of the tragic deaths of Trayvon Martin, George Floyd, and Breonna Taylor, among others.

What this means for business is that companies must be even more vigilant in addressing issues of discrimination as the workforce composition continues to change. While whites continue to make up the majority of the U.S. labor force (77 percent), Hispanics or Latinos make up 70 percent of the recent growth in the labor market.[12] As of 2019, African Americans and Asians constitute an additional 13 and 6 percent of the labor market, respectively.[13] Women now comprise half of the U.S. labor force (50.4 percent); however, in each state women are still less likely to be in the workforce than men.[14]

Job losses related to the COVID-19 pandemic hit women harder than men, according to one Gallup poll. Explanations from respondents included that the types of jobs women hold were disproportionately affected, as well as that there were greater family demands on women than men related to child care and school closures.[15] The lesbian, gay, bisexual, and transgender/transsexual (**LGBT**) workforce, while also growing, also faced difficulties during the pandemic. While stigma and methodological barriers make it difficult to get an accurate count of the LGBT workplace population, one survey estimated that more than five million LGBT employees may have been affected by the pandemic.[16] A major challenge for business going forward will be to assimilate this increasingly diverse workforce. Federal legislation to bar discrimination based on sexual orientation and gender identity passed in the U.S. House and was under consideration in the Senate, as of this writing.[17] These changes create challenges for firms with operations throughout the country. Diversity issues will continue to evolve with time and employers must stay aware of shifts in this changing landscape. And again, businesses must be vigilant in addressing any hint of discrimination.

One way to understand the changing public policy with respect to employment discrimination is to examine the evolution of federal laws prohibiting discrimination. Once we have a better appreciation of the legal status of protected groups, we can more completely understand the complex issues that have arisen with respect to the evolving meaning of discrimination and its relationship to related workforce issues.

13.2 Federal Laws Prohibiting Discrimination

This section provides an overview of the major laws that have been passed in the United States to protect workers against discrimination. We will focus our discussion on legislation at the federal level that has been created in the past 60 years; while there are state and local laws that address many of these same topics, lack of space does not permit their consideration here. We will discuss issues arising from the various forms of discrimination in more detail later in this chapter. Our purpose in this section is to provide an overview of antidiscrimination laws and the major federal agencies that enforce those laws.

13.2a Title VII of the Civil Rights Act of 1964

Title VII of the Civil Rights Act of 1964, as amended, prohibits discrimination in hiring, promotion, discharge, pay, fringe benefits, and other aspects of employment on the basis of race, color, religion, sex, or national origin. It was extended to cover federal, state, and local employers and educational institutions by the Equal Employment Opportunity Act of 1972. The amendment to Title VII also gave the Equal

Employment Opportunity Commission (EEOC) the authority to file suits in federal district court against employers in the private sector on behalf of individuals whose charges had not been successfully conciliated. In 1978, Title VII was amended to include the Pregnancy Discrimination Act, which requires employers to treat pregnancy and pregnancy-related medical conditions in the same manner as any other medical disability with respect to all terms and conditions of employment, including employee health benefits.[18]

Title VII also prohibits firms from retaliating against employees who file discrimination claims. In 2006, the U.S. Supreme Court strengthened the anti-retaliation provisions of Title VII. The High Court ruled that an employee could establish a retaliation claim even when they were not terminated or demoted. While the parameters of Title VII have not changed much in recent years, the applications of Title VII have changed in response to social changes. In 2020, the U.S. Supreme Court expanded Title VII to prohibit employment discrimination based on homosexuality or transgender status—effectively bringing sexual preference and transgender status under the protected classes definition. In 2020, the EEOC received 1,857 charges that included allegations of sex discrimination related to sexual orientation and/or gender identity/transgender status, and they resolved most of these through voluntary agreements and approximately $6 million in monetary relief for workers.[19] Figure 13-1 presents an overview of Title VII's coverage.

Figure 13-1 Title VII of the Civil Rights Act of 1964

EMPLOYMENT discrimination based on race, color, religion, sex, or national origin is prohibited by Title VII of the Civil Rights Act of 1964.

Title VII covers private employers, state and local governments, and educational institutions that have 15 or more employees. The federal government, private and public employment agencies, labor organizations, and joint labor–management committees for apprenticeship and training also must abide by the law.

It is illegal under Title VII to discriminate in:

- Hiring and firing;
- Compensation, assignment, or classification of employees;
- Transfer, promotion, layoff, or recall;
- Job advertisements;
- Recruitment;
- Testing;
- Use of company facilities;
- Training and apprenticeship programs;
- Fringe benefits;
- Pay, retirement plans, and disability leave; or
- Other terms and conditions of employment.

Under the law, pregnancy, childbirth, and related medical conditions must be treated in the same manner as any other non-pregnancy-related illness or disability.

Title VII prohibits retaliation against a person who files a charge of discrimination, participates in an investigation, or opposes an unlawful employment practice.

Employment agencies may not discriminate in receiving, classifying, or referring applications for employment or in their job advertisements.

Labor unions may not discriminate in accepting applications for membership, classifying members, referrals, training and apprenticeship programs, and advertising for jobs. It is illegal for a labor union to cause or try to cause an employer to discriminate. It is also illegal for an employer to cause or try to cause a union to discriminate.

Source: U.S. Equal Employment Opportunity Commission, https://www.eeoc.gov/statutes/title-vii-civil-rights-act-1964, accessed May 28, 2021.

13.2b Age Discrimination in Employment Act of 1967

This law protects workers aged 40 years and older from arbitrary age discrimination in hiring, discharge, pay, promotions, fringe benefits, and other aspects of employment. It is designed to promote employment of older people based on ability rather than age and to help employers and workers find ways to meet problems arising from the impact of age on employment. The act does not protect employees under age 40 from age discrimination, but it does protect anyone from retaliation for complaining about age discrimination or being closely associated with someone who does.[20]

Like the provisions of Title VII, the **Age Discrimination in Employment Act (ADEA)** does not apply where age is a **bona fide occupational qualification (BFOQ)**—a qualification that might ordinarily be argued as being a basis for discrimination but for which a company can legitimately argue that age is job-related and necessary. For example, there are mandatory retirement ages for bus drivers and airline pilots for safety reasons.[21] The act also does not bar employers from differentiating among employees based on reasonable factors other than age.[22] To prove unlawful discrimination, employees must prove that their age was a determining factor in the employer's decision to take an adverse employment action. For example, courts and the federal EEOC have found that an employer's use of age-related code words such as "energetic," "new blood," "fresh," and "set in their ways" when describing candidates and employees may be examples of age discrimination.[23]

Unfortunately, many employers might not even realize that they are being discriminatory with such language. This could be an example of **ethical blindness** that occurs when decision makers behave unethically without even being aware of it—a temporary inability to see the ethical dimension of a decision at stake.[24] It could also be an example of **implicit bias**. Implicit bias occurs when individuals act on the basis of prejudice and stereotypes without intending to

do so.[25] Nevertheless, the law in this case protects against the phenomenon of ethical blindness or implicit bias.

13.2c Equal Pay Act of 1963

As amended, this act prohibits sex discrimination in payment of wages to women and men who perform substantially equal work in the same establishment. Passage of this landmark law marked a significant milestone in helping women, who were the chief victims of unequal pay, to achieve equality in their pay checks.[26] While progress has been made on narrowing wage gaps, it is still fairly wide, with women on average earning about 17 percent less than men. And women of color fare worse, with the pay gap for black women at 39 percent and for Hispanic or Latina women at 47 percent.[27]

To address these issues and more, the Paycheck Fairness Act has been introduced and reintroduced at different times since 1997, but it has failed to pass both chambers of Congress.[28] The legislation, if enacted, would require employers to prove that pay disparities between men and women are job-related. Lobbyists and special interest groups representing small and midsized businesses have expressed their concerns about how the act would restrict their ability to base pay decisions on performance. At this writing, the act was passed by the U.S. House of Representatives, but the fate of the act is unclear.

Figure 13-2 summarizes other details of the **Equal Pay Act of 1963**.

While proposed federal legislation surrounding a Paycheck Fairness Act continues to stall, several states including California, Connecticut, Delaware, North Dakota, and Oregon have passed new laws designed to repair pay discrimination, or at least prohibit employers from discriminating or retaliating against employees who discuss wages.[29] However, these laws are not without controversy. Some critics say that they are based on false accounting of the pay gap, which, when controlled for many factors that explain earnings differences like hours worked, career choice, and

Figure 13-2 Equal Pay Act of 1963

The Equal Pay Act (EPA) prohibits employers from discriminating between men and women on the basis of sex in the payment of wages where they perform substantially equal work under similar working conditions in the same establishment. The law also prohibits employers from reducing the wages of either sex to comply with the law.

A violation may exist where a different wage is paid to a predecessor or successor employee of the opposite sex. Labor organizations may not cause employers to violate the law.

Retaliation against a person who files a charge of equal pay discrimination, participates in an investigation, or opposes an unlawful employment practice also is illegal.

The law protects virtually all private employees, including executive, administrative, professional, and outside sales employees who are exempt from minimum wage and overtime laws. Most federal, state, and local government workers also are covered.

The law does not apply to pay differences based on factors other than sex, such as seniority, merit, or systems that determine wages based on the quantity or quality of items produced or processed.

Many EPA violations may be violations of Title VII of the Civil Rights Act of 1964, which also prohibits sex-based wage discrimination. Such charges may be filed under both statutes.

Sources: *Information for the Private Sector and State and Local Governments: EEOC* (Washington: Equal Employment Opportunity Commission), 9. Also see U.S. Department of Labor, Equal Pay Act of 1963, as amended, http://www.dol.gov/oasam/regs/statutes/equal_pay_act.htm, accessed May 28, 2021.

family roles, goes away.[30] Other critics see that there will be unintended consequences of rising compliance costs and check listing that, in the end, will only hurt women.[31] However, what is not disputable is that businesses must do everything that they can to ensure that women are treated fairly in the workforce, and they need to address and remove any obstacles to equal treatment. We discuss this further in the section on Issues in Employment Discrimination below.

13.2d Rehabilitation Act of 1973, Section 503

This law, as amended, prohibits job discrimination on the basis of a disability. It applies to employers holding federal contracts or subcontracts. In addition, it requires these employers to engage in affirmative action to employ the disabled, a concept we will discuss later in this chapter. Related to this act is the Vietnam Era Veterans Readjustment Assistance Act of 1974, which also prohibits discrimination and requires affirmative action among federal contractors or subcontractors.[32]

13.2e Americans with Disabilities Act

The **Americans with Disabilities Act (ADA)** of 1990, as amended in 2008, prohibits discrimination based on physical or mental disabilities in private places of employment and public accommodation, in addition to requiring transportation systems and communication systems to facilitate access for the disabled. The ADA was modeled after the Rehabilitation Act of 1973, which applies to federal contractors and grantees.[33] The basic provisions of the ADA are detailed in Figure 13-3.

Essentially, the ADA gives individuals with disabilities civil rights protections similar to those provided to individuals based on race, sex, national origin, and religion. The ADA applies not only to private employers but also to state and local governments, employment agencies, and labor unions. Employers of 15 or more employees are covered.

The ADA prohibits discrimination in all employment practices, including job application procedures, hiring, firing, advancement, compensation, training, and other terms, conditions, and privileges of employment. If a person's disability makes it difficult for them to function, firms are expected to make **reasonable accommodations** if doing so does not represent an **undue hardship** for the firm. The act covers qualified individuals with disabilities. Qualified individuals are those who can perform the **essential functions** of the job.[34] The definition of essential function is sometimes difficult to determine. A case in point occurred with golfer Casey Martin when he applied to the PGA for permission to ride a cart in PGA tournaments when other players were walking the course. Much controversy ensued over whether walking the golf course was an essential function of playing

Figure 13-3 The Americans with Disabilities Act

Title I of the Americans with Disabilities Act of 1990 prohibits private employers, state and local governments, employment agencies, and labor unions from discriminating against qualified individuals with disabilities in job application procedures, hiring, firing, advancement, compensation, job training, and other terms, conditions, and privileges of employment. The ADA covers employers with 15 or more employees, including state and local governments. It also applies to employment agencies and to labor organizations. The ADA's nondiscrimination standards also apply to federal sector employees under Section 501 of the Rehabilitation Act, as amended, and its implementing rules.

An individual with a disability is a person who:

- Has a physical or mental impairment that substantially limits one or more major life activities;
- Has a record of such an impairment; or is regarded as having such an impairment.

A qualified employee or applicant with a disability is an individual who, with or without reasonable accommodation, can perform the essential functions of the job in question. Reasonable accommodation may include, but is not limited to:

- Making existing facilities used by employees readily accessible to and usable by persons with disabilities;
- Restructuring jobs (for parallelism), modifying work schedules, and reassigning to a vacant position;
- Acquiring or modifying equipment or devices; adjusting or modifying examinations, training materials, or policies; and providing qualified readers or interpreters.

An employer is required to make a reasonable accommodation to the known disability of a qualified applicant or employee if it would not impose an "undue hardship" on the operation of the employer's business. Undue hardship is defined as an action that requires significant difficulty or expense when considered in light of factors such as an employer's size, financial resources, and the nature and structure of its operation.

An employer generally does not have to provide a reasonable accommodation unless an individual with a disability has asked for one. If an employer believes that a medical condition is causing a performance or conduct problem, it may discuss with the employee how to solve the problem and ask if the employee needs a reasonable accommodation. Once a reasonable accommodation is requested, the employer and the individual should discuss the individual's needs and identify the appropriate reasonable accommodation. Where more than one accommodation would work, the employer may choose the one that is less costly or is easier to provide.

It is also unlawful to retaliate against an individual for opposing employment practices that discriminate based on disability or for filing a discrimination charge, testifying, or participating in any way in an investigation, proceeding, or litigation under the ADA.

Sources: EEOC Facts about the Americans with Disabilities Act https://www.eeoc.gov/eeoc/publications/fs-ada.cfm, accessed May 28, 2021. Also see Department of Justice, Americans with Disabilities Act of 1990, as amended, http://www.ada.gov/, accessed May 28, 2021.

professional golf. The Supreme Court subsequently ruled that he could use a cart because providing the cart was a reasonable accommodation and his use of the cart would not fundamentally alter the game.

The ADA requires that firms make their places of business accessible to people with disabilities as long as doing so does not create an undue hardship. Recently, the ride sharing company Lyft reached a settlement agreement with the U.S. Department of Justice (DOJ) over allegations that the Lyft drivers discriminated against people who use foldable walkers and wheelchairs, in violation of the ADA.[35] The DOJ found that while Lyft had a policy requiring drivers to "make every reasonable effort to transport a passenger and their wheelchair," they did not require drivers to review the company's policy.

Pregnancy discrimination and genetic information nondiscrimination are two issues that also fit under the issue of disabilities discrimination. In fact, the law treats pregnancy as a temporary disability. Genetic discrimination occurs when people are treated differently by their employer or insurance company because they have a gene mutation that causes or increases the risk of an inherited disorder. The protection of that private information guards people from discrimination based on possible future disabilities, and so we discuss it in the context of disabilities as well.

Pregnancy Discrimination. For some time, maternity leave has been an issue for women. In 1987, the Supreme Court upheld a California law that granted pregnant workers four months of unpaid maternity leave and guaranteed that their jobs would be waiting for them when they returned. Justice Thurgood Marshall argued, "By taking pregnancy into account, California's statute allows women, as well as men, to have families without losing their jobs."[36]

The **Pregnancy Discrimination Act of 1978**, an amendment to Title VII, requires employers to treat pregnancy and pregnancy-related medical conditions the same way as any other medical disability with respect to all terms and conditions of employment. While some may think that issues of pregnancy discrimination have subsided since the 1978 act, current statistics show that this is not true. In the last 10 years, more than 50,000 pregnancy discrimination claims were filed with the EEOC and Fair Employment Practices Agencies in the United States.[37]

New ethical and legal issues have surfaced relative to the application of the Pregnancy Discrimination Act (PDA) in the workforce. These issues were prompted by a recent Supreme Court case, *Young v. UPS*, which we discuss in the Ethics in Practice case on reasonable accommodation. The EEOC continues to provide guidance in situations where employers have accommodation obligations under

---

Ethics In Practice Case

Better Check Your Old Yearbooks and Social Media Posts

In 2019, Governor Ralph Northam of Virginia faced perhaps the biggest crisis of his political career when a photo of the governor from his 1984 medical school yearbook showed a man dressed in blackface and one in a Ku Klux Klan robe and hood. When the photo came to light, the governor first apologized, then said it was not him, and then divulged that he had once darkened his skin as part of a Michael Jackson costume. Eventually, he acknowledged appearing in the "clearly racist and offensive photograph" and asked his constituents to forgive him.

This was not the first political figure to have his character questioned, based on old yearbook information. Supreme Court Justice Brett Kavanaugh was questioned extensively during his appointment hearing, when his personal yearbook page boasted, "100 Kegs or Bust," and some interpreted his references to a young woman as boasting about a conquest. Justice Kavanaugh vehemently denied the allegation before the Senate Judiciary Committee.

Of course, old yearbook pictures are not the only potential source of reputational damage. Inflammatory tweets and social media postings are as well.

Incidents like this that involve offensive and damaging images surrounding race, gender, sexual orientation, or sexual acts increase the need for human resources departments to improve their due diligence when vetting employees. Additionally, in light of heightened social movements like the Black Lives Matter movement and increasing sensitivity to racial justice issues, many employers are doing background checks and screening candidates' social

media histories as part of their hiring processes. In fact, some of these screenings for senior level and board hires can go back 25 years or more.

1. What are the ethical issues here?
2. Is it fair to hold someone accountable for something they did years ago? Should there be a statute of limitations on how far back it is fair to go?
3. What is an appropriate way to respond to allegations from old yearbook testaments or social media posts? Is it okay to say "I was (just) young at the time"? What is the appropriate response to such allegations?

Sources: Lauren Weber and Vanessa Fuhrmans, "Executives Need to Revisit Old Yearbooks," *The Wall Street Journal* (February 6, 2019), B4; Lauren Vozzella, Jim Morrison, and Gregory Schneider, "Governor Ralph Northam Admits He Was in 1984 Yearbook Photo Showing Figures in Blackface, KKK Hood," *The Washington Post* (February 1, 2019), https://www .washingtonpost.com/local/virginia-politics/va-gov-northams -medical-school-yearbook-page-shows-men-in-blackface-kkk- robe/2019/02/01/517a43ee-265f-11e9-90cd-dedb0c92dc17_story .html, accessed May 28, 2021; Kate Kelly and David Enrich, "Kavanaugh's Yearbook Page Is 'Horrible, Hurtful' to a Woman It Named," *The New York Times* (September 24, 2018), https:// www.nytimes.com/2018/09/24/business/brett-kavanaugh- yearbook-renate.html, accessed May 28, 2021; Rachel Feintzeig and Vanessa Furhmans, "Hiring Hazard: Social Media," *The Wall Street Journal* (August 6, 2018), B1.

Ethics In Practice Case

What Is Reasonable Accommodation for Pregnancy?

Peggy Young worked for UPS as a pickup and delivery driver. When she became pregnant, her doctor restricted her from lifting more than 20 pounds during her first 20 weeks of pregnancy and 10 pounds for the remainder. UPS placed Young on leave without pay because her job required her to be able to lift parcels weighing up to 70 pounds. UPS said they followed a "pregnancy-blind" policy that is nondiscriminatory by nature when they put her on leave. Young filed suit, claiming that her co-workers were willing to help her, and that UPS had a policy of accommodating other, non-pregnant drivers who suffered from disabilities or who lost their Department of Transportation certifications. She brought suit against UPS under the Pregnancy Discrimination Act of 1987 and the Americans with Disabilities Act of 1990.

The U.S. Supreme Court found in Young's favor after two lower courts had taken UPS's side; however, they did not completely agree with her logic. Young said that employers are required to accommodate pregnant women when they provide an accommodation to any other non-pregnant employee who is similar in ability to work. The Court, however, said that under a "disparate treatment" theory of liability, the employee must show that she was intentionally discriminated against. They said that Young must demonstrate that the employer's policies impose a "significant burden" on pregnant workers, and that the employer has not raised a "sufficiently strong" reason to justify that burden. In Young's case, she had to show that UPS accommodates most non-pregnant employees with lifting limitations while categorically failing to accommodate pregnant employees with lifting limitations.

The Court clarified, however, that there is a high legal burden employers will have to meet in order to justify their policies or practices that provide accommodations to some categories of employees, but not to pregnant women. While the Supreme Court remanded the case to the lower court to determine whether UPS can meet this burden, the ramifications from the case have already changed EEOC guidelines for applying the Pregnancy Discrimination Act. What this means for businesses is that employers will have to be very careful if they accommodate some groups of employees without also accommodating pregnant employees.

1. Why do you think some employers are still refusing to comply with pregnant workers' requests for temporary accommodations? Are such refusals justified? Why or why not?
2. How is this an example of the integration of ethics and the law? What ethical principles are at stake here?
3. What would you have done if you were Peggy Young?

Sources: *Young v. United Parcel Service, Inc.* (n.d.)., *Oyez.* https://www.oyez.org/cases/2014/12-1226, accessed May 28, 2021; *Young v. United Parcel Service, Inc.*, Supreme Court of the United States (Argued December 3, 2014–Decided March 25, 2015), http://www.supremecourt.gov/opinions/14pdf/12-1226_k5fl.pdf, accessed May 28, 2021; U.S. EEOC, "Enforcement and Guidance: Pregnancy Discrimination and Related Issues," https://www.eeoc.gov/laws/guidance/pregnancy_guidance.cfm.

---

the PDA—essentially importing the ADA's accommodation obligations into the PDA.[38]

For example, EEOC guidelines say that employers must treat employees temporarily unable to perform the functions of their job because of their pregnancy-related condition in the same manner as it treats other employees similar in their ability or inability to work.[39] They can do this by providing modified tasks, alternative assignments, or fringe benefits such as disability leave and leave without pay. Additionally, parental leave that is offered to new parents so that they may bond with or care for a new child must be provided to everyone on equal terms.[40] These are just a few of the guidelines designed to ensure that pregnant people and their families are treated respectfully and fairly—which is the right thing to do, both legally and ethically.

Fetal Protection Policies. Another related form of discrimination was identified when the Supreme Court ruled that **fetal protection policies** constituted sex discrimination. The decisive case was *UAW v. Johnson Controls, Inc.* Johnson Controls, like a number of other major firms, developed a policy of barring women of childbearing age from working in sites in which they, and their developing fetuses, might be exposed to such harmful chemicals as

lead. Johnson Controls believed it was taking an appropriate action in protecting the women and their unborn children from exposure to chemicals. The U.S. Supreme Court found that the policy was on its face discriminatory and that the company had not shown that women were more likely than men to suffer reproductive damage from lead.[41]

Even though the Supreme Court ruled that injured children, once born, would not be able to bring lawsuits against the company, several experts think it is possible that such lawsuits will indeed be filed in the future. OSHA has identified reproductive health hazards as an area likely to experience an increase in litigation over time.[42] One thing is clear; companies must take care to assure that their employees are fully informed of all potential risks in the workplace.[43]

Genetic Information Nondiscrimination Act. The **Genetic Information Nondiscrimination Act (GINA)** prohibits employers from requiring, requesting, purchasing, or disclosing employees' genetic information; however, it does not prohibit employees from voluntarily disclosing genetic information to co-workers or to superiors.[44] GINA protects former employees as well as current ones and applies only to employers with 15 or more employees.[45]

Genetic information is defined broadly and so it includes not only the information from employee genetic tests and medical history but also information from family members' tests and medical history.[46] Family members need not be blood relatives.

GINA is unique in that it is the first *preemptive* civil rights law in U.S. history.[47] Antidiscrimination laws typically respond to discrimination that has already happened. Genetic testing is so new that there is no significant history of discrimination; instead, GINA represents an effort to prevent genetics-based discrimination before it occurs. The EEOC knew that employers might discriminate against employees, spouses, and children because of concerns about health-care costs, so GINA was put in place to protect employees and their families.

Currently, more than 26 million consumers have added their DNA to commercial ancestry and health databases with two companies, Ancestry and 23andMe, holding some of the world's largest collections of DNA.[48] However, many people avoid the test because of a major omission in the GINA law that allows life, disability, and long-term insurers to access the results of genetic testing.[49] Even if most insurers are not asking for the genetic tests specifically, they can seek out medical records and can use genetic test results listed there.[50] Therefore, issues of privacy and the potential that employees could be discriminated against because of their genetic makeup have sparked concerns from employee and consumer activists.

13.2f Civil Rights Act of 1991

The primary objective of the **Civil Rights Act of 1991** was to provide increased financial damages and jury trials in cases of intentional discrimination relating to sex, religion, race, disability, and national origin. Under the original Title VII, monetary awards were limited to such items as back pay, lost benefits, and attorney fees and costs. This 1991 act permitted the awarding of both compensatory and punitive damages. In addition, charges of unintentional discrimination were more difficult for employers to defend, because the act shifted the burden of proof back to the employer.[51]

13.2g Equal Employment Opportunity Commission

As the major federal body created to administer and enforce U.S. job bias laws, the **Equal Employment Opportunity Commission (EEOC)** deserves special consideration. Several other federal agencies also are charged with enforcing certain aspects of the discrimination laws and executive orders, but we will restrict our discussion to the EEOC because it is the major agency.

The EEOC has five commissioners and a general counsel appointed by the president and confirmed by the Senate. The five-member commission is responsible for making equal employment opportunity policy and approving all litigation the commission undertakes. The EEOC staff receives and investigates employment discrimination

Ethics In Practice Case

Using DNA to Catch a Killer

In 2018, the "Golden State Killer," a California man accused of a series of decades-old rapes and murders, was found when law enforcement agencies compared a sample of his DNA to information provided through shared data from DNA testing companies like 23andMe and Ancestry. While testing companies like these emphasize that DNA data is "de-identified" for privacy, data shared with researchers can be re-identified for other uses, like responding to law enforcement requests in an investigation or responding to other requests from the federal government, the State Department, or the U.S. military.

While catching a killer is a good thing, the use of such techniques is highly controversial, including a number of unintended privacy effects like outing family secrets and uniting the children of previously anonymous sperm donors. In fact, Pentagon leadership has encouraged military personnel not to take 23andMe tests due to privacy concerns. In addition to civil liberty concerns, there are concerns about a disproportionate impact on communities of color, because they are already disproportionately in contact with the police, and a focus on using these databases to identify criminals could create more unease and distrust. With DNA testing companies like 23andMe soon to be going public, fresh privacy and equity questions are being raised about the information of millions of customers.

1. Do you think that DNA data from private testing companies should be used to identify criminals? What about use in employment decisions?
2. 23andMe has "opt in" consumer agreements that allow external sharing of data. Does this mitigate any concerns about privacy?
3. Should GINA laws be expanded to take into account issues of potential genetic discrimination when law enforcement agencies tap DNA through consumer testing companies to capture criminals?
4. What ethics issues apply here?

Sources: Jocelyn Kaiser, "We Will Find You: DNA Search Used to Nab Golden State Killer," *Science* (October 11, 2018), https://www.sciencemag.org/news/2018/10/we-will-find-you-dna-search-used-nab-golden-state-killer-can-home-about-60-white, accessed May 28, 2021; Eric Rosenbaum, "5 Biggest Risks of Sharing Your DNA with Consumer Genetic-Testing Companies," *CNBC* (June 16, 2018), https://www.cnbc.com/2018/06/16/5-biggest-risks-of-sharing-dna-with-consumer-genetic-testing-companies.html, accessed May 28, 2021; "Fears over DNA Privacy as 23andMe Plans to Go Public in Deal with Richard Branson," *The Guardian* (February 9, 2021), https://www.theguardian.com/technology/2021/feb/09/23andme-dna-privacy-richard-branson-genetics, accessed May 28, 2021.

> **Spotlight on Sustainability**
>
> ### Are Sustainability Advocates a New Protected Class?
>
> As head of sustainability for Grainger, one of Britain's largest property firms, Tim Nicholson would sometimes get in conflicts with other executives at the firm. For example, when one top executive left his mobile phone in London and then ordered a staff person to get on a plane, retrieve it, and bring it back to him, Nicholson believed that wasting jet fuel to return a mobile phone and other such environmentally inappropriate actions were evidence of contempt for his sustainability beliefs. When he was later laid off, Nicholson filed suit.
>
> The judge decided that if one genuinely holds a belief in human-caused climate change, and its alleged resulting moral imperatives, that it could be considered a "philosophical belief." Grainger contended that Nicholson was let go when organizational restructuring made his position redundant. In the United Kingdom, it is unlawful to
>
> discriminate against a person on the grounds of their religious or philosophical beliefs. After a judge ruled he could use employment equality (religion and belief) regulations to make his claim, he reached a settlement with the company. In the words of Mr. Nicholson's solicitor, "He is pleased to have created an important point of law to support those individuals, like him, who hold a strong belief in the urgent need to combat climate change."
>
> Sources: Karen McVeigh, "Judge Rules Activist's Belief on Environment Akin to Religion," guardian.co.uk (November 9, 2009), http://www.theguardian.com/environment/2009/nov/03 /tim-nicholson-climate-change-belief, accessed May 28, 2021; "Climate Change Worker Tim Nicholson Reaches Settlement," BBC News (April 15, 2010), http://news.bbc.co.uk/2/hi/uk_news /england/oxfordshire/8621703.stm, accessed May 28, 2021.

charges/complaints. If the commission finds reasonable cause to believe that unlawful discrimination has occurred, its staff attempts to conciliate the charges/complaints. When conciliation is not achieved, the EEOC may file lawsuits in federal district court against employers.[52] In 2020, the EEOC received 70,804 private sector workplace discrimination charges; retaliation (37,632), disability (24,324), race (22,064), and sex discrimination, including sexual harassment and pregnancy (21,398), represented the charges that were filed most frequently.[53]

13.3 Expanded Meanings of Employment Discrimination

Over the years, it has been left to the courts to define the word *discrimination*, because it was not defined in Title VII. Over time, it has become apparent that two specific kinds of discrimination exist: **disparate treatment** and **disparate impact**.

13.3a Disparate Treatment

Disparate treatment refers to intentional discrimination, wherein people in a protected class are deliberately treated differently.[54] Examples of disparate treatment might include refusing to consider black citizens for a job, paying women less than men are paid for the same work, or supporting any decision rule with a racial or sexual premise or cause.[55]

While the message of disparate treatment is clear, businesses continue to face different contexts where this kind of discrimination might occur. Take the case of Samantha Elauf, a job applicant for Abercrombie & Fitch (A&F). When she applied for a job, the clothier refused to hire her because she was wearing a hijab, or head scarf, which

A&F said was at odds with the company's "neutral look policy" and dress code that forbade caps.[56] The Council on American-Islamic relations filed a complaint on her behalf with the EEOC, who tried to resolve the issue with A&F informally, but ended up suing the retailer for religious discrimination. Abercrombie claimed that Elauf was not turned down because of her faith; rather, she was in violation of the dress code and she did not specifically ask for any religious accommodation. This case went all the way to the Supreme Court, where the Court ruled that companies could not discriminate against job applicants or employees for religious reasons, even if an accommodation is not requested. As noted by Justice Scalia, "The rule of disparate-treatment claims based on a failure to accommodate a religious practice is straightforward. An employer may not make an applicant's religious practice, confirmed or otherwise, a factor in employment decisions."[57]

13.3b Disparate Impact

Disparate impact refers to discrimination that is unintentional, where the procedures are the same for everyone, but people in a protected class are negatively affected.[58]

The *Griggs v. Duke Power Company* case established the legal precedent for disparate-impact lawsuits involving racial discrimination.[59] Duke Power Company had required that employees transferring to other departments have a high school diploma or pass a standardized intelligence test. This requirement excluded a disproportionate number of minority workers. The court noted that there were non-minorities who performed satisfactorily and achieved promotions though they did not have diplomas. The court then reached the ground-breaking conclusion that it was the *consequences* of an employer's actions, not only its intentions, which determined whether discrimination had taken place. If any employment practice or test had an adverse or differential effect on minorities, it was a discriminatory practice.

An unequal impact, or disparate impact, means that fewer minorities are included in the outcome of the test or the hiring or promotion practice than would be expected by their numerical proportion in society. The court also held that a policy or procedure with a disparate impact would be permissible if the employer could demonstrate that it was a business- or job-related necessity. In the *Duke Power* case, however, a high school diploma and good scores on a general intelligence test did not have a clearly demonstrable relationship to successful performance on the job under consideration.[60]

The concept of disparate impact is quite significant, because it runs counter to so many traditional employment practices. For example, the minimum height and weight requirements of some police departments have unequal impact and have been struck down by courts because they tended to screen out women, people of Asian heritage, and Latinos disproportionately.[61] Several Supreme Court rulings have addressed the issue of the kind of evidence needed to document or prove discrimination. Typically, if a member of a minority group does not have a success rate of at least 80 percent compared to the majority group, the practice may be considered to have an adverse impact unless business necessity can be proven.[62] When this **four-fifths rule** is triggered, the firm will not necessarily be found guilty of having a disparate impact. However, it will be incumbent upon the firm to show that the selection practice is job related and necessary for the business.[63] Figure 13-4 summarizes the characteristics of disparate treatment and disparate impact.

13.4 Issues in Employment Discrimination

The essentials of the major federal laws on discrimination have been presented, and we have traced the evolution of the concept of discrimination. Now it is useful to discuss briefly some of the specific issues and problems in employment discrimination including issues of race, color, ethnicity, gender, and other targets of discrimination that result in inequality, inequities, and other harms.

13.4a Race, Color, and Ethnicity

Although racial discrimination was one of the first forms of discrimination to attract the focus of the civil rights legislation, it remains a major problem in workplaces in the United States and throughout the world. Racial discrimination is always hurtful; however, the nature of its form and impact has been different for people of different races. Race discrimination includes discrimination based on ancestry or physical or cultural characteristics associated with a certain race, such as skin color, hair texture or styles, or certain facial features.[64] Color discrimination is also identified separately by the EEOC and involves treating someone unfavorably because of skin color complexion.[65]

As noted at the beginning of the chapter, the racial discrimination events of the past few years will forever shape the future approaches that businesses take toward addressing those who are at risk of discrimination and face inequities in the workplace. People of color make up nearly 40 percent of the U.S. population yet remain acutely underrepresented in most influential fields, including business, law, and the STEM areas (e.g., science, technology, engineering, mathematics).[66] Perhaps a move in the right direction is that many large U.S. companies are providing more detailed diversity data than ever before, in large part due to voluntary, but new, Securities and Exchange Commission regulations along with investor interest. Of the more than 160 annual reports filed by the S&P 500 companies in 2020, about three-quarters disclosed at least some information on racial and equity diversity. For example, Pepsico reported that 43 percent of its U.S. workers were "racially/ethnically diverse individuals." [67]

Simply increasing the numbers of diverse candidates in business does not necessarily address issues of discrimination—at least in the short run. Companies cannot fix problems of discrimination without measuring the extent of it first, and most companies do not do this until it reaches a point where allegations are made and/or charges are filed. The consequences to businesses and society can be disturbing. Despite some progress over the decades, exclusion and injustice and the "long reach of racism" has been said to extend to the tenuous economic base of Black Americans, for example, and its downward mobility, as the black poverty rate is 2.5 times the white rate.[68]

People who are Hispanic or Latino are also faced with significant discrimination that can take the form of racial, national origin, and/or color discrimination. In a 2021

Figure 13-4 Two Kinds of Employment Discrimination

Disparate Treatment	Disparate Impact
Primary discrimination	Secondary discrimination
Different treatment	Different results
Intentional discrimination	Unintentional discrimination
Biased actions	Neutral actions, biased impact
Different standards for different groups	Different consequences for different groups

Source: EEOC, "Employment Tests and Selection Procedures," http://www.eeoc.gov/policy/docs/factemployment_procedures.html, accessed May 28, 2021.

Gallup Poll, 61 percent of Hispanic or Latino workers who have experienced discrimination say that it was related to their race or ethnicity.[69] And the perception of discrimination for these workers resulted in feelings of exclusion, lack of value, and a loss of autonomy.[70]

Asian Americans have also faced significant discrimination in the workplace. This was heightened during the COVID-19 pandemic, when racist rhetoric blaming Asians for the pandemic infused hate incidents and violence toward Asians around the world. Whether because of outright bias, implicit bias, or stereotypes, Asian Americans are virtually absent in the executive suites. They represent 12 percent of the country's professional workforce, yet less than 1 percent of the S&P 500 CEOs are of East Asian descent.[71] They are also less likely than any other racial group to be promoted to management, according to one study.[72]

While these examples represent only a few of the groups and discriminatory issues that protected class members experience in the workforce, businesses need not only to be vigilant but also to be proactive in promoting racial and ethnic justice and antidiscriminatory practices. Beyond putting out corporate statements, donating monies to racial justice initiatives, and changing leadership, businesses can make concrete changes within their businesses. To that end, HR experts and sociologists suggest the following for business managers:[73]

- Do a full audit: Go beyond employee and board representation numbers and examine vendors, bankers, and even technology for bias. Examine for discrimination at every level of the organization from the board of directors down.
- Rethink leadership: Continue to review leaders for insensitive and discriminatory comments or behaviors, and then replace any leaders who practice such behaviors with those who prioritize how they value diversity and inclusion.
- Standardize hiring (and train hiring managers): Work on unconscious and implicit bias issues. Hiring managers should ask set questions and all candidates should be evaluated on the same scorecard tied to the qualifications of the job.
- Create a pipeline: Pipeline programs at universities are good sources for creating pipelines for diversity in business, and they also provide exemplary training on recognizing signs of discrimination. The LEAD program at Wharton School of Business, for example, serves students from underserved communities and helps them pursue careers in business.
- Do not assume an annual diversity training will be enough: Go beyond "checking the box" and think about systemic change.
- Know that real change takes time: Pause and look internally, analyzing where you and your company have prioritized diversity and where you fall short.
- Consider where exactly you can make a difference: Examine hiring, retention, funding, training, and development to address discrimination and racial justice concerns.
- Be dedicated to consistency.

In sum, companies must be proactive, not just reactive, in addressing issues of discrimination. To that point, companies often engage in activism to address social issues like racial discrimination.

As we have discussed in earlier chapters, companies that approach their employees with the best practices of business ethics and stakeholder management in the end will benefit. In this way, business and society work together to address the changing social issues around them.

13.4b Gender

Issues surrounding sex discrimination are different from those involving race, color, and national origin. Gender issues include discrimination against men, women, gay, lesbian, bisexual, and transgender/transsexual (LGBT) employees alike. We focus on women first with managerial positions and pay, as this has received a lot of attention in both research and the media. We then expand our gender classifications in the areas of sexual harassment, sexual orientation, and gender identity discrimination. However, we note that the major issues for women today can also apply across all gender classifications.

The major issues for women today include (1) getting into professional and managerial positions and out of traditional female-dominated positions, (2) achieving pay commensurate with that of men, (3) eliminating sexual harassment, and (4) being able to take maternity leave without losing their jobs. Some progress is being made on each of these fronts, but as we discuss, more work remains to be done.

Women in Professional/Managerial Positions. In 2020, the number of women CEOs rose to a historic high, with 7.8 percent of S&P 500 firms headed by women. Further, the *Women CEOs in America Report*, published by the Women in Business Collaborative, C200, and Catalyst, predicted that this would rise to 15 percent by 2025, with 10 percent of those being women of color.[74] However, while this is certainly a drastic improvement at the executive levels, women are still challenged with a **gender gap** in the workplace. One study points to the fact that while women and men enter the workforce in roughly equal numbers, women fall behind in promotions from "the very first stop onto the management ladder."[75] By senior-manager level, men outnumber women two to one, and in the C-suite, just 22 percent are women.[76]

Some argue that it takes decades to become a CEO and so the pipeline for female CEOs is just starting to fill.[77] Sheryl Sandberg raised a media furor with her 2013 book, *Lean In*, which suggests women sabotage themselves by lacking self-confidence and not grabbing opportunities as they arise.[78] However, after establishing the nonprofit LeanIn.Org to support women in their career ambitions, Sandberg modified her stance to focus on what companies can and should do to reduce the gender gap. As noted by Sandberg and writer Rachel Thomas, "The future of women in the workplace hangs in the balance, and good intentions aren't good enough anymore. Women are leaning in. Companies need to lean in, too."[79]

Women also suffered disproportionately during the COVID-19 pandemic, wiping out many of the recent gains that women had made in the workplace. One McKinsey study showed that women accounted for 54 percent of initial virus-related job losses, with many unable to work due to childcare burdens, as well as burnout and anxiety in trying to balance work and home life.[80]

Gender discrimination remains a key explanation for the disparity, and that explanation is supported by the scores of studies that show the significant pay discrepancy between men and women in the workplace.[81] One thing is clear: The explanation is not performance driven. Women-run hedge funds outperform those run by men, male retail investors outtrade but underperform women, and women-led companies in the S&P 1500 outperform those run by men.[82]

Equal Pay and Promotion. As we noted earlier, equal pay and specifically the gender pay gap is a hot-button issue for gender discrimination. While we noted that some critics have tried to explain the discrepancy by arguing that these statistics include women who lost both time and experience through extended maternity leave, the Bureau of Labor statistics, as well as research done by the compensation firm PayScale, shows that the gap exists at the start of women's careers as well as for women who work full time.[83] The gap also exists for women in professional and technical occupations.[84] This issue affects families as well as the worker involved.

It might seem surprising that issues of gender pay inequality, like other forms of discrimination, still exist today, with more legislation and court cases trying to address the issues. However, in the case of gender pay inequality, a study conducted by women in the San Francisco Bay Area, called the "Elephant in the Valley," found that the workplace requires more than "equal pay for equal work" covered under the Equal Pay Act.[85] For example, they found that women were presented with fewer business opportunities, excluded from key social networking events, and had colleagues address questions to their male peers that should have been addressed to them.[86]

While these may be examples of more subtle versions of discrimination against women, current research shows that subtle forms are just as damaging as more overt forms, with a host of adverse work-related outcomes at the individual and organizational levels.[87] Additionally, both subtle and overt forms of discrimination against women have been said to contribute to a "toxic work world" where only the young, childless, and eldercare-less employees are valued (since it is mostly women who handle care giving in families).[88] In sum, employers must be prepared to address both overt and subtle forms of gender discrimination, just as they have to do with racial, ethnic, and other forms of discrimination.

Sexual Harassment. Sexual harassment in the workplace is a worldwide problem with negative consequences that are pervasive and ongoing. A meta-analysis of sexual harassment studies found that victims of sexual harassment

suffered a range of negative outcomes such as decreased job satisfaction, lower organizational commitment, withdrawal from work, poor physical and mental health, and even symptoms of posttraumatic stress disorder.[89]

The EEOC defines **sexual harassment** in the following way:

Unwelcome sexual advances, requests for sexual favors, and other verbal or physical conduct of a sexual nature constitute sexual harassment when submission to or rejection of this conduct explicitly or implicitly affects an individual's employment, unreasonably interferes with an individual's work performance, or creates an intimidating, hostile, or offensive work environment.

Implicit in this definition are two broad types of sexual harassment. First is what has been called **quid pro quo** harassment. This is a situation where something is given or received for something else. For example, a supervisor may make it explicit or implicit that a sexual favor is expected if the employee wants a pay raise or a promotion. Second is what has been referred to as **hostile work environment** harassment. In this type, nothing is given or received, but the employee perceives a hostile or offensive work environment by virtue of uninvited sexually oriented behaviors or materials being present in the workplace. Examples of this might include sexual teasing or jokes or sexual materials, such as pictures or cartoons, being present in the workplace.

One study of EEOC settlements over a ten-year period found that almost all of the cases (98.5 percent) included a hostile environment aspect and most of the cases (89.1 percent) only involved a hostile environment, that is, did not include a quid pro quo complaint.[90] By statistics, sexual harassment filings with the EEOC have decreased over the last several years; however, reports of retaliation in connection with sexual harassment have risen as well, suggesting that fear of retribution may be holding employees back from filing charges.[91] To clear up common misconceptions, the EEOC indicates that sexual harassment can occur in a variety of circumstances that include but are not limited to the following:[92]

- The victim as well as the harasser may be a woman or a man or LGBT.
- The victim does not have to be of the opposite sex.
- The harasser can be the victim's supervisor, an agent of the employer, a supervisor in another area, a co-worker, or a nonemployee.
- The victim does not have to be the person harassed but could be anyone affected by the offensive conduct.
- Unlawful sexual harassment may occur without economic injury to or discharge of the victim.
- The harasser's conduct must be unwelcome.

Figure 13-5 lists examples of sexual harassment complaints. These are made by women, men, and LGBT employees. The stereotypical view of sexual harassment is that of a male supervisor harassing a female subordinate. However, this is

Figure 13-5 Examples of Sexual Harassment Complaints

- Being subjected to sexually suggestive remarks and propositions
- Being subjected to sexual innuendo and joking
- Being touched by a supervisor while working
- Co-workers' "remarks" about an employee sexually cooperating with the supervisor
- Suggestive looks and gestures
- Deliberate touching and "cornering"
- Suggestive body movements
- Sexually oriented materials being circulated around the office, e-mail, or social media
- Pornographic cartoons and pictures posted or present in work areas
- Pressure for dates and sexual favors
- Retaliation by supervisor after sexual advances are resisted

Note: It should be noted that these are "complaints." Whether each item turns out to be sexual harassment or not in the eyes of the law is determined in an official hearing or trial.

not always the case. In 2020, the EEOC had 6,587 charges filed alleging sexual harassment, with 16.8 percent filed by males.[93] Of the 1,857 sex discrimination cases that we noted above filed by LGBT members in 2020, a majority of them appear to involve sexual harassment.[94]

Many people do not realize that Title IX offers protection against sexual harassment in a way that is essentially similar to Title VII. Title IX, the law that bans sex discrimination at schools receiving federal funds, is best known in its sports context for the formula that determines if schools are providing women with fair opportunities to play sports. Schools can be sued for monetary damages under Title IX for knowingly allowing sexual harassment to take place.

There are four parts to the burden of proof: (1) the school must be aware of the sexual harassment, (2) the school must fail to take steps to stop it, (3) the harassment must deny access to an educational opportunity, and (4) the harassment must take place in an educational setting.[95]

Supreme Court rulings underscore the importance of companies' being diligent in their efforts to discourage harassing behavior. For example, the Supreme Court ruled that employers might be held liable even if they did not know about the harassment or their supervisors never carried out any threatened job actions.[96] Clearly, employers must develop comprehensive programs to protect their employees from harassment. When businesses develop comprehensive and clear programs to prevent sexual harassment, they are legally rewarded. The Supreme Court ruled that good faith efforts to prevent and correct harassment are one prong of an "affirmative defense" that companies can employ when charged with harassment. The second prong is proving the employee failed to take advantage of opportunities the firm provided for correction or prevention.[97]

13.4c Other Forms of Employment Discrimination

Much of the attention surrounding employment discrimination has focused on racial, ethnic, gender, and sexual discrimination. However, other important forms of discrimination represent critical issues for business today. Whether for legal or ethical reasons, it is important for managers to

understand the many forms that discrimination can take in an increasingly diverse workforce and where courts currently stand on those issues.

Religious Discrimination. Religious discrimination is one that is growing quickly; complaints more than doubled in the past 20 years, totalling 2,404 cases in 2020.[98] According to the EEOC, violations of religious discrimination involve a variety of patterns, including:[99]

1. Refusing to hire or firing workers after learning their religion;
2. Discharging workers who take leave for religious-related events (such as observing the Sabbath);
3. Failing to accommodate religious-related garb choices; and
4. Retaliating against employees who requested religious accommodation or complained about religious discrimination.

Research has shown that religious discrimination is a continuing problem, as we noted in the recent Abercrombie & Fitch case. In many cases, corporate policies are at issue. For example, in 2020 an owner of 11 McDonald's restaurants in Florida agreed to settle a religious discrimination suit after he refused to hire a Jewish applicant as a part-time maintenance worker. The worker would not shave his beard to comply with McDonald's "completely clean-shaven" grooming policy, due to his religious practices. He offered to wear a beard net as a solution but was denied. The EEOC filed suit because the denial of the accommodation request violated Title VII of the Civil Rights Act of 1964.[100]

Retaliation. As noted earlier, most cases filed with the EEOC are in response to retaliation. The same laws that protect individuals from discrimination protect them from being retaliated against for filing a discrimination claim. They also provide legal protection for someone who is not the target of the discrimination but is retaliated against for supporting a person who files a claim. **Retaliation** can take many forms, including firing, demotion, or harassment. Retaliation also can include intimidation, threats,

Ethics In Practice Case

Bigotry in the Bakery?

Since my junior year in high school, I have been working in the same local supermarket. My main job was to get the bread set up ready before the following day. After working in the bakery for quite some time, I began to notice the difference between how I have been treated compared to other co-workers. At first, I didn't notice the differences, but as time passed, I saw how they were making me do work that others in my department have never done. For example, the manager of the store realized that the ceiling of the bakery department was dirty and had accumulated pesticides. He told me to go up and clean the ceiling; he gave me no mask to protect myself from the pesticides. He just told me to go up and use Windex and clean the ceiling. I was hesitant at first but I completed the task without asking why. At the time, I was still new so I didn't want to mention anything to my boss so I just did as I was told.

Now as this continued to happen, I asked my co-workers, who were white, if they were ever told to complete this task. They all answered saying that none of them have ever been told to clean the ceiling and don't know of anyone in the store who has. They couldn't believe that I was cleaning the ceilings full of pesticides. For the past four years, they have been making me do this and it's not my

job to do so. For this job, they should be hiring a cleaning crew to come in at night and clean the store. So, I asked another Latino in the store who has been working there for more than ten years how he is treated. He answered saying that they have asked him do things around the store that aren't under his job description as well. Over the years, I've seen that the manager feels like it is okay for me to clean the ceilings even though that can potentially harm my health. It is not only happening to me but other Hispanic employees as well. However, I try to be a good employee and listen. The same is true for the other Latinos in the store who have not said anything to the manager and continue to perform these tasks.

1. Is discrimination taking place in this job assignment situation?
2. If it is, what should I do next? This job is important to me and I don't want to lose it.
3. Will the fact that I agreed to perform these dirty and dangerous tasks affect my case? I was always taught to work hard and earn the money I am paid. Was that the wrong thing to do?

Contributed anonymously

and untrue negative evaluations, denial of a promotion, negative references, increased surveillance, or any other kind of treatment that would make a person hesitate to file a claim. This prohibition against retaliation only applies to those who file claims on their own behalf and those who oppose discrimination by supporting victims, testifying at proceedings, or calling attention to unlawful practices. It does not apply to whistle-blowers who call attention to illegal acts other than discrimination (although other whistle-blower protections may apply in those instances). In addition to this being a legal issue, it also represents an important ethical issue. Ethical principles discussed earlier in the text, for example, fair treatment, rights, and due process, would preclude responsible companies taking retaliatory actions against workers for seeking to protect their job.

Sexual Orientation and Gender Identity Discrimination. Corporations have been faster than governments in instituting protections for lesbian, gay, bisexual, and transgender (LGBT) employees. However, an important change came in the form of a recent Supreme Court case, *Bostock v. Clayton County, Georgia* (No. 17-1618), where the Court held that firing individuals because of their sexual orientation or transgender status violates Title VII's prohibition on discrimination based on sex.[101]

Other changes have been made beyond case law. As of 2020, 96 percent of the Fortune 500 companies include **sexual orientation** in their nondiscrimination policies and a majority (57 percent) provides domestic partner health

insurance benefits to employees.[102] The greatest growth has been in prohibition of gender identity discrimination in the *Fortune* 500. In 2000, only three companies prohibited discrimination based on gender identity, but in 2020, 94 percent prohibited gender identity discrimination.[103]

A combination of new state legislation, private protections, case law, and federal litigations have provided some momentum in ensuring employment protection for LGBT workers, but in the 29 states with no antidiscrimination laws based on sexual orientation and gender identity, the possibility of overt discrimination still exists, and this is especially true for transgender employees. A recent survey of younger transgender workers found that 61 percent of them reported harassment on the job.[104] And transgender workers are subject to different types of harassment than other LGBT workers, including bathroom accessibility, being deliberately referred to by incorrect pronouns, and having to tolerate inappropriate questions.[105]

Business has been generally supportive of proposed federal and state legislation that would extend LGBT protections. Corporate advocacy has also extended to protests against state bills that businesses like Mars, Inc, Nestle SA, and Unilever perceived as targeting LGBT workers.[106] The year 2021 was labelled by some as the "worst year in recent history for LGBTQ state legislative attacks" when 17 new state bills were enacted into law limiting things like trans sports and trans medical care.[107] Hence, there is a renewed call for businesses to pressure legislatures to reform state laws, including boycotts against companies that do not speak out against such legislation.[108]

Gender identity, among other issues, addresses the special challenges for business of the treatment of transgender and transsexual employees. *Transgender* is an umbrella term that refers to people who express a gender that does not match the one on their original birth certificate or physically change their gender through surgery. *Transsexual* refers specifically to a person who is undergoing or has undergone sex-change surgery.[109] This is not a new workplace issue; it has been around for a couple decades.

The concept of gender identity and its legal protections continues to evolve, but the trend against gender stereotyping carries implications for future protections for various gender identity issues. *InsideCounsel* legal magazine offers employers the following advice: "Employers across the nation should be scrutinizing their policies and practices with regard to discrimination against transgender and transsexual people as states pass laws prohibiting discrimination on the basis of gender identity and courts interpret existing civil rights laws to protect those individuals."[110]

13.5 Diversity and Inclusion in the Workforce

Workplace diversity refers to the variety of differences between people in an organization. It encompasses race, gender, ethnicity, age, religion, personality, tenure, education, and more. Most businesses refer to **diversity management** as assembling and then retaining workers from different backgrounds and experiences that together create a more innovative and productive workforce.

In the 1990s, businesses began making the connection of diversity to work perspectives through an integration-and-learning paradigm.[111] The focus was on integrating the goals of equal opportunity, acknowledgment of cultural differences and value, as well as letting the organization internalize differences, learn, and grow because of them in a long-term transformative process. However, today, as companies try to rectify a legacy of discrimination and racial justice problems that span generations, firms are facing increasing demands for more and better diversity and inclusion programs. For example, a global survey of more than 16,000 employees in 14 countries found that members of majority groups continue to underestimate the obstacles that diverse employees face.[112] Over half said that they do not believe their companies have the right mechanisms in place to ensure that major decisions such as promotion or stretch assignment decisions are free from bias.

According to the survey, the top ranked employer interventions include:

- Robust, well-crafted, and consistently followed antidiscrimination policies
- Effective training to mitigate biases and increase cultural competency
- Removing bias from evaluation and promotion decisions

Additionally, female employees wanted to see visible role models in the leadership team and help with work/life balance. Approximately half of LGBTQ employees surveyed were still closeted at work and were looking for efforts to create inclusive day-to-day experiences.

The focus of businesses regarding diversity management is on providing inclusive corporate cultures that, according to the Society for Human Resource Management, "foster ways to accommodate, empower and motivate each employee."[113] When diverse employees feel unheard and/or undervalued then they do not feel included. As noted by one set of experts, "Diversity *plus inclusion* is the source of real value."[114]

While companies are making concerted efforts to recruit diverse employees, and more organizations providing staff exclusively dedicated to this function, the challenge of developing an inclusive and innovative culture to complement such efforts can be tough.[115] Most diversity and inclusion experts agree that it begins with a commitment at the top of the organization. According to consultant group BCG, the next steps must follow: (1) setting clear expectations for managers supported by training, (2) identifying best practices and disseminating them while also celebrating them publicly, (3) setting clear standards while holding people accountable, and (4) tracking progress to determine where more time and focus are needed. While difficult to change an organization's culture, it is easy to see how such steps can help businesses practice business ethics and stakeholder management in addressing racial, gender, ethnic, and other forms of discrimination in their businesses.

Despite progress in managing a diverse workforce, challenges abound. With most companies providing diversity training programs and actively recruiting for diverse employees, there is some thought that there is "**diversity fatigue**" when companies fail to rethink their management styles and simply engage in "box-ticking."[116] In addition, despite increases in workforce diversity, many companies are setting discrete goals and tying those numbers to pay and performance, particularly regarding hiring and retaining women.[117] While there is still a stigma associated with quotas in the United States, this is not the case in other countries, as we discussed in Chapter 9. Overall, there is much work to be done in the diversity and inclusion efforts by businesses. However, before we leave this topic, it is important to address the topic of affirmative action, which continues to be timely, particularly in the context of college admissions policies.

13.6 Affirmative Action in the Workplace

Affirmative action was originally introduced as the process of taking positive steps to hire and promote people from groups previously discriminated against. The concept was formally introduced to the business world in 1965, when former president Lyndon B. Johnson signed Executive Order 11246, the purpose of which was to require all firms doing business with the federal government to engage in affirmative actions to accelerate the movement of minorities into the workforce. Companies today have affirmative action programs because they do business with the government, have begun the plans voluntarily, or have entered into them through collective bargaining agreements with labor unions.

The meaning of affirmative action has changed since its introduction. It originally referred only to special efforts to ensure equal opportunity for members of groups that had been subject to discrimination. Eventually, the term came to refer to programs in which members of such groups are given some degree of definite preference in determining access to positions from which they were formerly excluded.[118] It is important to remember that affirmative action is not just one thing; it can be anything in a range of programs. Today, when people speak of affirmative action, they are typically referring to some degree of preferential selection. It has most recently been applied to admissions practices in higher education, where race and ethnicity have been used in admissions decisions.

One federal case may make it soon to the U.S. Supreme Court. In 2018, Students for Fair Admissions (SFFA) filed a suit against Harvard University, claiming that the University discriminates against Asian American applicants through race-conscious admissions policies that favor other protected classes. According to the SFFA, "Using race and ethnicity in college admissions is unfair, unconstitutional and is fraying the social fabric that holds our nation together."[119] In November 2020, a federal appeals court ruled that Harvard's admissions process did not violate civil rights law; however, many speculate that the issue will come before the U.S. Supreme Court, based on public sentiment.

In 2019, a Pew Research survey found that 73 percent of Americans said race or ethnicity should not be a factor in college admissions. Harvard said during its 2018 trial that it considered race as one of many factors, and not the determining one, which was allowed under previous Supreme Court rulings. Nevertheless, the plaintiffs argued that Harvard systematically discriminated against Asian-American applicants by holding them to higher standards and invoking racial stereotypes about studious, shy Asians that were used against them in the selection process.

Figure 13-6 summarizes the key Supreme Court decisions to date on affirmative action.

The underlying rationale for affirmative action is the principle of **compensatory justice**, which holds that whenever an injustice is done, just compensation or reparation is owed to the injured party or parties.[120] The principal objection to affirmative action and the reason it has become and remained controversial is that it leads to **reverse discrimination**. The

Figure 13-6 Key Supreme Court Decisions on Affirmative Action

Year	Case	Issue	General Finding
2016	*Fisher v. University of Texas*	Admission to the university	U.S. Supreme Court upheld the affirmative action program at the University of Texas
2013	*Fisher v. University of Texas*	Admission to the university	Remanded the case to the lower court finding, it did not apply the standard of strict scrutiny
2009	*Ricci v. DeStefano*	Firefighter lieutenant and captain exams	Unconstitutional to discard exams due to concerns about disparate impact
2006	*Parents v. Seattle* and *Meredith v. Jefferson*	School integration	Unconstitutional to consider race when assigning students to schools
2003	*Grutter v. Bollinger*	Admission to law school	Race can be a factor (invalidates *Hopwood*)
1996	*Hopwood v. University of Texas Law School*	Admission to law school	Rejected legitimacy of diversity as a goal for AA
1995	*Adarand Constructors, Inc. v. Peña*	Federal affirmative action set asides	AA must pass "strict scrutiny" test of compelling interest and narrow tailoring
1989	*City of Richmond v. Croson*	Construction set asides for black-owned firms	AA unconstitutional unless racial discrimination proven widespread in industry
1987	*United States v. Paradise*	Hiring of state trooper in Alabama	Strict quotas accepted only because there was persistent and pervasive racism
1986	*Wygant v. Board of Education*	Layoff policy that protected minorities	Preferential layoffs unacceptable—greater injury than hiring policy
1980	*Fullilove v. Klutznick*	Set asides for minority contractors	Set asides acceptable due to narrow focus and limited intent
1979	*United Steelworkers v. Weber*	Admission to private employer training program (Kaiser)	Quotas acceptable if temporary and addressing a clear imbalance
1978	*Regents of the University of California v. Bakke*	Admission to medical school	Race deemed a legitimate factor but ruled against strict quotas

possibility of reverse discrimination is at the core of the controversy surrounding affirmative action. In the 2013 case of *Fisher v. University of Texas*, a young white female, Abigail Fisher, was rejected for admission to the university and said that her rights were violated by UT Austin's consideration of race and ethnicity in admissions decisions. The 2013 and 2014 Court of Appeals rulings on the case allowed colleges to continue the practice, but it raised the bar for colleges in how they must justify the consideration of race and ethnicity in admissions. In 2016, the Supreme Court reviewed the Fisher case again and upheld the constitutionality of affirmative action in admissions practices, thereby allowing the University of Texas to continue to use its "race-conscious" admissions program.[121]

Some have suggested that college admissions should focus on favoring preferences for low-income students as a way of achieving diversity; however, the University of Michigan, where affirmative action has not been allowed in admissions since 2009, has argued that it does not work. A study by The Century Foundation points to a different solution. It found that states that banned affirmative action in higher education have been successful in recruiting minorities by implementing new methods of promoting racial, ethnic, and socioeconomic diversity, including (1) guaranteeing admission to public colleges for top graduates from each high school in the state, (2) adding socioeconomic factors to admissions, (3) funding new financial aid programs, (4) improving recruitment and support, and (5) dropping legacy preferences.[122]

What is the future of affirmative action for higher education and businesses? The spirit of affirmative action, and diversity, continues to be endorsed by businesses. In fact, following the *SFFA v. Harvard* ruling, 14 companies, mostly tech and pharmaceutical companies, filed briefs in support of Harvard's admissions policies. Companies including Apple, Twitter, and Verizon said they need workers who are diverse and who thrive "in an inclusive environment" and that a "race conscious admissions policy" produces the graduates they need.[123]

13.7 The Future of Diversity Management

We began this chapter by noting that diversity and inclusion is a top priority in businesses today as they actively pursue diversity management strategies in their companies. With the buying power of minority groups in the United States increasing dramatically, there is further incentive for business's achieving greater diversity. Additionally, Gen Z employees are demanding change, with fairness and equity embedded firmly and authentically into their workplace behaviors.[124]

New analytical tools can provide opportunities to identify gender and race inequalities in the workforce and offer some new opportunities for diversity management. New software tools allow companies to detect potential gender and race gaps in outcomes like pay, recruitment, and promotion, given different inputs like training, mentoring, and company policies and practices.[125] These offer opportunities to provide "real fixes" for workplace bias that can be institutionalized in the design of the businesses themselves, and perhaps, even to put an end to discrimination.[126] While it is early to see if these tools can truly make the workplace fairer, more inclusive, and productive, they provide one more way to ensure that underrepresented groups receive a fair shot in the workforce.

Summary

This chapter addresses several subgroups of employee stakeholders whose job rights are protected by law, and whose issues are ethically important, as well as vital to effective stakeholder management. We noted that managing diversity in the workforce has evolved from a paradigm of recruitment and retention of protected class members to one that promotes active integration and inclusion of diverse members into the workforce. As companies have sought to become better corporate citizens, the movement toward diversity has become a hallmark of these companies.

This movement toward fair treatment of all workers and a diverse workforce was initiated by and has been supported by numerous laws, beginning with the Civil Rights Act of 1964, which prohibited discrimination based on race, color, religion, sex, or national origin. Laws covering age and disabilities then followed. Other protections related to disability are prohibitions against pregnancy discrimination and genetic information discrimination. The EEOC was created to assume the major responsibility for enforcing the discrimination laws. Like other federal agencies, the EEOC has had problems. However, on balance, it has done a reasonable job of monitoring the two major forms of discrimination: disparate treatment and disparate impact. Discrimination issues discussed in this chapter include issues of racial discrimination, women moving into professional/managerial positions, pay equity, sexual harassment, pregnancy discrimination, fetal protection policies, age discrimination, and religious discrimination. In addition, new and evolving discrimination issues such as sexual orientation, gender identity, and color bias as separate from race were discussed.

Affirmative action, the taking of positive steps to hire and promote people from groups previously discriminated against, was one of the government's answers to the problem of discrimination. There is evidence that attitudes toward affirmative action are changing as the global economy brings a more diverse workforce and customer base.

However, psychological and sociological aspects of people being people may mean that achieving diversity will be an elusive goal. Firms should follow best practices when designing diversity programs, and there is the potential for new analytical software tools to help them with this. Moral management and sound stakeholder management require companies to strive to be fair in their employment practices.

Key Terms

affirmative action, p. 308
Age Discrimination in Employment Act (ADEA), p. 297
Americans with Disabilities Act (ADA), p. 298
bona fide occupational qualification (BFOQ), p. 297
Civil Rights Act of 1991, p. 301
compensatory justice, p. 309
disparate impact, p. 302
disparate treatment, p. 302
diversity, p. 294
diversity fatigue, p. 308
diversity management, p. 308

Equal Employment Opportunity Commission (EEOC), p. 301
Equal Pay Act of 1963, p. 297
essential functions, p. 298
ethical blindness, p. 297
fetal protection policies, p. 300
four-fifths rule, p. 303
gender gap, p. 304
gender identity, p. 308
Genetic Information Nondiscrimination Act (GINA), p. 300
hostile work environment, p. 305
implicit bias, p. 297

inclusion, p. 294
LGBT, p. 295
Pregnancy Discrimination Act of 1978, p. 299
protected groups, p. 294
quid pro quo, p. 305
reasonable accommodations, p. 298
retaliation, p. 306
reverse discrimination, p. 309
sexual harassment, p. 305
sexual orientation, p. 307
Title VII of the Civil Rights Act of 1964, p. 296
undue hardship, p. 298

Discussion Questions

1. What are protected groups, and how have these evolved over time?
2. Is it important for a company to promote diversity and inclusion in the workforce? Why or why not?
3. Identify the major federal discrimination laws and indicate what they prohibit. Which agency is primarily responsible for enforcing these laws?
4. Give two different definitions of discrimination, and provide an example of each.
5. How have social movements affected business's approach to discrimination, diversity, and inclusion?
6. How has the Americans with Disabilities Act (ADA) evolved since its inception?
7. How is it that women in business still face gender and pay gaps?
8. Do you agree with the Genetic Nondiscrimination Act? Do companies have a right to know and use genetic information about employees? Why or why not?
9. Have the concepts of diversity management, diversity, and inclusion supplanted the concept of affirmative action in leading companies today?

Endnotes

1. Arian Campo-Flores, Joshua Jamerson, and Douglas Belkin, "A Year after Floyd Killing, Debate on Race Simmers," *The Wall Street Journal* (May 26, 2021), A1.
2. Camille Lloyd, "One in Four Black Workers Report Discrimination at Work," Gallup (January 12, 2021), https://www.gallup.com/topic/category_discrimination_in_the_workplace.aspx. Accessed May 26, 2021.
3. Ibid.
4. U.S. Equal Employment Opportunity Commission, "Who Is Protected," https://www.eeoc.gov/employers/small-business/3-who-protected-employment-discrimination. Accessed May 26, 2021.
5. Human Rights Campaign, "Statewide Employment Laws and Policies," https://www.hrc.org/resources/state-maps. Accessed May 26, 2021.
6. See Lloyd, 2021; "Diversity + Inclusion," *Built In* (2021), https://builtin.com/diversity-inclusion. Accessed May 26, 2021.
7. Josh Bersin, "Why Diversity and Inclusion Will Be a Top Priority for 2016," *Forbes* (December 6, 2015), http://www.forbes.com/sites/joshbersin/2015/12/06/why-diversity-and-inclusion-will-be-a-top-priority-for-2016/#37dc803f4bd4. Accessed May 31, 2016.
8. Dieter Holger, "The Business Case for More Diversity," *The Wall Street Journal* (October 28, 2019), R11.
9. Ibid.
10. William F. Glueck and James Ledvinka, "Equal Employment Opportunity Programs," in William F. Glueck, *Personnel: A Diagnostic Approach*, rev. ed. (Dallas, TX: Business Publications, 1978), 593–633.

11. "Equal Opportunity: A Scorecard," *Dun's Review* (November 1979), 107.

12. See U.S. Bureau of Labor Statistics (2019), https://www.bls.gov/cps/demographics.htm. Accessed May 27, 2021; Soi Trujillo, "The 'Latino Factor' Will Save America's Economy," *The Wall Street Journal* (August 30, 2018), A15.

13. Ibid.

14. Tara Law, "Women Are Now the Majority of the U.S. Workforce—but Working Women Still Face Serious Challenges," *Time* (January 16, 2020), https://time.com/5766787/women-workforce/. Accessed May 28, 2021.

15. Jonathan Rothwell and Lydia Saad, "How Have U.S. Working Women Fared During the Pandemic?" *Gallup* (March 8, 2021), https://news.gallup.com/poll/330533/working-women-fared-during-pandemic.aspx. Accessed May 28, 2021.

16. Catalyst, "Lesbian, Bisexual, Transgender Workplace Issues" (June 1, 2021), https://www.catalyst.org/research/lesbian-gay-bisexual-and-transgender-workplace-issues/. Accessed May 28, 2021.

17. JDSupra, "Federal Legislation to Bar Discrimination Based on Sexual Orientation and Gender Identity Passes in the U.S. House, Is Under Consideration in the Senate," March 9, 2021, https://www.jdsupra.com/legalnews/federal-legislation-to-bar-9922287/. Accessed May 31, 2021.

18. EEOC, "Title VII: Enforces Job Rights" (Washington, DC: The U.S. Equal Employment Opportunity Commission, Office of Communications, October 1988), 1.

19. U.S. Equal Employment Opportunity Commission, "LGBT-Based Sex Discrimination Charges," https://www.eeoc.gov/statistics/lgbt-based-sex-discrimination-charges. Accessed May 28, 2021.

20. U.S. Equal Opportunity Commission, "Age Discrimination," http://www.eeoc.gov/youth/age.html. Accessed May 28, 2021.

21. *Legal Dictionary.net*, "Bona Fide Occupational Qualification," http://legaldictionary.net/bona-fide-occupational-qualification/. Accessed May 28, 2021.

22. EEOC, "Age Discrimination," 2020, https://www.eeoc.gov/age-discrimination. Accessed May 28, 2021.

23. R. Scott Oswald and Tom Harrington, "What It Takes to Prove an Age Discrimination Case," *Forbes* (September 28, 2015), http://www.forbes.com/sites/nextavenue/2015/09/28/what-it-takes-to-prove-an-age-discrimination-case/#760a34a27dbe. Accessed June 1, 2016.

24. Guido Palazzo, Franciska Krings, and Ulrich Hoffrage, "Ethical Blindness," *The Journal of Business Ethics* (Vol. 109, 2012), 323–338.

25. Stanford Encyclopedia of Philosophy, "Implicit Bias," 2019, https://plato.stanford.edu/entries/implicit-bias/. Accessed May 28, 2021.

26. EEOC, "Equal Work, Equal Pay" (Washington, DC: The U.S. Equal Employment Opportunity Commission, Office of Communications, October 1988), 1.

27. Eric Bachman, "Today Is Equal Pay Day. Here's What You Need to Know about the Equal Pay Act," *Forbes*, (March 24, 2021), https://www.forbes.com/sites/ericbachman/2021/03/24/today-is-equal-pay-day-heres-what-you-need-to-know-about-the-equal-pay-act/?sh=76326d6e658e. Accessed May 28, 2021.

28. Allen Smith, "U.S. House of Representatives Passes Paycheck Fairness Act," SHRM (April 15, 2021), https://www.shrm.org/resourcesandtools/legal-and-compliance/employment-law/pages/house-passes-paycheck-fairness-act-2021.aspx. Accessed May 28, 2021.

29. "Pay Equity and State-by-State Laws," Paycor (December 4, 2020), https://www.paycor.com/resource-center/articles/pay-equity-and-state-by-state-laws/. Accessed May 28, 2021.

30. Elissa Sangster, "The Pay Gap Is Real. Don't Let Anyone Convince You Otherwise," *Forbes* (March 24, 2021), https://www.forbes.com/sites/elissasangster/2021/03/24/the-pay-gap-is-real-dont-let-anyone-convince-you-otherwise/?sh=4818cd2d7ceb. Accessed May 28, 2021.

31. Ibid.

32. EEOC, "Equal Employment Opportunity Is the Law" (Washington, DC: The U.S. Equal Employment Opportunity Commission, Office of Communications 1986), 1.

33. Henry H. Perritt Jr., *Americans with Disabilities Act Handbook* (New York: John Wiley & Sons, 1990), vii.

34. U.S. Department of Justice, Office on the Americans with Disabilities Act, *The Americans with Disabilities Act: Questions and Answers,* https://adata.org/guide/americans-disabilities-act-questions-and-answers. Accessed May 28, 2021.

35. Kim Lyons, "Lyft Settles with Justice Department over Rider Accessibility Complaints," *The Verge* (June 25, 2020), https://www.theverge.com/2020/6/25/21302866/lyft-settles-wheelchair-accessibility-complaints-justice-department. Accessed May 28, 2021.

36. Beth Brophy, "Supreme Court Gives Motherhood Its Legal Due," *U.S. News & World Report* (January 26, 1987), 12.

37. Bryan Robinson, "Pregnancy Discrimination In the Workplace Affects Mother and Baby Health," *Forbes* (July 11, 2020), https://www.forbes.com/sites/bryanrobinson/2020/07/11/pregnancy-discrimination-in-the-workplace-affects-mother-and-baby-health/?sh=7a10987cac69. Accessed May 28, 2021.

38. VedderPrice, "EEOC Guidance on Pregnancy Discrimination Acts Stirs Controversy in Form and Content," http://www.vedderprice.com/eeoc-guidance-on-pregnancy-discrimination-act-stirs-controversy-in-form-and-content/. Accessed July 9, 2021.

39. Ibid.

40. Ibid.

41. "Under a Civil Rights Cloud, Fetal Protection Looks Dismal," *Insight* (April 15, 1991), 40–41.

42. U.S. Department of Labor, "Safety and Health Topics," http://www.osha.gov/SLTC/reproductivehazards/. Accessed July 9, 2021.

43. Dan Markiewicz, "Avoid a Costly Court Challenge." *Industrial Safety & Hygiene News* 47.2 (2013): 18.

44. Andrea Davis, "GINA Can't Prevent Employee Disclosure," *Employee Benefit News* 27.1 (2013), 9–10.

45. Thomas H. Christopher, Louis W. Doherty, and David C. Lindsay, "EEOC Issues Final Regulations on Genetic Discrimination in the Workplace," *Employee Relations Law Journal* 36.4 (2011), 45–49.

46. Ibid.

47. Jessica L. Roberts, "Preempting Discrimination: Lessons from the Genetic Information Nondiscrimination Act." *Vanderbilt Law Review* 63.2 (2010): 437–490.

48. Antonio Regalado, "More than 26 Million People Have Taken an At-Home Ancestry Test," *MIT Technology Review* (February 11, 2019), https://www.technologyreview.com/2019/02/11/103446/more-than-26-million-people-have-taken-an-at-home-ancestry-test/. Accessed May 28, 2021.

49. Kira Peikoff, "Fearing Punishment for Bad Genes," *The New York Times* (April 7, 2014), http://www.nytimes.com/2014/04/08/science/fearing-punishment-for-bad-genes.html?_r=0. Accessed July 9, 2021.

50. Ibid.

51. John D. Rapoport and Brian L. P. Zevnik, *The Employee Strikes Back* (New York: Collier Books, 1994), 233–234.

52. EEOC, "What You Should Know: The EEOC, Conciliation and Litigation," https://www.eeoc.gov/laws/guidance/what-you-should-know-eeoc-conciliation-and-litigation. Accessed May 28, 2021.

53. EEOC Charge Statistics, https://www.eeoc.gov/eeoc/statistics/enforcement/charges.cfm. Accessed May 28, 2021.

54. Raynes, Lawn, and Hehmeyer, "What Is the Difference Between Disparate Impact and Disparate Treatment Discrimination?" https://rayneslaw.com/what-is-the-difference-between-disparate-impact-and-disparate-treatment-discrimination/. Accessed May 28, 2021.

55. James Ledvinka, *Federal Regulation of Personnel and Human Resource Management* (Boston, MA: Kent, 1982), 37. Also see W. N. Outten, R. J. Rabin, and L. R. Lipman, *The Rights of Employees and Union Members* (Carbondale, IL: Southern Illinois University Press, 1994), chapter VIII, 154–156.

56. See Jess Bravin, "Employers Watch Court in Religious-Garb Case," *The Wall Street Journal* (February 23, 2015), B1; Richard Wolf, "Muslim Girl Wins in Job Dispute," *USA Today* (June 2, 2015), 8A.

57. Ibid.

58. Raynes, Lawn, and Hehmeyer.

59. *Griggs v. Duke Power Company*, 401 U.S. 424, 1971.

60. Theodore Purcell, "Minorities, Management of and Equal Employment Opportunity," in L. R. Bittel (ed.), *Encyclopedia of Professional Management* (New York: McGraw-Hill, 1978), 744–745.

61. Wu Yiyang, "Scaling the Wall and Running the Mile: The Role of Physical-Selection Procedures in the Disparate Impact Narrative," *University of Pennsylvania Law Review* 160.4 (2012): 1195–1238.

62. Mary-Kathryn Zachary, "Discrimination without Intent," *Supervision* (May 2003), 23–26.

63. Biddle Consulting Group, "Uniform Guidelines on Employee Selection Procedures," http://www.uniformguidelines.com/questionandanswers.html. Accessed July 9, 2021.

64. EEOC, "Race/Color Discrimination," https://www.eeoc.gov/racecolor-discrimination. Accessed May 29, 2021.

65. Ibid.

66. Paul Newkirk, "Diversity Has Become a Booming Business," *Time* (October 21–28, 2019), p. 38.

67. Theo Francis, Inti Pacheco, and Thomas Gryta, "Companies Detail Diversity Data," *The Wall Street Journal* (March 2, 2021), B5.

68. Orlando Patterson, "The Long Reach of Racism in the U.S.," *The Wall Street Journal* (June 5, 2020), B4.

69. Gallup, 2021.

70. Ibid.

71. See Christopher Tang, "Why Successful Asian Americans Are Penalized at the Workplace," *The Los Angeles Times* (May 6, 2021), https://www.latimes.com/opinion/story/2021-05-06/asian-bias-discrimination-corporate-culture-glass-ceiling. Accessed May 29, 2021; N'dea Yancey-Bragg, "'Stop Killing Us': Attacks on Asian Americans Highlight Rise in Hate Incidents Amid COVID-19," *USA Today* (February 24, 2021), Accessed May 29, 2021.

72. Ibid.

73. Rachel Feintzeig, "Diversity Is a Higher Priority: Now What?", *The Wall Street Journal* (July 20, 2020), A13.

74. Ibid.

75. Vanessa Fuhrmans, "What #Metoo Has to Do with the Workplace Gender Gap," *The Wall Street Journal* (October 23, 2018), R1.

76. Ibid.

77. Regina Herzlinger, "Has the Glass Ceiling Been Shattered for Women Leading Major Companies?" *The Huffpost Business* (June 2, 2013), http://www.huffingtonpost.com/regina-e-herzlinger/has-the-glass-ceiling-bee_b_3001344.html. Accessed June 2, 2016.

78. Jodi Kantor, "A Titan's How-To on Breaking the Glass Ceiling," *The New York Times* (February 21, 2013), http://www.nytimes.com/2013/02/22/us/sheryl-sandberg-lean-in-author-hopes-to-spur-movement.html?pagewanted=all. Accessed July 9, 2021.

79. Sheryl Sandberg and Rachel Thomas, "Women Are Leaning In. Now Companies Need to Lean In, Too," *The Wall Street Journal* (October 23, 2018), R2.

80. Lauren Weber and Vanessa Fuhrmans, "The Coronavirus Setback," *The Wall Street Journal* (September 30, 2020), R1.

81. See "The State of the Gender Pay Gap in 2021," *Payscale* (March, 2021), https://www.payscale.com/data/gender-pay-gap. Accessed May 29, 2021; Steven M. Davidoff, "Why So Few Women Reach the Executive Rank," *The New York Times* (April 2, 2013), http://dealbook.nytimes.com/2013/04/02/why-so-few-women-reach-the-executive-rank/. Accessed May 29, 2021.

82. Ibid.

83. Ibid.

84. Ibid.

85. Sam Turner, "Gender Inequality in the Workplace Goes Beyond the 'Pay Gap'," *NewsOK* (January 20, 2016), https://www.oakdaleleader.com/business/business-news/gender-inequality-in-the-workplace-goes-beyond-the-pay-gap/. Accessed July 9, 2021.

86. Trae Vassalo, Ellen Levy, Michele Madansky, Hillary Mickell, Bennett Porter, Monica Leas, and Julie Oberweis, *The Elephant in the Room Study*, http://www.elephantinthevalley.com/. Accessed July 9, 2021.

87. Kristen P. Jones, Chad I. Peddie, Veronica Gilrane, Eden King, and Alexis Gray, "Not So Subtle: A Meta-Analytic Investigation of the Correlates of Subtle and Overt Discrimination," *Journal of Management* (DOI: 10.1177/0149206313506466, 2013).

88. Anne-Marie Slaughter, "A Toxic Work World," *The New York Times* (September 201, 2015), SR1.

89. Chelsea R. Willness, Piers Steel, and Kibeom Lee, "A Meta-Analysis of the Antecedents and Consequences of Workplace Sexual Harassment," *Personnel Psychology* (Spring 2007), 127–162.

90. Jana Szostek, Charles J. Hobson, Andrea Griffin, Anna Rominger, Marilyn Vasquez, and Natalie Murillo (2012), "EEOC Sexual Harassment Settlements: An Empirical Analysis," *Employee Relations Law Journal* 38, no. 1: 3–13.

91. See "Charges Alleging Sexual Harassment FY 2010-2020," EEOC, https://www.eeoc.gov/statistics/charges-alleging-sex-based-harassment-charges-filed-eeoc-fy-2010-fy-2020. Accessed May 29, 2021; Lauren Weber, "Harassment Claims Still Bring Retaliation," *The Wall Street Journal* (December 18, 2018), B6.

92. Ibid.

93. EEOC, "Charges Alleging Sex-Based Harassment FY2010–FY2020," https://www.eeoc.gov/statistics/charges-alleging-sex-based-harassment-charges-filed-eeoc-fy-2010-fy-2020. Accessed June 4, 2021.

94. Ibid.

95. Erik Brady, "Colorado Scandal Could Hit Home to Other Colleges," *USA Today* (May 26, 2004), http://usatoday30.usatoday.com/sports/college/football/big12/2004-05-26-colorado-cover_x.htm?csp=34. Accessed July 9, 2021.

96. Susan B. Garland, "Finally, a Corporate Tip Sheet on Sexual Harassment," *Businessweek* (July 13, 1998), 39.

97. Anita Cava, "Sexual Harassment Claims: New Framework for Employers," *Business and Economic Review* (July–September 2001), 13–16; Ted Meyer and Linda Schoonmaker, "Employers Must Think outside the Sexual Harassment Box," *Texas Lawyer* (February 12, 2001), 36.

98. EEOC, "Religion-Based Charges FY 1997–FY 2020," https://www.eeoc.gov/statistics/religion-based-charges-charges-filed-eeoc-fy-1997-fy-2020. Accessed June 4, 2021.

99. EEOC, "Fact Sheet on Recent EEOC Religious Discrimination Litigation," https://www.eeoc.gov/fact-sheet-recent-eeoc-religious-discrimination-litigation. Accessed June 4, 2021.

100. "McDonald's Franchisor Settles EEOC Religious Discrimination Suit," *JDSupra* (August 19, 2020), https://www.jdsupra.com/legalnews/mcdonald-s-franchisor-settles-eeoc-98554/. Accessed May 29, 2021.

101. EEOC, "What You Should Know: The EEOC and Protections for LGBT Workers," EEOC, https://www.eeoc.gov/laws/guidance/what-you-should-know-eeoc-and-protections-lgbt-workers. Accessed May 29, 2021.

102. See *Catalyst* 2020, "Lesbian, Gay, Bisexual, Transgender Workplace Issues" (May 1, 2021) https://www.catalyst.org/research/lesbian-gay-bisexual-and-transgender-workplace-issues/. Accessed May 29, 2021; *Catalyst* 2016, "Lesbian, Gay, Bisexual, Transgender Workplace Issues," http://www.catalyst.org/knowledge/lesbian-gay-bisexual-transgender-workplace-issues. Accessed May 29, 2021.

103. Ibid.

104. Dawn Ennis, "Survey: More Than 1 in 3 LGBTQ Youth Experience Discrimination at Work," *Forbes* (March 30, 2021), https://www.forbes.com/sites/dawnstaceyennis/2021/03/30/survey-more-than-1-in-3-lgbtq-youth-experience-discrimination-at-work/?sh=5a08bc555519. Accessed May 29, 2021.

105. Ibid.

106. Carolina Gonzalez, "US Corporate Leaders Speak Out Against Anti-LGBTQ Bills," Aljazeera (April 7, 2021), https://www.aljazeera.com/economy/2021/4/7/us-corporate-leaders-speak-out-against-states-anti-lgbtq-bills. Accessed May 29, 2021.

107. Human Rights Campaign, "2021 Officially Becomes the Worst Year," https://www.hrc.org/press-releases/2021-officially-becomes-worst-year-in-recent-history-for-lgbtq-state-legislative-attacks-as-unprecedented-number-of-states-enact-record-shattering-number-of-anti-lgbtq-measures-into-law. Accessed July 9, 2021.

108. Joshua Green, "Corporate Activism on Voting Rights Echoes Role in LGBTQ Battles," *Bloomberg Businessweek* (April 29, 2021), https://www.bloomberg.com/news/articles/2021-04-29/corporate-activism-on-voting-rights-echoes-role-in-lgbtq-battles. Accessed May 29, 2021.

109. Human Rights Campaign, "Sexual Orientation and Gender Identity Definitions," http://www.hrc.org/resources/entry/sexual-orientation-and-gender-identity-terminology-and-definitions. Accessed July 9, 2021.

110. David L. Chappell, "If Affirmative Action Fails …What Then?" *The New York Times* (May 8, 2004), B7; Terry H. Anderson, *The Pursuit of Fairness: A History of Affirmative Action* (New York: Oxford University Press, May 2004).

111. Ibid.

112. Matt Krentz, "Survey: What Diversity and Inclusion Policies Do Employees Actually Want?" *Harvard Business Review* (February 5, 2019), https://hbr.org/2019/02/survey-what-diversity-and-inclusion-policies-do-employees-actually-want. Accessed May 29, 2021.

113. Society for Human Resource Management, "Workplace Diversity Series Part I: Moving Forward with Diversity" (March 1, 2016), https://www.shrm.org/research/articles/articles/pages/workplacediversityseriespartimovingforwardwithdiversity.aspx. Accessed May 29, 2021.

114. Matt Krentz, Justin Dean, and Gabrielle Novacek, "Diversity Is Just the First Step. Inclusion Comes Next," *BCG* (April 24, 2021), https://www.bcg.com/en-us/publications/2019/diversity-first-step-inclusion-comes-next. Accessed May 29, 2021.

115. Society for Human Resource Management Diversity and Inclusion Report (April 8, 2014), https://www.shrm.org/research/surveyfindings/articles/pages/diversity-inclusion.aspx. Accessed May 29, 2021.

116. See Valorie Waldon, "Diversity Farigue: What It Is and Why It Matters," Employers Council (September 3, 2020), https://blog.employerscouncil.org/2020/09/03/diversity-fatigue-what-it-is-and-why-it-matters/. Accessed May 29, 2021; "Diversity Fatigue," *The Economist* (February 13, 2016), http://www.economist.com/news/business/21692865-making-most-workplace-diversity-requires-hard-work-well-good-intentions-diversity. Accessed July 9, 2021.

117. Rachel Feintzeig, "More Companies Say Targets Are the Key to Diversity," *The Wall Street Journal* (September 30, 2016), http://www.wsj.com/articles/more-companies-say-targets-are-the-key-to-diversity-1443600464. Accessed May 29. 2021.

118. Daniel Seligman, "How 'Equal Opportunity' Turned into Employment Quotas," *Fortune* (March 1973), 160–168.

119. See Anemona Hartocollis, "Harvard Victory Pushes Admissions Case Toward a More Conservative Supreme Court," *The New York Times* (November 12, 2020), https://www.nytimes.com/2020/11/12/us/harvard-affirmative-action.html. Accessed May 29, 2021.

120. Markkula Center for Applied Ethics, "Justice and Fairness," https://www.scu.edu/ethics/ethics-resources /ethical-decision-making/justice-and-fairness/. Accessed June 4, 2021.

121. Adam Liptak, "Supreme Court Upholds Affirmative Action Program at University of Texas," *The New York Times* (June 23, 2016), http://www.nytimes.com/2016/06/24/us /politics/supreme-court-affirmative-action-university-of -texas.html?=&_r=0. Accessed May 29, 2021.

122. Halley Potter, "What Can We Learn from States That Ban Affirmative Action?" *The Century Foundation* (June 26, 2014), https://tcf.org/content/commentary /what-can-we-learn-from-states-that-ban-affirmative- action/?version=meter%20at%207&module=meter- Links&pgtype=article&contentId&mediaId&referrer =https%3A%2F%2Fwww.google.com&priority=true&act ion=click&contentCollection=meter-links-click. Accessed May 29, 2021.

123. Peter Coy, "What Big Companies Say about the Harvard Affirmative Action Case," Bloomberg Businessweek (November 13, 2020), https://www.bloomberg.com/news /articles/2020-11-13/what-big-companies-say-about-the -harvard-affirmative-action-case. Accessed May 29, 2021.

124. Carmen Morris, "Shaping a New Normal for Diversity and Inclusion Is Key for Future Success," *Forbes* (August 18, 2020), https://www.forbes.com/sites /carmenmorris/2020/08/18/shaping-a-new-normal -for-diversity-and-inclusion-is-key-for-future- success/?sh=6c4d18ce75bb. Accessed May 29, 2021.

125. Iris Bohnet, "Real Fixes for Workplace Bias," *The Wall Street Journal* (March 11, 2016), https://www.wsj.com /articles/real-fixes-for-workplace-bias-1457713338. Accessed June 4, 2021.

126. Ibid.

Part 6

External Stakeholder Issues

Chapter 14

Consumer Stakeholders: Information Issues

Chapter 15

Consumer Stakeholders: Product and Service Issues

Chapter 16

Community Stakeholders and Corporate Philanthropy

14

Consumer Stakeholders: Information Issues

Chapter Learning Outcomes

After studying this chapter, you should be able to:

1. Describe the consumer movement and identify the Consumer's Magna Carta and explain its meaning.
2. Identify product information issues that are affected by business's social and ethical responsibilities. Identify the major abuses of advertising and discuss specific controversial advertising issues.
3. Describe the role and functions of the Federal Trade Commission (FTC).

4. Explain important consumer-related legislation that has been passed—Credit Card Act (CARD) and the Consumer Financial Protection Bureau (CFPB).
5. Discuss the strengths and weaknesses of self-regulation of advertising. How does self-regulation vary from being socially responsible and ethical?
6. Identify the three moral models and their likely perspectives on consumer stakeholders.

As businesses have been striving to come out of the worldwide pandemic, they all have been fighting for the hearts and minds of consumers. Consumers around the world have been trying to determine what their new normal will be in terms of spending. There is noticeable variance in consumer sentiments and behavior across countries.[1] In the United States, as the big changes from the global pandemic continue to evolve—digital transformation, emergence of a homebody economy, and a shock to consumer loyalty—signs are appearing that consumers are in a spending recovery. Discretionary spending has continued to increase since summer of 2020, especially in the "essentials" category. Consumer spending is expected to continue increasing into 2021 and beyond.[2] Despite intermittent lockdowns, European optimism about consumer spending recovery remains steady.[3] Consumer spending and behavior are the primary drivers of the business-and-consumer stakeholder relationship, and most economies are built upon these relationships growing and remaining strong. By all measures, however, it is clear that businesses need to be paying careful attention to customer stakeholders if they expect to survive and grow.

In general, consumers are expecting the economy to improve as the pandemic fades.[4] However, predictions are that habits formed during the pandemic are likely to continue into the years ahead. Euromonitor, a global market-research firm based in London, predicts more brand activism, more emphasis on spontaneity and convenience, more open-air activities, an increased digital world, thoughtful frugality, an obsession with safety, and greater self-awareness.[5] Other expected trends established in 2020 are expected to continue, including an increased

concern for privacy, a return to instant gratification, homebody products and services, clean-air activism, local pride, and reuse as the new recycle.[6] In other words, businesses are now facing consumers who have not only traditional, conventional needs but also newly imagined ones.

In light of these changes, one cannot help but ask the perennial question: How important are consumers as stakeholders? According to management expert Peter Drucker, there is only one valid definition of business purpose: *to create a customer*.[7] *Retaining* customers is essential, too. In fact, small increases in customer retention rates can lead to dramatic increases in profits.[8] Clearly, businesses must create and retain customers if they are to succeed in today's competitive marketplace. It is not surprising, therefore, that **customer relationship management (CRM)** continues to be an important part of marketing.[9] Customer relationship management is "the ability of an organization to effectively identify, acquire, foster, and retain loyal profitable customers."[10] CRM is digitized and managed through software platforms from companies such as Salesforce, SAP, and Oracle.

One vital key to successful business–customer relationships is the concept of **customer engagement**.[11] Customer engagement is all about the emotional connection companies are able to establish between their customers and the company. Gallup, in its research, focuses on three assessments that customers make: whether the company always delivers what it promises, the pride the customer feels by being a company's customer, and the judgment made that the company is the best match for the customer.[12] Research has shown that simply satisfying customers is no longer the key to increasing sales. Engaging them is the key. Fully engaged customers bring in 30 to 45 percent more annual revenues.[13]

In practice, however, a focus on customer satisfaction seems to be more prevalent than a focus on customer engagement. As one expert notes, "satisfied customers tell three friends, but angry customers tell 3,000."[14] There are many reasons why customers are not satisfied today. One reason seldom gauged is that consumers are exhausted at all the choices they face and the decisions they must make in their roles as consumers. Whether the consumer is attempting to buy a new mobile device or a cup of coffee, the choices are dizzying. And, when it comes to paying for products and services, there is too much fine print to read, much less understand. In short, as companies have sought to satisfy customers, they have frustrated them with too much complexity, whether it be in the products or services offered or the information related to the decision, or the after-purchase experience.[15] Exhausted customers are seldom satisfied customers.

As it is apparent, the business-and-consumer stakeholder issue is at the forefront of discussions about business and its relationships with, and responsibility to, the society in which it exists because we are all consumers and companies are not sustainable without us. Products and services are the most visible manifestations of business in society. For this reason, the whole issue deserves careful examination. Consequently, we devote two chapters to consumer stakeholders. In this chapter, we focus on the consumer movement and product/service information issues—most notably, advertising. In the next chapter, we focus on the product or service itself, especially issues such as quality and safety.

14.1 The Consumer Movement

The basic expectations of the modern consumer movement were found in the **Consumer's Magna Carta**, or the four basic consumer rights spelled out by President John F. Kennedy in his "Special Message on Protecting the Consumer Interest."[16] Those rights included the right *to safety*, the right *to be informed*, the right *to choose*, and the right *to be heard*. In addition to these basic rights, consumers today want "fair value" for money spent, a product that will meet "reasonable" expectations, a product (or service) with full disclosure of its specifications, a product (or service) that has been truthfully advertised, and a product that is safe and has been subjected to appropriate product safety testing. Consumers also expect that if a product is too dangerous, it will be removed from the market or some other appropriate action will be taken.

According to marketing expert Philip Kotler, today's consumers' lives are characterized by a number of changes that have had major impacts on the consumer movement. A few of these changes include the following:[17]

- A digital revolution with computers, Internet, smartphones, Wikipedia, and social media
- An ability to order almost anything to be delivered by Amazon, Walmart, or other vendors with accelerated speed

- A determination by major companies to please their customers and meet or exceed consumer expectations
- More companies trying to please their employees as well as consumers indicating that stakeholder capitalism is evident
- More companies willing to take a stand on public issues and demonstrate their values

In spite of these many positive changes, consumers continue to express disappointments indicating they are often neglected or mistreated.

From a historical perspective, the roots of consumer activism in the United States date back to 1906, when Upton Sinclair published *The Jungle*, his famous exposé of unsanitary conditions in the meatpacking industry.[18] The contemporary wave of consumer activism, however, has been growing for many decades, although in a variety of forms.[19] Today it is called consumerism, consumer activism, or the consumer movement.

The following definition of **consumerism** captures the essential nature of the consumer movement:

> Consumerism is a social movement seeking to augment the rights and powers of buyers in relation to sellers.[20]

Although the modern consumer movement is often said to have begun with the publication of Ralph Nader's criticism of General Motors in his book *Unsafe at Any Speed*,[21] the impetus for the movement was actually a complex combination of circumstances. Doubtless, the factors of affluence, education, awareness, and rising expectations mentioned in Chapter 1 also have been at work. And, since everyone is a consumer, this sector of corporate social responsibility (CSR) will naturally continue and never go away.

Ralph Nader's contribution to the birth, growth, and nurturance of the consumer movement cannot be overstated. Nader arrived on the scene more than 50 years ago, and he is still the acknowledged "father of the consumer movement." The impact of Nader's auto safety exposé, *Unsafe at Any Speed*, was momentous. His book not only gave rise to auto safety regulations and devices (safety belts, padded dashboards, stronger door latches, head restraints, air bags, etc.) that we take for granted today, but it also created a new era—that of the consumer. Nader, personally, was thrust into national prominence.

Nader put his time, energy, and money to work and built an enormous and far-reaching consumer protection empire. His legions of zealous activists became known as "Nader's Raiders." Nader popularized public interest law and his activism generated significant growth in the popularity of law schools. Nader and the consumer movement were the impetus for consumer legislation being passed in the 1970s.[22]

Nader continues to be a provocative activist for the consumer voice. Consumer complaints did not disappear with the advent of Nader's activism; instead, they intensified. One of Nader's greatest contributions is that he made consumer complaints respectable. Though less active today in part due to age, in 2016, Nader opened the American Museum of Tort Law in his hometown of Winsted, Connecticut, celebrating class action lawsuits and tort law.[23]

14.1a Consumerism Today

There is not a unified consumer movement today though consumer activism is alive, well, and diversified. Many groups make up the loose confederation known today as the consumer movement. Consumerism involves grassroots organizations, social media activism, and the rise of many different nonprofit organizations and websites that increasingly specialize in one aspect of consumer products or services.[24] At a broad level, the consumer movement is represented by advocacy organizations such as the Consumer Federation of America, Public Citizen, American Council on Consumer Interests, and Consumer's Union of United States, Inc., which publishes *Consumer Reports,* a highly respected magazine focused on evaluating products and services in the marketplace. Some of the more specialized organizations that focus on specific consumer issues include Center for Auto Safety, Center for Science in the Public Interest, and the Better Business Bureau.[25]

Many of today's consumers' issues extend beyond the traditional customer complaints we often read about. Some of these issues include the following[26]:

- Lack of clean water and healthy living conditions and a shortage of stores characterizes many underprivileged communities today.
- The prices of many important products are too high. This includes pharmaceuticals, health-care insurance, college education, and other product areas.
- There is considerable packaging waste affecting landfills and water quality in many communities.
- There are too many brands lacking differentiation, resulting in stores carrying too many goods and stores are larger than they need to be.
- There is a lack of healthier foods contained less sugar, salt, and fat.

In spite of these broader issues, the consumer movement is still driven by traditional consumer problems and consumer complaints. Figure 14-1 lists some of the most frequently cited examples of consumers' problems with business. In addition to this list of general consumer problems, the Consumer Federation of America each year lists its top ten consumer complaints, by category, and its most recent listing included issues related to the following[27]:

- Autos—misrepresentations in advertising, lemons, faulty repairs
- Home improvement/construction—shoddy work, failure to start/complete
- Credit/debit—billing/fee disputes, predatory lending, abusive collection
- Retail sales—false advertising, deceptive practices, problems with rebates and coupons
- Services and communications—misrepresentations, shoddy work, failure to perform
- Landlord/tenant—unhealthy/unsafe conditions, failure to make repairs, deposits
- Telecommunication sales—misrepresentations, deceptive practices, failure to deliver
- Health products/services—misleading claims, unlicensed practitioners
- Fraud—bogus sweepstakes, work-at-home scams, fake check scams
- Household goods—misrepresentations, failure to deliver, faulty repairs

Before we consider more closely the corporate response to the consumer movement and the consumer stakeholder, it is fruitful to examine some of the issues that have become prominent in the business–consumer relationship and the role that the major federal regulatory bodies have assumed in addressing these issues. Broadly, we may classify the major kinds of issues into two groups: *product/service information* and the *product/service itself.* As stated earlier, in this chapter we focus on product/service information issues such as advertising, warranties, packaging, and labeling. The next chapter focuses on the product or service itself.

Figure 14-1 Examples of Typical Consumer Problems with Business

- The high prices of many products
- The poor quality of many products
- The complexity of products
- Misleading and deceptive advertising, often on social media
- Hidden fees
- Poor quality of after-sales service
- Too many products breaking or going wrong after you bring them home
- Misleading packaging or labeling
- Slack filling
- The feeling that it is a waste of time to complain about consumer problems because nothing substantial will be achieved
- Inadequate guarantees and warranties
- Failure of companies to handle complaints properly
- Too many products that are dangerous or unsafe
- The absence of reliable information about various products and services
- Not knowing what to do if something is wrong with a product you have bought

14.1b Product and Service Information Issues

Why have questions been raised about business's social and ethical responsibilities in the area of product and service information? Most consumers know the answer. Companies understandably want to portray their products in the most flattering light. However, efforts to paint an appealing portrait of a product can easily cross the line into misinformation or deception regarding the product's attributes. Consumer Reports conducts independent tests of products and report their findings in their print and online editions of *Consumer Reports (CR)*.[28] "Selling It" is a featured segment in *Consumer Reports*; it is designed to "memorialize the excesses in the world of marketing." These are goofs, glitches, and gotchas spotted by their readers. Quite often the ads are contradictory. The following items are examples of recent often-humorous absurdities they chronicle:[29]

> A sign on the wall of a car wash reads: Free Vacuum—$7. *Apparently, free doesn't mean what it used to.*
>
> The label on a bottle of hand sanitizer reads: Edible | Alcohol. *This container of sanitizer was eventually recalled.*
>
> At the top of a label of dishwashing liquid, the label read: "New & Improved Scent." Further down the label, it read "Original Scent." *Sometimes the new and improved is the same as the old one!*

These cases are actual examples of the questionable and careless use of **product information**, usually in an ad, flyer, or on a sign. It is doubtful whether the firms that created these communications were intending to deceive; however, the information they provided did not match the reality of the product or service. Business has a legal and an ethical responsibility to provide fair and accurate information about its products or services.

The primary ethical issue with product or service information falls in the realm of advertising. Other information-related areas include warranties or guarantees, packaging, labeling, instructions for use, and the sales techniques used by direct sellers. Information about after-sale service is also a critical issue.

14.1c Advertising Issues

The 4Ps of marketing include product, place, price, and promotion.[30] Companies are looking for effective ways to promote their products and services, and advertising is the primary tool they employ. The advertising industry represents the face of big business to consumers. Advertising expenditures were down in 2020 due to the pandemic, but forecasts are for advertising to grow significantly through 2022 and beyond. Half of this is expected to be digital media advertising.[31] As a result of its huge impact, the debate over the role of advertising in society has been going on for decades. Most observers have concentrated on the economic function of advertising in our market system, but opinions vary as to whether advertising is beneficial or detrimental as a business function. Critics charge that it is a wasteful and inefficient tool of business and that our current standard of living would be even higher if we could be freed from the negative influences of advertising.[32] In response, others have claimed that advertising is a beneficial component of the market system and that the increases in the standard of living and consumer satisfaction may be attributed to it.[33] The debate over whether advertising is a productive or wasteful business practice will undoubtedly continue. As a practical matter, however, advertising has become the lifeblood of the free enterprise system.

While *providing information* is one legitimate purpose of advertising in our society, another legitimate purpose is *persuasion*. Most consumers today expect that business advertises for the purpose of persuading them to buy their products or services, and they accept this as a part of the commercial system. Indeed, many people enjoy companies' attempts to come up with interesting ways to sell their products. It is commonplace for people to talk with one another about the latest appealing or entertaining advertisement they have seen but at the same time complain about others.

Awards are given for outstanding advertisements. The most famous ones today seem to be the ranking of the top ads that appear on Super Bowl Sunday. They generate considerable interest and talk before, during, and after the big game. But, just as excellent ads are recognized, so are the bad ones.[34] Ethical issues in advertising arise as companies cross over the line in their attempts to inform and persuade, and sometimes entertain, consumer stakeholders. The frequently heard phrase "the seamy side of advertising" alludes to the economic and social costs that derive from advertising abuses of which the reader is probably able to supply ample personal examples.

The Ethics in Practice (EIP) case titled "Can We Tell the Customer Anything to Make the Sale?" predated the Wells Fargo case at the end of the text. It is presented to clarify that these events in organizations have been occurring for some time. What are the parallels between this EIP and the end-of-text case?

Advertising Abuses. At this time, it is important to outline some of the major advertising abuses. There are four general types of advertising abuses in which ethical issues arise. These include situations in which advertisers are ambiguous, conceal facts, exaggerate, or employ psychological appeals.[35] These four types of deceptive appeals cover most of the common criticisms leveled at advertising.

Ambiguous Advertising One of the simplest ways that companies deceive is through **ambiguous advertising**, in which something about the product or service is not made clear because it is stated in a way that may mean several different things.

An ad can be made ambiguous in several ways. One way is to make a statement using **weasel words**, which leaves it

Ethics In Practice Case

Can We Tell the Customer Anything to Make the Sale?

While working as a customer service representative at a bank, a huge part of our job is to sell financial products to customers. We have to meet our goal every quarter by opening as many accounts as we can and to sell the bank's products. The branch manager is very tough, and we can be written up if we don't reach our goal; then, eventually, we can be terminated from the job if it continues.

As part of our jobs, we are supposed to make sure the customer is aware of the banking products they are getting or the accounts they are opening. Also, the customer service representative needs to explain the product fully to the customer and leave it up to them to decide if they want to open the account or not.

Some of my co-workers don't explain everything in detail to the customer unless the customer asks. However, I have overheard the whole conversation of one of my co-workers—telling a customer to open a lot of accounts combined together because they come as a package. This means the customer will have to open Checking, Savings, Debit Card, Apply for Overdraft Protection, and Credit Card.

My co-worker didn't give the customer an option to choose from but told her she had to open everything because it's a package—which is not true. The customer had no option because she trusted the employee because he knows better than her. The employee is the one that has more knowledge of what they are doing. The customer ended up opening all the accounts.

I was really in shock because I knew what was going on and what I have heard is totally wrong. I also knew that we are supposed to explain the products to the customer and leave the decision up to them as to what accounts they would like to open. I felt so bad that the customer just went by what the employee had said and opened everything, even though she didn't want it, but she believed she had to. In addition, the same co-worker always got recognized for selling a lot of products and always reaching his goal. I was in shock and I didn't know how to react.

1. Is not telling the whole story a deceptive practice? Are we being accurate, unambiguous, and clear? What's the harm if the customer opens all the accounts?
2. Should I have gone over to my co-worker's desk while he was with the customer and stopped what was going on and made sure the customer got the correct information? Or, should I have waited until the customer left and then gone to my co-worker to tell him that what he had done was wrong and unethical?
3. Is this misinformation given to the customer important enough for me to approach my manager and tell her everything I heard, even though the manager pushes us to sell accounts and do whatever it takes?
4. Is it possible my co-worker felt pressure from management to meet unrealistic goals and that this pressure was behind the deception?

Contributed by Haidy Elfarra

to the viewer to infer the message. Weasel words are inherently vague and the company could always claim it was not misleading the consumer. An example of a weasel word is *help*. Once an advertiser uses the qualifier "help," almost anything could follow, and the company could claim that it was not intending to deceive. We see ads that claim to "help us keep young," "help prevent cavities," or "help keep our houses germ free." Think how many times you have seen expressions in advertising such as "helps stop," "helps prevent," "helps fight," "helps you feel," "helps you look," or "helps you become."[36] Other weasel words include *like, virtually,* and *up to* (e.g., stops pain "up to" eight hours—which simply means it won't stop pain for more than eight hours). The use of such words makes ads ambiguous. Another way to make an ad ambiguous is through use of legalese, or other excessively complex and ambiguous terminology. To make matters worse, often the legalese and complex language is found in the fine print, which consumers are not inclined to read anyway.

Concealed Facts A type of advertising abuse called **concealed facts** refers to the practice of not telling the whole truth or deliberately not communicating information the consumer ought to have access to in making an informed choice. Another way of stating this is to say "a fact is concealed when its availability would probably make the desire,

purchase, or use of the product less likely than its absence."[37] This is a difficult area because few would argue that an advertiser is obligated to tell "everything," even if that were humanly possible. For example, a pain reliever company might claim the effectiveness of its product in superlative terms without stating that there are dozens of other products on the market that are just as effective.

Ethical issues arise when a firm, through its advertisements, presents facts in such a selective way that a false belief is created. For example, a burrito restaurant in a college town ran a humorous newspaper ad with "FREE BEER" in large block letters; underneath in small letters were the words "will not be served." No one accused this company of unlawful deception; however, not all instances of concealed facts are considered benign. Other concealed facts often occur with respect to hidden fees or surcharges on services. Today, you have to be a sophisticated consumer willing to do timely detective work to root out the rules and policies governing fees companies charge.

An increasingly popular form of concealed advertising is **product placement**, also known as embedded marketing, which is the practice of embedding products in movies and TV shows. Critics call this "stealth advertising." Product placements are everywhere—an Apple store in the background, an iPhone, a Coke, a Pepsi, Reebok shoes, Nike sweats, a GM car, and so on.[38] An unusual situation occurred when some films were delayed by a year or more due to the pandemic. By the time the film was ready to be released, the product models that had been placed in the film were outdated. Who wants to see James Bond talking on a phone model that's not the latest? Some of the films' product placements had to be edited or redone.[39]

Nonprofit activist groups have called this practice of sneaking in product pitches egregious and deceptive.[40] In a variation of product placement, termed **plot placement**, sponsors have paid to make their products integrated into the plotline of a TV show. Today, product and plot placement have given way to **brand integration**. With predictive analytics based on artificial intelligence, companies can now bring unparaled brand integration and customization across influencer marketing, streaming, TV, and film. Companies using brand integration today include KFC, General Mills, Disney, Bose, and P&G.[41]

Exaggerated Claims Companies can also mislead consumers by exaggerating the benefits of their products and services. **Exaggerated claims** are claims that simply cannot be substantiated by any kind of evidence. A few specific examples are helpful. The Dannon company claimed it was "scientifically proven" that its Activia yogurt helps regulate digestion and boost the immune system. A judge concluded they had not proven their case and were forced to pay $45 million to settle. Coca-Cola falsely claimed that its vitaminwater products could promote healthy joints and reduce the incidence of eye disease. The company agreed to change its labels. 5-Hour Energy claimed that its energy drink shots were more effective than coffee and that doctors recommended it. The claims were found to be exaggerated and the company was required to pay $4.3 million in penalties and fees.[42]

The general form of exaggeration is known as **puffery**, a euphemism for hyperbole or exaggeration that usually refers to the use of general superlatives. Is Budweiser really the "King of Beers"? Is Wheaties the "Breakfast of Champions"? Does "better ingredients" mean Papa John's has "Better Pizza"? Normally, a claim of general superiority is considered puffery and is allowable. However, companies walk a fine line when engaging in puffery. They need to be certain that no direct comparison is being made.

Most people are ambivalent about puffery, because the claims usually are so general and so frequent that any consumer would know that the firm is exaggerating and simply doing what many do by claiming their product is the best. However, exaggeration continues to be a deceptive practice.

Psychological Appeals In advertising, **psychological appeals** are those designed to persuade on the basis of human emotions and emotional needs rather than reason. There is perhaps as much reason to be concerned about ethics in this category as in any other category. One reason is that the products can seldom deliver what the ads promise (i.e., power, prestige, sex, masculinity, femininity, approval, acceptance, and other such psychological satisfactions).[43]

Another reason is that psychological appeals can stir emotions in a way that is manipulative and appears designed to take advantage of the consumer's vulnerability. For example, many home security salespeople will watch the newspapers and social media for reports of home break-ins and then call the homeowner with a sales pitch for a new home security system (appeal to fear).

Studies have demonstrated that emotional and psychological appeals resonate with consumers more than product functions or features. Thus, ads that employ a psychological aspect typically outsell others that focus on product functions. Demonstrating how a new computer will change your life for the better generally sells more computers than ads that explain how the computer works. Fear, uncertainty, and doubt are often used by businesses to motivate consumers to change their behavior.[44]

Though most advertising strives to appeal to our sight, an increasingly popular form of sensual advertising has been focusing on consumers' hearing. Neuromarketers have concluded, on the basis of research, that the most effective sounds in terms of their psychological appeals are babies giggling, cell phones vibrating, ATM machines dispensing cash, steaks sizzling on a grill, and a soda being popped and poured.[45] Such ploys represent questionable uses of psychological persuasion.

14.1d Specific Controversial Advertising Issues

We have considered four major kinds of deceptive advertising—ambiguous advertising, concealed facts, exaggerated claims, and psychological appeals. There are many other variations on these themes, but these are sufficient to make the point. Later in this chapter, we will discuss the FTC's attempts to keep advertising honest. But even in that discussion, we will see that the whole issue of what constitutes deceptive advertising is an evolving and amorphous concept, particularly when it comes to the task of proving deception and recommending appropriate remedial action. This is why the role of business responsibility is so crucial if business honestly desires to deal with its consumer stakeholders in a fair and truthful manner.

There are several specific advertising issues that have become particularly controversial in recent years because of borderline and questionable ethics. These merit further consideration: comparative advertising, use of sex in advertising, advertising to children, marketing to the poor, advertising of alcoholic beverages, cigarette advertising, health and environmental claims, ad creep, and social media advertising.

Comparative Advertising. One of the earliest forms of advertising that became controversial and threatened to affect advertising adversely is **comparative advertising**. This refers to the practice of directly comparing a firm's product or service with the product or service of a competitor—typically going so far as to name the competitor's

Ethics In Practice Case

What Does the Word *Free* Mean? Should It Be Banned in Advertising?

A recent article brought home a significant point. It said the "best things in life are free—unless they're not." What is your reaction when you see the word free in advertisements? Unless you are an inexperienced novice, you are probably uttering "what's the catch?" In other words, consumers today are skeptical when they are told something is free and yet marketers continue to find clever ways to make us "think" something is free.

Many different industries use the "free" offer as a key part of their advertising. One prominent industry that does this is the travel industry. Many of their advertisements include phrases such as "free tickets," "free checked bags," "free upgrades," and "kids eat free." One woman checked into a hotel that told her she had "free Internet." Turns out she did have free Internet but it was a basic, sluggish Internet connection and she kept getting pop-up ads asking her to upgrade to a premium version at an added charge. The woman did not believe she had gotten anything free, though the ad had drawn her in to this hotel.

The airlines are famous for their "free" offers. It turns out that no matter what, you end up paying for what you are getting—it's costing you tons of miles from your frequent flyer plan; it's costing you taxes and fees you never anticipated, and so on. You apply for a "free" item online and all they want, you find out, is all of your personal information along with complete contact information. Is this free? Or will the advertiser be using your data or selling your personal information to a third-party advertiser?

Chip Bell, author of *9½ Principles of Innovative Service*, has explained three types of "free." The first type is "truly free." This you get without any preconditions. You can walk into the store, pick it up, and walk out. A second type is "free with purchase." You buy this item and you'll get one of these. The third type is "free with strings." The cable provider offers you a "free" $300 rewards card to spend as you like. All you have to do is to convert to their service. The Big Print offers you a free printer. The Small Print says you have to buy your printer ink from their company for a year.

1. What questions should you ask yourself as you strive to understand what is a "free" offering?
2. Describe an experience you have had on social media where you thought you were getting something free, but it was not? If you pursued it, how did it turn out?
3. What ethical guidelines should an advertiser use to not be accused of exploiting the word *free*?
4. Is the word *free* so abusive in advertising that it should be banned by the FTC?

Sources: DirJournal, "Is There Anything Really Free Out There?" https://www.dirjournal.com/blogs/is-there-anything-really-free-out-there/, accessed April 21, 2021; Chip Bell, "9 ½ Principles of Innovative Service," https://www.simpletruths.com/personal-inspiration/nine-one-half-principles-of-innovative-service.html, accessed April 21, 2021; Christopher Elliott, "Best Things in Life Are Free—Unless They're Not," *USA Today*, August 4, 2014, 3B; Federal Trade Commission, "What Makes an Advertisement Deceptive?" https://www.ftc.gov/tips-advice/business-center/guidance/advertising-faqs-guide-small-business, accessed April 21, 2021.

brand or product. Some classic examples of past high-profile comparative campaigns include Coke versus Pepsi, PC versus Mac, Whopper versus Big Mac, Avis versus Hertz, and Sprint versus Verizon.

Is comparative advertising legal? The short answer is that "yes," it is legal as long as the company can prove its claims and they are not otherwise deceptive or misleading. The long answer is that there are some specific guidelines

Spotlight on Sustainability

Are Consumers Willing to Pay More for Sustainability?

Two companies joined together to publish a report on how consumers viewed the concept of sustainability. Consumers were asked about sustainability with respect to four product categories: purchased food and beverages, household cleaning products, personal care products, and over-the-counter medications. Consumers most often said that sustainability meant "the ability to last over time" and "the ability to support oneself." Consumers also linked the concept with "environmental concerns." The consumers also said that terms such as *eco-conscious* and *green* unduly limited the concept of sustainability because they do not account for the variety of economic, social, and environmental issues that real people believe are important in sustaining themselves, their communities, and society as a whole.

The consumers surveyed went on to say that they would pay a 20 percent premium for sustainable products. In another study, 40 percent of consumers said they would not purchase a product if the company did not communicate its sustainability results.

In another study, Nielsen found that consumers are trying to be responsible citizens when it comes to purchasing. Consumers are increasingly doing their homework before buying. They are checking labels, checking websites, and paying attention to public opinion. Nielsen found that 66 percent of global respondents were willing to pay more for sustainable products. They especially sought out fresh, natural, or organic ingredients. They also sought out companies that were environmentally friendly.

Sources: RealLeaders, "Consumers Want to Buy Eco-friendly Products, but Don't Know How to Identify Them," March 26, 2021, https://real-leaders.com/consumers-want-to-buy-eco-friendly-products-but-dont-know-how-to-identify-them/, accessed April 21, 2021; Remi Rosemarin, "Sustainability Sells," April 22, 2020, https://www.businessinsider.com/sustainability-as-a-value-is-changing-how-consumers-shop, accessed April 21, 2021; NielsenIQ, "The Sustainability Imperative," https://nielseniq.com/global/en/insights/analysis/2015/the-sustainability-imperative-2/, accessed April 21, 2021.

issued by the FTC about how you compare yourself to the competition. What you say about yourself, what you say about your competitor, and where you say it all enter into whether your competitor can sue you and succeed.[46]

Comparative advertising sometimes generates unexpected and undesirable conflicts among companies and raises ethics questions. Whether out of pride or general business interest, more and more companies are fighting back when they think the competition has gone too far. Companies may take their adversaries to court, before the FTC, or before voluntary associations, such as the National Advertising Division of the Council of Better Business Bureaus, that attempt to resolve these kinds of disputes. Though there can

be good reasons to launch comparative ads, they sometimes come at a cost.

Use of Sex Appeal in Advertising. The use of sex appeal in U.S. advertising has been an ongoing ethical issue for decades. It has not been quite as controversial in some other countries. The issue took center stage years ago when several women's groups were offended by a series of television commercials sponsored by a major airline. Today, sexual references and innuendos in advertising have become commonplace, moving beyond women these days and featuring different gender groups, and the issue continues to spark some controversy. Companies can go too far, and

---

Ethics In Practice Case

Advertising Traps: Do They Represent Ethical Advertising?

There are many assertions and promises companies make in their advertising. These occur in magazines, newspapers, online websites, and social media. In most cases they represent deceptive or misleading promotions of a product or a service. Sometimes they represent only partial truths. Some of the most frequently used ad traps are discussed below.

"We Will Not Be Undersold"

This declaration is commonly understood to mean that the company promoting the product or service is making an offer that cannot be beat by anyone else. Sometimes the declaration means that the company will lower its price to meet that of any competitor. Sometimes not. Usually, the true meaning of this expression cannot be found without significant effort on the consumer's part.

"Satisfaction Guaranteed"

This expression can mean many different things. Sometimes companies will advertise to give you your money back if you are not "satisfied." Often, there are limitations on the "satisfaction guaranteed" promise. You must return the product in ten days; in original packaging; only for an exchange, not a refund; money back after we deduct a restocking fee; and so on. Again, the truth is often in the fine print, sometimes not easily available.

"Lifetime Warranty"

Whose or what lifetime is being referred to here? The purchaser's lifetime? The product's lifetime? Only as long as the company stocks the product? Only with the original receipt? (Who keeps those?) Is the offer "unconditional"? Are there strings attached? Maybe the product has to be registered online first? Maybe a shipping fee is required when returning the product.

"Going out of Business" Sale

What does "going out of business" really mean? In some retail sectors it is not uncommon to go out of business under one company name only to open up soon thereafter in the same location under a different name. Does "going out of business" mean you will get a better price? Not always. Are products sold under these terms still "guaranteed" once the company goes out of business? Researchers have learned that sometimes prices go up during a sale of this type.

"Free"

Is there any offer that has been abused more than being offered something "free"? This ubiquitous offer has been misused and abused probably more than any other ad trap. "Free" is one of those "gotcha" offers that may be qualified in many different ways. The FTC has said that if the word free is used in an ad, then it must be absolutely free without condition. But, how many times have you wondered if related products have been jacked up to cover the cost of the free item? Or, what about the offer of "buy one, get one free"? Has the one you bought been overpriced? What if you only want one? Will it be half priced? Sometimes yes; sometimes no.

Other Abused Words Used as "Ad Traps"

Other words that are often used as ad traps include the following: *New, Save, Proven, Results, Easy,* and *You,* as in "let's talk about *you*" or "this will make *you* rich."

Questions

1. Which of the above advertising traps have you been caught in? Explain how it happened.
2. Does use of these ad traps represent deceptive advertising? What would make each one of them a fair advertisement?
3. Should agencies such as the FTC, Food and Drug Administration (FDA), Consumer Product Safety Commission, and others have official definitions of these terms before they may be used?
4. How should companies monitor themselves to be sure they are treating consumers fairly when using these marketing terms?
5. What steps should you take as a consumer to make sure you are not being deceived by these terms?

Sources: Federal Trade Commission Act Section 5: Unfair or deceptive acts or practices, December 2018, https://www.fdic.gov /resources/supervision-and-examinations/consumer-compliance-examination-manual/documents/7/vii-1-1.pdf, accessed April 21, 2021; "Don't Let These Ad Traps Catch You," *Consumer Reports,* March 2014, 13; Gumas, "The Ten Most Powerful Words in Advertising," https://gumas.com/the-ten-most-powerful-words-in-advertising/, accessed April 21, 2021.

some believe we have moved into an arena in which we are becoming numb to things that would have offended many of us years ago.[47]

A troubling trend in using sex appeal advertising campaigns is to target younger and younger girls and boys with the idea that they can be sexy too. Ads are targeting younger and younger girls to diet and get hair extensions, eye-lash extensions, and push-up bras. Critics say this is subtly training girls to focus on their external appearance at the expense of developing a fuller identity. It is argued that girls are being overly sexualized in our culture long before they are cognitively and emotionally prepared.[48] In addition, boys are being sexualized in ads too at a younger and younger age.[49]

Most studies have shown that the use of sex in advertising works.[50] Studies seem to show, however, that though many oppose the use of sex appeal in ads, their purchasing decisions reflect that sex appeal works. However, at least one study has raised questions about the effectiveness of the "sex sells" mantra. This study found that sexual content within an ad causes consumers to have a less favorable attitude toward the brand, but it does not result in a decline in sales.[51]

Research has also shown that ads that portray young women as sex objects can have a serious impact on the physical and mental health of girls. A task force report from the American Psychological Association (APA) studied this issue and found that the media's sexualization of young women can lead to a lack of confidence with their bodies as well as depression, eating disorders, and low self-esteem.[52] In spite of the fact that sex in advertising is widespread today, the practice still carries serious ethical questions about its appropriateness, and responsible companies must be careful and sensitive to these concerns.

Advertising to Children. A continuously debated ethical issue over the past several decades has been advertising to children, especially on television, but increasingly on social media and computer games. Once you have children, you better understand why this can be an ethical issue. This practice has sometimes been called "kid-vid" advertising. A typical weekday afternoon or Saturday morning in America finds millions of kids sprawled on the floor, glued to the TV, or staring at the computer.[53] These same trends occur in other countries as well.

Children are the consumers of the future, and companies are eager to get their foot in the door of their spending habits. Merchandisers are trying to instill brand loyalty at a young age. Mattel, with its iconic Barbie doll, is a case in point. Since her debut decades ago, Barbie has survived critique, censure, competition, and the advent of social media. Six decades later, America's most controversial doll looks very different from its earlier versions.[54]

Mattel has long been criticized for its Barbie doll's unrealistic body proportions—a young woman who appears impossibly thin, tall, and busty.[55] In 2016, Mattel made Barbie available in different body shapes and different skin tones. By 2021, Mattel had taken Barbie into the digital age.

Barbie is now a gamer, vlogger, and bread-making sensation, and sales reached record levels. In the post–COVID-19 period, Mattel is planning for Barbies to be EMTs, physicians, and firefighters.[56] According to Mattel, it wanted to make Barbie more relevant to girls today. In addition to its diverse line, it now has a line of "Shero" Barbies that represent real women role models.[57] In spite of all of Mattel's adaptations of Barbie, critics still say playing with Barbies is still a bad influence on young girls. One female sociologist summarized: "playing with Barbie dolls negatively affects young girls' self-esteem, body image, and even career aspirations."[58] The sociologist also claimed that in spite of the diversification, the key message embodied in the doll remains sexualized and gendered.[59]

Toying with the consciousness of children is particularly troubling given an American Psychological Association (APA) finding that children under the age of eight do not have the cognitive development to understand persuasive intent, making them easy targets.[60] Children have proved to be receptive targets as well. A phenomenon called **age compression** or "kids getting older younger" (KGOY) has marketers targeting eight- and nine-year-olds with products once meant for teenagers. With the overabundance of ads to which they are exposed, children are tiring of toys much earlier and looking for products that they see teenagers using.[61]

The Children's Advertising Review Unit (CARU) of the Council of Better Business Bureaus was established to respond to public concerns. CARU developed "Self-Regulatory Guidelines for Children's Advertising."[62] The function of the CARU guidelines is to delineate those areas that need particular attention to help avoid deceptive and/or misleading advertising messages to children. The basic activity of CARU is the review and evaluation of child-directed advertising in all media. When advertising to children is found to be misleading, inaccurate, or inconsistent with the guidelines, CARU seeks changes through the voluntary cooperation of advertisers. It does not always get cooperation, and sometimes the advertiser appeals to the National Advertising Review Board (NARB).

The advertising to children of food products that contain sweets and unhealthy ingredients has become a burning issue as well. As the obesity epidemic among children has become widely known and debated, special interest groups have been criticizing companies for their marketing of these products to children. Obesity researchers now say they have data documenting that the least healthy cereals are the ones that are marketed most aggressively to children. The obesity crisis among children in the United States is now established, and researchers believe that TV advertising is a significant contributing factor.[63]

To their credit, some leading cereal makers have responded by reducing calories, fat, and sugar and increasing fiber and vitamins. Kellogg, General Mills, and Quaker's parent company, PepsiCo, are among about 12 of the largest food companies that have promised to market only "better for you" foods to kids under age 12. While this seems to indicate some promise that cereal companies will take responsibility for their advertising, skeptics are concerned because the companies themselves are deciding what constitutes "better for you" standards.[64]

Regulatory bodies have been trying for decades to get greater supervisory authority with respect to children's advertising. In 1990, the **Children's Television Act (CTA)** was passed. This act prohibited the airing of commercials about products or characters during a show about those products or characters and limited the number of commercial minutes in children's shows. However, much has changed since that act was passed. With the rise of the Internet, social media, and smart toys, companies have found new ways to advertise to children. More than two-thirds of the children and teen Internet sites rely on advertising for their revenue. Banner ads were not successful in reaching children, and so these Internet sites have employed games, e-mail, and wireless technology in creative ways. In response, the FCC has added new regulations over the last decade that address cable and Internet webpages.[65]

The issue of obesity and advertising to children continues to pick up steam. New York Mayor Michael Bloomberg introduced an anti-obesity campaign that sought to ban large-serving sugary drinks, especially sodas, but this law was struck down in the courts.[66] Further, it has been observed that companies disproportionately target black and Latino youth in their TV ads for young children.[67] Meanwhile, advertising to children continues to be a questionable activity for companies today.

Advertising to the Poor. Many businesses have found that significant profits can be obtained from advertising and marketing to poor people. In the subprime credit industry, businesses provide financing to high-risk borrowers at high interest rates. While this gives poorer people greater access to cars, credit cards, computers, and homes, it often ends with the borrower buried under a mountain of debt. The past decade has been the worst ever in home mortgage foreclosures and loan defaults. Many of these have come from the subprime mortgage market where relatively poor people were lured into loans they had little hope of repaying. Several of the deceptive marketing practices mentioned earlier have been involved in these loans: concealed facts, ambiguous advertising, and psychological appeals.

Another technique by which business profits from the poor is in the form of *payday loans*, loans that provide borrowers with an advance on their pay checks. As the FTC warns, these loans represent costly cash; for example, a borrower might write a personal check for $115 to borrow $100 for up to two weeks. The payday lender agrees to hold the check until the person's next payday. Then, depending on the plan, the lender deposits the check, which the borrower can redeem by paying the $115 in cash. Alternatively, the borrower can roll over the check by paying a fee to extend the loan for another two weeks. In this example, the cost of the initial loan is a $15 finance charge and 391 percent annual percentage rate (APR). If they roll over the loan three times, the finance charge would climb to $60 to borrow $100.[68] The

---

Ethics In Practice Case

Food Advertising to Children—Should It Be Banned?

There continues to be an ongoing battle between those who think marketing food and beverages to children should be halted and those who think it's up to parents to make these decisions not Big Government. Some companies have been attempting to come up with their own standards to decrease unhealthy ingredients and make kids' foods more nutritious. It is now estimated that one-third of children in the United States are overweight or obese. It has been argued by a number of experts that sugar in soft drinks and fast foods are the major culprits. Additionally, commercial advertising for food products assaults children with TV commercials, ads in schools, product placements, and digital marketing. Research shows that this advertising works.

Founded in the year 2000, a nonprofit organization Campaign for a Commercial Free Childhood (CCFC) is seeking to address the rapidly escalating problem of commercialism encroaching on the lives of children. Starting out as a small group of concerned parents, health professionals, and educators, CCFC has grown into a powerful force seeking to end what it calls the exploitative practice of child-targeted advertising.

CCFC has taken on the following issues: marketing to children, advertising in schools, commercializing toys and play, food marketing and childhood obesity, marketing to babies and toddlers, sexualizing childhood, and media violence. In 2021, CCFC began urging Mark Zuckerberg to abandon any plans for an Instagram for children. They claim that now, more than ever, children really need time to just play, learn, and socialize away from digital devices.

1. Should food and beverage advertising to children be banned? What about for other types of products as well?
2. Is it unethical for food companies to target their ads toward children? In a period when most parents are working, how are children to be protected?
3. Should the federal or state government begin restricting food ads targeted at children? What about for other products?
4. Can companies do enough on their own to adequately address these problems?
5. Of the list of issues CCFC has taken on (listed above), which do you see as the most serious and why?

Sources: Campaign for a Commercial Free Childhood, https://commercialfreechildhood.org/about-us/, accessed April 21, 2021; American Psychological Association, "The Impact of Food Advertising on Childhood Obesity," https://www.apa.org/topics/kids-media/food, accessed April 21, 2021.

special case of payday loans is explored further in Case 8 at the end of the text. Similar tactics are used by many credit card companies, rent-to-own outfits, and used-car dealers.

The primary issue with marketing and advertising to the poor is the vulnerability of this consumer segment. All consumers are vulnerable to a certain extent because business has more information about its product or service than does the consumer. However, poor people are especially vulnerable because they are likely to be less educated and thus less aware of the true price of the products or services being advertised to them. Nevertheless, businesses continue to push these products. Another vulnerable group of consumers is the elderly, and some of the same tactics are used on them that are used on the poor.[69]

Advertising Alcoholic Beverages. The advertising of alcoholic beverages, especially to a younger demographic profile, has been an issue for decades.[70] In addition to the concern for the health effects, critics have argued that many alcohol ads link drinking with valued personal attributes such as sociability, elegance, and physical attractiveness that might relate to outcomes such as success, romance, relaxation, and adventure.[71] It has been found that, in general, adolescents are drawn to alcohol ads, especially those with celebrity endorsers, humor, animation, and popular music. Further, it has been shown that lifestyle or image advertising results in more favorable attitudes toward alcohol when compared with strictly product-oriented or informational advertising.[72] Recently, advertising alcohol on social media has been a huge issue that needs to be watched closely. TikTok is the hottest social media site around today, and advertisers are excited about getting their ads in front of 2 billion users. The social media sites are proposing sample policies that might serve to curtail alcoholic beverage advertising to the younger demographic.[73] As self-regulations, however, it remains to be seen how effective these policies will be.

Although efforts to curb advertising abuses of alcohol continue, consumer advocates may find they face an uphill battle. There seems to be less public opposition today to alcohol advertising but the industry will need to remain vigilant, because any attempts at exploitation of youth, for example, are likely to meet considerable criticism and resistance. As a result of the pandemic, alcohol drinking at home increased. According to one study, alcohol and marijuana use among teenagers rose some during the pandemic. Many are wondering whether these consequences could outlast the pandemic.[74]

Cigarette Advertising. No industry has been under greater criticism and regulation than the cigarette industry for its products and its marketing and advertising practices. Cigarette makers have been under fire from all sides for decades. Two particularly important issues dominate the debate about cigarettes and their advertising. First, there has been general opposition to the promotion of a dangerous product. As the World Health Organization (WHO)

puts it, cigarettes remain the only legal product that kills half of its regular users when consumed as intended by the manufacturer.[75]

The second issue concerns the ethics of the tobacco industry's longstanding advertising to young people and to less-educated consumer markets. Research shows that these ads are popular with young people and that they strongly influence children and teens. Many teens are going through developmental changes in which they become more concerned with their popularity and image. They want to be accepted by friends. One study found that cigarette ads may make teens feel more like smoking because they would be more popular, sophisticated, attractive, or tough.[76]

In 2009, Congress gave the FDA oversight of the tobacco industry when it passed the Tobacco Control Act. The Tobacco Control Act was intended to protect the public and to create a healthier future for all citizens.[77] This act authorized the FDA to regulate the manufacture, distribution, and marketing of tobacco products. Among other actions, the FDA restricts tobacco marketing and sales to youth, requires smokeless tobacco products to carry warning labels, and require disclosures of ingredients in tobacco products.[78]

In the past several years, electronic-cigarettes (e-cigs) and vaping have become increasingly popular, and the tobacco companies have been working hard to promote them. The e-cigarette industry is a multi-billion-dollar industry that now includes disposable e-cigs and rechargeable e-cigs with prefilled cartridges and flavored e-liquids (e.g., fruit, candy, mint).[79] E-cigs vaporize nicotine without burning tobacco and are the fastest-growing rival to traditional cigarettes.[80] The Centers for Disease Control and Prevention (CDC) is concerned about how e-cigs are attracting more teenagers, as the rate of usage has nearly tripled in recent years. The CDC is particularly concerned about addiction, lung damage, and the effects on the developing brains of youth.[81]

Opponents of tobacco and tobacco-related products continue their campaigns against cigarettes, e-cigarettes, and their advertising. The Campaign for Tobacco-Free Kids, an advocacy group, has been urging the FDA to consider more regulation.[82] According to their statistics, there are more than 480,000 deaths annually in the United States that are tobacco-related and the annual health care costs have reached $170 billion. They estimate that worldwide deaths due to tobacco have reached 7 million annually.[83] While the industry seems to be striving to make products that are more palatable and appealing, there is still the concern that the smokeless varieties carry significant health risks.

The future will be somewhat determined by what actions and decisions the FDA decides to take regarding existing products and whatever new products come on the market. Beginning in 2016, the FDA announced its first ad campaign on the dangers of smokeless tobacco. Its "The Real Cost" campaign focused on educating teenagers about the negative health consequences of smokeless tobacco to include nicotine addiction, gum disease, tooth loss, and multiple types of cancer. Their central message was "smokeless doesn't mean harmless."[84] The ethical issues surrounding tobacco products and their advertising increase in complexity with new products and new media outlets to be monitored.

Health and Environmental Claims. We now live in a health-conscious and environmentally aware society. Consumers' interest in products that are healthful and sustainable has grown significantly, and so it is not too surprising that these issues have gained so much attention. Because health and environmental sustainability claims attract customers, marketers are tempted to advertise claims that are not really true. Consumers today are undoubtedly bewildered as they scan health claims on so many products. The fronts of boxes are shouting out claims about different nutrients—sugar free, extra fiber, all natural, zero transfats, multi-grain, organic, free range, gluten free, added vitamins, fat free, and healthy for your heart.

The market for more healthy food products is growing, and a few companies have been taking it upon themselves to progressively plan for the future. One highly visible example is that of PepsiCo, which under former CEO Indra Nooyi was instrumental in restructuring and diversifying PepsiCo toward healthier products. During her stint as CEO from 2006–2018, she wanted PepsiCo to be "a model of how to conduct business in the modern world."[85] With respect to her company's products, she wanted to help customers wean off of sugar, salt, and fat. Nooyi unveiled a series of goals to improve the healthiness of PepsiCo products. In 2016, PepsiCo announced it had met its 2020 goal of reduction in foods with saturated fats in the United States, the United Kingdom, and Turkey.[86] Astutely, Nooyi observed that she wanted to prevent the food companies from going the way of the tobacco firms.[87]

Advertising and labeling practices that make claims about health and environmental safety have taken on growing importance in the past decade. One reason that these issues have come to the forefront is the renewed enforcement activities of the FDA, the FTC, and state attorneys general in cracking down on misleading or unsubstantiated claims. Beginning in 2016, the FDA announced it was taking a fresh look at "healthy" labeling because many of the regulations governing it date back to the 1990s.[88] The FTC has also cracked down on false advertising in health-related products, including vitamin supplements, weight-loss plans, and beauty products.[89] The FTC has noted that Americans spend billions of dollars each year on foods, supplements, and devices that claim to improve their health and fitness. Many of these products do not live up to their advertising claims that they can help people lose weight, combat disease, or improve their cognitive abilities. The FTC also seeks to monitor truth in advertising for tanning salons, personal care products, disinfectant devices, and body slimming creams.[90]

Organic food claims are another arena in which deceptive advertising claims are often made. One of the most challenging questions is, what exactly does organic mean?

Organic foods or ingredients are generally defined to be those that meet certain criteria. The United States Department of Agriculture (USDA) for example, claims that to be "Certified Organic" or carry the "USDA Organic" label, the item must have an ingredients list and the contents should be at least 95 percent or more "certified organic," which means free of synthetic additives like pesticides, chemical fertilizers, and dyes and must not be processed using industrial solvents, irradiation, or genetic engineering.[91]

If you see the alternative label, "100 percent organic," it must meet the standards listed above. Or, it could say "Made with Organic," in which case it means it must contain 70 percent of more organic ingredients.[92] The volume of organic products now available and the low penalties assessed for violations has led to some scepticism as to whether the USDA is fully enforcing its own requirements. Some now worry that *organic* has turned into a marketing and advertising term with little meaning.[93] If this is the case, consumers will have to shop carefully and hope that the reputation of the seller is high enough to be conveying the truth.

Closely related to organic products are a set of products that claim to be "natural." Many natural food companies also promote their products as environmentally friendly, or "green." What is the difference between organic and natural? Though similar in perception, organic and natural do not mean exactly the same thing, and this poses more challenges for consumers trying to understand the various health claims of products. **Natural products** are generally meant to be foods that are minimally processed and do not contain any hormones, antibiotics, or artificial flavors or colors.[94] In the United States, the FDA and the USDA do not have rules for products that claim to be natural. By contrast, for a food to be labeled organic, it must meet more tightly regulated standards. The result has been some confusion between organic and natural, and many natural product claims turn out to be murky.[95]

Green advertising is another major controversial advertising practice wherein companies are claiming that their products and/or their product packages are environmentally friendly, sustainable, or safe. For some time now, many companies have been ramping up their advertising claims about the sustainability of their products—that their products are "green." Though popular, two factors cause consumers to be careful about such purchases: their price premiums and communication challenges. Consumers have a hard time judging and trusting sustainability claims, so this confusion poses a special challenge for marketers.[96]

The FTC now issues guidelines for "eco-friendly" labeling saying that companies better be able to back up their claims.[97] The FTC called these their **Green Guides**.[98] The FTC's Green Guides are intended to help marketers avoid making environmental claims that are misleading to consumers. The guidance they provide includes (1) general principles that pertain to all environmental marketing claims, (2) information on how consumers are likely to interpret particular claims and how companies can substantiate their claims, and (3) how marketers can qualify their claims to avoid deceiving consumers.[99]

One of the most egregious violations involving green advertising is the now well-known Volkswagen's "clean diesel" vehicle advertising. In addition to facing issues of criminal fraud and deception regarding its product wherein it admitted it rigged more than half a million vehicles with software to cheat emissions regulations, the FTC added to VW's legal problems by filing a complaint that the company's advertising falsely claimed its diesel vehicles were environmentally friendly.[100] Volkswagen did reach a deal with consumers in which it would agree to buy back the cars affected, and the buyback could cost VW more than $7 billion. The FTC's most recent update of the Green Guides is designed to make it easier for companies to understand and use them. The changes include new guidelines on "renewable" energy sources and "carbon offset" claims.[101]

Consumers' willingness to pay more for green products is sometimes hard to gauge. Consumers' expressed concerns do not always translate into actual purchases. Recent research in the United States has indicated that fewer than half of consumers are inclined to purchase eco-friendly products and the estimated market share of green products will only reach 25 percent of store sales by 2021.[102] In Europe, however, there seems to be more support for purchasing sustainable brands. Many Europeans are frustrated because many brands claim to be sustainable but do not take enough action on climate issues. It has been reported that those companies that fail to take action may expect creative disrupters, investors, and activists to sabotage their brand equity.[103]

To offset much of the health and green advertising, an industry of what might be called **green watchdogs** has been growing also. The fact that these monitoring groups are actively at work, however, suggests this is an issue that needs to be watched closely by consumers lest they be duped about the health or eco-friendliness of products they buy.[104] Some of the recent issues being monitored include sugary drinks and calorie labeling on DoorDash, GrubHub, and other third-party ordering platforms.[105]

Advertisers have come on so fast and strong with their environmental- and health-friendly claims that there is a growing sense of **green fatigue** developing among some consumers who are growing weary of such claims.[106] The evidence seems to be that being green is not enough. Products need to be wallet-friendly as well, especially for those struggling during tight economic times. For some time now, marketers even have noticed a green backlash among consumer attitudes.[107] Companies and advertisers will need to watch carefully the quality of their claims or a real cynicism about health and green claims may develop.

Companies today are striving to transition from **green marketing** to marketing for health and environmental sustainability.[108] Part of this challenge is to create a stronger case along with documentation. Four insights along these lines have been presented:

- First, more reliable metrics are needed to translate "green" commitments into customer value.

- Second, verifiable product standards and certifications help to communicate this value.
- Third, these standards need to be developed in concert with multiple stakeholders if they are to be trustworthy.
- Fourth, environmental sustainability brand value needs to be embedded in sincere, systemic, and organization-wide commitments.[109]

It will be challenging for companies to make this transition, but the market potential is growing, and the possibilities for questionable practices will be present all along the way.

Ad Creep. Ad creep refers to the way that advertising has increasingly crept into everywhere one looks. Both produce placement and plot placement, discussed earlier, are special cases of ad creep. Ads are now going into places that once were not considered acceptable for advertisements. School buses, textbooks, doctors' offices, ATMs, garbage cans, Google searches, and historical monuments have all been festooned with advertisements. The traditional term for advertising that is located in nontraditional places is **ambient advertising**, but *ad creep* reflects both the way the ads have grown and the way people often feel about its creators.[110]

A variety of factors contribute to ad creep. A declining network TV audience and increased dispersion from cable and Internet outlets combine with soaring network television rates to make it difficult to blanket the population with an advertising message. The rise of social media and electronic products of all varieties make them fertile ground for ad creep. The biggest issue today is the extent to which ads are creeping into places once thought to be private—trails in public parklands, on kids' report cards, for example.[111]

Furthermore, ad creep generates more ad creep because people become numb to messages in traditional places and so unique new venues are sought—just to get the consumer's attention.[112]

Social Media Advertising. Though **social media advertising** is used in virtually all the advertising issues discussed above, special consideration should be given to it as a controversial category on its own because of its rapid growth in recent years and some of the questionable uses to which it has been employed. Traditional TV ads will continue, but today consumers seem to be more interested in social media advertising and the industry is taking notice. Social media as an approach to marketing and advertising is exploding and the industry is continuing to grow.[113]

As social media advertising grows, so does the opportunity for deceptive advertising via social media rise as well. In fact, Social Media and Marketing Daily has called social media and deceptive advertising the "new frontier."[114] Companies that communicate using social media face legal, ethical, and reputational risks in the realms of false and deceptive advertising just like traditional companies.

One of the most recent applications of deceptive social media advertising has been in the use of **social media bots**. Bots are automated software that appear on platforms and use a set of algorithms that simulate human behavior. Harmful and fraudulent uses of such bots are widespread and can involve the creation of false accounts that amplify false or deceptive product reviews. Or, they can automatically inflate a product's online popularity.[115] Recently, the FTC has begun investigating social media bots, especially in the category of their deceptive advertising uses. Ninety percent of social media bots are used for commercial purposes, and improper use occurs when influencers use them to boost the popularity of products by increasing the number of clicks an ad receives, among other deceptions, thus increasing revenues. Because of their widespread use, the FTC is recommending that new, specific requirements be established, possibly with the intervention of Congress.[116]

The nine controversial advertising issues discussed above are simply the tip of the iceberg. Issues continue to be raised about the marketing of pharmaceutical drugs directly to patients through magazine and television ads and social media. These ads encourage patients to ask their doctor for the prescription drug, to the frustration of doctors everywhere. Concerns have also been raised about the marketing of guns and ammunition, particularly in family stores like Walmart and Kmart. Channel One, a television station that beams educational programming to schools across the country, has been sharply criticized for its commercials, which students end up watching along with the educational programming. Ads have crept onto smartphones and social media apps as well, and as handheld devices grow

Ethics In Practice Case

Product Names and Racial Bias

Recently, a number of companies have been criticized for having product or brand names that are racially biased, spurred in large part by recent social movements addressing racial injustice, equity, and inclusion. These criticisms include corporate names, product names, logos, and mascots. At least 20 top brands have been identified as having questionable naming. Many of these accusations of racism came in the aftermath of the George Floyd killing in Minneapolis and Black Lives Matter (BLM) protests.

Some of the accused racist brands include the following:

Product names: *Aunt Jemima* and *Eskimo Pies*
Logos/Branding: *Mrs. Butterworth's* curvy bottle shape suggesting a racial caricature stereotype of Black women
Product descriptions: Both Johnson & Johnson and L'Oreal have been accused of product wording that may suggest a racial bias; for example, skin-lightening creams that use words like "whitening," "fair," and "light"
Mascots: It is said that P&G should remove the "Senior Sleepy" mascot from their *Spic & Span* cleaning products. The suggestion is that the word "spic" and the brown-skinned mascot is a racial stereotype of Latinx people.

Companies have responded to these accusations in a variety of ways, but many of the companies have seemed willing to change their product names to accommodate the accusations, although most have claimed that no racial bias was intended. For example, Pepsico announced that its *Aunt Jemima* brand will be changed to Pearl Milling Co. Mars, Inc. is changing the name of its *Uncle Ben's* rice to Ben's Original rice.

Unilever's Fair & Lovely skin-lightener cream brand has been exceptionally popular in India. In 2020, it was announced that the product generated more than $560 million in annual sales and is considered to be a safe alternative to dangerous bleaching products. In mid-2020, Unilever announced that it would the removing certain words—*fair, fairness, white, whitening, light,* and *lightening*—from its product communications. Johnson & Johnson announced that it will take its *Clean & Clear Fairness* skin-whitening products off the shelves in India because of criticism from BLM. L'Oreal announced that it will remove racially insensitive phrases like "fair," "light," and "whitening" from its skin products. Their decision was made in support of social justice and equality.

A high school student in California accused the popular grocer Trader Joe's of having racist names for some of its ethnic products, citing examples like "Trader Ming's," "Arabian Joe's," "Trader Jose," and "Trader Giotto." After agreeing to change these names, Trader Joe's reversed its position and stated it would not change the names based on someone's petition.

Accusations of bias in product branding and advertising extend beyond just race. Someone recently asked whether certain brands need to change due to gender bias favoring men. Examples might include Manpower Group, Five Guys Burgers, Two Men & a Truck, Pizza Guys, and The Termite Guy pest control service. As current trends continue, it is expected that many companies will be re-examining their product names and slogans to be sure that possible bias will be eliminated.

1. Do the product's names mentioned suggest racial bias, or are these allegations just getting to be too hypersensitive?
2. Did Trader Joe's make the right move by changing its decision about product names thought by petitioners to be racist?
3. What should the companies do when such allegations are made? Should they discontinue the product line? Change the product's name and image? How do they decide where to draw the line?
4. At what point do companies resist being pressured to alter product communications due to pressure from special-interest groups?

Sources: Saabira Chaudhuri, "Unilever's Skin-Lightening Cream Attracts Louder Social Criticism," *The Wall Street Journal*, June 24, 2020, B2; Marci Robin, "Following Pressure to Discontinue Skin-Lightening Cream, Unilever Will Rename Fair & Lovely," June 26, 2020, https://www.allure.com/story/fair-and-lovely-unilever-name-skin-lightening-cream, accessed April 27, 2021; Onig, "20+ Top Brands Changing Their Name to Avoid Racial Bias," https://blog.ongig.com/diversity-and-inclusion/alleged-racist-brands/, accessed April 27, 2021; Hannah Rimm, "Trader Joe's Changes Its Mind: Will Not Remove Controversial Packaging," July 31, 2020, https://www.refinery29.com/en-us/2020/07/9943628/trader-joes-racist-names-statement-controversy, accessed April 27, 2021.

in popularity, this will be yet another burgeoning area where advertisers may run the risk of raising questionable issues.

There is no end to the list of concerns about deceptive or misleading advertising practices undertaken today. Businesspeople must tread carefully to make certain they do not cross the line where their customers become more annoyed with their practices than be attracted to their products. Further, serious ethical questions continue to arise about the types and placements of advertising in the future.

14.1e Warranties and Guarantees

From the glamorous realm of advertising, we now proceed to the less glamorous and often neglected issues of warranties and guarantees. Warranties were initially used by manufacturers to limit the length of time they were expressly responsible for products. Over time, they came to be viewed by consumers as mechanisms to protect the buyer against faulty or defective products. Most consumers have had the experience of buying a cell phone, a hair dryer, a computer, a refrigerator, an automobile, a washing machine, a chain saw, or any of thousands of other products only to find that it did not work properly or did not work at all. That is when warranties and guarantees take center stage.

Warrantees and guarantees are promises made to consumers by manufacturers or sellers. A **warranty** is usually a written, contractual promise that attests to the quality or durability of a product purchased for a period of time. Should a product become defective while it is still under warranty for some limited time, say a year, the company agrees to repair or replace the product.[117] A **guarantee** is also a promise regarding product quality, but guarantees are less likely to be written. Vendors will sometimes verbally guarantee a product with unsatisfied customers getting a full or a partial refund. Warrantees and guarantees are similar, but usually the warranty is the written contract that is legally enforceable.[118] But not all types of warrantees are in writing.

The law recognizes two types of warranties: implied and express. An **implied warranty** is an unspoken promise that there is nothing significantly wrong with the product and that the product can be used for the purposes intended. An **express warranty** is explicitly offered at the time of the sale. The nature of express warranties can range from advertising claims to formal certificates, and they may be oral or written.[119]

The passage of the Magnuson–Moss Warranty Act (1975) helped clarify the nature of warranties for consumers. It is still the basic law of the land, although the FTC has amended, clarified, and interpreted it over the years.[120] This act was aimed at clearing up a variety of misunderstandings about manufacturers' warranties—especially whether a **full warranty** was in effect or whether certain parts of the product or certain types of defects were excluded from coverage, resulting in a **limited warranty**.[121] The Warranty Act set standards for what must be contained in a warranty and the ease with which consumers must be able to understand it. If a company, for example, claims that its product has a full warranty, it must contain certain features, including repair

"within a reasonable time and without charge."[122] The law holds that anything less than this unconditional assurance must be promoted as a limited warranty. With the rise of e-commerce, warranties have become a much more important issue to consumers. Companies find that warranties or guarantees are essential when marketing by mail.

Another issue of increasing ethical concern is **extended warranties**, service plans that lengthen the warranty period and are offered at an additional cost. Consumer advocates advise against buying most extended warranties because they often cost as much as the original item bought would eventually cost to replace. Eric Antum, editor of *Warranty Week*, explains that retailers might make only $10 on a $400 television, but will then make $50 on a $100 extended warranty.[123] Not surprisingly, the lure of big profits has led to some hardball sales tactics.

Consumers spend billions of dollars on extended warranties.[124] They have become popular with car purchases, perhaps because customers are keeping their cars longer. Some customers view the warranties to be insurance, and they are willing to take the risk. A serious problem today are third-party vendors who are selling extended warranties on products such as autos, and some of them may go out of business when a car owner tries to collect, and some represent scams that never intend to pay off for anyone.[125] Opponents of extended warranties offer the following reasons not to buy them: the manufacturer's warranty is usually sufficient; extended warranties are not always effective; the necessity of repairs is rare; warranties are not cost-effective; and credit cards can offer better protection.[126]

If companies simply offer complete satisfaction, with no fine print, the warranty problem is not such a problem. Few companies offer this. L.L.Bean once had a warranty that virtually lasted forever, but even it had to place limits on its warranties due to customers taking advantage of it. Today their warranty is limited to one year. However, they continue to say that after one year they will consider any items under warranty that need to be returned due to defective materials or craftsmanship.[127]

Closely related to warranties and guarantees are the **returns policies** that merchants use to provide customers with a chance to return the product if they are not satisfied. The returns policy is often a part of the warranty, but it could be a separate document. The returns policy usually spells out the terms under which the merchant will accept returns and how that process should be handled.[128] Most merchants use reasonable returns policies, but the consumer should always check carefully as to what the policy is before making a purchase. In recent years, customer abuses of returns policies and fraud have become a huge issue for merchants. Amazon has taken a tougher position when it declared that it would close customers' accounts because of too many returns.[129]

14.1f Packaging and Labeling

Abuses in packaging and labeling were fairly frequent until the passage of the Federal Packaging and Labeling Act (FPLA).

The purpose of this act was to prohibit deceptive labeling of certain consumer products and to require disclosure of certain important information. This act, which is administered by the FTC, requires the FTC to issue regulations regarding net contents disclosures, identity of commodity, and name and place of manufacturer, packer, or distributor. Both the FTC and the FDA have direct responsibilities under this act. The act authorizes additional regulations when necessary to prevent consumer deception or to facilitate value comparisons with respect to the declaration of ingredients, slack filling of packages, "downsizing" of packaging, and use of "cents off" designations. The act gives the FTC responsibility for consumer commodities.

The FDA administers the FPLA with respect to foods, drugs, cosmetics, and medical devices.[130]

As mentioned in an earlier section, the packaging and labeling issue is drawing renewed interest because of health and environmental claims and advertising law in specific product categories such as pharmaceuticals, food, tobacco, alcohol, and advertising directed at children. Consumer interest groups as well as lawsuits have been bringing the issue of labeling and packaging to the forefront in recent years. It should be added that the advertising of products with labeling or packaging issues also represents the additional charge of deceptive advertising, a topic discussed earlier.

Ethics In Practice Case

The Growing Business of Return Fraud

Consumers love warranties, guarantees, and excellent return policies on the products they purchase. From the merchant's perspective, these policies help keep customers satisfied and coming back. However, a problem merchants are facing more and more is the burgeoning business of **return fraud**. Return fraud typically occurs when consumers purchase a product, use it for some limited period of time, and then return it wanting their money back. One estimate is that return fraud is costing American businesses almost $9 billion annually and rising.

One type of return fraud began when merchants such as L.L.Bean or REI, Inc., offered lifetime warranties with the privilege of returning anything, anytime, for any reason. REI, the privately held sporting goods chain, had to change its return policy because so many people took unreasonable advantage of it. At one REI store, a customer returned a 9-year-old backpack that he had used for mountain climbing because it was getting old and dirty and the customer didn't like it any more. In another case, a woman returned a worn pair of sandals designed for hiking and wading in rivers because she had concluded they were not sexy enough.

Customers have returned clothing or shoes that have been torn, charred in a fire, or otherwise abused in extreme sports and have expected and gotten refunds. Some stores have gotten shredded clothing returned that was cut loose from customers when rescue workers had to cut through the fabric while saving them from a mishap. Both REI and L.L.Bean have had to change their returns policies in the past few years by limiting returns to one year except in unusual circumstances.

Another form of returns fraud also has been occurring, often in high-end clothing stores such as Bloomingdales, when women purchase fancy dresses, wear them once to a wedding or party, and then return them, sometimes soiled with sweat, and want their money back. Jewelry purchases are also being abused. The merchants call this practice "wardrobing" and are starting to take a firmer stand with respect to returns because of all the returns abuse they have been experiencing. In one recent year, 65 percent of retailers reported they were victims of wardrobing.

Bloomingdale's finally started a policy of placing a 3-inch b-tag in a highly visible place, such as on the hemline of dresses costing $150 or more, as they are being purchased. Then, the customer can try the dress on at home without disturbing the tag and return it if it doesn't fit. Once the customer removes the tag to wear the dress in public, however, the garment cannot be returned. The company says it is using the "b-tags" to reinforce their policy that once garments have been worn, washed, damaged, used, or altered, they cannot be returned. Recently, Bloomingdale's had to announce that it does not accept face masks for return or exchange.

Return fraud began exploding in 2020–2021 partially due to the pandemic. By then, the industrialization of return fraud had been achieved by illicit fraudsters who had decided to turn it into a profitable business. Merchants have been experiencing return fraud for years, but now it is a growing business. Professional fraudsters are now operating to take it to a whole new level. As a result, otherwise respectable consumers who wish to return a product now may be viewed as suspicious by concerned merchants.

1. How do excellent customers, ones who do not abuse return policies, regard what merchants are currently having to face today? What can you do to protect yourself?
2. Do consumers have a "social responsibility" to merchants? How would you spell it out?
3. Is it unethical for customers to take advantage of returns policies, or is this just the cost of doing business today? Is it unethical for companies to take the actions they are now having to take?
4. What is your appraisal of some of the actions companies have to take with respect to their return policies? Are they justified? Is the consumer no longer "always right"?

Sources: Merchant Risk Council, "Return Fraud: Why 2021 Is the Perfect Storm," February 19, 2021, https://merchantriskcouncil .org/news-and-press/mrc-blog/2021/refund-fraud-why-2021 -is-the-perfect-storm?utm_content=buffer42f41&utm_medium =social&utm_source=facebook.com&utm_campaign=buffer, accessed April 27, 2021; Matthew Hudson, "How to Recognize Retail Return Fraud," January 27, 2020, https://www .thebalancesmb.com/recognizing-return-fraud-2890255, accessed April 27, 2021; Cotten Timberlake, "Don't Even Think about Returning That Dress," *Bloomberg Businessweek*, September 30–October 6, 2013, 29–31.

An important issue in labeling today is ingredient labeling. Consumers now want to know more about what ingredients are in the products they are using, especially food and health-related products. We discussed the consumer's desire for GMO labeling in Chapter 8 because it was an ethical issue being raised in the realm of biotechnology and business ethics. But, GMO labeling certainly falls within the purview of this discussion as well. Due to recent actions taken by the FDA, GMO labeling is set to be required by 2022, but most companies are already beginning to label their products accordingly and thus removing, to some extent, the complaints about GMO ingredients in products.[131] This issue will not go away, but movements in a more transparent direction are underway.

With respect to ingredients labeling, generally, more transparency is now expected by consumers. In response, the FDA continues to revise its Nutrition Facts label panel that has been standard on most food products since 1994. The FDA's recent changes include a redesign to make calorie information more prominent and also a change to what is considered a single serving size to reflect the increase in portion sizes that people have begun eating over the past two decades.[132] Some researchers have said that the labels are an improvement but still are not clear enough to convey what the net value of a food may be.[133]

As consumers demanded to know more about food ingredients, the Grocery Manufacturers Association (GMA) announced its *SmartLabel* initiative that is supported by more than 30 companies including Hershey, PepsiCo, and General Mills among others.[134] As part of this initiative, the companies are using smartphone scanning technology so that shoppers can quickly get a detailed picture of their product's ingredients. The SmartLabel uses a quick response (QR) code that shoppers can scan while in the stores, and using an app this will take them to the company's website where more nutrition information regarding ingredients will be available. The GMA says they have a survey that reveals that 75 percent of consumers would likely use the new label.[135] The Center for Food Safety, an environmental-and-health nonprofit, however, has said that conveying information in this way is insufficient because some consumers cannot afford smartphones or know how to use the scanning feature. They say the QR code labeling discriminates against the poor, minorities, rural populations, and the elderly.[136]

In the area of product packaging, the issue of **slack fill** has been the topic of much recent criticism. Slack fill, known in regulatory terms as *nonfunctional slack fill*, is the practice of companies putting less product in the package while often keeping the container size the same but raising the price.[137] In toilet paper packaging, the practice has been called "de-sheeting" as the number of sheets on a roll are reduced. The slack fill practice has been going on for years in products such as cereal, candy bars, deodorants, and virtually all consumer products.

Prominent companies that often carry strong social responsibility records are not exempt from charges of deceptive packing. Whole Foods Market was accused of overcharging customers in New York after officials discovered

the company had mislabeled weights of freshly packaged foods like vegetable platters and chicken tenders that lead to overcharges of $1 to $15 per item.[138] Starbucks faced a lawsuit from a woman in Chicago who claimed Starbucks regularly overfills its cold drinks with ice instead of using the advertised amount of coffee or other liquid in its plastic cups. The lawsuit alleged that an iced beverage advertised at 24 ounces contains about 14 ounces of product and the rest is ice. The lawsuit sought class action status so it could include customers from the past decade to join in.[139] The Starbucks case could be viewed as both a deceptive advertising and packaging example. Both Starbucks and Whole Foods have had strong CSR records, so these examples illustrate how no companies are exempt from close scrutiny and have to watch carefully their own practices.

14.1g Other Product Information Issues

It is difficult to catalog all the consumer issues in which product information is a key factor. Certainly, advertising, warranties, guarantees, packaging, and labeling constitute the bulk of the concerns. In addition to these, however, we must briefly mention several others. Sales techniques in which direct sellers use deceptive information must be mentioned. Some other major laws that address information disclosure issues include the following:

1. *Equal Credit Opportunity Act*, which prohibits discrimination in the extension of consumer credit.
2. *Truth-in-Lending Act*, which requires all suppliers of consumer credit to fully disclose all credit terms and to permit a three-day right of rescission in any transaction involving a security interest in the consumer's residence (e.g., in the case of home equity loans).
3. *Fair Credit Reporting Act*, which ensures that consumer-reporting agencies provide information in a manner that is fair and equitable to the consumer.
4. *Fair Debt Collection Practices Act*, which regulates the practices of third-party debt collection agencies.

14.2 The Federal Trade Commission (FTC)

We have discussed three main areas of product information: (1) advertising, (2) warranties and guarantees, and (3) packaging and labeling. Both the FTC and the FDA are actively involved in these issues. It is important now to look more closely at the federal government's major instrument, the **Federal Trade Commission (FTC)**, for ensuring that business lives up to its responsibilities in these areas. Actually, the FTC has broad and sweeping powers, and it delves into several other areas that we refer to throughout the book. The Consumer Product Safety Commission (CPSC) and the FDA are major regulatory agencies, too, but we consider them more carefully in the next chapter, where we discuss products and services more specifically.

Figure 14-2 The Federal Trade Commission

FTC's Mission	To prevent business practices that are anticompetitive or deceptive or unfair to consumers; to enhance informed consumer choice and public understanding of the competitive process; and to accomplish this without unduly burdening legitimate business activity.
FTC's Vision	A U.S. economy characterized by vigorous competition among producers and consumer access to accurate information, yielding high-quality products at low prices and encouraging efficiency, innovation, and consumer choice.
FTC's Strategic Goals	1. *Protect Consumers*: Prevent fraud, deception, and unfair business practices in the marketplace. 2. *Maintain Competition*: Prevent anticompetitive mergers and other anticompetitive business practices in the marketplace. 3. *Advance Performance*: Advance the FTC's performance through organizational, individual, and management excellence.
FTC's Benefits to Consumer	As a consumer or businessperson, you may be more familiar with the work of the Federal Trade Commission than you think. The FTC deals with issues that touch the economic life of every American. The FTC is the only federal agency with both consumer protection and competition jurisdiction in broad sectors of the economy. The FTC pursues vigorous and effective law enforcement; advances consumers' interests by sharing its expertise with federal and state legislatures and U.S. and international government agencies; develops policy and research tools through hearings, workshops, and conferences; and creates practical and plain-language educational programs for consumers and businesses in a global marketplace with constantly changing technologies.

Sources: Federal Trade Commission, "About the FTC," https://www.ftc.gov/about-ftc, accessed April 28, 2021; Federal Trade Commission, "Protecting Consumers," mail.google.com/mail/u/0/?tab=wm#inbox/FMfcgxwLtkSFKzTFlrZFlxwQZcgHxplW, accessed April 28, 2021.

The FTC was created in 1914. Its purpose was to prevent unfair methods of competition in commerce as part of the battle to "bust the trusts." Over the years, Congress passed additional laws giving the agency greater authority in the policing of anticompetitive prices. In 1938, Congress passed a broad prohibition against "unfair and deceptive acts or practices." Since then, the FTC has also been directed to administer a wide variety of other consumer protection laws including Truth-in-Lending, Fair Packaging and Labeling, Fair Credit Reporting, and Equal Credit Opportunity Acts.[140] Over the course of its history, the FTC has been more or less active depending on the administration that was in office and the zeal of the chairperson. Figure 14-2 provides additional information about the FTC's mission, vision, and how it helps consumers.

Today, the FTC is playing a more active role as government's consumer data watchdog. Though it has long used computer scientists and technically knowledgeable lawyers, in 2010 the FTC embarked on yet another mission in its quest to keep current with rapid changes in technology. The agency created a new position, that of chief technologist, and in the past several years it has been investigating whether companies truly are keeping customers' personal data secure and private.[141] The FTC's chief technologist has challenged the tracking of shoppers online and in stores, though this has drawn criticism from an online-advertising trading group.[142]

The FTC also has created a special unit called the Office of Technology Research and Investigation so that it can keep on top of new technologies and ensure that consumers are better protected from invasive approaches.[143] The FTC expects the unit to investigate a wider array of emerging technologies including Internet-connected automobiles, connected home devices, and mobile payment systems, and in particular, their implications for data security and privacy.[144] In one of its investigations, the agency filed a complaint against a retail-tracking company that uses mobile phone signals to track shoppers' movements in stores but has failed to live up to its commitment to inform shoppers about the in-store surveillance and permit them to opt out.[145]

14.3 Consumer Financial Protection Bureau (CFPB)

Though the FTC supervises most consumer regulations with respect to product and service information and advertising, and other laws have been passed that address specific issues, it is useful to briefly consider the most recent federal consumer legislation that has been passed in the last few years. The Dodd–Frank Wall Street Reform and Consumer Protection Act of 2010 (Dodd–Frank Act) established the **Consumer Financial Protection Bureau (CFPB)**. Congress established the CFPB to protect consumers by implementing and enforcing federal consumer financial laws. Among other activities, the CFPB:[146]

- Writes rules, supervises companies, and enforces federal consumer financial protection laws
- Restricts unfair, deceptive, or abusive acts or practices
- Takes consumer complaints
- Promotes financial education
- Researches consumer behavior
- Monitors financial markets for new risks to consumers
- Enforces laws that outlaw discrimination and other unfair treatment in consumer finance

The CFPB has had considerable support because many consumers and political leaders believed that such an agency was needed in light of the financial misdealings and deceptions of the previous decade. One aim of the agency was that it would police and write rules for financial firms' retail products such as mortgages, bank accounts, and credit cards. In fact, the CFPB was given authority to administer the **Credit Card Act of 2009** that spelled out new regulations governing credit cards. Officially, the act was named the *Credit Card Accountability, Responsibility, and Disclosure Act 2009 (CARD)* and it was passed by Congress and enacted in February 2010.[147] The CFPB is user-friendly for consumers and addresses the multitude of questions and issues that consumers might have in connection with credit cards.

According to the CFPB's 2020 Annual Report, credit and consumer reporting complaints accounted for more than 58 percent of complaints received. This was followed by debt collection (15%), credit cards (7%), checking or savings (6%), and mortgage (5%). Beginning in April 2020, consumers began to submit more than 3,000 complaints mentioning coronavirus keywords nearly every month. In general, overall complaints to CFPB were up 54 percent from the previous year.[148]

The CFPB has not been without its critics. One of the primary criticisms is that the agency is run by political appointees and thus can reflect the position of the administration in office. For example, the CFPB had become less forceful during President Donald Trump's time in office, but it is expected to embrace a much more aggressive role during the Biden administration. According to reports, the revitalized CFPB is expected to issue more fines, try to recover more money for consumers, and give priority to protecting people hurt by the COVID-19 recession.[149]

14.4 Self-Regulation in Advertising

Cases of deceptive or unfair advertising in the United States are handled primarily by the FTC. In addition to this regulatory approach, however, self-regulation of advertising has become an important business response. Under the regulatory approach, advertising behavior is controlled through various governmental rules that are backed by the use of penalties. **Self-regulation**, on the other hand, refers to the control of business conduct and performance by the business itself, or business associations, rather than by government or by market forces.[150] The idea behind self-regulation is that companies will carefully monitor their own advertising for legal and ethical issues and take the initiative in correcting deficient advertising without the regulatory agencies having to get involved. Self-regulation is a form of firms engaging in CSR practices and striving to be proactive and ethical rather than reactive.

The most prominent instance of voluntary self-regulation by business in the advertising industry is the program sponsored by the National Advertising Division (NAD) of the Council of Better Business Bureaus, Inc.[151] The NAD monitors national advertising in all media, enforces high standards of truth and accuracy, and efficiently resolves disputes to build consumer trust and support fair competition. NAD reviews advertising based on challenges from business, complaints from consumers, or on its own initiative covering a wide spectrum of industries and issues. NAD's decisions represent the single largest body of advertising decisions in the United States.[152] At the global level, the International Council for Advertising Regulation is a global platform promoting responsible ads through the implantation of self-regulatory standards.[153]

14.5 Moral Models and Consumer Stakeholders

It is useful to conclude this chapter by providing insights into how the three types of moral manager models, introduced in Chapter 5, would view consumer stakeholders. Figure 14-3 presents a brief statement as to the likely orientations of immoral, amoral, and moral managers to this vital stakeholder group. As can be seen in these descriptions, the moral management model best represents the highest ethical standards of consumer treatment and is, therefore, the recommended model for business to follow.

Figure 14-3 Three Moral Management Models and Their Orientations toward Consumer Stakeholders

Model of Management Morality Orientation to Consumer Stakeholders

Immoral Management Customers are viewed as opportunities to be exploited for personal or organizational gain. Ethical standards in dealings do not prevail; indeed, an active intent to cheat, deceive, and/or mislead is present. In all marketing decisions—advertising, pricing, packaging, distribution, warrantees—the customer is taken advantage of to the fullest extent.

Amoral Management In this model, management does not think through the ethical consequences of its decisions and actions toward consumers. It simply makes decisions with profitability within the letter of the law as a guide. Management is not focused on what is fair from the perspective of the customer. The focus is on management's rights. No consideration is given to ethical implications of interactions with customers.

Moral Management Customers are viewed as equal partners in transactions. The customer brings needs and expectations to the exchange transaction and is treated honestly and fairly. Managerial focus is on giving the customer fair value, full information, fair guarantee, and satisfaction. Consumer rights are liberally interpreted and honored.

Summary

Consumer stakeholders have always been at the top of the list of business's stakeholders. Some of the newer challenges, such as social media advertising, advertising and labeling for more healthy food options, the expanding use of e-cigarettes, and new government agencies that are beginning to have influence, are important features of this chapter.

The issue of consumer stakeholders is always at the forefront of the economy's status. More and more, businesses are realizing that the economy is built on consumer spending and that they need to do all they can do to get consumers spending again. This has been especially true following the COVID-19 pandemic as many companies were locked down, greatly down-sized, or went out of business. In a consumption-driven society, business must be especially attentive to the issues that arise in its relationships with consumers. It is a paradox that consumerism arose during the very period that the business community discovered the centrality of the marketing concept to business success. The consumer's Magna Carta includes the rights to safety, to be informed, to choose, and to be heard. Consumers, however, expect more than this, and hence the consumer movement, or consumerism, was born. Ralph Nader, considered the father of this movement, made consumer complaining respectable. Since then, the consumer movement has been among the most active of the stakeholder categories and promises to be important in the future.

Product and service information issues comprise a major area in the business–consumer stakeholder relationship. Foremost among these is advertising. Many issues have arisen because of perceived advertising abuses, such as ambiguity, concealed facts, exaggerations, and psychological appeals. Specific controversial spheres have included, but are not limited to, comparative advertising, use of sex appeal in advertising, advertising to children, marketing to the poor, advertising of alcoholic beverages, advertising of cigarettes, health and environmental claims, ad creep, and social media advertising.

Other product information issues include warranties, guarantees, packaging, and labeling. The major governmental body for regulating product information issues is the FTC. The FDA and the state attorneys general have become active as well. Important consumer protection legislation has included the Credit Card Act and the rising importance of the Consumer Financial Protection Bureau, intending to give consumers greater protection, especially with financial service industry products. On its own initiative, business has introduced a variety of forms of self-regulation with respect to its product and service information, especially advertising. The National Advertising Division coordinates self-regulation in the advertising industry. This is a global movement as well. Moral models with respect to consumer stakeholders were presented, and the moral management model in which customers are viewed as equal partners in transactions was held out to be the best practice.

Key Terms

ad creep, p. 329

age compression, p. 325

ambient advertising, p. 329

ambiguous advertising, p. 320

brand integration, p. 322

Children's Television Act (CTA), p. 326

comparative advertising, p. 322

concealed facts, p. 321

Consumer Financial Protection Bureau (CFPB), p. 334

consumerism, p. 318

consumer's Magna Carta, p. 318

Credit Card Act of 2009, p. 335

customer engagement, p. 317

customer relationship management (CRM), p. 317

exaggerated claims, p. 322

express warranty, p. 331

extended warranties, p. 331

full warranty, p. 331

green advertising, p. 328

green fatigue, p. 329

Green Guides, p. 328

green marketing, p. 329

green watchdog, p. 329

guarantee, p. 331

Federal Trade Commission (FTC), p. 333

implied warranty, p. 331

limited warranty, p. 331

natural products, p. 328

organic food, p. 328

plot placement, p. 322

product information, p. 320

product placement, p. 321

psychological appeals, p. 322

puffery, p. 322

return fraud, p. 332

returns policies, p. 331

self-regulation, p. 335

slack fill, p. 333

social media advertising, p. 329

social media bots, p. 329

warranty, p. 331

weasel words, p. 320

Discussion Questions

1. In addition to the basic consumer rights expressed in the Consumer's Magna Carta, what other expectations or rights do you think consumer stakeholders have of business? Do consumers have some moral rights that have not yet been formalized into law? If so, what are these and what are their justifications?

2. What is your assessment of today's consumerism movement? Is it "alive and well" or is it fading away? Why has consumerism been such an enduring movement for so long?

3. Give an example of a major abuse of advertising via social media from your own observations and experiences. How do you feel about this as a consumer?

4. Are companies genuinely interested in marketing sustainable products or is this just a marketing strategy that is popular today? Do you think "green fatigue" has set in? If so, what should companies now do?

5. Does the new Consumer Financial Protection Bureau make sense? How do you keep politics out of government agencies? In a free market, why shouldn't consumers be left to fend for themselves with respect to consumer financial products?

Endnotes

1. McKinsey & Company, "Global Surveys of Consumer Sentiment during the Coronavirus Crisis," October 26, 2020, https://www.mckinsey.com/business-functions /marketing-and-sales/our-insights/global-surveys-of -consumer-sentiment-during-the-coronavirus-crisis. Accessed April 20, 2021.

2. McKinsey & Company, "Survey: U.S. Consumer Sentiment during the Coronavirus Crisis," March 24, 2021, https://www.mckinsey.com/business-functions/marketing -and-sales/our-insights/survey-us-consumer-sentiment- during-the-coronavirus-crisis. Accessed April 20, 2021.

3. McKinsey & Company, "Survey: European Consumer Sentiment during the Coronavirus Crisis," March 31, 2021. Accessed April 20, 2021.

4. Gwynn Guilford, "Consumers Expect Economy to Improve as Pandemic Fades," *The Wall Street Journal*, December 12–13, 2020, A3.

5. Ellen Byron, "Pandemic Habits Shift Consumer Trends in 2021," *The Wall Street Journal*, January 19, 2021, A11.

6. Ellen Byron, "Top Consumer Trends for 2020," *The Wall Street Journal*, January 15, 2020, A11.

7. Peter F. Drucker, *Management: Tasks, Responsibilities, Practices* (New York: Harper & Row, 1973), 61.

8. Frederick F. Reichheld, *The Loyalty Effect* (Cambridge, MA: Harvard Business School Press, 1996).

9. Salesforce, "What Is CRM?" https://www.salesforce.com /crm/what-is-crm/. Accessed April 20, 2021.

10. "The Customer Is Often Ignored," *Marketing Week* (September 27, 2001), 3, https://www.marketingweek. com/the-customer-is-often-ignored/. Accessed April 20, 2021.

11. Gallup, "Customer Engagement," https://www.gallup .com/services/169331/customer-engagement.aspx? g_source=CUSTOMER_ENGAGEMENT&g _medium=topic&g_campaign=tiles. Accessed April 20, 2021.

12. Ibid.

13. Ibid.

14. Pete Blackshaw, *Satisfied Customers Tell Three Friends, Angry Customers Tell 3,000* (New York: Crown Business, 2008).

15. Joe Queenan, "America Is Having Way too Much of a Good Thing," *The Wall Street Journal*, April 27–28, 2019, C6.

16. Robert J. Holloway and Robert S. Hancock, *Marketing in a Changing Environment*, 2nd ed. (New York: John Wiley & Sons, 1973), 558–565.

17. Philip Kotler, "Where Does Consumerism Stand Today?" *Journal of Creating Value*, 2020, 6(2), 144–148.

18. Ruth Simon, "You're Losing Your Consumer Rights," *Money* (Vol. 25, No. 3, 1996), 100–111.

19. For more on the history of the consumer movement, see Archie B. Carroll, Kenneth J. Lipartito, James E. Post, Patricia H. Werhane, and Kenneth E. Goodpaster, executive editor, *Corporate Responsibility: The American Experience* (Cambridge: Cambridge University Press, 2012).

20. Philip Kotler, "What Consumerism Means for Marketers," *Harvard Business Review* (May–June 1972), 48–57.

21. Ralph Nader, *Unsafe at Any Speed* (New York: Grossman Publishers, 1965).

22. PBS, "How Ralph Nader Defined Consumer Rights," December 22, 2015, https://www.pbs.org/newshour/extra /daily-videos/how-ralph-nader-defined-consumer-rights/. Accessed April 20, 2021.

23. American Museum of Tort Law, "About the Tort Museum," https://www.tortmuseum.org/about-us/. Accessed April 20, 2021.

24. Kerryn Higgs, "How the World Embraced Consumerism," BBC, January 20, 2021, https://www.bbc.com/future /article/20210120-how-the-world-became-consumerist. Accessed April 20, 2021.

25. *Wikipedia*, "Consumer Organizations," February 11, 2021, https://en.wikipedia.org/wiki/Consumer _organization#United_States. Accessed April 20, 2021.

26. Kotler, 2020, ibid.

27. Consumer Federation of America, "2019 Consumer Complaint Survey Report," July 27, 2020. Accessed April 20, 2021.

28. Consumer Reports, https://www.consumerreports.org/cro/index.htm. Accessed April 20, 2021.

29. Consumer Reports, "Selling It," https://www.consumerreports.org/advertising-marketing/selling-it-may-2021/. Accessed April 20, 2021.

30. Purely Branded, "The 4 P's of Marketing," https://www.purelybranded.com/insights/the-four-ps-of-marketing/. Accessed April 26, 2021.

31. Marketing Charts, "Digital Expected to Hit Half of All Global Ad Spend This Year," February 17, 2021, https://www.marketingcharts.com/advertising-trends/spending-and-spenders-116193#:~:text=After%20a%20challenging%20year%20last,ad%20spending%20growth%20of%205.8%25. Accessed April 20, 2021.

32. Rizwan Amjed, "10 Disadvantages of Advertising," ToughNickel, June 10, 2020, https://toughnickel.com/industries/DISADVANTAGES-OF-ADVERTISING. Accessed April 20, 2021.

33. Ibid.

34. Megan McCluskey and Rachel Greenspan, "These Were the Best Super Bowl 2020 Commercials," *Time*, February 2, 2020, https://time.com/5772692/best-super-bowl-commercials-2020/. Accessed April 20, 2021.

35. Shaw and Barry, ibid.

36. Ibid., 404.

37. Daniel Hopper, "How Product Placement Puts Your Brand in Front of Your Target Customers," Sales & Marketing, January 2, 2021, https://www.business2community.com/branding/how-product-placement-puts-your-brand-in-front-of-your-target-customers-02373480. Accessed April 20, 2021.

38. Justine Goodman, "5 Hilariously Blatant Examples of Product Placement," November 14, 2012, http://www.maxim.com/movies/5-hilariously-blatant-examples-of-product-placement. Accessed April 30, 2013.

39. Jon Porter, "Bond Film Delays Are Reportedly Causing Product Placement Havoc for Brands," January 27, 2021, https://www.theverge.com/tldr/2021/1/27/22252018/james-bond-no-time-to-die-hmd-global-nokia-phones-product-placement. Accessed May 10, 2021.

40. Tom Lowry and Burt Helm, "Blasting Away at Product Placement," *Businessweek* (October 26, 2009), 60.

41. BEN, "Brand Integration, Built on AI," https://ben.productplacement.com/?utm_source=google&utm_medium=cpc&utm_campaign=754092460&utm_term=advertising%20placement&gclid=Cj0KCQjw9_mDBhCGARIsAN3PaFO-BgidjHfW7mxlVdvnoR24T8A4Od4xxqM1SkxWhAtPw1l_Nzcf6CYaAs6JEALw_wcB. Accessed April 20, 2021.

42. Grant Suneson and John Harrington, "What Products Were Among Those Marketing with the Most Outrageous Claims of All Time?" *USA Today*, June 9, 2020, https://www.usatoday.com/story/money/2020/06/09/39-most-outrageous-false-product-claims-of-all-time/111913486/. Accessed April 21, 2021.

43. Shaw and Barry, Ibid.

44. Fast Company, "Five Psychological Tactics Marketers Use to Influence Consumer Behavior," https://www.fastcompany.com/3032675/5-psychological-tactics-marketers-use-to-influence-consumer-behavior. Accessed April 21, 2021.

45. Jeffrey Kluger, "Now Hear This," *Time* (March 1, 2010), https://www.martinlindstrom.com/timecnn-now-hear-this/. Accessed April 21, 2021.

46. Ted Vrountas, "Comparative Advertising: The Legality, When to Use It & Best Practices for Optimal Campaign Results (Examples)," https://instapage.com/blog/comparative-advertising, April 15, 2020. Accessed April 21, 2021.

47. Business News Daily Editor, "Why Sex Sells…More Than Ever," February 24, 2020, https://www.businessnewsdaily.com/2649-sex-sells-more.html. Accessed April 21, 2021.

48. Jill Weber, "Sexy Teen Lingerie Sends All the Wrong Messages," *USA Today*, March 13, 2013, 8A, https://www.usatoday.com/story/opinion/2013/03/12/sexy-teen-lingerie-victorias-secret/1983047/. Accessed April 21, 2021.

49. Johnny Shannon, "The Impact of Over Sexualization of Our Teens," https://www.jonnyshannon.com/blog/how-medias-sexualisation-has-affected-our-teens. Accessed April 21, 2021.

50. BusinessNewsDaily, "Why Sex Sells…More Than Ever," ibid.

51. About-Face, "Does Sex Really Sell?" https://about-face.org/does-sex-really-sell/. Accessed April 21, 2021.

52. American Psychological Association, "Sexualization of Girls," https://www.apa.org/pi/women/programs/girls/report. Accessed April 21, 2021.

53. "The Ethics of Advertising Aimed at Children," HubPages, http://brandconsultant.hubpages.com/hub/advertisingtochildren. Accessed May 4, 2016.

54. Mattie Kahn, "There's Something about Barbie," Glamour, March 17, 2019, https://www.glamour.com/story/barbie-diversity-60-anniversary. Accessed April 21, 2021.

55. Michael Pearson, CNN, "Barbie's New Body: Curvy, Tall and Petite," January 28, 2016, https://www.cnn.com/2016/01/28/living/barbie-new-body-feat/index.html. Accessed April 21, 2021.

56. Erich Schwartzel, "Barbie Maker Mattel Tackles Playtime in a Post-Covid World," *The Wall Street Journal*, May 6, 2021, https://www.wsj.com/articles/barbie-maker-mattel-tackles-playtime-in-a-post-covid-world-11620316872. Accessed May 10, 2021.

57. Sarah Cavill, "It's a Barbie World—and This Time It's Digital," DMS Insights, February 8, 2021, https://insights.digitalmediasolutions.com/articles/barbie-digital-mattel. Accessed April 21, 2021.

58. Sherlyn Seah, "Barbie Turns 60: True Icon of Empowerment or Bad Influence for Girls?" March 10, 2019, https://www.todayonline.com/singapore/barbie-turns-60-true-icon-empowerment-or-bad-influence-girls. Accessed April 21, 2021.

59. Ibid.

60. American Psychological Association, "Children," https://www.apa.org/search?query=children. Accessed April 21, 2021.

61. Jayne O' Donnell, "As Kids Get Savvy, Marketers Move the Age Scale," https://www.usatoday.com/search/?q=As+kids+get+savvy%2C+marketers+move+the+age+scale. Accessed April 21, 2021.

62. Children's Advertising Review Unit, Better Business Bureau, "Self-Regulatory Program for Children's Advertising," 2009, https://bbbnp-bbbp-stf-use1-01.s3.amazonaws.com/docs/default-source/caru/self-regulatory-program-for-childrens-advertising-revised-2014-.pdf. Accessed April 21, 2021.

63. "Bruce Bradley, "Marketing to Kids: Collateral Damage in Big Food's Profit Hunt," October 11, 2020, https://www.brucebradley.com/food/marketing-to-kids-collateral-damage-in-big-foods-profit-hunt/. Accessed April 21, 2021.

64. Annie Gasparro, "A Spoonful of Sugar Helps the Sales Go Up: Cereal Makers Return to the Sweet Stuff," *The Wall Street Journal*, April 5, 2018, https://www.wsj.com/articles/a-spoonful-of-sugar-helps-the-sales-go-up-cereal-makers-return-to-the-sweet-stuff-1522937066. Accessed April 21, 2021.

65. Federal Communications Commission, "Children's Educational Television—rules and orders," July 10, 2019, https://www.fcc.gov/general/childrens-educational-television-rules-and-orders. Accessed April 21, 2021.

66. Michael L. Marlow, "The Skinny of Anti-Obesity Soda Laws," *The Wall Street Journal*, April 1, 2013, A11.

67. Robin Ortiz, ABCNews, "Companies Disproportionately Target Black, Latino Youth in TV Ads for Unhealthy Foods," January 18, 2019, https://abcnews.go.com/Health/companies-disproportionately-target-black-latino-youth-tv-ads/story?id=60418243. Accessed April 21, 2021.

68. Federal Trade Commission, "Payday Loans," https://www.ftc.gov/news-events/media-resources/consumer-finance/payday-lending. Accessed April 26, 2021.

69. Martha T. S. Laham, "One in 5 Seniors Has Fallen Prey to a Financial Swindle, but This Is Just the Tip of the Iceberg," https://seniorlifechoices.com/1-in-5-seniors-has-fallen-prey-to-a-financial-swindle-but-this-is-just-the-tip-of-the-iceberg/. Accessed April 26, 2021.

70. Dana Silversteen, "The Ethics behind Advertising Alcohol to the Teenage Demographic," Business Government and Society, https://bizgovsoc2.wordpress.com/2012/04/09/the-ethics-behind-advertising-alcohol-to-the-teenage-demographic/#:~:text=The%20Ethics%20Behind%20Advertising%20Alcohol%20to%20the%20Teenage%20Demographic,-Posted%20by%20Dana&text=Kids%20who%20start%20drinking%20young,in%20an%20alcohol%20related%20crash.&text=By%20focusing%20on%20a%20profit,rate%20of%20teen%20alcohol%20consumption. Accessed April 26, 2021.

71. Joel W. Grube, "Alcohol in the Media: Drinking Portrayal, Alcohol Advertising, and Alcohol Consumption by Youth," https://www.ncbi.nlm.nih.gov/books/NBK37586/. Accessed April 26, 2021.

72. Ibid.

73. JDSupra, "Advertising on Social Media: Key Considerations for Alcohol Brands," March 19, 2021, https://www.jdsupra.com/legalnews/advertising-on-social-media-key-9669603/. Accessed May 10, 2021.

74. Andrew Thurston, "Alcohol Consumption Has Spiked during the Pandemic. Could the Consequences Outlast the Coronavirus?" March 25, 2021, http://www.bu.edu/articles/2021/alcohol-consumption-has-spiked-during-the-pandemic-could-the-consequences-outlast-coronavirus/. Accessed May 10, 2021.

75. World Health Organization, "Tobacco," https://www.who.int/news-room/fact-sheets/detail/tobacco. Accessed April 26, 2021.

76. Carol Duh-Leong, MD, "How Cigarette Advertising Influences Teens," December 14, 2020, https://www.healthychildren.org/English/family-life/Media/Pages/How-Cigarette-Advertisements-Influence-Teens.aspx. Accessed April 26, 2021.

77. U.S. Food and Drug Administration, "Tobacco Control Act," June 3, 2020, https://www.fda.gov/tobacco-products/rules-regulations-and-guidance/family-smoking-prevention-and-tobacco-control-act-overview. Accessed April 26, 2021.

78. Ibid.

79. CDC, "E-cigarette Unit Sales, by Product and Flavor Type—United States, 2014-2020," September 18, 2020, https://www.cdc.gov/mmwr/volumes/69/wr/mm6937e2.htm. Accessed April 26, 2021.

80. Ibid.

81. Ibid.

82. "Campaign for Tobacco Free Kids," https://www.tobaccofreekids.org/what-we-do. Accessed April 26, 2021.

83. Ibid.

84. U.S. Food and Drug Administration, "The Real Cost Campaign," February 26, 2021, https://www.fda.gov/tobacco-products/public-health-education/real-cost-campaign. Accessed April 26, 2021.

85. "Pepsi Gets a Makeover: Taking the Challenge," *The Economist* (March 27, 2010), 67.

86. Pepsico, "2019 Sustainability Report," https://www.pepsico.com/sustainability/focus-areas/product. Accessed April 26, 2021.

87. *The Economist*, 2010, Pepsico, http://www.pepsico.com/Purpose/Human-Sustainability/Product-Choices. Accessed May 4, 2016.

88. Food and Drug Administration, "Use of the Term Healthy on Food Labeling," October 22, 2018, https://www.fda.gov/food/food-labeling-nutrition/use-term-healthy-food-labeling. Accessed April 26, 2021.

89. Federal Trade Commission, "Truth in Advertising: Health Claims," https://www.ftc.gov/news-events/media-resources/truth-advertising/health-claims. Accessed April 26, 2021.

90. Ibid.

91. Alan Henry and Elizabeth Yuko, "Are Organic Foods Really Worth the Money?" June 10, 2020, https://lifehacker.com/what-does-organic-really-mean-and-is-it-worth-my-money-5941881#:~:text=Put%20simply%2C%20if%20you%20see,dyes%2C%20and%20must%20not%20be. Accessed April 26, 2021.

92. Ibid.

93. Ibid.

94. Rodale Institute, "Natural vs Organic: Does the Label Matter?" October 1, 2019, https://rodaleinstitute.org/blog/natural-vs-organic-does-the-label-matter/. Accessed April 26, 2021.

95. Ibid.

96. PRNewswire, "Global Survey Asks 30,000+ Consumers about Views on Sustainability," February 12, 2020, https://www.prnewswire.com/news-releases/global-survey-asks-30-000-consumers-about-views-on-sustainability-301003468.html. Accessed April 26, 2021.

97. Federal Trade Commission, "Green Guides," https://www.ftc.gov/system/files/documents/public_events/975753/ftc_-_environmental_claims_summary_of_the_green_guides.pdf. Accessed April 26, 2021.

98. Ibid.

99. Ibid.

100. Federal Trade Commission, "FTC Charges Volkswagen Deceived Consumers with Its Clean Diesel Campaign," March 29, 2016, https://www.ftc.gov/news-events/press-releases/2016/03/ftc-charges-volkswagen-deceived-consumers-its-clean-diesel. Accessed April 26, 2021.

101. Federal Trade Commission, "Green Guides," ibid.

102. Gary Mortimer, "Climate Explained: Are Consumers Willing to Pay More for Climate-Friendly Products?" The Conversation, September 29, 2020, https://theconversation.com/climate-explained-are-consumers-willing-to-pay-more-for-climate-friendly-products-146757. Accessed April 25, 2021.

103. Forrester, "Greener Consumers Demand Sustainable Brands," March 22, 2021, https://www.forrester.com/report/Greener+Consumers+Demand+Sustainable+Brands/-/E-RES162635. Accessed April 27, 2021.

104. Center for Science in the Public Interest, "Celebrating 50 Years of America's Food and Health Watchdog," https://www.cspinet.org/. Accessed April 21, 2021.

105. Ibid.

106. Gayle Macdonald, "Are You Suffering from Green Fatigue?" March 14, 2020, https://www.theglobeandmail.com/life/article-are-you-suffering-from-green-fatigue-heres-how-to-overcome-it/. Accessed April 26, 2021.

107. Megan Basham, "Green Fatigue," *World* (March 27, 2010), 59–60, https://wng.org/articles/green-fatigue-1617334449. Accessed April 26, 2021.

108. Debra L. Scammon and Jenny Mish, "From Green Marketing to Marketing for Environmental Sustainability," in Pratima Bansal and Andrew J. Hoffman (editors), *The Oxford Handbook of Business and the Natural Environment* (Oxford: Oxford University Press, 2012), 347–402.

109. Ibid, 353. Also see James Story, "What Is Sustainable Marketing and How Should You Use It?" October 23, 2019, https://www.smartinsights.com/online-brand-strategy/brand-positioning/sustainable-marketing-how-should-you-use-it/#:~:text=Sustainable%20marketing%20is%20the%20promotion,%2C%20practices%2C%20and%20brand%20values.&text=Businesses%20can%20use%20sustainable%20marketing,that%20has%20nailed%20sustainable%20marketing. Accessed April 26, 2021.

110. Daisuke Wakabayashi, "How Ad Creep Has Transformed the Google Search," April 24, 2017, https://www.afr.com/companies/how-ad-creep-has-transformed-the-google-search-20170424-gvr1m8. Accessed April 26, 2021.

111. Kelly Sarabyn, "The Dangers of Ad Creep," https://bookclubbabble.com/the-dangers-of-ad-creep-an-interview-with-mark-bartholomew/. Accessed April 26, 2021.

112. Ibid.

113. MediaPost, "The New Frontier: Social Media and Deceptive Advertising," May 11, 2015, https://www.mediapost.com/publications/article/249403/the-new-frontier-social-media-and-deceptive-adver.html. Accessed April 26, 2021.

114. Ibid.

115. JDSupra, "FTC Report on Social Media Bots and Deceptive Advertising," https://www.jdsupra.com/legalnews/ftc-report-on-social-media-bots-and-48242/. Accessed April 26, 2021.

116. Ibid.

117. Diffen, "Guarantee vs. Warranty," https://www.diffen.com/difference/Guarantee_vs_Warranty. Accessed April 27, 2021.

118. Ibid.

119. Ibid.

120. Federal Trade Commission, "Businessperson's Guide to Federal Warranty Law," https://www.ftc.gov/tips-advice/business-center/guidance/businesspersons-guide-federal-warranty-law. Accessed April 27, 2021.

121. "The Guesswork on Warranties," *Businessweek* (July 15, 1975), 51; "Marketing: Anti-Lemon Aid," *Time* (February, 1976), 76.

122. Ibid.

123. Jacob Stein, "What You Probably Didn't Know about Extended Warranties," August 21, 2018, https://www.joinclyde.com/blog/extended-warranties-what-you-didnt-know. Accessed April 27, 2021.

124. Ibid.

125. Cervantes, "Please Spare Me the Extended Warranty," October 15, 2009, https://abluteau.wordpress.com/2009/10/15/please-spare-me-the-extended-warranty/. Accessed April 27, 2021.

126. Moneycrashers, "6 Reasons Why You Should Never Purchase an Extended Warranty," April 24, 2012, https://finance.yahoo.com/news/6-reasons-why-never-purchase-202002517.html. Accessed April 27, 2021.

127. L.L.Bean, "Returns and Exchanges," https://www.llbean.com/llb/shop/510624?nav=ln-510624. Accessed April 27, 2021.

128. Kate Robinson, "The Ins and Outs of Warranties and Return Policies for Ecommerce Stores," September 1, 2015, https://www.prestashop.com/en/blog/ins-outs-warranties-returns-policies-ecommerce-stores. Accessed April 27, 2021.

129. Khadeeja Safdar and Laura Stevens, "Amazon Bans Customers for Too Many Returns," *The Wall Street Journal*, May 23, 2018, A1.

130. Federal Trade Commission, "Fair Packaging and Labeling Act," https://www.ftc.gov/enforcement/rules/rulemaking-regulatory-reform-proceedings/fair-packaging-labeling-act-regulations-0. Accessed April 27, 2021.

131. WatchUsGrow, "Everything You Need to Know about GMO Labeling in 2020," https://www.watchusgrow.org/2019/01/08/everything-you-need-to-know-about-gmo-labeling-in-2019/. Accessed April 21, 2021.

132. Riley Johnson, "Food Labels and What to Look For," 2018, https://www.food-finders.org/food-labels-and-what-to-look-for/. Accessed April 27, 2021.

133. Ibid.

134. SmartLabel, "Welcome to SmartLabel," 2021, http://www.smartlabel.org/. Accessed April 27, 2021.

135. Ibid.

136. Ibid.

137. Paul Ziobro, "Same Package, Same Price, Less Product," *The Wall Street Journal*, June 12, 2015, B1.

138. Annie Gasparro, "Whole Foods Sales Sour after Pricing Scandal," *The Wall Street Journal*, July 30, 2016, B1.

139. Associated Press, "Lawsuit: Starbuck's Overfills Cold Drinks with Ice," *Atlanta Journal Constitution*, May 3, 2016, A2.

140. Federal Trade Commission, "Our History," https://www.ftc.gov/about-ftc/our-history. Accessed April 28, 2021.

141. Alfred Ng, "Government Watchdog Finds Weak Enforcement of U.S. Privacy Regulations," CNET, February 13, 2019. Accessed April 28, 2021.

142. Ibid.

143. Federal Trade Commission, "Office of Technology Research and Investigation," https://www.ftc.gov/about -ftc/bureaus-offices/bureau-consumer-protection/office-technology-research-investigation. Accessed April 28, 2021.

144. Ibid.

145. Ibid.

146. Consumer Financial Protection Bureau, "Consumer Resources," https://www.consumerfinance.gov/consumer -tools/. Accessed April 28, 2021.

147. Consumer Financial Protection Bureau, "Credit Cards," https://www.consumerfinance.gov/consumer-tools/credit -cards/. Accessed April 28, 2021.

148. Consumer Financial Protection Bureau, "CFPB Annual Complaint Report Highlights More than a half-Million Complaints Received in 2020," March 24, 2021, https:// www.consumerfinance.gov/about-us/newsroom/cfpb-annual -complaint-report-highlights-more-than-a-half-million-complaints-received-in-2020/. Accessed April 28, 2021.

149. Orla McCaffrey and AnnaMaria Andriotis, "Lenders Fear a Biden Win Would Embolden Consumer Watchdog," *The Wall Street Journal*, October 22, 202, A3.

150. International Chamber of Commerce, "The Benefits of Advertising Self-Regulation in Ensuring Responsible and Compliant Advertising," https://iccwbo.org/publication /the-benefits-of-advertising-self-regulation-in-ensuring -responsible-and-compliant-advertising/#:~:text =Whatever%20the%20model%2C%20the%20 goals,advertising%20practice%20to%20promote% 20consumer. Accessed April 28, 2021.

151. Better Business Bureau, "National Advertising Division," https://bbbprograms.org/programs/all-programs/national -advertising-division. Accessed April 28, 2021.

152. Ibid.

153. International Council for Ad Self-Regulation, "About ICAS," https://icas.global/about/. Accessed April 28, 2021.

15

Consumer Stakeholders: Product and Service Issues

Chapter Learning Outcomes

After studying this chapter, you should be able to:

1. Describe and discuss the two major product and service issues: quality and safety. How are they both related?
2. With respect to product safety, what are the key laws and concepts governing them?
3. Explain the role and functions of the Consumer Product Safety Commission (CPSC). Provide an example of a recent action taken by the CPSC.
4. Explain the role and functions of the Food and Drug Administration (FDA). Provide an example of a recent action taken by the FDA.
5. Outline and describe business's responses to consumer stakeholders, including customer service programs, and quality initiatives such as Total Quality Management (TQM), Six Sigma, Lean Six Sigma, Kaizen, and ISO 9000.

Sam Walton, founder of Walmart, got it right when he said, "There is only one boss. The customer. And the customers can fire everybody in the company from the chairman on down, simply by spending their money somewhere else." Customers today have more access to information and, at a click or a swipe, they may make their decisions to shop elsewhere or buy different products and services.[1] Therefore, consumers are more empowered than they have ever been before to weigh in on the quality and safety of products.

Product information, as discussed in the previous chapter, is a pivotal issue between business and consumer stakeholders, but product and service issues such as *quality* and *safety* are more central to consumers' concerns. In other words, the product or service *itself* is a more compelling concern than information about it. Sure, customers may be misled or deceived through advertising, packaging, and warranties, but the center of their attention is on the products and services themselves.

Americans spend around $13 trillion on products every year. These consumers expect that their purchases will function as intended without causing any harm.[2] Hence, the quest to improve product and service quality has been driven by the demands of a competitive global marketplace and an increasingly sophisticated consumer base. With product safety, an additional driving force has been the threat of product liability lawsuits and the damage these can inflict on both the balance sheet and the firm's reputation. The marketers' challenge is to meet these market-driven needs as well as the social and ethical expectations consumers have of them.

Several recent cases illustrate how the issue of product safety and quality, often inseparable, can become critical to consumers and costly to companies. First is the case of Johnson & Johnson's talc powder being implicated in ovarian cancer cases. In 2018, a Missouri jury awarded $4.6 billion to 22 victim plaintiffs for its faulty talcum powder, which was said to cause ovarian cancer in women who regularly used the product.[3] For J&J, the threats that have been posed by current and future lawsuits are significant. Though the company has long had a record of outstanding corporate social responsibility, the lawsuits came on the heels of other product liability lawsuits involving off-label prescription drug marketing, faulty hip and knee parts, and consumer product recalls of children's Tylenol.[4]

In another recent case, Monsanto Corporation was hit with $289 million in damages because its Roundup weed killer product caused a plaintiff to develop non-Hodgkin's lymphoma. Part of this award was punitive damages against Monsanto for failure to warn consumers about the cancer-causing properties of Roundup.[5]

Both the Johnson & Johnson and Monsanto cases illustrate vividly how a company's products can cause serious life and health consequences for consumers and financial and reputational harm to the company that may take years to overcome. Typically, these cases are in the news for years as legal action takes time. And, most relevant here, it was because of quality and safety issues in their widely respected products.

Other products in and of themselves can be harmful to consumers, including tobacco products and opioids. Tobacco products have been under legal scrutiny for decades for their addictive and harmful consequences, and in 2021 it appeared that the Biden administration was going to crack down on tobacco companies even more. Two actions being considered included reducing the amount of nicotine allowed to make them less addictive and banning menthol cigarettes.[6]

One of the most recent and serious product safety issues has arisen in the pharmaceutical industry, with pharma companies accused of misrepresenting the risks associated with opioids. Indeed, it has been said that there is an opioid crisis in the United States and the world. Purdue Pharma, the owners of Oxycontin, in 2021 agreed to pay $4.28 billion to resolve lawsuits charging the company with helping to fuel the opioid epidemic. The wave of lawsuits drove the company into bankruptcy.[7] There is a proposed bill being considered in Congress titled the Opioid Crisis Accountability Act, but it has not yet passed. The purpose of the bill is to hold the pharmaceutical industry accountable for dubious marketing and distribution of opioid products and for their role in creating and exacerbating the opioid epidemic in the United States.[8]

Consumers face many issues with companies, their products, and their marketing, but this chapter focuses attention on two essential product characteristics: quality and safety issues. Product quality and safety are business, legal, and ethical issues. After our discussion of product quality, safety is examined. In connection with safety, we consider the product liability issue and the ongoing calls for tort reform. The Consumer Product Safety Commission (CPSC) and the Food and Drug Administration (FDA) are the federal government's primary regulatory bodies with respect to these issues, and they are also discussed. Finally, business's responses to consumer stakeholders regarding the manufacturing and marketing issues introduced in Chapter 14 and in this chapter are considered. Companies' concern for these issues are integral to their current and future strategies toward operating as highly ethical and socially responsible enterprises.[9]

15.1 The Issue of Quality

The two central issues in this chapter—quality and safety—represent the overwhelming attention given to product and service issues over the past decade. As the J&J and Monsanto examples so clearly suggest, quality and safety are not separate concepts; safety is one aspect of quality. Its importance, however, merits separate attention.

The concept of *product* quality means different things to different people. Some consumers are interested in the composition and design of a product. Others are more concerned with the product's features, functionality, and durability. All are essential aspects of quality. In general, quality is considered the totality of characteristics and features of a product and may embrace both reality and perceptions of

excellence, conformance to specifications, value, and the degree to which the product meets or exceeds the consumer's expectations.

With respect to *service* quality, customers are typically concerned that the service is performed the way expected or advertised, that it is completed on time, that all that was promised has been delivered, that courtesy was extended by the provider, and that the service was easily obtained and consistent from use to use. Some of these issues involve personal judgment and perception, and so one can see how difficult it often is to judge quality.

There are several important reasons for the current and ongoing concerns with product and service quality. A concern for quality has been driven by the average consumer household's family income and consequent demand for good value. With both adults often working outside the home, consumers expect a higher lifestyle. In addition, no one has surplus time to hang around repair shops or wait at home for service representatives to show up. This results in a need for products to work as they should, to be durable and long lasting, and to be easy to maintain and fix.

The Internet and social media have also made it possible for customers to communicate immediately with other customers about their satisfaction, or dissatisfaction, with a product, and this has heightened consumers' exchange of information and expectations. Product review sites such as TripAdvisor, Yelp, Amazon, and Google My Business depend heavily on consumer reviews as part of their quest to keep quality up and to inform consumers interested in other customers' experiences. One downside to this has been revelations that an industry of fibbers and promoters has arisen to sell positive recommendations and raves for a price.

Closely related to rising household expectations is the global competitiveness that has dominated business transactions for the last decade or more. Businesses now compete in a hypercompetitive landscape in which multinational strategies have given way to global strategies, and the solutions that once worked no longer will.[10] As firms jockey for position in these hypercompetitive markets, they vie to attract customers by increasing the value of the product or service.

Each time a competitor raises the quality and/or lowers the price of a product or service, other competitors scramble to catch up, and the bar is raised.[11] The greater the competition, the more firms will be jockeying for position and the more often the bar will be raised. Firms that do not continually improve their quality are certain to be left behind. The above-mentioned stories about J&J and Monsanto show how quickly, in this highly competitive atmosphere, well-respected companies can derail. Once derailed, it is difficult to catch up because of a lag in reputations. Chipotle's food contamination case discussed earlier in the book illustrates clearly how long it can take for a company to snap back from a product safety or quality crisis. Often, consumer perceptions of quality do not catch up to actual changes in quality for years after the quality improvements have been made.[12]

Service Quality. Our discussion of quality here includes service as well as products. The topic is so important it merits its own section. The United States and many developed nations have visibly become more service-based in their economies, and poor quality of service has become one of the great consumer frustrations of all time. The American Customer Satisfaction Index (ACSI) measures customer satisfaction with purchasing, and this index has declined steadily between 2018 and 2020 with the future uncertain. Global CSI is used in some countries to index customer satisfaction, but it is not as widespread as in the United States.[13]

Consumers today often swap horror stories about poor service. Consider the following typical examples: repeated trips to the car dealer, poor installation of appliances, poor customer service from the cable company, fouled-up travel reservations, poorly installed carpeting, no human answering a customer service line, and on and on. Over the past decade or so, service seems to have gone downhill as companies began outsourcing their call centers to developing nations where workers earn very little, are disconnected from the companies they represent, and often face language barriers.[14] But poor service comes at a price. One study showed that 54 percent of the people interviewed would lose all loyalty to a company that had rude or unhelpful staff. One in ten said they would walk away if a company did not seem to listen.[15]

So, what does good customer service look like? Good customer service is a function of customer-centric employees who are good at the following:[16]

- Responding quickly
- Acting on feedback
- Demonstrating empathy
- Maintaining customer self-service options
- Providing omnichannel support
- Going the extra mile

The following are excellent customer service examples that demonstrate companies' sincere interest in making the consumer number one: JetBlue thanks frequent customers with small gestures; Adobe responds to customer service complaints before they happen; Trader Joe's helps those in time of need by delivering though that is not part of their business;

Zappos provides a personal response to every e-mail; Tesla meets customers where they are by going to their homes to fix issues with their cars; and Ritz-Carlton permits their employees to spend up to $2,000 to fix any guest problem, no questions asked.[17] These companies see service quality as an integral part of selling their products and retaining customers.

Dimensions of Quality. It might seem intuitive to identify what quality is in a product, but it often is not that simple. To develop a more comprehensive understanding of quality, some of its key dimensions are worth noting. At least eight critical dimensions of product or service quality must be understood and acted on if business is to respond strategically and fairly to this factor.[18] These include (1) performance, (2) features, (3) reliability, (4) conformance, (5) durability, (6) serviceability, (7) aesthetics, and (8) perception. *Performance* refers to a product's primary operating characteristics. For an automobile, this would include such items as handling, steering, and comfort. *Features* are the "bells and whistles" of products that supplement their basic functioning. *Reliability* reflects the probability of a product malfunctioning or failing. *Conformance* is the extent to which the product or service meets established standards.

Durability is a measure of product life. *Serviceability* refers to the speed, courtesy, competence, and ease of repair. *Aesthetics* is a subjective factor that refers to how the product looks, feels, tastes, and so on. Finally, *perceived quality* is a subjective inference that the consumer makes on the basis of a variety of tangible and intangible product characteristics. It should be emphasized that these quality dimensions are not distinct. Depending on the industry, situation, type of contract, or specification, several dimensions may be interdependent.[19] To address the issue of product or service quality, a manager must be astute enough to appreciate these different dimensions of quality and the subtle and dynamic interplays among them.

Ethical Underpinnings. An important question is whether quality is a social or an ethical issue or just a competitive factor that a business needs to be successful in the marketplace. For many consumers, quality is seen to be something more than just a business issue, although it is definitely a business

---

Ethics In Practice Case

The Pirated Popcorn

Last year, I worked in a local movie theater to earn money during the summer. Part of my job was to clean the theater between showings, collecting discarded cups, napkins, and popcorn tubs. I thought it was odd when my manager asked that I empty and then bring him discarded popcorn tubs that were in fairly good shape. He would then reuse them—refilling them with popcorn for unsuspecting customers.

I soon learned that the theater paid for its popcorn concession by the number of tubs it used. By reusing the tubs, the theater was able to lower its costs. However, I was fairly

certain that customers would have been upset if they knew what was happening (I knew that I would be).

1. How would you characterize the practice in which the movie theater engaged? Does this practice represent fair customer service? How are customers hurt or adversely affected?

2. Should I have followed my manager's orders and gone along with his request? Was it really such a terrible thing to do?

issue. Consumers expect ethical and responsible companies to provide quality service. Three ethical theories based on the concept of duty that informs our understanding of the ethical dimensions of quality include (1) contractual theory, (2) due care theory, and (3) social costs theory. The **contractual theory** focuses on the contractual agreement between the firm and the customer. Firms have a responsibility to comply with the terms of the sale, inform the customers about the nature of the product, avoid misrepresentation of any kind, and not coerce the customers in any way. The **due care theory** focuses on the relative vulnerability of the customer, who has less information and expertise than the firm, and the ethical responsibility this places on the firm or its salesperson. Customers must depend on the firm providing the product or service to live up to the claims about it and to exercise due care to avoid customer injury. The third theory, **social costs theory**, extends beyond contractual theory and due care theory to suggest that, if a product causes harm, the firm should pay the costs of any injury, even if the firm had met the terms of the contract, exercised all due care, and taken all reasonable precautions. This perspective serves as the underpinning for strict liability and its extension into absolute liability, which is discussed later.[20] In short, quality is an ethical issue as well as a business issue regardless of which ethical justification is considered.

15.2 The Issue of Safety

Business clearly has a duty to consumer stakeholders to sell them safe products and services. The concept of safety, in a definitional sense, means "free from harm or risk" or "secure from threat of danger, harm, or loss."[21] Practically speaking, however, the use of virtually any consumer product or service entails some degree of risk or some chance that harm will come to the consumer who uses the product or service. Today,

it is thought to be important that even financial services do not cause damage or financial harm. It is for this reason that the Consumer Financial Product Bureau discussed in Chapter 14 was passed. An important question that never goes away is, How safe should a product be made? Difficult judgments about this question often thrust the issue of safety into the ethical category by many consumers.

Throughout most of history the prevailing legal view has been *caveat emptor* ("let the buyer beware"). The basic idea behind this concept was that buyers had as much knowledge of what they wanted as the seller and, in any event, the marketplace would punish any violators. The caveat emptor doctrine gradually lost its favor and rationale, because it was frequently impossible for the consumer to have complete knowledge about manufactured goods.[22] In addition, the explosive increase in the number of lawyers and the emergence of a litigious society ensured that those harmed by products would have their day in court. Today, businesses are held responsible for all products placed on the market. Thus, we have the doctrine known as *caveat vendor* (or *caveat venditor*)—"let the seller beware."[23]

Through a series of legal developments as well as changing societal values, business has become increasingly and significantly responsible for product safety. Court cases and legal doctrine now hold companies financially liable for harm to consumers. Yet this still does not answer the difficult question, "How safe are manufacturers obligated to make products?" It is not possible to make products totally "risk free:" experience has shown that consumers seem to have an uncanny ability to injure themselves in novel and creative ways, many of which cannot be anticipated. The challenge to management, therefore, is to make products as safe as possible while at the same time making them affordable and useful to consumers. And consumers today expect that if products are found to be unreasonably dangerous, they will be removed from the market.

Spotlight on Sustainability

Sustainable Products Meet Long-Term Market Needs

Companies today are seeking to develop sustainable products. Sustainable products are made to last for an indefinite period and have the least damaging effects on the environment. They are products providing environmental, social, and economic (ESG) benefits as compared with other commercial products. An excellent example is the Levi's® Eco jeans by Levi Strauss Europe designed to tap into the consumers' interest in organic and sustainable products. Levi's also brought out a line of recycled blue jeans.

Another example of a company that is promoting its sustainable products is Unilever. Unilever's *Sustainable Living Brands* are promoted as having both purpose and product in action. Unilever says that its program provides more growth, less cost, less risk, and more trust. Examples of products that the company promotes as sustainable brands include Dove soap, one of the first brands to offer compressed aerosol deodorants that reduce carbon footprint; Knorr sauces, soups, and seasonings that use 100 percent

sustainable sourcing; and Lipton teas that are sourced from Rainforest Alliance Certified estates. Unilever is striving to embed sustainability into its products, and the company is counting on its *Sustainable Living Brands* to drive current and future growth. Unilever has led its sector in the Dow Jones Sustainability World Indexes for many years. In 2020, it announced it would remove fossil fuels from cleaning products as part of a €1 Billion clean future program.

Sources: Levi Strauss & Co., "Sustainability: Using Recycled Denim to Make a Difference," December 16, 2020, https://www .levistrauss.com/2020/12/16/recycled-denim-makes-difference/, accessed May 3, 2021; FastCompany, "Your New Levi's Will Now Be Part Old, Recycled Levi's," July 31, 2020, https://www .fastcompany.com/90529709/these-new-levis-are-made-in-part-from-recycled-jeans, accessed May 3, 2021; ESGToday, Unilever, https://www.esgtoday.com/?s=unilever, September 3, 2020, accessed May 3, 2021.

Figure 15-1 Product Safety Best Practices

In addition to meeting legal requirements, manufacturers or importers should take additional steps to be sure that products not only meet but exceed the requirements of all safety laws. The following are some Product Safety Best Practices issued by the Consumer Product Safety Commission (CPSC).

- Practice safety by design. Make safety a priority at the product design state.
- Build safety in your supply chain. Use suppliers who can reliably and consistently provide compliant materials and subassemblies.
- Be knowledgeable and aware of the business and regulatory environment. Review and monitor consumer feedback reported by customers using SaferProducts.gov.

- Be prepared. Have a recall plan in place should you need to act quickly.
- Document, Document, Document. Document the work you have done toward meeting compliance standards.
- Challenge yourself to manufacture the safety possible consumer product. Go above and beyond the mandatory and voluntary standards. Seek an outside perspective.

Source: U.S. Consumer Product Safety Commission, "Best Practices," https://www.cpsc.gov/business--manufacturing/business-education/business-guidance/BestPractices, accessed May 3, 2021.

Figure 15-1 presents product safety best practices that companies can emphasize to ensure safety and avoid product recalls.

Today the public is concerned about a variety of potential or perceived hazards, such as the rise in genetically modified foods (GMOs), discussed in Chapter 8, and the dangers of living near toxic waste dumps or nuclear plants. Food and drug scares have occupied much of the public's attention in the past several years as questions have been raised about food safety all over the world.

Ethics In Practice Case

Are Video Games a Harmful Product?

Video games can be subcategorized into computer games and console games. In recent years, however, the growth of social networks, smartphones, and tablets has introduced new categories such as mobile and social games. Video games today offer photo-realistic graphics and simulate reality to a breath-taking degree.

The video game market worldwide is estimated to be around $200 billion in 2023. The market size of video games in the United States in 2021 was about $65.5 billion. It is estimated that, worldwide, there will be 3 billion gamers by 2023. The coronavirus pandemic led to an increase in game usage, but this is expected to taper off. Clearly, it represents a large market sector that ought to be subjected to expectations of business ethics and corporate social responsibility (CSR).

Though these issues apply to many age groups, the target concern here are children and youth under age 18. It is estimated that 70 percent of this age group are active gamers. Many parents are increasingly concerned about the intense violence, blood and gore, strong sexual content, and use of drugs that appear frequently as central parts of these games. The American Academy of Pediatrics (AAP) maintains that exposure to violent media, including video games, can contribute to real-life violent behavior and harm children in other ways. One psychologist believes that the aggressive behavior that is rewarded in games affects the players' aggressiveness in real life and their worldview. Other researchers have argued that most youth are not affected by violent games.

Researchers also have said that overdoing video games can affect other issues as well such as friendships and how well a child does in school. Two Montreal researchers conducted a study in which it was concluded that playing action video games may be damaging to the child's brain.

The good news is that playing video games some of the time can be okay if quality games are chosen and screen time is restricted. Age appropriateness is a key factor also.

1. Though studies are mixed, can many video games be dangerous and bad for your health, especially for young people?
2. Is it unethical to produce and sell video games that may cause harm?
3. Should video games be more strictly regulated in terms of content and ages to purchase and use?
4. What should the video game makers be doing to produce a safer and more ethical product?
5. Could a parent file a lawsuit against a video game maker and charge the company with producing a harmful, hazardous product? Would the doctrine of strict liability apply?

Sources: J. Clement, "Video Game Industry—Statistics and Facts," April 29, 2021, https://www.statista.com/topics/868/video-games/#dossierSummary, accessed May 4, 2021; Blake Droesch, "The U.S. Gaming Ecosystem 2021," March 17, 2021, https://www.emarketer.com/content/us-gaming-ecosystem-2021, accessed May 5, 2021; Finances Online, "Number of Gamers Worldwide 2021/2022: Demographics, Statistics and Predictions," https://financesonline.com/number-of-gamers-worldwide/#:~:text=2021%20figures%20are%20forecast%20to,from%20its%201.5%20billion%20gamers, accessed May 5, 2021; Harvard Mental Health Letter, "Violent Video Games and Young People," October 2010, https://www.health.harvard.edu/newsletter_article/violent-video-games-and-young-people, accessed May 5, 2021; Laura Hirsch, MD, Kid's Health, "Are Video Games Bad for Me?" https://kidshealth.org/en/kids/video-gaming.html, accessed May 5, 2021; Stephen Smith, "Playing Action Video Games May Be Bad for Your Brain, Study Finds," August 8, 2017, https://www.cbc.ca/news/canada/montreal/shooting-video-games-health-1.4237361#:~:text=Montreal-,Playing%20action%20video%20games%20may%20be%20bad%20for%20your%20brain,concluded%20after%20a%20new%20study, accessed May 5, 2021; Julie Jargon, "Talking with Your Kids about Violent Videogames," *The Wall Street Journal*, February 10, 2021, A13.

Food Safety. In the United States, food safety issues, especially tainted or contaminated foods, have dominated the news for years and have been the safety issue most troubling to consumers. Each year food products are recalled due to contamination or some other foodborne issue. Just in the past year, the FDA and the Centers for Disease Control and Prevention (CDC) have forced a number of food recalls tied to outbreaks in foodborne illnesses. Some of the largest recalls have been due to salmonella contamination in produce, and this is closely followed by illnesses caused by listeria as well as several other undeclared allergens on products put out by major food companies. Generally, these products are quickly identified and recalled quickly.[24]

One of the most highly visible food recalls occurred with Blue Bell Creameries after a deadly listeria outbreak forced a massive recall of ice cream. In 2016, the company claimed that it only partly knew what went wrong. But these issues sometimes have a long life and carry with them ethical and legal implications. In the fall of 2020, Blue Bell president Paul Kruse was charged in connection with the listeria outbreak that actually began in 2015. Kruse was charged with wire fraud and conspiracy to commit wire fraud related to his efforts to conceal from customers what the company knew about the listeria contamination in its products. Kruse allegedly orchestrated a scheme to deceive some Blue Bell customers by directing his employees to remove potentially contaminated products from store freezers without notifying retailers or consumers about the real reason for removing the products. The company apparently did not immediately recall the product or issue any formal communication to inform customers about the potential contamination.[25] Kruse's trial has been scheduled for late 2021 or early 2022.[26] Blue Bell has stated that it now has programs in place to effectively control for the bacteria.[27]

In another high-profile case, Chipotle Mexican Grill has been struggling to survive a food safety scandal for quite some time now, and its efforts to get back on track have been highly visible.[28] We describe this in more detail in Case 3 at the end of the text. Chipotle agreed to pay a $25 million federal fine for its role in some of the outbreaks between 2015 and 2018; however, another lawsuit was filed against the company in 2020 for an incident traced to one of its Columbus, Ohio, locations.[29] To address these issues, Chipotle recommitted to new, progressive food safety programs and procedures, while also bringing on board new executive leaders. In fact, it had a stellar year in 2020 and announced it was planning to build a couple hundred more stores beginning in 2021.[30] Figure 15-2 summarizes some of the food safety issues in the news today.

The government's regulation of food safety is primarily driven by the **Food Safety Modernization Act (FSMA)**. The FSMA is enforced by the FDA. The purpose of the legislation is to ensure that the food supply is safe by shifting from responding to contaminations to preventing them.[31] After a two-year delay in getting approvals, the FDA tightened its food safety rules so that the FSMA could be more fully implemented.[32] The rule tightening focused on requiring companies to create and implement written plans for keeping food safe. Companies will have to identify hazards in manufacturing, create measures to reduce the risk of contamination, and design methods to verify that the controls are working. If they do not comply, then the FDA is authorized to access a company's plans and take action.[33]

Food safety advocates have complimented the new rules of the FDA because they attempt to transform a regulatory system that used to be mostly reactive to one that is focused on prevention of food contamination. The new rules were announced shortly after the Blue Bell ice cream company resumed sales following its recall in 2016. According to FDA records, Blue Bell did not have in place safety practices that might have prevented the listeria outbreak, including the implementation of a comprehensive food safety program that food manufacturers now have to have in place because of the tighter FDA rules.[34]

Figure 15-2 Food Safety Issues in the News

Company or Product	Food Safety Issue
Breese Hollow Dairy milk	Listeria monocytogenes contamination
Michelina's Spaghetti	Undeclared allergen and misbranding
Shetler farm products	Raw milk butter, not pasteurized
Art's Food Market beef	Beef tainted with *Escherichia coli (E. coli)* bacteria
Baby foods, some organic, sold as Parent's Choice, Sprout Organic Foods, Campbell Soup Company	Contaminated with heavy metals, including arsenic, lead, and cadmium
Real Water, Inc.	Outbreak of nonviral hepatitis
Peanut Corporation of America	Deadly salmonella outbreak
Chipotle Mexican Grill	E. coli outbreak
Blue Bell Ice Cream	Listeria infections
Pilgrim's Pride	Chicken contamination with multiple materials

One writer on public health has argued that the rise in food contamination reports has actually been a good thing because it means that the more we hear about it, the more the food supply will be getting safer.[35] The speed with which outbreaks have been identified, along with public notifications, has risen significantly. This is partially attributable to advances in the government's pathogen-tracking system, known as *PulseNet*. *PulseNet* has allowed regulators to get information faster and more accurately. The Blue Bell outbreak was only one of a number of different contamination notifications that were speeded up because of *PulseNet*. Previously, some contamination communications took much longer or were not solvable without the new technology.[36]

Safe drinking water goes hand-in-hand with safe food products. In most developed countries, safe drinking water is taken for granted and does not tend to raise as many issues as food products. However, safe drinking water is a critical issue at the world level. Today, 2.2 billion people lack access to safely managed drinking water services, and 4.2 billion lack safely managed sanitation services. The impact on child mortality rates is devastating with more than 297,000 children under the age of 5 who die annually from diarrhoeal diseases due to unsafe drinking water, poor sanitation, and poor hygiene.[37] This issue poses enormous CSR opportunities to global corporations to get involved in the desperately needed realm of human safety.

Other Safety Issues. Manufacturing is a high-profile industry for which product safety is of paramount concern. Over the past decade, the following are the major product liability lawsuits filed for dangerous or defective products: transvaginal mesh; GM faulty ignition switches; Monsanto Roundup; Takata defective air bags; 3M earplugs; J&J talcum powder; and Zantac heartburn medicine.[38] Other recent recalls have included infant/child products, sports and recreation products, and household products.[39] Manufactured products create hazards not only because of unsafe product design but also as a result of consumers being given inadequate information regarding the hazards associated with using the products. Consequently, in product liability claims, it is not surprising to find charges based on one or more of several allegations. First may be the charge that the product was *improperly manufactured*, wherein the producer failed to exercise due care in the product's production, which contributed directly to the accident or injury. Second could be the charge that, though manufactured properly, the product's *design could have been defective*, in that alternative designs or devices, if used at the time of manufacture, may have prevented the accident. Third could be that the producer failed to provide *satisfactory instructions and/or warnings* that could have helped avert accident or injury. Fourth may be that the producer failed to *foresee a reasonable and anticipated misuse* of the product and warn against such misuse.[40]

Another major category of concern that has arisen is with the use of artificial intelligence (AI) and, for example, robots and autonomous, self-driving vehicles. It is inevitable that accidents related to these products will arise and some could cause catastrophic injuries. In 2021, a California man was arrested for driving his Tesla from the backseat, with no one behind the wheel. He was charged with reckless driving. After he got out of jail, he did it again. Though autonomous driving may have a bright future, it is currently illegal.[41] It is important to note that not only a product defect may occur, but possible cyberattacks against these products, or an entire network, fleet, or industry could be possible.[42] These are clearly safety issues that will have to be addressed in the near future.

Safety in the provision of services, as well as products, is also an issue. A sector in which this has the potential to develop is that of telemedicine or telehealth. Telemedicine generally refers to the provision of medical services through electronic or other technological means. Telehealth, often used interchangeably, refers to the broader area that includes information and communications technologies, including remote patient monitoring devices and patient and public health information. Telemedicine focuses more on the curative aspect of health care, whereas telehealth focuses on the preventative and promotional aspects as well as the curative aspects.[43]

Though spurred on by uses during the pandemic, telemedicine is expected to become a new norm for delivering health care services. This raises the issue of both service quality and safety. Legislation governing telemedicine is still at the early stages, but already the question of what constitutes a generally accepted "standard of care" is being raised. The safety and liability dimensions of these services pertains to the possibility of malpractice charges and liabilities being leveled against health care providers. In response to the rapid expansion of telemedicine and telehealth, discussions of what will constitute acceptable standards of care by which to measure quality and liability are already underway.[44]

To appreciate the "big picture" of dangerous products, it should be noted that the Consumer Product Safety Commission keeps track of injuries treated in hospital emergency rooms and has identified the following categories of consumer products as being the most frequently associated with hospital-treated injuries:[45]

- Sports and Recreation
- Chemicals
- Toys and Children's Products
- Fuel, Lighters, and Fireworks
- Furniture and Décor
- Home Maintenance and Construction
- Kitchen and Dining
- Public Facilities and Products
- Older Adults

Whether we deal with consumer products (where there is potential for harm following accidents or misuse) or with food products (where not-so-visible threats to human health may exist), the field of product safety is a significant responsibility and a growing challenge for the business community. No matter how careful business is with regard to these

Ethics In Practice Case

Was "Pink Slime" a Victim of Social Media Frenzy? Unethical Reporting?

The "pink slime" case is a cautionary tale of what can happen to a company that gets involved in a hot button issue when challenged by a contingent of online tweeters with social media accounts.

In the early 1990s, Eldon Roth started a meat processing company named Beef Products, Inc. (BPI). The company would buy tons of fatty meat scrap that was left over after cattle were carved into steaks and roasts. Roth developed a centrifuge that would spin the fat away. The remaining product was then treated with a puff of ammonia hydroxide as a safety measure to kill bacteria. Then he would quick freeze the remaining meat into a pink pulp that when mixed in with ground beef made it leaner. This product became known as "lean finely textured beef" or LFTB in the industry. Roth's company would then package the product in the form of frozen bricks and sell them to companies as an additive to ground beef, making the resulting beef leaner and cheaper. Among others, McDonald's, Burger King, Taco Bell, Kroger, and Walmart would then use the product.

Roth's company was so successful that it opened plants in Kansas, Texas, Iowa, and Nebraska, employing about 1,500 workers. In fall 2011, Roth was inducted into the Meat Industry Hall of Fame. Roth had been called a genius who ran a company that was on the vanguard of food safety.

In March 2012, someone labeled Roth's product "pink slime," and a food blogger launched an online petition to have it removed from the federal lunch program. ABC News and other media jumped on the story, and soon the product was being assailed as unsafe and gross as the story went viral on the blogosphere. On Twitter, uses of the term *pink slime* rapidly occurred and went on for several months. As the social media frenzy increased, many customers quickly abandoned his product, and Roth was forced to suspend production at three plants and lay off half his workers. After the ABC News reports, BPI initiated an extensive PR campaign seeking to get the truth out. BPI also filed a $1.9 billion lawsuit against ABC News and the reporters. The company claimed more than 200 false or disparaging statements were made about BPI.

In the United States, pink slime eventually came back in favor as beef prices soared and retailers began seeking cheaper trimmings.

For the record, LFTB is not an unsafe product even in the eyes of food safety advocates. It is an ingredient we have all eaten many times. The USDA insisted the product was safe but would let schools decide whether to buy meat with or without the textured beef. Iowa Governor Terry Branstad, whose state hosts a BPI plant, said he would call for a congressional investigation of the "smear campaign" against BPI.

The lawsuit against ABC News went to trial in 2017 but before it could be completed, ABC settled the suit with BPI for an undisclosed amount. A judge dismissed the claims against Diane Sawyer, an anchor at ABC, before the start of the jury trial. Due to a South Dakota food libel law that provides for triple damages against those found to have knowingly lied about the safety of a food product, ABC was facing a potential $6 billion in damages. In 2019, BPI won a long-sought semantic victory when the USDA announced that LFTB could now officially be called "ground beef," just like what we know as ground beef today.

1. How can a product that has been characterized as "lean" and less expensive be treated in such a disparaging way? Was ABC unethical in using this terminology?
2. Do you think LFTB and Roth's company had been treated fairly up until the final settlement by ABC? Has this product gotten a bad rap by overzealous social media critics? Was this a case of "fake news"?
3. Should those who labeled the product "pink slime" and questioned it unfairly be disciplined in any way? Or, is this just the social media "market at work" and nothing should be done?
4. Was Eldon Roth an innovative genius to come up with this product? Did he deserve to be placed in the Meat Industry Hall of Fame?
5. Given the final resolution of this case, what lessons are learned about business ethics in the news with respect to reporting on food safety?

Sources: "'Pink Slime' Uproar Overshadows More Serious Food Safety Threats," USA Today, April 17, 2012, 8A; "Was a Food Innovator Unfairly Targeted?" *Bloomberg Businessweek*, April 16–April 22, 2012, 18–20; Jacob Bunge and Kelsey Gee, "Pink Slime Back in Favor as Prices Soar for U.S. Beef," *The Wall Street Journal*, May 24–25, 2014, A1; Patrick Fitzgerald and Jacob Gershman, "ABC Settles Suit over 'Pink Slime,'" *The Wall Street Journal*, June 29, 2017, B5.

issues, the threat of product liability lawsuits has become an industry unto itself and intimately linked with product safety discussions. Therefore, we now turn our attention to this vital topic. Product liability has been a monumental consumer issue in the United States for many decades.

15.3 Product Liability

In recent years, the product liability issue (sometimes called products liability) has been one of the most important legal and ethical responsibilities businesses have faced. What is

at stake is the responsibility for harm caused by products. **Product liability**, as a legal concept, includes the liability of all parties in the chain of manufacture and sale of a product and for any damage caused by that product. This includes the manufacture, assembly, wholesaling, and retailing of the product. Products containing defects that result in harm to a consumer or someone to whom the product was loaned or given are the subjects of product liability lawsuits. Defective products might include, for example, faulty auto brakes, contaminated baby food, exploding bottles of beer, flammable children's pajamas, or products that lack proper warning labels.[46]

Reasons for Concern about Product Liability.

Product, or products, liability has become a major issue because of the *sheer number of cases* involving products that have resulted in illness, harm, or death. More than in other countries, U.S. residents tend to file lawsuits and pursue litigation when faced with situations in which they are harmed or dissatisfied.

Another cause for concern has been the *size of the financial awards* that have been given by the courts. Some of the largest U.S. product liability cases in recent years have included the well-known companies listed earlier.[47] In a recent year, the average product liability awards were in excess of $7.6 million, and this category of award exceeded all other personal injury awards.[48]

It has been estimated that litigation's *cost to society* runs into the hundreds of billions per year, more than half of which goes to legal fees and costs, some of which could be spent to hire more teachers, police officers, and firefighters. A decrease in innovation has been another issue. This *decrease in innovation* due to tort litigation carries lasting consequences for competitiveness.[49]

Doctrine of Strict Liability.

Though one should consult law books and lawyers for all of the intricacies and complexities of legal concepts, it is useful to have an overview of what the basic concepts mean. The key legal concept in tort law that governs product liability cases is the **doctrine of strict liability**. A **tort** is a wrongful act that gives rise to injury or harm to another and amounts to a civil wrong for which the courts may impose liability. The primary purpose of **tort law** is to provide relief to injured parties for harms caused by others, to impose liability on parties responsible for the harm, and to deter others from committing harmful acts.[50] In its most general form, the doctrine of strict liability holds that anyone in the value chain of a product is liable for harm caused to the user if the product as sold was unreasonably dangerous because of its defective condition. This applies to anyone involved in the design, manufacture, or sale of a defective product. Beyond manufacturing, courts have ruled against plaintiffs from a broad array of functions, such as selling, advertising, promotion, and distribution.[51] Strict liability law has been controversial. Some have held that it is not fair for a defendant to be held accountable for something unrelated to the defendant's intentions.[52] But, it is the law.

The doctrine of strict liability and the expansion of this concept in the courts have been at the heart of the litigation explosion in the United States. As mentioned previously, the social costs theory of product quality underlies the concept of strict liability and its extensions. In addition, some hold the strict liability view as utilitarian; that is, society has made a determination that it is better to hold persons responsible for certain actions even without a showing of negligence because the benefits derived (e.g., safety, improved products, accountability)

outweigh the burden placed on the defendant in a strict liability lawsuit. In the area of consumer product development, strict liability laws have fostered meaningful safety developments that have prevented innumerable deaths and injuries. Strict liability is not without its cost, however, and the price of consumer goods today reflects this cost-shifting consequence.[53]

Extensions of Strict Liability Rule.

Courts in several states and certain countries have established a standard that is much more demanding than strict liability. This concept is known as **absolute liability**. The ruling that established this concept was handed down by the New Jersey Supreme Court in *Beshada v. Johns Manville Corporation* (1982). The plaintiffs in the *Beshada* case were employees of Johns Manville and other companies who had developed asbestos-related diseases as a result of workplace exposure.[54] The court ruled in this case that a manufacturer could be held *strictly liable* for failure to warn of a product hazard, even if the hazard was scientifically unknowable at the time of manufacture and sale. Therefore, a company cannot use as its defense the claim that it did its best according to the state of the art in the industry at that time. Under this ruling, the manufacturer is liable for damages even if it had no way of knowing that the product might cause a problem later.[55]

Product liability law can be extremely complex and managers should seek legal advice when faced with uncertain situations. The recommended course of action, of course, is to create safe products and be guided by law and ethics in all phases of the design, production, and distribution process.

As part of their social and ethical responsibilities, companies might elect to develop a **product liability risk management program**.[56] Five steps may be followed in such a program.

- Transfer risk through management of suppliers. This helps the business avoid financial vulnerability to damages and claims due to liabilities caused or contributed by others.
- Manage supplies and imported goods. Companies that import products and components later provided to an end user may bear responsibility for safety requirements. The company may be responsible for assuring that the imported product complies with applicable industry standards and government regulations and documenting that proper safety warnings, labels, and instructions are provided to the end user.[57]
- Build safety into the product's design. Hazards may often be eliminated in the product design stage.
- Keep essential records for documentation purposes should product liability issues arise.
- Enable and review customer feedback. If the company makes it easy for customers to share their concerns, they will have information that may improve on product exposures and issues.[58]

Product Tampering and Product Extortion. Two other concerns that have contributed to the product liability risks that companies face today are *product tampering* and *product extortion*. The most well-known case of **product tampering** involved Tylenol in the 1980s—first in 1982, when seven Chicago people died from taking tainted Tylenol® Extra Strength capsules, and again in 1986, when cyanide-laced bottles of Tylenol were found in New York, and one woman died. James Burke, J&J chairperson at the time, characterized the case as "terrorism, pure and simple."[59] In response to these and other incidents, firms began to employ tamper-evident packaging. Although improvements in packaging have slowed the rate of pharmaceutical product tampering, they have not stopped it.

In addition to the Tylenol case, other notable cases of product tampering have involved Jell-O pudding, bottled water, oranges, candy, baby food, and Girl Scout cookies.[60] In addition to invading packaging, there are other approaches to product tampering as well. In 2016, a man walked into a Michigan Whole Foods Market and sprinkled a mysterious substance on the grocery store's buffet. The substance turned out to be a mixture of hand cleaner, water, and mouse poison. An observant employee saw the incident and all of the food was thrown away. The man was captured and arrested. He contaminated the buffet at two other stores.[61]

Though product tampering of food and pharmaceuticals are not common today, it still happens occasionally.

Ethics In Practice Case

Sleep Tight and Don't Let the Bedbugs Bite

Ronald Gorny awoke one morning in his home and noticed several tiny insects scampering about on his newly upholstered headboard. Ronald decided to investigate further as he pulled back his sheets. To his surprise, he found dozens more bugs. He also noticed what appeared to be stains on surrounding fabric. Ronald called in the exterminators and they confirmed that the creatures were Cimex lectularius, otherwise known as bed bugs.

Ronald decided to visit the website of *Pissed Consumer* (https://www.pissedconsumer.com/) to see if anyone else had reported similar problems. To his surprise, he discovered that many other consumers had reported similar problems with their bedding purchased from Wayfair, the online housewares company from whom they purchased the headboard.

Gorny's attempt to get satisfaction ended up in a class-action lawsuit that was halted by a judge when Wayfair informed him of the arbitration clause. Unknown to Gorny, when he made the purchase he had agreed to the "terms of use," 4,600 words of legalese, in which he found the operative provision: "Any dispute between you and Wayfair ... will be settled by binding arbitration."

A 2019 study published in a law review found that 81 of the 100 largest U.S. companies are now using arbitration in their disputes with customers. Other studies have revealed that most consumers don't know they've agreed to arbitration when they purchase products and quickly agree to the terms of the agreement; who wants to read thousands of words? Just check the box and move on. *Consumer Reports* decided to investigate to find out which major brands use arbitration agreements. Some of the stellar firms included Sleep Number Beds; Kitchen Aid microwaves; LG smartphones; Bose and Skullcandy headphones; Microsoft laptops; Samsung TVs; and Epson printers. As it turns out, in each of these product categories many firms are using the arbitration agreements.

The major implication of companies writing their own arbitration clauses and using them is that consumers are less likely to prevail when the grievances are handled via arbitration rather than in the courts. It is not surprising, therefore, to learn that a massive debate is transpiring over the fairness of arbitration clauses; sadly, the only ones who know about it are the ones getting stuck with them when a dispute arises. As a side note, many employment contracts today contain arbitration clauses so it's not only consumers but also employees who may be losing their rights. One judge was quoted as saying that these mandatory arbitration clauses are like giving companies a "get out of jail free" card for all their potential transgressions. In 2017, the Consumer Financial Protection Bureau began regulating arbitration agreements in contracts for specified "consumer financial products and services."

1. Did you know that when you quickly agree to the "terms of use" when you make a purchase that deep into the thousands of words is likely to be an arbitration clause? Do most consumers?
2. Is the law that allows companies to write their own arbitration clauses as a condition of a sale a fair one? Why is it fair? Why is it unfair?
3. Do arbitration clauses negate liability law in which companies may be held accountable? How can the two be reconciled?
4. How can consumers protect themselves when there exist arbitration clauses in purchasing contracts?
5. Should the Federal Trade Commission or some other appropriate regulatory body pass regulations to govern the use of arbitration clauses for consumer products that do not fall into the category of "financial products and services"? Would this be fair to both companies and consumers?

Sources: Katherine Stone and Alexander Colvin, "The Arbitration Epidemic," Economic Policy Institute, December 7, 2015, https://www.epi.org/publication/the-arbitration-epidemic/#:~:text=Moreover%2C%20once%20a%20dispute%20is,arbitration%20clause%20in%20their%20contracts.&text=For%20one%20thing%2C%20arbitration%20may,discovery%20that%20a%20court%20would, accessed May 6, 2021; Scott Medintz, "Clause for Concern," *Consumer Reports*, March 2020, pp. 38–45; Consumer Financial Protection Bureau, "Arbitration Agreements," July 10, 2017, https://www.consumerfinance.gov/rules-policy/final-rules/arbitration-agreements/, accessed May 6, 2021.

Product extortion occurs when someone threatens to damage, destroy, or contaminate products in an effort to leverage ransom monies from the affected companies.[62] Though there have not been many recent cases in the United States, product extortions have occurred around the world in a variety of markets. The problem has occurred frequently enough, however, that insurance companies now exist that specialize in product extortion insurance.[63] Unlike product tampering and contamination, product extorters do not try to do reputational harm to the company. They are typically just interested in ransom from the company.[64] In fact, ransomware attacks such as the one against the Colonial Pipeline in 2021 are spiking, and companies have a new threat against which they need to be prepared.[65]

Product Liability (or Tort) Reform. The problems discussed up to this point have combined to generate calls from many groups for **product liability reform**, also known as **tort reform**. As indicated earlier, a tort is an act that injures someone in some way and for which the injured person may sue the wrongdoer for damages. Legally, torts are civil wrongs, not criminal wrongs.[66] The U.S. tort system costs U.S. consumers hundreds of billions of dollars every year. Built into the price of every product is a component to pay for liability insurance and lawsuit defense. Tort risks are the second most important factor when a company decides where to relocate or expand operations or build a new plant or introduce a new product.[67]

The business community's criticisms of the current system illustrate some of the aspects of the controversy. Currently, there is a patchwork of state laws, with the law varying significantly from state to state. Business wants a uniform federal code to govern product liability. It also argues for no punitive damages unless the plaintiff meets tougher standards of proof because meeting government standards is no defense in most states. Business thinks it should have an absolute shield against punitive damages for drugs, medical devices, and aircraft that meet government regulations. Business also wants a cap placed on how high punitive awards can be. Finally, business wants victorious plaintiffs to be able to recover damages only to the extent that defendants are liable.[68]

On the other side of the issue are consumer and citizen groups and others who support the current system and say the critics of the product liability laws have exaggerated the problems. These supporters of the current system point out that some of the most infamous injuries inflicted on consumers were remedied mainly through lawsuits, not regulatory action. Examples include the Pinto's exploding gas tank; the damage to workers exposed to asbestos; many tobacco cases; and many lesser-known cases.[69] To be sure, the health-care arena is one of the primary stages upon which the tort system's reform is being played out.[70]

A special situation involving tort law arose during the pandemic era regarding the major companies that quickly manufactured the COVID-19 vaccines. Under the Public Readiness and Emergency Preparedness Act (PREP), the federal government gave companies such as Pfizer and Moderna immunity from liability if something unintentionally goes wrong with their vaccines. Pharmaceutical companies typically are not given this type of immunity, but due to the urgent need for the vaccines the companies were given this added protection. In addition, consumers cannot sue the FDA who approved the drug. This is part of the sovereign immunity law. The companies, however, continue to assure the public that no shortcuts were taken in producing the products.[71] Only time will tell what will turn out to be the long-term implications of this decision and whether the courts will change their minds if unpredicted situations emerge.

The debate over product liability reform is ongoing. The American Tort Reform Association (ATRA) has been working for decades to bring about modifications in product liability legislation. ATRA is an organization that represents a nationwide network of state-based liability reform coalitions backed by many grassroots supporters. The issue of tort reform is so heated, controversial, and complex, however, that little progress seems to be made.[72] From an ethical perspective, if businesses internalize the notion of product safety and take responsibility for the products and services they sell, the need for legal redress is precluded and the entire business–consumer relationship is far better served.

There are two major government agencies that are dedicated to product safety and both have become more activist in recent years: the CPSC and the FDA.

15.4 Consumer Product Safety Commission

The **Consumer Product Safety Commission (CPSC)** is an independent regulatory agency that was created by the Consumer Product Safety Act of 1972. CPSC works to reduce the risk of injuries and deaths from consumer products by[73]:

- developing <u>voluntary standards</u> with industry
- issuing and enforcing <u>mandatory standards</u>; banning consumer products if no standard would adequately protect the public
- obtaining the <u>recall</u> of products and arranging for their repair, replacement, or a refund
- conducting <u>research</u> on potential product hazards
- informing and educating consumers through the media, state and local governments, private organizations, and by responding to consumer inquiries.

Figure 15-3 summarizes the laws passed by Congress that are administered by the Consumer Product Safety Commission.

Figure 15-3 Laws Passed by Congress That Are Administered by the CPSC

- Consumer Product Safety Act (CPSA): The umbrella statute enacted in 1972
- Consumer Product Safety Improvement Act (CPSIA): Amended CPSA in 2008; gives the CPSC authority to pursue recalls and to ban products under certain circumstances
- Public Law 112-28: Updates to CPSIA: Amended in 2011 to give CPSC greater authority
- Children's Gasoline Burn Prevention Act (CGBPA): Governs portable gasoline containers to conform to child resistance packaging
- Federal Hazardous Substance Act (FHSA): Regulates electrically operated toys, cribs, rattles, pacifiers, bicycles, and children's bunk beds, among other products
- Child Safety Protection Act (CSPA): Amends FHSA to regulate flammable clothing and interior furnishings. Additional standards set.
- Flammable Fabrics Act (FFA): Regulates manufacture of flammable clothing and interior furnishings
- Other Laws: Labeling of Hazardous Art Materials Act (LHAMA); Poison Prevention Protection Act (PPPA); Refrigerator Protection Act (RPA); Virginia Graeme Baker Pool and Spa Safety Act (VBGA); Child Nicotine Poison Prevention Act (CNPPA); Drywall Safety Act (DSA)

Source: U.S. Consumer Product Safety Commission, "Statutes," https://www.cpsc.gov/Regulations-Laws--Standards/Statutes, accessed May 7, 2021.

The CPSC was created at the zenith of the consumer movement as a result of initiatives taken in the late 1960s. Over the decades, the CPSC has experienced ups and downs and degrees of activism as various administrations came into office. During some administrations, it was significantly bolstered in its power and budget, and during other administrations, it was downplayed and underemphasized. As with all government agencies, their directors are appointed by the presidents in office at the time and their powers are greatly affected by the budgets given them by Congress.

Since the CPSC was created, the most comprehensive piece of legislation given to the CPSC for enforcement was the **Consumer Product Safety Improvement Act (CPSIA) of 2008**. This act provided the CPSC with new regulatory and enforcement tools. CPSIA addresses, among other things, lead, phthalates, toy safety, third-party testing and certification, imports, ATVs, civil and criminal penalties, and SaferProducts.gov.[74] In 2011, CPSIA was updated to provide stronger regulatory and enforcement tools.[75]

The CPSC continues to play a vital role in protecting consumers from unsafe products. Since the passage of CPSIA, the cap on civil penalties has been increased from just under $2 million to $15 million for violations of the consumer safety laws.[76] Up until 2016, no penalty higher than $5 million had been issued. The huge penalty was a way of sending a message to non-U.S. companies that if they sell, manufacture, or distribute consumer goods in the United States, they must meet their reporting and product certifications that must be accurate and up-to-date under the U.S. consumer protection laws or face record high consequences.[77]

An example of the CPSC's recall power was illustrated in 2021 when Peloton, the exercise-equipment maker, was asked to halt sales of and recall its Tread+ treadmill model because of injury statistics the CPSC has been accumulating. Peloton rebuffed the recall at first but eventually gave in and agreed to recall all its treadmills. Peloton has said that its machines are no more dangerous than other treadmills if not used properly, so the CPSC said it would investigate the other brands as well.[78] Examples such as this make it obvious why companies need to carefully focus on the safety of their products.

Despite all that the CPSC does in administering its various laws, many dangerous products enter and stay on the market. Of the 15,000 product categories the government oversees, only a few require testing before being released onto the market. According to a *Consumer Reports* study in 2020, 96 percent of American consumers think products they buy for their homes must adhere to a safety standard. In reality, only 1 percent of these product categories must comply with a mandatory safety standard. Most of the standards are voluntary and many manufacturers do not comply with the rules, and this leaves a huge hole in the safety net.[79] It is little wonder then that product safety continues to be a major issue in the marketplace and consumers need to be wary and diligent regarding the purchases they make. Companies need to focus their CSR and ethics initiatives upon one of the most important stakeholder groups they have: consumers.

15.5 Food and Drug Administration

The **Food and Drug Administration (FDA)** is one of the U.S. federal government's most important consumer-related regulatory agencies. The FDA evolved from the **Food and Drugs Act of 1906**, which set the stage, and the agency was renamed in 1931 when it became the Food and Drug Administration.[80] Today, the FDA is responsible for protecting public health by assuring the safety, efficacy, and security of human and veterinary drugs, biological products, medical devices, the nation's food supply, cosmetics, tobacco products, and products that emit radiation.[81] The scope of the FDA's regulatory authority is broad and is closely related to some other regulatory agencies. As a result, it is often frustrating and confusing to consumers to determine the appropriate regulatory body to contact.[82] The FDA conducts an enormous amount of business as it carries out its mission, and like the CPSC it has been controversial over the decades and its zeal in pursuing its mission has varied widely depending on the administration in office.

Figure 15-4 provides the most recent information about the FDA's mission.

Figure 15-4 U.S. Food and Drug Administration's (FDA)—Mission

- The FDA is responsible for protecting the public health by ensuring the safety, efficacy, and security of human and veterinary drugs, biological products, and medical devices; and by ensuring the safety of our nation's food supply, cosmetics, and products that emit radiation.
- The FDA also has responsibility for regulating the manufacturing, marketing, and distribution of tobacco products to protect the public health and to reduce tobacco use by minors.
- The FDA is responsible for advancing the public health by helping to speed innovations that make medical products more effective, safer, and more affordable and by helping the public get the accurate, science-based information they need to use medical products and foods to maintain and improve their health.
- The FDA also plays a significant role in the Nation's counterterrorism capability. The FDA fulfills this responsibility by ensuring the security of the food supply and by fostering development of medical products to respond to deliberate and naturally emerging public health threats.

Source: U.S. Food and Drug Administration, "FDA Mission," https://www.fda.gov/about-fda/what-we-do, accessed May 12, 2021.

In addition to regulating food, discussed earlier, in recent years, the FDA's primary foci have included tobacco products and drugs, to include biologics and vaccines. The FDA's work with respect to cigarettes, e-cigs, and tobacco products seems to consume its time and energies. Once research and the FDA concluded that tobacco products were not safe products, it then had to decide how far to carry its activities toward monitoring and regulating them. The FDA is always on the attack against Big Tobacco and its efforts are combined with state legal action and class action lawsuits.[83] In 2020, the FDA prioritized its enforcement against certain unauthorized flavored e-cigs that appeal to young people.[84] In 2021, the FDA decided to begin the process of banning menthol cigarettes.[85]

Today, the FDA is spending considerable time monitoring and regulating drugs and biologics, including vaccines. After giving emergency approval for COVID-19 vaccines, the pandemic has brought to a halt in-person inspections of many pharmaceutical manufacturing facilities around the world. In mid-2021 the FDA had a backlog of more than 1,000 audits to clear and were under great pressure to move toward virtual inspections of foreign drug plants, a practice they have resisted for years. Unless the FDA is able to speed up the pace of inspections, they will face bottlenecks for years to come, and this is hardly in the public's best interests.[86] At the same time, Pfizer/BioNTech are asking the FDA for full vaccine approval and are expected to get it.[87]

On top of all this, another active issue in the drug category is the opioid crisis, which we discuss as well in Chapter 12 relative to employee use of opioids. Many Americans, and others the world over, have been affected by the serious harms associated with these medications, including oxycodone, hydrocodone, and morphine, among others. Opioids have become one of the highest priorities because their use and abuse have been claiming lives at a staggering rate. Overdoses of opioids are reducing the life expectancy of citizens everywhere.[88]

Though the FDA and the other regulatory agencies do a fine job, there are critics who say they often operate out of their own self-interest. Milton Friedman, the famous economist, once said that to understand an organization's actions you need to follow its self-interest. A major part of regulators' self-interest is in staying out of trouble. One way to do that is not to approve new products in record time that might experience unanticipated problems. Some have observed that a consequence of this caution is often slow movement of new products toward approval and market, although the FDA's quick response to pandemic vaccines shows that they certainly can move quickly.[89]

15.6 Business's Response to Consumer Stakeholders

Business's response to consumerism and consumer stakeholders has varied over the years. It has ranged from poorly conceived public relations ploys at one extreme to well-designed and implemented programs focusing on customer relations, customer satisfaction, customer engagement, and customer relationship management at the other extreme. Business's response has also included programs focusing on quality and continuous improvement initiatives such as Total Quality Management (TQM), Kaizen, ISO Certification, and Lean Six Sigma programs.[90] Though particular programs may become less fashionable to businesses over time, the core activities that are involved in being responsive to consumers remain.

The history of business's response to consumers parallels its perceptions of the seriousness, pervasiveness, effectiveness, and longevity of the consumer movement. When the consumer movement first began, business's response was casual, perhaps symbolic, and hardly effective. Today, the consumer movement has matured, and formal interactions with consumer stakeholders have become more and more institutionalized. Business has realized that consumers today are more persistent than in the past, more assertive, and more likely to use or exhaust all appeal channels before being satisfied. Armed with considerable power and influence, consumer activists have been a major stimulus to more sincere efforts on behalf of business to provide consumers with a forum. These efforts have included the creation of toll-free hot lines, user-friendly websites, consumer service representatives, and more extensive customer service training. Today, virtually all successful companies have customer service programs, irrespective of whether they are selling products or services.

15.7 Customer Service Programs

It is ironic that the United States is said to now be a service economy and yet poor customer service, especially the AI aspects, seem to be a topic on every consumer's minds today.[91] In recent years, retailers of all types have been pushing the idea of self-service, and many consumers continue to be upset with how businesses keep pushing this concept whether it be checking out your own groceries, following a computer voice protocol to fix your own cable TV or Internet connection problem, or downloading your own boarding pass at home.

But the other type of consumer dissatisfaction is simply with the way merchants and retailers who claim they are providing good, quality service do not do a very good job, and sometimes they behave unethically. Too many companies seem to be finding new ways to plague the consumer with lousy service.[92]

Despite customer frustrations with poor to mediocre and erratic service, consumers today continue to expect high-quality, safe products and responsive customer service regarding the products and services they buy. Nothing is more frustrating than spending money on a product only to encounter after-sale problems or issues that are not quickly and easily remedied. Experts today argue that companies should strive to develop loyal customers who will always come back and that the key to customer retention is customer service. Building lifelong devotion among customers takes serious commitment and hard work. It also requires that a company create a culture and employees who are motivated and committed to delivering outstanding service.

One way to think about good customer service is to identify what constitutes bad customer service. Bad customer service occurs when buyers feel that their expectations were not met. According to one report, almost half of customers will switch to a competitor after just one bad support experience. This same study found that about 80 percent of the customers will leave after more than one disappointing customer service episode.[93] During the pandemic, more customers were shopping online and they were looking to connect with positive customer service experiences. Consequently, the stakes are high for delivering positive customer service, though many companies fail to do so.

Following are five examples of poor customer service and general ideas about how to fix the problem.[94]

1. Lack of empathy: the company doesn't seem to feel bad for the upset customer. Solution: Bake empathy into the company ethos.
2. The company is difficult for the customer to reach. Solution: Allow customers to reach the company on the channel of their choice.
3. Poor automated phone prompts: They are hurting more than they are helping. Solution: Use AI to upgrade support messages.
4. Long wait times: They are ridiculously long. Solution: Use technology to cut down on wait times.
5. Being transferred on calls too many times: The callers get whiplash. Solution: Use the right software to manage customer data.

These recommended solutions seem overly generalized and simplistic, but many times it just takes time, effort, and common sense to recognize the enormity of the problems and address them.

One major factor that holds out hope for better customer service is the fact that there are a number of companies that not only give good customer service but also have become well known for excellence in customer service. One notable example is Zappos, the e-commerce company.[95] Zappos has become a model for how to build a culture of employees that know how to serve their customer base while also enjoying their work. One of the keys to Zappos's success is the careful hiring process they use to make sure the employees will fit in with and can adapt to the customer-centric culture.[96]

Companies address customer service in a variety of ways, and it is often dependent on the nature of the products or services and the competitiveness of the market that drives commitment on the part of companies. Companies provide customer service through money-back guarantees, warranties, and offices of consumer affairs in which are found customer service representatives whose full-time job is to make customers happy. The effective execution of customer service depends on a host of factors, but it is absolutely critical that top management be committed to providing a service as part of its ongoing relationship with the consumer. Management's job is to attract, maintain, and retain customers, and this requires a high degree of dedication and commitment.[97]

There are many principles that drive high-quality customer service and many guidelines for creating a customer-oriented company. Figure 15-5 presents some key customer service principles and guidelines for developing customer-oriented companies. If companies followed these, customers would justifiably think they have been treated fairly, ethically, and in a socially responsible manner.

Customer service and strong business ethics are intrinsically linked, and successful companies will employ both. Some companies have gone so far as to create a customer service code of ethics that identifies and promotes their values as well as spells out how values drive the company's actions. In essence, a customer service code of ethics involves putting ethics into action.[98]

Customer service programs are very important and so are programs that focus on quality such as Total Quality Management (TQM) and Six Sigma. These programs have become important strategic responses to both product quality and safety issues. Lean Six Sigma, Kaizen, and ISO 9000 are also popular quality enhancement programs. These responses are not only concerned with quality but also customer satisfaction and ethical treatment. They merit brief consideration.

Figure 15-5 Customer Service Principles and Customer-Oriented Companies

---

Seven Principles of Customer Service[a]

1. **Keeping your word is where it all begins.** Keeping your word builds trust. Trust is the foundation of all successful relationships.
2. **Always be honest and tell it like it is.** By being honest and telling your customers the truth, you are much more likely to get a positive response to any situation.
3. **Always think proactively, looking around the corner.** Thinking proactively when it comes to customer service boils down to addressing concerns prior to you having to hear from the customer that something needs to be done.
4. **Deal with problems as best you can yourself, never passing the buck.** The more authority employees have to address customer problems, the better it is because nothing upsets customers more than being passed from department to department.
5. **Do not argue with a customer because it is a lose/lose situation.** The best question to ask yourself is: What can be done to make the customer feel happy and cared for?

6. **Accept your mistakes, learn from them, and do not repeat them.** Accept that you have made a mistake, evaluate the situation, learn the lesson, and move on. Don't get stuck in an indefinite state of denial.
7. **Consistency is the name of the game for lasting success.** When the customer service principles discussed above are practiced consistently, customers realize over time that the integrity of how you choose to run your business is not to be compromised.

Creating a Customer-Oriented Company[b]

1. Top–down culture and commitment are essential.
2. Identify internal champions and uphold them.
3. Commit resources to the task.
4. Hire the right people.
5. Empower your employees.
6. Make customer service training a priority.

---

[a]Summarized from Imran Rahman, "Seven Service Principles Guaranteed to Create Raving Fans," https://www.slideshare.net/obeisantartist303/seven-service-principles-guaranteed-to-create-raving-fans-by-imran-rahman, accessed May 14, 2021.

[b]Summarized from John Allen, "Creating a Service-Oriented Company Takes Commitment," *Houston Business Journal*, https://www.bizjournals.com/houston/stories/2009/04/13/smallb3.html, accessed May 14, 2021.

15.8 Total Quality Management Programs

Total Quality Management (TQM) has many different characteristics, but it essentially means that all of the functions of the business are blended into a holistic, integrated philosophy built around the concepts of quality, teamwork, productivity, customer understanding, and satisfaction.[99] The purpose of TQM is to satisfy customers by focusing on product quality and safety issues. To be successful, a strong TQM program needs to employ principles, practices, and techniques that focus on the customer, use continuous improvement, and employ teamwork.[100] It should be noted that the customer, or consumer stakeholder, is at the center of the process. The positive impact TQM can have on safety in the workplace has been established for decades.[101]

To be successful, TQM must emphasize eight key elements—Ethics, Integrity, Trust, Training, Teamwork, Leadership, Recognition, and Communication. The first three—Ethics, Integrity, and Trust—constitute the foundation on which all else is built. These three elements foster openness, fairness, and sincerity, and they create the foundation for involvement by everyone.[102]

A vital assumption and premise of TQM is that the customer is the final judge of quality. Therefore, the first part of the TQM process is to define quality in terms of customer expectations and requirements. Quality means different things to different people, and this makes its achievement challenging, but the four attributes of quality that most often seem to be used include *excellence, value, conformance to specifications,* and *meeting and/or exceeding expectations.*[103] It is important to remember that customers' *perception* of quality is not always the same as *actual* quality and so firms may have to wait for customers to realize that genuine quality improvements have been made.[104]

Opportunities for recognition have helped propel quality efforts. In the United States and the rest of the industrialized world, the Malcolm Baldrige Award, ISO Quality Management standards, and the Deming Quality Award have enhanced the reputations of firms that undertake quality initiatives and complete them successfully.[105] As often occurs with new management approaches, TQM became a management buzzword, and many of its slogans, such as "Getting it right the first time," became viewed as clichés. It is against this backdrop that other tools developed and became popular, such as Just in Time (JIT) strategy and Business Process Reengineering (BPR). Some analysts have argued that sustainability and TQM are intimately related. And, TQM is often characterized as a predecessor to Six Sigma and other approaches, though it is still practiced in its fundamental principles.

The need for a more rigorous definition of quality was part of the appeal of Six Sigma, and other approaches, which we discuss next.

15.9 Six Sigma Strategy and Other Processes

Six Sigma is a development within TQM that has become a standard process for many corporations. *Sigma* is a statistical measure of variation from the mean; higher

Figure 15-6 A Consumer Stakeholder Satisfaction Model

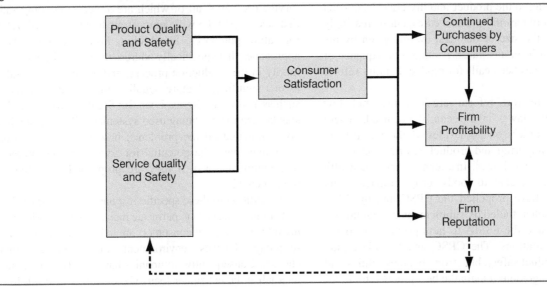

values of sigma mean fewer defects. The six-sigma level of operation is 3.4 defects per million. Most companies operate around the four-sigma level, that is, 6,000 defects per million.[106]

Six Sigma also is viewed as a general heading under which is grouped a body of strategies, methodologies, and techniques. Six Sigma continues as a popular way of improving quality and reducing costs.[107] Deere & Company, Amazon, GE, Vanguard Group, and Bank of America are but a few of the major corporations that have adopted the Six Sigma methodology.[108] Although some observers deride Six Sigma as "TQM on steroids," it has brought new commitment and energy to the quest for quality well beyond the new millennium.[109]

While Six Sigma is a comprehensive quality program, a newer program, **Lean Six Sigma (LSS)**, began being practiced in conjunction with it. Although Six Sigma focused on improving quality, Lean Six Sigma focused on removing waste. As a combined quality management approach, LSS amplifies the strengths and minimizes the weaknesses of both approaches.[110] TQM and Six Sigma are often used in conjunction with the Japanese concept of **Kaizen**, which means "improvement," and refers to

activities that are continuously involving all employees, management, and workers toward process improvement. Kaizen is also seen as a companywide improvement mindset that is focused on customer satisfaction.[111] Accompanying these approaches to quality improvement, **ISO standardization** is often used as well. ISO is a family of international standards on quality management and quality assurance that have a customer focus. The standards are based on quality management principles that senior management can apply for organizational improvement.[112] It should be emphasized as well that there is a close relationship between the quality management approaches described and sustainability. Research has demonstrated that quality-oriented practices have a positive and significant impact on corporate sustainability.[113]

The ultimate goal of these quality or safety approaches is the satisfaction of the consumer and positive, overall societal impact. Figure 15-6 outlines a **consumer stakeholder satisfaction model** that depicts how product and service quality and safety lead to consumer satisfaction and the consequences for the firm's profitability, reputation, and continued purchasing by consumers.

Summary

Consumer stakeholders have become concerned with product quality and safety, largely because businesses have failed to meet their needs reliably on these two fronts. The situation has been the same with both manufacturing and services. One major challenge has been to identify and understand the different dimensions of the quality issue. Today, quality includes performance, features, reliability, conformance,

durability, serviceability, aesthetics, perceived quality, or some combination of these dimensions. Product and service quality is both a business and an ethics issue.

An extremely important legal and ethical issue has been the consumer's right to safety. Product safety, especially food safety, has become one of the most crucial consumer issues of the day. The product liability crisis has been an outgrowth of business's lack of attention to quality and safety. Other factors contributing to the product liability crisis have been the sheer number of harmful-product cases, our increasingly litigious society, the size of financial awards given by the courts, and rising insurance rates. A major consequence of these phenomena has been calls for product liability reform or tort reform.

Discussions of tort reform are ongoing, but few changes in these laws have recently occurred. There are many stakeholders on both sides of the tort reform issue. Product tampering and product extortion have also become safety-related issues. In recent years, the health and safety issues related to foods, drugs, tobacco, and medical devices have propelled the CPSC and the FDA into prominent roles, fueled by supplementary regulations like the CPSIA and the FSMA to help provide protocols and enforce regulations. The CPSC and the FDA play vital roles in product safety, but strong business ethics and responsible management remain the best practice for dealing with these issues.

Companies today employ a host of different customer service programs, all of which are aimed at creating satisfied customers who will demonstrate loyalty and will return for future purchases. In addition, firms use a variety of approaches that specifically address the issue of quality, primarily in the production process, and these embrace safety as one significant feature. Quality improvement initiatives such as TQM, Six Sigma, Lean Six Sigma, Kaizen, and ISO standardization are being used systematically, but they have not eliminated all the problems; however, they and other techniques have the potential for addressing the problems in a significant way if they are properly formulated and implemented.

In addition to these specific responses, a consumer focus and orientation needs to permeate management decision making if the concerns of consumers are to be handled effectively. In today's business environment, consumers have many choices. Consequently, companies have no alternative but to internalize the consumer focus if they are to succeed. In the process, other societal stakeholders are better off as well.

Key Terms

absolute liability, p. 350	doctrine of strict liability, p. 350	product liability reform, p. 352
caveat emptor, p. 345	due care theory, p. 345	product liability risk management
caveat venditor, p. 345	Food and Drug Administration (FDA),	program, p. 350
caveat vendor, p. 345	p. 353	product tampering, p. 351
Consumer Product Safety Commission	Food and Drugs Act of 1906, p. 353	Six Sigma, p. 356
(CPSC), p. 352	Food Safety Modernization Act	social costs theory, p. 345
Consumer Product Safety	(FSMA), p. 347	tort, p. 350
Improvement Act (CPSIA) of 2008,	ISO standardization, p. 357	tort law, p. 350
p. 353	Kaizen, p. 357	tort reform, p. 352
consumer stakeholder satisfaction	Lean Six Sigma (LSS), p. 357	Total Quality Management (TQM),
model, p. 357	product extortion, p. 352	p. 356
contractual theory, p. 345	product liability, p. 349	

Discussion Questions

1. Identify the major dimensions of quality. Give an example of a product or service in which each of these characteristics is important.
2. What ethical theories can help us better understand the issue of quality? Discuss.
3. Identify the principal reasons why we have a product liability crisis. Have any reasons been omitted? Discuss.
4. Differentiate the doctrine of strict liability from the doctrines of absolute liability and market share liability. What implications do these views have for the business community and for future products and services that might be offered?

5. Given the current business and consumer climate, what do you anticipate the future to be for the CPSC and the FDA? What role does politics play in your answer?
6. What is your assessment of business's response to product and service quality and safety? Have they done enough? What is missing from their approaches?
7. How do consumers as well as society benefit from quality and safety initiatives in products and services? How are these related to sustainability?

Endnotes

1. Knowledge@Wharton Essentials, *The Customer of Tomorrow*, 2016, https://www.goodreads.com/book /show/25479938-the-customer-of-tomorrow. Accessed May 17, 2021.
2. Dordullian, "15 of the Largest Product Liability Lawsuits in the United States," November 4, 2020, https://www .dlawgroup.com/top-product-liability-lawsuits/. Accessed April 30, 2021
3. Ibid.
4. Ibid.
5. Ibid.
6. *The Wall Street Journal*, "Danger for Cigarette Stocks Re -Emerges," April 21, 2021, B14.
7. Jonathan Randles and Sara Randazzo, "Purdue Pharma Family Raises Offer," *The Wall Street Journal*, March 17, 2021, B1.
8. Congress.gov, "Opioid Crisis Accountability Act of 2019," https://www.congress.gov/bill/116th-congress /house-bill/2917/text?q=%7B%22search%22%3A% 5B%22opioid+and+distribution%22%5D%7D&r=1&s=1. Accessed May 26, 2021.
9. Archie B. Carroll, "Corporate Social Responsibility: Perspectives on the CSR Construct's Development and Future," *Business & Society*, 2021, 1–21.
10. Francisco Diaz Hermelo and Roberto Vassolo, "Institutional Development and Hypercompetition in Emerging Economies," *Strategic Management Journal* 31.13 (2010): 1457–1473.
11. Rajaram Veliyath and Elizabeth Fitzgerald, "Firm Capabilities, Business Strategies, Customer Preferences, and Hypercompetitive Arenas," *Competitiveness Review* (Vol. 10, 2000), 56–82.
12. Debanjan Mitra and Peter N. Golder, "Quality Is in the Eye of the Beholder," *Harvard Business Review* (April 2007), 26–28.
13. American Customer Satisfaction Index, "U. S. Overall Customer Satisfaction," https://www.theacsi.org/national -economic-indicator/us-overall-customer-satisfaction. Accessed May 1, 2021.
14. Sharon Terlep, "Please Continue to Fume," *The Wall Street Journal*, August 3–4, 2019, B1
15. "Customers Turned Off by Poor Service Levels," *Marketing Week* (March 5, 1998), 11. Also see "Bad Customer Service? Most Consumers Will Dump Your Brand," May 24, 2020, https://www.businessnewsdaily .com/10024-bad-customer-service.html. Accessed May 1, 2021.
16. Qualtrics, "Eleven Examples of Companies Delivering Great Customer Service," September 30, 2020, https:// www.qualtrics.com/blog/customer-service-examples/. Accessed May 1, 2021.
17. Ibid.
18. Ron Pereira, "8 Dimensions of Quality," May 14, 2020, https://blog.gembaacademy.com/2008/05/28/8 -dimensions-of-quality/. Accessed May 1, 2021.
19. Ibid.
20. Manuel G. Velasquez, *Business Ethics: Concepts and Cases* (Upper Saddle River, NJ: Prentice Hall, 2002), 335–344.
21. Merriam Webster, "Safety," https://www.merriam-webster .com/dictionary/safety. Accessed May 3, 2021.
22. Yair Aharoni, *The No Risk Society* (Chatham, NJ: Chatham House Publishers, 1981), 62–63.
23. YourDictionary, "Caveat Venditor," https://www .yourdictionary.com/caveat-venditor. Accessed May 3, 2021.
24. Mura Dominko, "8 Major Food Recalls You Need to Know about Now," September 7, 2020, https://www.eatthis.com /major-summer-food-recalls-you-need-to-know-about/. Accessed May 4, 2021.
25. U. S. Department of Justice, "Former Blue Bell President Charged in Connection with 2015 Ice Cream Listeria Contamination," October 21, 2020, https://www.justice .gov/opa/pr/former-blue-bell-creameries-president-charged- connection-2015-ice-cream-listeria#:~:text=In%20an%20 indictment%20filed%20in,in%20certain%20Blue%20- Bell%20products. Accessed May 4, 2021.
26. Dan Flynn, "Jury Trial for Retired Blue Bell President Not Likely Until Late 2021," November 17, 2020, https:// www.foodsafetynews.com/2020/11/jury-trial-for-retired -blue-bell-president-not-likely-until-late-2021/. Accessed May 4, 2021.
27. Jesse Newman, "Blue Bell: Outbreak's Sources Partly Known," *The Wall Street Journal*, April 4, 2016, B3.
28. Alexandra Sifferlin, "Why the Rise in Food-Poisoning Reports Is Actually a Good Thing," *Time*, March, 28, 2016.
29. Amanda Macdonald, "Chipotle Is Being Sued Again for Food Poisoning," November 13, 2020, https://www.eatthis .com/chipotle-sued-again-for-food-poisoning/. Accessed May 4, 2021.
30. Quality Assurance and Food Safety, "Chipotle's Bounce Back," October 12, 2020, https://www .qualityassurancemag.com/article/chipotles-bounce-back/. Accessed May 4, 2021.
31. U.S. Food and Drug Administration, "Food Safety and Modernization Act (FSMA)," January 4, 2021, https:// www.fda.gov/food/guidance-regulation-food-and- dietary-supplements/food-safety-modernization-act-fsma, Accessed May 4, 2021.
32. Jesse Newman, "FDA Tightens Its Food Safety Rules," *The Wall Street Journal*, September 15, 2015, B3.
33. Ibid.
34. U.S. FDA, Food Safety and Modernization Act (FSMA), January 4, 2021.
35. Sifferlin, 2016, Kowitt, 120–121.
36. Sifferlin, Ibid.
37. United Nations, "Water, Sanitation and Hygiene," https:// www.unwater.org/water-facts/water-sanitation-and- hygiene/. Accessed May 4, 2021.
38. Jeff Craig, "7 Major Product Liability Lawsuits of the Past Decade," August 5, 2020, https://texasjustice.com/blog /major-product-liability-lawsuits-past-decade/. Accessed May 4, 2021.
39. U.S. Consumer Product Safety Commission, "Recall List," https://www.cpsc.gov/Recalls. Accessed May 4, 2021.
40. E. Patrick McGuire, "Product Liability: Evolution and Reform" (New York: The Conference Board, 1989), 6. Also see Michele Mirman, "3 Types of Product Liability Claims," January 31, 2020, https://mirmanlawyers.com /blog/3-types-of-product-liability-claims/. Accessed May 4, 2021.

41. Jesse Gary, "I'm Very Rich: Back Seat Tesla Rider Pulls Same Stunt, but in New Car After Jail Release," May 12, 2021, https://www.ktvu.com/news/back-seat-tesla-rider-pulls-same-stunt-but-in-new-car-after-jail-release. Accessed May 26, 2021.

42. Stephen Wu, "AI Product Liability Issues and Associated Risk Management," August 20, 2019, https://www.americanbar.org/groups/business_law/publications/blt/2019/09/risk-mgmt/. Accessed May 5, 2021.

43. White & Williams, LLP, "Liability in the Telehealth Era," June 19, 2020, https://www.jdsupra.com/legalnews/liability-in-the-telehealth-era-65973/. Accessed May 6, 2021.

44. Ibid.

45. U.S. Consumer Product Safety Commission, "Research & Statistics," https://www.cpsc.gov/Research--Statistics. Accessed May 4, 2021.

46. Cornell University Law School, Legal Information Institute, "Product Liability," https://www.law.cornell.edu/wex/product_liability. Accessed May 4, 2021.

47. Investopedia, "The 5 Largest Product Liability Lawsuits," April 26, 2021, https://www.investopedia.com/the-5-largest-u-s-product-liability-cases-4773418. Accessed May 4, 2021.

48. Insurance Information Institute, "Facts + Statistics: Product Liability," https://www.iii.org/fact-statistic/facts-statistics-product-liability. Accessed May 26, 2021.

49. Alberto Galasso and Hong Luo, "Tort Reform and Innovation," Harvard Business School Working Paper, 2016, https://www.hbs.edu/ris/Publication%20Files/16-093_14c952bf-4842-4ed7-b785-f4b8ae39875b.pdf. Accessed May 4, 2021.

50. Cornell Law School Legal Institute, "Tort," https://www.law.cornell.edu/wex/tort. Accessed May 5, 2021.

51. Fred W. Morgan and Karl A. Boedecker, "A Historical View of Strict Liability for Product-Related Injuries," *Journal of Macromarketing* (Spring 1996), 103–117.

52. Cornell Law School Legal Institute, "Strict liability," https://www.law.cornell.edu/wex/strict_liability. Accessed May 5, 2021.

53. Cornell Law School Legal Institute, "Strict Liability as Applied to Tort Law," https://www.law.cornell.edu/wex/strict_liability. Accessed May 5, 2021.

54. Terry Morehead Dworkin and Mary Jane Sheffet, "Product Liability in the 1980s," *Journal of Public Policy and Marketing* (1985), 71.

55. "Business Line: India Supreme Court Ruling on Damage Liability of Common Carrier," *Businessline* (June 30, 2000), 1.

56. Travelers, "Five Steps for Product Liability Risk Management," https://www.travelers.com/resources/business-topics/product-service-liability/5-steps-for-product-liability-risk-management. Accessed May 5, 2021.

57. Ibid.

58. Ibid.

59. "Tampering with Buyers' Confidence," *U.S. News & World Report* (March 3, 1986), 46.

60. Iva Cheung, "Ten Notorious Cases of Product Tampering," March 1, 2020, https://listverse.com/2010/12/27/10-notorious-cases-of-product-tampering/. Accessed May 4, 2021.

61. Hayley Pederson, "FBI Arrests Man Who Poured Mouse Poison on Whole Foods' Buffets," May 4, 2016, https://www.businessinsider.com/fbi-arrests-man-who-poured-poison-on-whole-foods-items-2016-5#:~:text=FBI%20The%20FBI%20has%20arrested,Foods%20in%20Ann%20Arbor%2C%20Michigan.&text=The%20FBI%20was%20alerted%20to,down%20its%20food%20bars%20afterward. Accessed May 4, 2021.

62. "Product Extortion Insurance," http://www.koeberich-fl.com/grobritannien-uk/financial-lines/produkterpressung/index.html. Accessed May 6, 2021.

63. Ibid.

64. Orion, "Product Recall and Extortion," https://www.orionins.com/product-recall-extortion/. Accessed May 6, 2021.

65. Brenda Sharton, "Ransomware Attacks Are Spiking: Is Your Company Prepared?" *Harvard Business Review*, May 20, 2021, https://hbr.org/2021/05/ransomware-attacks-are-spiking-is-your-company-prepared. Accessed May 26, 2021.

66. "Tort," law.com, https://dictionary.law.com/default.aspx?selected=2137. Accessed May 6, 2021.

67. Angela Logomasini, "Consumers Pay the Price for Mass Torts Driven by Junk Science," November 23, 2020, https://cei.org/blog/consumers-pay-the-price-for-mass-torts-driven-by-junk-science/. Accessed May 6, 2021.

68. Michele Galen, "The Class Action against Product Liability Laws," *Businessweek* (July 29, 1997), 74. Also see Center for Justice and Democracy, "The ABCs of Tort Reform," https://centerjd.org/content/abcs-tort-reform. Accessed May 6, 2021.

69. HG.org, "The Case Against Tort Reform," https://www.hg.org/legal-articles/the-case-against-tort-reform-7095. Accessed May 6, 2021.

70. American Academy of Orthopaedic Surgeons, "Tort Reform: Where Are We Now?" February 11, 2021, https://www.aaos.org/aaosnow/2021/feb/advocacy/advocacy02/. Accessed May 6, 2021.

71. MacKenzie Sigalos, "You Can't Sue Pfizer or Moderna if You Have Severe Covid Vaccine Side Effects. The Government Likely Won't Compensate You for Damages Either," December 17, 2020, https://www.cnbc.com/2020/12/16/covid-vaccine-side-effects-compensation-lawsuit.html. Accessed May 6, 2021.

72. American Tort Reform Association, "At a Glance," https://www.atra.org/about/. Accessed May 6, 2021.

73. U.S. Consumer Product Safety Commission, "Who We Are—What We Do for You," https://www.cpsc.gov/Safety-Education/Safety-Guides/General-Information/Who-We-Are---What-We-Do-for-You. Accessed May 7, 2021.

74. U.S. Consumer Product Safety Commission, "Consumer Product Safety Improvement Act of 2008," https://www.cpsc.gov/Regulations-Laws--Standards/Statutes/The-Consumer-Product-Safety-Improvement-Act. Accessed May 7, 2021.

75. Ibid.

76. Baker McKenzie, "CPSC Signals Civil Penalties Will Reach New Heights after Chinese Entities Agreed to Pay a Landmark $15.45 Million Settlement," April 11, 2016, https://www.lexology.com/library/detail.aspx?g=ff3db2a3-6d2a-4b44-b4b6-73ed2f9d2265. Accessed May 7, 2021.

77. Ibid.

78. Sharon Terlep and Allison Prang, "Peloton Recalls all Its Treadmills," *The Wall Street Journal*, May 6, 2021, B1.

79. Rachel Rabkin Peachman, "Is It Safe to Buy This Product? How Dangerous Products Get and Stay on the Market," *Consumer Reports*, May 4, 2021, https://www.consumerreports.org/product-safety/is-this-safe-to-buy-how-dangerous-products-get-and-

stay-on-the-market/?EXTKEY=NWT15TSA1&utm_source=acxiom&utm_medium=email&utm_campaign=20210507_nsltr_whatsnew_newsletter&utm_nsltr=whatsnew. Accessed May 7, 2021.

80. U.S. Food and Drug Administration, "About the FDA," https://www.fda.gov/about-fda. Accessed May 11, 2021.

81. FDA, "What We Do," http://www.fda.gov/AboutFDA/WhatWeDo/default.htm. Accessed May 11, 2016.

82. Ibid.

83. Sy Mukherjee, "The Fight Against Big Tobacco," *Fortune*, October 2019, 18.

84. U.S. FDA, "FDA Finalizes Enforcement Policy on Unauthorized Flavored Cartridge-Based e-cigarettes That Appeal to Children, Including Fruit and Mint," January 2, 2020, https://www.fda.gov/news-events/press-announcements/fda-finalizes-enforcement-policy-unauthorized-flavored-cartridge-based-e-cigarettes-appeal-children. Accessed May 12, 2021.

85. American Medical Association, "FDA Agrees to Ban Menthol to Protect African Americans," April 29, 2021, https://www.ama-assn.org/press-center/press-releases/fda-agrees-ban-menthol-protect-african-americans. Accessed May 12, 2021.

86. *Bloomberg Businessweek*, "Keeping a Close Watch, from Far Away," April 19, 2021, 15–17.

87. "Pfizer, BioNTech Ask FDA for Full Vaccine Approval," *The Wall Street Journal*, May 8–9, 2021, A6.

88. U.S. FDA, "Opioid Medications," March 29, 2021, https://www.fda.gov/drugs/information-drug-class/opioid-medications. Accessed May 12, 2021.

89. Henry J. Miller, "Follow the FDA's Self-Interest," *The Wall Street Journal*, October 28, 2018, A21.

90. Mike Collins, "Why So Many Management Strategies Become Fads That Fade Away," *Forbes*, June 11, 2015, http://www.forbes.com/sites/mikecollins/2015/06/11/why-so-many-management-strategies-become-fads-that-fade-away/#54bf6486cf68. Accessed May 13, 2016.

91. Swetha Amaresan, "40 Customer Service Stats to Know in 2021," https://blog.hubspot.com/service/customer-service-stats. Accessed May 26, 2021.

92. Bill Saporito, "Staying Power: New Ways Companies Are Getting Us to Stick with Lousy Service," *Time*, February 4, 2013, 56, http://content.time.com/time/subscriber/article/0,33009,2134518,00.html. Accessed May 13, 2021.

93. Erin Hueffner, "Five Examples of Bad Customer Service (and How to Be Great Instead)," March 24, 2021, https://www.zendesk.com/blog/what-is-bad-customer-service/. Accessed May 14, 2021.

94. Ibid.

95. Buzz Knight, "Culture Breeds Excellent in Customer Service," https://radioink.com/2016/04/25/culture-breeds-excellence-in-customer-service/. Accessed May 14, 2021.

96. Roxanne Warren, "10 Things to Know about Zappos Customer Service," April 17, 2020, https://www.zappos.com/about/stories/customer-service-things-to-know. Accessed May 14, 2021.

97. Ibid.

98. Lindsay Kramer, "Customer Service Ethics," August 8, 2019, https://bizfluent.com/info-7759527-business-ethical-considerations.html. Accessed May 14, 2021.

99. K. Ishikawa, *What Is Total Quality Control?* (Milwaukee, WI: Quality Press, 1985). Also see Kat Boogaard, "The Ultimate Guide to Total Quality Management (TQM)," January 20, 2021, https://www.wrike.com/blog/total-quality-management-tqm-guide/. Accessed May 15, 2021.

100. James W. Dean Jr. and David E. Bowen, "Management Theory and Total Quality: Improving Research and Practice through Theory Development," *Academy of Management Review* (Vol. 19, No. 3, July 1994), 395.

101. Boogaard, 2021, ibid.

102. Nayantara Padhi, "The Eight Elements of TQM," https://www.isixsigma.com/methodology/total-quality-management-tqm/eight-elements-tqm/. Accessed May 15, 2021.

103. Carol A. Reeves and David A. Bednar, "Defining Quality: Alternatives and Implications," *Academy of Management Review* (Vol. 19, No. 3, July 1994), 437.

104. Debanjan Mitra and Peter N. Golder, "Quality Is in the Eye of the Beholder," *Harvard Business Review* (April 2007), 26–28.

105. ISO 9000 Family, "Quality Management," https://www.iso.org/iso-9001-quality-management.html. Accessed May 15, 2021.

106. *iSixSigma*, "What Is Six Sigma?" https://www.isixsigma.com/new-to-six-sigma/getting-started/what-six-sigma/#:~:text=Six%20Sigma%20at%20many%20organizations,%E2%80%9D%20or%20%E2%80%9CCustomer%20Perfection.%E2%80%9D. Accessed May 15, 2021.

107. Michael Hammer and Jeff Godling, "Putting Six Sigma in Perspective," *Quality* (October 2001), 58–62, https://go.gale.com/ps/anonymous?id=GALE%7CA79515895&sid=googleScholar&v=2.1&it=r&linkaccess=abs&issn=03609936&p=AONE&sw=w. Accessed May 15, 2021.

108. Wilipedia, "List of Six Sigma Companies," https://en.wikipedia.org/wiki/List_of_Six_Sigma_companies. Accessed May 15, 2021.

109. Hammer and Godling, 58.

110. "New to Lean Six Sigma?" https://www.moresteam.com/new-to-lean-six-sigma.cfm. Accessed May 15, 2021.

111. Mind Tools Team, "Kaizen," https://www.mindtools.com/pages/article/newSTR_97.htm. Accessed May 15, 2021.

112. ISO Family, ibid., https://www.iso.org/iso-9001-quality-management.html. Accessed May 15, 2021.

113. Jawad Abbas, "Impact of Total Quality Management on Corporate Sustainability through the Mediating Effect of Knowledge Management," *Journal of Cleaner Production* 244, January 2020, https://www.sciencedirect.com/science/article/abs/pii/S0959652619336765. Accessed May 15, 2021.

16

Community Stakeholders and Corporate Philanthropy

Chapter Learning Outcomes

After studying this chapter, you should be able to:

1. Discuss reasons for community involvement, various types of community projects, and management of community stakeholders.
2. Explain the pros and cons of corporate philanthropy, provide a brief history of corporate philanthropy, and explain why and to whom companies give.

3. Differentiate between strategic philanthropy, cause-related marketing, and cause branding.
4. Characterize the detrimental impacts of business in the community, including the loss of jobs in the contexts of offshoring, reshoring, and plant closings.

The COVID-19 pandemic of 2020–2021 facilitated a platform for businesses to engage in generous community relations. Most communities were hit hard and the effects were often devastating. Hospitals had to deal with shortages of personal protective equipment and ventilators. Restaurants and businesses locked down. Countless residents lost jobs and struggled with food shortages. Nonprofit organizations saw their contributions decline. Communities were vulnerable as they did not have access to preventive items such as face masks and hand sanitizer. Many companies suffered and struggled financially, having to shut down and lay off many employees.

In spite of the stresses and challenges communities faced, a multitude of companies made commitments to donate money, equipment, employee time, and other items needed to help communities and their residents to cope with the adverse circumstances being experienced.[1] A few examples illustrate how companies demonstrated their concern for the communities in which they resided and often for other communities as well. Hanes partnered with Invisible People to donate 1 million masks. Nestle donated $500,000 to Meals on Wheels. Allbirds donated $500,000 worth of shoes to health-care workers. Dyson donated 5,000 ventilators to meets the needs of victims of the pandemic. Talkspace gave 1,000 months of free online therapy to medical workers.[2] In short, businesses across the United States and most countries demonstrated their citizenship responsibilities toward their community stakeholders during this time of crisis.

There are many definitions of the word *community*; however, they all share an underlying theme of commonality.

A shared geographic locale, a shared profession, a shared ideology, or even a shared recreational pastime can join communities. The actions of business affect a range of communities, and it is important that managers be aware of these impacts so they can manage them in a way that respects the interests and needs of community stakeholders. This chapter focuses on business and community stakeholders, typically on the business's immediate locale—the town, city, or state—in which a business resides. We should remember, however, that today's instant communication, speedy travel, and social networking often expand the relevant community to include the region, the nation, the world, and even the virtual world.

Though not specifically designed for crises or the pandemic, the company Reddit has created a community of users and an online bulletin board where registered community members can submit content, such as text posts or direct links. The company has demonstrated how a concern for community may extend via the Web to bring people together for mutual interests. Top Reddit users have the ability to shape or close large parts of the website, beyond their own personal pages or profiles. Content entries are organized by areas of interest called "subreddits." The subreddit topics include news, gaming, movies, music, books, fitness, food, photo sharing, and other topics community members hold in common. In essence, Reddit has created an online virtual community that may also affect and be affected by business.[3] As an example of how powerful this type of community can be, Reddit's volunteer users/moderators shut down large portions of the link-sharing website to protest the sudden firing of a popular Reddit employee.[4]

Often, companies respond to crises that may occur in or near their facilities or in nearby regions or countries. For example, it is not uncommon for large retail stores to chip in when crises arise. But few actually prepare for crises the way Amazon has recently done in the Atlanta area. In preparation for the 2021 hurricane season, Amazon announced in June 2021 that it was opening its first Disaster Relief Hub, a facility in metro Atlanta that will store emergency supplies. Atlanta's close proximity to the Gulf Coast, the Caribbean, and Central America was also a factor in determining its location.[5] The hub will initially support six global humanitarian aid organizations including American Red Cross, Direct Relief, the International Federation of Red Cross and Red Crescent Societies, and Save the Children.[6] Amazon's leaders say this kind of community help is part of their mission and therefore it only makes sense to prepare for it.[7]

When we think of businesses responding to their social responsibilities with community stakeholders, two major kinds of relationships come to mind. One is the positive contribution business can make to the community. Examples of these positive contributions include volunteerism, financial and in-kind company contributions, and support of programs in education, culture, urban development, the arts, civic activities, and health and welfare endeavors. Strategic management expert Michael Porter observed that companies can even benefit their communities by simply doing more business close to home.[8]

On the other hand, business can also cause harm to community stakeholders. It can pollute the environment or put people out of work by offshore outsourcing or closing a plant. Business can abuse its power and exploit consumers and employees. When business causes harm, as has occurred during financial crises, it is incumbent upon business to work harder to have a positive impact on the community. To this point, each year *The Civic 50*, an initiative of the Points of Light (in partnership with Bloomberg LP), honors the 50 most community-minded companies based on the results from a survey of employees in the United States.[9] The four levels of criteria for the award include[10]:

- Investment—How extensively the company applies its resources, like employee time, skills, cash, and in-kind giving and leadership, to community engagement.
- Integration—How the company "does well by doing good" through its business functions.
- Institutionalization—How the company supports community engagement through its institutional policies, systems, and incentives.
- Impact—How the company measures the social and business impact of its engagement program.

It is easy to see that the companies that make this list are those that purposefully integrate community engagement into their strategies. Honorees for 2020 included companies such as Allstate, Aflac, General Mills, and the Hershey Company. On the other side, there are companies that are not community minded and they either ignore members of the community or, worse, harm them.

In terms of our four-part concept of corporate social responsibility (CSR), focusing on economics, legal responsibilities, ethics, and philanthropy, community stakeholders primarily fit into the ethics and philanthropic categories. Specifically, this chapter concentrates on community involvement and corporate philanthropy as community stakeholder issues. In addition, it discusses the potential downside effects of company actions, especially the topics of offshore outsourcing and business or plant closings as community stakeholder concerns. These discussions should provide us with an opportunity to explore both the positive and the detrimental effects that characterize business–community relationships. Let us begin with the positive.

In addition to being profitable, obeying the law, and being ethical, a company may create a positive impact in the community by giving in two ways: (1) donating the time and talents of its managers and employees and (2) making financial contributions. The first category, **community engagement**, manifests itself in a wide array of voluntary activities in the community. The second category involves **corporate philanthropy** or business giving. We should note that there is significant overlap between these two categories, because companies quite frequently donate their time and talent and give financial aid to the same general projects and stakeholders. First, we discuss community engagement and the various ways in which companies get involved to enhance the quality of life in their communities.

16.1 Community Involvement and Engagement

Business must—not only for a healthier society but also for its own well-being—be a strong corporate citizen by being willing to give the same serious consideration to human needs that it gives to its own needs for operations and profits. These sentiments are echoed in the thoughts and actions of Salesforce CEO Marc Benioff, who has pushed fellow tech giants in the San Francisco area to give back to the community by donating money, funding research grants, and subsidizing housing rents for underprivileged families.[11] Noting that "we no longer live in a world that can tolerate maximizing shareholder values," Benioff states that Salesforce pursues a "stakeholder value" approach with consideration to balancing the interests of investors with the welfare of "employees, the people in the community and the city's children."[12] Salesforce's community engagement plan is particularly timely as the San Francisco community has been trying to adapt to the tech boom influx of young, wealthy individuals who have contributed to rising housing prices and subsequent high eviction rates. Additionally, Benioff cites the fact that his industry "has a history of stinginess," and he is determined to change that.[13]

Business involvement in the community represents enlightened self-interest because businesses are in a position to help their companies in the process of helping others. These dual objectives of business clearly illustrate that making profits and addressing social concerns are not mutually exclusive endeavors. When companies draw on their strengths and resources, they can make deep and lasting contributions to the communities they serve. Furthermore, when they make community service part of their identities, they can develop greater trust and community. John Lechleiter, former Eli Lilly chairman, president, and chief executive officer, has driven this point home:

> The business community can—and must—play a vital role in addressing complex societal problems. It's clear that writing a check or donating product alone doesn't have a lasting impact. A growing body of evidence demonstrates that when a company engages with partners in an area in which the company has deep expertise and a vested interest, society benefits and the company enhances its own performance.[14]

In fact, research has shown that employees receive tremendous satisfaction from **community involvement**, allowing them to achieve a sense of identification with the organization through social exchange with the community that translates into better productivity and ultimately better firm performance.[15] Other rationales for business engagement in community affairs provide ethical justification, beyond that of enlightened self-interest. For example, utilitarian arguments can support corporate giving in that improvement of the social fabric creates the greatest good for the greatest number. This need not contradict the mandates of self-interest because the corporation is one of the community members that will benefit.[16]

Although justifications for corporate engagement in the community are possible from various perspectives, one thing is clear: Business has an ethical responsibility to build a relationship with the community and to be sensitive to its impacts on the world around it. The Center for Corporate Citizenship at Boston College has developed a set of six management practices, processes, and policies that represent a global standard of excellence in corporate community involvement. These are listed in Figure 16-1.

16.1a Volunteer Programs

One of the most pervasive examples of business involvement in communities is a volunteer program. Corporate volunteer programs reflect the resourcefulness and responsiveness of business to communities in need of increasing services. They also have become essential for attracting and retaining the best talent in the workforce.[17] Employees not only want to work for "the good guys," they want to be the good guys too.[18] According to Kellie McElhaney of the Haas School of Business, "For today's millennials entering the workforce, engagement in sustainability is a must-have, not a nice-to-have. They don't want to be told what the company is doing. They want to do it."[19]

In their 2020 edition of "Giving in Numbers," a coalition of CEOs in the world's largest companies called the **Chief Executives for Corporate Purpose (CECP)** reported recent data about the impact of their community volunteerism. According to their survey, 89 percent of their companies offered paid release time for volunteer programs, 43 percent represented the top quartile participation rate, and overall, 29 percent of employees participated in volunteer work.[20]

According to the CECP, **Paid Release Time** is the most common type of service program.[21] This is supported by companies like Deloitte Consulting, whose philosophy of community engagement and unlimited hours of paid time off for employee volunteering contributed to their being voted one of the "100 Best Companies to Work For" by *Fortune* magazine.[22] Another popular volunteer option is a **Company-Wide Day of Service**, where employees

---

Figure 16-1 Standards of Excellence in Corporate Community Involvement

Standard 1: Leadership

My company is committed to the mutual success of business and the community and demonstrates leadership around this issue both internally and externally.

Standard 2: Strategy

My company takes a strategic approach to community involvement to add demonstrable value to the business and to society.

Standard 3: Relationship Building

My company builds and maintains trusting and productive stakeholder relationships in the community to advance both business and community goals.

Standard 4: Infrastructure

My company provides the resources and support needed to ensure the successful execution of its community involvement strategy.

Standard 5: Measurement and Evaluation

My company measures and evaluates the results and effectiveness of its community involvement programs to improve performance.

Standard 6: Communication

My company effectively and transparently communicates about its community involvement, mission, strategy and performance.

Sources: Center for Corporate Citizenship at Boston College, "New Standards of Excellence and Diagnostic Tool," https://ccc.bc.edu/content/ccc/blog-home/2009/04/blog-2009-04-conference-exclusive-new-standards-of-excellence-and-diagnostic-tool.html, accessed June 5, 2021; Boston College Center for Corporate Citizenship, "Updating the Standards of Excellence," https://ccc.bc.edu/content/ccc/blog-home/2009/01/blog-2009-01-updating-the-standards-of-excellence.html, accessed June 5, 2021.

mobilize volunteers for a day. During the recent pandemic, Vertex used their day of service by partnering with Points of Light to create custom remote and virtual employee volunteering opportunities in eight countries.[23] **Skills-Based Pro Bono Service** allows employees to volunteer with their specific skills—like tax accountants from KPMG and Deloitte who volunteer to help seniors prepare tax returns. Finally, **Dollars for Doers** involve contributions in recognition of a certain level of employee volunteer service.

This last type of volunteer program is worth mentioning in detail. The Dollars for Doers program magnifies the service contributions of the employee by matching employee volunteer hours with a corporate donation.[24] Unlike the traditional matching grant that matches employee donations with corporate funds, Dollars for Doers matches hours of service. For example, Campbell Soup donated $500 to nonprofits for every 25 hours an employee volunteered, and IBM provided nonprofits with equipment and services to match employee volunteer hours.[25] In return, companies are likely to get healthier and happier employees.

There are numerous examples of corporations making a difference in communities through volunteer activities. AT&T has had success with their employee volunteer program. For 2020, for example, AT&T employees volunteered 521,460 hours, and the total value of employee volunteerism was $14.5 million.[26]

Big Data has also been helpful in making employee community engagement more beneficial for both employees and the community. For example, Capital One used volunteerism data to help link employees to the best experience and also identify gaps in participation rates and build targeted strategies. When they identify an employee who has not logged in volunteer hours or participated in a company-sponsored program, they send those employees a targeted message on how to sign up to volunteer. They also use the data to personalize volunteerism options.[27]

Many of the benefits derived from employee volunteerism are summarized in Figure 16-2.

16.1b Managing Community Engagement

For organization and discussion purposes, we are separating our treatment of *managing community engagement* from that of *managing corporate philanthropy*. In reality, however, this separation is impossible to fully achieve because there are significant overlaps between these two areas. Corporate philanthropy involves primarily the giving of financial resources. Community involvement focuses on other issues in the business–community relationship, particularly the contribution of managerial and employee time and talent. This section addresses these broader community issues; a later section of this chapter deals with the more specific issue of managing corporate philanthropy.

Business Stake in the Community. When one speaks with corporate executives in the fields of community and civic affairs and examines community affairs manuals and other corporate publications, one sees a broad array of reasons why companies need to keep abreast of the issues, problems, and changes expressed as community needs. Self-interest and self-preservation provide one rationale. Companies typically have a significant physical presence in the community and so they want to protect that investment. Issues of interest to companies include zoning regulations, the threat of neighborhood deterioration, corporate property taxes, the community tax base, and the availability of an adequately trained workforce. For example, when J.C. Penney began to sell its 1.8 million-square-foot office headquarters and downsize its 20-year-old offices and 40 surrounding acres in Plano, Texas, it was careful in its rezoning request to preserve a small pond and suggest an urban village mixed-use project like one that was already popular with locals.[28]

Companies can support their communities through their daily activities in a variety of ways, including sourcing from local businesses, joining public policy debates, investing in local banks, serving on local business-government committees, and locating facilities in places that benefit community development. In addition, companies can develop community action programs that transcend daily operations. For global corporations, the world is the community and so engagement must be at both the global and the local levels. Figure 16-3 presents how four different companies gave back through volunteerism on the National Day of Service.

Figure 16-2 Benefits of Employee Volunteerism

For the Employee
- Improves morale
- Increases meaningfulness of work
- Develops teamwork and leadership skills
- Improves mental and physical health

For the Corporation
- Builds company image and reputation
- Improves employee attraction and retention
- Develops employee skills
- Builds relationship with and loyalty from consumers

For the Community
- Addresses community needs
- Saves community resources
- Builds pool of future volunteers and contributors
- Builds awareness of community needs

Figure 16-3 Giving Back Through Volunteerism on National Day of Service, 2021

Company	Giving Back Program
Raytheon Technologies	In 2021, Raytheon served as the presenting sponsor for *The Mission Continues* "2021 MLK Jr. National Day of Service." This was a series of in-person and virtual volunteering events across the United States. The Day of Service events are sponsored through Raytheon Technologies' new partnership with *The Mission Continues*, a nonprofit that provides military veterans with a way to continue serving their country through community improvement projects.
Verizon Wireless Co.	The company invited employee volunteers to work on issues ranging from digital inclusion and climate protection to food insecurity and African American history. Activities included writing a letter to *Feeding America* volunteers that are working to end hunger, sharing expertise on ed-tech nonprofit *UPchieve*'s blog to help low-income students achieve their academic goals, and recording sky observations for scientists to help ground-truth NASA satellite images.
Qualcomm Semiconductor Co.	The company's employee and community engagement efforts extended around the world. The company organizes "giving committees" that determine how the organization's funds are distributed throughout local communities. Qualcomm's giving committees are located in more than 25 countries and have donated to more than 70 local organizations.
Pfizer Pharmaceutical Co.	Through its *Give Forward* initiative, the company offers its employees an opportunity to volunteer their time, money (through a matching gift program), or expertise. With each hour volunteered, Pfizer offers "rewards" that employees can donate to an eligible nonprofit of their own choice.

Sources: U.S. Chamber of Commerce Foundation, "Giving Back on the National Day of Service," January 14, 2021, https://www.uschamberfoundation.org/blog/post/giving-back-national-day-service, accessed June 7, 2021; U.S. Chamber of Commerce Foundation, "Community Improvement," https://www.uschamberfoundation.org/topics/community-improvement, accessed June 7, 2021.

Developing a Community Action Program. The motivation for developing a **community action program** is evident when one considers the stake a firm has in the community. Likewise, the community represents a major stakeholder of business. Therefore, business has an added incentive to be systematic about its relationship with the community. First, the business must *get to know the community* in which it intends to become involved. The next step is then *to assess the company's resources* to determine what the company is best able to give. Then the company can *design a community action program* by matching the community needs to the resources the company has available. Finally, as with all corporate endeavors, management should *monitor the performance* of the community action program carefully and make adjustments where needed.

An excellent example of a community project that follows these guidelines is the Ronald McDonald House Charities (RMHC) program sponsored by McDonald's Corporation. The three core programs of RMHC—the Ronald McDonald House, Ronald McDonald Family Room, and Ronald McDonald Care Mobile—are focused on helping families in need. The well-known Ronald McDonald House program provides a "home away from home" for families of seriously ill children receiving treatment at nearby hospitals. Since its inception more than 38 years ago, millions of families around the world have received shelter and solace through the program.[29] Another example of careful action planning was the Amazon Disaster Relief Hub discussed earlier.

16.2 Corporate Philanthropy or Business Giving

In addition to community involvement and engagement, businesses carry out their corporate citizenship responsibilities to their communities by way of philanthropy. The word *philanthropy* comes from the Greek *philien*, which means "to love," and *anthropos*, which means "mankind."[30] Thus, **philanthropy** is defined as "goodwill to members of the human race" or an "active effort to promote human welfare."[31] Corporate philanthropy is also called "business giving." In this section, we concentrate on the voluntary giving of financial resources by business. One problem with the dictionary definition of philanthropy is that the motive for the giving is usually characterized as charitable, benevolent, or generous, seeking to promote human welfare. In actual practice, it is difficult to assess the true motives behind businesses'—or anyone's—giving of themselves or their financial resources. Some companies give out of a true sense of benevolence or altruism and many companies give for practical reasons—just to be good corporate citizens in the community and to enhance their reputational capital.

According to Giving in Numbers, the total giving by businesses in 2020 reached $24.8 billion. This was down slightly from the 2019 level of $26 billion but this could be traceable to the pandemic when many companies were stressed.[32] Employee giving is counted separately, but 89 percent of companies surveyed match employee giving.[33] Though corporate giving is often for straight humanitarian purposes, most corporate giving is becoming increasingly focused with

---

Ethics In Practice Case

Matters of Good Intentions

A high-level finance computer programmer is sitting at his cubicle working on an upgrade that his management assigned to him. As he works on his project, he overhears one of his co-workers talking to his partner, who has a major role at an important charity organization in the community. He hears how his fellow co-worker is explaining about how he had created an account dedicated to funding a charity because the company does not make any contributions at all. He hears his co-worker also say that he did this without getting any approval from his senior-level management and explain that the way the program works is that it takes very small fractions of cents that have been rounded off and over multiple transactions dumps the fractions of cents into this account made for charity. As he hears his co-worker explain this to his partner, he wonders to himself, "What

should I do? Should I tell management? He is my friend and technically it is for a good cause ... right?"

1. Who are the stakeholders in this situation and what are their stakes?
2. Should the listener report the conversation he overheard to management?
3. Is your answer affected by the fact that the money is going to a good cause?
4. Is your answer affected by the fact that the company gives no money to charity?
5. Is there some alternative way this situation should be handled? Explain.

Contributed by Steve Coiscou

---

companies giving in a way that is consistent with their core business strategies, skills, and resources.[34] Yet, the motivations and drivers of corporate giving are still debated by academics, as these can range from the motivations of individual top-level executives, to organizational- and industry-level drivers.[35]

Today, the use of Big Data is also helping companies to be more deliberate or strategic in their philanthropy. One company, Mission Measurement, helps companies quantify the business benefit they get from philanthropy and community engagement.[36] Companies like Coke and Disney have taken advantage of this data. Coke has been in business in Africa for years, but through mining data, they figured out a way to create a program where local women could buy Coke products at wholesale prices and take the products to sell by carts, bicycles, and mopeds.[37] Similarly, Disney is using consumer data research to help identify social causes connected to the families that visit their theme parks.[38] Even churches have been able to increase their tithing numbers with mobile apps that make it easier to collect donations.[39] In sum, philanthropy has gotten more strategically in line with companies' missions and easier to do. We discuss "strategic philanthropy" in more detail later in the chapter.

16.2a A Brief History of Corporate Philanthropy

Business philanthropy of one kind or another can be traced back to the 1920s when the most significant effort to "translate the new social consciousness of management into action" emerged in the form of organized corporate philanthropy.[40] Since about 1960, corporate giving has grown to encompass a variety of initiatives. Now in the 21st century, broader social initiatives continue, but the nature of business giving has taken a turn. The corporate philanthropy watchword is now *strategic* philanthropy, philanthropy that benefits both society and the corporation that is giving.

Recent trends in philanthropy also include newer communities of philanthropists. For example, a group of self-described "**philanthropy hackers**" has evolved with the enrichment of social media and a new group of very wealthy individuals from that domain. As explained by Sean Parker, the founding president of Facebook, a board member of Spotify, and the chair of the Parker Foundation, this group shares common values that translate easily into charity: "An anti-establishment bias, a belief in radical transparency, a nose for sniffing out vulnerabilities in systems, a desire to 'hack' complex problems using elegant technological and social solutions, and an almost religious belief in the power of data to aid in solving those problems."[41] Rather than favoring gifts to well-established institutions like major universities, they want to interact directly with the scientists, field workers, and academics through tools like GiveDirectly that allow them to send cash payments to worthy causes directly through cell phones.[42]

16.2b A Call for Transparency in Corporate Philanthropy

A major debate has arisen over proposals for legislation that would require companies to disclose which charities they support and how much money they give. Although companies are required to disclose the money they give through foundations because of the tax benefits derived from the foundation's tax-exempt status, companies need not disclose direct donations.

The disclosure issue has renewed the age-old debate about the role of business in society. Proponents of disclosure contend that the money belongs to the shareholders and they alone have the right to determine where it will go. Law professors sometimes argue that philanthropy often only serves to glorify corporate managers and that, unless the philanthropy clearly benefits the company, it represents a waste of corporate assets. A few nonprofits, such as the

American Red Cross, also agree that disclosure would be good public policy. Surprisingly, the National Society of Fundraising Executives even supports disclosure, arguing that it would help the image of philanthropy, which has been hurt by scandals in recent years.[43]

This broad-based support notwithstanding, most corporations and nonprofits have expressed concern that disclosure would have a chilling effect on corporate donations. Their arguments include that charitable giving is a business decision, that it would provide competitors with information about a firm's strategy, that it might incite controversy with special-interest groups, and that the paperwork would become an administrative burden.[44] No real closure on the issue of corporate philanthropy transparency has been achieved; however, concerns about knowing the source of political donations has given the issue new life.

The fact that corporations are under no obligation to report their charitable donations has led to the rise of "dark money," that is, political funding received from undisclosed sources, an issue that will be discussed in Chapter 18. Shareholder rights advocates, public pension systems, and the AFL-CIO advocate for greater transparency, while a coalition of the Chamber of Commerce, the Business Roundtable, and the National Association of Manufacturers, as well as other groups, continue to lobby against it.[45]

16.2c Giving to the Nonprofit Sector

According to philanthropist John D. Rockefeller III, business giving is necessary to support what has been called the **third sector**—the nonprofit sector. The first two sectors—business and government—receive support through profits and taxes. The third sector (which includes hundreds of thousands of churches, museums, hospitals, libraries, private colleges and universities, and performing arts groups) depends on corporate and personal philanthropy for support. Philanthropy gives these institutions the crucial margin that assures them of their most precious asset—their independence.[46]

Why Do Companies Give? Perhaps it would be more worthwhile to know why companies give to charitable causes rather than to know how much they give. There are several ways to approach this question. We get initial insights when we consider the three categories of corporate contributions programs identified by the CECP.[47] The motivations are:

- *Charitable*: Community giving for which there is little or no expected benefit for the business,
- *Community Investment*: Gifts that support long-term strategic business goals while also meeting a critical community need, and
- *Commercial*: Giving that benefits the business wherein the benefit is its primary motivation. CECP's annual report showed an increase in community investment giving and a decrease in charitable giving.[48]

Others identify the motives for business giving differently. For example, Goodbox, an organization dedicated to excellence for charities, argues there are three motives for corporate giving. First, to shine a light on the company and its business. Corporate giving makes the business look good to the public. Second, to help the community. To be sure, local communities, especially, count on business giving to enhance the quality of life where the business is located. Third, to enhance team morale. It has been found that if employees do good, they feel good about their employers and its work. One study showed that employee happiness makes workers 12 percent more productive.[49] A different study of Canadian workers found that employees feel good about the way their organizations "give back" to the community. The study's findings: 18 percent are more likely to stay; 45 percent are more likely to be brand ambassadors; 83 percent are more likely to put in more effort; and 57 percent say they are more likely to feel valued.[50]

As economic pressures and increased international competitiveness force companies to be more careful with their earnings, we should not be surprised to see the profit motive coexisting with loftier goals in corporate contributions programs. In a subsequent section of this chapter, we illustrate more fully how philanthropy can be "strategic," and the ways in which corporate giving can be aligned with the firm's economic or profitability objectives.

Giving Patterns. During the course of any budget year, companies receive numerous requests for contributions from a wide variety of applicants. Most of them are official nonprofit organizations, but some are not. Companies must then weigh both quantitative and qualitative factors to arrive at decisions regarding the recipients of their gifts. By looking at the beneficiaries of corporate contributions, we can estimate the value business places on various societal needs in the community. However, we should note that, because of the lack of transparency in corporate giving that we discussed earlier in the chapter, data regarding giving are simply estimates, and estimates from different sources will vary.

According to the Conference Board, the majority of annual business giving is distributed primarily among five major categories of recipients in the following order of emphasis: (1) health and human services, (2) community and economic development, (3) education, (4) civic and public affairs, and (5) culture and the arts.[51]

The giving patterns and trends in corporate philanthropy are often more important than the specific groups to whom companies and their foundations give. Due to the pandemic, the year 2020 was a difficult one for corporate giving; however, many companies increased their giving despite the tough times they faced. This generosity is a testament to the importance these companies place on supporting their local communities.[52] Based on a survey of Conference Board members, the outlook for 2021 and beyond is optimistic. Almost half the companies that had increased their giving during the 2020 pandemic said they planned to maintain this higher level of giving, and 22 percent indicated they would increase their level of giving going forward.[53]

Spikes in giving are often seen in response to natural disasters or other crises. But the spikes during the pandemic were the most significant since 9/11. The increase was attributed to four concurrent crises: (1) the pandemic, (2) the state of the economy, (3) humanitarian needs, and (4) racial justice.[54] Just under 60 percent of the donations were used to address COVID-19 issues. These included health care, safety nets such as food banks, housing support, and the move to virtual learning in the schools. Close to 55 percent of the balance of donations went to help eradicate racial injustice and support equity initiatives for people of color.[55]

Giving in Times of Crisis. It is evident from the above-mentioned patterns that corporate giving in times of crisis is an important trend that seems to be central to what many companies are doing today. According to data gathered by The Conference Board, crisis giving, sometimes referred to as disaster giving, involves both in-kind giving and employee volunteerism in addition to actual cash donations. In addition to cash, the following are the top three types of crises or disaster relief giving and the percentage of companies surveyed engaging in this type of giving[56]:

- Employee giving with company matching gifts (76.5% of companies)
- In-kind donation of company's products or services (73% of companies)
- Hands-on employee volunteering (66.1% of companies)

It is important for companies that are giving during crisis periods to realize that smaller and medium-sized charities have deep relationships in communities and often are better positioned to deliver needed remedies. In addition, most of these nonprofits and charities have credibility and are best positioned to understand the appropriate ways to help their communities. The urgency and the uncertainty of the COVID-19 pandemic serves as a perfect example for corporations to demonstrate their new purpose by structuring their philanthropy with a keen eye toward supporting not only large charities but also small and midsized ones as well.[57]

Some of the suggestions for reordering matters of policy and practice during crises include the following.[58]

- Fund Innovation. What worked in the past may not work now and in the future. Therefore, it is crucial that innovative ideas be given support. Watch for organizations that are trying to do something different and support them.
- Give to Crisis-Adjacent Charities. Using COVID-19 as an example, once the immediacy of the crisis has passed, it is important to understand that new and related challenges will arise as people and organizations try to get back to normal. With respect to the pandemic, for example, such adjacent issues as the following are likely to continue: homelessness, food insecurity, and lack of job readiness.

- Be Open to Funding New Needs. Consider funding to support emerging approaches to social issues. Examples might include the new challenges that might be faced in virtual education and those related to undocumented workers who may be afraid to access traditional health-care resources.
- Support Inclusive Leadership. Charities run by people of color receive just a fraction of the funding granted to those organizations run by white counterparts.
- Sponsor Special Events. Many nonprofits operate based on funds received during special events held during the year. Sponsorships of entire events as well as table purchases at these events are critical to many of the smaller charities.

The Council on Foundations has recommended that companies realign their corporate philanthropy programs away from what might be called the "current paradigm" to what they see to be the "emerging paradigm." Some of the key changes they see underway within the broad corporate philanthropy field, with most organizations being in the middle of the transformation from the current to the emerging paradigm, include the following[59]:

- From "values" to "values and value created"
- From "charity" mindset to an "investment mindset"
- From "responsive" to "proactive and responsive"
- From "transactions" to "relationships"
- From "needs focused" to "outcomes focused"
- From "organizations" to "issues"
- From "short term" to "short and long term"
- From "isolated" to "aligned and integrated"
- From "cash, employees" to "cash, employees, full value chain"
- From "reports" to "knowledge"
- From "managerial" function to "leadership" function

In short, the Council on Foundations maintains that companies need to create a new narrative for corporate philanthropy as an investment in society. Companies need to improve collaboration, communication, and knowledge sharing. They need to professionalize the field, and they need to mobilize "field level" leadership behind this agenda.[60] If these ideas are brought to fruition, corporate philanthropy will be better off both for the corporate givers involved and for the recipients of the business giving.

Figure 16-4 illustrates how foundations creatively helped to save a city.

16.2d Managing Corporate Philanthropy

We have touched on important ideas regarding the management of corporate philanthropy. It is appropriate to explore this idea further. As performance pressures on business have continued and intensified, companies have had to ramp up their attention to *managing* corporate philanthropy. Early on, managers did not subject their contributions to the same kinds of rigorous analysis given to expenditures for plants and equipment, inventory, product

Figure 16-4 The Motor City and the Arts

When the city of Detroit declared Chapter 9 bankruptcy in 2013, the Detroit Institute of Arts (DIA) played a central part in its recovery plan. The DIA was a municipal department linked to the finances of the city. The Bankruptcy Court formed a "grand bargain" plan supported by $800 million from foundations, the Detroit Institute of Arts (DIA), private donors, and the state of Michigan to protect the DIA from having to auction off its art. Foundations and others saw the importance of preserving Detroit's historical art pieces and agreed to make contributions to the grand bargain to reduce public employee pension cuts if the DIA's survival could be guaranteed.

It worked. One year later, Detroit was out of bankruptcy. The first grand bargain payment of $23.3 million was paid to the General Retirement System and the Police and Fire Retirement Systems in December 2014, including $18.3 million from foundations and $5 million from the DIA.

A total of 20 payments would ultimately be made to the City of Detroit from the Foundation for Detroit's Future. Twelve foundations committed a total of $366 million over 20 years to the grand bargain. In addition to contributing $100 million, the DIA also became an independent charitable trust, like most large American museums, instead of being owned by the city.

The grand bargain also helped Detroit out of bankruptcy by creating a new entity, called the Foundation for Detroit's Future, governed by a five-member board of directors. Going forward, money from foundations, private donors, and the state of Michigan will go through The Foundation for Detroit's Future, and the foundation will then funnel the money to the city. This novel and creative way to approach a city's bankruptcy and preserve its art may pave the way for other cities to see business and the arts as true partners in a community.

Sources: National Committee for Responsive Philanthropy, "One Year Later: Reflecting on Detroit's Philanthropy-Driven 'Grand Bargain'," adapted from *Philamplify*, https://www.alliancemagazine.org/blog/one-year-later-reflecting-on-detroits-philanthropy-driven-grand-bargain/, accessed June 9, 2021; Randy Kennedy, "'Grand Bargain' Saves the Detroit Institute of Arts," *The New York Times*, https://www.nytimes.com/2014/11/08/arts/design/grand-bargain-saves-the-detroit-institute-of-arts.html, accessed June 9, 2021; Quinn Klinefelter, "Detroit's Big Comeback: Out of Bankruptcy, A Rebirth," December 28, 2018, https://www.npr.org/2018/12/28/680629749/out-of-bankruptcy-detroit-reaches-financial-milestone, accessed June 9, 2021.

development, marketing, and a host of other budgetary items. This began to change because cutbacks in federal spending on charitable causes created an increasing need for contributions by business. Over time and through the vicissitudes of the economy, it became increasingly clear that business had to reconcile its economic and social goals, both of which were essential.[61]

Even though this realization of merging economic and social goals became evident and many companies have adapted, the pressure on businesses to be more business-like in their philanthropy remains. There are two aspects to this. The first is to base giving on business skills, resources, and capabilities to enhance philanthropic outcomes. The second is to focus on philanthropy that will enhance corporate profitability while also making a

positive difference in the community at large. To facilitate this process, most large companies today have an executive and a department dedicated to corporate giving. Those who are leading these efforts usually carry titles such as vice president for corporate giving, director for corporate philanthropy, or manager for corporate relations.

Following a strategic approach to managing philanthropy requires an ethic of enlightened self-interest, and this trend is clearly on the rise. Most data show that companies are engaging in more focused giving, targeted to their core strategic interests, and this has become even more important in the post–COVID-19 world.[62] By all indications this trend will continue. Community partnerships is one important way these ideas are being implemented.

Spotlight on Sustainability

Corporate Philanthropy through Greening the Workforce

Community colleges have always been skilled at preparing two-year graduates to enter practical professions because their close ties with industry enable them to be more responsive to industry's needs. These attributes make the two-year college the perfect venue for preparing students to enter green-economy jobs. Recognizing the fit between community colleges and eco-economy job training, businesses are entering into partnerships with community colleges to prepare workers to meet their growing eco-workforce demands. For example, GE donated a small wind turbine to Mesalands Community College in Tucumcari, New Mexico, for their wind energy technician program and promised to hire their first three years of graduates. Johnson Controls constructed a 2,500 solar

panel farm at Milwaukee Area Technical College, enabling students there to be trained as the photovoltaic designers and installers that Johnson Controls needs to hire. Experts predict that the expected expansion of environmental policies could increase renewable energy jobs from 9 million in 2007 to 19.5 million in 2030.

Sources: Mina Kimes, "Get a Green Job in Two Years," CNN Money, https://money.cnn.com/2009/11/16/news/economy/community_colleges_green_jobs.fortune/, accessed June 9, 2021; Mesaland Community College, "Wind Energy Technology," https://www.mesalands.edu/wind-energy/, accessed June 9, 2021; Juan Somavia, "Greening the Workforce," United Nations, https://www.un.org/en/chronicle/article/greening-workforce, accessed June 9, 2021.

Community Partnerships. As a broad response to this growing need to reconcile financial and social goals, the concept of **community partnerships** evolved. A community partnership occurs when a for-profit business enters into a cooperative arrangement with a nonprofit organization for their mutual advantage. Businesses see in community partnerships the opportunity for simultaneous achievement of economic and philanthropic objectives. Business skills and resources are often exactly what a community nonprofit organization needs to achieve its mission. A good example of this is National Safe Place.

National Safe Place (NSP) is a youth outreach program with two purposes: (1) educating young people about the dangers of running away or trying to resolve difficult, threatening situations on their own and (2) providing safe havens and resources for youth in crisis.[63] NSP has created a variety of Safe Place locations (e.g., schools, fire stations, libraries, grocery and convenience stores, public transit, YMCAs, and other appropriate public buildings) where young people can get help and be safe. The locations display the yellow and black diamond-shaped Safe Place sign. Corporations that have skills and resources that can help with the Safe Place programs have partnered with the nonprofit. These include UPS, Sprint, CSX Movers, Southwest Airlines, QT, and the National Association of Convenience Stores.[64]

Community partnerships take on many different forms. Partnership options include sponsorships, vendor relationships, licensing agreements, and in-kind donations.[65] Other ways of building alliances are based on strategic philanthropy and cause-related marketing. We consider strategic philanthropy and cause-related marketing in more detail.

Strategic Philanthropy. **Strategic philanthropy** is an approach by which corporate or business giving and other philanthropic endeavors of a firm are designed in a way that best fits with the firm's overall mission, goals, and values.[66] This implies that the firm has some idea of what its overall strategy is and that it is able to articulate its missions, goals, or objectives. One goal of all firms is profitability. Therefore, one requirement of strategic philanthropy is to make as direct a contribution as possible to the financial goals of the firm. Philanthropy has long been thought to be in the long-range economic interest of the firm. Strategic philanthropy simply presses for a more direct or immediate contribution of business giving to the firm's economic success.[67]

An important way to make philanthropy strategic is to bring contribution programs into sharper alignment with business endeavors. This means that each firm should pursue those social or community programs that have a direct rather than an indirect bearing on its success. Thus, a local bank should logically pursue people-oriented projects in the community in which it resides; a manufacturer might pursue programs having to do with environmental protection or technological advancement.

A third way to make philanthropy strategic is to ensure that it is well planned and managed rather than handled haphazardly and without direction. Planning implies that it has clearly delineated goals, is properly organized and staffed, and is administered in accordance with certain established policies.[68] Figure 16-5 presents recommendations for best practices in the implementation of a philanthropy program.

Strategic philanthropy must find the place of overlap where the philanthropy provides both social and economic benefits. In an important article, Michael Porter and Mark Kramer argued that few companies have effectively taken advantage of the competitive advantage that corporate philanthropy can provide.[69] Similarly, Pablo Eisenberg, a *Chronicle of Philanthropy* columnist, wrote that "Strategic philanthropy might be less worrisome if it were not practiced so often by very large foundations run by small, insular boards that do little to tell the public how they make decisions."[70]

To be truly strategic, Porter and Kramer argue that philanthropy must be congruent with a company's competitive context, which consists of four interrelated elements: factor conditions, demand conditions, the context for strategy and rivalry, and related and supporting industries.[71]

Factor (Supply) Conditions These are the available inputs for production. Porter and Kramer point to DreamWorks as an example of a company that uses strategic philanthropy to improve its factor/supply conditions effectively. They created a program that provides training to low-income and disadvantaged youth in the skills needed to work in the entertainment industry. The societal benefits of an improved educational system are clear. While providing these social benefits, DreamWorks also enhances the labor pool from which they can draw. This not only strengthens the company but the industry as a whole as well.[72]

Figure 16-5 Attributes of an Effective Strategic Philanthropy Program

An effective strategic philanthropy program should have the following attributes:

1. The program should fit with the company's strategic goals and mission.
2. The program should be connected with the community involvement programs.
3. The budget and infrastructure should be sufficient to meet goals.
4. Company policies and guidelines should be made clear.
5. Employees should be involved in philanthropy-related activities.
6. Stakeholders should be made fully aware of the program.
7. Long-term business–nonprofit partnerships should be developed.

Demand Conditions These are concerned with the nature of the company's customers and the local market. Philanthropy can influence the local market's size and quality. Porter and Kramer point to Apple's long-held policy of donating computers to public schools. By introducing young people and their teachers to computers, Apple expands their market. They also increase the sophistication of their customer base, which benefits a differentiated product such as the ones Apple sells.[73] Similarly, Burger King focuses its philanthropic efforts on highly focused programs to help students, teachers, and schools.[74] This program enhances name recognition in its target population of consumers.

The demand for capitalism with a conscience is growing. In response to a global survey by public relations firm Edelman, 47 percent of respondents said that every month they buy a product from a company that supports a good cause: That is a 47 percent increase in two years.[75] In another study, 84 percent of consumers globally say they seek out responsible products whenever possible, though 81 percent cite availability of these products as the largest barrier to not purchasing more.[76] The upsurge in social consciousness is partly in response to the influence of Millennials, people born from 1982 to 2004, who were burned by economic conditions and have learned to use social media to be more informed consumers.[77]

Whole Foods has developed a strategic philanthropy program that affects both factor and demand conditions, enabling the company to reap benefits along the length of the value chain. In the factor market, Whole Foods has designed a system for sourcing products from developing countries while maintaining product standards. It developed a strict set of criteria for its suppliers to adhere to and contracted with TransFair USA and the Rainforest Alliance, two respected third-party certifiers, to ensure the suppliers met these criteria. These certified products receive a Whole Trade logo so that customers know which products come from the developing world and meet the criteria. Its customers value these attributes and so Whole Foods' demand conditions also improve as a result of their efforts.[78]

Context for Strategy and Rivalry The business's context, or environment, can be influenced by strategic philanthropy. Porter and Kramer point to the many corporations that support Transparency International as examples of firms using philanthropy to create a better environment for competition. As discussed in Chapter 7, Transparency International's mission is to deter and disclose corporate corruption around the world. The organization measures and publicizes corruption while pushing for stricter codes and enforcement. By supporting Transparency International, corporations are helping to build a better competitive environment—one that rewards fair competition. [79]

Related and Supporting Industries These can also be strengthened through strategic philanthropy, thereby enhancing the productivity of companies. American Express provides an excellent example of a firm that uses philanthropy to strengthen its related and supporting industries. For more than 20 years, American Express has funded travel and tourism academies in secondary schools. The program trains teachers, supports curricula, and provides both summer internships and industry mentors. A strong travel industry translates into important benefits for American Express.[80]

Now let us turn our attention to a special kind of strategic philanthropy that has become quite prevalent in recent years: cause-related marketing.

Cause-Related Marketing. There is some debate as to whether cause-related marketing is really philanthropy. It is seen by some as a form of strategic philanthropy. Porter and Kramer argue that it is marketing and nothing more.[81] However, because cause marketing represents a close linkage between a firm's financial objectives and corporate contributions, it is discussed here as philanthropy-related.

Stated in its simplest form, **cause-related marketing** is the direct linking of a business's product, service, or brand to a specified charity. Each time a consumer uses the service or buys the product, a donation is given to the charity by the business.[82] Thus some observers refer to cause-related marketing as "quid pro quo strategic philanthropy." Cause-related marketing is typically located in the marketing department of companies, and thus some have a hard time thinking of it as philanthropy.[83] Regardless, the outcomes are often the same: some charity or nonprofit benefits by the company's actions, and the company's image or reputation is enhanced.

The term *cause-related marketing* was coined by the American Express Company to describe a program it began years ago in which it agreed to contribute a penny to the restoration of the Statue of Liberty every time a customer used one of its credit cards to make a purchase. The project generated $1.7 million for the statue restoration and a substantial increase in usage of the American Express card.[84] Since that time, companies have employed this same approach to raise millions of dollars for a wide variety of local and national causes.

Cause-related marketing has given way to a new concept, **cause branding**. Cause branding represents a longer-term commitment than cause marketing. It also relates more directly to the firm's line of business and the target audience. Avon Products, Inc., has become a recognized leader in cause branding. Its target audience is women, and so it has developed an array of programs to raise awareness of breast cancer, a disease that mostly affects women. The company raises money for programs that provide low-income women with education and free screening. Avon sells products featuring the pink ribbon that is worn for breast cancer awareness and then donates the proceeds from these products to nonprofit and university programs. In 2021, Avon contributed more than $800 million to breast cancer crusades, educated millions of women about breast health, and founded nearly 20 million mammograms and clinical breast exams.[85]

Ethics In Practice Case

Competition in the Nonprofit Workplace

I have been interning for a multibillion-dollar nonprofit organization since January. As a supply chain intern, my primary responsibility is to analyze potential suppliers. I use data to determine the cheapest supplier that can properly provide my organization with a product or service. These analyses have saved my organization thousands of dollars each year. This money can be placed back into our grant-making program to help people who are in need of our assistance.

Recently, my boss has hired a second intern to assist with the supplier analyses. My boss split my desk in half and told me that I would be sharing my office with the new intern. I welcomed the notion of having someone to work with and to discuss ideas.

My boss instructed that we share supplier information with each other, but not our opinions. Instead, he preferred that we come to our own separate conclusions. When the analyses are due, the other intern and I present our findings to my boss. If we come to different conclusion and choose different suppliers, my boss carefully weighs both options and chooses the best supplier.

When my co-intern first started at the foundation, I willingly shared all of my supplier research such as the price, capabilities, references, and financial status. Although the other intern had not shared information with me, I merely thought he was still growing accustomed to his new position. However, when presenting our findings to my boss, my co-intern used data and statistics that he had *never* shared with me. My boss often asked why I had not included this data in my analyses.

On several occasions, I would ask my co-intern why he had withheld information from me. He would ignore or avoid the question each time. I know that my co-intern is withholding information from me because he is competitive and wants to impress my boss.

I feel that my co-intern is taking advantage of my research in order to outperform me. I often want to withhold my research as well, but I do not want to hinder potential cost savings for my nonprofit organization. I do not want to sacrifice possible grant-making money for my own benefit, but I also do not want my boss to think my work is below average.

1. Is it productive to have competition in the workplace, especially in a nonprofit that focuses on helping others? Is there a conflict of interest here?
2. Is my boss right in assigning the same project to my co-intern and me? Are there better options to increase our productivity?
3. Should I sacrifice my performance for the benefit of my organization?
4. What actions do you recommend I should take to resolve this competition?

Contributed by Zachary Greytsman

Cause branding has become a successful marketing tool. In a relevant Cone Communications/Ebiquity survey, 90 percent of U.S. consumers said they would switch brands to one associated with a cause, given comparable price and quality.[86] The benefits do not apply only to consumers; employees react to cause branding as well. This is important because finding good employees has become a real challenge. The findings of the latest Cone/Roper Executive Study found that cause branding strengthens internal corporate cultures and has a dramatic influence on employee pride, morale, and loyalty. Experts have concluded that there is no turning back now. Cause branding falls at the intersection of company strategy and good citizenship, and it is fast becoming a "must do" practice for organizations today.[87]

Global Philanthropy. The size of a company's workforce in international markets is the greatest determinant of the size of their charitable contributions to that market. It should come as no surprise, then, that as corporate operations have become increasingly globalized, so has corporate philanthropy. According to Chief Executives for Corporate Purpose (CECP), in 2020 two-thirds of their surveyed companies made donations to international recipients.[88] In terms of topics, two areas of impact have dominated the news in terms of global philanthropy: dealing with disasters and, more recently, dealing with the international consequences of the COVID-19 pandemic. In general, serving the underserved is also a common theme in corporate global giving.[89]

Businesses want to protect the communities in which they operate, keeping them healthy and environmentally sound. Businesses also develop infrastructure to facilitate the flow of goods and services. According to Stephen Jordan of the U.S. Chamber of Commerce Business Civic Leadership Center, companies are increasing their corporate philanthropy to "create a culture of opportunity" in the developing world. He said, "Ninety-six percent of opportunity is outside our borders.… Increasingly, companies… want to grow their customer base in emerging markets."[90]

16.3 Detrimental Impacts on Communities

Firms not only have positive, constructive impacts on communities, but they also can have detrimental impacts as well. Some of these could be negative environmental impacts, but they might also include the impact that occurs when a business decides to downsize or close a plant or branch. Among the most important impacts is the issue of job losses in the community, and we will focus on that primarily. Other losses include all the positive benefits discussed earlier in the chapter—most importantly, community involvement, volunteerism, and corporate philanthropy.

In turning our attention to the loss of jobs, which represents the most direct and significant detrimental impact, we see a most pervasive example of these negative effects when mass job layoffs occur because jobs are moved elsewhere or when a business or plant closes and management does not carefully consider the community stakeholders affected. We will address the issue of offshoring and reshoring first, because many of the recent job losses are attributable to this issue, and then we take a more in-depth look at business and plant closings.

16.3a Offshoring and Reshoring

Offshoring refers to the relocation of business processes to a different country, whereas **reshoring** is the returning of business processes to their original location. Offshoring became popular when new technologies such as high-speed data links and the Internet made it easier to do work overseas, where labor was cheaper.

Some decades ago, concerns over offshore outsourcing focused on skilled labor occupations, primarily factory workers, and it was mostly a problem in the United States. **Outsourcing** refers to the relocation of business processes to a different company. Then, the Internet boom of the 1990s made it a professional services issue with information technology workers being particularly affected.[91] Then, a programmer who made $11,000 in India or $8,000 in Poland and Hungary could do the work of a programmer who made $80,000 in the United States.[92] This represented huge savings for firms dealing with global competition.

In spite of the savings for companies involved with offshoring, it has not been a panacea for all companies. Often, the problems that developed from shipping jobs overseas often ended up outweighing the cost savings. Capital One ended a contract for a 250-person call center in New Delhi when they found that workers would boost their sales by offering unauthorized lines of credit.[93] Similarly, Dell brought a tech support center back to the United States after customers complained about poor service.[94] Stanley Furniture moved its manufacturing facilities back to the United States after a recall of cribs made in Slovenia.[95] In short, major detriments of offshoring jobs include time zone differences and proximity, communication and language differences, cultural and social differences, the possibility of geopolitical unrest, and the displacement of jobs.[96]

COVID-19 wreaked havoc on offshoring, outsourcing, and reshoring. This issue was highlighted during the COVID-19 pandemic when much needed medical equipment heightened the urgency of shortening the supply chain and increasing domestic production of previously imported goods.[97] Reshoring requires a "robust, comprehensive strategy that coordinates policies in trade, currency valuation, investment, financing, energy, technology, tax, education, training, government procurement, and labor."[98] Current trends indicate that reshoring will continue, most likely for industries that have access to global markets and can take advantage of cheaper natural gas—as well as those industries that have products that change rapidly, like fashion apparel and technology that uses relatively little labor.[99]

Despite the popularity of reshoring, many companies in the United States and in other developed nations continue to relocate plants to other countries where labor costs are significantly less. And, due to these continuing relocations and job losses, the detrimental impacts on communities by corporations will continue. Our next section on business and plant closings discusses how this continuing factor has detrimental impacts on communities.

16.3b Business and Plant Closings

In March 2019, General Motors CEO Mary Barra announced that the company was closing down its Lordstown, Ohio, plant. After producing 16 million new vehicles for 52 years, the assembly plant was shut down. This decision was made by GM to avoid the errors it made a decade prior in not responding to the changing market.[100] As customers have gravitated to trucks and SUVs and away from cars, GM decided to close five plants in the United States and Canada, and Lordstown was the first to shutter. This was not seen as a surprise because the plant produced the slow-selling Cruze sedan. Shutting down five plants resulted in the loss of 14,000 jobs. The shutdown had a devastating effect on employees, other businesses, and the community as it wondered what would happen next.[101]

Although the right to close a business or plant has long been regarded as a management prerogative, the business shutdowns of the past two decades—especially their dramatic effects—have called attention to the question of what rights and responsibilities business has in relation to employee and community stakeholders. The literature on business social responsibility and policy has documented corporate concern with the detrimental impact of its actions. Indeed, business's social response patterns have borne this out. Management expert Peter Drucker suggested the following business position regarding social impacts of management decisions:

> Because one is responsible for one's impacts, one minimizes them. The fewer impacts an institution has outside of its own specific purpose and mission, the better does it conduct itself, the more responsibly does it act, and the more acceptable a citizen, neighbor, and contributor it is.[102]

This raises the question of whether business's social responsibilities in the realm of plant closings and offshoring and their impacts on employees and communities are any different from the host of CSR obligations that have already been assumed in areas such as employment discrimination, diversity, employee privacy and safety, honesty in advertising, product safety, and concern for the environment.

Business essentially has two opportunities to be responsive to employee and community stakeholders in shutdown situations. It can take certain actions *before the decision* to close is made and other actions *after the decision* to close has been made.

Before the Decision to Close Is Made. Before a company makes a decision to close down, it has a responsibility to itself, its employees, and its community to thoroughly and diligently study whether the closing is the only or best option available. A decision to leave a community that has come to depend on them should be preceded by critical and realistic investigations of economic alternatives such as diversification, seeking new ownership, or employee ownership.

Diversification Sometimes it is possible to find other revenue streams to help the company cope with the slim margins of manufacturing. For example, manufacturer SRC Holdings was making only 2 to 3 percent a year but needed a profit of 4 percent to compete effectively. The company's CEO explained, "We took our manufacturing discipline into the service sector to develop new sources of revenue.... Without creating these other businesses, we couldn't have survived. Manufacturing has very slim margins but if a company innovates the margins can be incredible."[103] Having weathered multiple economic storms, SRC took pride in becoming "the oldest employee-owned remanufacturer to OEM's in North America."[104] In 2021, it was acknowledged as a Top 25 Best Small Company in America.[105] Sometimes a company cannot avoid closure, but its suppliers need to diversify to survive. This was the case with many suppliers of the GM Oshawa plant closure in Toronto in 2019. Suppliers had been anticipating the possibility of a closure and began their diversification initiatives well ahead of time. Their result was survival and a minimal impact on jobs and the community.[106]

New Ownership After a careful study of alternatives has been made, it may be concluded that finding new ownership for the plant or business is the only feasible alternative. Two basic options exist at this point: (1) find a new owner or (2) explore the possibility of employee ownership.[107] A company has an obligation to its employees and the community to try to sell the business as a going unit instead of shutting down. This is often not possible, but it is an avenue that should be explored. Quite often, the most promising new buyers of a firm are residents of the state who have a long-term stake in the community and are willing to make a strong commitment. Ideally, local organizations and the government will be able to offer incentives to companies willing to bring jobs to the areas.

For example, when the Grumman Olson facility closed in Lycoming County, Pennsylvania, several parties joined together to bring jobs back to the area. The local chamber of commerce worked with the state to develop an incentive package that included job creation tax credits and customized job training at the local college. Specialized Vehicles Corporation (SVC) bought the facility, promising to offer jobs first to the displaced workers of Grumman Olson.[108]

Employee Ownership The idea of a company selling its business or a plant to the employees as a way of avoiding a closedown is appealing at first glance. In the United States, over a thousand companies are **employee owned**. Most of these companies are very small. The National Center for Employee Ownership (NCEO) lists the 100 largest employee-owned companies in the United States, defined as having over 50 percent employee ownership. Many of these are 100 percent employee owned. In 2021, some of these companies included Publix Super Markets, W. L. Gore & Associates, Graybar Electric, Abt Associates, and Performance Contracting, Inc.[109] Although employee ownership is not a major trend in the current environment, it is instructive to understand its history and record of success and failure to appreciate fully the pros and cons of employee ownership.

Employee ownership experiences have not always been favorable.[110] In numerous cases, employees have had to take significant wage and benefit reductions to make the business profitable. Some companies, however, have met with better success. Publix Supermarkets is the largest employee-owned company in the United States.[111] Most observers credit their employee ownership with earning Publix the number-one supermarket ranking on the American Customer Satisfaction Index for many years.[112] Publix employees are known for bending over backward to please customers and have won awards for their community involvement.[113]

After the Decision to Close Is Made. In 2020, the State of Ohio announced that it would force GM to pay $60 million for its closure of the Lordstown auto plant in 2019. The state says that GM received tens of millions in tax breaks to operate the assembly plant. Ohio officials said that the plant closure violated the terms of two state economic development agreements that GM signed a decade earlier.[114] Apparently, the company had pledged to maintain operations at Lordstown until at least 2027. GM is asking the state to take into consideration the collapsed market for small cars, the specialty of Lordstown, and the economic downturn begun by the pandemic.[115]

In 2019, GM sold the Lordstown plant to Lordstown Motors, an electric truck startup. Lordstown Motors said it would produce the Endurance electric pickup truck there.[116]

There are a multitude of actions that a business can take once the decision has been made that a closedown or relocation is unavoidable. The overriding concern should be that the company seriously attempts to mitigate the social and economic impacts of its actions on employees and the community. Regardless of the circumstances of the move, some basic planning can help alleviate the disruptions felt by those affected. Ideally, there are several actions that management can take, including:[117]

- Conducting a community-impact analysis;
- Providing advance notice to the employees or community;
- Providing transfer, relocation, and outplacement benefits;
- Phasing out the business gradually; and
- Helping the community attract replacement industry.

Community-Impact Analysis Because management is responsible for its impacts on employees and the community, a thorough community-impact analysis of a decision to close down or move is always in order. The initial action should be to identify realistically those aspects of the community that would be affected by the company's plans. This entails asking questions such as the following:[118]

- What groups will be affected?
- How will they be affected?
- What is the timing of initial and later effects?
- What is the magnitude of the effect?
- What is the duration of the impact?
- To what extent will the impact be diffused in the community?

Once these questions have been answered, management is better equipped to modify its plans so that negative impacts can be minimized and favorable impacts, if any, can be maximized.

Advance Notice One of the most often discussed responsibilities in business- or plant-closing situations is the provision of advance notice to workers and communities. The national advance-notice law is called the **Worker Adjustment and Retraining Notification Act (WARN)**. Figure 16-6 provides an overview of the WARN Act.

Employers faced many challenges and threats of closings during and immediately after the pandemic, and several consequences, including plant closings and/or mass layoffs, triggered WARN notifications. However, there are three circumstances under which companies may not be required to give the required 60-day notice. First is the case of a faltering company that is seeking financial support in good faith and believes the warning could adversely affect its ability to raise funds. Second are unforeseeable circumstances that are not reasonably foreseeable at the time the 60-day notice would be required. Third is the case of a natural disaster. This applies when a plant closing or mass layoff is the direct result of a natural disaster such as a flood, earthquake, drought, storm, tidal wave, or similar effects of nature. In this case, notice may be given after the event.[119] As is typical with government requirements, however, there are many definitional and circumstantial details that must be attended to and followed by companies. Seeking legal advice is usually recommended.

Employees who sue successfully under WARN may get back pay and benefits for up to 60 days. The penalty for not giving adequate notice is $500 per day. The only acceptable reasons for not providing a 60-day notice are (1) action being taken by the employer, which, if successful, would have postponed or eliminated the need for layoffs, (2) business circumstances that the employer could not reasonably have foreseen, and (3) natural disasters.[120]

Since the bill's inception, legislators have tried to strengthen the law by closing loopholes and giving it some teeth. One key problem is that the Labor Department has no enforcement power over the WARN Act, and so displaced employees must hire their own attorneys to hold their former employers accountable.[121]

Good communication is critical when a company is thinking about a business closing and subsequent layoffs. Communication expert Hugh Braithwaite offers important advice on communicating with employees being laid off.[122]

- **Be complete.** Employees will try to fill any holes in your story, and that is how rumors begin.
- **Be consistent.** Information will become muddled if the story keeps changing.
- **Inform affected employees first.** Provide a thorough "exit kit" that provides all information the employee might need to smooth their transition.
- **Inform retained employees.** Recognize that survivors have challenges too and provide ample opportunity for their questions to be asked and answered.

Transfer, Relocation, and Outplacement Benefits Enlightened companies are increasingly recognizing that the provision of separation or outplacement benefits is in the

---

Figure 16-6 The Worker Retraining and Adjustment Act (WARN)

The Worker Adjustment and Retraining Notification Act (WARN) seeks to protect workers, their families, and communities by requiring most employers with 100 or more employees to provide notification 60 calendar days in advance of plant closings and mass layoffs.

Employees entitled to notice under WARN include managers and supervisors, as well as hourly and salaried workers. WARN requires that notice also be given to employees' representatives, the local chief elected official, and the state dislocated worker unit.

Advance notice gives workers and their families some transition time to adjust to the prospective loss of employment, to seek and obtain other jobs, and, if necessary, to enter skill training or retraining that will allow these workers to compete successfully in the job market.

- Generally, WARN covers employers with 100 or more employees, not counting those who have worked less than six months in the last 12 months and those who work an average of less than 20 hours a week.
- Employees entitled to advance notice under WARN include managers and supervisors as well as hourly and salaried workers.
- Regular federal, state, and local government entities that provide public services are *not* covered by WARN.

The Department of Labor's (DOL) Employment and Training Administration (ETA) administers WARN at the federal level, and some states have plant closure laws of their own. DOL has no enforcement role in seeking damages for workers who did not receive adequate notice of a layoff or received no notice at all. However, they can assist workers in finding a new job or learning about training opportunities that are available.

Source: The United States Department of Labor, WARN Act Compliance Assistance, https://www.dol.gov/agencies/eta/layoffs/warn, accessed June 11, 2021.

long-range best interest of all parties concerned. Everyone is better off if disruptions are minimized in the lives of the firm's management, the displaced workers, and the community. Outplacement benefits have been used for years as companies have attempted to remove redundant or marginal personnel with minimum disruption and cost to the company and maximum benefit to the individuals involved. Now these same benefits are being used in business and plant closings.[123]

Gradual Phase-Outs Another management action that can significantly ameliorate the effects of a business shutdown is the gradual phasing out of the business. A gradual phase-out buys time for employees and the community to adjust to the new situation and to solve some of their problems. Unfortunately, these types of programs are few and far between. The tech industry, for example, has a history of doing major layoffs too frequently and with poor execution.[124] As one exception, when the semiconductor industry took a deep downturn, Sony Electronics found it necessary to close its plant in San Antonio. They let their employees go in phases as they gradually wrapped up their customer orders. Affected workers were given 60 days' notice. This did not come as a surprise because, as one worker noted, "It was fairly well-known that the company was sick for a quite a while."[125] When asked about worker reactions, one employee said, "There were a few who were upset but some of them actually requested to be included in Phase 1 (job cuts). They wanted to get their severance packages and get on with their lives."[126] Sony provided workers with severance pay based on years on the job. They also extended benefits packages, outplacement services, and job transfers, where possible, to other Sony plants in the United States.

Helping to Attract Replacement Industry The principal responsibility for attracting new industry falls on the community, but the management of the closing firm can provide cooperation and assistance. The closing company can help by providing inside information on building and equipment characteristics and capabilities, transportation options based on its experience, and contacts with other firms in its industry that may be seeking facilities. Helping the community attract replacement industry has the overwhelming advantage of rapidly replacing large numbers of lost jobs. In addition, because attracted businesses tend to be smaller than those that closed, this strategy enables the community to diversify its economic base while regaining jobs.[127]

General Motors moved quickly to find a replacement industry when it decided to close its Lordstown assembly plant. It is not clear how Lordstown Motors Corporation was identified so quickly, but the plant was sold and the potential for future growth was established. As of May 2021, Lordstown Motors struggled to get its plant up to forecasts. Also in May 2021, Lordstown Motors CEO Steve Burns said that the company had encountered some challenges and that it expected to produce only half the number of vehicles it initially forecast for 2021.[128] In June 2021, CEO Burns and CFO Julio Rodriguez resigned amid inaccurate preorder disclosures. A board committee was established to investigate allegations made that the company had misled investors about the strength of its preorders and progress about starting up production.[129] The challenges faced by Lordstown Motors demonstrate that even when plant closings are potentially remedied by selling the plant, there are no guarantees as to what eventual effects the sale will have on the community, employees, and other stakeholders.

Survivors: The Forgotten Stakeholders. When job losses occur, attention is understandably placed on the workers who lose their employment and the many repercussions that loss holds for them and their communities. Employee needs must come first because they withstand the worst of the impact. However, those who retain their jobs—whether they are the remaining employees at a downsized plant or the workers at a plant that survived consolidation—are in need of support as well. Even the managers who conducted the layoffs will not emerge unscathed. One study of managers who issued WARN notices found that they had an increase in health and sleep problems: They reported feelings of depersonalization, and a greater intent to quit, with emotional exhaustion playing a role in their difficulties.[130]

All survivors of business closings are likely to evidence a variety of negative actions, perceptions, and behaviors. These include depression, guilt, stress, uncertainty, decreased loyalty, and lower enthusiasm.[131] Firms must attend to these concerns of survivors if they are to emerge stronger after job cuts. They can do this by providing[132]:

1. Emotional support—assuring employees that they are important.
2. Directional support—communicating the direction the company is going and the employees' place in that journey.
3. Tactical support—presenting new goals and objectives for the employees.
4. Informational support—answering all questions about the layoff and future plans.

We have just touched the surface of the stakes and stakeholders involved in the business-closing issue, the impacts that business closings have on employees and communities, the public's reaction to the problem, and types of corresponding actions that management might take. During the recent COVID-19 pandemic, business closings were rampant, and it may be years before we understand their full effect on communities and employees. According to one study, 60 percent of the business closures due to the COVID-19 pandemic will be permanent.[133] To be sure, many of these are small businesses; however, they served as important places of employment for many workers, significant investments for owners, and as key economic and social elements in communities. Business closings and their adverse consequences are issues that business must continue to address in the future, lest yet another public problem culminates in new laws or another knotty regulatory apparatus.

Summary

Community stakeholders are extremely important to companies and the variable economic conditions have heightened the importance of business's attending to community stakeholder needs. In many ways, business can provide support in difficult times. Companies may donate the time and talents of managers and employees (volunteerism). Because business has a vital stake in the community, it engages in a variety of community projects. Community engagement programs are a key part of managing community involvement.

Business also contributes to community stakeholders through corporate philanthropy or business giving. The third sector, or nonprofit sector, depends on business's support. Companies give for a variety of reasons—some altruistic, some self-interested. Major recipients of business giving include health and welfare, education, civic activities, and culture and the arts. Giving in times of crisis also is important to companies and communities.

As companies have attempted to manage their philanthropy, two major types of corporate giving have been emphasized: (1) strategic philanthropy, which seeks to improve the overall fit between corporate needs and charitable programs, and (2) cause-related marketing, which tightens the linkage between a firm's profits and its contributions. Cause-related marketing represents a unique joining of business and charity with the potential for great benefit to each. Cause branding also has become an important element of philanthropy.

Just as firms have beneficial effects on community stakeholders, they can have detrimental effects as well. Businesses offshoring and then reshoring can wreak havoc for employees, although most stakeholders recognize that these decisions are not made lightly. Business or plant closings are another example of these detrimental effects. Loss of jobs is the primary way in which these effects are manifested. They frequently occur due to offshoring decisions or changes in demand for products. Plant closings have a pervasive influence in the sense that a multitude of community stakeholders—employees, local government, other businesses, and the general citizenry—are affected. There is no single reason why these closings occur, but among the major reasons are economic conditions, consolidation of company operations, outsourcing, outmoded technology or facilities, changes in corporate strategy, and international competition. Reshoring has become a recent trend, but it has not offset the number of firms that continue to relocate in other countries.

Before management makes the decision to close a facility, it has a responsibility to itself, its employees, and the community to study thoroughly whether closing is the only or the best option. Finding a new owner for the business and pursuing the possibility of employee ownership are reasonable and desirable alternatives. After the decision to close has been made, responsible actions include community-impact analysis; giving advance notice; providing transfer, relocation, or outplacement benefits; phasing out operations gradually; and helping the community attract replacement industry. Finally, the needs of survivors must be met as the firm continues operations. Companies have an added incentive to be responsive to the business-closing issue, because state and federal governments are closely watching the manner in which firms are handling this problem.

Key Terms

cause branding, p. 372
cause-related marketing, p. 372
Chief Executives for Corporate
    Purpose (CECP), p. 364
community action program, p. 366
community engagement, p. 363
community involvement, p. 364
community partnerships, p. 371

Company-Wide Day of Service, p. 364
corporate philanthropy, p. 363
Dollars for Doers, p. 365
employee owned, p. 375
offshoring, p. 374
outsourcing, p. 374
Paid Release Time, p. 364
philanthropy, p. 366

philanthropy hackers, p. 367
reshoring, p. 374
Skills-Based Pro Bono Service, p. 365
strategic philanthropy, p. 371
third sector, p. 368
Worker Adjustment and Retraining
    Notification Act (WARN), p. 376

Discussion Questions

1. Have you participated in community involvement at work? What type of program did the company endorse? Outline what you experienced to be the benefits of employee volunteerism.

2. Explain the pros and cons of corporate philanthropy, and explain why and to whom companies give.

3. Differentiate among strategic philanthropy, cause-related marketing, and cause branding. Provide an example of each not discussed in the text.

4. Identify and discuss briefly what you think are the major trade-offs that firms face as they think about offshoring and reshoring. When

substantial layoffs are involved, what are firms' responsibilities to their employees and their communities?

5. How serious is the plant and business closing phenomenon? Are their responsibilities companies

have to their communities that extend beyond those discussed in the chapter? Explain.

6. In your opinion, why does a business have a responsibility to employees and community stakeholders in a business- or plant-closing decision?

Endnotes

1. Gabrielle Olya, "30 Major Companies Giving Back During COVID-19," August 10, 2020, https://www.yahoo.com/news/30-major-companies-giving-back-090033889.html?guccounter=1&guce_referrer=aHR0cHM6Ly93d3cuZ29vZ2xlLmNvbS8&guce_referrer_sig=AQAAABDQ-cC4P3ZXvJbCMTF-L6L20el1D63sE3Sn80erSDdtAEx0PnXtIOCV_fStH0VtF8VBl5_1u4BxESMqahfhF8y9GVGH0VkzOOGHiI_WJuclgH-sOiFSPHIgFTsT592QaeMH_VVSw9EcYem3puXXSId8btXDRp6wawo8-fwr8wee. Accessed June 5, 2021.

2. Ibid.

3. Jeff Elder, "Reddit Revolt Shows Challenge of Harnessing Community of Volunteers," *The Wall Street Journal* (July 6, 2015), https://www.wsj.com/articles/BL-DGB-42542. Accessed June 5, 2021.

4. Ibid.

5. Tim Darnell, "Amazon Opens First Disaster Hub in Metro Atlanta," *Atlanta Journal Constitution*, https://epaper.ajc.com/popovers/dynamic_article_popover.aspx?guid=baafed18-a9fb-4691-9080-908c25caf1f1&pbid=8e0858ee-1443-484d-9e94-f8b8a1eaaaff&utm_source=app.pagesuite&utm_medium=app-interaction&utm_campaign=pagesuite-epaper-html5_share-article. accessed June 7, 2021.

6. Ibid.

7. Ibid.

8. Michael E. Porter, "Michael Porter on Inner City Business," May 27, 2010, https://www.bloomberg.com/news/articles/2010-05-27/michael-porter-on-inner-city-businessbusinessweek-business-news-stock-market-and-financial-advice. Accessed June 5, 2021.

9. Points of Light, "The Civic 50 Honorees," https://www.pointsoflight.org/the-civic-50-honorees/. Accessed June 5, 2021.

10. Points of Light, "Corporate Civic Engagement Framework," https://www.pointsoflight.org/the-civic-50/. Accessed June 5, 2021.

11. Brad Stone, "Marc Benioff's Philanthropic Mission: San Francisco," Bloombergbusinessweek, https://www.bloomberg.com/news/articles/2014-12-23/marc-benioff-to-tech-industry-give-back-to-san-francisco. Accessed June 5, 2021.

12. Ibid.

13. Ibid.

14. Biospace, "Eli Lilly and Company Plans $30 Million Attack on Diabetes," September 13, 2011, https://www.biospace.com/article/releases/eli-lilly-and-company-plans-30-million-attack-on-diabetes-/. Accessed June 5, 2021.

15. David Jones, "Does Serving the Community Also Serve the Company? Using Organizational Identification and Social Exchange Theories to Understand Employee Responses to a Volunteerism Programme," *Journal of Occupational and Organizational Psychology*," 83(4), 857–878.

16. Bill Shaw and Frederick Post, "A Moral Basis for Corporate Philanthropy," *Journal of Business Ethics* (October 1993), 745–751.

17. J.B. Rodell, H. Breitsohl, M. Schröder, and D. J. Keating, "Employee Volunteering a Review and Framework for Future Research," *Journal of Management* (Vol. 1, No. 42, 2016), 55–84.

18. Susanne Gargiulo, "Why Everyone Wants to Work for the 'Good Guys'," CNN.com (November 8, 2012), https://www.cnn.com/2012/11/07/business/global-office-csr-volunteer/index.html. Accessed June 7, 2021.

19. Ibid.

20. CECP 2020, "Strength in Solutions: Giving in Number Brief 2020," https://cecp.co/wp-content/uploads/2020/10/Giving-in-Numbers-Infographic-2020.pdf. Accessed June 7, 2021.

21. Ibid.

22. Benjamin Snyder, "These 10 Companies Offer Big Incentives for Volunteering," *Fortune* (March 21, 2015), https://fortune.com/2015/03/21/companies-offer-incentives-for-volunteering/. Accessed June 7, 2021.

23. Points of Light, "Virtual Volunteering: How to Companies Shifted their Days of Service Online Amidst the Pandemic," October 29, 2020, https://www.pointsoflight.org/blog/virtual-volunteering-how-2-companies-shifted-their-days-of-service-online-amidst-the-pandemic/. Accessed June 7, 2021.

24. Ryan Scott, "Is Your Company Doubling Down on Its Employee Volunteers?" *Forbes*, https://www.forbes.com/sites/causeintegration/2012/10/09/is-your-company-doubling-down-on-its-employee-volunteers/?sh=20b475146f32. Accessed June 7, 2021.

25. Ibid.

26. AT&T, "Community Engagement," https://about.att.com/csr/home/reporting/issue-brief/community-engagement.html. Accessed June 7, 2021.

27. CECP 2020, "Capital One," https://cecp.co/?s=capital+one. Accessed June 7, 2021.

28. Steve Brown, "J.C. Penney Seeks Approval for Big Plano Office and Retail Complex at Legacy," *The Dallas Morning News* (March 7, 2016), https://www.dallasnews.com/business/2016/03/07/j-c-penney-seeks-approval-for-big-plano-office-and-retail-complex-at-legacy/. Accessed June 7, 2021.

29. Ronald McDonald House of Charities, "Our Impact," https://www.rmhc.org/about-us/our-impact. Accessed June 7, 2021.

30. Cecily Railborn, Antoinette Green, Lyudmila Todorova, Toni Trapani, and Wilborne E. Watson, "Corporate Philanthropy: When Is Giving Effective," *The Journal of Corporate Accounting and Finance* (November/December 2003), 47–54.

31. Merriam-Webster, "Philanthropy," https://www.merriam -webster.com/dictionary/philanthropy#:~:text=1%20 %3A%20goodwill%20to%20fellow%20members,set%20 aside%20for%20humanitarian%20purposes. Accessed June 8, 2021.

32. CECP, "Giving in Numbers," https://cecp.co/home/ resources/giving-in-numbers/?tid=1398. Accessed June 8, 2021.

33. Ibid.

34. Railborn et al., Ibid.

35. Arthur Gautier and Ann Claire Pache, "Research on Corporate Philanthropy: A Review and Assessment," *Journal of Business Ethics* (Vol. 126, Issue 3, 2015), 343–369.

36. Matt Krantz, "How Coke, Disney Use Data to Donate Smarter," *USA Today* (March 11, 2016), 6B, https://www .usatoday.com/story/money/markets/2016/03/11/how- coke-disney-use-data-donate-smarter/81646052/. Accessed June 8, 2021.

37. Ibid.

38. Ibid.

39. Rebecca Greenfield, "I Gave Online," *Bloomberg Businessweek* (March 14–20, 2016), 82.

40. Morrell Heald, *The Social Responsibilities of Business: Company and Community 1900–1960* (Cleveland: Case Western Reserve University Press, 1970), 112.

41. Sean Parker, "Philanthropy for Hackers," *The Wall Street Journal* (June 25, 2016), https://www.wsj.com/articles /sean-parker-philanthropy-for-hackers-1435345787. Accessed June 8, 2021.

42. Ibid.

43. Adam Bryant, "Companies Oppose Disclosure of Details on Gifts to Charity," *The New York Times* (April 3, 1998), A1, https://www.nytimes.com/1998/04/03/business /companies-oppose-disclosure-of-detail-on-gifts-to-charity .html. Accessed June 8, 2021.

44. Ibid.

45. Nicholas Confessore, "S.E.C. Is Asked to Require Disclosure of Donations," *The New York Times* (April 23, 2013), https://www.nytimes.com/2013/04/24/us/politics /sec-is-asked-to-make-companies-disclose-donations.html. Accessed June 8, 2021.

46. John D. Rockfeller III, "In Defense of Philanthropy," *Business and Society Review* (Spring 1978), 26–29.

47. CECP, "Investing in Society," https://cecp.co/iis/. Accessed June 8, 2021.

48. Ibid.

49. Goodbox, "How Being a Good Business Leads to Good Business," November 25, 2019, https://www.goodbox .com/2019/11/why-do-companies-give-to-charity/. Accessed June 8, 2021.

50. Elizabeth Dove and Alison Grenier, "66,000 Employees Have Spoken: They Want to Work for Companies that Give Back," Triple Pundit, December 9, 2019, https:// www.triplepundit.com/story/2019/community-investment -employee-engagement/85851. Accessed June 8, 2021.

51. The Conference Board, "Giving in Numbers," file:///C:/ Users/Owner/Desktop/2018%20Giving%20in%20 Numbers.pdf. Accessed June 9, 2021.

52. The Conference Board, "Corporate Giving Looks to Be Strong in 2021," January 26, 2021, https://conference -board.org/blog/corporate-citizenship/2021_corporate_ giving. Accessed June 9, 2021.

53. Ibid.

54. Ibid.

55. Ibid.

56. Robert Schwarz, "Disaster Philanthropy Practices: 2020 Edition," The Conference Board, 2020, p. 14.

57. The Wakeman Agency, "Rewriting the Rules of Corporate Giving During a Crisis," May 9, 2020, https://www .thewakemanagency.com/rewriting-rules-corporate-giving -crisis/. Accessed June 9, 2021.

58. Ibid.

59. Council on Foundations, "Increasing Impact, Enhancing Value," https://www.cof.org/sites/default/files/documents /files/CorporateGuide.pdf. Accessed June 9, 2021.

60. Ibid.

61. James J. Chrisman and Archie B. Carroll, "Corporate Responsibility: Reconciling Economic and Social Goals," *Sloan Management Review* (Winter 1984), 59–65.

62. Brenda Bouw, "Focus on Strategic Philanthropy Increasing Amid COVID-19 Crisis," December 11, 2020, https:// www.theglobeandmail.com/investing/globe-advisor /advisor-news/article-focus-on-strategic-philanthropy -increasing-amid-covid-19-crisis/. Accessed June 9, 2021.

63. National Safe Place Network, https://www.nspnetwork.org /programs. Accessed June 9, 2021.

64. Ibid.

65. Richard Steckel and Robin Simons, *Doing Best by Doing Good* (New York: Dutton Publishers, 1992); also see Anne Bahr Thompson, *Do Good: Enhancing Brand Citizenship to Fuel Both Purpose and Profit* (New York: AMACOM, 2018).

66. Archie B. Carroll, "Strategic Philanthropy," in Robert Kolb (ed.), *The Sage Encyclopedia of Business Ethics and Society* (Thousand Oaks, CA: SAGE, 2018).

67. Ibid.

68. Ibid.

69. Michael Porter and Mark Kramer, "The Competitive Advantage of Corporate Philanthropy," *Harvard Business Review* (December 2002), 56–69.

70. Tom Watson, "Philanthropy Is on a Collision Course with Presidential Campaign Politics," *The Chronicle of Philanthropy* (January 12, 2016), https://philanthropy.com /article/Opinion-Philanthropy-Is-on-a/234886. Accessed April 13, 2016.

71. Porter and Kramer, pp. 56–69.

72. Ibid.

73. Ibid.

74. Everythingwhat, "What Does Burger King Do for the Community," January 22, 2020, https://everythingwhat. com/what-does-burger-king-do-for-the-community. Accessed June 9, 2021.

75. Bruce Horovitz, "Be Kind and They Will Come," *USA Today International Edition* (March 27, 2013), A1–A2, https://www.pressreader.com/usa/usa-today-us-edit ion/20130326/281479273867151. Accessed June 9, 2021.

76. Cone Communications/Ebiquity, "Millennial CSR Study," https://www.conecomm.com/research-blog/2015-cone -communications-millennial-csr-study. Accessed June 9, 2021.

77. Ibid.

78. Whole Foods Market, "Standards That Are Not Standard Anywhere Else," https://www.wholefoodsmarket.com /quality-standards. Accessed June 9, 2021.
79. Porter and Kramer, 56–69.
80. Cited in Ibid.
81. Ibid.
82. Patricia Caesar, "Cause-Related Marketing: The New Face of Corporate Philanthropy," *Business and Society Review* (Fall 1986), 16.
83. Gayle Sullk, "Cause Marketing Is Not Philanthropy," *Psychology Today*, October 27, 2013, https://www. psychologytoday.com/us/blog/pink-ribbon-blues/201310 /cause-marketing-is-not-philanthropy. Accessed June 9, 2021.
84. Martin Gottlieb, "Cashing In on a Higher Cause," *The New York Times* (July 6, 1986), 6-F.
85. Avon, "Breast Cancer Crusade," 2021, https://www.avon .com/breast-cancer-crusade. Accessed June 9, 2021.
86. Cone Communications/Ebiquity, "Global CSR Study," https://www.conecomm.com/research-blog/2015-cone- communications-ebiquity-global-csr-study. Accessed June 9, 2021.
87. Carol Cone, "Cause Branding in the 21st Century," https:// www.psaresearch.com/cause-branding-in-the-21st- century/, https://www.psaresearch.com/cause-branding-in -the-21st-century/. Accessed June 9, 2021.
88. CECP. "Giving in Numbers Brief 2020," https://cecp .co/wp-content/uploads/2020/10/Giving-in-Numbers- Infographic-2020.pdf. Accessed June 10, 2021.
89. Center for Disaster Philanthropy, "Announcing Round 10 of COVID-19 Grants Totalling More Than $4.7 million," April 29, 2021, https://disasterphilanthropy.org/blog /diseases/announcing-round-10-of-covid-19-grants- totaling-more-than-4-7-million/. Accessed June 10, 2021.
90. U.S. Chamber of Commerce Foundation, "Corporate Citizenship Center," quote by Elizabeth Kelleher, https:// www.uschamberfoundation.org/corporate-citizenship- center. Accessed June 10, 2021.
91. "Where America's Jobs Went," *The Week*, January 11, 2015, https://theweek.com/articles/486362/where- americas-jobs-went. Accessed June 10, 2021.
92. Dale Kasler, "Outsourcing Reaps Winners, Losers in U.S. Economy," *The Sacramento Bee* (April 26, 2004).
93. Brad Stone, "Should I Stay or Should I Go," *Newsweek* (April 19, 2004), 52–53.
94. Ibid.
95. Sarah Kabourek, "Back in the USA," *Fortune* (September 28, 2009), 30.
96. Rural Sourcing, "5 Cons of Offshoring," https://www .ruralsourcing.com/blogs/5-disadvantages-of-offshoring/? creative=469811773643&keyword=&matchtype=b&network =g&device=c&gclid=Cj0KCQjw8IaGBhCHARIsAGIRR YrCdDGN1hxJwQjAYnaddbe8HzQAVVUwHSRhvwSSL2a HU0ALkLsra5UaAgxjEALw_wcB. Accessed June 10, 2021.
97. Owen Herrnstadt, "Ending Offshoring and Bringing Jobs Back Home Will Take More Than Tweets, Press Releases, and Op Eds," May 20, 2020, https://www.epi.org/blog /ending-offshoring-and-bringing-jobs-back-home-will -take-more-than-tweets-press-releases-and-op-eds/. Accessed June 10, 2021.
98. Ibid.
99. Michael Sainato, "U.S. Corporations Continue Sending Jobs Abroad During Pandemic," *The Guardian*, September 12, 2020, https://www.theguardian.com/business/2020 /sep/12/us-corporations-sending-jobs-abroad-offshoring -pandemic. Accessed June 10, 2021.
100. Phil LeBeau, "GM's Lordstown Factory Goes Dark as Authomaker Idles Underused Plants," CNBC, March 6, 2019, https://www.cnbc.com/2019/03/06/gms-lordstown -factory-goes-dark-as-automaker-closes-underused-plants. html. Accessed June 14, 2021.
101. Ibid.
102. Peter F. Drucker, *Management: Tasks, Responsibilities, Practices* (New York: Harper & Row, 1974), 327–328.
103. Susan Diesenhouse, "Business: To Save Factories, Owners Diversify," *The New York Times* (November 30, 2003), 5, https://www.nytimes.com/2003/11/30/business/business -to-save-factories-owners-diversify.html. Accessed June 10, 2021.
104. SRC Holdings, "Who We Are," https://www.srcholdings .com/about. Accessed June 10, 2021.
105. Ibid.
106. John Irwin, "Diversification Key to Suppliers Surviving GM Oshawa Closure," May 6, 2019, https://canada .autonews.com/automakers/diversification-key-suppliers- surviving-gm-oshawa-closure. Accessed June 10, 2021.
107. Archie B. Carroll, "When Business Closes Down: Social Responsibilities and Management Actions," *California Management Review* (Winter 1984), 131.
108. Specialized Vehicles, Inc., "History," https://svi-results .com/history/. Accessed June 10, 2021.
109. ADD NOTE TEXT HERE.
110. Terri Minsky, "Gripes of Rath: Workers Who Bought Iowa Slaughterhouse Regret That They Did," *The Wall Street Journal* (December 2, 1981), 1.
111. Publix, "Facts and Figures," http://corporate.publix.com /about-publix/company-overview/facts-figures. Accessed June 10, 2021.
112. "The Opposite of Wal-Mart," *The Economist* (May 5, 2007), 79. Also see ACSI, "Customer Satisfaction Reports 2020-2021," https://www.theacsi.org/news-and-resources /customer-satisfaction-reports/reports-2021. Accessed June 10, 2021.
113. Publix, ibid.
114. Dan O'Brien, "GM Closed the Lordstown Auto Plant. Now Ohio May Force a $60 Million Repayment," June 15, 2020, https://www.propublica.org/article/gm-closed-the -lordstown-auto-plant-now-ohio-may-force-a-60-million -repayment. Accessed June 14, 2021.
115. Ibid.
116. Jamie LaReau, *Detroit Free Press*, "GM Sells Its Lordstown Assembly Plant to Electric Truck Startup," November 7, 2019, https://www.freep.com/story/money /cars/general-motors/2019/11/07/gm-lordstown-assembly -workhorse/2521887001/. Accessed June 14, 2021.
117. Carroll, 132.
118. Grover Starling, *The Changing Environment of Business* (Boston: Kent, 1980), 319–320.
119. Delaney Busch and Emma Follansbee, "The WARN Act and COVID-19: What Are Employers Obligated to Do?" May 14, 2020, https://www.mintz.com/insights-center /viewpoints/2226/2020-04-02-warn-act-and-covid-19 -what-are-employers-obligated-do. Accessed June 11, 2021.
120. Loretta W. Prencipe, "Impending Layoffs Need Warning," *Info World* (April 9, 2001), 15.

121. James Drew and Steve Eder, "Different Workers Face the Same Problem with the WARN Act," *The Blade* (July 17, 2007), https://www.toledoblade.com/business/2007/07/17/Different-workers-face-the-same-problem-with-the-WARN-Act/stories/200707170035. Accessed June 14, 2021.

122. Kelly M. Butler, "Going above and beyond Advance WARNing," *Employee Benefit News* (February 2009), 7.

123. Eric Cormier, Insperity, "Outplacement: Is This a Service You Should Offer?" https://www.insperity.com/blog/providing-outplacement/, https://www.insperity.com/blog/providing-outplacement/. Accessed June 14, 2021.

124. Rob Enderle, "How to Do Layoffs Right (When You Absolutely Have To)," *CIO.com* (September 18, 2015), https://www.cio.com/article/2984682/how-to-do-layoffs-right-when-you-absolutely-have-to.html. Accessed June 14, 2021.

125. MyPlainview, "Sony Lays Off 120 at San Antonio Plant," https://www.myplainview.com/news/article/Sony-lays-off-120-at-San-Antonio-plant-8877331.php. Accessed June 14, 2021.

126. Ibid.

127. Cornell University Workshop Report, 28–30.

128. Michael Wayland, CNBC, "Lordstown Motors Shares Tumble After Company Slashes 2021 Production Plans, Says It Needs More Capital," May 24, 2021, https://www.cnbc.com/2021/05/24/lordstown-slashes-21-production-plans-says-more-capital-needed.html. Accessed June 14, 2021.

129. Ben Foldy and Micah Maidenberg, "Lordstown Motors Executives Resign Amid Inaccurate Preorder Disclosures," *The Wall Street Journal*, June 14, 2021, https://www.wsj.com/articles/lordstown-motors-chief-executive-finance-chief-resign-11623676356?mod=hp_lead_pos1. Accessed June 14, 2021.

130. Leon Grunberg, Sarah Moore, and Edward S. Greenberg, "Managers' Reactions to Implementing Layoffs: Relationship to Health Problems and Withdrawal Behaviors," *Human Resource Management* (Summer 2006), 159–178, https://onlinelibrary.wiley.com/doi/abs/10.1002/hrm.20102. Accessed June 14, 2021.

131. Suzanne M. Behr and Margaret A. White, "Layoff Survivor Sickness," *Executive Excellence* (November 2003), 18.

132. Ibid.

133. Anjali Sundaram, "Small Business: Yelp Data Shows 60% of Business Closures Due to the Coronavirus Pandemic Are Now Permanent," CNBC, December 11, 2020, https://www.cnbc.com/2020/09/16/yelp-data-shows-60percent-of-business-closures-due-to-the-coronavirus-pandemic-are-now-permanent.html. Accessed June 14, 2021.

Part 7

Business and Government Relations

Chapter 17
Business, Government, and Regulation

Chapter 18
Business Influence on Government and Public Policy

17

Business, Government, and Regulation

Chapter Learning Outcomes

After studying this chapter, you should be able to:

1. Articulate a brief history and changing nature of the government's role in its relationship with business.
2. Appreciate the complex roles of government and business.
3. Identify the elements in the complex interactions among business, government, and the public.
4. Identify and describe the government's nonregulatory influences, especially the concepts of industrial policy and privatization.
5. Identify and describe the government's regulatory influences on business including the major reasons for regulation, the types of regulation, and issues arising out of deregulation.

How can business and government work effectively together? The pendulum of government involvement in business swings from minimal intervention to active participation depending on a variety of factors, including the political parties in office at the time. The depth, scope, and direction of government's involvement in business have made the relationship of government to business one of the most hotly debated issues today. Issues of privatization, government monitoring of e-mails, data and phone calls, tax rates, regulation and deregulation, the scope of state versus federal laws, and so on: these are some of the hot-button issues in the business/government relationship that businesses face today. Some argue that government interferes too much in the process of value creation and hinders, rather than helps, business, whereas others argue that business, and particularly big tech, are the "robber barons" that the government needs to control.[1]

In a 2021 Gallup poll, 57 percent of Americans polled thought that more regulation is needed for firms including Amazon, Facebook, and Google, with concerns over misinformation on the Internet, the size and power of large tech companies, online hate speech, foreign interference in U.S. elections and the privacy of personal data online.[2] Additionally, concerns over opioid addiction and the role of pharmaceutical companies caused many to advocate for more government regulation. In the COVID-19 pandemic, support for more government regulation occurred when businesses needed bailouts and subsidies. And yet, many also advocate for different or less regulation in the forms of (1) "smarter" regulation in assessing costs and benefits; (2) self-regulation of businesses, particularly when complicated technologies are involved; and

(3) deregulation of businesses to revive industries and bring back competition.[3]

The bottom line is that business and government need each other. Governments rely on businesses to drive economic growth and create jobs while businesses need government for legal systems and security. Government also educates workers, creating infrastructure that supports a market system. It is important to understand that the government is also a customer of business—the typical government spending in a developed country represents around 30 to 40 percent of gross domestic product (GDP).[4] Therefore, the government is a major stakeholder with which business must establish an effective working relationship if it is to survive and prosper.

The increased level of government involvement in business is likely to remain for some time. As an exemplar of a free-market economy, the United States serves as a case in point, and therefore much of this chapter focuses on the U.S. government. However, general discussions about business/government relationships apply across many different types of markets and political economies.

This chapter and the next examine the relationship between business and government, with the public assuming an important role in the discussion as well. Exploring this relationship carefully will provide an appreciation of the complexity of the issues surrounding business or government interactions. From a manager's standpoint, one needs an understanding of the forces and factors involved in these issues before beginning to talk intelligently about strategies for dealing with them. This chapter discusses how government, as a major stakeholder, influences business, whereas Chapter 18 discusses how business influences government.

17.1 The Pendulum of Government's Role in Business

To be certain, the government involvement pendulum has swung back and forth for years. Business has never been fond of its stakeholder, government, having an activist role in establishing the ground rules under which it operates. In contrast, public sentiment has been cyclical, going through periods when it has thought that the federal government had too much power and other periods when it has thought that government should be more activistic in its business dealings. For example, in the United States and other Western nations, large-scale government and military programs helped seed many industries during and after World War II; however, the pendulum swung back to less government involvement in the 1980s when the governments got out of businesses like telecoms, utilities, and transports.[5] Following the 2008 global financial crisis, there was less skepticism toward big government. More recently, the COVID 19 pandemic necessitated more government intervention, and, as noted by one banking group, "the role of the state in the economy will probably loom considerably larger" as a result of the massive bail-outs for businesses and broader economies that accompanied the pandemic.[6]

The changing areas in which government has chosen to initiate legislation have been accompanied by cries for less or more regulation—with many of these messages on the "less" side. It is not surprising that businesses often argue for fewer regulations, citing the additional costs and administrative burdens of compliance. However, even some small business operators acknowledge that the benefits from regulations can often outweigh the costs. Responding to the news of a possible hike in the minimum wage in his locale, one entrepreneur noted, "I feel if the minimum wage was more than it is now then people could afford to buy more, and if people were able to afford more, then it would pass on to all or most businesses."[7] One of the challenges in assessing the ideal level of involvement of government in business is that the arguments are often couched in partisan politics.

The multiplicity of roles that government has assumed has increased the complexity of its relationship with business. Government is not only a regulator of business that can determine the rules of the game but also a major purchaser with buying power that can affect a business or industry's likelihood of survival. It can elevate some businesses and industries while devaluing others through the setting of government policy. For example, fees on crude oil production may facilitate government support for new climate change initiatives.[8] The government can even create new businesses and industries through subsidization and privatization. In 2021, for example, the United States approved legislation that provided billions of dollars in federal incentives like tax credits to promote semiconductor manufacturing and research in the throes of heavy competition from China.[9]

The range of government roles illuminates the crucial interconnectedness between business and government and the difficulty both business and the public have in fully understanding (much less prescribing) what government's role ought to be in relation to business. In short, we might say that government is a "mixed blessing" stakeholder, in terms introduced earlier in Chapter 3.

17.2 The Roles of Government and Business

It is not our intention to philosophize in this chapter on the ideal role of government in relation to business, because this is outside our stakeholder frame of reference. However, we will strive for an understanding of current major issues as they pertain to this vital relationship. For effective management, government's role as a stakeholder must be understood.

The fundamental question underlying our entire discussion of business and government relationships is, "What should be the respective roles of business and government in our socioeconomic system?" More specifically, we ask, "Given all the tasks that must be completed to make our society work, which of these tasks should be handled by government and which by business?" These questions pose the issue clearly, but other questions remain unanswered. If we decide, for example, that it is best to let business handle the production and distribution roles in our society, the next question becomes, "How much autonomy are we willing to allow business?" If our goals in business are simply the production and distribution of goods and services, we would not have to constrain business severely.

In modern times, however, other goals have been added to the production and distribution functions—a safe working environment for those engaging in production, equal employment opportunities, racial justice and equity in the workforce, fair pay, clean air, safe products, employee rights, and so on. When we superimpose these goals on basic economic goals, the tasks of business become much more complex and challenging.

Because businesses do not automatically factor these more socially oriented goals into their decision making and processes, it often falls on the government to ensure that those goals that reflect social concerns be achieved. Thus, whereas the marketplace dictates economic production decisions, government becomes one of the citizenry's designated representatives charged with articulating and protecting the public interest. Of course, the concepts of corporate social responsibility, sustainability, and business ethics urge businesses to factor these considerations into their practices so that it is not left to government alone to deal with these issues. In spite of this, some measure of government involvement is typically needed.

Figure 17-1 The Clash of Ethical Systems between Business and Government

Business Beliefs	Government Beliefs
• Individualistic ethic	• Collectivistic ethic
• Maximum concession to self-interest	• Subordination of individual goals and self-interest to group and group interests
• Minimizing the load of obligations society imposes on the individual (personal freedom)	• Maximizing the obligations assumed by the individual and discouraging self-interest
• Emphasizes inequalities of individuals	• Emphasizes equality of individuals

A Clash of Ethical Belief Systems. A clash of emphases partially forms the crux of the antagonistic relationship that has evolved between business and government over the years. Although this clash will vary between different countries and cultures, the underlying tension between business and government still holds true. This problem has been termed "a clash of ethical systems." The two ethical systems (systems of belief) are the **individualistic ethic of business** and the **collectivistic ethic of government**. Figure 17-1 summarizes the characteristics of these two philosophies.[10]

The clash of these two ethical systems partially explains why the business and government relationship is adversarial in nature. The goals and values of a pluralistic society continue to be complex, numerous, interrelated, and difficult to reconcile. At the same time, economic and social conditions often compel governments around the world to take a more active role in the economy.[11] This was evident during the COVID-19 pandemic when collective action was essential to fighting against the spread of the virus.

As conflicts among diverse interest groups increase, it becomes more difficult to reconcile trade-off decisions and establish social priorities. Establishing social priorities also involves staying current with sociocultural and demographic

issues. For example, a national survey by researchers at Harvard Kennedy School's Carr Center for Human Rights Policy found that events in 2020–2021, such as the pandemic and economic and racial justice issues, led bipartisan majorities of Americans to "think differently about the role and responsibility of government in protecting rights."[12] Similarly, with more and more public support for climate change and ESG disclosures, it has been speculated and debated in the United States that there will be more regulations like those in Europe that impose enhanced ESG disclosure requirements on public companies.[13] In sum, the relative pros and cons of government intervention in business continue to serve as fuel for debates.[14]

17.3 Interaction of Business, Government, and the Public

This section offers a brief overview of the influence relationships among business, government, and the public. This should be helpful in understanding both the nature of the public policy decision-making process and the current problems that characterize the business–government relationship. Figure 17-2 illustrates the interactive pattern of these

Figure 17-2 Interaction among Business, Government, and the Public

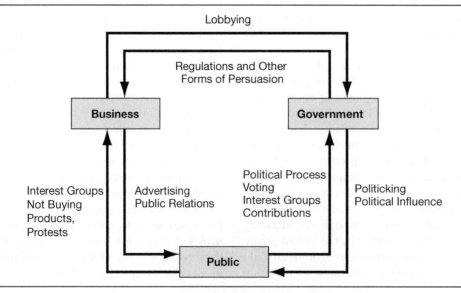

influence relationships as we focus on government-business, public-government, and business-public relationships, outlined below.

17.3a Government–Business Relationship

Government influences business through regulations, taxation, and other forms of persuasion that we will consider in more detail in the next section. Business, likewise, has its approaches to influencing government, which we discussed in Chapter 12. Lobbying, in one form or another, is business's primary means of influencing government. In 2020, for example, Facebook and Amazon were the two biggest corporate lobbying spenders in the United States, spending a combined $38 billion in federal lobbying.[15]

17.3b Public–Government Relationship

One might rightly ask, "Why include the public as a separate entity? Isn't the public represented by government?"

In an ideal world, perhaps this would be true. However, there are functions of government that are separate from the public. Additionally, the public has its own unique methods of influence. The public uses the political processes of voting and electing officials (or removing them from office) to influence government. It also exerts its influence by forming special-interest groups (farmers, small business owners, educators, senior citizens, truckers, manufacturers, etc.) to wield more targeted influence. Increasingly, this public influence is wielded using social media. Government, in turn, uses politicking, public policy formation, and other political influences to have an impact on the public.

17.3c Business–Public Relationship

Business influences the public through advertising, public relations, and other forms of communication. The public influences business through the marketplace or by forming

---

Ethics In Practice Case

The NCAA, the Players, and the Government: Should College Athletes Be Paid?

For years, the National Collegiate Athletic Association (NCAA) in the United States has designed, implemented, and enforced the rules and regulations surrounding college athletes—acting like the "sheriff of college sports." The NCAA considers college athletes "amateurs" and does not allow athletes to earn any money from their athletic fame, although they help to generate millions for their schools and their coaches. A 2020 study by the National Bureau of Economic Research (NBER) found that less than 7 percent of the revenue generated by the NCAA—more than $8 billion annually—finds its way to football and basketball players through scholarship and living stipends. And the dollars that are foregone by the athletes are substantial. In 2021, for example, former Clemson University quarterback Trevor Lawrence, the anticipated No.1 pick for the NFL draft, was estimated to be worth $2 million annually in social media value alone when he graduated from college. However, none of that was available to him while he was at Clemson. One athlete, Hunter Woodhall, a double-amputee track star for the University of Arkansas, had enough with the NCAA restrictions and went professional even though he had a year of eligibility left, stating, "I got so tired of waiting, tired of their hypocrisy."

Recently, state and federal politicians have proposed dozens of bills that would let college athletes earn money from their name, image, and likeness, which is currently forbidden under NCAA policy. A handful of states, including Florida and California, have opposed the NCAA and have given college athletes in their states the right to earn money. Some say that this creates the risk that top athletes will gravitate to schools in states where they could make the most money, eroding the competitive fairness that is the cornerstone of college sports.

Recently, the NCAA has been challenged in the courts as well. In 2021, the U.S. Supreme Court agreed to hear arguments in a case, *Alston v. NCAA*, where former West Virginia football player Shawne Alston and other athletes alleged anticompetitive practices by the NCAA in capping their educational benefits. The court case could decide the scope of the NCAA's rule-making authority, although it is not expected to weigh in on what the specific rules should be for college athletes.

The NCAA, spending millions in legal fees each year to fend off athlete lawsuits, has called for federal legislation to override a patchwork of state laws. Meanwhile, the issue has received increased attention with the backdrop of racial-justice issues, as many point out that NCAA rules restrict the earnings of largely Black football and men's basketball players while mostly white head coaches take home high public salaries.

1. What are the ethical issues in this case? What values are involved? What are the arguments on both sides of the issue?
2. Should an organization like the NCAA have so much power? What are the alternatives to this type of authority?
3. If college athletes are allowed to make money off of their sport, how would companies secure group licensing agreements for a video game, for example? What are the issues here?
4. Is federal law a better option for this issue? Who would benefit? Are there other alternatives to resolving these tensions?

Sources: Rachel Bachman and Lane Higgins, "NCAA Faces Reckoning on Pay," *The Wall Street Journal* (March 30, 2021), A1-10; Tommy Beer, "NCAA Athletes Could Make $2 Million a Year if Paid Equitably, Study Suggests," *Forbes* (September 1, 2020), https://www.forbes.com/sites/tommybeer/2020/09/01/ncaa-athletes-could-make-2-million-a-year-if-paid-equitably-study-suggests/?sh=57e2c6d35499, accessed March 31, 2021; Kurt Streeter, "He's the Ideal College Athlete. So Why Did He Quit?" *The New York Times*, (March 29, 2021), accessed March 31, 2021.

special-interest groups (e.g., AARP, Friends of the Earth, American Civil Liberties Union, Consumers Union) and protest groups.

Earlier we raised the question of whether government really represents the public. This question may be stated another way: "Who determines what is in the public interest?" In our pluralistic society, determining the public interest is not a simple matter. While government may be the official representative of the public, we should not assume that representation occurs in a straightforward fashion. As we saw in Figure 17-2, the public takes its own initiatives both with business and with government. The three major groups, therefore, are involved in a dynamic interplay of influence processes that strive to define the current public interest.

A primary concern in this chapter is with government's role in influencing business, and we now turn our attention to that topic. We will begin to see more clearly how government is a major stakeholder of business. Government's official priority is in representing the public interest as it sees and interprets the public's wishes. However, like all large bureaucratic organizations, government also takes on a life of its own with its own goals and agenda.

17.4 Government's Nonregulatory Influence on Business

Broadly speaking, we may categorize the kinds of influence government has on business as *nonregulatory* and *regulatory*. We limit our treatment to the federal government's influence on business, but we must remain mindful of the presence and influence of state, local, and other governments as well. In the next section, we focus on government regulation, but in this section, let us consider the wide range of *nonregulatory* influences that government has on business.

Two major issues merit consideration before we examine some of the specific policy tools or mechanisms government uses to influence business. These two major issues are (1) industrial policy and (2) privatization. Industrial policy is concerned with the role that government plays in shaping the national economy, and privatization focuses on the question of whether current public functions (e.g., public education, public transit, social security, fire service) should be turned over to the private (business) sector for more effective and efficient administration. Both issues have important implications for the business–government relationship.

17.4a Industrial Policy

Industrial policy is "every form of state intervention that affects industry as a distinct part of the economy."[16] Industrial policy has differed over time and across countries in both its philosophy and its actions, but it has generally addressed ailing industries that governments wanted to support.[17] Current examples of this new form of industrial policy abound in the United States today. For example, over the past few years the U.S. government has supported the development and growth of the electric car industry. Similarly, the U.S. federal government also provides grants or tax credits to cover a percentage of the cost of solar installations, benefiting companies like SolarCity, which reported receiving more than $500 million in direct grants from the Treasury Department.[18] This type of industrial policy is not limited to the United States. The European Union, for example, provides subsidies to support various sectors of the energy industry, with the largest amounts going to renewables such as solar, onshore wind, biomass, and hydropower.[19]

The COVID-19 pandemic compelled governments around the world to take an active part in reviving economic growth and restoring financial stability.[20] To do this, governments needed not only to focus on economic reform but also on ways to work together to address public health issues.[21] In sum, while nonregulatory influences continue in industrial policy, economic and safety concerns often swing the pendulum of government intervention toward more regulation.

Government intervention in business continues, sometimes in ways that are appropriate and sometimes not. Various interventions such as "voluntary" restrictions on imports, occasional bailouts for nearly bankrupt companies, and a wide array of subsidies, loan guarantees, and special tax benefits for particular firms and industries constitute an industrial policy by default.[22] And there are significant administrative costs to these programs. For example, we mentioned earlier that SolarCity, one of the Tesla subsidiaries, had received grants from the U.S. government. Several years ago, the government accused SolarCity of overstating the costs of their solar energy systems in order to receive inflated grant payment. SolarCity ended up settling the case and paying $29.5 million in fines.[23] Thus, it is important to think carefully about the role of government in business so that a default industrial policy does not emerge. Industrial policy (whether coordinated or by default) is a powerful nonregulating approach by government to influence business that is certain to be debated for years to come.

17.4b Privatization

Privatization, generally speaking, refers to the process of converting a public organization to private control or ownership.[24] It is the second major, nonregulatory means by which government might influence business. The intent of privatization is to capture both the discipline of the free market and a spirit of entrepreneurial risk-taking.[25] However, it is a highly contested issue, as we discuss below.

The Privatization Debate. Proponents of privatization in both the United States and Europe suggest that the functions of entire bureaucracies need to be contracted out to the private sector. They maintain that government at all levels is involved in thousands of businesses in which it has no real comparative advantage and no basic reason for being involved. They also argue that publicly owned enterprises are less efficient and less flexible than are competitive private firms.[26] Opponents of privatization contend that certain activities cannot be handled safely or effectively by the private sector.[27] For example, many point to the **federalization** of airport security (the return of airport security to the government sector) following the attack on the World Trade Center. The argument for privatization has played out recently in discussions about privatizing the U.S. Postal System, which has been financially unstable for years, in part because of government-approved, pre-funded pension liabilities.[28]

Successful privatization can achieve both financial efficiency and broad social goals. When Argentina privatized its national water system, the results were impressive. Service expanded to reach areas that were previously underserved.[29] Furthermore, far fewer children died from infections and parasitic diseases, and investment in this endeavor soared.[30] Privatization efforts are always undertaken with the hope that they will lead to improvements in efficiency and overall performance. In some cases, these hopes are realized, but in others, they are not. However, differences in post-privatization performance can also result from differences in the ways that firms implement privatization programs. The nature of top management, the functioning of the board, and the strategic actions the firms undertake will all contribute to the likelihood of a privatization strategy's success.[31] This was supported by the findings of a study on the efficiency and effectiveness of privatized urban transit services after 25 years of operation. They found no difference between public and private provision of services and concluded that the situation specifics are better predictors of performance than whether the service was public or private.[32]

The two issues, industrial policy and privatization, continue to be discussed and debated. As we have seen, the success of these efforts is largely dependent on their context—both the environments in which they are adopted and the ways in which they are implemented. Regardless, they both illustrate the nonregulatory influences that government can have on business. We now return to our discussion of the ways in which government uses various policies and mechanisms for influencing business.

17.4c Other Nonregulatory Governmental Influences on Business

Government has a significant impact on business in many ways, including:

- as a major employer
- as a large purchaser of goods and services
- as a source of debt
- as a provider of subsidies and transfer payments
- as a competitor of business
- as an entity that levies taxes
- as a financier linked to monetary policy
- as a persuader of business

We explain these below.

Government has a significant impact on business because it has a large payroll and is a *major employer* itself. At all levels, government employs millions of people who, as a consequence of being government employees, see things from the government's perspective. Government is also in the position of being a standard setter; for example, the eight-hour workday began in the federal government.

Government is one of the largest *purchasers* of goods and services produced in the private sector. The U.S. government awards more than $500 billion in contracts every year.[33] Some key industries, such as aerospace, electronics, and shipbuilding, are dependent on government purchasing. Government can exert significant influence over the private sector by its insistence that minorities be hired, depressed areas be favored, small businesses be favored, and so on. Changes in government policy can dramatically change a firm's business environment. For some firms in narrow markets, such as defense, the government dominates and controls whether or not those firms have a good year—indeed, whether or not they survive at all.[34]

Government influences the behavior of business by using *subsidies* in a variety of ways. Subsidies are made available to industries such as agriculture, fishing, transportation, nuclear energy, and housing and to groups in special categories, such as minority-owned enterprises and businesses in depressed areas. Quite often, these subsidies have special qualifications attached. Government also influences business, albeit indirectly, by virtue of its *transfer payments*. Government provides money for social security, welfare, and other entitlement programs that totals hundreds of billions of dollars every year. These impacts are indirect, but they do significantly affect the market for business's goods and services.[35]

Government also is a major *competitor* of business. The Tennessee Valley Authority (TVA) in the United States competes with private suppliers of electricity, the Government Printing Office competes with private commercial publishers and printing firms, and the U.S. Postal Service competes with private delivery services. In areas such as health, education, recreation, and security, the competition between government and private firms crosses federal, state, and local levels.

Government loans and *loan guarantees* are sources of influence as well. Government lends money directly to small businesses, housing providers, farmers, and energy companies. Often such loans are made at lower interest rates than those of private competitors. During the COVID-19 pandemic, many governments provided relief loan packages to small businesses and nonprofit organizations experiencing temporary losses of revenue.

Taxation is another example of a nonregulatory government influence. Tax deductibility, tax incentives, depreciation policies, and tax credits are tools that are all at the disposal of the government. International tax policy can increase or decrease competitiveness for business. It can make a country more attractive, relative to other countries, as a site for new investment and new jobs.

For many years a controversial issue in the United States was that of "tax inversions," where U.S.-operating companies could choose to re-incorporate in another country like Ireland where corporate tax rates were lower. The United States is one of the few countries in the world where U.S.-domiciled companies must pay taxes on all their global income—not just the income earned in the United States. Hence, a tax inversion is a strategy companies employed to reduce their tax burden. Over the past few years, the practice has been less prevalent, particularly with 2017 legislation that cut U.S. corporate tax rates.[36] However, as we noted above, the relationship between business and government is volatile and political. Should corporate taxes rise again, tax inversions may once again be popular.

Monetary policy can have a profound effect on business. In the United States, the Federal Reserve System is independent of the executive branch; however, it often responds to presidential leadership or initiatives. Hence, there are concerns of increasing government influence over the Federal Reserve in areas of balance sheet and financial market operations and, particularly, interest rate setting, which affects business. Many have called for pressures—either setting the rates lower when elections are coming up or setting the rates higher as part of partisan politics.[37]

Finally, *moral suasion* is a tool of government. This refers to the government's attempts to "persuade" business to act in the public interest by taking or not taking a particular course of action. These public interest appeals might include a request to roll back a price hike, show restraint on wage and salary increases, or exercise "voluntary" restraints of one kind or another. For example, the U.S. Education Department Office for Civil Rights uses

moral suasion through "Dear Colleague" letters to education leaders on topics. In 2021, they issued a letter on preventing and addressing potential discrimination associated with COVID-19 and the bullying of students perceived to be of Asian descent.[38] Moral suasion tactics are often controversial, with some believing that they become like "bullying," particularly when they are framed under some authority.[39]

17.5 Government's Regulatory Influences on Business

In many ways, government regulation has been the most controversial issue in the business–government relationship. Government regulation has affected virtually every aspect of how business functions. It has affected the terms and conditions under which firms have competed in their respective industries. It has touched almost every business decision ranging from the production of goods and services to packaging, distribution, marketing, and service. Most people agree that some degree of regulation has been necessary to ensure that consumers and employees are treated fairly and are not exposed to unreasonable hazards and that the environment is protected. However, many also think that government regulation has often been too extensive in scope, too costly, and inevitably burdensome in terms of paperwork requirements and red tape. One thing is clear: the level of regulation continues to rise.

The annual page count in the *Federal Register* is an imperfect measure of regulatory intensity, but the overall upward trend tells us something about the nature of government and business in the United States. The *Federal Register* celebrated its 90th birthday in 2016. In 1936, it contained 2,620 pages; by 2020, the page count had grown to 70,000 pages.[40] The page count seems to stay high irrespective of the party in office. The highest count was 83,294 in 2010 at the end of the Clinton presidency.

17.5a Regulation: What Does It Mean?

Generally, **regulation** refers to the act of governing, directing according to rule, or bringing under the control of law or constituted authority. Although there is no universally agreed-on definition of federal regulation, a federal regulatory agency is generally described in the *Federal Register* as one that:[41]

1. Has decision-making authority.
2. Establishes standards or guidelines conferring benefits and imposing restrictions on business conduct.
3. Operates principally in the sphere of domestic business activity.
4. Has its head and/or members appointed by the president (generally subject to Senate confirmation).
5. Has its legal procedures generally governed by the Administrative Procedures Act.

The commerce clause of the U.S. Constitution grants to the government the legal authority to regulate. Within the confines of a regulatory agency as outlined here, the composition and functioning of regulatory agencies differ. Some are headed by an administrator and are located within an executive department—for example, the Federal Aviation Administration (FAA). Others are independent commissions composed of a chairperson and several members located outside the executive and legislative branches, such as the Interstate Commerce Commission (ICC), the Federal Communications Commission (FCC), and the Securities and Exchange Commission (SEC).[42]

17.5b Reasons for Regulation

Regulations have come about over the years for a variety of reasons. Some managers probably think that government is just looking for reasons to impose upon their business. There are several legitimate reasons why government regulation has evolved, although these same businesspeople may not entirely agree with them. For the most part, government regulation has arisen because **market failure** (failure of the free enterprise system) has occurred and government, intending to represent the public interest, has chosen to take corrective action. We should make it clear, however, that many regulations resulted from special-interest groups lobbying successfully for them. Four major reasons or justifications for regulations are typically offered: (1) controlling natural monopolies, (2) controlling negative externalities, (3) achieving social goals, and (4) other reasons.

Controlling Natural Monopolies. One of the earliest circumstances in which government felt a need to regulate occurred when a natural monopoly existed. A **natural monopoly** exists in a market where the economies of scale are so great that the largest firm has the lowest costs and thus is able to drive out its competitors. Such a firm can supply the entire market more efficiently and cheaply than can several smaller firms. Local electrical service and sewer services are an example, because parallel suppliers would involve waste, duplication, and cost. Monopolies such as this may seem "natural," but when left to their own devices they could restrict output and raise prices. This potential abuse justifies the regulation of monopolies. Therefore, we see public utilities, for example, regulated by a public utility commission. This commission determines the rates that the monopolist may charge its customers.

Related to the control of natural monopolies is the government's desire to intervene when it thinks companies have engaged in anticompetitive practices, often called "antitrust" cases that are in violation of the Sherman Antitrust Act. Many of these circumstances arise when companies vertically integrate and make their companies dependent on them, or when there has been considerable consolidation in an industry, sparking concerns over limiting competition.

U.S. technology companies have faced a mountain of antitrust litigation in recent years both in the United States and abroad following increasing industry consolidation. Concerns largely surround big platforms' market power and their ability to restrain competition. The Big Four tech giants—Google, Facebook, Amazon, and Apple—have all faced potential or actual antitrust cases.[43] Google has been targeted for its online search dominance and digital advertising monopoly that creates an unfair advantage over publishers and rivals. Facebook has engaged in a pattern of acquisitions (e.g., Instagram, WhatsApp) that cause regulators to question if they are buying start-ups to kill emerging rivals, which is illegal. Additionally, in 2019, the United States levied a record $5 billion fine against Facebook for privacy violations, leading regulators to question whether they acquired monopoly power through deceptive promises about privacy. Amazon has been targeted for squeezing suppliers, removing some vendors from its site, and harming rival sellers. Apple has been accused of using its platform for iPhone apps to favor its own products, hurting other rivals' offerings, including music streaming services such as Spotify.[44]

All in all, despite tech giants' claims that such litigation hurts their ability to innovate, many governments are increasingly scrutinizing these tech companies and considering stricter rules and more regulation. In fact, after Twitter was fined 450,000 euros for breaking the European Union's (EU's) data privacy laws, the EU and British authorities released another set of draft laws to improve competition.[45]

Controlling Negative Externalities. Another important rationale for government regulation is that of controlling the negative externalities (or spillover effects) that result when the manufacture or use of a product gives rise to unplanned or unintended side effects on third parties (the producer and the consumer are first and second parties). As we noted in Chapter 4, examples of these negative externalities include air pollution, water pollution, and improper disposal of toxic wastes. The consequence of such negative externalities is that neither the producer nor the consumer of the product directly "pays" for all the "costs" that are created by the manufacture of the product. The "costs" that must be borne by the public include an unpleasant or a foul atmosphere, illness, and the resulting health-care costs. These also have been called social costs, because they are absorbed by society rather than incorporated into the cost of making the product.

Preventing negative externalities is enormously expensive, and few firms are willing to pay for these added costs voluntarily. Additionally, externalities often create value conflicts. This may be seen when considering the issues of data privacy that confront the digital communities. Providing privacy protection comes with trade-offs, which became highlighted during the COVID-19 pandemic. Apple and Google developed software for a contact tracing system to assist with the identification of individuals and populations that had been in contact with the virus. However, restrictions on privacy prevented the tool from being as effective it could be.[46] In such situations, therefore, industry incumbents may even welcome government regulation because it requires all firms competing in a given industry to operate according to the same rules. Additionally, by forcing all firms to incur the costs, regulation can level the competitive playing field.

Just as companies do not voluntarily take on extra expenditures for environmental protection, individuals often behave in the same fashion. For example, automobile emissions are one of the principal forms of air pollution, but how many private individuals would voluntarily request an emissions control system if it were offered as optional equipment? In situations such as this, a government standard that requires everyone to adhere to the regulation is much more likely to address the public's concern for air pollution.[47]

Achieving Social Goals. Government not only employs regulations to address market failures and negative externalities but also seeks to use regulations to help achieve certain social goals it deems to be in the public interest. Some of these social goals are related to negative externalities in the sense that government is attempting to correct problems that might also be viewed as negative externalities by particular groups. An example of this might be the harmful effects of a dangerous product or the unfair treatment of minorities resulting from employment discrimination. These externalities are not as obvious as air pollution, but they are just as real.

Another important social goal of government is to keep people informed. One could argue that inadequate

information is a serious problem and that government should use its regulatory powers to require firms to reveal certain kinds of information to consumers. Thus, the Consumer Product Safety Commission requires firms to warn consumers of potential product hazards through labeling requirements. Other regulatory mandates that address the issue of inadequate information include grading standards, weight and size information, truth-in-advertising requirements, and product safety standards.

Other important social goals that have been addressed include preservation of national security (deregulation of oil prices to lessen dependence on imports), considerations of fairness or equity (employment discrimination laws), protection of those who provide essential services (farmers), allocation of scarce resources (gasoline rationing), and protection of consumers from excessively high price increases (natural gas regulation).[48]

17.5c Types of Regulation

Broadly speaking, government regulations address two basic types of goals, economic and social; therefore, it has become customary to identify two different types of regulation: economic regulation and social regulation.

Economic Regulation. The classical or traditional form of regulation is economic regulation. This type of regulation is best exemplified by old-line regulatory bodies in the United States such as the Interstate Commerce Commission (ICC), which was created in 1887 by Congress to regulate the railroad industry; the Civil Aeronautics Board (CAB), which was created in 1940; and the Federal Communications Commission (FCC), which was established in 1934 to consolidate federal regulation of interstate communications and, later, the radio, telephone, and telegraph. These regulatory bodies divide along industry lines: They regulate business behavior through the controlling and influencing economic or market variables such as prices (maximum and minimum), entry to and exit from markets, and types of services offered.[49]

Public support for economic regulation has varied over the years. For example, according to a Pew Research Center survey, economic concerns were at the top of the public's agenda in 2021 after declining in relative importance in prior years.[50] This is logical, given that the COVID-19 pandemic stopped the U.S. economy in its tracks, as well as negatively impacted the global economy.[51]

Later we discuss deregulation, a trend that has significantly affected the old-line form of economic regulation that dominated business–government relations in the last century.

Social Regulation. The 1960s ushered in a new form of regulation that has come to be known as social regulation, because its major thrust is the furtherance of societal objectives quite different from the earlier focus on markets and economic variables. While economic regulation focuses on

Ethics In Practice Case

The Regulatory Dilemma Regarding Marijuana

In the United States in 1996, California's voters legalized the sale of marijuana for medical use. Since then, 40 more states and territories have done the same; however, it not yet approved on the federal level. This provides a dilemma for businesses in those states that regularly test employees for substance abuse. In *Coats v. Dish Network*, a Colorado employee who is quadriplegic and used medical marijuana outside of working hours sued for wrongful termination of his job after he tested positive for marijuana. The confusing legal landscape led to his claim that Colorado labor laws (i.e., state laws) deemed his use of marijuana legal and thus his termination illegal. The Colorado Supreme Court ruled against Mr. Coats, however, because Mr. Coats broke the law by using a product that is illegal under the federal Controlled Substances Act.

This case highlights the confusing and complex issues of drug policy and law in the United States. Contradictions between state and federal statutes also cross over to the sales of recreational marijuana. By early 2021, 15 states, plus Washington D.C., had legalized marijuana for recreational use for adults over the age of 21. Proponents for the legalization of marijuana at the federal level note that regulated markets protect consumers, raise revenues, reduce the costs of enforcement, promote fairness, and put criminals out of business. Arguments against the federal legalization of marijuana capture those from the states who have historically opposed it: the public-health effects of marijuana, the increased tax burden, the danger of cannabis "edibles" with young children, and its potentially addictive nature.

The legalization of marijuana has been more of a debate in the United States than in other countries, particularly because of the contradictions between state and federal laws. Much of Europe has embraced the sale of medical marijuana, as has Australia. France, however, has some of the harshest cannabis laws in Europe. Jamaica has legalized "ganja" for broadly defined religious purposes, and Spain allows users to grow and buy it through small collectives. Canada legalized marijuana for recreational use in 2019, with many viewing it as a step toward building a fairer justice system for black and indigenous Canadians who were often caught up in the criminal system, beginning with minor cannabis possession charges.

1. What are the ethical issues in this case? Who are the stakeholders, and what are their stakes?
2. How are the two issues different—the legalization of marijuana for medical use versus the legalization of marijuana for recreational use?
3. U.S. state versus federal law makes this issue particularly complex. What are other examples of industries where U.S. state and federal law are seemingly at odds?
4. What actions should the federal government take to help resolve this conflict between federal and state laws?

Sources: "Reefer Regulatory Challenge," *The Economist* (February 13, 2016), 18; Ian Austen, "2 Years After Legalizing Cannabis, Has Canada Kept Its Promises?," *The New York Times* (January 23, 2021), https://www.nytimes.com/2021/01/23/world /canada/marijuana-legalization-promises-made.html, accessed March 31, 2021; Alex Ledsom, "Is France Moving Towards A Legalization of Cannabis?" *Forbes* (January 19, 2021), https:// www.forbes.com/sites/alexledsom/2021/01/19/is-france-moving -towards-a-legalization-of-cannabis/?sh=62e44a8275cb, accessed March 30, 2021.

---

markets, social regulation focuses on business's impacts on people. This emphasis on people addresses the needs of people in their roles as employees, consumers, and citizens.

Social regulations include regulating ESG reporting, providing rules and enforcement about climate change, promoting cybersecurity, regulating data privacy issues, and standardizing reporting on diversity and inclusion in the workforce.[52] Generally speaking, social regulations govern product dangers, safety and health laws, employment conditions, pollution laws, and so on. In fact, amid a general climate of distrust with the U.S. government, a 2020 Pew research survey found that over 50 percent of respondents thought that the federal government was doing well in the following social areas[53]:

- Responding to natural disasters
- Keeping the country safe from terrorism
- Ensuring safe food and medicine
- Maintaining infrastructure

However, the survey also noted that less than 50 percent of respondents felt good about ensuring access to health care, protecting the environment, handling threats to public health, helping people get out of poverty, and managing the immigration system.[54]

Figure 17-3 summarizes the nature of economic versus social regulations along with pertinent examples. While economic regulation aims primarily at companies competing in specific industries, the social regulation tends to addresses business practices affecting all industries. However, there are social regulations that are industry specific, such as the National Highway Traffic Safety Administration (automobiles) and the Food and Drug Administration (food, drugs, medical devices, and cosmetics). We note the current trend of **reregulation**—the process of imposing regulations and restrictions on an industry or area that was previously deregulated. For example, following the election of U.S. President Joe Biden, the *Columbia University Earth Institute* began tracking "Climate Reregulation," by looking at the measures taken by the Biden-Harris administration to reinstate federal climate mitigation and adaptation measures that were rolled or eliminated in the preceding four years under the Trump administration.[55]

Figure 17-3 Comparison of Economic and Social Regulations

	Economic Regulations	Social Regulations
Focus	Market conditions, economic variables (entry, exit, prices, services)	People in their roles as employees, consumers, and citizens
Industries affected	Selected (railroads, aeronautics, communications)	Virtually all industries
Examples	Civil Aeronautics Board (CAB)	Equal Employment Opportunity Commission (EEOC)
	Federal Communications Commission (FCC)	Occupational Safety and Health Administration (OSHA)
	Federal Trade Commission (FTC)	Consumer Product Safety Commission (CPSC)
		Environmental Protection Agency (EPA)
Current trend	Reregulation (e.g., Financial Stability Oversight Board)	Reregulation (e.g., Paris Climate Agreement)

17.5d Issues Related to Regulation

It is important to consider some of the issues that have arisen out of the increased governmental role in regulating business. In general, managers have been concerned with what might be called "regulatory unreasonableness."[56] We could expect that business would just as soon not have to deal with these regulatory bodies; therefore, some of business's reactions are simply related to the nuisance factor of having to deal with a complex array of restrictions. Small businesses, moreover, are hit hard by unreasonable and costly regulations. However, other legitimate issues that have arisen over the past few years also need to be addressed.

Ethics In Practice Case

To Mask or Not to Mask? COVID-19 Mandates

The COVID-19 pandemic brought a host of new issues for business/government relationships. The highly contagious virus spread more easily than the flu and caused more serious illnesses than had been seen since the flu epidemic in 1918. Health measures such as universal mask wearing, social distancing, good ventilation, and hand hygiene were promoted by scientists during the COVID-19 pandemic, but exactly how to enforce these was difficult for businesses to navigate. Public reactions to mask requirements ranged from full compliance to blatant defiance when mask-wearing became increasingly mandatory in public places like stores and public transit. Anti-mask protest rallies took place throughout the world, even as medical experts pointed to the efficacy of mask-wearing in stopping the spread of the virus.

Many protested that the threat of COVID-19 had been exaggerated. Some pointed to early communication from the World Health Organization (WHO), the Centers for Disease Control and Prevention (CDC), and other health organizations that masks were ineffective and caused people to touch their faces, thereby increasing their chances of infection. Others pointed to the high variability across states and businesses about where and when masks might or might not be required. Business employees and managers were increasingly confused and tired of the backlash from those who either supported or defied the use of masks. As noted by one restaurant owner who was reluctant to go mask-less when the state of Texas dropped COVID-related restrictions after nine months of a mask mandate,

"I already get screamed at when people don't want to wear their mask.... If that happens with the mandate how am I going to manage without it?"

1. What are the issues in the case? Who are the stakeholders involved?
2. How might public health issues be different from other issues when it comes to business/government relations?
3. As governments around the world began to vaccinate individuals toward herd immunity, some businesses, colleges, and universities decided to require COVID-19 vaccinations for those returning to offices and campuses. Do you agree with this mandate? What are the ethics issues here?

Sources: Centers for Disease Control and Prevention, "Workplace Vaccination Program" (March 25, 2021, https://www.cdc.gov /coronavirus/2019-ncov/vaccines/recommendations /essentialworker/workplace-vaccination-program.html, accessed April 3, 2021; Sharon Terlep, "Starbucks, Target Among Companies to Still Mandate Masks in Texas Despite Lift on COVID-19 Restrictions," *The Wall Street Journal* (March 3, 2021), https://www.wsj.com/articles/starbucks-target-among -companies-to-still-mandate-masks-in-texas-despite-lift-on -covid-19-restrictions-11614800113, accessed April 3, 2021; Steven Taylor and Gordon J. G. Asmundson, "Negative Attitudes about Facemasks during the COVID-19 Pandemic," medRxiv (November 17, 2020), https://www.medrxiv.org /content/10.1101/2020.11.17.20233585v1.full, accessed April 3, 2021.

To be certain, there are benefits of government regulations. Businesses treat employees more fairly and provide them with safer work environments. Consumers are able to purchase safer products and receive more information about them. Citizens from all lifestyles have cleaner air to breathe and cleaner water in lakes and rivers. These benefits are real, but their exact magnitudes are difficult to measure. Costs resulting from regulation also are difficult to measure. For example, the costs of complying with COVID-19 regulations were substantial for businesses, ranging from following regulatory alerts that averaged 217 updates a day, to increasing their compliance teams and their budgets.[57]

The **direct costs** of regulation are most visible when we look at aggregate expenditures and growth patterns of the budgets of federal agencies responsible for regulation. Figure 17-4 shows the rise in spending for both economic and social regulation over the last 60 years in millions of constant year 2000 dollars.

In addition to the direct costs of administering the regulatory agencies, there are **indirect costs** such as forms, reports, and questionnaires that business must complete to satisfy the requirements of the regulatory agencies. Businesses call them "red tape." These indirect costs of government regulation are passed on to the consumer in the form of higher prices. There are also **induced costs**. The induced effects of regulation are diffuse and elusive, but they constitute some of the most powerful consequences of the regulatory process. In actuality, then, these induced effects are also costs. Three induced effects are worthy of elaboration.[58]

1. *Innovation may be affected.* To the extent that firms must devote more of their scientific resources to meeting government requirements, fewer resources are available to dedicate to new product and process research and development and innovation. However, the relationship is anything but clear. A study showed that deregulation actually had a dramatic negative impact on public interest environmental research by public utilities, whereas regulation can have a positive impact on pollution abatement research by profit maximizing firms.[59] The moral of these findings seems to be that organizations will pursue their own interests.

2. *New investments in plant and equipment may be affected.* To the extent that corporate resources must be used for regulatory compliance purposes, these funds are diverted from uses that are more productive. Environmental and job safety requirements lessen productivity and uncertainty about future regulations and diminish motivation for introducing new products and processes.[60] Once again, the incentives will play a major part. Investments that aid the firms in complying with regulations are likely to be continued or increased, whereas those that are beyond the scope of the regulation are likely to diminish.

3. *Small business may be adversely affected.* Although it is not intentional, federal regulations often have a disproportionately adverse effect on small firms because of economies of scale. Large firms have more money, personnel, and resources with which to get the work of government done than do small firms. They can spread the costs over a larger base, whereas small companies can find their resources drained from their efforts to comply.

Robert Reich's advice to executives who feel the government is *breathing* down their necks has been, "Get used to it."[61] That advice is true today, as companies worldwide will be dealing with regulatory concerns for the foreseeable

Figure 17-4 Regulatory Spending in the United States

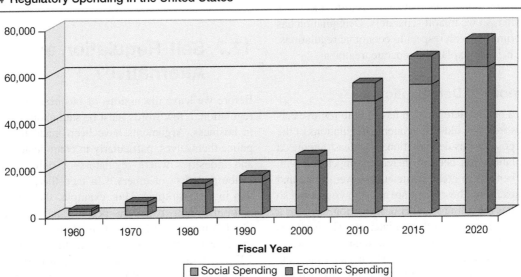

Source: Mark Febrizio and Melinda Warren, "Regulators' Budget: Overall Spending and Staffing Remain Stable," George Washington University Regulatory Studies Center. https://regulatorystudies.columbian.gwu.edu/regulators-budget-overall-spending-and-staffing-remain-stable, accessed April 1, 2021.

future. In financial services, governments in the United States, Europe, and Japan now hold equity in banks. In housing, the U.S. government has taken over a large portion of outstanding mortgage loans. In the auto industry, the United States, Canada, Germany, Sweden, and Japan provided tens of billions of dollars in loans and equity. The United States, Europe, and Japan are all subsidizing non-carbon-based energy development. The United States is enacting health-care reforms that will affect both the health-care and pharmaceutical industries, and it is investing in greater broadband coverage that will affect the telecom industry.

17.6 Deregulation

Quite frequently, trends and countertrends overlap with one another. Such is the case with regulation and its counterpart, **deregulation**. From an economic perspective, a continual striving for the balance of freedom and control for business will be best for society. From a political perspective, there is an ongoing interplay of different societal goals and means for achieving those goals. The outcome is a mix of economic and political decisions that seem to be in a constant state of flux. Thus, in the economy at any point in time, trends that appear counter to one another can coexist. These trends are the natural result of competing forces seeking some sort of balance or equilibrium.

This explains how the trend toward deregulation has evolved in a highly regulated environment. Deregulation represents a counterforce aimed at keeping the economy in balance. It also represents a political philosophy that prevailed during the period of its origin and growth. Depending on the political party in office, support for deregulation comes and goes.

Deregulation is one kind of regulatory reform. It is unique and quite unlike the regulatory reform measures discussed earlier, so we treat it separately. Deregulation has taken place primarily with respect to economic regulations, and this, too, helps to explain its separate treatment.

17.6a Purpose of Deregulation

The basic idea behind deregulation has been to remove certain industries from the old-line economic regulations of the past. The purpose of this deregulation, or at least a reduced level of regulation, has been to increase competition with the expected benefits of greater efficiency, lower prices, and enhanced innovation. These goals are not always met and so debate continues regarding whether deregulation works as a method of maximizing society's best interests. The positives of deregulation include that it allows more innovation while allowing the free market to set prices. The negatives include that it can allow asset bubbles to build and burst (like a housing crisis) and industries that have large initial infrastructure costs may have a difficult time getting started.[62]

17.6b The Changing World of Deregulation

A trend toward deregulation began in the 1980s, most notably exemplified in the financial industry, the telecommunications industry, and the transportation (trucking, airline, railroad) industry, and represented business's first major redirection in 50 years.[63] The result seemed to be a mixed bag of benefits and problems. On the benefits side, prices fell in many industries, and better service appeared in some industries along with increased numbers of competitors and innovative products and services.

Several problems arose also. Although prices fell and many competitors entered some of those industries, more of those competitors were unable to compete with the dominant firms. They were failing, going bankrupt, or being absorbed by the larger firms. Entry barriers into some industries were enormous and had been greatly underestimated. Most dramatically, deregulation in the repeal of the Depression-era Glass–Steagall Act has been accused of causing the global recession that began in 2008.[64]

Deregulation was a key feature of the Trump administration in the United States from 2016–2020, coupled with tax cuts and trade reform. In the three years to 2019 the administration said it eliminated $51 billion of regulatory costs.[65] Key areas included the deregulation of the entry of generic drugs to the market, financial deregulation including raising the threshold above which banks must carry out "stress tests," and lifting or weakening certain environmental regulations including oil, natural gas, and extraction bans.[66]

The dilemma with deregulation is how to enhance the competitive nature of the affected industries without sacrificing the applicable social regulations, that is, to allow for freer competition without lowering health and safety requirements. Unfortunately, the dog-eat-dog competition unleashed by economic deregulation can force many companies to cut corners in ways that endanger the health, safety, and/or welfare of their customers.

17.7 Self-Regulation as an Alternative?

Before we leave discussions of business, government, and regulation, a few words must be said about **self-regulation** in business. Arguments have been made to let industries police themselves, particularly in complicated technologies and industries where regulators or policymakers default to the expertise of others.[67] In fact, there is precedent for this in the workplace. For example, the Federal Aviation Administration routinely permits airline manufacturers like Boeing to certify that their products are safe. This led to some terrible consequences in the crash of two of its 737 Max jetliners.[68] The National Highway Traffic and Safety Administration (NHTSA) also came under fire when a former Navy SEAL died when his Tesla Model S on autopilot drove under a semi-trailer crossing a Florida highway. Until that accident, the NHTSA had taken a hands-off approach to regulating autonomous vehicle technology.[69] However, self-regulation might make sense when agency inspectors cannot keep pace with rapid technological advances and/or standards might be developed by industry trade groups that stay current with technologies and trends.

Self-regulation has also been suggested for industries that are at risk for government regulation, like social media companies, television, movies, and video games that have been targeted for publishing socially harmful content.[70] Taking a proactive approach, self-regulation in developing standards around content can help companies avoid some of the costs associated with impending regulation, while also showing society that they care about limiting things like violent, profane, or sexual content and curbing inappropriate or harmful activities. In short, self-regulation is a lot like companies and industries pursuing highly ethical decisions and strategies.

Summary

Any discussion of business and society must consider the paramount role played by government. Although the two institutions have opposing systems of belief, they interconnect in their functioning in our socioeconomic system. In addition, the public assumes a major role in a complex pattern of interactions among business, government, and the public. Government exerts a host of nonregulatory influences on business. Two influences include industrial policy and privatization. A more specific influence is the fact that government is a major employer, purchaser, subsidizer, competitor, financier, and persuader. These roles permit government to affect business significantly.

One of government's most controversial interventions in business is direct regulation. Government regulates business for several legitimate reasons, including controlling natural monopolies, controlling negative externalities, and achieving social goals. Social regulation continues to grow and is more dominant than economic regulation. Social regulations apply across all industries and often focus on important issues such as employee safety and well-being and product safety. Creating fairness in the business and stakeholder relationship is an important objective of social regulation. There are many benefits and various costs of government regulation. One response to the problems with regulation has been deregulation. However, bad or mixed experiences in key industries such as trucking, airlines, telecommunication, financial services, and utilities have led to some reregulation and caused many to wonder what the optimal mix of regulation and deregulation should be. Finally, self-regulation is an alternative that businesses should consider because this approach is consistent with the pursuit of higher ethical standards.

Key Terms

collectivistic ethic of government, p. 386
deregulation, p. 395
direct costs, p. 395
economic regulation, p. 392
federalization, p. 389
indirect costs, p. 395

individualistic ethic of business, p. 386
induced costs, p. 395
industrial policy, p. 388
market failure, p. 391
natural monopoly, p. 391
negative externalities, p. 392
privatization, p. 388

regulation, p. 391
reregulation, p. 393
self-regulation, p. 396
social costs, p. 392
social goals, p. 392
social regulation, p. 392

Discussion Questions

1. Briefly explain how business and government represent a clash of ethical systems (belief systems). With which do you find yourself identifying most? Explain. With which would most business students identify? Explain.

2. Explain why the public is treated as a separate group in the interactions among business, government, and the public. Doesn't government represent the public's interests? How should the public's interests be manifested?

3. What is regulation? Why does government see a need to regulate? Differentiate between economic and social regulation. What social regulations do you think are most important, and why? What social regulations ought to be eliminated? Explain.

4. Outline the major benefits and costs of government regulation. In general, do you think the benefits of government regulation exceed the costs? In what areas, if any, do you think the costs exceed the benefits?

5. What are the trade-offs between privatization and federalization? When would one or the other be more appropriate? What problems might you foresee and what future events would merit a shift in the current mix?

6. What are deregulation and reregulation? Under what circumstances should each be considered? When might self-regulation be considered for business?

Endnotes

1. See Kevin Carty, "Tech Giants Are the Robber Barons of Our Time," *The New York Post* (February 3, 2018), https://nypost.com/2018/02/03/big-techs-monopolistic-rule-is-hiding-in-plain-sight/. Accessed March 23, 2021; Philip Coggan, "A World of Robber Barons," *The Economist* (Vol. 410, No. 8875, February 22, 2014).

2. Megan Brenan, "Views of Big Tech Worsen; Public Wants More Regulation," Gallup (February 18, 2021), https://news.gallup.com/poll/329666/views-big-tech-worsen-public-wants-regulation.aspx. Accessed March 23, 2021.

3. See Cass R. Sunstein, "A Quiet Revolution Has Given the U.S. Smarter Regulations," *The Wall Street Journal* (October 22, 2018), A19; Dimitra Kessenides, "The Problem with Self-Regulation," *Bloomberg Businessweek* (April 1, 2019), 16–17; "There's a Brawl Coming Over Government Regulation," *The Washington Post* (January 12, 2020), https://www.washingtonpost.com/opinions/theres-a-brawl-coming-over-government-regulation/2020/01/12/5328e798-33e4-11ea-91fd-82d4e04a3fac_story.html. Accessed March 23, 2021.

4. See Coggan, 2014; *International Monetary Fund*, https://www.imf.org/en/Home. Accessed March 23, 2021.

5. Tom Fairless and Stella Yifan Xie, "More Western Nations Adopt State Support of Businesses," *The Wall Street Journal* (November 6, 2020), A10.

6. "Starting Over Again: The COVID-19 Pandemic Is Forcing a Rethink in Macroeconomics," *The Economist* (July 25, 2020), https://www.economist.com/briefing/2020/07/25/the-covid-19-pandemic-is-forcing-a-rethink-in-macroeconomics. Accessed March 25, 2021.

7. SCORE.org, "Infographic: How Do Small Business Owners Feel about Minimum Wage Increases?" *SCORE* (December 11, 2019), https://www.score.org/resource/infographic-how-do-small-business-owners-feel-about-minimum-wage-increases. Accessed March 23, 2021.

8. Kayla Tausche, Stephanie Dhue, and Emma Newburger, "American Petroleum Institute Endorses Carbon Pricing," *CNBC* (March 25, 2021), https://www.cnbc.com/2021/03/25/climate-change-american-petroleum-institute-endorses-carbon-pricing.html. Accessed March 26, 2021.

9. "Semiconductor Industry Applauds NDAA Enactment," *Semiconductor Industry Association* (January 1, 2021), https://www.semiconductors.org/semiconductor-industry-applauds-ndaa-enactment-urges-full-funding-for-semiconductor-manufacturing-and-research-provisions/. Accessed March 28, 2021.

10. L. Earle Birdsell, "Business and Government: The Walls Between," in Neil H. Jacoby (ed.), *The Business—Government Relationship: A Reassessment* (Santa Monica, CA: Goodyear, 1975), 32–34.

11. Nancy Killefer, "The New Business of Government," *McKinsey Quarterly* (Issue 3, 2009), 7.

12. James Smith, "Poll Finds Strong Bipartisan Support for Rights, and Concern that Rights Are Under Threat," Harvard Kennedy School (September 14, 2020), https://www.hks.harvard.edu/faculty-research/policy-topics/human-rights/poll-finds-strong-bipartisan-support-rights-and-concern. Accessed March 27, 2021.

13. Emily Glazer, "Companies Get Ready for New ESG Rules," *The Wall Street Journal* (January 19, 2021), R9.

14. See Robert D. Putnam and Shaylyn Romney Garrett, "The Power of 'We'," *Time* (December 14, 2020), 36; "Should the Government Intervene with Free Market and Save Failing Businesses?," *Debate.org*, http://www.debate.org/opinions/should-the-government-intervene-with-the-free-market-and-save-failing-businesses. Accessed March 22, 2021.

15. Jane Chung, "Big Tech, Big Cash: Washington's New Power Players," *Public Citizen* (March 24, 2021), https://www.citizen.org/article/big-tech-lobbying-update/. Accessed March 31, 2021.

16. James Foreman-Peck and Giovanni Frederico, *European Industrial Policy: The Twentieth-Century Experience* (Oxford University Press, 1999).

17. Karl Aiginger, "Industrial Policy: A Dying Breed or a Reemerging Phoenix?" *Journal of Industry, Competition & Trade* (December 2007), 297–323.

18. Jerry Hirsch, "Elon Musk's Growing Empire Is Fueled by $4.9 Billion in Government Subsidies," *The Los Angeles Times* (May 30, 2015), http://www.latimes.com/business/la-fi-hy-musk-subsidies-20150531-story.html. Accessed March 31, 2021.

19. European Commission Interim Report on Energy Costs and Subsidies for EU28 across Power Generation Technologies (October 13, 2014), European Commission Press Release, http://europa.eu/rapid/press-release_IP-14-1131_en.htm. Accessed March 31, 2021.

20. Emily Barone, "How the New COVID-19 Pandemic Relief Bill Stacks Up to Other Countries," *Time* (December 21, 2020), https://time.com/5923840/us-pandemic-relief-bill-december/. Accessed March 25, 2021.

21. Ibid.

22. Anshu Siripurapu, "Is Industrial Policy Making a Comeback?" *Council on Foreign Relations* (March 16, 2021), https://www.cfr.org/backgrounder/industrial-policy-making-comeback. Accessed April 2, 2021.

23. Ben Lane, "SolarCity Agrees to Pay $29.5 million to Settle Allegations of Lying to the Government," HousingWire (September 22, 2017), https://www.housingwire.com/articles/41370-solarcity-agrees-to-pay-295-million-to-settle-allegations-of-lying-to-government/. Accessed March 30, 2021.

24. http://www.merriam-webster.com/dictionary/privatize. Accessed March 31, 2021.

25. Shaker A. Zahra, R. Duane Ireland, Isabel Gutierrez, and Michael A. Hitt, "Privatization and Entrepreneurial Transformation: Emerging Issues and a Future Research Agenda," *Academy of Management Review* (July 2000), 509–524.

26. Michael Lewis, "What Is Privatization of Public Services – Definition, Pros & Cons," Money Crashers (2021), https://www.moneycrashers.com/privatization-definition-public-works/. Accessed April 2, 2021.

27. Ibid.

28. See Nicole Goodkind, "USPS Could Privatize as Early as Next Year," *Fortune* (December 27, 2019), https://fortune.com/2019/12/27/usps-privatization-postal-service-going-private/. Accessed March 30, 2021; Erik Sherman, "7 Reasons Why Privatizing the Postal System Is Ridiculous and Foolish," *Forbes* (August 7, 2020), https://www.forbes.com/sites/eriksherman/2020/08/17/7-reasons-privatizing-postal-system-usps/?sh=3dceb03b5303. Accessed March 29, 2021.

29. Eduardo Porter, "When Public Outperforms Private in Services," *The New York Times* (January 15, 2013), http://www.nytimes.com/2013/01/16/business/when-privatization-works-and-why-it-doesnt-always.html. Accessed March 30, 2016.

30. Ibid.

31. Alvaro Cuervo and Bélen Villalonga, "Explaining the Variance in the Performance Effects of Privatization," *Academy of Management Review* (July 2000), 581–590.

32. Suzanne Leland and Olga Smirnova, "Reassessing Privatization Strategies 25 Years Later: Revisiting Perry and Babitsky's Comparative Performance Study of Urban Bus Transit Services," *Public Administration Review* (September/October 2009), 855–867.

33. U.S. Small Business Administration, "How to Do Business with the Federal Government," *SBA* (February 3, 2020), https://content.govdelivery.com/accounts/USSBA/bulletins/27934ad. Accessed April 1, 2021.

34. Murray L. Weidenbaum, *Business, Government and the Public*, 3d ed. (Englewood Cliffs, NJ: Prentice Hall, 1986), 5–6.

35. Ibid., 6–8.

36. Tom Giovanetti, "Whatever Happened to Corporate Inversions?" The Institute for Policy Innovation (August 12, 2020), https://www.ipi.org/ipi_issues/detail/whatever-happened-to-corporate-inversions. Accessed March 31, 2021.

37. "Why Giving Politicians Influence over Monetary Policy Is a Bad Idea," *The Economist* (March 10, 2016), http://www.economist.com/blogs/economist-explains/2016/03/economist-explains-7. Accessed April 30, 2016.

38. U.S. Department of Education, "OCR Coronavirus Statement," (March 4, 2020), https://content.govdelivery.com/accounts/USED/bulletins/27f5130. Accessed March 31, 2021.

39. Jacob E. Gersen, "How the Feds Use Title IX to Bully Universities," *The Wall Street Journal* (January 24, 2016), http://www.wsj.com/articles/how-the-feds-use-title-ix-to-bully-universities-1453669725. Accessed March 31, 2021.

40. Ballotpedia, "Federal Register Tops 70,000 Pages," *Ballotpedia.org* (November 6, 2020), https://ballotpedia.org/Federal_Register_tops_70,000_pages_(2020). Accessed March 31, 2021.

41. U.S. National Archives, "Code of Federal Regulations," *Federal Register*, https://www.archives.gov/federal-register/cfr. Accessed April 2, 2021.

42. Ibid.

43. See Isobel Asher Hamilton, "A New Antitrust Bill Could Pose Huge Threat to Google, Amazon, Apple and Facebook," *Business Insider* (February 4, 2021), https://www.businessinsider.com/amy-klobuchar-antitrust-bill-apple-amazon-google-facebook-fines-2021-2. Accessed April 2, 2021; Keach Hagey, "Publishers Laud Google Antitrust Suit," *The Wall Street Journal* (December 23,2020), B1; Brent Kendall and John McKinnon, "Facebook Hit with Antitrust Suits," *The Wall Street Journal* (December 10, 200), A1; James V. Grimaldi and Brent Kendall, "The Government v. the Tech Giants," *The Wall Street Journal* (September 10, 2019), B4.

44. Ibid.

45. Adam Satariano, "Big Fines and Strict Rules Unveiled Against 'Big Tech' in Europe," *The New York Times* (December 15, 2020), https://www.nytimes.com/2020/12/15/technology/big-tech-regulation-europe.html. Accessed March 30, 2021.

46. Kristian Stout, "The Negative Externalities of Protecting Privacy," *Truth on the Market* (May 7, 2020), https://www.businessinsider.com/amy-klobuchar-antitrust-bill-apple-amazon-google-facebook-fines-2021-2. Accessed April 2, 2021.

47. U.S. Environmental Protection Agency, "Air Pollution: Current and Future Challenges," https://www.epa.gov/clean-air-act-overview/air-pollution-current-and-future-challenges. Accessed March 31, 2021.

48. See Office of the Federal Register, National Archives and Records Administration, 2021, https://www.govinfo.gov/app/collection/fr/2021. Accessed March 30, 2021.

49. Weidenbaum, 178–179.

50. "Economy and COVID-19 Top the Public Policy Agenda for 2021," *Pew Research Center* (January 28, 2021), https://www.pewresearch.org/politics/2021/01/28/economy-and-covid-19-top-the-publics-policy-agenda-for-2021/. Accessed March 31, 2021.

51. Alex Sherman, "Five Charts that Show How COVID-19 Stopped the U.S. Economy in Its Tracks," *CNBC* (March 11, 2021), https://www.pewresearch.org/politics/2021/01/28/economy-and-covid-19-top-the-publics-policy-agenda-for-2021/. Accessed March 31, 2021.

52. PwC, "Top Policy Trends 2021," PwC https://www.pwc.com/us/en/services/consulting/risk-regulatory/library/top-policy-trends.html. Accessed March 31, 2021.

53. Pew Research Foundation, "Americans' View of Government: Low Trust, but Some Positive Performance Ratings," https://www.pewresearch.org/politics/2020/09/14/americans-views-of-government-low-trust-but-some-positive-performance-ratings/. Accessed March 31, 2021.

54. Ibid.

55. Sabin Center for Climate Change Law, Columbia Law School, "Climate Reregulation Tracker," 2021, https://climate.law.columbia.edu/content/climate-reregulation-tracker. Accessed March 31, 2021.

56. Graham K. Wilson, *Business and Politics: A Comparative Introduction*, 3d ed. (Chatham, NJ: Chatham House, 2003).

57. Susannah Hammond and Mike Cowan, "2020 Cost of Compliance: New Decade, New Challenges," *Thomson Reuters*, 4.

58. Ibid., 12–14.

59. Paroma Sanyal, "The Effect of Deregulation on Environmental Research by Electric Utilities," *Journal of Regulatory Economics* (June 2007), 335–353.

60. Ibid., 12.

61. Reich, 98.

62. Kimberly Amadeo, "Deregulation: Definition, Pros, Cons, Examples," *AboutNews* (February 8, 2016), http://useconomy.about.com/od/glossary/g/deregulation.htm. Accessed March 12, 2016.

63. "Deregulating America," *Businessweek* (November 28, 1983), 80–89.

64. Alison Vekshin, "U.S. Senators Propose Reinstating Glass–Steagall Act," *Bloomberg.com* (December 16, 2009), http://www.bloomberg.com/apps/news?pid=newsarchive&sid=aQfRyxBZs5uc. Accessed April 9, 2016.

65. "How to Judge President Trump's Economic Record," *The Economist* (October 17, 2020), https://www.economist.com/leaders/2020/10/17/how-to-judge-president-trumps-economic-record. Accessed April 1, 2021.

66. See Casey B. Mulligan, "Trump's Vast Deregulatory Landscape Goes Unnoticed by the Experts," *E21 Manhattan Institute* (January 13, 2020), https://economics21.org/trump-deregulation-unnoticed-experts. Accessed April 1, 2021; "An Assessment of the White House's Progress on Deregulation," *The Economist* (October 14, 2017), https://www.economist.com/business/2017/10/14/an-assessment-of-the-white-houses-progress-on-deregulation. Accessed April 1, 2021; Cayli Baker, "The Trump Administration's Major Environmental Deregulations," *The Brookings Institute* (December 15, 2020), https://www.brookings.edu/blog/up-front/2020/12/15/the-trump-administrations-major-environmental-deregulations/. Accessed April 1, 2021.

67. Kessenides, 2019.

68. Ibid.

69. Ibid.

70. Michael Cusumano, Annabelle Gawar, and David B. Yoffie, "Social Media Companies Should Self-Regulate. Now." *Harvard Business Review* (January 15, 2021), https://hbr.org/2021/01/social-media-companies-should-self-regulate-now. Accessed April 1, 2021.

18

Business Influence on Government and Public Policy

Chapter Learning Outcomes

After studying this chapter, you should be able to:

1. Understand the many elements of political corporate social responsibility (PCSR).
2. Describe the three elements of corporate political participation, including the different levels at which business lobbying occurs.
3. Identify the different levels and types of business lobbying.
4. Define and discuss corporate social activism.
5. Discuss corporate political spending and the arguments for and against it.

6. Describe the different types of political action committees (PACs), in terms of their historical growth, and the magnitude of their activity.
7. Describe the agency issues involved with corporate political spending and some of the contexts where these might arise.
8. Discuss the issues of corporate political accountability and disclosure.
9. Outline the types of strategies for corporate political activity.

As our previous discussion of industrial policy showed, government is a central stakeholder of business. Government's interest, or stake, in business is broad and multifaceted, and its power is derived from its legal and moral right to represent the public in its dealings with business. Government not only establishes the rules of the game for business functions but it also influences business in its roles as competitor, financier, purchaser, supplier, watchdog, and so on.

Businesses, on the other hand, also have considerable influence on government. Attempts by business to influence government are a major and accepted part of the public policy process in the United States and in many countries. Opportunities for business and government to cooperate in a mutual pursuit of common goals are present to some extent, but the major opportunity for business is in developing strategies for effectively working with government in such a way that businesses achieve their own objectives. In doing this, business has the responsibility of obeying the laws of the land and of being ethical in its responses to government expectations and mandates. To do otherwise raises the specter of abuse of power.

The active interaction of businesses and government in the United States is considered by many to be an issue of **political corporate social responsibility (PCSR)**, as we noted in Chapter 2. The logic behind PCSR is that if citizens expect companies to be socially responsible, then businesses *need* to be political actors and take on responsibilities traditionally

left to governments in order to meet societal expectations. It goes beyond corporate citizenship because it entails those responsibilities that turn corporations into political actors.[1] This is a newer concept for businesses in the United States relative to European or other contexts where businesses have historically assumed a larger political role in society. There are many challenges to managing political corporate social responsibility—the dynamics, the different national settings and institutional contexts, the role of business leaders in engaging in different strategies, and even the role of digital technologies and the way businesses frame their political responsibilities.[2] PCSR is a growing issue that businesses around the world must consider.

Society would be best served if the system maintained a balance of power; however, business's power to drive the political agenda in the United States is supported by largely business-sponsored lobbyists. In 2020, these lobbyists numbered over 11,000, although this was down from a high of almost 15,000 in 2007.[3] Industries that spend the most on lobbying include pharmaceuticals, real estate, electronics manufacturing, and insurance.[4]

During election years, the influence of business may also be seen in the amount of money spent on elections. For example, spending by businesses and unions on presidential and congressional races more than doubled from 2000 to 2020.[5] These numbers speak to the staggering amounts that help businesses to gain access to legislators and agencies. Throw in the other monies that businesses plow into lobbying—an estimated $3.5 billion in 2020—and it is obvious that business has tremendous influence on government.[6]

Power comes with the duty to use it responsibly and so the need for business to be mindful in its approach to influencing government is greater than ever. Given its inherent wealth and power, business must navigate the political waters thoughtfully, taking care to understand the range of corporate political activity's consequences, for society as well as for business. This qualifies as enlightened self-interest because business too needs a healthy and balanced society to thrive.

18.1 Corporate Political Participation

Political involvement by business is broadly defined as participation in the formulation and execution of public policy at various levels of government. As decisions about the current and future shape of society and the role of the private sector shift from the marketplace to the political arena, corporations, like all interest groups, find it imperative to increase their political involvement and activity.[7]

Some, like author Nicholas Lemann, see this as a broad response to the social consequences of the financial revolution in the late 20th century and a "new economic politics" that looks for more government interventions to counter inequalities.[8] Lemann points to the increasingly politicized roles that Big Tech companies play in the government/business arena, which parallel those of railroads, Standard Oil, and other money trusts in earlier days, and that eventually required antitrust interventions.[9]

Regardless of the cause, it is obvious that corporate political participation is here to stay. This was certainly seen in 2020, when companies formally re-committed to making

politics their business following public protests on racial inequality and justice issues, as well as the divisive 2020 U.S. presidential election and U.S. capitol rioting.[10] Many companies suspended their political funding while simultaneously upping their commitments to becoming more socially active.[11]

While the antecedents and consequences of corporate political activity might be debated, it is widely understood that business is increasingly politicized. In this chapter, we focus on the following major approaches to corporate political activity: (1) corporate social activism, (2) lobbying, and (3) political spending. As we begin, our perspective will be largely descriptive as we seek to understand these approaches, their strengths and weaknesses, and business's successes and failures with them. We will then explore normative issues in corporate political activity, highlighting areas where there are possible abuses of power and violations of sound ethics.

18.2 Corporate Social Activism

Corporate social activism is a form of political involvement by business. It refers to an advocacy position taken by a company to impact public policy for social change. Beginning in spring 2021, corporate activism was said to be "having a moment" as companies weighed in to address racial inequities and injustice in the wake of the controversial 2020 deaths of Breonna Taylor in Kentucky and George Floyd in Minneapolis, both at the hands of police officers.[12] The Black Lives Matter (BLM) movement also spurred companies to action following the acquittal of the man who shot and killed Trayvon Martin, a black teenager, in Florida. In response to these issues, Netflix posted on Twitter that "to be silent is not an option," while Walmart brokered a

Ethics In Practice Case

A Scoop of Social Justice with Ice Cream, Please

In 2020, as the Black Lives Matter social movement was gaining traction, Ben & Jerry's featured a new ice cream, "Justice ReMix'd," that was flavored with cinnamon and chocolate and was accompanied by a statement about the Advancement Project, a nonprofit that addresses "human rights struggles for equality and justice." This is just one example of Ben & Jerry's legacy of corporate social activism, as it commits money and time to promoting causes ranging from racial justice to immigration and climate change.

Environmental concerns have long been part of the company's targeted social issues. In the late 1980s it released an ice cream called "Rainforest Crunch" that incorporated nuts responsibly sourced from the Amazon, which prompted international discussions about deforestation. There is still a dilemma for Ben & Jerry's in the fact that it makes its profits from a notably unhealthy product at a time when obesity is considered a public health crisis. However, its long track record of activism may help mitigate those criticisms. As noted by Ben & Jerry's board chair,

Anuradha Mittal, "If we [the customers and the company] share values on climate, same-sex marriage rights, racism, I think that's a deeper bond than sugar and fat."

1. Do you agree that businesses like Ben & Jerry's should take on political and social issues?
2. How vulnerable are businesses to criticism when they take public political and social stances?
3. Would you buy a product in support of a company's social activism?
4. Who are the stakeholders involved when companies make decisions to be socially active?

Sources: Jordyn Holman and Thomas Buckley, "I Scream, You Scream, We All Scream for Social, Economic, and Environmental Justice," *Bloomberg Businessweek* (July 27, 2020), 35–39; John D. Stoll, "Lessons on Activism from Ben & Jerry," *The Wall Street Journal* (July 6/7, 2020), B5; The Advancement Project, https://advancementproject.org/, accessed April 11, 2021.

deal to move a confederate soldier statue in its hometown of Bentonville, Arkansas.[13]

Corporate social activism offers an opportunity for businesses to use their power and influence for change. In 2021, retail brands Nike and H&M joined other retailers in taking a stance to not use cotton from China's Xinjiang region, where the government is accused of abuses including forced labor and the imprisonment of Uyghurs and other minority groups.[14] In this case, corporate activism seemed to be effective, as earlier in the year the U.S. government restricted 11 Chinese companies from buying goods because of links to Xinjiang-related human rights abuses.[15]

The challenge for businesses engaging in corporate social activism is that their actions must be sincere and not just promoted as an opportunity to be on the right side of history. For example, when McDonald's Corporation issued a statement in support of Black Lives Matter that each black victim was "one of us," the American Civil Liberties Union (ACLU) asked why it was denying thousands of black workers access to paid sick and family leave during the global pandemic.[16] Additionally, there is always the possibility of boycotts and backlash when other stakeholders disagree with a business's stance.

Corporate social activism allows businesses to voice their concerns and push governments to change, but it is also increasingly expected by employees, customers, and other stakeholders that companies take a bigger role in social and political events. The ice cream maker Ben & Jerry's has long been known for its corporate activism and is seen by some as an exemplar of corporate activism, as we highlight in the Ethics in Practice case. Known as a company founded by "a pair of hippies" in the late 1970s, it has been active in social justice issues for decades, even after being acquired by food conglomerate Unilever.

18.3 Business Lobbying

Lobbying is the process of influencing public officials to promote or secure the passage or defeat of legislation or to help candidates get elected or defeated. Lobbyists are intensely self-interested. Their goals are to promote legislation or candidates that are in their organizations' interests and to defeat legislation or candidates that run counter to their interests. Business interests, labor interests, ethnic and racial groups, professional organizations, and those simply pursuing ideological goals they believe to be in the public interest are lobbying at the federal, state, and local levels. Our focus is on business lobbying at the federal level, although we must remember that this process is also occurring daily at the state and local levels.

Lobbying has been defined as the professionalization of the art of persuasion.[17] Lobbying serves several purposes. It is not just a technique for gaining legislative support or institutional approval for some objective such as a policy shift, a judicial ruling, or the modification or passage of a

law. Lobbying may be directed toward the reinforcement of established policy or the defeat of proposed policy shifts. As a tool to get the votes they want, lobbyists can also target the election or defeat of national, state, and local legislators.[18] A lobbyist may be a lawyer, a public relations specialist, a former head of a public agency, a former corporate executive, or a former elected official.

Lobbying has been called "one of America's most despised professions," and sometimes the label fits.[19] In 2010, Jack Abramoff was a lobbyist convicted of a variety of charges related to corrupt lobbying and influence peddling of legislators that also defrauded Native American tribes of millions of dollars.[20] His crimes were so notorious that he became the subject of the documentary *Casino Jack and the United States of Money* as well as a feature film, *Casino Jack*, with Kevin Spacey in the title role. Abramoff served time in prison but then ended up heading back to jail in 2020 after secretly meeting with members of Congress on behalf of the marijuana and cryptocurrency industries without registering as a lobbyist.[21] He was charged with violating the Lobbying Disclosure Act. Ironically, this was the same act that was amended after details emerged of his earlier scheme.

Given the large amounts of money involved, it is not surprising that people will cross the legal and ethical line. In 2020, lobbyists spent approximately $3.5 billion advocating for a range of interests.[22] One study examined lobbying for multinational tax breaks and found that the return on investment was 22,000 percent.[23] We should note, however, that lobbying is not inherently malicious. Some lobbyists work for nonprofit organizations, supporting causes about which the public would forget without someone representing them in Washington. They become involved in issues surrounding education, for example, like the lobbyist groups that square off in debate about the best ways to increase the quality of education.[24] Other lobbyists work for companies that care about doing the right thing, like supporting ESG and sustainability initiatives.[25] Lobbyists can serve as educators, providing needed information to elected officials and the public.

Businesses, as well as other special-interest groups, are increasingly turning to lobbyists to facilitate their involvement in the public policy process. As we mentioned in Chapter 17, Big Tech giants including Google, Facebook, Microsoft, Facebook, and Apple have faced increasing regulatory scrutiny, which has triggered a rise in lobbying by these companies in the United States and abroad. In 2020, these tech companies spent a combined 19 million euros lobbying the European Union (EU).[26] In the United States, Facebook and Amazon topped all other companies in federal lobbying expenditures, totalling $20 million and $18 million, respectively.[27]

The coronavirus pandemic also spurred a rush of companies looking for help through the lobbying business. In 2020, more than 3,200 companies, trade groups, and other organizations stepped up their lobbying in an effort to influence the federal government's response to coronavirus and the $2.2 trillion relief bill.[28] In sum, lobbying provides

Ethics In Practice Case

The Politics and Business of Blue Jeans

As companies become more and more involved in political issues, the popularity of their brands often divides along political lines. This is best exemplified in the Levi's versus Wrangler's "blue jeans versus red jeans" discourse. Consumer research data show that Democrats are affiliated with purchases of Levi's while Republicans are affiliated with purchases of Wrangler's blue jeans. While both companies got their start as the "go-to jeans" for those who pioneered the American West, it seems that the companies' affiliations with particular social and political stances play a role in the divided consumer purchases.

Levi's, for example, is noted for its San Francisco location and support of more liberal stances such as gun control and immigration reform. Wrangler's, headquartered in North Carolina, is less known for social stances, but it markets its cowboy/western heritage, which appeals to more rural consumers and Republicans. The data on purchases supports the divide, as from 2004 to 2018, Levi's customer base to the Democrats grew by 3 percent, while Wrangler's customer base moved by 13 percent toward the Republicans.

1. Do you think that brands should be associated with a political party? Should they promote such an association or leave that unspoken?
2. Brands these days are more often publicizing their social and political stances. Do you think this is good business practice?
3. What are some of the ethical challenges that businesses face when they take a political or social stand?
4. What are some other companies that have become politically active with their brands?

Sources: Suzanne Kapner and Dante Chinni, "Blue Jeans vs Red Jeans: Retail's Partisan Divide," *The Wall Street Journal* (November 20, 2019), A1; Rachel Tashjian, "How Buying Jeans Became a Political Act," *GQ* (November 20, 2019), https://www.gq.com/story/political-fashion-fatigue, accessed April 8, 2021.

a means for businesses to voice their concerns about a variety of issues. Such attempts by business to influence government are a major and accepted part of the public policy process in the United States and abroad. The active participation of interest groups striving to achieve their own objectives drives the political system. The business sector is behaving, therefore, in a normal and expected fashion when it assumes an advocacy role for its interests. Other groups, be they labor organizations, consumer groups, farmers' groups, doctors' organizations, real estate broker organizations, military groups, women's rights organizations, environmental groups, church groups, and so on, also strive to pursue their special interests with government. Today's pluralism encompasses the idea that all of these groups take advantage of their opportunity to influence government.

18.3a Organizational Levels of Lobbying

The business community engages in lobbying at several organizational levels. At the broadest level are **umbrella trade associations**, which represent the collective business interests of the United States. The best examples of umbrella trade associations in the United States are the U.S. Chamber of Commerce and the National Association of Manufacturers (NAM). Both have been considered for decades to be the unmatched voices of industry in the United States, although there is some evidence that their voice is waning relative to other advocacy coalitions.[29] Other umbrella organizations represent subsets of business in general, such as the Business Roundtable, which we mentioned in earlier chapters represents the largest firms in America.

At the next level are **sectoral trade associations**, which are composed of many firms in a given industry or line of business. Examples include the American Hospital Association, the Pharmaceutical Research and Manufacturers Association, and the National Association of Realtors, the latter of which spent $84 million on lobbying in 2020, more than any other organization.[30] In addition, there are individual **company lobbying** efforts. Here, firms such as Oracle, Microsoft, Qualcomm, and Delta Airlines lobby on their own behalf. Typically, companies use their own personnel, establish Washington offices for the sole purpose of lobbying, or hire professional lobbying firms or consultants located in Washington or a state capital. Finally, companies sometimes form **ad hoc coalitions** to address particular issues for a period. For example, the Plastic Pollution Coalition is a global alliance of more than 1,200 organizations and individuals in 75 countries working toward stopping plastic pollution.[31]

It should be noted, however, that there is some opportunity for all levels of lobbying to come together for a specific purpose. Take, for example, the moves by Monsanto Corporation in defense of genetically modified foods (aka GMOs, which we discussed in Chapter 8). In this case, Monsanto formed an alliance with the (umbrella organization) Biotechnology Industry Organization, as well as the (sectoral) Grocery Manufacturers Association and various (ad hoc coalitions) universities to make their case in the safety debate surrounding GMOs.[32]

Figure 18-1 depicts examples of the broad range of lobbying and political interest organizations used by businesses. As noted above, there has been considerable growth in company-level lobbying over the years.

It is now useful to discuss lobbying in greater detail, beginning with the use of professional lobbyists.

Figure 18-1 Examples of the Range of Lobbying Organizations Used by Businesses

Broad Representation: Umbrella Trade Associations

- Busines Roundtable
- Chamber of Commerce of the United States
- National Association of Manufacturers (NAM)

Midrange Representation: Sectoral Trade Associations and Coalitions

- National Automobile Dealers Association
- National Association of Realtors
- American Petroleum Institute American Trucking Association

Narrow/Specific Representation: Company-Level Lobbying

- Washington and State Capital Offices
- Law Firms Specializing in Lobbying
- Public Affairs Specialists
- Political Action Committees (PACs)
- Grassroots Lobbying
- Company-Based Coalitions
- Former Government Officials

Professional Lobbyists. Lobbyists, sometimes derisively referred to as "influence peddlers," operate under a variety of formal titles and come from a variety of backgrounds. Officially, they are lawyers, government affairs specialists, public relations consultants, or public affairs consultants. Some are on the staffs of large trade associations based in Washington. Others represent specific companies that have Washington-based offices dedicated to the sole purpose of representing those companies in the capitol city. Still others are professional lobbyists who work for large law firms or consulting firms in Washington that specialize in representing clients to the lawmakers.

The Washington lobbyist is frequently a former government official. Called **revolving door lobbyists**, some are former congressional staff members or former members of Congress.[33] Others are former presidential staff assistants or other highly placed government officials. In fact, lobbying is the single most popular career choice for retiring members of Congress in the United States.[34] To be formally considered a lobbyist, an ex-legislator must be engaged in lobbying activities for 20 percent or more of their time for an individual client.

Under a Revolving Door Ban Executive Order on Ethics, executive agency appointees must wait for two years from the date of appointment before they participate in lobbying.[35] However, by spreading services among many clients, or by providing "strategic advice" rather than "lobbying services," any ex-lawmaker can effectively evade the ban.[36] This practice has given rise to the term **stealth lobbying** or **shadow lobbying**. The "cooling off" periods between government

Spotlight on Sustainability

What Green Rankings Don't Tell You

A corporation's political activities can have a greater impact on the environment than the work it does to make its operations greener. Green rankings can be misleading because they focus on operational impacts, compliance with regulations, and overall practices, while ignoring the firm's political advocacy activities. A recent study compared companies' green rankings to their ranking on political transparency and noted a weak correlation: some of the companies with higher-than-average green rankings had lower-than-average political transparency rankings.

Companies with higher environmental transparency rankings included firms in the highly environmentally regulated mining, chemical, and energy industries. Firms in those industries typically lobby for more relaxed regulations and so some question whether these companies have environmentally friendly political activity to match their environmental transparency. Because disclosure of corporate political activity is not required, there is no way to know the nature of their efforts. What is the solution? Some suggest that future green rankings should include voluntary disclosure of environment-related lobbying and donations. Otherwise, firms may receive credit for being green when, behind closed doors, they are working against the interests of the environment with their corporate political activity.

Sources: Aaron Chatterji and Michael Toffel, "What Green Rankings Don't Tell You," *Newsweek* (October 22, 2012), http://www.hbs.edu/faculty/Publication%20Files/Chatterji%20Toffel%202012%20DailyBeast_c01da612-2a82-462c-ad67-33cea6af3d2b.pdf, accessed April 10, 2021; Auden Schendler and Michael Toffel, "The Factor Environmental Ratings Miss," *MIT Sloan Management Review* 53.1 (Fall 2011): 17–18; "The Problem with Green Rankings," *The Guardian* (December 20, 2011), https://www.theguardian.com/environment/2011/dec/20/problem-with-green-rankings, accessed April 10, 2021.

and lobbying work apply only to the agency where an ex-official used to work—so contacting other agencies during that time is still allowable.[37]

What do business lobbyists actually do? Lobbyists offer a wide range of services that include drafting legislation, creating slick advertisements and direct-mail campaigns, consulting, and, most importantly, getting access to lawmakers. Access, or connections, seems to be the central product that the new breed of lobbyist is selling—the returned phone call, the tennis game with a key legislator, or lunch with the Speaker of the House. With so many competing interests in Washington today, the opportunity for businesses to get their points across to regulators in any format is a significant advantage. Lobbyists also play the important role of showing busy legislators the virtues and pitfalls of complex legislation.[38] According to consultant Edward Segal, keys to success for companies employing lobbyists involve the following:[39]

1. Find the best advocate: one who does not ask for favors, but rather helps policymakers succeed.
2. Focus not on winning, but making progress on an issue.
3. Cultivate relationships for two-way discussions.
4. Prioritize your issues.

In sum, lobbyists can buy influence and allow companies to make sure the government has all the information they need on an issue.

Grassroots Lobbying. In addition to lobbying directly through the use of professional lobbyists, firms and trade associations use what is called **grassroots lobbying**, which refers to the process of mobilizing the "grassroots"—individual citizens who might be most directly affected by legislative activity—to political action. The better corporate grassroots lobbying programs usually arise in companies whose leaders recognize that people are a firm's most potent political resource. Although firms cannot direct or require people to become politically involved, they persuade and encourage them. In addition to using social media, trade associations often use grassroots support by organizing rallies and developing instant advertisements.[40]

Grassroots lobbying has become such an effective tool for such a wide range of individual firms and associations that the Public Affairs Council holds an annual Advocacy/Grassroots Conference.[41] The 2021 agenda included participation from companies as diverse as eBay and General Motors, as well as trade groups such as the Association of American Medical Colleges.

Other forms of grassroots lobbying have emerged with the growth of technology. For example, **cyberadvocacy** is a computer-based form of grassroots campaigning. Computers and the Internet have made communication, and thus grassroots lobbying, infinitely easier. Books and consulting services have sprung up to assist organizations in using the Internet to both amass grassroots support and enable grassroots supporters to contact their legislators. Social media

platforms have made it a little easier to gain access to influencers, with sites like LinkedIn and apps facilitating connections.[42] For example, the driver service Uber used its app to rally riders to go to City Hall and challenge New York City Mayor Bill de Blasio's proposal to cap the number of livery vehicles.[43] Uber offered free rides to the venue and then got customers to send 17,000 e-mails in opposition to the new rules. Competitor Lyft also mobilized users to support less-restrictive regulations, as did home-sharing company Airbnb, and e-commerce company eBay, which was fighting online sales taxation.[44]

However, this new modality of gathering support has also created its own set of ethics and stakeholder issues in lobbying. In 2020, several state lawmakers and regulators enacted new regulations in efforts to curb lobbyists delivering messages to public officials through social media with concerns about conflicts of interest and the tax-exempt, nonprofit status of many of the grassroots organizations.[45] In response, many advocacy groups started posting "legal tips" on using social media for advocacy.[46]

Grassroots lobbying can be highly effective, but the grassroots response should be genuine. Some organizations and trade associations have created fake groups that appear to be grassroots but are largely created and funded by an organization or trade association. These phony "**astroturf lobbying**" efforts give the impression of being the result of a genuine public groundswell but are actually orchestrated and funded by professional organizations. Over time, astroturfing has grown more sophisticated and is estimated to be a billion-dollar industry in Washington.[47]

In 2021, the Council for Citizens Against Government Waste (CCAGW) lobbied against a federal program known as 340B that allows for discounted drug sales to medical facilities that serve the poor. Allegations of astroturfing by Big Pharma surfaced when people began questioning how the cause fit with CCAGW's mission of eliminating waste. Additionally, an affiliate of CCAGW was found to have received $265,000 from the Pharmaceutical Research and Manufacturers Association (PhRMA) since 2014. Is it astroturfing? Maybe. Today's astroturf organizations are more subtle and less likely to be showing their true origins without investigation from an outside source. Even professional journalists have been duped by astroturf organizations.[48] Until transparency requirements are in place, consumers of information will have to be vigilant in expecting lobbying groups to be transparent and accountable.

Trade Associations. Lobbying at the association level is frequent today. **Trade associations** are established by individual industries or professions to help businesses in the same industry or profession to interact with each other and benefit from those interactions. In 2021, for example, trade associations representing drone makers like Amazon and the Alphabet subsidiary Wing were trying to expedite approval for airborne deliveries.[49] Trade associations sometimes find themselves in the undesirable role of battling with each other in their attempts to lobby government officials. For example, during the COVID-19 pandemic, trade associations from the hotel and hospitality industries were actively lobbying state and local governments in New York to include their workers in early rounds of virus vaccines as essential workers.[50] Meanwhile, a trade group representing landlords of rent-stabilized buildings in New York City issued a release asking that superintendents and building maintenance staff members receive vaccines quickly.[51] Other trade groups representing teachers, school nurses, truck drivers, morticians, and even zookeepers joined the fray for vaccine priority. In the end, although trade associations may on the surface seem collaborative, they are just as competitive as professional and grassroots lobbyists in promoting their causes.

Umbrella Organizations. The umbrella organizations are trade associations, too; however, an umbrella organization has a broad base of membership that represents businesses in several different industries of various sizes. Two major umbrella organizations in the United States have been the Business Roundtable and the Chamber of Commerce of the United States. Each of these groups has political action as one of its central objectives.

Business Roundtable Formed in 1972, the Business Roundtable (BRT) is often regarded as an umbrella organization, although it has a more restricted membership. It is an association of chief executive officers of leading corporations with a combined workforce of more than 20 million employees in the United States and $9 trillion in revenues.[52] The Business Roundtable differs from most umbrella organizations, in the limitation of participation to chief executive officers (CEOs). Rather than pushing narrow issues that benefit narrow interests, the organization generally selects broader concerns on which to focus, including issues of climate change and U.S. immigration policies.[53]

One of the targets of the BRT's lobbying activities is the shareholder empowerment movement. Not surprisingly, the BRT's association of CEOs prefers that the decision-making power reside in top management. The BRT shifted focus in 2019 toward a broader stakeholder movement, as we noted in Chapter 9 on corporate governance, when they issued the "Statement on the Purpose of the Corporation" affirming their commitment to all stakeholders that has been described as "stakeholder capitalism."[54] How they are going to embark on this commitment remains to be seen, and critics have questioned the statement. As noted by one critic, "With shareholders disempowered and no other form of vigilance empowered, how will the risk that stakeholder capitalism becomes an agency of CEO empowerment be avoided?"[55]

Chamber of Commerce of the United States The National Chamber of Commerce was founded in 1912 as a federation of businesses and business organizations. In addition to firms, corporations, and professional members, the chamber has thousands of local, state, and regional chambers of commerce, including the International Chamber of Commerce and several thousand trade and professional associations. Its diversity of membership shows why it is referred to as an umbrella organization.

Historically, the U.S. Chamber of Commerce had been a legislative powerhouse in its ability to influence public policy. More recently, as noted above, its power and influence seems to be dwindling.[56] The Chamber's reputation for supporting legacy industries like tobacco, firearms, and oil has been particularly controversial as these industries' interests often collide with other industries.[57] The Chamber's position on climate change led Apple to resign from the organization and Nike to withdraw from the board, remaining as a member to "debate climate change from within."[58] Nevertheless, the U.S. Chamber of Commerce continues to lead the pack of lobbyists, spending more than any other interest group in Washington.[59] Other major umbrella groups in the United States include the National Association of Manufacturers (NAM) and the National Federation of Independent Businesses (NFIB).

Coalitions A noteworthy and growing mechanism of political involvement in the public policy process is the creation and use of **coalitions** to influence government processes. A coalition forms when distinct groups or parties realize they have something in common that might warrant their joining forces, at least temporarily, for joint action. More often than not, an issue that various groups feel similarly about creates the opportunity for a coalition. For example, the coalition FlyersRights.org was formed when a family was stranded for nine hours on the tarmac in Austin, Texas. Today, with more than 40,000 members, it is the largest nonprofit consumer organization in the United States representing airline passengers.[60] During the early days of the COVID-19 pandemic, it was involved in petitioning the Department of Transportation (DOT) to mandate mask wearing by all persons on planes and at airports.[61] A coalition can work cooperatively with government or it can lobby government when that government does not share the coalition's priorities.

Coalition formation has become a standard practice for firms interested in accomplishing political goals or influencing public policy. If a company or an association wants to pass or defeat particular legislation, it can strengthen its position by enlisting support from an individual or organization that has a similar position on the issue. Coalitions enable members to share their resources and pool their energies when they confront difficult issues. Coalitions also can provide cover for a company that wants to push for its own agenda without necessarily having its name attached to the campaign.

One example of coalition building around a specific issue is the Global Business Coalition against Human Trafficking. Members include Carlson, Delta Air Lines, Exxon Mobil, LexisNexis, ManpowerGroup, Microsoft, NXP, and Travelport.[62] These corporations have joined to share their resources and expertise to work with business and government to fight the growing problem of modern-day slavery.[63]

Another example of a coalition is Partnering for Racial Justice in Business, which was spearheaded by the World Economic Forum in 2021, following protests all over the world about the lack of inclusion and inequities regarding Black and other racially diverse individuals.[64] The coalition focuses on changing practices in the workforce including work, wages, education, skills and learning, and economic growth for diverse employees, among other topics. It was endorsed by 48 corporate leaders and their corporations with the overarching goal of setting new global standards for racial and ethnic justice in business.[65]

18.4 Corporate Political Spending

To this point, our discussion of business's political involvement has focused primarily on interpersonal contact and powers of persuasion. We now turn our attention to corporate political spending and its implications for businesses and their stakeholders.

In the United States, the Federal Election Campaign Act (FECA) prohibits corporations from making direct contributions to candidates.[66] However, the law has always permitted corporations to form **political action committees (PACs)**—committees that are organized to raise and spend money for political candidates, ballot initiatives, and proposed legislation; it is neither a party committee nor the committee of a candidate.[67]

Figure 18-2 shows the top ten PAC contributors to federal candidates. Most PACs have a political point of view, either conservative or liberal, but many simply focus on a specific issue and try to do so in a nonpartisan manner.[68]

In addition to the traditional PACs, companies can contribute corporate funds to trade associations and other tax-exempt groups that will subsequently support a particular candidate or cause. Companies can also contribute to Super PACs, political parties, and political committees, both connected and nonconnected to candidates. Unlike PACs formed by legislation, **Super PACs** resulted from judicial decisions.[69] Super PACs are a type of political committee that can raise monies from corporations, unions, and individuals but cannot contribute to or coordinate directly with parties or candidates. The first judicial decision in support of Super PACs occurred in 2010 when the U.S. Supreme Court ruled in *Citizens United v. FEC* that corporations and labor unions could use the funds from their treasuries to support or oppose political candidates as long as the spending is independent, that is, not coordinated with, or donated directly to, a candidate.[70] The Federal Court in *Speechnow v. FEC* further clarified the implementation of *Citizens United* by ruling that any government restrictions on the amount corporations can spend would be unconstitutional.[71]

These two rulings spurred the creation of Super PACs, and these committees have since transformed the political landscape. As of April 2021, 2,276 groups have been organized as Super PACs, with total receipts of $3.4 billion and expenditures of $2.1 billion in the 2019–2020 cycle.[72] Of course, many people question the actual independence of the Super PAC expenditures. Typically, Super PACS are headed by former aides and associates who know the candidate well and so do not need to confer with the candidate to know what the candidate would want the Super PAC to do. In addition, the candidate can simply speak to the media and then the Super PAC can simply follow the news for clues as to where to spend the money.

With this range of options and few meaningful restrictions on corporate involvement, corporate political spending

Figure 18-2 Top Ten PAC Contributors to Candidates (2019–2020)

PAC	Total Amount ($)	Democrat Percentage	Republican Percentage
National Association of Realtors	3,960,998	52	48
National Beer Wholesalers Assn.	3,147,500	53	47
Credit Union National Assn.	2,849,800	53	47
AT&T, Inc.	2,742,000	46	54
American Crystal Sugar	2,702,500	55	45
Comcast Corp	2,664,500	46	54
American Bankers Association	2,661,200	31	69
Operating Engineers Union	2,599,700	82	18
Sheet Metal, Air, Rail & Transportation Union	2,488,150	92	8
Majority Cmte PAC*	2,460,100	0	100

*A Leadership PAC affiliated with U.S. Congressman Kevin McCarthy (R-Calif)

Source: OpenSecrets.org, https://www.opensecrets.org/political-action-committees-pacs/top-pacs/2020?filter=P&pac=A&party=A#candidates, accessed April 11, 2021.

has become "dangerous terrain."[73] Instead of just worrying about contributions to candidates and political parties, firms must now deal with requests from Super PACs, trade associations, and 501(c)(4) "social welfare" associations, and they must do so carefully.[74] As Bruce Freed and Karl Sandstrom explain:[75]

> Political spending should not be a casual decision, a choice defaulted to companies' government-relations managers—or to trade associations or c4s. The spending, whether done directly or through third-party groups, needs to reflect the deliberate choices of senior managers and the board. When it comes to political engagement, a company must adhere to its values, keep its broader interests in mind, and understand that giving money to candidates or entities whose behavior is uncertain or at odds with those values and long-term business interests ultimately harms the company and its shareholders. To understand political spending fully is to understand its full consequences.

Target Corporation, the huge retailer, did not understand the full consequences of its political spending and ended up paying a price. The company contributed to Minnesota Forward, a pro-economic growth political action group, in order to help it support pro-growth political candidates.[76] However, one of those candidates opposed gay marriage, a position that neither Target nor Minnesota Forward endorsed. This led to a boycott of Target stores by gay-marriage activists. Target later apologized for the contribution, noting that the company endorsed the candidate's stance on economic issues and not social issues. Target learned the hard way that corporate political spending contains repercussions that extend beyond any single issue.

Regardless of how you feel about corporate political spending campaigns, it is clear that "money matters." Particularly during presidential elections, money is a "necessary but not a sufficient condition" for winning an election because while money might not buy elections, it allows the candidates to stay in the race.[77] It is important to note that we focus on corporate contributions because the purpose of this chapter is to explore the impact of business on government. However, Super PACS do not stem only from business—unions and other interested organizations may also form them.

In sum, the reputational risks of corporate political contributions are substantial, with the possibility of creating polarization and distrust.[78] Hence, businesses would be wise to consider carefully their political spending and do their homework to make sure that their monies are going toward issues that align with their values.

18.4a Arguments for Corporate Political Spending

The most visible and ultimately influential defenders of corporate political spending are the five U.S. Supreme Court justices who shared in the majority opinion in *Citizens United*, the controversial 2010 U.S. Supreme Court ruling that declared government may not restrict independent corporate political expenditures. The logic behind the ruling is that the First Amendment establishes the right to free speech and that not only individuals but also groups of individuals have that right. From this perspective, limiting a group's right to political advocacy would violate the free speech of the people who belong to that group. It follows from this logic then that corporations, as well as unions and other groups of people, have the right to express their political opinions and their candidate preferences. Business has an important part to play in society and part of that is speaking up for the needs of business and sharing an economic perspective. In pluralistic societies, business provides a counterbalance to other interest groups who express their own agendas.

18.4b Arguments against Corporate Political Spending

Senator John McCain (R-AZ) became one of the most often quoted critics of corporate campaign spending when he called the *Citizens United* decision "one of the worst decisions I have ever seen.… I predict to you that there will be huge scandals associated with this huge flood of money."[79] The late Senator McCain's comments crystallize one of the key arguments against corporate political spending: Corporations have access to large amounts of money and that creates a serious imbalance of power. Another concern is the possibility of agency problems as managers may promote their own interests rather than the shareholders' interests, or the interests of stakeholders, when promoting candidates or issues.

Even when promoting shareholder welfare, the innate self-interest of business gives people pause as business is not likely to focus on the common good. Justice Stevens shared these apprehensions in the dissenting opinion on *Citizens United*, "The financial resources, legal structure and instrumental orientation of corporations raise legitimate concerns about their role in the electoral process. Our lawmakers have a compelling constitutional basis, if not also a democratic duty, to take measures designed to guard against the potentially deleterious effects of corporate spending in local and national races."[80] The **Golden Rule of Politics** sums up the concerns of those who argue against corporate political spending: "He who has the gold, rules."[81]

18.4c Agency Issues

As we discussed in Chapter 9, agency problems arise when the actions of managers are not in the shareholders' best interests. Corporate political spending, like all corporate spending, should have the best interests of the firm, its shareholders, and its stakeholders in mind. Political spending should not provide an opportunity for managers to pursue their personal preferences because the money those managers are spending is not their own. Political spending should have a clear association with the firm's best interests rather than the managers' personal points of view.

Agency problems can also arise when managers give the firm's money to a third party, such as a trade association or nonprofit group. These organizations might donate to a candidate whose actions do not serve the interests of the firm's shareholders and stakeholders. Several major drug companies found themselves in this predicament after donating money to PhRMA, the trade association that represents their industry.[82] The trade association gave $4.8 million to two 501(c)(4) associations that subsequently used that money to support 23 congressional candidates successfully. After being elected, all 23 voted to limit access to and cut federal funding for birth control, as well as to cut medical research funds on which pharmaceutical companies rely.[83] Bayer AG, Johnson & Johnson, Merck, and Pfizer are all leading manufacturers of contraceptives. In essence, through the trade association, they had inadvertently supported politicians who voted both to shrink their market and to reduce funding on which they depend. Angry investors berated the firms' managers for belonging to a trade association that used "its members' payments against those same members' best interests."[84]

18.5 Political Accountability and Transparency

Political accountability is an assumption of responsibility for political actions and a willingness to be answerable for them. In today's political landscape, corporations have unprecedented freedom to pursue their political agendas. Restrictions on the money they can spend are virtually gone and multiple opportunities exist to hide the nature of their activities from public view. This freedom, and the power it gives, brings forth a duty for corporations to be responsible and, to that end, a movement to promote corporate political accountability has formed.

Some efforts are aimed at putting limits on what companies can spend; these include shareholder resolutions and lawsuits against big spenders. Since the *Citizens United* decision, investors have filed more than 500 shareholder resolutions calling for more transparency in corporate political activity.[85] In 2020 alone, 48 shareholder proposals calling for greater disclosures of corporate political and lobbying activity gathered more than 20 percent support.[86] Interestingly, the impact of shareholder engagement on political disclosure has been positive for future transparency. Companies with a history of shareholder resolutions on political disclosure, and who subsequently reach an agreement with shareholders, have significantly better disclosure policies, according the CPA-Zicklin Index of Political Disclosure and Accountability at the Center.[87]

Transparency has become a major issue in political accountability because much corporate political activity today is outside the public view. The Sunlight Foundation coined the term **dark money** to refer to the political contributions from undisclosed donors.[88] Well over $1 billion was spent by dark money donors in 2020, including $660 million in donations from opaque political nonprofits and shell

companies to outside groups.[89] The *Citizens United* ruling made it easier for donors to stay hidden, and this can occur several different ways:

- Tax-exempt "social welfare organizations," known as **501(c)(4)** groups, are not required to disclose their donors, and so it is impossible to trace the money candidates receive from them back to the source.[90]
- Tax-exempt **527 groups** are groups organized under section 527 of the Internal Revenue Code to raise money for political activities, but they are only required to file with the FEC if they are a PAC or political party that expressly advocates for or against a federal candidate.[91]
- Super PACs are required to disclose their donors but often their donors hide behind other nonprofit groups, creating a vicious cycle of secrecy.[92]
- **Hybrid PACs** are also called **Carey Committees**, named after Retired Rear Admiral James Carey who brought suit against the Federal Election Commission (FEC) in 2011. These are hybrid political actions committees not affiliated with a candidate and can operate both as a traditional PAC (contributing funds to a candidate's committee) and as a super PAC, which makes independent expenditures. It can collect unlimited contributions from almost any source for its independent expenditure account.[93]
- Trade associations are another conduit for dark money. In *Hidden Rivers*, the Center for Political Accountability dubbed trade associations "the Swiss bank accounts of American politics." This in-depth examination of the nation's trade associations showed how they have become conduits for unlimited corporate political spending of dark money. Of major concern is the fact that trade associations "are subject to even less disclosure than the much-criticized spending of independent political committees (527s)."[94]

The arguments against dark money are undeniable. Advocacy is best understood when one knows the motives of the person making the arguments. Sound ethics would suggest that voters have a right to know who is putting forth arguments for and against a candidate or an issue, and dark money denies them that right. In addition, it is a well-known fact that people behave more ethically when their actions are visible to others.

Advocates of transparency at the federal level have tried repeatedly to enact legislation to require that donors be identified. Getting a handle on dark money is not easy because dark money spending often comes in layers. In California, state law requires nonprofit organizations to disclose donors who give money in order to fund political activities. However, in 2021, the U.S. Supreme Court justices agreed to hear an appeal from two groups, the Americans for Prosperity Foundation funded by the Koch brothers and the Thomas More Law Center, that argued that the state's policy violates the First Amendment and deters people from giving. At the time of this writing, the case was not decided. However, groups advocating for more transparency worry that should the Supreme Court overturn the state law, it would endorse the dark money spending that continues to grow in the United States.[95]

18.6 Strategies for Corporate Political Activity

We have discussed the principal approaches by which business has become politically active—through corporate social activism, lobbying, and political spending. To be sure, there are other approaches, but these are the major ones. In our discussion, we have unavoidably referred to the use of these approaches as part of a strategy. To develop the idea of strategy for political activism, it is important to understand that managers must not only identify useful approaches but also address when and under what conditions these various approaches should be used or would be most effective. We do not want to carry this idea too far, because it is beyond the scope of this book. On the other hand, as managers devise and execute political strategies, it is useful to see political strategy as consistent with their development of stakeholder management, sound ethics, and ethical leadership.

The purpose of political strategy is "to secure a position of advantage regarding a given regulation or piece of legislation, to gain control of an idea or a movement and deflect it from the firm, or to deal with a local community group on an issue of importance."[96] As with all strategies, it is important to approach political activity in a well-thought-out and ethical manner, paying attention not only to the procedures to follow but also to the values inherent in the sought-after outcomes and any repercussions that could follow. As we discussed in Chapters 1 and 2, business is often accused of abusing its power and its political power is enormous. Companies therefore need to watch carefully that their power is not abused or used unethically.

Researchers Amy Hillman and Michael Hitt offer three distinct types of strategies that companies use to interact with decision makers in the political arena.[97] They are:

- *Information Strategy*—providing information to policymakers through activities such as lobbying, research projects, position papers, and being an expert witness

- *Financial Incentives Strategy*—making direct financial contributions, providing desired services, reimbursing travel, or paying fees to policymakers
- *Constituency Building Strategy*—mobilizing grassroots or business cohort to work together through public relations, political education, press conferences, and advertising

Firms may use any or all of them at any given time. These are all proactive strategies, in which the firm makes a conscious decision to be politically active.[98] They also align with the concept of political corporate social responsibility, discussed earlier. For example, in a study examining the relationship between corporate community programs and corporate political activity, researchers found that businesses could gather more information and engage in more constituency-building political strategies through community programs that enhance a firm's human, organizational, and geographic capital.[99] Firms can also sit by the sidelines and passively react to changes in the political environment, but that strategy is unlikely to serve the business world in today's rapidly changing political environment. That is why, perhaps, CEOs are considered "the new lawmakers."[100]

18.6a Financial Performance Outcomes

Many studies have been conducted to calculate whether corporate political spending influences political decisions and, ultimately, firm performance. These studies have mixed results. Some find strong support, others find none, and a third group has mixed or marginal findings.[101] An important meta-analysis found that corporate political activity had a consistent positive relationship with firm financial performance.[102] However, generic results are of limited value because the outcomes of corporate political activity occur in a variety of contexts and so researchers have looked for contingencies that might explain differences in returns. The mixed results of these studies make it difficult to draw a definite connection between corporate political activity and firm performance. Clearly, context matters, and so strategies that work in one situation will not necessarily transfer to another. Yet, despite the uncertainty of results, companies seem to believe that political activity pays off because they keep doing it at unprecedented levels.

Summary

The world is still feeling the after-effects of a global pandemic as well as the divisive politics of transition governments. In this challenging environment, corporate political participation and political corporate social responsibility have taken on renewed importance.

We discussed the different ways that corporations can participate in political activity, including social activism, different levels of lobbying, the different types of PACs, and

how each can be used responsibly. The 2010 Supreme Court ruling in *Citizens United v. Federal Election Commission* has changed the rules significantly, particularly in terms of corporate political spending. In the midst of these ebbs and flows in restrictions, corporate social activism, lobbying, and corporate political spending remain a permanent part of the political landscape. Business advocating for its interests is an important part of maintaining the balance of power needed in a pluralistic society. To maintain a true balance of power, however, businesses must advocate in a way that is both ethical and legal. Business has a duty to temper the freedom it now has with responsibility, accountability, and transparency.

While we describe corporate political strategies at a macro level, they each contain a variety of different ways for corporations to take political action. We should remember that politically active firms are inclined to combine various strategies. Companies make political contributions, set up their own lobbyists in Washington offices, contract with outside lobbyists to represent their interests, and join like-minded organizations to push for change through trade associations and coalitions. Corporate social activism, political spending, and lobbying are not separate strategies; they are part of an overall approach.

Business's political activity continues to be controversial with the public. As we discussed in Chapters 1 and 2, business often receives criticism for using and abusing its power. Nowhere is this more evident than in corporate lobbying and its outcomes. As new excesses develop, new regulations and rulings come to address the problems they present. In the meantime, responsible businesses are focused on determining how they can pursue an ethical approach to political participation. This is the ongoing "back and forth" that characterizes the political process.

Key Terms

501(c)(4)s, p. 410
527 groups, p. 410
ad hoc coalitions, p. 404
astroturf lobbying, p. 406
Carey Committees, p. 410
Citizens United v. FEC, p. 408
coalitions, p. 407
company lobbying, p. 404
corporate social activism, p. 402
cyberadvocacy, p. 406

dark money, p. 410
Golden Rule of Politics, p. 409
grassroots lobbying, p. 406
hybrid PACs, p. 410
lobbying, p. 403
political accountability, p. 410
political action committees (PACs), p. 408
political corporate social responsibility (PCSR), p. 401

political involvement, p. 402
revolving door lobbyists, p. 405
sectoral trade associations, p. 404
shadow lobbying, p. 405
stealth lobbying, p. 405
Speechnow v. FEC, p. 408
Super PACs, p. 408
trade associations, p. 406
transparency, p. 410
umbrella trade associations, p. 404

Discussion Questions

1. Explain the different ways that businesses can influence government. Which do you think is most effective? Why?
2. Describe lobbying in your own words. Identify and explain the different levels at which lobbying takes place. Why is there a lack of unity among the umbrella organizations?
3. What is a PAC? How is it different from a Super PAC? What are the major arguments in favor of PACs? What are the major types of PACs and how

do they differ? In your opinion, are PACs a good way for business to influence the public policy process? What changes would you recommend for PACs?
4. Discuss *Citizens United* and *Speechnow* and their likely effects on future elections. What, if any, reforms would you recommend?
5. What does corporate accountability mean to you? How important is corporate political transparency?
6. What are the limits of corporate political strategy? Are there lines that companies should not cross?

Endnotes

1. Andreas G. Scherer, Andreas Rasche, Guido Palazzo, and Andre Spicer, "Managing for Political Corporate Social Responsibility: New Challenges and Directions for PCSR 2.0," *Journal of Management Studies* (Vol. 53, No. 3, May 2016), 273–298; Michael Hadani, Jean -Philippe Bonardi, and Nicolas M. Dahan, "Corporate Political Activity, Public Policy Uncertainty, and Firm Outcomes: A Meta-Analysis." *Strategic Organization* 15, no. 3 (2017): 338–366.
2. Ibid.
3. Erin Duffin, "Number of Registered Active Lobbyists in the U.S. from 2000 to 2020," *Statista* (March 4, 2021), https://www.statista.com/statistics/257340/number-of -lobbyists-in-the-us/. Accessed April 8, 2021.
4. Ibid.
5. William Horncastle, "The Scale of US Election Spending Explained in Five Graphs," *The Conversation* (October 15, 2020), https://theconversation.com/the-scale -of-us-election-spending-explained-in-five-graphs-130651. Accessed April 8, 2021.

6. Erin Duffin, "Total Lobbying Spending in the United States from 1998 to 2020," *Statista* (March 4, 2021), https://www.statista.com/statistics/257337/total-lobbying-spending-in-the-us/. Accessed April 8, 2021.

7. S. Prakash Sethi, "Corporate Political Activism," *California Management Review* (Spring 1982), 32.

8. Nicholas Lemann, *Transaction Man: The Rise of the Deal and the Decline of the American Dream* (New York: Farrar, Strauss and Giroux, 2019)

9. Nicholas Lemann, "When Corporations Changed Their Social Role – And Upended Our Politics," *The Wall Street Journal* (September 7/8, 2019), C1.

10. See Emily Glazer and Chip Cutter, "Companies Are Making Politics Their Business," *The Wall Street Journal* (January 16/17, 2021), B1; Emily Glazer, Theo Francis, and Chip Cutter, "Companies Suspend Political Funding," *The Wall Street Journal* (January 11, 2021), A4.

11. Ibid.

12. John D. Stoll, "Lessons on Activism from Ben & Jerry's," *The Wall Street Journal* (June 6/7, 2020), B5.

13. Ibid.

14. Nathaniel Taplin, "Hypernationalism on Xinjiang Poses Risks for Chinese Brands, Too," *The Wall Street Journal* (April 9, 2021), B12

15. Michelle Toh, "Activists Are Urging Big Brands to Eradicate Traces of Human Rights Abuse in Xinjiang," CNN Business (July 28, 2020). Accessed April 11, 2021.

16. Jordyn Holman and Thomas Buckley, "I Scream, You Scream, We All Scream for Social, Economic and Environmental Justice" (July 27, 2020), 35–40.

17. H. R. Mahood, *Interest Group Politics in America* (Englewood Cliffs, NJ: Prentice Hall, 1990), 52.

18. See "The Hill's Top Lobbyists 2020," *The Hill* (December 10, 2020), https://thehill.com/business-a-lobbying/top-lobbyists/529550-the-hills-top-lobbyists-2020. Accessed April 8, 2021; David D. Kirkpatrick, "Lobbyists Get Potent Weapon in Campaign Ruling," *The New York Times* (January 21, 2010), http://www.nytimes.com/2010/01/22/us/politics/22donate.html?_r=0. Accessed April 8, 2021.

19. Elizabeth Dwoskin, "Lobbyist on Incremental Mission to Restore Lobbying's Good Name," *Bloomberg Businessweek* (June 7, 2012), 78.

20. Nathaniel Popper, "Disgraced Lobbyist Jack Abramoff Headed Back to Jail," *The New York Times* (June 25, 2020), https://www.nytimes.com/2020/06/25/us/politics/jack-abramoff-marijuana-cryptocurrency.html. Accessed April 9, 2021.

21. Ibid.

22. Lobbying Database, OpenSecrets.org, https://www.opensecrets.org/federal-lobbying. Accessed April 9, 2021.

23. Raquel Meyer Alexander, Stephen W. Mazza, and Susan Scholz, "Measuring Rates of Return for Lobbying Expenditures: An Empirical Case Study of Tax Breaks for Multinational Corporations," *Journal of Law and Politics* (Vol. 25, No. 401, 2009), 401.

24. Peter Elkind, "Business Gets Schooled," *Fortune* (January 1, 2016), 49.

25. Joel Makower, "State of Green Business 2021," *Greenbiz* (January 25, 2021), https://www.greenbiz.com/article/state-green-business-2021. Accessed April 9, 2021.

26. Elena Sanchez Nicolas, "'Big Five' Tech Giants Spent €19m Lobbying EU in 2020," *EU Observer* (March 7, 2021), https://euobserver.com/science/151072. Accessed April 9, 2021.

27. Ryan Tracy, Chad Day, and Anthony De Barros, "Facebook and Amazon Boosted Lobbying Spending in 2020," *The Wall Street Journal* (January 24, 2021), https://www.wsj.com/articles/facebook-and-amazon-boosted-lobbying-spending-in-2020-11611500400. Accessed April 9, 2021.

28. Theodoric Meyer, "Coronavirus Fuels K Street Lobbying Gush, New Disclosures Show," *Politico* (April 22, 2020), https://www.politico.com/news/2020/04/22/coronavirus-lobbying-gush-199951. Accessed April 9, 2021.

29. Brody Mullins and Alex Leary, "Washington's Biggest Lobbyist, the U.S. Chamber of Commerce, Gets Shut Out," *The Wall Street Journal* (May 2, 2019), https://www.wsj.com/articles/washingtons-biggest-lobbyist-the-u-s-chamber-of-commerce-gets-shut-out-11556812302. Accessed April 9, 2021.

30. Karl Evers-Hillstrom, "Lobbying Spending Nears Record High in 2020 Amid Pandemic," *OpenSecrets* (January 27, 2021), https://www.opensecrets.org/news/2021/01/lobbying-spending-nears-record-high-in-2020-amid-pandemic/. Accessed April 9, 2021.

31. See Plastic Pollution Coalition, https://www.plasticpollutioncoalition.org/the-coalition. Accessed April 10, 2021.

32. Eric Lipton, "Emails Reveal Academic Ties in a Food War," *The New York Times* (September 6, 2015), 1.

33. Michael Hiltzik, "The Revolving Door Spins Faster," *The Los Angeles Times* (January 6, 2015) (http://www.latimes.com/business/hiltzik/la-fi-mh-the-revolving-door-20150106-column.html. Accessed March 21, 2016.

34. Russell Berman, "The Most Unrealistic Proposal in the Democratic Presidential Primary," *The Atlantic* (May 28, 2019, https://www.theatlantic.com/politics/archive/2019/05/lobbying-ban-bennet-warren-2020/590182/. Accessed April 9, 2021.

35. "Executive Order on Ethics Commitments by Executive Branch Personnel," *The White House* (January 20, 2021), https://www.whitehouse.gov/briefing-room/presidential-actions/2021/01/20/executive-order-ethics-commitments-by-executive-branch-personnel/. Accessed April 10, 2021.

36. Hilzik, 2015.

37. Josh Gerstein, "How Obama Failed to Shut Washington's Revolving Door," *Politico* (December 31, 2015), http://www.politico.com/story/2015/12/barack-obama-revolving-door-lobbying-217042. Accessed March 23, 2016.

38. Evan Thomas, "Peddling Influence," *Time* (March 3, 1986), 27.

39. Edward Segal, "How and Why Corporate Lobbying Will Continue to Matter During the Biden Administration," *Forbes* (January 26, 2021), https://www.forbes.com/sites/edwardsegal/2021/01/26/how-and-why-corporate-lobbying-will-continue-to-matter-during-the-biden-administration/?sh=6a05bde544dd. Accessed April 10, 2021.

40. Jane M. Keffer and Ronald Paul Hill, "An Ethical Approach to Lobbying Activities of Businesses in the United States," *Journal of Business Ethics* (September 1997), 1371–1379.

41. Public Affairs Council, The Advocacy Conference 2021, https://pac.org/events/the-advocacy-conference/agenda/. Accessed April 10, 2021.

42. Deanna Fox, "Social Media Powers Young Lobbyists," *Timesunion* (January 13, 2016), http://www.timesunion.com/tuplus-local/article/Social-media-powers-young-lobbyists-6753277.php. Accessed April 10, 2021.

43. Edward T. Walker, "The Uber-ization of Activism," *The New York Times* (August 6, 2015), https://www.nytimes.com/2015/08/07/opinion/the-uber-ization-of-activism.html. Accessed April 12, 2021.

44. Ibid.

45. Kim Miller and Jeff Hunter, "Lobbying and Campaign Finance Laws in 2020," *MultiState* (March 4, 2021), https://www.multistate.us/insider/2021/3/4/these-states-made-changes-to-lobbying-and-campaign-finance-laws-in-2020. Accessed April 10, 2021.

46. See for example, *The Alliance for Equal Justice* "Communications Toolkit," http://allianceforequaljustice.org/for-the-alliance/alliance-resources-and-tools/communications-toolkit/. Accessed April 10, 2021.

47. Daniel Stone, "The Browning of Grassroots," *Newsweek* (August 20, 2009), http://www.newsweek.com/id/212934. Accessed March 8, 2013.

48. SourceWatch, "Journalists Who Have Been Taken in by Astroturfing" (2019), http://www.sourcewatch.org/index.php/Journalists_who_have_been_taken_in_by_astroturfing. Accessed April 13, 2021.

49. David McCabe, "How Tech Lobbyists Are Using the Pandemic to Make Gains," *The New York Times* (April 3, 2020), https://www.nytimes.com/2020/04/03/technology/virus-tech-lobbyists-gains.html. Accessed April 10, 2021.

50. J. David Goodman and Luis Ferre-Sadurni, "'Big Fight' Breaks Out Over Which Interest Groups Get Vaccine First," *The New York Times* (December 20, 2020), https://www.nytimes.com/2020/12/20/nyregion/essential-worker-coronavirus-vaccine.html. Accessed April 10, 2021.

51. Ibid.

52. *Business Roundtable*, http://businessroundtable.org/about. Accessed April 11, 2021.

53. See "Business Roundtable Statement on Introduction of the U.S. Citizenship Act of 2021," *Business Roundtable* (February 18, 2021), https://www.businessroundtable.org/business-roundtable-statement-on-introduction-of-the-us-citizenship-act-of-2021. Accessed April 11, 2021; "Addressing Climate Change," *Business Roundtable* (September 16, 2020), https://www.businessroundtable.org/climate. Accessed April 11, 2021.

54. Lawrence H. Summers, "If the Business Roundtable CEOs Are Serious About Reform, Here's What They Should Do," *The Washington Post* (September 2, 2019), https://www.washingtonpost.com/opinions/if-business-roundtable-ceos-are-serious-about-reform-heres-what-they-should-do/2019/09/02/53b05014-cdc0-11e9-8c1c-7c8ee785b855story.html. Accessed April 11, 2021.

55. Ibid.

56. Mullins and Leary, 2019.

57. See Mullins and Leary, 2019; David Brodwin, "The Chamber's Secrets," *US News* (October 22, 2015), http://www.usnews.com/opinion/economic-intelligence/2015/10/22/who-does-the-us-chamber-of-commerce-really-represent. Accessed April 11, 2021.

58. Jane Sasseen, "Who Speaks for Business?" *Businessweek* (October 19, 2009), 22–24.

59. Mullins and Leary, 2019.

60. http://www.flyersrights.org/. Accessed April 11, 2021.

61. PR Newswire, "FlyersRights Petitions DOT to Protect the Public with a Mask Rule" (August 14, 2020), https://www.prnewswire.com/news-releases/flyersrights-petitions-dot-to-protect-the-public-with-a-mask-rule-301112523.html. Accessed April 11, 2021.

62. Global Business Coalition Against Human Trafficking, GBCAT, https://www.gbcat.org/. Accessed April 11, 2021.

63. Ibid.

64. Alex Altman, "Why the Killing of George Floyd Sparked an American Uprising," *Time* (June 4, 2020), https://time.com/5847967/george-floyd-protests-trump/. Accessed April 11, 2021.

65. Sheryl Estrada, "Major U.S. Companies Join Global Coalition for Racial Justice in Business," *HR Dive* (February 2, 2021), https://www.hrdive.com/news/major-us-companies-join-global-coalition-for-racial-justice-in-business/594358/. Accessed April 11, 2021.

66. "Court Won't Hear Campaign Contributions Appeal," *Boston Herald* (February 25, 2013), http://www.bostonherald.com/news_opinion/us_politics/2013/02/court_wont_hear_campaign_contributions_appeal Accessed February 26, 2016.

67. Federal Election Commission, "Who Can and Can't Contribute," https://www.fec.gov/help-candidates-and-committees/candidate-taking-receipts/who-can-and-cant-contribute/. Accessed April 11, 2021.

68. OpenSecrets.org, https://www.opensecrets.org/political-action-committees-pacs/top-pacs/2020?filter=P&pac=A&party=A#candidates. Accessed April 11, 2021.

69. R. Sam Garrett, "Super PACs in Federal Elections: Overview and Issues for Congress," *Congressional Research Service* (April 4, 2013), http://www.fas.org/sgp/crs/misc/R42042.pdf. Accessed April 11, 2021.

70. Adam Liptak, "Courts Take on Campaign Finance Decisions," *The New York Times* (March 26, 2010), http://www.nytimes.com/2010/03/27/us/politics/27campaign.html. Accessed April 11, 2021.

71. Ibid.

72. OpenSecrets.org, https://www.opensecrets.org/political-action-committees-pacs/super-pacs/2020. Accessed April 11, 2021.

73. See Amelia Ahl, "The Risks of 'Business as Usual' Corporate Political Contributions," TriplePundit (February 22, 2021), https://www.triplepundit.com/story/2021/corporate-political-contributions/718861, Accessed April 11, 2021; Bruce F. Freed and Karl J. Sandstrom, "Dangerous Terrain: How to Manage Corporate Political Spending in a Risky New Environment," *The Conference Board Review* (Winter 2012), 20–27.

74. Ibid.

75. Bruce F. Freed and Karl J. Sandstrom, "Navigating Politics," *The Conference Board Review* (Winter 2013), http://www.tcbreview.com/tcbr-leadership/navigating-politics.html. Accessed April 11, 2021.

76. Josh Duboff, "Target Issues Apology After Donation to Anti-Gay, Conservative Republican," *New York Intelligencer* (August 8, 2010), https://nymag.com/intelligencer/2010/08/target_issues_apology_after_do.html. Accessed April 13, 2021.

77. Kirby Goidel and Keith Gaddie, "Money Matters (in Presidential Elections)," *Huffington Post* (February 8, 2016), http://www.huffingtonpost.com/kirby-goidel/money-matters-in-presiden_b_9190198.html. Accessed March 23, 2016.

78. Ahl, 2021.

79. Staff, "McCain Raps High Court's Campaign Finance Ruling," *Associated Press* (January 12, 2012), https://www.yahoo.com/news/mccain-raps-high-courts-campaign-finance-ruling-123521384.html. Accessed April 11, 2021.

80. Michael Beckel, "Supreme Court Gives Corporations, Unions Power to Spend Unlimited Sums on Political Messaging," *OpenSecretsblog* (January 21, 2010), http://www.opensecrets.org/news/2010/01/supreme-court-gives-corporatio.html. Accessed April 11, 2021.

81. Larry J. Sabato, "PAC-Man Goes to Washington," *Across the Board* (October 1984), 16.

82. Freed and Sandstrom, 2013.

83. Ibid.

84. Ibid., 26.

85. See *Proxy Preview*, https://www.proxypreview.org/proxy-preview-2018/social-issues/corporate-political-activity?rq=transparency. Accessed April 11, 2021; Kelly Ngo, "Political Spending Shareholder Resolutions: The Big Ten," *Citizenvox* (April 22, 2015, http://www.citizenvox.org/2015/04/22/political-spending-shareholder-resolutions-the-big-ten/ Accessed April 11, 2021.

86. Tory Newmyer, "Activist Shareholders Pressing Companies to Disclose More of Their Political Activity after Capitol Attack," *The Washington Post* (February 23, 2021), https://www.washingtonpost.com/business/2021/02/23/corporate-political-giving-capitol-attack/. Accessed April 11, 2021.

87. The CPA-Zicklin Index of Corporate Political Disclosure and Accountability, http://files.politicalaccountability.net/index/CPA-Zicklin_Index_Final_with_links.pdf. Accessed April 11, 2021.

88. Sunlight Foundation, http://sunlightfoundation.com/. Accessed March 24, 2016.

89. Anna Massoglia and Karl Evers-Hillstron, "'Dark Money' Topped $1 Billion in 2020, Largely Boosting Democrats," *OpenSecrets.org* (March 17, 2021), https://www.opensecrets.org/news/2021/03/one-billion-dark-money-2020-electioncycle/. Accessed April 11, 2021.

90. Brian C. Mooney, "Ruling Allows Major Political Donors to Hide Identities," *The Boston Globe* (February 15, 2012), http://www.bostonglobe.com/news/nation/2012/02/15/major-political-donors-can-hide-identities/JrQx1lLgLQNJ1Mfuz5LbjN/story.html?camp=pm. Accessed April 11, 2021.

91. OpenSecrets.org, "527 Basics," https://www.opensecrets.org/527s/basics.php. Accessed April 11, 2021.

92. See Kate Ackley, "Super PACs After 10 Years: Often Maligned but Heavily Used," *Roll Call* (Janaury 16, 2020, https://www.rollcall.com/2020/01/16/super-pacs-after-10-years-often-maligned-but-heavily-used/. Accessed April 11, 2021; John Dimsdale, "Required Super PAC Disclosures Don't Reveal All," *Marketplace* (February 1, 2012), http://www.marketplace.org/topics/elections/campaign-trail/required-super-pac-disclosures-dont-reveal-all. Accessed April 11, 2021.

93. OpenSecrets.org, "527 Basics," https://www.opensecrets.org/527s/types.php. Accessed April 11, 2021.

94. Center for Political Accountability, "Hidden Rivers (2006): How Trade Associations Conceal Corporate Political Spending, Its Threat to Companies, and What Shareholders Can Do," http://politicalaccountability.net/reports/cpa-reports. Accessed April 11, 2021.

95. Andrew Ross Sorkin, Jason Karaian, Michael J. de la Merced, Lauren Hirsch, and Ephrat Livni, "Please Don't Follow This Money," *DealBook, The New York Times* (January 19, 2021), https://www.nytimes.com/2021/01/19/business/dealbook/supreme-court-dark-money.html. Accessed April 11, 2021.

96. Mahon, 1989.

97. Amy J. Hillman and Michael A. Hitt, "Corporate Political Strategy Formulation: A Model of Approach, Participation, and Strategy Decisions," *Academy of Management Review* (Vol. 24, No. 4, 1999), 825–842.

98. Ibid.

99. Douglas A. Schuler and Kathleen Rehbein, "Linking Corporate Community Programs and Political Strategies," *Business & Society* (Vol. 54, No. 6, 2015), 794–821.

100. Jim VandeHei, "CEOS are the New Lawmakers," *Axios* (April 5, 2021), https://www.axios.com/ceo-corporations-voting-rights-laws-8978f793-1927-4831-a3a9-88c095ab656a.html?utm_campaign=organic&utm_medium=socialshare&utm_source=email. Accessed April 12, 2021.

101. See Michael Hadani and Douglas Schuler, "In Search of El Dorado: The Elusive Financial Returns on Corporate Political Investments," *Strategic Management Journal*, February 2013, 165–181; Sean Lux, T. Russell Crook, and Terry Leap. "Corporate Political Activity: The Good, the Bad, and the Ugly," *Business Horizons*, May 2012, 307–312.

102. Sean Lux, T. Russell Crook, and David J. Woehr, "Mixing Business with Politics: A Meta-Analysis of the Antecedents and Outcomes of Corporate Political Activity," *Journal of Management* (Vol. 37, No. 1, 2011), 223–236.

Case

Case 1
Walmart: The Main Street Merchant of Doom

Case 2
Walmart's Labor Practices

Case 3
Chipotle's Struggle with Food Safety: Back on Top Again?

Case 4
The Theranos Story and Fake Blood Testing: Culture, Crime, and Hubris

Case 5
Direct-to-Consumer Advertising for Pharmaceuticals: Is It Ethical?

Case 6
The COVID-19 Pandemic: Herculean Challenges for Business and CSR

Case 7
Volkswagen's Diesel Deception and Its Aftermath

Case 8
Payday Loans: A Needed Product or a Financial Scam?

Case 9
Big Tech's Power Plays

Case 10
An Epidemic of Cheating in College

Case 11
Climate Change and Corporate Activism: Is It All Just Hot Air?

Case 12
Family Business

Case 13
What Makes a Good CEO? The Waiter Rule, Humility, and Amazon

Case 14
Nike, Sweatshops, and Other Issues

Case 15
The Rana Plaza Factory Collapse

Case 16
Big Food, Big Problem: Nestlé in Brazil

Case 17
The Dark Side of Going Green: Tesla's Ethical Dilemma

Case 18
Coke and Pepsi in India: Water, Issues, and Crisis Management

Case 19
An Ethical Dilemma for Chiquita in Colombia

Case 20
Dark Money and Corporate Political Spending on Campaigns

Case 21
Big Pharma's Marketing Tactics

Case 22
Purdue Pharma, OxyContin, and the Opioid Crisis

Case 23
McDonald's: The Coffee Spill Heard 'Round the World

Case 24
Boeing's Two Flight Crashes

Case 25
Should States Woo Big Business with Tax Incentives? Amazon Thinks So!

Case 26
Everlane: Ethical Chic and Radical Transparency in Global Supply Chains

Case 27
Slow and Sustainable Fashion

Case 28
The Perils of Student Loan Debt

Case 29
"Dead Peasant" Life Insurance Policies

Case 30
The Case of the Fired Waitress

Case 31
Two Vets, Two Dogs, and a Deadlock

Case 32
Are Criminal Background Checks Discriminatory?

Case 33
To Take or Not to Take

Case 34
Workplace Spying

Case Analysis Guidelines

The guidelines presented below have been designed to help you analyze the Cases that follow. The guidelines are presented in three stages, but they are not intended to be a rigid format. Each question is designed to elicit information that will help you in analyzing and resolving the Case. Each Case is different, and some parts of the guidelines may not apply to every Case. The questions for discussion at the end of each Case should be addressed in any complete Case analysis. Use the Issue/Problem Identification and Analysis/Evaluation steps to focus on generating and defending the most effective set of recommendations possible because the objective of Case analysis is making recommendations. In all stages of the Case analysis, use the stakeholder, ethics, sustainability, and corporate social responsibility (CSR) concepts presented in the text.

Issue/Problem Identification

1. **Facts and Assumptions.** What are the *central facts* of the Case and the assumptions you are making on the basis of these facts?

2. **Major Overriding Issues/Problems.** What are the *major overriding issues* in this Case? (What major questions/issues does this Case address that merit(s) their/its study in this course and in connection with the chapter/material you are now covering?)

3. **Subissues and Related Issues.** What *subissues* or *related issues* are present in the Case that merit consideration, discussion, and action?

Analysis/Evaluation

4. **Stakeholder Analysis.** Who are the *stakeholders* in this Case, and what are their stakes? (Create a stakeholder map to depict relationships.) What challenges, threats, or opportunities does each stakeholder face? What stakeholder characteristics are at work (legitimacy, power, urgency)?

5. **CSR Analysis.** What CSRs (*economic, legal, ethical, philanthropic*) does the company have, and what exactly are the nature and extent of these responsibilities to the various stakeholders?

6. **Evaluations.** If the Case involves a company's or manager's actions, evaluate what the company or manager did or did not do correctly in handling the issue affecting it. How should actions have been handled?

Recommendations

7. **Recommendations and Implementation.** What *recommendations* would you make in this Case? If a company's or a manager's strategies or actions are involved, should they have acted the way they did? What actions should they have taken? What actions should the company or manager take now, and why? Be specific and include a discussion of alternatives (*right now, short term,* and *long term*). Identify and discuss any important *implementation considerations*.

Case 1

Walmart: The Main Street Merchant of Doom*

Sam Walton, founder, owner, and mastermind of Walmart,[1] passed away on April 5, 1992, leaving behind his spirit to ride herd on the colossal Walmart organization. To the consumer in the small community, his store, Walmart, was seen as a friend when it came to town. On the flip side, many a small-town merchant had been the victim of Sam's blazing merchandising tactics. So, what is Walmart to the communities it serves? Is Walmart the consumer's best friend, the purveyor of the free-enterprise system, the "Mother of All Discount Stores," or, conversely, is it really "The Main Street Merchant of Doom"?

The Man Named Sam

Samuel Moore Walton was born on March 29, 1918, near Kingfisher, Kansas.He attended the University of Missouri in the fall of 1936 and graduated with a degree in business administration. At age 22, Sam joined JCPenney. One of his first tasks was to memorize and practice the "Penney Idea." Adopted in 1913, this credo exhorted the associate to serve the public; not to demand all the profit the traffic will bear; to pack the customer's dollar full of value, quality, and satisfaction; to continue to be trained; to reward people in the organization through participation in what the business produces; and to test every policy, method, and act against the question, "Does it square with what is right and just?"[2]

Sam's First Store

In 1962, at age 44, Sam Walton opened his first Walmart store in Rogers, Arkansas. He took all the money and expertise he could gather and applied the JCPenney idea to Middle America. Sam first targeted small, underserved rural towns with populations of no more than 10,000 people. The people responded, and Walmart soon developed a core of loyal customers who loved the fast, friendly service coupled with consistently low prices. Later, Sam expanded his company into the larger cities, often with numerous Walmarts spread throughout the city.

The Store That Sam Built

By 2001, Walmart Stores, Inc., had become the world's largest retailer with $191 billion in sales. The company employed one million associates worldwide through nearly 3,500 facilities in the United States and more than 1,000 stores throughout nine other countries. Walmart claimed that more than 100 million customers per week visited Walmart stores. The company had four major

retail divisions: Walmart Supercenters, Discount Stores, Neighborhood Markets, and Sam's Club warehouses. As it entered the 2000s, Walmart had been named "Retailer of the Century" by *Discount Store News*, made *Fortune* magazine's lists of the "Most Admired Companies in America" and the "100 Best Companies to Work For," and was ranked on *Financial Times*' "Most Respected in the World" list.[3] Fiscal year 2020's revenue was $524 billion and Walmart employed more than 2.2 million associates worldwide. The company is quick to say that its financials were significantly affected by the COVID-19 outbreak.[4]

The Walmart Way

Sam's approach was to promote the associate—the hourly employee—to a new level of participation within the organization. Sam, as the head cheerleader, saw his job as the chief proponent of the "Walmart Way." The Walmart Way reflected Sam's idea of the essential Walmart culture that was needed for success. Sam felt that when a customer entered Walmart in any part of the country, the customer should feel at home. Examples of the culture included "exceeding customer expectations" and "helping people make a difference." He was a proponent of the "Ten-Foot Rule," which meant that if a customer came within ten feet of an associate, the associate would look the customer in the eye, greet the customer, and ask if the customer needed help.[5]

Sam, the CEO, hired the best managers he could find. He let them talk him into buying an extensive computer network system. This network corporate satellite system enabled Sam to use round-the-clock inventory control and credit card sales control and provided him with information on total sales of which products where and when. This computer control center was about the size of a football field and used a satellite for up-linking and down-linking to each store.

Early Social Awareness initiatives

Sam, the innovator, was responsible for two early social responsibility innovations: Walmart's "Buy American" plan and its "Environmental Awareness" campaign.

Walmart's "Buy American" plan was in response to Sam's realization that his company was adding to the loss of American jobs by buying cheaper foreign goods. This concern drove him to find a solution. In February 1986, about 12 months after the Buy American plan had begun, Sam held a press conference. He showed off all the merchandise Walmart was now buying domestically. He estimated that Walmart's Buy American plan had restored 4,538 jobs to the American economy and its people.[6] The Buy American plan was one of Walmart's early efforts at

---

*This case, originally prepared by William T. Rupp, Austin Peay State University, was revised and updated by Archie B. Carroll, University of Georgia, in 2021.

corporate social responsibility. Ironically, Walmart eventually abandoned this program and became one of the largest purchasers of products made overseas. In fact, the company in time became the country's largest purchaser of Chinese goods in any industry. Some say that by taking its orders abroad, Walmart forced many U.S. manufacturers out of business.[7]

Awareness of the environment was on the rise also, and Sam looked for a way to involve Walmart in the environmental movement. In August 1989, an ad in *The Wall Street Journal* proclaimed Walmart's "commitment to our land, air and water." Sam envisioned Walmart as a leader among American companies in the struggle to clean up the environment. Walmart wanted to use its tremendous buying power to aid in the implementation of the campaign. In the stores, shelf tags made from 100 percent recycled paper informed customers of the environmental friendliness of the highlighted product. As a result of these shelf tags and Walmart's advertising, customer awareness had increased, and some environmentally safe product manufacturers were reaping the rewards of increased Walmart orders.

The Early Merchants of Main Street Resist

Not everyone was excited to see Sam and his mechanized Walmart army arrive and succeed. Small merchants across America shuddered when the winds of the "Walmart Way" began to blow in their direction. Kennedy Smith of the National Main Street Center in Washington, D. C., said, "The first thing towns usually do is panic." Once Walmart comes to town, Smith says, "Downtowns will never again be the providers of basic consumer goods and services they once were."[8]

Some towns learned to "just say 'no'" to Walmart's overtures. Steamboat Springs, Colorado, was one such city. Colorado newspapers called it the "Shootout at Steamboat Springs." Walmart was denied permission to build on a nine-acre parcel along U.S. Route 40. Owners of upscale shops and condos were concerned with the image of their resort and ski community, and Walmart, with its low-cost reputation, did not fit the community ambiance. The shootout lasted for two years, and finally Walmart filed a damage suit against the city. Countersuits followed. A petition was circulated to hold a referendum on the matter. This was the shot that made Walmart blink and back down. Years later, Steamboat Springs finally got a Walmart. It won't be found on the tourist's lists of shopping places, but it's there.

Meanwhile, in Pawhuska, Oklahoma, as a result of Walmart's entry in 1983 and other local factors, the local "five-and-dime," JCPenney, Western Auto, and a whole block of other stores closed their doors. Four years later, Dave Story, general manager of the local *Pawhuska Daily Journal Capital*, wrote that Walmart was a "billion-dollar parasite" and a "national retail ogre."[9]

Walmart managers had become active in Pawhuska and surrounding communities since that time. A conversation with the editor of the Pawhuska paper, Jody Smith, and her advertising editor revealed that Walmart sponsored the local rodeo, gave gloves to the local coat drive, and was involved with the local cerebral palsy and multiple sclerosis fundraisers. On the other hand, Fred Wright, former owner of a TV and record store, said, "Walmart really craters a little town's downtown."[10]

Opposition Gets Organized

By the 1990s, there were dozens of organized groups actively opposing Walmart's expansion.[11] Some of these groups were and still are run by social activists who are reliving the 1960s and 1970s. Instead of protesting the Vietnam War, nuclear proliferation, or the destruction of the environment, they turned their efforts to Walmart specifically and capitalism in general. One of these activists, Paul Glover, who was an antiwar organizer, defined Walmart as the epitome of capitalism, which he despises. For Glover and others, Walmart stands for "everything they dislike about American society—mindless consumerism, paved landscapes, and homogenization of community identity."[12]

In Boulder, Colorado, Walmart tried to counter these allegations by proposing a "green" store. Steven Lane, Walmart's real estate manager, said that a "green store" would be built that would be environmentally friendly, with a solar-powered sign out front. His efforts were trumpeted by Spencer Havlick, an organizer of the first Earth Day in 1970, suggesting that the entire store be powered by solar energy. Mr. Lane did not respond to this suggestion.[13]

Protest organizers united against the spread of the "Walmart Way" differ from the downtown merchants in that these protesters have no financial stake though they still regard themselves as stakeholders. These activists attacked Walmart on a higher, philosophical plane. The accusations rang with a tone of argument that was made by other activists protesting polluting industries (e.g., the coal, nuclear, and chemical industries). These activists accused Walmart of "strip-mining" towns and communities of their culture and values.

One possible root of this culture clash may be attributed to the unique aspects of the internal corporate culture at Walmart's headquarters. This is a place where competition for the reputation as the "cheapest" was practiced. An example is the competition among employees in procuring the cheapest haircut, shoes, or necktie. Consequently, as a result of the internal culture of Walmart and the external environment, some analysts believe that a clash of priorities and values was inevitable as Walmart moved into larger, more urban settings.

Some of the most vigorous opposition to Walmart's growth came from the New England area. This area held great promise for Walmart because of the large, dense population and the many underserved towns. These towns are typically underserved in three ways: in variety of product choices, in value, and in convenience. The opposition to Walmart entering these New England markets includes some high-profile names, such as Jerry Greenfield, co-founder of Ben & Jerry's Homemade ice cream, and Arthur Frommer, a well-known travel writer.[14] In addition to New England, other areas, such as resort areas, opposed Walmarts because they have wanted to insulate their unique cultures from what they considered to be the offensive consumerism that is usually generated by Walmart's presence.

Continuing Challenges and Issues

Despite opposition and criticism, Walmart has continued its aggressive diversification and growth pattern. Each year seems to bring something new about Walmart and its competitiveness. In 2021, Walmart began signaling that it is getting serious about financial technology, hiring several executives from Goldman Sachs to build its consumer banking platform in the quest for cost savings as well as efficient payment processing. At the same time, it was expanding into online advertising and other businesses.[15] More broadly, Walmart has sought to diversity its profit base as it has expanded its third-party marketplace on its website along with its Walmart+ subscription service and online advertising. Much of Walmart's recent growth, perhaps related to the pandemic, has been in its e-commerce operations. Walmart has tried to compete with Amazon.com. Additionally, much attention continues to be focused on whether Walmart will seek a banking charter.[16]

In spite of its many achievements, article titles from newspapers and magazines have consistently raised questions about Walmart's size, power, and impact in the United States and around the world. In the 2020 Fortune 500 listing, Walmart has held on to its #1 position in terms of revenues: $524 million.[17] Some of these article titles reveal the public's thinking about the giant corporation: "Planet Walmart," "One Nation under Walmart," and "The Wal-Martization of America."[18] Sheer size has become a huge problem for Walmart because many citizens equate size with power. Being so highly visible makes the company a natural target of critics.

Some of the continuing issues that Walmart faces in the 2020s include global growth, bribery scandals, labor practices, crime problems at their stores, and charges that they helped to fuel an opioid crisis. Their global growth has been supersized, and the sheer size of their international business poses strategic challenges more than social and ethical challenges. Walmart's $16 billion stake in India's Flipkart turned out to be the largest e-commerce deal to date.[19]

Related to their global expansion, however, have been charges of bribery and corruption as the company has attempted to enter countries in which bribery and kickbacks are often standard practice. In 2019, Walmart finally agreed to pay $282 million in settlement to resolve years-long criminal and regulatory allegations into whether it paid bribes in various countries. The company agreed that it had lax policies that perhaps allowed potential corruption. The SEC said that the company violated the U.S. Foreign Corrupt Practices Act, which prohibits U.S. firms from paying bribes to win business abroad.[20] The Walmart probe began with some questionable operations in Mexico but moved on to its practices across the globe, including Brazil, China, and India. The SEC said that the company's low-cost philosophy contributed to its inadequate policies to combat corruption and that the company failed to employ careful compliance policies and repeatedly failed to see red flags regarding corruption risks.[21]

Walmart's labor practices continue to be a constant source of challenge, but these topics are identified and discussed more completely in Case 2 on "Walmart's Labor Practices."

Crime in Stores

Another issue that Walmart has faced for some years now is its store-related crime problems. Every day a violent crime occurs at a U.S. Walmart, and many of the police departments have reported that they are fed up with it.[22] The crimes at Walmarts range from the petty ones such as shoplifting, trying to use phony gift cards, customers failing to scan products at self-checkout, and customers trying to walk out the door without paying to more serious crimes, including armed robberies, parking lot shootouts, attempted kidnappings, stabbings, and an occasional murder. These do not occur at all stores, and the store's location has a lot to do with crime severity and frequency.[23]

An example of how frequent crimes may occur at some stores is illustrated by the Walmart in Tulsa, Oklahoma. One Tulsa police officer stays at the store ten hours a day because there is constantly something going on. People, including colleagues, are now calling him "Officer Walmart." The officer stations himself in a small security office where four Walmart employees are watching monitors. There also is a hired security officer on duty. Some police departments say they are frustrated and exhausted by having to constantly be on duty or be called to various Walmarts throughout the day.[24]

Part of the problem is that Walmarts are open 24 hours, often staffed by low-paid employees who have not been properly trained, and this is a natural draw for after-hours crimes to take place. Some say that the crime is also enhanced because Walmart allows overnight camping and recreational vehicle parking in store parking lots, potentially inviting homeless people to dwell there. Some critics say this all began 20 years ago when Walmart's cost-cutting crusade allowed many stores to deteriorate. Many stores eliminated their famed greeters, and this opened the door to problems because one fewer deterrent existed. Self-checkout scanners replaced many employees, and there are fewer people to monitor things.[25]

When Doug McMillon, current CEO, took charge in 2014, he began an ambitious program to fix up long-neglected stores, making them cleaner and stocking them better. Critics say they just aren't doing it fast enough. A major problem is money. Experts say most store managers could clean up their problems quickly if given adequate resources. But Walmart's low-cost philosophy creates tension. Some complain that Walmart's board just doesn't have enough retail experience to fund what needs to be done in the realms of safety and security. They are too focused on profits, some allege. More technology, more investments in hiring security, higher wages, and better training are all avenues that have been proposed.[26]

Opioids

In 2020, a new issue arose regarding Walmart's policies and practices on filling opioid prescriptions at its pharmacies. Some critics have accused Walmart of fueling the opioid crisis occurring in the United States. Sensing that the federal government was planning to take legal action against the firm, Walmart sued the U.S. government in an effort to head off opioid penalties.[27] Walmart was seeking to strike a preemptive blow against what it thought was an inappropriate, impending lawsuit from the Justice Department. As expected, the U.S. Justice Department did accuse Walmart of helping to fuel the country's opioid crisis by insufficiently screening questionable prescriptions.[28]

The Justice Department's lawsuit claims that Walmart tried to boost its profits by understaffing its pharmacies and putting pressure on pharmacists to fill prescriptions quickly. The lawsuit alleges that Walmart's pressure on employees caused pharmacies to inadequately reject invalid prescriptions, thus enabling widespread drug abuse nationwide.[29] Walmart defended itself by saying that the Drug Enforcement Administration (DEA) is to blame by letting some doctors overprescribe drugs. Walmart says that the Justice Department wants to penalize it for filling authorized prescriptions from doctors who have DEA registrations to issue such prescriptions.

Walmart has argued that blaming pharmacies for not second-guessing the doctors that the DEA approved to prescribe opioids is a transparent attempt to shift blame from the DEA's well-documented failures in keeping bad doctors from prescribing opioids in the first place. As it turns out, Walmart is just one of several large companies that have been targeted in such lawsuits that have been filed by more than two dozen states and many local governments claiming that their aggressive marketing of prescription painkillers has helped fuel the crisis.[30]

In spite of such issues, shoppers around the world continue to support Walmart. On a global scale, Walmart has more than 11,500 stores, and during the pandemic, its e-commerce went up by 74 percent. Each week, Walmart stores host around 256 million customers.[31] In addition to its retail size and power, many consider the company to be socially responsible in addition to being a provider of thousands of jobs, low prices, and high value and service. Walmart has numerous corporate citizenship and sustainability initiatives at the local and national levels. Walmart and the Walmart Foundation together provide more than $1 billion in cash and in-kind donations to support programs that align with their philanthropic priorities.[32] In 2021, they committed $100 million over five years to fund research,

advocacy, innovation of practices, and stakeholder convening to address racial inequity through Walmart.org's Center for Racial Equity.[33] Walmart's reputation for philanthropy goes back to 1998, when the Walton Family Charitable Support Foundation, the charitable program created by Sam Walton's family, announced what at the time was the largest ever single gift made to an American business school: $50 million to the College of Business Administration of the University of Arkansas. Helen R. Walton, the "first lady" of Walmart, said that she and her husband established the foundation to support specific charities, including the university.[34] To no one's surprise, it is now called the Sam M. Walton College of Business.[35] Locally, Walmart stores continue to underwrite college scholarships for high school seniors, raise funds for children's hospitals through the Children's Miracle Network Telethon, provide local fundraisers money and workforce, and educate the public about recycling and other environmental topics.[36]

Global Responsibility and Sustainability

In its 2020 Environmental, Social and Governance (ESG) Report, Walmart featured and summarized some of its recent goals and achievements:[37] Walmart states that it prioritizes ESG issues that offer the greatest potential to create shared value. The company focuses on issues that are highly relevant to their business and stakeholders. The company performed its first ESG materiality assessment in 2014, heavily engaging stakeholders, and the results informed their plans reaching out to 2025. These include goals related to associate/employee opportunity, environmental and social challenges in supply chains, and community resilience. The company performs regular updates through ongoing stakeholder engagement. Climate change is another top priority. The company has called for public and private sector engagements and has reaffirmed its own commitments through science-based targets for emissions reductions and Project Gigaton, an initiative for working with suppliers to reduce or avoid one gigaton of emissions in its supply chain by 2020.[38]

Epilogue to Sam's Story

Sam learned his lessons well. The people who bought at his stores have been mostly satisfied. The downtown merchants who survived learned to coexist with the company's associates. The changes had come rapidly. The social fabric of the small town was changed forever. The larger towns continued to fight but had only limited success. The search for new locations became more complicated as opposition rose, but the spirit of Sam continued to ride on. In fact, much of Sam's spirit appears to be playing out through current CEO Doug McMillon, as we describe next.

Doug McMillon, CEO

Doug McMillon, 49, a two-decade veteran at Walmart, was appointed CEO in 2014, succeeding Mike Duke who was CEO from 2009–2014.[39] McMillon immediately sensed the monumental task he faced as the new head of the world's largest employer. McMillon moved quickly during his first 18 months on the job. He accelerated new investments in e-commerce, made news by raising the minimum wage for Walmart employees, and experimented with one of the company's newest retail models, Walmart Pickup Grocery, where the trial run for this business model took place right in the company's headquarters in Bentonville, Arkansas.[40] In 2018, McMillon signaled that the company's transformation was about building new capabilities to meet changing customer expectations and equipping associates with the tools and training to compete in the evolving workplace.[41] However, Walmart faced its biggest challenge with the COVID-19 pandemic and its implications for the Walmart and Sam's Club stores. The year 2020 was a big year for Walmart as it continued to provide essential products and services for millions of citizens. The company grew its revenue by $35 billion, and its e-commerce business grew by triple digits. Also in 2020, Walmart launched its Walmart+ venture along with Walmart Connect, express delivery, and curbside pickup at Sam's Club.[42] For his achievements, CEO McMillon was named 2021 CEO of the Year by the Safe America Foundation for his work in protecting 2 million employees and millions of consumers in 2020.[43] It is little wonder that when he was appointed CEO, Fortune magazine dubbed him the "chosen one" and said that he may be the best-prepared executive to lead Walmart since Sam Walton himself.[44] The years ahead will be interesting to watch as Walmart plays out its "business in society" role.

Questions for Discussion

1. What are the major issues in this case? What does Walmart's experience tell you about the business and society relationship?
2. What happened to the "Penney Idea," Sam's ten-foot rule, and the Buy America Plan? Were these discontinued over time or did they fade away and get lost when Sam died?
3. Assess Walmart's corporate social responsibility using the four-part CSR model. Is Walmart socially responsible even though it has had a devastating impact on many small merchants and various stakeholder groups, and some communities do not want it?
4. What about Walmart's impact on communities in terms of sprawl, traffic congestion, and impact on the appearance of the environment? Regarding these issues, what responsibility, if any, does the company have to the communities it enters?
5. Sam Walton has been called a motivational genius. After reading this case, and with what you have observed at your local Walmart store, do you think his motivational genius is still felt by the associates? What is the "Walmart Way"? How would you characterize the store's culture now that Sam is no longer around?
6. Walmart was an early leader in the area of corporate social responsibility. Is the company's detrimental impact on merchants, and current opioid, labor, and bribery scandals, offset by the benefits of its recent corporate citizenship and sustainability initiatives?
7. Walmart continues to find resistance to its expansion in some communities. What are the true goals of the opponents of Walmart? Include a consideration of the following: (a) stopping Walmart's expansion, (b) preserving the status quo (e.g., downtown community and social fabric), (c) developing a cause that will pay their bills, (d) fighting for an ideology, or (e) something else. What should Walmart do when it encounters resistance?
8. When Walmart does have to close stores due to the economy and/or competition, does it have any social responsibilities to the communities it is leaving? If so, what would those responsibilities be?
9. When you are the largest company in the world, how do you protect yourself against the kind of criticism Walmart has received? Does it seem that no matter how hard you try, it's difficult to make things better?

Endnotes

1. Walmart Stores, Inc. (NYSE: WMT) is the legal name of the corporation. The name "Walmart," expressed as one word and without punctuation, is a trademark of the company and is used analogously to describe the company and its stores.
2. Ibid., 34.
3. Walmart, "Company Facts," https://corporate.walmart.com/newsroom/company-facts. Accessed June 25, 2021.
4. Walmart's earnings release, Q1, FY21, https://corporate.walmart.com/media-library/document/q1-fy21-earnings-release/_proxyDocument?id=00000172-29ed-d3ff-a3f6-bded2c350000. Accessed May 26, 2021.
5. For up-to-date information on Walmart's culture, Walmart, "Our Business," https://corporate.walmart.com/our-story/our-business. Accessed June 25, 2021.
6. Ibid., 261.
7. "Store Wars: When Walmart Comes to Town," IMDb, Accessed May 18, 2016.
8. Dan Koeppel, "Wal-Mart Finds New Rivals on Main Street," *Adweek's Marketing Week* (November 10, 1990), 5.
9. Karen Blumenthal, "Arrival of Discounter Tears the Civic Fabric of Small-Town Life," *The Wall Street Journal* (April 14, 1987), 1, 23.
10. Ibid., 23.
11. Bob Ortega, "Aging Activists Turn, Turn, Turn Attention to Wal-Mart Protests," *The Wall Street Journal* (October 11, 1994), A1, A8.
12. Ibid., A1.
13. Ibid., A8.
14. Joseph Pereira and Bob Ortega, "Once Easily Turned Away by Local Foes, Wal-Mart Gets Tough in New England," *The Wall Street Journal* (September 7, 1994), B1.

15. Telis Demos and Jingoo Lee, "Walmart Diversification Goes into Overdrive with Goldman Hires," *The Wall Street Journal*, March 1, 2021, https://www.wsj.com/articles/walmart-diversification-goes-into-overdrive-with-goldman-hires-11614631326. Accessed June 2, 2021.

16. Ibid.

17. Fortune, "Global 500," https://fortune.com/global500/. Accessed May 28, 2021.

18. *The New York Times* (November 15, 2003), A26; *Fortune*, March 3, 2003, 66–78; and "First," *Fortune*, May 3, 2010.

19. Beth Kowitt, "The World According to Walmart," *Fortune*, October 1, 2018, 70–76.

20. Dave Michaels and Sarah Nassauer, "Walmart to Pay $282 Million in Settlement of Bribery Probe," *The Wall Street Journal*, June 21, 2019, B3.

21. Ibid.

22. Shannon Pettypiece and David Voreacos, "Walmart's Crime Problem," *Bloomberg Businessweek*, August 17, 2016, 40–45.

23. Ibid.

24. Ibid.

25. Ibid.

26. Ibid.

27. Brent Kendall and Sara Randazzo, "Walmart Sues U.S. Aiming to Head Off Opioid Penalties," *The Wall Street Journal*, October 23, 202, A1.

28. Timothy Puko and Sadie Gurman, "U.S. Sues Walmart over Opioid Epidemic," *The Wall Street Journal*, December 23, 2020, A1.

29. Ibid.

30. Puko and Gurman, ibid.

31. Szabolcs Szec, "39 Walmart Statistics to Showcase the Retailer's Giant Power," Capital Counselor, April 3, 2021, https://capitalcounselor.com/walmart-statistics/. Accessed May 28, 2021.

32. Walmart.org, "Working Together to Spark Change," https://walmart.org/. Accessed June 27, 2021.

33. Ibid.

34. University of Arkansas, Sam Walton College of Business, http://walton.uark.edu/about/walton-atrium.php. Accessed May 18, 2016.

35. Walton College, University of Arkansas, https://walton.uark.edu/. Accessed May 21, 2016.

36. Walmart, "Sustainability," https://corporate.walmart.com/global-responsibility/sustainability/. Accessed May 28, 2021.

37. Walmart, 2020 Walmart Environmental, Social and Governance Report, https://corporate.walmart.com/esgreport/. Accessed June 2, 2021.

38. Ibid.

39. Brian O'Keefe, "The Chosen One," *Fortune*, June 15, 2015, 134–144. Also see Doug McMillon, "Walmart CEO: To Tackle Today's Challenges, to Listen with Open Ears and an Open Heart," *Fortune*, October 6, 2020, https://fortune.com/2020/10/06/walmart-ceo-doug-mcmillon-leadership-collaboration-dialogue/. Accessed June 30, 2021.

40. O'Keefe, Ibid.

41. Walmart, "CEO McMillon Says Walmart Embracing Change , Positioning for Continued Success," June 1, 2018, https://corporate.walmart.com/newsroom/2018/06/01/ceo-mcmillon-says-walmart-embracing-change-positioning-for-continued-success. Accessed June 25, 2021.

42. Sharon Edleson, "Walmart CEO Talks Wage Increases, Employee Covid Vaccine Mandates at Annual Meeting," *Forbes*, June 2, 2021, https://www.forbes.com/sites/sharonedelson/2021/06/02/sustainability-people-are-highlights-of-walmarts-2020-annual-meeting/?sh=35ee917460c6. Accessed June 25, 2021.

43. *Marietta Daily Journal*, "Walmart CEO McMillon named 2021 CEO of the Year by Safe America Foundation," May 5, 2021, https://autos.yahoo.com/walmart-ceo-doug-mcmillon-named-035900715.html. Accessed June 25, 2021.

44. Krantz, 134.

Case 2

Walmart's Labor Practices*

Historically, the primary criticism of Walmart, the world's largest company, has been its impact on communities and small merchants. Anti-sprawl activists and small-town merchants, in particular, have taken issue with the company moving into their communities.[1] In *Case 1—Walmart: The Main Street Merchant of Doom*, these issues were presented in some detail as well as other recent social issues the company is facing.

In particular, Walmart's labor practices and treatment of its employees over the past decade or so have raised many concerns in public and business discussions. Paradoxically, Walmart refers to its employees as "associates," a term intended to bestow a loftier status on its human resources than the term "employees."

Figure 1 presents some interesting facts about Walmart and its employees.

*This case was prepared by Archie B. Carroll, University of Georgia. Revised and updated in 2021.

Many consumers and citizens view Walmart as an excellent provider of jobs in communities, and despite criticisms that have been raised, people continue to seek out employment with Walmart. Though it has high turnover, it is viewed by countless job seekers as a stable place to work, and some individuals have sought to establish careers at the company. To the surprise of some, Walmart's 2021 ranking in *Fortune's* list of World's Most Admired Companies was #11, up from #18 in 2020, and ranked slightly higher than Nike (#13) and Johnson & Johnson (#15). This was Walmart's highest ranking since 2011.[2] Seventeen years earlier, *Fortune* writer Jerry Useem had asked, "Should we admire Walmart?" He went on to say, "Some say it's evil. Others insist it's a model of all that's right with America. Who are we to believe?"[3]

Many different employee-related issues with respect to Walmart have been the focus of news coverage over the years, and it is the purpose of Case 2 to explore those issues in more detail. The company has been accused of hiring too many part-time workers; offering jobs that are actually dead-end; paying low wages and poor benefits; forcing workers to work "off-the-clock," that is, to work overtime without overtime pay; and taking advantage of undocumented immigrants. Over the years, the company has also been accused of gender discrimination against women, who occupy most jobs at the company. Coupled with allegations of employee mistreatment, the company, which currently is not unionized, has fought unions and unionization everywhere it locates.

Over the past several years, income inequality has become an important issue in the United States and worldwide, and this has exacerbated the low wage accusations against all merchants, especially the big box stores.[4] In addition, the minimum wage debate has continued in the United States as a number of cities and states have moved to a $15 per hour minimum wage level.[5] The "living wage" movement has continued to lobby for minimum wage increases, and this movement seems to be gaining some momentum even in the face of a mixed economy and some companies having to lay off workers due to

the pandemic or because they cannot afford higher minimum wages.[6] These national trends have created a backdrop against which Walmart and other stores that rely on many entry-level jobs have had to deal in recent years. However, most of Walmart's employee challenges began years ago.

Low Pay, Hard Work, Questionable Treatment

Walmart is the nation's largest employer. It employs 2.2 million worldwide, with 1.6 million in the United States alone.[7] As such, it is not surprising that it has a large number of interactions with employees, and these interactions will be both positive and negative. Walmart claims to offer "good jobs, [and] good careers," but a number of employees have become vocal in recent years about their working conditions at the company. As with many retailers and service industries, Walmart is accused of offering low pay and few benefits. Many of these employees have been angered by the disparity between their low wages, few benefits, and the company's profits.[8] Related working complaints include not getting enough hours, scheduling inconsistencies, and difficulty getting decent raises.[9]

Working Off the Clock and without Breaks

One of the most troubling allegations of unfair treatment reported by some Walmart employees has been that of being asked to "work *off* the clock." This means that employees are pressured to do overtime work for which they do not get paid. One employee reported that they were asked to work off the clock by both the store manager and the assistant manager. According to several employees, managers would wait until an employee had clocked out and then say something like, "Do me a favor. I don't have anyone coming in—could you stay here?" Before they knew it, four to five hours passed before they could away.[10] In 2017, both current and former Walmart employees won a case that claimed the company failed to pay them for off-the-clock work, including time passing through security checks as well as meal breaks and overtime. Later that year, Walmart agreed to pay $60.8 million to settle the lawsuit.[11]

Labor Union Resistance

Because of employee complaints and desires to have higher wages and more generous benefits, Walmart employees have been the subject of union organizers for decades. Walmart's huge size and number of employees allows the firm to increasingly set the standard for wages and benefits throughout the U.S. economy.[12]

Across the country, workers in many states have tried to get unions organized, but so far they have not had much success. According to one report, employees at more than 100 stores in 25 states have been trying to get union representation. Walmart has tried in various ways to fight the union organizing efforts. The company has engaged in some actions that have been judged to be in violation of federal labor laws. Walmart has been held to be in violation of the law in ten separate cases in which the National Labor Relations Board has ruled that it has engaged in illegal activities such as confiscating union literature, interrogating workers, and discharging union sympathizers.[13]

Success in Union Resistance

There are several reasons why the unions have not been successful in unionizing Walmart. First, many employees feel intimidated by the company and fear signing on with a union. They fear retaliation of some kind, and many of the employees cannot afford to lose their jobs. Second, Walmart has mastered the art and science of fighting unionization. At one point, the company had a "union avoidance program." In this program, the company, with its vast resources, would wear people down and even destroy their spirit.[14]

One consultant said that each Walmart manager had been taught to take attempts at union organizing personally and to consider that supporting a union is like slapping the supervisor in the face.[15] Walmart is considered to be a sophisticated adversary when it comes to fighting unionization. At one point managers had been asked to call a 24-hour hotline if they ever see a hint of unionization taking place, and a labor team can be dispatched to a store under threat at a moment's notice.[16] Third, many Walmarts are located in southern states that do not have a history and tradition of unionization.[17] Regardless, unions in cities in the north continue, especially in Chicago, ferociously fighting the company's plans to locate in historically union territory, but they have not had great success. These cities are hungry for jobs and cheap products, and these factors seem to win out.[18]

In 2014, Anonymous, a network of hacker activists, leaked two internal Walmart PowerPoint slideshows. Walmart confirmed the slides' authenticity. One was a Labor Relations Training presentation for store managers on which it was suggested that labor unions were money-grubbing outfits that cared little about the workers' welfare.[19] Another slide went on to say that the unions just want the associates' money and that they spend the dues money on other things than representing them.[20] After the slideshow episode, one of Walmart's orientation videos was leaked, and it revealed more of Walmart's anti-union efforts. Walmart stated that it showed the videos to new hires between 2009 and 2014.[21] With respect to its position, a Walmart spokesperson says that the company is not anti-union, it is "pro-associate."[22] According to writer Karen Olsson, "Walmart has made it clear that keeping its stores union-free is as much a part of the culture as door greeters and blue aprons."[23]

A History of Gender Discrimination Charges

The most serious employee issues Walmart has faced in the past decades have been accusations of gender discrimination against women. In 2001, six women filed a gender bias lawsuit against Walmart, claiming they were discriminated against. The case, *Dukes v. Walmart*, started as an EEOC complaint by Betty Dukes, the lead plaintiff, who claimed she had been trying to get promoted from the cashier ranks for nine years.[24] In a landmark decision in June 2004, a federal judge in San Francisco ruled that the sex discrimination lawsuit could proceed as a class-action lawsuit, affecting as many as 1.6 million current and former female employees who have worked for the company since December 26, 1998.[25] In February 2007, a federal appeals court upheld the 2004 decision that Walmart must face the class-action bias claim. Walmart appealed the decision but lost. It was said that the company could lose billions of dollars should it be found guilty of sex discrimination in a class action lawsuit.[26] The lawsuit, which has been called the "largest private civil rights case ever,"[27] had the potential to go on for years and doubtless would have significant repercussions for Walmart and other companies in the retail and other industries.

A summary of the major allegations against Walmart included three major areas. First, women claimed they had been denied equal promotions. Second, women claimed they had been paid less for the same jobs, even when they have more experience. Third, women claimed they were subjected to sexist actions and gender stereotyping.[28]

Lawyers for the plaintiffs argued that top managers at Walmart knew about the sex bias that was taking place in the company. The lawyers argued that women complained to corporate executives, including then-CEO Lee Scott, about pay disparities or sexism and received little response. They also argued that information was shared with board members and that outsiders complained and got little or no response from corporate offices.[29]

The Company's Defense

Walmart has long argued that it treats its female employees fairly. The company has said that women do not apply for promotion as often as men, and this accounts for the under representation of women.[30] The main argument by the company was its opposition to the lawsuit being categorized as a class-action lawsuit. The company argued that decisions about employees are made at the individual store level and that a class-action lawsuit is too unwieldy because it thinks it should be able to present evidence defending itself against each individual plaintiff's claims and that this would not be possible in a class-action trial. Walmart claimed that in a class-action lawsuit of this size, it means that store managers will not be given the opportunity to explain how they made individual compensation and promotion decisions.

The company argued in its appeal of the class-action judgment that the class was certified under laws intended to provide injunctive relief, that is, to stop a particular practice, but that the judge ruled that the class can also seek monetary damages that the company does not think applies to the case. Part of the monetary relief could be punitive damages, but for these to apply, it has to be proven that Walmart management "fostered or recklessly ignored discriminatory practices." The judge concluded that whereas the individual decisions were made at specific store locations, there was some evidence of a corporate culture of gender stereotyping that may have affected the decisions made at the store level.[31] Judge Martin Jenkins was not ruling on the merits of the case but was simply saying there was some evidence of a corporate culture permeating the organization that may be related to the discrimination, and thus he allowed the case to move forward as a class action.

In April 2010, a federal appeals court ruled that the gender discrimination lawsuit could move forward as a class action. It was estimated that if the company lost this lawsuit, it could cost Walmart upward of $1 billion. In addition, a loss would be a terrible blow to its reputation and much-improved corporate image.[32] Walmart appealed this case and it went to the U.S. Supreme Court. In 2011, the court rendered its decision in a 5–4 decision in favor of Walmart.[33] The court ruled that the class action suit could not move forward and that each woman would have to file her claim individually. The ruling did not decide whether Walmart was guilty of discrimination or not, but the Supreme Court decision would have far-reaching effects on the future of class action lawsuits.[34]

Changes Made After Sex Discrimination Case
Partially as a result of criticism and bad publicity Walmart had been receiving, the company announced some changes that were planned to improve conditions for its workers. In 2004, then-CEO Lee Scott outlined the changes that would be made but indicated it may take several years before the true impact of the changes take place are felt throughout the company.[35]

One change would include the creation of a compliance group to oversee workers' pay, hours, and breaks. The company also began testing a new program that would alert cashiers when it is time for them to take a meal break. Another change was the implementation of a new system that would require employees to sign off on any changes that are made to their time cards. The company also planned to implement software that would force managers to adhere to state employment rules regarding areas such as how late teenagers can work. While announcing these new policies, Scott mentioned several times that he was tired of the adverse publicity that the company was getting.[36]

Walmart Strives to Improve Its Image and Policies
In 2015, led by new CEO Doug McMillon, Walmart decided to upgrade its investments in its employees over a two-year period, a criticism that had been hanging over the company for several years. The company committed $2.7 billion in wage increases, scheduling improvements, and employee training.[37] After years of complaints about low wages and poor employee treatment, Walmart increased its minimum wage to $9 an hour in 2015 and then to $10 per hour in 2016.[38] However, the company has repeatedly resisted the current trend of raising the minimum wage to $15 per hour, preferring to raise the average—not the minimum—associate wage to more than $15 per hour.[39]

Employee Law Suits Won't Go Away
As the world's largest employer and the largest nongovernmental employer, Walmart gets sued 20 times a day, close to 5,000 times every year.[40] Many of these lawsuits are filed by its employees over employment discrimination issues or wage and hour claims, often regarding overtime. More often than not, these lawsuits are settled out of court.[41] One of the most frequent categories of lawsuits involves discrimination against women. In addition to sex discrimination, Walmart often is sued on the basis of discrimination based on sexual orientation, gender identity, race, and age.

In one of its most recent large lawsuits, Walmart agreed to pay $20 million to settle a nationwide hiring discrimination lawsuit filed by the Equal Employment Opportunity Commission (EEOC). As a result of the settlement, Walmart agreed to discontinue using a Physical Abilities Test that disproportionately excluded female order filler applicants. The EEOC said that the parties were able to reach a quick resolution because of Walmart's willingness to engage in settlement discussions.[42]

Many law firms seem to relish taking cases against Walmart. Some even create separate "Walmart" pages on their websites, perhaps to attract clients.[43] It is important to understand that other large retailers also face many lawsuits every year. Walmart happens to be the largest and thus gets most of the attention because of its high profile. For example, Costco faced a gender class action lawsuit by 700 women employees in 2012; Dollar General has faced lawsuits alleging malicious and reckless conduct; Dollar Tree has been sued based on allegations of unpaid overtime and wages; and other companies facing employee lawsuits include virtually every major retailer.[44] Regardless, Walmart has been and likely will remain the primary headliner when it comes to employee-related lawsuits as it strives to satisfy and manage millions of employees around the world.

Questions for Discussion

1. Identify and describe the major labor relations issues facing Walmart and the likely stakeholders to be affected.
2. Walmart has been said to have excessive power in its relationship with communities. How is its manifestation of power with employees similar to or different than with communities? Which is the most serious issue? Why?
3. Are many of the allegations by employees at Walmart just reflections of the changing social contract between companies and their workers? Are many of the so-called problems just the free-enterprise system at work? Discuss.
4. Is the practice of being required to "work off the clock" an unethical practice or just "to be expected" in the modern world of work? After all, many salaried employees are expected to work "until the job is done" no matter how many hours it takes.
5. Is it wrong for Walmart to fight unionization? Sam Walton always felt the company should function as one big happy family and that unions were to be resisted. What is your evaluation of the union opposition?
6. If Walmart can effectively argue that women are contributors to their plight by not applying for promotions or for seeking fewer responsibilities to accommodate family priorities, should the company be held to be in violation of sex discrimination laws because the statistics reveal differences between women and men?
7. Regarding the various labor practices discussed in this case, do they reflect questionable treatment of associates or just the business system at work in a large corporation?
8. Have increased competitiveness, globalization, higher wages, technology, and changing social trends affected Walmart's relations with its associates?
9. Conduct Internet research on Walmart and update allegations and lawsuits against the company.

Endnotes

1. Charles Fishman, "The Wal-Mart Effect and a Decent Society: Who Knew Shopping Was So Important," *Academy of Management Perspectives* (August 2006), 6–25.
2. *Fortune*, "World's Most Admired Companies, 2021," https://fortune.com/worlds-most-admired-companies/2021/search/. Accessed June 16, 2021.
3. Jerry Useem, "Should We Admire Walmart?" *Fortune* (March 8, 2004), 118–120.
4. Pew Research Center, "Trends in Income and Wealth Inequality," January 9, 2020, https://www.pewresearch.org/social-trends/2020/01/09/trends-in-income-and-wealth-inequality/. Accessed June 16, 2021.
5. U.S. Department of Labor, "State Minimum Wage Laws," May 1, 2021, https://www.dol.gov/agencies/whd/minimum-wage/state. Accessed June 16, 2021.
6. John Morrison, "A CEOs Take on the Living Wage," World Economic Forum, March 15, 2021, https://www.weforum.org/agenda/2021/03/living-wage-business-government-changes/. Accessed June 16, 2021.
7. Macrotrends, "Walmart: Number of Employees 2006–2021," https://www.macrotrends.net/stocks/charts/WMT/walmart/number-of-employees. Accessed June 16, 2021.
8. Nicholas Hines, "Workers Reveal What It's Really Like Working at Walmart," October 21, 2020, https://www.mashed.com/265058/workers-reveal-what-its-really-like-to-work-at-walmart/. Accessed June 16, 2021.
9. Ibid.
10. Herman Law, "Walmart Employees Allege Off-the-Clock Work," September 12, 2018, https://paycheckcollector.com/off-the-clock-work/. Accessed June 16, 2021.
11. Phillip Mattera, "Walmart Stores," Corporate Research Project, https://www.corp-research.org/wal-mart. Accessed June 16, 2021.
12. The Center for Popular Democracy, "How Walmart Persuades Its Workers Not to Unionize," https://www.populardemocracy.org/news/how-walmart-persuades-its-workers-not-unionize. Accessed June 16, 2021.
13. Ibid.
14. Hugo Meunier, "Walmart Has Everything – Except Unions," November 15, 2019, https://thewalrus.ca/walmart-has-everything-except-unions/. Accessed June 16, 2021.
15. Karen Olsson, "Up Against Walmart," *Mother Jones*, March/April 2003, 56, https://www.motherjones.com/politics/2003/03/against-wal-mart/. Accessed June 16, 2021.
16. Cora Daniels, "Up Against the Walmart Think Your Job Is Tough? Meet the People Whose Job it is to Unionize the World's Biggest Company," *Fortune*, May 17, 2004, 116.https://money.cnn.com/magazines/fortune/fortune_archive/2004/05/17/369617/index.htm, Accessed June 16, 2021.
17. Ibid.
18. "Unions vs. Wal-Mart: Belaboured," *The Economist* (May 29, 2010), 30–32.
19. Steven Greenhouse, "How Walmart Persuades Its Workers Not to Unionize," *The Atlantic*, June 8, 2015, https://www.theatlantic.com/business/archive/2015/06/how-walmart-convinces-its-employees-not-to-unionize/395051/. Accessed June 16, 2021.
20. Ibid.
21. Ibid.
22. Ibid.
23. Olsson, 58.
24. Cora Daniels, "Women vs. Walmart," *Fortune* (July 21, 2003), 79–82.
25. Ann Zimmerman, "Judge Certifies Walmart Suit as Class Action," *The Wall Street Journal* (June 23, 2004), A1.

26. David Kravets, "Wal-Mart Must Face Class-Action Bias Trial: Female Workers Say Men Were Paid More," *USA Today* (February 7, 2007), 3B.

27. Stephanie Armour and Lorrie Grant, "Walmart Suit Could Ripple Through Industry," *USA Today* (June 23, 2004), 4B.

28. Stephanie Armour, "Rife with Discrimination: Plaintiffs Describe Their Lives at Walmart," *USA Today*, June 24, 2004, 3B.

29. Stephanie Armour, "Women Say Wal-Mart Execs Knew of Sex Bias," *USA Today* (June 25, 2004), 1B.

30. "Wal-Mart: Trial by Checkout," *The Economist* (June 26, 2004), 64.

31. Zimmerman, 2004, B2.

32. Sean Gregory, "Walmart Faces a Gender Discrimination Suit," *Time* (April 29, 2010), http://www. time.com/time/business/article /0,8599,1985549,00.html. Accessed July 31, 2010.

33. Nina Martin, "The Impact and Echoes of the Walmart Discrimination Case," ProPublica, September 27, 2013, https://www.propublica.org /article/the-impact-and-echoes-of-the-wal-mart -discrimination-case. Accessed June 16, 2021.

34. Oyez, "Walmart Stores versus Dukes," https://www .oyez.org/cases/2010/10-277. Accessed June 16, 2021.

35. Constance L. Hays, "Walmart Plans Changes to Some Labor Practices," *The New York Times* (June 5, 2004), B2.

36. *Ibid*.

37. Haley Peterson, "Walmart Spent $2.7 Billion Fixing a Major Weakness," *Business Insider*, May 19, 2016, https://www.seacoastonline.com /business/20160519/walmart-spent-27-billion -fixing-major-weakness. Accessed June 16, 2021.

38. Matt Krantz, "Walmart's Wages Get CEO's Attention," *USA Today*, March 2, 2015, 2B.

39. Thomas Buckley, "Walmart's Fight Against a $15 Minimum Wage Could Thrust It Into the Inequality Debate," *Bloomberg Businessweek* (April 27, 2021), https://www.bloomberg.com/news/articles/2021 -04-27/walmart-wmt-fights-against-15-minimum -wage-as-inequality-debate-rages. Accessed June 27, 2021.

40. "Walmart Store Settlements and Lawsuits," Miller & Zois, https://www.millerandzois.com/wal-mart -injury-settlements.html. Accessed June 25, 2021.

41. Ibid.

42. U.S. EEOC, "Walmart to Pay $20 Million to Settle EEOC Nationwide Hiring Discrimination Case," September 10, 2020, https://www.eeoc.gov /newsroom/walmart-inc-pay-20-million-settle-eeoc -nationwide-hiring-discrimination-case. Accessed June 25, 2021.

43. PLBSH, Ibid.

44. Barbara Farfan, "Employee Lawsuits in the Retail Industry," November 20, 2019, https://www .thebalancesmb.com/retail-employee-lawsuits -4061835. Accessed June 25, 2021.

Case 3

Chipotle's Struggle with Food Safety: Back on Top Again?*

When five customers of a Seattle, Washington, Chipotle entered the restaurant in July 2015, they placed their normal orders…burritos, bowls, tacos—you name it. These customers expected to indulge in what they had come to love over the years, what Chipotle has preached since opening its doors in 1993, "Food with Integrity." Real, fresh, responsibly raised ingredients that "just taste better."[1]

Unfortunately, for these five patrons, integrity was not served up on that summer day. Approximately three days after consumption, the symptoms of an *Escherichia coli* (*E. coli*) bacterial infection began to set in—upset stomach, body aches, sporadic cramping, and, worst of all, persistently bloody stools. The infected were able to trace their

ingestion of bacteria back to their beloved Chipotle meals.[2] However, the source ingredient of this particular outbreak was not immediately determined. Unfortunately, this incident was just a precursor of the crisis to come.

Months later, in December 2015, Boston College students flocked to their local Brighton, Massachusetts, Chipotle restaurant, looking for a quick and hearty meal. Members of the varsity men's basketball team, club hockey players, and many others were expecting to have their cravings satisfied, per usual, and placed their orders without hesitation. However, like the Chipotle patrons in Seattle, the students became ill shortly after they ate their food. Unbeknownst to the diners, the chicken that had been prepared in the restaurant was not kept at a warm enough temperature in the assembly line. The lack of heat combined with workers showing physical symptoms of illness provided the perfect breeding grounds for a norovirus to

---

*This case was originally prepared by Thomas Hart, Bentley University, and was revised and updated by Jill A. Brown, Bentley University, in 2021.

spread. Like an *E. coli* infection, a norovirus infection is not instantaneous, so these folks still enjoyed their meals, but they certainly paid for them later on. The students soon found themselves with persistent diarrhea, painful stomach cramps, fevers, and vomiting.[3]

The problems did not stop with this incident. Within weeks of the Boston incident, outbreaks of *E.coli* from Chipotle meals began to occur across the nation with no explanation as to their origins. The company's stock price began to slide, making the fall of 2015 a difficult quarter for Chipotle. Overall, from July to December 2015 there were more than ten reported outbreaks nationwide, ranging from *E. coli* to norovirus to salmonella. At least 500 people across 13 states were affected by the outbreaks—luckily, no deaths were reported.[4] Sales tumbled, along with Chipotle's share price. Chipotle closed more than 40 stores, primarily in the northeast region of the United States. However, food safety issues continued to plague Chipotle beyond these incidences, with more than 1,100 people sickened between 2015 and 2018. The Justice Department eventually charged Chipotle with violating federal law and negligence in maintaining health standards. The chain paid $25 million in criminal fees to avoid conviction—the largest fine of its kind to date.[5]

The History of Chipotle

Steve Ells, the founder of Chipotle, is a man who has always enjoyed cooking. Ells began cooking at a young age, as his mother would put him to work in the kitchen helping her bake and prepare meals. As he grew, it was not uncommon in high school and college for Ells to host elaborate dinner parties for his friends and family, where he would serve them with delicious meals. On completion of his undergraduate degree and unsure of where he was going to go next, the aspiring chef made a deal with his father. He had to work for a year in the restaurant industry to ensure that he truly wanted to be in the business, and then his father would pay for culinary school—but, it had to be "the best culinary college in America."[6]

Ells held up his end of the bargain and went on to the Culinary Institute, graduating in 1990. After graduating, Ells soon moved to San Francisco where he gained both experience as a sous-chef and an appreciation for Mission-style burritos. Ells was not just attracted to San Francisco's Mexican food itself, but the way it was prepared and packaged, the simplicity of a foil wrap with everything tucked away inside. After receiving a loan from his father and locking down a storefront, Ells opened the first Chipotle restaurant in Denver in July of 1993.

No recipes, no calculated formulas, just fresh ingredients for customers to look at and choose from: this is the way Ells designed his business so that it would be extremely simple to manage and operate, because, in his words, "I didn't want to spend much time there."[7] The first restaurant had no individual menus and no menu board as you see when you walk into a current-day Chipotle. Customers were supposed to order what they wanted based on what they saw in front of them. Although reportedly some customers walked back outside confused, the majority were happy that they had so many fresh food options. Ells was fast to respond to customer demands and quickly created the concept of the burrito bowl when he was trying to shed the tortilla. He wanted all of his customers to enjoy their meals, leaving them with a desire to come back again.

It was not long before the business started to take off. The first few Chipotle restaurants were established with the help of Ells's parents; however, Ells soon realized that larger investors would be necessary to continue to fuel the company's growth. Ells's parents were able to gather just over $1 million from close friends, and then they began to hunt for larger contributors. In 1998, when Chipotle had just 13 stores opened, McDonald's invested approximately $50 million.

More significant than the cash received, Chipotle gained access to McDonald's supply chain, construction knowledge, and vast industry knowledge because of the buy-in. The two chains had an interesting relationship in that the only common menu items were the soft drinks. From 1998 to McDonald's divestiture in Chipotle in 2006, the chain grew to more than 500 restaurants, and its growth did not cease after parting ways with McDonald's.[8] Today, Chipotle boasts more than 2,622 locations.[9]

Managing the "Perfect (Public Relations) Storm"

Some experts believe that Chipotle managed the crisis well. Chipotle was noted to be "aggressive and forthcoming" in its approach to closing affected stores for deep cleaning, going so far as to close all stores on one day to hold a companywide meeting to discuss the changes.[10] In addition, the company revealed it would provide fully paid sick days to ill employees who are now required to stay home an additional five days from the time their symptoms disappear. *Fortune* magazine referred to this as a "one-two approach" that not only addressed norovirus concerns but also proved Chipotle's loyalty to its employees.[11] The chain also hired former Taco Bell CEO Brian Niccol to run the chain in 2018. And these changes seemed to pay off for the long term. Chipotle's share price has recovered and tripled since the final resolutions to the outbreaks. By June 25, 2021, Chipotle shares (NYSE:CMG) were trading at $1,494.25 a share, outperforming many of its competitors. Even in the midst of the COVID-19 pandemic, Chipotle made its debut on the *Fortune 500* at 464 in a year when *Fortune* magazine noted, "much of the restaurant industry was wrecked by COVID-19 pandemic."[12]

Many have said that the chain's ability to be upfront and honest with the public through the years has been the key to its success, as well as key to helping them stay afloat during times of crisis. Chipotle was founded and grown as an "anti-fast food" fast-food restaurant, sacrificing efficiencies and cost savings to prioritize quality and customer satisfaction—"people-before-profits" —and this message resonated even during the food safety issues.[13] The chain posted information to its website regarding the outbreaks and released information to media when appropriate.

Following the food safety crisis, Chipotle implemented a new food safety program to assess the safety risks of every ingredient on its menu. This included DNA-based testing of its ingredients before being shipped to Chipotle locations and changes to food prep and handling, including new training for safety standards for workers. They provided new safety updates on their website under "safety advancements" and created new models in the supply chain to further mitigate risk.[14] The goal continued to be to provide the freshest food possible at a low cost to customers, despite the challenges of using local supply chains. Nevertheless, one article about Chipotle, postcrisis, was titled "Chipotle Struggling to Get Customers Back."[15] It cited the need for Chipotle to "tweak" its food safety changes and beef up its advertising. That month, Chipotle issued free burritos to any customer who texted a code to a designated phone number. This marketing campaign proved successful, with 5.3 million people texting the number, and 67 percent of those people redeeming the coupon.[16] By combining damage control tactics, new leadership, positive press, and driving traffic to its locations, Chipotle seemed to have successfully gained back its lost customer loyalty and trust.

Nevertheless, the foodborne illness scare and other issues continue to follow Chipotle. In 2020, Chipotle employees in New York City restaurants reported to the National Consumers League, a nonprofit consumer advocacy group, that the company was not complying with food standards.[17] In May 2021, the Colorado Department of Public Health and Environment (CDPHE) investigated a Chipotle near Denver for possible norovirus outbreaks when eight patrons and employees fell ill.[18]

Also in 2021, problems with employee labor practices surfaced when New York City workers complained about labor law violations, including insufficient notice about schedules, lack of break periods between shifts, failure to provide extra pay for multiple shifts, denying requests for time off, failure to pay for sick leave, and more. In April 2021, New York City filed suit against Chipotle for these alleged violations of New York City's Fair Workweek Law, which took effect in 2017, as well as the city's Paid Sick Leave Law, which was enacted in 2014.[19] According to the complaint, workers are owed more than $150 million in relief for the violations that took place between 2017 and 2019.

Chipotle has responded with vigorous denial of the allegations, saying that it is a "dramatic overreach."[20] The lawsuit acknowledges that Chipotle attempted to comply with the law since 2019, but that violations are ongoing. The big question remains, however: Will Chipotle survive this latest crisis, as it did following the norovirus outbreaks between 2015 and 2018? To date, the shareholders seem to think so; however, much will depend on whether Chipotle can avoid allegations of poor food safety practices and labor law violations in the future.

Questions for Discussion

1. What are the ethical issues of this case?
2. How would you describe Chipotle's handling of the food safety crisis? How does this compare/contrast to its current handling of labor issues in New York City?
3. In Chapter 10, we identified that Chipotle did not seem to have time to completely develop a plan to manage its crises. Looking back at Chapter 10's" *5 Steps in Managing Crises,"* what might the Chipotle management team have done differently? How might these steps be applied to current issues?
4. What is the role of the Centers for Disease Control and Prevention (CDC) in food safety situations? How did it help or hurt Chipotle in managing the crisis?
5. Think about the conventional approach to business ethics that we discussed in Chapter 6. Do you think that these food safety and labor issues are common in the retail food business? What standards and norms apply here? How would a principles approach and an ethical tests approach enhance the ethical decision making of Chipotle management on labor issues?

Endnotes

1. Chipotle, "Food with Integrity" (Chipotle, 2016), https://www.chipotle.com/food-with-integrity. Accessed June 25, 2021.
2. Susan Berfield, " Inside Chipotle's Contamination Crisis," *Bloomberg* (December 22, 2015), http://www.bloomberg.com/features/2015-chipotle-food-safety-crisis/. Accessed June 25, 2021.
3. Maggie Fox, "Norovirus Caused Chipotle Outbreak in Boston, Officials Say," *NBC News* (December 8, 2015), http://www.nbcnews.com/health/health-news/chipotle-outbreak-grows-80-boston-college-students-n476316. Accessed June 25, 2021.
4. Coral Beach, "Nothing Ruled Out Yet as Cause of Chipotle E. coli Outbreaks," Food Safety News (January 22, 2016), http://www.foodsafetynews.com/2016/01/122728/#.V1oVM-SUQmQ. Accessed June 25, 2021.
5. Mura Dominko, "Workers Reveal the Reasons Behind Rampant Food Safety Issues at the Chain," *Eat This, Not That*! (May 24, 2021), https://www.eatthis.com/news-workers-reveal-reasons-behind-chipotle-food-safety-issues/. Accessed June 25, 2021.
6. Kyle Stock and Vanessa Wong," Chipotle: The Definitive Oral History" (February 2, 2015), http://www.bloomberg.com/graphics/2015-chipotle-oral-history/. Accessed June 25, 2021.
7. Ibid.
8. Ibid.
9. Chipotle Locations, https://locations.chipotle.com/. Accessed June 25, 2021.
10. Daniel B. Kline, "Here's Everything Chipotle Has Done to Handle its E.Coli Crises; Is It Enough?" *The Motley Fool* (February 10, 2016).
11. Tyler Barnett," Chipotle Knows What It's Doing by Closing Its Stores," *Fortune* (February 10, 2016), http://fortune.com/2016/02/10/chipotle-temporarily-closing-pr/. Accessed June 25, 2021.

12. Beth Kowitt, "How Chipotle Survived a Food Safety Crisis and a Pandemic to Debut on the This Year's Fortune 500," *Fortune* (June 3, 2021), https://fortune.com/2021/06/02/chipotle-fortune-500-ceo-brian-niccol-interview/. Accessed June 25, 2021.

13. Geoff Williams, "Chipotle's E.coli Crisis: P.R. Experts Say It's Handling It Right," *Forbes* (November 4, 2015), http://www.forbes.com/sites/geoffwilliams/2015/11/04/can-chipotle-survive-its-e-coli-crisis-pr-experts-seem-to-think-so-and-offer-advice/#6d8544ab1644. Accessed June 25, 2021.

14. Chipotle, "Our Safety Advancements," https://www.chipotle.com/foodsafety. Accessed June 25, 2021.

15. Sam Oches, "Chipotle Struggling to Get Customers Back," *QSR* (March 17, 2016), https://www.qsrmagazine.com/news/chipotle-struggling-get-customers-back. Accessed June 25, 2021.

16. Ibid.

17. "Chipotle Employees Blow the Whistle on Food Safety Problems," *Bad Food Recall* (February 11, 2020), https://www.badfoodrecall.com/2020/02/chipotle-employees-blow-whistle-food-safety-problems/. Accessed June 27, 2021.

18. NewDesk, "State Investigates Chipotle near Denver for Likely Norovirus Outbreak," *Food Safety News* (May 19, 2021), https://www.foodsafetynews.com/2021/05/chipotle-mexican-grill-cmg-location-near-denver-investigated-for-likely-norovirus-outbreak/. Accessed June 27, 2021.

19. See Mary Meisenzahl, "Chipotle Has Been Sued by New York City Over Claims It Violated Scheduling Sick Leave Laws, and Now Owes Over $150 Million to Workers," *Business Insider.com* (April 28, 2021), https://www.businessinsider.com/nyc-lawsuit-chipotle-over-labor-law-violations-2021-4. Accessed June 27, 2021; Noah Scheiber, " Chipotle Is Sued by New York City Over Scheduling Practices," *The New York Times* (April 28, 2021), https://www.nytimes.com/2021/04/28/business/chipotle-new-york-illegal-scheduling.html. Accessed June 27, 2021.

20. Ibid.

Case 4

The Theranos Story and Fake Blood Testing: Culture, Crime, and Hubris*

Stanford University dropout Elizabeth Holmes was desperate to make her mark in the business world. In 2003, she dropped out of Stanford's electrical and chemical engineering program at the age of 19 to create a company to develop a revolutionary blood-testing machine. She raised nearly $6 million through family connections, formed a company called Theranos, and hired a PhD student at Stanford as her first employee.

Over the next several years, investors poured more than $400 million into the company, which by 2016/2017 was valued at $9 billion.[1] The Theranos corporate board was populated with prestigious directors, including former U.S. Secretaries of State George Shultz and Henry Kissinger, former U.S. Senator Sam Nunn, former CEO of Wells Fargo Richard Kovacevich, and former director of the Centers for Disease Control and Prevention William H. Foege.[2] Holmes struck up partnerships with Walgreens and Safeway to use the new technology in their stores. Like many hot startup "unicorns," Theranos seemed well on its way to an initial public offering.

One problem popped up, however. Despite best efforts, including a team of former Apple researchers that Holmes wooed to the company, the blood-testing machine called Edison did not work. Worse yet, it seemed that Holmes and her chief operating officer/president and romantic partner Ramesh "Sunny" Balwani were involved in a deep cover-up of Edison's failures.[3] A *New Yorker* magazine profile of Holmes called Holmes's explanations of the Theranos technology "comically vague."[4] *Wall Street Journal* reporter John Carreyrou led the charge to expose the Theranos scam, and eventually 70 former employees helped reconstruct the story, which Carreyrou turned into a book, *Bad Blood: Secrets and Lies in a Silicon Valley Startup.*[5]

The Edison was going to revolutionize blood testing—offering more than 240 tests ranging from cholesterol to cancer—with technology that would work with just a finger prick.[6] However, in 2014–2015, several Theranos employees went to regulators complaining that the company was exaggerating its achievements and failing to report test results that raised questions about the accuracy of the Edison system.[7] Their complaints seemed to fall on deaf ears. In 2015, President Barack Obama named Holmes a U.S. ambassador for global entrepreneurship.[8] That same year she was awarded the prestigious Horatio Alger Award by the Horatio Alger Association of Distinguished Members, which is said to symbolize "the Association's values, including personal initiative and perseverance, leadership and commitment to excellence."[9] Additionally, the award-winning members are said to be "similar to characters in stories by Horatio Alger, Jr.; they traditionally have started life in 'humble' or economically challenging circumstances."[10] Holmes was also

_____

*This case was written by Jill A. Brown, Bentley University, in 2021.

named one of the 100 Most Influential People in the World by *Time* magazine, and *Glamour* magazine anointed her one of its eight Women of the Year.[11]

By 2018 the story had turned, however, and Elizabeth Holmes, once the "darling of Silicon Valley," was being investigated by the Securities and Exchange Commission and the federal government for defrauding investors out of hundreds of millions of dollars and deceiving hundreds of patients and doctors.[12] Balwani was also indicted. The SEC charges of wire fraud were settled in 2018 and the company ceased operations in September that year.

The Edison was supposed to imitate what a chemist does in a lab: take samples, dilute them, add antibodies and a reagent, and reveal a result.[13] Inside the Edison, which was designed to look like an Apple product, a robotic arm was supposed to do the work. Tyler Shultz, a former Theranos employee and one of the first whistleblowers, told *60 Minutes* in 2018 that it just did not work.[14] Pieces of the machine would fall off, doors would not close, and the temperature could not be regulated. In 2016, Theranos wiped out two years of blood tests because federal regulators said they were putting patients' health and safety at risk.[15]

The stories about the cover-up speak to a culture of secrecy, intimidation, and fear, allegedly led by Balwani and Holmes. Carreyrou, in his book, points to the culture of secrecy inspired by Apple because Holmes was obsessed with Apple and idolized Steve Jobs (Holmes reportedly wore black turtlenecks and allegedly lowered her voice to sound more like Jobs).[16] According to Carreyrou, potential whistleblowers were threatened with lawsuits, and those who were critical of leadership practices were either fired or marginalized.[17] Holmes came to be described as a "smart, charming bully" with parallels to Bernie Madoff.[18]

The rise and fall of the Theranos blood-testing company seems like something out of a novel on how business should *not* be done. And yet, Elizabeth Holmes's lawyers, during her early defense hearing, suggested that Theranos succumbed to the "Silicon Valley startup culture" that invites exaggeration in the funding process.[19] Prosecutors consequently warned the judge about giving Holmes too much room to argue that her actions were not any different than any other start-ups, and Judge Edward Davila agreed.

As of 2021, Holmes was still awaiting trial on federal charges. In March 2021, Holmes announced she was pregnant with her husband, hotel heir Billy Evans, and she was expected to give birth in July 2021, further delaying her trial.[20] If convicted, Holmes could be sentenced up to 20 years in prison. The Theranos story, with its intriguing founder and Silicon Valley connections, remains a popular topic for the media. In addition to Carreyrou's book, which received critical claim and several awards, the story was adapted for a movie called *Bad Blood*, starring Jennifer Lawrence as Holmes, due out in late 2021–2022. In 2019, HBO released the documentary *The Inventor: Out for Blood in Silicon Valley*, and ABC News produced a podcast, *The Dropout*, hosted by Rebecca Jarvis, which is scheduled to be made into a limited series on Hulu. More limited series and podcasts have followed, as the world tunes in to see what the consequences will be for Holmes and Balwani in the wake of the "bad blood" scandal.

Questions for Discussion

1. What are the major issues in this case?
2. Consider the corporate culture of Theranos. How might this have influenced the decisions that Holmes and Balwani made to keep forging ahead, even as the Edison continued to fail?
3. What do you think of the defense strategy that puts blame on the "Silicon Valley startup culture"?
4. Is there any justification for the actions of Holmes and Balwani?
5. Consider the actions of whistleblower Tyler Shultz. Would you have gone to regulators if you were in his position? Why or why not?

Endnotes

1. See John Carreyrou, "Hot Startup Theranos Has Struggled with Its Blood-Test Technology," *The Wall Street Journal* (October 16, 2015), https://www.wsj.com/articles/theranos-has-struggled-with-blood-tests-1444881901; Avery Hartmans and Paige Leskin, "The Rise and Fall of Elizabeth Holmes, the Theranos Founder Whose Federal Fraud Trial Is Delayed Until 2021," *Business Insider* (August 11, 2020), https://www.businessinsider.com/theranos-founder-ceo-elizabeth-holmes-life-story-bio-2018-4. Accessed June 29, 2021.
2. Lydia Ramsey Pflanzer, "How Elizabeth Holmes Convinced Powerful Men like Henry Kissinger, James Mattis, and George Shultz to Sit on the Board of Now Disgraced Blood-Testing Startup Theranos," *Business Insider* (March 19, 2019), https://www.businessinsider.com/theranos-former-board-members-henry-kissinger-george-shultz-james-mattis-2019-3. Accessed June 29, 2021.
3. Kate Knibbs, "How John Carreyrou Exposed the Theranos Scam," *The Ringer* (May 22, 2018), https://www.theringer.com/2018/5/22/17378494/bad-blood-theranos-john-carreyrou-interview. Accessed June 29, 2021.
4. See Sheelah Kolhatkar, "The Founder of Theranos Tries to Change the Subject," *The New Yorker* (August 2, 2016), https://www.newyorker.com/business/currency/the-founder-of-theranos-tries-to-change-the-subject. Accessed June 29, 2021; Ken Auletta, "Blood Simpler," *The New Yorker* (December 8, 2014), https://www.newyorker.com/magazine/2014/12/15/blood-simpler. Accessed June 29, 2021; Zaw Thiha Tun, "Theranos: The Fallen Unicorn," *Investopedia* (June 16, 2021), https://www.investopedia.com/articles/investing/020116/theranos-fallen-unicorn.asp. Accessed June 29, 2021.
5. John Carreyrou, *Bad Blood: Secrets and Lies in a Silicon Valley Startup* (Penguin Random House, 2018).

6. Carreyou, 2015.
7. Ibid.
8. James B. Stewart, "The Narrative Frays for Theranos and Elizabeth Holmes," *The New York Times* (October 29, 2015), https://www.nytimes.com/2015/10/30/business/the-narrative-frays-for-theranos-and-elizabeth-holmes.html. Accessed June 29, 2021.
9. Horatio Alger Association, https://horatioalger.org/haa_news/21-surprising-facts-about-billionaire-entrepreneur-elizabeth-holmes/. Accessed June 29, 2021.
10. Ibid.
11. Stewart, 2015.
12. Reed Abelson, "Theranos Founder Elizabeth Holmes Indicted on Fraud Charges," *The New York Times* (June 15, 2018), https://www.nytimes.com/2018/06/15/health/theranos-elizabeth-holmes-fraud.html. Accessed June 29, 2021.
13. Cory Stieg, "What Exactly Was the Theranos Edison Machine Supposed to Do?," Refinery29 (March 12, 2019), https://www.refinery29.com/en-us/2019/03/224904/theranos-edison-machine-blood-test-technology-explained. Accessed June 29, 2021.
14. "On 60 Minutes, in His First TV Interview, Whistleblower Tyler Shultz Explains How Theranos Deceived Investors and the Public with Its Blood Testing Device," CBS News (May 18, 2018),
15. Tun, 2021.
16. See John Carreyrou, *Bad Blood: Secrets and Lies in a Silicon Valley Startup* (2018); Knibbs, 2018.
17. Melissa Lorrain Chua, "Bad Blood: 5 Lessons in Company Culture from the Rise and Fall of Theranos," *Medium* (October 15, 2019), https://medium.com/swlh/company-culture-lessons-from-theranos-5dfc7cfba072. Accessed June 29, 2021.
18. Taylor Dunn, Victorial Thompson, and Rebecca Jarvis, "Ex-Theranos Employees Describe Culture of Secrecy at Elizabeth Holmes' Start-Up: 'The Dropout' Podcast Ep.1" (March 12, 2019), https://abcnews.go.com/Business/theranos-employees-describe-culture-secrecy-elizabeth-holmes-startup/story?id=60544673. Accessed June 29, 2021.
19. Yasmin Khorram and Scott Cohn, "Elizabeth Holmes Back in Court for First Time in 15 Months, Putting Silicon Valley Culture Under Scrutiny," CNBC (May 4, 2021), https://www.cnbc.com/2021/05/04/elizabeth-holmes-reappears-in-court-as-attorneys-spar.html. Accessed June 29, 2021.
20. Yasmin Khorram, "Elizabeth Holmes Trial Pushed to August Following Surprise Pregnancy Announcement," CNBC (March 17, 2021), https://www.cnbc.com/2021/03/17/elizabeth-holmes-trial-pushed-to-august-after-surprise-pregnancy-announcement.html. Accessed June 29, 2021.

https://www.viacomcbspressexpress.com/cbs-news/releases/view?id=50209. Accessed June 29, 2021.

Case 5

Direct-to-Consumer Advertising for Pharmaceuticals: Is It Ethical?*

What do Ozempic® and Prolia® have in common? They are both gold medal winners for their direct-to-consumer advertising (DTCA) in the pharmaceutical industry.[1] Although their brand-name recognition does not rival that of Coca-Cola, their names are familiar to consumers across the nation. As flag bearers of the DTCA efforts of the pharmaceutical industry, they are at the forefront of the DTCA debate. At this writing, the United States and New Zealand are the only developed countries that permit DTCA of pharma drugs. While over the years there has been discussion about opening up the United Kingdom and the European Union to such marketing practices, there has been little progress on that front. In fact, during a "tell all" television interview of Prince Harry and Meghan Markle by Oprah Winfrey in 2021, British viewers seemed to be more shocked by the prescription drug advertisements during the telecast than the big reveals about the British Royal Family.[2]

Why debate DTCA? In his testimony before the Senate Commerce Subcommittee on Consumer Affairs, Dr. Sidney Wolfe, director of the Public Citizen's Health Research Group, expressed the following concern: "There is little doubt that false and misleading advertising to patients and physicians can result in prescriptions being written for drugs that are more dangerous and/or less effective than perceived by either the doctor or the patient."[3] Beyond safety concerns, there are also concerns over the additional costs that consumers bear with DTCA, as well as the emotional impact and tone of images used in the advertising. For the past six years, the American Medical Association has called for a ban on DTCA practices for prescription drugs and medical devices with concerns that the growing proliferation of ads is driving demand for expensive treatments, despite the effectiveness of less costly alternatives.[4]

*This case, originally written by Ann K. Buchholtz, Rutgers University, was revised and updated by Jill A. Brown, Bentley University, in 2021.

The findings of a CMI/Compas survey of 104 physicians across multiple specialties underscore these concerns: 89 percent of the physicians indicated that a patient requested a prescription because of seeing a DTCA and 43 percent of the physicians reported changing their prescribing as a result.[5] Only 20 percent agreed (5 percent strongly and 15 percent somewhat) that DTCA improves the relationship between a clinician and the patient.[6] However, it seems that consumers feel differently. In 2019, the research arm of the Food & Drug Administration (FDA) published research based on a survey of more than 1,700 U.S. adults and found that most patients do not believe DTCA has a negative influence on the patient-provider interaction. A majority (76 percent) said they were likely to ask a health-care provider about advertised drugs and 26 percent of that group had already done so.[7]

On the positive side, DTCA can help patients. In the CMI/Compas Survey, 48 percent of the same physicians agreed (5 percent strongly and 43 percent somewhat) that DTCA educates patients, and 52 percent agreed (9 percent strongly and 43 percent somewhat) that DTCA lessened the stigma of some diseases.[8] Dr. Richard Dolinar, an endocrinologist, says that the ads empower consumers: "Direct-to-consumer advertising is getting patients with diabetes into my office sooner so they can be treated."[9] Professor Dhaval Dave of Bentley University conducted a study for the National Bureau of Economic Research (NBER) and found that "advertising directed at consumers can expand the total market for drug treatment by educating consumers with regard to treatment options for their symptoms, by facilitating contact between the patient and the physicians, and by reminding patients who already have prescribed medications to adhere to their drug therapy."[10]

With strong arguments for and against DTCA, many people find their opinions evolving. John LaMattina, the former president of Pfizer Global Research and Development, is an expert on the pharmaceutical industry. In a *Forbes* article titled "Maybe It's Time for Drug Companies to Drop TV Ads," he questioned whether the negatives of DTCA are starting to outweigh the benefits.[11] He was an early supporter of DTCA based on its education value for the consumer and he still believes that some benefits remain; however, he now thinks that the ads are having too many negative effects due to industry missteps. For example, some of the commercials are not age appropriate for children and so are subject to tighter industry standards.[12] Researchers Denis Arnold and James Oakley found that, over a four-year period, five major pharmaceutical companies violated industry standards in their marketing of erectile dysfunction drugs, leading to children being exposed to sexually themed advertising more than one billion times.[13] Another issue LaMattina raised is that the endless listing of negative side effects creates problems. He quotes Elizabeth Rosenthal's *New York Times* article:[14]

> When the Food and Drug Administration in the 1990s first mandated that drug makers list medicines' side effects in order to advertise prescription drugs, there

was a firestorm of protest from the industry. Now the litany of side effects that follows every promotion is so mind-numbing—drowsiness, insomnia, loss of appetite, weight gain—as to make the message meaningless.

It seems that the message is that the potential benefits of DTCA must be balanced with the potential for harms. In fact, this is what a recent literature review of studies on DTCA concluded.[15] The review showed that the benefits of exposure to DTCA include patients' enhanced information-seeking, increased patient requests for appropriate prescriptions, and patients' perceptions of higher-quality interactions with prescribers. Harms of DTCA, however, included patients receiving drug prescriptions that were not appropriate for them or that the patients did not need, and the potential for DTCA to interfere with medical adherence in some populations, such as those with mental illness.[16]

Questions for Discussion

1. What are the ethical issues related to DTCA?
2. Should DTCA be judged by the same criteria as other advertising? If not, how should it be judged differently?
3. What public policy changes would you advocate regarding DTCA? Should the United States and New Zealand ban them? Should the United Kingdom and the European Union (EU) allow them?
4. How will changes in technology and viewing habits change the DTCA issue?

Endnotes

1. DTC National Hall of Fame, https://dtcperspectives.com/dtcn/dtc-national-award-winners/. Accessed June 25, 2021.
2. See Hannah Frishberg, "UK Viewers Horrified by US Drug Ads During Harry and Meghan Interview," *The New York Post* (March 9, 2021), https://nypost.com/2021/03/09/uk-shocked-by-us-drug-ads-during-harry-and-meghan-interview/. Accessed June 25, 2021; The Washington Post, "U.K. Viewers Baffled by Pharmaceutical Ads During Oprah," *The Washington Post* (March 8, 2021), https://www.washingtonpost.com/world/2021/03/08/harry-meghan-oprah-interview-pharmaceutical-ads/. Accessed June 25, 2021.
3. Sidney M. Wolfe, "Direct-to-Consumer (DTC) Ads: Illegal, Unethical, or Both," *Public Citizen's Health Research Group Health Letter* (September 2001), 3–4.
4. See Barbara McAneny, "AMA on Proposal to Increase Transparency in Drug Ads," American Medical Association (October 15, 2018), https://www.ama-assn.org/press-center/ama-statements/ama-proposal-increase-transparency-drug-ads. Accessed June 25, 2021; "AMA Calls for Ban on Direct to Consumer Advertising of Prescription Drugs and Medical Devices," American Medical Association News Room (November 17, 2015), http://www.ama-assn.org/ama/pub/news/news/2015/2015-11-17-ban-consumer-prescription-drug-advertising.page. Accessed June 25, 2021.

5. "CMI/Compas Survey Finds Doctors' True Opinions of DTC Advertising" (May 1, 2013), http://www.prweb.com/releases/2013/5/prweb10733538.htm. Accessed June 25, 2021.

6. Ibid.

7. See Helen Sullivan, Kathryn Aikin, Jennifer Berktold, Karen Stein, and Victoria Hoverman, "Direct-to-Consumer Prescription Drug Advertising and Patient-Provider Interactions," *Journal of the American Board of Family Medicine* (March 2020), Vol. 33(2), pp. 279-283; Kathryn Aikin, Kevin Betts, Amie O'Donoghue, and Helen Sullivan, *Office of Prescription Drug Promotion (OPDP) Research*, https://www.fda.gov/about-fda/center-drug-evaluation-and-research-cder/office-prescription-drug-promotion-opdp-research#communicating. Accessed June 25, 2021.

8. CMI/Compas, 2013.

9. Ira Teinowitz, "DTC Regulation by FDA Debated," *Advertising Age* (July 30, 2001), 6.

10. Coalition for HealthCare Communication, "Study Cites Benefits of Pharma's Promotional Efforts" (March 4, 2013), http://www.cohealthcom.org/2013/03/04/study-cites-benefits-of-pharma%E2%80%99s-promotional-efforts/. Accessed June 25, 2021.

11. See Reenita Das, "Are Direct-to-Consumer Ads for Drugs Doing More Harm than Good?", *Forbes* (May 14, 2019), https://www.forbes.com/sites/reenitadas/2019/05/14/direct-to-consumer-drug-ads-are-they-doing-more-harm-than-good/?sh=2fcdff434dfc. Accessed June 25, 2021; John LaMattina, "Maybe It's Time for Drug Companies to Drop TV Ads," *Forbes* (February 15, 2012), http://www.forbes.com/sites/johnlamattina/2012/02/15/maybe-its-time-for-drug-companies-to-drop-tv-ads/. Accessed June 25, 2021.

12. Ibid.

13. Arnold and Oakley, 2013.

14. Elizabeth Rosenthal, "I Disclose. . . Nothing," *The New York Times* (January 21, 2012), SR1. Cited in LaMattina, 2012.

15. Jessica Frank, Nancy Berkman, Leila Kahwati, Katherine Cullen, Kathryn Aikin, and Helen Sullivan, "Direct-to-Consumer Advertising of Prescription Drugs and the Patient-Prescriber Encounter: A Systematic Review," *Health Communication* (April 11, 2019), https://doi.org/10.1080/10410236.2019.1584781. Accessed June 25, 2021.

16. Ibid.

Case 6

The COVID-19 Pandemic: Herculean Challenges for Business and CSR*

When the pandemic Spanish flu, otherwise known as the Great Influenza Pandemic, broke out in 1918, businesses suffered as retail sales declined and manufacturing activity slowed. By the end of the pandemic, in 1920, an estimated 40 million people, or 2.1 percent of the global population, had died.[1] According to researchers from the National Bureau of Economic Research, the COVID-19 pandemic will not even be close to reaching the devastating social and economic impacts of the 1918 pandemic, but it has substantially affected those who have lost loved ones and brought significant challenges to businesses and business/society relationships.[2]

As businesses struggled to stay afloat during the COVID-19 pandemic, many issues played out regarding a firm's *economic responsibilities*. Lockdowns in countries, states, and cities shuttered many businesses, damaged supply chains, and created widespread unemployment. Labor supply was reduced as many workers fell ill, and layoffs and loss of income reduced household consumption and business investments. The pandemic caught many supply chains off guard, exposing vulnerabilities at first in the medical supplies arena and then, later, across most industries. The hospitality sector dried up as airlines and hotels struggled to stay solvent. COVID-19 pandemic brought a financial shock that went beyond individual businesses to the global economy. By the end of 2020, at the height of the pandemic, the global economy contracted by 3.5 percent, reshaping world trade and triggering a health and fiscal support that the Brookings Institute termed "unprecedented in terms of speed and magnitude."[3]

Additionally, the global recession highlighted more than ever the disparities of the impact of COVID-19 pandemic around the world. While inequality is notoriously hard to measure, when taking into account differences in gross domestic product (GDP) per capita weighted population, inequality between countries increased dramatically during 2020, with poorer countries suffering significantly both in terms of mortality and economic performance.[4] To make matters worse, job and income losses hit lower-skilled and uneducated workers the hardest, as well as exacerbating preexisting racial and gender inequalities that already existed in the labor markets.[5]

For businesses during COVID-19, their economic objective was to survive and to provide the goods and

---

*This case was written by Jill A. Brown, Bentley University, in 2021.

services that consumers and employees needed. In the United States, roughly 200,000 businesses closed permanently during the first year of the outbreak, which was much lower than originally anticipated. Many point to the Paycheck Protection Program (PPP), which provided $525 billion in forgivable loans to small businesses in 2020 and reopened in January 2021 with an additional $284 billion in funding.[6] Some businesses and their founders and employees found opportunities to move to other businesses during that time. For example, when San Francisco–based juicing/smoothie company Good Use went out of business, a few employees took on a "nothing to lose" attitude and went on to start other businesses, including a dog-walking business, a property management company, a line of Mexican beverages, and a tiny home manufacturing company.[7]

Businesses'*legal responsibilities* have changed along with recent regulation related to COVID-19. While the PPP support helped businesses, legal debates blossomed during the pandemic. A "mask debate" ensued in the United States when federal health guidance and the Centers for Disease Control and Prevention (CDC) seemed to fluctuate on recommended and required mask procedures, further complicated when states, cities, counties, and local jurisdictions provided their own mandates.[8] The debate seemed to divide along political lines, with conservatives generally bristling at being told they should wear face coverings and liberals generally embracing it.[9] Confrontations at stores ensued, leaving store employees managing confrontations and apprehending shoppers. When the CDC eased restrictions on wearing masks in May 2021, businesses such as supermarkets and retailers had to deal with employees who were fearful of exposure after months of wearing masks on the job.[10]

If mask-wearing mandates were not enough of a challenge for businesses during COVID-19, the issue of mandating vaccinations continues to be a hotly debated issue. By June 2021, 39 percent of people in the United States had been fully vaccinated against COVID-19, well short of President Biden's stated 70 percent target by July that year.[11] But vaccine hesitancy, particularly in rural and/or remote areas, continued to impede vaccination goals. While reasons for hesitancy ranged from apathy, to fear, to skepticism about the quick vaccine rollout, the challenge for businesses became what to do when employees returned to work. Unlike many past vaccinations, the new vaccine is completely voluntary. Can businesses mandate that their employees be vaccinated? In June 2021, Morgan Stanley CEO James Gorman told its workers that they would not be allowed to return to the New York City and Westchester offices unless they were vaccinated. Additionally, he said that he would be "very disappointed" if they did not find their way into the office by Labor Day.[12] It was also reported that he'd "take a dim view of employees who did not work regularly in the office" and told his employees, "If you want to get paid New York rates, you work in New York."[13]

For businesses, navigating this new environment is tricky. According to the Equal Employment Opportunity Commission, companies can legally require vaccines as a condition of employment, and ask employees about their vaccination status, as long as the data are kept confidential.[14] However, businesses continue to face some tough decisions about whether or not they want to make it a formal requirement going forward.

With economic and legal challenges paramount to survival during the coronavirus, it is no wonder that business's *ethical responsibilities* have also been put to the task across many different stakeholder groups. Worker health and well-being, the rationing of medical care, the ethical management of crises, the hazards posed to essential workers, the disruption to domestic lives as children learned online and families adjusted to hybrid online/in-office modalities—these are just a few of the issues brought on by the pandemic. Zoom fatigue plagued employees as well as brought out feelings of isolation and depression associated with working from home. Women were disproportionately affected by the COVID-19 crisis, driving as many as 2 million women to consider leaving the workforce or stepping back from their careers.[15] Black U.S. entrepreneurs faced unequal access to capital, and Asians were the subject of hate crimes and discrimination because the COVID-19 outbreak was first detected in China.[16] With so many areas that required businesses to view their stakeholders with an ethical lens, the term "moral courage" became a touted theme for business-and-ethics conferences.[17]

However, lest things seemed dismal for businesses trying to be socially responsible in the midst of a pandemic, a shining light seemed to be businesses' commitment to their *philanthropic responsibilities*. While disasters often stimulate philanthropy, businesses' charitable responses to COVID-19 surpassed all other recent disasters to date. More than $20 billion was awarded for COVID-19 globally in 2020, with 44 percent of funding coming from corporations.[18] While only 5 percent were designated for Black, Indigenous and People of Color (BIPOC) communities, organizations focused on civil rights and the environment saw the biggest increase compared with pre-pandemic levels.[19]

The pandemic also, remarkably, did not derail businesses' commitment to environmental initiatives and addressing climate change. McKinsey & Company noted that pandemics and climate risk are similar in that they both represent physical shocks and share similar attributes.[20] As such, they both represent untested vulnerabilities and are therefore risk multipliers that require fundamental shifts in thinking.[21] In June 2021, the G-7 nation leaders—the United States, Germany, Japan, France, Italy, Canada, and Britain—along with other world leaders seemed to agree, as they renewed commitments to addressing climate change.[22] And Larry Fink, CEO and chair of Blackrock, continued to increase the pressure on boards at the height of the pandemic to put climate change on the top of their agendas, even as they struggled to guide their companies through pandemic issues.[23]

In sum, the COVID-19 global pandemic has brought intense and, yes, Herculean challenges for business/society relationships, as well as some opportunities. However, for businesses that have embraced CSR as part of their corporate missions and strategies, the pandemic might be viewed as just a different context for them to apply their CSR principles along economic, legal, ethical, and philanthropic dimensions.[24] While losses have been many, particularly across employee, consumer, and community stakeholders, the lessons learned from the COVID-19 pandemic might actually spur businesses to rethink their CSR strategies as they navigate the murky waters of a global pandemic.

Questions for Discussion

1. What is your assessment of how businesses approached the pandemic? Can you name some businesses that have practiced good issue and crisis management during COVID-19?
2. Of the dimensions of CSR, which one do you see as most/more relevant regarding how businesses should prioritize their strategic actions during a crisis like a pandemic?
3. CSR inevitably involves tensions between its different dimensions: legal versus ethical, economic versus philanthropic, etc. Where do you see these tensions with regard to businesses' actions during the pandemic?
4. Are there some helpful lessons for businesses to learn from the pandemic? What are these lessons? Which pertain to crisis management and which pertain to ongoing management?

Endnotes

1. Steve Maas, "Social and Economic Impacts of the 1918 Influenza Epidemic," *National Bureau of Economic Research* (May 5, 2020), https://www.nber.org/digest/may20/social-and-economic-impacts-1918-influenza-epidemic. Accessed June 28, 2021.
2. Howard Bodenhorn, "Business in a Time of Spanish Influenza," National Bureau of Economic Research (July 2020), Working Paper #27495, DOI 10.3386/w27495, https://www.nber.org/papers/w27495. Accessed June 28, 2021.
3. Eduardo Levy Yeyati and Federico Filippini, "Special and Economic Impact of COVID-19," *Brookings Institute* (June 8, 2021), https://www.brookings.edu/research/social-and-economic-impact-of-covid-19/. Accessed June 28, 2021.
4. Francisco H.G. Ferreira, "Inequality in the Time of COVID-19," *International Monetary Fund* (Summer 2021), https://www.imf.org/external/pubs/ft/fandd/2021/06/inequality-and-covid-19-ferreira.htm. Accessed June 28, 2021.
5. Ibid.
6. Ruth Simon, "COVID-19's Toll on Business? 200,000 Extra Closures in Pandemic's First Year," *The Wall Street Journal* (April 16, 2021), https://www.wsj.com/articles/covid-19s-toll-on-u-s-business-200-000-extra-closures-in-pandemics-first-year-11618580619?mod=article_inline. Accessed June 28, 2021.
7. Lauren Weber, "When COVID Sank This Small Business, Here's How Its Workers Rebounded," *The Wall Street Journal* (May 17, 2021), https://www.wsj.com/articles/job-search-small-business-pandemic-careers-good-use-11621014650. Accessed June 28, 2021.
8. Mitch Smith, "Mask? No Mask? New Rules Leave Americans Recalibrating, Hour by Hour," *The New York Times* (May 15, 2021), https://www.nytimes.com/2021/05/15/us/cdc-mask-guidance-americans.html. Accessed June 28, 2021.
9. Ibid.
10. Jaewon Kang, "New Face-Mask Rules Put Grocery Workers Back at the Center of the Debate," *The Wall Street Journal* (May 22, 2021), https://www.wsj.com/articles/new-face-mask-rules-put-grocery-workers-back-at-center-of-the-debate-11621675803. Accessed June 28, 2021.
11. Jim Carlton, "Vaccinating America Means Convincing Skeptics in Rural Nebraska," *The Wall Street Journal* (April 29, 2021), https://www.wsj.com/articles/vaccinating-america-means-convincing-skeptics-in-rural-nebraska-11619706865?mod=article_inline. Accessed June 28, 2021.
12. Jack Kelly, "Morgan Stanley Told Its Employees They Need to be Vaccinated to Return to Work: Here's a Theory as to Why the Bank Is Doing This," *Forbes* (June 23, 2021), https://www.forbes.com/sites/jackkelly/2021/06/23/morgan-stanley-told-its-employees-they-need-to-be-vaccinated-to-return-to-work-heres-a-theory-as-to-why-the-bank-is-doing-this/?sh=5e9964883bac. Accessed June 28, 2021.
13. Ibid.
14. U.S. Equal Employment Opportunity Commission, "EEOC Issues Updated COVID-19 Technical Assistance," *EEOC* (May 28, 2021), https://www.eeoc.gov/newsroom/eeoc-issues-updated-covid-19-technical-assistance. Accessed June 30,2021.
15. McKinsey Quarterly Five Fifty, "The Pandemic's Gender Effect," *McKinsey.com*, (December 4, 2020), https://www.mckinsey.com/featured-insights/diversity-and-inclusion/five-fifty-the-pandemics-gender-effect. Accessed June 28, 2021.
16. McKinsey & Company, "COVID-19: Implications for Business," *McKinsey.com* Executive Briefing (June 23, 2021), https://www.mckinsey.com/business-functions/risk/our-insights/covid-19-implications-for-business. Accessed June 28, 2021.
17. Nebraska......
18. David Maurrasse, "Philanthropy During COVID-19," *Columbia Climate School* (April 30, 2021), https://news.climate.columbia.edu/2021/04/30/philanthropy-during-covid-19/. Accessed June 28, 2021.
19. Coral Murphy Marcos, "Charitable Giving Rose in 2020, with Civil Rights and Environmental Groups Benefiting," *The New York Times* (June 15, 2021), https://www.nytimes.com/2021/06/15/business

/philanthropy-2020-pandemic.html. Accessed June 28, 2021.

20. Dickon Pinner, Matt Rogers, and Hamid Samandari, "Addressing Climate Change in a Post-Pandemic World," *McKinsey & Company Quarterly* (April 7, 2020), https://www.mckinsey.com /business-functions/sustainability/our-insights /addressing-climate-change-in-a-post-pandemic -world. Accessed June 28, 2021.

21. Ibid.

22. Richard Perez-Pena, "The G7 Leaders Get Down to Business, Taking on Climate Change and the Pandemic," *The New York Times* (June 12, 2021), https://www.nytimes.com/2021/06/12/world/europe

/leaders-biden-pandemic-climate.html. Accessed June 28, 2021.

23. Michael Peregrine, " Larry Fink Turns Up Climate Change Pressure on Boards," *Forbes* (January 26, 2021), https://www.forbes.com /sites/michaelperegrine/2021/01/26/larry -fink-turns-up-climate-change-pressure-on -boards/?sh=82300463010e. Accessed June 28, 2021.

24. Archie B. Carroll, "Corporate Social Responsibility (CSR) and the COVID-19 Pandemic: Organizational and Managerial Implications," *Journal of Strategy and Management,* forthcoming, 2021.

Case 7

Volkswagen's Diesel Deception and Its Aftermath*

Former Volkswagen (VW) CEO Martin Winterkorn and other company executives will pay the company a total of $351 million to settle lawsuits for their alleged roles in an emissions scandal, often referred to as "Dieselgate," that lasted for close to a decade. This announcement came in June 2021. The emissions fraud continues to cast a shadow over the company after it was finally disclosed six years prior.[1] Mr. Winterkorn became CEO in 2007 but was forced to step down in 2015, shortly after the company was charged with defrauding customers and violating U.S. environmental laws due to company rigging of nearly 11 million vehicles to cheat emissions tests and then covering it up. It was alleged that Winterkorn learned of the full extent of the deception as early as 2014 but did nothing as CEO to stop the practice or bring it to the attention of the authorities.[2] Winterkorn still faces criminal charges due to his role in the fraud.[3] The diesel scandal cost VW about $35 billion.[4]

The company's decision to seek damages from Winterkorn and other top executives followed an internal investigation that began six years earlier, when U.S. authorities charged VW with conspiracy to commit fraud, making false statements on goods brought for sale in the United States, and obstruction of justice. The U.S. investigation revealed a decade-long deception by VW to rig millions of diesel-powered vehicles to cheat emissions tests and later attempted to cover up the deception. The scandal turned out to be one of the largest frauds ever committed by a European company. Executives from the company admitted that the emissions cheating that was disclosed in the

United States had begun in Germany and that over a decade VW engineers had installed illegal software on 11 million cars so that they would pass emissions tests even though they emitted toxic tailpipe emissions in violation of environmental laws.[5] This case represented one of the most significant in the history of business in which the CEO and other top-level executives were implicated and held to account for their actions.

Background

Between 2009 and 2015, Volkswagen manufactured and marketed clean diesel automobiles that were designed to provide high performance without the polluting emissions commonly associated with diesel engines. These turbocharged direct injection (TDI) clean diesel vehicles were very popular in Western Europe, where environmentally conscious or "green" consumers found they could have fast, responsive cars that seemed to sip diesel. On September 18, 2015, the U.S. Environmental Protection Agency (EPA) announced that it was suing the Volkswagen Group for selling more than 482,000 diesel Volkswagens and Audis with software "defeat devices" that caused the vehicles to be far more polluting than expected during normal driving. The vehicles would be recalled for repairs.[6]

In the following weeks, U.S. and German investigators swarmed into Volkswagen offices, including the company's international headquarters in Wolfsburg, Germany, and the corporate offices of the company's U.S. subsidiary, Volkswagen Group of America (VWoA).[7] The Volkswagen group manufactures and markets automobiles, vans, and trucks around the world in a variety of brands. The Volkswagen marque is the company's most popular brand. Prestige brands such as Audi, Porsche, and

---

*This case was written by William A. Sodeman, Seven Hills Foundation, Worcester, Massachusetts. Revised and updated by Archie B. Carroll, University of Georgia, in 2021.

Bentley have significantly lower sales volumes, but much higher margins.[8] The following year, in May 2016, VW reported a quarterly profit on Volkswagen-branded cars of only €73 million for the first quarter of 2016, a significant decrease from the €514 million profit it posted in the first quarter of 2015. Much of the profits were erased by dealer incentives and consumer rebates that supported sales of gasoline-powered Volkswagen-branded vehicles. As a whole, Volkswagen Group posted a quarterly profit of €2.4 billion; Audi and Porsche accounted for two-thirds of that profit.[9]

Volkswagen's History and Culture

Founded in 1937, Volkswagen's initial intention was to produce a "people's car," designed by Ferdinand Porsche, for the citizens of the Third Reich. The town of Wolfsburg was established in 1938 for VW employees. U.S. distribution of the VW Beetle, a modified version of the original "people's car" design, began in 1949. The company founded Volkswagen Group of America (VWoA) in 1955 and created the Audi marque in 1969.[10] VW's international success helped spur the recovery of West Germany.[11] VW opened a US$1 billion manufacturing facility in Chattanooga, Tennessee, in 2008. To secure Volkswagen's commitment, the state of Tennessee offered Volkswagen a package of tax incentives that grew to almost $US1 billion by 2015.[12] Porsche took over VW in 2009[13] after decades of cooperation and conflict between the Porsche family and Volkswagen management.[14]

In 2015, Volkswagen was tightly controlled by the billionaire descendants of Ferdinand Porsche, who owned 50 percent. Independent shareholders owned about 12 percent of the stock. The north German state government of Lower Saxony, where Wolfsburg is located, and Qatar's sovereign wealth fund[15] owned the rest. A network of powerful German labor unions participated in management decisions, as compensation for funds that were confiscated after World War II.[16] Volkswagen had a fleet of corporate jets, including an Airbus A319; VW owned more than 100 factories in 31 countries[17] across 12 different brands and the Volkswagen air services subsidiary that flew company executives as needed.

"Be aggressive at all times" was how one Volkswagen executive described the company's confident approach to global competition. Volkswagen chief executives including Ferdinand Piëch, a grandson of Ferdinand Porsche, and Piëch's successor, Martin Winterkorn, heavily promoted clean diesel technology as part of the company's environmental commitment. Winterkorn had promised that Volkswagen would surpass Toyota to become the world's largest automobile manufacturer and that clean diesel vehicles, not hybrids, were the key to global domination.[18]

Soon after the EPA recall announcement in September 2015, Winterkorn resigned. In December 2015, the new CEO, Mathias Müller, and the chair of Volkswagen's supervisory board announced in a press conference that Volkswagen employees had created the emissions test scheme in 2005, after realizing the company's diesel technology could not pass U.S. environmental standards.[19] CEO Müller announced that the company might have to sell the corporate Airbus A319 corporate jet, among other major changes. The company set aside €6.7 billion to cover the costs of repairing faulty diesel cars, including the option of repurchasing some diesel vehicles from consumers.[20] While Volkswagen planned to keep its 12 different brands, plans for a €100 million corporate design center intended for Wolfsburg were scrapped.[21]

In January 2016, members of the Porsche and Piëch families, who owned half of Volkswagen, made public statements endorsing Müller after his controversial visit to the United States.[22] In an NPR interview recorded during a visit to Detroit, Müller apologized for the scandal and promised to "deliver appropriate solutions to [VWoA] customers."[23] Earlier in the interview, Müller claimed that Volkswagen did not lie to the American public:

> Frankly spoken, it was a technical problem. We made a default, we had a ... not the right interpretation of the American law. And we had some targets for our technical engineers, and they solved this problem and reached targets with some software solutions which haven't been compatible to the American law. That is the thing. And the other question you mentioned—it was an ethical problem? I cannot understand why you say that.[24]

NPR interviewed Müller the next day, and the CEO attempted to mitigate the damage of his previous statements:

> We have to accept that the problem was not created three months ago. It was created, let me say, 10 years ago. ... We had the wrong reaction when we got information year by year from the EPA and from the [California Air Resources Board]. ... We have to apologize for that, and we'll do our utmost to do things right for the future.[25]

In April 2016, Volkswagen agreed to repurchase almost all the affected two-liter diesel vehicles in the United States and further agreed to provide owners with additional compensation. This buyback program was estimated to cost US$7 billion, but it did not include three-liter diesel vehicles from Audi and Porsche.[26] Later in April, Müller personally apologized to President Barack Obama for the emissions scandal.[27] The following month, Volkswagen challenged the U.S. Department of Justice's authority in the matter, claiming that the affected cars were sold not by the European parent companies, but by local businesses in the United States.[28] While Volkswagen's European operations designed the automobiles and their emissions systems, many of the affected diesel automobiles were manufactured in Volkswagen's Chattanooga facility.[29]

Cheating the System

The emissions control systems used in the affected Volkswagen, Audi, and Porsche cars included software designed by Volkswagen engineers to deceive or cheat emissions tests. Automakers often use common body frames, engines, components, and software across multiple brands to reduce duplication and costs. Emissions tests usually involve running at several different speeds while the wheels of the vehicle rest on a treadmill. When testing a front-wheel-drive model, the back wheels remain stationary.[30] To test an all-wheel-drive or four-wheel-drive vehicle, treadmills are placed under both axles. The vehicle is connected to a dynamometer, a device that measures the torque or power of an engine.[31] Sensors attached to the vehicle's exhaust pipe measure the vehicle's emissions.

The test or "dyno" mode used in the engine control unit (ECU)[32] of VW diesel vehicles was activated only when the following conditions were met:

the steering wheel was not being moved;

the vehicle was operating at a constant speed; and

the atmospheric barometric pressure was steady.[33]

In April 2016, German newspapers and television broadcasts revealed that an early version of this "dyno" mode plan was found in a 2006 PowerPoint presentation that had been prepared by a German Volkswagen executive.[34] Under normal driving conditions, the vehicle's braking and stability control systems might take over the vehicle because a lack of steering column movement; this is one indication of a loss of vehicular control, such as a skid. Therefore, the test or "dyno" mode performed a useful function by allowing the vehicle to be driven normally on a dynamometer.

The ECU, braking, and stability control modules for VW diesel vehicles were manufactured by Bosch, a major manufacturer of automotive components.[35] These components were programmed by VW engineers, using proprietary code developed within the company. The EPA performs emission testing on only about 10 to 15 percent of new cars each year and relies on automobile manufacturers to certify the emissions performance of its vehicles. According to Columbia University law professor Eben Moglen, "[s]oftware is in everything… proprietary software is an unsafe building material. You can't inspect it."[36] In the summer of 2015, the EPA announced that it opposed inspection of proprietary automobile software, supporting automobile manufacturers who claimed that people might try to reprogram their vehicles systems to increase performance in unsafe ways.[37]

Volkswagen engineers took advantage of "dyno" mode by programming the ECU to shift the vehicle's emissions control systems into a full power mode that significantly reduced emissions but used significantly more fuel to operate.[38] Diesel engines produce emissions that include nitrogen oxides (NO_x) and ozone. These are chemical compounds that, according to the EPA, can cause "adverse respiratory effects including airway inflammation in healthy people and increased respiratory symptoms in people with asthma," especially inside vehicles and near roads.[39] Emissions control systems are installed in vehicles to reduce the production and/or emissions of compounds.

Volkswagen started selling diesel cars in the United States in 1977, taking advantage of increased consumer interest in diesel fuel economy.[40]

One form of Volkswagen's diesel emissions control systems used a technology called selective catalytic reduction (SCR).[41] This method used a solution of 70 percent water and 30 percent urea to convert NO_x emissions to nitrogen, oxygen, water, and carbon dioxide (CO_2).[42] A computerized controller sprayed an optimal amount of liquid as the emissions passed through the exhaust system. The liquid is sold in the United States as AdBlue.[43] This system required drivers to have the urea tank refilled periodically at a service center.

A different system was installed in the Golf and other small cars, partly because the SCR system required more space than was available. This version did not require refills; it used a nitrogen oxide trap located before the exhaust valve and catalytic converter to capture and reduce emissions. The vehicle used about 4 percent more diesel fuel when the trap was operating at full power.[44] Some industry experts claimed that traps were less effective than urea-based systems.[45]

VW engineers changed the vehicle's software to turn off the nitrogen oxide trap or catalytic scrubbers[46] during the "on road" mode that was used for normal operation of the vehicle.[47] This boosted the vehicle's overall speed and acceleration but reduced fuel economy while increasing NO_x emissions by a factor of 40. VW's diesel emissions control systems also increased the price of each vehicle between US$5000 to $8000.[48]

Catching the Cheat

Government reliance on manufacturer testing can be problematic. According to Zeynep Tufekci, an assistant professor at the University of North Carolina, smart cars and other smart devices should be tested in realistic conditions, not in a controlled environment. Companies should not be able to use copyright and intellectual property laws to restrict inspection of proprietary software, especially when the code is used in important processes such as voting and public safety. Developers should also include logs and audit trails in their software, to help document its operation.[49]

Volkswagen's "dyno" or cheat mode was discovered in 2014 by researchers at West Virginia University (WVU) who measured the emissions of VW diesel vehicles during long-distance driving tests. One vehicle had a nitrogen oxide trap, while two other vehicles used urea-based SCR systems. WVU was contracted by a nogovernmental organization (NGO), the International Council on Clean Transportation (ICCT), to perform these tests after European investigators noticed discrepancies in their emissions tests of VW and BMW diesel vehicles. U.S. emissions testing is more stringent than European testing, and California automobile emissions standards are more stringent that federal standards.[50]

While the WVU report only mentioned Volkswagen once,[51] it was clear that the VW diesel vehicles produced much higher levels of NO$_x$ emissions during the WVU road tests than were seen in dynamometer tests performed by the California Air Resources Board.[52] ICCT posted the findings to its website in May 2014 and notified the EPA. Investigations by CARB and the EPA led to the EPA's September 2015 announcement. The regulators refused to certify VW's 2016 diesel vehicles for sale, leaving VW and its North American dealers with billions of dollars in new car inventory that could not legally be sold.[53] On September 21, VW's stock price dropped 23 percent.[54]

More than 11 million diesel vehicles worldwide had engines that were affected by VW's unorthodox technology; 660,000 were sold in the United States. The EPA ordered a recall of more than a dozen diesel-powered models.[55]

U.S. consumers were assured that they could continue to drive their affected vehicles while the recall was being organized. For 2015 and 2016 model year vehicles that used the nitrogen oxide trap, the repair was most likely a software patch, installed by a dealer.[56] More extensive modifications were needed for SCR models.

Marketing the Clean Diesel

Between 2009 and 2015, VWoA bought significant amounts of advertising for diesel vehicles in the United States, which was one of Volkswagen's most profitable markets. Diesel vehicle sales accounted for about 5 percent of the North American market,[57] but about 25 percent of VW's sales were in the diesel category.[58] While VW is a market leader in China, diesel engines are unpopular there. There are stringent emissions control rules in European countries, especially in cities such as Paris, but diesel vehicles held a 50 percent market share in Western Europe.[59] Between January and September 2015, VW spent $77 million on U.S.television advertising for diesel vehicles, which was about 45 percent of the company's total in that market.

VW diesel ads used humor to emphasize the high performance and clean emissions of its diesel cars. In a 2015 campaign, three older women discussed the drawbacks of diesel cars while being driven in a VW diesel vehicle. The series, titled "Old Wives Tales," focused on consumer complaints regarding diesel cars, including sluggish performance, loud noise, and the scarcity of diesel fuel. The passengers in the commercials were always surprised when their VW vehicle overcame the problems they discussed.[60] Another 2015 VW advertisement showed precocious boys who caused chaos in a convenience store, to the sounds of Waylon Jennings's country music song "Mommas, don't let your babies grow up to be cowboys." Their mother notices the boys are missing while she refuels their vehicle outside. A VW diesel Jetta drives by, and the viewers see the mother who is driving that vehicle while her three boys sit quietly.[61]

Another benefit that VW and Audi emphasized in their marketing was decreased diesel fuel consumption. During the 2010 Super Bowl, Audi ran a television advertisement for its A3 TDI hatchback that showed the car as the only vehicle that could pass through a fictional "green police" checkpoint.For the 2015 diesel Jetta, VW aired a television advertisement that claimed "When you're driving, things aren't always what they appear to be." The advertisement only aired a few times before it was pulled in September 2015.[62] After the EPA's September 18 announcement, VWoA paused its national advertising through October 11, including the company's non-diesel vehicles.[63] Advertising for gasoline and electric vehicles resumed slowly, as VWoA managers and ad agencies scrambled to create new campaigns and content.

Government Investigations

More than 450 VW and third-party investigators conducted a probe during late 2015 and early 2016, coordinated by the accounting firm Deloitte and a U.S.-based law firm, Jones Day. There were many obstacles in VW's internal reports and documentation on the affected diesel systems. VW engineers used dozens of code words such as "acoustical software" when referring to the emission control countermeasures. The investigators turned their focus on about 20 VW employees. Many persons interviewed during the investigation were "reluctant to provide insight because they were afraid of the legal consequences".[64] The German employees under investigation were not executives. However, the idea that VW executives were unaware of the diesel defeat designs "just doesn't pass the launch test," to quote John German, a former EPA official who became a senior fellow at ICCT and helped begin that group's investigation of VW in 2013.[65] French authorities launched their own investigation into intentional fraud by VW.[66]

German law exempts companies from being prosecuted for crimes; the German Penal Code or *Strafgesetzbuch* (*StGB*) stipulates that only individuals can be held liable for criminal acts. Six Volkswagen employees were under investigation for charges of corporate tax evasion. In the United States, Senators Ron Wyden (D-OR) and Orrin Hatch (R-UT) accused Volkswagen and VWAG of accepting as much as US$51 million in tax incentive credits for diesel vehicles.[67] Margo Oge, who was director of the EPA Office of Transportation and Air Quality in 2011, revealed that German Volkswagen executives had pressured the EPA for "special fuel economy credits for environmental friendliness" that were equivalent to those awarded to zero-emissions vehicles such as electric cars.[68] Oge perceived that the German Volkswagen executives believed their diesel technology was superior to electric motors: "I never had a problem dealing with the Americans. The U.S. Volkswagen people would always come and apologize to US after meeting with the Germans. My sense was that things were being dictated by Germany."[69]

Whistleblowers also came forward. David Donovan, who worked at VWoA in electronic discovery and information management, claims he was fired in December

2015 after he reported his concerns to the company's legal department.[70] Volkswagen acknowledged that there were at least 50 other whistleblowers.[71]

The legal responsibilities of Volkswagen and VWoA executives is also of concern. CIOs are responsible for finding and archiving data, messages, and other corporate information. In September 2015, U.S. Deputy Attorney General Sally Quillian Yates announced that the U.S. Department of Justice planned to increase its efforts to prosecute corporate executives for their involvement in corporate misconduct.[72] Investors criticized Volkswagen's executive compensation practices. Billionaire investor Christopher Hohn of TCI Fund Management wrote in a letter to Volkswagen's executive supervisory boards that top management compensation appeared to be "excessive" and was "unlinked to transparent metrics and paid in cash with no vesting or deferral, and has encouraged aggressive management behavior, contributing to the diesel scandal."[73]

Michael Schrage, a research fellow at MIT's Center for Digital Business, noted that Volkswagen had brought the crisis on itself by failing to acknowledge societal and technological change. The emergence of the Internet of Things (IoT), in which products are embedded with sensors and smart systems, coupled with societal acceptance of social media, made the revelation of corporate deception far more likely than ever before.[74]

Questions for Discussion

1. Consider the corporate culture of Volkswagen in Germany. How did it affect this situation?
2. Why did Volkswagen engineers decide to cheat on the emissions tests? Should the engineers have consulted with executives?
3. What is your assessment of VW's sense of business ethics and fair play as manifested in the emissions cheating scandal?
4. VW has always been perceived to be a socially responsible corporation. In light of this, how could an emissions cheating scandal like this occur?
5. Assume that you are a consumer who purchased one of the affected diesel vehicles in 2014, before the EPA made its announcement. What might your reaction have been? What forms of restitution would you have sought from VWoA and Volkswagen?
6. Is it appropriate that CEO Winterkorn and top-level executives be held financially responsible for their involvement in this fraud?
7. Do research into what has taken place in the VW case since the end of this case. Are circumstances looking better or worse for the company?

Endnotes

1. William Boston, "VW to Receive Dieselgate Settlement from Former CEO, Executives," *The Wall Street Journal* (June 9, 2021), https://www.wsj.com /articles/vw-to-receive-dieselgate-settlement-from -former-ceo-executives-11623248510. Accessed June 23, 2021.
2. William Boston, "VW's Ex-CEO Must Stand Trial Over Emissions Scandal," *The Wall Street Journal* (September 10, 2020), B3.
3. Boston, 2021, Ibid.
4. William Boston, "Volkswagen Goes After Former CEO," *The Wall Street Journal* (March 27-28, 2021), B3.
5. Ibid.
6. Nathan Bomey. "EPA Accuses Volkswagen, Audi of Evading Emission Laws." *USA Today* (September 18, 2015), https://www.USatoday.com/story/money /cars/2015/09/18/epa-accUSes-volkswagen-audi -evading-emission-laws/72400018/. Accessed June 22, 2021.
7. Danielle Ivory and Keith Bradsher, "Regulators Investigating 2nd VW Computer Program on Emissions." *The New York Times* (October 8, 2015), https://www.nytimes.com/2015/10/09 /bUSiness/international/vw-diesel-emissions -scandal-congressional-hearing.html. Accessed June 22, 2021.usUS
8. Jack Ewing and Graham Bowley, "The Engineering of Volkswagen's Aggressive Ambition," *The New York Times* (December 13, 2015), https://www.nytimes .com/2015/12/14/bUSiness/the-engineering-of -volkswagens-aggressive-ambition.html. Accessed June 22, 2021.
9. Jack Ewing, "Volkswagen Reports Profit Drop as It Grapples with Emissions Scandal," *The New York Times* (May 31, 2016), https://www.nytimes .com/2016/06/01/bUSiness/international/volkswagen -q1-earnings.html. Accessed June 22, 2021.
10. Zachary Wilson, "The History of Volkswagen," *Fast Company* (February 1, 2010), https://www .fastcompany.com/1512941/history-volkswagen. Accessed June 22, 2021.
11. Tim Bowler, "Volkswagen: From the Third Reich to the Emissions Scandal," October 2, 2015, https:// www.bbc.com/news/business-34358783. Accessed June 22, 2021.
12. Sue Sturgis, "Reminder: Here's What One State Paid to Lure Lawbreaking VW," *Blue Nation Review* (September 25, 2015).
13. Wilson, Ibid.
14. Luca Ciferri, "Winners and Losers in the VW Scandal," *Automotive News* (November 9, 2015).
15. Dietmar Hawranek, "The Porsche Story: The Downfall of a Corporate Upstart," *Der Speigel* (July 22. 2009), https://www.spiegel.de/consent-a -?targetUrl=https%3A%2F%2Fwww.spiegel.de%2 Finternational%2Fbusiness%2Fthe-porsche-story -the-downfall-of-a-corporate-upstart-a-637542 .html&ref=https%3A%2F%2Fwww.google .com%2F. Accessed June 22, 2021.us
16. Ewing and Bowley.
17. Bowler, ibid.
18. Danny Hakim, Aaron M. Kessler, and Jack Ewing, "As Volkswagen Pushed to Be No. 1, Ambitions Fueled a Scandal," *The New York Times* (September 26, 2015), https://www.nytimes.com/2015/09/27/business/as-vw -pushed-to-be-no-1-ambitions-fueled-a-scandal.html. Accessed June 22, 2021.

19. Ibid.
20. Ewing and Bowley.
21. Rauwald, Ibid.
22. Jan Schwartz,"Porsch, Piech Families Support Embattled Volkswagen CEO: Sources," *Reuters* (January 17, 2016). https://www.reuters.com/article/us-volkswagen-emissions-porsche/porsch-piech-families-support-embattled-volkswagen-ceo-sources-idUSKCN0UV0JW. Accessed June 22, 2021.
23. Sonari Glinton,"'We didn't lie,' Volkswagen CEO Says of Emissions Scandal," *NPR* (January 11, 2016), https://www.npr.org/sections/thetwo-way/2016/01/11/462682378/we-didnt-lie-volkswagen-ceo-says-of-emissions-scandal. Accessed June 22, 2021.
24. Glinton, ibid.
25. Glinton, ibid.
26. Jack Ewing,"Volkswagen Reaches Deal in U.S. over Emissions Scandal," *The New York Times* (April 21, 2016), https://www.nytimes.com/2016/04/22/business/international/volkswagen-emissions-settlement.html#:~:text=Volkswagen%20agreed%20on%20Thursday%20to,equipped%20with%20illegal%20emissions%20software.&text=And%20there%20are%20many%20more,still%20to%20be%20dealt%20with. Accessed June 22, 2021.
27. Jack Ewing, "VW Chief 'Personally' Apologized to Obama Over Cheating," *The New York Times* (April 28, 2016), https://www.nytimes.com/2016/04/29/business/international/volkswagen-legal-costs-emissions-cheating.html. Accessed June 22, 2021.
28. Hiroko Tabuchi,"Volkswagen Challenges U.S. Jurisdiction in Emissions Scandal," *The New York Times* (May 25, 2016), https://www.nytimes.com/2016/05/26/business/volkswagen-challenges-us-jurisdiction-in-emissions-scandal.html. Accessed June 22, 2021.
29. Geoffrey Smith,"Scandal Halts VW's Diesel Passat Production in the United States," *Fortune* (November 11, 2015), https://fortune.com/2015/11/11/scandal-halts-vws-diesel-passat-production-in-u-s/#:~:text=German%20automaker%20Volkswagen%20AG%20(VLKAY,its%20doctoring%20of%20emissions%20data. Accessed June 22, 2021.
30. Jon Linkov,"Volkswagen Emissions Cheat Exploited 'Test Mode'," *Consumer Reports* (September 25, 2015), https://www.consumerreports.org/cro/cars/volkswagen-emissions-cheat-exploited-test-mode. Accessed June 22, 2021.
31. Tom Lish,"What Is a Dynamometer and How Does It Work?" https://www.setra.com/blog/test-and-measurement-dynamometer. Accessed June 22, 2021.
32. Linkov, ibid.
33. Jim Dwyer,"Volkswagen's Diesel Fraud Makes Critic of Secret Code a Prophet," *The New York Times* (September 22, 2015), https://www.nytimes.com/2015/09/23/nyregion/volkswagens-diesel-fraud-makes-critic-of-secret-code-a-prophet.html#:~:text=Volkswagen's%20Diesel%20Fraud%20Makes%20Critic%20of%20Secret%20Code%20a%20Prophet,-By%20Jim%20Dwyer&text=A%20Columbia%20University%20law%20professor,stories%20a%20few%20days%20earlier. Accessed June 22, 2021.
34. Jack Ewing,"VW Presentation in '06 Showed How to Foil Emissions Tests," *The New York Times* (April 26, 2016). http://www.nytimes.com/2016/04/27/busUSiness/international/vw-presentation-in-06-showed-how-to-foil-emissions-tests.html. Accessed June 10, 2016.
35. Linkov, Ibid.
36. Dwyer, Ibid.
37. Dwyer, Ibid.
38. Ian Mouawad and Sydney Ember,"VW's Pitch to Americans Relied on Fun and Fantasy," *The New York Times* (September 27, 2015), https://www.nytimes.com/2015/09/28/business/media/vws-pitch-to-americans-relied-on-fun-and-fantasy.html. Accessed June 22, 2021.
39. EPA, "Nitro Oxygen (NO2) Pollution," https://www.epa.gov/no2-pollution.Accessed June 22, 2021.
40. Mouawad and Ember, Ibid.
41. Ewing, d015, Ibid.
42. Eric Niiler,"VW Could Fool the EPA, But It Couldn't Trick Chemistry," *Wired* (September 22, 2015), https://www.wired.com/2015/09/vw-fool-epa-couldnt-trick-chemistry/#:~:text=When%20engineers%20at%20Volkswagen%20allegedly,to%20this%20existential%20automotive%20conflict. Accessed June 22, 2021.
43. Jack Ewing,"VW Says Emissions Cheating Was Not a One-Time Error," *The New York Times* (December 10, 2015), https://www.nytimes.com/2015/12/11/business/international/vw-emissions-scandal.html#:~:text=WOLFSBURG%2C%20Germany%20E2%80%94%20The%20chairman%20of,States%20clean%20air%20standards%20legally. Accessed June 22, 2021.us
44. Ewing (2015), Ibid.
45. Ewing (2015), Ibid.
46. Gilbert Gates, Jack Ewing, Karl Russell, and Derek Watkins,"Explaining Volkswagen's Emissions Scandal," *The New York Times* (June 1, 2016),http://www.nytimes.com/interactive/2015/bususiness/international/vw-diesel-emissions-scandal-explained.html. Accessed June 6, 2016.
47. Linkov, Ibid.
48. Niiler., Ibid.
49. Zeynep Tufekci,"Volkswagen and the Era of Cheating Software," *The New York Times* (September 23, 2015), https://www.nytimes.com/2015/09/24/opinion/volkswagen-and-the-era-of-cheating-software.html. Accessed June 23, 2021.
50. Jeff Plungis and Dana Hull,"VW's Emissions Cheating Found by Curious Clean-Air Group," *Bloomberg* (September 20, 2015), https://www.bloomberg.com/news/articles/2015-09-19

/volkswagen-emissions-cheating-found-by-curious
-clean-air-group. Accessed June 23, 2021.

51. Gregory G. Thompson, Daniel K. Carder, Marc C. Besch, Arvind Thiruvengadam, and Hemanth K. Kappanna,"In-Use Emissions Testing of Light -Duty Diesel Vehicles in the United States," *Center for Alternative Fuels, Engines & Emissions, West Virginia University* (May 15, 2014), https://theicct .org/publications/use-emissions-testing-light-duty -diesel-vehicles-us. Accessed June 23, 2021.us

52. Ibid.

53. Plungis and Hull, Ibid.

54. Naomi Kresge and Richard Weiss,"Volkswagen Drops 23% After Admitting Diesel Emissions Cheat," Bloomberg (September 21, 2015),https:// www.bloomberg.com/news/articles/2015-09-21 /volkswagen-drops-15-after-admitting-u-s-diesel -emissions-cheat. Accessed June 23, 2021.

55. Gates et al.

56. Jeff S. Bartlett,"Guide to the Volkswagen Emissions Recall," *Consumer Reports* (April 28, 2016).https:// www.consumerreports.org/cars-guide-to-the -volkswagen-dieselgate-emissions-recall/. Accessed June 23, 2021.

57. Ciferri, Ibid.

58. Mouawad and Ember, Ibid.

59. Ciferri, Ibid.

60. Mouawad and Ember, Ibid.

61. Volkswagen Passat TDI TV Spot, Mom song by Waylon Jennings,https://www.ispot.tv/ad/78QS /volkswagen-passat-tdi-mom-song-by-waylon -jennings. Accessed June 23, 2021.

62. Mouawad and Embry, Ibid.

63. Bond, Ibid.

64. Volkswagen code words trip up diesel investigators, *Automotive News* (April 25, 2016), https://www.autonews.com/article/20160425 /LEGALFILE/304259968/volkswagen-code-words -trip-up-diesel-investigators. Accessed June 23, 2021.

65. Ewing and Bowley, Ibid.

66. Jack Ewing, "Volkswagen Inquiry Expands to 17 Suspects," *The New York Times* (March 8, 2016). https://www.nytimes.com/2016/03/09/business /international/volkswagen-inquiry-germany.html. Accessed June 23, 2021.

67. Kelly Phillips Erb, "Germany Investigating Volkswagen Employees for Emissions Scandal Related Tax Evasion," *Forbes* (December 1, 2015), https://www.forbes.com/sites/kellyphillipserb /2015/12/01/germany-investigating-volkswagen -employees-for-emissions-scandal-related-tax -evasion/?sh=c8f60291d7dc. Accessed June 23, 2021.

68. Aaron M. Kessler, "Volkswagen Sought a Green Seal for Its Diesel Cars," *The New York Times* (October 6, 2015), https://www.nytimes.com/2015/10/07/business /international/volkswagen-sought-a-green-seal-for -its-diesel-cars.html. Accessed June 23, 2021.

69. Kessler, Ibid.

70. Kim S. Nash and Steven Norton, "Electronic Discovery Can Bring CIOs to Court," *The Wall Street Journal* (March 25, 2016), https://www.wsj.com /articles/BL-CIOB-9414. Accessed June 23, 2021.

71. Ewing and Bowley, Ibid.

72. Nash and Norton, Ibid.

73. Antoine Gara. "Billionaire Christopher Hohn Says Lavish Bonuses Contributed to Volkswagen's Emissions Scandal," *Forbes* (May 6, 2016), https:// www.forbes.com/sites/antoinegara/2016/05/06 /billionaire-christopher-hohn-says-exec-bonuses -contributed-to-volkswagens-emissions -scandal/?sh=1d52832059fb. Accessed June 23, 2021.

74. Michael Schrage, "Is VW's Fraud the End of Large-Scale Corporate Deception? *Harvard Business Review* (September 29, 2015), https://hbr .org/2015/09/is-vws-fraud-the-end-of-large-scale -corporate-deception#:~:text=Consequently% 2C%20I%20believe%20Volkswagen's%20debacle, multi%2Dbillion%20dollar%20global% 20fraud. Accessed June 23, 2021.

Case 8

Payday Loans: A Needed Product or a Financial Scam?*

Ethan Dorsett was a retired and disabled Marine living in Missouri.[1] He struggled for five years trying to pay back a $2,500 payday loan that had escalated to $50,000 in interest due. Ethan's plight began when his wife, Emily, slipped on ice and broke her ankle. Needing surgery, she was unable to work in her retail job for several months. Her medical bills came to $26,000, and she was ineligible for insurance at her work. With two children in college, Ethan found himself unable to pay his wife's medical bills. Ethan tried borrowing the money from family, friends, banks, and credit unions. He had a "fair" credit rating, but it was not good enough to borrow such a large sum of money.[2]

Out of desperation, Ethan turned to storefront lenders (another name for payday loan companies). He took out five $500 loans and paid interest every week. Every two weeks,

*This case was written and updated in 2021 by Archie B. Carroll, University of Georgia.

each of the five loans carried $95 in interest for a total of $475, and he had to take out new loans to cover the old ones.[3] Eventually, through taking various jobs over the five years, Ethan somehow got the loans paid off. It was tough. Ethan said, "We ended up losing our home. We lost our car."[4]

Ethan was one of the fortunate ones. Not everyone is able to get out from under the burden of high-interest loans. Quite often, these storefront loans are given to people in more desperate circumstances who are not able to pay off their loans like Ethan did.

Many consumers who take out payday loans are not as good a credit risk as Ethan. More frequently, payday loan borrowers are living on the ragged edge financially and end up borrowing, paying interest, and borrowing some more. Many end up going to title loan companies, which are somewhat similar to payday loans, where they end up signing over the title to their cars. One 66-year-old woman and her jobless son in Las Vegas took out a $2,000 title loan and pledged his 2002 Ford F-150 truck as collateral. Both said no one verified whether she or her son would be able to repay the loan, which carried 121.5 percent interest. When they finally paid the loan off, she said the company did not give them the truck title back; rather, the company talked them into borrowing another $2,000.[5]

What is a Payday Loan?

A payday loan is a short-term loan, generally for $500 or less, that is usually due on your next payday.[6] Payday loans typically have the following characteristics. In addition to these loans typically being for a small amount and due on your next payday, they generally require that the lender is given access to the borrower's checking account, or they must write a check for the full balance in advance so the lender has the option of depositing the check when the loan comes due (on the borrower's payday).[7]

Payday loans often have features other than those described. Though they are usually paid off in one lump sum, it is possible to set them up so that the borrower pays interest-only payments resulting in "renewals" or "rollovers" that may result in installment payments over a longer period of time.[8]

The borrower may receive a loan in a variety of ways. It could be given as cash or a check; it could be received through funds loaded onto a prepaid debit card; or, the borrower could have the funds electronically deposited into a checking account. The finance charge for the loan (the cost of borrowing) may range from $10 to $30 for each $100 borrowed, which equates to an Annual Percentage Rate (APR) of almost 400 percent. To appreciate this rate, compare it with the APR on a credit card where the range usually runs 12 percent to 30 percent, depending on the card holder's credit rating.[9]

Example: Let's say you need to borrow $300 until your next payday which is two weeks away. To pay it back, you will owe $345 assuming a fee of $15 per each $100 borrowed. Let's assume you need to renew or roll over your loan. You get charged a $45 fee when the extension is over. That comes to a $90 charge for borrowing $300 for several weeks.[10]

In addition to the fixed fees for a payday loan, other fees may be added on. If you renew or roll over your loan, for example, you will be charged an added fee and you still owe the original amount. In addition, if you do not repay the loan on time, you might be charged a late fee or a returned check fee. If your loan is loaded onto a prepaid debit card, there are other possible fees. These could include fees to add the funds to your card, fees for checking your balance, fees each time you use your card, and/or regular monthly fees.[11]

States Push Back

Payday loans are governed by state laws. Some states do not permit payday lending storefronts because the loans are not permitted by state laws. Or, some payday lending businesses may opt not to do business in a state because of its regulations.[12] Twenty-two states have already regulated the industry, but in some states the industry has protected itself from regulations by making huge donations to the state lawmakers. Further, those donations are carefully targeted at key leaders in the legislature and to members of important committees when legislation has stalled or died in recent years.[13]

Some states, such as Colorado and Indiana, say they have found a balanced approach to payday lending that keeps the payday loans available but heavily regulates them.[14] In Colorado, many have praised the state for effectively reducing the interest rates on such loans by two-thirds and slowing down the rate that the lenders can roll over the loans. Some say Colorado is the most consumer-friendly payday loan market in the United States, but others say that there is still evidence of repeat reborrowing and high default rates.[15]

One credit counselor observed that before Colorado's new rules, families with numerous payday loans, all from different lenders, would spend Saturdays driving all over town rolling over their loans, but now that doesn't happen much anymore. According to Colorado state data, the number of payday loan stores has dropped from 486 before 2010 to 188. In addition, 15 states have effectively banned payday loans by imposing strict caps on interest rates.[16]

Regulations Proposed but not Passed

Beginning in 2015, the relatively new Consumer Financial Protection Bureau (CFPB) began studying ways that payday lenders would be required to make sure that borrowers can pay back their loans.[17] By spring 2016, it was becoming evident what the new CFPB regulations might look like. The draft of the new regulations issued by CFPB director Richard Corday was 1,300 pages long.[18] Under the new regulations, payday lenders would be required to run full credit checks on prospective borrowers to check out their sources of income, need for the loan, and ability to keep paying their living expenses while paying the loan back.[19] In short, potential borrowers would be subject to the same kinds of screens that banks and credit unions now use and for which the typical payday borrower cannot qualify. An anonymous CFPB official was quoted as saying that if this new rule were enacted, it would have excluded almost two-thirds of potential borrowers from receiving this type of loan.[20] As of March 2021, the proposed federal payday loan regulations had not yet been passed or enacted.[21]

The new regulations would have made it difficult or impossible for the typical payday loan borrower to take advantage of the service because they likely will not meet the requirements for the loans. In addition, huge record-keeping requirements being foisted on the industry will likely force the small, local lenders who have dominated the industry out of business, and favor the large firms and consolidators who can afford and manage the regulatory overhead.[22]

The Google Ban

Just before the CFPB announced its proposed regulations on the payday lending industry, Google announced that it would no longer run ads for payday loans, a decision that would impact significantly the online-lending sector of the industry. Online loans account for about half of the payday lending market.[23] The payday loan industry did not respond well to Google's decision. They claimed the new policy was "discriminatory and a form of censorship."[24] The president and CEO of the Online Lenders Alliance said that Google's new policy "will prohibit legal loans for many Americans who otherwise do not have access to the financial system."[25] She added, "The policy discriminates against those among us who rely on online loans."[26] In its defense, Google said that it hopes that fewer people will be exposed to misleading or harmful products.[27]

According to a *Wall Street Journal* (*WSJ*) editorial, Google may be getting plaudits from some observers, but maybe Google's motivations are not entirely pure. Apparently, the venture capital arm of Google's parent company, Alphabet, has invested in LendUp, a company that offers short-term loans at high interest rates and competes with the payday lenders. Google responded that it planned to block LendUp's ads too. The *WSJ* editorial also pointed out that Google had invested about $125 million in the online Lending Club and posed the question of how much that firm would pick up in business due to the ban.[28] As it turned out, payday lending companies were finding ways to change their messaging in ways that met Google's policies.[29]

Don't Rush In

Supporters of the payday lending industry point out that the government should not rush into payday loan regulations. One writer pointed out that when the CFPB conducted a study of consumer complaints, less than 1 percent of the consumer complaints were related to payday lending. This was a small percentage compared to the complaints related to mortgages, debt collection, and credit cards, which made up about two-thirds of the complaints.[30]

A further issue is that the proposed new regulations would further reduce alternatives for consumers who already lack access to the banking system. The CEO of the Community Financial Services Association of America, which represents the storefront payday lenders, said, "payday loans represent an important source of credit for millions of Americans who live from paycheck to paycheck."[31] He went on to say that we need to find ways to increase, not limit, the ways that these people can get access to the credit they need.[32] Pew Charitable Trusts research found that some consumers turn to pawning their belongings or borrowing further from families and that these were not good options for people in a financial pinch.[33]

The Pandemic

The COVID-19 pandemic that hit the economy hard starting in 2020 could have presented a windfall opportunity for payday lenders. Unemployment and financial stress hit low-income citizens hard. However, the opposite happened because the federal government pushed trillions of dollars of federal relief, including direct cash payments and enhanced unemployment benefits, into the economy, thus reducing demand for the payday loans.[34] Demand for payday loans fell 67 percent in the midst of the pandemic lockdowns and has yet to recover to pre–COVID-19 levels. Further, community banks and other community development financial institutions have surfaced as competitors, but it remains to be seen how much this new competition will cut into the payday lending industry. In addition, the Biden administration is also likely to impose new restrictions through an emboldened CFPB.[35]

Questions for Discussion

1. Who are the stakeholders in this case and what are their stakes?
2. Have you ever taken out a payday loan or title loan? What was your experience?
3. What is your evaluation of the corporate social responsibility of the payday lending industry, using the four-part definition of CSR? Is payday lending an exploitive industry that snares borrowers in a never-ending cycle of debt?
4. Could it be that the industry is socially responsible but some of its members are engaging in questionable practices? What questionable practices are most troublesome?
5. Given the strong demand for payday loans on the part of some citizens, should the industry be regulated so that borrowers are further protected? What are borrowers to do who do not meet new federal regulations if they are passed?
6. Some states have regulated the payday lending industry. Should the federal government be getting involved with regulating this industry? What will be the effects of new CFPB regulations?

7. What is your assessment of the Google ban? Does Google have a conflict of interest in imposing this ban?

8. Should the CFPB back off and let the marketplace and the states handle payday lending issues?

Endnotes

1. Susanna Kim, ABCNews, "Missouri Man Paid $50,000 in Interest after Taking $2,500 in Payday Loans," May 21, 2016, https://abcnews.go.com /Business/missouri-man-paid-50000-interest-taking -2500-payday/story?id=39253982. Accessed June 23, 2021.Note: the name given him in this case has been changed.
2. Ibid.
3. Ibid.
4. Ibid.
5. Fred Schulte, "Title Loan Companies Grow, Fend Off Regulation.," *USA Today*, December 9, 2015, https://www.usatoday.com/story/news/2015/12/09 /title-loan-companies-investigated-across-usa /76911572/. Accessed June 23, 2021.
6. Consumer Financial Protection Bureau, "What Is a Payday Loan?" https://www.consumerfinance.gov /ask-cfpb/what-is-a-payday-loan-en-1567/. Accessed June 23, 2021.
7. Ibid.
8. Ibid.
9. Ibid.
10. Ibid.
11. Ibid.
12. Ibid.
13. Kyle Whitmire, "Which Lawmakers Go Payday Cash for Free?" *The Huntsville Times*, March 29, 2015, A10.
14. Yuka Hayashi, "States Push Back on Payday," *The Wall Street Journal*, March 17, 2016, C2.
15. Ibid.
16. Ibid.
17. Alan Zibel, "Payday Loans Face New Controls," *Wall Street Journal*, January 5, 2015, C1.
18. Holman W. Jenkins Jr., "Payday Loans a Crony Capitalist Target," *The Wall Street Journal*, June 4–5, 2016, A11.
19. Ibid.
20. CFPB, "CFPB Proposes Changes to Payday Loan Regulations," credit.com, March 16, 2021, https:// www.credit.com/blog/cfpb-proposes-changes-to -payday-loan-regulations-189860/. Accessed June 23, 2021.
21. Ibid.
22. Ibid.
23. Yuka Hayashi, "Google to Pull Plug on Ads for Payday Lenders," *Wall Street Journal*, May 12, 2016, C1.
24. Ibid.
25. Ibid.
26. Ibid.
27. "Google's Payday Lending Ban," *The Wall Street Journal*, May 31, 2016, A12.
28. Ibid.
29. Ginny Marvin, "Why Are Payday Lending Ads Still Showing on Google after the Ban?" October 5, 2016, https://searchengineland.com/payday-loan -ads-still-showing-google-ban-258945. Accessed June 23, 2021.
30. Dennis Shaul, "We Shouldn't Rush into Payday Lending Regulations," *The Huntsville Times*, March 29, 2015, A13.
31. Ibid.
32. Ibid.
33. Sarah Skidmore Sell, Associated Press, "Payday Loans 101," *Athens Banner-Herald*, June 12, 2016, B8.
34. Peter Robison, "Hard Times Aren't Helping Payday Lenders," *Bloomberg Businessweek*, May 10, 2021, 25–27.
35. Ibid.

Case 9

Big Tech's Power Plays*

The last few years have seen a glut of attention paid to an assemblage of huge companies known as Big Tech. One article summed up the concern directly by posing the question, "Is Big Tech Now Just Too Much to Stomach?"[1] Big Tech is comprised of five major firms that have come to dominate the business sector, especially information technology: Facebook, Amazon, Apple, Microsoft, and Google (Alphabet).

The total value of the tech giants approximates $5 trillion. Goldman Sachs has anointed the big five with the acronym FAAMG, standing for the first letter in each of their names.

These five companies make up about 13 percent of the value of the whole S&P500 by market capitalization. FAAMG have grown through mergers and acquisitions. For example, even though 2020 was an economic disaster for much of the business sector, the Big Tech five were able to acquire 20 other companies.[2] In addition, these leading

---

*This case was prepared by Archie B. Carroll, University of Georgia, 2021, for this 11th edition.

companies bring sociocultural evolution to a large scale, including driving social change at full speed.[3] Similar to Big Oil, Big Tobacco, and Big Pharma, Big Tech is here to stay and will shape today's society in more ways than just technology.[4] Further, the global tide of public opinion has been turning against the tech companies, often led by activists who for years have been sounding the alarm that the companies, collectively, are too powerful.[5]

There are several allegations that have been made about Big Tech. These include their sheer size and market power, their privacy practices, and the bias built into their artificial intelligence (AI) algorithms. Additionally, censorship and political bias also have been alleged. To understand the problems associated with Big Tech, it is necessary to consider some of these issues in more detail.

Size and Market Power

First, consider their size and market power. This gets into the economic and financial dimensions of their influence. The Big Tech companies were already huge before the COVID-19 pandemic hit. The pandemic made them bigger—a lot bigger. The companies' combined market value at the end of 2019 was $4.9 trillion. At the end of 2020 it had grown to $7.5 trillion.[6] Because of the dizzying growth of technological products and services, and during one of the most punishing economic downturns on record, spending surged on products such as computers, video games, online retail, cloud-computing services, and digital advertising. Big Tech's aggregate profit rose even faster at a 24 percent rate.[7] The five companies now account for nearly one quarter of the total stock market value of the S&P500. As the *Wall Street Journal* observed, there's "Regular-Big," and now there's "Pandemic-Big."[8]

It is little wonder, therefore, that Big Tech is now at the center of an antitrust debate in Washington. An investigation by the House of Representatives in 2020 accused the companies of abusing their dominance to thwart competition and recommended a series of reforms to antitrust laws that anti-monopoly activists have long supported. Among these would be restricting which markets the companies can operate in and requiring them to treat other businesses on their platforms fairly and without favoritism. Federal antitrust officials and state attorneys general have sued Google and Facebook for what they say are monopoly abuses.[9]

Though it may be some time before these issues are resolved, at least five bipartisan House proposals seek to lessen the power of tech's biggest players.[10] Amazon was hit with an antitrust suit by the District of Columbia that alleges that the company blocks sellers on its marketplace from offering better deals elsewhere, leading to higher prices for consumers.[11] The European Union (EU) also has gotten into the fray. The EU has launched an antitrust probe into Google's use of advertising technology. They are looking into an array of suspected anticompetitive business practices involving the company's brokering of ads and sharing user data with advertisers across websites and mobile apps, one of the newest areas of antitrust scrutiny for the company.[12] In May 2021, it was announced that Google was nearing a settlement with France in an antitrust case alleging it had abused its power in online advertising and was likely to pay a fine and be required to make operational changes.[13] In June 2021, the Federal Trade Commission (FTC) announced that it would review Amazon's proposed acquisition of Hollywood studio MGM. The FTC is now led by chair Lina Khan, who made a name for herself in antitrust circles by criticizing Amazon.[14] In June 2021, a federal judge threw out two antitrust cases against Facebook, claiming the FTC had not made its case. One allegation was that Facebook held a monopoly over social networking. The judge gave the agency 30 days to refile with more detail and stronger arguments. These rulings struck a major blow to the government's attempts to rein in Big Tech.[15]

Privacy Issues

One of the longest-standing arguments has been that Big Tech violates the privacy of consumers through its digital dominance and unrestrained policies. The tech companies operating digital platforms where personal information is gathered are said to be the primary culprits. A $5 billion penalty against Facebook in 2019 for privacy missteps may have provided a wakeup call to Big Tech, but concerns about privacy continue.[16] The FTC investigation of Facebook began after reports that personal data of tens of millions of users improperly ended up in the hands of data firm Cambridge Analytica. The user data at issue went beyond those of direct users who downloaded the app but also included data about their Facebook friends as well.[17]

Who has not used Facebook, Amazon, Google, or your Apple iPhone, and related apps, and wondered what happens to all the personal information that is gathered? Further, surveillance and collection of information is an ongoing enterprise in the digital age. Shoshana Zuboff, author of *The Age of Surveillance Capitalism*,[18] argues that the massive concentrations of data these companies collect manipulate our commercial and political lives and threaten our democracy.[19] Zuboff claims that these companies are black boxes, operating outside of societal influence and democratic control, and they simply claim the right to treat our private lives as raw material for their profits.[20]

Zuboff observes that important new legislative proposals in the EU and the United Kingdom would for the first time insist that the largest digital platforms be accountable to audit and oversight, the rule of law, and established rights of citizens.[21] In June 2021, a European Union privacy regulator proposed a $425 million fine against Amazon; if it passes, it could be the biggest-yet penalty under the EU's privacy law. The EU's data protection commission, the CNPD, is Amazon's main privacy regulator in the EU, and the case relates to alleged violations of Europe's General Data Protection Regulation (GDPR) focused on protection of personal data.[22] Ireland's Data Protection Commission leads GDPR's enforcement for Facebook, Alphabet/Google, and Apple because their EU headquarters are in their country. They expect to make draft decisions for half a dozen privacy cases involving Big Tech in 2021.[23] In spite of its efforts, Ireland, which leads enforcement for the EU and the biggest of the U.S. tech companies, has come under fire from activists and politicians for not having issued more decisions against the companies. To date, their one major decision was in late 2020, fining Twitter €450,000.[24]

The United States has lagged behind the EU in attempting to regulate Big Tech and their privacy violations. It is likely that the U.S. regulators will step in eventually, but some of their current practices intended to protect consumers are already being criticized as inadequate. From the consumer's perspective, the current "consent model," when consumers are asked to agree to share their personal data, gives the illusion of control to the consumer but really does not offer it. In proposed legislation, consent requirements are to be presented in plain language so consumers can understand how their personal data will be used, but the consent clauses typically run for several pages and are seldom read by users because of their length and legalese. Further, these provisions simply "give notice" to consumers, they don't actually regulate how this information is used.[25]

Some Big Tech CEOs say they welcome regulation, but Silicon Valley lobbyists in Washington are working day and night to block any restrictive legislation that might affect their profits. Facebook spent $20 million and Amazon spent $18 million on federal lobbying in 2020, more than in the same time period in any previous year.[26] Once again, the power of Big Tech dominates the debates about how many, if any, new regulations need to be considered.

Algorithms Used

Behind many of the digital abuses that Big Tech has been accused of lies the issue of the algorithms they use. An algorithm is a process or set of rules to be followed in calculations and other problem-solving operations, especially those that are computer-driven.[27] Search engines such as Google, Yahoo, and Bing are the biggest players, but all of the Big Tech companies use them.[28] Algorithms are used by virtually all companies to make decisions, but that does not necessarily mean that they are impartial or operate fairly. Combined with Big Data, algorithms increasingly affect individuals, organizations, and society, and they drive recommendations that influence what we buy, which movies we watch, what businesses we frequent, what websites we access, and the social media networks in which we engage.[29] Today, there is a call for algorithmic transparency or accountability. Behind this is the issue of algorithmic abuse or bias.

When algorithms are used on citizens and consumers via Big Tech, one can see quickly that some uses might be legitimate, but others are questionable or quite illegitimate. Along these lines, University of Georgia researchers Hugh Watson and Conner Nations have proposed a "Creepiness Scale" to categorize various algorithm uses. In their scheme, algorithmic uses might range from "this is helpful," to "this is creepy," to "this is so wrong."[30] "Helpful" uses might include movie suggestions on Netflix, LinkedIn's matching of job recruiters and applicants, and traffic information from Google Maps before going somewhere. "Creepy" applications might include Google telling you how long it will take to get to your destination without you saying where you are going, ads from Instagram based on how you use your phone's microphone, or researching a sickness you might have and then seeing ads for specialists. Finally, "wrong" applications might be Facebook's ability to influence your worldview through news feeds, screening job applicants based on analyzing their smiles, or visiting a hospital emergency room and then receiving ads from personal injury lawyers.[31] Obviously, each person's assessments of these uses might vary.

Allegations about algorithmic bias include beliefs that they are racist, sexist, political, or otherwise too heavily relying on narrow input data. One accusation is that AI and algorithm construction are dominated primarily by white men and that blacks or Latinos/Latinas are underrepresented, and this fact shows bias in the resulting design.[32] Another example was when Amazon was developing a tool to screen résumés so that it could screen job applicants more quickly. It built an algorithm based on data it had been collecting for a decade but those previous résumés came primarily from men. That meant the system was designed to discriminate against women, though not intentionally. It also ended up using proxies for gender such as whether a person went to a women's college or not.[33] In short, algorithmic bias can easily be built into Big Tech's decision models either unintentionally or intentionally.

Algorithmic transparency appears to be one of the helpful policies or processes to guard against bias. The Association for Computing Machinery (ACM), for example, has published accountability principles designed to offset bias. Among these are principles of awareness, accountability, access and redress, explanation, auditability, validation, and testing.[34] Their promulgation, however, does not ensure their use.

Censorship Issues

Related to the issue of algorithmic bias is another issue that has arisen regarding Big Tech, that of the censorship of free speech.[35] Many of these censorships are alleged to be because of political differences. For example, when most of the Silicon Valley tech companies permanently banned former President Donald Trump from its platforms in 2021, a backlash of accusations about censorship took place around the world.[36] Government leaders, many ideologically opposed to the policies of Trump, raised objections against what they claimed to be the power and arrogance of Big Tech. Many groups have stated that the tech giants have accumulated too much power to censor.[37]

During the height of the COVID-19 pandemic, China officials censored doctors for sharing what the doctors thought about the coronavirus. They labeled it as dangerous misinformation being disseminated on social media. In turn, according to a *Wall Street Journal* editorial board commentary, the social media giants have silenced doctors who hold contrarian views regarding the virus's origins, in what they and others have considered an effort to shut down scientific debate. According to the *Wall Street Journal*, some fact-checking on Facebook's fact checkers is in order.[38] Scientists often disagree as to how evidence should be interpreted, and debate is how ideas are refined. But it is alleged that Facebook is using its own fact checkers to present their opinions as facts and to silence scientists whose viewpoints challenge their own.[39] Sadly, science has been politicized in recent years, and it is difficult to nail down facts.

Managers of social media platforms have been accused of suppressing or deleting what ought to be considered legitimate public debate. Their power is driven by their own content filters that filter what they consider to be "hate speech," "misinformation," and "authoritative" versus "non-authoritative" sources.[40] One academic reported that he got a notice from LinkedIn (owned by Microsoft) that his account had been blocked in China and that his profile that detailed his career history had been blocked as "prohibited" content. He asserted that LinkedIn is "pulling people's material off without telling them why." It has been reported that LinkedIn made a trade-off to accept Chinese censorship when it entered China in 2014 and that it has typically censored human-rights activists and deleted content that it thought were considered sensitive to the Chinese government.[41]

During 2021, Facebook said that its content-oversight board overturned four instances where it found the company unfairly infringed on users' speech on the platform or misapplied vague rules on content that could cause imminent harm.[42] However, the question remains, who is monitoring the monitors? According to one technology correspondent, if Big Tech is allowed to develop unchecked and unregulated, it will eventually have the power to suppress the news, opinions, and political movements. This would mean the end of democracy as we know it because the public would be placed forever under the thumb of an "unaccountable oligarchy."[43]

To be sure, Big Tech provides many benefits to consumers, and these should not be overlooked. However, the economic, social, and ethical issues that have been raised may potentially lead companies to embark on new self-controls, such as higher ethical standards. Alternatively, consumers may decide they have had enough and vote with their pocketbooks to avoid purchasing goods and services from Big Tech. Finally, as seen in Europe, the United States may decide to invoke harsher government regulations. Whole books have been written about these issues and many more will be also.[44] Will Big Tech be allowed to stay so Big? The future is uncertain.

Questions for Discussion

1. Is Big Tech too big? Does it have too much power? What type of power does it have? Should it be controlled or regulated as a monopoly? Should any of the large companies be broken up?
2. Is Big Tech socially responsible? Analyze one of the Big Tech companies using the four-part definition of CSR presented in Chapter 2: economic, legal, ethical, and philanthropic responsibilities. Check the news about them for the past year or so as your source.
3. Big Tech provides many benefits. Do its benefits outweigh the costs citizens are experiencing?
4. Which of Big Tech's issues is most problematic for society? Market power? Privacy practices? AI bias? Censorship? Political bias?
5. Have you personally experienced any of Big Tech's powers used against you? Explain.

Endnotes

1. Jasper Jolly, "Is Big Tech Now Just Too Much to Stomach?" *The Guardian*, February 6, 2021, https://www.theguardian.com/business/2021/feb/06/is-big-tech-now-just-too-big-to-stomach. Accessed June 23, 2021.
2. Nicolas Lekkas, "The Big Five Tech Companies: Big Tech Facts," September 7, 2020, https://growthrocks.com/blog/big-five-tech-companies-acquisitions/. Accessed June 23, 2021.
3. Jolly, Ibid.
4. Lekkas, Ibid.
5. Billy Perrigo, "Building a Better Internet," *Time*, February 1–8, 2021, pp. 80–83.
6. Wall Street Journal Staff, "How Big Tech Got Even Bigger," *The Wall Street Journal*, February 6–7, 2021, B6.
7. Ibid.
8. Wall Street Journal Staff, "In Tech, There's Regular-Big and There's Pandemic Big," *The Wall Street Journal*, May 1–2, 2021, B5.
9. David McLaughlin, "The Limits of Lina Khan's Power," *Bloomberg Businessweek*, June 28, 2021, 36–37.
10. Dana Mattioli and Ryan Tracy, "Bills Aim to Split Amazon, Curb Tech Giants," *The Wall Street Journal*, June 12–13, 2021, A1.
11. Ryan Tracy, "D.C. Sues Amazon, Alleging Monopoly That Raises Prices," *The Wall Street Journal*, May 26, 2021, A1.
12. Sam Schechner and Parmy Olson, "EU Launches Antitrust Probe into Google's Use of Ad Tech," *The Wall Street Journal*, June 23, 2021, A1.
13. Sam Schechner and Keach Hagey, "Google, France Near Antitrust Settlement," *The Wall Street Journal*, May 28, 2021, A1.
14. Brent Kendall, "FTC to Review Amazon-MGM Deal," *The Wall Street Journal*, June 23, 2021, B1.
15. Cecilia Kang, "Judge Throws Out Two Cases Against Facebook," *The New York Times*, June 29, 2021, https://www.nytimes.com/2021/06/28/technology/facebook-ftc-lawsuit.html?action=click&module=Top%20Stories&pgtype=Homepage. Accessed June 29, 2021.

16. Emily Glazer, Ryan Tracy, and Jeff Horwitz, "Facebook Penalty Is Set at $5 Billion," *The Wall Street Journal*, July 13–14, 2019, A1.

17. Ibid.

18. Soshana Zuboff, *The Age of Surveillance Capitalism* (New York: PublicAffairs, 2019).

19. Quoted in Perrigo, Ibid.

20. Ibid.

21. Ibid.

22. Sam Schechner, "Amazon Faces Fine Over Privacy," *The Wall Street Journal*, June 11, 2021, B1.

23. Ibid.

24. Scott Ikeda, "First Cross-Border GDPR Fine Comes in; Twitter Will Pay €450,000," *CPO Magazine*, December 23, 2020, https://www.cpomagazine.com/data-protection/first-cross-border-gdpr-fine-comes-in-twitter-will-pay-e450000/. Accessed June 28, 2021.

25. David Roe, "Regulators May Finally Get to Tame Big Tech," *CMS Wire*, March 5, 2021, https://www.cmswire.com/information-management/regulators-may-finally-get-to-tame-big-tech/. Accessed June 28, 2021.

26. Perrigo, p. 83.

27. "Algorithms," *Merriam-Webster*, https://www.merriam-webster.com/dictionary/algorithm. Accessed June 28, 2021.

28. Ibid.

29. Hugh J. Watson and Conner Nations, "Addressing the Growing Need for Algorithmic Transparency," *Communications of the Association for Information System*, 2019.

30. Ibid.

31. Ibid.

32. Rebecca Heilweil, "Why Algorithms Can Be Racist and Sexist," *Vox*, February 18, 2020, https://www.vox.com/recode/2020/2/18/21121286/algorithms-bias-discrimination-facial-recognition-transparency. Accessed June 28, 2021.

33. Ibid.

34. Watson and Nations, Ibid.

35. LibertiesEU, "How Big Tech Censorship Is Harming Free Speech," May 5, 2021, https://www.liberties.eu/en/stories/big-tech-censorship/43511. Accessed June 28, 2021.

36. Allum Bokhari, "Who Is in Control? The Need to Rein in Big Tech," *Imprimis*, January 2021.

37. Ibid.

38. "Fact-Checking Facebook's Fact Checkers," *The Wall Street Journal*, March 6–7, 2021, A12.

39. Ibid.

40. Bokhari, Ibid.

41. Liza Lin, "LinkedIn Accounts for Several Scholars Are Blocked in China," *The Wall Street Journal*, June 23, 2021., B4.

42. Jeff Horwitz, "Facebook Panel Overturns Some Content Decisions," *The Wall Street Journal*, January 29, 2021, B9.

43. Bokhari, Ibid., pp. 4–5.

44. Floyd Brown and Todd Cefaratti, *Big Tech Tyrants* (Post Hill Press, 2019); Josh Hawley, *The Tyranny of Big Tech* (Regnery Publishing, 2021); Alan Dershowitz, *The Case Against the New Censorship* (Hot Books, 2021); Franklin Foer, *World Without Mind: The Existential Threat of Big Tech* (Penguin Books, 2018).

Case 10

An Epidemic of Cheating in College*

While we spend plenty of time critiquing businesses, governments, and other institutions for their flawed ethics, it is also important to consider college students' ethics, especially in the form of academic dishonesty. A year of remote learning during the pandemic gave students ample opportunity to take ethical shortcuts on their assignments. Many students were isolated at home during the 2020–2021 year and taking online classes, which some say created a situation where academic dishonesty had never been easier.[1]

Texas A&M reportedly had a 50 percent increase in cheating allegations in the fall of 2020 from a year prior. One incident involved 193 students who self-reported their academic misconduct so they could receive lighter punishment. The University of Pennsylvania witnessed cheating investigations rise by 71 percent during the 2019–2020 year, according to school data.[2]

In 2021, the U.S. Military Academy at West Point concluded investigations into the largest cheating scandal in at least four decades. The academy punished dozens of cadets found to be cheating on an exam while studying remotely. The irony is that these students had been required to memorize an honor code warning them to "not lie, cheat, steal, or tolerate those who do." These words are inscribed in marble at the Honor Plaza that thousands of future officers walk by every day.[3]

To be sure, there is nothing new about student cheating. However, there is strong evidence that during the pandemic when classes switched to virtual modalities, cheating increased. After fall semester 2020, a survey by *Yale News*

*This case was written by Archie B. Carroll, University of Georgia, 2021.

was conducted that found that 50 percent of those admitting to academic dishonesty said they did it for the first time during the virtual learning semesters.[4] According to one student at Yale, the exceptional grades received by many in one of his courses were not the result of intelligence or hard work but due to the academic dishonesty of the students, made easier by the online format of the course.[5]

So, why do students cheat? There are many answers to this question, and psychologists and professors have addressed it many times. First, it must be said that students know that cheating is wrong. Unless you come from a different culture where cheating is accepted or tolerated, it is clear that cheating is not a defensible practice. It is a question of simple fairness and honesty. Most of the students who cheat in college also cheated in high school. There is a distinct pattern.[6] According to Professor David Rettinger, director of the Center for Honor, Leadership and Service, dedicated to integrity, students who cheat still see themselves as principled people by rationalizing their cheating for reasons they see as legitimate. Some do it because they do not see the value of their assigned work. Some do it because they perceive an overemphasis on content linked to high-stakes tests.[7]

Although some students cheat on assignments they do not believe have value, other students are able to rationalize their cheating on assignments they do see as having value. Some high-achieving students feel pressured to attain perfection so they can be admitted to prestigious graduate schools. They do not want a single test score to sabotage months of hard work. Others claim there is a cutthroat environment that is driving rampant dishonesty. Others do it because of peer pressure. Cheating is seen by some as being contagious among students, in addition to serving as a social adhesive in environments where it is widely practiced and tolerated. One student said that he did not want to help his friends cheat, but once he started it was hard to stop.[8]

There is no question that technology has made cheating easier and perhaps more frequent. Research by Professor Donald McCabe found that more than 60 percent of the students he surveyed who had cheated considered digital plagiarism to be trivial. In essence, the students did not see it as cheating at all.[9]

There are many other reasons students cheat on exams and assignments. Some blame their cheating on unfair professors or tests. Some feel an obligation to help friends: a fraternity brother, a sorority sister, a hallmate. Some students cheat because they see themselves as being in competition with other students for grades. Some cheat because they think they can get away with it. Some students may cheat when they feel anonymous in class, such as in large lecture sections. Some students may cheat because they cannot manage their study time and they do not adequately prepare for assignments.[10]

Some students may cheat because they witness their parents doing it, for example, in the college admissions process. The college admissions scandal, dubbed Operation Varsity Blues, chronicles how wealthy parents paid Rick Singer to help get their children into respected colleges. In one case, a CEO paid Singer $850,000 to create fake résumés to make his kids appear to be athletes and to pay bribes to get them into prestigious universities.[11] The possible reasons for cheating are endless.

All of this is important because college students are the future leaders in business, government, education, and other institutions of "tomorrow." According to research, students who engage in unethical acts in college are more likely to engage in dishonest acts in the workplace.[12] But, it is interesting to note that some research also has found that a higher percentage of nonbusiness majors report cheating on tests and home work than business majors.[13] This is interesting but of little consolation since employers hire a variety of college graduates, not just business majors. Regardless, it has been recommended that employers use preemployment screening that might include testing applicants' honesty, but that has been problematic. However, employers do need to take an active interest in curbing academic dishonesty by working with students, faculty, and administrators to encourage ethical student behavior.[14] These are thought-provoking questions and issues that are likely to be around for some time.

Questions for Discussion

1. Do college students understand what constitutes "cheating" in college? If so, why do so many engage in academic dishonesty? Is cheating seen as a norm and not really all that bad?
2. Is academic dishonesty as widespread as news articles seem to be reporting?
3. Is it worse for students at one of the military academies to cheat than those in a public or private college or university?
4. Why *do* students cheat? Why do students *not* cheat? What are the reasons and factors that come into play?
5. Do students "mature" when they graduate and start behaving more honestly in their work and lives?
6. What changes can be made in college and college courses that would diminish the temptation to cheat in classes?
7. How is it possible for those who engage in questionable practices in college to critique others in business or other organizations who do the same?

Endnotes

1. Tawnell D. Hobbs, "Cheating at School Is Easier Than Ever—and Its Rampant," *The Wall Street Journal*, May 12, 2021, https://www.wsj.com/articles/cheating-at-school-is-easier-than-everand-its-rampant-11620828004. Accessed June 22, 2021. Also see D. L. McCabe, L. K. Treviño, and K. D. Butterfield, "Cheating in academic institutions: A Decade of Research," *Ethics & Behavior*, *11*(3), 2001, 219–232.
2. Ibid.
3. Tawnell, D. Hobbs, "West Point Scandal Spurs End to Leniency," *The Wall Street Journal*, April 17–18, 2021, A1.

4. Madison Hawamy and Kevin Chan, "As Pandemic Continues Cheating Gains Speed," *Yale News*, April 28, 2021, https://yaledailynews.com /blog/2021/04/28/as-pandemic-continues-cheating -gains-speed/. Accessed June 25, 2021.
5. Ibid.
6. Andrew Simmons, "Why Students Cheat—and What to Do about It," *Edutopia*, April 27, 2018, https://www.edutopia.org/article/why-students -cheat-and-what-do-about-it. Accessed June 25, 2021.
7. Ibid.
8. Ibid.
9. Ibid.
10. Carnegie Mellon University, "Solving a Teaching Problem," https://www.cmu.edu/teaching /solveproblem/strat-cheating/index.html. Accessed June 25, 2021.
11. Joe Nocera, "He Pleaded Guilt in 'Varsity Blues', Then Fought the Sentence," *Bloomberg Businessweek*, March 29, 2021, p. 68.
12. S. Nonis and C. Swift, "An Examination of the Relationship Between Academic Dishonesty and Workplace Dishonesty: A Multicampus Investigation," *The Journal of Education for Business*, 2001, 76(6), pp. 69–77.
13. Sharron Graves, "Student Cheating Habits: A Predictor of Workplace Deviance," *Journal of Diversity Management* 3(1), 2008, pp. 15–22.
14. Ibid.

Case 11

Climate Change and Corporate Activism: Is It All Just Hot Air?*

Climate change is on everyone's mind, including most businesses. Beyond exercising market power, businesses today have access to digital and financial platforms that allow them to exercise significant power and influence to weigh in on social issues like climate change. As one writer framed it, the climate crisis "is pushing companies toward social and political activism."[1]

The evidence of corporate climate change activism is everywhere. Here are a few examples:

- **The Paris Accord**. In December 2020, prior to President Biden's decision to rejoin the Paris Accord, 42 major companies, including Amazon, JPMorgan Chase, and General Motors, joined forces with the Center for Climate and Energy Solutions (C2ES) to express support for bipartisan climate policies and to push for rejoining the accord.[2] The push worked. On January 20, 2021, President Joe Biden signed an executive order to have the United States reenter the Paris Climate Agreement.

- **Shareholder Resolutions Filed in Support of Climate Change Policies**. In the first quarter of 2021, shareholders in the United States had filed 79 climate-related resolutions, compared with 72 for all of 2020 and 67 in 2019. Resolutions included calls for companies like Exxon to provide emissions limits, pollution reports, and climate audits.[3]

- **BlackRock**. Shareholder resolutions are increasingly backed by large investors like BlackRock, the world's largest investor with $8.7 trillion under management.

For example, BlackRock backed a shareholder resolution at Procter & Gamble's annual general meeting, which asked the company to report on efforts to eliminate deforestation. In 2020, BlackRock backed 6 percent of shareholder environmental proposals, 7 percent of social proposals, and 17 percent of governance proposals.[4]

- **More BlackRock**. Each year BlackRock CEO Larry Fink writes a letter to CEOs. In 2021, he brought the issue of climate change front and center with a bold statement linking climate change to the COVID-19 pandemic: "*I believe that the pandemic has presented such an existential crisis—such a stark reminder of our fragility—that it has driven us to confront the global threat of climate change more forcefully and to consider how, like the pandemic, it will alter our lives.*"[5]

He further noted: "*In the past year, people have seen the mounting physical toll of climate change in fires, droughts, flooding and hurricanes. They have begun to see the direct financial impact as energy companies take billions in climate-related write-downs on stranded assets and regulators focus on climate risk in the global financial system. They are also increasingly focused on the significant economic opportunity that the transition will create, as well as how to execute it in a just and fair manner. No issue ranks higher than climate change on our clients' lists of priorities. They ask us about it nearly every day.*"

Despite such bold statements by the giant investment firm, some critics say that corporate activism on climate change

---

*This case was written by Jill A. Brown, Bentley University, in 2021.

is filled with big promises (also known as "hot air") that are not backed by enough action. For example, BlackRock has been criticized for omitting crucial details behind its pledge, including what proportion of the companies BlackRock invests in will be zero-emission businesses by 2050.[6] Numerous other businesses that endorse and espouse climate change have also struggled to cut emissions, including Costco, Netflix, Cargill, and Levi Strauss. And "power-hungry data centers" that are used by tech companies like Google and Microsoft continue to challenge their abilities to achieve their "moonshot" objectives.[7]

One climate change expert noted that while sustainability reports for many companies look great, "there is not a lot of substance behind the commitments."[8] Some attribute the lack of substance to the limitations of sustainability reporting, which focuses companies on measurement and reporting, rather than implementing important structural transformations. Researcher Kenneth Pucker calls this "overselling sustainability reporting," with the result that companies confuse output with impact.[9] According to Pucker, "The real danger is when politicians and CEOS are making it look like real action is happening when in fact almost nothing is being done."[10]

The environmental activist group Greenpeace recently called out Amazon and the other big cloud companies on their use of renewable energy credits (RECs) related to solar and wind projects to offset their use of fossil fuels—making them look better on paper than they are in practice. They noted that Amazon's "whopping 44.4 million tons of CO2e carbon footprint" provides a huge challenge to reducing their carbon footprint, and that Amazon "remains the least transparent among the big three cloud companies, failing to provide even basic information about its energy demand."[11] When then-CEO Jeff Bezos said he would spend $10 billion to launch a new entity called the Bezos Earth Fund, climate activists accused Bezos of hypocrisy, since his businesses still support oil and gas firms.[12]

Whether or not you believe that corporate activism on climate change is sincere or just "hot air," the topic is obviously important to shareholders, and therefore many CEOs see it as an agenda item that they must pursue. A recent study noted that shareholder activism, measured by the number of environment-related shareholder proposals submitted to a company, does induce firms to voluntarily disclose climate change risks.[13] And the stock market responds favorably to such disclosures. Hence, CEOs of publicly traded companies and large-scale investors like BlackRock will likely continue to show support for climate change initiatives, and shareholders will continue to demand more transparency… and action.

Questions for Discussion

1. What are the benefits related to corporate political activism and climate change? What are the costs?

2. Beyond climate change issues, what other social issues do you see corporations targeting for activism?

3. How does corporate activism compare to activism by individuals and/or nonprofit, nongovernmental agencies?

4. What can businesses do to avoid being criticized for being hypocritical or not taking action regarding climate change?

5. Are there some businesses and industries that are not seen as sincere regarding climate change because of what they do?

Endnotes

1. Amelia Ahl, "The Climate Crisis Is Pushing Companies toward Social and Political Activism," *TriplePundit* (October 2, 2020), https://www.triplepundit.com/story/2020/climate-crisis-companies-activism/706231. Accessed July 9, 2021.

2. Edward Segal, "In Latest Example of Corporate Activism, Companies Are Working with Environmentalists to Fight Climate Change," *Forbes* (December 2, 2020), https://www.forbes.com/sites/edwardsegal/2020/12/02/in-latest-example-of-corporate-activism-companies-are-working-with-environmentalists-to-fight-climate-change/?sh=1b5b55575924. Accessed July9, 2021.

3. Simon Jessop, Matthew Green, and Ross Kerber, "Show Us the Plan: Investors Push Companies to Come Clean on Climate," *TriplePundit* (February 24, 2021), https://www.reuters.com/article/us-climate-change-agm-insight-idUKKBN2AO0IR. Accessed July 9, 2021.

4. Dawn Lim, "BlackRock Starts to Use Voting Power More Aggressively," *The Wall Street Journal* (April 30, 2021), https://www.wsj.com/articles/blackrock-takes-aggressive-posture-on-esg-proxy-votes-11619775002. Accessed July 9, 2021.

5. BlackRock, "Larry Fink's 2021 Letter to CEOs" (January 2021), https://www.blackrock.com/corporate/investor-relations/larry-fink-ceo-letter. Accessed July 9, 2021.

6. Peter Eavis and Clifford Krauss, "What's Really Behind Corporate Promises on Climate Change?," *The New York Times* (February 22, 2021), https://www.nytimes.com/2021/02/22/business/energy-environment/corporations-climate-change.html. Accessed July 9, 2021

7. Ibid.

8. Ibid.

9. Kenneth Pucker, "Overselling Sustainability Reporting," *Harvard Business Review* (May–June 2021), https://hbr.org/2021/05/overselling-sustainability-reporting. Accessed July 9, 2021.

10. Ibid.

11. Elizabeth Jardim, "Microsoft, Google, Amazon —Who's the Biggest Climate Hypocrite?," Greenpeace (January 27, 2020), https://www.greenpeace.org/usa/microsoft-google-amazon-energy-oil-ai-climate-hypocrite/. Accessed July 9, 2021.

12. Charlie Wood, "Climate Activists Accuse Bezos of Hypocrisy Over His $10 Billion Environmental Pledge Because Amazon Works with Oil and Gas Firms," *BusinessInsider* (February 18, 2020), https://www.businessinsider.com/greenpeace-amazon-activists-accuse-jeff-bezos-hypocrisy-climate-pledge-2020-2. Accessed July 9, 2021.

13. Caroline Flammer, Michael Toffel, and Kala Viswanathan, "Shareholders Are Pressing for Climate Risk Disclosures. That's Good for Everyone," *Harvard Business Review* (April 22, 2021), https://hbr.org/2021/04/shareholders-are-pressing-for-climate-risk-disclosures-thats-good-for-everyone. Accessed July 10, 2021.

Case 12

Family Business*

Jane had just been hired as the head of the payroll department at R&S Electronic Service Company, a firm comprising 75 employees. She had been hired by Eddie, the general manager, who had informed her of the need for maintaining strict confidentiality regarding employee salaries and pay scales. He also told her that he had fired the previous payroll department head for breaking that confidentiality by discussing employee salaries. She had also been formally introduced to Brad, the owner, who had told her to see him if she had any questions or problems. Both Brad and Eddie had made her feel welcome.

Greg's High Commissions

After three months of employment, Jane began to wonder why Greg, a service technician and Eddie's brother, made so much more in commissions than the other service technicians. She assumed that he must be highly qualified and must work rapidly because she had overheard Brad commending Greg on his performance on several occasions. She had also noticed Brad, Eddie, and Greg having lunch together frequently.

One day, Eddie gave Jane the stack of work tickets for the service technicians for the upcoming week. The

technicians were to take whatever ticket was on top when they finished the job they were working on. After putting the tickets where they belonged, Jane remembered that she had a doctor's appointment the next morning and returned to Eddie's office to tell him she would be reporting late for work.

Eddie Shows Favoritism

When she entered Eddie's office, she saw Eddie give Greg a separate stack of work tickets. As she stood there, Eddie told her that if she mentioned this to anyone, he would fire her. Jane was upset because she understood that Eddie was giving the easier, high commission work to his brother. Jane also realized that Eddie had the authority to hire and fire her. Because she had been at the company for only a short time, she was still a probationary employee. This was her first job since college. She wondered what she should do.

Questions for Discussion

1. What are the ethical issues in this case?
2. Is a family business different from other types of businesses with respect to employee treatment?
3. What was Jane's ethical dilemma?
4. What should Jane have done? Why? How would you have handled this situation if you were Jane? What ethical principles or concepts apply?

*This case was written by Marilyn M. Helms, University of Tennessee at Chattanooga. Permission to reprint granted by Arthur Andersen & Co., SC.

Case 13

What Makes a Good CEO? The Waiter Rule, Humility, and Amazon*

As the topic of corporate governance has been in the news more and more during the past several decades, it is useful

*This case was originally prepared by Archie B. Carroll, University of Georgia, and was revised and updated by Jill A. Brown, Bentley University, in 2021.

to reflect on what boards of directors have to do in terms of their roles and responsibilities. Acting on behalf of shareholders, one of the board's most important jobs is selection of the CEO, who will provide strategic direction for the firm and, in turn, hire the top management team. But how does a board go about hiring a CEO? Certainly, this has got to be one of the toughest jobs of selection in the business world.

In recent years, so many contentious issues have surrounded CEOs that the board's task is no small one. Many CEOs have been implicated in ethics scandals, and many of them have been criticized for what the public considers to be excessive compensation. Today especially, boards want to be sure they hire CEOs with high integrity and impeccable character. It is a lofty goal and things do not always turn out the way boards wish. With a record number of CEO firings in the past several years, it is little wonder boards of directors are always seeking insights as to how to make these selection decisions.

Business managers are always on the alert for guidance, for suggestions, for tips that would make their hiring more successful or run more smoothly. But if an elusive quality such as character is so important, how does one gauge a prospective CEO's or top executive's character? Or, for that matter, how can we gauge the character of anyone at any level of management?

Swanson's Unwritten Rules

In an important *USA Today* article, it was revealed that Bill Swanson, CEO of Raytheon, the defense contractor based in Waltham, Massachusetts, that has 80,000 employees and more than $22 billion in annual sales, had published a booklet containing 33 brief leadership observations.[1] The booklet was titled *Swanson's Unwritten Rules of Management*. The book is filled with commonsense maxims, observations, rules, and guidelines. Among the 33 guidelines or rules compiled in the booklet is one rule that Swanson has said never fails in terms of helping to assess someone's character: The "Waiter Rule."

The Waiter Rule

Known as the "Waiter Rule," the observation says that "A person, who is nice to you but rude to the wait staff, or to others, is not a nice person."[2] A number of CEOs and other corporate executives have all agreed with the Waiter Rule. They basically concur that how a privileged corporate executive treats people in subordinate roles, whether they be waiters, clerks, maintenance workers, golf caddies, or any other service-type worker, reveals insights into the executive's character that should be taken into consideration in hiring decisions.

Former Office Depot/OfficeMax CEO Steve Odland recalls that when he was working in a restaurant in Denver many years ago, he spilled a glass of purple sorbet all over the expensive white gown of an apparently important and rich person. Though it occurred more than 30 years ago, he cannot get the spill out of his mind. But what struck him most was their reaction to his careless spill. The person responded in a very kind and understanding way. They kept their composure and in a calm voice said, "It's okay. It wasn't your fault." Years later, Odland recalled what he learned about this incident: "You can tell a lot about a person by the way they treat the waiter."[3]

Character Revealed

As it turns out, just about every CEO has a waiter story to tell. The opinion they hold in common, moreover, is that the Waiter Rule is a valid way to gain insights into the character of a person, especially someone who may be in a position of authority over thousands of workers. Ron Shaich, the cofounder of Au Bon Pain, the leading urban bakery and sandwich café, eventually became CEO of Panera Bread. He tells the story of interviewing a person for general counsel who was kind to him but turned "amazingly rude" to the person cleaning tables. The person did not get the job.[4] They had failed the Waiter Rule.

The Waiter Rule seems to align with the idea that good leaders practice humility. In the bestselling book *Good to Great: Why Some Companies Make the Leap... And Others Don't*, author Jim Collins points out that the highest level of leadership invokes both willpower and humility.[5] Recent research also supports the importance of humility, such as learning from criticism and admitting mistakes, which can create an environment of inclusiveness in the workforce.[6]

However, it is difficult to assess others on their levels of humility, or integrity, or any other aspirational personal characteristic, for that matter. One leadership expert suggests rating potential candidates on a ten-point scale for four factors: Integrity (including humility), Judgment, Drive, and Emotional Intelligence.[7] They suggest rating the candidates based on observations that include whether the person "sweats the small stuff" and does not take credit for the accomplishments of others (Integrity); seems to be an aggressive, self-directed learner (Judgment); initiates and brings things to closure (Drive); and leads more with questions than answers, really listens, and connects with people (Emotional Intelligence). Of course, the reliability of these types of rating systems is always at question, as one person's assessment of whether someone is a listener, for example, can differ from another person's assessment of that same person.

Amazon's Successor: Andy Jassy

When Jeff Bezos stepped down as CEO from Amazon, he was arguably the most successful CEO in corporate history. Having founded the company more than 27 years ago as an online book retailer, Bezos grew the company to its current spot as the leading e-retailer in the United States, with more than $380 billion in 2020 net sales, and around 1.3 million employees across the world.[8] Did Bezos practice the Waiter Rule at Amazon? It is difficult to say. According to one professional networking platform, Bezos scores very low on a personality assessment for humility.[9] However, his successor, CEO Andy Jassy, is described by former Amazon employees as "more even-keeled with employees than Mr. Bezos" as well as "soft-spoken and approachable."[10] He is known for his frugality and, while seen to be demanding, he is known for his most common response to emails: "Nice!"[11]

Bezos has often spoken of humility, however. According to Bezos, the key to success as a manager is "intellectual humility," the ability to embrace a number of ideas and opinions and "accept the possibility that you're wrong."[12] He has noted that "the smartest people are constantly revising their understanding, reconsidering a problem they thought they'd already solved. They're open to new points of view, new information, new ideas, contradictions, and challenges to their own way of thinking."[13] Bezos has also commended his employees on their humility. In an email to his employees where he announced his transition from CEO to executive chair, he said, "When times have been good, you've been humble. When times have been tough, you've been strong and supportive, and we've made each other laugh."[14] As Amazon transitions to its new leadership, it will be interesting to see how humility plays out in the executive ranks of Amazon over the next decade or so.

The CEO Bubble

In a recent interview, former Boston Consulting Group CEO Rich Lesser, also known as "The CEO Whisperer," reflected on his career advising CEOs.[15] He pointed to several challenges in finding good CEOs. First, he notes that CEOs need to have a "learning mindset" that requires them to listen not just to people they are comfortable with but also to those they are not comfortable with. He calls it the "CEO bubble," when CEOs fall into a bubble where they listen to the same people over and over, and then people begin screening what they say to the CEO. Second, Lesser notes that it is not easy to be a CEO these days, particularly in a multi-stakeholder world where society, the climate, customers, employees, and others are all high priorities. In the end, Lesser says, learning broadly and quickly with a team mindset, and recognizing the importance of technology are key factors to be a successful CEO these days. However, he also notes that the CEO job is becoming increasingly political, which requires CEOs to figure out when to speak up and when to be political. He advises CEOs to focus on those issues that are aligned with a company's purpose and values.

Questions for Discussion

1. Is humility an essential ingredient in ethical leadership? Why is it especially important in managers? In leadership, especially among CEOs, is character important? Why?
2. Do you agree with the Waiter Rule? Does it provide useful insights into who might be an ethical or unethical leader?
3. Should corporate boards consider character when hiring someone for the top position? What are some of the challenges to hiring for character?
4. Some might say that hiring for character at the CEO level means foregoing hiring an outsider, and instead, promoting someone from within the organization who is familiar to the rest of the employees (e.g., an insider). Do you agree? Reflecting back on Chapter 9 corporate governance

concepts, what are the pros and cons of hiring a CEO from within, as done by Amazon?
5. Is using the Waiter Rule too simplistic a guideline for hiring people in important positions such as CEO? Is it too simplistic a guideline for judging one's ethics?
6. Have you found yourself in situations where you have been in a "bubble" —listening to the same people and not keeping yourself open to different perspectives?

Endnotes

1. Del Jones, "CEOS Vouch for Waiter Rule: Watch How People Treat Staff," *USA Today* (April 14, 2006), B1.
2. William H. Swanson, *Swanson's Unwritten Rules of Management* (Raytheon, 2005).
3. Jones, Ibid.
4. Ibid.
5. Jim Collins, *Good to Great: Why Some Companies Make the Leap…And Others Don't* (Harper Collins, 2001).
6. See Jeanine Prime and Elizabeth Salib, "The Best Leaders Are Humble Leaders," *Harvard Business Review*, https://hbr.org/2014/05/the-best-leaders-are-humble-leaders. Accessed July 6, 2021; C. Caldwell, R. Ichiho, and V. Anderson, "Understanding Level 5 Leaders: The Ethical Perspectives of Leadership Humility," *Journal of Management Development* (May 12, 2014), https://hbr.org/2014/05/the-best-leaders-are-humble-leaders, Accessed July 6, 2021.
7. Timothy Clark, "How to Choose the Right Executive," *Forbes* (September 18, 2020), https://www.forbes.com/sites/timothyclark/2020/09/18/how-to-choose-the-right-executive/?sh=35ae133b71b6. Accessed July 6, 2021.
8. See Jeff Bezos, "Email from Jeff Bezos to Employees" (February 2, 2021), *Amazon.com*, https://www.statista.com/topics/846/amazon/. Accessed July 6, 2021; Daniela Coppola, "Amazon Statistics & Facts," *Statista* (July 5, 2021), https://www.statista.com/topics/846/amazon/. Accessed July 6, 2021.
9. Chris Hodges, "The Top Personality Traits of the World's Richest Man, Jeff Bezos," GoGig (March 8, 2018), https://www.gogig.com/blog/top-personality-traits-of-the-worlds-richest-man-jeff-bezos. Accessed July 6, 2021.
10. Aaron Tilley, Dana Mattioli, and Kirsten Grind, "The Man Who Is Primed to Take the Wheel," *The Wall Street Journal* (July 3–4, 2021), B1.
11. Ibid.
12. John McMahon, "Jeff Bezos Says This Is the Number 1 Sign of High Intelligence," *Boss Hunting* (September 27, 2018), https://www.bosshunting.com.au/hustle/careers/jeff-bezos-high-intelligence/. Accessed July 6, 2021.
13. Quoted in McMahon (2018).
14. Bezos (2021).
15. Rich Lesser, "The CEO Whisperer," *The Wall Street Journal* (June 26–27, 2021), B8.

Case 14

Nike, Sweatshops, and Other Issues*

Nike, Inc. is no stranger to sweatshop allegations. Since the mid-1990s, the company has been imperiled by negative press, lawsuits, and demonstrations on college campuses alleging that the firm's overseas contractor's subject employees to work in inhumane conditions for low wages. As Philip Knight, the cofounder of Nike, once lamented, "The Nike product has become synonymous with slave wages, forced overtime, and arbitrary abuse."[1]

Philip Knight started his own athletic shoe distribution company in 1964. Using his Plymouth Reliant as a warehouse, he began importing and distributing track shoes from Onitsuka Company, Ltd., a Japanese manufacturer. First-year sales of $8,000 resulted in a profit of $254. After eight years, annual sales reached $2 million, and the firm employed 45 people. However, Onitsuka saw the huge potential of the American shoe market and dropped Knight's relatively small company in favor of larger, more experienced distributors. Knight was forced to start anew. Instead of importing and distributing another firm's track shoes, he decided to design his own shoes and create his own company. The name he chose for his new company was "Nike."[2]

Nike's Use of Contract Labor

When the company began operations, Knight contracted the manufacture of Nike's shoes to two firms in Japan. Shortly thereafter, Nike began to contract with firms in Taiwan and Korea. In 1977, Nike purchased two shoe-manufacturing facilities in the United States—one in Maine, the other in New Hampshire. Eventually, the two U.S. plants became so unprofitable that the firm was forced to close them. The loss due to the write-off of the plants was approximately $10 million in a year in which the firm's total profit was $15 million. Despite such a setback, the firm had a successful IPO in 1980, eight years after the company was founded. Nike became the largest athletic shoe company in the world.[3]

Nike does not own a single shoe or apparel factory. Instead, the firm contracts the production of its products to independently owned manufacturers. Today, practically all Nike subcontracted factories are in countries such as Indonesia, Vietnam, China, and Thailand, where the labor costs are significantly less than those in the United States. Worldwide, more than 530,000 people are employed in factories that manufacture Nike products. In an earlier calculation of labor costs for a pair of shoes, the labor costs amounted to less than 4 percent of the consumer's price for the shoes.[4]

Even in today's hi-tech environment, the production of athletic shoes is still a labor-intensive process. Although most leaders in the industry are confident that the entire production process will someday be automated, it may still be years before the industry will not have to rely on inexpensive human labor. After some bad press in the early 1990s, Nike sought to improve the working conditions of its plants by establishing a code of conduct for its suppliers.[5] This was not seen as impactful enough by outside critics, however. Nike's use of overseas contractors is not unique in the athletic shoe and apparel industry. All other major athletic shoe manufacturers also contract with overseas manufacturers, albeit to various degrees.

Nike spends heavily on endorsements and advertising and pays several top athletes millions of dollars a year in endorsement contracts. Michael Jordan, the now iconic basketball star, changed things forever for Nike. Jordan met with Nike when he entered the NBA and signed with the company. It may be the most successful marketing partnership in history.[6] To this day, Nike and Jordan have a lucrative partnership. It has been reported that Jordan has earned over $1.3 billion from Nike.[7] Nike later signed other great athletes such as Derek Jeter of the New York Yankees and legendary golfer Tiger Woods.[8]

The Anti-Sweatshop Movement

There is one pivotal event largely responsible for introducing the term "sweatshop" to the American public. In 1996, Kathie Lee Gifford, cohost of the formerly syndicated talk show "Live with Regis and Kathie Lee," endorsed her own line of clothing for Walmart. During that same year, labor rights activists disclosed that her "Kathie Lee Collection" was made in Honduras by seamstresses who earned 31 cents an hour and were sometimes required to work 20-hour days. Traditionally known for her pleasant, jovial demeanor and her love for children, Kathie Lee was outraged. She tearfully informed the public that she was unaware that her clothes were being made in so-called sweatshops and vowed to do whatever she could to promote the anti-sweatshop cause.[9]

Nike Is Accused

In a national press conference, Gifford named Michael Jordan as another celebrity who, like herself, endorsed products without knowing under what conditions the products were made. At the time, Michael Jordan was Nike's premier endorser and was reportedly under a $20 million per year contract with the firm.[10] Nike, the number-one athletic shoe brand in the world, soon found itself under attack by the rapidly growing anti-sweatshop movement.

---

*This case was written initially by Bryan S. Dennis, Idaho State University. Revised and updated by Archie B. Carroll, University of Georgia, in 2021.

Shortly after the Gifford story broke, Joel Joseph, chairperson of the Made in the USA Foundation,[11] accused Nike of paying underage Indonesian workers 14 cents an hour to make the company's line of Air Jordan shoes. He also claimed that the total payroll of Nike's six Indonesian subcontracted factories was less than the reported $20 million per year that Jordan was receiving from his endorsement contract with Nike. The Made in the USA Foundation is one of the organizations that ignited the Gifford controversy and is largely financed by labor unions and U.S. apparel manufacturers that are against free trade with low-wage countries.[12]

Nike quickly pointed out that Air Jordan shoes were made in Taiwan, not Indonesia. Additionally, the company maintained that employee wages were fair and higher than the government-mandated minimum wage in all of the countries where the firm has contracted factories. Nike avowed that the entry-level income of an Indonesian factory worker was five times that of a farmer. The firm also claimed that an assistant line supervisor in a Chinese subcontracted factory earned more than a surgeon with 20 years of experience.[13] In response to the allegations regarding Michael Jordan's endorsement contract, Nike stated that the total wages in Indonesia were $50 million a year, which is well over what the firm pays Jordan.[14]

Nike soon faced more negative publicity. Michael Moore, the movie director whose documentary *Roger and Me* shed light on the plight of laid-off autoworkers in Flint, Michigan, and damaged the reputation of General Motors chairperson Roger Smith, interviewed Nike CEO Philip Knight for his movie *The Big One*. On camera, Knight referred to some employees at subcontracted factories as "poor little Indonesian workers."[15] Knight, the only CEO interviewed in the movie, received harsh criticism for his comments. Nike alleged that the comments were taken out of context and were deceitful because Moore failed to include Knight's pledge to make a transition from a 14- to a 16-year-old minimum age labor force. Nike prepared its own video that included the entire interview.[16]

Thomas Nguyen, founder of Vietnam Labor Watch, inspected several of Nike's plants in Vietnam in 1998 and reported cases of worker abuse. At one factory that manufactured Nike products, a supervisor punished 56 women for wearing inappropriate work shoes by forcing them to run around the factory in the hot sun. Twelve workers fainted and were taken to the hospital. Nguyen also reported that workers were allowed only one bathroom break and two drinks of water during each eight-hour shift. Nike responded that the supervisor who was involved in the fainting incident had been suspended and that the firm had hired an independent accounting firm to look into the matters further.[17]

Nike Responds

In 1997, Nike hired former Atlanta mayor Andrew Young, a vocal opponent of sweatshops and child labor, to review the firm's overseas labor practices. Neither party disclosed the fee that Young received for his services. Young toured 12 factories in Vietnam, Indonesia, and China and was reportedly given unlimited access. However, he was constantly accompanied by Nike representatives during all factory tours. Furthermore, Young relied on Nike translators when communicating with factory workers.[18]

In his 75-page report, Young concluded, "Nike is doing a good job, but it can do better." He provided Nike with six recommendations for improving the working conditions at subcontracted factories. Nike immediately responded to the report and agreed to implement all six recommendations. Young did not address the issue of wages and standards of living because he felt he lacked the "academic credentials" for such a judgment.[19]

In 1998, Nike hired Maria Eitel to the newly created position of vice president for corporate and social responsibility. Eitel was formerly a public relations executive for Microsoft. Her responsibilities were to oversee Nike's labor practices, environmental affairs, and involvement in the global community. Although this move was applauded by some, others were skeptical and claimed that Nike's move was nothing more than a publicity stunt.[20]

Later that same year, Philip Knight gave a speech at the National Press Club in Washington, D.C., and announced six initiatives that were intended to improve the working conditions in its overseas factories. The firm chose to raise the minimum hiring age from 16 to 18 years. Nike also decided to expand its worker education program so that all workers in Nike factories would have the option to take middle and high school equivalency tests.[21] The director of Global Exchange, one of Nike's staunchest opponents, called the initiatives "significant and very positive." He also added, "we feel that the measures—if implemented could be exciting."[22]

The Fair Labor Association

In 1996, a presidential task force of industry and human rights representatives was given the job of addressing the sweatshop issue. The key purpose of this task force was to develop a workplace code of conduct and a system for monitoring factories to ensure compliance. In 1998, the task force created the Fair Labor Association (FLA) to accomplish these goals. This organization was made up of consumer and human rights groups as well as footwear and apparel manufacturers. Nike was one of the first companies to join the FLA. Many other major manufacturers (Levi Strauss & Co., Liz Claiborne, Patagonia, Polo Ralph Lauren, Reebok, Eddie Bauer, and Phillips-Van Heusen) along with hundreds of colleges and universities also joined the FLA.[23]

Members of the FLA must follow the principles set forth in the organization's Workplace Code of Conduct. The Code of Conduct is based on international labor and human rights standards—primarily Conventions of the International Labor Organization (ILO)—and prohibits discrimination, the use of child or forced labor, and harassment or abuse. It also establishes requirements related to health and safety; freedom of association and collective bargaining; wages and benefits; hours of work; and overtime compensation.[24]

The Worker Rights Consortium

The Worker Rights Consortium (WRC) was organized as an alternative to the FLA. The WRC asserts that the prevailing industry or legal minimum wage in some countries is too low and does not provide employees with the basic human needs they require. They proposed that factories should instead pay a higher "living wage" that takes into account the wage required to provide factory employees with enough income to afford housing, energy, nutrition, clothing, health care, education, potable water, child care, transportation, and savings. Additionally, the WRC supports public disclosure of all factory locations and the right to monitor any factory at any time. As of 2021, 153 colleges and universities had joined the WRC and agreed to adhere to its policies.[25]

Nike, a member and supporter of the FLA, did not support the WRC. The firm stated at the time that the concept of a living wage is impractical as "there is no common, agreed-upon definition of the living wage. Definitions range from complex mathematical formulas to vague philosophical notions." Additionally, Nike was once opposed to the WRC's proposal that the location of all factories be publicly disclosed. Nike also has claimed that the monitoring provisions set out by the WRC are unrealistic and biased toward organized labor.[26]

The University of Oregon, Philip Knight's alma mater, joined the WRC in the year 2000. Alumnus Knight had previously contributed more than $50 million to the university—$30 million for academics and $20 million for athletics. Upon hearing that his alma mater had joined the WRC, Knight was shocked. He withdrew a proposed $30 million donation and stated that "the bonds of trust, which allowed me to give at a high level, have been shredded" and "there will be no further donations of any kind to the University of Oregon."[27,28]

Nike Comes Around

In 2001, Harsh Saini, Nike's corporate and social responsibility manager, acknowledged that the firm may not have handled the sweatshop issue as well as it could have and stated that Nike had not been adequately monitoring its subcontractors in overseas operations until the media and other organizations revealed the presence of sweatshops.

> We were a bunch of shoe geeks who expanded so much without thinking of being socially responsible that we went from being a very big sexy brand name to suddenly becoming the poster boy for everything bad in manufacturing.[29]

She added, "We realized that if we still wanted to be the brand of choice in 20 years, we had certain responsibilities to fulfill."[30]

In early 2001, Oregon's state board of higher education cast doubt on the legality of the University of Oregon's WRC membership, and the university dissolved its ties with the labor organization.[31] In September of the same year, Philip Knight renewed his financial support. Although the exact amount of Knight's donation was kept confidential, it was sufficient to ensure that the $85 million expansion of the university's football stadium would go through as originally planned.

Nike released its first corporate social responsibility report in October 2001. According to Knight, "[I]n this report, Nike for the first time has assembled a comprehensive public review of our corporate responsibility practices." [32] The report cited several areas in which the firm could have done better, such as worker conditions in Indonesia and Mexico. The report, compiled by both internal auditors and outside monitors, also noted that Nike was one of only four companies that had joined a World Wildlife Fund program to reduce greenhouse admissions. Jason Mark, a spokesperson for Global Exchange, one of Nike's chief critics, praised the report and stated that Nike is "obviously responding to consumer concerns."[33]

Critics Quiet Down But Don't Go Away

Nike's critics never go away, but they did quiet down as the company took steps to address many of the criticisms made over the years. One organization that remains semi-active in taking Nike to task is "Team Sweat." Team Sweat identifies itself as an "international coalition of consumers, investors, and workers committed to ending the injustices in Nike's sweatshops around the world." It goes on to say, "Team Sweat is striving to ensure that all workers who produce Nike products are paid a living wage."[34] One other organization that conducts an ongoing campaign against Nike's and other companies' sweatshops is Oxfam Australia. Among other charges, Oxfam complained about Nike paying Tiger Woods $25 million a year while the workers who make its products receive poverty wages and endure harsh working conditions.[35] In addition to Nike, Oxfam pursues its initiatives against Puma, adidas, and Fila and the companies that sell their products.[36]

Nike Turns It Around But Sweatshops Don't Go Away

By 2005, Nike was the first company in its industry to adopt a policy of transparency and to publish a complete list of its contract companies.[37] Once the company publicly proclaimed it would change, it seemed to take this mandate seriously and eventually became a company that would be regarded as one of the leaders in CSR.[38] Since that time, the company has continued to post its commitments, standards, and audit data as part of its CSR reports.[39] Its 2020 report was called its Impact Report and in it the company discusses how it has set and met standards in meeting stakeholder's expectations.[40] By 2021, Nike was ranked #18 in 3BLMedia's "100 Best Corporate Citizens of 2021." [41]

In spite of turnarounds such as that witnessed at Nike, sweatshops have not gone away, and protest groups continue to monitor what Nike and other companies are doing and raise issues about their questionable practices. Since the tragic Rana Plaza factories collapse in Bangladesh in 2013 (see Case 15) that resulted in more than 1,100 deaths, the world's awareness of what has been going on in the shoe and apparel industries has been significantly energized.[42]

In 2021, questions began being raised about Nike's relationship with China.[43] The United States and China are two of Nike's most important markets, and Greater China is the company's fastest growing market. However, sales in Greater China came in below expectations soon after a social media backlash occurred there. Nike, H&M, and Adidas were among the Western brands that were caught up in an online boycott in China after some nationalist users on social media noticed that the brands had released statements expressing concern about reports of forced labor in China's Xinjiang region.[44] A survey of Chinese consumers by Citgroup found that about 34 percent of the respondents said the Xinjiang controversy made them "significantly less likely" to buy foreign brands.[45] Though Nike and Adidas remain in the No. 1 and 2 positions in China's sportswear market, the trend among the younger Chinese consumers is domestic brands. Questions are now being raised: Could the love affair between Nike and China be in trouble? Will the backlash in China have long-term consequences for Nike?[46]

Other Issues

If dealing with sweatshop issues and the huge Chinese market were not enough, Nike has faced other controversial issues in recent years. In 2018, Nike entered highly charged political territory when it put NFL quarterback-turned-activist Colin Kaepernick at the center of its advertising campaign, risking backlash from many consumers.[47] Kaepernick drew considerable opposition when he began kneeling on the field during the playing of the national anthem as a sign of protest over racial injustice and social inequities.[48] After a period of turbulence, sales did not seem to be affected. The company has a history of making controversial ads and many young consumers support them.[49]

A year later, a business writer offered the perspective that when it comes to Kaepernick, the flag, and Nike, it's just business. He argued that Nike's core customer in the United States has different expectations of the sports apparel company and that they basically approved of Kaepernick's employment.[50] Later, Kaepernick, without being asked, expressed disapproval of Nike's plan to bring out a Betsy Ross flag sneaker for the Fourth of July because he was concerned with the flag's association with an era of slavery. Nike promptly stopped the product, but there were extensive repercussions. For example, a proposed Nike factory got caught in the Betsy Ross flag shoe fight. The mayor of Goodyear, Arizona, said officials wanted Nike to open a factory in their city, but the governor of the state pulled his support in protest of Nike's decision to not make and sell the Betsy Ross flag shoe. Nevertheless, the Goodyear city council approved of Nike's locating there in spite of the controversy and objections. They saw it as an economic issue outweighing social concerns.[51]

Another controversial issue kicked off when Nike was accused of protecting managers accused of sexual harassment. The company began receiving reports and complaints about inappropriate workplace behavior and sexual harassment and two veteran executives were forced out by March 2018.[52] It had been alleged that inside Nike a "Boys-Club" culture was allowed to grow and exist. Former employees had said that such a culture had existed for years.[53] Former employees also said that due to no fear of reprisal, this created an environment where male employees could pursue and continue sexual relationships with subordinates and assistants. Nike said it tried to prevent this inappropriate behavior but the company did not prohibit it.[54]

Several female employees described experiences of encountering slights and offenses as they moved up the ladder. One woman said her senior-director boss had derogatory nicknames for female staffers and would favor men on the team with the better opportunities. Another former manager said that a male colleague had multiple complaints of bullying made against him to human resources but the only punishment he experienced was a delayed promotion. Out of frustration with Nike's handling of these incidents, several women left the company.[55] Later that year, two Nike women, ex-employees, filed a discrimination lawsuit against the company claiming it held back their pay and career advancement.[56] Amid pressure, Nike did decide to review and tweak their pay and bonus practices and at least 11 executives departed, including the man who was CEO heir apparent.[57]

Finally, some of Nike's deals with superstar endorsers have had unpleasant endings. In 2021, Nike discontinued its sponsorship agreement with Neymar, after the Brazilian soccer player refused to cooperate with an investigation that he had sexually assaulted a female employee of the company from years prior.[58] Neymar disputed Nike's reason for the ending of the soccer star's endorsement deal and denied the employee's allegation of sexual assault.[59]

In summary, over the years, Nike has had some difficult issues to deal with and to this day is still dealing with several of them. Questions about the use of inexpensive labor in developing nations will continue to plague shoe and apparel makers. The hiring of controversial athletes seems to be a major part of Nike's marketing strategy, and it is unlikely to abandon it. This promotional strategy will continue to be questioned by some. The company seems to be striving to eliminate its male-dominated culture and be fairer to women employees. In spite of the many challenges the company has faced, Nike has turned its reputation around and is viewed in a much more positive light now than before. Because it is a huge, high-profile, global company, however, it can expect to be in the critical limelight for virtually any action it takes.

Questions for Discussion

1. What are the ethical and social issues in this case?
2. Should Nike and other companies be held responsible for what happens in factories that they do not own? Does Nike have a responsibility to ensure that factory workers receive a "living wage"?
3. Is it socially responsible and fair for Nike to pay endorsers millions while its factory employees receive a few dollars a day?
4. Is Nike's responsibility to monitor its subcontracted factories a legal, economic, social, or philanthropic responsibility?
5. What was behind the turnaround at Nike? Is it "good business" for Nike to acknowledge its past errors and become more socially responsible?
6. What is your assessment of Nike using controversial athletes such as Colin Kaepernick?
7. In light of Nike's success, what do you make of its alleged "Boys Club" culture and discriminatory practices?
8. Nike seems to be a much more respected company today than it was back when the anti-sweatshop movement began. What has changed in Nike and the world to explain this?

Endnotes

1. Bien Hoa, "Job Opportunity or Exploitation," *Los Angeles Times* (April 18, 1999), https://www.latimes.com/archives/la-xpm-1999-apr-18-fi-28567-story.html. Accessed July 3, 2021.
2. Philip Knight, "Global Manufacturing: The Nike Story Is Just Good Business," *Vital Speeches of the Day* 64(20): 637–640.
3. Ibid.
4. These data were presented on an earlier Nike website that is no longer available. The site was http://nikeinc.com/.
5. "Working Conditions in Factories: When the Jobs Inspector Calls," *The Economist*, March 31, 2012, 73—74.
6. Madilyn Zeegers, "Nike Spends More Than Any Other Company to Endorse Athletes," Showbiz Cheatsheet, June 10, 2020, https://www.cheatsheet.com/entertainment/nike-spends-more-than-any-other-company-to-endorse-athletes.html/. Accessed July 3, 2021.
7. Ibid.
8. Ibid.
9. David Bauman, "After the Tears, Gifford Testifies on Sweatshops—She Turns Lights, Cameras on Issue," *Seattle Times* (July 16, 1996), A3.
10. Del Jones, "Critics Tie Sweatshop Sneakers to 'Air' Jordan," *USA Today* (June 6, 1996), 1B.
11. Made in USA Foundation, https://www.madeintheusa.org/. Accessed July 6, 2021.
12. Ibid.
13. Nike press release (June 6, 1996).
14. Del Jones, 1B.
15. Garry Trudeau, "Sneakers in Tinseltown," *Time*, April 20, 1998, 84, http://content.time.com/time/subscriber/article/0,33009,988194,00.html. Accessed July 3, 2021.
16. William J. Holstein, "Casting Nike as the Bad Guy," *U.S. News & World Report* (September 22, 1997), 49.
17. Verena Dobnik, "Nike Shoe Contractor Abuses Alleged," *The Atlanta Journal-Constitution* (March 18, 1997), A14.
18. Simon Beck, "Nike in Sweat over Heat Raised by Claims of Biases Assessment," *South China Morning Post* (July 6, 1997), 2.
19. Matthew C. Quinn, "Footwear Maker's Labor Pledge Unlikely to Stamp Out Criticism," *The Atlanta Journal-Constitution* (June 25, 1997), F8.
20. Bill Richards, "Nike Hires an Executive from Microsoft for New Post Focusing on Labor Policies," *The Wall Street Journal* (January 15, 1998), B14, https://www.wsj.com/articles/SB884842235627510500. Accessed July 6, 2021.
21. Knight, 640.
22. Patti Bond, "Nike Promises to Improve Factory Worker Conditions," *The Atlanta Journal-Constitution* (May 13, 1998), 3B.
23. Fair Labor Association, https://www.fairlabor.org/. Accessed July 6, 2021.
24. Fair Labor Association Workplace Code of Conduct, https://www.fairlabor.org/our-work/code-of-conduct. Accessed July 6, 2021.
25. Worker's Rights Consortium, "Mission," https://www.workersrights.org/about/. Accessed July 3, 2021.
26. Nike website, http://www.nikebiz.com/labor/index.shtml. Current website is:https://www.nike.com/. Accessed July 6, 2021.
27. Philip Knight Press Release (April 24, 2000). Found at http://www.nikebiz.com/media/n_uofo.shtml. (Website no longer active.)
28. Louise Lee and Aaron Bernstein, "Who Says Student Protests Don't Matter?" *BusinessWeek* (June 12, 2000), 96, https://www.bloomberg.com/news/articles/2000-06-11/commentary-who-says-student-protests-dont-matter. Accessed July 6, 2021.
29. Ravina Shamdasani, "Soul Searching by 'Shoe Geeks' Led to Social Responsibility," *South China Morning Post* (May 17, 2001), 2, https://www.scmp.com/article/347186/soul-searching-shoe-geeks-led-social-responsibility. Accessed July 6, 2021.
30. Ibid.
31. Greg Bolt, "University of Oregon Ends Relationship with Antisweatshop Group," *The Register Guard* (March 6, 2001).
32. William McCall, "Nike Releases First Corporate Responsibility Report," *Associated Press State & Local Wire* (October 9, 2001), https://www.csrwire.com/press_releases/24905-nike-releases-first-corporate-responsibility-report. Accessed July 6, 2021.
33. Ibid.

34. Team Sweat, https://www.facebook.com /BehindtheSwoosh/about/?ref=page_internal. Accessed July 3, 2021.

35. Oxfam Australia, "Nike," https://www.oxfam.org .au/what-we-do/economic-inequality/workers-rights /nike/. Accessed July 3, 2021.

36. Ibid.

37. Andrea Newell, "How Nike Embraced CSR and Went from Villain to Hero," *TriplePundit*, June 19, 2015, https://www.triplepundit.com/story/2015 /how-nike-embraced-csr-and-went-villain -hero/57726. Accessed July 6, 2021.

38. Ibid.

39. Max Nisen, "How Nike Solved Its Sweatshop Problem," *Business Insider*, May 9, 2013, https:// www.businessinsider.com/how-nike-solved-its -sweatshop-problem-2013-5. Accessed July 6, 2021.

40. Nike, "2020 Impact Report, Breaking Barriers," https://purpose-cms-preprod01.s3.amazonaws .com/wp-content/uploads/2021/04/26225049 /FY20_NIKE_Inc_Impact_Report2.pdf. Accessed July 3, 2021.

41. 3BLMedia, "100 Best Corporate Citizens of 2021," https://100best.3blmedia.com/. Accessed July 3, 2021.

42. Judy Gearhart, "Remembering Rena Plaza, Advancing Women Workers' Rights in Global Supply Chains," Huffpost Women, April 27, https:// laborrights.org/blog/201604/remembering-rana -plaza-advancing-women-workers%E2%80%99 -rights-global-supply-chains. Accessed July 6, 2021.

43. Jinjoo Lee, "Nike Doesn't Want to Step in It with China, *The Wall Street Journal*, June 26–27, 2021, B14.

44. Ibid.

45. Ibid.

46. Marc Bain, "Is Nike Too Cool to Suffer in China?" *Quartz*, March 29, 2021, https://qz.com/1990163

/will-nike-suffer-long-term-in-china-over-its -xinjiang-stance/. Accessed July 5, 2021.

47. Andrew Beaton and Khadeeja Safdar, "Nike's Plunge into NFL Battle Draws Quick Backlash," *The Wall Street Journal*, September 9, 2018, A1.

48. Ibid.

49. Khadeeja Safdar, "Nike Shows Boycotts Just Don't Do It," *The Wall Street Journal*, September 17, 2018, B1.

50. John Stoll, "When It Comes to Kaepernick, the Flag and Nike, It's Just Business," *The Wall Street Journal*, July 5, 2019, B1.

51. Charlie McGee, "Nike Factory Caught in Flag Fight," *The Wall Street Journal*, July 5, 2019, B2.

52. Sara Germano and Joann Lublin, "Complaints Lead to 2ndNike Exit," *The Wall Street Journal*, March 17–18, 2018, B3.

53. Sara Germano and Joann Lublin, "Inside Nike, a Boys-Club Culture," *The Wall Street Journal*, April 2, 2018, B1.

54. Matt Townsend and Esme Deprez, "Is the Corporate Bully the Next Workplace Pariah?" *Bloomberg Businessweek*, May 14, 2018, 22–23.

55. Ibid.

56. Stu Woo, "Nike Ex-Employees Sue, Alleging Discrimination," *The Wall Street Journal*, August 11–12, 2018, B3.

57. Sara Germano, "Nike Rethinks Pay, Bonus Practices," *The Wall Street Journal*, July 24, 2018.

58. CBSNews, "Nike Ends Deal with Neymar Over Sexual Assault Accusation by Company Employee," May 28, 2021, https://www.cbsnews.com/news /neymar-nike-footballer-soccer-sexual-assault -accusation/. Accessed July 5, 2021.

59. Joshua Robinson and Khadeeja Safdar, "Neymar Dispute's Nike's Account for Breakup," *The Wall Street Journal*, May 29–30, 2021, B3.

Case 15

The Rana Plaza Factory Collapse*

On April 24, 2013, an eight-story garment factory building collapsed in Rana Plaza on the outskirts of Dhaka, Bangladesh. The Rana Plaza building is located in Savar, near Dhaka. The collapse occurred just after work had begun that morning in several companies that were all housed in the building. Roughly 5,000 workers, mostly women, worked in the complex. By that evening, 1,000 people had been rescued, and it was reported the next day that at least 119 were killed. This building collapse

occurred months after more than 100 workers had died in a fire at the Tazreen Fashions factory near Dhaka.[1]

As the weeks passed, the death toll continued to rise. A month later, it was apparent that more than 1,100 garment workers perished in the collapse of the substandard factory building. The gruesome calamity has been called the worst industrial accident since the Bhopal/Union Carbide gas leak disaster in 1984, and the worst ever in the garment industry.[2]

What makes the disaster especially tragic is that it involves the decades-long debate over the use of sweatshops in the supply chains of multinational companies to manufacture cheap products for the Western world. At

---

*This case was written by Archie B. Carroll, University of Georgia, and updated in 2021.

issue are the safety, health, and security of the employees at these work sites.

Since the building collapse occurred and the total costs in lives, injuries, and property losses have been tallied, logical questions about responsibility for the tragedy have been raised. In a complex disaster such as this, there is considerable finger-pointing as many stakeholders are identified as being responsible. According to some reports, the owners of the building had been warned that it was unsafe, and one response by the owners was to threaten to fire the people who did not just keep working.[3] Within a month of the building collapse, the government created a panel to study the accident, and the panel issued a 400-page report claiming that substandard building materials, failure to comply with building regulations, and the use of heavy equipment on upper floors were key factors in the disaster. The panel also recommended that the owner of Rana Plaza, Sohel Rana, and the owners of the five garment factories located in the building should be charged with "culpable homicide" for allegedly forcing the employees to return to work after cracks had been seen on the exterior of the building the previous day.[4] A Bangladesh court only sentenced the owner of the building to three years in jail.[5]

The Bangladeshi government was pressured by many diverse groups to take action to overhaul workplace safety in the aftermath of the building collapse. A more serious problem was the lack of acceptable regulations and enforcement on the part of the government itself. Many blamed the government for not setting and enforcing safety standards in the same way regulations work in more developed countries.

Finally, the government took some steps in the aftermath of the tragedy. It shut down 20 sites for safety improvements.[6] One reason the government started working quickly after the tragedy was because it feared losing millions of jobs to another country if companies exited en masse.[7] The government also said it would broker talks for higher garment industry minimum wages, residing at $38 per month on average at the time of the accident. At the time, the country of Bangladesh was second only to China in terms of garment manufacturing for the developed world; however, its minimum wages were paltry in comparison to the $138 per month received on average by workers in China at the time. In December 2013, a new minimum wage of about $95 per month was established following international pressures.[8]

As so often is the case involving sweatshops and their consequences, however, the primary public discussion about the Rana Plaza disaster quickly turned to U.S. and other wealthy nations' corporations who had taken advantage of the low costs in Bangladesh and were thought to be indifferent to the working conditions of supplying countries. Product remnants of two companies were found in the rubble of the building collapse: Primark, a cut-rate British brand, and Canada's Loblaw, including its Joe Fresh brand.[9]

Following the tragedy, other national brands were also pressured to take action regarding worker safety, even though they had not been linked to the Rana Plaza fire. Among these companies were such familiar names as Walmart, Gap, Dress Barn, H&M, Benetton, J. C. Penney, Mango, Target, Sears, Walt Disney Co., and Nike. These companies were not new to sweatshop allegations and challenges as they had been using them for decades. And, many of them had been striving for years to improve workplace conditions, but the challenges posed in countries such as Bangladesh are formidable. Walmart had started a fire-safety training academy there even before the disaster. Gap had already announced a plan to help factory owners upgrade their plants. The clothing industry had already held meetings with NGOs and governments seeking to develop a strategy to improve safety in Bangladesh's 5,000 factories.[10]

However, following the Rana Plaza tragedy, questions arose for multinational companies and their global supply chains: To ensure safe and good practices, does a company need to check the supplier of its supplier's supplier? Is seeing a certificate that a factory is safe an adequate assurance? Should the company send people in to check every safety feature of the building and to observe working conditions? If so, how often and for how long?[11] Two major approaches surfaced for companies to respond to the serious workplace safety situation in Bangladesh: (1) form a group, or an accord, and act together or (2) each company act independently and go its own way.

European Accord on Fire and Building Safety in Bangladesh

In mid-May 2013, some of Europe's largest retailers took the first approach and decided to create and sign an accord to improve fire and building safety conditions in Bangladesh. The accord was a legally binding five-year agreement not to hire manufacturers whose factories failed to meet safety standards. The group also agreed to pay for necessary factory repairs and renovations. This agreement was negotiated with global worker-safety advocates, overlapping with the Bangladeshi government in its efforts to raise the minimum wage and making it easier for workers to join unions.[12] Leaders of the accord said they needed widespread participation to make the agreement work.

Two of the companies leading the proposed European accord were Sweden's Hennes & Mauritz AB (H&M) and Spain's Inditex. H&M is the leading buyer of clothing from Bangladesh's $20 billion (at the time) garment industry. Observers have said that H&M had no choice but to take the lead since the volume it requires from global suppliers is so large.[13] Other signers of the accord included Italy's Benetton Group, Spain's Mango MNG Holdings SL, France's Carrefour SA, and the UK's Marks & Spencer.[14]

Companies Acting Independently

When the European-led accord was being developed, two leading companies, Walmart and Gap, indicated they would not join the accord but would put together their own safety plans for improving conditions in Bangladesh. One major objection they had to the accord was that it was legally binding; additionally, details were unclear. Other companies were reluctant to sign the accord for the same reasons.

Walmart's initial plan, which it called a commitment, involved hiring outside auditors to inspect 279 Bangladesh factories and publish the results on its website. When warranted, Walmart said it would require the factory owners to make needed renovations or risk being removed from its list of authorized factories. Walmart said that it believed its safety plan would meet or exceed the accord's plan and would get results faster. The company also reported that it had already met and revoked authorization for more than 250 factories in the country. Another part of Walmart's plan was to set up an independent call center for workers to call and report unsafe conditions. Walmart also committed to conducting safety training for every worker in plants making its products.[15]

Though Gap did not agree with the European-led accord, the company indicated that if certain revisions were made to the legally binding agreement, it might join the accord. Other companies initially indicated they would craft their own safety plans for Bangladesh; these companies included J. C. Penney, Sears, and Japan's Fast Retailing Co., operator of the Uniqlo casual clothing chain.[16]

Several companies decided to downplay their use of manufacturing in Bangladesh because of the risks involved. Nike, for example, said that Bangladesh is a high-risk country for them and they planned to keep their footprint limited there. Nike said that only eight of the 896 factories it worked with were in Bangladesh. To ensure compliance with its safety requirements, Nike has its own system of grading or judging the suppliers.[17] Walt Disney Co. had told its licensees in March, before the building collapse, that they could no longer produce Disney-branded products in Bangladesh because some boxes of Disney sweatshirts were found at the site of the Tazreen factory fire that had occurred in Bangladesh the previous November. Disney and Walmart claimed that they did not know their goods were being produced at the plant that burned and that it was not an authorized manufacturer.[18]

United States' Retailers Alliance for Bangladesh Worker Safety Formed

Just over a month after saying they would act alone, it was announced in late June 2013 that Walmart, Gap, VF Corp., Macy's, Sears Holdings, and other large U.S. retailers would establish their own accord to improve safety conditions in Bangladesh garment factories. The agreement became known as the Alliance for Bangladesh Worker Safety. The agreement was a $50 million, five-year fund for improving safety conditions. There were several key differences between the European-led and the U.S.-led proposals. Whereas the European plan did not require participation of the Bangladesh government, the U.S. plan required the government's participation. Another major difference was in the realm of legal liability. The European plan required signatories to accept broad legal liability whereas the U.S. plan called for limited legal liability.[19]

The $50 million U.S.-led plan was contingent on the Bangladesh government meeting certain criteria ensuring accountability and compliance for safety improvements. This was included because many safety codes were often ignored by governmental officials responsible for enforcing them. As for legal liability, the U.S. proposal stipulated that signatories to their plan not have broad but rather limited legal liability. In the U.S. proposal, firms could be held legally liable if they agreed to commit resources and then reneged, or if they continued to use the unsafe factories.[20] Another major difference between the two plans was the amount of resources required for improvements. Under the European plan, companies were required to pay for all upgrades to factories at an estimated cost of $600,000 per factory. In the U.S. plan, companies set up a $50 million fund to help cover the upgrade costs.

The European Accord Continues Its Work

The European Accord continued its work and reported periodically on its progress on its website.[21] The accord's initiatives included inspections, remediation, and workplace programs. The remediation process required the factory owner and the companies to develop a Corrective Action Plan that specified what remedial actions will be taken along with clear deadlines and a financial plan signed off by each party.[22] In its March 2016 quarterly report, the accord showed that real and important progress was being made in the remediation of safety hazards identified.[23] In spite of progress being made, the report indicated that the majority of factories monitored by the accord were behind schedule with remediation. The accord reported that it has been accelerating the pace of remediation.[24] In its 2018 report, the European Accord announced that it would continue its accord for three more years. Inspections at plants revealed 130,000 safety violations, ranging from structural damage to unsafe fire escape routes. By 2020, most of these issues had been resolved.[25]

On June 1, 2020, the Bangladesh office of the accord transitioned its functions to a newly established local organization, Ready-Made-Garment Sustainability Council (RSC).[26] The RSC was set up to go forward as the implementing agency of the accord's established safety programs in Bangladesh. The RSC was not intended to replace the accord itself. Company and Brand obligations under the accord remained in effect and would continue until the accord's expiration scheduled for 2021. In June 2021, the accord was continued for another three months while negotiations continued for a lasting solution.[27] The Worker Rights Consortium (WRC) will continue to play a critical role in implementing and enforcing the accord.[28]

The U.S.-Led Alliance for Worker Safety Made Progress

The Alliance for Bangladesh Worker Safety is a collaborative process involving apparel companies and stakeholders including the U.S. and Bangladeshi governments, policymakers, NGOs, labor organizations, and members of civil society.[29] The alliance's initiatives include standards and inspections, remediation, worker empowerment, worker helpline, training, and sustainability/capacity building. The alliance claims it coordinates and collaborates with all groups that are committed to bringing about the sustainable transformation of the garment sector in Bangladesh.[30] After five years, in the 2018, 5th Annual and Final Report, the alliance provided a snapshot of the progress that had been made along with key statistics in its programmatic areas.[31] Among the progress reported was the following:

- A total of 428 factories had achieved completion of their initial Corrective Action Plans.
- Nearly 1.6 million workers had been trained in fire safety.
- More than 28, 000 security guards had been trained in fire safety and emergency evacuation procedures.
- More than 1.5 million workers had been given access to the alliance's 24-hour confidential worker helpline; 87 percent of helpline issues had been resolved.
- Worker Safety Committees had been formed and were operating in 181 factories,giving workers a seat at the table with management in resolving safety issues.

In 2021, eight years after the Rana Plaza disaster, many activists fear that Bangladesh's factory workers may be in danger again, particularly after the alliance was disbanded and the accord was extended for three months while negotiations continued. According to Christie Miedema, a spokesperson for the Clean Clothes campaign, a network that works to improve conditions for workers in the global garment industry, the workers' lives have not changed that much. She does say there is increasing awareness in the industry that companies are responsible for their complete supply chain and that they need to carry out due diligence. But she argues that many companies do not practice what they preach. Her major concern is that the workers and their buildings are not covered by any legally binding program and that Bangladesh's garment industry could go back to where it was before and risk another Rana Plaza–type disaster.[32]

On July 9, 2021, dozens died as another factory fire struck Bangladesh. Reports are that at least 51, maybe more, workers died in a fire in an industrial building outside of Dhaka, the capital. Two people inside the building leapt to their death trying to escape the fire. Despite public complaints about the previous fires, and the progress that had been made, many factories remain unchanged and fires are common.[33]

Despite the progress that has been made, bringing about a high level of safety in the sweatshop industry in underdeveloped countries will be an ongoing challenge for large global buyers and smaller suppliers alike.

Are Consumers the Responsible Party?

By implication, the world's consumers of "fast fashion" and other cheaply produced products are identified by some as responsible parties in the tragedy in Bangladesh. Though surveys report that consumers will reward responsible business practices or punish violators, this doesn't happen often. *USA Today* writer Jayne O'Donnell reported on a 23-year-old woman who said she would pay a little more for her clothes if she knew the companies were "socially responsible in the way that they gave their workers safe conditions and adequate pay." But O'Donnell observes that this woman may be the exception; consumers will be troubled by these news accounts, but they quickly forget. Consumer psychologist Kit Yarrow was quoted as observing that "denial is a pretty powerful thing if something is beautiful and you really want it."[34]

Questions for Discussion

1. Who are the stakeholders in this case and what are their stakes? What are the ethical issues?
2. Based on your study of the building collapse in Bangladesh, which party or parties do you think are primarily responsible and why?
3. What role does the government of Bangladesh assume in this building collapse and other safety violations?
4. Do Western companies have an obligation to safeguard the safety of workers in foreign lands where the products they sell are made?
5. What are the pros and cons of companies working together in an accord to address safety violations versus taking independent action to address the issues in the plants they use? Do both approaches represent sound global corporate citizenship?
6. Which plan seemed best for addressing the factory safety problem in Bangladesh: the European-led accord or the U.S.-led alliance? What are the pros and cons of each?
7. What is your appraisal of companies that decide Bangladesh is too risky a country for them to do business in?
8. What is the responsibility of consumers to the employees in other countries where their products are made? Is it true that "we quickly forget" ? What can consumers do to address this mindset?

Endnotes

1. Syed Zain Al-Mahmood and Shelly Banjo, "Deadly Collapse," *The Wall Street Journal*, April 25, 2013, A1.
2. "Disaster at Rana Plaza," *The Economist*, May 4, 2013, 12, https://www.economist.com /leaders/2013/05/04/disaster-at-rana-plaza. Accessed July 2, 2021.
3. Ibid.
4. Syed Zain Al-Mahmood, "Shoddy Materials Are Blamed for Building Collapse," *The Wall Street Journal*, May 24, 2012, B4.
5. ABCNews, "Rana Plaza: Bangladesh Jails Owner of Factory Building That Collapsed in 2013 for Corruption," August 29, 2017, https://www.abc .net.au/news/2017-08-29/rana-plaza-owner-of -collapsed-bangladesh-building-jailed/8854240. Accessed July 8, 2021.
6. Syed Zain Al-Mahmoud, "Bangladesh Factory Toll Passes 800," *The Wall Street Journal*, May 9, 2013, A10.

7. Adam Davidson, "Clotheslined," *The New York Times* Magazine, May 19, 2013, 16.
8. Syed Zain Al-Mahmood, "Bangladesh to Raise Workers' Pay," *The Wall Street Journal*, May 13, 2013, B4; Reuters Staff, "Bangladesh Raises Wages for Garment Workers," September 13, 2013, https://www.reuters.com/article/us-bangladesh-garments/bangladesh-raises-wages-for-garment-workers-idUSKCN1LT2UR. Accessed July 2, 2021.
9. *The Economist*, May 4, 2013, ibid.
10. Ibid.
11. Ibid.
12. Shelly Banjo and Christina Passariello, "Promises in Bangladesh," *The Wall Street Journal*, May 14, 2013, B1, https://www.wsj.com/articles/SB10001424127887323716304578480883414503230. Accessed July 2, 2021.
13. Jens Hansegard, Tripti Lahiri, and Christina Passariello, "Retailers' Dilemma: Cut Off or Help Fix Unsafe Factories," *The Wall Street Journal*, May 29, 2013, B1.
14. Shelly Banjo, Ann Zimmerman, and Suzanne Kapner, "Wal-Mart Crafts Own Bangladesh Safety Plan," *The Wall Street Journal*, May 15, 2013. B1, https://www.wsj.com/articles/SB10001424127887323716304578480883414503230. Accessed July 2, 2021.
15. Ibid.
16. Mayumi Negishi, "Uniqlo Won't Join Accord on Bangladesh Labor Safety," *The Wall Street Journal*, May 28, 2013, B1, https://www.wsj.com/articles/SB10001424127887324125504578508670666933426. Accessed July 2, 2021.
17. "Nike's Game Plan for Policing Its Suppliers: Try to Avoid Bangladesh," *The Wall Street Journal*, November 30, 2012, https://www.wsj.com/articles/SB10001424127887324020804578149591783958054. Accessed July 2, 2021.
18. Hansegard et al., ibid.
19. Shelly Banjo, Ann Zimmerman, and Suzanne Kapner, "Walmart Lays Out Its Own Bangladesh Safety Plan," *The Wall Street Journal*, May 14, 2013, https://www.wsj.com/articles/SB10001424127887324216004578483381921421300. Accessed July 2, 2021.
20. Ibid.
21. Accord on Fire and Building Safety in Bangladesh, http://bangladeshaccord.org/about/. Accessed June 20, 2016.
22. Ibid, Remediation Process, http://bangladeshaccord.org/remediation/. Accessed June 20, 2016.
23. Quarterly Aggregate Report, March 31, 2016, http://bangladeshaccord.org/wp-content/uploads/Quarterly-Aggregate-Report-11-May-2016.pdf. Accessed June 20, 2016.
24. Ibid.
25. Worker Rights Consortium, "Bangladesh Accord," https://www.workersrights.org/our-work/bangladesh-accord/. Accessed July 2, 2021.
26. Ibid.
27. Ecotextile, "Accord Agreement Extended for Three Months," June 1, 2021, https://www.ecotextile.com/2021060127863/materials-production-news/accord-agreement-extended-for-three-months.html. Accessed July 8, 2021.
28. Worker Rights Consortium, "Bangladesh Accord," Ibid.
29. Alliance for Bangladesh Worker Safety, "About the Alliance," https://www.bangladeshworkersafety.org/who-we-are/about-the-alliance. Accessed July 2, 2021.
30. Ibid.
31. Ibid., Alliance for Bangladesh Worker Safety, November 2018, https://www.bangladeshworkersafety.org/files/Alliance%20Fifth%20Annual%20Report%202018.pdf. Accessed July 2, 2021.
32. Ana Salva, "8 Years After Rana Plaza Disaster, Activists Fear Bangladesh's Workers Are in Danger Again," *The Diplomat*, May 19, 2021, https://thediplomat.com/2021/05/8-years-after-rana-plaza-disaster-activists-fear-bangladeshs-garment-workers-are-in-danger-again/. Accessed July 2, 2021.
33. Saif Hasnat and Emily Schmall, "Dozens Die as Another Fire Strikes Bangladesh," *The New York Times*, July 9, 2021, https://www.nytimes.com/2021/07/09/world/asia/bangladesh-factory-fire.html. Accessed July 10, 2021.
34. Jayne O'Donnell, "Treat Workers Well, or Kiss Our Cash Goodbye," *USA Today*, May 23, 2013, 5B.

Case 16

Big Food, Big Problem: Nestlé in Brazil*

With the motto of "Good Food, Good Life," Nestlé wants its customers to see its products as nutritious and healthy.

Likewise, the company prides itself on caring for its customers' well-being.

However, public health experts accuse Nestlé of causing a major health crisis in developing countries such as Brazil. In fact, experts claim that Nestlé's aggressive marketing of

*This case was prepared by Sabine E. Turnley and William H. Turnley, Kansas State University.

cheap ultra-processed food and drinks is contributing to the rapidly rising obesity rate in Brazil and other countries. While people tend to think of hunger or starvation as the world's greatest food-related problem, there are now more people across the world who are obese than underweight. Specifically, according to the *New England Journal of Medicine*, there are currently more than 700 million obese people worldwide, with 108 million of them being children.[1]

In recent years, Nestlé has experienced a weaker demand for processed food in wealthy countries.[2] In response, it has redirected its efforts toward developing economies such as Brazil. Nestlé has used the power of its brands and a unique sales model to reach as many customers as possible, even in some of the most remote areas of Brazil. As a result, the traditional Brazilian diet is being replaced with a reliance on ultra-processed foods, which are industrial formulations of highly palatable mixtures of synthetic flavorings and cheap commodity ingredients that require little, if any, cooking.[3]

Critics worry that Nestlé's promotion of its processed food is not driven by nutritional science and wellness but, instead, by a focus on profit and growth at the expense of some of the world's most vulnerable populations. While Nestlé is trying to reimage itself into a "nutrition, health and wellness" company, it still makes and vigorously promotes KitKat bars, Hot Pockets, and a host of other highly processed foods.

Company Background

Nestlé S.A., headquartered in Switzerland, is the world's largest processed-food company. The Swiss company employs 273,000 people worldwide, operates 376 factories in 81 countries, and has a portfolio of 2,000 brands sold in 186 countries.[4] The food giant ranked #39 in the 2021 edition of the Forbes Global 2000 list of the most powerful public companies, up two spots from last year.[5] Nestlé has a primary listing on the SIX Swiss Exchange (ticker: NESN) and its market cap is USD 333.2 billion.

Nestlé sells a large product portfolio including baby food, breakfast cereals, coffee, water, confectioneries, dairy products, frozen food, pet foods, and snacks. It owns several global brands such as Stouffers, Nescafé, KitKat, and Carnation as well as many local brands such as Ninho and *Passatempo*. More than 30 of its brands have annual sales of over CHF 1 billion (USD 1.1 billion) including Nespresso, Smarties, and Nesquik. While Nestlé claims that its key categories are coffee, infant nutrition, water, and pet care, it should be noted that only about half of its sales (53 percent) are generated from those categories, leaving about 47 percent of Nestlé sales to come from other products.

In 2020, 44.7 percent of Nestlé's revenue came from the Americas (North America, Central America, and South America), while 29 percent originated in the EMENA Zone (Europe, Middle East,and North Africa) and 26.3 percent came from Asia, Oceania, and Sub-Saharan Africa. The United States, Nestlé's biggest market, accounted for nearly 30.8 percent of its 2020 revenue.[6]

According to the company's website, Nestlé's purpose is to enhance the quality of individuals' lives. Nestlé also says that it wants to inspire people to live healthier lives.[7] Their mission is encapsulated is the motto "**Good Food, Good Life.**" Nestlé aims to provide consumers with the best tasting, most nutritious choices in a wide range of food and beverage categories, at all times of the day, and for all stages of life, delivered in a convenient and time-saving manner.[8]

The Big Food Industry

The term "Big Food" generally refers to the large transnational corporations that increasingly control the production and distribution of ultra-processed food and beverages throughout the world.[9] The Big Food industry is heavily concentrated. Ten companies control the vast majority of food and beverage brands in the world.[10] Nestlé has held the title of top food company for more than a decade. Collectively, the top ten Big Food companies generate close to USD 400 billion in sales annually.

Ultra-processed food and drink products are defined as industrial formulations with five or more ingredients.[11] Ultra-processed foods contain several manufactured ingredients that are not generally used when cooking from scratch, including natural and artificial flavors or colors, sweeteners, preservatives, and other additives.[12] Ultra-processed foods are formulated and packaged to have a long shelf-life and to eliminate the need for culinary preparation. They are meant to be convenience foods that can be consumed anywhere, either immediately or almost immediately. Because ultra-processed foods are made to be eaten on the run or as snacks, their use tends to erode the tradition of family meals. It is also believed that ultra-processed foods encourage overeating, both because they are engineered by food scientists to induce cravings and because Big Food manufacturers spend lavishly on marketing. Finally, because the manufacturing of these products is tied to the industrial farming of staples like corn and soy instead of the produce of family farmers, the Big Food industry is transforming the kinds of food that is grown around the world.[13]

Growth has been hard to come by in the Big Food industry in recent years, making the industry hyper competitive. Specifically, the global packaged food industry (Food Processing Sector NAICS 311) has struggled in wealthy markets that have become more hostile to their products: millennial consumers intrinsically distrust mainstream legacy brands with mysterious ingredients and instead are seeking healthier, less processed foods.

However, in early 2020, the fortune of the entire Big Food industry changed almost overnight because of the COVID-19 pandemic. The coronavirus profoundly altered how people spend their money and ultra-processed food made a huge comeback in wealthy countries like the United States.Consumers found themselves eating most of their meals at home instead of at restaurants, and they seemed to prefer comfort foods that are cheap and convenient to make. Groceries are the lone spending category that has grown since the outbreak of the virus in the United States.[14] In fact, year-over-year grocery sales were up as much as 79 percent during some weeks in 2020. Sales have since fallen from those historic levels, but they remain higher than normal. Food companies, including Hormel Foods Corp., Tyson Foods, Inc., and Kraft Heinz Co., have announced an increase in production by as much as 40 percent in order to keep up with rising demand during the pandemic.[15]

As a result, 2020 became a banner year for the processed food industry. Experts believe that consumption and sales of packaged food will continue to grow at high levels due to the high unemployment rate, restaurant closures, and inflation facing many nations.[16]

Brazil: A "Growing" Market

Brazil is the largest country in South America and, more broadly, in Latin America. It has approximately 213 million people, making it the world's sixth most populous country. Brazil is projected to have the world's 13th largest GDP in 2021.[17]

As the Brazilian economy has grown, the country is now faced with a stark new public health challenge: hunger has been replaced by obesity as the major food-related health issue. Over the last decade, the country's obesity rate has nearly doubled and the percentage of people who are overweight has nearly tripled. Today, 58 percent of Brazil's population is overweight and 20 percent of Brazilians are obese.[18] Thus, nearly 80 percent of Brazilians are either overweight or obese. Particularly worrisome is the fact that about 33 percent of children from 5 to 9 years old are overweight, and 14.3 percent are obese.[19] Though Brazil's obesity rate still falls short of that of the United States or Mexico, the obesity rate in Brazil now surpasses that of most European countries according to the Organisation for Economic Co-operation and Development (OECD).[20]

Obesity is widely recognized as a risk factor for many health issues including diabetes, heart disease, hypertension, stroke, and several cancers. Its rise in Brazil presents a serious problem, not only for the individuals themselves but also for the country's public health-care system. The obesity epidemic will come with a hefty cost to the Brazilian government and taxpayers.

According to the Brazilian Ministry of Health, data demonstrate that those who consume highly processed foods are more likely to become obese. Walmir Coutinho, one of Brazil's leading endocrinologists, is so concerned with the obesity epidemic that he stated that if Brazil does not change its ways, it could become the most obese nation in the world in the next 15 years.[21]

Over the past decade, food has become cheaper and more widely available throughout most of the world. However, the most accessible foods are often high in calories, salt, sugar, and fat, and low in nutrients. Three-fourths of world food sales are processed foods. In particular, sales of ultra-processed food in Brazil have more than doubled in the past ten years, and Big Food companies have successfully pushed their brands into the most remote parts of this large country. For instance, in 2010, Nestlé started supplying boats to serve as floating supermarkets for communities residing along the Amazon River. Remote communities could therefore buy branded ultra-processed foods in place of local farm produce.[22] Consequently, the traditional food systems and Brazilian dietary patterns are quickly being displaced by ultra-processed products made by transnational food corporations.[23]

The Brazilian government, under pressure to address this public health issue, tried to introduce legislation to preserve its traditional diet and curb the obesity epidemic. Some regulatory proposals included advertising warnings to consumers about foods high in sugar, salt, and saturated fats, as well as advertising restrictions on marketing aimed at children. However, the rising clout of the Big Food firms translated into intense lobbying efforts that prevented the passage of the legislation. According to the organization Transparencia Brasil, the Big Food industry donated $158 million to members of Brazil's National Congress in 2014, a threefold increase over 2010. More than half of Brazil's federal legislators received donations from the food industry before the Supreme Court banned corporate contributions in 2015.[24] Nestlé's executives sit on the board of the Brazilian Association of Food Industries, which is a lobbyist group. It is believed that these lobbyists and some Big Food corporate lawyers waged an effective multipronged campaign to derail legislative proposals to fight the obesity crisis.[25] Moreover, the current president of Brazil, Jair Bolsonaro, is a business-friendly politician, whose allies in Congress are currently seeking to chip away at the handful of regulations and laws intended to encourage healthy eating.

Nestlé Brasil Ltda

Nestlé Brasil Ltda is a subsidiary of Nestlé SA. It employs more than 20,000 individuals and sells more than 800 items in 20 different market categories.

In 2020, Brazil was Nestlé's fifth leading market after the United States, China, France, and the United Kingdom. Nestlé Brasil was responsible for nearly 3.3 percent of the food giant's total revenue.[26] Research shows that 95 percent of Brazilian households consume at least one Nestlé product every day.[27] It should be noted that out of the 800 products that Nestlé Brazil provides through its door-to-door vendors, customers are mostly interested in about two dozen of them, virtually all sugar-sweetened snack items such as Kit-Kats; Nestlé Greek Red Berry, a 3.5-ounce cup of yogurt with 17 grams of sugar; and *Chandelle Pacoca*, a 3.5-ounce peanut-flavored pudding that has 20 grams of sugar, nearly the entire daily limit as recommended by the World Health Organization (WHO).[28]

Sales Model to Reach the Poor

In Brazil, Nestlé uses several specific sales strategies to more deeply penetrate the market. By relying on a door-to-door direct sales force, the food giant can reach the most remote areas of the country. This door-to-door delivery model makes it easy for the poorest Brazilians to access processed food, even when there are no grocery stores nearby.

Nestlé currently uses 200 micro-distributors and 7,000 saleswomen across Brazil, selling products to 700,000 low-income consumers each month.[29] Despite the continuing economic crisis in Brazil, this direct sales program has been growing at 10 percent annually because Nestlé gives customers a full month to pay their bills. Its local, female-only sales force is highly effective because the vendors are known by the community members and are trained to sing the products' praises. Moreover, they are aware of when their customers receive *Bolsa Familia*, the monthly government allowance for 14 million low-income households.[30]

Nestlé also came up with a creative way to increase its presence in the backcountry of Brazil. It sponsored a river barge to create a "floating supermarket" for the remote villages along the Amazon River. The "supermarket" boat, which measures 1,076 square feet, journeyed to 18 cities and served up to 800,000 consumers on the Para and Xingu Rivers. Since 2010, this boat has delivered tens of thousands of cartons of milk powder, yogurt, chocolate pudding, cookies, and candy. The boat was taken out of service in July 2017, but private boat owners have taken over to fill the demand and continue the distribution of Nestlé products.[31]

In 2019, Nestlé opened its own-brand supermarket, Emporió, near its headquarters in Sao Paulo. Emporió stocks more than 1,500 products including chocolate candy and snacks, coffee, cereals, beverages, and dairy foods. Nestlé has also partnered with Supermercado Now for delivery service of its products purchased at Emporió.

All in all, it is clear that Nestlé is aggressively targeting as many Brazilians as possible. Nestlé products are not only being sold door-to-door in the poorest areas of Brazilian cities but also on trains and subway stations, in retail chains, its own stores, and also on "floating supermarkets."[32]

Nestlé's Response to the Obesity Crisis in Brazil

When asked about Nestlé's role in spurring changes to the Brazilian diet, the company stated that its products have helped eradicate hunger and are providing important nutrients to a needy population. It is true that hunger is no longer a major problem in Brazil, but the country is now dealing with a new type of condition in which people are both overweight and undernourished. Sean Westcott, head of Nestlé food research and development, said that rising obesity was an unintended side effect of making the company's processed foods more commonplace.[33]

Nestlé is responding to the criticism in several different ways, including R&D projects, product reformulations, and education programs.

The food giant created the Nestlé Research Centre in Switzerland, which is the world's largest privately owned facility for research on food and nutrition. More recently, Nestlé opened two more units—Nestlé Health Science SA and the Nestlé Institute of Health Sciences—to do research on products that could prevent or treat chronic ailments such as obesity and diabetes. According to the head of marketing and communications in Brazil, Frank Pflaumer, Nestlé Brasil allocated 400 million reals (USD 99.66 million) to innovation in the last five years. Last year, Nestlé opened a new quality assurance lab and launched its first organic food line in Brazil.[34]

At the same time, however, Nestlé continues to invest in unhealthy food products (such confectionaries and chocolate) and is aggressively expanding its product penetration in emerging markets. This makes it hard to understand how this marketing strategy aligns with Nestlé's professed commitment to nutrition and science.

Regarding product reformulations, Nestlé states that it has removed 350 tons of sodium, 5,000 tons of saturated fats, and 6,900 tons of sugar from the products it sells in Brazil since 2014.[35] For example, Nestlé reduced sugar in yogurts by 23 percent. In addition, Nestlé reduced sugar by 15 percent and saturated fat by 515 in its best-selling cookie brand in Brazil, *Passatempo*.[36] Nestlé S.A.'s 2020 objectives were to reduce the sodium it adds to its products by 10 percent,[37] to reduce added sugar by 5 percent, and to reduce saturated fat by 10 percent.[38] Due to COVID-19 pandemic, those objectives were only partially achieved (3.8 percent reduction in added sodium, 4.5 percent reduction in added sugar, and 10 percent reduction in saturated fat).[39] Yet, one wonders if product reformulations will be enough to combat the obesity epidemic in Brazil. Some of Nestlé's products may have less salt, sugar, and fat than before, but overconsumption by a vulnerable population is not being addressed. This point is even more relevant considering the fact that, according to the research, the Brazilian population consumes serving sizes that are up to 9.2 times larger than the suggested serving size on the product label.[40] In Western economies, the new marketing message being touted by Big Food companies is to treat these highly processed foods as an indulgence or as treats to be enjoyed on special occasions and in small quantities. In contrast, in Brazil and other developing countries, cookies, chocolates, pudding, and other unhealthy products are often seen as part of a daily diet.

Nestlé is also trying to quiet its critics by sponsoring programs to educate the Brazilian consumer about healthy eating. For example, Nestlé has created a website called "Nutrir," where school-age kids can play games about nutrition and health. Nestlé claims that they have reached three million children since 1999, but it should be noted that many of the poorest children in developing countries do not have access to computers.

Moreover, it should be remembered that Nestlé is familiar with being the target of public uproar over its strategic decisions. In the 1970s, after providing incentives to doctors and nurses in developing countries to promote the use of its baby formula instead of breast milk, Nestlé faced a lot of negative publicity and eventually an international boycott that spread to the United States, Europe, and Asia. To respond to the public outcry about marketing infant formula in developing countries, nine manufacturers created an infant formula manufacturer code of ethics but refused to admit any responsibility for marketing abuses. The manufacturers' code was virtually useless as it contained few, if any, new restrictions for the industry.

In 1981, the World Health Assembly, which is the most prominent global health policy-setting body, adopted the WHO International Code of Marketing of Breastmilk Substitutes (The Code). The WHO Code restricted marketing practices of infant formula makers, but it existed only as a recommendation and was not legally binding or enforceable. Nestlé initially claimed that since the code was a recommendation targeted at governments, the industry itself was under no legal obligation to enforce the agreement. So, an international boycott against Nestlé lasted for seven years and took a significant financial toll on the company. Eventually, Nestlé pledged to fully implement the WHO Code. Specifically, Nestlé promised not to engage in advertising or give free samples of infant formula to mothers. Nestlé also provided assurances that it would include statements with its product declaring the superiority of breastfeeding and promised to translate product labels and warnings into local languages with pictorial messages when appropriate. Although Nestlé did take some steps to change its practices, it appears that the company persisted in violating some of the advertising and marketing guidelines of the WHO Code. Evidence showed that mothers were regularly receiving free formula. A second boycott against the company was started in 1988 for failing to comply with the code.[41] Now, more than 30 years after the WHO Code was adopted, Nestlé is still suspected of regularly breaching the code and received a poor score of just 36 percent regarding compliance with the code.[42] For example, Nestlé introduced follow-on formulas and growing-up milks to avoid code-derived legislation in countries that only prohibited the advertising of formula aimed at younger infants.

As the world's largest food company, how much responsibility should Nestlé take to support the health of families around the globe? Should a company whose motto is "Good Food, Good Life" provide food that is actually healthy? Should a company that claims to be driven by nutritional science remove junk food from its portfolio or change its marketing practices, especially in developing country?

Questions for Discussion

1. What are the key ethical issues revealed in this case?
2. Conduct a stakeholder analysis to identify Nestlé's key stakeholders and the risks that Nestlé's actions (or inaction) create for them. In the wake of recent news stories about the obesity epidemic, how should the company prioritize its stakeholders' needs?
3. What strategic actions should Nestlé's board of directors take moving forward, specifically in relation to its product offerings in Brazil?
4. What are the ethical obligations of companies who sell perfectly legal, but unhealthy, products? Do these companies' ethical obligations change when they are dealing with vulnerable populations or when entering markets in less-developed countries? Explain.
5. Even if Nestlé continues to sell its full array of products in Brazil, are there specific types of marketing actions from which it should voluntarily refrain? Are there specific actions the company should pursue? Explain.

Endnotes

1. Andrew Jacobs and Matt Richtel, "How Big Business Got Brazil Hooked on Junk Food," *The New York Times*, September 16, 2017, https://www.nytimes.com/interactive/2017/09/16/health/brazil-obesity-nestle.html. Accessed June 9, 2021.
2. *Nestlé S.A. Website*, "Nestlé S.A. Full-Year Results 2017 Press Conference," https://www.nestle.com/media/mediaeventscalendar/allevents/2017-full-year-results. Accessed June 9, 2021.
3. Bridget Huber, "Welcome to Brazil, Where a Food Revolution Is Changing the Way People Eat," *The Nation*, July 28, 2016, https://www.thenation.com/article/slow-food-nation-2/. Accessed June 9, 2021
4. *Nestlé S.A. Website*, https://www.nestle.com/ask-nestle/our-company. Accessed June 9, 2021.
5. Andrea Murphy, Eliza Haverstock, Antoine Gara, Chris Helman, Nathan Vardi, "Global 2000: How the World's Biggest Public Companies Endured the Pandemic," *Forbes*, May 13, 2021, https://www.forbes.com/lists/global2000/#419469065ac0. Accessed June 9, 2021.
6. *Nestlé S.A. Website*, "2020 Consolidated Financial Statement of the Nestlé Group," p. 31, https://www.nestle.com/sites/default/files/2021-02/2020-financial-statements-en.pdf. Accessed June 9, 2021.
7. *Nestlé S.A. Website*, https://www.nestle.com/aboutus. Accessed June 9, 2021.
8. Ovidijus Jurevicius, Strategic Management Insight, "Mission Statement of Nestlé," *Strategic Management Insight*, https://strategicmanagementinsight.com/mission-statements/nestle-mission-statement.html. Accessed June 9, 2021.
9. Carlos A. Monteiro, Geoffrey Cannon, "The Impact of Transnational 'Big Food' Companies on the South: A View from Brazil", *PLOS MEDICINE*, July 3, 2012, https://www.ncbi.nlm.nih.gov/pmc/articles/PMC3389019/. Accessed June 9, 2021.
10. Kate Taylor, "These 10 Companies Control Everything You Buy," *Business Insider*, April 4, 2017, https://www.businessinsider.com/10-companies-control-food-industry-2017-3. Accessed June 9, 2021.

11. *British Nutrition Foundation*, "Ultra-Processed Foods – Are they to Blame for Obesity?" February 9, 2018,https://www.nutrition.org.uk /nutritioninthenews/headlines/ultraprocessedfoods .html/ Accessed June 10, 2021.

12. Ashley Welch, "Ultra-Processed Foods a Huge Chunk of American Diet," *CBS News*, March 10, 2016, https://www.cbsnews.com/news/ultra -processed-foods-calories-american-diet/. Accessed June 10, 2021.

13. Bridget Huber, "Welcome to Brazil, Where a Food Revolution Is Changing the Way People Eat," *The Nation*, July 28, 2016, https://www.thenation.com /article/slow-food-nation-2/. Accessed June 10, 2021.

14. Lauren Leatherby and David Gelles, "How the Virus Transformed the Way Americans Spend Their Money," *The New York Times*, April 11, 2020, https://www.nytimes.com/interactive/2020/04/11 /business/economy/coronavirus-us-economy -spending.html?smtyp=cur&smid=tw-nytimes. Accessed June 10, 2021.

15. Sam Sosland, "US Packaged Foods Growth Expected to Far Exceeded Expectations," *Food Business News*, March 30, 2020, https://www .foodbusinessnews.net/articles/15709-us-packaged -foods-growth-expected-to-far-exceed-expectations. Accessed June 10, 2021.

16. *Seeking Alpha*, "2020 Will Be a Banner Year for the Packaged Food Sector," April 13, 2020, https:// seekingalpha.com/article/4337339-2020-will-be -banner-year-for-packaged-food-sector. Accessed June 10, 2021.

17. *Statistics Times*, "Projected GDP Ranking," June 3, 2021, https://statisticstimes.com/economy /projected-world-gdp-ranking.php. Accessed June 10, 2021.

18. Leanna Garfield, "There's a War between Two Food Systems and the Big Food Conglomerates Are Winning," *Business Insider*, September 19, 2017, http://www.businessinsider.com/big-food -companies-obesity-epidemic-world-2017-9. Accessed June 10,2021.

19. Natalia Cancian, "Obesidade quase dobra entre os jovens brasileiros en des anos," *Folha de S. Paulo*, August 9, 2017, https://www1.folha.uol.com .br/equilibrioesaude/2017/08/1908212-obesidade -dispara-entre-jovens-do-pais.shtml. Accessed June 10, 2021.

20. *OECD*, "Obesity Update," June 2014,http://www .oecd.org/els/health-systems/Obesity-Update-2014. pdf. Accessed June 10, 2021.

21. Ana Paula Picasso, "This Country Is on Track to Dethrone the US as the Most Obese in the World," *Business Insider*, October 5, 2015,https://www .businessinsider.com/brazil-on-track-to-be-most -obese-in-world-2015-10. Accessed June 10, 2021.

22. Meera Senthillingam, "Brazil's Burgeoning Obesity Problem," *CNN*. July 9, 2014, https://www.cnn .com/2014/07/09/health/beating-the-bulge-brazil -obesity/index.html. Accessed June 10, 2021.

23. Carlos A. Monteiro, Geoffrey Cannon, "The Impact of Transnational 'Big Food' Companies on the South: A View from Brazil" , *PLOS MEDICINE*, July 3, 2012,https://journals.plos.org/plosmedicine /article?id=10.1371/journal.pmed.1001252. Accessed June 10, 2021.

24. Andrew Jacobs and Matt Richtel, "How Big Business Got Brazil Hooked on Junk Food," *The New York Times*, September 16, 2017, https://www .nytimes.com/interactive/2017/09/16/health/brazil -obesity-nestle.html. Accessed June 10, 2021.

25. Andrew Jacobs and Matt Richtel, "How Big Business Got Brazil Hooked on Junk Food," *The New York Times*, September 16, 2017, https://www .nytimes.com/interactive/2017/09/16/health/brazil -obesity-nestle.html. Accessed June 10, 2021.

26. *Nestlé S.A. Website*, "2020 Consolidated Financial Statement of the Nestlé Group," p. 31, https://www .nestle.com/sites/default/files/2021-02/2020 -financial-statements-en.pdf. Accessed June 10, 2021.

27. Carlos Adese, "In Good Taste: Nestlé Tweaks Products for Different Parts of Brazil and Latin America to Boost Sales," Latin Trade, July 2007.

28. Andrew Jacobs and Matt Richtel, "How Big Business Got Brazil Hooked on Junk Food," *The New York Times*, September 16, 2017, https://www .nytimes.com/interactive/2017/09/16/health/brazil -obesity-nestle.html. Accessed June 10, 2021.

29. *Nestlé S.A. Website*, "How Nutritious Are Nestlé foods in Brazil?" https://www.nestle.com/ask -nestle/health-nutrition/answers/obesity-junk-food -brazil. Accessed June 10, 2021.

30. Bridget Huber, "Welcome to Brazil, Where a Food Revolution Is Changing the Way People Eat," *The Nation*, July 28, 2016, https://www.thenation.com /article/slow-food-nation-2/. Accessed June 10, 2021.

31. Leanna Garfield, "Nestlé Sponsored a River Barge to Create a Floating Supermarket That Sold Candy and Chocolate Pudding to the Backwoods of Brazil," *Business Insider*, September 19, 2017,https://www .businessinsider.com/nestl-expands-brazil-river -barge-2017-9. Accessed June 10, 2021.

32. Carlos A. Monteiro and Geoffrey Cannon, "The Impact of Transnational 'Big Food' Companies on the South: A View from Brazil," *PLOS MEDICINE*, July 3, 2012, https://journals.plos.org/plosmedicine /article?id=10.1371/journal.pmed.1001252. Accessed June 10, 2021.

33. Andrew Jacobs and Matt Richtel, "How Big Business Got Brazil Hooked on Junk Food," *The New York Times*, September 16, 2017, https://www .nytimes.com/interactive/2017/09/16/health/brazil -obesity-nestle.html. Accessed June 11, 2021.

34. Gabriela Mello, "Nestlé to Boost Healthy Food Products in Brazil, Eyes Partnerships," Reuters, May 17, 2019, https://www.reuters.com/article /us-nestle-brazil-health/nestle-to-boost-healthy -food-products-in-brazil-eyes-partnerships -idUSKCN1SN1SU. Accessed June 11, 2021.

35. *Nestlé S.A. Website*, "How Nutritious Are Nestlé foods in Brazil?" https://www.nestle.com/ask-nestle/health-nutrition/answers/obesity-junk-food-brazil. Accessed June 11, 2021.

36. *Nestlé S.A. Website*, "How Nutritious Are Nestlé foods in Brazil?" https://www.nestle.com/ask-nestle/health-nutrition/answers/obesity-junk-food-brazil. Accessed June 11, 2021.

37. *Nestlé S.A. Website*, "What Are You Doing to Reduce Salt in Your Products?" https://www.nestle.com/ask-nestle/health-nutrition/answers/what-are-you-doing-to-reduce-salt-in-your-products. Accessed June 11, 2021.

38. *Nestlé S.A. Website*, "Reducing Sugars, Sodium and Fat," https://www.nestle.com/csv/impact/tastier-healthier/sugar-salt-fat. Accessed June 11, 2021.

39. *Nestlé S.A. Website*, "Reducing Sugars, Sodium and Fat," https://www.nestle.com/csv/impact/tastier-healthier/sugar-salt-fat. Accessed June 11, 2021.

40. Mariana Vieira dos Santos Kreamer, Priscila Pereira Machado, Nathalie Kliemann, David Alejandro Gonzalez Chica, Rossana Pacheco da Costa Proenca, "The Brazilian Population Consumes Larger Serving Sizes Than Those Informed on Labels, *The British Food Journal*, February 2, 2015, https://www.emeraldinsight.com/doi/abs/10.1108/BFJ-11-2013-0339. Accessed June 11, 2021.

41. Nancy Ellen Zelman, "The Nestlé Infant Formula Controversy: Restricting the Marketing Practices of Multinational Corporations in the Third World," *Global Business and Development Law Journal*, January 1, 1990, https://scholarlycommons.pacific.edu/cgi/viewcontent.cgi?article=1212&context=globe. Accessed June 11, 2021.

42. *Changing Markets Foundation*, "Busting the Myth of Science-based Formula: An Investigation into Nestle Infant milk products and claims" , February 2018, http://changingmarkets.org/wp-content/uploads/2018/02/BUSTING-THE-MYTH-OF-SCIENCE-BASED-FORMULA.pdf. Accessed June 11, 2021.

Case 17

The Dark Side of Going Green: Tesla's Ethical Dilemma*

Society has unknowingly grown dependent on a blue-colored mineral called cobalt because it is used in the rechargeable lithium-ion batteries powering our phones, laptops, and electric vehicles. Sixty-four percent of the world's cobalt is extracted from the Democratic Republic of Congo (DRC), an African country plagued by conflict, poverty, and dysfunction.[1] More than 100,000 Congolese, including up to 40,000 children, work in unregulated, unmonitored, and unsafe makeshift mines.[2] Without protective gear or adequate tools, they often work 12-hour shifts in hand-dug and unsupported tunnels to unearth this most coveted mineral.

Tesla, Inc., the electric car and energy company based in Palo Alto, California, produces more lithium-ion batteries than all other carmakers combined. Tesla's strategic intent is to become the world's biggest and most highly regarded producer of electric-powered motor vehicles (EVs) and, by doing so, to accelerate the world's transition to sustainable energy.[3] With its Model 3 as the first mass-produced electric car, Tesla is now targeting a broad market of customers.

While it is clear that today's consumers want to curb carbon emissions and want to see companies use clean and renewable energy, consumers and activists are also concerned with social issues such as extreme poverty, human right violations, and child labor. Tesla finds itself at the juncture of this ethical dilemma.

Tesla's zero-emission electric cars are marketed as an environmentally conscious alternative to traditional fossil-fueled automobiles. Yet, the batteries powering these vehicles use cobalt. Going green is great, but what happens if that comes at the expense of some of the most vulnerable people in Africa?

> "Without radical changes, the batteries which power green vehicles will continue to be tainted by human rights abuses."
> Kumi Naidoo, Amnesty International's Secretary General

Is Tesla profiting from the clean energy revolution while turning a blind eye to the problems of working conditions, child labor, and environmental contamination that are prevalent in the cobalt mining industry?

Company Background

Tesla, Inc. was founded in July 2003 by Silicon Valley engineers Martin Eberhard and Marc Tarpenning, but the company didn't release its first car, the Roadster, until five years later. Tesla caught the attention of PayPal cofounder Elon Musk, who invested millions in the company during the early rounds of funding. Musk eventually became the chair of the board for the company before taking on the

*This case was written by Sabine E. Turnley and William H. Turnley, Kansas State University.

role of chief executive officer. Tesla has become a widely recognized brand, known for innovation and cutting-edge technology in the EV industry.

Tesla's stated mission is to "accelerate the world's transition to sustainable energy."[4] Its strategic intent is to be the world's biggest and most highly regarded producer of electric-powered motor vehicles. Tesla already produces more batteries in terms of kWh than all other car manufacturers combined,[5] and its lithium-ion battery technology is one of its biggest competitive advantages.

As of the end of 2020, Tesla had 70,757 full-time employees.[6] Tesla's 2021 product line includes the Model S sedan, the Model X sports utility vehicle, the Model Y midsized SUV, and a smaller and more affordable midsized sedan, the Model 3, which is expected to be its mainstream model.[7] After 13 years in the market, Tesla ranks as the world's best-selling plug-in passenger car maker with a market share of 11 percent.[8] In addition, with the opening of the Gigafactories and the acquisition of SolarCity, Tesla also offers a suite of energy products that incorporates solar, storage, and grid services.

Tesla has pursued a high degree of vertical integration in an effort to gain a competitive advantage. For example, it designs and manufactures its own lithium-ion battery in partnership with Panasonic, a Japanese company that is the world's largest automotive lithium-ion battery manufacturer.

In 2020, Tesla reported its first full-year profit, a feat 18 years in the making. Tesla earned $721 million in 2020, in contrast to a loss of $862 million in 2019, nearly $1 billion in 2018, and close to $2 billion in 2017. Tesla announced that they sold 499,550 cars in 2020, with China being the largest market for EVs.[9]

The company has invested heavily in its infrastructure with the construction of its Gigafactory 1 in Reno, Nevada, Gigafactory 2 in Buffalo, New York, Gigafactory 3 in Shanghai, China, Gigafactory 4 in Berlin, Germany (to open in 2021), and Gigafactory 5 in Austin, Texas (to open in 2021).[10]

Tesla believes it could sell more than 800,000 cars in 2021 as it expands output at its Chinese factory and opens another plant in Berlin and in Austin, Texas.[11]

The Cobalt Industry

Cobalt is a critical component in lithium-ion batteries because it provides thermal stability and high energy density. In other words, cobalt allows batteries to operate more safely and for longer periods of time.

Almost all land-based deposits of cobalt are found in combination with nickel or copper. Thus, cobalt is often a byproduct of nickel and copper mining.

In 2020, global production of cobalt was 140,000 metric tons.[12] The EV industry generates most of the demand for cobalt. On average, an electric-vehicle battery requires about 18 pounds of cobalt—more than 1,000 times as much as the quarter-ounce of cobalt used in a smartphone.[13]

Demand for cobalt for use in lithium-ion batteries is expected to double by 2025, and then double again by 2030, according to the London-based cobalt-trading company

Darton Commodities.[14] Cobalt is the most expensive material in the EV battery. Its price peaked at $43/lb in March 2018[15] and is expected to remain relatively high due to the limited supply and the soaring demand.

Cobalt is geographically concentrated in one sliver of territory known as the Copperbelt, which is located in the southern region of the DRC. Sixty-four percent of the world cobalt supply comes from the DRC.[16] This area is at the epicenter of the modern-day "Gold Rush" for cobalt. In fact, the DRC's mining of cobalt has nearly tripled since 2008.[17]

The path that cobalt takes from the moment it is mined in the DRC to its place in the end-product sold to consumers is complicated and nearly impossible to trace. After cobalt is extracted from makeshift tunnels, Congolese miners load up the mineral into bags and then onto bikes, animals, or wagons. These bags are not labeled and offer no information to trace them to a specific mine.[18] It is therefore impossible to determine whether the cobalt was mined by children. The minerals are then transported to the local marketplace, where shops purchase the minerals for extremely low prices. Acting as intermediaries, the shops then resell the minerals to Congo DongFang Mining (CDM). CDM is a subsidiary of the powerful Chinese conglomerate Zhejiang Huayou Cobalt, which processes the cobalt mineral into a usable form for manufacturing. The processed cobalt from Huayou is ultimately sold to battery manufacturers.

Other countries such as Russia, Cuba, Australia, the Philippines, and Canada also produce cobalt, but at a much smaller scale and at a much higher cost.[19]

It is important to note that not only is the production of cobalt highly concentrated (mostly in the DRC) but that the downstream industry (smelter/refinery stage) is also beginning to resemble a monopoly. Zhejiang Huayou Cobalt controls 80 percent of the world's refined cobalt.[20] Essentially, a single Chinese company tightly controls the overwhelming bulk of the refined cobalt available to the EV battery industry, making it impossible for automakers in the United States, South Korea, Japan, and Europe to all secure the amount of cobalt needed should they choose to avoid this supplier. In this regard, the geopolitical environment and trade wars between the United States and China make the global supply chain even more complicated.

Cobalt is not mined just for making batteries. It is also used for other applications. It can be integrated into superalloys to make materials extremely temperature stable as well as corrosion and wear resistant. These materials can then be used in blades for gas turbines and jet aircraft engines, in orthopedic implants and prosthetics, and even in the manufacturing of jewelry. Compounds of cobalt are also used to color porcelain, glass, pottery, and tile due to the blue color it produces.[21] Radioactive Cobalt-60 is used in the treatment of cancer.

The Democratic Republic of the Congo (DRC)

The Democratic Republic of the Congo (DRC) is located in sub-Saharan central Africa. It is the second largest country in Africa in terms of size. Once a Belgian colony exploited for its natural resources, the DRC has been independent for nearly 50 years. The DRC is one of the poorest countries in the world and has suffered from decades of civil war and corruption. Being such a mineral-rich country, the DRC's economy is dependent on mining. In fact, mining is its largest source of export income and accounts for about 80 percent of the DRC's earnings.[22] The DRC ranked near the bottom on the UN Human Development Index in 2015, at 176th out of 188 countries, and it does not fare any better on the anti-corruption index of the NGO Transparency International.[23]

Life is difficult for the 87 million Congolese who have no running water or electricity at home. The average life expectancy is about 60 years and nearly half of the population is under 15 years old. With few formal jobs available, hundreds of thousands of Congolese men, women, and children have been driven to dig their own mines to earn their livelihood. The average Congolese worker earns just $700 a year[24] and families often have to rely on their children to work in the mines. These children are therefore denied an education. While living in desperate poverty, Congolese adults and children also service giant tech and auto companies, whose products they will never be able to own.

At the root of the concerns over cobalt sourcing are the so-called artisanal mines, which are not owned by a mining company but instead are hand-dug by people with few other options for supporting their families. These makeshift mines are not regulated or monitored. The government claims that artisanal mines are only responsible for 20 percent of the cobalt exported from the DRC, but, according to Amnesty International, the true figure is likely much higher.[25] The artisanal mines produce cheaper cobalt than industrial mines. As demand for cobalt rises, new sites are created across the region. It is estimated that there are more than 100,000 cobalt miners that work in these "artisanal" mines, including up to 40,000 children.[26] Individuals working in these mines only earn about $1—$3 per day for the bags of cobalt they sell at the marketplace. Children as young as seven also scavenge for rocks containing cobalt in the discarded byproducts of industrial mines. They then wash and sort the ore before it is sold.[27]

The conditions in the artisanal mines are extremely hazardous. There are typically no industrial tools available for use, no safety gear or equipment for the workers, and no oversight or safety measures. The miners usually work barefoot with no gloves or facemasks, and they work long hours in dangerous conditions. In addition to the health problems caused by inhaling cobalt dust (which can lead to lung disease), the miners also face the risk of their hand-dug tunnels caving in or catching on fire. Deaths and injuries are common among miners. The surrounding communities have also seen a rise in health issues ranging from breathing problems to birth defects, as well as higher levels of water pollution. Exposure to toxic metals is not only created by the highly toxic dust stirred up from the mines but also by the process of washing the minerals, which contaminates the rivers that are also used for irrigation, fishing, and bathing.[28]

Due to ongoing corruption and the endless conflict between local militias, the DRC government lacks the resources or the will to help the miners and their communities. This leaves the artisanal miners to be taken advantage of by the local buyers who pay them a low price for the mineral and then resell it to the Chinese refineries. Then, the industrial mine operators mix the cheap artisanal cobalt with their industrially extracted cobalt, while government officials turn a blind eye to this known, but underground, system. For Tesla and other companies who state that they have a zero-tolerance policy for child labor, it is impossible to determine if their supply chain has actually been involved with child labor.

Tesla's Need for Cobalt

In response to questions about the source of its cobalt, Tesla provided two arguments to support the ethicality of its sourcing practices: (a) Tesla says it uses less cobalt in its EV batteries than its competitors, and (b) Tesla claims that it will only source its cobalt from North America.

Tesla's mastery of battery technology is one of its biggest strengths. Having started more than a decade ago, Tesla is years ahead of the competition. And, it is true that since the development of the Roadster in 2009, Tesla has reduced the amount of cobalt required for its batteries by 59 percent. The Roadster required about 11 kg of cobalt per vehicle, while the 2018 Model 3 only required about 4.5 kg per vehicle.[29] While Tesla has achieved a significant reduction in the amount of cobalt required, there is a limit to how much the use of this key material can be reduced without compromising the performance and stability of the battery. Tesla claims that it is working on slashing the cobalt content of its next generation battery even more, with its ultimate goal being to introduce a cobalt-free battery. However, even if this materializes, this technological breakthrough would still be years away. More importantly, Tesla is transitioning from being a niche player targeting early EV adopters to a more mainstream competitor in the EV industry. Mass-producing electric vehicles will require a massive amount of cobalt, even if less cobalt is used per-battery than the current industry standard.

Moreover, mining industry analysts reject the claim that all the cobalt required by Tesla can be acquired in North America. It is estimated that 7,800 tons of cobalt would be needed to produce 500,000 Model 3s. This quantity is not currently available in North America. And, while there are plans to break ground on new cobalt mines in North America, they are not expected to begin producing the mineral for at least 5 years. In fact, the United States produced 500 metric tons of cobalt in 2019 and an estimated 600 in 2020. Canadian mines produced 3,800 metric tons of cobalt in 2019 and an estimated 3,600 in 2020.[30] Tesla will need to be much more transparent about identifying where its cobalt is sourced. In comparison to the other EV makers who purchase their batteries from Chinese manufacturers, Tesla has a greater responsibility because it actually owns battery manufacturing facilities (Gigafactories) where it produces batteries in a partnership with Panasonic.

Slow Progress Toward a Solution

In response to the investigations done by journalists at the Washington Post, CBS, and other news organizations, and to reports written by international ethics organizations such as Amnesty International, many companies have created initiatives to reduce the use of child labor and to improve the working conditions for cobalt miners. Unfortunately, there is an evident lack of progress resulting from these efforts.

In 2010, the United States Conflict-Minerals Law was passed to "stem the flow of money to Congo's murderous militias, focusing on the artisanal mining of four minerals."[31] However, cobalt was excluded from this law. It was speculated that cobalt was excluded because "any crimp in the cobalt supply chain would devastate" U.S. tech companies as well as military and industrial manufacturing.[32]

In 2012, the Organization for Economic Cooperation and Development (OECD) issued a guideline that "manufacturers should be able to say who their smelters or refiners are and should make public their own assessment of whether the smelter's due diligence practices are adequate in identifying and addressing human rights risks and abuses." Unfortunately, not a single car manufacturer has done this.[33]

In 2016, the Responsible Cobalt Initiative was formed to "help the industry conduct due diligence in line with the OECD standards, and tackle the issue of child labor" in the DRC.[34] This initiative includes Apple, HP, Sony, Samsung SDI (a battery manufacturer), Huawei (a Chinese telecom giant), and Huayou Cobalt (the smelter and refinery who purchases cobalt from artisanal mines). It should be noted that despite the spikes in demand for cobalt for the EV industry, no car manufacturer has joined this initiative.

Meanwhile, the DRC government announced that it would take action to eliminate child labor in its mines by 2025 and appealed for international help. However, because previous government promises have come to nothing, most watchdog organizations remain skeptical.

To complicate things even more, one solution that could prove disastrous for the people of the DRC would be for these companies to simply stop buying from the artisanal mines. This would devastate the already impoverished communities that rely on mining.

Many companies have their own responses to questions about their cobalt supply, with Apple claiming to have cut ties with the largest artisanal cobalt supplier, Microsoft stating that it has partnered with nongovernmental organizations to eliminate child labor, and Samsung announcing that it is undertaking the effort of mapping its supply chain. Tesla has responded by stating that it performs audits; however, few details have been shared regarding the results of these audits.[35] Thus, many questions regarding the sourcing of cobalt remain for Tesla and other users of this important mineral.

Questions for Discussion

1. What is the ethical dilemma faced by Tesla's customer base?
2. When conducting a stakeholder analysis, what obligations does Tesla have to each of its key stakeholders? What influence, if any, do these stakeholders have over Tesla, and how likely are they to exert this influence?
3. Is there any way that Tesla can ensure the cobalt it needs to manufacture its electric cars is sourced ethically and in a socially responsible manner? If so, how can this be accomplished?
4. Virtually everyone agrees that child labor and dangerous working conditions for adults represent work practices that should be avoided. However, shutting down the artisanal mines would devastate already impoverished communities and families. How should these conflicting concerns be addressed and balanced?

Endnotes

1. Angela Chen, "Elon Musk Wants Cobalt out of His Batteries – Here's Why That's a Challenge," *The Verge*, June 21, 2018, https://www.theverge .com/2018/6/21/17488626/elon-musk-cobalt-electric -vehicle-battery-science. Accessed June 14, 2021.
2. Antonio Cascais, "Child Labor Still Rife in Democratic Republic of Congo", *DW*, June 11, 2017, https://www.dw.com/en/child-labor-still -rife-in-democratic-republic-of-congo/a-39194724. Accessed June 14, 2021.
3. *Tesla Inc. Website*, https://www.tesla.com/about. Accessed June 14, 2021.
4. *Tesla Inc. Website*, https://www.tesla.com/about. Accessed June 14, 2021.
5. *Tesla Inc. Website*, https://www.tesla.com /gigafactory. Accessed June 16, 2021.
6. *Statista*, "Number of Tesla employees from July 2010 to December 2020," https://www.statista .com/statistics/314768/number-of-tesla-employees/. Accessed June 14, 2021.
7. *Tesla Inc. Website*, https://www.tesla.com/about. Accessed June 14, 2021.
8. Grace Kay, "Tesla's Global Market Share Fell to Its Lowest Level in over 2 years as Electric Car Competition Heats up," *Business Insider*, June 3, 2021,https://www.businessinsider.com/tesla -market-share-april-lowest-level-2-years-increased -competition-2021-6#:~:text=Tesla%20stock%20 surged%20in%202020,loss%20has%20been%20 Ford's%20gain.Accessed June 14, 2021.
9. Neal E. Boudette, "Tesla Has First Profitable Year, But Competition Is Growing," *The New York Times*, January 7, 2021, https://www.nytimes .com/2021/01/27/business/tesla-earnings.html. Accessed June 14, 2021.
10. Scooter Doll, "Tesla's Factory Locations: Where They Are and Would Soon Be," *Electrec*, January 12, 2021, https://electrek.co/2021/01/12/tesla-factory -locations-where-they-are-and-could-soon-be/. Accessed June 14, 2021.

11. Neal E. Boudette, "Tesla Has First Profitable Year, But Competition Is Growing," *The New York Times*, January 7, 2021, https://www.nytimes .com/2021/01/27/business/tesla-earnings.html. Accessed June 14, 2021.

12. *Statista*, "Worldwide Mine Production of Cobalt from 2008 to 2020," https://www.statista.com /statistics/339759/global-cobalt-mine-production /#:~:text=In%202020%2C%20total%20worldwide %20mine,cobalt%20totaled%20140%2C000%20 metric%20tons. Accessed June 14, 2021.

13. Vivienne Watt, "Blood, Sweat, and Batteries," *Forbes*, August 23, 2018, http://fortune.com /longform/blood-sweat-and-batteries/. Accessed June 14, 2021.

14. Vivienne Watt, "Blood, Sweat, and Batteries," *Forbes*, August 23, 2018, http://fortune.com /longform/blood-sweat-and-batteries/. Accessed June 14, 2021.

15. Nick Martin, "Glencore's Closure of Congolese Cobalt Mine Could Backfire", *DW*, August 20, 2019, https://www.dw.com/en/glencores-closure-of -congolese-cobalt-mine-could-backfire/a-50101698. Accessed June 14, 2021.

16. Angela Chen, "Elon Musk Wants Cobalt out of His Batteries – Here's Why That's a Challenge", *The Verge*, June 21, 2018, https://www.theverge.com /2018/6/21/17488626/elon-musk-cobalt-electric -vehicle-battery-science. Accessed June 14, 2021.

17. M. Garside, "Cobalt – Mine Production by Major Countries 2010-2020," Statista, February 16, 2021, https://www.statista.com/statistics/264928/cobalt -mine-production-by-country/. Accessed June 15, 2021.

18. Jacob Kushner, "In Congo, Lure of Quick Cash Turns Farmers into Miners," *North Country Public Radio*, March 28, 2013, https://www .northcountrypublicradio.org/news/npr/175577518 /www.cloudsplitter.org. Accessed June 14, 2021.

19. *Statista*, "Major Countries in Worldwide Cobalt Mine Production from 2010 to 2020," https://www .statista.com/statistics/264928/cobalt-mine -production-by-country/. Accessed June 15, 2021.

20. Jack Farchy and Hayley Warren, "China Has a Secret Weapon in the Race to Dominate Electric Cars," *Bloomberg*, December 2, 2018, https:// www.bloomberg.com/graphics/2018-china-cobalt/. Accessed June 14, 2021.

21. M. Garside, "Cobalt – Mine Production by Major Countries 2010-2020," Statista, February 16, 2021, https://www.statista.com/statistics/264928/cobalt -mine-production-by-country/. Accessed June 15, 2021.

22. M. Garside, "Cobalt – Mine Production by Major Countries 2010-2020," Statista, February 16, 2021, https://www.statista.com/statistics/264928/cobalt-mine -production-by-country/. Accessed June 15, 2021.

23. Vivienne Watt, "Blood, Sweat, and Batteries," *Forbes*, August 23, 2018, http://fortune.com /longform/blood-sweat-and-batteries/. Accessed June 14, 2021.

24. Vivienne Watt, "Blood, Sweat, and Batteries," *Forbes*, August 23, 2018, http://fortune.com /longform/blood-sweat-and-batteries/. Accessed June 14, 2021.

25. *Amnesty International*, "This is What We Die For: Human Rights Abuses in the DRC Power the Global Trade in Cobalt," January 19, 2016, https://www .amnesty.org/en/documents/afr62/3183/2016/en/. Accessed June 14, 2021.

26. Antonio Cascais, "Child Labor Still Rife in Democratic Republic of Congo," *DW*, June 11, 2017, https://www.dw.com/en/child-labor-still -rife-in-democratic-republic-of-congo/a-39194724. Accessed June 14, 2021.

27. *Amnesty International*, "This Is What We Die For: Human Rights Abuses in the DRC Power the Global Trade in Cobalt" , January 19, 2016, https://www .amnesty.org/en/documents/afr62/3183/2016/en/. Accessed June 14, 2021.

28. Annie Kelly, "Pollution Causing Birth Defect in Children of DRC Cobalt Miners – Study," *The Guardian*, May 6, 2020, https://www .theguardian.com/global-development/2020 /may/06/pollution-causing-birth-defects-in -children-of-drc-cobalt-miners-study. Accessed June 14, 2021.

29. Simon Alvarez, "Tesla Is Leading Electric Car Batteries Away from Cobalt Mining Industry," *Teslarati*, May 7, 2018, https://www.teslarati .com/tesla-battery-tech-cobalt-mining-industry/. Accessed June 14, 2021.

30. *Statista*, "Major Countries in Worldwide Cobalt Mine Production from 2010 to 2020," https://www .statista.com/statistics/264928/cobalt-mine -production-by-country/. Accessed June 15, 2021.

31. Todd C. Frankel, "The Cobalt Pipeline: Tracing the Path from Deadly Hand-Dug Mines in Congo to Consumers' Phones and Laptops," *The Washington Post*, September 30, 2016, https://www .washingtonpost.com/graphics/business/batteries /congo-cobalt-mining-for-lithium-ion-battery/. Accessed June 14, 2021.

32. Katherine Martinko, "What You Should Know about the Cobalt in Your Smartphone," *Treehugger*, May 27, 2020, https://www.treehugger.com /corporate-responsibility/what-you-should-know -about-cobalt-your-smartphone.html. Accessed June 14, 2021.

33. Mark Dummett, "The Dark Side of Electric Cars: Exploitative Labor Practices," Amnesty International, September 29, 2017, https://www .amnesty.org/en/latest/news/2017/09/the-dark -side-of-electric-cars-exploitative-labor-practices/. Accessed June 14, 2021.

34. Mark Dummett, "The Dark Side of Electric Cars: Exploitative Labor Practices," Amnesty International, September 29, 2017, https://www .amnesty.org/en/latest/news/2017/09/the-dark -side-of-electric-cars-exploitative-labor-practices/. Accessed June 14, 2021.

35. *Amnesty International*, "This is What We Die For: Human Rights Abuses in the DRC Power the Global Trade in Cobalt," January 19, 2016, https://www .amnestyusa.org/files/this_what_we_die_for_-_ report.pdf. Accessed June 14, 2021.

Case 18

Coke and Pepsi in India: Water, Issues, and Crisis Management*

There is nothing new about multinational corporations (MNCs) facing challenges as they do business around the world, especially in developing nations or emerging markets. Royal Dutch Shell had to greatly reduce its production of oil in Nigeria due to guerrilla attacks on its pipelines. Cargill was forced to shut down its soy-processing plant in Brazil because of the claim that it was contributing to the destruction of the Amazon rainforest. Tribesmen in Botswana accused De Beers of pushing them off their land to make way for diamond mines.[1] Google was kicked out of China only to be later restored. Global business today is not for the faint-hearted.

It should not come as a surprise, therefore, that MNC giants such as Coca-Cola and PepsiCo—highly visible, multibillion-dollar corporations with well-known, iconic brands around the world—would encounter challenges in the creation and distribution of their products in some countries. After all, soft drinks are viewed as discretionary and sometimes luxurious products when compared to the staples of life that are often scarce in developing countries. One of those scarce staples is water. Many observers think a shortage of water is the next burgeoning global resource crisis.[2]

Whether it is called an issue, an ethics challenge, or a scandal, the situation confronting both Coke and Pepsi in India, beginning in 2003, richly illustrates the many complex and varied social challenges companies face once they decide to embark on another country's shores. Their experiences in India may predict other issues they may eventually face elsewhere or trials other companies might face as well. With a billion-plus people and an expanding economy, and with markets stagnating in many Western countries, India, along with China and Russia, represent immense opportunities for growth for virtually all businesses. Hence, these companies cannot afford to ignore these burgeoning markets.

Initial Allegations

Coke and Pepsi's serious problems in India began in 2003. In that year, India's Center for Science and Environment (CSE), an independent public interest group, made allegations that tests they had conducted revealed dangerously high levels of pesticide residue in the soft drinks being sold all over India. The director of CSE, Sunita Narain, stated that such residues could cause cancer and birth defects as well as harm nervous and immune systems if the products were consumed over long periods of time.[3] Further, CSE stated that the pesticide levels in Coke's and Pepsi's drinks were much higher than that permitted by European Union standards. On one occasion, Narain accused Pepsi and Coke of pushing products that they wouldn't dare sell at home.[4]

In addition to the alleged pesticides in the soft drinks, another special interest group, India Resource Center (IRC), accused the companies of over-consuming scarce water and polluting water sources due to their operations in India.[5] IRC intensely criticized the companies, especially Coca-Cola, by detailing a number of different "water woes" experienced by different cities and regions of the country. IRC's allegations even more broadly accused the companies of water exploitation and of controlling natural resources, and thus communities. Examples frequently cited were the impact of Coke's operations in the communities of Kerala and Mehdiganj.[6]

In 2004, IRC continued its "Campaign to Hold Coca-Cola Accountable" by asserting that communities across India were under assault by Coke's practices. Among the continuing allegations were communities' experiencing severe water shortages around Coke's bottling plants, significant depletion of the water table, strange water tastes and smells, and pollution of groundwater as well as soil. IRC said that in one community Coke was distributing its solid waste to farmers as fertilizer and that tests conducted found cadmium and lead in the waste, thus making it toxic waste. And the accusation of high levels of pesticides continued. According to IRC, the Parliament of India banned the sale of Coca-Cola in its cafeteria.[7] In December 2004, India's Supreme Court ordered Coke and Pepsi to put warning labels on their products. This caused a serious slide in sales for the next several years.[8]

Sunita Narain

One major reason that Indian consumers and politicians took seriously the allegations of both CSE and IRC was CSE's director, Sunita Narain—a well-known environmental activist in New Delhi. Narain was born into a family of freedom fighters whose support of Mahatma Gandhi goes back to the days when Gandhi was pushing for independence in India more than 60 years ago. She took up environmental causes in high school. One major cause she adopted was to stop developers from cutting down trees. Her quest was to save India from the ravages of industrialization. She became the director of CSE in 2002.[9]

Narain strongly holds forth on the topic of MNCs exploiting the natural resources of developing countries, especially India. She manifests an alarmist tone that tends toward the end-is-near level of fervency. She is skilled at getting media attention. In 2005, she won the Stockholm Water Prize, one of a number of environmental accolades she has received.[10] In addition, she has been successful in taking advantage of India's general suspicion of huge MNCs, dating back to its tragic Bhopal gas leak in 1984. Narain claims she does not intend to hurt companies but only to spur the country to pass stricter regulations.[11]

*This case was prepared by Archie B. Carroll, University of Georgia. Updated and revised in 2021.

Sacred Water

Coke's and Pepsi's problems in India have been complicated by the fact that water carries considerable significance in India. We are often told about cultural knowledge we should have before doing business in other countries. Water is one of those issues in India. Although the country does not have the best water in the world, due to poor sewage, pollution, and pesticide use, according to UN sources, water carries an almost-spiritual meaning to Indians. Bathing is viewed by many of them to be a sacred act, and tradition for some residents holds that one's death is not properly noted until one's ashes are scattered in the Ganges River. In one major poll, Indians revealed that drinking water was one of their major life activities to improve their well-being.[12] Indians' sensitivity to the subject of water has undoubtedly played a role in the public's reactions to the allegations.

Coke's and Pepsi's Early Responses

Initially, Coke and Pepsi denied the allegations of CSE and IRC, primarily through the media. It was observed that their response was limited at best as they got caught up in the technical details of the tests. Coke conducted its own tests, the conclusion of which was that their drinks met demanding European standards.[13] Over the next several years the debate continued as the companies questioned the studies and conducted studies of their own. The companies also pointed out that other beverages and foods in the Indian food supply, and indeed water, had trace pesticide levels in it, and they sought to deflect the issue in this manner.

The IRC also attacked Coke and Pepsi for not taking the crisis seriously. They argued that the companies were "destroying lives, livelihoods, and communities" while viewing the problems in India as "public relations" problems that they could "spin" away. IRC pointed out that Coca-Cola had hired a new public relations firm to help them build a new image in India, rather than addressing the real issues. IRC also pointed out that Coke had just increased its marketing budget by a sizable amount in India. IRC then laid out the steps it felt Coke should take to effectively address its problems.[14]

Pesticide Residue and Partial Bans

The controversy flared up again in 2006 when the CSE issued a new study. The new test results showed that 57 samples from 11 Coke and Pepsi brands contained pesticide residue levels 24 times higher than the maximum allowed by the Indian government. Public response was swift. Seven of India's 28 states imposed partial bans on the two companies, and the Indian state of Kerala banned the drinks completely. Officials there ignored a later court ruling reversing the ban.[15] During 2006, the United Kingdom's Central Science Laboratory questioned the CSE findings. Coca-Cola sought a meeting with CSE that was denied. Also that year, India's Union Health Ministry rejected the CSE study as "inconclusive."

The Companies Ratchet up Their Responses

As a result of the second major flurry of studies and allegations, both Coke and Pepsi ratcheted up their responses, sometimes acting together, sometimes taking independent action. They responded almost like different companies than they were before. Perhaps they finally reckoned this issue was not going to go away and had to be addressed more forcefully.

Coke's Response

Coke started with a more aggressive marketing campaign. It ran three rounds of newspaper ads refuting the new study. The ads appeared in the form of a letter from more than 50 of India's company-owned and franchised Coke bottlers, claiming that their products were safe. Letters with a similar message went out to retailers and stickers were pressed onto drink coolers, declaring that Coke was "safety guaranteed." Coke also hired researchers to talk to consumers and opinion leaders to find out what exactly they believed about the allegations and what the company needed to do to convince them the allegations were false.[16]

Based on its research findings, Coke created a TV ad campaign that featured testimonials by well-respected celebrities. One of the ads featured Aamir Khan, a popular movie star, as he toured one of Coke's plants. He told the people that the product was safe and that if they wanted to see for themselves, they could personally do so. In August and September 2006, more than 4,000 people took him up on his offer and toured the plants. Opening up the plants sent the message that the company had nothing to hide, and this was very persuasive.[17]

The TV ads, which were targeted toward the mass audience, were followed by giant posters with movie star Khan's picture drinking a Coke. These posters appeared in public places such as bus stops. In addition, other ads were targeted toward adult women and housewives, who make the majority of the food-purchasing decisions. One teenager was especially impressed with Khan's ads because she knew he was selective about which movies he appeared in and that he wouldn't take a position like this if it wasn't appropriate.[18]

In a later interview, Coke's then-CEO Neville Isdell said he thought the company's response during the second wave of controversy was the key reason the company began turning things around. After the 2003 episode, the company changed management in India to address many of the problems, both real and imagined. The new management team was especially concerned about how it would handle its next public relations crisis. Weeks later, in December 2006, India's Health Ministry said that both Coke's and Pepsi's beverages tested in three different labs contained little or no pesticide residue.

Pepsi's Response

Pepsi's response was similar to Coke's. Pepsi decided to go straight to the Indian media and try to build relationships there. Company representatives met with editorial boards, presented the company's own data in press conferences, and also ran TV commercials. Pepsi's commercials featured the then-president of PepsiCo India, Rajeev Bakshi, shown walking through a polished Pepsi laboratory.[19]

In addition, Pepsi increased its efforts to cut down on water usage in its plants. Employees in the plants were organized into teams and used Japanese-inspired *kaizens*, and suggested improvements, to bring waste under control. The company also employed lobbying of the local government.

Indra Nooyi becomes CEO. Pepsi had an advantage in rebuilding its relationships in India, because in October 2006, an Indian-born woman, Indra Nooyi, was selected to be CEO of the multinational corporation. It is not known whether Pepsi's problems in India were in any way related to her being chosen CEO, but it definitely helped. After graduating from the prestigious Indian Institute of Management, and later Yale University, Nooyi worked her way up the hierarchy at PepsiCo before being singled out for the top position.[20] She previously held positions at the Boston Consulting Group, Motorola, and ABB Group.

Prior to becoming CEO, Nooyi had a number of successes in Pepsi and became the company's chief strategist. She was said to have a perceptive business sense and an irreverent personal style. One of Nooyi's first decisions was to take a trip to India in December 2006. While there, she spoke broadly about Pepsi's programs to improve water and the environment. The Indian media loved her, beaming with pride, and covered her tour positively as she shared her own heartwarming memories of her life growing up in India. She received considerable praise. Not surprisingly, Pepsi's sales started moving upward.[21]

While all the criticism of Coke and Pepsi was going on, roughly from 2003 to 2006, both companies were pursuing corporate social responsibility (CSR) initiatives in India, many of them related to improving water resources for communities, while the conflict was center stage.

Hostility Toward MNCs?

Because of all the conflicting studies and the stridency of CSE and IRC, one has to wonder what was going on in India to cause this developing country to so severely criticize giant MNCs such as Coke and Pepsi. Many developing countries would be doing all they could to appease these companies. It was speculated by a number of different observers that what was at work was a form of backlash against huge MNCs that come into countries and consume natural resources.[22] Why were these groups so hostile toward the companies? Was it really pesticides in the water and abuse of natural resources? Or was it environmental interest groups using every opportunity to bash large corporations on issues sensitive to the people? Were CSE and IRC strategically making an example of these two hugely successful companies and trying to put them in their place?

Late in 2006, an interesting commentary appeared in *BusinessWeek* exploring the topic of what has been going on in India with respect to Coke and Pepsi.[23] This commentary argued that the companies may have been singled out because they are foreign-owned. It appears that no Indian soft drink companies were singled out for pesticide testing, though many people believe pesticide levels were even higher in Indian milk and bottled tea. It was pointed out that pesticide residues are present in most of India's ground-water, and the government has ignored or has been slow to move on the problem. The commentary went on to observe that Coke and Pepsi have together invested $2 billion in India over the years and have generated 12,500 jobs and support more than 200,000 indirectly through their purchases of Indian-made products including sugar, packing materials, and shipping services.[24]

Continuing Protests, Renewed Priorities, and Strategies

Eventually, the open conflict settled down and sales took an upturn for both companies, but the issue lingered. In June 2007, the IRC continued its attacks on Coca-Cola. It accused the company of "greenwashing" its image in India.[25] The IRC staged a major protest at the new Coke Museum in Atlanta on June 30, 2007, questioning the company's human rights and environmental abuses. They erected a 20-foot banner that read "Coca-Cola Destroys Lives, Livelihoods, Communities" in front of the New World of Coke that opened in May 2007. Amit Srivastava of the IRC was quoted as saying, "This World of Coke Museum is a fairy tale land and the real side of Coke is littered with abuses." A representative of the National Alliance of People's Movements, a large coalition of grassroots movements in India, said, "The museum is a shameful attempt by the Coca-Cola Company to hide its crimes."[26]

The protestations by these groups apparently motivated other groups to take action against Coke. It was reported that United Students Against Sweatshops also staged a "die-in" around one of Coke's bottling facilities in India. And more than 20 colleges and universities in the United States, Canada, and the United Kingdom removed Coca-Cola from campuses because of student-led initiatives to put pressure on the company. In addition, the protests in Atlanta were endorsed by a host of groups that participated in the U.S. Social Forum.[27]

Coke's Renewed Priorities

Undaunted, Coca-Cola continued its initiatives to improve the situation in India and around the world. Coke faces water problems around the world because it is the key natural resource that goes into its products. The company had 70 clean-water projects in 40 countries aimed at boosting local economies. It was observed that these efforts were part of a broader strategy on the part of CEO Neville Isdell to build Coke's image as a local benefactor and a global diplomat.[28]

The criticism of Coke has been most severe in India. CEO Isdell admitted that the company's experience in India taught some humbling lessons. Isdell, who took over the company after the crisis had begun, said, "It was very clear that we had not connected with the communities in the way we needed to." He indicated that the company has now made "water stewardship" a strategic priority, and in a recent 10-K securities filing had listed a shortage of clean water as a strategic risk.[29] In August 2007, Coca-Cola India unveiled its "5-Pillar" growth strategy to strengthen its bonds with India. Coke's new strategy focuses on the pillars of People, Planet, Portfolio, Partners, and Performance. The company also announced a series of initiatives under each of the five pillars and its "Little Drops of Joy" proposal, which tried to reinforce the company's connection with stakeholders in India.[30]

Though most of the attention focused on Coca-Cola, it should also be noted that Pepsi continued taking steps on a number of projects as well. One novel initiative was that the company began gathering rainwater in excavated lakes and ponds and on the rooftops of its bottling plants in India. The company sponsored other community water projects as well.[31]

Indian Beverage Association Formed

Though Coke and Pepsi are typically fighting each other in their longstanding "cola wars," due to their mutual problems in India they formed the Indian Beverage Association (IBA) in the summer of 2010. Other beverage companies were quick to join.[32] Because of continuous hostility from regulators and activist groups, the two companies decided that a joint effort to address issues might make sense.[33]

The IBA was formed to address the issues related to the government of Kerala's charge that Coke is polluting the groundwater in the state and other taxation issues that affect both companies. Their issues had been ongoing, but Kerala's government decided to form a tribunal against Coca-Cola, seeking $48 million in compensation claims for allegedly causing pollution and depleting the groundwater level there. Another important issue was the value added tax (VAT) by the Delhi government. The IBA brought in other bottlers and packaging firms that had similar interests and issues in India.[34]

Water Issues Never Go Away

Coke's and Pepsi's issues in India, especially involving the issue of water, never seem to go away. Beginning in fall 2011, the India Resource Center (IRC) alleged that Pepsico's water claims had been "deception with a purpose."[35] According to the IRC, Pepsico's claims of achieving "positive water balance" were misleading and did not stand up to scrutiny. IRC accused that PepsiCo (1) severely underestimates the amount of water it uses in India, (2) has flawed water balance accounting techniques, (3) just doesn't get it that water issues are local issues in India, (4) has one in four of its plants operating in a water stressed area, and (5) lacks commitment to local water stewardship in India.[36]

In 2012–2013, the IRC's campaigns against Coca-Cola continued as well. According to IRC, 15 village councils (panchayats) called on their government to reject Coca-Cola's application for expansion because it would further worsen the water conditions in the area. They also called for an end to Coca-Cola's groundwater extraction in Mehdiganj in Varanasi district in India. The 15 village councils are located within a five-kilometer radius of the Coca-Cola bottling plant and are affected by Coca-Cola's bottling operations.[37] On a continuing basis, the IRC has been extremely activist toward Coca-Cola and continues its "Campaign to Hold Coca-Cola Accountable."[38]

In February 2016, Coke announced that it was closing a bottling plant in north India. Activists campaigning against the plant said that the facility was depleting groundwater and undermining agriculture in the area.[39] The opposition to Coke was led by the Indian Resource Center and several other activist groups that had been targeting the company for more than a decade. One activist claimed that "Coke has drained us of water." He went on to say that "water meant for poor farmers and their fields was time and again diverted to the factory."[40] A Coca-Cola spokesperson in India said that the plant only uses a miniscule share of the water there and that it was using less than one percent of the area's water.[41] In spite of the challenges, Coca-Cola said it planned to inject $5 billion into the country by the year 2020.[42] In May 2016, PepsiCo was put on notice that it is contributing to the water shortage in parts of India, and the company is being asked to stop its operations for some months until the situation improves.[43]

In 2021, it was announced that cola giants Coke and Pepsi were unlikely to reclaim their pre-pandemic levels of sales. Lockdowns and restrictions have taken their toll on beverage sales and it may be some time before a full recovery.[44] In spite of this downturn, bottlers of Pepsi and Coke command a combined market share of 80 percent of India's non-alcoholic beverage sales. Recovery is expected as the pace of vaccinations picks up.[45]

Perhaps in part due to its experiences in India, Coca-Cola announced in March 2021 its 2030 water security strategy. This is a global framework focusing on regenerative water used in bottling operations, improved watershed health, and enhanced community water resilience.[46] In its 2020 Sustainability Report, Pepsi announced that water would be one of its primary focus areas.[47] Pepsi is focused on improving operational and agricultural water-use efficiency, local water replenishment in high water risk areas, and advocacy for smart water policies and regulations and best practices. It stated that by 2025 all its high-risk water facilities would meet the Alliance for Water Stewardship standard.

Questions for Discussion

1. Identify the ongoing issues in this case with respect to global business ethics, crisis management, and stakeholder management. Rank these in terms of their priorities for Coca-Cola and for PepsiCo.

2. Assess the corporate social responsibility (CSR) of Coke and Pepsi in India.

3. Are these companies ignoring their responsibilities in India, or is something else at work?

4. Did these companies mistakenly view their issues as just public relations rather than legitimate crises?

5. Why does it seem that Coke has become a larger and more frequent target than Pepsi in India? Did having an Indian-born CEO help Pepsi's case?

6. By their sales, it appears both companies are popular with the people. If so, what is driving the activist groups? Are they just going after "deep pockets"?

7. How do companies defend themselves against the nonstop allegations of activist groups that have made them a permanent target? Is any form of stakeholder management workable?

8. IRC seems to have made it its life's work to defeat Coca-Cola. Is IRC an interest group that has just gone too far? How should Coke deal with IRC?

9. What lessons do Coke's and Pepsi's experiences in India present for multinationals in their global business and society relationships? Enumerate three to five lessons and give examples from the case to document them.

Endnotes

1. "Beyond India, More Battles," *BusinessWeek* (June 11, 2007), 52.
2. Annie Chernich, "Is Water the Next Resource Crisis?" PRI, https://www.pri.org/stories/2016-02-18/water-next-resource-crisis. Accessed July 6, 2021.
3. Duane D. Stanford, "Coke's PR Offensive in India Pays Off," *Atlanta Journal Constitution* (December 3, 2006), D1, D9.
4. Diane Brady, "Pepsi: Repairing a Poisoned Reputation in India," *Bloomberg BusinessWeek* (June 11, 2007), 50, https://www.bloomberg.com/news/articles/2007-05-31/pepsi-repairing-a-poisoned-reputation-in-indiabusinessweek-business-news-stock-market-and-financial-advice. Accessed July 2, 2021.
5. Amit Srivastava, "Communities Reject Coca-Cola in India," *India Resource Center* (July 10, 2003), https://www.corpwatch.org/article/communities-reject-coca-cola-india#:~:text=Coca%2DCola%20is%20in%20trouble%20in%20India.&text=The%20communities%20are%20left%20thirsting,the%20scarce%20water%20that%20remains.Accessed July 2, 2021.
6. Ibid.
7. Ibid.
8. Stanford, D1.
9. Diane Brady, 2007, Ibid. 46-54.
10. Ibid.
11. Sunita Narain, *Time*, April 21, 2016, https://time.com/collection-post/4299642/sunita-narain-2016-time-100/. Accessed July 2, 2021.
12. Brady, 50.
13. Stanford, D9.
14. "Campaign to Hold Coca-Cola Accountable: Coca-Cola Crisis in India," *India Resource Center*, http://www.indiaresource.org/campaigns/coke/. Accessed July 2, 2021.
15. Stanford, D9.
16. Stanford, D9.
17. Ibid.
18. Ibid.
19. Brady, 54.
20. Ibid., 46.
21. Ibid., 54.
22. Ibid., 48.
23. Brian Bremner and Nandini Lakshman, with Diane Brady, "Commentary India: Behind the Scare over Pesticides in Pepsi and Coke," Bloomberg *Businessweek* (September 4, 2006), 43, https://www.bloomberg.com/news/articles/2006-09-03/commentary-india-behind-the-scare-over-pesticides-in-pepsi-and-coke. Accessed July 2, 2021.
24. Ibid.
25. Christopher Zara, "Coca-Cola Company Busted for Greenwashing: PlantBottle Marketing Exaggerated Environmental Report, Consumer Report," *International Business Times*, September 3, 2013, https://www.ibtimes.com/coca-cola-company-ko-busted-greenwashing-plantbottle-marketing-exaggerated-1402409. Accessed July 2, 2021.
26. India Resource Center, "Major Protest at Coke Museum in Atlanta" (June 30, 2007), http://www.indiaresource.org/news/2007/1049.html. Accessed July 2, 2021.
27. Ibid.
28. Betsy McKay, "Why Coke Aims to Slake Global Thirst for Safe Water," *The Wall Street Journal* (March 15), 2007, https://www.wsj.com/articles/SB117392644638537761. Accessed July 2, 2021.
29. Ibid.
30. Ibid.
31. McKay.
32. India Beverage Association, http://www.in-beverage.org/. Accessed July 2, 2021.
33. Anuradha Shukla, "Taxation Issues Bring Arch Rivals Coke and Pepsi on the Same Platform," *India Today*, July 6, 2010, https://www.indiatoday.in/business/india/story/taxation-issues-bring-archrivals-coke-pepsi-on-same-platform-78120-2010-07-06. Accessed July 2, 2021.
34. Ibid.
35. India Resource Center, "November 30, 2011, "Deception with Purpose: Pepsico's Water Claims in India," http://www.indiaresource.org/news/2011/pepsipositivewater.html. Accessed July 2, 2021.
36. Ibid.
37. India Resource Center, "Coca Cola Crisis in India," http://www.indiaresource.org/campaigns/coke/index.html. Accessed July 2, 2021.
38. Ibid.
39. Preetika Rana, "Coca-Cola Closes Plant in India," *Wall Street Journal*, February 10, 2016, https://www.wsj.com/articles/coca-cola-closes-plant-in-india-1455122537#:~:text=Preetika%20Rana,-Biography&text=NEW%20

DELHI%E2%80%94Coca%2DCola%20 Co,world's%20second%2Dmost%20populous%20 nation. Accessed July 2, 2021.

40. Ibid.
41. Ibid.
42. Ibid.
43. *The Economic Times*, "After Coke, Palakaad Now Wants PepsiCo to Shut Its Plant Due to Water Crisis," https://economictimes.indiatimes.com /industry/cons-products/food/after-coke-palakkad -now-wants-pepsico-to-shut-its-plant-due-to-water -crisis/articleshow/52204403.cms?from=mdr. Accessed July 2, 2021.
44. John Sarkar, "Covid-19 Second Wave Takes Fizz Out of Coke and Pepsico's India Business,"

The Times of India, May 21, 2021, https://timesofindia .indiatimes.com/business/india-business/covid-19 -second-wave-takes-fizz-out-of-coke-and-pepsicos -india-business/articleshow/82832651.cms. Accessed July 2, 2021.

45. Ibid.
46. Coca-Cola Company, "Coca-Cola Unveils Its 2030 Water Security Strategy," March 22, 2021, https:// www.coca-colacompany.com/news/2030-water -security-strategy. Accessed July 2, 2021.
47. Pepsico, "2020 Sustainability Report," https:// www.pepsico.com/docs/album/sustainability -report/2020-csr/2020_sustainability_report _summary.pdf?sfvrsn=2b435ae0_6. Accessed July 2, 2021.

Case 19

An Ethical Dilemma for Chiquita in Colombia*

Assume that you are the top executive for a firm doing business in Colombia, South America. If a known terrorist group threatens to kill your employees unless you pay extortion money, should the company pay it?

If you answer "no," how would you respond to the family of an employee who is later killed by the terrorist group?

If you answer "yes," how would you respond to the family of an innocent citizen who is killed by a bomb your money funded?[1]

Background

In many parts of the world, doing business is a dangerous proposition. Such has been the case in the country of Colombia in South America, particularly leading up to 2017, when civil conflict between the government and the leaders of the Revolutionary Armed Forces of Colombia (known as FARC) reached levels of terrifying violence, kidnappings, and acts of terror. The danger has been described in the following way: "In Colombia's notoriously lawless countryside, narco-terrorists ran roughshod over the forces of law and order—or collaborated with them in a mutual game of shakedowns, kidnappings, and murders."[2]

Foreign companies that choose to do business in many parts of the world are often considered easy targets for corruption because they have resources, they care about their employees, and many of them have been willing to

negotiate with terrorists and just consider it one of the costs of doing business. Security in many of these countries is available only at a price.[3]

Formerly known as United Fruit Company and then United Brands, Chiquita Brands International, headquartered in Charlotte, North Carolina, has faced the kind of situation described above. Today, Chiquita is a global food company that markets and distributes bananas and pineapples and packaged salads sold under the Fresh Express and other brand names. Chiquita employs more than 18,000 employees across 70 countries in six different continents, and their 2020 sales were over $730 million.[4] The company has strong brand-name recognition and premium positioning in the United States and Europe, and it operates with-solid logistics and an efficient supply chain.[5]

Buying Security: Protecting Its Employees

According to then-CEO Fernando Aguirre, Chiquita started making payments to paramilitary groups in Colombia beginning in 1997 and extending into 2004. The payments came to a total of about $1.7 million. The company felt it was forced to make these payments because the lives of its employees were at stake.[6] During the period 2001–2004, the company was making payments to the terrorist group United Self-Defense Forces of Colombia (AUC). AUC was the group's Spanish acronym, by which the group was primarily known. A major complication during this period was that the U.S. government had declared AUC to be a specially designated terrorist organization, making it illegal to provide funds for them, and the Bush administration had vowed to go after any company that funded terrorist groups.[7]

_____

*This case was originally written by Archie B. Carroll, University of Georgia, and revised and updated by Jill A. Brown, Bentley University, in 2021.

Chiquita Turns Itself In

Chiquita turned itself in and reported to the government that it had made the payments to AUC during the years indicated.

In 2007, CEO Fernando Aguirre released a public statement outlining what he called "an excruciating dilemma between life and law."[8] Following are some excerpts from his statement:

- In February 2003, senior management of Chiquita Brands International learned that protection payments the company had been making to paramilitary groups in Colombia to keep our workers safe from the violence committed by those groups were illegal under U.S. law.
- The company had operated in Colombia for nearly a century, generating 4,400 direct and an additional 8,000 indirect jobs. We contributed almost $70 million annually to the Colombian economy in the form of capital expenditures, payroll, taxes, social security, pensions, and local purchases of goods and services.
- However, during the 1990s, it became increasingly difficult to protect our workforce. Among the hundreds of documented attacks by left- and right-wing paramilitaries were the 1995 massacre of 28 innocent Chiquita employees who were ambushed on a bus on their way to work, and the 1998 assassination of two more of our workers on a farm while their colleagues were forced to watch.
- Despite the harsh realities on the ground, the discovery that our payments were violating U.S. law created a dilemma of more than theoretical proportions for us: the company could stop making the payments, complying with the law but putting the lives of our workers in immediate jeopardy; or we could keep our workers out of harm's way while violating American law.[9]
- Each alternative was unpalatable and unacceptable. So, the company decided to do what we believe any responsible citizen should do under the circumstances: We went to the U.S. Department of Justice and voluntarily disclosed the facts and the predicament. The U.S. government had no knowledge of the payments and, had we not come forward ourselves, it is entirely possible that the payments would have remained unknown to American authorities to this day.[10]

In a plea deal, the company was fined $25 million, and in September 2007 it made its first installment payment of $5 million. Chiquita's general counsel said that "this was a difficult situation for the company and that the company had to do it to protect the wellbeing of our employees and their families." The Department of Justice prosecutor called the payments "morally repugnant" and said that the protection payments "fueled violence everywhere else."[11]

Board Knowledge Revealed

During the investigation of this incident, it was discovered that the Board of Directors of the company came to know that the questionable payments were going on. A prosecution document, according to the *Miami Herald*, presented the following timeline of events:[12]

2000—Chiquita's audit committee, composed of board members, heard about the payments and took no action.

2002—Soon after AUC had been designated a terrorist organization; a Chiquita employee learned about this and alerted the company.

2003—Chiquita consulted with a Washington attorney who told the company, "Bottom line: Cannot make the payment."

2003—Two months later, Chiquita executives reported to the full board of directors that the company was still making payments. One board member objected and the directors agreed to make the payments known to the Department of Justice.

Chiquita's Social Responsibility Initiatives

An interesting description of the company's track record in the area of corporate social responsibility (CSR) makes this case particularly unusual. Jon Entine's account of Chiquita's turnaround as a company is enlightening. Apparently, Chiquita spent at least 15 years living down its longstanding reputation as a "ruthless puppeteer manipulating corrupt Latin American banana republics."[13] Once operating as United Fruit, the company began turning itself around in 1990 and remade itself into a model food distributor, complete with high environmental and ethical standards.

Better Banana Project

In the early 1990s, the company separated itself from its competitors by teaming up with the Rainforest Alliance on sustainability and labor standards. This became known as the Better Banana Project.[14] Rainforest Alliance had the following to say about Chiquita's adoption of the Better Banana Project: "The Rainforest Alliance monitors and verifies that Chiquita's farms abide by strong environmental and social standards, which have positive impacts on rural communities and tropical landscape."[15] The Better Banana Project's ability to be responsive to environmental concerns without threatening the livelihood of companies and employees earned it the 1995 Peter F. Drucker Award for Nonprofit Innovation. Chiquita also became well known through its publications of its corporate social responsibility reports. The company issued public reports on its CSR and sustainability efforts each year starting in 2000.[16]

Regarding its CSR initiatives and payments to terrorist groups, CEO Fernando Aguirre pointed to the fact that the company came forward voluntarily to disclose the payments to the paramilitaries as an indication that Chiquita is "completely committed to corporate responsibility and compliance."[17] He noted too that the voluntary action involved considerable cost. In June 2004, Chiquita sold its

Colombian farms at a loss of $9 million to bring closure to the issue and remove itself from a difficult situation.[18] The company settled its case with the U.S. Justice Department for $25 million.[19]

Lawsuits Against Chiquita

After this, Chiquita faced a host of lawsuits related to its time in Colombia. These included one from families of six U.S. citizens who were kidnapped and killed by Colombia's notorious FARC paramilitary group.[20] The lawsuit suggested that Chiquita's connection with FARC may have been more proactive than just paying protection money. The suit also claimed that Chiquita used its network of local transportation contractors to transport weapons to the group.[21] The case went on for years and was finally settled out of court for an undisclosed amount in 2018.[22]

These same charges propelled the largest lawsuit, based on the Alien Torts Claims Act (ATCA), filed by family members of thousands of Colombians who were tortured or killed by paramilitaries in Colombia. In 2014, Chiquita won dismissal of this lawsuit by 4,000 Colombians who sought to hold the company responsible for the deaths of relatives. The court said it lacked the power to review the claims because all relevant conduct took place outside the United States, and Chiquita's mere presence in the United States did not confer jurisdiction.[23]

However, other cases still abound. In 2017, cases from around the country were consolidated and put before a South Florida federal judge.[24] Chiquita asked the judge to dismiss the case, arguing that, as a victim of extortion, Chiquita was not responsible for the crimes that the paramilitary groups committed.[25] U.S. District Judge Kenneth A. Marra granted Chiquita's motion to dismiss terrorism-related claims; however, he allowed the plaintiffs to move forward with claims against Chiquita for torture, war crimes, and crimes against humanity.[26] A 2019 case filed on behalf of ten Colombians who were murdered was thrown out of court by Judge Marra based on failure to link their loved ones' brutal deaths to a specific group, much less Chiquita.[27] It was considered a "bellwether case" —that is, a case to give those involved an idea of their chances of winning their claims in hopes of spurring settlement talks. Hence, the ruling seemed to be an effort to bring an end to litigation. Nevertheless, filings continue, including a 2020 case filed by EarthRights International representing more than 200 Colombian plaintiffs whose family members were murdered by paramilitary death squads.[28]

Although things have improved in the last ten years, Transparency International recently scored Colombia as a 39 out of 100 for transparency, noting that there is an "alarming concentration of power in the executive branches" that has "contributed to an explosion in irregularities and corruption cases," particularly in the wake of COVID-19 supply chain issues.[29] However, Colombia is not unique in its corruption and security challenges for global businesses. In fact, the global market for private security services continues to grow, with many security firms advertising security for "crisis zones" around the world, with employees providing "highly trained armed personnel and logistical support."[30]

A Tale of two Companies

The Chiquita payment controversy has been called a "tale of two companies."[31] One face of Chiquita comes across as a defiant, secretive multinational, with lots of resources, determined to break the law to keep its employees safe and its businesses running. The other face of Chiquita builds partnerships with groups such as Rainforest Alliance to support the Better Banana Project and issues frequent corporate social responsibility reports to keep its stakeholders pleased and informed. The company tried to extricate itself by turning itself in, paying huge fines or settlements, suffering tremendous embarrassment and loss of reputational capital, and finally selling its farms to help reach closure. Which is the real Chiquita?

Questions for Discussion

1. Go to the ethical dilemma at the beginning of the case. Which position did you take and why? Did your position change after you read the case?

2. Was Chiquita justified in making the extortion payments to protect its employees? Was the company really between a rock and a hard place? What should it have done differently?

3. Using your knowledge of business ethics and global practices, what concepts, principles, or ideas from your study have a bearing on this case? Explain how some of them might have guided Chiquita toward better decisions.

4. What is your assessment of then-CEO Aguirre's statements? Did he come across as sincere or just making excuses?

5. What is your analysis of the Chiquita board of directors' handling of this case? Do you think selling the farms at a loss in Colombia was the right thing to do? Why?

6. If you were the judge in the consolidated case, what would you decide?

7. How does this case exemplify what global businesses face in different parts of the world? How does this case inform the current trend of businesses hiring private security?

8. In the "tale of two companies," which do you think is the real Chiquita and why?

Notes

1. Denis Collins, Edgewood College, Madison, Wisconsin, posed these questions in an e-mail to an International Association for Business and Society ListServ discussing the Chiquita Banana situation on June 18, 2007. Used with permission.
2. See Christopher H. Stubbert, Stephen F. Pires, and Rob Guerette, "Crime Science and Crime

Epidemics in Developing Countries: A Reflection on Kidnapping for Ransom in Colombia, South America," *Crime Science* (2015), DOI 10.1186 /s40163-015-0034-5; Rushworth M. Kidder, "Ethical Bananas," *Ethics Newsline* (March 19, 2007), a publication of the Institute for Global Ethics, http://www.globalethics.org /newsline/2007/03/19/. Accessed May 27, 2016.

3. Ibid.
4. "Chiquita Brands International Stock Forecast, Price & News," *MarketBeat* (July 7, 2021), https:// www.marketbeat.com/stocks/NYSE/CQB/. Accessed July 8, 2021.
5. Ibid.
6. Kidder, 2007.
7. See Katy Byron, "Chiquita to Plead Guilty to Ties with Terrorists," *CNN* (March 14, 2007), https:// money.cnn.com/2007/03/14/news/companies /chiquita/. Accessed July 8, 2021; Jane Bussey, "Chiquita Disregarded Warnings, Records Show," *The Miami Herald* (April 16, 2007).
8. Fernando Aguirre, "An Excruciating Dilemma between Life and Law: Corporate Responsibility in a Zone of Conflict," *The Corporate Citizen* (U.S. Chamber of Commerce, April 2007), 1–2.
9. Ibid.
10. Ibid.
11. Pablo Bachelet, "Chiquita Pays Fine for Supporting Colombian Terrorist Group," McClatchy Washington Bureau, McClatchy Newspapers, http:// www.mcclatchydc.com/news/nation-world/world /article24469555.html#.Ua4Fe9LVB8E. Accessed July 7, 2021.
12. See Byron, 2007, and Jane Bussey, "" Documents: Chiquita Paid Up Despite Warnings," *Miami Herald*, April 17, 2007, http://www.miamiherald .com/news/nation-world/world/americas /article1927938.html. Accessed May 27, 2016.
13. Jon Entine, "Chiquita Counts the Cost of Honesty," *Ethical Corporation* (May 2007), 74.
14. Ibid.
15. Earth Times, "The Rainforest Alliance Helps Chiquita Produce a Better Banana and Transforms an Industry," http://www.sdearthtimes.com/et1200 /et1200s10.html. Accessed July 8, 2021.
16. Chiquita, "Sustainability. Behind the Blue Sticker," Chiquita.com (2019), https://www.chiquita.com /sustainability/. Accessed July 8, 2021.
17. *The Corporate Citizen* (April 2007).
18. Ibid.
19. Associated Press, "Chiquita Settles Case on Payments to Rebel Groups," *The New York Times* (March 15, 2007), http://www.nytimes.com /2007/03/15/business/worldbusiness/15bananas .html?ref=chiquitabrandsinternationalinc. Accessed July 8, 2021.

20. See Business & Human Rights Resource Centre "Chiquita Lawsuits" (July 2021), https://www .business-humanrights.org/en/latest-news/chiquita -lawsuits-re-colombia/. Accessed July 8, 2021; Daniel Tencer, "Lawsuit: Chiquita Fruit Company Funded Death Squads in Colombia," *The Raw Story* (April 7, 2010), http://www.rawstory.com /rs/2010/04/07/chiquita-funded-death-squads -colombia/. Accessed May 27, 2016.
21. Ibid.
22. Brendan Pierson, "Chiquita Settles with Families of U.S. Victims of Colombia's FARC," *Reuters* (February 5, 2018), https://www.reuters.com /article/us-usa-court-chiquita/chiquita-settles -with-families-of-u-s-victims-of-colombias-farc -idUSKBN1FP2VX. Accessed July 8, 2021.
23. Jonathan Stempl, "Chiquita Wins Dismissal of U. S. Lawsuits over Colombian Abuses," *Reuters* (July 24, 2014), https://www.reuters.com/article /chiquita-colombia-decision/chiquita-wins -dismissal-of-u-s-lawsuits-over-colombian -abuses-idUSL2N0PZ28P20140724. Accessed July 8, 2021.
24. Associated Press, "Chiquita Sued Over Colombian Paramilitary Payments," Syracuse.com (May 30, 2011), http://www.syracuse.com/news/index .ssf/2011/05/chiquita_sued_over_colombian_p .html. Accessed July 8, 2021.
25. CNN Wire Staff, "Florida Judge Allows Suits Against Chiquita to Move Forward," *CNN* (June 4, 2011), http://edition.cnn.com/2011 /WORLD/americas/06/03/florida.colombia.chiquita .lawsuits/. Accessed July 7, 2021.
26. Ibid.
27. Jane Musgrave, "WPB Judge Tosses Suits Accusing Chiquita of Helping Terrorists Kill Colombians," *The Palm Beach Post* (September 13, 2019), https:// www.palmbeachpost.com/news/20190913/wpb -judge-tosses-suits-accusing-chiquita-of-helping -terrorists-kill-colombians. Accessed July 8, 2021.
28. Business & Human Rights Resource Centre, 2021.
29. Transparency International, "CPI 2020: Americas" (January 28, 2021), *Transparency.org*, https:// www.transparency.org/en/news/cpi-2020-americas. Accessed July 7, 2021.
30. See SecurityDegreeHub.com, "30 Most Powerful Private Security Companies in the World," 2021, https://www.securitydegreehub.com/most-powerful -private-security-companies-in-the-world/. Accessed July 8, 2021; Claire Provost, "The Industry of Inequality: Why the World Is Obsessed with Private Security," *The Guardian* (May 12, 2017), https:// www.theguardian.com/inequality/2017/may/12 /industry-of-inequality-why-world-is-obsessed -with-private-security. Accessed July 8, 2021.
31. Jon Entine, 74.

Case 20

Dark Money and Corporate Political Spending on Campaigns*

Recent election cycles have brought new challenges for corporations and their boards of directors. For example, in the 2020 presidential election campaign, candidate Joe Biden unveiled a plan to lower drug prices by letting Medicare negotiate payment for certain high-cost drugs.[1] Yet ironically, the pharmaceutical industry was one of the most generous industry donors to the Biden campaign, as well as those of the other candidates. In fact, the health industry overall (including health professionals, hospitals, HMOs, and pharmaceutical companies) donated more than $80 million to the presidential candidates in 2020, with the pharmaceutical industry donating more to Democrats than Republicans in the lead up to the final election.[2] In essence, the pharmaceutical companies and health-care professionals spent money to promote policies that went against their own financial interests.

This happened in congressional elections as well. In 2020, the pharmaceutical industry's trade group, PhRMA, donated funds to nonprofit groups that used those funds to hit back on House Democrats' plan to approve the drug pricing plan to lower prescription drug costs.[3] Some of those funds came from firms including Pfizer, Bayer, and Merck, all manufacturers of contraceptives.

Political spending is also an issue with individual companies. Target Corporation, a company that had positioned itself as an LGBT-friendly corporation, found itself the target of angry employees and customers when they learned about Target's political spending. Target, a sponsor of the annual Twin Cities Gay Pride Festival, donated money to a business group that supported an anti–gay rights candidate for Minnesota governor. Angry employees and consumers conducted protests outside Target stores and threatened a boycott.[4]

These examples show how political spending can have dramatic consequences for corporations. Politicians take positions on a range of policies, and so the same politician may hold some positions that support and other positions that damage a corporation's best interests. This problem was exacerbated when the U.S. Supreme Court's *Citizen United* decision changed the political spending landscape for corporations. Before that decision, political spending was constrained to political action committees (PACs), and PAC political activity had to be disclosed to the FEC (Federal Election Commission). Now firms can make unlimited contributions directly to candidates or indirectly to 501c4 nonprofits and trade associations, who can then hide both the donors who provided the money and the way the money was spent. These are called "Dark Money"

donations, where companies and trade groups can spend millions to shape elections without revealing where their money comes from. Firms are now freer to become politically involved but, as Target and the pharmaceutical companies found out, that freedom comes with risk. Shareholders and other stakeholders are asking firms to be transparent in their political spending. They want to judge those expenditures for themselves to avoid agency problems and other conflicts of interest.

The Center for Political Accountability, located in Washington, D.C., in conjunction with the Zicklin Center for Business Ethics Research at The Wharton School (University of Pennsylvania), annually rates leading U.S. public companies on their political disclosure and accountability policies and practices for election-related spending.[5] Interestingly, they found that recent elections have seen much better and stronger policies of disclosure and accountability by businesses regarding their election-related spending. They commented, "Especially striking are the increases in company adoption of board oversight and more detailed committee review of political spending."[6] It seems that there is some upside for society, in that while the Dark Money continues to pour into campaigns, at least there is a movement toward more transparency and accountability.

Ira M. Millstein, founder of the Ira M. Millstein Center for Global Markets and Corporate Ownership at Columbia Law School, proposed that boards of directors need to step up and institute more measures for accountability regarding corporate political spending. He suggests the following: (1) Companies should require trade associations of which they are members to report to them on their political spending. (2) Companies should require trade associations of which they are members to disclose the donors who provide the money for their political spending. (3) Companies should then disclose the information they receive from their trade associations when they disclose their other spending to shareholders and other stakeholders.[7] Millstein's message is clear. If businesses do not implement such measures to deal with "Dark Money," then they must face the reputational repercussions… just like Target and other companies who may be unaware of the flow of political spending through trade groups.

Questions for Discussion

1. What is your reaction to the issue of political spending? What would you do if you were the CEO of a pharmaceutical company? Would you still belong to PhRMA? Would your membership in PhRMA have any conditions attached?
2. What is your reaction to the Target situation? How would you handle it if you were the CEO?
3. It seems like corporate political campaign spending is becoming more transparent. Do you agree?

*This case was originally written by Ann K. Buchholtz, Rutgers University, and revised and updated in 2016 and 2021 by Jill A. Brown, Bentley University.

4.   Should Dark Money spending be more regulated? If so, how?

5.   Do you agree with Ira Millstein? Should companies require trade associations to disclose this information before they join? Should companies then disclose the information they receive? If a trade association refuses to provide that information, should the company refuse to join?

Notes

1.   Fraiser Kansteiner, "Biden's 2022 Budget Re-ups Prospect of Medicare Drug Pricing Negotiations," Fierce Pharma (June 1, 2021), https://www .fiercepharma.com/pharma/president-biden-s-2022 -budget-re-ups-bid-for-medicare-drug-pricing -negotiations. Accessed July 8, 2021.

2.   See Open Secrets, "2020 Presidential Race," OpenSecrets.org, 2021, https://www.opensecrets .org/2020-presidential-race/industry-totals?highlight =y&ind=H04&src=a. Accessed July 8, 2021; Open Secrets, "Pharmaceuticals/Health Products," https://www.opensecrets.org/industries/indus. php?cycle=2020&ind=H04. Accessed July 8, 2021; Conor Kavanagh, "Pharmaceutical Industry Donating More to Democrats than Republicans in the Lead Up to 2020 Election," *Pharmafile* (December 10, 2020), http://www.pharmafile.com /news/561370/pharmaceutical-industry-donating -more-democrats-republicans-lead-2020-election. Accessed July 8, 2021.

3.   See Emmarie Huetteman, Jay Hancock, and Elizabeth Lucas, "Pharma Cash Donations Target 'Vulnerable' Lawmakers as Industry Tries to Defend Itself," *USA Today* (August 26, 2019), https://www .usatoday.com/story/news/politics/2019/08/26 /pharma-industry-ups-donations-senate-republicans -mcconnell/2116231001/. Accessed July 8, 2021; Krystal Hur, "Pharma-backed 'Dark Money' Group Hits House Dems on Drug Pricing Plan," OpenSecrets.org (May 13, 2021), https://www .opensecrets.org/news/2021/05/american-action -network-hits-house-dems/. Accessed July 8, 2021.

4.   Stephanie Condon, "Target Apologizes for Controversial Political Donation," *CBS News* (August 5, 2010), https://www.cbsnews.com /news/target-apologizes-for-controversial-political -donation/. Accessed July 8, 2021.

5.   Center for Political Accountability, "CPA-Zicklin Index," http://www.politicalaccountability.net/cpa -zicklin-index-/#. Accessed July 8, 2021.

6.   Ibid, p. 12.

7.   Bruce F. Freed and Karl Sandstrom, "Political Spending: Big Risk for Boards," *Directors & Boards*, 2013 Annual Report, Vol. 37 (4), pp. 25–26.

Case 21

Big Pharma's Marketing Tactics*

"Big Pharma" is the name the business press uses for the gigantic pharmaceutical industry. Most of us are familiar with Big Business, Big Government, and, now, Big Tech (see Case 9). Big Pharma has been around for quite a while, and it continues to be in the news regarding its marketing, advertising, pricing, and sales tactics. The pharmaceutical industry has been under attack by consumers and patient groups for more than a decade.

In 2015 and 2016, two companies, Valeant Pharmaceuticals International and Turing Pharmaceuticals, became headliners in an issue that has touched many families and has energized a national debate about the drug industry and especially drug pricing. Valeant would buy patents for unique, lifesaving drugs, raise their prices steeply, and watch the profits roll in.[1] While raising prices is a common industry practice, it all boils down to the degree. Valeant was doubling and tripling its prices of new drugs while other companies used smaller price hikes imposed over a number of years.

Valeant got into trouble because it did not follow the industry practice called the rule of three: If you are raising prices, do it quietly, modestly, and over time.[2] The immediate response was outrage by the public and some members of Congress. In 2015, drug companies jacked up the prices on their brand-name products an average of 16.2 percent.[3] In 2018, Valeant changed its company name to Bausch Health Companies, Inc. to distance itself from the public outrage associated with the massive price increases introduced by Valeant.[4]

In 2015, Turing Pharmaceuticals and its 32-year-old founder and CEO Martin Shkreli bought a drug named Daraprim, the lifesaving HIV drug, and quickly raised its price more than 5,000 percent.[5] Tablets that once cost $13.50 per pill were jacked up to $750 per tablet, raising the annual cost for some patients to hundreds of thousands of dollars.[6] Shkreli, a former hedge fund manager, quickly drew the wrath of consumers and has since been called the "bad boy" of Big Pharma.[7] Two years later, Shkreli was found guilty of securities fraud stemming from his management of two hedge funds and a separate drug company and was sentenced to seven years in prison.[8] The Valeant

---

* This case was written and revised by Archie B. Carroll, University of Georgia. Updated in 2021.

and Turing cases are just part of the recent backdrop in the ongoing controversial pharmaceutical industry.

From 2016 to 2021, Purdue Pharma was in the glaring spotlight for its aggressive and questionable marketing of OxyContin and its contributions to the opioid crisis in America. This case was scheduled to be settled in 2021 after the company declared bankruptcy, and the Sackler family, founders and owners, agreed to personal payments of $4.28 billion and dissolution of the company (see Case 22).[9]

As *Time* magazine has stated, it is hard to empathize with the drug industry because of the high cost of our prescriptions.[10] Consistently negative public perceptions of the pharmaceutical industry have become standard and have added to its problems. Big Pharma has ranked poorly in the eyes of the public for more than a decade, and by 2019, Big Pharma ranked at the bottom of the Gallup poll on U.S. Industry Rankings of 25 industries in America.[11] This meant it is the most poorly regarded industry. By 2021, Big Pharma's rankings had improved, but that was primarily due to the role of a couple companies in quickly developing vaccines for the COVID-19 pandemic. Also, Big Tech companies had by then stolen the negative spotlight and were drawing the ire of the public. The two industries swapped places in the nationwide popularity contest.[12]

Putting aside Pharma's recent popularity because of the COVID-19 vaccine, many of the allegations regarding Big Pharma continued as they had in the past. Big Pharma has been aware that it faces challenges to its marketing, pricing, and sales tactics. One gets the impression that the industry does not try to repair its negative image as much as it calls on its huge army of lobbyists in Washington, D.C., to protect its interests. According to OpenSecrets, Big Pharma ranked at the top of industries in lobbying and in 2021 was spending around $92.3 million on lobbying, far more than any other industry.[13] Though the public values the drugs that the industry makes available for sale, on a continuing basis, the multibillion-dollar industry's social responsibilities and business ethics continue to be questioned.

The Pharmaceutical Industry

The pharmaceutical industry is one of the healthiest and wealthiest in America. However, astronomical drug prices have continued to result in pushback against the industry. A 2021 survey conducted by the Rand Corporation, surveying 32 nations, indicated that prescription drug prices in the United States are 2.5 times higher than in other countries. According to experts, brand-name drugs are the primary driver of the high prices.[14] The prices have been steadily increasing for a while. In total, all countries in the study spend around $800 billion annually with the U.S. portion of that total being around 58 percent.[15]

The top ten pharmaceutical companies in the world, according to revenue data, include the familiar names, with the most profitable at the top of the list:[16]

1. Johnson & Johnson: $56.1 billion
2. Pfizer: $51.75 billion
3. Roche: $49.23 billion
4. Novartis: $47.45 billion
5. Merck: $46.84 billion
6. GlaxoSmithKline: $44.27 billion
7. Sanofi: $40.46 billion
8. AbbVie: $33.26 billion
9. Takeda: $30.52 billion
10. Shanghai Pharmaceuticals Holding: $26.69

Among this group, only Johnson & Johnson (J&J) was ranked among *Fortune*'s "most admired companies in the world in 2021."[17] And, in spite of its relatively high ranking (#15), J&J has continuously experienced various allegations of questionable business practices, which have resulted in large settlements. For example, in addition to large lawsuits, J&J has been at the center of scandals and government investigations and has had to issue recalls on some of its drugs and devices.[18] A Huffington Post investigation called J&J "America's most admired lawbreaker."[19]

Depending on the study considered and how expenses are calculated, the pharmaceutical industry spends much more on marketing and sales than on research and development.[20] In spite of its size and success, Big Pharma has been called into question for a number of years now for its dubious marketing, advertising, pricing, and sales techniques. The charges have included questionable direct-to-consumers (DTCA) advertising (see Case 5) and questionable ethics, and a number of them have resulted in lawsuits.

By one estimate, Big Pharma has paid out more than $30 billion during a recent decade to resolve government allegations and to settle criminal and civil lawsuits involving illegal marketing practices, Medicaid overcharges, and kickbacks.[21] Dr. Eric Campbell, a medical school professor, stated that the settlements and fines these companies pay "far outstrip any penalties they pay."[22] Campbell argues that the pharmaceutical firms view these payments as a cost of doing business, and this appears to be the business model the firms are using.[23]

Sales Over Science

A continuing criticism of Big Pharma is that the industry has abandoned science for sales.[24] That is, the industry has become more concerned with pushing pills than for developing new and important drugs. An example of this was provided in the aggressive marketing by Novartis of its fourth biggest selling drug. Was this drug a lifesaver? No, it is Lamisil, a pill for toenail fungus. Yes, toenail fungus can turn a nail yellow, but apparently no one has died of this illness. On the other hand, a few people may have died taking the drug, as regulators linked the drug to at least 16 cases of liver failure, including 11 deaths. In its defense, Novartis claimed most of these patients had preexisting illnesses or were on other drugs.[25]

One group calculated that Novartis spent $236 million on Lamisil ads over three years, but Novartis denies this figure. In the first run of one commercial, regulators thought the ad so overstated the drug's benefits that the company had to pull that version of the ad. It was reported that the drug cured the problem in only 38 percent of patients, but Lamisil's sales increased 19 percent after it.[26] In short, it was alleged that the industry spends a fortune on remedies to cure trivial maladies while its drug research pipelines are running dry. This allegation has been dubbed "salesmanship over science."[27] Others have said it represents marketing and profits being considered more important than consumer safety and wellness.[28]

Charges and Lawsuits Span Multiple Issues

Pricing

Though Valeant and Turing dominated the news for years about skyrocketing drug prices, it is an industrywide problem that does not go away. These two companies gave the entire industry a black eye and have invited increased regulatory scrutiny.[29] *Bloomberg Businessweek* ran an article that summed up the situation nicely: "Big Pharma's Favorite Prescription: Higher Prices."[30]

Between 2007 and 2018, drug corporations raised prices on prescription drugs by 160 percent.[31] In the midst of the coronavirus pandemic, while receiving billions of dollars to develop vaccines, the major pharmaceutical companies raised prices on 800 medicines, hoping no one would notice. But that is nothing new as past history indicates.It is little wonder that lowering drug prices is politically popular and many are hoping for increased regulations governing drug prices.[32] As a result of high prices, one-third of Americans have said they have skipped refilling prescriptions, and one in ten admitted to self-rationing medications in the past. The Lower Drug Costs Now Act has been introduced in Congress, and some think it is long overdue.[33]

What is driving prices up? Many companies raise prices just because they can. There are no simple answers. The United States has the highest drug prices in the world, and the high prices are a function of a complex set of circumstances including the complicated interplay between the insurance industry, the Affordable Care Act, Medicare, and Medicaid systems. Medicare is the single largest payer for health care in the United States, and it is barred by law from negotiating directly with drug companies. As a result, the United States is a drugmakers' gold mine. According to recent statistics, the U.S. drug spending was more than twice that of France, Germany, Italy, and Britain combined.[34]

In July 2021, President Biden issued an executive order that was designed to promote business competition and lay out a series of steps to lower prescription drug prices, and to take legal action against Big Pharma companies that have tried to keep generic medicines off the market.[35] What is not in the executive order, however, is any directive that would allow the federal Medicare agency to negotiate prices with the drug companies. Currently, federal law generally bars the agency from negotiating prices though everyone agrees this would be the best solution.[36] Unless the law is changed, this option does not appear to be available.

Mergers and acquisitions in the drug industry have reduced the number of competitors, and this has been an influential factor in drug pricing, especially among generic drugs. The recent price increases of many medicines have climbed so steeply in the last couple years that some analysts see a crisis looming. More and more, insurers, health maintenance organizations, pharmacy associations, and patient groups are sounding the alarm that prices are becoming unsustainable.[37]

Off-Label Marketing and Prescribing

Another questionable and illegal practice that some companies are charged with involve promoting drugs for uses for which they were not approved of by the FDA or run counter to state consumer protection laws. The result of this is that doctors may be prescribing, and patients may be using, drugs for conditions for which those medicines were not intended, are not appropriate, or might hurt patients.[38]

A major danger in this unlawful practice is that physicians and consumers may be misled to believe that an off-label use of a prescription drug is safe or effective.[39] Big Pharma employs a variety of techniques to illegally promote their drugs for unapproved indications. The most common strategies include (1) promoting off-label use to doctors, (2) providing free samples and encourage off-label use, (3) offer financial incentives and kickbacks, (4) teaching and research activities to promote off-label use, (5) helping doctors receive reimbursements for off-label use, (6) offering patients gifts or incentives to encourage use, and (7) reviewing patients charts to see targets of off-label promotions.[40]

The FDA and state attorneys general have been unhappy about drug companies marketing their products for "off-label" uses and continue to pursue companies for these violations. The anomaly is this: doctors may prescribe drugs for off-label use when they believe they are appropriate, but it is illegal for the drug companies to market or promote the drugs for off-label use.[41] Meanwhile, issues of the law and practice of off-label prescribing and promotion continues to be debated.[42]

Improper Payments and Bribes

Sometimes the questionable marketing of drugs entails improper payments or bribes. In a landmark case, the Securities and Exchange Commission (SEC) announced that the drug maker Schering-Plough Corporation would pay a $500,000 penalty to settle claims that one of its subsidiaries made improper payments to a Polish charity in a quest to get a Polish government health official to buy the company's products.[43]

The SEC claimed that Schering-Plough Poland donated about $76,000 to a Polish charity over a three-year period. Chudnow Castle Foundation, the charity, was headed by a health official in the Polish government. Apparently, this information came to light while regulators were investigating several pharmaceutical companies for compliance with the U.S. Foreign Corrupt Practices Act. The SEC charged that the payments were not accurately shown on the company's books and that the company's internal controls failed to prevent or detect them. The SEC said that the charity was legitimate but that the company made the contributions with the expectation of boosting drug sales. In addition to paying the fine, the company also agreed to hire an independent consultant to review the company's internal control system and to ensure the firm's compliance with the Foreign Corrupt Practices Act (FCPA).[44]

Johnson & Johnson is another company that has been pursued for improper payments. In its case, the improper payments were in connection with the sale of medical devices in two foreign countries. Johnson & Johnson turned itself in, and the worldwide chairperson of medical devices and diagnostics took responsibility and retired.[45] In a related case, the company was being investigated for possible bribery in its medical device unit in Shanghai, in which it is alleged that the company bribed the deputy chief of the Chinese state FDA.[46]

In 2020, Alexion Pharmaceuticals agreed to pay $21 million to resolve charges it made payments to foreign government officials, in violation of the U.S. Foreign Corrupt Practices Act, to secure favorable treatment for one of its primary drugs.[47] Alexion was charged with making payments to government officials to improperly influence them to approve patient prescriptions and to improve the regulatory treatment for their drug.[48]

Questionable Payments to Doctors

Few cases more vividly illustrate the questionable marketing tactics of Big Pharma than that of making payments to doctors. About half of all U.S. doctors accept money or gifts each year from drug and device companies, totaling more than $2 billion.[49] The conflicts of interest created by these payments are clear, but the medical community has resisted doing anything about it. They argue that these payments do no harm to patients and possibly help them.[50]

"Shadowy" Financial Lures

Interviews with 20 doctors, industry executives, and observers close to the investigation of Schering-Plough and other drug companies revealed a "shadowy system of financial lures" that the companies had been using to convince the physicians to favor their drugs. In the case of Schering-Plough, the tactics included paying doctors large sums of money to prescribe its drug for hepatitis C and to participate in the company's clinical trials that turned out to be thinly disguised marketing ploys that required little on the part of the doctors. The company even barred doctors from participating in the program if they did not exhibit loyalty to the company's drugs.[51]

One doctor, a liver specialist, and eight others who were interviewed said that the company paid them $1,000 to $1,500 per patient for prescribing Intron A, the company's hepatitis C medicine. The doctors were supposed to gather data, in exchange for the fees, and pass it on to the company. Apparently, many doctors were not diligent in record-keeping, but the company did little. Another liver disease specialist said that the trials were "merely marketing gimmicks."[52] According to some doctors, the company would even shut off the money if one of the doctors wrote prescriptions for or spoke favorably about competing drugs. Other doctors reported being signed up for consulting services and being paid $10,000, and the only purpose was to keep them loyal to the company's products.[53]

In response to the allegations against the company, former Schering-Plough CEO Fred Hassan reported that the violations took place before he took office. He went on to outline steps he was taking to get the company on track. This included instituting an "integrity hotline" for employees to report wrongdoing and the creation of a chief compliance officer to report directly to the CEO and the board. Hassan said that compliance has to become "part of the DNA" of a drug company.[54] Another company official said that the company has been "undergoing a company-wide transformation since the arrival of new leadership in mid-2003," which is a "commitment to quality compliance and business integrity."[55]

As it turns out, most doctors take money from drug and device companies. A ProPublica analysis concluded that Big Pharma companies have paid doctors billions of dollars for consulting, promotional speeches, meals, and much more. In their study, they found that for 32 of 50 drugs studied, at least 10 percent of the doctors prescribing the drug received payments tied to the drug from the company that made it.[56]

Gifts Take Many Forms

Not only do pharmaceutical companies give cash payments to doctors under a variety of justifications, but many payments also come in the form of meals, tickets to shows and sporting events, ski and beach vacations disguised as medical education seminars, consulting "jobs" for which the doctors do no work, and other gifts as part of their marketing strategies. The companies expect something in return. They expect the doctors to prescribe their medicines. It is estimated that there is an army of more than 90,000 pharmaceutical reps, many of them young and beautiful, supplying the doctors and their staffs with gifts and freebies. It is argued that these gifts damage the doctors' integrity.[57]

One survey of doctors found that 94 percent of them had some type of relationship with the drug industry. The most frequent drug-industry ties were food and drinks in the workplace (83 percent), drug samples (78 percent), payments for consulting (18 percent), payments for speaking (16 percent), reimbursement for meeting expenses (15 percent), and tickets to cultural or sporting events (7 percent).[58] Some argue that these financial relationships between doctors and companies reflect a conflict of interests making it appear that the drug companies are rewarding the doctors for prescribing their lucrative drugs to patients. Others in the industry say that doctors have a right to make this money because they are providing research and access for the drug companies.[59]

A new requirement, instituted by the Affordable Care Act, is that the Centers for Medicare and Medicaid Services (CMS) must collect information from applicable manufacturers and group purchasing organizations about their financial relationships with doctors and hospitals. The Open Payments website allows the public access to their data.[60] Whether this effort to provide transparency will make a difference or not remains to be seen.

Promotional Gifts to Med Students

In addition to gifts to physicians, Big Pharma starts its promotional techniques while the doctors are still students in medical school. Companies start early trying to persuade the young doctors-to-be to prescribe their products by inundating them with logo-infested products and other gifts, including free lunches, pens, and notepads. Some medical students have become fed up with the practice and have resisted the free gifts and have started movements to stop the practice from occurring in the first place.[61]

One former med student in Toronto reported what he learned while he was in med school. He learned that his major textbook on gastroenterology was actually published by the pharmaceutical company AstraZeneca, and the company was donating the textbooks to the med school he attended.[62] He was not pleased with this. Along with another classmate, he started a petition against the pharma-funded material and began questioning whether the industry was too involved in educating future doctors. His concern was that the companies had a financial conflict of interest in helping the students.[63]

To their credit, some states and some med schools have banned pharmaceutical reps from giving gifts to physicians and students, and some improvements in their graduates being more objective later in terms of prescribing medicines has been evident.[64] Some experts believe not enough has been done on this issue and that the time has come for a ban on all gifts to med students and physicians because of the conflict of interest involved.[65]

Big Pharma = Big Lobbying

How is Big Pharma able to ward off most government regulations and actions to control it? The answer is through the power of its huge lobbying force. According to the Center on Public Integrity, Big Pharma has a stranglehold on Washington. The pharmaceutical industry spends more each year on lobbying than any other industry, and that includes the nation's defense and aerospace industries and Big Oil.[66] We might call this process Big Pharma doing Big Lobbying. The pharmaceutical lobby has defeated most attempts over the years to restrain drug marketing.

It was revealed both by the *New York Times* and *The Wall Street Journal* how successfully Big Pharma had lobbied for its own self-interest and won in the passage of the Affordable Care Act (Obamacare).[67] According to the *New York Times*, the administration's unlikely collaboration with the drug industry forced unappealing trade-offs. Of particular importance was the industry's writing into the proposed law the provision that the Medicare program could not negotiate prices with the drug industry. The result was there would be no lower prices for drugs in the new legislation.[68]

Congress has been fighting this provision for years but has not been successful in its dealings with Big Pharma because of the industry's lobbying power. The Medication Prescription Drug Price Negotiation Act of 2015 was assigned to a committee in January 2016. This bill has been stalled in Congress since its introduction in 2011.[69] More recent legislation has been proposed, titled Prescription Drug Pricing Reduction Act of 2019, but it too is stalled in committee.[70] What is clear is that Big Pharma's behind-the-scenes lobbying has paid big dividends for the industry—it has been able to continue its marketing tactics essentially unimpeded.

Questions for Discussion

1. What are the ethical issues in this case?
2. Who are the primary stakeholders in these incidents and what are their stakes?
3. Is there any justification for the marketing and pricing tactics described in the case? Which tactics are acceptable and which are questionable?
4. What ethical principles may be violated by the marketing tactics described? Do any of these ethical principles *support* the companies' actions?
5. Big Pharma needs enormous sums of money to conduct R&D and to advance its innovations. Do the ends justify the means because the citizenry's health is at stake?
6. What response do you think physicians should take when approached regarding some of the schemes presented in this case? Are doctors in a conflict-of-interest situation when taking Big Pharma's money?
7. What strategy should a sociallyconscious Big Pharma company adopt if it wanted to address the questionable tactics discussed? Is it likely that a more responsible company will initiate such action? Why? Why not?

Endnotes

1. Haley Sweetland Edwards, "Public Outrage: What's Behind the Gouging?" *Time*, May 30, 2016, 38–43, https://time.com/4341416/why-cant-drug-costs-be-reined-in/. Accessed July 12, 2021.
2. Ibid., 42.
3. Ibid., 40.
4. Wikipedia, "Bausch Health," https://en.wikipedia.org/wiki/Bausch_Health, https://en.wikipedia.org/wiki/Bausch_Health. Accessed July 7, 2021.
5. Ben Elgin and Robert Langreth, "Pharma's Play," *Bloomberg Businessweek*, May 23–29, 2016, 44–49.

6. Andrew Pollack, "Drug Goes from $13.50 a Tablet to $750 Overnight," *The New York Times*, September 20, 2015, https://www.nytimes.com/2015/09/21/business/a-huge-overnight-increase-in-a-drugs-price-raises-protests.html. Accessed July 7, 2021.

7. Julie Creswell and Andrew Pollack, "The Bad Boy of Pharmaceuticals Hits Back," *The New York Times*, December 6, 2015, 1BU.

8. Jason Slotkin, "Pharma Bro, Martin Shkreli Denied Release from Prison to Research Coronavirus Cure," *NPR*, May 17, 2020, https://www.npr.org/sections/coronavirus-live-updates/2020/05/17/857612249/pharma-bro-martin-shkreli-denied-release-from-prison-to-research-coronavirus-cur. Accessed July 7, 2021.

9. Jonathan Randles and Sara Randazzo, "Purdue Pharma Family Raises Offer," *The Wall Street Journal*, March 17, 2021, B1.

10. Daren Fonda and Barbara Kiviat, "Curbing the Drug Marketers," *Time* (July 5, 2004), 40–42.

11. Justin McCarthy, "Big Pharma Sinks to the Bottom of U.S. Industry Rankings," Gallup Poll, September 3, 2019, https://news.gallup.com/poll/266060/big-pharma-sinks-bottom-industry-rankings.aspx. Accessed July 7, 2021.

12. Nicole Wetsman, "Pharma Is Winning the Big Business Popularity Contest," *The Verge*, June 12, 2021, https://www.theverge.com/2021/6/12/22529863/pharma-tech-opinion-pandemic-vaccines. Accessed July 7, 2021.

13. OpenSecrets, "Industries," 2021, https://www.opensecrets.org/federal-lobbying/industries. Accessed July 7, 2021.

14. Christopher Curley, "Prescription Drug Prices in the U.S. Are Twice as High: Here's Why," *Healthline*, February 2, 2021, https://www.healthline.com/health-news/prescription-drug-prices-in-the-u-s-are-twice-as-high-heres-why. Accessed July 9, 2021.

15. Ibid.

16. Pharmaceutical Technology, "Top Ten Pharma Companies in 2020," June 1, 2021, https://www.pharmaceutical-technology.com/features/top-ten-pharma-companies-in-2020/. Accessed July 9, 2021.

17. *Fortune's* World's Most Admired Companies 2021, https://fortune.com/worlds-most-admired-companies/2021/search/?ordering=asc. Accessed July 9, 2021.

18. Drugwatch, "Johnson & Johnson," https://www.drugwatch.com/manufacturers/johnson-and-johnson/. Accessed July 9, 2021.

19. Ibid.

20. Rebecca Farley, "Do Pharmaceutical Companies Spend More on Marketing than Research & Development?" PharmacyChecker.com, April 28, 2021, https://www.pharmacychecker.com/askpc/pharma-marketing-research-development/#! Accessed July 9, 2021.

21. Consuella Pachio, "Billions of Dollars Paid Out for Illegal Marketing Practices," *Legalreader*, May 8, 2016, http://www.legalreader.com/billions-of-dollars-paid-out-for-illegal-marketing-practices/. Accessed June 6, 2016.

22. Ibid.

23. Ibid.

24. Robert Langreth and Matthew Herper, "Pill Pushers: How the Drug Industry Abandoned Science for Salesmanship," *Forbes* (May 8, 2006), 94–102; Concordia University, "A Presciption to Cure Big Pharma's Image Problem," October 20, 2015, https://www.eurekalert.org/pub_releases/2015-10/cu-apt102015.php. Accessed July 9, 2021.

25. Landgreth and Herper, Ibid., 94.

26. Ibid.

27. Ibid., 96.

28. Dani Veracity, "Pharmaceutical Fraud: How Big Pharma's Marketing and Profits Come before Consumer Safety and Wellness," https://www.naturalnews.com/020345_drug_marketing_racket.html. Accessed July 9, 2021.

29. Knight Kiplinger, "Are Drug Prices Unethically High?" *Kiplinger's Personal Finance*, January 2016, 18, https://www.kiplinger.com/article/insurance/t027-c013-s002-are-drug-prices-unethically-high.html. Accessed July 9, 2021.

30. "Big Pharma's Favorite Prescription: Higher Prices," *Bloomberg Businessweek*, May 12–18, 2014, 22–24.

31. Margarida Jorge, "Opinion: Inflation in Drug Prices is Soaring and Its Time to Break Big Pharma's Grip on Our Health," *Marketwatch*, May 29, 2021, https://www.marketwatch.com/story/empowering-medicare-to-negotiate-cheaper-drug-prices-could-finally-break-big-pharmas-grip-on-our-health-11622095288. Accessed July 9, 2021.

32. Ibid.

33. Ibid.

34. Laura Lorenzetti, "The U.S. Has the Highest Drug Prices in the World. And Hating Martin Shkreli Won't Be Enough to Change It," *Fortune*, November 1, 2015, 17, https://fortune.com/2015/10/26/drug-prices-daraprim-turing-scandal/. Accessed July 9, 2021.

35. Thomas Burton, "Steps Laid Out to Cut Drug Prices," *The Wall Street Journal*, July 10–11, 2021, A6.

36. Ibid.

37. Lorenzetti, Ibid, 10.

38. Carolyn Susman, "False Marketing of Drugs Raises Red Flags," *Cox News Service* (May 25, 2004).

39. WhistleblowerInternational, "Off Label Use," https://www.whistleblowersinternational.com/types-of-fraud/pharmaceutical/off-label-marketing/. Accessed July 12, 2021.

40. Ibid., "Off-Label Marketing Strategies."

41. Joseph V. Gulfo, "Ending the Prescribe-Don't-Tell Charade for Off-Label Drugs," *The Wall Street Journal*, March 28, 2016, A15, https://www.wsj.com/articles/ending-the-prescribe-dont-tell-charade-for-off-label-drugs-1459114978. Accessed July 12, 2021.

42. Shariful A. Syed, Brigham A. Dixson, Eduardo Constantino, and Judith Regan, "The Law and Practice of Off-Label Prescribing and Physician Promotion," *Journal of the American Academy of Psychiatry and the Law Online*, November 2020. Accessed July 12, 2021.

43. Judith Burns, "SEC Settles Bribery Case vs. Schering-Plough Corp.," *The Wall Street Journal* (June 9, 2004);also see https://www.sec.gov /litigation/litreleases/lr18740.htm. Accessed July 12, 2021.

44. Burns, Ibid.

45. Peter Loftus, "Ex-health Executives Go on Trial," *The Wall Street Journal*, May 23, 2106, B1. Muck Rack, Peter Loftus, https://muckrack.com/loftus/ articles. Accessed July 12, 2021.

46. Jim Edwards, "J&J's Other Headache: Foreign Bribery Probe Targets Shanghai Unit," CBS Moneywatch, June 25, 2010, https://www.cbsnews .com/news/j038js-other-headache-foreign-bribery -probe-targets-shanghai-unit/. Accessed July 12, 2021.

47. U.S. SEC, "SEC Charges Alexion Pharmaceuticals with FCPA Violations," July 2, 2020, https://www .sec.gov/news/press-release/2020-149. Accessed July 12, 2021.

48. Ibid.

49. Aaron Mitchell and Deborah Korenstein, "Drug Companies' Payments and Gifts Affect Physician's Prescribing. It's Time to Turn Off the Spigot," STAT, December 4, 2020. https://www.statnews.com/2020 /12/04/drug-companies-payments-gifts-affect -physician-prescribing/. Accessed July 12, 2021.

50. Ibid.

51. Edwards,Ibid.

52. Ibid.

53. Ibid.

54. Fonda and Kiviat, 41.

55. Reuters (June 28, 2004).

56. Hannah Fresques, "Doctors Prescribe More of a Drug if They Receive Money from a Pharma Company Tied to It," ProPublica, December 20, 2019, https://www.propublica.org/article/doctors -prescribe-more-of-a-drug-if-they-receive-money -from-a-pharma-company-tied-to-it. Accessed July 12, 2021.

57. "Gifts from Drugmakers Damage Doctors' Integrity," *USA Today* (February 8, 2006), 10A; also see John Fauber, "A Surge in Risky, Expensive Drug Prescriptions: What's Behind It?" August 7, 2019, https://www.usatoday.com/story/news /investigations/2019/08/07/biologic-drug-makers -pay-doctors-prescriptions/1943331001/. Accessed July 12, 2021.

58. Reported in Rita Rubin, "Most Doctors Get Money, Gifts from Industry," *USA Today*

(April 26, 2007), 4D. Also see Mitchell and Korenstein, 2020, ibid.

59. Amy Davis, "Is Your Doctor Taking Money from Drug Companies?" Click2Houston, February 20, 2019, https://www.click2houston.com/consumer /2019/02/20/is-your-doctor-receiving-money-from -drug-makers/. Accessed July 12, 2021.

60. CMS.gov, "Open Payments," https://www.cms.gov /openpayments. Accessed July 12, 2021.

61. Laura Hensley, "Big Pharma Pours Millions into Medical Schools: Here's How It Can Impact Education," August 12, 2019, GlobalNews, https:// globalnews.ca/news/5738386/canadian-medical -school-funding/. Accessed July 9, 2021.

62. Ibid.

63. Ibid.

64. Kevin B. O'Reilly, "Pharma Gift Bans for Budding Doctors Have Long Term Impact," https://amednews.com/article/20130218 /profession/130219950/6/. Accessed July 9, 2021; also see Naveed Saleh, "A Physician's Guide to Acceptable Pharma Swag," MDLinx, May 19, 2019, https://www.mdlinx.com/article/a-physician -s-guide-to-acceptable-pharma-swag/lfc-3715. Accessed July 14, 2021.

65. Aaron Mitchell and Deborah Korenstein, "Drug Companies Payments and Gifts Affect Physician's Prescribing. Its Time to Turn Off the Spigot," STAT, December 4, 2020, https://www.statnews .com/2020/12/04/drug-companies-payments-gifts -affect-physician-prescribing/. Accessed July 9, 2021.

66. Wendell Potter, "Opinion: Big Pharma's Stranglehold on Washington," Center for Public Integrity, https://publicintegrity.org/health /opinion-big-pharmas-stranglehold-on-washington/. Accessed July 12, 2021.

67. Peter Baker, "Obama Was Pushed by the Drug Industry, E-mails Suggest," *The New York Times*, June 8, 2012, https://www.nytimes.com/2012/06/09 /us/politics/e-mails-reveal-extent-of-obamas-deal -with-industry-on-health-care.html. Accessed July 12, 2021; Jonathan Gruber, "ObamaCare's Secret History," *The Wall Street Journal*, June 14, 2017, https://www.wsj.com/articles/obamacares-secret -history-1497482858, Accessed July 12, 2021.

68. Baker, Ibid.

69. Govtrack.us, "S.31: Medicare Prescription Drug Price Negotiation Act of 2015," https://www .govtrack.us/congress/bills/114/s31. Accessed July 12, 2021.

70. National Committee to Preserve Social Security and Medicare, "Rebuild the Middle Class," June 10, 2021, https://www.ncpssm.org/documents /medicare-policy-papers/meeting-demand-for -lower-drug-prices-in-medicare/. Accessed July 12, 2021.

Case 22

Purdue Pharma, OxyContin, and the Opioid Crisis*

Purdue Pharma is the company that many say fueled the opioid epidemic. Purdue did this through aggressive marketing, which has been a notable problem for Big Pharma, in general (see Case 21). In Purdue's case, the company claimed it was unaware until years later that its highly addictive product, OxyContin, was being misused and abused. However, a Justice Department report suggested that the company was aware early on that the drug was being crushed and snorted for its powerful narcotic effect, but the company continued to market it as less addictive.[1] This report documented that the company knew about "significant" abuse early on after the drug's introduction in 1996. Further, it concealed this information.[2]

A memo to the sales force at Purdue in 1999 showed how aggressively the company was pushing sales of the addictive, pain-relieving drug. Sales representatives were told that their bonuses would be calculated so that OxyContin sales counted for considerably more bonus money than other drugs. The memo said, "Your priority is to sell, sell, sell OxyContin."[3] One way that Purdue pushed prescriptions of OxyContin was to create relationships with pain specialists and position the drug as helping to solve an epidemic of chronic pain in the United States. In one email, Richard Sackler, one of the founding members of the Sackler family, emphasized what a great relationship he was developing with pain doctors.[4]

The Sacklers

The Sackler family, founders and owners of Purdue Pharma, is a huge family, and many of them are involved financially in the business. The three main brothers of the family were Arthur, Mortimer, and Raymond, but they are all deceased now. Their adult children are the primary executives in charge of the company.[5] The Sackler family is a sprawling, feuding clan, famous in philanthropic circles for decades of generous philanthropy toward some of the world's leading institutions such as the Guggenheim Museum and the Serpentine Gallery and the Royal Academy in Great Britain.[6] But as the world now knows, most of their wealth came from the blockbuster prescription painkiller, OxyContin.[7] Seven members of the Sackler family were on the Board, but they would not disclose who owns how many shares in the company. Disclosures of wealth released to the government indicate that the family members are collectively worth $11 billion.[8]

OxyContin, the Drug

The brand name, OxyContin, is the name for Oxycodone, a narcotic, controlled substance, developed to remedy moderate to severe pain. Oxycodone works in the brain to change how your body feels and responds to the pain. Higher strengths of the drug (more than 40 milligrams per tablet) may cause overdose or death.[9] Though it is effective in what it does, it often may cause addiction, and this risk may be higher if the person has a substance abuse disorder such as overuse or in addition to drugs/alcohol.[10] Individuals abuse OxyContin for the euphoric effect it produces—an effect similar to that associated with heroin use. OxyContin tablets have a controlled-release feature and are designed to be swallowed whole. To bypass the controlled release, abusers chew or crush the tablets. Crushed tablets can be snorted or dissolved in water and injected. The most common names for the drug are OCs, ox, or oxy. Street names include Blue, Hillbilly heroin, Kicker, and Oxycotton.[11]

OxyContin's Marketing

When Purdue Pharma started marketing OxyContin in 1996, Dr. Richard Sackler, a family member who started and controlled the company as its executive, announced to those gathered at the launch party that its release would be "followed by a blizzard of prescriptions that will bury the competition."[12] As questions were being asked about the risk of addiction and overdose five years later, Sackler laid out a strategy that critics say the company has used often by diverting the blame to others, especially those who had become addicted to the opioids. Sackler wrote in an email, "We have to hammer on the abusers in every way possible." He continued, "They are the culprits and the problem. They are the reckless criminals."[13]

As the opioids crisis was unfolding, in September 2017, the new CEO Craig Landau jotted down some notes, perhaps to pass the blame onto others. The notes read:

> There are:
>
> Too many Rxs being written
>
> Too high a dose
>
> For too long
>
> For conditions that don't often require them
>
> By doctors who lack the requisite training in how
>
> to use them appropriately.[14]

It is said by many, including those filing lawsuits against the company, that Purdue played a major role in the U.S. opioid crisis. Reports from the U.S. Centers for Disease Control and Prevention are that more than 130 Americans die every day of opioid overdoses, which usually follow an addiction. The center has also said that more than 200,000 Americans have died from opioid-related overdoses in the last two decades.[15] These numbers do not include those who died in many different countries during this period and are difficult to account for.

*This case was written by Archie B. Carroll, University of Georgia, for the 11th Edition, 2021.

Lawsuits and Bankruptcy

Purdue first faced a lawsuit over its aggressive marketing of OxyContin in 2007. Then it reached settlements over criminal charges that it had misled the public about the risk of addiction. However, more lawsuits followed. A State of Massachusetts's legal complaint in 2019 contended that the Sacklers were pushing Oxycodone into more hands through their marketing, at higher doses and for longer periods of time, while reaping billions of dollars even as the company blurred the risks of addiction and overdose that came with the drugs.[16] In the state's lawsuit against Purdue Pharma, it concluded by saying, "The opioid epidemic is not a mystery to the people who started it. The defendants knew what they were doing."[17]

In September 2019, the company filed for bankruptcy protection as part of its efforts to deal with the thousands of lawsuits that were accusing the company of fueling the opioid crisis. The lawsuits claimed that the Sackler family had aggressively marketed OxyContin, while at the same time misleading doctors and patients over the addiction and overdose risks.[18] The Chapter 11 bankruptcy postpones a company's obligations to its creditors as it is given time to reorganize its debts or sell parts of the business. The bankruptcy deal called for Purdue to be dissolved and an amount of money of about $10–$12 billion, along with $3 billion from the Sackler family, be set aside to settle the lawsuits. The Sacklers also offered to add an additional $1.5 billion that would come from the sale of Mundipharma, another company owned by the family.[19]

Several of the states involved oppose the deal because they do not know how the Sacklers came up with these amounts. Some of the prosecutors claim that the Sacklers have been moving billions of dollars offshore to different banks including some in Switzerland. The states want the Sackers to increase the amount of their own money that goes into the fund.[20] An increasing number of complainants are warning that the proposed settlement would short-circuit broader discussions about how to use Purdue's assets to address the addiction epidemic.[21]

Outside of its bankruptcy case, Purdue pleaded guilty in November 2020 to three federal felonies, including paying illegal kickbacks and deceiving drug-enforcement officials.[22] In the latest case, Purdue is set to plead guilty to three felony accounts including conspiracy to defraud the United States and conspiracy to violate federal anti-kickback laws as part of their settlement. The agreement also calls for Purdue to transform itself into a company to be run for the benefit of the public.[23] In addition, the Sackler family has agreed to pay $4.28 billion, a larger sum than the $3 billion previously agreed on.[24]

In June 2021, it appeared that the Sackler family was poised to win immunity from future opioid lawsuits. A federal judge in White Plains, New York, moved the deal forward despite objections from dozens of state attorneys general. According to legal documents filed, the immunity from further liability would extend to dozens of family members and other entities associated with the Sacklers.[25] The Sackler family will give up control of the company. The more than 400 civil cases already filed against family members would be halted. Members of the Sackler family testified at a hearing months prior claiming that they had done nothing wrong. David Sackler, who served on Purdue's board for six years, testified, "The family and the board acted legally and ethically."[26] Meanwhile, Massachusetts Attorney General Maura Healy said that giving the Sackler's immunity would "set a terrible precedent."[27]

Regardless of the outcome, the Sackler name will forever be associated with the opioid crisis. In December 2019, Tufts University in Boston removed the Sackler name from five facilities and programs, much to the chagrin of family members.[28] Other universities that have received significant donations from the Sackler family, including Tel Aviv University, Cornell, and Columbia, are being pressured by activist groups, students, and politicians to do the same.

Questions for Discussion

1. Identify the ethical issues in this case and the stakeholders affected.
2. What is wrong with aggressive marketing of drugs such as OxyContin? Shouldn't a company be free to market its products as it sees fit?
3. What marketing tactics they engaged in do you think are questionable?
4. The Sackler family owned and controlled Purdue Pharma. What is your assessment of their claim they did nothing wrong legally or ethically? It's the "company's" liability, they seem to be saying.
5. What is your assessment of the proposed settlement with the Sackler family? Should this end it all?

Endnotes

1. Barry Meier, "Origins of an Epidemic: Purdue Pharma Knew Its Opioids Were Widely Abused," *New York Times*, May 29, 2018, https://www.nytimes.com/2018/05/29/health/purdue-opioids-oxycontin.html. Accessed July 6, 2021.
2. Ibid.
3. Shraddha Chakradhar and Casey Ross, "The History of OxyContin, Told Through Unsealed Purdue Documents," *STAT*, December 3, 2019, https://www.statnews.com/2019/12/03/oxycontin-history-told-through-purdue-pharma-documents/. Accessed July 6, 2021.
4. Ibid.
5. Joanna Walters, "Meet the Sacklers: The Family Feuding Over Blame for the Opioid Crisis," *The Guardian*, February 13, 2018, https://www.theguardian.com/us-news/2018/feb/13/meet-the-sacklers-the-family-feuding-over-blame-for-the-opioid-crisis. Accessed July 6, 2021.
6. Ibid.
7. Ibid.
8. Sara Randazzo, "Purdue's Sackler Family Owners Worth $11 Billion, Documents Show," *The Wall*

Street Journal, April 20, 2021, https://www.wsj.com /articles/purdues-sackler-family-owners-worth-11 -billion-documents-show-11618962513. Accessed July 14, 2021.

9. WebMD, "Oxycontin," https://www.webmd.com /drugs/2/drug-2798/oxycontin-oral/details. Accessed July 6, 2021.

10. Ibid.

11. U.S. Department of Justice, "OxyContin Fast Facts," https://www.justice.gov/archive/ndic /pubs6/6025/6025p.pdf. Accessed July 7, 2021.

12. Andrew Joseph, "A Blizzard of Prescriptions: Documents Reveal New Details about Purdue's Marketing of OxyContin," *STAT*, January 15, 2019, https://www.statnews.com/2019/01/15 /massachusetts-purdue-lawsuit-new-details/. Accessed July 7, 2021.

13. Ibid.

14. Ibid.

15. BBCNews, "Purdue Pharma Files for Bankruptcy in the U.S." September 16, 2019, https://www.bbc .com/news/business-49711618. Accessed July 7, 2021.

16. Ibid.

17. Ibid.

18. BBCNews, Ibid.

19. Ibid.

20. Ibid.

21. Peg Brickley, "Purdue's Opioid Deal Faces Opposition," *The Wall Street Journal*, November 12, 2020, B9.

22. Randles and Randazzo,2021, B2.

23. Ibid.

24. Ibid.

25. Brian Mann, "Sackler Family Empire Poised to Win Immunity from Opioid Lawsuits," NPR, June 2, 2021, https://www.npr.org/2021/06/02/1002085031 /sackler-family-empire-poised-to-win-immunity -from-opioid-lawsuits. Accessed June 7, 2021.

26. Ibid.

27. Aaron Katersky and Meredith Deliso," Purdue Pharma Bankruptcy Plan, Which Would Give Sackler Family Immunity, Moves Forward," *ABC News* (June 3, 2021), https://abcnews.go.com /Business/purdue-pharma-bankruptcy-plan-give -sackler-family-immunity/story?id=78072454. Accessed July 14, 2021.

28. Ellen Barry, "Tufts Removes Sackler Name Over Opioids: 'Our Students Find It Objectionable," *The New York Times* (December 5, 2019), https://www .nytimes.com/2019/12/05/us/tufts-sackler-name -opioids.html. Accessed July 14, 2021.

Case 23

McDonald's: The Coffee Spill Heard 'Round the World*

The 1992 McDonald's coffee spill case is perhaps the most famous consumer lawsuit in the world. The details involved with it continue to be debated in many different venues—classrooms, websites, blogs, law schools, and business schools. Regardless, it serves as one of the best platforms in the world for considering what companies owe their consumer stakeholders and what responsibilities consumers have for their own well-being. Consumers, lawyers, students,and analysts are still debating the world-famous coffee spill case.[1]

The 2011 documentary film *Hot Coffee*, which analyzed the famous coffee spill, set the facts straight and revitalized the ongoing debate about the impact of tort reform on the U.S. judicial system. The film premiered at the 2011 Sundance Film Festival and aired on HBO during June 2011.[2] The film won many awards because it represented an iconic case. As of 2021, the film *Hot Coffee* was still available on Amazon Prime. What makes the case so intriguing? The issues of harm, liability, responsibility, and transparency are all involved in deciding whether or not McDonald's hot coffee is too hot and whether the company handled this case in the best manner.

Stella Liebeck

Stella Liebeck and her grandson, Chris Tiano, drove her son, Jim, to the airport 60 miles away in Albuquerque, New Mexico, on the morning of February 27, 1992. Because she had to leave home early, she and Chris missed having breakfast. After dropping Jim off at the airport, they proceeded to a McDonald's drive-through for breakfast. Stella, an active, 79-year-old, retired department-store clerk, ordered a McBreakfast, and Chris parked the car so she could add cream and sugar to her coffee.[3]

What occurred next was the coffee spill that has been heard 'round the world. A coffee spill, serious burns, a lawsuit, and an eventual settlement made Stella Liebeck (pronounced Lee-beck) the "poster lady" for the bitter tort reform discussions that have dominated the news for more than 30 years. To this day, the issue is still debated, with cases similar to Stella's continuing to be filed.

Third-Degree Burns

According to Liebeck's testimony, she tried to get the coffee lid off her coffee. She could not find any flat surface in the car, so she put the cup between her knees and tried to get it off that way. As she tugged at the lid, scalding coffee

---

*This case was written by Archie B. Carroll, University of Georgia, and updated in 2021.

spilled into her lap. Chris jumped from the car and tried to help her. She pulled at her sweatsuit, but the pants absorbed the coffee and held it close to her skin. She was squirming as the 170-degree coffee burned her groin, inner thigh, and buttocks. Third-degree burns were evident as she reached an emergency room. A vascular surgeon determined she had third-degree (full thickness) burns over 6 percent of her body.

Following the spill, Liebeck spent eight days in the hospital and about three weeks at home recuperating under the care of her daughter, Nancy Tiano. She was then hospitalized again for skin grafts. Liebeck lost 20 pounds during the ordeal and at times was practically immobilized. Another daughter, Judy Allen, recalled that her mother was in tremendous pain both after the accident and during the skin grafts.[4]

According to a *Newsweek* magazine report, Liebeck wrote to McDonald's in August 1994, asking them to turn down the coffee temperature. Though she was not planning to sue, her family thought she was due about $2,000 for out-of-pocket expenses, plus the lost wages of her daughter who stayed at home with her. The family reported that McDonald's offered her $800.[5]

Stella Files a Lawsuit

After this, the family went looking for a lawyer and retained Reed Morgan, a Houston attorney, who had won a $30,000 settlement against McDonald's in 1988 for a woman whose spilled coffee had caused her third-degree burns. Morgan filed a lawsuit on behalf of Liebeck, charging McDonald's with "gross negligence" for selling coffee that was "unreasonably dangerous" and "defectively manufactured." Morgan asked for no less than $100,000 in compensatory damages, including pain and suffering, and triple that amount in punitive damages.

McDonald's Motion Rejected

McDonald's moved for summary dismissal of the case, defending the coffee's heat and blaming Liebeck for spilling it. According to the company, she was the "proximate cause" of the injury. With McDonald's motion rejected, a trial date was set for August 1994.

As the trial date approached, no out-of-court settlement occurred. Morgan, the attorney, said that at one point he offered to drop the case for $300,000 and was willing to settle for half that amount, but McDonald's would not budge. Days before the trial, the judge ordered the two parties to attend a mediation session. The mediator, a retired judge, recommended McDonald's settle for $225,000, using the argument that a jury would likely award that amount. Again, McDonald's resisted settlement.[6]

The Trial

The trial lasted seven days, with expert witnesses dueling over technical issues, such as the temperature at which coffee causes burns. Initially, the jury was annoyed at having to hear what at first was thought to be a frivolous case about

spilled coffee, but the evidence presented by the prosecution grabbed its attention. Photos of Liebeck's charred skin were introduced. (These dramatic photos are shown in the documentary *Hot Coffee*.) A renowned burn expert testified that coffee at 170 degrees would cause second-degree burns within 3.5 seconds of hitting the skin.

The Defense Helped Liebeck

Defense witnesses inadvertently helped the prosecution. A quality-assurance supervisor at McDonald's testified that the company did not lower its coffee heat despite 700 burn complaints over ten years. A safety consultant argued that 700 complaints—about one in every 24 million cups sold—were basically trivial. This comment was apparently interpreted to imply that McDonald's cared more about statistics than about people. An executive for McDonald's testified that the company knew its coffee sometimes caused serious burns, but it was not planning to go beyond the tiny print warning on the cup that said, "Caution: Contents Hot!" The executive went on to say that McDonald's did not intend to change any of its coffee policies or procedures, saying, "There are more serious dangers in restaurants."

In the closing arguments, one of McDonald's defense attorneys acknowledged that the coffee was hot and that that is how customers wanted it. She went on to insist that Liebeck had only herself to blame as she was unwise to put the cup between her knees. She also noted that Liebeck failed to leap out of the bucket seat in the car after the spill, thus preventing the hot coffee from falling off her. The attorney concluded by saying that the real question in the case is how far society should go to restrict what most of us enjoy and accept.[7]

The Jury Decides

The jury deliberated about four hours and reached a verdict for Liebeck. It decided on compensatory damages of $200,000, which it reduced to $160,000 after judging that 20 percent of the fault belonged to Liebeck for spilling the coffee. The jury concluded that McDonald's had engaged in willful, reckless, malicious, or wanton conduct, which is the basis for punitive damages. The jury decided on a figure of $2.7 million in punitive damages.

Company Neglected Customers

One juror later said that the facts were overwhelmingly against the company and that the company just was not taking care of its customers. Another juror felt the huge punitive damages were intended to be a stern warning for McDonald's to wake up and realize its customers were getting burned. Another juror said he began to realize that the case was really about the callous disregard for the safety of customers.

Public-opinion polls after the jury verdict were squarely on the side of McDonald's. Polls showed that a large majority of Americans—including many who usually support the little guy—were outraged at the verdict.[8] But the public did not hear all the details presented in the trial.

Judge Reduces Award

The judge later slashed the jury award by more than 75 percent to $640,000. Liebeck appealed the reduction, and McDonald's continued fighting the award as excessive. In December 1994, it was announced that McDonald's had reached an out-of-court settlement with Liebeck, but the terms of the settlement were not disclosed due to a confidentiality provision. The settlement was reached to end appeals in the case. We will never know the final ending to this case because the parties entered into an undisclosed settlement that has never been revealed to the public. Since this was a public case, litigated in public and subjected to extensive media reporting, some lawyers think that such secret settlements, after public trials, should not be condoned.[9]

Debate Over Coffee Temperature

Coffee suddenly became a hot topic in the industry. The Specialty Coffee Association of America put coffee safety on its agenda for discussion. A spokesperson for the National Coffee Association said that McDonald's coffee conforms to industry temperature standards. A spokesperson for Mr. Coffee, the coffee-machine maker, said that if customer complaints are any indication, industry settings may be too low. Some customers like it hotter. A coffee connoisseur who imported and wholesaled coffee said that 175 degrees is probably the optimum temperature for coffee because that's when aromatics are being released. Coffee served at home is generally 135–140 degrees. McDonald's continued to say that it is serving its coffee the way customers like it. As one writer noted, the temperature of McDonald's coffee helps explain why it sells a billion cups a year.[10]

Later Incidents

In August 2000, a Vallejo, California, woman sued McDonald's, saying she suffered second-degree burns when a handicapped employee at a drive-through window dropped a large cup of coffee in her lap.[11] The suit charged that the handicapped employee could not grip the cardboard tray and was instead trying to balance it on top of her hands and forearms when the accident occurred in August 1999. The victim, Karen Muth, said she wanted at least $10,000 for her medical bills, pain and suffering, and "humiliation." But her lawyer, Dan Ryan, told the local newspaper that she was entitled to between $400,000 and $500,000. Attorney Ryan went on to say, "We recognize that there's an Americans with Disabilities Act, but that doesn't give them [McDonald's] the right to sacrifice the safety of their customers."[12] It is not known how this lawsuit was settled.

Suits Go Global

It was also announced in August 2000 that British solicitors had organized 26 spill complainants into a group suit against McDonald's over the piping-hot nature of its beverages. One London lawyer said, "Hot coffee, hot tea, and hot water are at the center of this case. We are alleging they are too hot." Since that time other lawsuits have been filed around the world.[13]

Burned By a Hot Pickle

In a related turn of events, a Knoxville, Tennessee, woman, Veronica Martin, filed a lawsuit in 2000 claiming that she was permanently scarred when a hot pickle from a McDonald's hamburger fell on her chin.[14] She claimed the burn caused her physical and mental harm. Martin sued for $110,000. Martin's husband, Darrin, also sought $15,000 because he "has been deprived of the services and consortium of his wife." According to Veronica Martin's lawsuit, the hamburger "was in a defective condition or unreasonably dangerous to the general consumer and, in particular, to her." The lawsuit went on to say, "while attempting to eat the hamburger, the pickle dropped from the hamburger onto her chin. The pickle was extremely hot and burned the chin of Veronica Martin." Martin had second-degree burns and was permanently scarred, according to the lawsuit. One report was that the McDonald's owner settled this case out of court.[15]

Issue Won't Go Away

The Stella Awards

For 30 years now, the coffee spill heard 'round the world continues to be a subject of heated debate. The coffee spill and subsequent trial, publicity, and resolution "prompted a tort reform storm that has barely abated."[16] One school of thought held that it represents the most frivolous lawsuit of all time. In fact, a program called the "Stella Awards" was begun to recognize each year's most outrageous lawsuit. The awards were the creation of humorist Randy Cassingham, and his summaries of award-winning cases may be found on the Stella Awards website.[17] In actuality, most of the lawsuits he chronicles are far more outrageous than the coffee spill in which Stella Liebeck did get seriously injured. On the other hand, consumer groups are still concerned about victims of what they see as dangerous products, and they continue to assail McDonald's callous unconcern for Stella Liebeck.

In the ensuing decades, lawsuits over spilt beverages have continued to come and go, but most of them have been resolved with less fanfare than Stella's case. As for S. Reed Morgan, the lawyer who successfully represented Stella Liebeck, he has handled only three cases involving beverages since Liebeck's suit. Morgan has turned down many plaintiffs but said he is interested in such cases only if they involve third-degree burns.[18]

A Lawsuit in Moscow

Coffee spill cases have gone global. In fact, a long-running case against McDonald's in Moscow was closed in 2006 by a Moscow court after the claimant withdrew her $34,000 lawsuit. Olga Kuznetsova filed a lawsuit against the company after hot coffee was spilled on her in a Russian

McDonald's. Kuznetsova claimed that a swinging door hit her while she was walking out onto the restaurant's terrace with a full tray. She demanded 900,000 rubles (then about $34,000) in damages. McDonald's lawyers said she had nobody to blame but herself because the paper cup carried a warning that the coffee was hot, which prompted her to go to court.[19]

Coffee Spill Suits Continue

There is likely no end in sight for coffee-spill cases. For example, in 2017 a Florida personal injury plaintiff was awarded $100,000 after she suffered serious burns from the coffee she bought at a Starbucks drive-through in Jacksonville.[20] She claimed that the lid on the cup was faulty, causing the hot coffee to spill in her lap, causing first- and second-degree burns. Evidence presented at the case revealed that the company had received more than 80 complaints about coffee lids popping off.[21]

Stella Liebeck never regained the energy and strength she had before the coffee spill. Stella passed away in 2004, at the age of 91, but the memory of her case continues on.[22] Since her case was filed, consumers have pursued hot coffee claims not just with McDonald's but also Burger King, Dunkin' Donuts, Starbucks, Continental Airlines, and other companies. McDonald's now serves its coffee at 10 degrees lower than before Stella's lawsuit.[23]

Consumers can learn more about the Stella Liebeck case and many others by visiting Ralph Nader's American Museum of Tort Law in Winsted, Connecticut, his hometown.[24] The new museum features groundbreaking civil cases on auto safety, tobacco, asbestos, and, yes, spilled coffee, along with many others.[25]

Questions for Discussion

1. What are the major issues in the Liebeck case and in the following incidents? Was the lawsuit "frivolous" as some people thought, or was it serious business regarding safety and treatment of consumers?
2. What are the social (economic, legal, and ethical) responsibilities toward consumers by McDonald's in the Liebeck case and the other cases? What are consumers' responsibilities when they buy a product such as hot coffee or hot hamburgers? How does a company give consumers what they want and yet protect them at the same time?
3. What are the arguments supporting McDonald's position in the Liebeck case? What are the arguments supporting Liebeck's position? Should McDonald's have settled this case when it had a chance?
4. If you had been a juror in the Liebeck case, which position would you most likely have supported? Why? What if you had been a juror in the pickle burn case?
5. What are the similarities and differences between the coffee burn cases and the pickle burn case? Does one represent a more serious threat to

consumer harm? What should McDonald's, and other fast-food restaurants, do about hot food, such as hamburgers, when consumers are injured?
6. Why did Stella Liebeck win this case, and what implications does it pose for businesses' responsibilities toward consumers?
7. What is your assessment of the "Stella Awards"? Is this making light of a serious problem?
8. Do we now live in a society where businesses are responsible for customers' accidents or carelessness in using products? We live in a society that is growing older. Does this fact place a special responsibility on merchants who sell products to senior citizens?

Endnotes

1. Andy Simmons, "Remember the Hot Coffee Lawsuit? It Changed the Way McDonald's Heats Coffee Forever," RD.com, February 23, 2021, https://www.rd.com/article/hot-coffee-lawsuit/. Accessed July 12, 2021.
2. Hot Coffee, http://www.hotcoffeethemovie.com/. Accessed June 8, 2016.
3. Andrea Gerlin, "A Matter of Degree: How a Jury Decided That a Coffee Spill Is Worth $2.9 Million," *The Wall Street Journal* (September 1, 1994), A1, A4.
4. Theresa Howard, "McDonald's Settles Coffee Suit in Out-of-Court Agreement," *Nation's Restaurant News* (December 12, 1994), 1.
5. Aric Press and Ginny Carroll, "Are Lawyers Burning America?" *Newsweek* (March 20, 1995), 30–35, https://www.newsweek.com/are-lawyers-burning-america-180680. Accessed July 13, 2021.
6. Howard, 1.
7. "Coffee-Spill Suits Meet ADA," Overlawyered.com, August 10, 2000, https://www.overlawyered.com/archives/00aug1.html. Accessed July 13, 2021.
8. Gerlin, A4.
9. "The Actual Facts about the McDonald's Coffee Case," The 'Lectric Law Library, https://www.lectlaw.com/files/cur78.htm/. Accessed July 13, 2021.
10. Ibid.
11. *The Los Angeles Times*, "Woman Scalded by Cup of Coffee Dropped in Her Lap Sues McDonalds," August 8, 2000. https://www.latimes.com/archives/la-xpm-2000-aug-08-mn-668-story.html. Accessed July 13, 2021.
12. Ibid.
13. Wikipedia, "McDonald's Legal Cases," May 8, 2020, https://en.wikipedia.org/wiki/McDonald%27s_legal_cases. Accessed July 13, 2021.
14. Chicago Tribune, "Woman Settles Suit Over Hot Pickle," April 15, 2001, https://www.chicagotribune.com/news/ct-xpm-2001-04-15-0104150365-story.html. Accessed July 13, 2021.
15. Associated Press, "Couple Seeks $125,000 for Pickle Burn on Chin," *Athens Banner Herald* (October 8, 2000), 6A. Also see "Woman, McDonalds Settle Lawsuit Over a Hot Pickle,"

Deseret News, April 14, 2001, https://www
.deseret.com/2001/4/14/19580722/woman
-mcdonald-s-settle-lawsuit-over-a-hot-pickle.
Accessed July 13, 2021.

16. Matt Fleisher-Black, "One Lump or Two?" *The American Lawyer* (June 4, 2004).

17. StellaAwards.com, https://stellaawards.com/.
Accessed July 13, 2021.

18. Carlson Law Firm, "The Verdict: How the Hot Coffee Lawsuit Led to Tort Reform," September 10, 2020,
https://www.carlsonattorneys.com/news-and-update
/liebeck-v-mcdonalds. Accessed July 13, 2021.

19. "Moscow McDonald's Coffee-Spill Case Closed,"
RIA Novosti (January 11, 2006), http://en.rian.ru
/russia/20061101/55304783.html.Accessed June 8,
2016.

20. Halberg and Fogg, "Another Hot Coffee Case?
Florida Injury Lawyer Explains What Many
Misunderstand," October 2, 2020, https://www
.southfloridainjurylawyerblog.com/another-hot
-coffee-case-florida-injury-lawyer-explains-what
-many-misunderstand/. Accessed July 13, 2021.

21. Ibid.

22. Simmons, 2021, Ibid.

23. Ibid.

24. American Museum of Tort Law,https://www
.tortmuseum.org/liebeck-v-mcdonalds/. Accessed
July 13, 2021.

25. PBS News Hour, "Inside Ralph Nader's American
Museum of Tort Law," https://www.pbs.org
/newshour/show/to-teach-tort-law-ralph-nader
-builds-a-museum. Accessed July 13, 2021.

Case 24

Boeing's Two Flight Crashes*

On October 29, 2018, Lion Air's Boeing 737 MAX plane crashed into the Java Sea, off the coast of Jakarta, Indonesia, just 13 minutes after takeoff, killing 189 people.[1] An investigation by Indonesian investigators said that the flight was doomed by a combination of aircraft design flaws, inadequate pilot training, and maintenance issues.[2] The final accident report concluded that the flight from Indonesia's capital, Jakarta, to the island of Sumatra crashed because the pilots were never told how to quickly respond to malfunctions in the jet's automated flight-control system.[3]

The final accident report concluded that the flight should have been grounded before it took off because of an earlier cockpit issue. Because the issue had not been properly recorded, the plane was allowed to take off without being fixed.[4] In addition, investigators found that a crucial sensor, which had been bought from a repair shop in Florida, had not been properly tested. The sensor was to feed information into the plane's Maneuvering Characteristics Augmentation System (MCAS). The purpose of this software is to help prevent the 737 Max from stalling. Indonesian investigators found that the system repeatedly pushed the plane's nose down while the pilots were fighting for control.[5]

The investigators also discovered that the plane's first officer, who reportedly performed poorly during training, had to struggle to read through a list of emergency steps that he was supposed to have memorized. The first officer was flying the plane at the time but the report said that the captain had not suitably briefed him when he handed over the controls as they struggled to keep the plane in the air.[6] The report also found that 31 pages of the plane's maintenance log were missing. Investigators from Indonesia had previously said that design and mechanical problems were key factors in the plane's crash.[7]

After the accident, Boeing provided documents to investigators that revealed an exchange of messages about the plane's automated safety system when the plane was being certified in 2016. One pilot reported that he had run into unexpected troubles during tests and said further that he had basically lied to the regulators unknowingly.[8]

Five months after the Indonesian crash, the same kind of malfunction caused a Boeing 747 MAX to crash in Ethiopia, resulting in the deaths of all 157 people on board.[9] Ethiopian Airlines flight 302 plunged to the ground six minutes after takeoff on March 10, 2019.[10] Flight 302 took off from the Ethiopian capital, Addis Ababa, enroute to Nairobi.[11] An Ethiopian investigation cited design flaws with MCAS, just as in the Indonesian investigation. It was also conveyed that Boeing had not provided adequate training to the crew using the MAX's unique systems.[12]

The Ethiopian Airlines and Lion Air disasters of 2018 and 2019 raised concerns around the world about the safety of the Boeing 747 MAX fleet, and the whole fleet of aircraft was grounded on March 13, 2019, as a result.[13] In addition to the human tragedy, Boeing's business suffered a huge blow. The company had thousands of orders for the 747 MAX on the books. Also, it was discovered that there were other concerns with the plane's flight control computer, wiring, and engines.[14]

A congressional investigation in the United States concluded that the two fatal crashes were partly due to Boeing's

*This case was written by Archie B. Carroll, University of Georgia, in 2021 for the 11th Edition.

unwillingness to share technical details with those needing to know. The investigation blamed a "culture of concealment" at Boeing but also said that the government's regulatory system was flawed as well.[15] The U.S. report was highly critical of both Boeing and the regulatory agency, the Federal Aviation Association (FAA). The 250-page report found that Boeing had failed in its design and development of the MAX, and the FAA failed in its oversight and certification of the aircraft. The report also alleged "regulatory capture," wherein an overly close relationship had developed between Boeing and the FAA that compromised the process of gaining safety certification.[16] The report said that the FAA was, in effect, in Boeing's pocket and that FAA's management had actually overruled its own technical and safety experts "at the behest of Boeing."[17]

Even though there was evidence that Boeing knew about the aircraft's problems before the accidents, the company cooperated with the investigations. Just eight days after the first crash, Boeing issued a safety warning advising 747 MAX operators to deactivate MCAS if the flight crew encountered conditions like those identified in the Lion Air crash. Boeing expressed sympathy to the victim's families and pledged $100 million in support.[18] After the Lion Air crash, Boeing CEO Dennis Muilenburg reported that the company would address the safety concerns even as some called for his resignation. Muilenburg appeared before two congressional committees and admitted that Boeing knew of the test pilot's concerns expressed in 2019.[19] During the hearings, Muilenburg offered repeated apologies to the families of the victims of the crashes.[20] Boeing also said it would pay $144,500 to families who lost relatives in the crashes. The money was to come from a $50 million financial assistance fund that the company created in July 2019.[21]

On December 23, 2019, Boeing announced that Muilenburg resigned from his position effective immediately. The company's board of directors named David Calhoun, its current chair, as successor.[22] Boeing had been under intense stress and scrutiny since the plane crashes, and the crises were threatening the stability of the company. In a press release, Boeing's board announced that the changes in leadership were made so that the company could restore confidence and to rebuild relationships with regulators, its customers, and other stakeholders.[23]

Several observers want to hold the board of directors responsible, in part, for not carefully monitoring the safety issue. A Boeing investor lawsuit claimed that the board had been negligent because it did not carefully provide safety oversight both before and after the two deadly crashes.[24] The lawsuit also alleged that the board deliberately misled the public through interviews with various media. The lawsuit quotes internal e-mails and board meeting records maintaining that the company's board repeatedly moved in tandem with the company's management rather than challenging decisions based on safety considerations.[25] The lawsuit asserted further that the board failed to fulfill its proper role, that they missed red flags they should have

noted, and they failed to question CEO Muilenburg about how he handled the crisis. The shareholder lawsuit seeks to hold the board members personally accountable for paying the company back for damages incurred because of their breach of duties.[26] In early 2021, the Justice Department did announce that Boeing had agreed to pay $2.5 billion to settle a criminal charge that the company had conspired to defraud the FAA during its review of the 737 MAX.[27]

By June 2021, the 737 MAX was finally cleared to fly again in most of the world. Safety agencies in most countries had ordered Boeing to make repairs to the flight control system, update operating manuals, and increase pilot training.[28] Earlier in 2020, however, Boeing had fixed a date to discontinue its flagship 737-8 model of aircraft in favor of aircraft that are more efficient, have better range, and are more flexible. The Boeing 737 MAX is now being passed over by the smaller, nimbler, Boeing 787 Dreamliners and the Airbus A350s. By 2021, the airlines found themselves in the midst of the most severe financial aviation crisis ever faced, due to the pandemic and worldwide lockdowns. However, they continue to fly the old 737-8 line and plan to retire them as quickly as possible.[29]

Questions for Discussion

1. Identify the legal, ethical, and management issues involved with the two Boeing 747 MAX crashes.
2. Who is most accountable for the Boeing crashes? Boeing executives? The pilots? The Boeing maintenance crews? The FAA? The Boeing Board?
3. Do you think the "culture of concealment" and "regulatory capture" issues were instrumental to the crashes? Could these have been avoided through sound ethics management? What ethical principles should Boeing have followed?
4. What is your assessment of how Boeing handled the crashes from a human relations, business ethics, and crisis management perspective?
5. What could Boeing's leadership have done differently or better in terms of dealing with the crises?
6. Based on your reading, do you think the Boeing 747 MAX is now safe to fly? Will customers back off now when they realize they are scheduled to fly on a 747 MAX? Or, will things quickly return to "business as usual"?

Endnotes

1. Associated Press and Reuters, "Indonesia Report Finds Fatal Lion Air Jet Crash Due to Boeing, Pilots, Maintenance," NBCnews, October 25, 2019, https://www.nbcnews.com/news/world/indonesia-report-finds-fatal-lion-air-jet-crash-due-boeing-n1071796. Accessed July 13, 2021.
2. Ibid.
3. Ibid.
4. BBC News, "Boeing 737 MAX Lion Air Crash Caused by a Series of Failures," October 25, 2019, https://www.bbc.com/news/business-50177788. Accessed July 13, 2021.
5. Ibid.

6.   Ibid.
7.   Ibid.
8.   BBC News, "Boeing Staff Texted about 737 MAX Issue in 2016," October 18, 2019, https://www.bbc.com/news/business-50101766. Accessed July 13, 2021.
9.   Associated Press and Reuters, October 25, 2019, Ibid.
10.   Jeff Wise, "" Six Minutes of Terror: What Passengers and Crew Experienced Aboard Ethiopian Airlines Flight 302," April 9, 2019, https://nymag.com/intelligencer/2019/04/what-passengers-experienced-on-the-ethiopian-airlines-flight.html. Accessed July 13, 2021.
11.   Ilaria Grasso Macola, "Ethiopian Airlines Crash: What's Happened in the Last Two Years?" Airport Technology, June 10, 2021, https://www.airport-technology.com/features/ethiopian-airlines-crash-what-happened-last-two-years/. Accessed July 13, 2021.
12.   Kent German, "Two Years After Being Grounded, the Boeing 737 MAX is Flying Again," June 19, 2021, https://www.cnet.com/news/boeing-737-max-8-all-about-the-aircraft-flight-ban-and-investigations/. Accessed July 13, 2021.
13.   Ibid.
14.   Ibid.
15.   BBC News, "Boeing's Culture of Concealment to Blame for the 737 Crashes," September 16, 2020, https://www.bbc.com/news/business-54174223. Accessed July 13, 2021.
16.   Ibid.
17.   Ibid.
18.   German, 2021, Ibid.
19.   Ibid.
20.   Brakkton Booker, "Boeing CEO Muilenburg Is Out," *NPR*, December 23, 2019, https://www.npr.org/2019/12/23/790750329/boeing-ceo-dennis-muilenburg-to-step-down. Accessed July 13, 2021.
21.   BBC, "Boeing to Pay Bereaved 747 Families $144,500 Each," September 23, 2019, https://www.bbc.com/news/business-49803068. Accessed July 13, 2021.
22.   Booker, Ibid.
23.   Ibid.
24.   Douglas MacMillan, "Investors Allege Boeing Board of Directors Misled Public About Company's Safety Oversight After Crashes," *The Washington Post*, February 16, 2021, https://www.washingtonpost.com/business/2021/02/16/boeing-investor-lawsuit/. Accessed July 17, 2021.
25.   Ibid.
26.   Ibid.
27.   Ibid.
28.   German, 2021, Ibid.
29.   Andrew Curran, "Boeing Set to End the 747 After Over a Half Century of Production," Simple Flying, July 2, 2020, https://simpleflying.com/boeing-to-end-747-production/. Accessed July 13, 2021.

Case 25

Should States Woo Big Business with Tax Incentives? Amazon Thinks So!*

Often, state and local governments use tax cuts (abatements) or other types of incentives to entice firms to locate within their area. While tax abatements remain useful incentives to help governments achieve job creation goals, those same cuts may create undue burdens for other stakeholders such as taxpayers and local businesses who do not benefit from tax cuts. Additionally, some argue that legacy local businesses end up suffering, particularly when facing new competition from large companies that are usually the recipient of such incentives.

Amazon is a company that has received numerous such incentives, causing one *Fortune* reporter to write, "Why are local governments paying Amazon to destroy Main Street?"[1] Over the last decade, Amazon has opened up new facilities all across the country with the help of local governments offering various incentives. For example, Glenwillow, Ohio, reduced the taxes on Amazon's new distribution center by nearly half for 15 years.[2] Similar stories abound in Whiteland, Indiana, Arlington Heights, Illinois, and Windsor, Connecticut. Overall, as of 2020, Amazon received more than $3 billion in subsidies from state and local governments that were excited to woo the big e-commerce giant to their areas.[3]

Most local officials pushing for such tax breaks believe it will bring jobs and revenue to their cities and towns. However, according to the Economic Policy Institute, new warehouses do not bring wider employment growth to the local economy; if they do, it is too small of an impact to even measure.[4] Nevertheless, state and local governments cannot seem to resist the lure of big business—even when it means lost tax revenue for their constituents. In 2020, watchdog group Good Jobs First (GJF) identified more than $20.1 billion in revenue lost to tax abatements, warning that the number is low because states and localities often

*This case was prepared by Linda Rodriguez, University of South Carolina-Aiken, and Jill A. Brown, Bentley University, in 2016 and updated by Jill Brown in 2021.

do not fully disclose the amounts.[5] The case of Amazon in South Carolina (SC) may be one such example of how tax abatements can come with some unintended consequences.

Amazon in South Carolina

In 2012, Amazon decided to build a fulfillment center in Lexington, South Carolina." Fulfillment centers," where goods and services are held and then distributed, are instrumental to Amazon's success in their distribution strategy.[6] Amazon started with two fulfillment centers in Seattle and Delaware; currently they have approximately 110 centers in the United States and another 185 globally, amounting to more than 333 million active square feet of storage space.[7]

Lexington, South Carolina, was an ideal location for its southeast distribution network. Along with plans to do the same in Tennessee, it began to negotiate with the SC state legislature. Specifically, Jeff Bezos said that he would not open a fulfillment center in South Carolina unless the state agreed that Amazon would not have to collect sales tax from SC residents.[8] He had negotiated this deal with other states under a 1992 U.S. Supreme Court ruling holding that the Constitution's commerce clause prevents state officials from requiring retailers who have no physical presence in their states to collect their sales taxes.[9]

South Carolina agreed with his request after initially voting it down.[10] They did this, in part, because Amazon immediately canceled $52 million in procurement contracts and removed all job postings from their website when they encountered opposition.[11] To incentivize the company to locate to Lexington, the state legislature of South Carolina, in conjunction with Lexington County, granted Amazon approximately 90 acres of land, a five-year exemption from charging SC residents state sales tax, capital property tax cuts, and state job tax credits. Further, the long-standing Sunday-morning sales restrictions were lifted so that Amazon could fill orders around the clock.[12]

At the time of the negotiations, South Carolina had been experiencing some of the highest unemployment in the country. The Bureau of Labor listed South Carolina's unemployment in August 2011 as 10.9 percent, causing the state to be ranked at 48 out of 50 in unemployment.[13] The lure of new job opportunities through Amazon was hard for the SC legislature to resist. Amazon agreed that in return for building and tax concessions, they would hire primarily from within SC, adding 1,250 jobs in the first year, with an additional 750 jobs over the next five years. However, the deal was highly debated.

At first, then-governor Nikki Haley staunchly opposed the SC sales tax exemption because many local businesses believed that the exemption would create an unfair tax advantage for Amazon relative to other SC firms. At least 20 SC lawmakers agreed, including SC State Representative Gary Simrill (R-York), who claimed that the sales tax break gave Amazon an unfair advantage over local brick and mortar businesses.[14]

However, the SC legislature let the deal pass, and Governor Haley capitulated by not vetoing the bill. In the end, the legislature supported the bill with the notion that building the distribution center would support job creation, and the staffing of the distribution center from local labor pools would help South Carolina's economic recovery. Further, South Carolina expected to net $11 million in payroll and property taxes per year regardless of losing the SC state sales tax revenues from Amazon.[15] In essence, the legislature, the governor, and Amazon stuck to "quid pro quo" negotiations, essentially ignoring many local stakeholder interests and the opposing voices from the community.

Nikki Haley, Then-Governor of South Carolina

Nikki Haley, in 2011, was the nation's youngest governor at age 39.[16] Governor Haley ran as a fiscal conservative becoming South Carolina's first female and ethnic minority governor.[17] She was born in Bamberg, SC, to Indian immigrants, where her first job was in her family's clothing store as a bookkeeper; she started the job when she was 13. She attended and graduated from Clemson University with a bachelor of science degree in accounting. After graduation, she worked as an accounting supervisor for FCR Recycling, Inc. and five of its subsidiaries. Eventually she returned to the family business, growing it into a multimillion-dollar operation.

At the time of the Amazon deal, Governor Haley was in a tough position. Former governor Mark Sanford, who finished his office under the scandal of an extramarital affair, had promised Amazon the tax breaks in late 2010.[19] When Governor Haley relented to the decision of the SC legislature, she said that although she opposed the tax breaks, she would honor the commitments made by the previous administration. However, she vowed, "we will never have a change like this in tax policy under the Haley administration in order to get jobs. It is bad policy and it is not something we are going to have happen."[20]

Amazon's Opposition

Local groups and businesses most opposed to the bill becoming law spent nearly $166,000 for lobbyists to halt the sales tax break.[21] To fight back, Amazon spent nearly $200,000 for their own set of lobbyists; various reports said the total amount was more because neither side was compelled to disclose total costs. Some claimed that the costs to battle the sales tax break approached $2 million.[22] Among those opposed to the Amazon.com deal was the SC Alliance for Main Street Fairness, which formed a coalition of local businesses.[23]

The Result

In 2012, Amazon built the fulfillment center in Lexington, South Carolina, at a total cost of around $2 million.[24] Then, it announced plans to open a second fulfillment center in Spartanburg County, South Carolina, such that the total investment in South Carolina fulfillment centers would be close to $50 million.[25] Vice President of Amazon Global Customer Fulfillment David Clark announced, "We had a great first holiday season in Lexington County and we look forward to serving our customers from both Lexington and Spartanburg Counties by the fall.[26] By 2020, Amazon had hired thousands of workers for the South Carolina fulfillment centers, with one county council person noting, "Amazon exceeded all of our expectations."[27]

Corporate Welfare

The subject of tax and other incentives to lure businesses to an area is an example of what has been called "corporate welfare." Corporate welfare are those actions that governments take that provide benefits to a corporation or industry and may include things such as grants, tax breaks, regulatory preference, and the like.[28] However, the example of Amazon in South Carolina shows how contentious corporate welfare might be. Some say that the uncollected sales tax from Amazon costs each state quite a bit of lost revenue. According to a report by the National Conference of State Legislatures, South Carolina lost out on an estimated $254 million in taxes from out-of-state sales, mostly online.[29] One expert estimated that in total, Amazon's sales-tax-free status has cost states almost $8.6 billion in tax revenues.[30]

On New Year's Day, 2016, the sales tax breaks the South Carolina Legislature gave Amazon in 2011 expired. Amazon began collecting sales tax for products it sold in South Carolina but pushed back on collecting taxes on third-party marketplace sales. Amazon maintained that the seller is responsible for determining if sales tax is required and for collecting and remitting it. In 2019, the South Carolina Department of Revenue took Amazon to court to collect more than $12 million in back taxes, penalties, and interest for third-party sales for the first quarter of 2016. South Carolina argued that under state law, Amazon is considered the seller because the company controls a large part of the sales process for its third-party merchants. The State of South Carolina won the lawsuit, but as of 2021, Amazon was still appealing the ruling. The lawsuit has the potential to affect more than just Amazon transactions, as third-party collections and state taxes have been issues for other online retailers and distributors, including Wayfair. A decision in the 2018 Supreme Court case *South Dakota v. Wayfair* provided precedent for South Carolina's case requesting that sellers like Amazon collect and pay taxes.[31]

If Governor Haley Had A Crystal Ball...

If Governor Haley had the opportunity to see into the future, would she have still supported the Amazon tax abatements? There is no question that the fulfillment centers have employed many South Carolinians and brought tax monies to the area. However, the potential negative impact on small businesses and the ongoing tax fights provide some challenges to hosting a powerful business like Amazon. Nevertheless, Governor Haley responded to the initial announcement of Amazon's hiring at the Lexington, SC,facility with the following message:

> For a company like Amazon to make the decision to expand its operations in South Carolina, it is a special source of pride and a reason to celebrate because it

proves what we already know—that we have a world class work force and competitive business environment. The 500 new jobs this expansion will create is terrific news for the Midlands community, and we look forward to watching Amazon continue to grow here for many years to come.[32]

Questions for Discussion

1. Who is helped and who gets hurt in the use of tax incentives? Draw a stakeholder map for Amazon and the governments involved. Who was excluded, or who could have been included?
2. Did Amazon, the South Carolina State Legislature, and the county of Lexington, SC, arrive at creating shared value for the greatest number of stakeholders?
3. What is the nature of the various stakeholder stakes? Are they owners or community members? Analyze their legitimacy, power, and urgency characteristics.
4. Was Amazon abusing its power when it cancelled procurement contracts and job postings if it did not get its way?
5. Could the state of South Carolina, or Lexington County, have asked for more, or were they fortunate to get what they got?
6. Do "corporate welfare" deals like this give Amazon an unfair advantage over other businesses that do not receive tax breaks? What are the ethical issues involved in this decision?
7. What updates can you find about this tax break issue in South Carolina or in other states?

Endnotes

1. Pat Garofalo, "Why Are Local Governments Paying Amazon to Destroy Main Street?," *Fortune* (August 23, 2020), https://fortune.com/2020/08/23/amazon-coronavirus-taxes-local-governments/. Accessed July 14, 2021.
2. Ibid.
3. Ibid.
4. Ibid.
5. Richard McGahey, "Amazon Gets Billions While State and Local Government Budgets Collapse," *Forbes* (December 17, 2020), https://www.forbes.com/sites/richardmcgahey/2020/12/17/amazon-gets-billions-while-state-and-local-government-budgets-collapse/?sh=163c3b5d42db. Accessed July 14, 2021.
6. Dan Berthiaume, "Amazon's Expanding Footprint Includes New Fulfillment Centers, College Pickup Locations," *Retailing Today* (April 27, 2016), http://www.retailingtoday.com/article/amazons-expanding-footprint-includes-new-fulfillment-centers-college-pickup-locations. Accessed June 22, 2016.
7. Ramish Zafar, "Amazon Grows 333 Million Square Foot Operating Footprint Via New Deal," WCCFTech (June 23, 2020), https://wccftech.com/amazon-warehouse-lease-new-york/. Accessed July 14, 2021.
8. Tim Flach, "Amazon Packing after South Carolina Tax Vote," *McClatchyDC*, http://www.mcclatchydc.com/news/nation-world/national/economy/article24626677.html. Accessed July 15, 2021.

9. Janet Novack, "Amazon's Special Deals with States Unconstitutional, Law Profs Say," *Forbes* (December 4, 2011), http://www.forbes.com /sites/janetnovack/2011/12/04/amazons-special -deals-with-states-unconstitutional-law-profs -say/#4ddfcf2c73c7. Accessed July 15, 2021.
10. Ibid.
11. Ibid.
12. Charles Reynolds, "Sunday Blue Laws Ended in Lexington County," *The Examiner* (December 23, 2010), http://www.examiner.com/article/sunday -blue-laws-ended-lexington-county. Accessed July 15, 2021.
13. Bureau of Labor Statistics, "State Unemployment Rates 2011," http://www.bls.gov/opub/ted/2012 /ted_20120313.htm. Accessed July 15, 2021.
14. Cassie Cope, "Controversial Amazon SC Tax Break Set to Expire in 2016," *The State* (December 28, 2014), http://www.thestate.com/news/local /article13930880.html. Accessed July 15, 2021.
15. Ibid.
16. K Severson, "South Carolina's Young Governor Has a High Profile and Higher Hopes," *Spartanburg Herald Journal* (July 3, 2011), 1, https://www .nytimes.com/2011/07/03/us/03haley.html. Accessed July 15, 2021.
17. Leah Jessen, "29 Facts About Nikki Haley," The Daily Signal (January 12, 2016), http://dailysignal .com/2016/01/12/29-facts-about-nikki-haley-who -will-give-the-gop-response-to-the-state-of-the -union/. Accessed July 15, 2021.
18. Ibid.
19. Rosalie Thompson, "Nikki Haley Will Leave Amazon Tax Breaks Up to Legislature," *Examiner* (April 6, 2011), http://www.examiner.com/article /nikki-haley-will-leave-amazon-tax-breaks-up-to -legislature. Accessed July 15, 2021.
20. Ibid.
21. Tim Flatch, "Reports Hint at High Cost of Amazon Tax-Break Battle," *The State 2011* (July 12, 2011), 1.
22. Ibid.
23. Ibid.
24. John Cook, "Amazon Fulfillment Centers Planned for India, South Carolina," *Geekwire* (January 23, 2012), http://www.geekwire.com/2012/amazoncom -plans-distribution-centers-india-south-carolina/. Accessed July 15, 2021.
25. Ibid.
26. "Amazon Announces New Facility in Spartanburg County, South Carolina," South Carolina Department of Commerce (January 23, 2012), http://sccommerce.com/news/press-releases /amazon-announces-new-facility-spartanburg -county-south-carolina. Accessed July 15, 2021.
27. See Sarah Ellis, "Amazon Is Hiring Thousands of Workers Heading into the Holiday Season," *The State* (October 27, 2020), https://www.thestate.com /news/local/article246746871.html. Accessed July 14, 2021; Terry Ward, "As Amazon Grows, So Will Lexington County," ColaDaily (February 6, 2017), https://www.coladaily.com/communities/cayce /archive/as-amazon-grows-so-will-lexington -county-workforce/article_511c5015-b10b-5743 -921a-fd64c31c80b7.html. Accessed July 14, 2021.
28. C.E. Dawkins, "Corporate Welfare, Corporate Citizenship and the Question of Accountability," *Business & Society* (Volume 41, Issue 3, 2002), 269–291.
29. "No More Tax Breaks for S.C. Amazon Shoppers," *WYFF4.com* (January 3, 2016), http://www.wyff4 .com/news/No-more-tax-breaks-for-S-C-Amazon -shoppers/37242228. Accessed July 15, 2021.
30. Peter Cohan, "Amazon's Sales-Tax-Free Status Cost States $8.6 Billion," *Forbes* (October 17, 2012), http://www.forbes.com/sites/petercohan /2012/10/17/amazons-sales-tax-free-status-cost -states-8-6-billion/#1a0fcc452234. Accessed July 15, 2021.
31. "State of Wayfair: Amazon Pushes Back in South Carolina Tax Fight," *Bloomberg Tax* (October 16, 2019), https://news.bloomberglaw.com/daily-tax -report-state/state-of-wayfair-amazon-pushes-back -in-south-carolina-tax-fight?context=article-related. Accessed July 14, 2021.
32. "Amazon Expanding Lexington County Operations," South Carolina Department of Commerce (March 10, 2015), http://sccommerce. com/news/press-releases/amazon-expanding -lexington-county-operations. Accessed July 15, 2021.

Case 26

Everlane: Ethical Chic and Radical Transparency in Global Supply Chains*

Global supply chains have been wrought with controversy for decades now. Images and stories of global

---

*This case was prepared by Jill A Brown, Bentley University, in 2016 and updated in 2021.

manufacturing, and particularly textile manufacturing, have highlighted issues of unsafe working conditions, child labor, unfair wages, and corruption.

Enter a company called Everlane, an online clothing company founded in 2010 and committed to "radical transparency." Its founder, Michael Preysman, wanted to develop a clothing brand that was both ethical and trendy, commonly known as *ethical fashion*, or, as Preysman described it, a brand that followed the "look of Céline and the ethics of Patagonia."[1] He started with venture capital money to offer high-quality clothes at lower prices that would be sold online under the mission to provide radical transparency. This included providing customers with information about how Everlane found "the best factories in the world" to ensure a factory's integrity.[2]

Preysman then began publicizing the costs of making Everlane shirts on Facebook, which broke tradition from the unspoken protocol of keeping this information as a trade secret.[3] He noted that in "traditional retail," a designer shirt is marked up eight times by the time it reaches the customer, and he promised to be fairer to the consumer by passing on the cost savings of being an online-only store to the customer.[4] More transparency followed, focusing in on its global supply chain partners. For example, in response to the Rana Plaza collapse in Bangladesh in 2013, when more than 1,100 workers died in factories that supplied clothes to European and American retailers, Everlane posted videos and photos of the workers and factories that it uses for production.

To do business with Everlane, factories have to be willing to be photographed and have their costs and audit scores made public. They must supply information about their workers' dorms, including the availability of hot water, heating, and air conditioning. All of this information reinforces Everlane's commitment to radical transparency, noted on its website byline as," Know your factories. Know your costs. Always ask why."[5]

Ethical Fashion

Companies like Everlane are part of a bigger fashion trend that supports the concept of ethical fashion and sustainable practices. This trend is associated with a rise in conscious consumerism that has driven many companies to make serious changes to their global supply chains and increase their reputation as good corporate citizens.[6] Some companies have chosen to be Fair Trade certified through the non-profit corporation Fair Trade USA, which introduced more than 334 compliance criteria for textile factories in 2012, and whose certification now appears on multiple brands, including Patagonia and Bed Bath & Beyond.[7] Others have chosen to pursue a "slow fashion" trend that involves taking the time to source organic materials and articles made by artisans and craftspeople around the globe, and viewing apparel as a more long-term investment.[8] This trend has sparked an annual "Fashion Revolution Day" to generate awareness of slow fashion and a call for accountability through all steps in the clothes-making process."[9]

Supply Chain Challenges

The supply chain has always been a focus of Everlane and its commitment to an ethical production process, as opposed to using organics or fair trade collections, or "artisan made" classifications, which are other alternatives for ethical fashion.[10] Everlane searches for factories certified by independent outside organizations—in fact, Preysman himself spends time with each factory's owner to get some idea about whether they are "a decent human being."[11] Duringone review of one of their Chinese suppliers, Everlane was deciding whether to break ties with the factory after it twice failed an independent audit that tried to reconcile workers' hours with wages paid.[12] Everlane was trying to work with the supplier to raise its audit scores, rather than simply cut ties with the organization,in part because of a sense of loyalty to the relationship, but also because Everlane has struggled over the years to find good suppliers in China that were willing to take on a smaller company. Even as Everlane grew to a company with more than $100 million in revenues by 2017, it continued to face supply chain challenges in comparison to larger, global competitors such as Nike (revenues of $37 billion in 2020) and Adidas (revenues of €19.8 billion in 2020).[13]

Sourcing goods and suppliers in China, which still offers the lowest relative costs of manufacturing, can be difficult, particularly for smaller U.S. companies.[14] Some Business-to-Business sourcing platforms have endorsed service provider lists and supplier blacklists that can be helpful, but it is often a question of access for smaller companies like Everlane.[15] Executives from Everlane, including Preysman, often visit Chinese suppliers after the Lunar New Year holiday in February, when they can get a sense of how many workers return to work after the holiday—an important indicator of how well the factory treats them.[16] While Everlane faces some significant challenges in holding to its mission of ethical production through transparency, it feels comfortable with a model that allows it some control over cost and quality. According to Preysman, "We look for partners with the same aesthetics."[17] Most recently, Everlane partnered with Chinese companies for marketing and distribution, including Alibaba-owned online delivery service Ele.me and Shanghai boutique roaster Seesaw Coffee, to produce an environmentally friendly lunch set that included a bento box and T-shirt made from recycled materials.[18]

Some suggest that companies like Everlane should become even more integrated with Chinese companies and offer Chinese suppliers the opportunity for them to move up the value chain by offering more design input, more make-on-demand, and venturing into higher technology components.[19] However, Everlane likes the ability to control costs and quality in its current model. It shares production costs with customers, and when it sees an increase in costs, it tries to figure out how to lower them.[20] Therefore, while it is difficult for Everlane to get in the door with suppliers who agree to be transparent, once it is in the door, it works hard to train their suppliers to be efficient as well.

Ethical Challenges for Everlane as it Grows

Some worry that Everlane's ambitions to be ethical and transparent cannot keep up with its growth.[21] Preysman argues that the bigger his company is, the more impact he can make.[22] However, in 2020 it seemed that Everlane was facing growing pains and more. The financial fallout from the COVID-19 pandemic began to affect Everlane sales.[23] Additionally, after a period of growth, and despite regular audits, Everlane received a "not good enough" rating from the brand ratings platform Good on You.[24] Everlane was critiqued for not tracking greenhouse gases across its entire line, as well as not reducing water use and not providing initiatives to guarantee living wages. Since then, the company has decided to produce a corporate and social responsibility report, as well as worked toward third-party certifications—a big reversal from its earlier stance on not pursuing certifications. It also committed to ensuring all of its cotton comes from certified organic sources and eliminate virgin plastic in its supply chain.[25] It seems like as Everlane sales grew, the demands for accountability and transparency also grew, forcing Everlane to change its tactics.

Internally, things also seemed to unravel for Everlane in 2020. Former employees accused the company of poor company culture, including using insensitive and inappropriate terms when referring to people of color and failing to implement formal processes to deal with harassment or discrimination.[26] When a group of remote workers announced they were unionizing, subsequent layoffs at the company seemed like retribution for the union push, although Everlane denied such intentions.[27] Everlane responded by making organizational changes and opening up a board seat for a black board member, as well as adding a black person to senior leadership and rolling out antiracism training for the entire company.[28]

In late 2020 it was announced that Everlane had garnered $85 million in new funding from LVMH-linked consumer-focused private equity firm L Catterton.[29] Many saw this as a stabilizing endorsement of the company, its founder, and its platform of radical transparency in sustainable fashion.[30] Whether or not it will help Everlane regain its reputation for ethical fashion remains to be seen.

Questions for Discussion

1. What are the ethical and social issues in this case?
2. How difficult is it for a company like Everlane to follow through on its mission? What are the challenges to its commitment to radical transparency in global supply chains?
3. What are the different ways that a fashion company can be ethical?
4. What interest groups might support an ethical fashion group like Everlane? How could they do this?
5. What are the other stakeholder groups that are involved with Everlane? How would each stakeholder view Everlane's quest for transparency and ethical production?
6. How does Everlane's approach to its supply chain differ from a large global buyer like Nike?
7. How hard is it to create and sustain a positive corporate culture when working with remote workers and unions?
8. Is the Everlane business model sustainable? Or is it just temporarily popular because it is unique? Are competitors likely to follow?

Endnotes

1. Susan Berfield, "Making Ethical Chic," *Bloomberg Businessweek* (December 7–13, 2015), 58.
2. Everlane, https://www.everlane.com/about .Accessed July 13, 2021.
3. Berfield, 2015.
4. Ibid.
5. Ibid.
6. Nayelli Gonzalez, "A Brief History of Sustainable Fashion," *TriplePundit* (February 19, 2015), http://www.triplepundit.com/special/sustainable -fashion-2014/brief-history-sustainable-fashion/#. Accessed July 13, 2021.
7. Andria Cheng, "'Fair Trade' Becomes a Fashion Trend," *The Wall Street Journal* (July 7, 2015), http://www.wsj.com/articles/fair-trade-becomes-a -fashion-trend-1436307440. Accessed June 21, 2016.
8. See Laura Wise, "Industry Leaders Discuss Whether Sustainable Fashion is Possible," *Triple Pundit* (September 10, 2019); Colleen Kane, "Who Made Your Clothes? A 'Slow Fashion' Revolution Rises," *Fortune* (April 24, 2015), http://fortune .com/2015/04/24/clothes-slow-fashion-zady/. Accessed July 13, 2021.
9. Ibid.
10. Fair Trade Winds and The Good Trade, "35 Fair Trade and Ethical Clothing Brands That Are Betting Against Fast Fashion," *The Good Trade* (2015), http://www.thegoodtrade.com/features/fair-trade -clothing. Accessed July 13, 2021.
11. Stephanie Clifford, "Some Retailers Say More About Their Clothing's Origins," *The New York Times* (May 8, 2013), http://www.nytimes .com/2013/05/09/business/global/fair-trade -movement-extends-to-clothing.html. Accessed July 13, 2021.
12. Berfield, 2015.
13. "Everland – An eCommerce That Grew from $0 to $100M+ In Just 6 Years!," PixelPhant (November 3, 2020), https://pixelphant.com/blog/ecomstories -everlane-ecommerce. Accessed July 13, 2021.
14. Rick Frasch, "Sourcing Goods and Suppliers in China: A How-to-Guide for Small Businesses," *Forbes* (January 6, 2014), http://www.forbes.com /sites/allbusiness/2014/01/06/sourcing-goods -and-suppliers-in-china-a-how-to-guide-for-small -businesses/#126f84fb5e5b. Accessed July 13, 2021.
15. Ibid.
16. Ibid.
17. Ibid.
18. Avery Booker, "A&A: Everland Taps China's Burgeoning Eco-Friendly Consumer," *Jing Daily* (October 20, 2020), https://jingdaily.com/everlane -chinas-burgeoning-eco-friendly-consumer/. Accessed July 13, 2021.

19. Michael Zakkour, "Supply Chain Key to Success in China-Outlook 2014," *Forbes Asia* (February 6, 2014), http://www.forbes.com/sites/michaelzakkour/2014/02/06/supply-chain-key-to-success-in-china-outlook-2014/#70dedbc12e35. Accessed July 13, 2021.
20. Berfield, 2015.
21. Ibid.
22. Ibid.
23. See "Amidst Tumult, Everlane Raises $85 Million," Newspaper (September 11, 2020), https://www.24x7news.live/amidst-tumult-everlane-raises-85-million/. Accessed July 13, 2021.
24. Jessica Testa, Vanessa Friedman, and Elizabeth Paton, "Everlane's Promise of 'Radical Transparency' Unravels," *The New York Times* (July 26, 2020), https://www.nytimes.com/2020/07/26/fashion/everlane-employees-ethical-clothing.html. Accessed July 13, 2021.
25. Ibid.
26. Ibid.
27. Ibid.
28. "Amidst Tumult," 2020.
29. Sarah Kent, "Amidst Tumult, Everlane Raises $85 Million," *Business of Fashion* (September 11, 2020), https://www.businessoffashion.com/articles/retail/amidst-tumult-everlane-raises-85-million. Accessed July 13, 2021.
30. Sarah Kent, "Beyond Disruption: Everlane's Next Chapter," *Business of Fashion* (May 3, 2021), https://www.businessoffashion.com/articles/retail/beyond-disruption-everlanes-next-chapter. Accessed July 13, 2021.

Case 27

Slow and Sustainable Fashion*

Consumers are increasingly embracing the concept of sustainable brands and eco-friendly shopping. A recent McKinsey study showed that 57 percent of shoppers have made significant changes to their lifestyles to lessen their environmental impact.[1] As a result, the sustainable fashion market is expected to reach $9.81 billion in 2025 and $15.17 billion in 2030, despite some of the supply chain and purchasing challenges brought to the industry by the COVID-19 pandemic.[2]

One particular type of fashion that is gaining ground for its sustainability is the concept of slow fashion. Slow fashion applies to both the producers and consumers. On the producer side, slow fashion refers to the concept of designers forsaking traditional fast retail schedules and creating staples made to last, and often available year-round.[3] "Hand-made pieces," "made-to-last materials," and "ethically sourced" materials are some of the descriptions applied to this type of fashion. On the consumer side, slow fashion refers to being more thoughtful about purchasing pieces that a person will have for a lifetime.[4] Hence, the terms "vintage," "retro," and "enduring styles" are often used to describe consumer purchases of slow fashion. Slow fashion is also more apt to be described by what it does NOT embrace. It does not treat clothing as disposable, and it does not employ materials that harm the environment. Hence, slow fashion is truly the opposite of fast fashion. Fast fashion is described as inexpensive clothing that is rapidly produced by mass-market retailers for the latest trends.[5]

On average, Americans buy a new piece of clothing every five days, endorsing the idea of fast fashion that has fueled enviable growth for some companies.[6] Companies like Zara benefited from the fast fashion trend for the past few decades by producing more than 840 million pieces of clothing for sale in its 6,000+ stores around the world each year.[7] However, recently fast fashion has been criticized for creating monumental environmental and social side effects. Zara's workers have been said to have wages below the poverty line. Water discharges from garment factories in China, India, and Bangladesh have been said to have polluted the waters. Plastic microfibers from synthetic clothing manufacturers have allegedly negatively affected water and food chain supplies.[8]

Hence, new slow fashion brands like Toronto-based Encircled, Paris-based Tricot, and U.S.-based Paloma Wool, Studio One Eighty Nine, Pact, and Opok have been supported by consumers interested in being more socially and environmentally conscious. Other slow fashion brands include Southern Star (U.S.), Dear Frances (UK), and AYR (U.S). The slow fashion trend benefited to a certain extent from the COVID-19 pandemic, as designers began preselling their collections and producing only what was purchased.[9] In the words of one designer, "slow has never been so chic."[10]

However, experts warn that while slow fashion and sustainability may be the hottest thing in fashion right now, the term "sustainable," which is often attached to slow fashion, may be a misnomer for some products. One fashion expert equates it to using the term "natural" to describe food—it is very broad.[11] Slow fashion retailers often use materials such as linen, organic cotton, or Tencel to make sturdy pieces that

*This case was prepared by Jill A Brown, Bentley University, in 2021.

keep environmental impact down. Additionally, slow fashion producers often produce clothing in-house or locally to allow for full control of the supply chain.[12] So the onus is on consumers who want to be socially and environmentally conscious to make sure the brands they purchase are truly eco-conscious. The upside is that joining the slow fashion movement, for producers or consumers, is fairly easy. As noted by one, "the barrier to entry is fairly low—anyone can join."[13]

Questions for Discussion

1. What are the arguments *for* slow fashion? What are the arguments *against* slow fashion?
2. What incentivizes consumers to make socially conscious purchasing decisions, especially with clothing?
3. Do you think slow fashion is just a trend that will go away, particularly as the world recovers from the COVID-19 pandemic?
4. Are the companies that produce slow fashion clothing really "true believers" or are they just targeting a market niche?
5. Would you be willing to pay more and wait longer for slow fashion products?

Endnotes

1. McKinsey & Company, "The State of Fashion 2020," https://www.businessoffashion.com /reports/news-analysis/the-state-of-fashion-2020 -bof-mckinsey-report-release-download. Accessed July 17, 2021; McKinsey & Company, "The State of Fashion 2021," https://www.mckinsey.com /industries/retail/our-insights/state-of-fashion. Accessed July 16, 2021.
2. Good on You, "7 Sustainable Fashion Trends for 2021," https://goodonyou.eco/sustainable-fashion -trends-2021/. Accessed July 16, 2021.
3. Haley Phelan, "What Is Slow Fashion? We Explain," *The New York Times* (October 11, 2017), https://www.nytimes.com/2017/10/11/fashion/what -is-slow-fashion.html. Accessed July 17, 2021.
4. Ibid.
5. Oxford English Dictionary.
6. Natalie Remy, Eveline Speelman, and Steven Swartz, "Style That's Sustainable: A New Fast-Fashion Formula," McKinsey Sustainability (October 26, 2016), https://www.mckinsey.com /business-functions/sustainability/our-insights /style-thats-sustainable-a-new-fast-fashion-formula. Accessed July 17, 2021.
7. Christopher Marquis, "What Does Slow Fashion 'Actually' Mean?" , (May 14, 2021), https://www .forbes.com/sites/christophermarquis/2021/05/14 /what-does-slow-fashion-actually-mean/?sh =2105f41c73b4. Accessed July 17, 2021.
8. Ibid.
9. Natalie Theodosi, "Slow Fashion for the Instant Gratification Generation," YahooNews! (September 2, 2020), https://news.yahoo.com/slow-fashion -instant-gratification-generation-113022409.html. Accessed July 17, 2021.
10. Phelan, 2021.
11. Sara Bosworth, "The Best Sustainable Fashion Brands—if You're Sick of Fast Fashion," *The Wall Street Journal* (February 2, 2021), https://www.wsj .com/articles/what-are-the-best-sustainable-fashion -brands-for-actually-stylish-clothes-11612295743. Accessed July 17, 2021.
12. Audrey Stanton, "What Does Slow Fashion Actually Mean?," *The Good Trade* (March 2, 2020), https://www.thegoodtrade.com/features/what-is -slow-fashion. Accessed July 17, 2021.
13. Ibid.

Case 28

The Perils of Student Loan Debt*

Following the lessons learned in the 2008–2009 mortgage crisis, one would think that issues of egregious lending practices would have gone away. Instead, they have taken a different twist in the context of student loans. Take the example of Steven Burns.[1]

Steven Burns was excited when he opened the letter that said he had been accepted to an Ivy League university. He had worked very hard in high school, determined to be the first from his family to attend an Ivy League institution.

He accepted his offer, sent in a deposit to hold his slot, and figured that he would apply for student loans and grants to facilitate his tuition payments. He filled out his FAFSA (Free Application for Federal Student Financial Aid) form and waited to hear about his options. Although both of Steven's parents had gone to college and had good full-time jobs, there was no way that they could pay for Steven's $70,000 annual estimated tuition and expenses. However, Steven was not too worried. He wanted to do it on his own, anyway. He felt confident that if he did well in college, he would get a great job later and repay his loans over the next few years.

*This case was prepared by Jill A Brown, Bentley University, in 2016 and updated in 2021.

Five years and $207,000 of debt later, Steven graduated with an engineering degree. He began working at a large engineering company with a starting salary of $75,000 per year before taxes. His monthly payments toward his FAFSA student loans ran approximately $2,000 a month. The interest rates on his loans were 4 percent, but payments became due right after he graduated. Before he knew it, his interest began compounding and he was struggling to meet his payments while covering his rent for an apartment plus transportation to work in the metropolitan area where his firm was located.

Embarrassed and humiliated, Steven asked his parents if he could move back in with them. Even though he would have a long commute to work, he had no choice because he was risking his credit rating if he fell behind with his payments. As it stood, his parents had to guarantee his credit on his apartment because he was not deemed "credit worthy" with the extensive loans taken out under his name.

Steven's story is actually a more fortunate one than many other students' debt stories. At least his university was accredited and provided him an excellent education and the opportunity to be recruited for a good job. Additionally, his loans were Federal Direct Subsidized student loans, at a reasonable interest rate. There are horror stories of students being recruited by colleges with deceptive marketing tactics to attend less-than-legitimate colleges that misrepresent graduates' job prospects.[2] Additionally, private lenders, including banks, colleges, private organizations, and state government agencies, charge higher rates than those of federal loans, and these might rise over time. Finally, private collection agencies, some of whom were hired by the U.S. Education Department, have been accused of using illegal, high-pressure debt-collection tactics.[3] Worse yet, federal investigators caught private lenders including Sallie Mae, Citibank, and Bank of America allegedly paying financial aid officers to steer students to their loans, which had significant mark-ups over federal loans.[4]

The Numbers

Student loans have surpassed credit cards to become the second largest source of outstanding debt in the United States after mortgages, with Americans owing more than $1.7 trillion in student loans.[5] The economic recession in 2008-2009 drove many people back to school, and the demand for student loans exploded. Since then, U.S. student debt has increased by more than 100 percent.[6] Federal student loans can be in the form of direct loans for undergraduates, direct loans for graduate students, and "Plus" loans for parents and graduates.[7] The federal student loan rates are set by Congress in the spring for the upcoming academic year based on the auction of ten-year Treasury notes.[8]

Private debt collection agencies are employed by the Education Department to collect on federal student loans. The government lends to students and parents without any sort of credit check, but the risks are limited because it can garnish wages, Social Security benefits, and tax refunds to collect the money.[9] Parents and graduate students can borrow up to the full cost of attendance as long as they have not defaulted recently on a loan, declared bankruptcy, or had any other problems on a credit report in the past two years.[10] As a result, it is not just students who are at risk of perennial debt. In fact, there are 8.7 million borrowers age 50 and up who have student debts because they financed their own schooling and/or their children's, and the total outstanding education loans held by people 50 or older is more than $370 billion.[11] Retirees who still owe money can even have loan repayments deducted from their social security income. In fiscal year 2019, the Department of Education recouped $4.9 billion of debts owed by deducting from benefits like social security that are due under government programs.[12]

In 2020, student debt holders received a bit of a break when the CARES Act was passed during the COVID-19 pandemic. All debt collections on defaulted government-held federal student loans were temporarily suspended under the act, and federal student-loan payments were put on hold and interest rates set to zero.[13] This helped about 89 percent of student loan borrowers—approximately 42 million borrowers—who held federal (not private) loans.[14] The pause on interest accumulation alone saved borrowers roughly $4.8 billion a month.

Pushback

Students and parents are beginning to push back. Many are seeking loans to be forgiven based on an obscure 1994 federal "forgiveness" law that allows debts to be forgiven if fraud has occurred.[15] Prior to 2015, the law had rarely been applied because it is vague, with little guidance about what proof is needed to demonstrate that a school committed fraud. However, in 2021, under President Biden's platform to address student loan debt, the U.S. Department of Education engaged in several rounds of forgiveness, including (1) discharging student loans totaling $55.6 million by students who attended a number of identified troubled schools, (2) forgiving $1 billion in student debt held by defrauded borrowers from students who attended ITT Technical Institute, Corinthian Colleges, and American Career Institute, and (3) forgiving $1.3 billion held by Americans with permanent disabilities.[16]

A Way Forward

Federal regulators, and specifically the Consumer Financial Protection Bureau, have been trying for years to put in place new rules to change a number of practices in the student loan industry. Under consideration are:[17]

- Putting requirements on student-loan servicers to help lower monthly payments and lessen the chances of default
- Addressing debt-collection tactics when borrowers fall behind
- Reviewing the oversight of federal student lending, which is handled by the Education Department
- Addressing poor customer service and routine transfers of student loan servicing rights from one company to another

- Making sure that service providers provide borrowers with adequate information about affordable repayment options, including income-driven repayment plans
- Reviewing private student loan providers to ensure they are providing information about how they could receive federal income tax benefits
- Reviewing procedures for co-signers who may be having difficulty when they try to get out of a loan years after student borrowers are making payments

Ongoing Problems

Nobody disputes the fact that the U.S. student loan system needs overhauled. However, debates continue over the source of the problems and the solutions. Most recently, President Biden called for $10,000 per person in student debt forgiveness, with some other legislators such as Senator Elizabeth Warren calling for as much as $50,000 per person in debt forgiveness.[18] However, some feel that the federal safety net of forgiving student loans will become outrageously costly down the road for taxpayers who had nothing to do with the student loan system. For example, one former executive of JP Morgan did an analysis for the U.S. Department of Education and projected that taxpayers could be on the hook for roughly a third of the outstanding federal student loan portfolio—potentially more than $500 billion.[19] Further, there are already safety programs in place that are both underutilized and costly, like the Income Driven Repayment Plan (IDRP), originally passed under President Bill Clinton, and the Public Service Loan Forgiveness Plan (PSLF), started under President George W. Bush.

The IDRP allows debtors to cap their monthly payments at a maximum of 15 percent of their discretionary income. After a maximum of 25 years, any remaining balance is wiped off. The PSLF plan allows debtors with federal direct loans to have their remaining balance on student loans forgiven after 10 years of full-time government or nonprofit service. Critics of these plans point out that they act as a powerful, indirect subsidy for the $500 billion higher education industry, which then has no incentive to lower tuition costs.[20]

Other debates are more philosophical. Some debate whether everyone is qualified to go to college and whether the United States has encouraged millions of unprepared people to enroll in college, who then end up dropping out and defaulting on student loans.[21] They point to the fact that most borrowers who have defaulted owe relatively little—a median of $17,000—but cumulatively they contribute to the growing problem.[22] Others point to the idea that a college education is the most effective intervention to help people obtain economic security.[23] Therefore, they argue, the student loan problem is a systems failure of for-profit institutions and community colleges that increase their rates in line with the total amount of federal loans their students receive.[24] Finally, some argue that fixing the system will probably involve significant costs to the taxpayers, including raising money for the new Student Aid Enforcement Unit to adjudicate claims of deceptive practices.[25]

What can be done to solve the student loan problem? It is obvious that the system needs an overhaul. Meanwhile, students are begging for debt relief, moving back home with their parents, delaying buying homes, and contemplating other career options. Additionally, some say there is less obvious damage to the economy that occurs as well. For example, with rising student debt, small business creation suffers because young entrepreneurs cannot afford to take on any more liabilities.[26] In any case, the student loan business continues to see increasing defaults, with lenders like the U.S. government scrambling to collect. And, it is the taxpayers who end up funding any losses.

Questions for Discussion

1. What are the ethical issues involved with student loans? How do these issues parallel those that were involved with the mortgage lending crisis of 2008–2009?
2. As a matter of public policy, should the federal government be getting involved in providing these funds for education?
3. Who are the stakeholders involved in student lending?
4. Should large sums of money (tens of thousands of dollars) be loaned to students and parents without any sort of credit check? Should qualifying for a student loan be any different than qualifying for a home mortgage? Why or why not?
5. How can responsible lending take place in this sort of environment? Is it ethical and responsible for private lenders to make such loans just because they are backed by taxpayer money?
6. Should the federal government be involved in guaranteeing loans provided by private lending groups? Why or why not?
7. Should student loan forgiveness be limited to situations where a college has engaged in deceptive practices? If so, why should taxpayers be responsible for bad judgments being made?
8. If the federal government engages in a broad student loan relief program, how might they determine the amount of per person forgiveness? What issues of procedural and distributive justice are at play here?
9. What do you think about the IDRP and PSLF programs for student loan relief?

Endnotes

1. Names have been changed to protect the identity of the student.
2. Josh Mitchell and Douglas Belkin, "New Office Will Probe Colleges," *The Wall Street Journal* (February 9, 2016), A2.
3. See National Consumer Law Center, "2021 Federal Priorities: The U.S. Government Must Act Now to Address the Student Debt Crisis," (December 2020), https://www.nclc.org/issues/student-loans .html. Accessed July 16, 2021.

4. Danielle Douglas-Gabriel, "How the Attempt to Fix Student Loans Got Bogged Down by the Middlemen," *The Washington Post* (August 23, 2016), https://www.washingtonpost.com/business /economy/how-the-education-department-turned -into-a-massive-bank/2015/08/23/7618f2fa-1442 -11e5-9ddc-e3353542100c_story.html. Accessed June 21, 2016.

5. See Abigail Johnson Haas, "U.S. Student Debt Has Increased by More Than 100% Over the Past 10 Years," CNBC.com (December 22, 2020), https:// www.cnbc.com/2020/12/22/us-student-debt-has -increased-by-more-than-100percent-over-past -10-years.html. Accessed July 16, 2021; Natalie Kitroeff, "The Student Debt Collection Mess," *Bloomberg Businessweek* (June 8, 2016), 45.

6. Ibid.

7. Ibid.

8. Tom Anderson, "The Fed and the Future of Student Loan Rates," *Forbes* (March 17, 2016), http://www .forbes.com/sites/tomanderson/2016/03/17/the-fed -and-the-future-of-student-loan-rates/#2ecb6ea300. Accessed June 21, 2016.

9. Douglas-Gabriel, 2016.

10. Ibid.

11. Natalie Kitroeff, "Hey, Pops, My Student Loans Are Due," *Bloomberg Businessweek* (December 21, 2015), 24.

12. Alexandre Tanzi and Madison Paglia, "Older Americans Are on the Front Line of the Student Debt Crisis," *Bloomberg Businessweek* (June 17, 2021), https://www.bloomberg.com/news /articles/2021-06-17/student-loan-growing-share -of-1-7-trillion-debt-pile-held-by-older-americans. Accessed July 16, 2021.

13. Amber Burton and Julia Carpenter, "A Year Without Student-Loan Payments," *The Wall Street Journal* (March 20, 2021), https://www.wsj.com/articles/a -year-without-student-loan-payments-11616252402. Accessed July 16, 2021.

14. Burton and Carpenter, 2021.

15. Tanzi andPaglia, 2021.

16. See Lance Lambert, "Biden Administration Wipes Out More Student Loan Debt," *Fortune* (July 12, 2021), https://fortune.com/2021/07/12/student -loans-debt-forgiveness-biden/. Accessed July 16,

2021; U.S. Department of Education, "Department of Education Approves Borrower Defense Claims Related to Three Additional Institutions" (July 9, 2021), https://www.ed.gov/news/press-releases /department-education-approves-borrower-defense -claims-related-three-additional-institutions. Accessed July 17, 2021.

17. AnnaMaria Andriotis, "Regulator to Revamp Student-Loan Rules," *The Wall Street Journal* (September 30, 2015), C4.

18. Stephen Roll, Jason Jabbari, and Michal Grinstein -Weiss, "Student Debt Forgiveness Would Impact Nearly Every Aspect of Peoples' Lives," *The Brookings Institute* (May 18, 2021), https://www .brookings.edu/blog/up-front/2021/05/18/student -debt-forgiveness-would-impact-nearly-every -aspect-of-peoples-lives/. Accessed July 16, 2021.

19. Josh Mitchell, "Is the U.S. Student Loan Program Facing a $500 Billion Hole? One Banker Thinks So," *The Wall Street Journal* (April 29, 2021), https://www.wsj.com/articles/is-the-u-s-student -loan-program-in-a-deep-hole-one-banker-thinks -so-11619707091. Accessed July 16, 2021.

20. Ibid.

21. See Committee on Small Business, "Velazquez Introduces Bill to Launch Student Loan Debt Forgiveness Program for Entreprenuers," Smallbusiness.House.gov (June 30, 2021), Accessed July 17, 2021; Neal McCluskey, "We End Up Hurting the Students We Are Trying to Help," *The Wall Street Journal* (February 29, 2016), R7.

22. Zack Friedman, "Student Loan Debt Statistics in 2020: A Record $1.6 Trillion," *Forbes* (February 3, 2020), https://www.forbes.com /sites/zackfriedman/2020/02/03/student-loan-debt -statistics/?sh=28a12fbd281f. Accessed July 17, 2021.

23. Sara Goldrick-Rab, "Lenders Shouldn't Pick Which Students Get an Education," *The Wall Street Journal* (February 29, 2016), R7.

24. Ibid.

25. Jorge Klor de Alva and Mark Schneider, "The Feds and Students vs. Taxpayers," *The Wall Street Journal* (March 4, 2016), A13.

26. "The Student-Loan Siphon," Op-Ed, *The Wall Street Journal* (August 29, 2015), A10.

Case 29

"Dead Peasant" Life Insurance Policies*

Caroline Murray was mourning the death of her husband, Mike, when she received a call from the employee benefits

*This case was written by Jill A. Brown, Bentley University, updated in 2021.

division of his company requesting a copy of the death certificate.[1] After asking why they needed the certificate, Caroline was surprised to learn that her husband's company had purchased a life insurance policy on her husband. Especially surprising was the fact that Caroline had no record of the policy, and apparently, neither did her husband. This particular policy listed only the company as beneficiary and allowed the company to borrow against Mike's policy, write off the loan's interest on its taxes, and receive a tax-free payout upon Mike's death. Mike's position at the company was not an executive one; he was the security guard at a local manufacturing company, and his company received $80,000, tax-free, upon his death. His family received nothing. How did this happen? Through the company's purchase of a life insurance policy nicknamed "dead peasant" life insurance.

Corporate-Owned Life Insurance Policies

Corporate-owned life insurance policies (COLI) have been around for years. They are used as funding mechanisms for protecting businesses against the loss of its "human capital." Additionally, until the 1990s, these policies provided financial gains for companies as a form of "tax arbitrage" where they could deduct the interest on leveraged insurance transactions while simultaneously avoiding tax payments on the interest credited to the policies' cash values. In the mid-1990s, the federal government closed most of the tax loopholes and opportunity for arbitrage;however, the tax-free benefits and tax deferrals on the policies still exist as financial incentives for companies. It is estimated that about a quarter of the Fortune 500 either have or had "broad-based" COLI policies covering about 5 million employees.[2]

The pseudonym "broad-based" refers to the policies' coverage of both executive and lower-level employees. Until the mid-1980s, most states required that an employer have an "insurable interest" in the lives of the employees that they insured, so these plans were limited to executives. Because of federal tax law changes that limited the amount that companies might deduct per insured employee, many states relaxed the "insurable interest" requirement, and businesses began taking life insurance policies out on rank-and-file workers to retain profitability on their policies. Hence, the term "dead peasants" was used to reference the lower social status of some employees.

In 2009 a Michael Moore documentary, *Capitalism: A Love Story*, highlighted this practice and drew attention to some of the problems. Families of deceased employees challenged the practice and began suing corporations and their insurers for allegedly misrepresenting what the policies offer. Many cases settled out of court, including a 2004 class action suit against Walmart that settled for $10.3 million and another in 2006 that settled for $5 million.[3] However, the practice continues today, albeit with some changes. Dead peasant life insurance is still legal, but highly regulated, largely by the Internal Revenue Service (IRS) under the Penson Protection Act of 2006.[4] Today, if employers take out COLIs on employees, the employees must be notified and give written consent. Additionally, COLI can only be taken out on the top 35 percent of the highest-earning employees. Finally, employers cannot retaliate against an employee who refuses to participate in the plan.[5]

Currently, top employers still take out COLIs on employees and have received significant cash value and tax benefits from them over the years, including Wells Fargo (+$17 billion), Bank of America (+$17 billion), JP Morgan Chase (+$11 billion), Winn-Dixie, Citi Bank, Walt Disney, Walmart, American Electric Company, Dow Chemical, Procter & Gamble, and many others.[6] In a horrible twist of fate, in 2011, police in Ohio arrested the owner of an oil-change business and charged him with trying to hire a hit man to kill a former employee to collect on a $250,000 COLI policy.[7]

The Laws Regarding Colis

How is it that companies were able to take life insurance out on employees without their knowledge prior to IRS regulations? Part of the confusion was with the different state laws back in the 1980s and 1990s when these policies became popular. Some state laws, like those in Texas, required that employees "consent" to having their lives insured while other states, like Georgia, did not require consent. Additionally, some employees "consented" without knowing it. In one Texas lawsuit, Walmart employees alleged that they consented without knowing it when they were offered a special $5,000 death benefit when Walmart launched the program. Walmart disputed the claim by stating that the policies were signed in Georgia with an insurance management company located in Georgia, and therefore the more lenient Georgia law applied, regardless of the consent issue.[8] However, the term "consent" was, and is still, vague because some states consider consent granted if an employee *does not object* to a notice of the employer's intent to purchase a policy.[9]

In the mid-2000s, regulators stepped in to address the practice. The IRS cracked down on companies deducting interest on loans taken by companies on these policies, Congress approved stricter consent laws, and state laws were modified.[10] Insurance law is regulated by states, and some have responded by passing "insurable interest" laws, which require that employers have the possibility of financial loss because of an employee's death before they can take out a life insurance policy on them.[11] In 2006, The COLI Best Practices Provision, within The Pension Protection Act of 2006, was signed into federal law. The law was designed to codify the industry and identify "best practices." In fact, many policies for which employers did not obtain consent are still in effect, because those purchased before the law became effective in 2006 were grandfathered from its provisions.[12] Additionally, as noted above, what constitutes "consent" could simply be employees not noticing that they had to "opt out." Currently, millions of employees of major firms may be covered today by dead peasant policies that were taken out on employees before 2006.[13]

The COLI Debate

Critics of COLI insurance policies point to the disincentives for employee safety; after all, if a company is going to collect money on an employee's death, what incentives do they really have to protect that employee? Additionally, critics point to the comparison to slaveholders' policies, the loss of tax revenues, and the use of these policies to fund exorbitant executive compensation programs.[14]

Supporters of these insurance policies cite the fact that it is no different than insuring a business asset and it is perfectly legal. For years, companies have protected their interests with life insurance policies on their CEOs, top management team members, and executives whose deaths could seriously affect a company's bottom line. Finally, many supporters point out that these insurance policies provide a beneficial-vehicle for funding the growing costs of retiree benefits, so there is financial soundness to these policies that offer benefit to all employees of the companies. However, there is room for more debate in that the proceeds are often directed toward funding executive benefits, not for general retirees.

Business Backs Off of Dead Peasants but COLIS Continue

While different states continue to set the parameters for the legalities of these policies, some companies have decided to cancel these COLI policies to avoid the risk of lawsuits from family members of the deceased who say that they are the rightful owners of the policies. Walmart canceled most of these policies after several lawsuits with similar companies resulted in stiff penalties and settlements. Walmart continues to settle claims from the estates of deceased Walmart employees.

In 2011, President Obama's proposed budget included further decreases in the amount of allowable interest deductions for borrowing against COLI policies. Although this did not outlaw the practice, it was designed to influence businesses to put a halt to these policies. By 2015, with the removal of many tax incentives, it was estimated that COLI insurance policies might go away, although it has fostered larger debates about life insurance schemes and corporate tax loopholes.[15] In fact, a 2019 lawsuit filed by the federal agency Pension Benefit Guaranty Corporation said that a dead peasant COLI scheme cooked up by executives of the newspaper *Orange County Register* was designed to make up for shortfalls that executives owed the newspaper's pension fund.[16] In the end, the insurance scheme lost millions of dollars for the newspaper's pension fund. While lawsuits over the use of these COLI policies may continue in the future, at least with the IRS regulations in place, the widows and widowers of "dead peasants" like Caroline Murray will be able to mourn the death of their loved ones without surprise calls from benefits divisions.

Questions for Discussion

1. What are the major ethical issues involved in this case? Is it ethical for an employer to benefit from the death of an employee if they took out and paid for the policy?
2. How does the idea that these policies help fund executive compensation and/or retiree benefits affect your answer to #1?

3. Should Congress create more stringent guidelines, beyond "best practices," for the administration and use of COLI policies?
4. Should states be pressured to conform to stricter "consent" policies for those current policies that are grandfathered under the old "no consent" rules?
5. What are other ways that federal and state governments could encourage businesses to avoid these COLI policies?

Endnotes

1. Fictional characters based on a true story.
2. David Gelles, "An Employee Dies and the Company Collects the Insurance," *Dealb%k* (June 22, 2014), http://dealbook.nytimes.com/2014/06/22/an-employee-dies-and-the-company-collects-the-insurance/?_r=1. Accessed July 15, 2021.
3. Michelle Fablo, "Can Your Employer Make Money on Your Death? Corporate-Owned Life Insurance Policies," *Legal Zoom* (August 2010), https://www.legalzoom.com/articles/can-your-employer-make-money-on-your-death-corporate-owned-life-insurance-policies. Accessed July 15, 2021
4. Elizabeth Rivelli, "Dead Peasant Insurance," Bankrate (November 12, 2020), https://www.bankrate.com/insurance/life-insurance/dead-peasant/. Accessed July 15, 2021.
5. Amanda Shih, "What Is Dead Peasant Life Insurance?," *Policygenius* (February 23, 2021), https://www.policygenius.com/life-insurance/dead-peasant-insurance/. Accessed July 15, 2021.
6. Gelles, 2014.
7. Jay MacDonald, "Does a Sneaky Boss Have Life Insurance on You?", *Bankrate.com* (June 26, 2014), http://www.bankrate.com/finance/insurance/dead-peasant-life-insurance.aspx. Accessed July 15, 2021.
8. Sixel, L. "Profiting from Death? Lawsuit Filed in WalMart Life Insurance Case," *The Houston Chronicle*, April 25, 2002, 1.
9. Ibid.
10. Fablo, 2010.
11. Ibid.
12. David McCann, "'Dead Peasant Insurance' Still Alive in Corporate America," *CFO.com* (January 31, 2014), http://ww2.cfo.com/tax/2014/01/dead-peasant-insurance-still-alive-corporate-america/. Accessed July 15, 2021.
13. Michael Hiltzik, "Feds Say the O.C. Register's Ghoulish Purchase of Life Insurance on its Employees Cost it Millions," *The Los Angeles Times* (February 19, 2019), https://www.latimes.com/business/hiltzik/la-fi-hiltzik-register-insurance-20190219-story.html. Accessed July 15, 2021.
14. McCann, 2014.
15. Warren S. Hersch, "4 Threats to the Insurance Industry: Tax Reform (and three others)," *LifeHealthPro* (May 20, 2016), http://www.lifehealthpro.com/2016/05/20/4-threats-to-the-insurance-industry-tax-reform-and. Accessed July 15, 2021.
16. Michael Hiltzik, 2019.

Case 30

The Case of the Fired Waitress*

Ruth Hatton, a waitress for a Red Lobster restaurant in Pleasant Hills, Pennsylvania, was fired from her job because she was accused of stealing a guest-comment card that had been deposited in the customer comment box by a disgruntled couple.[1] The couple, who happened to be black, had been served by Hatton and was unhappy with the treatment they felt they got from her. At the time of her firing, Hatton, age 53, had been a 19-year veteran employee. She said, "It felt like a knife going through me."

The Incident

The couple had gone to the Red Lobster restaurant for dinner. According to Hatton, the woman had requested a well-done piece of prime rib. After she was served, she complained that the meat was fatty and undercooked. Hatton then said she politely pointed out to the woman that prime rib always has fat on it. Hatton later explained, based on her experience with customers in the working-class area in which the restaurant was located, that the customer might have gotten prime rib confused with spare rib.

Upset Customers Leave

Upon receiving the complaint, Hatton explained that she returned the meat to the kitchen to be cooked further. When the customer continued to be displeased, Hatton offered the couple a free dessert. The customer continued to be unhappy, doused the prime rib with steak sauce, and then pushed it away from her plate. The customer then filled out a restaurant comment card, deposited it in the customer comment box, paid her bill, and left with her husband.

Inadvertently Thrown Out

Hatton explained that she was curious as to what the woman had written on the comment card, so she went to the hostess and asked for the key to the comment box. She said she then read the card and put it in her pocket with the intention of later showing it to her supervisor, Diane Canant. Hatton said that Canant, the restaurant's general manager, had commented earlier that the prime rib was overcooked, not undercooked. Apparently, the restaurant had had a problem that day with the cooking equipment and was serving meat that had been cooked the previous day and so it was being reheated before being served. Later, Hatton said that she had forgotten about the comment card and had inadvertently thrown it out. It also came out that it is against Red Lobster's policy to serve reheated meat, and the chain decided to no longer serve prime rib.[2]

---

*This case was prepared by Archie B. Carroll, University of Georgia. Updated in 2021.

Hatton Is Fired

Canant said that she fired Ruth Hatton after the angry customer complained to her and to her supervisor. Somehow, the customer had learned later that Hatton had removed the comment card from the box. Canant recalled, "The customer felt violated because her card was taken from the box and she felt that her complaint about the food had been ignored." Referring to the company's policy manual, Canant said Hatton was fired because she violated the restaurant's rule forbidding the removal of company property.

Another person to comment on the incident was the hostess on duty, Dawn Brown, then a 17-year-old student, who had been employed by the restaurant for the summer. Dawn stated, "I didn't think it was a big deal to give her the key (to the comment box). A lot of people would come and get the key from me."[3]

The Peer Review Process

Hatton felt she had been unjustly fired for this incident. Rather than filing suit against the restaurant, however, she decided to take advantage of the store's peer review process.[4] The parent company of Red Lobster, Darden Restaurants, four years earlier had adopted a peer review program as an alternative dispute resolution (ADR) mechanism. Many companies across the country have adopted the peer review method as an alternative to lengthy lawsuits and as an avenue of easing workplace tensions. In addition to peer review, other types of ADR mechanisms include mediation, Ombuds, Fact Finding Experts, and Settlement Conferences.[5]

Success of Peer Review

Executives at Red Lobster observed that the peer review program had been "tremendously successful." It helped to keep valuable employees from unfair dismissals, and it had reduced the company's legal bills for employee disputes by $1 million annually. Close to 100 cases had been heard through the peer review process, with only ten resulting in lawsuits. Executives at the company also said that the process had reduced racial tensions. In some cases, the peer review panels have reversed decisions made by managers who had overreacted to complaints from minority customers and employees.[6]

Hatton's Peer Review Panel

The peer review panel chosen to handle Ruth Hatton's case was a small group of Red Lobster employees from the surrounding area. The panel included a general manager, an assistant manager, a hostess, a server, and a bartender, all of whom had volunteered to serve on the panel. The peer review panel members had undergone special peer review training and were being paid their regular wages and travel expenses. The peer review panel was convened about three weeks after Hatton's firing. According to Red Lobster policy, the panel was empowered to hear testimony and to even overturn management decisions and award damages.

The panel met in a conference room at a hotel near Pittsburgh and proceeded to hear testimony from Ruth Hatton, store manager Diane Canant, and hostess Dawn Brown. The three testified as to what they believed had happened in the incident.

Through careful deliberations, the panelists tried to balance the customer's hurt feelings with what Hatton had done and why, and with the fact that a company policy may have been violated. Initially, the panel was split along job category lines, with the hourly workers supporting Hatton and the managers supporting store management. After an hour and a half of deliberations, however, everyone was finally moving in the same direction and the panel finally came to a unanimous opinion as to what should be done.[7]

Questions for Discussion

1. What are the ethical issues in this case from an employee's point of view? From management's point of view? From a customer's point of view?
2. Who are the stakeholders in this case, and what are their stakes? What are their legitimacy, power, and urgency characteristics?
3. As a peer review panel member, how would you judge this case? Do you think Hatton "stole" company property or inadvertently threw it away? Was the discharge too harsh a penalty for a 19-year, veteran employee? Do you think the discharge should be upheld?
4. Is the peer review method of resolving work complaints a desirable substitute for lawsuits? What are its strengths and weaknesses?
5. If you had been Hatton, would you be willing to turn your case over to a peer review panel like this and then be willing to live with the results?

Endnotes

1. Margaret A. Jacobs, "Red Lobster Tale: Peers Decide Fired Waitress's Fate," *The Wall Street Journal* (January 20, 1998), B1, B4, https://www.wsj.com/articles/SB885259114196095000. Accessed July 13, 2021.
2. Ibid.
3. Ibid.
4. U. S. Equal Employment Opportunity Commission, "Peer Review," https://www.eeoc.gov/federal-sector/peer-review. Accessed July 13, 2021.
5. EEOC, "Types of ADR Techniques," https://www.eeoc.gov/federal-sector/types-adr-techniques. Accessed July 13, 2021.
6. Jacobs, Ibid.
7. Ibid.

Case 31

Two Vets, Two Dogs, and a Deadlock*

When a roadside explosion in Afghanistan blew up his Humvee, Russ Murray sustained brain and back injuries as well as posttraumatic stress disorder that made it difficult to leave his home in Watkinsville, Georgia. Getting Ellie, his service dog, made it possible for him to leave the house, and the two became inseparable.[1] When he visited Clyde's Armory Gun Shop in a nearby town, however, he was told by the owner, Andrew Clyde, that Ellie could not come in the store because she was disturbing the owner's security dog, Kit. Kit is a Doberman Pinscher who roams freely from the store to the warehouse and, according Clyde, "does not interact well with other dogs."[2] Dobermans are regarded among the best security or guard dogs. They are strong, fast, and brave.[3]

Clyde, a veteran himself, served three combat missions in Iraq. Clyde maintained that he had a right not to allow

Murray in with his dog because "[t]he store was private property, therefore, the owner of the facility decides who is allowed to enter."[4] Clyde also said that he wanted his store to be a safe environment, "but when someone becomes confrontational and refuses to follow instructions, at that point the only recourse is to ask them to leave."[5] Clyde said that he is a disabled veteran too but that he is allowed to ask a customer with a service dog to leave if the dog is being disruptive. Murray agreed that Clyde told him that Ellie was disturbing his security dog, Kit.[6]

Murray received his service dog from the Dog Tag program of Puppies Behind Bars, an organization that trains prison inmates to raise service dogs for disabled Afghanistan and Iraq war veterans.[7] Ellie, a black lab, is able to respond to about 80 commands; she can pick up items, help with laundry, and call 911.[8] According to Gloria Stoga, president of Puppies Behind Bars, the organization has placed about 54 dogs with wounded veterans. She notes that the dogs they place are "fully trained service dogs."[9]

---

*This case was prepared by Ann K. Buchholtz, Rutgers University. Updated by Archie B. Carroll in 2021.

Murray said he intended to file a complaint under the Americans with Disabilities Act of 1990 (ADA), adding, "I don't want this to happen to anyone else."[10]

Clyde asked Murray to leave the store, and when he refused, two employees escorted him out. Murray then called the police and an officer was dispatched to the scene. In the officer's presence, Clyde told Murray he was barred from the store for two years.[11] Murray later told reporters that he thought Clyde would be in trouble with the law for asking him to leave. Clyde said Murray's final warning to him was, "Don't worry, I won't be back until I own the place." Clyde reported that he thought Murray had a vendetta against him because Murray had contacted several news outlets about the issue.[12]

Questions for Discussion

1. Before doing any more research on service dogs and the ADA, think about what happened. Was this a violation of the ADA or does the store owner also have rights that confound matters in terms of providing a clear answer?
2. When Clyde said the service dog, Ellie, was disturbing his security dog, Kit, could this have been construed that he thought the service dog was out of control? If he did think the service dog was out of control, does this influence his decision about removing them from his store?
3. Should Clyde have accommodated Murray in any way? If so, how? Should Murray have complied and left his service dog, Ellie, outside as requested?
4. Now check out the ADA policy on service animals.[13] Taking this into consideration, whose rights should have prevailed in the above scenario? Is it clear? Does your answer change from the one you gave in Question #1? Explain.

Endnotes

1. Fox News, "Disabled Vet, Service Dog, Reportedly Kicked Out of Georgia Gun Shop," April 10, 2013,https://www.foxnews.com/us/disabled-vet-service-dog-reportedly-kicked-out-of-georgia-gun-store. Accessed July 14, 2021.
2. Wayne Ford, "Two War Vets Disagree Over 'Service Dog' in Athens Gun Store," Online Athens (April 10, 2013), https://www.onlineathens.com/local-news/2013-04-10/two-war-vets-disagree-over-service-dog-athens-gun-store. Accessed July 20, 2021.
3. Amina Lake Abdelrahman, "The 15 Best Guard Dogs to Protect Your Family and Home," GoodHousekeeping Institute, April 15, 2020, https://www.goodhousekeeping.com/life/pets/g22997516/best-guard-dogs/?slide=8. Accessed July 16, 2021.
4. Ford, Ibid.
5. Ibid.
6. Fox News, Ibid.
7. Puppies Behind Bars, https://www.puppiesbehindbars.com/. Accessed July 20, 2021.
8. Ford, Ibid.
9. Ford, Ibid.
10. Ford, Ibid.
11. Ford, Ibid.
12. Ford, Ibid.
13. U.S. Department of Justice, Civil Rights Division, Disability Rights Section, ADA Requirements, "Service Animals," https://www.ada.gov/service_animals_2010.htm#:~:text=A%20service%20animal%20must%20be,safe%2C%20effective%20performance%20of%20tasks. Accessed July 15, 2021.

Case 32

Are Criminal Background Checks Discriminatory?*

At Nehemiah Manufacturing Company in Cincinnati, Ohio, workers with criminal records make up around 80 percent of the company's 180 employees.[1] The company that makes consumer products like Boogie Wipes and Saline Soothers started hiring workers with criminal records in 2011. While there were significant challenges in the beginning, the private company has had much success with its hiring model, finding that their hires who had criminal backgrounds were their most loyal employees. With sales over $60 million and an operating income of $5.7 million, it appears that their "second chance" employee population is doing well.

However, the reality is that Nehemiah Manufacturing's hiring model is an exception to the norms of workplace hiring. Many companies require a criminal background check before they will make a hiring decision. And many will not hire those with a criminal background. It is not illegal for an employer to ask questions about an applicant's or employee's background (except for restrictions related to medical or genetic information), or to require a background check.[2] However, it *is* illegal to check the background of applicants and employees when that decision is based on a

*This case was prepared by Ann K. Buchholtz, Rutgers University, and updated by Jill Brown, Bentley University, in 2016 and 2021.

person's race, national origin, color, sex, or other protected class criteria.[3] In fact, the Equal Employment Opportunity Commission (EEOC) has repeatedly warned that the use of criminal background as a basis for excluding an applicant must be "job related and consistent with business necessity."[4] The EEOC acknowledges that arrest and incarceration rates are high for black and Hispanic men, and so a blanket exclusion of applicants with criminal backgrounds is likely to have disparate impact and thus be a violation of Title VII of the Civil Rights Act of 1964.[5]

Such was the case when the EEOC filed lawsuits against Dollar General and a BMW manufacturing plant in South Carolina. Both companies were accused of discriminating against African Americans. In the case of BMW, the issue arose when a new logistics service was hired. The previous service had a policy of only screening convictions that occurred in the past seven years. BMW did not have a screening time limit and ordered the new logistics service to do a new screening. Employees with convictions that violated the BMW policy of no time limit were terminated, even if they had worked for the company for years.[6] The Dollar General case involved two applicants. One had her conditional job offer revoked due to a six-year-old conviction, even though she disclosed the conviction in the interview and worked for another retailer in a similar position for four years.[7]

Reaction to the filing of the lawsuits was swift. *The Wall Street Journal* (*WSJ*) opined, "We would have thought that criminal checks discriminate against criminals, regardless of race, creed, gender or anything else."[8] The editorial goes on to say that one can argue that criminals deserve a second chance but "business owners and managers ought to be able to decide if they want to take the risk of hiring felons."[9] An EEOC spokesperson told the Associated Press, "Overcoming barriers to employment is one of our strategic enforcement priorities. We hope that these lawsuits will further educate the public and the employer community on the appropriate use of conviction records."[10]

The BMW Manufacturing Company settled the EEOC lawsuit and agreed to pay $1.6 million to the 56 known claimants and other black applicants.[11] They also implemented a new criminal background check policy under the guidance of the EEOC. In 2019, a federal judge approved a settlement of the EEOC Dollar General case that alleged discrimination against black workers with criminal histories. Dollar General agreed to paying $6 million to the applicants and agreed to hire a criminologist to develop a new background check process.

Nevertheless, cases alleging discrimination in using criminal background checks continue. Recently, the rideshare company Uber was sued in a class action lawsuit filed in New York alleging the company's use of background checks discriminates against black and Latino/Latina drivers.[12] The plaintiff launching the suit claimed that his criminal history consisted of a single 2013 misdemeanor speeding violation, which Uber discovered in a 2020 background check. The driver had been driving for them without incident from 2014–2020. However, one day after they did the background check, he was deactivated. According to the plaintiff, Job Golightly, a black resident of Bronx County, he had passed previous background checks done by the New York City Taxi and Limousine Commission, but when Uber began using another credit reporting agency, the 2013 ticket popped up. According to Golightly, there are approximately 80,000 potential class members who have been denied the opportunity to drive for Uber based on criminal history.

Questions for Discussion

1. Do you agree with the EEOC position or the *WSJ* position regarding criminal background checks? Explain why based on legal or ethical principles.
2. Are blanket exclusions of people with criminal backgrounds discriminatory or should businesses be given the discretion to make the employment decision when a potential or current employee is found to have a criminal background?
3. How would you determine whether a conviction record is "job related and consistent with business necessity"? Identify the type of jobs wherein "job related and business necessity" would be relevant and justified.
4. What factors would affect your decision? Would it vary by the nature of the conviction? If so, how would it vary? Would it vary by the nature of the business and industry? If so, how would it vary?

Endnotes

1. Ruth Simon, "The Company of Second Chances," *The Wall Street Journal* (January 25, 2020), https://www.wsj.com/articles/the-company-of-second-chances-11579928401. Accessed July l7, 2021.
2. U.S. Equal Employment Opportunity Commission, "Background Checks: What Employers Need to Know," *EEOC.gov*, https://www.eeoc.gov/laws/guidance/background-checks-what-employers-need-know. Accessed July 17, 2021.
3. Ibid.
4. "Consideration of Arrest and Conviction Records in Employment Decisions under Title VII of the Civil Rights Act of 1964," http://www.eeoc.gov/laws/guidance/arrest_conviction.cfm. Accessed July 17, 2021.
5. Ibid.
6. Tess Stynes, "EEOC Files Suits against BMW Manufacturing, Dollar General," *The Wall Street Journal* (June 11, 2013), http://www.advfn.com/nasdaq/StockNews.asp?stocknews=UTIW&article=57945371. Accessed July 17, 2021.
7. Scott Thurm, "Employment Checks Fuel Race Complaints," *The Wall Street Journal* (June 11, 2013), http://www.wsj.com/articles/SB10001424127887323495604578539283518855020. Accessed July 17, 2021.
8. "Banning Background Checks: The EEOC Says That Screening For Felonies Is Discriminatory, *The Wall Street Journal* (June 15, 2013), A14.

9. Ibid.
10. Bruce Kennedy, "BMW, Dollar General Hit With Discrimination Suits," *MSN Money* (June 12, 2013), http://money.msn.com/now/blog--bmw-dollar-general-hit-with-discrimination-suits. Accessed July 17, 2021.
11. U.S. Equal Employment Opportunity Commission, "Significant EEOC Race/Color Cases," *EEOC.com* (2021), https://www.eeoc.gov/initiatives/e-race/significant-eeoc-racecolor-casescovering-private-and-federal-sectors. Accessed July 17, 2021.
12. Madalyn Doucet and Kevin White, "Gig Employer Hit with Background Check Class Action," Hunton Employment Perspectives (April 14, 2021), https://www.huntonlaborblog.com/2021/04/articles/criminal-background-checks/gig-employer-hit-with-background-check-class-action/. Accessed July 17, 2021.

Case 33

To Take or Not to Take*

As a state employee, I am restricted from receiving excessive gifts because of my opportunity to direct business toward certain vendors. Currently, the state forbids acceptance of gifts that exceed $100 in value. Regardless of the limit, I make it a personal policy not to receive gifts of any value to be equitable to all vendors.

Recently, however, a vendor to whom I frequently provide business (because of the great value in their products and services) offered me two tickets to a sold-out concert for a group that my wife greatly enjoys. With our anniversary approaching, I had tried unsuccessfully to purchase the tickets on my own. The face value of the two tickets does not exceed the $100 limit, but I still do not feel comfortable taking them. I am torn because of the joy it would bring my wife to attend the concert.

Questions for Discussion

1. What are the ethical issues in this case?
2. Am I being too hard on myself? Should I accept the tickets? On what are you basing that decision? What rationalization can I use?
3. Should I change my practice of refusing all gifts?
4. Should the state's policies be modified regarding gifts? If so, how should they be modified?

*This case was prepared by Ken Crowe.

Case 34

Workplace Spying*

Investment banking company Goldman Sachs flags employee e-mails that contain inappropriate "swear" words.[1] Bank of America's call centers track employee movements.[2] Ikea trawls data on employee's bank accounts and even tracks what kind of car they drive.[3] Other companies check their employees' browser histories, log their keystrokes for productivity checks, and pinpoint their locations. In fact, Boston-based Sociometric Solutions provides companies with employee ID badges fitted with microphones, location sensors, and accelerometers (to track the motions of employees).[4] Amazon recently patented an electronic wristband to monitor employees' tasks.[5] And, during the COVID-19 pandemic, employers' monitoring of remote workers became the norm, with one in five companies admitting to spying on their employees working from home.[6] How is it that employers can track employees in this way? Moreover, what are the consequences of employee monitoring?

In general, it is legal for a company to monitor the usage of its own property, including equipment, computers, laptops, and cell phones. The two main federal restrictions on workplace monitoring are the Electronic Communications Privacy Act of 1986 (ECPA) and common-law protections against invasion of privacy.[7] Only two states, Connecticut and Delaware, require employers to notify employees that

*This case was prepared by Jill A Brown, Bentley University, in 2016 and updated in 2021.

their e-mail is being monitored, although California and Illinois require employers to get consent from third parties before accessing employee e-mails.[8] Professional lawyers suggest a clear and reasonable monitoring policy that is linked to a firm's mission and goals.[9] However, regardless of the legality, many feel that workplace monitoring has gone too far.

Some say that this is the case at United Parcel Service (UPS). The company claims to save millions of dollars each year by using a computer analysis program that guides drivers to avoid time-and-fuel wasting left turns and even steers them to drive past a stop and come back later if it is more efficient.[10] The "telematics" tracking system involves putting sensors on the trucks that report everything from an open door to a buckled (or unbuckled) seatbelt.[11] With more than 200 sensors on each delivery truck, the data are fed in real time to a supervisor.[12] At the end of each day, the data are sent to a central data center where computers crunch the data.[13] However, reports abound of stressed UPS drivers being called to account for their every movement.[14]

UPS drivers allege "metrics-based harassment," including supervisors posting printouts of drivers' data every day to keep the pressure on for better efficiency.[15] The drivers also note potential safety hazards from such monitoring, such as when workers use tricks to keep up—like sitting on top of already-fastened seat belts to save time.[16] Inevitably, drivers end up over their allotted times by at least an hour or two due to traffic or other holdups. The real concern for UPS safety, however, may be the handful of trainees who come in as much as two hours under. As one UPS supervisor stated in an interview with *Harper's Magazine*," there's no way drivers could be beating their time quotes by that much without sprinting the entire day and recklessly cutting corners on safety."[17] She pointed to the telematics as the source of the pressure:" It's like when they ship animals. But this is a mental whip."[18]

Many say that privacy laws are playing "catch up" with the newer technologies that allow for such monitoring. For companies monitoring remote-working employees, these technologies include keylogger software that gather data on keystrokes, video surveillance, attention tracking webcams, geolocation tracking, web browsing and app utilization software, e-mail and social media monitoring software, and collaboration tools such as Slack that track internal communications.[19] Companies provide the justification for using such tools by noting the productivity benefits to the firm. But the question remains: How much is too much in the use of employee monitoring tools for better firm performance? And, might some of these tools actually hurt firm performance in the long run?

Questions for Discussion

1. What are the benefits of employee monitoring? What are the downside consequences?
2. Do you consider any of the company practices reported in this case to be ethically questionable? Which ones and why?
3. What is the correct balance of monitoring of, and discretion for, employees? When does workplace spying cross the line?
4. Should companies place this much stress on their employees?
5. Is this an example of dehumanizing employees?
6. Do you think workplace monitoring can be an effective part of an employee engagement program?
7. If workplaces adopt a more flexible work-at-home schedule post-COVID pandemic, is the privacy trade-off worth it, with businesses spying on employees at home?

Endnotes

1. See Sarah Krause, "The New Ways Your Boss Is Spying on You," *The Wall Street Journal* (July 19, 2019), https://www.wsj.com/articles/the-new-ways-your-boss-is-spying-on-you-11563528604. Accessed July 18, 2021; "The Rise of Workplace Spying," *The Week* (July 5, 2015), http://theweek.com/articles/564263/rise-workplace-spying. Accessed June 24, 2016.
2. Ibid.
3. Caroline Pailliez, "IKEA Fined $1.2 Million for Spying on French Employees," *Reuters* (June 15, 2021), https://www.reuters.com/business/retail-consumer/ikea-found-guilty-fined-12-mln-french-employee-spy-case-2021-06-15/. Accessed July 18, 2021.
4. Ibid.
5. Andrea Miller, "More Companies Are Using Technology to Monitor Employees, Sparking Privacy Concerns," ABC News (March 10, 2018), https://abcnews.go.com/US/companies-technology-monitor-employees-sparking-privacy-concerns/story?id=53388270. Accessed July 18, 2021.
6. Mehreen Kasana, "Companies Admit They've Spied on Remote Workers During COVID-19," *Input* (January 20, 2021), https://www.inputmag.com/culture/one-in-five-companies-say-they-spy-on-remote-workers-during-covid-19. Accessed July 18, 2021.
7. Department of Justice, Electronic Communications Act of 1986 (ECPA), https://bja.ojp.gov/program/it/privacy-civil-liberties/authorities/statutes/1285. Accessed July 18, 2021.
8. See Jemimah Suemo, "12 Most Asked Questions on U.S. Employee Monitoring Laws," *Worktime* (October 5, 2020), https://www.worktime.com/12-most-asked-questions-on-us-employee-monitoring-laws#C1. Accessed July 18, 2021; "USA Employee Monitoring Laws: What Are Employers Allowed and Not Allowed Doing in the Workplace?" *WorkTime* (June 2016), http://www.worktime.com/usa-employee-monitoring-laws-what-can-and-cant-employers-do-in-the-workplace/. Accessed July 18, 2021.
9. Ibid.
10. See Miller, 2018; Lee Michael Katz," Monitoring Employee Productivity: Proceed with Caution," Society for Human Resource Management (SHRM)

(June 1, 2015), https://www.shrm.org/publications
/hrmagazine/editorialcontent/2015/0615/pages
/0615-employee-monitoring.aspx. Accessed
July 18, 2021.

11.   Jessica Bruder," These Workers Have a New
Demand: Stop Watching Us," The Nation
(May 27, 2015), https://www.thenation.com/article
/these-workers-have-new-demand-stop-watching
-us/. Accessed June 23, 2016.

12.   Esther Kaplan, "The Spy Who Fired Me," *Harper's
Magazine* (March 2015), http://harpers.org
/archive/2015/03/the-spy-who-fired-me/2/.
Accessed July 18, 2021.

13.   Jacob Goldstein," To Increase Productivity, UPS
Monitors Drivers' Every Move," South Carolina

Public Radio (April 17, 2014), http://www.npr.org
/sections/money/2014/04/17/303770907/to-increase
-productivity-ups-monitors-drivers-every-move.
Accessed July 18, 2021.

14.   Ibid.
15.   Ibid.
16.   Ibid.
17.   Kaplan, 2015.
18.   Ibid.
19.   Darrell M. West, "How Employers Use Technology
to Surveil Employees," *Brookings Institute*
(January 5, 2021), https://www.brookings.edu
/blog/techtank/2021/01/05/how-employers-use
-technology-to-surveil-employees/. Accessed
July 18, 2021.

Subject Index

A

Abbott Labs, 215
ABC News, 349
Abercrombie & Fitch (A&F), 302
AB InBev, 72
Absolute liability, 350
Accenture, 45
Accord on Fire and Building Safety in
  Bangladesh, 157
Accounting bias, 109
Accounting Reform and Investor Protection
  Act of 2002. *See* Sarbanes-Oxley Act of
  2002 (SOX)
AccountingWeb, 144
ADA. *See* Americans with Disabilities Act
  (ADA)
Ad creep, 329
ADEA. *See* Age Discrimination in
  Employment Act (ADEA)
Ad hoc coalitions, 404
Adidas Group, 159
Adobe
  position title for lead CSR position, 20
  response to customer service complaints,
    344
ADR. *See* Alternative dispute resolution (ADR)
Ad traps, 324
Advance notice, 376
Advertising, 320–331
  abuses, 320–322
    ambiguous advertising, 320–321
    concealed facts, 321–322
    exaggerated claims, 322
    psychological appeals, 322
  controversial issues in, 322
    ad creep, 329
    advertising to children, 325–326
    advertising to poor, 326–327
    alcoholic beverage advertising, 327
    cigarette advertising, 327–328
    comparative advertising, 322–324
    health and environmental claims, 328–329
    sex appeal, use of, 324–325
    social media advertising, 329–331
  ethical issues in, 320, 321
  productive or wasteful business practice,
    debate on, 320
  purpose of, 320
  self-regulation in, 335
  traps, 324
  word "free" in, 323, 324
Advocacy/Grassroots Conference, 406
Affirmative action, 308–310
  key Supreme Court decisions on, 309f
Affluence, 7
  education and, 7–8
Affordable Care Act, 492
Aflac Cancer Center and Blood Disorders
  Service, 23
Aflac, Inc., 23, 27
AFL-CIO, 206, 285, 368
Age compression, 325
Age discrimination, 297

Age Discrimination in Employment Act
  (ADEA), 297
Agency culture, 60
Agency problems, 203
The Age of Surveillance Capitalism
  (Zuboff), 448
Age-related code words, 297
Ag-gag laws, 59
Agriculture
  biotech, 191
  sustainable, 35
AI. *See* Artificial intelligence (AI)
Air Act of 1981, 85
Airbnb, 406
Air pollution, 75–77
Alamo, 76
Alcatel-Lucent, 140
Alcoholic beverages, advertising of, 327
Alcohol in workplace, 285
Alexion Pharmaceuticals, 491
Algorithms use, by Big Tech companies, 449
Alibaba Group Holding, 70
Alien Tort Claims Act (ATCA), 160–161, 485
Allbirds, 230, 362
Alliance for Bangladesh Worker Safety, 157,
  465–466
Alliance for Board Diversity, 211
Allis Chalmers, 167
Alphabet, 204, 446
  shareholder lawsuits against, 216
  shareholder resolutions, 215
Alston v. NCAA, 387
Alternative dispute resolution (ADR), 259–261
  common approaches, 260
  future of, 260–261
  mechanism, 516
  ombudsman, 260
  peer review panel, 260
The Amazing Race, 101
Amazon, 180, 391, 447
  broadcasting employee bad behavior, 277
  community help by, 363
  employee tracking tools, use of, 276
  investment in renewable energy
    technology, 78
  lobbying expenditures, 403
  peer-review process, 260
  on raising minimum wage, 252
  Six Sigma methodology, adoption of, 357
  stakeholder capitalism, 45
  tax incentives case, 503–506
  violation of labor law, 261
Ambient advertising, 329
Ambiguity, 109
Ambiguous advertising, 320–321
American Academy of Pediatrics (AAP), 346
American Civil Liberties Union (ACLU), 403
American College of Occupational and
  Environmental
  Medicine (ACOEM), 280
American Council on Consumer Interests, 319
American Customer Satisfaction Index
  (ACSI), 344

"American dream," 8
American Express, 372
American Hospital Association, 404
American Medical Association, 433
American Museum of Tort Law, 319
American National Standards Institute, 191
American Psychological Association
  (APA), 325
  survey, 282
American Red Cross, 368
Americans for Prosperity Foundation, 410
American Society for the Prevention of Cruelty
  to Animals (ASPCA), 49
Americans with Disabilities Act (ADA), 276,
  295, 298–301, 518
  basic provisions of, 298f
  fetal protection policies, 300
  pregnancy discrimination, 299–300
American Tort Reform Association
  (ATRA), 352
Amoral management, 109–111, 111f
  characteristics of amoral managers, 110f
  consumer stakeholders and, 335f
  employee stakeholders and, 256f
  illustrative cases, 110–111
  intentional, 109
  operating strategy of, 110
  as organizational problem, 112
  unconscious biases, 109–110
  unintentional, 109–110
Ancestry, 301
Anderson Cancer Center, 109
Anglo-American model, 201–202. *See also*
  Shareholder-primacy model, of
  corporate governance
  separation of ownership from control in,
    203–204, 203f
Animal cloning, 191–192
Anthem, 145
Anthropocene extinction, 84
Anticorruption movement, 162, 164
Anti-Phishing Working Group, 185
Antitrust cases, 391
Apple, 128, 186, 202, 372, 391, 407, 447
  core values, 231
  green bonds, 88
  investment in renewable energy
    technology, 78
  as mainstream adopter, 27
  recycling process, 79
  shareholder resolutions, 215
  stakeholder capitalism, 45
  sustainability initiatives, 74
  Tim Cook statements, 74
Approval, 109
Arbitration agreements, 351
Ardnak Plastics Inc., 62
Aretaic theories, 126
Aretaic theory of ethics, 129. *See also*
  Virtue ethics
Argentina, privatized water system in, 389
Aristotle, 126
Arthur Andersen firm, 97

Artificial intelligence (AI), 177–178
  screening tools, 279
Asian Americans, 304
Aspen Institute, 253
Associated Press (AP), 158
Association for Computing Machinery
    (ACM), 449
Association of American Medical Colleges,
    406
Association of Certified Fraud Examiners, 143
AstraZeneca, 492
Astroturf lobbying, 406
ATCA. *See* Alien Tort Claims Act (ATCA)
AT&T, 130, 365
  Greenleaf s career at, 130
  as mainstream adopter, 27
  position title for lead CSR position, 20
Attachment, 109
Au Bon Pain, 456
Audit committee, 212
Australia
  Earth Hour, 155
  ozone layer, 77
  wildfires and air quality, 75
Authors Guild, 187
Automation, 189
Autonomous driving, 348
Autonomy, principle of, 127

B
Backdating, 205
Background checks, 275, 518–520
  guidelines on use of, 275–276
Bad-apple theory, 122, 123
Bad-barrel theory, 122, 123
Bad Blood, 123, 432
*Bad Blood: Secrets and Lies in a Silicon Valley
    Startup* (Carreyrou), 431
Bad-orchard theory, 122, 124
Bank of America, 357
  shareholder lawsuits against, 216
Ban-the-box, 275
Barbie dolls, 325
Barclay's PLC, 143
Barnes & Noble, 159
Bausch Health Companies, Inc., 488
Baxter International, 239
B Corps. *See* Benefit corporations
Bed Bath & Beyond, 158
Beef Products, Inc. (BPI), 349
Behavioral ethics, 136–137
Benefit corporations, 26–27, 230
  mission of, 230
  pros and cons of, 230f
Ben & Jerry's, 26, 227
  acquisition by Unilever, 227
  as benefit corporation, 230
  social activism, 402, 403
Berkshire Hathaway Inc., 216
Beshada v. Johns Manville Corporation, 350
Best practices, 137
  for improving organizational ethics,
    137–146, 137f
Better Banana Project, 484–485
Better Business Bureau, 319
Bezos Earth Fund, 454
Bhopal tragedy, 156–157
Bias
  conformity, 136
  implicit, 297
  overconfidence, 136

  in product branding and advertising, 330
  self-serving, 136
  unconscious, 109–110
Big Data, 177–178, 181
  advantages of, 177
  downsides and challenges, 177
  employee community engagement, role in,
    365
  and employee health, 274
  and ethical issues, 178
Big Food industry, 468–469
Big Four test, 132, 132f
The Big One, 459
Big Pharma's marketing tactics (case), 488–494
Billions, 8
Bio-based product, 73f
Biodiversity, 81
Biodiversity Summit, by United Nations, 81
Bioethics, 190–191
Biofuel, 73f
Biometric Information Privacy Act (BIPA), 274
Biometrics, 188–189
Biotech crops, 191
Biotechnology, 190–193
  bioethics, 190–191
  genetically modified organisms, 192–193
  genetic engineering, 191–192
Biotechnology Industry Organization
    (BIO), 191
B Lab, 230
Black, Indigenous and People of Color
    (BIPOC) communities, 436
Black Lives Matter movement, 295, 299, 402
BlackRock, 75, 206, 212, 436, 453, 454
Bloomberg, 234
Bloomberg Businessweek, 10, 490
Bloomingdales, 332
Blue Bell Creameries, 213, 347
Board independence, 205
Board of directors, 202
  committees, 212–213
  diversity, 211–212
  duty of, 204
  female representation, 212
  leadership and oversight, 145–146
  member liability, 213
  relationship with CEO, 213
  under shareholder-primacy model, 202
The Body Shop International, 26
Boeing, 20, 205, 241
Boeing's two flight crashes (case), 501–503
Boise, Inc., 56
Bona fide occupational qualification
    (BFOQ), 297
"Born Loser" comic strip, 102
Bostock v. Clayton County, Georgia, 307
Botnets, 185
Botnet scams, 185
Bots, 329–330
Bottom-line mentality, 117
Bottom of pyramid (BOP), 229
Bounded ethicality, 136
BP PLC, 75
Brand integration, 322
Brand names, racially biased, 330
Bribery, 161
  bribes and grease payments compared,
    162f
  costs of bribes, 161–162

  opinions in favor of, 161
  reasons against giving, 161
BRT. *See* Business Roundtable (BRT)
Brundtland Commission, 69
Building collapse in Bangladesh, 157
Bullet-dodging, 205
Burger King, 55, 372
Burgerville, 35
Burnout, 283
Business
  COVID-19 pandemic, impact of, 2, 226,
    235, 317
  criticism of, 6–13
    business response to, 12–13
    power–responsibility balance and, 12
    social environment and, 6–10
    use and abuse of power, 10–12
  defined, 4
  as digital enterprises, 5
  economic responsibilities, 21–22
  fragile mandate of, 201
  influence on government and public policy,
    401–412
  interaction with government and public,
    386–388, 386f
  involvement in communities, 363–366
    (*See also* Communities)
  legitimacy of, 201
  response to consumer stakeholders, 354–355
  roles of government and, 385–386
  and stakeholder relationships, 6f
  sustainable, 69
  total social responsibility of, 25
Business analytics, 177
Business and plant closings, 374–377
  actions after decision to close, 375
    advance notice, 376
    community-impact analysis, 376
    gradual phase-outs, 377
    helping to attract replacement
      industry, 377
    transfer, relocation, and outplacement
      benefits, 376–377
  actions before decision to close, 375
    diversification, 375
    employee ownership, 375
    new ownership, 375
  needs of survivors, 377
Business and society relationship, 2–3, 20
  business criticism and corporate response,
    6–13, 7f
  business defined, 4
  COVID-19 pandemic, impact of, 2, 4
  in macroenvironment, 4–5
  pluralistic society and, 5–6
  social contract and, 12–13
  society defined, 4
  special-interest society and, 5–6
  sustainability in, 3
Business case for CSR, 29, 30f
Business criticism–social response cycle,
    19, 19f
Business ethics, 13, 97–99
  conventional approach to, 100–103,
    101f, 133f
  customer service an, 355
  defined, 99–100
  descriptive *vs.* normative, 100
  ethical judgments, 101–103
  ethical models (*See* Management
    ethics models)

ethical tests approach to, 131–133, 133f
ethics and morality, relationship
      between, 99
examples of ethical issues, 99f
law and, 103–104
macro effects, 97
major scandals, 98f
media reporting on, 98
micro effects, 97
moral judgment and, 112–117
poor, 122
principles approach to, 125–131, 133f
public's opinion of, 97–98
sources of ethical norms, 101f
and technology, 176–194 (*See also*
      Technology)
today *vs.* earlier periods, 98f
training, 143–145
Venn model, 104, 105f
Business for Social Responsibility (BSR),
      18–19, 61
Business giving. *See* Corporate philanthropy
Business–government relationship. *See*
      Government–business relationship
Business in the Community Ireland, 29
Business judgment rule, 213
Business-level strategy, 228
Business lobbying. *See* Lobbying
Business power, 10, 11
balance of responsibility and, 12
defined, 10
levels of, 10–11
spheres of, 12
Business Process Reengineering (BPR), 356
Business–public relationship, 387–388
Business Roundtable (BRT), 45, 202, 404, 407
Business scandals, 3
Business-to-business (B2B) transactions,
      183, 184
Business-to-consumer (B2C) transactions, 184
Business use of technology. *See* Technology
BusinessWeek, 480
on social contract, 13
BYOD—"bring your own device," 188

C

California Consumer Privacy Act of 2018, 185
Cambridge Analytica, 177, 237
Campaign for a Commercial Free Childhood
      (CCFC), 326
Campaign for Tobacco-Free Kids, 327
Campaign to Hold Coca-Cola Accountable,
      478
Campbell Soup, 365
Candor, 139
Cap and trade, 84
Capitalism: A Love Story, 10, 514
Capital One, 365, 374
Carbon dioxide, 73f
Carbon emission, 73f
Carbon footprints, 73f, 75
calculator, 88
Carbon neutral, 73f, 88
Carbon offsets, 73f, 75, 76
Carbon pricing, 75, 237
Career ambassador, 260
CareerBuilder, 105
Caremark, 213
Caremark Law, 213
Carey Committees. *See* Hybrid PACs
Caring, principle of, 129

Carrefour, 159
Car rental companies, 76
Carroll's corporate social performance model,
      32–33, 33f
Carrying capacity, 73f
Case analysis guidelines, 417
Casino Jack, 403
Casino Jack and the United States of Money,
      403
Castlight, 274
Caterpillar Tractor, 167
Cause branding, 372–373
Cause-related marketing, 372–373
Caux Round Table, 166
Principles, 167, 168f
Caveat emptor ("let the buyer beware"), 345
Caveat vendor doctrine, 345
Cell phone use, 189–190
Center for Auto Safety, 319
Center for Corporate Citizenship at Boston
      College, 34, 364
standards of excellence in corporate
      community involvement, 364f
Center for Food Safety (CFS), 192, 333
Center for Science in the Public Interest, 319
Centers for Disease Control and Prevention
      (CDC), 245, 327, 347, 394
Centers for Medicare and Medicaid Services
      (CMS), 492
CEO pay, excessive, 206
CEO pay–firm performance relationship, 205
CEO Pay Ratio, 205
Ceres (Coalition for Environmentally
      Responsible Economies), 61, 70–71,
      234
CFPB. *See* Consumer Financial Protection
      Bureau (CFPB)
Chamber of Commerce of the United States,
      407
Channel One, 330
Character Counts program, 130
Character education, 130
Charter, 202
Chasing Madoff, 211
Cheating in college (case), 451–453
"Check the box" exercise, 144
Chesapeake blue crab, 80
Chevron Corporation, 161, 214
Chick-fil-A, 23
Chief executive officers (CEOs)
board's relationship with, 213
CEO duality, 213
retirement packages, 206–207
What makes a good CEO? (case), 455–457
Chief Executives for Corporate Purpose
      (CECP), 364, 373
Chief privacy officers (CPOs), 186, 281
Chief sustainability officer (CSO), 71
Chief technology officer (CTO), 176
Child-directed advertising, 325–326
Children, advertising to, 325–326
Children's Advertising Review Unit (CARU),
      325
Children's Online Privacy Protection Act, 185
Children's Television Act (CTA), 326
Chipotle
conscious capitalism by, 38
E. coli outbreak, 240, 243, 428
struggle with food safety (case), 428–431
Chipotle Mexican Grill, 347
Chiquita Brands International, 167, 483

Chlorofluorocarbons (CFCs), 73f, 77
Chronicle of Philanthropy, 371
Cigarette advertising, 327–328
Cigna Corporation, 274
Circular business model, 72
Circular economy, 72, 72f, 73f, 79
Cisco's 2020 sustainability report, 233
Cisco Systems, 45
Citizens United v. FEC, 408–410
The Civic 50, 363
Civil Aeronautics Board (CAB), 392
The Civil Corporation (Zadek), 29
The Civil Rights Act, 278–279
Civil Rights Act of 1964, 255, 295
Civil Rights Act of 1991, 301
Civil rights movement, 295–296
Civil Service Reform Act 1938, 264
Claim, 46
Clarkson Principles, 63
Clash of ethical systems, 386
Classical economics
on corporate social responsibility, 28
"invisible hand" and, 20
Classified boards, 214
Clawback provisions, 206
Clean Air Act, 75, 82, 84
Clean capitalism, 206
Clean Clothes campaign, 466
Clean Water Act, 84
Climate Action 100+, 87
Climate change, 56, 70, 71, 74–75
and corporate activism (case), 453–455
Climate crossroads, 75
Cloning of animals for food, 191–192
Clubhouse, 183
CMI/Compas survey, 434
Coalitions, 407–408
Coats v. Dish Network, 393
Cobalt industry, 474
Cobots, 189
Coca-Cola Co., 69
code of conduct, 141, 167
exaggerated claims by, 322
hybrid truck use by, 56
in India (case), 478–483
as mainstream adopter, 27
position title for lead CSR position, 20
stakeholder engagement on sustainability,
      61–62
suspension of activities in India, 169
water shortages concern, 79
Codes of conduct, 141–142
disciplining violators of, 142
Codes of ethics, 141–142
COLI. *See* Corporate-owned life insurance
      policies (COLI)
Collective bargaining, 255
Collectivistic ethic of government, 386
College admissions industry, 125
Color discrimination, 303
Columbia University Earth Institute, 393
Common Sense Media, 176
Common sense test, 131, 132f
Communication
in business closing and subsequent layoffs,
      376
crisis, 244–245
of ethical messages, 139
Communities
business stake in, 365
companies concern at time of crisis, 362–363

Communities (continued)
    companies giving back program, 366f
    COVID-19 pandemic impact on, 362
    detrimental impacts on, 373–377
        business and plant closings, 374–377
        offshoring and reshoring, 374
    involvement and engagement, 363–366
        managing, 365–366
        standards of excellence in, 364f
        volunteer programs, 364–365
Community action program, 366
Community colleges and eco-economy job
        training, 370
Community engagement, 363
Community Financial Services Association of
        America, 446
Community-impact analysis, 376
Community involvement, 364
Community-minded companies, 363
Community partnerships, 371
Community stakeholders, and corporate
        philanthropy, 362–377
Company issue management groups, 237
Company lobbying, 404
Company tweeters, 182
Company-Wide Day of Service, 364–365
Comparative advertising, 322–324
Compensation committee, 212–213
Compensatory justice, 128, 309
Competing rights, 128
Competition in nonprofit workplace, 373
Compliance officer, 140
Compliance orientation, 136
Compliance strategy, 110
Comprehensive Environmental Response,
        Compensation, and Liability Act of
        1980 (CERCLA), 84
Concealed facts, 321–322
Cone Communications/Ebiquity survey, 373
Confidentiality, 139
Conflict of interest, 125, 215–216
Conformity bias, 136
Congo DongFang Mining (CDM), 474
Congressional Budget Office (CBO) report,
        252
Conscious capitalism, 3, 18, 20, 37–38.
        See also Corporate social
        responsibility (CSR)
Consequences of action, 126
Consequential principle, 126
Constituency building strategy, 411
Consumer activism, 318
Consumer complaints, 318
Consumer Federation of America, 192, 319
Consumer Financial Protection Bureau
        (CFPB), 12, 334–335, 351, 445
Consumerism, 318. See also Consumer
        movement
    today, 319
Consumer movement, 318–333
    advertising issues, 320–331
    changes impacting, 318
    consumerism today, 319
    disclosure issues, 333
    father of, 318
    general consumer problems, 319, 319f
    Nader and, 318
    packaging and labeling, 331–333
    product and service information issues,
        320–333
    warranties and guarantees, 331

Consumer privacy
    business initiatives in protection of, 185–186
        chief privacy officers, 186
        data security, 186
        ethical leadership, 185
        privacy policies, 185–186
    government's involvement in protection of,
        185
    invasion of, 184–188, 184f
    questionable businesses and practices, 186
        illegal downloading, 186–187
        monitoring technology, 187–188
Consumer Product Safety Act of 1972, 352
Consumer Product Safety Commission
        (CPSC), 12, 333, 392
    laws administered by, 353f
    product safety best practices by, 346f
    role and functions of, 352–353
Consumer Product Safety Improvement Act
        (CPSIA) of 2008, 353
Consumer Protection Act, 204
Consumer reports, 275
Consumer Reports, 319, 320, 351, 353
Consumer reviews, 343
Consumer rights, basic, 318
Consumer's Magna Carta, 318
Consumer stakeholders, 317–336
    Consumer Financial Protection Bureau and,
        334–335
    consumer movement and, 318–333
    Federal Trade Commission and, 333–334
    information issues, 317–336
        Consumer Financial Protection Bureau,
            334–335
        consumer movement, 318–333
        Federal Trade Commission, 333–334
        moral models, 335
        self-regulation in advertising, 335
    moral models and, 335
    product and service issues, 342–358
        business's responses to, 354–355
        Consumer Product Safety Commission,
            352–353
        customer service programs, 355
        Food and Drug Administration, 353–354
        product liability, 349–352
        quality issue, 343–345
        safety issue, 345–349
        Six Sigma Strategy and Process, 356–357
        Total Quality Management (TQM)
            programs, 356
    satisfaction model, 357, 357f
    self-regulation in advertising, 335
Consumer's Union of United States, Inc., 319
The Container Store, 38
Content analysis, 239
Continental-European model, 202
Contractual theory, 345
Conventional approach, 125
    to ethics, 100–103, 101f (See also Business
        ethics)
Conventional level of moral development,
        113–114
Cookies, 184
Core values, 231
    importance of, 231
Corporate activism on climate change (case),
        453–455
Corporate affairs (CA), 235–236
Corporate citizenship, 18, 20, 33–35, 227. See
        also Corporate social responsibility (CSR)

    broad and narrow views of, 33–34
    definition of, 33
    global, 34
    global CSR and, 34–35
    stages of, 34
Corporate community relations, 34. See also
        Corporate citizenship
Corporate culture, 59
Corporate donations, 367–368
Corporate egoist culture, 60
Corporate gadflies, 215
Corporate governance, 200–219, 228
    alternative models of, 217–218
    components of, 201–204
    COVID-19 pandemic and, 202
    definition of, 201
    hierarchy of authority, 202f
    improving, 210–213
        board diversity, 211–212
        board member liability, 213
        board's relationship with CEO, 213
        changes in boards of directors, 211, 211f
        legislative initiatives for, 210
        outside directors, 212
        role of SEC, 210–211
        use of board committees, 212–213
    investor relations and shareholder
        engagement, 216–217, 217f
    legitimacy and, 200–204
    problems in, 204–210
        board independence and, 205
        compensation issues, 205–208
        insider trading, 208–210
        mergers and acquisitions, 208
    purpose of, 201
    role of shareholders, 214–216
    shareholder activism and, 215
    shareholder democracy in, 214–215
    shareholder-primacy model of, 202–203
Corporate Knights, 206
Corporate Knights, 69
Corporate-level strategy, 228
Corporate-owned life insurance policies
        (COLI), 514–515
Corporate performance, sustainable, 233–235
Corporate philanthropy, 363, 366–367
    brief history of, 367
    call for transparency in, 367–368
    cause-related marketing, 372–373
    community partnerships, 371
    giving in times of crisis, 369
    giving patterns and trends in, 368–369
    global, 373
    managing, 369–373
    motives for, 368
    nonprofit sector and, 368–369
    spikes in giving, 369
    strategic philanthropy, 371–372
    through greening the workforce, 370
Corporate political activity, strategies for, 411
Corporate political participation, 402
    corporate social activism, 402–403
    lobbying, 403–408
    political spending, 408–410
Corporate political spending, 408–410
    agency issues, 409–410
    arguments against, 409
    arguments for, 409
    case, 487–488
    Golden Rule of Politics, 409
Corporate public affairs, 227

Corporate Reputation Watch study, 7
Corporate responsibility, 20. *See also* Corporate
    social responsibility (CSR)
    committees, 213
Corporate social activism, 201, 402–403
Corporate social impact (CSI), 18, 32
Corporate social performance (CSP), 18, 32
    Carroll's CSP model, 32–33, 33f
Corporate social policy, 226
    defined, 227
    idea behind, 227
    as part of enterprise-level strategy, 228
        (*See also* Enterprise-level strategy)
    strategic management and, 226–227
    sustainability in, 227
Corporate social responsibility (CSR), 18–19,
    31–32
    arguments against, 28
    arguments in support of, 28–29
    beginnings of, 20–21
    business case for, 29, 30f
    business criticism–social response cycle,
        19, 19f
    concept of, 19–27, 20f
    definitions of, 21
    evolutionary trajectory, 38f
    evolving views of, 21
    explicit CSR *vs.* implicit CSR, 34
    four-part definition, 21–23
    greenwashing, 31
    measuring sustainability and, 233–235
    political, 31
    in practice, 26–27
    pyramid of, 24–26, 24f
    responsive CSR, 232
    social-financial-reputation relationship,
        35–37
    strategic CSR, 232–233
        Porter–Kramer framework, 232–233
Corporate social responsiveness, 18, 31–32
Corporate Strategy and the Search for Ethics,
    227
Corporate sustainability, 68. *See also* Corporate
    citizenship;
        Corporate social responsibility (CSR);
        Sustainability
Corporate sustainability committees, 213
Corporate sustainability policy, 227. *See also*
    Corporate social policy
Corporate transparency, 145
Corruption, 161–165. *See also* Bribery
Corruption Perception Index (CPI), 164
Costco, 59, 252
    conscious capitalism by, 38
Cost of service revenue model, 390
Council for Citizens Against Government
    Waste (CCAGW), 406
Council of Better Business Bureaus, 325
Council of Institutional Investors (CII), 206
The Council on Foundations, 369
COVID-19 pandemic, 2, 21, 25, 70, 189
    business, impact on, 4, 20, 226, 235, 317
    communities, impact on, 362
    corporate governance and, 202
    as external risk, 237
    and Herculean challenges for business
        (case), 435–438
    job losses related to, 295
    mask wearing during, 394
COVID Response Alliance for Social
    Entrepreneurs, 229

Cox Oil, 204
CPA-Zicklin Index of Political Disclosure and
    Accountability, 410
CPSC. *See* Consumer Product Safety
    Commission (CPSC)
Cradle-to-Cradle Fashion Positive certification,
    87
Creating shared value (CSV), 18, 20, 37.
        See also Corporate social responsibility
        (CSR)
Credit Card Act of 2009, 335
Creepiness Scale, 177
Criminal background checks in hiring, 276,
    518–520
Criminal crises, 242
Crisis
    defined, 242
    types of, 242
Crisis drills, 244
Crisis management, 236, 241–245
    crisis communications, 244–245
    managing business crises, 242–244
        developing plan for dealing with threats,
            243
        forming crisis teams, 243–244
        identifying areas of vulnerability, 243
        learning from experience, 244
        simulating crisis drills, 244
    nature of crises, 241–242
    political model of, 244
Crisis pills, 208
Crisis teams, 243–244
CSP. *See* Corporate social performance (CSP)
CSR. *See* Corporate social responsibility (CSR)
CSR exemplar firms, 26
    mainstream adopters, 27
    social entrepreneurship firms, 26–27
    social intrapreneurship firms, 27
CSR Greenwashing, 31
CSV. *See* Creating shared value (CSV)
Cultural relativism, 166
Cultural values, 115–116
Cummins Engine Company, 63
Customer-centric employees, 344
Customer engagement, 317
Customer-oriented companies, guidelines for
    development of, 356f
Customer relationship management (CRM),
    317
Customer satisfaction, 318
Customer service principles, 356f
Customer service programs, 355
Cutter & Buck, 159
CVS Caremark, 108
CVS Health, 108–109
Cyberadvocacy, 406
Cybercrime, 181
Cyber risk, 145
Cybersecurity, 181–182, 237

D

*Damage Control: Why Everything You Know
    about Crisis Management Is Wrong*
    (Dezenhall and Weber), 244
Danfoss, 77
Dannon company, 322
Dark money, 410
    case, 487–488
Dark Waters, 71, 235, 264
Data breaches, 186
Data security, 181, 186

"Dead peasant" life insurance policies,
    513–515
Decentralization of power, 5
The Declaration of Independence, 127
Deere & Company, 357
Defend Trade Secrets Act, 264
Deforestation, 80–81
Dell, 374
Del Monte, 161
Deloitte, 365, 441
Deloitte Consulting, 364
"Deloitte & Touche USA Ethics & Workplace"
    survey, 107
Delphi technique, 239
Delta Airlines, 404
Deontological theories, 126
Department of Transportation (DOT), 407
Deregulation, 396
    changing world of, 396
    purpose of, 396
Descriptive ethics, 100
    vs. normative ethics, 100
Descriptive value, 52
De-sheeting, 333
Detroit Institute of Arts (DIA), 370f
Digital amnesia, 179
Digital citizenship, 176
Digital enterprise, 176. *See also* Technology
Digital technology, 176. *See also* Technology
Digital transformation, 176
Dilbert comic strip, 106
Direct costs, 395
Director-primacy model, of corporate
    governance, 218
Directors
    inside, 205
    neglectful, 255
    outside, 205, 212
Directors & Officers (D&O), 213
Direct-to-consumer advertising (DTCA), for
    pharmaceuticals (case), 433–435
Disability rights movement, 295
Disclosure, 216, 367–368
Disclosure rule, 131
Discount Store News, 418
Discrimination, 294. *See also* Employment
    discrimination
    disparate impact, 302–303, 303f
    disparate treatment, 302, 303f
Disney, 75, 158, 237, 367
Disparate impact, 302–303, 303f
Disparate treatment, 302, 303f
Distributive justice, 128
Diversification initiatives, 375
Diversity, 294
    and inclusion in workforce, 294, 308
Diversity fatigue, 308
Diversity management, 308
    future of, 310
DNA testing, 301
Doctrine of strict liability, 350
Dodd–Frank Wall Street Reform and Consumer
    Protection Act, 206, 207, 210, 215, 334
    whistle-blower protections under, 264
Dog Tag program of Puppies Behind Bars, 517
Dole Food Company, 213
Dollars for Doers program, 365
Do Not Track mechanism, 185
Don Quixote (Cervantes), 125
Dove soap, 345
Dow Chemical Company, 157

Dow Jones Sustainability Indexes, 69
Downloading, illegal, 186–187
DreamWorks, 371
The Dropout, 432
Drug Enforcement Administration (DEA), 421
Drugs in workplace, 285
Drug testing, 279–281
  arguments against, 280
  arguments for, 280
  employee assistance programs, 280–281
  ethical aspects of, 281f
  guidelines for, 280
  state and federal legislation on, 280
Due care theory, 345
Due process, employees' right to, 259
Duke Power Company, 302
Dukes v. Walmart, 425
DuPont, 69, 77, 215
  as mainstream adopter, 27
  and sustainability reporting, 235
  use of toxin PFOA by, 71, 286–287
Duty, 126
DWY (driving while yakking), 190
Dynamic Products Co. (DP), 163
Dyson, 362

E

EAPs. *See* Employee Assistance Programs
  (EAPs)
Earth Day, 74
Earth Hour, 155
Earth Liberation Front (ELF), 58
eBay, 257, 406
E-business. *See* Electronic commerce
Ecology of Commerce (Hawken), 107
E-commerce. *See* Electronic commerce
Economic crises, 242
Economic environment, 4
Economic model, of business responsibility, 20
Economic Policy Institute, 205
The Economic Policy Institute, 252
Economic regulation, 392, 394f
Economic responsibilities, 21–22, 23f, 25
The Economist, 7, 189, 259
Ecosystem, 73f
Ecosystem of sustainable brands, 74
Eco-terrorists, 58
ECPA. *See* Electronic Communication Privacy
  Act (ECPA)
Edelman, 372
EDF. *See* Environmental Defense Fund (EDF)
Education, affluence and, 7–8
EEOC. *See* Equal Employment Opportunity
  Commission (EEOC)
Electronic-cigarettes (e-cigs), 327
Electronic commerce, 182–188
  business transactions via, 183
  and ethics issues, 183
    access, 184
    intellectual property, 184
    privacy and informed consent, 184
    protection of children, 184
    security of information, 184
    trust, 184
  growth of, 183
  invasion of consumer privacy via, 184–188,
    184f
  online scams, 183
Electronic Communication Privacy Act
  (ECPA), 273, 276, 520
Elements of moral judgment, 106

EM Armored Car Service, Inc., 123
Embedded marketing, 321
Emergency Planning and Community Right-to-
  Know Act (EPCRA), 84, 286
Emissions trading, 84
Employee Assistance Programs (EAPs),
  280–281
  broad brush EAP, 280
Employee data for health tracking, use of, 274
Employee ownership, 375
Employee Polygraph Protection Act (EPPA),
  278
Employee Privacy Bill of Rights, 281
Employees
  abuse by customer, 287
  background checking, 275
  co-workers *vs.* friendship, 279
  dismissing with care, 258–259
  engagement, 254
  LGBT, 306, 307
  monitoring, 272
  privacy issues, 274
    collection and use of employee
      information, 274–276
    drug testing, 279–281
    employee monitoring, 276–278
    integrity testing, 278–279
  rights, 254–256
  rights to privacy, 273–281
  under shareholder-primacy model, 203
  transgender, 307
  transsexual, 308
  work-life balance, 283–284
Employee stakeholders
  employee rights movement, 254–256
  freedom of speech in workplace and,
    261–267
  management morality models and, 256f
  new social contract and, 252–254
  practice of employee engagement, 254
  right not to be fired without cause, 256–259
  right to due process and fair treatment,
    259–261
  and workplace issues, 251–267
Employee volunteerism, benefits of, 365, 365f
Employer promises, 255
Employment-at-will doctrine, 256–258
  concept of, 256
  legal challenges to, 256–257
  moral and managerial challenges to, 257–258
Employment discrimination
  civil rights movement and, 295–296
  disparate impact, 302–303, 303f
  disparate treatment, 302, 303f
  expanded meanings of, 302–303
  federal laws prohibiting, 296–302 (*See also*
    specific laws)
  issues in, 303–308
    gender, 304–306
    race, color, and ethnicity, 303–304
    religious discrimination, 306
    retaliation, 306–307
    sexual orientation and gender identity
      discrimination, 307–308
Endangered Species Act (ESA), 1973, 85
Energy inefficiency, 77
Enlightened self-interest, 28
Enron Corporation, 200, 204, 210
  bankruptcy of, 200, 210
  immoral management at, 106–107
  scandal, 20, 97, 106–107, 210

Enterprise, 76
Enterprise-level strategy, 228–231
  in action, 230
  benefit corporation, 230
  bottom of pyramid, 229
  core values, importance of, 231
  social entrepreneurship, 229
Enterprise rights, 255
Enterprise strategy, 227
Entitlement mentality, 9
Entrepreneurs, social, 229
Entropy, 73f
Environment, 71, 73f. *See also* Natural
  environment
  terms related to, 73f
Environmental and sustainability (E&S)
  initiatives, 257
Environmental Defense Fund (EDF), 56, 61,
  85, 88
  partnership with Google Earth Outreach, 72
Environmental ethics, 81–82
Environmental interest groups, 85–86
Environmentalism, waves of, 72
The environmentalist movement, 85
Environmental literacy, 72–73
Environmental pollution, 29
Environmental Protection Agency (EPA), 55,
  82, 192, 438, 441
  carbon footprint calculator, 88
  Clean Air Act, 75, 82
Environmental scanning, 238
Environmental, social, and governance (ESG)
  investing, 38–39, 87
Environmental, social, and governance (ESG)
  practices, 227
Environment Protection Act of 1986 (EP Act),
  85
Equal Credit Opportunity Act, 333
Equal Employment Advisory Council, 260
Equal Employment Opportunity Act of 1972,
  296
Equal Employment Opportunity Commission
  (EEOC), 273, 275, 276, 282, 296,
  301–302, 426, 436
  background checks and, 519
  on sexual harassment, 305
  on violations of religious discrimination, 306
Equal Pay Act of 1963, 297–298, 297f
Equifax, 97
Equilar survey, 204
ESG reports. *See* Sustainability reports
Espinoza v. Zuckerberg, 209
Essential functions, 298
Estee Lauder, data breaches of, 186
Ethical blindness, 297
Ethical Consumer, 169
Ethical decision making, 141
  ethics screen, use of, 141, 142f
Ethical dilemma for Chiquita in Colombia,
  483–486
Ethical dilemmas, 122. *See also* Ethics
  competing rights and, 128
  industry or profession level, 124–125
  managerial- and organizational-level,
    123–124
  personal-level, 123
Ethical due process, 128
Ethical failures in business, 122
Ethical impact statements, 170
Ethical imperialism, 166
Ethical investing, 38

Ethical judgments, 101–103
  elements in making of, 101, 102f
Ethical lag, 180
Ethical leadership, 185
  strong, 138–139
  two pillars of, 138
  weak, 138
Ethical messages, communication of, 139
Ethical ombudsperson, 143
Ethical organization, barriers to, 137
Ethical relativism, 103
Ethical responsibilities, 22, 23f, 25
Ethical scandals, 122
Ethical supply chains, 159
Ethical tech, 180
Ethical tests, 100
  approach to decision making, 131–133
  Big Four test, 132, 132f
  common sense test, 131, 132f
  gag test, 132, 132f
  making something public test, 131, 132f
  one's best self test, 131, 132f
  purified idea test, 132, 132f
  using several tests in combination, 132–133
  ventilation test, 132, 132f
Ethic of reciprocity, 130
Ethics
  defined, 99
  duty approach to, 126
  and global strategy, 167–169
  issues, 122–123
    industry or profession level, 124–125
    managerial and organizational levels,
      123–124 (See also Organizational
      ethics)
    personal level, 123
    societal and global level, 125
  managerial, 125
  and morality, distinction between, 99
  principles approach to, 125–131
  strategic management and, 227
  technology and, 179–180 (See also
    Technology)
  and values, 115 (See also Values)
  virtue, 129–130
Ethics and Compliance Initiative (ECI), 135,
  140, 262
  2020 survey, 123–124
Ethics and compliance (E&C) officers, 140, 146
Ethics and compliance programs, 139, 140f
Ethics audit, 145
Ethics hotlines, 143, 144
Ethics industry, 97, 98
Ethics of care, 115, 129
Ethics officer, 140
Ethics orientation, 136
Ethics principles, 125
  types of, 126
Ethics program risk analyses, 145
Ethics screen, 141, 142f
Etsy, 230
The EU Novels Food Regulation 2015/2283,
  192
Euromonitor, 317
Europe, 25, 329, 386
  implicit CSR in, 34
  political CSR in, 39
  privatization in, 388
  Say on Pay requirements in, 206
  sustainable development in, 85
  use of wind and solar energy, 78

European accord, 464, 465
European Commission, 85, 185, 192
European Union (EU), 448
European Union Directive, 233
Everlane, 71, 160, 506–509
Exaggerated claims, 322
Exchange-traded funds (ETFs), 78
Executive pay, excessive, 206
Executive retirement packages, 206–207
Expert panels, 239
Explicit CSR, 34
Express warranty, 331
Extended warranties, 331
Externalities, 71
External risks, 237
Extinction, 70
Exxon, 75

F
Facebook, 20, 169, 177, 181, 206, 209, 237,
  367, 391, 447
  data breaches of, 186
  investment in renewable energy technology, 78
  lobbying expenditures, 403
Factory fire in Dhaka, 157
Fair Chance to Compete for Jobs Act of 2019, 275
Fair Compensation Strategy, 159
Fair Credit Reporting Act (FCRA), 185, 275,
  333
Fair Debt Collection Practices Act, 333
Fair Labor Association (FLA), 159, 160, 459
Fairness principle, 128–129
Fairtrade International (FTI), 158
Fair-trade movement, 158
Fair Trade USA (FTUSA), 158
"Fair weather" concept, 36
False Claims Act (FCA), 266
False consciousness, 136
Families First Coronavirus Response Act
  (FFCRA), 284
Family and Medical Leave Act (FMLA), 273,
  284, 284f
Family business (case), 455
Family-friendly workplace, 283–284
Fast Company, 8, 257
FBI. See Federal Bureau of Investigation (FBI)
FBI Whistleblower Protection Enhancement
  Act, 264
FCC. See Federal Communications
  Commission (FCC)
FCPA. See Foreign Corrupt Practices Act (FCPA)
FCRA. See Fair Credit Reporting Act (FCRA)
FDA. See Food and Drug Administration (FDA)
Federal Aviation Administration (FAA), 391, 396
Federal Bureau of Investigation (FBI), 128, 278
Federal Communications Commission (FCC),
  391, 392
Federal Election Campaign Act (FECA), 408
Federal Election Commission (FEC), 410
Federal Packaging and Labeling Act (FPLA),
  331–332
Federal Register, 390–391
Federal Reserve System, 390
Federal Sentencing Guidelines, 140
Federal Trade Commission (FTC), 12, 182, 275
  on false advertising in health-related
    products, 328
  guidelines for "eco-friendly" labeling (Green
    Guides), 328
  Office of Technology Research and
    Investigation, 334

role and functions of, 333–334, 334f
  on social media bots, 330
FedEx, 56
Fetal protection policies, 300
Fidelity, 55
  in communication, 139
Fiduciary duties, 216
Financial incentives strategy, 411
Financial performance outcomes, 411
Financial Services Modernization Act
  (Gramm–Leach–Bliley Act), 185
Financial Times, 242
Finite Carbon, 75
First Solar, 71
Fisher v. University of Texas, 310
Fissuring, 259
Fitbit, 238, 240
501(c)(4) groups, 410
527 tax-exempt group, 410
FLA. See Fair Labor Association (FLA)
Flex Perks, 204
Flint City, Michigan water crisis, 80, 82
FlyersRights.org, 407
Food advertising to children, 325–326
Food and Drug Administration (FDA), 12, 327,
  328, 347, 393
  drugs and vaccines approval and monitoring,
    354
  mission of, 354f
  role and functions of, 353–354
Food and Drugs Act of 1906, 353
Foodkeeper app, 83
Food safety issues, 347–348, 347f
Food Safety Modernization Act (FSMA), 347
Ford Motor Company, 161, 234
Foreign Corrupt Practices Act (FCPA), 162, 491
  bribes vs. grease payments, 162, 163
  examples of violations of, 163f
Forest Stewardship Council (FSC), 51
Formulation, in issue management process, 240
Fortune, 12, 70
Forum for Sustainable and Responsible
  Investing, 38–39
Fossil fuels, 73f, 77–78
Four-fifths rule, 303
FPLA. See Federal Packaging and Labeling Act
  (FPLA)
Fracking, 73f, 77
Fragile mandate of business, 201
Framing, 136
Frank & Ernest comic strips, 100–101
Fraud!Alert, 183
Fraud risk assessments, 145
Frauds over Internet, 183
Freakonomics (Levitt), 105
Freedom of speech in workplace, 261–267
Friends of the Earth, 47, 49
Fringe stakeholders, 48
FTC. See Federal Trade Commission (FTC)
Full disclosure, 216
Full warranty, 331
Futures research, 238

G
Gag test, 132, 132f
Gallup poll, 3, 98, 200, 254, 384
  on discrimination, 294, 304
  of employee engagement, 254
  on job losses related to COVID-19
    pandemic, 295
Gap, Inc., 20, 79, 158, 160

Gender discrimination, 304–305
Gender gap, 304
Gender identity, 308
Gender pay inequality, 305
General Data Protection Regulation (GDPR), 185, 240
General Electric (GE), 357
    eco-workforce demands and, 370
    as mainstream adopter, 27
    Six Sigma and, 357
General Mills, 159
    "better for you" foods to kids, 325
    food during COVID-19 pandemic, 23
    as mainstream adopter, 27
General Motors (GM), 3, 4, 161, 261, 374, 406
    and Ceres relationship, 61
    conduct codes, 261
    electric vehicles by, 78
    Nader's criticism of, 318
    plant closings, 374
    scandals, 3
Generation Z, 253
Generation Z employees survey, 87
Genesis Healthcare, 206–207
Genetically engineered foods (GEFs), 192
Genetically modified foods (GMFs), 192, 346
    labeling of, 193
Genetically modified organisms (GMOs), 192–193
    labeling of, 192–193
Genetic engineering, 191–192
    cloning animals for food, 191–192
    definition of, 191
    genetic profiling, 192
    genetic testing, 192
Genetic Information Nondiscrimination Act (GINA), 192, 300–301
Genetic profiling, 192
Genetic testing, 192
Geopolitical issues, 153
Ghost tweeters, 182
Gifts acceptance, 520
Gig economy, 253
Giki app, 83
GINA. See Genetic Information Nondiscrimination Act (GINA)
Giving in Numbers, 366
Giving Voice to Values, 264
Glass Lewis, 215
The Global Anticorruption Movement, 162, 164
2020 Global Busines Ethics Survey, 135
Global business citizen, definition of, 34
Global Business Citizenship, 34
Global Business Coalition against Human Trafficking, 407
Global Business Ethics Survey (GBES), 262
Global carbon dioxide emissions, growth in, 76f
Global codes of conduct, 167, 168f
    corporate global codes, 167
    by international organizations, 167, 168f
Global competitiveness, 4, 28
Global corporate citizenship, 34
Global economy, 153. See also Global ethical issues
Global ethical issues, 153–171
    challenges in global environment and, 154–155
    corruption, bribery, and questionable payments, 161–165
    human rights, sweatshops, and labor abuses, 157–161

improving, 165–170
    marketing practices, 155–156
    multinational corporation and, 154–155
    plant safety, 155–157
    strategies to improve business ethics, 166–170
        ethical impact statements and audits, 170
        global codes of conduct, 167, 168f
        linking ethics with global strategy, 167–169
        suspension of business, 169–170
        traditions of home and host countries, 165–166, 165f
    transnational economy and, 153–154
Global financial crisis, 153, 210
Global 100 index, 69
Global Initiative for Sustainability Ratings (GISR), 234
Globalization, 153
Global outsourcing guidelines, 160
Global philanthropy, 373
Global positioning system (GPS) technology, 276
Global Reporting Initiative (GRI), 85, 234–235
    guidelines, 167, 168f
    mission of, 235
Global Sullivan principles of social responsibility, 167, 168f
Global warming, 74–75, 80
GM. See General Motors (GM)
GMFs. See Genetically modified foods (GMFs)
GMO labeling, 333
GMOs. See Genetically modified organisms (GMOs)
GNC Holdings, Inc., 201
Golden parachutes, 208
Golden Rule, 130
Golden Rule of Politics, 409
Goldman Sachs, 86, 138, 420, 447, 520
    violations of Foreign Corrupt Practices Act by, 163f
Goodbox, 368
"Good boy/nice girl" morality stage, 113
Good cause norm, 256
Good faith principle, 257
GoodGuide app, 83
Good to Great: Why Some Companies Make the Leap... And Others Don't (Collins), 456
Google, 20, 187, 206, 391, 447
    Chinese censorship and, 169
    codes of conduct, 141
    investment in renewable energy technology, 78
    lobbying by, 403
    safe and productive work environment for employees by, 273
Google Effect, 179
Gourmet magazine, 35
Government
    clash of ethical systems between business and, 386, 386f
    influence of business on, 401–412
    interaction with business and public, 386–388, 386f
    involvement pendulum, 385
    nonregulatory influence of (See Nonregulatory governmental influences on business)
    regulation (See Government regulation)
    roles of business and, 385–386
Government–business relationship, 387

Government regulation, 390–396
    direct costs of, 395
    economic regulation, 392, 394f
    indirect costs of, 395
    induced effects of, 395
    issues related to, 394–396
    natural monopolies and, 391
    negative externalities and, 391–392
    reasons for, 391–392
    regulation defined, 391
    social goals and, 392
    social regulation, 392–393, 394f
    warding off, 28–29
Gradual phase-out, 377
Grainger, 302
Grandma test, 131
Grassroots lobbying, 406
Gravity, Inc., 207
Grease payments, 162
Green advertising, 328–329
GreenBiz Group, 71
Greenbiz report, 242
Green consumers, 87
Green employees, 87
Green fatigue, 329
Green Guides, 328
Greenhouse effects, 74–75
Greenhouse gas, 73f
Green investors, 87
Green marketing, 329
Greenpeace, 47, 49, 85, 454
Green to Gold (Esty and Winston), 69
Greenwashing, 73f, 75
Green watchdogs, 329
GRI. See Global Reporting Initiative (GRI)
Grievance committee, 260
Griggs v. Duke Power Company, 302–303
Grocery Manufacturers Association (GMA), 333
Groundwater depletion, 79
Group's stakes, 55–56. See also Stakeholders
    nature/legitimacy of, 55
    power of, 55
    subgroups within generic group, 55–56
Grumman Olson, 375
Guarantees, 331
Guardian newspaper, 107
Gucci, 159

H
Haas School of Business, 364
Hanes, 362
Harvard Business Review, 251, 260
Harvard Business School, 29
Harvard Kennedy School's Carr Center for Human Rights Policy, 386
Hazardous wastes, 79
Health-care industry, ethical challenges faced by, 124–125
Healthy Forever, 163
Hearing procedure, 260
Hennes & Mauritz AB (H&M), 86, 403, 464
    chief sustainability officer in, 71
Herbalife, 163f
Hershey Company, 141
Hidden Rivers, 410
Home Depot
    stakeholder capitalism, 45
    stakeholder power, 51
Honesty testing. See Integrity testing
Hormel Foods Corp., 469
Hostile takeovers, 208

Hostile work environment, 305
Hot Coffee, 497
HP, 208
Human rights violations, 158–161
Human Rights Watch 2018 report, 158
Hurt avoidance, 115
Hybrid PACs, 410
Hypercompetition, 4
Hypernorms, 166
Hyundai Motor Co., 266

I

IBM, 161, 204, 365
    stakeholder capitalism, 45
    suspension of activities in India, 169
Identity theft, 185
The Identity Theft Resource Center, 275
"Idolatry of data," 177
Ikea, 77, 78
Ill-conceived goals, 137
Illegal corporate behavior, 104
Illegal downloading, 186–187
ILO. *See* International Labor Organization
    (ILO)
IMAGINE, 71
Immoral management, 106–107, 111f
    characteristics of immoral managers, 106f
    consumer stakeholders and, 335f
    defined, 106
    employee stakeholders and, 256f
    everyday questionable practices, 107
    illustrative cases, 106–107
    management's motives selfish, 106
    operating strategy of, 106
Impact investing, 38–39
Implementation, in issue management process,
    240
Implicit bias, 297
Implicit CSR, 34
Implied contract exception, 257
Implied warranty, 331
Impulse society, 9
Inclusion, 294
"Income inequality" movement, 129
Incrementalism, 136
India
    Bhopal tragedy, 156–157
    Coke and Pepsi in (case), 478–483
    energy demand in, 77
    legal rights to nature, 51
    National Action Plan on Climate Change
        (NAPCC), 85
Indian Beverage Association (IBA), 481
India Resource Center (IRC), 478, 480, 481
India's Center for Science and Environment
    (CSE), 478
India's National Action Plan on Climate
    Change (NAPCC), 85
Indirect blindness, 137
Indirect costs, 395
Inditex, 464
Individual hypothesis, 112
Individualistic ethic of business, 386
Indoor air pollution, 77
Induced costs, 395
Industrial policy, 388
Infant Formula Action Coalition (INFACT),
    156
Infant formula controversy, 155–156
Influence peddlers, 405
The Informant!, 264

Information asymmetry, 210
Information crises, 242
Information strategy, 411
Information technology (IT), 181–190
    cybersecurity, 181–182
    electronic commerce, 182–188
    invasion of consumer privacy, 184–188
    social media and, 181
    workplace and digital technology, 188–190
Ingka Group, 78
Ingredient labeling, 333
InsideCounsel, 308
Inside directors, 205
The Insider, 264
Insider trading, 208–210, 209f
Instagram, 181, 183
Institute of Finance and Management (IOFM),
    287
Institutional owners, 55
Institutional Shareholder Services (ISS), 215
Instrumentalist culture, 60
Instrumental value, 52
Integrated reports (IRs). *See* Sustainability
    reports
Integration of managerial and moral
    competence, 118
Integrity, 122
Integrity strategy, 108
Integrity testing, 278–279
Intel Corporation, 217
Intentionally amoral managers, 109
Interface Carpet, 107
Interfaith Center on Corporate Responsibility
    (ICCR), 156, 215
Internal carbon tax, 73f
Internal Revenue Code, 410
Internal Revenue Service (IRS), 162
International Baby Food Action Network
    (IBFAN), 156
International Chamber of Commerce, 166
International Council for Advertising
    Regulation, 335
International Council on Clean Transportation
    (ICCT), 440, 441
"International Day for Clean Air for Blue
    Skies," 77
The International Integrated Reporting Council
    (IIRC), 233
Internationalization of business, 153. *See also*
    Global ethical issues
International Labor Organization (ILO),
    158, 459
International Standards Organization (ISO),
    167, 189
    standards, 167, 168f
International tax policy, 389
Internet of Things (IoT), 183
Interstate Commerce Commission (ICC),
    391, 392
Invasion of consumer privacy, 184–188, 184f
The Inventor: Out for Blood in Silicon Valley,
    123, 432
Investor relations, 216–217
Invisible People, 362
IRecycle, 83
Iron Law of Responsibility, 12
Irreversibility, 73f
ISO. *See* International Standards Organization
    (ISO)
ISO 37001—Anti-Bribery Management
    Systems, 167, 168f

ISO 26000—Social Responsibility, 167, 168f
ISO standardization, 357
Issue
    analysis of, 238–239
    categories, 238f
    defined, 237
    development life cycle process, 240, 241f
    identification, 238
    management process, model of, 238–240, 239f
        evaluation, monitoring and control in, 240
        formulation and implementation of
            responses, 239–240
    ranking/prioritization of, 239
Issue management, 237–240
Issue Management Council, 237
Issue managers, 237
IT. *See* Information technology (IT)

J

J.C. Penney, 158, 205, 365, 418
JetBlue, 344
Job loss
    business and plant closings, 374
    COVID-19 pandemic and, 295
    outsourcing, offshoring, reshoring, 374
Johnson Controls, 300
Johnson & Johnson (J&J), 37, 57, 77, 133, 140,
    330, 489, 491
    board committees, 213
    steps to address air pollution, 77
    talc powder in ovarian cancer cases, 342
    Tylenol poisoning crisis, 57
Johnson's Wax, 167
Jones Day, 441
JPMorgan Chase, 3, 86, 138, 145, 274
The Jungle (Sinclair), 318
Just Capital, 72
Justice
    compensatory, 128
    distributive, 128
    principle of, 128–129
    procedural, 128
Just in Time (JIT) strategy, 356

K

Kaizen, 357
Kant's categorical imperative, 126–127
Kapersky Labs, 179
Key performance indicators (KPIs), 68
KFC, 55
Kia Corporation, 266
Kids getting older younger (KGOY), 325
Kid-vid advertising, 325
Kmart, 158, 330
Kohlberg's levels of moral development,
    112, 113f
    conventional level, 113–114
    ethics of care as alternative to, 115
    Gilligan s criticisms of, 115
    postconventional level, 114
    preconventional level, 113
KPMG, 227, 365
KPMG Survey of Corporate Responsibility
    Reporting 2020, 233
Kraft Heinz Co., 79, 469
Kronos Inc., 278
Kyoto Protocol, 84

L

Labor rights and abuses, 157–159
Labor unions, 254

Law
    and ethics, 103–104
    social contract and, 13
Law-and-order morality stage, 113
LEAD program at Wharton School of
    Business, 304
Lean In (Sandberg), 304
Lean Six Sigma (LSS), 357
Legal model, of business responsibility,
    20–21
Legal responsibilities, 22, 23f, 25
Legal rights, 127, 127f
Legal values, 116
Legitimacy, 200–201
    and corporate governance, 200–204
Legitimation, 201
    macro level of, 201
    micro level of, 201
Lego, 79
LendUp, 446
Lesbian, gay, bisexual, and transgender/
    transsexual (LGBT) workforce, 295
Less-developed countries (LDCs), ethical
    challenges in, 155
Levi Strauss & Co., 160, 166
    Eco jeans, 345
    ethics in strategic decision making, 169
    global sourcing guidelines, 169
    23-page Worldwide Code of Business
        Conduct, 169
    political stance with brand, 404
    Sustainability Guidebook, 169
License for piece of music, 187
Limited warranty, 331
LinkedIn, 181, 450
Little white lies, 103
L.L.Bean, 63, 331, 332
Lobbying, 401, 403–408
    astroturf, 406
    defined, 403
    grassroots, 406
    organizational levels of, 404, 405f
    professional lobbyists, 405–406
    purposes of, 403–404
    stealth, 405
    trade associations and, 406–407
    umbrella organizations and, 407–408
Lobbying Disclosure Act, 403
Lobbyists, 405–406. *See also* Lobbying
Locavore, 83
London's Financial Times Stock Exchange
    (FTSE), 206
The Lord of the Rings, 130
Lordstown Motors Corporation, 377
L'Oreal, 330
Louisiana Court of Appeals, 132
LPEC (Leading Professional in Ethics and
    Compliance), 139
Lumber Liquidators, 77
Lyft, 299, 406

M
Macroenvironment, 4
    society as, 4–5
Mad Men (TV series), 7
Magnuson–Moss Warranty Act, 331
Mainstream adopters, 27
Majority vote, 214
Making something public test, 131, 132f
Management
    amoral, 109–111, 111f

crisis, 241–245
    immoral, 106–107, 111f
    moral, 108–109, 111f
    risk, 236–237
    under shareholder-primacy model, 203
    stakeholders, 15
    strategic (*See* Strategic management)
Management ethics models, 106–112, 111f
    amoral management, 109–111, 112
    emphases on CSR and, 112f
    hypotheses regarding, 111–112
        individual hypothesis, 112
        population hypothesis, 111–112
    immoral management, 106–107
    moral management, 108–109
Managerial approach, 13
Managerial ethics, 125
Managerial view of the firm, 47, 48f
Managers
    amoral, 110f
    factors affecting morality of, 134f
    immoral, 106f
    issue, 237
    moral, 108f, 146, 147f
Mandatory arbitration, 261
Marginal stakeholder, 57, 58f
Margin Call, 8
Marijuana use, 280, 282, 285
    legalization of, 393
Marine Protection, Research, and Sanctuaries
    Act of 1972, 84
Market failure, 391
Marketing practices, questionable, 155–156
Marketing, 4Ps of, 320
Marriott, 145
Mask wearing, during COVID-19 pandemic, 394
Massachusetts Right to Know Law, 255
Material information, 208
Mattel Toy Company, 170
    Barbie doll adaptations by, 325
McDonald's Corporation, 205
    black workers and, 403
    coffee spill lawsuit (case), 497–501
    engagement with stakeholders, 61
    PETA's protests, 54–55
    Ronald McDonald House Charities (RMHC)
        program by, 366
McKinsey & Company, 153, 186, 436, 509
McKinsey Global Institute, 153
McKinsey study, 55, 81, 294
McNeil Laboratories, 133
Measurement system, 63
Medication Prescription Drug Price
    Negotiation Act of 2015, 492
Medtronic, 122
    code of conduct, 167
Mental health
    athletes and, 283
    coronavirus pandemic impact on, 282
    stigma of, 283
    in workplace, 282
Merck & Co., 109
Mercy for Animals, 59
Merit System Protection Board, 264
#MeToo movement, 295
MGM Resorts, data breaches of, 186
Michigan's Whistleblowers Protection Act of
    1981, 264
Microsoft Corporation, 75, 182, 183, 237,
    404, 447
    carbon offsets by, 75

codes of conduct, 141
    as exemplar of social responsibility and
        sustainability, 27
Millennials, 253, 257
Minnesota Forward, 409
Mis-leaders, 138
Mission Measurement, 367
Mixed-blessing stakeholder, 58, 58f
Moderna, 70, 352
Monitoring technology, 187–188
Monsanto Corporation
    cancer from Roundup weed killer product, 342
    lobbying by, 404
Montreal Protocol, 77, 85
Moral action, 119
Moral awareness, 119
Moral decisions, 146, 147f
Moral development, 113
    Kohlberg s levels of (*See* Kohlberg s levels
        of moral development)
Moral equilibrium, 136
Moral evaluation, 117
*Moral Freedom: The Search for Virtue in a
    World of Choice* (Wolfe), 116
Moral hazard, 75
Moral identification and ordering, 117
Moral imagination, 117
Moral intent, 119
Moralist culture, 60
Moral judgment, 112–117, 119
    elements of, 117–118, 118f
Moral management, 108–109, 111f, 137–139
    characteristics of moral managers, 108f
    consumer stakeholders and, 335f
    employee stakeholders and, 256f
    habits of moral leaders, 108
    illustrative cases, 108–109
    operating strategy of, 108
Moral managers, 139, 146, 147f
Moral minimums, 166
Moral organizations, 146, 147f
Moral person, attributes of, 139
Moral rights, 127, 127f
Morals, 99
    and ethics, distinction between, 99
Moral suasion, 390
Moral tone, 137
Morgan Stanley, 436
Mosquito in the tent strategy, 87f
Motivated blindness, 137
Motorola, 63
Motor Vehicle Safety Whistleblower Act, 264
MSCI, 234
Multifiduciary approach to stakeholders, 52
Multinational corporation (MNC), 154
    achieving corporate legitimacy by, 154
    BOP concept and, 229
    challenges faced by, 154–157
    dilemma of, 154, 154f
    home and host country ethical standards,
        154, 166
Multinational enterprise (MNE). *See*
    Multinational corporation (MNC)
Mutual fund organizations, 55

N
Nader's Raiders, 318
The Naked Corporation, 61
*The Naked Employee: How Technology Is
    Compromising Workplace Privacy*
    (Lane III), 281

National, 76
National Academy of Sciences (NAS), 193
National Advertising Division (NAD), of
    Council of Better Business Bureaus,
    Inc., 335
National Advertising Review Board (NARB),
    325
National Aeronautics and Space Administration
    (NASA), 77
National Association of Manufacturers (NAM),
    404, 407
National Association of Realtors, 404
National Bureau of Economic Research
    (NBER), 387, 434, 435
National Center for Employee Ownership
    (NCEO), 375
National Collegiate Athletic Association
    (NCAA), 387
National Consumers League, 183, 430
National Council of Churches, 156
National Environmental Education Foundation
    (NEEF), 257
National Environmental Policy Act (NEPA), 82
National Federation of Independent Businesses
    (NFIB), 407
National Football League's Rooney Rule, 212
National Green Tribunal Act of 2010, 85
National Highway Traffic Safety
    Administration (NHTSA), 266, 393,
    396–397
National Hockey League, 88
National Labor Relations Act (NLRA), 261
National Priorities List, 84
National Resources Defense Council (NRDC),
    85
National Safe Place (NSP), 371
National Society of Fundraising Executives, 368
Natural disasters, 242
Natural environment, 68, 71–73
    air pollution and toxins, 75–77
    business and environmental partnerships, 88
    climate change and global warming, 74–75
    deforestation and biodiversity, 80–81
    energy and fossil fuels, 77–78
    environmental interest groups, 85–87
    governmental role in issues about, 82–85
    impact of business on, 73–74
    oceans and fisheries, 79–80
    responsibility for, 81–82
    as stakeholder, 47, 51
    sustainability interest groups, 87–88
    waste management, 79
    water, 78–79
Natural gas, 77
Natural monopoly, 391
Natural products, 328
The Nature Conservancy, 88
Negative externalities, 392
Negative right, 128
Negative social screens, 39
Neglectful director, 255
Nestlé, 69
    donation to Meals on Wheels, 362
    health crisis in Brazil, 467–473
    questionable marketing practices, 156
    water shortages concern, 79
Nestlé Brasil Ltda, 469
Netflix, 208
Newcastle University, United Kingdom, 116
"New economic politics," 402
New England Journal of Medicine, 468

New workplace, 251
New York City Human Rights Law
    (NYCHRL), 275
New York Stock Exchange (NYSE), 212
New York Times, 74, 492
NGOs. See Nongovernmental organizations
    (NGOs)
NHTSA. See National Highway Traffic Safety
    Administration (NHTSA)
Nielsen survey, 29
Nike Corporation, 87, 158, 160, 403, 407
    cheap-labor factories and, 159
    chief sustainability officer in, 71
    sweatshops and (case), 458–463
9½ Principles of Innovative Service
    (Bell), 323
Nissan, 200
Nominating committee, 212
Nonfunctional slack fill, 333
Non-GMO Project, 193
Nongovernmental organizations (NGOs), 6,
    47, 49, 88
Nonmarket players (NMPs), 49
Nonregulatory governmental influences on
    business, 388
    as competitor of business, 389
    industrial policy, 388
    as large purchaser of goods and services, 389
    loans and loan guarantees, 389
    as major employer, 389
    monetary policy, 390
    moral suasion, 390
    privatization, 388–389
    subsidies and transfer payments, 389
    taxation, 389
Nonsupportive stakeholder, 57–58, 58f
No One Would Listen, 211
Normative ethics, 100, 103
    vs. descriptive ethics, 100
Normative value, 52
Novartis, 163f
Novo Nordisk, 77
Nvidia, 70

O
The Oath Project, 116–117
Obesity
    and advertising to children, 325, 326
    crisis in Brazil, 469
Occidental Petroleum of Los Angeles, 161
Occupational Safety and Health Act, 285
Occupational Safety and Health Administration
    (OSHA), 285
    Hazard Communication Standard, 286
    recommendations for preventing workplace
        violence, 288f
Oceans and fisheries, 79–80
OECD. See Organisation for Economic
    Co-operation and Development (OECD)
OECD Antibribery Initiatives, 164
OECD guidelines for responsible business
    conduct, 167, 168f
Office of General Counsel, 264
Offshoring, 374
Ohio Environmental Council, 55
Ohio's Environmental Protection Division, 55
Old yearbook pictures, 299
Olive Garden, 158
Olympus Corporation, 144
Ombuds. See Ombudsman
Ombudsman, 260

Ombudsperson. See Ombudsman
One's best self test, 131, 132f
1099 economy, 253
Online Lenders Alliance, 446
Online scams, 183
Opacity, 145
Open-door policy, 260
Operation Varsity Blues: The College
    Admissions Scandal, 125
Opioid crisis, 354
Opioid Crisis Accountability Act, 343
Oracle, 404
Organic cotton labeling, 87
Organic food, 328
Organisation for Economic Co-operation and
    Development (OECD), 85, 164, 254, 476
Organizational ethics, 132
    best practices for improving, 137–146, 137f
    board of director leadership and oversight,
        145–146
    business ethics training, 143–145
    codes of ethics or conduct, 141–142
    communication of ethical messages, 139
    compliance vs. ethics orientation, 136
    corporate transparency and, 145
    disciplining violators of ethics standards, 142
    ethical decision making, 141
    ethics and compliance programs and officers,
        139–140
    ethics audits and risk assessments, 145
    ethics hotline and whistle-blowing, 143
    factors affecting ethical climate, 133–135
    improving ethical culture, 135–136
    realistic objectives and, 140–141
    top management leadership, 137–139
Organizational Sentencing Guidelines, 136
Organizational technoethics, 179
Organizational values, 231
Organization's moral climate, 133–134. See
    also Organizational ethics
    factors affecting morality of managers and
        employees, 134f
    levels of moral climate, 134f
OSHA. See Occupational Safety and Health
    Administration (OSHA)
OSHA's Whistleblower Protection Program, 262
Out-of-context tweeters, 182
Outplacement benefits, 376–377
Outside board director compensation, 207
Outside directors, 205
Outsourcing, 374
Overcoming values, 137
Overconfidence bias, 136
Overfishing, 80
Ozone, 77
    depletion, 77
"Ozone Watch," 77

P
Pacific Investment Management Company
    (Pimco), 260
Packaging and labeling, 331–333
PACs. See Political action committees (PACs)
Paid Release Time, 364
Paid tweeters, 182
Panasonic, 474
Pandora Media, 206
Panera, 27, 38
Paper Karma, 83
Paris Accord, 453
2016 Paris Agreement on Climate Change, 75

Paris Climate Conference (COP21), 85
Parker Foundation, 367
Parmalat, 200
Partnering for Racial Justice in Business, 408
Patagonia, 72, 87, 158, 159, 230
    as benefit corporation, 230
    as exemplar of social responsibility and
        sustainability, 27
    sustainability initiatives, 74
Pawhuska Daily Journal Capital, 419
Pax World, 55
Paycheck Fairness Act, 297
Paycheck Protection Program (PPP), 436
Payday loans, 326
    case, 444–447
PayScale, 305
PCSR. *See* Political corporate social
        responsibility (PCSR)
Peer review panel, 260
Peer review process, 516
Peloton, 353
Penson Protection Act of 2006, 514
People for the Ethical Treatment of Animals
        (PETA), 49, 50, 56, 61
    campaign against McDonald's Corporation,
        54–55
    as nonsupportive stakeholders, 58
PepsiCo, 69, 79, 328, 330
    "better for you" foods to kids, 325
    on healthier products, 328
    in India (case), 478–483
Perks, 204
Personal devices in workplace, use of, 188
Personal information, collection and use of, 184
Personality test, 278
Personal liability, 213
*Persona: The Dark Truth Behind Personality
        Tests,* 279
Personnel crises, 242
Person's values, sources of, 115–117
PETA. *See* People for the Ethical Treatment of
        Animals (PETA)
Pew Research Center, 189, 392
Pew Research survey, 309
Pfizer, 70, 140, 243, 352, 366f
Pfizer Global Research and Development, 434
Pharmaceutical Research and Manufacturers
        Association (PhRMA), 404, 406
Philanthropic responsibilities, 22–23, 23f, 25
Philanthropy, 23, 366. *See also* Corporate
        philanthropy
Philanthropy hackers, 367
Philips Foundation, 77
Philosophical beliefs, 302
Philosophical values, 115
Phishing, 185
Phone cams, 277
Photovoltaic (PV) panels, 73f
PhRMA, 410. *See* Pharmaceutical Research and
        Manufacturers Association (PhRMA)
Physical crises, 242
"Pink slime" case, 349
Pivot, 260
Planning integrativeness, 61
Plastic Pollution Coalition, 404
Plato, 206
Plot placement, 322
Pluralism, 5
Pluralistic societies, 5–6
Points of Light, 365
Poison pills, 208

Political accountability, 410–411
Political action committees (PACs), 408, 408f
Political corporate social responsibility
        (PCSR), 31, 401
Political environment, 5
Political involvement, 402
Political spending, 408–410. *See also*
        Corporate political spending
Polygraph, 278
Ponzi scheme, 211
Poor customer service, 355
Poor people, advertising and marketing to,
        326–327
Population hypothesis, 111–112
Porter–Kramer framework, 232–233
Positive right, 128
Positive social screens, 39
Postconventional level of moral development, 114
Power, Inc., 10
Powerwall solar battery pack, 74
Pratt & Whitney aircraft, 237
Preconventional level of moral development, 113
Precursor events, use of, 239
Pregnancy Discrimination Act (PDA), 296, 299
Prescription Drug Pricing Reduction Act of
        2019, 492
Preventable risks, 237
Primary nonsocial stakeholders, 48
Primary social stakeholders, 48
Principle of autonomy, 127
Principle of caring, 129
Principle of ends, 127
Principles approach to ethics, 100, 103, 125–131
    ethics of care, 129
    ethics principles, 125
        types of, 126
    Golden Rule, 130
    Kant's categorical imperative, 126–127
    principle of justice, 128–129
    principle of rights, 127–128
    principle of utilitarianism, 126
    servant leadership, 130–131
    virtue ethics, 129–130
Principles of stakeholder management, 63
Privacy Act of 1974, 274
Privacy, in workplace, 273–281
Privacy policies, 185–186
Private property, 254
Private Securities Litigation Reform Act of
        1995, 216
Privatization, 388–389
Proaction, 29
Procedural due process, 259
Proceduralism, 191
Procedural justice, 128
Process fairness, 128
Procter & Gamble, 81, 295
    chief sustainability officer in, 71
    suspension of activities in Nigeria, 169
Product and service information issues,
        320–333
    advertising, 320–331
    other, 333
    packaging and labeling, 331–333
    warranties and guarantees, 331
Product and service quality, 343–345
    dimensions of quality, 344
    ethical dimensions of quality, 344–345
        contractual theory, 345
        due care theory, 345
        social costs theory, 345

good customer service, 344
    product quality, 343
    reasons for concerns with, 343
    service quality, 343, 344
Product extortion, 352
Product information, 320
Production view of the firm, 47, 48f
Product liability, 349–352
    absolute liability, 350
    doctrine of strict liability and, 350
    product extortion and, 352
    product tampering and, 351
    reasons for concern about, 350
Product liability reform, 352
Product liability risk management program,
        350
Product placements, 321–322
Product review sites, 343
Product tampering, 351
Professional lobbyists, 405–406
Professional values, 116–117
Project ROI, 29
Protected groups, 294
Proxy access, 215
Proxy advisory firms, 215
Proxy Preview, 87, 214
Psychological appeals, 322
Public affairs (PA), 235–236
Public affairs management, 227
Public awareness, through media, 7–8
    movies, 8
    social media, 8
    24/7 television programming, 7–8
Public Citizen, 319
Public Citizen's Health Research Group, 433
Public–government relationship, 387
Public issues scanning, 238
Public policy exception, 257
Public Readiness and Emergency Preparedness
        Act (PREP), 352
Public Relations Society of America, 116
Public support for CSR, 29
Publix Supermarkets, 375
Puffery, 322
Pulpex Limited, 79
PulseNet, 348
Puma, 159
Purdue Pharma, 489
    accused for exacerbating opioid epidemic, 343
    OxyContin and opioid crisis (case), 495–497
    role in opioid drug crisis, 200
    scandal, 3
Purified idea test, 132, 132f
Purpose-driven business, 18, 20, 38. *See also*
        Corporate social responsibility (CSR)
PwC's 2020 annual corporate directors survey,
        211
Pyramid of corporate social responsibility,
        24–26, 24f

Q

QR code labeling, 333
Qualcomm Semiconductor Co., 366f, 404
Quality, 343, 356. *See also* Total Quality
        Management (TQM)
    ethical dimensions of, 344–345
    key dimensions of, 344
    product, 343
    service, 343, 344
QualityCom, 163
Quality of code content, 141

Quest Diagnostics, 280, 285
Questionable marketing practices, 155–156
Quid pro quo harassment, 305

R

Race conscious admissions policy, 310
Racial discrimination, 303–304
Rainforest Action Network (RAN), 56, 58, 86
Rana Plaza building collapse, in Bangladesh, 157, 463–467
Rand Corporation survey, 489
Rawls's principle of justice, 128–129
Raytheon Technologies, 366f
Reaction-to-punishment stage, 113
Ready-Made-Garment Sustainability Council (RSC), 465
"The Real Cost" campaign, 327
Realistic objectives, 140–141
Real-time monitoring, 187
Reasonable accommodations, 298
Recording Industry Association of America (RIAA), 186
Recycled PET, 87
Recycling, 79
Reddit, 362–363
Redefining the Corporation: Stakeholder Management and Organizational Wealth, 46
Red Lobster, 158, 516–517
Red tape, 395
Reduce, Reuse, and Recycle, 79
Reebok, 158, 166
Regulation FD (fair disclosure), 210
Rehabilitation Act of 1973, Section 503, 298
REI, Inc., 332
Relationship maintenance, 115
Religious discrimination, 306
Religious values, 115
Remote work, 272
Renewable energy credits (RECs), 454
The Report, 264
RepRisk, 234
Reputational crises, 242
Reregulation, 393
Reshoring, 374
Resource adequacy, 61
Resource Conservation and Recovery Act (RCRA), 84
Respect for person's principle, 127
Responsible Cobalt Initiative, 476
Responsible Supply Chain Commitment (RSCC), 170
Responsive CSR, 232
Restricted stock, 206
Rest's four component model of ethical decision making and behavior, 119
Résumé inflation and deception, 105
Retaliation, 306–307
Return fraud, 332
Returns policies, 331
Reverse discrimination, 309
Revolving Door Ban Executive Order on Ethics, 405
Revolving door lobbyists, 405
Rights
    competing, 128
    legal, 127, 127f
    moral, 127, 127f
    negative, 128
    positive, 128
    principle of, 127–128

Rights movement, 9
Right to due process and fair treatment, 259–261
Right-to-know laws, 286–287
Rising expectations, 8–9
Risk committees, 213
Risk management, 236–237
    external risks, 237
    preventable risks, 237
    strategic risks, 237
    and sustainability, 237
Risks
    external, 237
    preventable, 237
    strategic, 237
Risk shifting, 237
Ritz-Carlton, 344
Roboethics, 189
Robotics, 189
Roger and Me, 459
Role modeling through visible action, 138
Role morality, 136
Ronald McDonald House Charities (RMHC) program, 366
Royal Dutch/Shell Group, 63
R&S Electronic Service Company, 455
Russell 3000 index, 211

S

Safe drinking water, 348
Safe Drinking Water Act of 1974, 84
Safety issues, 345–349
    artificial intelligence use and, 348
    consumer products associated with hospital-treated injuries, 348
    drinking water, 348
    food safety, 347–348
    manufactured products, 348
    product safety best practices, 346f
    telemedicine and, 348
Salesforce
    community engagement plan, 363
    stakeholder capitalism, 45
Sarbanes–Oxley Act (SOX), 145, 204, 205, 210, 260
    effectiveness of, 210
    penalties for noncompliance with, 210
    whistle-blower protections under, 264
Sarbanes–Oxley law, 140
"Save the Planet with Capitalism," 2–3
Say on Pay movement, 206
Scenario building, 239
Schering-Plough Corporation, 490
Schneider Electric, 69, 70
Screen addiction, 176
Seafood industry, slavery in, 158
Seafood Watch app, 83
SEC. *See* Securities and Exchange Commission (SEC)
Secondary nonsocial stakeholders, 48–49
Secondary social stakeholders, 48
Sectoral trade associations, 404
Secular Faith (Smith), 116
Securities and Exchange Commission (SEC), 162, 205, 210–211, 391
    Climate and ESG Task Force, creation of, 210
    examples of violations of FCPA charged by, 163f
    Post-Madoff Reforms, 211
Seed Biotechnology Center, 191

Seeking-of-rewards stage, 113
Selective catalytic reduction (SCR), 440
Self-checkouts, 124
Self-regulation, 396–397
    in advertising, 335
Self-serving bias, 136
Sense of moral obligation, 118
Sensual advertising, 322
Serial whistle-blowers, 262
Servant leadership, 130–131
Service dogs, veterans and (case), 517–518
The Seven Habits of Highly Effective People (Covey), 108
Sex appeal use, in advertising, 324–325
Sex discrimination in payment of wages, 297
Sexual harassment
    complaints, 306f
    definition of, 305
    LGBT employees and, 306
    in workplace, 101, 305–306, 306f
Sexual orientation, 307
SFFA v. Harvard, 310
Shadow lobbying, 405
Shared understandings, social contract and, 13
Shared value, 229
Shareholder-Director Exchange (SDX), 216
Shareholder empowerment movement, 407
Shareholder engagement, 216–217
Shareholder lawsuits, 216
Shareholder-primacy model, of corporate governance, 202–203, 202f, 217
    board of directors, 202
    employees, 203
    management, 203
    shareholders, 202
Shareholder resolutions, 87, 214, 215–216
    and sustainability, 214
Shareholders
    activism, 215
    democracy, 214–215
    engagement, 216–217
    role in corporate governance, 214–216
    under shareholder-primacy model, 202
Shell, 75
Sherman Antitrust Act, 391
SHRM. *See* Society for Human Resource Management (SHRM)
Side Effects, 8
Siemens Mobility, 77
Sierra Club, 55, 86
Silent Spring (Carson), 74
Six Sigma, 356–357
Sixth mass extinction, 84
Skills-Based Pro Bono Service, 365
Slack fill, 333
Slippery slope, 137
Slow and sustainable fashion, 86, 509–510
SmartLabel initiative, 333
Smartphone use and texting, 189–190
SMC. *See* Stakeholder management capability (SMC)
Smell test, 131
Smithfield Foods, 88
Smoking in workplace, 284–285
The Snowden Files, 264
Social Accountability 8000 (SA8000), 159, 160
Social Accountability International (SAI), 159
Social activism, 201
Social audits. *See* Sustainability reports

Social contract, 12, 252
  between business and society, 12–13, 13f
  evolution of, 252–254, 253f
Social-contract orientation, 114
Social costs, 392
Social costs theory, 345
Social enterprises. *See* Social entrepreneurship
      firms
Social entrepreneurship, 229
Social entrepreneurship firms, 26–27
Social environment, 4
  affluence and education, 6–7
  awareness through media, 7–8
  factors in, 6–10, 7f
  rights movement, 9
  rising expectations, 8–9
Social forecasting, 238
Social goals, 392
Social intrapreneurship firms, 27
Socialization process, 117
Socially responsible firms, 25
  practices of, 26, 26f
Socially responsible investing (SRI), 38–39
Social media, 181
  advertising alcohol on, 327
  and business criticism, 8
  for business purposes, 181
  platforms, 181
Social media advertising, 329–303
  deceptive, 329
Social media bots, 329–330
Social mission, 229
Social model, of business responsibility, 21
The Social Network, 8
Social problem, 9, 9f
Social regulation, 392–393, 394f
Social responsibility, 19–21. *See also*
      Corporate social responsibility (CSR)
Social responsibility reports. *See* Sustainability
      reports
Social screening, 39
Societal-level strategy, 228
Society
  defined, 4
  as macroenvironment, 4–5
  pluralistic, 5–6
  special-interest, 5–6
Society for Human Resource Management
      (SHRM), 260, 308
SoftBank Group, 208
SolarCity, 78, 388
Solar Electric Light Fund, 88
SolarWinds hack, 181–182, 183
Solid Waste Disposal Act of 1965, 84
Sony, 145, 377
Southwest Airlines 1380 disaster, 241, 244
S&P 500, 211
Spam, 184
Special interest groups, 4, 6
Special-interest society, 5–6
Specialized Vehicles Corporation (SVC), 375
Speechnow v. FEC, 408
SpencerStuart, 235
S&P 500 ESG Index, 87
Spotify, 187
Spring-loading, 205
SRC Holdings, 375
Stages of corporate citizenship, 34
Staggered boards. *See* Classified boards
Stake, 46
Stakeholder–bottom line, 37

Stakeholder capitalism, 3, 45
Stakeholder Capitalism (Schwab), 45
Stakeholder communications, 61
Stakeholder corporation, 62–63
  model for, 46
Stakeholder crisis, 56
Stakeholder culture, 59–60
  continuum of, 60, 60f
Stakeholder dialogue, 62
Stakeholder engagement, 61–62, 240
  ladder of, 61
  stakeholder dialogue in, 62
  on sustainability, 61–62
  transparency in, 61
Stakeholder governance model, 218
Stakeholder identification, 53–55
Stakeholder inclusiveness, 62
Stakeholder management capability (SMC),
      60–61
  process level of, 61
  rational level of, 60
  transactional level of, 61
Stakeholder map, 48, 49f
Stakeholder mindset, 59
Stakeholder model, of business responsibility, 21
Stakeholder orientation, 59
Stakeholder pressure, 50
Stakeholder responsibility matrix, 57, 57f
Stakeholders, 5, 15, 45
  approach to business-and-society
        relationship, 46–64
  attributes, 49–51
    legitimacy, 50, 51
    power, 50, 51
    proximity, 50
    urgency, 50, 51
  business's, 47
  defined, 46
  engaging on sustainability, 60, 61–62
  fringe, 48
  generic and specific, 54, 54f
  group's stakes, 55–56
  indirect, 47
  management, 15, 52–58
    challenge of, 52
    as core competence, 63
    and engagement, 58–63
    in firm's governing philosophy, 63
    functions of, 52
    global, strategic steps toward, 63
    implementation of, 63
    indicators of, 63
    principles of, 63
    questions for, 52–58, 53f
    stakeholder thinking and, 59
  marginal, 57, 58f
  mixed-blessing, 58, 58f
  multifiduciary approach, 52
  nonsupportive, 57–58, 58f
  opportunities and challenges, 56
  organization's, 53–55, 54f
  origins of concept of, 46
  performance measurement system, 63
  plants and flowers as, 51
  potential for cooperation, 56
  potential for threat, 56
  primary, 48–49
  responsibilities to, 56–57, 57f
  secondary, 48–49
  stake in value, 46
  strategic approach, 52

  supportive, 57, 58f
  synthesis approach to, 52
  three views of the firm and, 47–48, 48f, 49f
  types and recommended strategies, 57–58, 58f
  types of stakes, 47f
  typology of, 50f, 51
  values of stakeholder model, 52
    descriptive value, 52
    instrumental value, 52
    normative value, 52
Stakeholders, 46
Stakeholder symbiosis, 63
Stakeholder thinking, 59
Stakeholder trustee, 63
Stakeholder utility, 64
Stakeholder view of the firm, 46, 47–48, 49f
Stanley Furniture, 374
Starbucks, 214
  charges of deceptive advertising and
        packaging on, 333
  conscious capitalism by, 37
  ethics in corporate strategies, 169
  as exemplar of social responsibility and
        sustainability, 27
  Mental Health Fundamentals program, 282
State charter, 202
State Street, 212
Statutory rights, 255
Stealth advertising, 321
Stealth lobbying, 405
Stock options, 205
Strategic approach to stakeholders, 52
Strategic control, 233. *See also* Sustainability
      reports
Strategic corporate social responsibility,
      232–233
Strategic management, 226
  and corporate social policy, 226–227
  defined, 226
  ethics and, 227
  key strategy levels, 226–231
    business-level strategy, 228
    corporate-level strategy, 228
    enterprise-level strategy, 228
    functional-level strategy, 228
    hierarchy of, 227, 228f
  process, 231–235
    corporate public policy and, 231, 232f
    defined, 231
    measuring sustainable corporate
          performance, 233–235
    strategic corporate social responsibility,
          232–233
  public affairs as part of, 235–236
Strategic philanthropy, 371–372
  attributes of effective strategic philanthropy
        program, 371f
  context for strategy and rivalry, 372
  demand conditions, 372
  factor conditions, 371
  related and supporting industries, 372
Strategic risks, 237
Street ready hybrid trucks, 56
Strict liability law, 350
Strong ethical leadership, 138–139
Student loans, 125, 510–513
Students for Fair Admissions (SFFA), 309
Subordinates, pressure on, 134
Subsidies, 389
Sulphur dioxide pollution, 84
Sunburst, 182

The Sunlight Foundation, 410
SunTrust Bank, 123
Superfund, 84
Super PACs, 408, 410
Supportive stakeholder, 57, 58f
Survivor, 101
Suspension of business in foreign country, 169–170
Sustainability, 15, 18, 20, 68–69, 227. *See also* Corporate social responsibility (CSR)
    consumers view of, 323
    in corporate social policy, 227
    engaging stakeholders on, 60, 61–62
    focus of, 69
    goal of, 68–69
    in hiring and retention of employees, 257
    imperative, 69–71
    myths and misconceptions about, 37
    risk management and, 237
    shareholder resolutions and, 214
    triple bottom line and, 68
Sustainability (nonprofit advocacy organization), 27
Sustainability audit, 145
Sustainability reports, 233–234
    in context of strategic control, 233, 234f
    DuPont and, 235
    globalization as driver for, 234
    impetus for, 234
    importance of, 233
Sustainability software, 83
"Sustainability Stakeholder Engagement" conferences, 61
Sustainable Agriculture Guiding Principles (SAGP), 62
Sustainable Apparel Coalition, 87
Sustainable business, definition of, 69
Sustainable corporations, in COVID-19 pandemic crisis, 242
Sustainable development, 15, 29
Sustainable Development Goals (SDGs), 69, 70f, 167, 228
Sustainable products, 345
Sustainable supply chains, 159
Sustainalytics, 234
Swanson's Unwritten Rules of Management, 456
Sweatshops, 158–160
    Nike Inc. and (case), 458–463
Synthesis approach to stakeholders, 52

T
Takata Corporation, 3
Talkspace, 362
Tap app, 83
Target Corporation, 158, 409, 487
    cyberattacks at, 145
    repercussions of corporate political spending, 409
Tax inversions, 390
Tazreen Fashions, Ltd., 157
Team production model of corporate governance, 218
Team Sweat, 460
Technoethics, 179
Technological determinism, 180
Technological environment, 5, 178
Technology, 176–194, 217
    benefits of, 178–179
    Big Data and artificial intelligence, 177–178
    biotechnology, 190–193
    and business communication, 181

costs of, 178–179
and ethics, 179–180
information (*See* Information technology (IT))
meaning of, 178
monitoring, 187–188
social media and, 181
surveillance cameras, 180
technological environment and, 178
undesirable side effects of, 178–179
unemployment, 179
Telemedicine, 348
Teleological theories, 126
Television, business criticism on, 7–8
Tenet Healthcare, 140
Tennessee Valley Authority (TVA), 389
TerraChoice, 31
TerraPass, 76
Tesla, 71, 78, 208–209, 344
    ethical dilemma (case), 473–477
    sustainability initiatives, 74
Texting, 189–190
Theranos, 97, 123
    fake blood-testing kits, 200
    fraud charges against, 123
    story and fake blood testing (case), 431–433
There's No Such Thing as "Business" Ethics: There's Only One Rule for Making Decisions (Maxwell), 130
Think Dirty app, 83
Third sector, 368
"This Is No Time to Go Wobbly on Capitalism," 3
Thomas More Law Center, 410
Thomson Reuters, 234
TikTok, 183, 327
Timberland
    as exemplar of social responsibility and sustainability, 27
    Path of Service Program, 23
    Pillar Service Events Program, 23
Time magazine, 176
Tippee, 209
Tipper, 209
Title VII of the Civil Rights Act of 1964, 296
The Tobacco Control Act, 327
Tobacco industry, 12
Tobacco use, deaths from, 327
Toilet paper packaging, 333
Tolerance of moral disagreement and ambiguity, 118
Toms, 26, 30
Top management leadership, 137–139
Tort, 350, 352
Tort law, 350, 352
Tort reform, 352
Toshiba, 3
Total Quality Management (TQM), 356
Toxic substances, 77
Toxic Substances Control Act, 1976, 84
Toyota, 82, 238
Trade associations, 406–407
Tragedy of the commons, 81
Transfer payments, 389
Transgender, 308
Transgender movement, 295
Transnational economy, 153. *See also* Global ethical issues
Transparency, 145, 146, 216
Transparency, in political accountability, 410
Transparency International (TI), 164, 372
Transsexual, 308

Transsexual employees, 308
Trend extrapolation, 239
Triple bottom line, 68
    components of, 68
    goal of, 68
Truth-in-Lending Act, 333
Turing Pharmaceuticals, 488
23andMe, 301
Twitter, 61, 169, 181, 391
    ethics in business, 182
    mission statement, 63
Tylenol poisonings, 57, 351
Type 1 error, 279
Type 2 error, 279
Tyson Foods, Inc., 59, 81, 469

U
UAW v. Johnson Controls, Inc., 300
Uber, 406
    lawsuit against use of background checks, 275
Ultra-processed food, 468
Umbrella organizations, 407–408
    Business Roundtable, 407
    Chamber of Commerce of the United States, 407
    coalitions, 407–408
Umbrella trade associations, 404
Unconscious biases, 109–110
    discounting, 110
    escalation, 110
    familiarity, 110
UN Convention against Corruption (UNCAC), 164–165
Under Armour, 159
Undue hardship, 298
U.N. Environment Programme (UNEP), 234
UNGC. *See* United Nations Global Compact (UNGC)
UNGC 2030 Agenda for Sustainable Development, 69
UN Global Compact, 167, 168f
    principles, 228
Uniform Law Commission, 273
Unilever, 71, 403
    Ben & Jerry's acquisition by, 227
    board committees, 213
    Fair & Lovely skin-lightener cream brand, 330
    as mainstream adopter, 27
    purpose and principles, 231f
    Sustainable Living Brands program, 345
Unintentional amoral management, 109–110
Union Carbide, 156–157, 285, 286. *See also* Bhopal tragedy
United for Respect, 252
United Nations Children's Fund (UNICEF), 156
United Nations Conference on Environment and Development, 1992, 79
United Nations Environment Programme (UNEP), 85
United Nations Global Compact (UNGC), 69, 85
    COVID-19 pandemic impact on goals of, 70
    sustainable development goals, 69, 70f
    UNGC 2030 agenda, 69–70
United Parcel Service (UPS), 56, 300, 521
    as mainstream adopter, 27
United Self-Defense Forces of Colombia (AUC), 483
United States
    air quality legislation, 82, 84
    benefit corporation movement in, 230

United States *(continued)*
  endangered species and biodiversity
    legislation, 84–85
  explicit CSR in, 34
  land-related legislation, 84
  National Environmental Policy Act (NEPA),
    82
  water quality legislation, 84
Universal-ethical-principle orientation, 114
University of Tennessee–Chattanooga (UTC), 261
Unsafe at Any Speed (Nader), 318
UPS. *See* United Parcel Service (UPS)
USA Patriot Act, 274
USA Today, 466
U.S.-based Sustainability Accounting
    Standards Board (SASB), 233
U.S. Chamber Institute for Legal Reform, 216
U.S. Chamber of Commerce, 404
U.S. Department of Agriculture (USDA),
    192, 328
  National Bioengineered Food Disclosure
    Standard, 193
U.S. Department of Labor (DOL) Wage and
    Hour Division, 259
U.S. Drug Enforcement Administration, 280
U.S. Federal Trade Commission, 185
U.S. Foreign Corrupt Practices Act, 420
U.S. NASDAQ, 212
U.S. National Highway Safety Transportation
    Agency (NHSTA), 189
U.S. Postal Service, 56, 389
U.S. Sentencing Commission (USSC), 136, 140
U.S. Supreme Court
  absolute liability concept, 350
  affirmative action decisions, 309f
  Bostock v. Clayton County, Georgia, 307
  Citizens United v. FEC, 408, 409
  on employment discrimination, 296, 302
  on fetal protection policies, 300
  Fisher v. University of Texas, 310
  on pregnancy discrimination, 299
  privacy of personal e-mails on company's
    computer, 273
  rights movement and, 9
  on scope of Alien Torts Act, 161
  on sexual harassment, 306
  on Title VII of Civil Rights Act, 296
Utilitarianism, principle of, 126
Utility regulation, 390

V
Valeant Pharmaceuticals International, 488
Value proposition, 233
Values
  cultural, 115–116
  external sources of, 115–116
  internal sources of, 117
  legal, 116
  organizational, 231
  philosophical, 115
  professional, 116–117
  religious, 115
  sources of, 115–117
Values statement, 63
Vanguard, 55, 357
Venn model, for ethical decision making,
    104, 105f
Ventilation test, 132, 132f
Verizon, 206, 214, 366f
  position title for lead CSR position, 20
Vertex, 365

VF, 159
Video camera surveillance, 180
Video games, 346
Video Investigator, 180
Vietnam Era Veterans Readjustment Assistance
    Act of 1974, 298
Viral news test, 131
Virtue ethics, 129–130
Volkswagen, 4, 20, 212, 242
  clean diesel vehicle advertising, 329
  diesel deception (case), 438–444
  emissions scandal, 3, 97, 107, 109
  immoral management, 107
Volkswagen Group of America (VWoA),
    438, 439
Volunteer programs, 364–365

W
"Waiter Rule," 456
Walker Information, 26
WALL-E, 68
Wall Street, 8
Wall Street financial crisis, 20, 97
Wall Street Journal, 144, 177, 294, 446,
    450, 492
Wall Street: Money Never Sleeps, 8
Walmart, 37, 83, 157, 158, 166, 330, 342
  "Buy American" plan, 418–419
  case about, 418–423
  labor practices (case), 423–428
  as mainstream adopter, 27
  position title for lead CSR position, 20
  on raising minimum wage, 252
  Sustainability Index System (THESIS), 63
  use of employee data for health tracking, 274
  violations of Foreign Corrupt Practices Act
    by, 163f
Walmart Way, 418
Walt Disney, 159, 205
  privacy policy, 185–186
Wardrobing, 332
Warranties, 331
  express, 331
  extended, 331
  full, 331
  implied, 331
  limited, 331
Waste management, 79
Water bankruptcy, 79
Water pollution, 78–79
Watershed, 79
Waters of the United States (WOTUS) rule, 84
Waves of environmentalism, 72
Weak ethical leadership, 138
Weasel words, 320–321
Web-based marketing. *See* Electronic commerce
Webcams, 277
WEF. *See* World Economic Forum (WEF)
Wegmans, 230
Weight of Gold, 282
Wellness programs for mental health, 282
Wells Fargo, 20
  accounts scandal, 3, 97, 107
  fraud/fake accounts scandal, 200
  immoral management, 107
  unintentionally amoral management, 110–111
WeWork, 208
WhatsApp, 181, 189, 209
What Would You Do?, 102
Whistle-blower, 262. *See also* Whistle-blowing
  serial, 262

The Whistleblower, 264
Whistleblower Protection Act, 264
Whistle-blowing, 262
  checklist for, 263f
  consequences of, 262–263
  employee responsibility and, 262f
  False Claims Act, 266
  federal laws protecting, 264–265, 265f
  key elements of process of, 262
  management responsiveness to, 266–267
  movies about, 264f
Whistle-blowing mechanisms, 143
WHO International Code of Marketing of
    Breastmilk Substitutes
    (The Code), 471
Whole Foods Market, 22, 37, 158, 193
  charges of deceptive packing on, 333
  conscious capitalism by, 37
  Higher Purpose Statement, 63
  labeling of genetically modified foods,
    193
  strategic philanthropy program, 372
Who Speaks for the Trees (Sama, Welcomer,
    and Gerde), 81
Wicked problems, 81
Wildfires, and air pollution, 75
Williams-Sonoma, 158
WinShape Centre® Foundation, 23
The Wolf of Wall Street, 8
Women as sex objects, in advertising, 325
Women CEOs in America Report, 304
Women, issues for, 304
  equal pay and promotion, 305
  getting into professional/managerial
    positions, 304–305
  sexual harassment, 305–306, 306f
Worker Adjustment and Retraining Notification
    Act (WARN), 376, 376f
Worker Rights Consortium (WRC), 460, 465
Workers Memorial Day, 285
"Working in America: Absent Workforce"
    study (Kronos Inc.), 278
Work-life balance, 253, 283–284
Workplace
  accidents, 286
  affirmative action in, 308–310
  alcohol use in, 285
  diversity, 308
  drugs in, 285
  family-friendly, 283–284
  freedom of speech in, 261–267
  health and wellness in, 282–285
  mental health in, 282
  privacy in (*See* Workplace privacy)
  safety, 285–288
  sexual harassment in, 305–306, 306f
  smoking in, 284–285
  trends, 251
  vaping in, 284–285
Workplace monitoring, 276–278
  consequence of, 277
  guidelines on issue of, 277–278
  technology use for, 276, 277
  what can be monitored, 276–277
Workplace privacy, 273–281
  drug testing and, 279–281
  employee information collection and use,
    274–276
  employee monitoring, 276–278
  integrity tests, 278–279
  policy guidelines, 281

Workplace safety, 285
    problem, 285–286
    right-to-know laws, 286–287
    today, 286
Workplace sensibilities, 273
Workplace spying, 520–521
Workplace surveillance, 272
Workplace technology issues, 188–190
    automation and robotics, 189
    biometrics, 188–189
    cell phones and texting, 189–190
    company actions, 190
    unethical activities by employees, 190
Workplace violence, 287–288
    from co-workers, 287
    deaths due to, 287
    guidelines on prevention of, 288
    workers at increased risk of, 287–288

WorldCom, 97, 200, 204, 210
World Economic Forum (WEF), 45, 161, 408
    on air pollution issues, 76–77
World fossil carbon dioxide emissions, 76f
World Health Assembly, 471
World Health Organization (WHO), 156,
        193, 394
    on air pollution, 75
    on cigarette use, 327
    on health and wellness, 282
World Water Day, 79
World Wide Fund for Nature (WWF), 155
Worn Wear, 72
Wrangler, 404

X
Xerox, 37, 208
    as mainstream adopter, 27

Y
Yahoo, 105
Young v. UPS, 299, 300
Youth activism, 70
YouTube, 181

Z
Zady, 86
Zappos, 344, 355
Zara, 86
Zero Trust, 183
Zhejiang Huayou Cobalt, 474
Zoom, 145
    data breaches of, 186
Zoom fatigue, 272, 436

Name Index

A

Abramoff, Jack, 403
Ackerman, Robert, 31
Agle, B. R., 50
Aguirre, Fernando, 483, 484
Alston, Shawne, 387
Amarelo, Monica, 235
Amos, Daniel, 11
Anderson, Ray, 107
Andester, Nikita, 76
Andreessen, Marc, 209
Antum, Eric, 331
Ariely, Dan, 112
Aristotle, 115, 126, 129
Arnold, Denis, 434
Asmundson, Gordon J. G., 394
Austen, Ian, 393
Axelrod, Bobby, 8

B

Bachman, Rachel, 387
Bachs, Skinner, 88
Baer, Justin, 138
Bainbridge, Stephen, 218
Bakshi, Rajeev, 480
Ballingee, Ryan, 243
Balwani, Ramesh, 123, 431, 432
Barclay, William, 115
Barnett, Michael, 36
Barra, Mary, 11, 374
Bauer, Raymond, 31
Bebchuk, Lucian, 218
Beer, Tommy, 387
Bell, Chip, 323
Benioff, Marc, 47, 363
Bentham, Jeremy, 115, 126
Bernstein, Blair, 243
Berridge, Rob, 214
Bezos, Jeff, 254, 277, 454, 456, 504
Biden, Joe (President), 75, 85, 393, 436, 453,
    487, 490, 512
Bieler, Des, 243
Bilot, Rob, 235
Blackman, Reid, 277
Blair, Elizabeth, 86
Blair, John D., 58
Bloomberg, Michael, 326
Boles, Erskine, 209
Bolsonaro, Jair, 469
Booker, Brakkton, 80
Boren, Cindy, 243
Bosman, Julie, 80, 258
Boston, William, 78
Bowie, Norman E., 257
Bradley, Ryan, 230
Braithwaite, Hugh, 376
Branstad, Terry, 349
Broughton, Philip, 30
Brown, Amy, 242
Brown, Jill A., 428, 431, 433, 435, 453, 455,
    483, 487, 503, 506, 509, 510, 513, 518
Buchholtz, Ann K., 433, 487, 517, 518
Buckley, Thomas, 252, 402
Buffett, Warren, 11, 216

Bunge, Jacob, 349
Burke, James, 351
Burns, Steve, 377
Burns, Steven, 510
Bush, George W. (President), 512

C

Calhoun, David, 502
Campbell, Eric, 489
Carey, James, 410
Carreyrou, John, 431, 432
Carroll, Archie B., 21, 24, 32–33, 104, 108,
    111, 418, 423, 438, 444, 447, 451,
    455, 458, 463, 478, 483, 488, 495,
    497, 501, 516
Carson, Rachel, 74
Cartwright, Dorwin, 11
Casselman, Ben, 252
Cataldi, Carlotta, 86
Cervantes, Miguel de, 125
Challenger, John A., 213
Chan, Thomas, 278
Chatterji, Aaron, 405
Chaudhuri, Saabira, 330
Chiappardi, Matt, 209
Chinni, Dante, 404
Chouinard, Yvon, 74
Chu, Kathy, 160
Ciulla, Joanne, 131
Clancy, Heather, 230
Clark, David, 504
Clarkson, Max, 63
Clinton, Bill (President), 512
Cohen, Ben, 26
Cohen, Sasha, 283
Coiscou, Steve, 367
Colias, Mike, 78
Collins, Denis, 207
Collins, Jim, 456
Colvin, Alexander, 351
Conner, Steve, 116
Cook, Tim, 11, 74
Cooper, David, 252
Corday, Richard, 445
Covey, Stephen, 108
Cowen, Tyler, 206
Crew, Jonathan, 230
Crowe, Ken, 520
Cudmore, Dale, 27
Curry, Lynne, 278
Cutter, Chip, 258

D

Dauncey, Guy, 88
Dave, Dhaval, 434
David, Ruth, 138
Davila, Edward, 432
Davis, Gray, 107
De Blasio, Bill, 256, 406
Dees, J. Gregory, 229
Dennis, Bryan S., 458
DePasquale, Matthew, 10
Depinho, Ronald, 109
Derry, Robbin, 129

Desmond-Hellman, Sussan, 209
Detert, James, 266
Dezenhall, Eric, 244
DiCaprio, Leonardo, 8
Dickson, Maureen, 86
Diess, Herbert, 11
Dimon, Jamie, 3
Donaldson, T., 166
Donaldson, William, 145
Donovan, David, 441
Dorsett, Ethan, 444–445
Douglas, Michael, 8
Draper, Don, 7
Droesch, Blake, 346
Drucker, Peter, 317, 374
Dubinsky, Joan, 141
Dunfee, T., 166
Dwyer, Angela, 182
Dwyer, Ben, 124

E

Easterbook, Gregg, 177
Eberhard, Martin, 473
Edwards, Richard, 255
Efrati, Amir, 105
Eisenberg, Pablo, 371
Eitel, Maria, 459
Elauf, Samantha, 302
Elfarra, Haidy, 321
Elliott, Christopher, 323
Ellis, Lee, 122
Ells, Steve, 243, 429
Enrich, David, 299
Epstein, Marc, 122, 134, 153
Esty, Daniel, 69

F

Farra, Emily, 86
Fastow, Andy, 107
Faury, Guillaume, 11
Febrizio, Mark, 395
Feintzeig, Rachel, 299
Fernandez, Clara Rodriguez, 190
Fink, Larry, 75, 436, 453
Fitzgerald, Patrick, 349
Floyd, George, 295, 330, 402
Foege, William H., 431
Foldy, Ben, 266
Fombrum, Charles, 33
Fox, Emily Jane, 277
Freed, Bruce, 409
Freeman, R. Edward, 48
French, John, 11
Friedman, Milton, 28, 118
Frommer, Arthur, 420
Fuhrmans, Vanessa, 237, 299

G

Gardner, Gregg, 266
Gee, Kelsey, 349
Gentile, Mary C., 265
George, Bill, 122
Gerde, Virginia W., 81
German, John, 441

Gershman, Jacob, 349
Gerwitz, Lisa, 87
Gibbs, Nancy, 176
Gifford, Kathie Lee, 458
Gilbert, Lewis, 215
Gilligan, Carol, 115, 129
Gini, Al, 138
Glover, Crystal, 86
Glover, Paul, 419
Goodpaster, Kenneth, 51
Gorman, James, 436
Gorny, Ronald, 351
Graham, Donald, 209
Greenfield, Jerry, 26, 419
Greenleaf, Robert K., 130
Green, Ronald M., 138
Greytsman, Zachary, 373
Gunther, Marc, 87
Guterres, Antonio, 70
Gwang-ho, Kim, 266

H
Hager, George, 206
Haley, Nikki, 504
Hanson, Kirk, 122, 134, 153
Harrison, Jeffrey S., 46
Harrison, Steve, 258
Harris, Sophia, 124
Hart, Stuart L., 229
Hart, Thomas, 428
Hartung, John, 243
Hassan, Fred, 491
Hastings, Reed, 209
Hatch, Orrin, 441
Hatton, Ruth, 516
Havlick, Spencer, 419
Hawaleshka, Danylo, 88
Hawken, Paul, 107
Haynes, Todd, 71
Heisler, Steve, 244
Helms, Marilyn M., 455
Higgins, Lane, 387
Hill, Catey, 204
Hillman, Amy, 411
Hirsch, Laura, 346
Hitt, Michael, 411
Hodgson, Paul, 209
Hohn, Christopher, 442
Holcomb, Steve, 283
Holman, Jordyn, 402
Holmes, Elizabeth, 123, 431–432
Hood, Bryan, 78
Horch, A. J., 283
Horta E Costa, Sofia, 138
Hudson, Matthew, 332
Humphreys, Kenneth K., 263
Husted, Bryan, 36

I
Icahn, Carl, 208
Irfan, Umair, 76
Isaacson, Walter, 190
Isdell, Neville, 479, 480

J
Janin, Alex, 283
Jargon, Julie, 346
Jarvis, Rebecca, 432
Jassy, Andy, 456
Jenkins, Anthony, 143

Jeter, Derek, 458
Jobs, Steve, 123, 432
Johnson, Lyndon B., 309
Jones, Lolo, 283
Jones, Patricia E., 58
Jordan, Michael, 159, 458
Jordan, Stephen, 373
Joseph, Joel, 459

K
Kaepernick, Colin, 461
Kaiser, Jocelyn, 301
Kanal, Vijay, 37
Kant, Immanuel, 115, 126–127
Kaplan, Robert, 237
Kapner, Suzanne, 404
Kavanaugh, Brett, 299
Kavulla, Travis, 390
Keegan, Paul, 207
Kelly, Gary, 241
Kelly, Kate, 299
Kennedy, John F., 318
Kennedy, Randy, 370
Khan, Aamir, 479
Khan, Lina, 448
Kiefer, Halle, 283
Kimes, Mina, 370
Kindervag, John, 183
King, Martin Luther, Jr., 295
King, Mervyn, 233
Kissinger, Henry, 431
Klinefelter, Quinn, 370
Knight, Philip, 458–460
Kohlberg, Lawrence, 113
Kohn, Stephen Martin, 263
Kotler, Philip, 318
Koum, Jan, 209
Kourabas, Michael, 235
Kovacevich, Richard, 431
Kramer, Mark R., 26, 37, 229, 232–233, 371–372
Krisher, Tom, 266
Kruse, Paul, 347
Kullman, Ellen, 215
Kuznetsova, Olga, 499–500

L
LaMattina, John, 434
Landau, Craig, 495
Lane, Frederick S., 281
Lane, Steven, 419
Lantos, Geoffrey P., 62
Larkin, Bob, 103
Lawrence, Jennifer, 123, 432
Lawrence, Trevor, 387
Lay, Ken, 107
Lebron, Andrea, 287
Lechleiter, John, 364
Ledsom, Alex, 393
Lee, Allison Herren, 210
Lemann, Nicholas, 402
Lemonick, Michael D., 37
Leonard, Darius, 283
Lesser, Rich, 457
Levitt, Steven, 105
Lewis, Danny, 116
Lewis, Phillip, 133
Liebeck, Stella, 497
Liedtka, Jeanne, 129
Locke, John, 115, 127

Loeb, Dan, 215
Loftus, Peter, 263
Lores, Enrique, 226
Lowery, David, 187
Lublin, J. S., 105, 211
Lucas, Suzanne, 188
Lynch, Karen, 11

M
Mackee, George, 62
Mackey, John, 37
MacMillan, Ian C., 58
Macron, Emmanuel, 153
Madoff, Bernard, 97, 211
Makower, Joel, 242
Malone, Chris, 261
Mark, Jason, 460
Markle, Meghan, 433
Markopolos, Harry, 211
Marshall, Jack, 124
Martin, Casey, 298
Martin, Trayvon, 402
Martin, Veronica, 499
Matten, Dirk, 34
Mattoli, Dana, 243
Maxwell, John C., 130
McCabe, Donald, 452
McCain, John, 409
McCarthy, Gina, 80
McCarthy, Kevin, 408
McElhaney, Kellie, 364
McMillon, Doug, 252, 420–422, 426
McVeigh, Karen, 302
Mears, Tom, 35
Medintz, Scott, 351
Meibauer, Madeline, 279
Melo, Sandra, 188
Miceli, Marcia P., 262
Miedema, Christie, 466
Mill, John Stuart, 126
Millstein, Ira M., 487
Mitchell, R. K., 50
Mittal, Anuradha, 402
Moglen, Eben, 440
Mokhiber, Zane, 252
Moon, Jeremy, 34
Moore, Michael, 10, 459, 514
Morgan, Reed, 498
Morrison, Jim, 299
Moyo, Jane, 160
Muilenburg, Dennis, 205, 502
Mulcahy, Anne, 37
Müller, Mathias, 439
Murphy, Dan, 87
Murray, Caroline, 513
Murray, Russ, 517
Musk, Elon, 11, 208–209, 473
Mustafa, Nadia, 30
Muth, Karen, 499
Mycoskie, Blake, 26, 30

N
Nader, Ralph, 318–319
Naisbitt, John, 176
Narain, Sunita, 478
Near, Janet P., 262
Nelson, Gaylord, 74
Neumann, Adam, 208
Nguyen, Thomas, 459
Niccol, Brian, 429

Nicholson, Tim, 302
Nix, Timothy W., 58
Nooyi, Indra, 328, 480
Northam, Ralph, 299
Nunn, Sam, 431

O
Oakley, James, 434
Obama, Barack (President), 431, 515
Odland, Steve, 456
O'Donnell, Jayne, 466
Oge, Margo, 441
Ohno, Apolo, 283
Olsson, Karen, 425
Olupinyo, Grace, 257
Osawa, Juro, 144

P
Paine, Lynn Sharp, 108, 110
Palazzo, G., 31, 154
Papa, Joseph, 11
Parker, Sean, 367
Parks, Rosa, 104, 295
Peltz, Nelson, 215
Perry, Andrew, 242
Peterson, Joel, 258
Pfeffer, Jeffrey, 11
Pflaumer, Frank, 470
Phelps, Michael, 282
Picchi, Aimee, 274
Pichai, Sundar, 204
Piëch, Ferdinand, 439
Plato, 129
Plumer, Brad, 74
Pollack, Bridget, 27
Polman, Paul, 71
Porsche, Ferdinand, 439
Porter, Michael E., 26, 29, 37, 229, 232–233, 363, 371–372
Post, James, 63
Powers, Charles W., 117, 119
Prahalad, C. K., 229
Pratt, Mary, 183
Preysman, Michael, 507
Price, Dan, 207
Prince Harry, 433
Profita, Cassandra, 390
Pucker, Kenneth, 454

Q
Quiñones, John, 102

R
Radin, Tara J., 257
Rasche, A., 31
Raven, Bertram, 11
Rawls, John, 128
Raymond, Rick, 278
Reesman, Ann, 260
Reich, Robert, 395
Rest, James, 112, 119
Rettinger, David, 452
Reynolds, Scott, 142
Rich, Nathaniel, 235
Rimm, Hannah, 330
Robertson, Derek, 80
Robin, Marci, 330
Roche, Julia La, 138
Rockefeller, John D., 368
Roddick, Anita, 26
Rodriguez, Julio, 377

Rodriguez, Linda, 503
Rometty, Ginni, 204
Rosemarin, Remi, 323
Rosenbaum, Eric, 301
Rosenthal, Elizabeth, 434
Roth, Eldon, 349
Ruffalo, Mark, 71–72, 235
Rupp, William T., 418
Ryan, Dan, 499

S
Sackler, David, 496
Sackler, Richard, 495
Saini, Harsh, 460
Salomon, Robert, 36
Sama, Linda M., 81
Sandberg, Sheryl, 209, 304
Sandstrom, Karl, 409
Sanford, Mark, 504
Santoro, Michael, 210
Savage, Grant T., 58
Sawyer, Diane, 349
Schendler, Auden, 405
Scherer, A. G., 31, 154
Schneider, Gregory, 299
Schrage, Michael, 442
Schwab, Klaus, 45
Schwartz, John, 74
Schwartz, Mark S., 104
Schwarzenegger, Arnold, 107
Scott, Lee, 425, 426
Segal, Edward, 406
Sewing, Christian, 11
Shaich, Ron, 456
Sherman, Alex, 11
Shkreli, Martin, 488
Shultz, George, 431
Shultz, Tyler, 432
Sillanpää, Maria, 62
Silverman, Rachel Emma, 274
Sinclair, Upton, 318
Singer, Paul, 215
Skilling, Jeffrey, 107
Smith, Adam, 20
Smith, Jeffrey, 215
Smith, Jody, 419
Smith, Kelly Anne, 252
Smith, Kennedy, 419
Smith, Lorraine, 146
Smith, Mark, 116
Smith, Mitch, 258
Smith, Rebecca, 390
Smith, Roger, 459
Smith, Stephen, 346
Sniderman, Brenna, 180
Snyder, Rick, 80
Sodeman, William A., 438
Solheim, Jostein, 227
Soltau, Jill, 205
Somavia, Juan, 370
Sowell, John, 207
Spacey, Kevin, 403
Spang, Victoria, 288
Spence, Laura, 27
Spicer, A., 31
Spitznagel, Eric, 278
Srivastava, Amit, 480
Starik, Mark, 47, 60
Stempel, Jonathan, 209
Sterling, Donald, 261
Stewart, Martha, 244

Stoga, Gloria, 517
Stoll, John D., 402
Stone, Katherine, 351
Story, Dave, 419
Straus, Rachel, 143
Strauss, Ronald, 210
Streeter, Kurt, 387
Surowiecki, James, 230
Swanson, Bill, 456
Swift, Taylor, 186
Szecsei, Szabolcs, 424

T
Tankersley, Jim, 252
Tapscott, Don, 61
Tarpenning, Marc, 473
Tashjian, Rachel, 404
Taylor, Breonna, 402
Taylor, David, 295
Taylor, Steven, 394
Terlep, Sharon, 394
Thiel, Peter, 209
Thomas, Rachel, 304
Thompson, Scott, 105
Thunberg, Greta, 70
Ticoll, David, 61
Timberlake, Cotten, 332
Toffel, Michael, 405
Toffler, Barbara Ley, 143
Treanor, Jill, 143
Treviño, Linda, 142
Tricoire, Jean-Pascal, 70
Trump, Donald (President), 261, 335, 431
Tufekci, Zeynep, 440
Turner, Jane, 264
Turnley, Sabine E., 467, 473
Turnley, William H., 467, 473

U
Ubben, Jeff, 215
Useem, Jerry, 424

V
VanSandt, Craig, 133
Vargas, Catalina, 135
Vera, Amir, 243
Visser, Wayne, 24
Vogel, David, 117, 119
Vozzella, Lauren, 299

W
Wahba, Phil, 277
Walton, Helen R., 421
Walton, Sam, 342, 418–419
Ward, Andrew, 263
Warren, Elizabeth, 512
Warren, Melinda, 395
Warzel, Charlie, 182
Watson, Hugh, 177
Weaver, Gary, 142
Weber, John, 244
Weber, Lauren, 299
Weil, David, 259
Weiss, Debra Cassens, 263
Welcomer, Stephanie A., 81
Werhane, Patricia, 257, 273
Westcott, Sean, 470
West, Tessa, 103
Wheeler, David, 62
Whitehead, Carlton J., 58
White, Shaun, 283

Wicks, Andrew C., 46
Williams, Bernadine, 76
Wilmot, Stephen, 78
Windsor, Duane, 33
Winston, Andrew, 69
Winterkorn, Martin, 438, 439
Wolfe, Alan, 116
Wolfe, Sidney, 433
Wood, Diane, 257
Wood, D. J., 50

Woodhall, Hunter, 387
Woods, Laura, 204
Woods, Tiger, 159, 242, 243, 458
Wright, Fred, 419
Wyden, Ron, 441

Y
Yang, Peter, 105
Yarrow, Kit, 466
Yates, Sally Quillian, 442

Young, Andrew, 459
Young, Peggy, 300

Z
Zadek, Simon, 29
Zarya, Valentina, 274
Zipperer, Ben, 252
Zuboff, Shoshana, 448
Zuckerberg, Mark, 8, 11, 209, 326

END OF TEXT CASE MATRIX

CASE #	End of Text Case Title	Chs. 1–2	Chs. 3–4	Chs. 5–6	Chs. 7–8	Chs. 9–10	Chs. 11–13	Chs. 14–16	Chs. 17–18
1	Walmart: The Main Street Merchant of Doom	X					X	X	
2	Walmart's Labor Practices			X			X		X
3	Chipotle's Struggle with Food Safety: Back on Top Again?	X	X					X	
4	The Theranos Story and Fake Blood Testing: Culture, Crime and Hubris	X	X		X	X			
5	Direct-to-Consumer Advertising for Pharmaceuticals: Is It Ethical?		X	X		X		X	
6	The COVID-19 Pandemic: Herculean Challenges for Business and CSR	X		X		X			
7	Volkswagen's Diesel Deception and Its Aftermath	X	X	X	X	X		X	X
8	Payday Loans: A Needed Product or a Financial Scam?	X	X		X	X		X	
9	Big Tech's Power Plays	X	X	X	X				X
10	An Epidemic of Cheating in College	X	X	X				X	
11	Climate Change and Corporate Activism: Is It All Just Hot Air?	X	X			X			
12	Family Business			X	X		X		
13	What Makes for a Good CEO? The Waiter Rule, Humility, and Amazon			X	X	X			
14	Nike, Sweatshops, and Other Issues			X	X	X			X
15	The Rana Plaza Factory Collapse				X	X			X
16	Big Food, Big Problem: Nestlé in Brazil		X			X		X	
17	The Dark Side of Going Green: Tesla's Ethical Dilemma		X	X	X				X
18	Coke and Pepsi in India: Water, Issues, Crisis Management		X	X	X			X	
19	An Ethical Dilemma for Chiquita in Colombia				X	X	X		X
20	Dark Money and Corporate Political Spending on Campaigns		X		X	X	X		X
21	Big Pharma's Marketing Tactics	X	X	X				X	X
22	Purdue Pharma, OxyContin, and the Opioid Crisis	X	X	X		X		X	X
23	McDonald's: The Coffee Spill Heard 'Round the World	X	X	X		X		X	
24	Boeing's Two Flight Crashes	X	X			X	X	X	X